PEARSON   ALWAYS LEARNING

Michael Bixby • Caryn Beck-Dudley • Patrick Cihon • Susan Park

The Legal Environment of Business

Fifth Edition

Previously published as:

The Legal Environment of Business
by Michael Bixby, Caryn Beck-Dudley, and Patrick Cihon
Copyright © 2001 by Prentice Hall
A Pearson Education Company
Upper Saddle River, New Jersey 07458

Pearson Learning Solutions, 501 Boylston Street, Suite 900, Boston, MA 02116
A Pearson Education Company
www.pearsoned.com

Printed in the United States of America

000200010270744728

RR/LP

ISBN 10: 1-256-15916-6
ISBN 13: 978-1-256-15916-2

We would like to dedicate this book to our students and families. Our students continually keep us alert and "on our toes" with their thoughts, comments, and ideas. The support and encouragement of our families have provided us with the energy and persistence needed to completely revise and update this book. We also appreciate the hard work and friendship of our co-authors.

MICHAEL BIXBY

CARYN BECK-DUDLEY

PATRICK J. CIHON

SUSAN PARK

COPYRIGHT ACKNOWLEDGMENTS

"Facebook Sets Stage for IPO Next Year," by Anupreeta Das, Geoffrey A. Fowler, and Liz Rappaport, reprinted from *The Wall Street Journal*, January 6, 2011, by permission of Dow Jones & Company, Inc.

"US and European Securities Officials Vow Cooperation," by Floyd Norris, reprinted by permission from *The New York Times*, June 5, 2004.

"Insider Trading: Why We Can't Help Ourselves," by Jason Zweig, reprinted from *The Wall Street Journal*, April 2, 2011, by permission of Dow Jones & Company, Inc.

"Wizard of ID," by Brant Parker and Johnny Hart, by permission of Brant Parker and Johnny Hart/Creators Syndicate.

"Steel Shortage Creating New Trials for Texas Contractors, Suppliers," by Joseph Dirik, reprinted from *Texas Construction*, May 2004, McGraw-Hill Construction.

"Insurer's Bad Faith Billing Practices Support Tort Liability, Justices Told," reprinted by permission of *Metropolitan News Enterprise*, June 3, 2004.

"We had a great Christmas—I just mailed 43 warranty cards," reproduced from *The Wall Street Journal*, Febuary 14, 1995, by permission of Cartoon Features Syndicate.

"Limited 90-day warranty—for Hewlett-Packard Personal Computer Mainframes, and Peripherals," by Hewlett-Packard Company (1995).

"Some Online Music Producers Allow Sharing," reprinted by permission of *Associated Press*, July 28, 2004.

"UAL Still Aloft One Year in Chapter 11," by David Kesmodel, reprinted from *Rocky Mountain News*, December 6, 2003.

"Better Off Deadbeat: Craig Cunningham Has a Simple Solution for Getting Bill Collectors Off His Back. He Sues Them," by Kimberly Thorpe, reprinted from *The Dallas Observer News*, January 21, 2010.

"Blockbuster and the Pushback by Unsecured Creditors," by Stephen J. Lubben, reprinted by permission from *The New York Times,* March 11, 2011.

"McDonald's Obesity Suit Tossed," by Jonathan Wald, reprinted by permission from *CNNMoney.com*, February 17, 2003.

"AT&T, Verizon Face Off in TV Ads," reprinted from *msnbc.com*, by permission of The Associated Press.

"HP Board of Directors in April 2011," by Hewlett-Packard Company.

"Hudson County, NJ, Trial Judge Declares Gestational Surrogacy Contract Involving Gay Male Couple Unenforceable," by Arthur S. Leonard.

"Lawyerese Goes Galactic as Contracts Try to Master the Universe," by James R. Hagerty, reprinted from *The Wall Street Journal*, October 29, 2009, by permission of Dow Jones & Company, Inc.

"Jury Rules in Favor of Bratz Dolls," by Gillian Flaccus, reprinted by permission of *Associated Press*, April 22, 2011.

"NLRB Actions Raise Political Controversies," reprinted from *www.nlrb.gov*.

ABOUT THE AUTHORS

MICHAEL B. BIXBY is a Professor of Legal Studies in Business at Boise State University, where in 2006 he was honored as "Outstanding Teacher of the Year" at Boise State University. Before joining the Boise State faculty, Professor Bixby practiced law for 11 years. Since then, in addition to writing and presenting more than 65 papers at academic conferences, he has authored 15 articles concerning various legal issues in business for *San Diego International Law Journal, The Oregon Law Review, Willamette Law Review, American Business Law Journal, Idaho Law Review*, and the *Journal of Public Policy and Marketing*. Professor Bixby is the past president of the Pacific Northwest Academy of Legal Studies in Business, and a member of the Governing Council of the Idaho Bar Association Business and Corporate Law Section and the State Bar of Michigan. Bixby's undergraduate and law degrees are from the University of Michigan.

CARYN L. BECK-DUDLEY is the Dean of the College of Business at Florida State University. She was formerly Dean at Utah State University. As a professor she taught business law, employment law and business ethics in the Department of Management and Human Resources at Utah State University, where she also served as Department Head. She has also taught at the University of Michigan School of Business and the Terry College of Business at the University of Georgia. Dean Beck-Dudley has given presentations and written on a variety of legal and ethical topics, including natural law jurisprudence, business organizations, employment law and insider trading. She is a past president of the National Academy of Legal Studies in Business.

PATRICK J. CIHON is an Associate Professor of Law and Public Policy at Syracuse University School of Management. He was with the Ontario Ministry of Labour before joining the Syracuse faculty. He received a BA from Pennsylvania State University, an LL.B. from Osgoode Hall Law School of York University in Toronto, and an LL.M. from Yale Law School. He was voted Outstanding Faculty Member by the Syracuse University Association of Graduate Business Students and by the Syracuse Chapter of Beta Gamma Sigma undergraduate honor society. His research interests are in the areas of employment law, labor relations, and employment discrimination law, and he has authored or co-authored a number of books and articles in those fields.

SUSAN PARK is a licensed attorney and has been a faculty member at Boise State University since 1997. She currently teaches Legal Environment of Business, Government & Society. She is the recipient of four Outstanding Teaching Awards and was named the 2006 Alpha Kappa Psi Professor of the Year. Her research interests include topics related to employment law, such as privacy, discrimination, and social media, as well as copyright and speech issues, and teaching pedagogy. She has published in the area of social networking and employment law, and is also the author of the study guide companion to this textbook. She is the 2011–12 President-Elect of the Pacific Northwest Academy of Legal Studies in Business, and is a member of the national Academy of Legal Studies in Business. Before joining the Boise State faculty, Professor Park practiced law in Boise, Idaho and clerked for the Chief Justice of the Idaho Supreme Court. She earned her J.D., *summa cum laude,* from the University of Idaho College of Law and a BA in English from the University of Colorado at Boulder.

BRIEF CONTENTS

CONTENTS

PREFACE

Welcome to the study of legal issues in business. Just as business students must learn the basic principles of accounting, marketing, economics, finance, management, statistics, and information systems, so must they master the fundamental knowledge of critical legal and regulatory issues affecting business. As a result of the authors' combined 70 years of experience in teaching and practicing law, *The Legal Environment of Business* presents both practical and academic insight into the primary legal issues that businesspeople need to understand. We believe this text is one that students will read, understand, remember, enjoy, and most importantly, use in their present or future careers.

The *Legal Environment of Business* will not create lawyers, nor should it. Rather, it will help prepare businesspeople to recognize and avoid legal problems. If each student can avoid one legal problem in the future because of something learned here, this book will have made a worthwhile contribution to the student and to society. Our text will help students address legal problems when they arise, know when to call a lawyer and what to discuss, and know how to participate in the solutions to legal problems.

This new edition of the textbook incorporates several features not present in previous editions. Every chapter has been updated, to include the latest cases and other legal developments. In addition to the edited cases, each chapter now contains one longer case report, written totally "in the language of the court." Although the case has been shortened, the entire excerpt contains only the actual words of the court—none have been re-written.

Since the last edition of the book, the business world has been rocked by the sub-prime mortgage crisis and the world-wide financial meltdown of 2008–2011. Many have called the economic situation in the United States the "Great Recession," only slightly less dire than the Great Depression of the late 1920s and 1930s. Also the economy is still recovering from the accounting and financial scandals involving Enron, WorldCom and many large corporations of 2001–2004. Congress enacted the Sarbanes-Oxley Act in response, which added significant new duties and responsibilities to corporate officers and directors. All of these topics are fully explained and explored in this new edition. Many new boxes contain thought-provoking Ethical and Social Issues, and several others highlight important "International Aspects." The chapter dealing with "International Legal Issues in Business" has been substantially updated to reflect contemporary legal concerns in the global marketplace. Also the chapter "Cyberlaw and Intellectual Property" has been edited and updated to examine in detail the rapidly changing world of intellectual property, including legal issues involving the internet, world wide web, as well as such important current topical issues as downloading of music, use and abuse of social media, piracy of intellectual property, data privacy and more. Many of the cases in the previous edition have been replaced by newer cases, while retaining the classic cases necessary to fully understand the legal principles. Also approximately $\frac{1}{2}$ of the chapter ending questions are new.

TARGET AUDIENCE

This textbook is primarily designed for business students and business men and women who have not taken a law course in recent years. Every aspect of this book has been developed to maximize the "real world" nature of the various legal principles presented. We have tried to take complex material and break it down into bite-sized chunks that can be easily digested. We are attempting to speak directly to the non-law student in a common-sense, practical manner. The coverage of important legal topics, while current and comprehensive, is clear and readable.

CONTENT COVERAGE AND ORGANIZATION

The Legal Environment of Business contains comprehensive coverage of private and public law topics. When possible, we have grouped subjects together in a manner that emulates their evolution as legal principles. For example, our discussion of contracts is followed by the discussion of laws of sales, warranties, and product liability, which represent modern adaptations and expansions of the earlier theories.

This practical approach allows us to demonstrate how and why topics in the law change over time. By doing this we better prepare students to become businesspeople who, by virtue of their understanding of legal evolution, are better prepared to anticipate and plan for future changes.

Among the key topics we address are the following:

- Judicial and alternative forms of dispute resolution (Chapters 2 and 3)
- The Constitution and business (Chapter 4), including recent court decisions that address the "Federalism" cases
- International Law (Chapter 6), including detailed discussions of the European Union, NAFTA, and the WTO
- Business ethics and corporate social responsibility. (Chapter 7)
- Agency and business organizations (Chapters 8 and 9), including treatment of limited liability partnerships and limited liability companies
- Business torts and business crimes (Chapter 11)
- Contracts (Chapter 12)
- Real, personal, property (Chapter 14)
- Cyberlaw and Intellectual Property (Chapter 16)

- Environmental law (Chapter 15)
- Employment law (Chapters 20, 21, 22 and 23), including extensive coverage of contemporary legal issues in employment, equal opportunity in employment, and labor management law and regulations.

STUDENT-ORIENTED FEATURES

The Legal Environment of Business contains the following features to help students better understand and retain the material:

Learning Objectives and Outlines begin each chapter and help students organize the chapter content and highlight key content.

Key Terms are defined in the margin as they are introduced in the text and are included in the glossary at the end of the book.

Social/Ethical Issues boxes appear throughout the chapters and raise questions concerning current social and ethical controversies in the legal environment of business. These questions require critical thinking and analysis and are good vehicles for class discussion.

"A Memo from the Legal Department" boxes offer practical advice concerning legal subjects covered in the chapters.

"In Consultation" features appear periodically throughout the text and offer students an opportunity to put themselves in business situations dealing with realistic legal issues.

Readings and Cartoons from *The Wall Street Journal, U. S. News and World Report*, and other sources help to explain the law and demonstrate its relevance to the business world.

Cases were chosen and edited for each chapter (three and four per chapter) on the basis of relevance, interest, and when possible currency. While some cases are very recent, others represent classic cases. Most cases are one or two pages long and have a Facts/Decision/Case Questions format. The case questions raise several legal and ethical questions designed to assist students in analyzing the case. The language used in most of the court cases (while often the court's own) is edited to ensure it includes only words and phrases explained elsewhere in the chapter. As mentioned earlier, one case in each chapter is longer, and contains only the language of the court (not re-written by the authors), in order for students to have the opportunity to look more closely and in depth at the legal reasoning process.

End-of-Chapter Problems raise both legal and ethical issues. Questions often arise from actual court cases, and in those cases the citations are included for optional reference.

Practical Exercises offer a unique learning tool. One of these exercises appears at the end of each chapter and allows students to either independently or collaboratively analyze a hypothetical situation based on the material presented in the chapter. Use in our own classrooms has shown that these "learning-by-doing" exercises can significantly aid students' retention and understanding of the material.

AACSB STANDARDS

The American Assembly of Collegiate Schools of Business (AACSB) standards state that the undergraduate and MBA curricula of all business colleges should reflect the particular mission that each school has developed. The AACSB states that, "Schools should assume great flexibility in fashioning curricula to meet their missions and to fit with the specific circumstances of particular programs." While no specific list of courses is required, the AACSB does state that:

> Topics typically found in general management degree programs include:
> - Global, environmental, political, economic, legal, and regulatory context for business.
> - Individual ethical behavior and community responsibilities in oganizations and society.
> - Management responsiveness to ethnic, cultural, and gender diversity.

How does *The Legal Environment of Business* deal with these issues? First, we thoroughly cover ethical and global issues in law. Chapter 6, *International Legal Issues in Business,* discusses the intricacies of doing business beyond the borders of the United States. Chapter 7 examines ethical theories and their relevance to corporate decision making as well as the increasingly important topic of corporate social responsibility. This chapter is practical in nature and shows students ways to analyze and apply ethical principles to real business situations. This chapter also examines the concept of corporate social responsibility, which many companies now see as a key strategic goal. Furthermore, both international and ethical issues are addressed in boxed features and cases within the chapters, as well as through exercises at the end of each chapter.

Second, political, social, legal and regulatory, environmental, and technological issues are all discussed within relevant chapters. The use of an "evolution of legal topics" organization uniquely demonstrates the interrelationship of law and these other societal influences. One chapter is devoted solely to Cyberlaw and Intellectual Property Issues.

Finally, our emphasis on the practical application of law to the "real world" along with a complete examination of equal opportunity laws and international issues will help in sensitizing students to issues involving diversity within organizations, and differences in customs, cultures, and laws around the world. In addition to coverage within the text narrative, issues involving diversity and international issues are presented in readings, feature boxes, and cases.

ACKNOWLEDGMENTS

The authors would like to express their appreciation to their families, first and foremost, without whose support, this text would not have been possible. We would also like to thank Kathleen Abraham, Rachel Rossi, and the staff at Pearson Custom Publishing for their excellent assistance in producing this new edition. We would also like to thank all the professors who have reviewed this and the previous editions of our textbook.

Michael Bixby
Caryn Beck-Dudley
Patrick Cihon
Susan Park

PART 1:
THE GLOBAL, LEGAL, REGULATORY, POLITICAL, AND SOCIAL ENVIRONMENT OF BUSINESS

CHAPTER 1

INTRODUCTION TO LAW

LEARNING OBJECTIVES

After you have read this chapter, you should be able to:

1. Understand the concept of jurisprudence, identify several different theories, and describe how they affect our understanding of the law.

2. Classify several different types of "law."

3. Discuss the sources of law and distinguish between statutory, administrative and common law.

4. Read and understand legal cases and answer questions about them.

CHAPTER OUTLINE

I. Why Study Legal Issues?

II. What Is Law?

III. Classifications of Law

IV. Sources of Law

At the end of every chapter in this book there will be a "Practical Exercise." These brief scenarios will ask you to discuss and use, in a "real life" situation, some of the terms and concepts explained in the chapter. The exercise at the end of this chapter involves a person who has had a difficult day, with many unfortunate happenings. You are asked to analyze some of the legal issues he may face.

1

WHY STUDY LEGAL ISSUES?

This book examines the most important legal issues affecting business—in other words, the "legal environment" in which American business firms operate. Laws, legal theories, and court decisions affect nearly every aspect of business. Suppose, for example, that Dan, Allison, and Matt decide to start a firm to develop business software during their third year in business school. One of their first decisions will be to select the form of business entity they want to use—a partnership, corporation, LLC, or some other form of entity. They then must secure space for their business by purchase or lease, obtain financing through a loan, from investors, or from their own funds, and acquire the equipment they need. Of course, they will then have to actually perform the service (design and develop software) that is the function of their business. The three owners may likely decide to hire employees to perform some services as well. Each of these business functions involves numerous legal issues.

As the business grows, many additional legal issues will arise. These include negligence and product liability concerns, occupational safety and environmental requirements, labor and employment laws, interactions with creditors and debtors, collection of debts and bankruptcy, and consumer protection and antitrust laws, to name just a few. This is the "legal environment" in which businesses operate.

Laws and legal issues are, and likely will always be, a major factor in business decisions. Many of us might wish that there were fewer laws, cases, and administrative regulations influencing business. But since the court system is the arena in which many traditional American doctrines and values have always been enforced, a high volume of cases and a steady outgrowth of new laws and regulations seem inevitable. American society has long valued individual rights, promoted individual responsibility, and steadfastly guaranteed such concepts as "due process of law," "enforcement of promises," and "equal justice for all." The continued development and fine-tuning of these theories through the legal system is unlikely to change in the future.

In addition, the United States Constitution sets forth the basic structure of our government, carefully carving out roles for the executive, legislative, and judicial branches through the concept of the "separation of powers." Generally, the legislative branch enacts laws, the executive branch enforces them, and the judicial branch interprets the laws when there are disputes. This basic structure has remained consistent for more than 200 years, and although we continue to improve its efficiency and to streamline some procedures, the general rules outlined in this book will almost certainly continue for many years to come.

All businesspeople at some point must deal with the three branches of government at both the federal and state levels. They will almost surely interact with an administrative agency, and perhaps with a local legislator concerning some actual or proposed legislation. And, sooner or later, most businesses must deal with the court system. Throughout the operation of the business, the owner should carefully monitor laws and regulations in order to *avoid* legal problems before they arise. As a businessperson you can throw up your hands and say, "There are too many laws, I just can't stand it!" Or instead you can attempt to gain a better understanding of how legal rules affects business and use this knowledge in a positive and proactive way for the benefit of the individual and the business. It is our hope that after you finish your study of these materials, you will adopt the latter approach.

This book will introduce you to the most critical legal issues and concepts that affect business, so that as businessmen and women you will be better able to:

1. Avoid legal problems in the first place.

2. Know when to engage the services of a lawyer if a legal problem does arise.

3. Converse intelligently with an attorney and actively participate in legal decisions that need to be made.

The material examined in this course will also assist you in dealing with important legal issues in other relationships—those between managers and employees within the business; those with other private business firms including suppliers, creditors, and competitors; interactions with government officials; and legal issues which arise in your personal life. Much like the introductory courses in accounting, statistics, economics, finance, marketing, and management, this **course will not make you an expert** in the subject but will provide basic information and education regarding fundamental elements of the topic. With this knowledge, you will **be able to make better business decisions** today and in the future.

During the past ten years, tremendous media attention has been devoted to reporting on the financial crisis of 2008–2010, the government bailout of prominent Wall Street financial and insurance firms, and the ensuing worldwide financial meltdown. It has been shown that many banks and financial institutions issued mortgage loans using improper and fraudulent procedures, followed by the bundling together and "securitization" of such mortgages, thereby helping to cause the financial crisis of 2008–2011, which affected business and the economy world-wide. A few years earlier, certain companies falsified accounting and financial records, and otherwise violated ethical and professional standards of corporate governance and record-keeping. Starting with Enron, and later with respect to WorldCom, Tyco, HealthSouth Corp. and others, the public has been shocked to find out that some of our largest companies and key executives ignored basic ethical principles followed by most of us—such as telling the truth. In the wake of the world-wide economic recession and the corporate scandals, thousands of employees have lost their jobs, and/or their pension and retirement funds, and millions of shareholders have seen the value of their investments fall dramatically. The cartoon below is what we hope <u>not</u> to do in this book.

"Your first responsibility is to prevent people from understanding the law."

From *The Wall Street Journal*, January 25, 1995. Reprinted with permission of Cartoon Features Syndicate.

It has become clear as more and more disclosures are made, that greed and arrogance blinded several top officials of large companies to their moral, ethical and legal duties to their employees, shareholders and the public. Congress responded to the financial meltdown and corporate misdeeds by enacting sweeping new laws, the Sarbanes-Oxley Act in 2002, the Dodd-Frank Wall Street Reform and Consumer Protection Act, which, among other things, eliminates loopholes that allow risky and abusive practices to go on unnoticed and unregulated, forces large financial firms to set aside more capital to cover losses, and forms a new agency to crack down on deceptive mortgages and other financial products. We will examine the significant new duties and liabilities which these laws have placed upon the officers, directors, accountants, attorneys and other officials of public companies, in several different chapters. As we go forward in this textbook, we will also analyze the ethical, as well as legal, responsibilities of business men and women. It is absolutely clear now—if it was ever in doubt—that ethical failings can and do have a tremendous effect on managers and businesses.

In order to offer broad coverage of the most important regulations and legal issues that influence business operations, this book has been divided into 23 chapters, grouped according to subject matter. This course covers many subjects in fairly quick succession. Each topic could certainly be explored more deeply—in fact, each chapter of this book comprises at least one full semester course in law school. Our goal with this textbook, however, is to provide the business student with significant, fundamental information regarding a wide range of important concepts comprising the "legal environment of business" while leaving the detail work to future classes.

Throughout this textbook, our emphasis is on **practical knowledge.** We attempt to explain important legal concepts in a clear, understandable fashion. We want our students to be able to use this information tomorrow and the next day, in their personal and business dealings. This textbook follows what we call an "organic" approach. In other words, we attempt to organize the topics in a way that emulates their evolution as legal principles. The early part of the book looks at the origins and sources of law, discusses the structure of legal systems in the United States and around the world, examines the importance of the U.S. Constitution in establishing American law, observes the role of and law established by administrative agencies, and studies how ethics and moral reasoning create and shape law. In subsequent chapters we will scrutinize a variety of specific legal topics, such as contracts, torts, environmental law, labor and employment law, and many others. But first, an analysis of this thing we call "law" is in order. What is it? Why do we have law? What exactly comprises "the law"?

WHAT IS LAW?

Every society has established rules to govern the conduct of its members. Sometimes these rules are informally developed and passed along verbally by elders to younger persons. In the United States our system of rules is quite formally established, based upon our Constitution, federal and state statutes, administrative regulations, and several hundred years of court decisions that form the basis of much of our law (known as *common law*). Of course, our families, religious training, organizations, and peers also contribute to our beliefs concerning the proper boundaries of conduct. However, American society leans heavily on law to establish and enforce the formal standards of acceptable conduct and to set a minimum level of behavior expected of its members.

JURISPRUDENCE

What is "**jurisprudence?**" *Black's Law Dictionary* defines jurisprudence as the "science of the law" or the "philosophy of the law." It has often been described as "the study of the philosophies of law." Jurisprudence helps lawyers and judges make decisions in complicated cases.

jurisprudence: The philosophy of the law.

There are several forms of competing jurisprudence in the United States. Occasionally the disagreements among jurisprudences are played out in the popular press, usually when a proposed Supreme Court Justice is testifying in Senate confirmation hearings. Most of the time, however, jurisprudence is not explicitly discussed but must be defined by court opinions and lawyers' arguments.

By most standards, the predominant jurisprudence in the United States is **positivism** or *legal formalism*. Positivism is organized around the concepts of power, position, and hierarchy, and it refers to "laws properly enacted by the appropriate authority in that nation," whether that be a king or a legislature. Positivism is rule and authority based. Moreover, positivism seeks to use something similar to the scientific method to resolve disputes. Therefore, a positivist will look to the exact wording of a statute or past court cases for the authority to determine what the law should be. Citation to previous legal authority is very important for positivist jurisprudence. Citing several cases decided by higher courts or citing the actual language of a statute is common when a judge or lawyer wants to make a positivist argument. Competing jurisprudences are *legal realism, law and economics, feminist jurisprudence, natural law, sociological jurisprudence, historical jurisprudence,* and *critical legal studies movement*.

positivism: The theory that law is the set of rules adopted by the lawful authority which governs that nation.

Legal realists argue that positivism merely reflects the biases of judges rather than any scientific method. They assert that any set of facts can be manipulated in such a way that a particular judge will not be bound by past authority. The great jurist Oliver Wendell Holmes was a proponent of legal realism. He argued that what was important was an understanding of the background and philosophy of judges, since in the final analysis the law reflected the bias of the judge who uttered it. He stated, "The prophecies of what the courts will do in fact, and nothing more pretentious, are what I mean by the law."

legal realists: Those who hold that law is simply the body of rules enforced by the courts and society.

Many proponents of the **law and economics** movement have been associated with the University of Chicago Law School, and it is therefore often referred to as the "Chicago school". This area of jurisprudence focuses on applying free enterprise economics to most areas of the law. One of the first categories in which this occurred was with antitrust law. Antitrust generally has to do with preventing anticompetitive agreements and various other practices by business firms that decrease competition.[1] Almost all antitrust cases are now resolved by looking at an economic analysis of the consequences of proceeding with a particular action. Law and economics proponents have also made inroads in property law. The "greatest good" in law and economics jurisprudence is efficiency, and proponents argue that where moral concepts and efficiency conflict, the case should be resolved in favor of efficiency.

law and economics movement: The theory that law is the set of rules which express the choices of people in a free market system.

Natural law was the predominant jurisprudence in the United States until it lost its hold to positivism around the turn of the 20th century. It is based on the belief that law should reflect morality. Traditional natural law

natural law: The theory that law is the basic system of moral principles developed through the power of reasoning, analysis, religion, and philosophy.

[1] This topic will be discussed more fully in Chapter 17.

proponents grounded their theories in the belief that a supreme being establishes the law and positivist laws must be judged against this "higher authority." Philosophers such as Aristotle, Plato, Socrates, and Thomas Aquinas have also contributed to the development of natural law theory through analysis of laws and actions as "right or wrong." Many current natural law proponents do not base their system of jurisprudence on a supreme being but on what is in the "common good" without regard to its efficiency. They rely heavily on morality and ethics to make these determinations.

feminist jurisprudence: The theory that law has been dominated by males and needs to adjust to more accurately include female views and experiences.

Feminist jurisprudence criticizes positivism as perpetuating male domination. It focuses on power, knowledge, morality, and self. For hundreds of years, women did not enjoy full legal rights, such as the right to vote, even in the United States. (It may come as a surprise to students to learn that the 19th Amendment to the Constitution, which finally guaranteed American women the right to vote, was only enacted in 1920) The Feminist theory maintains that the experiences of men are not necessarily the experiences of women, and therefore when the law views what is "reasonable," it may only be asking what is reasonable to men. For most of the past 200 years, the vast majority of American judges and legislators have been male. Feminist jurisprudence questions which underlying assumptions or descriptions of experience are made by the law. How does this affect women both practically and ideologically? In one sexual harassment case, *Ellison v. Brady,* 924 F.2d 872 (9th Cir. 1991), the court held "[w]e adopt the perspective of a reasonable woman primarily because we believe that a gender-blind reasonable person standard tends to be male-biased and tends to systematically ignore the experiences of women." This language is very much reflective of feminist jurisprudence.

sociological jurisprudence: The theory that law is the product of social forces and social movements involving different segments of the population.

Sociological jurisprudence seeks to understand the law from the basis of its impact on society and how the influence and needs of different groups affect the development of law. **Historical jurisprudence** draws upon historical events to explain the law and its place. Both types, however, use social science research to help courts make legal decisions. For example, in *Brown v. Board of Education,* the famous 1954 school desegregation case, the U.S. Supreme Court, when striking down racially segregated schools, relied heavily upon sociological research, which suggested that segregation promoted a feeling of "second-class" status among black children.

historical jurisprudence: The theory that law is produced and shaped by important historical facts and developments.

SOME IMPORTANT THEORIES OF JURISPRUDENCE

Positivism—Law is the set of rules adopted by the lawful authority that governs the country or jurisdiction.

Legal Realism—The law is merely that body of rules enforced by the courts and by society.

Law and Economics—Law is the set of rules that expresses the choices of people in a free market system.

Natural Law—Law is the basic system of moral principles developed through the power of reasoning and analysis, which may or may not coincide with the laws established by the government.

Sociological—Law is the product of social forces and social movements involving different segments of the population.

Historical—Law is produced and shaped by important historical factors and developments, such as the industrial revolution and the civil rights movement.
Feminism—Law has been largely made and shaped by males, and needs to adjust to more accurately include female views and experiences.
Critical Legal Studies—Law has been created and shaped by those who have political and economic power, and works to reinforce the current power structure.

The **Critical Legal Studies (CLS)** Movement may not refer to itself as a jurisprudence at all. It does, however, see positivism as responsible for maintaining those who are currently in power. Proponents of CLS rely heavily on disciplines such as sociology and anthropology for their studies of power, position, and wealth. Its advocates are highly critical of the status quo and seek to expose legal doctrines reinforcing the current power structure. Many of the leading CLS proponents over the past 20 years have been professors at major American law schools who have raised serious issues and generated much discussion concerning traditional forms of legal education in recent years.

When reading this text and the cases that are excerpted, pay particular attention to the type of jurisprudence that is actually being used. For example, an opinion may well appear to reflect positivism when in fact it is making a natural law argument.

> **Critical Legal Studies Movement:** The theory that laws, particularly those which represent a positivist view, are rules established by those who are currently in power.

CLASSIFICATIONS OF LAW

While jurisprudence takes an in-depth look at the underlying basis and philosophy of law, it is also possible to classify types of law and legal issues according to different aspects of their development and function.

CIVIL AND CRIMINAL LAW

The law can usually be classified as either criminal law or civil law. **Criminal law** concerns violations of the rules established by society that set the minimum acceptable standards for behavior. Criminal laws are all statutory—the elements of a crime must be precisely stated by the legislature—and the law must provide a penalty, or a range of penalties, for violations. Since criminal laws are meant to enforce society's standards, violation of such a law results in punishment of the criminal—generally by time in jail and/or a fine—but does not necessarily include compensation to the victim. In a legal sense, the victim is just one of the witnesses called at the trial to testify that the defendant broke a federal, state, or local criminal law.

Criminal cases are always brought by a governmental prosecutor, not an individual, and the decision whether to bring a case, to drop the case, or to settle the case (called "plea bargaining" in criminal matters) is made by the prosecutor. The case heading is titled something like *The People of the State of California v. Jones* or *The People of the United States of America v. Smith* to indicate that the prosecutor is actually representing the state, rather than any one individual. The chief county prosecutor—often called the

> **criminal law:** Violation of a specific statute, enacted by the legislature to protect society, which carries penalties such as a fine or imprisonment.

civil law: The body of law that allows one person or firm to sue a second person or firm for physical or economic damages caused by the second party.

plaintiff: The person who files a civil lawsuit against another.

defendant: The person against whom a civil or criminal lawsuit is brought.

District Attorney or County Prosecutor—is normally elected and therefore must be responsive to the general population. Although the best prosecutors always stay in touch with the "victims" of the crime, it should be clearly understood that the criminal law process is designed to enforce society's rules against a lawbreaker, and not primarily to compensate the victim of crime.

Civil cases, on the other hand, are brought by one individual or firm against another. Civil cases can be concerned with contracts, torts (any wrongful action that causes injury to another), labor or employment issues, product defects and liability, divorce and family matters, and many other topics. Since they are not criminal actions, no one will go to jail regardless of the result of the case. Society is not represented by a prosecutor in civil cases. Instead, the two parties both present their positions, citing previous cases and relevant statutes to support their legal arguments. Cases are brought by "**plaintiffs,**" not prosecutors. If the plaintiff wins the civil case, the result may be an award of money damages, or an injunction or some other court order directing the **defendant** to stop doing something.

SOCIAL/ETHICAL ISSUES

Do you think that a county or state prosecutor should owe a higher duty to the victim of crime? What if there are many victims? What if it is a so-called "victimless" crime? (Prostitution, gambling, and speeding are examples.) In several states, there are active victims' rights movements, which aim to increase the crime victim's role in criminal cases and to make it mandatory that victims receive adequate compensation as part of the criminal sentence. As will be discussed in the next section, civil cases can be filed by an injured person to gain compensation from one who has caused the injury. Should criminal actions get more involved in the compensation issue? What might be the positive and negative effects of such a development?

beyond all reasonable doubt: The standard of proof in a criminal case, which requires the prosecutor to prove each essential element to the point where no member of the jury has any reasonable doubt as to its existence.

In the American judicial system, there is usually no connection or relation between a civil case and a criminal case—a legal action is one type or the other. However, one event sometimes results in *both* civil and criminal cases. For example, suppose that Tom drinks four beers and then drives his car negligently in a way that strikes Kendra's car. Following an investigation by the police, or a complaint by Kendra, the prosecutor may decide to charge Tom with the crime of Driving Under the Influence of Alcohol (DUI). In order to prevail in a criminal case, the prosecutor must convince the judge or jury that all the elements of the crime (as specified in the statute) have been met "**beyond all reasonable doubt.**" If any member of the jury has any reasonable doubt about whether Tom committed any element of the crime, Tom should be found *"not guilty"*. If Tom is convicted at a criminal trial, he may be sent to jail or ordered to pay a fine to the state or both. Sometimes the defendant is ordered, as part of the sentence, to pay some sort of costs and/or expenses (called *"restitution"*) to the victim, but this amount is usually far less than full compensation. The focus of criminal cases is to punish the defendant for breaking society's rules, not to compensate the victim.

If Kendra wants to receive complete compensation for her injuries, medical expenses, lost wages, or damage to her car, she must file a separate civil case against Tom. This case will not be legally connected with the criminal case at all. It will be heard at a different time, in a different court, and the decision will hinge on principles of negligence law (which have developed through common law) and not on whether a criminal statute of the state was broken. To win this case, Kendra will merely need to prove to the court or jury that Tom was negligent by a **"preponderance of the evidence"**—that is, by more than 50 percent of the evidence. This is a much lower standard than is necessary in a criminal case. If Kendra wins the case, Tom will be ordered to pay her money damages, as determined by the judge or jury. He will not be sent to jail, however, no matter how the civil case results.

> **preponderance of the evidence:** Evidence which is of greater weight or more convincing than the evidence which is offered in opposition to it; the standard of proof in a civil case.

INTERNATIONAL PERSPECTIVE

In much of the world, there is not such a clear separation between civil and criminal cases, and in fact one court case may resolve both whether a crime has been committed, and whether the defendant must pay damages to the victim. In the United States, however, the two types of cases will be tried separately.

SUBSTANTIVE AND PROCEDURAL LAW

Another way to categorize law is to divide it into *substantive* and *procedural* parts. We will be studying primarily **substantive law** in this textbook—the key legal principles that govern a variety of different subject areas affecting business. For example, this book will examine the three main legal theories by which a manufacturer can be held liable for defective products and the essential features of each. The text will also analyze the legal requirements of five or six important environmental laws, the major labor laws, the main provisions of the laws regulating the sale of securities, and so on. These are substantive legal issues.

> **substantive law:** The legal principles that define one's rights in specific subject areas.

In actual cases, however, **procedural law** issues play a prominent part. For example, it is often critical whether a case is filed in the proper court and whether the complaint and answer were filed within the appropriate time period. When the case goes to trial, the result may be affected by the calling of witnesses, rulings of the judge concerning direct and cross-examination, and the objections of the attorneys to certain questions and introduction of evidence. Procedural legal issues such as these are definitely involved in most cases, but they are more properly dealt with by the lawyers in the case. So although Chapter 3 outlines the typical court system and provides some general information about legal procedures, this textbook is written for business students, and our primary focus is on substantive legal issues of importance to business, rather than procedural "rules of the game."

> **procedural law:** The legal rules governing court processes and procedures.

ACTIONS "AT LAW" AND "IN EQUITY"

When a business becomes involved in a legal dispute with another business firm or an individual, most often the result sought by the plaintiff is an award of money damages as compensation for the loss suffered due to the actions of

actions at law: Civil cases in which the plaintiff seeks money damages.

the other. In fact, the early English Courts of Law—on which the American court system is based—only had the power to award money damages as a remedy. The legal actions filed were called **actions at law.**

However, in some cases the aggrieved party wanted or needed something other than money. For example, suppose that Harold enters into a contract with June in which her business agrees to purchase a 12,000-acre commercial site. However, June later decides she does not want to go through with the agreement. It may be that what Harold most wants is not money damages for breach of the contract, but that June be ordered to fulfill the terms of the contract to which she agreed and transfer the property. When the early English Law Courts could not provide such relief, the king began to refer such matters to his important advisor, the chancellor. Thus, another court system was created in order to provide what was called "equity" or "equitable relief." For hundreds of years the Courts of Law and the Chancery courts remained separate in England.

actions in equity: Civil cases in which the plaintiff seeks to have the court order the defendant to do something or to not do something.

Today in the United States the powers of **equity**—to order a defendant to take or not to take some action—are a regular feature of most U.S. courts. Most U.S. courts have both law and equity powers. In the preceding example, Harold may file a court action against June, and if he proves the existence of a valid contract, he can ask the court for a decree of **"Specific Performance,"** a type of equitable order directing the defendant to fulfill the terms of a contract.

specific performance: A court order which requires a party to perform a contract as agreed.

Probably the most commonly sought equitable order is the **"injunction,"** which is an order issued by a court directing a party **not** to do something. It is sought by a plaintiff who wants the court to prevent another party from taking some particular action before it occurs. For example, if the local highway department plans to cut down a row of trees in front of your house, you might want the court to order the department not to cut down the trees, rather than awarding you damages after they are taken out. Other equitable orders include the **temporary restraining order** (a short-term injunction, used to preserve the status quo until the court can schedule a full hearing) and **rescission** (a court order canceling a contract).

injunction: A court order directing the defendant NOT to do something.

rescission: A court order cancelling a contract.

To receive an equitable order, however, the plaintiff must specifically request such relief when the case is filed, or soon thereafter. In general, courts prefer to award money damages, and equitable relief will only be given if the court is convinced that money damages are "inadequate" to fully compensate the plaintiff. Also, equity courts were designed to de-emphasize legal technicalities and promote fairness. The early English courts gave the chancellor considerable flexibility to fashion the relief necessary in order to produce a fair result. In furtherance of this goal, various doctrines previously developed by the English Chancery courts still govern use of the equitable powers in American courts today. For example, a plaintiff seeking equity must "come into equity with clean hands," and "he who desires equity must do equity." In other words, the person seeking the equitable order (injunction, for example) must not use the court to take advantage of someone or to perpetuate a wrong. There are no juries in cases seeking equitable orders, and thus all decisions are made by the judge.

SOURCES OF LAW

THE U.S. CONSTITUTION

In the United States, our hierarchy of legal authority begins with the U.S. Constitution. This amazing document, written in the summer of 1787, established the powers and duties of our federal government, divided the government into three branches, and also set out, in general terms, the roles of the federal and state governments. Four years later, largely in response to concerns raised during the debate for ratification of the Constitution, the first 10 amendments, known as the Bill of Rights, were added. These amendments set forth certain basic individual rights with which the government may not interfere (freedom of speech, freedom of press, freedom of religion, the right to be protected against unreasonable searches and seizures, and others). We will explore all of these issues in more depth in Chapter 4. At this early point in the book, our analysis will only examine how the Constitution, federal statutes, common law, administrative regulations, and court interpretations of all these legal sources produce "law."

HOW TO READ AND UNDERSTAND LEGAL CASES

In each chapter of this book there will be several actual legal cases interspersed with the discussion of legal principles in the text. The cases offer the opportunity to see how the legal principles explained in the text have been used and interpreted by courts in actual situations. For example, when we study contract law, there will be cases in the chapter in which courts have ruled on a contract dispute between two parties. All of the cases you will read have been edited by the authors of this book to make them shorter and easier to understand than the original decision rendered by the court—it is not unusual for court decisions to be 25 to 50 pages long. The cases in this book will contain the most important portions of the language used by the court, but a considerable amount has been deleted to make the cases easier for the student to read. In some of the court cases, the authors have summarized portions of the court's language, since the case included words and concepts not explained in this textbook. In other cases, (at least one per chapter) the authors have retained the "language of the court" and although the text of the case has been shortened, none of the court's language used has been re-written.

Each case included in this textbook has been carefully selected by the authors to help explain a particular point of law addressed in the chapter. (We did not throw darts at the law library to select the cases.) Each excerpted case dealing with a particular legal issue follows directly after the text discussion of that issue. The purpose of including cases is to give students a better understanding of how the precise legal principle being examined has been applied in a real situation.

Each case in this textbook will begin with a statement of **"Facts."** This section provides the history of the actions of each party that led up to the lawsuit. For example, the facts might include the analysis and determination of such issues as whether Arthur dumped hazardous waste onto Brittney's lawn or whether Melissa rode her bicycle without any brakes when she ran into Thomas. These are factual issues, which will play an important role in the outcome after being combined with appropriate legal principles. Almost all of the cases in this book are decisions of appellate courts, which are reviewing the result of a trial held in a lower court. The "Facts" section will conclude with a description of what type of lawsuit was filed and the decision of the lower court.

The second section of each excerpted case is called the **"Decision."** This portion describes the legal issues that were considered by the *appellate* court, the arguments of the parties, the decision made by the court, and most importantly, the **"rationale"** for the decision—in other words, the legal principles upon which it was based. As you read the cases, it is very important to ascertain and analyze the reasons for the decision. In this way, you will see how legal principles apply to actual cases, so that you can be better prepared to predict the results of future legal controversies—some of which may involve you!

Finally, every case will end with a few questions, called **"Case Questions,"** to help you focus on and analyze key issues in the case, and to provide a starting point for class discussion.

case citation: The heading of a court case, which contains the name of the parties, the volume and page of the set of books where it can be found, the court, and year of the decision.

The heading of each case (called the **citation**) gives the name of the parties, an abbreviation indicating the court which is making the decision reported here, and the year in which the decision was made. Each citation also contains the volume number of the set of books containing the case and the page of the volume on which the case begins. For example, the citation *Smith v. Jones, 5 Ill. 234 (2005)* indicates that the case Smith v. Jones was decided by the Illinois Supreme Court in 2005 and can be found in Volume 5 of the Illinois Reports on page 234.

Often there are several **plaintiffs** (those who are bringing the case) and **defendants** (those against whom the case is brought), but the citation only uses the names of the first plaintiff and first defendant. The citation "U.S." means the case was decided by the U.S. Supreme Court. A citation with "F.2d" or "F.3d" in place of a state name means that the case was decided by a federal (F) appeals court. Because there are so many federal decisions, the book publishers have started a second (F.2d) series, and a third (F.3d) series of books.

STATUTORY LAW AND STATUTORY INTERPRETATION

One of the primary functions of the court system is to interpret the meaning of laws enacted by Congress and the states. The Constitution, our most fundamental source of law, sets forth in elegant and timeless language the relationship between U.S. citizens and their government, and establishes certain fundamental rights of individuals. The phrases used are general, yet they establish clear boundaries on government intrusion into individual rights. For example, part of the Fifth Amendment contains this language:

> *No person shall be deprived of life, liberty, or property, without due process of law; nor shall private property be taken for public use, without just compensation.*

Although this language spells out certain basic rights of U.S. citizens, it obviously is too broad to indicate the precise result in any one case. For example, what exactly is "due process of law" or what is "public use"? Therefore, Congress and the state legislatures have enacted thousands of laws to specify in greater detail the legal rights and obligations of the citizens and the government.

Laws that are enacted by a legislature are called **statutes.** On the federal level, enacting laws is the primary function of Congress, and of course each state has its own legislature. Congress meets all year, and the state legislatures meet regularly (some people think they meet much too regularly!) and, after hearing ideas and requests from their constituents, legislators introduce bills that are then studied and debated and may be enacted into law. These statutes may later be amended or may be repealed completely by the legislative body that enacted them. Cities and towns also have the power to enact statutory laws governing their jurisdictions, and these laws are usually called **ordinances.**

Although Congress or a state legislature may have thought it had plainly stated what was intended when a statute was enacted, very often the exact meaning of a law will not be perfectly clear when it is applied to a difficult factual situation. Therefore, one of the main roles courts perform is statutory **interpretation.**

While statutes are more definite and less broad than Constitutional provisions, the exact meaning of such laws is often not clear until the courts have ruled on cases raising particular issues. One of the most important roles played by courts is to interpret how a statute passed by Congress or a state legislature should apply to a specific fact situation. The following case illustrates how a federal appellate court interpreted a federal law dealing with one of the many important "cyberlaw" issues which have arisen in recent years.

> **statute:** A law enacted by the U.S. Congress or by a state legislature.

> **ordinance:** A law enacted by a city or town council.

> **statutory interpretation:** The power of courts to interpret laws enacted by legislatures.

ZERAN V. AMERICA ONLINE

129 F. 3d 327 (4th Cir. 1997)

FACTS

A short time after the bombing of the federal building in Oklahoma City in April 1995, a message was posted anonymously on an America Online (AOL) bulletin board advertising "Naughty Oklahoma T-Shirts." The posting advertised the sale of shirts featuring offensive and tasteless slogans celebrating the tragic bomb blast, which killed 168 persons. The ad stated that interested buyers should call "Ken" at a phone number in Seattle. The phone number given was the actual number of Mr. Kenneth Zeran, who had nothing to do with the posting and most definitely had no such T-shirts for sale. It was apparently a nasty "prank" by someone who did not like Mr. Zeran.

During the following few weeks, Mr. Zeran received hundreds of phone calls and voice mail messages, almost all expressing extreme anger and outrage over his alleged actions.

These calls caused him a great deal of distress. Mr. Zeran notified AOL by telephone, letters, and e-mail about the bogus posting and harassment and asked AOL to immediately remove it and issue a public retraction. Although AOL did remove the original posting (the parties dispute how soon this occurred), soon thereafter, the unknown prankster posted another message advertising new T-shirts with more offensive slogans related to the Oklahoma City bombing, again giving Mr. Zeran's number and also stating, "Please call back if busy."

For the next few days, Mr. Zeran's phone rang almost every two minutes with irate messages. Meanwhile the perpetrator of the hoax continued to post new messages on AOL, advertising several new distasteful items (fictitious) such as bumper stickers and key chains celebrating the Oklahoma City massacre and again giving Mr. Zeran's phone number. An Oklahoma City radio station read the messages on the air and encouraged listeners to call Mr. Zeran to express their outrage. During the ensuing days, Zeran was deluged with even more calls, including several death threats. Finally an Oklahoma City newspaper ran an article exposing the T-shirt ads as a hoax, and the radio station issued an apology. The number of calls to Mr. Zeran's home then decreased to about 15 per day.

Kenneth Zeran, a 51-year-old entrepreneur who worked out of his home, was the victim of a terrible trick. "Someone pulled a sick joke," he later stated. "It was incredible. One minute I and the entire nation were grieving over the bombing, and the next thing you know, I was associated with it." In 1996, Mr. Zeran sued AOL, alleging that the Internet service provider (ISP) had been negligent in its slowness in removing the series of harmful postings after he had repeatedly notified AOL that the messages were a hoax. The federal district court later dismissed the suit, holding that a federal law, the Communications Decency Act (CDA) barred the suit. Mr. Zeran then appealed to the Fourth Circuit Court of Appeals.

DECISION

In considering Mr. Zeran's argument that the ISP should be held liable for negligence, the Court of Appeals had to consider the meaning and interpretation of Section 230 of the CDA. This section states, "No provider or user of an interactive computer service shall be treated as the publisher or speaker of any information provided by another information content provider."

Mr. Zeran argued that this section of the CDA was not intended to provide blanket immunity to ISPs but to apply only when an ISP acts in good faith to block material that causes harm. "Unless you can hold them [ISPs] accountable through civil liability . . . there is

no way to induce them to carry out their responsibilities in blocking defamatory messages," said Zeran's attorney. [Defamation is a legal theory—to be discussed fully in Chapter 11—that imposes liability on someone who makes or repeats false and damaging statements publicly about another person. The two primary types of defamation are libel (written) and slander (oral).]

The plaintiff further argued that the immunity granted by Congress in Section 230 was only intended to apply to "publishers" and that AOL was a cyberspace "distributor," similar to a vendor or bookseller that deals in magazines and books created by others. Although news distributors cannot generally be held liable for defamatory statements in the materials they sell, a distributor can be held liable when it has notice that it is distributing statements that are false and harmful, and does not take appropriate action, as Mr. Zeran had alleged in this case.

The Fourth Circuit Court of Appeals, however, rejected Mr. Zeran's arguments. Chief Judge Wilkinson wrote that the "plain language" of Section 230 created "a federal immunity to any cause of action that would make service providers liable for information originating with a third party user of the service." The court stated that Section 230 of the CDA precluded courts from entertaining claims that would place a computer service provider in a publisher's role. "Thus, lawsuits seeking to hold a service provider liable for its exercise of a publisher's traditional editorial functions—such as deciding whether to publish, withdraw, postpone or alter content—are barred," wrote Judge Wilkinson. The court noted:

The purpose of this statutory immunity is not difficult to discern. Congress recognized the threat that tort-based lawsuits pose to freedom of speech in the new and burgeoning internet medium. The imposition of tort liability on service providers for the communications of others represented, for Congress, simply another form of intrusive government regulation of speech.

Section 230 was enacted, in part, to maintain the robust nature of internet communication and, accordingly, to keep government interference in the medium to a minimum.

The appellate court also rejected Zeran's argument that AOL should be treated as a "distributor" rather than a publisher, finding that such liability was a "subset" of publisher liability. Once AOL received notice from Zeran about the false nature of the posting, it was put into the role of a publisher since AOL then had to decide whether to publish, edit, or withdraw the posted notices. AOL had argued in the case that it had 10 million subscribers creating millions of messages on its bulletin boards every day. Unlike a newspaper, it would be impossible for a service provider such as AOL to check all of its third-party ads and postings for accuracy. Moreover, AOL stated in its court briefs that if the company were subject to liability under Mr. Zeran's theory, it might be forced to get out of the bulletin board business altogether.

For the reasons stated, the Fourth Circuit Court of Appeals affirmed the dismissal of Mr. Zeran's case. He asked the U.S. Supreme Court to accept the case, but his request was denied.

CASE QUESTIONS

1. What federal statute was involved here?
2. Why did Congress provide immunity from lawsuits to ISPs?
3. What reasons did Mr. Zeran give to support his argument that AOL should be treated as a "distributor"?
4. Why did the appellate court rule that AOL should be treated as a "publisher"?
5. Do you agree with the decision's main point—that an ISP should not be responsible for postings made on its service?

Another important part of the Constitution, the **Commerce Clause** (Art. I, Sect. 8, cl. 3) provides that "[t]he Congress shall have Power . . . to regulate Commerce . . . among the several States." Although this statement contains an express grant of a specific power to the federal government, it has long been understood to have a "negative aspect" or "dormant clause" as well. Although states have the power to enact binding laws within their jurisdictions in order to promote the health and welfare of their citizens (as discussed more fully in Chapter 4), numerous cases have held that, by implication, the Commerce Clause prohibits the states from enacting laws that "discriminate against" or "unduly burden" the interstate flow of articles of commerce. The courts deciding these cases have reasoned that the power to regulate such commerce resides only with the federal government. Thus, courts often have to decide if a statute passed by a state legislature is unconstitutional because it restricts interstate commerce. In doing so, the court must interpret the meaning and effect of the state statute.

In 1994 the U.S. Supreme Court had to decide whether an Oregon state statute regarding the fees charged for disposal of solid waste conflicted with the provisions of the Commerce Clause. It is instructive to see how the Supreme Court considered and interpreted the United States Constitution, the Oregon statute, and previous court decisions in rendering its opinion in the next case.

OREGON WASTE SYSTEMS, INC. V. STATE OF OREGON

511 U.S. 93, 114 S. Ct. 1345 (1994)

FACTS

The state of Oregon enacted a comprehensive statute regulating the disposal of solid wastes within its borders, which law is administered by the Oregon Department of Environmental Quality. To assist in funding this agency, Oregon imposes a wide range of fees on landfill operators. In 1989 the Oregon Legislature passed a law adding a "surcharge" on "every person who disposes of solid waste generated out-of-state in an Oregon disposal site." The surcharge was set at $2.25 per ton by the administrative agency, which meant that waste from the state of Washington was charged $3.10 per ton by the landfill operator, while that from Oregon was charged only $0.85 per ton.

The law was challenged by an Oregon landfill operator (Oregon Waste Systems, Inc.) and a company that transports waste by barge from one county in Washington to the Oregon landfill owned by Waste Systems. (The Columbia River forms much of the boundary between Oregon and Washington). They argued that the law and the fee impermissibly discriminated against interstate commerce in violation of the Commerce Clause. The Oregon Court of Appeals and the Oregon Supreme Court upheld the law on the basis that the surcharge was justified as a "compensatory cost." The case was then appealed to the U.S. Supreme Court.

DECISION

In an opinion written by Justice Clarence Thomas, the Supreme Court reversed the decision of the Oregon Supreme Court and held that the state imposition of a larger tax on solid waste from out of Oregon was a violation of the "negative aspect" of the Commerce Clause of the U.S. Constitution.

The Supreme Court looked back to the writing of the Constitution and the purposes of the Interstate Commerce Clause, which gave the power to regulate such commerce to the federal government. "The Framers granted Congress plenary authority over interstate commerce in the conviction that in order to succeed, the new Union would have to avoid the tendencies toward economic Balkanization[2] that had plagued relations among the Colonies and later among the States under the Articles of Confederation." The Court quoted language from a 1949 Supreme Court case, which stated that "This principle that our economic unit is the Nation, which alone has the gamut of powers necessary to control the economy . . . has as its corollary that the states are not separable economic units." Justice Thomas even cited Federalist Paper No. 42, written by James Madison, at one point in the opinion.

By a 7-2 majority, the Supreme Court found that the Oregon law imposing the surcharge only on out-of-state solid waste was clearly discriminatory against interstate commerce. "As we use the term here," Justice Thomas stated, "discrimination . . . simply means differential treatment of in-state and out-of-state economic interests that benefits the former and burdens the latter." The court noted that it was "obvious" that the fee was discriminatory, since waste from other states was charged approximately three times more than in-state waste.

The Court stated that the only possible justification for such a discriminatory fee would be that it "advances a legitimate local purpose that cannot be adequately served by reasonable nondiscriminatory alternatives." Although such justifications are sometimes allowed, they will be looked at with the "strictest scrutiny," said the court. Extra fees might have been justified if, for example, (1) the out-of-state waste actually caused higher costs for Oregon than in-state waste or (2) if there were particular health and safety concerns posed by out-of-

---

[2] To "Balkanize" means to break up into small hostile states, as the Balkan states did during the Balkan wars (1912–13).

state waste. Such arguments were not made in this case, however.

Instead, the state of Oregon argued that the additional fees for out-of-state solid waste were necessary as a "compensatory tax" so that shippers of such waste paid their "fair share" of the costs imposed on Oregon. Several previous cases decided by the Supreme Court recognized that interstate commerce should "pay its own way" and pay its "just share" of state tax burdens. However, other cases stated that this principle did not allow states to exact "more than a just share" from interstate commerce. In a 1981 case the Supreme Court had allowed a tax on interstate commerce that was roughly approximate to a "substantially similar" tax on intrastate commerce in order to equalize the situation. However, there was no such tax in the Oregon case to justify the "compensatory tax." Thus, the tax was illegal and invalid under the Commerce Clause.

DISSENTING OPINION

Chief Justice Rehnquist, joined by Justice Blackmun (an unusual alliance of the most conservative and most liberal justices), dissented from the majority opinion.[3]

In this case, the dissenters argued that the Supreme Court opinion ignored the fact that landfill space is evaporating as solid waste accumulates. Justice Rehnquist pointed out

---

[3] In the Supreme Court and all U.S. appellate courts, decisions do not need to be unanimous but are made by majority vote. Often those judges or justices on the losing side decide to set out their reasons for not joining the court opinion in what is called a "dissenting opinion."

that Americans had generated nearly 196 million tons of municipal solid waste in 1990, which was expected to increase to 222 million tons by the year 2000. Finding environmentally safe disposal sites was a serious problem, which was getting worse. Rehnquist termed the majority opinion "myopic" in that it did not recognize that the state of Oregon had suffered a loss and had incurred additional costs when it accepted other states' waste. He argued that the purposes of the Commerce Clause were not met by striking down the additional tax here, since the states were not competing to get waste into their states. Rehnquist asserted that states that did not have adequate landfill space would use this decision to avoid the significant costs of developing, regulating, and cleaning up such sites, while their companies disposed of waste in neighboring states.

CASE QUESTIONS

1. What are the main purposes of the Interstate Commerce Clause in the U.S. Constitution?
2. How did the Supreme Court integrate the language of the Constitution and its purpose, the Oregon law and its purpose, previous case precedents, and logic to reach its conclusion?
3. What are "interstate" commerce and "intrastate" commerce? Why do you think the framers of the Constitution gave Congress (the federal government) the power to regulate interstate commerce?
4. What is the main argument of the dissenting justices? Do you agree? Why do justices write dissenting opinions?

ADMINISTRATIVE RULES AND REGULATIONS

Just as statutes are more specifically drawn than constitutions, so are administrative regulations more precise than statutes. For example, when Congress enacts a law concerning regulation of pollution in rivers and lakes, the statute will probably provide that the discharge of hazardous substances into waterways is illegal. But the statute will not normally state exactly what types of substances will violate the law, nor the exact amounts and over what period of time. Instead, Congress will typically put a clause right in the statute, delegating the power to make detailed regulations covering these matters to an administrative agency. In this case, the agency will likely be the Environmental Protection Agency (EPA), which has a large staff with expertise in various environmental and pollution matters. (The role and functions of administrative agencies will be fully explored in Chapter 5). The EPA will then develop precise rules and regulations concerning the specific actions that are to be prohibited, and those standards, once they are properly issued, will have the force of law.[4]

COMMON LAW

Despite the hundreds of statutes passed every year by the Congress and state legislatures and the thousands already "on the books," there are major areas of "the law" in the United States that are not controlled by statutes. For historical reasons, based upon our English legal heritage, a large portion of the legal principles that govern business and personal affairs has developed not from statutes, but from court decisions in individual cases. This body of law is called the **common law.**

common law:
Legal theories that arise from precedents established by court decisions, not legislative statutes.

The name *common* came about when English judges in the 13th century began to move from one court to another and to look to the rulings of other jurisdictions in making their decisions, so that the law became more "common" (similar) across the land. When the Founding Fathers of the United States established our legal system, they followed the English model that permits much of the law to develop solely through court decisions. In fact, not only did we borrow the system of common law development, but most of the major substantive principles that regulate the law of contracts, torts, and agency law today (all of which will be examined in detail later in this book) are primarily based upon English common law doctrines, as modified by more than 200 years of U.S. court decisions.

How does common law actually work? For example, look at contract law, clearly a very important part of the "legal environment" for any business. The principles of law governing contracts have essentially been created by hundreds of court decisions involving individuals where there was a dispute as to whether a valid contract had been created and, if so, whether it had been properly fulfilled. As the courts ruled on these cases, they wrote about what legal elements were necessary to constitute a valid contract offer or acceptance, or what factors were essential to make a contract binding, or what defenses to a contract action were available to the defendant. The court then applied the rules to the facts of the case at hand and rendered a decision.

Later, other courts facing contract questions used the principles developed in the earlier cases. Each case in this chain expounds upon and modifies the

---

[4] A detailed discussion of environmental laws is contained in Chapter 15 of this book, and a closer look at the powers and functions of administrative agencies is contained in Chapter 5.

theories further and thus clarifies the law. **Precedents** established in earlier cases are very important in deciding later cases within the same jurisdiction. The principle of **stare decisis,** "let the decision stand," means that decisions establishing legal principles made by higher courts in one jurisdiction must be followed and respected in subsequent decisions by lower courts within that jurisdiction. For example, if the Supreme Court of New Jersey rules in a contract case that the law of the state requires that both parties to a contract must promise to do something they were not previously required to do in order for the contract to be enforceable, this principle must be followed in subsequent cases by all lower courts in New Jersey. The entire body of U.S. contract, tort, and agency law, and other subjects as well, has developed in this way through common law evolution.

precedents: Judicial decisions used to establish standards for subsequent similar cases.

stare decisis: The legal principle that decisions of a higher court in previous cases establishing legal theories must be followed by lower courts in that jurisdiction.

SUMMARY

The law is a dynamic subject, consisting of many components from many origins, which greatly affects business and personal actions. The law includes constitutions, statutes, administrative regulations, and common law principles. It is shaped by moral, ethical, historical, sociological, and other forces. It represents society's rules of conduct and provides both tools of control for the powerful and rays of hope and the creation of rights for the less fortunate. Although many legal principles remain constant, others change with the times, as the result of new statutes passed by the legislature, or new common law interpretations by courts.

The system of law in the United States has been heavily influenced by the English model, from which we borrowed both structure and legal principles. These precepts have been augmented by the addition of American theories, beginning with the U.S. Constitution, and followed by hundreds of federal, state, and local statutes, administrative regulations, and court interpretations over more than 200 years of this country's history. In addition much of our law comes from the common law, which is based solely on decisions of courts, as each decision adds to principles established in earlier cases.

CHAPTER QUESTIONS

1. More than 20 years before the tragic explosion of the BP "Deepwater Horizon" oil facility off the Louisiana coast, which caused a huge oil spill, the oil tanker *Exxon Valdez* ran aground in Prince William Sound, Alaska. A leak in the hull then allowed the discharge of nearly 11 million gallons of crude oil into the pristine bay. Some 14,000 fishing professionals, Alaskan natives, and other businesses sued Exxon, claiming they had lost significant amounts of money and their way of life was changed due to Exxon's negligence. They sought several billion dollars in damages. The U.S. Environmental Protection Agency (EPA) and the state of Alaska also filed criminal charges against Exxon claiming violations of federal and state

laws. The ship captain, Joseph Hazelwood, was also charged with operating a ship while under the influence of alcohol. What will be the remedy if the fishing professionals and other businesses win their lawsuit? Is it civil or criminal? What might be the result of the EPA action? The action against Mr. Hazelwood? Are these civil or criminal cases?

2. In the Exxon case, the judge made a ruling prior to the trial that while those in the fishing industry could sue for damages for their lost fish harvests, they could not sue for the diminished value of their charter permits, or boats. The judge cited a 67-year-old maritime law and an even older court ruling by legendary Justice Oliver Wendell Holmes for support. In that case Justice Holmes had limited the claims of a man who sued because a ship he had chartered (hired or rented) was damaged while in dry dock. Holmes ruled that the claimant could not sue for economic losses while the boat was laid up because the ship was not his. What type of jurisprudence is at work here? Apply the theories discussed in the chapter to these facts. What would Justice Holmes be likely to say if he were alive today?

3. Several states have laws on their books prohibiting actions like swearing in public and tying horses up in downtown areas. Utah has a law prohibiting whale hunting and Alabama has a law making it illegal to wrestle a bear. These laws are almost never enforced, yet continue to exist as "the law." What type of jurisprudence is involved here? Why do the states not repeal these unenforced laws?

4. In recent years, Congress and the state legislatures have been unable or unwilling to pass legislation dealing with such serious public policy issues as the health costs of smoking, gun violence, and health maintenance organization (HMO) abuses. However, a number of major lawsuits have been filed that have resulted in large money judgments or settlements and significant changes in the policies of large businesses and governmental agencies. What are the "pros" and "cons" of this type of lawmaking? Why do Americans turn to the courts to resolve some of the nation's social problems? Is this likely to continue?

5. What type of jurisprudence is behind the establishment of laws against murder, rape, and theft? How about the Civil Rights Act of 1964 (which prohibits discrimination on the basis of race, color, sex, religion or national origin) ? the Clean Air Act and Clean Water Act? the federal laws prohibiting discrimination in employment on the basis of age and disability?

6. In 2003, the U.S. Supreme Court decided a case dealing with race discrimination. The Civil Rights Act of 1964 (discussed fully in Chapter 21) prohibits discrimination against a person based on race, color, sex, religion or national origin. When an employee files suit claiming such discrimination, the employer generally denies the claim and argues that the employee was demoted or not hired for some other reason, not related to discrimination. Previous Supreme Court cases had held that the employee could win so-called "mixed motive" cases, where both legitimate and non-legitimate rea-

sons motivated the employer's decision. In the 2003 case the Supreme Court decided that the plaintiff did not have to produce "direct evidence" of such discrimination in order to win such a case, but that "circumstantial" evidence might be enough. What function was the Supreme Court performing in deciding this case? What type of jurisprudence might be involved here? *Desert Palace, Inc. v. Costa, U.S. (2003)*

7. If the environmental action group Greenpeace files a lawsuit attempting to prevent an oil company from building an oil rig in the ocean off the California coast, what sort of remedy will it probably seek? Is this an action "at law" or "in equity"? What standard of proof will the plaintiffs need to establish in order to convince the judge to grant their request?

8. What is the purpose of the Commerce Clause of the U.S. Constitution? In what situations may a state regulate interstate commerce? Do any situations exist in which a state can impose an additional charge on out-of-state companies (as Oregon was not allowed to do in the *Oregon Waste Systems* case)?

9. What is the citation of the *Zeran* case? What court made the decision? What exactly does each number mean? What is the citation of the *Oregon Waste Systems* case? What do these numbers mean?

10. What is the difference between legal principles that are developed through common law and those that are established through statutes? Which type provides more stability and predictability? More flexibility? Why?

PRACTICAL EXERCISE

[*Note to students*: Each chapter will end with a practical exercise designed to enhance learning through the preparation of a written product, based on the material in the chapter. We hope that the exercises are interesting for you to do as well.]

Josh is riding his bicycle from his apartment to campus one day when a car following him on the street honks at him several times. Josh responds with an obscene gesture with his hand. Finally the car passes him, then immediately "cuts him off" by driving around him, bumping him as it passes, causing Josh to fall into the curb, which injures his arm. He gets up, rides fast and catches the car at the next corner. Josh and the driver of the car, Joyce, engage in an argument, which ends with Josh shoving Joyce against her car, breaking a finger.

Josh proceeds on to his job at a video store. After working for 5 hours, he is called into the manager's office, and is told that he is going to be terminated because the manager saw him take 3 DVDs out of the store last week without signing for them, and also giving 4 store videos to a friend without payment, and bypassing the store security system. Josh vigorously denies the allegations, but the manager says that he is terminated. Josh calls the manager a liar and a dishonest person and leaves the store.

Josh has obviously had a tough day. Please list the various legal problems he may have, and discuss whether each one is civil or criminal, and if it is statutory or common law. If Josh files a lawsuit over the problem, will he seek money damages or equity?

FURTHER INFORMATION

www.findlaw.com
A large Web site devoted to law and legal issues, including for example, a searchable database of all U.S. Supreme Court decisions issued since 1893.

www.law.cornell.edu
Another very large legal site with much legal information and links to many other sites.

www.supremecourtus.gov
The Supreme Court's own site includes opinions beginning with the 1999 term, as well as schedules, orders, rules of the Supreme Court, and transcripts of oral arguments before the Court since 2000.

CHAPTER 2

THE LEGAL SYSTEM IN THE UNITED STATES

After you have read this chapter, you should be able to:

1. Describe the organization of the state and federal court systems in the United States.

2. Discuss the factors involved in determining which court should hear and decide a case, including jurisdiction, venue, standing, and preemption.

3. List situations requiring professional legal advice.

4. Outline the issues to consider when choosing a lawyer, including the size and type of the firm, attorney's fees, and to understand various attorney/client ethical issues.

CHAPTER OUTLINE

At the end of Chapter 1, the "Practical Exercise" looked at some legal issues raised by Josh's bad day. What type of lawyer could help Josh? What sort of fee arrangement should he make with a lawyer? In what court might he file a case?

INTRODUCTION

The United States has been called "a nation of laws" by some, and "a nation overrun with lawyers" by others. Both statements contain elements of truth. We do have a large number of lawyers in this country—Americans have always placed great emphasis upon laws and courts as a way of resolving disputes, and as a means of protecting individual citizens from overreaching government officials. Our system of government, starting with the Constitution, has stressed concepts like "due process" and "equal protection." These principles guarantee each citizen the right to a fair hearing before an unbiased tribunal if that person believes that he or she is being treated unjustly. Equally important is the role law has played in this country in facilitating and regulating business and commercial practices.

In the past 30 years there has been a large increase in the number of students attending and graduating from law schools. The number of lawyers in the United States has therefore increased dramatically—to more than 1 million today. Our "free market" system allows people to choose whatever occupation they want, and it is apparent that many Americans want to practice law as a profession. Many of our most popular books, television shows, and movies deal with lawyers, justice, and the court system. Clearly, law and the legal system are major factors in our culture.

Americans, more so than people of many other cultures, tend to believe that when someone suffers a loss due to the wrongful conduct of another person, there should be a remedy. We are unwilling to simply accept as our "fate" that a careless driver ran into our automobile causing us personal injuries and property damage. Similarly, a business firm that enters into a contract with another company to furnish a certain amount of steel materials for its manufacturing process has the right to, and does expect, full performance of the contract at the time and place agreed upon. These basic American social, political, and legal expectations are unlikely to change in the near future, and it is thus important for businesspeople to understand the organization and nature of our court system.

STATE COURT SYSTEMS

Each state (and the District of Columbia) has developed its own court system, independent of all other states. Each state, of course, also has its own governor and legislature. No one state can dictate to another what type of courts or laws it should have, nor what the functions of each should be. Therefore, although this book will make some general observations about state courts, you should study your own state's court system to ascertain how it differs from the model.

Every state has at least one level of courts generically called "trial courts." Cases are started and trials are held at this level. These are the courts in which witnesses testify to the various facts that are relevant to the case, attorneys "object" to certain types of questions or evidence that they believe to be irrelevant to that particular case, and the witnesses and parties must deal with rulings from the trial judge. This is the level of the court system where there is a jury, if either party has asked for one. The trial courts often carry proper names such as District Court, Circuit Court, County Court, or Superior Court. (Different names are used in different states.)

In addition, several other specialized trial courts exist to handle specific functions. Many states have Juvenile Courts, which deal with adolescent crime and family matters; Traffic Courts, which deal with a wide variety of motor vehicle infractions; Probate Courts, which deal mainly with inheritance questions; and Small Claims Courts, which deal with disputes over a modest amount of money (and function much like the "People's Court" or "Judge Judy" seen on television). The jurisdiction of small claims courts typically is limited to cases involving less than $5,000—and the parties usually handle the cases themselves. In fact, many states do not permit lawyers to appear in small claims courts.

Each state also has at least one appellate court, which hears appeals from decisions of the trial courts. Most states have two levels of appellate courts—often called the Court of Appeals and the Supreme Court. These courts typically hear no trials and see no witnesses or evidence. The function of these courts is to review decisions made by the lower level trial courts. The appellate courts hear arguments from the parties (through their attorneys) regarding a case that has been decided in a trial court. One side, called the **appellant**, attempts to convince the appellate court that something was done incorrectly in the trial court, causing that party to lose the case or to receive an inadequate award. The other side, called the **appellee**, then seeks to persuade the court that the trial court did not make any errors, or if there were any that they were of minor importance. These arguments are made first in written documents, called "briefs" (although they are never very brief). Once each side has had the chance to respond to the other's written arguments, the court usually schedules an *oral argument* before a panel of appellate judges (usually three, five, or seven judges). The judges actively question the attorneys during the oral argument and then debate the matter among themselves and issue a written decision a few months later.

appellant: The party who appeals a case to a higher court, after a trial court decision.

appellee: The party who is defending the lower court decision in an appellate court.

The majority of states have intermediate courts of appeal, as pictured in Figure 2.1. The losing party in the trial court always has the right to have at least one appellate court review the trial court decision. Once the court of appeals has ruled on the case, the losing party may ask the state supreme court to hear a further appeal, but the supreme court generally has the option of declining to hear the case. In states where there is no intermediate appellate court, the state supreme court must hear an appeal from a trial court decision if one of the parties so requests.

THE FEDERAL COURT SYSTEM

The federal court system is a national system of courts divided into 94 districts, with one or more branches ("districts") in every state. Each federal district has several judges—some only 2 or 3, and some 20 or more, depending on population. Like the typical state court arrangement, there are trial courts (properly called "United States District Courts," or more commonly "federal district courts"), appellate courts (called "United States Courts of Appeals"), and the ultimate appellate court, the U.S. Supreme Court. Cases are normally

Figure 2.1
Chart of Typical State Court System

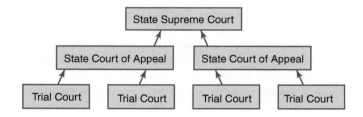

filed first in the U.S. District Courts, although there are some specialized federal trial courts (as there are in state court systems), like U.S. Bankruptcy Court, U.S. Claims Court, or U.S. Tax Court. All federal judges, at the District, Court of Appeals, and Supreme Court level, are appointed for life. Nominations are made by the President, and the U.S. Senate must "confirm" (approve) the appointment by a majority vote, after holding hearings on the prospective judge's qualifications. As of 2010, federal district judges were paid $174,000 per year, while Court of Appeals judges earned $184,500, and U.S. Supreme Court justices were paid $213,900, with the Chief Justice earning $223,500.

Following the decision of the federal district court, there is a right to appeal at least once to the appropriate U.S. Court of Appeals (there are 13 such courts). Eleven of these appellate courts hear appeals from federal District Courts within their designated geographic region. For example, the Court of Appeals for the 7th Circuit hears appeals from federal district court decisions in the states of Wisconsin, Illinois, and Indiana, and the 9th Circuit Court of Appeals hears appeals from federal district court decisions in nine western states and Guam. In addition, one of the Courts of Appeals is located in the District of Columbia, where it hears numerous appeals concerning actions taken by the federal government, as well as other cases. The final federal Court of Appeals (called the Court of Appeals for the Federal Circuit) hears

Figure 2.2
Diagram of Federal Circuit Court System

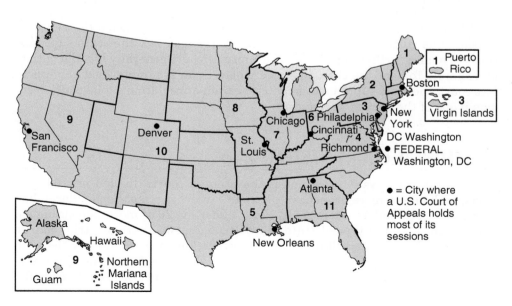

primarily cases involving intellectual property issues—that is, patent, trademark, and copyright matters, as well as some cases involving international trade law. Figure 2.2 illustrates the 13 federal judicial circuits.

In each U.S. Court of Appeals, there are many judges, and they usually hear appeals in panels of three. Following a decision of one of the federal Courts of Appeals, either party may request that the U.S. Supreme Court hear the case, which is usually done by filing a Petition for **Writ of Certiorari** with the Supreme Court. The nine justices of the U.S. Supreme Court decide which cases the court will hear (four of the justices must vote to accept a case), generally choosing cases of the most significance or cases where two of the Courts of Appeal have reached different conclusions as to the meaning of a particular law. In recent years, the U.S. Supreme Court has usually decided to hear only about 1 percent of the cases on which **certiorari** is requested, and the number of cases heard by the Supreme Court has been declining. The Court is now hearing less than half the number of cases it did 20 years ago. Recently, the Supreme Court has granted *certiorari* in only about 75–100 cases per year, out of some 7500 requests. So the odds of the Supreme Court accepting any one case for hearing is quite low.

certiorari: The request to the U.S. Supreme Court to hear a particular case.

There are a few categories where the Supreme Court must accept the case. For example, if a U.S. Court of Appeals has decided that a state statute is in violation of the Constitution or federal law, then there is a right to appeal. Also, a few cases per year may be appealed from the highest court of a state to the U.S. Supreme Court. This right arises if the state supreme court has found a federal statute invalid or has held a state statute unconstitutional or in violation of federal law. Otherwise, once a case is filed in a state court, it almost always stays in that state's appellate system, while cases filed in federal court stay in the federal appellate system. One party cannot appeal a state trial court decision to a federal court of appeals.

SOCIAL/POLITICAL CONSIDERATIONS

Since federal judges are appointed for life, and because the Supreme Court is hearing so few cases, the decisions of, and appointments to the thirteen federal Circuit Courts of Appeals have become increasingly important. The nomination and confirmation of federal appellate judges has become a major political issue in recent years. During the last two years of the Clinton administration, Senate Republicans blocked many of his suggested nominees for appellate positions, and later Democrats used filibuster tactics to block several of Pres. George W. Bush's nominees to federal appellate judgeships. During Pres. Bush's two terms in office, some 27 of his nominees to the Court of Appeals were challenged by Democrats, although 16 of them were later confirmed as judges. President Obama is finding even more serious resistance from Republicans to his nominations.

Although each judge makes his/her decisions based on the law as the judge sees it, clearly Republican and Democratic-appointed judges often have different interpretations. These views are not only evident in such major social issues as abortion rights or capital punishment, but many other topics such as rights of the disabled, access to corporate records and generally the role of the federal and state governments. That is why the power to name federal judges, given to the President with "consent" by the

Senate, is so important, and has become such a significant political struggle. The judicial appointment power allows the President to put people in positions where they can influence major policy and legal decisions for many years, long after the President leaves office.

What do you think about this process? Is this the way federal judges should be appointed? How far should the President and the Senate probe into a prospective judge's views on such controversial issues as abortion, or the rights of gays, or the legality of gun control laws? Should the questions relate more to the nominee's legal experience and qualifications?

JURISDICTION AND VENUE

jurisdiction: The power of a particular court to hear and decide a case.

The power of a court to hear and decide a case is called **jurisdiction.** In order for a court to properly hear a case it must have both **subject matter jurisdiction** and **personal jurisdiction.** Certain courts have been given power over specific subjects (e.g., juvenile courts or probate courts) and they may not hear cases that do not involve that particular subject. Also, trial courts are often given power to hear cases involving only a certain amount of money (e.g., less than $10,000) or particular types of criminal charges, with another court having jurisdiction of cases dealing with larger amounts of money or more serious criminal charges. Each court, therefore, only has the power to hear certain types of cases within its *"subject matter" jurisdiction.*

The power of the court over the parties is termed *"personal jurisdiction."* Generally courts located in one state (whether state or federal courts) have power only over those defendants whose home is in that state. So if John Jones, who lives in Michigan, wants to sue Susan Smith, who lives in Utah, John must normally file the lawsuit in either the state or federal court in Utah, so that the court hearing the case will have personal jurisdiction over the defendant.

long-arm statute: A law giving the courts of one state jurisdiction over a non-resident defendant.

However, most states have enacted laws, commonly called **long-arm statutes,** that allow a court to exercise personal jurisdiction over nonresident defendants where that person has had some sort of *"minimum contacts"* with the forum state. In the example above, the court system in the state of Michigan might have jurisdiction over Susan Smith, if she had been involved in a business operation in Michigan or had entered into contracts to supply goods and services in Michigan or had driven a car negligently in Michigan (even though she lived in Utah). In these cases, John can probably sue her in a Michigan court, using the *long-arm statute,* and she will have to come to Michigan, or at least hire a Michigan lawyer to appear in court and defend the case.

One interesting "cyberlaw" issue facing many courts today concerns the question of whether a company that maintains an interactive Web site is therefore subject to jurisdiction in any state where the site is accessed, even though it may have no office in that state. Courts have reached different results, depending on the level of activity with the state asserting jurisdiction and the "commercial nature" of such activity by the out-of-state firm. The following case involves whether a court in one state has jurisdiction over one of the nation's largest mail order merchants.

In the Language of the Court

GATOR. COM CORP. V. L.L. BEAN, INC.

341 F.3d 1072 (9th Cir. 2003)

Decision written by Judge Ferguson

FACTS

Defendant L.L.Bean is a Maine corporation with its principal place of business in that state. Its corporate offices, distribution facilities, and manufacturing facilities are all located in Maine. L.L. Bean sells clothing and outdoor equipment and has stores in 5 states. Bean sells over $1 billion worth of merchandise annually in all 50 states and 150 countries. A very large percentage of L.L. Bean's sales come from mail-order and internet business. The company ships more than 200 million catalogs each year and in 2000, its website sales accounted for over $200 million, or about 16% of its total sales. A New York Times story described L.L. Bean as "an e-commerce star that is out-performing all but a few companies in its categories on the web."

L.L. Bean is not authorized to do business in California, has no agent for service of process there, and is not required to pay taxes in California. However, L.L. Bean mails a substantial number of catalogs to California residents, maintains many "on-line" accounts for California consumers, and in 2000 alone, sold millions of dollars worth of products (6% of the total) in California. Like other consumers, California residents may view and purchase products on-line as well as interact with L.L. Bean customer service representatives "live" over the internet if they have questions or concerns. In addition, L.L. Bean maintains relationships with numerous California vendors from whom they purchase products.

Plaintiff Gator.com Corp. is a business which develops and distributes software to consumers who purchase goods or services over the Internet. Gator's principal place of business is in California. Gator has developed a program which stores computer user passwords to various websites and user personal information. Also when a user visits a website, the Gator program analyzes the URL associated with that webpage, and displays a "pop-up" window offering a coupon for a competitor. Gator users who visit L.L. Bean's website are offered coupons for Eddie Bauer, one of Bean's competitors, via a pop up window that at least partially obscures L.L. Bean's website.

In March 2001, L.L. Bean's corporate counsel mailed Gator a cease and desist letter requesting that Gator stop its pop-up windows from appearing when customers visited L.L. Bean's website. The lawyer stated that the pop-up windows "unlawfully appropriated the good will associated with L.L. Bean's famous trademark, created confusion about the source of the products . . . and suggested an affiliation between L.L. Bean and Eddie Bauer which does not in fact exist."

Gator refused to change its practices, and instead filed a lawsuit in federal district court in California seeking a declaratory judgment that the Gator program "does not infringe, or dilute, directly or contributorily, any trademark held by L. L. Bean and does not constitute unfair competition, a deceptive or unfair trade practice . . . or any other violation of law." L. L. Bean filed a motion to Dismiss the case, for lack of personal jurisdiction. In November 2001, the federal district judge granted L.L. Bean's motion finding that California did not have personal jurisdiction over L. L. Bean. After that ruling, Gator appealed to the Ninth Circuit Court of Appeals.

DECISION

Since there is no applicable federal statute governing personal jurisdiction we apply the law of the state in which the District Court sits. California permits the exercise of personal jurisdiction to the full extent permitted by due process. The assertion of personal jurisdiction satisfies due process so long as there are "minimum contacts" with the forum state such that "the maintenance of the suit does not offend traditional notions of fair play and substantial justice." *Int'l Shoe Co. v. Washington,* 326 U.S. 310, 66 S. Ct. 154 (1945).

We begin with an analysis of whether L. L. Bean's contacts with California were sufficient to confer general jurisdiction . . . Factors to be taken into consideration are whether the defendant makes sales, solicits or engages in business in the state, serves the state's markets, designates an agent for service of process, holds a license, or is incorporated there. We focus upon the "economic reality" of the defendants' activities, rather than a mechanical checklist." . . . Even if substantial, or continuous and systematic, contacts exist, the assertion of general jurisdiction must be reasonable [fair to the defendant].

In applying the "substantial" or "continuous and systematic" tests, courts have focused primarily on two areas. First, they look for some kind of deliberate "presence" in the forum state, including physical facilities, bank accounts, agents, registration, or incorporation . . . In addition, courts have looked at whether the company has engaged in active solicitation toward and participation in the state's markets, i.e., the economic reality of the defendant's activities in the state.

No Supreme Court cases and only a handful of Ninth Circuit cases have addressed the issue of when and whether general jurisdiction may be asserted over a company that does business on the internet. Given the high standard the Ninth Circuit has set, the presence of general jurisdiction is a close question. L.L. Bean has few of the factors traditionally associated with physical presence, such as an official agent or incorporation. Nevertheless, we find that there is general jurisdiction in light of L.L. Bean's extensive marketing and sales in California, its extensive contacts with California vendors, and the fact that, as alleged by Gator, its website is clearly and deliberately structured to operate as a sophisticated virtual store in California.

Bean meets the first set of factors of the "continuous and systematic contacts" test set out by previous cases. As alleged by Gator, L.L. Bean makes sales, solicits business in the state, and serves the state's markets . . . It targets its electronic advertising at California and maintains a highly interactive, as opposed to "passive" website from which very large numbers of California consumers regularly make purchases and interact with L.L. Bean sales representatives . . . Bean's contacts [with customer and vendors] are part of a consistent, ongoing and sophisticated sales effort that has included California for a number of years.

In short . . . the "consistent and substantial pattern of business relations" represented by these facts is sufficient to confer general jurisdiction. There is nothing "random, fortuitous, or attenuated" about subjecting L.L. Bean to the authority of the court as L. L. Bean has deliberately and purposefully availed itself, on a very large scale, of the benefits of doing business within the state.

Even if the only contacts L. L. Bean had with California were through its virtual store, a finding of general jurisdiction in the instant case would be consistent with the "sliding scale" test that ours and other circuits have applied to internet-based companies. This test requires the internet business contacts with the forum state be substantial or continuous and systematic. *Revell v. Lidov, 317 F3d 467 (5th Cir. 2002)* Recognizing that an online store can operate as the functional equivalent of a physical store, the test does not require an actual presence in the state . . . if the commercial activity is of a substantial enough nature to "approximate physical presence" *Bancroft & Masters, Inc. v. Augusta National, Inc., 223 F.3d 1082 (9th Cir. 2000).* The District of Columbia Circuit recently found general jurisdiction after finding that a defendant online brokerage firm was "through its website . . . doing business in the District of Columbia where customers could use the website to open accounts, transmit funds to those accounts electronically, use the accounts to buy and sell securities and enter into binding contracts with the defendant. *Gorman v. Ameritrade Holding Corp., 293 F.3d 506, 512–13 (D.C. Cir. 2002).*

It is increasingly clear that modern businesses no longer require an actual physical presence in a state in order to engage in commercial activity there. With the advent of "e-commerce," businesses may set up shop, so to speak, without ever actually setting foot in the state where they intend to sell their wares. Our conceptions of jurisdiction must be flexible enough to respond to the realities of the modern marketplace. "As technological progress . . . increases the flow of commerce between States, the need for jurisdiction over non-residents [undergoes] a similar increase." [citing an earlier Supreme Court case]

Businesses who structure their activities to take full advantage of the opportunities that virtual commerce offers can reasonably anticipate that these same activities will potentially subject them to suit in the locales that they have targeted. We find that the facts as alleged by Gator demonstrate that L.L. Bean has substantial or continuous and systematic contacts with California sufficient to support a finding of general jurisdiction. The decision of the District Court is reversed and the case is remanded for further proceedings.

CASE QUESTIONS

1. What was the central legal issue to be decided by the appellate court?
2. What did the court decide regarding this issue?
3. What were the key legal standards the court applied, in order to reach its decision?
4. What facts were most important to the court, in making its decision?
5. How did those facts fit in with the reasoning (rationale) of the court?
6. Do you agree with the decision? Is it fair to L.L. Bean?

Venue refers to the particular location of a specific court, within a given jurisdiction, which is the appropriate place to hear the case. In other words, once it has been decided that the trial court for the state of Texas has jurisdiction of a particular matter, the specific county where the case should be heard is a *venue* question. Each state has laws concerning venue, usually based on where the defendant lives or where the accident or crime occurred. Determining the appropriate venue is usually a practical matter involving such questions as: Where are the parties? Where is most of the evidence? Where is it possible to get an unbiased jury? It is not unusual for the defendant to be unhappy with the place the case has been filed by the plaintiff and to ask the court for a *change of venue*.

> **venue:** The particular court location within a specific court system, where a case should be heard.

FEDERAL JURISDICTION

The jurisdiction of the federal courts is limited. In order to file a case in federal district court, not only must there be personal jurisdiction over the defendant, but certain other requirements must be met as well. The two primary bases of federal jurisdiction are **federal question jurisdiction** and **diversity jurisdiction.** Unless the plaintiff (the party who has filed the case) can show that one of these tests is met, the federal courts will refuse to hear the case, although there are a few other laws that specifically grant federal jurisdiction.

Federal question jurisdiction exists if the plaintiff's case involves a claim "arising under" any federal law or the U.S. Constitution. For example, if Angela is claiming that her rights under the federal Truth-in-Lending Act were violated, she can file the case in federal district court. (She may also file the case

> **federal question jurisdiction:** Federal jurisdiction based on the fact that the case involves an issue of federal law.

in an appropriate state court.) Determining which one of the hundreds of federal courts around the United States is the appropriate one for her case is a venue question.

Diversity jurisdiction exists because as far back as the writing of the Constitution, lawmakers were concerned that there was the potential for bias if out-of-state plaintiffs were always required to sue defendants in the local state courts near their home. Local judges, who typically stand for election every few years, and local juries might tend to favor a local individual or prominent local business which is defending a lawsuit brought by a person or business from another state.

diversity jurisdiction: Federal jurisdiction based on the fact that the parties live in different states, and the case involves $75,000 or more.

Therefore, federal "diversity jurisdiction" allows a person to file suit against a defendant in the appropriate federal district court, rather than the state court, when the two parties are residents of different states or countries. In order to take advantage of this provision, however, the lawsuit must involve at least $75,000. There also must be complete diversity—that means that none of the parties on opposite sides of the case can be residents of the same state or foreign nation. Many lawsuits involve several plaintiffs and several defendants, and for "diversity" to exist, none of the plaintiffs and defendants can be residents of the same state or foreign nation, at the time the case is filed.

Federal judges are appointed for life, and thus do not face any re-elections. Therefore, theoretically at least, federal judges are less subject to local community pressures than state trial court judges. Also, federal court juries are typically drawn from a wider area of the state than local state court juries, which are typically composed of residents of a particular county.

If Alexa, a resident of California, wants to sue Adam, a resident of Florida, concerning a contract problem that had caused her $90,000 in damages, she can clearly choose to file the case in the federal district court in Florida (where Adam lives) or the appropriate state trial court in Florida. She might also be able to file the case in federal or state court in California, if the appropriate facts existed. If, for example, the contract had been signed and/or performed in California, she probably can file the suit there, using the "long arm" rules, as explained above, and Adam will have to answer and deal with the case in California.

concurrent jurisdiction: A type of case in which either the state or federal courts would have jurisdiction.

When both the state and federal courts have jurisdiction over a case, it is called **concurrent jurisdiction,** and it is initially the plaintiff's choice where to file. If the plaintiff files a case in a state court, and the defendant decides he or she would rather be in federal court, and there is a basis for either diversity or federal question jurisdiction, a **petition for removal** may be filed by the defendant with the federal court. If there is a proper jurisdictional basis, the case will be moved to the federal court. A defendant who wishes to remove a case to federal court, however, must institute procedures promptly after the case is filed. Once proceedings get underway in a court, the case will stay in that court system (state or federal) throughout.

THE CASE OR CONTROVERSY REQUIREMENT

American courts are limited by the Constitution to deciding actual "cases or controversies." This phrase means that courts will not give advisory opinions to a legislator or public official on whether a law is constitutional or not. The concept is based on the premise that the primary role of the courts is to decide disputes between parties, not to legislate. When two parties have truly adverse interests, they are more likely to thoroughly present the legal arguments and issues on both sides, allowing the court to make the decision. For example, a recent law passed by one state allowed police officers to use roadblocks to stop cars at random to look for drunk drivers. Although many people believed the law was unconstitutional (violation of the "search and seizure" rule of the Fourth Amendment), the courts could not rule on the question until someone was detained by the use of this technique and later challenged the legality of the arrest in court.

STANDING

The concept of **standing** is somewhat similar to the case or controversy requirement in that it also limits the number of disputes that courts can hear. The rule essentially holds that only those persons or businesses who have suffered some loss as the result of another's action or have a personal stake in the outcome of the dispute may sue. Only those persons directly affected have standing to argue the legal issues before the court. For example, if Sally hires Joe's Painting Service to paint her house, and Joe does a really poor job, some of Sally's neighbors might like to sue Joe because Sally's house is now unattractive enough to decrease the property values in the neighborhood. However, a court would probably rule that only Sally had standing to sue Joe for his breach of contract with her. The following case is a Supreme Court decision involving "standing."

standing: The requirement that one or more of the plaintiffs in a case show that they have actually suffered some direct effect or loss due to the defendant's actions.

STEEL CO. V. CITIZENS FOR A BETTER ENVIRONMENT
523 U.S. 83 (1998)

FACTS

Citizens for a Better Environment is a group interested in environmental protection. The organization sued Steel Co., a small manufacturing company in Chicago, for past violations of the Emergency Planning and Community Right-to-Know Act of 1986 (EPCRA). This federal law established a framework of state, regional, and local agencies that were to inform the public about the presence of hazardous and toxic chemicals, and to provide for emergency response when necessary.

The law (EPCRA) required users of specified toxic and hazardous chemicals to file annual reports containing much information about the company, the facility, the name and quantity of chemicals used, the waste disposal method employed, and more information. The law stated that it could be enforced against violators by the Environmental Protection Agency (EPA), or state and local governments, or even private citizens, when the EPA declined to act.

Citizens for a Better Environment sent a notice to the EPA and to local and regional governments in 1995, claiming (correctly) that Steel Co. failed to file the required reports every year since the law went into effect (1988). After the notices were received, Steel Co. was notified and then did file all the necessary overdue forms, and the EPA decided not to bring legal action. At that point, Citizens filed this lawsuit in federal district court. The district court dismissed the case, but that decision was later reversed by the Court of Appeals, which held that a citizens group could sue under the EPCRA for past violations. The case was then appealed to the U.S. Supreme Court, which decided that before reaching the substantive legal issues concerning the EPCRA, it must decide whether the plaintiffs had "standing" to bring the case.

DECISION

In an opinion written by Justice Antonin Scalia, the Supreme Court determined that the plaintiffs did <u>not</u> have standing. The court started its discussion of standing by noting that "Article III, Section 2 of the Constitution extends the 'Judicial Power' of the United States only to 'Cases' and 'Controversies.'" Justice Scalia said, "We have always taken this to mean cases and controversies of the sort traditionally . . . resolved by the court process."

The constitutional minimum of standing contains three elements. <u>First</u> and foremost, there must be alleged (and ultimately proved) an "injury in fact"—a harm suffered by the plaintiff that is "concrete" and "actual or imminent, not conjectural or hypothetical." <u>Second</u>, there must be causation—a fairly traceable connection between the plaintiff's injury and the conduct of the defendant. "And <u>third</u>, there must be redressability—a likelihood that the requested relief will redress the alleged injury."

Turning to the particular allegations of the plaintiffs' complaint in this case, the court found that the plaintiff states it is "an organization that seeks, uses, and acquires data reported under the EPCRA" and reports information to its members concerning storage and releases of toxic chemicals into the environment. The organization also prepares reports to its members and "advocates for changes in public policy to better protect the environment." It states that its members, who live in the area near the Steel Co. facility, will use the EPCRA information to learn about chemical releases and the use of hazardous substances in their communities to attempt to reduce the toxic chemicals in their area. The members' "safety, health, recreational, economic, aesthetic, and environmental interests" in the information "have been, are being, and will be adversely affected" by Steel Co.'s failure to file timely reports under the EPCRA, stated the group.

The Supreme Court then looked at the relief requested by the plaintiff organization, to determine whether any of the measures requested would redress the harm claimed. First, the request for a declaratory judgment, after the reports had been filed, was termed "worthless." Next, the plaintiffs' request for civil penalties (fines) would perhaps help redress the injuries, except that, by law, they are payable to the U.S. Treasury. The gratification that the plaintiffs might feel if the defendant were punished is not redress of the harm. Justice Scalia stated:

By the mere bringing of his suit, every plaintiff demonstrates his belief that a favorable judgment will make him happier. But although a suitor may derive great comfort and joy from the fact that the United States Treasury is not cheated, that a wrongdoer gets his just deserts, or that the Nation's laws are faithfully enforced, that psychic satisfaction is not an acceptable Article III [standing] remedy because it does not redress an Article III injury.

The court then examined the other remedies sought by the plaintiffs and found that none of them would redress the harms allegedly suffered. Even the request for an injunction ordering Steel Co. to provide copies of all EPA reports would not remedy any past wrong but looked to the future. Justice Scalia hinted that if the complaint by the Citizens group had alleged that the violations were continuing and were imminent in the future, perhaps the injunctive remedy would qualify as necessary redress, but no such allegation was in the complaint. Therefore, because the relief sought by the plaintiffs would not redress or compensate them for the harm they claimed, the case was dismissed for lack of standing.

CASE QUESTIONS

1. What is the purpose of the "standing" rule? How is it related to the constitutional requirement that courts only hear "cases and controversies"?
2. Why did Justice Scalia focus on the "redress" issue? How does this tie in with the standing requirement?
3. What did the Supreme Court find lacking in the plaintiff's requests here?
4. Translate the point being made by the Court in the paragraph set out in italics into your own words. What is the point?

CLASS ACTIONS

Sometimes a great number of persons are injured by another's actions or conduct. Suppose that 1 million people have been adversely affected by a nuclear accident at one company or that 100,000 people have purchased tires—many of which were slightly defective—from one company. According to the rules mentioned previously, each person may bring a separate lawsuit against the one defendant (because each one has suffered an injury). Thousands of lawsuits would cause tremendous problems for the court system. On the other hand, perhaps the injury to each person is so small ($50 for each tire) that no one will file a lawsuit, and the company will escape any penalty.

For these reasons, the **class action** lawsuit was developed. In such a case, a few individuals file a suit stating that they are representing "all others similarly situated." These individuals, through their attorneys, must convince the court that (1) the number of people involved is very large, (2) that the plaintiffs will adequately present the claims of the larger group, (3) that there are "common questions of law and fact" involved, and (4) that the plaintiffs' claims are typical of the rest of the class.

Obviously, when the claims of all the possible injured persons are added up, the damages sought become quite great. In the tire example, even though each consumer's damages were only $50, if each claim is multiplied by 100,000 people, the aggregated claims involve at least $5 million in damages. Businesses vigorously oppose such lawsuits. They sometimes argue that these cases are the creation of lawyers more interested in their fees (often 1/3 of the total recovery) than in helping injured persons. Consumer advocates, on the other hand, contend that businesses that make defective products must somehow be held accountable for the damage they cause, even if the amount incurred by each person is small.

As this edition of this book goes to press, one of the largest potential class actions in history is being argued at the U.S. Supreme Court—by the time you read this, the Court decision should be final. Six women plaintiffs filed a class action suit several years ago, purporting to represent as many as 1 million female employees, alleging that Wal-Mart systematically paid women lower wages and denied them promotions, in comparison to male employees. The plaintiffs claim that female employees were victimized by a "centralized corporate culture" that discriminated against women. Wal-Mart has argued that not only does it not discriminate, but class action status is inappropriate because personnel decisions are made by individual managers at its 3,400 stores and cannot be lumped together. The determination of whether a class action is proper in this case will have a huge impact on the success of the litigation.

The controversy has caused courts to closely supervise class actions. In most federal court class actions, the burden of notifying all of the members of the potential class about the lawsuit is put on the plaintiff. This requirement stops many class actions before they start, since the cost of mailing letters to thousands of people is quite significant. Sometimes in very large cases, the court will approve notices in a series of newspapers or some other method, but these instances are becoming less frequent and are vigorously opposed by the business defendants.

Once a person is notified that a class action has been approved by the court and is underway, he or she will be bound by the result unless the court is notified

class action: A type of lawsuit in which a few plaintiffs act to represent a much larger group, who have suffered the same type of injury.

that the individual has chosen to **"opt out"** and pursue his or her own remedies. If the plaintiffs win the class action case, or if a favorable monetary settlement is reached, as often happens, the award (after payment of costs and attorney fees) must be shared by all the class members, or at least as many as can be found. Those who have "opted out" will not receive part of the settlement, and are not bound by the decision and may pursue their own lawsuits.

SOCIAL/ETHICAL ISSUES

Do you think it is fair to allow four or five persons, through their lawyers, to say they represent hundreds or thousands of people, each of whom may have a relatively small monetary loss? Then, after starting a lawsuit, the plaintiffs attempt to notify all of these people to see if they want to join in, at no cost. When the claims are aggregated, the total may be several million dollars for which the firm that manufactured the product may be liable. And the attorneys bringing the lawsuit will take perhaps 1/3 or more of the total as attorneys fees.

In the absence of the class action procedure, how many of these people would ever have sued on their own? If very few would file suit, are such class actions therefore frivolous? On the other hand, if a manufacturer has made a product that has caused $25 or $30 of damage to 100,000 people, should it totally escape any financial liability because no one individual files a lawsuit?

FEDERALISM AND PREEMPTION

As we discussed in the section on jurisdiction, it is usually the plaintiff's choice whether to file a case in federal court or state court, although there are some limitations on the types of cases a federal court will hear. Additional federal/state interactions can arise, however, when the legal issue concerns a federal law and a state law that may be inconsistent with each other. The U.S. Constitution establishes a system of government based upon **federalism**, under which certain powers are given to the federal government while others are reserved to the states.

The **Supremacy Clause** of the U.S. Constitution states that "The Constitution, and the Laws of the United States which shall be made in Pursuance thereof; and all Treaties made . . . shall be the Supreme Law of the Land; and the Judges of every state shall be bound thereby. . . ." This clause has been interpreted in many cases over the past 217 years, and one important theory has developed that is known as the *preemption doctrine*.

The **preemption doctrine** holds that when the federal government acts to regulate an area in which it has been given power under the Constitution, its laws and regulations preempt (that is, displace or cancel) any state laws or actions that infringe directly or indirectly on the federal power. This doctrine only operates where (1) the federal government, usually through Congress, is acting in a substantive field as authorized by the Constitution (for example,

federalism: The sharing of power between the federal and state governments.

Supremacy Clause: The clause in the U.S. Constitution that establishes the Constitution as the final authority in the land, superior to conflicting state laws.

regulation of interstate commerce) and (2) the state law or action in question conflicts and infringes on the federal power.

The preemption doctrine does not apply if the state law merely supplements the federal law, rather than conflicts with it. For example, the federal government is specifically given the power to set up post offices and establish a copyright system by the Constitution. If a state were to pass a law establishing such a system, the law would be invalid on the basis of *preemption*. The issues become much more complex when the law regulates business and commerce, involving the Commerce Clause, as will be discussed in Chapter 4.

LAWYERS AND BUSINESS

This book is designed to help business students become more knowledgeable about the many legal issues that affect business. Rather than becoming lawyers, you will someday need to interact with attorneys in your own firm, if it is a large business, or deal with lawyers representing another company. Perhaps you will need to hire a lawyer to assist your own business. The aim of this book is to help you *avoid* legal problems before they become serious, to prepare you to choose an attorney wisely, and to be a more intelligent consumer of legal services—that is, to communicate better with the attorney chosen and to understand and participate more fully in each decision which must be made. So the next section will examine how one becomes a lawyer and will look more closely at the different types of lawyers.

WHAT IS A LAWYER?

There is an endless number of humorous answers to this question—there are probably more "lawyer jokes" (some of us trained as attorneys call them "anti-lawyer jokes") making the rounds than any other category—but let us be serious for now. First of all, in the United States the terms *lawyer* and *attorney* mean the same thing—there is no real difference. In England, on the other hand, there is an important difference between the terms *barrister* and *solicitor*. Only barristers argue cases in court, while solicitors handle many other legal matters out of court. In other countries, lawyers are sometimes termed *advocates*, or known by other titles, and each category may limit what one can do. In the United States any lawyer can assist people with the full range of legal concerns and appear in court in jurisdictions where that lawyer is licensed.

Licensing of American lawyers is done primarily on the state level, by the state **bar association** (the organization of lawyers in that state). There is no federal or national licensing of attorneys. It is necessary to apply for "admission to the bar" in the state where a lawyer wishes to practice law. A lawyer must be licensed in each state in which he or she wants to practice. Each state has its own independent Bar Association. You may have heard of the American Bar Association (ABA), a national organization with approximately 400,000 attorney members in 2010, which often speaks for the legal profession. The ABA is a voluntary organization, however, and lawyers are free to belong or not.

bar association:
An organization of attorneys—may be a local, statewide, or national group.

THE AMERICAN BAR ASSOCIATION

The national organization of lawyers is the American Bar Association. As mentioned above, the ABA membership includes approximately 400,000 lawyers and law students. Attorneys are not required to join the national group (they are required to belong to their state bar association), but many do so, to enhance their professional reputation and learn about new developments in law practice. Within the national organization, members may choose to join one or more Sections devoted to one legal subject area. The Sections hold meetings, publish newsletters and journals, and suggest improvements regarding that particular area of law. The largest sections of the ABA are "Litigation" and "Business Law," both with more than 60,000 members, and "Real Property, Probate and Trust Law," "Tort and Insurance Law," "Labor and Employment," "Taxation," "General Practice," and "Intellectual Property"—all with more than 20,000 members.

The ABA serves as the public voice of and for lawyers, speaking for the legal profession in public, before Congress and in other settings. In 2003 the ABA named the first African-American president in its long history. Dennis Archer of Michigan became the president after a long career in both the legal and political arenas. The president of the ABA in 2010–11 is Mr. Stephen Zack, who came to the United States from Cuba as a child. He is focusing his term in office on civic education about the law. The previous ABA president, Ms. Carolyn Lamm, had devoted considerable effort to increasing diversity in the legal profession.

The first step in becoming a lawyer is attending law school, which is normally a three-year course of study following graduation from undergraduate school. The person's undergraduate major is not particularly important—people with a wide variety of bachelors' degrees enroll in law school. After graduation from law school, a candidate must apply to the appropriate state Bar Association to take the "bar exam" in the state where he or she wishes to practice law. The exam is a difficult two- or three-day test in most states, and the "pass" rate varies considerably, from around 50 percent in some states up to 75 percent or 80 percent in other states. An unsuccessful applicant can usually attempt the test again at a future time.

If the law school graduate passes the test and his or her "character and fitness" investigation by the state bar association is positive, the applicant is then a "lawyer" and can begin to practice law in that state. Canada and many other nations require a period of apprenticeship with a practicing attorney before the new lawyer can practice alone. For better or worse, this procedure is not normally required in the United States.

Since licensing is controlled at the state level, if a lawyer licensed in one state wants to practice law in another state, he or she must seek formal permission from that state. Some states have "reciprocity" laws that allow lawyers practicing in other states to become members of that state's bar association simply by payment of the appropriate fees, as long as the background check does not disclose any previous problems (such as crimes or suspension from that state's bar association). However, many states, particularly in the West, have little or no reciprocity, so that if a lawyer who has been practicing law for 20 years in Georgia wishes to open a practice in California, he or she must sit for the bar exam just like a recent law school graduate. Not only is the initial licensing of lawyers carried out at the state level, but disciplinary actions including sanctions, suspensions, and ultimately "disbarment" of lawyers for misconduct is also done by the state bar associations.

WHEN YOU SHOULD RETAIN A LAWYER

Obviously, if you are sued for money damages or are formally charged with a crime, you need to consult a lawyer. But in many other circumstances, you are wise and financially astute to seek legal assistance long before a lawsuit is filed. It is a good idea for a businessperson to visit an attorney every year or so to review personal and business matters even if there are no immediate legal threats. Often people put off going to a lawyer for advice because they do not want to incur the cost. However, legal problems are much easier to avoid and head off—and much less expensive—if caught early.

Personal Legal Issues   It is advisable to have a will. Although this subject will be more thoroughly discussed later in this book, you should know that when a person dies without a will, that person's property will be distributed according to the laws of his or her state—usually to the closest heirs, such as children and parents. The property does not go to the state if one dies without a will—as some people think—unless there are essentially no relatives at all. One's property will be distributed to the closest heirs, such as uncles or cousins. But by preparing a will, a person can specify exactly to whom any or all assets will go and in what amount. A will can also establish a trust fund for children or specify that a certain amount be left to a church, the Humane Society, or other entity.

One reason many people with young children execute a will is to specify who will be named as guardian of their children if both parents should die. If there is no will, a court hearing will need to be held to determine, in the judge's view, who is the best person to care for the children. Sometimes these proceedings cause bitter family squabbles. However, if someone is named guardian of the children in a will and that person agrees to serve, courts will almost always follow these wishes.

Other family matters that often require the services of a lawyer include a divorce and adoption. Although it is possible to "do your own" divorce, if there are children or significant assets or debts involved, an attorney's help will be cost-effective in the long run. There may be complex legal issues involved in divorce that the untrained individual who just wants to "get out of this rotten marriage" may not perceive but which might cause problems later. Similarly, an adoption is an important legal event with substantial consequences for the child and the natural and adoptive parents.

Business Matters   For the person involved in business, many situations exist when one should seek legal assistance. As we mentioned at the beginning of this chapter, when starting a business, several pivotal legal decisions need to be made in which a lawyer's advice can be very valuable. Similarly, one should seek legal assistance when buying or selling an existing business. Hiring and firing employees, purchasing or renting property, entering into contracts, and solving tax issues are examples of occasions when an attorney's advice should definitely be sought.

Legal Issues Affecting Small Businesses

The National Federation of Independent Businesses has issued a booklet stating that Small Businesses definitely need to consult with an attorney in five particular situations. The NFIB says that consultation should occur: (1) When entering a partnership agreement; (2) When purchasing or leasing equipment; (3) When writing your company's sales/purchase contracts for customers; (4) When determining compliance with federal or local regulations for employee relations or workplace conditions; and (5) When preparing to raise funding of any kind, even from friends or relative.

HOW TO CHOOSE A LAWYER

When you have decided that a lawyer's advice is needed, how should you go about choosing one? First, get recommendations from friends you trust and whose opinion you value. In addition, business associates, supervisors, doctors, ministers, and perhaps accountants and bankers with whom your firm has dealt may be able to recommend an attorney. Obviously, recommendations from people who actually have worked with or used the services of the lawyer being considered are much more valuable than those who have just "heard something" about the person.

Most local bar associations (organized lawyer groups) have "referral services." These programs ask lawyers to sign up if they want to receive referrals and to list areas of legal work they engage in. Then, if an individual calls the bar association seeking a lawyer, the service may give out the name and number of an attorney from the list for a small fee. The referral service does not vouch for the expertise of the lawyer; rather, the service indicates that the lawyer has experience in a particular area. The individual needs to ask questions of the lawyer at the first meeting to make sure that he or she has the appropriate experience.

Lawyer advertising is now a regular feature of the telephone book and even the newspaper, radio, and television—especially in larger cities, where there is a large number of attorneys. While many lawyers have big, fancy offices, leather chairs, and long lists of corporate clients, there are numerous others making a modest living at best. Some of these attorneys are actively seeking new clients and new business and use advertising to publicize their image and their rates. Like other types of businesses, some lawyers feature low cost in their ads, while others stress their experience or expertise in particular matters.

Large, prestigious law firms typically do not advertise a great deal. These distinguished firms often believe that mass advertising lowers the public image of the legal profession. Also, these firms already have numerous clients and obtain most of their new business from referrals. Sometimes, large well-known law firms will have a yellow pages advertisement that simply lists the members of the firm.

After two young lawyers in Arizona were disciplined by the bar association in 1977 for advertising in violation of the state rules, the U.S. Supreme Court decided that the "Freedom of Speech" clause in the Constitution prohibited an outright ban on lawyer advertising. [See *Bates v. State Bar of Arizona,* 433 U.S. 350 (1977)]. The Court did allow states to enact regulations to protect the public against false or misleading advertising but not to ban attorney advertising totally. All the states have passed some kind of regulatory measures—some quite general and some very specific—but the regulations cannot prohibit informative, nondeceptive advertising. Consumers should keep in mind, however, that advertising is only that lawyer's own assertion as to his or her qualifications. The more informed the consumer, the better able he or she is to select and benefit from a lawyer's services.

LARGE FIRM OR SMALL FIRM?

Traditionally, the most sought-after jobs for law school graduates have been with large law firms in big cities. In general, these firms, often with hundreds of lawyers and several offices, pay the highest salaries, hire the top law school graduates, and have the most prestige in the law profession. In recent years, starting salaries for newly hired attorneys in large New York law firms have averaged $120,000 per year or more, with a large year-end bonus added for good performance. These lawyers are expected to work 60 or more hours per week, however, often under considerable time pressure. Salaries in other parts of the country are less than that, and vary considerably. Lawyers in large firms tend to specialize in one or two areas over the years, and such a firm will have experts in taxation, corporate and securities law, environmental law, antitrust law, employment law, and other fields. Large firms demand a lot from their lawyers and generally produce high-quality work.

America's 50 Largest Law Firms

Updated January 2011: Below you will find a listing of the 50 largest law firms in the U.S.

No.	Law Firm	Base Office	Attorneys
1.	Baker and McKenzie	Chicago	3,774
2.	DLA Piper	Chicago	3,448
3.	Jones Day	Washington	2,515
4.	Hogan Lovells	Washington	2,345
5.	Latham and Watkins	New York	2,006
6.	Skadden, Arps, Slate, Meagher and Flom	New York	1,886
7.	White and Case	New York	1,863
8.	Greenberg Traurig	New York	1,763
9.	KandL Gates	Pittsburgh	1,734
10.	Mayer Brown	Chicago	1,684
11.	Sidley Austin	Chicago	1,571
12.	Reed Smith	Pittsburgh	1,430
13.	Kirkland and Ellis	Chicago	1,419
14.	Morgan, Lewis and Bockius	Philadelphia	1,206

15.	Weil, Gotshal and Manges	New York	1,193
16.	Cleary Gottlieb Steen and Hamilton	New York	1,123
17.	Orrick, Herrington and Sutcliffe	San Francisco	1,079
18.	Dewey and LeBoeuf	New York	1,071
19.	Ropes and Gray	Boston	1,062
20.	Gibson, Dunn and Crutcher	Los Angeles	1,033
21.	Morrison and Foerster	San Francisco	1,004
22.	Holland and Knight	Washington	942
24.	Bryan Cave	St. Louis	928
23.	McDermott Will and Emery	Chicago	928
25.	Paul, Hastings, Janofsky and Walker	New York	924
26	Bingham McCutchen	Boston	918
27	Wilmer Cutler Pickering Hale and Dorr	Washington	907
28	Winston and Strawn	Chicago	899
29	Foley and Lardner	Milwaukee	895
30	O Melveny and Myers	Los Angeles	884
31	McGuireWoods	Richmond	872
32	Fulbright and Jaworski	Houston	855
33	Hunton and Williams	Richmond	846
34	Simpson Thacher and Bartlett	New York	814
35	Akin Gump Strauss Hauer and Feld	Washington	799
36	Covington and Burling	Washington	799
37	Shearman and Sterling	New York	798
38	King and Spalding	Atlanta	796
39	Alston and Bird	Atlanta	786
40	Goodwin Procter	Boston	776
41	Sullivan and Cromwell	New York	772
42	Dechert	Philadelphia	766
43	Lewis Brisbois Bisgaard and Smith	Los Angeles	764
44	Littler Mendelson	San Francisco	764
45	Paul, Weiss, Rifkind, Wharton and Garrison	New York	761
46	Squire, Sanders and Dempsey	Cleveland	761
47	Debevoise and Plimpton	New York	750
48	Wilson Elser Moskowitz Edelman and Dicker	New York	744
49	Davis Polk and Wardwell	New York	743
50	Seyfarth Shaw	Chicago	704

Source: Internet Legal Research Group

Because of their size, staff, and technical needs, large firms tend to charge higher rates than smaller firms, although there certainly are exceptions. They often pay higher salaries, have more secretaries and **paralegals** (nonlawyers working for a law firm under the supervision of a lawyer), and have higher library expenses. Your legal matter may be handled by a senior partner (at rates exceeding $300 per hour), or it may be given to an **associate** (a lawyer who is a salaried member of the firm but not yet a partner) at a lower hourly rate.

John Grisham's books, such as *The Firm, The Client, The Rainmaker, The Street Lawyer* and their movie adaptations have dramatically depicted the stress felt by young lawyers who join a large firm. His books clearly portray the tremendous pressure new associates in a large firm face to work long hours, produce a high number of "billable hours" (those that can be directly charged to clients), and please the supervising senior partner in order to "make partner" in six or seven years. Lawyers in large firms work long hours, generally produce excellent work, and earn the highest compensation in the legal field.

Smaller firms may not have experts in all types of legal problems, although they may be very proficient in certain specialties. They may not have an attorney who has previously handled exactly the same type of case as yours. Some small firms do concentrate on one particular area of the law, such as patent law or criminal law. In some cases, the services of a smaller firm will be more personalized, and the number of lawyers and size of the office less overwhelming. The client may get to know one lawyer well, rather than dealing with several different lawyers and paralegals. Regardless of the type of firm selected, it is important for the client to discuss early on the previous experience the particular attorney has with respect to the category of legal issue in question.

The *"sole practitioner"* is a lawyer who practices by him- or herself. Sometimes clients feel that they receive more personal attention from this attorney than from a large- or medium-sized firm. On the other hand, the law is becoming more complex every day, and the sole practitioner cannot possibly maintain expertise in all the areas of law that a larger firm can offer. The sole practitioner can be compared to the family doctor. Each one has a wide basic knowledge of many areas but may not be a specialist in any one. Some sole practitioners, however, do focus their energies on a few specific subject areas.

paralegals: Nonlawyers who work for a law firm under the supervision of a lawyer.

associate: A lawyer who is a salaried member of the firm but not yet a partner.

INTERNATIONAL PERSPECTIVE

Recently there has been a trend toward mergers among law firms, not only in the United States but also in Europe. The opening up of a unified European market and the removal of barriers to trade and to services across national borders has opened the door for combinations of law firms from different countries. In addition mergers are taking place between European law firms and giant U.S. accounting firms.

Despite the size of the largest U.S. law firms (see chart), the three largest law firms in the world, by revenue, are all based in the United Kingdom, as of late 2010. The huge British law firm Clifford Chance (the world's highest-grossing law firm) with its home office in London, now has more than 3,700 lawyers at 33 offices worldwide, In the United States, Clifford Chance has offices in New York, Washington, D.C., San Francisco, Palo Alto, Los Angeles and San Diego. The firm also maintains offices in Amsterdam, Bangkok, Barcelona, Beijing, Berlin, Brussels, Budapest, Dubai, Dusseldorf, Frankfort, Hong Kong, Luxembourg, Madrid, Milan, Moscow, Munich, Padua, Paris, Prague, Rome, Sao Paulo, Shanghai, Singapore, Tokyo and Warsaw.

Competition among accounting and auditing firms (and scandals) has reduced the number of huge accounting firms from 12 in 1990 to a "Big Four" today. These global firms are now seeking mergers with international law firms. While such mergers (called multidiscliplinary partnerships) are not allowed by American bar associations at this time, they are permitted in many, but not all, European nations. The power of the large accounting firms, which have legal divisions, makes them an attractive partner for a law firm with international clientele. All large corporations need sophisticated legal and accounting assistance.

FEES AND COSTS

There are three primary ways that attorneys charge for their services—(1) by the hour, (2) by a set fee or flat fee for a particular service, and (3) by a "contingent fee." The attorney and the client should discuss fees at the very first meeting and should agree on which type of fee will be used for this matter. The client should leave the office knowing how much he or she will be charged for the lawyer's time; paralegal time; and expenses and costs such as photocopying, court costs, and telephone charges; and if the fees depend on whether the case is won or lost.

The American rule: Each party in a lawsuit normally pays his or her own lawyer, whether the case is won or lost.

The general rule in the United States—the so-called **"American rule"**—is that both parties in a case pay their own lawyer fees, regardless of who wins the case. In many other countries, the rule is different—the winner normally is awarded compensation from the loser for his or her attorney fees, in addition to the other damages awarded. There are an increasing number of U.S. statutes that adopt this principle and allow the judge to assess attorney fees as part of the judgment in particular types of cases, but these are exceptions to the general American rule. The statutes where this principle has been adopted are usually those in which Congress has felt a need to encourage citizen enforcement actions such as civil rights, consumer protection, and environmental laws.

hourly fee: Where the lawyer charges the client a specified rate for each hour spent on the client's legal matters.

The most common way attorneys charge is **by the hour**. Each attorney sets his or her hourly rate—sometimes it is different for out-of-court time or in-court time. Attorneys' hourly rates vary considerably, and the client is wise to shop around, make calls, check references, and interview several attorneys before committing to a lawyer. Once the attorney begins to work for an individual, he or she will keep close account of all time spent working on that person's legal matter and will charge accordingly. This includes phone calls with the client and other attorneys or witnesses, as well as time spent on legal research, investigation, negotiation, and any other work on that case. It may not be wise to choose the attorney with the lowest hourly rate, but at least the client should be informed of the hourly fee right at the beginning, although the final cost will not be known at that time.

retainer: An advance payment to secure the services of a lawyer.

Sometimes at the beginning of the attorney–client relationship, the attorney will ask for a **"retainer."** This is a payment in advance of services being

"You're a partner now, Simpson. You shouldn't be drinking juice from a box."

From *National Law Journal*, 12/19/94. Cartoon © Mike Shapiro.

performed. This safeguards the attorney against doing a considerable amount of work and then having the client refuse to pay. However, there have been instances when attorneys have abused this type of fee arrangement, as the following case demonstrates.

MATTER OF COOPERMAN

611 N.Y.S.2d 465 (Ct.App. 1994)

FACTS

A New York attorney, Edward Cooperman, demanded that a number of his clients sign "nonrefundable retainer fee agreements." At the time Mr. Cooperman accepted a criminal case, he had the client sign a statement as follows: "My minimum fee for appearing for you in this matter is Fifteen Thousand Dollars ($15,000). This fee is not refundable for any reason whatsoever once I file a notice of appearance on your behalf." One month after signing this agreement, a client discharged Mr. Cooperman, but the lawyer refused to refund any portion of the fee. In another criminal case, the client signed a similar agreement (with a nonrefundable fee of $10,000) and then discharged the lawyer two days later, but Mr. Cooperman refused to refund any of the retainer fee.

In connection with accepting representation of a client in a probate proceeding, Mr. Cooperman required a client to sign the following statement: "For the MINIMAL FEE and NONREFUNDABLE amount of Five Thousand Dollars ($5,000), I will act as your counsel." Later in the agreement, this clause appeared: "This is the minimum fee no matter how much or how little work I do in this investigatory stage . . . and will remain the minimum fee and not refundable even if you decide prior to my completion of the investigation that you wish to discontinue the use of my services for any reason whatsoever." The client later discharged Mr. Cooperman, who refused to refund any portion of the retainer fee.

Several of these clients complained to the New York State Bar Association about Mr. Cooperman's practices. Mr. Cooperman had previously received a Letter of Caution from the Bar Association warning him not to use nonrefundable retainer agreements, but he had continued the procedure. The Grievance Committee of one district of the New York Bar Association brought formal charges against him, seeking his suspension or disbarment. The lower court, finding that his practices clearly violated the Code of Professional Responsibility governing lawyers in New York, suspended him from the practice of law for two years. Mr. Cooperman appealed to the New York Court of Appeals, New York's highest court.

DECISION

The Court of Appeals, in a decision authored by Justice Bellacosa, upheld the lower court decision. Beginning with a quote from Sir Francis Bacon that the "greatest trust between people is the trust of giving counsel," the court emphasized the unique fiduciary relationship created when clients hire attorneys to represent them. The court stated that this relationship is "imbued with ultimate trust and confidence." The attorney's obligations transcend those prevailing in the commercial marketplace.

Justice Bellacosa wrote that "the duty to deal fairly, honestly and with undivided loyalty superimposes onto the attorney–client relationship a set of special and unique duties, including maintaining confidentiality, avoiding conflicts of interest, operating competently, safeguarding client property and honoring the client's interests over the lawyer's."

Obviously, the matter of the fee is of significant importance to clients. Therefore, the Code of Professional Responsibility specifically states that an attorney "shall not enter into an agreement for, charge, or collect an illegal or excessive fee" (Rule 2-106A), and upon withdrawal from employment, the attorney shall "refund promptly any part of a fee paid in advance that has not been earned" (Rule 2-110A). Obviously, the "nonrefundable fee," where the entire amount of money paid by the client is retained by the lawyer regardless of the services performed, violates that section of the Rule.

The Court took note of the strong public policy recognizing a client's right to terminate the attorney–client relationship *at any time with or without cause*. This policy has long been enforced because of the special fiduciary relationship of lawyer and client, despite the usual legal principle that parties are bound by the terms of contracts they sign. The court stated, "Special nonrefundable retainer fee agreements diminish the core of the fiduciary relationship by substantially altering and economically chilling the client's unbridled prerogative to walk away from the lawyer."

If the court were to uphold nonrefundable retainers, clients would be "relegated to hostage status in an unwanted fiduciary relationship—an utter anomaly." Such circumstance would impose a penalty on a client for daring to invoke a hollow right to discharge. Interestingly, Mr. Cooperman even acknowledged that the essential purpose of the contract clause was to prevent clients from firing him as their lawyer. This purpose, stated the court, "directly contravenes the Code [of Professional Responsibility] and this State's settled public policy in this regard." Clients may therefore discharge their lawyers at any time without penalty.

The court pointed out that lawyers who are fired by their clients do have remedies available. Under traditional legal theories, supported by many court decisions, the discharged attorney is entitled to recover the reasonable value of services rendered. So Mr. Cooperman would have been entitled to keep whatever portion of the retainer fee he had earned at the time of the discharge, based on the efforts he expended, but the nonrefundable fee agreements were clearly illegal.

Mr. Cooperman's final argument was that he did not deserve to be suspended because he had acted "in good faith," based upon the "limited legal precedents at the time." The court was not persuaded, however, noting that "the conduct of attorneys is not measured by how close to the edge of thin ice they skate." The test instead is "whether the reasonable attorney, familiar with the Code and its ethical strictures," would have notice of what conduct is allowed. Given Mr. Cooperman's level of knowledge, as well as the previous warnings given him, his conduct did not measure up to the requirements. The Court of Appeals concluded that "Cooperman's case, therefore, constitutes a daring test of ethical principles, not good faith. He failed the test."

CASE QUESTIONS

1. What was Mr. Cooperman's reason for having his clients sign nonrefundable retainer fee agreements?

2. Does this case mean that, from now on, all "retainer fee" agreements are illegal in New York? If not, how do we discern which agreements are legal?

3. If there had been no previous case in New York directly concerning nonrefundable retainer fees, is not Mr. Cooperman correct when he said he was "acting in good faith, based on limited precedent"?

4. Do you think the penalty is too harsh? Too lenient?

Sometimes lawyers advertise a **set fee** for a service. Lawyer ads often state such services as "Uncontested Divorce—$300" or "Individual Bankruptcy—$400 ." If the client really does have a routine legal matter, these arrangements may be a good deal, since they can be performed efficiently by a lawyer who does many of them. If the case becomes more complicated, however, the set fee will not apply. Hopefully, the attorney and the client will have discussed the hourly rate that will be charged in addition to the set fee, should the matter become more involved. Clients become unhappy when they receive a large bill for extra services after the case "blows up" and they have not been warned of this possibility.

set fee: When a lawyer charges a fixed fee for a specific service.

Current Issue

The economic downturn, which some have called "the Great Recession," has caused many law firms to offer "alternative fee arrangements" in order to keep or gain corporate business. Such billing is often called "Value Billing" and can be structured as flat fees, fixed fees for services, "success" fees, or even a flat rate for work done over a whole year. (FindLaw.com, In House Counsel, March 8, 2011)

In cases where the client wants to sue someone for personal injuries, often the **contingent fee** is used. In these cases, there is a strong likelihood that some money will be recovered, either by settlement or at trial. The attorney can offer the client the choice of being charged by the hour (regardless of whether the case is won or lost) or of using a contingent fee. In this arrangement, the client pays no hourly fees at all to the lawyer, but instead agrees that the lawyer's fee will be a certain percentage of whatever judgment or settlement is received. Often the lawyer's fee is in the range of 33 percent to 40 percent of the money recovered. This way, if the case is lost and the client gets nothing, the

contingent fee: When the lawyer's fee is a certain percentage of the total money obtained by the client, at trial or by settlement.

How Much Can You Expect to Pay?

Rates for legal fees vary based on location, experience of the lawyer, and the nature of the matter. Believe it or not, rates may vary anywhere from $50 an hour to a $1,000 an hour or more. The following data regarding average attorneys' fees is based on information provided in the 2009 Billing Rates and Practices Survey; which was a study conducted by Incisive Legal Intelligence on the billing rates and practices of attorneys in small and mid-sized firms.

In rural areas and small towns, lawyers tend to charge less, and fees in the range of $100 to $200 an hour for an experienced attorney are probably the norm. In major metropolitan areas, the norm is probably closer to $200 to $400 an hour. Lawyers with expertise in specialized areas may charge much more. Here are some national averages to help you get a general idea.

- The national average billing rate is $284 per hour
- Firms with 2 to 8 lawyers have a national average billing rate of $262 per hour
- Firms with 76 to 150 lawyers have a national average billing rate of $295 per hour
- Firms with more than 150 lawyers have a national average billing rate of $333 per hour
- By Region: Northeast ($319 per hour), West ($296 per hour), South ($276 per hour) and Midwest ($264 per hour)

In addition, you can expect to be charged at an hourly rate for paralegals and other support staff. A good paralegal's time, for example, may be billed out at $50 to a $100 an hour or perhaps more. It would not be unusual for a legal secretary's time on things like document production to be billed out at perhaps $25 to $50 an hour.

Source: lawyers.com. Accessed March 24, 2011

---

lawyer also gets nothing. If the client wins $1 million, and the agreed contingent fee is 33 percent, the attorney will receive $333,333. Whether the case is won or lost, the client normally is expected to pay for actual costs, such as court fees, transcripts prepared by court reporters, and so on.

The contingent fee is sometimes controversial. Obviously, lawyers do not offer contingent fee contracts to clients unless they believe the case will be won or a good settlement reached, with money recovered. Some say that this encourages lawyers to file more cases and request more damages than they would if they were charging by the hour, and there certainly have been situations where lawyers have tried to "drum up" cases. On the other hand, many injured persons simply would not have the money to pursue a lawsuit against someone who had injured them, if they had to pay attorney fees of $200 or more/hour during the time the case was pending, win or lose. If lawsuits were not filed by injured persons because the costs were too high, those individuals or firms who caused the injuries would then escape liability for the harm they caused.

CORPORATE LEGAL DEPARTMENTS

About 10 percent of all American attorneys are employed full-time by corporations and the percentage is rising. These lawyers, called **in-house counsel** or **corporate counsel,** are regular salaried employees of the company, just like members of the corporate human resources or accounting department. They devote their full energies to the company's legal issues and normally do not have a private practice on the side. The economic recession of 2008–2010 has caused many companies to have more legal work done by their in-house counsel and less by more expensive private law firms.

> **corporate counsel** or **"in-house" counsel:** Lawyers who work full-time, at a salary, for a corporation.

Much legal work, of course, by both private law firms and corporate legal departments, does not involve court cases at all, but involves business planning, negotiating contracts, advising company officials and employees regarding compliance with governmental regulations, addressing tax issues, and assisting in other commercial legal matters. However, because of the lawyer certification rules explained previously, when a company does need to file a lawsuit against a defendant in another state, an attorney licensed in that state must be hired to institute the lawsuit. Often "in house counsel" for large corporations concentrate on the various specialized legal issues within the firm—such as employment, taxation, environmental compliance, and contracts—and hire private law firms to handle court litigation matters. According to a 2010 report, corporate counsel feel that they have more status and influence in their own companies in the post-recession world, and have more power over corporate legal matters than previously.

PHILADELPHIA MAGISTRATE JUDGE REDUCES HOURLY RATE FOR FEE AWARD FOR LAWYER'S ATROCIOUS WRITING

The lawyer won a jury verdict for a plaintiff in a Title VII employment discrimination case. But his written work was so bad that the magistrate judge cut his fee for that work from $300/hour to $150/hour. His pleadings were vague, incomplete and replete with typos. Problems with the lawyer's original complaint were so serious that the court had ordered the lawyer to file an amended complaint. But the amended complaint included portions that were "nearly unintelligible." Even in a letter to the court the lawyer misspelled the judge's first name as "Jacon," when it should have been "Jacob." In fact, there were even typos (quoted by the court) in the lawyer's response to the other side's attacks on the quality of his written work product. The court was unhappy and noted the following: " . . . Mr. [Lawyer's] complete lack of care in his written product shows disrespect for the court." In contrast to his written work, the court found the lawyer's courtroom work to be quite workmanlike and allowed $300/hour for that work. "[T]he court was impressed with the transformation."

ETHICAL ISSUES FOR ATTORNEYS

A longstanding rule of law is that the client's communications with his/her lawyer are confidential—that is, the lawyer may not disclose anything disclosed to him or her by the client during the time the client was represented by the lawyer, unless the client gives permission for the disclosure. For example, if Ben tells his lawyer Teresa that he had consumed 4 beers before his auto accident, Teresa may not repeat this information to anyone else without Ben's authorization. This rule is called the **attorney–client privilege**.

Although Teresa cannot repeat Ben's comment made to her as his attorney, that does not mean that she should assist Ben in lying, either in or out of court. Teresa should not tell the other attorney or the court what Ben told her, but if Ben is asked questions in court under oath, he is expected to tell the truth. As we saw earlier in this chapter with the *Cooperman* case in New York, each state has an ethical code of conduct that governs the professional behavior and conduct of attorneys licensed to practice in that state. These codes require that lawyers be "zealous" in representing their clients but prohibit attorneys from assisting the client in lying to the court. If a client insists on telling falsehoods in court, the attorney should ask the judge to be released from representing the client, in a private conference.

In a case decided in 1998, the U.S. Supreme Court held that the attorney–client privilege continues to exist after the client dies. The case received much publicity because the client who died was Vince Foster, a close friend and legal adviser to President Clinton. Mr. Foster died, apparently by suicide, in 1993. Nine days earlier he had consulted with his lawyer and may have discussed issues concerning the White House. Some years later, Independent Counsel Ken Starr (who was investigating President and Mrs. Clinton) tried to obtain notes taken by the lawyer during his conversation with Mr. Foster. The Supreme Court refused the request, finding that it has "been generally accepted for well over a century, that the attorney–client privilege survives the death of the client."

The public purpose for the attorney–client privilege is that the justice system works best when clients feel free to fully inform their lawyers of all facts they know, whether favorable or unfavorable to their case. Even if some of what the attorney knows is harmful to the client's cause, the attorney can better represent the individual if he or she knows both the strong and weak parts of the case. The American "adversary" system is designed to function so that when each side to a case is vigorously represented, the truth will emerge.

This privilege is not recognized in the same way around the world. In 2010, The European Court of Justice (top court in the European Union) decided that the "legal professional privilege" only applies to independent-lawyers, not those "in house" attorneys employed by a corporation. The court stated that its ruling was based in part on the fact that the in-house lawyer "does not enjoy the same degree of independence from his/her employer" as do attorneys working for an external law firm.

attorney–client privilege: An attorney may not disclose to anyone confidential statements made to him or her by the client.

ETHICAL ISSUES

The corporate scandals of 2002–03 (Enron, WorldCom, etc.) which disclosed the existence of massive fraudulent accounting and the issuance of financial reports which did not accurately state a corporation's profits and losses, have caused some changes in attorney ethical rules. Many of the misleading documents filed with the Securities and Exchange Commission (SEC) and provided to shareholders and banks were signed and approved by company lawyers and outside counsel. Many commentators faulted the legal profession, as well as accounting and auditing firms, for assisting in the perpetuation of the misleading financial information put forth by certain companies.

As the result of these ethical failings, new standards were established by the Sarbanes-Oxley Act and rules were later issued by the SEC applying to all attorneys who represent public companies regulated by the SEC. Under the final rule such attorneys are required to report evidence of material violations of the U.S. securities laws or a breach of fiduciary duty by a company or its agents to the chief legal officer (or chief legal officer and chief executive officer) of the company, or to report such evidence to a qualified legal compliance committee of the issuer.

Furthermore, attorneys must then report "up-the-ladder" to the audit committee, or another committee of independent directors, or directly to the board of directors in the event that the chief legal officer or chief executive officer fails to respond appropriately. Chief legal officers are required to investigate and take all reasonable steps to cause the issuer to adopt an appropriate response to the evidence of material violations. After considerable controversy and debate, the American Bar Association narrowly approved a similar version of rules as an addition to its code of ethics.

The SEC had originally proposed an additional step—that if the company Board of Directors failed to take responsible action, then the attorney must resign and inform the SEC of the violations of law and/or fiduciary duty. Organized attorney organizations and bar associations vigorously opposed this provision, (called the "noisy withdrawal" rule) arguing that such rules violated the attorney-client privilege, by requiring lawyers to disclose information given them in confidence by their clients. The SEC's final rule did not contain this section, but reserved the matter for further study.

In addition to guarding the confidential communications of clients as discussed previously, most state bar associations have attorney ethical codes that require the attorney to avoid any **conflict of interest.** Obviously, at the least, this means that the lawyer may not represent both the plaintiff and defendant in a case. Also an attorney should avoid any situation in which it appears that he or she may have obtained confidential information from one party that now he or she may attempt to use to benefit the other side.

conflict of interest: A situation that occurs when an attorney attempts to act for both his client and for one whose interest is adverse to that of his client.

Determining whether there is a conflict becomes more difficult when the lawyer represents a business or several businesses. In connection with doing legal work for a corporate client, the lawyer will likely have many private discussions with employees and officers of the corporation. As long as the interests of the corporation and the individuals are exactly the same, there is no problem, but the conflict-of-interest issue becomes sticky when those interests begin to diverge.

Suppose, for example, that the corporation fires the president and later the president wants to sue the company. Or when the audit is done, there is evidence of mismanagement of money by the controller. Or a member of the Board of Directors asks the attorney for some information that was given to the attorney by the company president. In each case the attorney must determine whether there is any conflict between the representation of the client (the company, in this example) and another party who desires legal advice (such as the board member or the president). The wise attorney declines to become involved in any situation in which there is a potential conflict of interest. She should clearly state that she is representing the company or the individual and recommend that the other party obtain legal counsel of their own.

Attorneys are also considered *"officers of the court."* Generally, this means that when licensed to practice law in a jurisdiction, an attorney not only owes allegiance to his clients but has an obligation to the legal system to behave in a way that promotes public confidence in justice. This responsibility involves obeying the court rules and ethical codes governing lawyers in that state and also requires that lawyers not take actions that jeopardize the public's faith in the fairness of the legal system. Attorneys have been disciplined not only for various forms of excessive and misleading advertising, but for various other actions, such as unduly harsh public criticism of a particular judge, which may cause the general public to question the fairness of the system.

MEMO FROM THE LEGAL DEPARTMENT

To: Students

From: Your Lawyer

1. When you decide to engage the services of an attorney, ask friends and business associates, bankers, accountants, and doctors for names of lawyers they can recommend. There is much competition in the legal arena today. You are the consumer and may shop around, ask for references, or ask questions about each attorney's experience with this type of case. You should do this before selecting an attorney.

2. Many attorneys (but not all) will offer one free consultation to discuss a prospective case. Make sure you know before you go into the office if there will be a fee for the first meeting. This is a good chance to see if you feel comfortable with the attorney and if the attorney seems sharp and listens to you.

3. The best attorneys know a lot about the law but usually are not confident that they have all the answers until they do some research. Every case is somewhat different. If an attorney tells you, "I know all about this; don't worry about a thing," it may be wise to get another opinion.

4. Discuss fee arrangements at the first meeting, and if you decide to retain (hire) the attorney, have the agreement put into writing. Make sure you understand what costs and other expenses you will be expected to pay and how much they will likely be. Find out how often you will be billed, and ask for a detailed billing statement.

5. Discuss who in the law firm will actually handle the case. Will it be this attorney or another or several? Will para-legals (nonlawyers who have studied law and assist the lawyer) be involved? Paralegals are often very knowledgeable and efficient, but you should know ahead of time if they will assist the attorney, and what the fees for their services will be.

6. If the lawyer wants a retainer (an "up-front" payment), clarify whether it will be refunded if the time needed is much less than expected and whether it counts against the first few hourly billings.

7. If you are thinking of suing someone, discuss at the first meeting with the lawyer whether it will be possible to collect a judgment from the person being sued. It makes little sense to sue someone who has few assets and no regular job. Courts do not award a "pound of flesh." Even if you are totally right and the other person is wrong, if the defendant has no money or assets and no insurance, you may win the case but never receive any monetary recovery. This is a very frustrating experience for both the lawyer and the client.

SUMMARY

The American legal system contains substantial state and federal components. Within each system—federal and state—there are trial courts, intermediate appellate courts, and a supreme court. In order for a court to hear and decide a case, it must have both personal and subject-matter jurisdiction. In addition, there must be an actual dispute between the parties, and the person bringing the case must have "standing" to make the arguments.

Business owners or managers will undoubtedly have occasion to employ the services of a lawyer at some time and should do so carefully and in an informed manner. The material in this chapter should help the businessperson make better decisions on when to retain a lawyer, to be able to make a more intelligent selection, and to work more effectively with the lawyer when one is selected. This chapter has examined the process of becoming a lawyer and some of the differences between types of lawyers, discussed the differences between "in-house" lawyers and attorneys in private practice, and compared large and small law firms. There are primarily three types of fee arrangements clients make with attorneys—hourly, contingent, and set fees. The more educated consumers are, the better choices they will make, when it is necessary to choose and work with an attorney. Since the attorney works for the client, it is important for the client to intelligently and actively participate in all decisions.

CHAPTER QUESTIONS

1. Describe the court system in your state. What are the names of the trial courts, and what type of jurisdiction does each have? Is there a small claims court, and what is its jurisdiction? What appellate courts are there?

2. Where is the nearest federal court? How many federal judges are there at that court? List their names and how long each one has been a judge. What federal appellate circuit are you in? Where would an appeal from a decision made by your local federal district court be heard?

3. A Texas partnership filed a lawsuit against a Mexican corporation in federal court seeking $1 million in damages as the result of a contract dispute. When the case was filed two of the partners in the partnership were Mexican citizens, but by the time the case went to trial, those 2 had left the firm. The lower federal court decided that diversity jurisdiction did exist at trial, and entered a judgment for $750,000 in favor of the partnership. The Mexican corporation appealed all the way to the U.S. Supreme Court, arguing that the lower court did not have federal jurisdiction because of a lack of "diversity". What should the Supreme Court decide? *Grupo Dataflux v. Atlas Global Group, LP,* 541 U.S. 567 (2004).

4. What is the difference between a lawyer in a private practice and one who is "in-house counsel" to a corporation? Are the ethical duties or the application of the lawyer–client privilege or conflict-of-interest rules any different depending on which type of lawyer the person is?

5. International Shoe Co. manufactures and sells shoes and other footwear. It is incorporated in Delaware and has its principal place of business in Missouri. For several years International Shoe had about 12 salespeople in the state of Washington who were compensated by commissions. The com-

pany had no offices and no inventory of shoes in Washington, although the salespeople occasionally rented space and rooms to show the shoes, for which they were reimbursed. The salespeople were given some samples, and after they showed the shoes, they solicited orders, which were sent to St. Louis for acceptance. If the contracts were accepted by International Shoe, the shoes were shipped directly from Missouri to the purchasers. The state of Washington decided that the salespeople were "employees" and sued International Shoe in state court in Washington to collect unpaid unemployment compensation contributions. The company argued that the state of Washington had no jurisdiction over it. How would you decide this case? Why? [See *International Shoe Co. v. Washington, 326 U.S. 310 (1945)*.]

6. The Funtime Corporation announced plans to develop a major amusement park in a marshy area of central Wisconsin. The park would feature "badger races," roller coasters, and other attractions and would create 500 new jobs. Some citizens were not thrilled, however. The local Sierra Club filed suit to block the development, claiming that the park would destroy the habitat for 30 species of migratory waterfowl and cause other damage to wildlife. In addition, George King, a local resident, complained that he has hiked and camped in that area for 30 years and does not want the project to be built. Does the club have "standing" to raise these issues? Does George? What are the issues? Please explain your answers.

7. William, a resident of Wilbraham, Massachusetts, was the president and major shareholder of a Massachusetts corporation, which was developing some real estate in New Hampshire. He made certain false statements to purchasers regarding some of the lots his company sold. Several of the unhappy buyers sued him in the New Hampshire state court. He claimed that the New Hampshire courts did not have jurisdiction over him. How would you decide this case? Why? What factors would lead you to change your answer?

8. John Wankum, a former city engineer, was terminated from employment and retained a lawyer to sue the city for wrongful discharge. Two years later the attorney was appointed to a judge position, and his cases were taken over by another lawyer. The new lawyer requested and received a $7,500 retainer from Mr. Wankum, but then failed to bring the case to trial within the 5-year time limit allowed for filing such cases. The lawyer also did not tell Mr. Wankum that the time for filing suit had run out, and he learned from another lawyer that it was now too late to sue. Has the lawyer committed malpractice? Will Mr. Wankum be successful in suing the attorney for damages?

9. Stephanie Lenz filed a lawsuit against Universal Music Corp claiming that it had sent a wrongful notice to You Tube under the Digital Millenium Copyright Act requesting removal of a video depicting a toddler dancing to Prince's "Let's Go Crazy." After the case was filed but before trial she wrote e-mails and blogs saying that her attorneys were "salivating about getting their teeth into Universal" and discussing her attorneys' strategy. The attorneys for Universal ask the court to order her to submit to further discovery on these topics, but she refused, citing her attorney–client privilege. Has she waived her attorney–client privilege by her actions? *Lenz v. Universal Music Corp.,* (D.C. Cal. 2010) reported at 79 USLW 1670 (Nov. 30, 2010).

10. Oxford is a British biotechnology company which owns a patent related to microarrays for analysis of polynucleotides. Oxford is not registered to do business in California, nor does it have any facilities, assets, employees,

or agents there. Autogenomics is a biotechnology company organized under the laws of California, with its main office in Carlsbad, California, and Autogenomics uses microarray technology in its business. Claiming that Autogenomics was infringing its patent, Oxford wrote to Autogenomics stating that a license should be obtained to use its patented technology. Autogenomics expressed some interest in taking a license, but alleged "serious issues with regard to novelty and obviousness" of the patent. Oxford responded by e-mail stating that "we are at a point whereby the commercial negotiations should begin to achieve a license for the Autogenomics product." In July 2007, two Oxford representatives flew to California to meet with representatives of Autogenomics, but the parties failed to agree on a license.

Oxford completed a collaborative agreement in 2007 with Agilent Technologies (Agilent) another California company, which involves "a collaborative agreement giving Oxford access to Agilent's microarray platform, confirming Oxford as an Agilent Certified Service Provider, and appointing Agilent as an OEM supplier for Oxford designed microarrays." The deal will purportedly allow the two companies to "jointly develop a Centre of (Microarray) Excellence." Autogenomics calls this a "joint venture," but Oxford executives characterize the relationship as a "close collaboration." Oxford representatives also attended three scientific conferences—trade shows in Autogenomics's terminology—in California in 2003, 2005, and 2007. The three conferences dealt with "nanotechnology," "bio-nanotechnology," and "modeling and simulation of microsystems," respectively and Oxford made presentations at these technical conferences.

When negotiations over the license were unsuccessful, Autogenomics sued Oxford in California, seeking a declaratory judgment that its patent was invalid. Oxford filed a motion to dismiss for lack of jurisdiction. What are the key issues and who should win? *Autogenomics, Inc. v. Oxford Gene Technology Limited,* 566 F.3d 1012 (Fed. Cir. 2009).

PRACTICAL EXERCISE

Using the factual situation outlined at the end of Chapter 1 (Josh's bad day), prepare a memo indicating: (1) what type of lawyer or law firm Josh might consult for his different legal problems; (2) what type of fee arrangement he might make with each lawyer; (3) what courts in your state would have jurisdiction over the various legal disputes involving Josh.

FURTHER INFORMATION

www.abanet.org
   Official site of American Bar Association.
www.law.com
   Large site containing daily reports on interesting legal issues.
www.uscourts.gov
   Home page of the federal court system.
Ethics and Lawyering Today
http://www.ethicsandlawyering.com
   Lively newsletter dealing with attorneys' ethical issues

CHAPTER 3

LITIGATION AND ALTERNATE DISPUTE RESOLUTION: GOING TO COURT, OR NOT

LEARNING OBJECTIVES

After you have read this chapter, you should be able to:

1. Understand and outline the steps involved in taking a civil case to court.
2. Describe the procedures of jury selection, including *voir dire* and the types of juror challenges.
3. Identify the different stages of a trial and the appellate process.
4. Summarize the various types of judgments and how courts enforce them.
5. Discuss the advantages and disadvantages of various forms of Alternate Dispute Resolution.

CHAPTER OUTLINE

I. Progress of a Civil Case from Filing to the Trial

II. Jury Procedures

III. The Trial

IV. The Appellate Process

V. Types of Judgments; Enforcing and Collecting Judgments

VI. Alternate Dispute Resolution

If a competitor ran advertisements making or implying false statements about your business, how would you respond in court? What allegations would you make in your complaint to effectively present your case?

"Get you off? You'll be lucky if I can defend you with a straight face!"

Source: From *The Wall Street Journal*, January 18, 1995. Reprinted with permission of Cartoon Features Syndicate.

INTRODUCTION

In the previous chapter we learned how the American legal system is structured, what types of cases should be filed in certain courts, and what powers and restrictions govern court jurisdiction. We also discussed the educational process required to become an attorney, the different types of lawyers and what their duties and responsibilities are, several ethical principles governing the attorney/client relationship, and the connection between lawyers and business. This chapter continues the explanation of the American legal system by examining the procedures used when a matter does arrive at the courthouse. We will also examine several types of alternate dispute resolution (ADR), which are methods of resolving disputes without actually going to court. Non-court resolution of disputes is becoming more important and popular with business each year. As before, our goal is not to turn you into an amateur lawyer but to provide you with more information on how the system works. With this knowledge, you will be a more informed consumer of legal services and will be able to participate more fully and more intelligently in business decisions involving legal issues.

THE PROGRESS OF A CIVIL CASE FROM FILING TO THE TRIAL

COMPLAINT AND ANSWER

complaint: The plaintiff's version of the events that led to the suit, and request for damages or other relief.

plaintiff: The person who files a civil lawsuit against another.

Once one of the parties to a dispute decides that he or she wishes to have a court make a decision in the matter, the proper court must be selected, as we have discussed in the previous chapter. The next step, usually taken with the assistance of a lawyer, is to prepare a **complaint.** This is the first document filed in the case; it sets forth, in numbered paragraphs, the arguments and factual assertions made by the **plaintiff** (the one filing the case). A sample complaint appears in Figure 3.1. The complaint must state enough facts so that the court can determine if it has jurisdiction of the case and also so the **defendant**

Figure 3.1
Complaint

State of Idaho
In The District Court for Ada County

Susan Jackson, Plaintiff
v.
Paul Brown, Defendant

COMPLAINT

1. The plaintiff, Susan Jackson, is a resident of Ada County in the state of Idaho.
2. The defendant, Paul Brown, is a resident of the city of Boise, Ada County, in the state of Idaho.
3. On May 2, 2010, plaintiff was driving her 2002 Chevrolet automobile in a lawful manner on Third Street in the city of Boise, Ada County, Idaho.
4. On the same date, defendant Paul Brown was driving his 1997 Ford pickup on Third Street in Boise.
5. At approximately 3:00 p.m. defendant Brown's vehicle was following behind the plaintiff's vehicle, when plaintiff applied her brakes to avoid hitting a dog which had run into the street.
6. Defendant brought his vehicle to a stop directly behind the plaintiff's car.
7. After stopping his truck, the defendant jumped out and ran toward plaintiff's car shouting angry obscenities at the plaintiff because she had stopped.
8. Plaintiff got out of her car to attempt to talk to the defendant, but before she could say anything, the defendant, still shouting, grabbed the plaintiff's shoulders and pushed her against the car.
9. Defendant acted intentionally, and his wrongful battery against plaintiff caused physical injury to her from which she still suffers and will continue to suffer in the future.
10. As the direct result of defendant's actions, plaintiff has suffered considerable pain and suffering, has incurred significant medical expenses, and has lost earnings due to her inability to work for several weeks after the battery by the defendant.

WHEREFORE, plaintiff requests that this Honorable Court award her damages from the defendant in the amount of $500,000 plus her attorney's fees.

_____
Susan Jackson
Plaintiff

(the person or persons against whom the case is filed) can understand and answer the claims made against him.

SUMMONS AND SERVICE OF PROCESS

In most states the complaint must be signed by the plaintiff; then, the original is taken to the appropriate court and filed with the clerk. At the same time, a **summons** is issued. This document technically comes from the court

summons: A document issued by the court when a civil case is filed. It notifies the defendant of the suit and tells him/her when an answer must be filed.

(although it is usually typed ahead of time by the plaintiff's attorney and then signed by the court clerk) and is directed to the defendant. It tells the defendant what court the case is in, what judge the case is assigned to (which is determined in some random method at the court when the case is filed), and how long the defendant has to respond.

service of process: Delivery of the complaint and summons to the defendant.

The next stage in the process is **service of process.** Fairness requires that if Joanna is going to sue Paul, she needs to inform him about the lawsuit, not just file the papers at the courthouse. Generally, service of process requires that a copy of the complaint and summons be personally delivered to the defendant—this is called "personal service." If the defendant is not served within a certain time, the case can be dismissed. In some cases, where the defendant's whereabouts are unknown, or the defendant is deliberately evading service, the law will allow some type of "substitute service," such as mailing the notice to him, posting the papers on the defendant's door, or publicizing it in a newspaper. Chapter 2 included a discussion about the need for personal jurisdiction over the defendant.

answer: The defendant's point by point response to the complaint.

After the defendant (Paul) receives the papers, he has a limited time (many state laws allow 20 days) to file an answer or take some other action. If Paul files an **answer,** it must contain a response, either admitting or denying each of the paragraphs of the complaint. A sample answer appears in Figure 3.2. Often, rather than filing an answer, the defendant will file a **motion to dismiss** (a request that the court terminate the case right then) or some other motion within the 20 days. Until the court rules on the motion, the defendant does not have to file an answer.

motion to dismiss: A request by the defendant that the case be dismissed because no valid legal claim has been made.

MOTIONS

The **motion to dismiss** requests that the court dismiss the case because the plaintiff has failed to properly state a valid legal claim. Most of the time these motions are denied; the court rules that the plaintiff has alleged a valid case and should be given the chance to prove it at trial. The defendant is then ordered to file an answer within a certain time. Occasionally, however, the plaintiff has failed to properly state a recognized legal claim, and the case is dismissed. For example, if Joanna files a lawsuit against Paul alleging a breach of contract, and she fails to state in her complaint sufficient facts to show that there ever was a valid contract existing between the two of them, her complaint would probably be dismissed.

If, after receiving service of process, the defendant fails to answer or bring some type of motion, the plaintiff will be entitled to take a **default** at the end of the time period. If the defendant is so angry upon being served with court papers (as many people are) that he or she tears them up or burns them, thinking that the case will go away, the defendant is badly mistaken. Every competent lawyer keeps track of the day when papers are served in each case and the date when answers are due and will ask the court for a **default judgment** in favor of the client soon after the time period for answers has passed.

default judgment: The court enters judgment for the plaintiff when the defendant fails to answer the complaint.

As the case moves along there may be many other kinds of motions filed by the parties. Most courts will not schedule a trial in a civil case for at least a year or two (or longer), so if either side wants some action taken by the court before then, the party must schedule a hearing to request a court order. For example, if one party believes the trial should be held elsewhere (a "change of venue," as

Figure 3.2
Answer

State of Idaho
In The District Court for Ada County

Susan Jackson, Plaintiff
v.
Paul Brown, Defendant

ANSWER

1. Defendant neither admits nor denies paragraph one of the complaint for lack of information, but leaves plaintiff to her proofs.
2. Defendant admits the allegations of paragraph two.
3. Defendant admits that plaintiff was driving her vehicle on the day in question, but denies that it was in a lawful manner.
4. Defendant admits the allegations of paragraph four.
5. Defendant admits that plaintiff suddenly and abruptly stopped her car in the middle of the street, but denies the remainder of paragraph five.
6. Defendant admits that he had to suddenly stop his vehicle in order to avoid hitting the plaintiff.
7. Defendant admits that he stepped out of his car and criticized plaintiff's driving, but denies the balance of paragraph seven.
8. Defendant denies the allegations of paragraph eight and leaves plaintiff to her proofs.
9. Defendant denies the allegations of paragraph nine and leaves plaintiff to her proofs.
10. Defendant denies the allegations of paragraph ten and leaves plaintiff to her proofs.

WHEREFORE, Defendant requests that the Court dismiss this complaint so wrongfully filed and award attorney fees and costs to defendant.

_____
Paul Brown
Defendant

---

discussed in Chapter 2), wants a temporary restraining order preventing the other side from selling the property that is the subject of the lawsuit, or desires a list of all doctors the plaintiff has seen, that party must file a motion for relief, and the court will set a date for a hearing on that motion. Most courts have at least one "motion day" per week, when the judge hears one motion after another, relating to the many cases pending in that judge's court.

COUNTERCLAIMS

In some cases, not only does the defendant assert that she did not do what the plaintiff has charged, but that the plaintiff has actually injured her. In this situation the defendant may file a **counterclaim**, which is in effect a complaint by the defendant against the plaintiff, to which the plaintiff will have to file an

counterclaim:
The defendant in a civil case files a counter action, alleging that the plaintiff has caused some injury to the defendant.

answer (usually called a "response"). When this is done, the court will eventually have to decide the two cases, one brought by the plaintiff and one by the defendant. One trial will be held, which will include the allegations on both claims.

For example, in our mythical *Jackson v. Brown* case, if Mr. Brown not only denies hurting Ms. Jackson, but in fact asserts that it was Ms. Jackson who hit him, the defendant (Brown) might not only file an *answer* as in our example, but might also file a *counterclaim*, seeking damages from Jackson.

While the decision about whether to file a counterclaim is usually an option for the defendant, sometimes the defendant *must* file a counterclaim or lose his or her legal right to file it later. The Federal Rules of Civil Procedure control federal court practice. Rule 13(a) states that if the defendant has any type of counterclaim arising out of the same transaction that is the subject of the plaintiff's complaint, she *must* assert it at the time of responding to the complaint, or she will lose the chance to make it at a later date. The legal phrase *res judicata* ("the thing has been decided") means that once a court has decided an issue between two parties in one case, it will not hear and decide that issue in another case. This rule may even apply to issues that *should have been* raised in the previous case, as the next case illustrates.

MARTINO V. MCDONALD'S SYSTEM, INC.

598 F. 2d 1079 (7th Cir. 1979)

FACTS

Louis Martino and his three brothers entered into a franchise agreement with McDonald's in 1962. They organized McDonald's Drive-in of Ottumwa, Iowa, Inc. and operated the business. The contract the Martinos signed with McDonald's provided that neither Martino nor any member of his immediate family would acquire a financial interest in a competing self-service food business without the written consent of McDonald's.

In 1968, however, Martino's son purchased a Burger Chef franchise in Pittsburgh, Kansas, with Martino providing the financing. McDonald's sued Martino and his brothers for this violation of their agreement, and the lawsuit ended with the parties reaching a consent judgment (settlement). The court entered the judgment on the record and included its findings of fact (one of which was that Martino had breached the contract). As part of the settlement, Martino sold the franchise back to McDonald's.

A few years later Martino brought this lawsuit against McDonald's, charging, among other things, that the franchise agreement violated the Sherman Antitrust Act as an illegal restraint on trade. McDonald's brought a motion to dismiss, based on the argument that Martino's claim should have been brought in the first case, because it was a compulsory counterclaim under Federal Rule 13(a). The lower court agreed and dismissed the case.

DECISION

Judge Pell wrote the opinion of the Court of Appeals:

Rule 13(a) says "a pleading shall state as a counterclaim any claim which at the time of serving the pleading the pleader has against the opposing party . . . ." However, in the earlier action, Martino filed no pleadings, as the word is defined in the federal rules. "Rule 13(a) is in some ways a harsh rule. It forces parties to raise certain claims at the time and place chosen by their opponents or to lose them. The rule, however, is the result of a balancing between competing interests. The convenience of the party with a compulsory counterclaim is sacrificed in the interest of judicial economy."

The drafters of Rule 13(a) did not choose the term "pleading" unadvisedly. It no doubt marks, although somewhat arbitrarily, the point at which "the judicial burden of the earlier lawsuit outweighs the opposing party's interest in bringing an action when and where it is most convenient."

Since the earlier action was concluded by a consent judgment before Martino filed an answer, Rule 13(a) does not apply here. McDonald's argues that the *time for an answer* had expired (even though no answer was filed), but there are other sanctions in the court rules to apply to that problem (i.e., a default judgment). Therefore, the antitrust claim is not barred by Rule 13(a).

There is another theory, however, that bars Martino's claim. The principles of *res judicata* establish a narrowly defined class of "common law compulsory counterclaims." Judge Pell stated that "a judgment on the merits of a case operates as an absolute bar to relitigation between the parties of every matter offered

and received to sustain or defeat the claim or demand and every matter been received for that purpose." Since the court in the earlier case had included judicial conclusions of law and fact (Martino's breach of contract), he should have, and could have, raised the antitrust claims then and cannot do so now. The judgment of dismissal entered by the district court was affirmed.

CASE QUESTIONS

1. What is the purpose of the compulsory counterclaim rule? Why does Judge Pell describe it as "in some ways a harsh rule"? What does he mean by the "interest of judicial economy"?
2. What pleadings were filed in the earlier case? By whom?
3. What is the *res judicata* rule? What is the purpose of this rule, which causes the court to rule in the end in favor of McDonald's? Where does the common law compulsory counterclaim rule come from?

MEMO FROM THE LEGAL DEPARTMENT

If you are ever sued in a civil case, as you are drafting your Answer to the Complaint with your lawyer, it is a good idea to think about the transaction or event that led to the lawsuit, to determine if you have a viable counterclaim against the plaintiff. DO NOT make anything up, but if you do feel that the plaintiff has done something to injure you, this is an excellent time to raise it. A lawsuit has already been filed against you, so you don't have to serve the other party—just prepare and file the counterclaim and mail a copy to the plaintiff's lawyer.

Since the vast majority of cases (95% or so) are settled before trial, a viable counterclaim will totally change the range of settlement negotiations, from "how much am I willing to pay" to settle the case, to "how much will the plaintiff pay me and how much will I have to pay the plaintiff." Again, this advice only applies to situations where you do have a real grievance—do not make up a story. But many business and personal disputes do have two sides, and a viable counterclaim is a powerful weapon.

AFFIRMATIVE DEFENSES

Another defensive document sometimes filed by the defendant is an **affirmative defense,** which claims that even if the plaintiff were to prove all he or she has alleged, there is some legal reason why he or she should lose the case. One example of a valid affirmative defense is the *statute of limitations,* which is a law

statute of limitations: A law that specifies how many years after an event a person has to bring a lawsuit.

that specifies how long after an event occurs the plaintiff has to file a lawsuit. In most states, for negligence or tort claims, the statute of limitations is two or three years. For example if the plaintiff waits five years to file a lawsuit after a traffic accident, the suit will be dismissed even if he or she has a strong case.

DISCOVERY

The next phase of the case is the *discovery* stage. This is the time when each side is entitled to learn about the other party's case—the names and addresses of the witnesses who will be called at trial, what they will say, what evidence the other side plans to introduce, and what medical records, bank records, charts, and other physical evidence support each side's claim. Some of the more important types of discovery procedures are set forth in the following sections.

deposition: An out-of-court procedure where the attorney for one side can ask direct questions of the opposing party.

Depositions   Each party is allowed to schedule the other for a **deposition**, a sort of minitrial or cross-examination. A deposition is held out of court, generally in one of the attorney's offices, or sometimes in the client's own office. The judge is not present, but a court reporter takes down and later types up all that is said. The court reporter administers the oath ("Do you swear to tell the truth . . ."), and then the person is questioned by the opposing attorney.

This proceeding gives both lawyers the opportunity to ask the opposing party any and all questions they may have about any issues that may pertain to the case. The deposition is the *only* chance for one side's attorney to directly ask the other side's key person a wide-ranging array of questions. Sometimes the questioning gets pretty far off the subject of the case. The party's own attorney is there, of course, to object to certain questions, but the judge is not present, so there is no ruling on the objections. On occasion, the atmosphere gets quite argumentative, which can make for some interesting reading when the court reporter prepares the transcript of the deposition. ("Mr. Johnson said to Ms. Martin (defendant's attorney) 'That is the most absurd, outrageous, irrelevant question I've ever heard another attorney ask a witness'.")

If an attorney really believes that a particular question is clearly improper, the attorney may tell the client, "I instruct you not to answer." The question may be presented later to the judge, who may or may not issue an order compelling an answer to the question. New federal civil procedure rules, explained below, have attempted to limit this tactic, and to encourage less argumentative depositions.

INTERROGATORIES

interrogatories: A set of written questions sent by one side to the opposing party.

Another widely used discovery tool is called **interrogatories**. These are sets of written questions sent by one side to the other, requesting information about the factual basis of the party's claim. These questions are often quite detailed, such as, "interrogatory 1: please list all bank accounts you have ever maintained with name and address of bank, date each account was opened and closed, and average balance." While parties must answer all *relevant* interrogatories, they do so in writing at a later date and after much consultation with their attorneys. The answers, therefore, tend to be the bare minimum required and often are as evasive as possible. Interrogatories are useful for getting at hard facts: names of witnesses, dates, and definite information of one kind or another.

Request for Production of Documents   If there are some important, relevant documents in the possession of one party that the other wants to see, a request for production of documents may be used. Often this request seeks copies of medical reports on the plaintiff's condition, prepared by his or her doctor. In addition, in cases where the plaintiff is alleging physical injury, the defendant is entitled to request the plaintiff to see a doctor of the defendant's choosing, in order to provide another opinion of the plaintiff's condition.

The reason all these discovery tools were developed is that the more each side knows about the other's case, the greater the likelihood that the case will be settled without the necessity of a full trial, thus saving considerable time and money. The discovery rules represent an attempt to move away from the "trial by surprise," which is likened to the movie or television scenario in which a previously unknown witness shows up late in the trial and offers dramatic and unexpected testimony. In real court cases, each side is required to provide, long before the trial, a list of witnesses who will be called at trial so the other side can adequately prepare for that testimony and perhaps interview or "depose" them. Every case is different, however, and problems sometimes occur that force the judge to make difficult decisions. The following case concerns a situation where the plaintiff's attorney did not comply with the discovery rules, causing the judge to dismiss the case.

DENNIE V. METROPOLITAN MEDICAL CENTER

387 N.W. 2d 401 (Minnesota Supreme Court, 1986)

FACTS

Mr. Francis Dennie entered Metropolitan Medical Center because of numbness in his right hand. Dr. Harold Nolan examined him and diagnosed carpal tunnel syndrome as well as other nerve diseases and difficulties. Surgery was performed on his hand to correct the carpal tunnel syndrome, and later that day a nurse gave Mr. Dennie a shot in the left buttock to relieve the pain.

In a few hours, however, he began to feel extreme pain in his entire left leg. Mr. Dennie, who was to have been discharged the next day, ended up staying in the hospital for 14 days and was bedridden for three months due to problems in his left leg. He has continued to experience pain in the leg.

About two years later, Mr. Dennie filed suit against the hospital, alleging that the nurse who gave him the shot did so negligently, causing permanent damage to the sciatic nerve in his leg. The hospital denied liability and was going to argue at trial that plaintiff's injury was caused either by an unavoidable accident or by his nerve problems.

Shortly after the case was filed in 1981, the defendant hospital served a set of interrogatories on the plaintiff. When no reply was received, the defendant asked the court for relief, and the Hennepin County District Court ordered the plaintiff to answer within 15 days. The plaintiff then answered that Dr. Nolan would appear as the expert witness at trial and would testify that the injection was given negligently. However, when his deposition was taken a few months later, in April 1982, Dr. Nolan stated that he did not believe that the injection was given negligently. In August 1982 the defendant filed a statement with the court indicating it was ready for trial, but the plaintiff did not respond. Under a court rule, no further discovery could be done thereafter without court permission.

In early 1983 the attorney who had been representing the plaintiff left the law firm and another lawyer took over. She made some efforts at reopening discovery but was unsuccessful. At the pre-trial conference she listed her witnesses as "Dr. Nolan, Steven Laven (the nurse), and a neurologist yet to be named." On May 3, 1984, the court scheduled the trial for June 18, 1984. Shortly thereafter, Dr. John Tulloch agreed to testify as the plaintiff's expert witness, and on June 11, the attorney so notified the court and defendant.

When the case was called for trial, defense counsel moved to suppress (prohibit) the testimony of both Dr. Tulloch and Mr. Laven because their identity had not been disclosed in advance, in violation of court rules, and there had been no opportunity for any discovery regarding what their testimony would be. The court denied the motion but instead ordered that their depositions be taken that afternoon, with the trial to start the following day.

Unfortunately, problems developed at the depositions. The plaintiff's attorney refused to let the defense counsel see the medical records reviewed by Mr. Laven. (Because she had put markings on them, she considered them part of the attorney's "work product.") Nor would she allow access to an opinion letter regarding the plaintiff prepared by Dr. Tulloch for the same reason.

The next morning in the court, the defendant's lawyer again asked that the court suppress the testimony of plaintiff's experts, and this time the motion was granted. Plaintiff's attorney asked the court to conduct its own review of the materials in dispute (called an *in camera* inspection), but the judge refused. After determining that the plaintiff had no expert testimony to present on the issue of negligence, the court dismissed the case with prejudice (which means "you cannot file it again— you are done"). On appeal to the Minnesota Court of Appeals, the dismissal was reversed. The court found that the remedy applied by the lower court was too harsh for the circum-

stances and was "an abuse of discretion" by the trial judge. The hospital then appealed the case to the Minnesota Supreme Court.

DECISION

Chief Justice Amdahl wrote the following opinion of the Supreme Court, affirming the Court of Appeals. "An order of dismissal on procedural grounds runs counter to the primary objective of the law to dispose of cases on the merits. . . . A dismissal with prejudice is the most punitive sanction that can be imposed for noncompliance with court rules. It therefore should be granted only under exceptional circumstances."

The Court noted that in this case the trial court had the difficult task of considering several problems that arose in the course of discovery. The general rule in Minnesota is that expert testimony should be suppressed for failure to make a timely disclosure of the expert's identity "only where the counsel's dereliction [in failing to make the disclosure] is inexcusable and results in disadvantage to the opponent." There are other sanctions available for violation of court rules, including assessing costs and attorneys' fees against the party at fault, which are much less prejudicial to the plaintiff.

After reviewing the problems that occurred in this case, the court decided that the trial court abused its discretion in suppressing both experts' testimony. Plaintiff's counsel had a reasonable legal basis for refusing defendant's attempt to discover the documents objected to at the deposition, and should at least have conducted an *in camera* inspection of the documents. The trial court should have considered the difficulty in preparing a case of this nature (getting doctors to testify against each other) and the limited time the plaintiff's attorney had been working on the case. Then, if the plaintiff's actions were held improper, court costs, fees, and other sanctions short of dismissing the case (such as postponing the trial but limiting the scope of the expert's testimony so as not to prejudice the defendant) should have been assessed. The decision of the Court of Appeals is affirmed.

CASE QUESTIONS

1. What was the trial judge's reason for dismissing the case? What is the public policy behind the reason?
2. Why were the plaintiff's lawyers constantly late in answering interrogatories, providing discovery, and preparing for trial? Was it a weak or difficult case? Poor lawyer preparation?
3. Is it right that an individual (i.e., Mr. Dennie) should lose his case because his lawyers messed up? If not, is it right that a business (i.e., the hospital) should continue to be dragged into court month after month on a case without knowing what the basis of the plaintiff's case is or who the experts are who are going to testify? Where is the proper balance between ensuring everyone his or her "day in court" and at the same time imposing some penalties on those who do not follow the rules?

In recent years, for the reasons brought out in the previous case and the case questions, a movement has begun to put some limitations on the length of time of discovery. As explained below, the rules governing practice in federal courts were amended in 2000 to put some limitations on the scope of discovery permitted, and the time allowed for depositions. While every lawyer would always like to know as much about the case as possible—no lawyer wants to go into a big trial less prepared than the other side—both clients are paying for each hour of attorney time used in the process, and the costs of discovery can be enormous. A significant business case can involve taking 20 or more depositions and sending several sets of interrogatories. Meanwhile, "the meter is running," that is, the attorneys for both sides are charging for each minute spent on the case—perhaps at $300 per hour or more. Many judges and courts—both state and federal—are putting limitations on the number of months or years allowed for discovery, as well as the number of depositions each side may take and the number and length of interrogatories.

Federal Discovery Rules

The Judicial Conference of the United States, the policymaking arm of the federal judiciary, launched a discovery study project in the late 1990s, after many years of complaints from the bar and the public about the costs associated with discovery. In the course of its study, the rules committee of the conference learned that in almost 40% of federal cases, discovery is not used at all. But in suits in which it was used, it represented 50% of litigation costs in the average case and up to 90% of litigation costs in cases in which it was used particularly exhaustively. The Conference thus proposed some new rules, which became effective in late 2000.

The new rules made some important changes to discovery procedures in federal courts. Rule 26 has narrowed the discovery that parties may seek. In the past, parties could obtain discovery relevant to the "subject matter" of the pending action. Now, the requested discovery must be "relevant to the claim or defense of any party." Only for "good cause" can the court allow more broad discovery as to general matters related to the "subject matter" of the case. This rule is intended to shorten some discovery efforts, which appeared to be so-called "fishing expeditions" where one side kept asking questions and seeking information somewhat unrelated to the case, in the hope of finding some damaging information.

Federal Rule 30 now states that objections cannot be argumentative or suggestive, and that the attorney can only instruct the client not to answer questions in limited circumstances. Rule 30 also places limits on the length of time allowed for depositions. The actual time of each deposition is limited to one 7 hour day per person, unless otherwise agreed by the parties or ordered by the court.

IN CONSULTATION

Marvin Manager has a problem. His company, ABC, Inc., is involved in litigation with a direct competitor called Othercorp. Othercorp filed suit against Marvin's company over who has an exclusive contract with a supplier they both use. Shortly after Othercorp filed its complaint, its lawyers sent Marvin several discovery requests. In addition to inquiring about the contract with the supplier, they also sent interrogatories and requests for the production of documents seeking the following information:
1. ABC's earnings for the past five years,
2. ABC's client list,
3. ABC's marketing strategy for the next two years,
4. ABC's financing arrangements with investors and banks, and
5. ABC's research and development plan for the next two years.

Marvin approached his company's in-house corporate counsel, asking whether he has to produce this information. Here is their conversation

Marvin:
1. The list of information that Othercorp seeks doesn't have anything to do with our supplier contract. Othercorp should not be able to obtain the information because it is irrelevant.
2. The materials sought by Othercorp are extensive, covering multiple years and several departments within the company. It will take weeks to compile everything and a forklift to deliver it. Isn't that an excessive burden?
3. The list contains proprietary commercial information that would cause a significant competitive disadvantage if it were to fall into Othercorp's hands. It is a direct competitor. Why should we hand them the nuts and bolts of our competitive edge when it has nothing to do with our supplier contracts?

Legal Department
1. Information obtainable during discovery is broader than evidence that may ultimately be presented at trial. Irrelevance may not be enough of a reason to prevent Othercorp from obtaining the information they seek. If our case is in federal court, however, the rules are somewhat more restrictive, and we would have a better chance of resisting some irrelevant discovery.
2. Perhaps, but not necessarily. The court must strike a balance between the seeking party's need for the information and our need to avoid undue burden and expense. If we really believe the requests are overly burdensome and "out of line" we might request a protective order from the court.
3. The court has the discretion to protect certain commercial information. I will review the applicable law to see if the items sought by Othercorp qualify for such protection. We will get back to you as soon as I have completed my research.

MEMO FROM THE LEGAL DEPARTMENT

To: Marvin Manager

Re: Scope of Discovery

Dear Marvin:

The initial answer to any question about information sought during discovery is that a party may obtain information regarding anything relevant to the lawsuit. Relevance is a broad standard that covers more than the specific issue in dispute. The purpose of discovery is to prevent "trial by surprise" and allow each party to adequately prepare all possible issues in the case. Discovery, therefore, requires a much wider scope than simply information that will be admissible at trial—especially in state courts. It is often impossible to know whether information is relevant until after you have produced it, so courts are disinclined to prevent discovery unless the irrelevance of the information is so obvious that it could not possibly have any relationship at all to the issues in dispute. Recent changes to the federal court procedural rules however, have tightened up the standards a bit. Discovery in federal cases now must be "relevant to the claim or defense of any party," rather than just relevant to the "subject matter" of the dispute.

In this case, for example, Othercorp's lawyers could argue that they need ABC's client list so they could find witnesses who have knowledge about ABC's production process. They could argue that they need marketing strategies so they can obtain evidence about the amount of supplies ABC will need. Othercorp may want research and development plans for similar evidence concerning future needs for supplies, demonstrating that information that may appear irrelevant may still be discovered.

Unfortunately, discovery is one of the biggest burdens of the entire litigation process. Complicated commercial litigation often involves substantial discovery with multiple documents, interrogatories, and depositions that inevitably consume hours of company time. New rules do limit each deposition to one 7 hour day, in most federal cases. Discovery, by definition, is disruptive and expensive. The only way to argue that the disruption and expense is inappropriate would be to prove that Othercorp is abusing the discovery process to harass ABC. Courts are disinclined to make a finding that a party is abusing the discovery process because of the court's keen interest in a full exchange of information with resulting trial preparedness.

In your third question, you mentioned that the materials sought are proprietary commercial information. This fact may offer ABC its best opportunity to avoid producing the items requested. We can file a document called a Motion for Protective Order, in which we will ask the court to protect ABC from being forced to produce the listed items. In order for our motion to prevail, we must be able to prove that the items are trade secrets that will harm our competitive edge if placed in the wrong hands. Trade secrets are broadly defined as information that has economic value, creates a competitive advantage, and is subject to efforts to maintain its secrecy. Othercorp wants to know about our earnings,

> client list, marketing strategy, financing arrangements, and research and development plans. If those materials give ABC a competitive edge and if we put programs in place to maintain their secrecy, the court may grant a Protective Order and prevent Othercorp from obtaining the information.

With regard to the discovery process, we should consider the following questions:
1. Describe the advantages and disadvantages of the broad standards for discovery. Explain whether you think trial preparedness is a sufficient justification for requiring parties to release such an extensive amount of information.
2. What could Marvin do to prepare the company for the burdens of the discovery process?
3. Recommend a trade secret program for ABC to ensure that its earnings, client list, marketing strategy, financing arrangements, research and development plans, and any other proprietary information are kept secret and protected from discovery.

SUMMARY JUDGMENT

summary judgment: The court enters a judgment in favor of one side, without a trial, when there are no "fact issues" in dispute, only legal questions.

At any time before the case goes to trial, but usually after quite a bit of discovery has been done, one side or both may bring a **motion for summary judgment.** This request basically asks the court to enter a summary (quick) judgment in favor of one side rather than proceeding to trial. In order to succeed on this motion, the moving party must convince the judge that there are no "genuine issues of material fact" in dispute—that is, the parties basically agree on the facts—and therefore the only remaining issues are legal questions.

Since legal issues are properly decided by the judge, it makes sense to avoid the time and costs of trial (and a possible erroneous decision by a jury) by having the judge decide the case now and entering a judgment for one party. Most of the time, however, there *are* significant differences between the parties regarding factual issues—for example, one party thinks the accident was caused by a red car going 30 mph, and the other thinks it was an orange car going 50 mph., or one party believes he fully and completely performed his contract to build a garage, while the other party believes that the performance was late and substandard. Therefore, summary judgment motions are usually denied, and the case is scheduled for trial. However, occasionally the important facts are not really in dispute, and the judge then decides the critical legal issues without a trial and enters a summary judgment in favor of one party.

PRE-TRIAL CONFERENCE

pre-trial conference: A meeting between the judge and the lawyers, prior to the trial, to discuss the issues in the case and set the date for the trial.

When the time for discovery has expired, the court will schedule a **pre-trial conference**. At this time the judge will meet privately in his/her office with the attorneys for both sides, discuss what the issues in the case are, and which ones can be agreed upon, where the major differences lie, whether there is a chance of settlement, how many witnesses each side wants to call, and how long the trial may last. Some judges are very aggressive in attempting to get a settlement at the pre-trial conference, asking questions like "What will you take to settle this case? What will you offer? That's all? Can't you go a little higher?"

In one case handled by one of this book's authors, the judge said at the pre-trial conference, "Go out and tell your client that I've heard 30 cases like this, and never has the plaintiff received more than $5,000. Now I'm not prejudging the case, of course, and maybe he will be the first one to win $15,000, but the chances are small. The defendant is offering to settle for $4,000, and that seems like a good offer to me." Since both clients are usually required to show up for the pre-trial (but do not get to go back in the judge's office with the lawyers to discuss the case), if a settlement is reached, everyone can go into the courtroom and put the agreement "on the record" by publicly stating it to the judge and having it taken down by the court reporter.

All judges are different. While some really push for settlement at the pre-trial conference, others simply ask what the real issues are in the case, how long each side wants to present its witnesses at trial, whether the attorneys have discussed settlement, and if they believe settlement is possible. At the close of the conference, the judge sets a date for the trial.

SOCIAL/ETHICAL ISSUES

Do you think a judge should aggressively push the parties toward a settlement? Is this a proper role for a judicial officer? Many believe the judge should remain passive and neutral and just make decisions as required. On the other hand, trials cost the state and the parties a considerable amount of money. Most court dockets are seriously overloaded and backlogged. If the judge can help some parties reach a settlement, others can go to trial sooner. What is the proper amount of pressure a judge should place on the parties to settle?

JURY PROCEDURES

If the case is not settled, it will eventually come to trial. The first decision to make is whether it will be a jury or nonjury trial. In a civil case if either party makes a formal request for a jury at the appropriate time (generally no later than the pre-trial conference), there will be a jury. If neither side requests a jury, the judge will hear the case without one. Sometimes in a complex or technical case, neither side wants to take the risk that the jury will become bored or antagonistic with the case, and the parties are happy to let the judge—who has heard lots of similar cases—decide the matter alone. However, in most personal injury and product liability cases, the plaintiff generally wants the case to be heard by a group of ordinary people who have not heard hundreds of such cases, and thus a jury is requested.

JURY SELECTION

If there is to be a jury trial, the selection of the members of the jury is an important step. In order to obtain a cross-section of the community, many persons are asked to come to the courthouse to serve as jurors. Some counties use voter registration lists or drivers license records and other means to make up their lists. Groups of potential jurors are then sent to the various courtrooms where trials are to take place. Before being chosen as a juror in a case, a person must answer a series of questions designed to indicate whether he or she has any bias for or against any of the parties to the case; knows any of the parties, witnesses, or attorneys involved; or has strong opinions about the issues involved in the case. This process is called *voir dire,* which means "to see and to say." (In Old French *voir* meant "truth"—that is, medieval jurors were actually witnesses.)

Voir dire is intended to produce jurors who can hear the evidence without bias. For example, if Bill is suing Michelle, he probably does not want her brother, her best friend, or her minister on the jury. Similarly, if Michelle is a newspaper reporter who has written something about Bill that he believes is false, he probably will prefer that no other newspaper reporters, or perhaps news media workers of any kind, sit on the jury. The judge will ask each prospective juror a series of questions designed to indicate if the person can view the case with an open mind, and often the attorneys ask questions as well.

As the questioning proceeds, one of the attorneys may ask the judge to remove a juror **for cause,** if he or she believes that the juror cannot be totally impartial, and the judge will rule on the request. The number of challenges for cause is not limited. In addition, each side has a certain number of **peremptory challenges,** which can be used to remove a juror without giving any reason and without any decision by the judge. The number of peremptory challenges is limited, and each side has the same number. For example, in Bill and Michelle's case, perhaps there is a prospective jury member who was a classmate of Bill's in high school but has not seen him in a number of years. When challenged for cause by Michelle's lawyer, he tells the court, "I'll be fair and view the case with an open mind," and the judge therefore turns down the challenge for cause. Michelle and her lawyer may decide they would just as soon not test his good faith and use one of their peremptory challenges to "thank and excuse" him from the jury. The following case concerns whether a judge should have dismissed a juror "for cause."

voir dire: The process of asking questions to potential jurors, to make sure they can be fair and impartial.

challenge for cause: One attorney asks the judge to remove a juror from the jury because of some possible bias. The judge decides.

peremptory challenge: Each side in a case is allowed to excuse a few potential jurors without giving a reason.

STATE V. SHIELDS

709 S.W. 2d 556 (Missouri Court of Appeals, 1986)

FACTS

In this criminal case, the defendant had been convicted of felonious restraint, burglary, and assault after a jury trial. The felonious restraint charges were filed after the defendant broke into his ex-wife's house and forced her and their two children to get dressed and go with him. He then drove them around in the car for five hours before releasing them.

About one month later, the defendant (Mr. Shields) again broke into his ex-wife's house and this time hit her several times with a stick. He also hit her mother across the back. Mr. Shields dragged his ex-wife outside and pushed her over a fence. A neighbor intervened to help the victim and chased Mr. Shields back to his truck where he got a gun and fired a shot at the neighbor. These actions led to the burglary and assault charges. Mr. Shields appealed his conviction, claiming that the judge should have dismissed one of the jurors.

DECISION

Judge Crist wrote the opinion of the court:

The defendant claims that the trial court erred by overruling his challenge for cause to one of the female jurors. It appears that some 17 years earlier the former wife of this woman's husband had forced her way into their home and had attacked her. The woman juror had not seen this person for some ten years, and she consistently told the court that she could give both sides in the case a fair trial under the evidence presented in court and would follow the instructions given by the court. When questioned by the defendant's attorney, she said her former experience "has nothing to do with what's going on here today."

While a defendant is entitled to a full panel of qualified jurors from which to make his preemptory challenges, "decisions concerning a juror's qualifications are consigned to the trial court's discretion and will be reversed only for a clear abuse of discretion," stated the Missouri Court of Appeals. The juror did not equivocate or waiver in her answers to the questions pro-

pounded on voir dire. "She insisted the experience would not affect her, and this insistence was reinforced by the amount of time which had passed between her experience and the trial. We can find no abuse of discretion." Judgment affirmed.

CASE QUESTIONS

1. Do you think the juror can judge the defendant fairly in this case? Why?
2. We all have experiences that shape the way we feel about the world. These experiences affect how we view such things as crime, drugs, marital violence, discrimination, and politics. How can we tell what prior events will influence a person's judgment in a given case? Try to fashion a rule that you would like applied to potential jurors in a case involving you.
3. Why did the defendant's attorney not use a peremptory challenge to bump the juror from the case after the challenge for cause was denied?

To help with jury selection in important cases, an entire industry of "jury selection consultants" has come into existence. Experts with sociological, psychological, and statistical backgrounds advise attorneys (for a substantial fee, of course) on what types of persons are supposedly more or less sympathetic to various kinds of people and arguments. In the mid-1990s, some six weeks were consumed solely with the selection of the jury for the sensational O.J. Simpson murder trial. Each side retained experts to assist it in jury selection and questioning and used mock juries to assess different people's reactions to various types of evidence.

 SOCIAL/ETHICAL ISSUES

Should lawyers use Facebook in jury selection? More than 500 million people now use Facebook, posting a wide variety of personal information, photos, "likes," opinions, and commentary about themselves and others on the popular social network site. Attorneys participating in jury selection have a duty to attempt to pick members of the jury that will be at least fair, and maybe even favorable toward their client. Should they use this new resource to find out as much as they can about potential members of the jury? Facebook users may think that their posts are available only to a limited number of "friends" but realistically the information can often be widely accessed. Is searching someone's Facebook pages without permission legal? Is it ethical? Another issue concerns whether the information people post on Facebook is reliable. One expert has said that people are often "projecting" when they post, and are posting "who they want to be, rather than who they are." What do you think?

MEMO FROM THE LEGAL DEPARTMENT

To: Students

From: Your Lawyer

Often, when called for jury duty, our first thought is how to "get out of" jury service. True, it is usually inconvenient to find the time to serve. The success of the jury system, however, requires that when called for jury service, employed persons and students try to find a way to serve rather than attempt to avoid serving. Otherwise, juries will not represent the entire community but will be composed of only retired or unemployed persons or others who have "all the time in the world" to serve on juries. Is that what we want?

While we take pride that our justice system accords an individual a trial before an "impartial jury of peers," what each side *really* wants is a jury that will decide in its favor. The attorneys, after all, are representing clients who want to win the case. It is important that judges stay closely involved in the jury selection process to ensure that juries do represent the community and that minorities are not systematically excluded from jury service. In fact, there have been U.S. Supreme Court decisions in recent years that have banned the use of peremptory challenges where they were used to exclude all minorities or women from the jury panel hearing a case.

THE TRIAL

THE OPENING STATEMENT

opening statement: At the beginning of a trial, each lawyer has an opportunity to tell the jury what the case is about.

Once the parties, the judge, and the jury are ready to begin, the first stage of the trial is the **opening statement** of the attorney for each side. At this time the attorney tries to "tell a story" to the jury—specifically the version of events that caused the lawsuit according to her client's point of view. The attorney describes in general what the key witnesses are expected to testify—being careful not to be too specific, because witnesses rarely tell the exact story to the court that they told the lawyer back in the office. This is probably the first time the jury has heard anything about the case, and the attorneys want to create interest and build sympathy for their clients. The plaintiff's attorney presents first, and the defendant's attorney either follows directly or waits until the plaintiff's witnesses have all testified to make the opening statement.

PRESENTATION OF EVIDENCE

After the opening statements, the plaintiff begins to present his case through the testimony of witnesses and introduction of evidence. This part of the trial is no doubt familiar to many of you through movies and television. "The plaintiff will call as his first witness, Dr. Samantha Jones," states the plaintiff's attorney, who will then ask Dr. Jones a series of questions pertinent to the case. This type of testimony, offered by "your witnesses," is called **direct examination.**

If the case concerns whether the plaintiff has suffered injuries and to what degree of severity and permanence, and Dr. Jones has treated the plaintiff, she will be asked to describe the injuries, the treatment, and her opinion of the severity and permanence. No "leading" questions are allowed on direct examination. The attorney uses "how," "when," and "where," open-ended questions to let the witness describe the events she observed.

The testimony must relate to the facts of the case at hand, however. If the plaintiff's attorney asked Dr. Jones about some other patient or some other medical problem of the plaintiff, the defendant's attorney might stand up and object to the question because it was "Irrelevant, your Honor." The standard of **relevance** means that only evidence that has some direct bearing on one of the issues in this case can be introduced in court. The judge's decision on the objection will depend on whether, in the judge's opinion, the question deals with an issue relevant to the case.

After the plaintiff's attorney has finished questioning Dr. Jones, the defendant's lawyer is given the opportunity to **cross-examine** the witness. While the questions from the plaintiff's attorney were probably friendly and open-ended ("Tell us about the injuries you saw, Dr. Jones"), the questions from the opposing attorney are likely to be hostile, tricky, and closed-ended ("Isn't it true, Dr. Jones, that you first treated the plaintiff while you were both at a party?"). The purpose of cross-examination is to test the truth of the nice, neat version of events the witness described on direct examination.

The American court system is called *adversarial* because it is expected that the truth will emerge through the examination and cross-examination of witnesses by the opposing attorneys under the general supervision of the judge. In some other countries the judge serves as more of an accuser and asks many questions. But in the United States the judge acts mostly as a referee to ensure fairness, although he or she can sometimes ask questions of witnesses, and all judges do so on occasion.

As the plaintiff's attorney calls one witness after another, there will be physical and documentary evidence that he or she will want to introduce (officially put before the court and jury for their consideration). Generally, each piece of evidence must be described and verified by a witness unless the parties have stipulated (agreed) to its admission. In other words, if the plaintiff's attorney wants to introduce the plaintiff's medical records, he or she must ask Dr. Jones or some other medical professional who is familiar with the records if these in fact are the plaintiff's records and if they have been maintained by the hospital in its regular manner. If the plaintiff's attorney wants to introduce a photograph of the plaintiff's wrecked car, either the person who took the picture or someone else who can testify that this is in fact an accurate depiction of the plaintiff's car right after the accident will have to be called as a witness. Otherwise, it is possible that some photo of another horribly wrecked car might be put before the jury.

direct examination: The series of questions asked by an attorney of a witness called by that attorney.

cross-examination: Questions asked by an attorney of a witness called by the opposing side.

MOTIONS FOR DIRECTED VERDICT AND CLOSING ARGUMENTS

directed verdict:
When the judge enters a verdict, after the evidence has been presented, because one side has failed to prove some essential element of the case.

After the plaintiff has called all her witnesses, and they have been cross-examined, the plaintiff "rests," which means "That's all I have." In other words, the plaintiff's side has presented all the witnesses and evidence it has chosen to offer. Often, at this point, the defendant will move for a **directed verdict,** which is a request to the judge to enter a decision in his or her favor because the plaintiff failed to prove his or her case or left out some essential element. Most of the time these motions are denied, and the case moves on, but once in a while the judge will grant the motion, and the case is over. If the motion is denied, then the defendant will begin calling witnesses, with each one being cross-examined by the plaintiff's attorney.

After both sides have completed the testimony of witnesses and introduction of evidence, each attorney will make a *closing argument* to the court. This is the time when the oratory of the experienced trial attorney reaches full flower. The attorneys can now refer to specific statements made by witnesses and highlight various items that have been introduced into evidence (e.g., waving the bloody shirt for the jury), without fear that a witness will change his or her story or be contradicted by another witness. Some attorneys are accomplished public speakers and make dramatic appeals to the jury's sense of justice and fairness. Others merely present factual, low-key recapitulations of the evidence favorable to their client's position.

JURY INSTRUCTIONS, DELIBERATIONS, AND VERDICT

jury instructions:
The judge gives the jury instructions on legal issues they must decide and rules they should apply to the case before them.

After both sides have presented all their evidence and given their closing arguments, the judge will give **instructions to the jury.** Each side will have previously given the judge a list of proposed instructions, which tell the jury about the burden of proof the plaintiff must meet, the definition of various legal terms relevant to the case, and how the jury should apply the law to the facts of the case. The judge will probably use some of the instructions suggested by the attorneys and may write some of his or her own. There are also standard lists of instructions on all legal topics developed by bar association committees in most states. The judge will have to decide which ones are most appropriate in this case.

After the instructions are given, the jury is excused and taken to a separate room to "deliberate," that is, to reach a decision. Traditionally, juries were composed of 12 persons, and their verdict was required to be unanimous, and this is still true in many cases—certainly in all major criminal cases. However, in recent years many courts in order to save time and money have used six-member juries and non-unanimous verdicts in certain types of cases. The jury is considered the *finder of facts,* that is, the jury decides who did what to whom, how fast the car was going, and so on. In almost all cases, different witnesses will give vastly different accounts of what happened, and the jury's duty will be to determine whom to believe. Most of the time the jury will be asked to deliver a *general verdict,* which is one that decides who should win and how much the damages are. In some cases, a *special verdict* will be requested, which requires the jury to reach an answer to a series of particular questions.

POST-TRIAL MOTIONS

After the jury renders its verdict, the losing side may bring a *motion for new trial* or *a motion for judgment notwithstanding the verdict* (which in Latin is

"Before announcing the verdict we would like to recommend that Harrison Ford play the defendant."

"Non Obstante Veredicto," and often therefore called **"Judgment N.O.V."**). The motion for new trial asks that the court order a new trial in the case because of some serious and prejudicial error that has occurred or because of the discovery of some important new evidence that was not available at the first trial. The motion for Judgment N.O.V. asks the court to enter a judgment opposite of the jury's decision because the jury's verdict is against the great weight of the evidence (i.e., "If the jury had followed your instructions, it could not possibly have reached the decision it did"). Most of these motions are denied, but every once in awhile, one is granted. Therefore, it often makes sense for the losing attorney to bring them. If nothing else, the denial of such a motion provides another legal basis for appeal of the trial court decision. After the post-trial motions have been argued, the judge will enter the final judgment in the case.

> **Judgment N.O.V.:**
> The judge enters a judgment different from the jury verdict.

THE APPELLATE PROCESS

Once the trial court judge has entered a judgment in the case, and any post-trial motions have been denied, the losing party's only recourse is to file an appeal. As we have discussed, there is at least one and often two levels of appellate courts in all states, which hear appeals from lower court decisions. The basis for the appeal must be that some serious legal error, made by the trial court judge, affected the outcome of the case and led to an unfair or unlawful result. The trial court judge may have made hundreds of rulings during the trial—whether to admit certain evidence, rulings on various objections to questions, instructions to the jury, and rulings on motions made by the parties—so that the losing side can generally find some issues on which to base an appeal.

brief: A written document containing the party's legal arguments.

The party desiring to appeal (**the appellant**) files a notice with the appropriate appellate court, indicating that he or she is appealing a lower court decision. At some specific time thereafter, the appellant must file a **brief** with the court, which will be a statement (but never very "brief"!) of the party's arguments concerning the errors made during the trial and citing past court decisions and laws supporting the appellant's position. Then, some 30–50 days later (whatever time period is specified by the law in that state), the other side (called **the appellee**) will file a brief in response, arguing that there was no significant error in the lower court and that the decision should stand. The appellee will also cite various supporting cases and statutes.

After both briefs have been filed, the appellate court will, in most cases, schedule a date for **oral argument**. At this time, the attorneys for both parties will appear before the appellate court (remember, there will be several judges on the panel) and attempt to convince the court of the strength of their arguments. Each lawyer will be given a short time—perhaps 30 minutes—to present his or her case, and the judges will interrupt and question the attorney whenever they choose to probe into various aspects of the case. There are no witnesses heard and no evidence presented to the appellate court. The focus is on the legal principles relevant to the case at hand and whether those principles were followed in the lower court. The discussion and debate over the proper legal principles to apply is doubly important because the decision will not only affect the parties to the case at issue, but will also affect all subsequent cases in that jurisdiction, raising similar issues through the rules of **precedent** and **stare decisis**, as discussed next.

PRECEDENT

The American legal system is very much a **common law** structure. One meaning of the term *common law* is that much of our law is not founded in the statutes passed by legislatures, but in the decisions of the courts. As part of the effort to make the principles of law predictable and stable, lower courts in one jurisdiction must follow the legal principles set out in decisions of higher (appellate) courts in their jurisdiction when they occur in similar situations. For example, if the Supreme Court of Montana has ruled in a 1976 case that driving an automobile while blindfolded was "negligence," and there is now a case being tried in Beaverhead County, Montana, involving similar facts, the trial court will be bound to follow the legal precedent of the 1976 case and find the driver negligent, if the jury decides that he was driving while blindfolded. This rule is called *stare decisis* ("Let the decision stand") and is premised on the idea that the law should be similar ("common") in all parts of a particular jurisdiction.

The rule of precedent or *stare decisis* only applies within the particular jurisdiction over which the higher court presides. Therefore, the decisions of the Montana Supreme Court on the interpretation of certain legal principles must be followed by trial and appellate courts in Montana, but need not be followed in Georgia, Vermont, or any other state. While a court in Georgia might be interested in the reasoning and language of a Montana Supreme Court decision concerning some legal principle, and might decide to adopt the same interpretation because the rationale made a lot of sense, the Georgia court has no obligation to do so. That court will have to follow principles established in earlier Georgia Supreme Court decisions, however.

Although lower courts within a jurisdiction are normally bound to follow the precedents set by earlier cases because of the *stare decisis* rule, sometimes the appellate courts decide that a rule of law has outlived its usefulness. The court that created the rule of law in the first place (the Montana Supreme Court in our earlier example) might decide that after several years of experience with the "driving blindfolded is negligent" rule, there are strong reasons for changing it. While the U.S. Supreme Court and the state supreme courts are reluctant to disregard *stare decisis* and change a longstanding rule, sometimes changes in society have made the old rule obsolete and out of place.

For example, most states used to have a common law rule that a patient could not sue a nonprofit hospital for damages even if the patient was injured while in the hospital. This rule arose at a time when most nonprofit hospitals were owned by religious or charitable groups, run largely be volunteers, and provided care at no charge to patients. That situation has changed considerably over the years. While there are still many nonprofit hospitals, they are often huge, powerful, and sophisticated businesses that employ large paid staffs and charge substantial sums for services. In response to this change, most state supreme courts have, in appropriate cases, overruled the old "charitable immunity" rule and held that nonprofit hospitals can be sued for negligence. When times change, some common law principles change as well, through later court decisions.

On the federal level, the decisions of the U.S. Supreme Court, regarding interpretations of the federal Constitution and federal statutes, are binding on all other courts in the nation. Decisions of the U.S. federal Courts of Appeal are binding on all lower federal courts within their geographical jurisdiction (see chart in Chapter 2). In diversity cases, the federal district court must follow the decisions on relevant legal principles (e.g., the definition of negligence) made by the highest court of the state where the incident took place.

APPELLATE COURT DECISIONS

After reading the briefs and hearing the oral arguments of the parties, the appellate court will likely do one of three things. It may **affirm** (uphold) the decision of the lower court; it may **reverse** the decision—that is, direct that the opposite party should win; or, more commonly, if the appellate court finds that some error occurred at the trial, it will reverse and **remand** the case to the lower court (send it back) with instructions for a new trial, or direct that some further proceedings are necessary. In each case, the appellate court will generally write a lengthy opinion, discussing the facts and legal issues involved in the case and carefully setting out its reasoning and explaining its view of the appropriate legal principles. This opinion will then become precedent to be used in all later cases raising similar issues.

Similarly, appellate court decisions often involve the interpretation of a statute ("*statutory interpretation*," discussed in Chapter 1). When an appellate court, for example, the Supreme Court of Ohio, issues a decision in a case that involves the interpretation of an Ohio law, that precedent will be binding on all lower courts in Ohio through the doctrine of *stare decisis*. Most of the cases in this textbook will be appellate court decisions, either interpreting a statute or the Constitution or examining a common law legal principle.

affirm: When an appellate court upholds a lower court decision.

reverse: The appellate court changes the ruling of the lower court.

remand: The appellate court sends the case back to the lower court for more hearings or a new trial.

TYPES OF JUDGMENTS; ENFORCING AND COLLECTING JUDGMENTS

In Chapter 1, we discussed the difference between "legal" (actions at law) and equitable (actions in equity) remedies. In general, legal remedies are those that require the losing party to pay the winning party a certain sum of money, while "equitable" remedies involve a court order to the defendant to do or not to do a specific action. Equitable remedies can only be obtained where the party convinces the court that money damages will be inadequate compensation. In most cases, courts prefer to award monetary damages to the prevailing party, as described in the next section.

MONEY JUDGMENTS (ACTIONS AT LAW)

The majority of civil actions are brought by people who want another to pay damages for something that the second one has done that injured the first person—actions at law. If the court finds for the plaintiff, it may award several types of money damages.

Compensatory Damages   Compensatory damages are the most common type of damages and are designed to compensate the plaintiff for the actual direct costs of the harm caused by the defendant. For example, if the defendant broke a contract he had made to pave the plaintiff's driveway, and the plaintiff had to pay someone else $1,500 more than the original contract to do the job, she would probably be entitled to $1,500 in compensatory damages from the defendant.

Consequential Damages   In some cases, the plaintiff alleges that in addition to the cost of the substitute performance, she has suffered further damages as a consequence of the defendant's actions. For example, in the situation just discussed, suppose that the plaintiff was the owner of a convenience store, and the defendant's failure to pave the driveway made it impossible for customers to reach the store until the other paving company did the job one week later. The store owner might want to ask for consequential damages to cover the additional loss (business profits) resulting from the defendant's breach of contract. Such damages are sometimes awarded when the consequences are foreseeable—that is, both parties understood what the damages would be if one or the other did not perform.

nominal damages: Very small damages ("in name only") to a winning plaintiff.

punitive damages: A large award of damages, in addition to compensatory damages, to "punish" the defendant for wilful or deliberately malicious actions.

Other Types of Money Damages   Courts sometimes award other money damages called nominal and punitive. **Nominal damages** are very small sums (perhaps $1) awarded when the plaintiff has won the case but has not established any monetary injury. **Punitive damages** may be awarded when the judge or jury finds that the defendant has acted maliciously or intentionally to harm the plaintiff. These damages may be very large, as they are intended to "make an example" of the defendant (indeed, such damages are often called "exemplary damages"), and go to the plaintiff in addition to whatever damages are awarded.

There has been much public debate recently about the role and use of punitive damages, including such questions as: (1) Is it fair to allow a jury to assess whatever amount of "punitive damages" they see fit, without regard to the amount of compensatory damages the plaintiff has been awarded? (2) Is it right to allow the plaintiff to receive a "windfall" of money over and above what he or she has proved in damages, solely to punish the defendant? (3) Is it appropriate to allow several courts to independently assess multi-million dollar punitive damage awards against a company (which may have made a defective drug, for example) for the same action, if that results in forcing the company into bankruptcy, thus making it impossible for other injured parties to collect anything? (4) Are punitive damages constitutional? Defendants against whom punitive damages have been awarded have argued that allowing a jury to assess any amount it chooses violates their right to "due process" of law.

Recent Punitive Damages Decisions The U.S. Supreme Court has decided several punitive damage cases in recent years. In a 2003 decision, *State Farm Mutual Insurance Co. v. Campbell,* the Court struck down a punitive damages award of $145 million where the compensatory damages awarded were $1 million. In doing so the Supreme Court continued its previous policy of "declining to set a bright-line ratio which punitive damages cannot exceed," in order to satisfy due process. In other words the Supreme Court refused to establish an exact ratio of punitive damages/compensatory damages which would be acceptable. However, the Court did set forth certain "guideposts" to be used by lower courts in reviewing punitive damages verdicts. Justice Kennedy wrote for the Court that "Our jurisprudence and the principles it has now established demonstrate, however, that in practice, few awards exceeding a single-digit ratio between punitive and compensatory damages, to a significant degree, will satisfy due process." In other words, the Supreme Court is unlikely to uphold any punitive damages awards which are more than 9 times the amount of compensatory damages.

In 1994, a jury in Anchorage returned a $5 billion punitive damages award against Exxon Mobil Corp. as punishment for the company's role in spilling 11 million gallons of oil into the pristine fishing waters of Alaska's Prince William Sound, causing extensive damage to fish, wildlife, and all who made their living from fishing in the region.

The company appealed the verdict. In 2006, the 9th U.S. Circuit Court of Appeals cut the award to $2.5 billion. Exxon then appealed that decision to the U.S. Supreme Court, and in 2008 the Court reduced the punitive damages to $507 million. While citing the *State Farm* case, the Court said that under maritime law the punitive damages should even be much lower than a 9-1 ratio, holding that "the punitive damages award against Exxon was excessive as a matter of maritime common law," and in this case the award should be limited to an amount equal to compensatory damages of $507 million.

The *State Farm* opinion cited two earlier Supreme Court cases which had described a 4-1 ratio as appropriate, and stated that ratios in excess of 9-1 (more than single digits) will be "presumptively unconstitutional." In the *State Farm* decision the Supreme Court cited with approval a 1996 U.S. Supreme Court decision *BMW of North America, Inc. v. Gore,* which had reversed a $2 million punitive damages award against the auto company BMW for selling a repainted BMW car as new. In that case, the Supreme Court had found the 500-to-1 ratio between punitive ($2 million) and compensatory damages ($4,000) to be "grossly excessive," and reversed the award. [In the actual *State Farm* case, following the Supreme Court ruling the case was sent back to the Utah Supreme Court for entry of a new judgment. Following the Supreme Court's reasoning the Utah court entered a new punitive damages award of $9 million, to go with the $1 million compensatory damages award.] No Supreme Court decisions have held that punitive damages are unconstitutional, however, and the lower courts

INTERNATIONAL IMPLICATIONS

Punitive damages are basically an American innovation. Almost all other nations around the world reject the idea of such "exemplary" damages. This affects the international enforcement of judgments entered in U.S. courts. Normally courts in other nations will enforce a money judgment properly obtained from an American court, against assets the defendant has in that other nation. However, since most countries do not recognize punitive damages, it is difficult for a person or firm that wins a large punitive damages award in the U.S. to obtain enforcement of the judgment in another country.

are still struggling with how to determine when punitive damages are appropriate and what types of awards are permissible. The awarding of punitive damages continues to be an important current legal issue for business, which we will discuss further in Chapter 11.

EQUITABLE REMEDIES

Sometimes the plaintiff does not want money compensation for what the defendant has done but instead wants the defendant ordered *to do* something or ordered *not to do* something. When a court enters such an order it is called an **equitable remedy.** Courts prefer to award money damages—order Bob to pay Jennifer $5,000—rather than order a person to do, or not do something. In general, in order to obtain equitable remedies, the plaintiff must persuade the court that *money damages are inadequate* to fully compensate the plaintiff for the harm done.

injunction: An equitable order from a court directing someone not to do something.

Perhaps, a business tenant in a downtown building hears that the building is going to be torn down to make way for a parking lot. The tenant does not want money compensation after the building is gone, but wants to stop the demolition. She may file a lawsuit against the owner seeking an **injunction,** an equitable order from the court directing the defendant not to tear down the building. Sometimes a plaintiff asks the court for a *preliminary injunction* early in the case, long before the trial, because she needs some immediate relief. Usually a court will grant such an injunction only when it is necessary to preserve the status quo pending the full trial of the case—in other words, where by the end of the case it might no longer be possible to grant the relief the winning party deserves (for example, if the building has been torn down during the time the case was pending). A **temporary restraining order** is a type of short-term injunction, generally lasting only until the court can hold a hearing on the case.

temporary restraining order: A short-term injunction used to preserve the status quo until the court can schedule a full hearing.

specific performance: An equitable order from a court directing someone to fully perform their contract obligations.

Another type of equitable relief is the order of **specific performance,** which directs a party to fulfill ("specifically perform") a contract he has agreed to. As we said above, in order to receive this type of order, the plaintiff must persuade the court **that monetary damages are inadequate** to fully compensate her for the injury. One type of proof of such inadequacy is where the item is "unique." For example, if Joe has made a contract to sell Tricia his 1933 Rolls Royce and then tries to back out of the deal, Tricia may be able to persuade the court that the item is "unique" and thus obtain an order of specific performance. She does not want money compensation, she wants that specific car, and it is unique. If the car were a 2003 Ford, however, the court would probably refuse specific performance and award Tricia money damages for her loss due to Joe's breach of contract. The courts have developed a common law rule that each parcel of real estate is unique, so specific performance is quite commonly awarded in cases involving the breach of contract to sell houses, land, and real estate.

Although specific performance orders may sometimes be issued to require parties to fulfill certain contract obligations, courts are reluctant to issue them to require people to perform personal services. While it is possible to require a business firm to deliver 1,000 gallons of gasoline as promised, it is problematic to require an artist to paint a picture, or a singer to perform a concert. Courts are more likely to award money damages in such situations where a contract has been breached. You might not want to attend the concert where an opera singer was performing only because of a court order.

ENFORCEMENT OF JUDGMENTS

Suppose Tara wins a $5,000 judgment against Nancy, but she does not pay it. What can Tara do? One quite surprising feature of our legal system is that court judgments are not automatically enforced by the court. Only when the noncompliance is brought to the court's attention by one of the parties (the one who wants to be paid) is action taken.

If a judgment has been entered ordering Nancy to pay Tara $5,000, but no payment is made, Tara may petition the court for several types of action. If Tara knows where Nancy works, she may ask the court for a **garnishment**, which is an order from the court to someone who owes Nancy money (her employer or her bank, for example) to pay a certain percentage of the wages due her (federal law limits the amount to 25 percent) to the court for transfer to Tara.

Another remedy, the **writ of execution**, directs the sheriff to take possession of some property which the defendant owns. The property (which may be either real estate or personal property like a car or machinery) is later sold, in accordance with the state law, and the proceeds are paid to the creditor toward satisfaction of the judgment. Until the judgment is paid, the creditor may return to court to continue her efforts to collect. If she does not know where the debtor works or if the debtor has assets, she may obtain a **discovery subpoena**, a court order directing the debtor to show up in court at a certain date and answer questions under oath about her assets.

In the early days of our country, nonpayment of debts sometimes resulted in a prison term, but this is no longer true. We no longer have "debtor's prison" in the United States. It is not a crime to owe money or even to fail to pay a court-ordered judgment. With the exception of court-ordered child support and alimony payments and taxes, the nonpayment of debts will not result in jail time. The creditor must, even after a court decision awarding a specific amount of money to her in a civil case, seek enforcement through the procedures outlined previously if the defendant does not pay. Courts may, however, issue warrants for the arrest of debtors who ignore discovery subpoenas and fail to appear in court to answer questions about their assets.

garnishment: An order from a court to an employer or other party who owes money to a defendant in a case who has not paid a judgment. The order tells the employer to pay part of the wages owed to the court.

ALTERNATE DISPUTE RESOLUTION

There are thousands of civil cases filed in federal and state courts every year. Many jurisdictions have a large backlog of cases to be tried. The resulting delays and the increasing legal costs associated with complex and lengthy litigation, as well as the substantial amount of time that business managers must devote to complicated lawsuits, have caused a great deal of interest in finding ways to resolve civil disputes other than "going to court." In general, the various types of **alternate dispute resolution (ADR)** are quicker and less costly than litigation, although there are exceptions.

ADR has other advantages besides being relatively quicker and less expensive than litigation. One significant advantage of ADR is that the hearings and paperwork are private. Most court proceedings and files are open to the press and the public, and anyone can attend trials and hearings. This is not true with ADR proceedings, which are confidential unless both parties agree to make them public. Another advantage of ADR is that the parties can tailor the procedures to fit their own situation through the terms of their agreement to use ADR.

Some of the more important types of ADR are arbitration, mediation, minitrials, and the private judge program. They will be discussed in some detail.

CONGRESS PROVIDES 9/11 VICTIM FUND AS ALTERNATIVE TO LITIGATION

In the days following the terrorist attacks of September 11, 2001, Congress established a victims' compensation fund to provide compensation for economic and non-economic losses to victims and families of deceased victims of the 9/11 attacks. The "September 11th Victim Compensation Fund" was created by Title IV of the Air Transportation Safety and System Stabilization Act, a legislative relief package for the airlines. The fund was designed as an alternative to tort litigation; a condition of claiming compensation through the fund, claimants had to waive their right to file a lawsuit seeking compensation for injuries sustained in the September 11th attacks. The only exception to the ban on lawsuits is a provision that allows civil suits against persons who knowingly participated in any conspiracy to hijack any aircraft or commit any terrorist act.

Persons claiming compensation from the fund had to file their claims by December 22, 2003; the fund was required to complete its deliberations on all claims by June 15, 2004. Kenneth R. Feinberg, a New York attorney, was appointed as Special Master of the fund, supervised the administration of the fund and the handling of the claims. The fund received 2,963 claims for compensation for wrongful death (approximately 98% of the total of 2,973 deaths attributed to the attacks); the average compensation award for a death claim was $2.1 million. The fund received 4,430 claims for compensation for injuries and it accepted 2,675 of them; the remainder of the injury claims were either withdrawn or rejected by the fund because of inadequate medical proof . The compensation for injury claims ranged from $500 to $8.6 million. The total compensation paid out by the fund was about $6.9 billion.

ARBITRATION

Perhaps the best-known of the ADR techniques is **arbitration,** in which the parties refer the dispute to an impartial third party, called the arbitrator, who listens to each side and then renders a decision, which is binding on both parties. Arbitration may arise because the parties have agreed earlier (in their contract) to arbitration of all disputes that may arise, or they may decide to arbitrate a dispute after it has arisen.

Arbitration is often—but not always—faster and less expensive than a court trial. Arbitrators can be selected who have specific expertise in the subject area in dispute (for example, an architect might be selected to arbitrate a disagreement about the construction of a house). The parties can agree on a specific person they want to be the arbitrator, or the parties can use the services of the American Arbitration Association, a national organization of people who perform arbitration, which has its own set of procedural rules, or other national arbitration organizations.

In most cases, getting to arbitration is a shorter process than court litigation. The arbitrator probably will not have a backlog of cases like a court and can hear the case sooner. In addition, the presentations of the parties are often limited to a few hours each (although some last several days) and the rules of evidence are much more relaxed than in a court. These factors generally result in the expenditure of less time by management and attorneys in resolving the dispute through arbitration, as opposed to litigation. The disadvantage is that the parties are generally bound by the decision, and even if they disagree with the result, by agreeing to binding arbitration, they have given up their right to appeal the decision in court.

MEDIATION

The process of mediation is different from arbitration in that the independent third party who is called upon to assist the two disputing parties does not render a decision, but merely attempts to aid them in reaching a settlement. The Federal Mediation and Conciliation Service has been used successfully to resolve certain well-publicized labor management disputes in recent years.

Many localities have also employed mediation to settle neighborhood disputes without resorting to the court system. Several manufacturers and business associations, like the Better Business Bureau, have utilized mediation as well in their attempts to handle consumer complaints.

There is also a process called *med-arb,* in which the neutral party tries to mediate the dispute first, but later may serve as an arbitrator.

MINITRIALS

One of the most recent additions to alternate dispute resolution techniques is the minitrial. In the 1980s, many corporations and government agencies began to settle disputes using this procedure. In a minitrial, the parties select a "neutral advisor" (who need not be a lawyer) who holds a short hearing—maybe one or two days—at which time the attorneys for each side present their best case. One of the key features of this process is that each side must have a top management official present for the minitrial, and the two managers meet immediately after the minitrial to attempt to settle the dispute.

Minitrials have proven quite successful. When the top managers fully hear both their side and the other side of the dispute, they are better able to ascertain the strengths and weaknesses of each. The process is quick, and the information is kept from public view. Minitrials use a businesslike decision-making procedure, reducing complicated issues down to the essential points of disagreement and then allowing the problem-solving and negotiation skills of top managers to find a solution to the dispute. Many complex business disputes that have dragged on for years have been settled quickly with a minitrial.

PRIVATE JUDGES

The Private Judge process taps into the expertise of the many retired judges in our country. These people know how to run a trial, how to handle attorneys, witnesses and evidence, and are comfortable with the dispute resolution process. Many retired judges have joined law firms and are practicing law full or part-time. The parties make arrangements to employ and pay a retired judge they select to hear a particular dispute. The dispute resolution hearings may be held in the law office conference room. The process will typically move much faster than if the case were in the regular court system, and the proceedings and information provided at the hearing will normally be kept private. The judge will make a decision that is normally binding on the parties.

ADR AND THE COURTS

ADR is an alternative to litigation in the courts, but what happens when one of the parties to an agreement to use ADR decides instead to take the case to a court? Because most such cases involve arbitration, the following discussion will focus on arbitration, but the legal principles are applicable to other forms of ADR as well.

Historically, courts had been suspicious of arbitration as a substitute for litigation; as in *Wilko v. Swan*, 346 U.S. 427 (1953), courts were reluctant to enforce agreements to arbitrate when one party to the agreement sought to take the claim to court. However, the Federal Arbitration Act, enacted in 1925, was an expression of Congressional support for arbitration when the parties had knowingly and voluntarily entered into an agreement to use arbitration as a means for resolving their disputes. After *Wilko*, the judicial approach to arbitration began to change; over the past 30 years, the U.S. Supreme Court has decided several cases enforcing arbitration agreements under the Federal Arbitration Act. Various efforts by plaintiffs to avoid arbitration, and file litigate their suits instead, have, for the most part, been rejected by the Supreme Court. The following case involves a claim by an employee, required to sign an arbitration agreement as a condition of employment, that he should be able to litigate his employment discrimination claim against his employer.

In the Language of the Court

CIRCUIT CITY STORES, INC. V. ADAMS

532 U.S. 105, 121 S.Ct. 1302, 149 L.Ed. 2d 234 (2000)

Opinion written by Justice Kennedy

FACTS

In 1995 Saint Clair Adams applied for a job with Circuit City Stores, a national retailer of consumer electronics. As part of the employment application, Adams signed a statement which provided in part:

> *I agree that I will settle any and all previously unasserted claims, disputes or controversies arising out of or relating to my application or candidacy for employment, employment and/or cessation of employment, with Circuit City, exclusively by final and binding arbitration before a neutral arbitrator. By way of example only, such claims include claims under federal, state, and local statutory or common law, such the Age Discrimination in Employment Act, Title VII of the Civil Rights Act . . .*

Mr. Adams was hired as a sales counselor in Circuit City's store in Santa Rosa, California. Then two years later, Adams filed an employment discrimination lawsuit against Circuit City in state court, asserting claims under California's Fair Employment and Housing Act, and other claims based on general tort theories under California law. Circuit City filed suit in the United States District Court for the Northern District of California, seeking to enjoin the state court action and compel arbitration of plaintiff's claims. The District Court entered the requested order. The respondent (Adams), the court concluded, was obligated to submit his claims to binding arbitration.

Mr. Adams appealed to the Ninth Circuit Court of Appeals. While this appeal was pending, the Ninth Circuit ruled on the key issue in this case. The court held that the Federal Arbitration Act (FAA) does not apply to contracts of employment. *Craft v. Campbell Soup Co.*, 177 F.3d 1083 (9th Cir. 1999). Following the rule announced in Craft, the 9th Circuit held, in the instant case (Adams) that the arbitration agreement between Circuit City was contained in a "contract of employment" and so was not subject to the FAA. Circuit City petitioned the Supreme Court to hear the case on appeal, noting that the Ninth Circuit's conclusion that all employment contracts are excluded from the FAA conflicts with every other Court of Appeals to have addressed the question. We granted certiorari to resolve the issue.

DECISION

Congress enacted the FAA in 1925. As the Court has explained, the FAA was a response to hostility of American courts to the enforcement of arbitration agreements, a judicial disposition inherited from then-longstanding English practice. See, *e.g., Allied-Bruce Terminix Cos. v. Dobson*, 513 U.S. 265 (1995); *Gilmer v. Interstate/Johnson Lane Corp.*, 500 U.S. 20 (1991). To give effect to this purpose, the FAA compels judicial enforcement of a wide range of written arbitration agreements. The FAA's coverage provision, § 2, *(9 U.S.C. § 2)* provides that

> *"[a] written provision in any maritime transaction or a contract evidencing a transaction involving commerce to settle by arbitration a controversy thereafter arising out of such contract or transaction, or the refusal to perform the whole or any part thereof, or an agreement in writing to submit to arbitration an existing controversy arising out of such a contract, transaction, or refusal, shall be valid, irrevocable, and enforceable, save upon such grounds as exist at law or in equity for the revocation of any contract."*

We had occasion in *Allied-Bruce,* to consider the significance of Congress' use of the words "involving commerce" in § 2. The analysis began with a reaffirmation of earlier decisions concluding that the FAA was enacted pursuant to Congress' substantive power to regulate interstate commerce and admiralty, and that the Act was applicable in state courts and preemptive of state laws hostile to arbitration, see *Southland Corp. v. Keating,* 465 U.S. 1 (1984). Relying upon these background principles and upon the evident reach of the words "involving commerce," the Court interpreted § 2 as implementing Congress' intent "to exercise [its] commerce power to the full." *Allied-Bruce.*

The instant case, of course, involves not the basic coverage authorization under § 2 of the Act, but the exemption from coverage under § 1. The exemption clause provides the Act shall not apply "to contracts of employment of seamen, railroad employees, or any other class of workers engaged in foreign or interstate commerce." Most Courts of Appeals conclude the exclusion provision is limited to transportation workers, defined, for instance, as those workers " 'actually engaged in the movement of goods in interstate commerce.' " As we stated at the outset, the Court of Appeals for the Ninth Circuit takes a different view and interprets the § 1 exception to exclude all contracts of employment from the reach of the FAA.

This comprehensive exemption had been advocated in *Gilmer,* where we addressed the question whether a registered securities representative's employment discrimination claim under the Age Discrimination in Employment Act of 1967., could be submitted to arbitration pursuant to an agreement in his securities registration application. Concluding that the application was not a "contract of employment" at all, we found it unnecessary to reach the meaning of § 1 There is no such dispute in this case; while Circuit City argued in its petition for certiorari that the employment application signed by Adams was not a "contract of employment," we declined to grant certiorari on this point. So the issue reserved in *Gilmer* is presented here.

Respondent, endorsing the reasoning of the Court of Appeals for the Ninth Circuit that the provision excludes all employment contracts, relies on the asserted breadth of the words "contracts of employment of . . . any other class of workers engaged in . . . commerce." Referring to our construction of § 2's coverage provision

in *Allied-Bruce*—concluding that the words "involving commerce" evidence the congressional intent to regulate to the full extent of its commerce power—respondent contends § 1's interpretation should have a like reach, thus exempting all employment contracts.

This reading of § 1, however, runs into an immediate and, in our view, insurmountable textual obstacle. Unlike the "involving commerce" language in § 2, the words "any other class of workers engaged in . . . commerce" constitute a residual phrase, following, in the same sentence, explicit reference to "seamen" and "railroad employees." Construing the residual phrase to exclude all employment contracts fails to give independent effect to the statute's enumeration of the specific categories of workers which precedes it; there would be no need for Congress to use the phrases "seamen" and "railroad employees" if those same classes of workers were subsumed within the meaning of the "engaged in . . . commerce" residual clause. The wording of § 1 calls for the application of the maxim *ejusdem generis,* the statutory canon that "[w]here general words follow specific words in a statutory enumeration, the general words are construed to embrace only objects similar in nature to those objects enumerated by the preceding specific words.". Under this rule of construction the residual clause should be read to give effect to the terms "seamen" and "railroad employees," and should itself be controlled and defined by reference to the enumerated categories of workers which are recited just before it; the interpretation of the clause pressed by respondent fails to produce these results.

We must, of course, construe the "engaged in commerce" language in the FAA with reference to the statutory context in which it is found and in a manner consistent with the FAA's purpose. These considerations, however, further compel that the § 1 exclusion provision be afforded a narrow construction. As discussed above, the location of the phrase "any other class of workers engaged in . . . commerce" in a residual provision, after specific categories of workers have been enumerated, undermines any attempt to give the provision a sweeping, open-ended construction. And the fact that the provision is contained in a statute that "seeks broadly to overcome judicial hostility to arbitration agreements," which the Court concluded in *Allied-Bruce* counseled in favor of an expansive reading of § 2, gives no reason to abandon the precise reading of a provision that exempts contracts from the FAA's coverage.

In sum, the text of the FAA forecloses the construction of § 1 followed by the Court of Appeals in the case under review, a construction which would exclude all employment contracts from the FAA. We should not adopt an expansive construction of the FAA's exclusion provision that goes beyond the meaning of the words Congress used . . . the text of § 1 precludes interpreting the exclusion provision to defeat the language of § 2 as to all employment contracts. Section 1 exempts from the FAA only contracts of employment of transportation workers

We see no paradox in the congressional decision to exempt the workers over whom the commerce power was most apparent. To the contrary, it is a permissible inference that the employment contracts of the classes of workers in § 1 were excluded from the FAA precisely because of Congress' undoubted authority to govern the employment relationships at issue by the enactment of statutes specific to them. By the time the FAA was passed, Congress had already enacted federal legislation providing for the arbitration of disputes between seamen and their employers . . . When the FAA was adopted, moreover, grievance procedures existed for railroad employees under federal law and the passage of a more comprehensive statute providing for the mediation and arbitration of railroad labor disputes was imminent, see Railway Labor Act of 1926 . . . It is reasonable to assume that Congress excluded "seamen" and "railroad employees" from the FAA for the simple reason that it did not wish to unsettle established or developing statutory dispute resolution schemes covering specific workers.

Furthermore, for parties to employment contracts not involving the specific exempted categories set forth in § 1, it is true here, just as it was for the parties to the contract at issue in *Allied-Bruce,* that there are real benefits to the enforcement of arbitration provisions. We have been clear in rejecting the supposition that the advantages of the arbitration process somehow disappear when transferred to the employment context. See *Gilmer.* Arbitration agreements allow parties to avoid the costs of litigation, a benefit that may be of particular importance in employment litigation, which often involves smaller sums of money than disputes concerning commercial contracts . . . The considerable complexity and uncertainty that the construction of § 1 urged by respondent would introduce into the enforceability of arbitration agreements in employment contracts would call into doubt the efficacy of alternative dispute resolution procedures adopted by many of the Nation's employers, in the process undermining the FAA's proarbitration purposes and "breeding litigation from a statute that seeks to avoid it."

The Court has been quite specific in holding that arbitration agreements can be enforced under the FAA without contravening the policies of congressional enactments giving employees specific protection against discrimination prohibited by federal law; as we noted in *Gilmer,* " '[b]y agreeing to arbitrate a statutory claim, a party does not forgo the substantive rights afforded by the statute; it only submits to their resolution in an arbitral, rather than a judicial, forum.' "

* * *

For the foregoing reasons, the judgment of the Court of Appeals for the Ninth Circuit is reversed, and the case is remanded for further proceedings consistent with this opinion.

It is so ordered.

CASE QUESTIONS

1. Did Adams agree to the arbitration requirement here? What choices were open to him?
2. Why did the Ninth Circuit refuse to enforce the arbitration agreement here?
3. How does the Supreme Court interpret § 1 of the Federal Arbitration Act? What does that mean for Adams here?
4. Can an employer require an employee or applicant to agree to arbitration as a condition of employment?

Arbitration agreements are becoming very common: stockbrokers require clients to agree to arbitrate any disputes arising from the handling of their accounts; banks require credit card holders to use arbitration to resolve any billing disputes; and, as in the *Circuit City* case, employees are required to agree, as a condition of employment, to arbitrate any disputes arising from their employment. But such agreements are not the result of a voluntary negotiations—the clients, consumers or employees are presented with the arbitration agreement on a "take it or leave it" basis—if they don't agree to the arbitration clause, they don't get a credit card, can't open a brokerage account, or don't get hired. Such "take it or leave it" contracts are known as contracts of adhesion. Contracts of adhesion don't involve the freely negotiated agreements envisioned by the Federal Arbitration Act; nevertheless, in cases such as *Circuit City v. Adams* and *Gilmer v. Interstate/Johnson Lane Corp.,* 500 U.S. 20 (1991) (cited by the Supreme Court in the *Circuit City* case) the Court has upheld and enforced such agreements.

Another interesting sidelight to the increasing use of alternate dispute resolution is that many professional arbitrators are developing financial dependency upon certain large companies that regularly use their services to arbitrate disputes with their customers. There is some pressure on these arbitrators to render decisions that do not seriously anger the companies in order to keep their business. Other issues related to arbitration have caused controversy, as described below.

RECENT LEGAL DEVELOPMENTS IN ARBITRATION

In most cases, when the agreement to arbitrate is fair to both sides, is clearly explained to the other party, does not give the company the right to "opt out" if it chooses, and otherwise grants equal rights to both parties, such agreements have been upheld—especially in business contracts and disputes. Such agreements keep cases out of the overburdened court system, and offer quick and less-expensive dispute resolution. In *Gilmer v. Interstate/Johnson Lane Corp.,* (mentioned earlier), the Supreme Court held that stockbroker Robert Gilmer was prevented from suing his employer for age discrimination because he had signed the security industry's standard form agreeing to arbitrate job claims. The Court said the agreement did not interfere with Gilmer's substantive rights under the age discrimination statute; it merely required that those rights be settled by arbitration rather than by the courts. Following *Gilmer* and *Circuit City,* The federal circuit courts enforced predispute arbitration agreements, so long as they are fair and provide the employees with a forum to vindicate their rights. Such decisions include *Koveleskie v. SBC Markets Inc.,* 167 F.3d 361 (7th Cir. 1999); *Seus v. Nuveen,* 146 F.3d 175 (3rd Cir. 1998); and *EEOC v. Luce, Forward & Hamilton,* 345 F.3d 742 (9th Cir. 2003).

PROCEDURAL FAIRNESS OF ARBITRATION

Because employees and consumers may be required to agree to arbitrate, the courts that are asked to enforce agreements to arbitrate will closely scrutinize those arbitration provisions to ensure that they are fair to both parties and are not being used by one party (the bank or employer) to deny legal rights to the other (the client or employee). This is especially true in *employment contracts*—particularly those that must be signed in order to receive various employee benefits, such as raises, promotions or transfers. The courts will refuse to enforce arbitration agreements that are one-sided, deny employees or consumers rights or limit remedies available to them. In *Ingle v. Circuit City Stores,* 328 F.3d 1165 (9th Cir. 2003), a case decided after the Supreme Court case involving Circuit City, the Ninth Circuit struck down Circuit City's form arbitration agreement, calling it "presumptively unconscionable." The Court said that the agreement contained an "insidious pattern of objectionable provisions" that required employees to forego statutory rights and remedies. The Ninth Circuit pointed to several terms (often found in employer arbitration agreements) that "unfairly limited" an employee's statutory rights and remedies or unilaterally granted the employer benefits not afforded to the employee, such as:

- The "one-sided coverage term," which limits the applicability of the agreement to claims brought by the employee, while imposing no such limitation on the employer.

- The strict one-year statute of limitations term, which deprives employees of arguing that the violation is continuing

- The bar on class-action arbitration, contrary to "firmly rooted principles" of both the federal and California legal systems

- The fee provision requiring that an employee pay the employer a $75 filing fee in order to initiate a complaint against the employer

- The employer's unilateral right to terminate or modify the agreement

- The limitation of otherwise available statutory remedies and the limits on an employee's damages otherwise provided by federal law.

In *Rosenberg v. Merrill Lynch, Pierce, Fenner & Smith Inc.,* 170 F.3d 1 (1st Cir. 1999), the employee signed a form agreeing to arbitrate claims after being hired by Merrill Lynch as a financial consultant. Rather than specifying the kinds of complaints she would have to submit to arbitration, the agreement said Rosenberg must abide by the arbitration rules of various industrial organizations, including the New York Stock Exchange. Rosenberg sued for sex and age discrimination after being fired, saying her work was better than that of four or more men in the same position who remained on the job. Merrill Lynch admitted it had agreed to inform Rosenberg of the industry arbitration rules, but "it did not keep its side of the bargain," the 1st Circuit Court said. The court specified that if the company had made a "modest effort" to make the information available to the employee, she would have been compelled to arbitrate.

In *Hooters of America v. Phillips,* 173 F.3d 933 (4th Cir. 1999), the Fourth Circuit Court of Appeals refused to enforce an arbitration agreement imposed on employees by Hooters Restaurants. The company told all employees in 1994 that if they wanted to be eligible for raises, transfers and promotions, they had to sign the agreement. Annette Phillips, a bartender at the Myrtle Beach, S.C. location had signed the agreement, and later threatened to sue Hooters after being sexually harassed by a manager. Hooters filed a court action seeking to force her to arbitrate her claim. The agreement gave Hooters control over the choice of arbitrators and allowed the company to change the arbitration rules at any time. The Court refused enforcement of the arbitration agreement, finding it "so one-sided as to undermine the neutrality of the proceeding."

The courts will also refuse to enforce arbitration agreements that restrict remedies available to employees less than those remedies available under the appropriate EEO statute, *Circuit City Stores, Inc. v Adams,* 279 F.3d 889 (9th Cir. 2002), *cert. denied,* 535 U.S. 1112 (June 3, 2002).

The California Supreme Court, in the case of *Armendariz v. Foundation Health Psychcare Services, Inc.* 99 Cal. Rptr.2d 745, 24 Cal.4th 83 (2000), set out requirements for enforcing agreements requiring arbitration of claims under California state employment discrimination legislation: (1) the arbitration must be by a neutral arbitrator; (2) the arbitration procedures must allow the parties access to witnesses and essential documents; (3) the arbitrator must provide a written decision; (4) the remedies available under the arbitration must be similar to those available in court; and (5) the employee may not be required to pay any arbitrators' fees or expenses or any unreasonable costs as a condition of going to arbitration. The *Armendariz* case was decided under state law, but some federal courts have adopted its analysis with regard to enforcing mandatory agreements to arbitrate.

From those cases, it is clear that giving the company control over the choice of arbitrators and allowing it to change the arbitration rules can be fatal to the contract. Failing to inform the employee of the arbitration rules seems to be another major flaw, as in *Prudential Insurance Co. v. Lai,* 42 F.3d 1299 (9th Cir. 1994). So is limiting available remedies. Safeguards to help ensure fairness include having a system for choosing an independent arbitrator and putting an independent administrator in charge of the arbitration system. In addition, due process procedures should be followed. Claimants must be able to vindicate themselves as fully before an arbitrator as if they were before a judge and jury.

Controversy has arisen in regard to arbitration in the securities industry because most arbitrators used in securities cases have previously worked as brokers or financial advisors. Studies have shown that brokers have won most of the arbitration cases filed by customers. Stock brokerage and securities associations are now studying possible reforms to make their arbitration procedures more customer-oriented.

COSTS OF ARBITRATION

In addition to reviewing the fairness of the arbitration procedures, courts may also review whether the arbitration agreement requires the employee or consumer to bear unreasonable costs. As mentioned in *Armendariz,* arbitration agreements that impose excessive costs on claimants could deter them from bringing complaints under EEO laws or consumer protection legislation. Because the employees or consumers may be required to arbitrate rather than litigate their claims, they are effectively denied the protection of those laws. Courts have therefore refused to enforce arbitration agreements requiring claimants to bear unreasonable arbitration expenses. In *Green Tree Financial Corp. v. Randolph,* 531 U.S. 79 (2000), the Supreme Court held that the party seeking to invalidate an arbitration agreement because it would be prohibitively expensive has the burden of demonstrating the likelihood of incurring such costs. After *Green Tree,* the courts have struggled to decide whether the cost requirements of arbitration are prohibitively or unreasonably expensive. Plaintiffs filing suits in the federal courts are generally required to pay a filing fee (currently less than $300) and must also bear the cost of legal representation; attorneys for plaintiffs are likely to take such cases on a contingency basis (they will only charge legal fees if the plaintiff wins the suit). Some legislation also provides that successful plaintiffs may recover legal fees as part of the statutory remedies available. In contrast, the claimants filing for arbitration will be required to pay a filing fee, will generally be held to pay at least half of the arbitrator's fees and expenses, and may have to additional fees for administrative costs for discovery proceedings, and for subpoenas of witnesses. A study of arbitration costs ["The Costs of Arbitration," conducted by Public Citizen, April 2002] estimated that the costs for arbitrating an employment dispute (assuming three days of hearings) would be between $3,950 and $10,925. Employees or consumers required to pay such expenses may effectively be prevented from pursing their legal rights; employers, brokers or banks may have an incentive to impose arbitration requirements with high costs to prevent claimants from filing claims. As a result, the courts have been sensitive to claims that the arbitration agreement imposes unreasonable costs on the employees or consumers.

In *Armendariz v. Foundation Health Psychcare Services, Inc.,* the California Supreme Court held that an arbitration agreement requiring the employee to pay any expenses beyond those required to file a suit in court would be held unreasonable and not enforceable. In *Morrison v. Circuit City Stores, Inc.* 317 F.3d 646 (6th Cir. 2003)(*en banc*), the court held that a "fee-splitting" clause (which required the employee and the employer to split the costs of the arbitration and the arbitrator's fees) would be unreasonable and unenforceable when it would deter a substantial number of potential claimants from exerting their statutory rights. In *Morrison,* the court required the employee to arbitrate her claim but held that the employer had to pay the costs of the arbitration. Other courts have held fee-splitting clauses were unreasonable *per se* and unenforceable because, by requiring the employee to pay at least some of the costs of arbitration, they automatically limit the remedies that would be available to the employee under Title VII, *Perez v. Globe Airport Security Services,* 253 F.3d 1280 (11th Cir. 2001), *Circuit City Stores, Inc. v. Adams,* 279 F.3d 889 (9th Cir. 2002), *cert. denied,* 535 U.S. 1112 (June 3, 2002), and *Ingle v. Circuit City Stores, Inc.,* 328 F.3d 1165 (9th Cir. 2003).

When determining whether the arbitration agreement would impose unreasonable costs on a claimant, the courts generally consider the income and resources available to the claimant, the potential costs of arbitration, and the costs of litigation as an alternative. The courts may reach different conclusions for different claimants–highly paid executives may be able to afford to pay half the costs of arbitration, but, as in *Morrison,* lower paid employees may not be required to pay the costs of arbitration.

ARBITRATION AGREEMENTS AND GOVERNMENT ENFORCEMENT

While the courts may enforce arbitration agreements against individual consumers and employees, such individual arbitration agreements will not prevent the government enforcement agencies such as the Equal Employment Opportunity Commission from bringing suits to enforce legislation prohibiting discrimination or protecting consumers. In *EEOC v. Waffle House, Inc.,* 534 U.S. 279 (2003), the Supreme Court held that the EEOC could bring legal action to enforce the EEO statutes, and could seek individual remedies (such as back pay and reinstatement) for the employee who had signed an arbitration agreement.

IN CONSULTATION

Marvin Manager has a problem. One of his employees is accusing his company, ABC, Inc., of disability discrimination under the Americans with Disabilities Act. The employee, Edwin, signed a contract when he was hired. Included in the contract is a clause that states:

> I understand that as a condition of employment and continued employment, I agree to submit any complaints to arbitration and to abide by and accept the final decision of the arbitration panel as the ultimate resolution of my complaint(s) for any and all events that arise out of my employment and/or termination of my employment.

Several months after joining ABC and signing this contract, Edwin filed his disability complaints with the Equal Employment Opportunity Commission (EEOC). Marvin was shocked by both the complaint and, more importantly, Edwin's EEOC filing. Marvin assumed that if any of his employees had employment complaints, they would pursue arbitration.

Edwin told Marvin that he did not consider himself bound by the arbitration clause in the contract. He alleged that he did not understand what he was signing away and he also did not feel that he had any power to negotiate because his job was on the line. He intended to pursue all of his rights under the Americans with Disabilities Act, including a jury trial.

Marvin approached his company's in-house corporate counsel,. He asked whether Edwin could evade the mandatory arbitration clause. Here is their conversation:

Marvin:

(1) Isn't an employment contract binding on both the employees and the employer?

(2) Then should we be able to force Edwin to go to arbitration?

(3) What about Edwin's allegation that he did not understand what he was signing and that he felt he had no bargaining power?

The company lawyer responds:

(1) Most employment contracts are binding so long as they are legal, signed by competent parties, and not contrary to public policy.

(2) Not necessarily. Mandatory arbitration clauses are controversial, and some assert they are against public policy.

(3) The court may take Edwin's allegations seriously. Mandatory arbitration clauses are closely scrutinized by the courts because they are often a condition of employment. Let me research the applicable law to see whether Edwin is bound by the arbitration clause in our contract. I'll get back to you.

MEMO FROM THE LEGAL DEPARTMENT

To: Marvin Manager

RE: Enforceability of mandatory arbitration clauses in employment contracts

Dear Marvin:

The presence of mandatory arbitration clauses has grown dramatically in recent years. Employers favor them because of the great reduction in costs they offer by providing a rapid solution to disputes without the expense of discovery and a trial. Courts, however, consider mandatory arbitration clauses in employment contracts suspect for several reasons. First, employment disputes often involve civil rights, which are strongly protected by statute and the Constitution. Courts are disinclined to allow employers to force employees to waive their full ability to protect their civil and statutory rights. Second, some courts assume that employees do not understand what they are waiving when they sign a contract containing an arbitration clause. Many employees apparently do not realize that arbitration is binding and that by agreeing to arbitration, they are giving up all access to the regular court system. Finally, courts are wary of employers who take advantage of their significant bargaining power with new hires and force people who need the job to sign away rights. Some courts find this practice oppressive for new employees who may not feel they have the ability to disagree with any clauses in their contract. The Supreme Court, in Circuit City, upheld the use of arbitration clauses in employment contracts in general, but other courts have found some particular clauses to be unfair.

In order to be valid, employees cannot be forced to waive substantive rights, so courts require that employees know what they are waiving. It would be very helpful if we could have more information about the circumstances under which Edwin signed his agreement. If we cannot establish that we explained the clause to him or even gave him the opportunity to ask questions, then we may not be able to enforce the arbitration provision. It would also assist our case if we could even establish that Edwin read the clause before signing the contract. Only if we can prove that Edwin knowingly and expressly waived his rights can we enforce our arbitration clause. And the EEOC may file its own case regardless of whether Edwin must arbitrate with us.

With regard to mandatory arbitration clauses in employment contracts, we should consider the following questions:
1. What are the arguments in support of mandatory arbitration in employment disputes?
2. What could Marvin and ABC have done differently to avoid the risk that the company's arbitration clause is unenforceable?
3. Why do you think the courts more closely scrutinize arbitration clauses in employment contracts as compared with other commercial agreements? Do you agree with the courts' concerns over fairness to employees and protection of employees' rights?

SUMMARY

The process of litigation in the American legal system is complex and sometimes lengthy. The procedures—from choosing a jury, to questioning witnesses, to deciding what evidence is relevant—are designed to ensure that each person has a full and fair hearing before an impartial decision maker. Fundamental features of the system are that it is "adversarial" (the parties and their attorneys make the arguments with the judge serving as a referee) and that "due process" (procedural fairness) is highly stressed. Although the American judicial system is a model for much of the world, there surely are situations where things do not work perfectly. Some cases seem to go on forever and at great cost to all involved. Persons convicted of horrible crimes sometimes do not go to jail or are allowed to appeal over and over. Juries occasionally render money verdicts that appear excessive to the rest of us. But for the most part the system is fair to all and works pretty well.

The material in this chapter is designed to assist you in becoming better informed about the procedural workings of the American court system. Although the system works in a fair and impartial manner most of the time, the more you know about how the procedures work, the better you will do when the need arises to use the court system. As business and community leaders in the future, many of you will also have the opportunity to participate in the ongoing attempt to improve the court system in your community—to make it work more efficiently while still guaranteeing due process to all.

The chapter has also examined the various forms of Alternate Dispute Resolution (ADR) by which the parties resolve their dispute outside of the formal court system. The use of ADR is growing rapidly, in both business and personal disputes. ADR offers, in most cases, a less-expensive, faster, and more private way of deciding the dispute. It should be remembered, however, that when the parties agree to settle their dispute using ADR, they are giving up their right to "go to court." Generally, courts will not interfere or review the decision made by the arbitrator or private judge, unless it can be shown that the process was somehow unfair to one side. Particularly in employment arbitration agreements drafted by the employer, the courts look carefully to make sure the terms are fair and that the nature of the agreement was fully explained to and understood by the employee before it is enforced.

CHAPTER QUESTIONS

1. A former employee at a Sam's Club (owned by Wal-Mart) in New Mexico brought a sexual harassment lawsuit alleging that a supervisor had made many sexual remarks to her and had inappropriately grabbed and touched her while she was operating a forklift. Wal-Mart tried to introduce photographs of the forklift at the trial, to show that such acts were impossible. However, Wal-Mart had not listed the photographs on the pretrial list of exhibits. Should the company be able to introduce them at the trial? [*Coates v. Wal-Mart Stores, Inc.,* 976 P. 2d 999 (N. Mex. 1999)]

2. Consolidated Aluminum Co. made ladders with polyethylene feet. Several persons were injured when ladders slipped while in use, causing the users to fall. Consolidated did not know that using polyethylene feet made the ladders defective and dangerous. What types of damages may the injured people recover? May they recover punitive damages? [*Sparks v. Consolidated Aluminum Co.,* 679 S.W. 2d 348 (Missouri Court of Appeals)]

3. When should a court grant a motion for directed verdict? How about a motion for judgment notwithstanding the verdict (Judgment N.O.V.)? A motion for new trial? Do these motions serve any purpose for the losing party, even if they are denied

4. In a business lawsuit, one attorney made repeated requests to conduct depositions of two of defendant's witnesses. On two occasions, deposition notices were sent, but defendant failed to produce the witnesses, one time writing a letter the day before stating they would not attend. The attorney failed to return phone calls requesting a date for new depositions. Finally, when the discovery period set by the court had expired, the Defendant said in effect

"I guess it's too late for you to depose them now." The court then entered an order barring the defendant from calling the two witnesses at trial. The defendant appealed, arguing that the sanction was too harsh, and "decimated our case." What should the decision be on appeal? Why? *Johnson v. J.B. Hunt Transport, Inc.,* 280 F.3d 1125 (7th Cir. 2002).

5. Gerald Martin filed a lawsuit in Idaho state court on May 4, 1995, alleging that the negligent driving of the defendant caused damages to him. His attorney initiated a series of telephone calls with the defendant's insurance company to discuss settlement of the case. The attorney told the insurance representative that they were not going to serve the summons and complaint on the defendant "until such time as we are unable to reach an agreement on settlement of this claim." Several letters and phone calls were exchanged over the next several months, without settlement. At the end of October, the plaintiff's attorney finally tried to obtain service on the defendant, but the sheriff reported that the defendant no longer lived at the address given and had apparently moved out of state some months earlier. The attorney then tried to obtain service on the defendant at an address given in the state of Washington, but found that it was only a mailbox address.

   Idaho law requires that service of process must be made on the defendant within six months of the date of the filing of a civil case, which did not happen here. The defendant's insurance company referred the case to an attorney who filed, on behalf of the defendant, a motion to dismiss the case for lack of service. The Idaho court rule states that if service of process is not made within six months and the plaintiff "cannot show good cause why such service was not made" within the time period, the case should be dismissed. What should the result be? Why? [*Martin v. Hoblit*, 987 P. 2d 284 (Id. 1999)]

6. What is the purpose of the *stare decisis* rule? What public policy reasons favor use of the rule? When should a court overturn a legal rule that has existed for many years? What effect will this have on individuals and businesses who have relied on the rule?

7. Mr. Brotby was hired as a consultant to do information technology work for Computer Task Group, Inc. (CTG) in Alaska. He signed a non-disclosure agreement and an agreement not to accept employment with any of CTG's customers. About two years later he did leave CTG and take a job with one of its customers, for whom he had been working as a consultant. CTG brought a lawsuit seeking an injunction and damages. During the course of discovery, Brotby consistently refused to answer many interrogatories, gave contradictory answers to others, filed "frivolous answers" and "baseless" motions, changed his story repeatedly, and refused to produce key documents. CTG filed 8 motions to compel discovery and the trial judge issued 5 orders to Brotby directing him to comply, but he failed to do so. Two years after the case was filed, CTG brought a motion to dismiss Brotby's counterclaims, strike his answer and enter judgment against him for discovery abuse. Should the court grant the motion? What are the arguments for and against such a sanction? *Computer Task Group, Inc. v. Brotby,* 364 F.3d 1112 (9th Cir. 2004).

8. An employee had worked for American General Financial (AGF) for 20 years when the company announced a new program that required that arbitration be used to resolve all employment disputes, unless prohibited

by law. The company distributed information to all employees that included a statement that if they continued their employment with the company that means that "you agree to resolve employment-related claims against the company through this process." A year or two later, the employee was fired. She sued, claiming the company violated her leave rights under the Family and Medical Leave Act. AGF moved to compel arbitration; the district court refused. AGF appealed. What should the result be and why? *Seawright v. American General Financial Services, Inc.*, 507 F.3d 967 (6th Cir., 2007).

9. A developer filed a lawsuit against a Delaware county after it refused to issue him a building permit for a shopping mall. He obtained a preliminary injunction from the federal district court prior to trial, ordering the county to issue the permit and restraining the county from "interfering with the construction" of the mall. The county appealed, arguing that this order violated the purpose and rationale for preliminary injunctions. What is the primary purpose of injunctions? What should be the result on appeal? [*Acierno v. New Castle County*, 40 F. 3d 645 (3rd Cir. 1994)]

10. Several plaintiffs filed a securities fraud class action in 2003 alleging that Merck & Co. knowingly misrepresented the heart-attack risks associated with its drug Vioxx, and that they purchased stock in the company (which price later declined) on the basis of the fraudulent misrepresentations. According to federal law, the complaint was timely if filed no more than two years after the plaintiffs "discover[ed] the facts constituting the violation." The lower court dismissed the case because it was filed after the Statute of Limitations (2 years) had run. The plaintiffs claimed that the running of the statute of limitations should be tolled (the time for filing should be extended) since, because of the fraud and deceit by Merck, they were unaware of the fraud at that time. What should the court decide and why? *Merck & Co. v. Reynolds*.

PRACTICAL EXERCISE

Christina and Carter are owners of competing pizza shops. For more than 10 years Carter has built up an excellent reputation in the community for the quality of his pizza, and his two shops are making a nice profit. Christina opened her business about one year ago and has aggressively marketed her pizza through flyers and television advertising. She is trying to build up her business. Recently she began to run a series of ads in both media, prepared by the local advertising firm "Fast and Slick," in which a customer exclaims "This is great!" while eating a slice of pizza out of a "Christina's" box. At another table, a man says "This tastes like cardboard" while eating a slice of pizza out of a clearly labeled "Carter's Pizza" box. "And you won't get sick after eating this one, either," says the first person.

Right after the ads began to run on television, Carter noticed a decrease in his business. He had received several "best pizza" awards from public polls in the past and has never had a problem with the health department or any complaints about people becoming ill after eating his pizza. Carter calls Christina and demands that she stop running the "false and misleading" ads, but she says "Too bad, this is just fair competition, buddy." Carter knows that you, his friend, are learning about legal issues in business. Prepare a complaint for Carter to file in local court against Christina and anyone else who may have taken action that unfairly damaged his business. The local county court is the Ada County District Court.

FURTHER INFORMATION

www.law.cornell.edu/supct/index/html
Cornell site—this part specializing in U.S. Supreme Court.

www.lawsource.com
The site contains a comprehensive list and links to "all on-line sources of American law., and a comparison of the legal system in the United States, Canada and Mexico.

www.law.emory.edu
Broad legal site, with many topics.

CHAPTER 4

THE CONSTITUTION AND BUSINESS

After you have read this chapter, you should be able to:

1. Discuss how the concepts of federalism, separation of powers, and judicial review affect the organization of the federal and state governments.

2. Describe the constitutional basis for the power of the federal government to regulate business.

3. Explain the concept of eminent domain and its applications.

4. List several of the fundamental rights and protections provided by the first ten amendments to the Constitution, known as the Bill of Rights.

Many American business firms now conduct drug tests, both prior to hiring and sometimes during employment. Such testing raises various constitutional issues, including the right to privacy and possible illegal search and seizure. The "Practical Exercise" at the end of this chapter is a situation involving these issues.

INTRODUCTION

The U.S. Constitution establishes the structure of the government and legal system in the United States. This remarkable document, drafted in 1787, created the three branches of the federal government, set forth the powers and duties of each, and formulated the basic relationship between the federal and state governments. Although there have been dramatic changes in every aspect of American business, culture, and society since 1787, the Constitution continues to be the primary source of guidance for resolving the most important legal issues of the day. In more than 200 years, the Constitution has been amended only 27 times. The first 10 amendments, called the Bill of Rights, were added within a few years after the Constitution was adopted and are practically part of the original document. Two of the other amendments (the prohibition of the sale of liquor and the repeal of that prohibition) cancelled each other out. Thus, there have really been only 15 other amendments added to the Constitution since 1791. It is an amazing document.

This chapter will begin with a discussion of the history of the writing of the Constitution and its ratification and then will look at the system of government it created and the provisions regulating business. Next, we will examine the concept of "eminent domain" by which government can take ownership of private property for public use. Finally, we will discuss a number of important concepts designed to preserve individual rights from being overcome by a powerful federal government—such as freedom of speech, press, and religion and the "due process" and "equal protection of the law" clauses.

HISTORY OF THE CONSTITUTION

Following the Revolutionary War, the American colonies entered into an agreement (ratified in 1781) called the Articles of Confederation. The purpose of this document was primarily to create an association between the former colonies rather than to develop a new central government. The colonists, having just obtained their freedom from a powerful sovereign (the King of England), were not eager to establish a strong federal government. However, within a few

Pepper . . . and Salt

THE WALL STREET JOURNAL

corlett

"Do you ever have one of those days when *nothing* seems constitutional?"

From *The Wall Street Journal.* Reprinted with permission of Cartoon Features Syndicate.

years it became apparent that changes were needed in the Articles of Confederation. The federal government had no power to levy taxes, to regulate commerce, or to create a federal court system. The colony-states were taxing or excluding each other's goods, issuing their own currency, and engaging in other forms of rivalry contrary to the best interests of the new nation.

Therefore, the states agreed to select delegates to meet in Philadelphia in the summer of 1787 in order to consider amendments to the Articles of Confederation. The expressed purpose was *not* to write a new Constitution—indeed if this had been indicated as the reason for the meeting, it is likely that many states would have refused to participate. However, when the delegates arrived, discussion soon turned, at the urging of James Madison, to the need for a completely new governmental structure.

The delegates were quite a group, consisting of 55 of what we might now term "the best and the brightest" men of the new nation, including George Washington, Alexander Hamilton, Roger Sherman, and Benjamin Franklin, as well as Madison. They were all men, and most were prominent landowners and political figures. Meeting all summer in the building now called Independence Hall in Philadelphia (with the windows of the meeting room nailed shut to ensure privacy), the delegates in September 1787 issued the proposed new Constitution.

The ratification process was not easy. The delegates had breached their instructions and had created a Constitution which established a strong federal government. Considerable opposition arose in many of the states to the federal government powers and to the resulting reduction in freedom and independence for the states. The system of federalism (described in the next section of this chapter) was a new concept to which many of the former colonists were opposed. Patrick Henry was particularly vociferous in his dissent. As "Tea Party" activists have reminded us in 2011. The arguments for ratification were led by Hamilton, Madison, and John Jay, who wrote a series of articles called *The Federalist Papers*, which were widely distributed (people actually read and debated them—there was no radio or television in those days). During the course of the debates, in order to improve the chances of ratification, particularly in New York, Rhode Island, and Virginia, the proponents of ratification promised to immediately begin work on a series of amendments designed to safeguard and guarantee individual rights, should the Constitution be ratified. The required number of states did ratify the Constitution by 1788, and the first Congress met in 1789. As promised, the first 10 amendments (the Bill of Rights) were added by 1791.

ORGANIZATION OF THE FEDERAL AND STATE GOVERNMENTS

FEDERALISM

enumerated powers: Those powers specifically given to the federal government in the Constitution.

One of the major compromises reached in the writing of the Constitution was the division of powers between the federal and state governments. As we have mentioned, the framers of the Constitution and the American citizens were quite apprehensive about an all-powerful federal government. Therefore, the Constitution specifically granted a series of powers to the federal government, which are termed **enumerated powers**, leaving other powers (not given to the federal government) to the states.

It has long been accepted, in theory at least, that Congress and the federal government may only exercise powers that were specifically granted them in the Constitution, such as "to lay and collect taxes," "to coin money," "to establish post offices and post roads," "to constitute tribunals inferior to the Supreme Court," and "regulate commerce with foreign nations and among the several states." To clarify this point, the 10th Amendment to the Constitution (added with the Bill of Rights) states, "The powers not delegated to the United States by the Constitution . . . are reserved by it to the states respectively, or to the people." This concept of dividing powers up between the federal and state governments is called **federalism.**

But you may be asking (as the Tea Party and other critics of federal power are doing today)—"if the federal government is limited to doing only the things specifically granted to it in the Constitution, how did it ever become as powerful and pervasive as it is today?" The answer lies in the way the Constitution has been interpreted, particularly with reference to two other important clauses of the Constitution itself. Article VI contains the **Supremacy Clause,** which states that the "Constitution and Laws of the United States which shall be made in pursuance thereof . . . shall be the supreme law of the land."

As was mentioned in Chapter 2, this clause has led to the doctrine of **preemption,** which holds that when a federal law and a state law govern the same subject and are conflicting, the federal law "preempts" (controls and displaces) the state law. As society has become more complex, the subjects that the federal government has chosen to regulate (especially under the Commerce Clause, as discussed later) have greatly expanded. Many of those same areas are dealt with in some way by state laws, and therefore, courts have had to determine on numerous occasions whether the state law should be preempted or not.

> **preemption:** The doctrine that holds that when a federal law and a state law are in direct conflict, the federal law prevails.

In addition, Article I, Section 8, of the Constitution grants Congress the right to make "all laws *necessary and proper* for carrying into execution" the enumerated powers. The **"necessary and proper clause"** has been interpreted hundreds of times by the courts. Often, judicial decisions have allowed Congress to pass laws to accomplish things not specifically authorized by the Constitution, where those actions are deemed necessary to carry out a power that was specifically assigned to the federal government. Actions taken under this theory are called **implied powers.** In 1819 the Supreme Court decided the first important case dealing with this type of power, *McCulloch v. Maryland.*

> **implied powers:** Laws and actions taken by the federal government that are "necessary and proper" to carry out enumerated powers.

MCCULLOCH V. MARYLAND

17 U.S. 316 (1819)

FACTS

Congress had passed a law establishing a national bank in 1816. The Maryland legislature attempted to tax all banks that were not chartered by the state, but the cashier of the national bank located in Baltimore refused to pay the tax. The state prosecutor brought criminal charges against the cashier. A main issue in the case became whether the federal government has the power to set up a bank.

The prosecution pointed out that none of the enumerated powers of the federal government authorize the formation of a national bank.

DECISION

Chief Justice Marshall decided that Congress did have the power to create a national bank. He wrote, "Among the enumerated powers, we do not find that of establishing a bank or creating a corporation. But there is no phrase in the instrument which, like the Articles of Confederation, excludes incidental or implied powers."

Much argument focused on the "necessary and proper" clause of the Constitution. The state argued that the word "necessary" meant that Congress could only pass laws which were "indispensable" to the exercise of the enumerated power. Marshall asked if this was the sense in which the word "necessary" was always used and decided that it was not. "We find that it frequently imports no more than that one thing is convenient, or useful, or essential to another . . . ."

Marshall wrote that there was no question but that the powers of the federal government were limited. But the court found that Congress should have some discretion about

the means by which the enumerated powers are carried out. Justice Marshall concluded, "Let the ends be legitimate, let it be within the scope of the constitution, and all means which are appropriate, which are plainly adapted to that end, which are not prohibited, but consistent with the letter and spirit of the constitution, are constitutional."

CASE QUESTIONS

1. Does the phrase "necessary and proper" mean something different than just the word "necessary"? What do you think were the intentions of the authors of the Constitution when they drafted that phrase?
2. Marshall states that if the "ends are legitimate" that the means for reaching the ends are within the discretion of Congress. What is the legitimate end served by the establishment of a national bank? Can you find an enumerated power that is being assisted by the national bank?
3. Think of as many "implied powers" of the federal government as you can. What are some of the things the government does that are not specifically mentioned in the Constitution?

FEDERALISM AND THE 11TH AMENDMENT

In 1999 the U.S. Supreme Court issued three significant decisions (all decided by a 5-4 majority) dealing with federalism and the 11th Amendment, which dramatically strengthened states' rights. The 11th Amendment to the Constitution reads:

"The judicial power of the United States shall not be construed to extend to any suit in law or equity, commenced or prosecuted against one of the United States by citizens of another state, or by citizens of any foreign state."

This "state immunity from lawsuit" amendment was enacted by Congress in 1794, one year after the Supreme Court decision in *Chisholm v. Georgia,* which had allowed a suit against a state for damages, pursuant to the Judiciary Act of 1789. The 11th Amendment was enacted specifically to overturn the result of the *Chisholm* case, and was quickly ratified by the states. If we recall the debate over ratification of the Constitution (discussed earlier) and specifically the apprehension that many state leaders had about relinquishing sovereignty to a strong federal government, it is possible to understand the angry reaction that followed the *Chisholm* decision, and the quick addition of the 11th Amendment to restore state immunity from certain lawsuits.

For over 150 years there were few decisions dealing with the scope of the 11th Amendment. In general, while states were held immune from suit by citizens of other states in federal court (which is what the 11th Amendment specifically provides), it was possible for citizens to sue their own states in state courts for various violations. However, under the leadership of Chief Justice Rehnquist, things began to change in the 1990s.

In 1996, the Supreme Court had held in *Seminole Tribe v. Florida* that Congress only had the power to authorize suits against states in federal court pursuant to its authority under Section 5 of the 14th Amendment (which allows Congress to enact laws to enforce the "due process," "equal protection," and other protections given there which specifically apply to the states). And in 1997 in *City of Boerne v. Flores,* the Court struck down the federal Religious Freedom Restoration Act, saying that Congress exceeded its power under Section 5 by "redefining rather than enforcing," the guarantees of the 14th Amendment. In 1999 the Supreme Court decided three cases severely restricting the power of the federal government by prohibiting nearly all lawsuits against a state for violation of federal law.

In *Alden v. Maine,* a group of state probation officers sued in state court under the Federal Fair Labor Standards Act to recover overtime pay allegedly owed them by the state of Maine. In an opinion by Justice Anthony Kennedy, the Supreme Court held that the officers could not sue the state of Maine in state courts, even if the federal wage and hour laws were violated.

After a lengthy review of the Constitution's structure and history (emphasizing the independent sovereignty of the states), and discussing several previous Supreme Court federalism decisions, Justice Kennedy explained that the 11th Amendment actually "confirmed rather than established" states' immunity from suit. State sovereign immunity preceded the Constitution's ratification, he stated, and was "implicit in the Constitutional design." Thus, the *Chisholm* case "deviated from the original understanding," which was "restored" by the 11th Amendment. Furthermore, since the immunity of the states existed prior to the 11th Amendment, it might be even broader than the words of that amendment and could cover suits in a state court by a state's own citizens, as well as suits by citizens of other states in federal court.

In the *Alden* case the Supreme Court, citing authority as far back as the *Federalist Papers*, confirmed that the states had always had a "residuary and inviolable sovereignty." Calling the question of the states' immunity from suit in their own state courts for violations of federal law "a matter of first impression," the Court found that history and prior cases indicated that states retained constitutional immunity from suit in their own courts.

The Supreme Court stated in strong language that "[f]ederalism requires that Congress accord States the respect and dignity due them as residuary sovereigns and joint participants in the Nation's governance. Immunity from suit in federal courts is not enough to preserve that dignity, for the indignity of subjecting a nonconsenting State to the coercive process of judicial tribunals at the instance of private parties exists regardless of the forum." In addition, "[p]rivate suits against nonconsenting states may threaten their financial integrity, and the surrender of immunity carries with it substantial costs to the autonomy, decisionmaking ability, and sovereign capacity of the States."

The result of the three 1999 cases is that individuals may not generally sue a state government, in either state or federal court, for its violations of federal law, unless the state chooses to give up its immunity. The *Alden* case involved alleged violation of federal wage, hour, and overtime rules, while the other two 1999 cases held that neither companies nor individuals could sue nonconsenting states for patent infringement or false advertising in violation of federal law. The only way for the federal government to remove this immunity was through use of the power it has under Section 5 of the 14th Amendment. But in two other cases decided the same day as *Alden,* the Court indicated that it would apply "strict scrutiny" analysis to any attempts by Congress to remove state immunity under the 14th Amendment.

The Rehnquist court's interpretation of the 11th Amendment has generated considerable comment and controversy. One commentator called the string of cases a return to "antebellum federal/state relations." On the other hand, other commentators maintained that it was merely "a continuation of a debate that began in the summer of 1787 and has never been fully resolved—the debate between a state-centered view of the American Constitution and a nationalist view."

Since announcing its new interpretation of the 11th Amendment in 1999, the Supreme Court has heard several more cases involving state/federal relations and the 11th Amendment. In 2000 in Kimel v. Florida Bd. of Regents, 528 U. S. 62, the Supreme Court held that the Age Discrimination in Employment Act could not be constitutionally applied to suits against the states. In Board of Trustees v. Garrett, decided in 2001, the Supreme Court held that states could not be sued by state employees for money damages for violations of Title 1 of the Americans with Disabilities Act (ADA). The Court concluded that the legislative record lacked the "pattern of unconstitutional discrimination" necessary to bring the law under the "equal protection" power of the 14th amendment.

However, the Supreme Court in later cases has signaled that there may be limits to how far the so-called "federalism revolution" would proceed. In 2003 Justice Sandra Day O'Conner (one of the 5 majority votes in the previous federalism cases), joined the other 4 justices in voting to allow certain lawsuits against states. The Court held in *Nevada Dept. of Human Resources v. Hibbs,* 538 U. S. 721, that the federal Family and Medical Leave Act did apply to and could be enforced against the states, as a valid means of fighting the well-documented history of employment discrimination.

And in 2004, the Supreme Court decided, in *Tennessee v. Lane,* that states could be sued under Title II of the ADA, for failing to provide reasonable access to the courts. This case also could have wider implications since the part of the law at issue bars discrimination in state government services, programs and activities. The lawsuit was brought by two paraplegics in wheelchairs, one of whom had to crawl up two flights of stairs to get to the courtroom for his first appearance on a misdemeanor charge.

In the Language of the Court

TENNESSEE V. LANE

124 S. Ct. 1978 (2004)

Justice Stevens delivered the opinion of the Court.

FACTS

Title II of the Americans with Disabilities Act of 1990 (ADA or Act), 104 Stat. 337, 42 U. S. C. §12131–12165, provides that "no qualified individual with a disability shall, by reason of such disability, be excluded from participation in or be denied the benefits of the services, programs or activities of a public entity, or be subjected to discrimination by any such entity." §12132. The question presented in this case is whether Title II exceeds Congress' power under §5 of the Fourteenth Amendment.

In August 1998, respondents George Lane and Beverly Jones filed this action against the State of Tennessee and a number of Tennessee counties, alleging past and ongoing violations of Title II. Respondents, both of whom are paraplegics who use wheelchairs for mobility, claimed that they were denied access to, and the services of, the state court system by reason of their disabilities. Lane alleged that he was compelled to appear to answer a set of criminal charges on the second floor of a county courthouse that had no elevator. At his first appearance, Lane crawled up two flights of stairs to get to the courtroom. When Lane returned to the courthouse for a hearing, he refused to crawl again or to be carried by officers to the courtroom; he consequently was arrested and jailed for failure to appear. Jones, a certified court reporter, alleged that she has not been able to gain access to a number of county courthouses, and, as a result, has lost both work and an opportunity to participate in the judicial process. Respondents sought damages and equitable relief.

The State moved to dismiss the suit on the ground that it was barred by the Eleventh Amendment. The District Court denied the motion without opinion, and the State appealed. The Court of Appeals entered an order affirming the District Court's denial of the State's motion to dismiss in this case. The order explained that respondents' claims were not barred because they were based on due process principles, not on equal protection grounds, as in *Garrett*. The Sixth Circuit later filed an amended opinion explaining that the Due Process Clause protects the right of access to the courts, and that the evidence before Congress when it enacted Title II "established that physical barriers in government buildings, including courthouses and in the courtrooms themselves, have had the effect of denying disabled people the opportunity to access vital services and to exercise fundamental rights guaranteed by the Due Process Clause."

DECISION

In *Garrett,* we concluded that the Eleventh Amendment bars private suits related to employment, seeking money damages for state violations of Title I of the ADA. We left open, however, the question whether the Eleventh Amendment permits suits for money damages under Title II

The ADA was passed by large majorities in both Houses of Congress after decades of deliberation and investigation into the need for comprehensive legislation to address discrimination against persons with disabilities. In the years immediately preceding the ADA's enactment, Congress held 13 hearings and created a special task force that gathered evidence from every State in the Union. The conclusions Congress drew from this evidence are set forth in the task force and Committee Reports, described in lengthy legislative hearings, and summarized in the preamble to the statute. Central among these conclusions was Congress' finding that

"individuals with disabilities are a discrete and insular minority who have been faced with restrictions and limitations, subjected to a history of purposeful unequal treatment, and relegated to a position of political powerlessness in our society, based on characteristics that are beyond the control of such individuals and resulting from stereotypic assumptions not truly indicative of the individual ability of such individuals to participate in, and contribute to, society." 42 U. S. C. §12101(a)(7).

Invoking "the sweep of congressional authority, including the power to enforce the fourteenth amendment and to regulate commerce," the ADA is designed "to provide a clear and comprehensive national mandate for the elimination of discrimination against individuals with disabilities." It forbids discrimination against persons with disabilities in three major areas of public life: employment, which is covered by Title I of the statute; public services, programs, and activities, which are the subject of Title II; and public accommodations, which are covered by Title III.

Title II prohibits any public entity from discriminating against "qualified" persons with disabilities in the provision or operation of public services, programs, or activities.

The Eleventh Amendment renders the States immune from "any suit in law or equity, commenced or prosecuted . . . by Citizens of another State, or by Citizens or Subjects of any Foreign State." Even though the Amendment "by its terms . . . applies only to suits against a State by citizens of another State," our cases have repeatedly held that this immunity also applies to unconsented suits brought by a State's own citizens. *Garrett,* 531 U. S., at 363; *Kimel v. Florida Bd. of Regents,* 528 U. S. 62, 72-73 (2000).

Our cases have also held that Congress may abrogate the State's Eleventh Amendment immunity. To determine whether it has done so in any given case, we "must resolve two predicate questions: first, whether Congress unequivocally expressed its intent to abrogate that immunity; and second, if it did, whether

Congress acted pursuant to a valid grant of constitutional authority The first question is easily answered here, since the ADA specifically provides for abrogation.

Regarding the second question, Congress can abrogate state sovereign immunity pursuant to a valid exercise of its power under §5 of the Fourteenth Amendment. That power is not, however, unlimited. In *City of Boerne v. Flores,* 521 U. S. 507, the Court set forth the test for distinguishing between permissible remedial legislation and unconstitutional substantive redefinition: Section 5 legislation is valid if it exhibits "a congruence and proportionality" between an injury and the means adopted to prevent or remedy it

The first step requires identification of the constitutional rights Congress sought to enforce when it enacted Title II. Like Title I, Title II seeks to enforce the Fourteenth Amendment's prohibition on irrational disability discrimination. But it also seeks to enforce a variety of other basic constitutional guarantees, including some, like the right of access to the courts here at issue, infringements of which are subject to heightened judicial scrutiny . . . Congress enacted Title II against a backdrop of pervasive unequal treatment of persons with disabilities in the administration of state services and programs, including systematic deprivations of fundamental rights.

The historical experience that Title II reflects is also documented in the decisions of this and other courts, which have identified unconstitutional treatment of disabled persons by state agencies in a variety of public programs and services . . . A Civil Rights Commission report before Congress showed that some 76% of public services and programs housed in state-owned buildings were inaccessible to and unusable by such persons.

The conclusion that Congress drew from this body of evidence is set forth in the text of the ADA itself: "[D]iscrimination against individuals with disabilities persists in such critical areas as . . . education, transportation, communication, recreation, institutionalization, health services, voting, and *access to public services.*" (emphasis added). This finding, together with the extensive record of disability discrimination that underlies it, makes clear beyond peradventure that inadequate provision of public services and access to public facilities was an appropriate subject for prophylactic legislation.

Title II is an appropriate response to this history and pattern of unequal treatment. Unquestionably, it is valid §5 legislation as it applies to the class of cases implicating the accessibility of judicial services. Congress' chosen remedy for the pattern of exclusion and discrimination at issue, Title II's requirement of program accessibility, is congruent and proportional to its object of enforcing the right of access to the courts. The unequal treatment of disabled persons in the administration of judicial services has a long history, and has persisted despite several legislative efforts to remedy the problem of disability discrimination. Faced with considerable evidence of the shortcomings of previous legislative responses, Congress was justified in concluding that this 'difficult and intractable problem' warranted "added prophylactic measures in response."

The remedy Congress chose is nevertheless a limited one. Title II does not require States to employ any and all means to make judicial services accessible to persons with disabilities, and it does not require States to compromise their essential eligibility criteria for public programs. It requires only "reasonable modifications" that would not fundamentally alter the nature of the service provided, and only when the individual seeking modification is otherwise eligible for the service.

In the case of facilities built or altered after 1992, the regulations require compliance with specific architectural accessibility standards. But in the case of older facilities, for which structural change is likely to be more difficult, a public entity may comply with Title II by adopting a variety of less costly measures, including relocating services to alternative, accessible sites and assigning

aides to assist persons with disabilities in accessing services.

This duty to accommodate is perfectly consistent with the well-established due process principle that, "within the limits of practicability, a State must afford to all individuals a meaningful opportunity to be heard" in its courts. Our cases have recognized a number of affirmative obligations that flow from this principle: the duty to waive filing fees in certain family-law and criminal cases, the duty to provide transcripts to criminal defendants seeking review of their convictions, and the duty to provide counsel to certain criminal defendants

Judged against this backdrop, Title II's affirmative obligation to accommodate persons with disabilities in the administration of justice cannot be said to be "so out of proportion to a supposed remedial or preventive object that it cannot be understood as responsive to, or designed to prevent, unconstitutional behavior." *Boerne,* 521 U. S., at 532; *Kimel,* 528 U. S., at 86. It is, rather, a reasonable prophylactic measure, reasonably targeted to a legitimate end.

For these reasons, we conclude that Title II, as it applies to the class of cases implicating the fundamental right of access to the courts, constitutes a valid exercise of Congress' §5 authority to enforce the guarantees of the Fourteenth Amendment. The judgment of the Court of Appeals is therefore affirmed.

CASE QUESTIONS

1. What was the precise legal issue in this case?
2. How is Title II of the ADA different from Title I?
3. How did the Supreme Court distinguish this case from the Garrett case and others where the 11th Amendment barred suits against the states?
4. What standard must be met, according to the Court, in order for Congress to pass a law that "abrogates" state immunity from suit?

SEPARATION OF POWERS

separation of powers: The division of federal power into three separate branches of the government.

Not only did the Constitution set forth the general roles of the federal and state governments, but it also divided the powers of the federal government into three separate branches. Due in part to the fear of excessive federal government power, the Framers created the (1) legislative branch, (2) the executive branch, and (3) the judicial branch of the federal government and gave each one different responsibilities. Through a system of *checks and balances*, each branch was given certain ways of preventing the other branches from assuming excessive power.

Article I of the Constitution grants *"all legislative powers"* to Congress, which "shall consist of a Senate and House of Representatives." Article I goes on to prescribe the necessary qualifications for Senator and Representative, the term of office, manner of election, duties of each body, powers of Congress, and various activities Congress and the states are prohibited from doing.

Article II vests the *"executive power"* in the President of the United States and sets forth the procedures for election of the president and vice-president. The president is directed to "take care that the Laws be faithfully executed" and is given the power to be "Commander in Chief of the Army and Navy," to make treaties, appoint ambassadors, judges of the Supreme Court, and other "officers of the United States," convene both houses of Congress, and shall give Congress "Information on the State of the Union" from time to time.

Article III grants the *judicial power* of the United States to "one Supreme Court, and such inferior courts as the Congress may from time to time ordain and establish." This article provides that judges shall have life terms "during good behavior" and establishes the jurisdiction of the federal courts. For example, one sentence in Article III states that "the judicial power shall extend to all Cases, in law and Equity, arising under this Constitution, the Laws of the United States, and Treaties made . . . under their authority. . . ." *Federal question jurisdiction*, as was discussed in Chapter 2, is based on this phrase in the Constitution. Article III also provides for juries in the "trial of all crimes," with the trial to take place in the state where the alleged crime has been committed.

For much of the past 223 years there has been tension among the three branches of government about the scope of the powers granted to each. Often, the president and executive branch officials complain that Congress is intruding on the power to control the armed forces or conduct international affairs. Likewise, many have argued that court decisions made by the judicial branch often do not merely interpret the laws passed by Congress, but change, alter, or add to them. Finally, senators and representatives have often criticized the extent of powers assumed by popular presidents and the growth in the number of agencies and personnel in the executive branch. This tension and tugging among the various branches is probably exactly what the framers hoped would happen when they created the branches and the "checks and balances" between them.

JUDICIAL REVIEW

Although the Constitution divides the federal powers into three parts, it does not specifically state what is to happen if one branch encroaches upon the responsibilities assigned to another or assumes powers not given to it by the Constitution. For example, suppose Congress passes a law that is signed by the President but that conflicts with a provision of the Constitution.

It did not take long after ratification of the Constitution for such an event to occur, and the resulting Supreme Court decision in *Marbury v. Madison* in 1803 is one of the most important legal decisions in United States history. Justice John Marshall's opinion in that case established the principle of **judicial review,** by which the judicial branch has the power to decide if actions of the legislative branch conform to the Constitution. The Court dealt with the question of what should happen if a law passed by Congress did not comply with the Constitution. Justice Marshall's rationale for the decision is one of the classic judicial opinions in American law, and has been followed for over 200 years. Justice Marshall's decision will be reported using the language of the court.

judicial review: The power of the judicial branch to review the actions of the executive and legislative branches to determine if their actions are Constitutional.

MARBURY V. MADISON

5 U.S. 137 (1803)

FACTS

In 1800 John Adams was defeated for reelection as President of the United States by Thomas Jefferson. Adams was a Federalist, and a supporter of a strong federal government, while Jefferson was an anti-Federalist who preferred more local and state government power. Shortly before leaving office, Adams appointed John Marshall, then his Secretary of State, as Chief Justice of the Supreme Court, and he was quickly confirmed. Congress also passed a law creating a number of new judgeships for the District of Columbia, and Adams quickly appointed 42 persons as judges, who were confirmed by the Senate (on Adams' last day in office).

However, four of the official commissions (papers appointing the Judges) were not delivered by the next day when Mr. Jefferson took office, and he stopped them from being delivered. One of the prospective judges, William Marbury, filed suit in the Supreme Court against James Madison, the new Secretary of State, seeking to force delivery of his commission.

Congress had passed a law, called the Judiciary Act of 1789, which authorized the Supreme Court to issue writs of *mandamus* (a court order directing an individual to do something) to government officials "in cases warranted by the principles and usages of law." This federal law added a new power to the duties of the Supreme Court, which primarily functions to hear appeals from lower court decisions. Marbury argued that this law gave the Supreme Court the power to order Madison to deliver his commission.

DECISION [IN THE LANGUAGE OF THE COURT]

Opinion of Chief Justice John Marshall:
When an instrument organizing fundamentally a judicial system, divides it into one supreme, and so many inferior courts as the legislature may ordain and establish, then enumerates its powers and proceeds so far to distribute them, as to define the jurisdiction of the supreme court by declaring the cases in which it shall take original jurisdiction, and that in others it shall take appellate jurisdiction; the plain import of the words seems to be, that in one class of cases its jurisdiction is original, and not appellate; in the other it is appellate, and not original . . . The authority, therefore, given to the supreme court, by the act establishing the judicial courts of the United States, to issue writs of mandamus to public officers, appears not to be warranted by the Constitution, and it becomes necessary to enquire whether a jurisdiction, so conferred, can be exercised.

The question, whether an act, repugnant to the Constitution, can become the law of the land, is a question deeply interesting to the United States; but happily, not of an intricacy proportioned to its interest. It seems only necessary to recognize certain principles, supposed to have been long and well established, to decide it.

That the people have an original right to establish, for their future government, such principles, as in their opinion, shall most conduce to their own happiness is the basis on which the whole American fabric has been erected. . . . The principles, therefore, so established, are deemed fundamental . . . and as the authority from which they proceed is supreme, they are designed to be permanent.

"This original and supreme will [the Constitution] organizes the government and assigns to different departments their respective powers . . . [with] certain limits not to be transcended by those departments. . . . The powers of the legislature are defined, and limited; and that those limits may not be mistaken, or forgotten, the constitution is written. To what purpose are powers limited, and to what purpose is that limitation committed to writing, if these limits may, at any time, be passed by those intended to be restrained? The distinction, between a government with limited and unlimited powers, is abolished, if those limits do not confine the persons on whom they are imposed, and if acts prohibited and acts allowed, are of equal obligation. It is a proposition too plain to be contested, that the Constitution controls any legislative act repugnant to it."

Between these alternatives there is no middle ground. The constitution is either a superior, paramount law, unchangeable by ordinary means, or it is on a level with ordinary legislative acts, and like other acts, is alterable when the legislature shall please to alter it. If the former be true, then a legislative act contrary to the constitution is not law; if the latter part be true, then written constitutions are absurd attempts, on the part of the people, to limit a power in its own nature illimitable.

Certainly all those who have framed written constitutions contemplate them as forming the fundamental and paramount law of the nations, and consequently the theory of every such government must be, that an act of the legislature, repugnant to the constitution, is void . . . If an act of the legislature, repugnant to the constitution, is void, does it, notwithstanding its invalidity, bind the courts, and oblige them to give it effect? Or in other words, though it be not law, does it constitute a rule as operative as if it was a law? This would be to overthrow in fact what was established in theory; and would seem, at first view, an absurdity too gross to be insisted on . . .

It is emphatically the province and duty of the judicial department to say what the law is. Those who apply the rule to particular cases must of necessity expound and interpret that rule. If two laws conflict with each other, the courts must decide on the operation of each.

So if a law be in opposition to the Constitution, if both the law and the Constitution apply to a particular case . . . the court must determine which of these conflicting rules governs the case. This is the very essence of judicial duty. If, then, the courts are to regard the Constitution; and the Constitution is superior to any ordinary act of the legislature, the Constitution, and not such ordinary act, must govern the case to which they both apply.

Must the courts close their eyes on the Constitution and see only the law? This doctrine would subvert the very foundation of all written constitutions. It would declare that an act which, according to the principles and theory of our government, is entirely void, is yet, in practice, completely obligatory. It would declare that if the legislature shall do what is expressly forbidden, such act, notwithstanding the express prohibition, is in reality effectual. . . . It is prescribing limits, and declaring that those limits may be passed at pleasure.

The Constitution states that [t]he judicial power is extended to all cases arising under the Constitution. Could it be the intention of those who gave this power, to say that in using it the Constitution should not be looked into?

That a case arising under the Constitution should be decided without examining the instrument under which it arises? This is too extravagant to be maintained.In some cases, then, the Constitution must be looked into by the judges. And if they can open it at all, what part of it are they forbidden to read or obey? There are many other parts of the constitution which serve to illustrate this subject.

It is declared that 'no tax or duty shall be laid on articles exported from any state.' Suppose a duty is imposed on the export of cotton, of tobacco, or of flour; and a suit instituted to recover it. Ought judgment to be rendered in such a case? Ought the judges to close their eyes on the Constitution, and only see the law?

The Constitution declares that no bill of attainder or ex post facto law shall be passed. If however, such a bill should be passed, and a person should be prosecuted under it; must the court condemn to death those victims whom the Constitution endeavors to protect?

From these, and many other selections which might be made, it is apparent that the Framers of the Constitution contemplated that instrument as a rule for the government of courts, as well as of the legislature. Why otherwise does it direct the judges to take an oath to support it? This oath certainly applies, in an especial manner, to their conduct in their official character. How immoral to impose it on them, if they were to be used as the instruments, and the knowing instruments, for violating what they swear to support?

It is not entirely unworthy of observation, that in declaring what shall be the *supreme* law of the land, the *Constitution* itself is first mentioned; and not the laws of the United States generally, but those only which shall be made in *pursuance* of the Constitution, have that rank. Thus, the particular phraseology of the Constitution of the United States confirms and strengthens the principle, supposed to be essential to all written constitutions, that a law repugnant to the constitution is void; and that courts, as well as other departments, are bound by that instrument.

CASE QUESTIONS

1. Did Mr. Marbury win or lose the case? Will he be installed as a judge?
2. Justice Marshall's ruling actually deprived the Supreme Court of a power that Congress had given it. What was that power? What was the basis of that power?
3. Although the *Marbury v. Madison* case technically took away one power given to the Supreme Court by Congress, what was the overall effect of the case upon the power of the judicial branch? Discuss the implications of this decision. Is it still important today?
4. How do you suppose former President Adams and Secretary of State Madison reacted to the *Marbury* decision made by their Federalist colleague Marshall? What do you imagine to be President Jefferson's response?
5. What was the foundation or basis of Marshall's opinion?

SOCIAL/ETHICAL ISSUES

Do you think it was appropriate for the Supreme Court to give itself the power to review the actions of the other branches of government? As a question of public policy, what would have happened if the Supreme Court did not have this power? What if each branch of the government had the power to decide if its actions were legal and constitutional?

Subsequent cases during the past 200 years have extended the rationale of the *Marbury* case and have established the principle that the judicial system may review not only acts of Congress but also actions of the other branches of government and even state laws to determine if they are in compliance with the Constitution.

THE POWER TO REGULATE BUSINESS ACTIVITIES

THE COMMERCE CLAUSE

Commerce Clause: The power given to Congress "to regulate commerce with foreign nations and among the several states." It has been interpreted to allow Congress to enact laws in any area that "affects interstate commerce."

Earlier in this chapter we discussed the "necessary and proper" clause, which allows Congress to pass laws necessary to carry out a power specifically given to the federal government ("enumerated powers"). Probably the greatest use of this principle has occurred in connection with Congress's power to "regulate commerce with foreign nations, and among the several states," found in Article I, section 8, of the Constitution. Through the **Commerce Clause**, Congress has enacted laws dealing with almost every facet of business enterprise in the United States. In fact, the legal authority for most of the federal laws and regulations discussed in the this textbook, dealing with subjects such as environmental law, securities law, labor–management relations, worker safety, employment discrimination, and consumer law was the federal government's power to regulate "commerce among the several states."

It was not always so. One of the earliest important cases to discuss the Commerce Clause was *Gibbons v. Ogden,* decided by the Supreme Court in 1824. The state of New York wanted to establish a monopoly license system for steamboats on its waters. Justice Marshall wrote the decision striking down the state law because navigation and commerce were interrelated, which meant that the federal government should regulate the matter (and, in fact, a related federal law existed). Marshall stated that the commerce power cannot be used to govern activities that are *wholly intrastate* (within one state), but Congress can regulate those intrastate matters that "affect the states generally" (that is, if they affect matters both within one state and outside that state).

During most of the 1800s, business activity proceeded without much federal regulation. However, by the turn of the next century, the industrial revolution had brought tremendous changes to American business, transportation, and communication. The increase in mass production, the expansion of the power and scope of industrial firms, and the emergence of labor organizations created new challenges and problems on a national level. Congress responded by passing new laws, dealing with labor, management, working conditions, and the economy.

From 1900 through the 1930s however, the Supreme Court struck down several such laws as being beyond the powers of Congress because they regulated activity that was not actually "in" interstate commerce. For example, a law regulating the hours and conditions of child labor was held unconstitutional as beyond the power of Congress.

But the stock market crash of 1929, the Depression of the 1930s and the election of President Franklin Roosevelt led to major social changes.

Roosevelt's "New Deal" called for greater federal government involvement in solving the country's problems, and the American public generally supported this approach.

By 1937 the mood of the country, the apparent need for more federal government action to solve society's problems, and Roosevelt's proposal to enlarge the Supreme Court (called the "Court-packing plan"), caused the Supreme Court to modify its views and to hold that *any activity that* **"affected"** *interstate commerce* was within the power of Congress to regulate. In 1937 the Supreme Court upheld the federal National Labor Relations Act, which provided substantial rights to employees to form unions and engage in collective bargaining, and in 1941 the Court upheld a federal law prohibiting manufacturers from shipping goods in interstate commerce unless they complied with federal minimum wage standards.

Since that time, the Supreme Court has almost always upheld the power of Congress to enact laws regulating business, if the activity being regulated somehow "affects" interstate commerce. In the American economy of today, where raw materials, workers, products, costs, and markets are all affected by developments in other states (and around the world), little business activity is so local in character that the federal government cannot regulate it if it chooses to do so.

However, in 1995, for the first time in 60 years, the U.S. Supreme Court declared a federal law unconstitutional on the grounds that the law exceeded the power of Congress under the Interstate Commerce Clause. In *U.S. v. Lopez,* 514 U.S. 549, 115 S. Ct. 1624 (1995), the court faced a challenge to the Gun-Free School Zones Act passed by Congress in 1990, which prohibited possession of a gun within 1,000 feet of a school.

Writing for a 5-4 majority, Chief Justice Rehnquist stated that the law was a "criminal statute that by its terms has nothing to do with commerce, or any sort of economic enterprise" and was thus beyond power of Congress to enact. Thus, even though the Commerce Clause has been given an expansive interpretation in modern times, the regulated activity must "substantially affect" interstate commerce in order for the federal law to be constitutional. The majority opinion noted that our dual system government (federal and state) requires that federal law not embrace effects upon interstate commerce so "indirect and remote" that it obliterates the distinction between what is local and what is national.

Writing for the four dissenters, Justice Breyer argued that Congress had a valid rational basis for concluding that the possession of firearms at or near schools was, in fact, having an effect on interstate commerce, and the sale and use of such guns in schools was a national problem. Furthermore, he stated that previous Supreme Court precedents had approved federal regulations with much less significant impact on interstate commerce.

Supporters of the *Lopez* decision hailed the end of the "dominance of the federal government" over the states. Other commentators pointed to language in the majority opinion that hinted that the court was close to allowing states to return to the powerful role they played under the Articles of the Confederation, before the Constitution established a strong federal government. Indeed, in 2000, in the case *United States v. Morrison,* 529 U.S. 598, 120 S. Ct. 1740 (2000) the Supreme

Court struck down the federal Violence Against Women Act, which established a federal civil cause of action for victims of gender-motivated violence. Citing *Lopez,* the Court found that "gender-motivated crimes of violence are not, in any sense of the phrase, economic activity . . . and thus far in our Nation's history our cases have upheld Commerce Clause regulation of intrastate activity only where that activity is economic in nature." The Court noted that the noneconomic, criminal nature of the conduct at issue was central to the decision in the *Lopez* case, and the *Morrison* case involved a similar situation.

In 2010–2011 many commentators have criticized the broad interpretation of the commerce clause as a leading cause of the expansion of federal power. However, in most instances since 1995, legislation enacted by Congress has been upheld against the challenge that such legislation was beyond its Commerce Clause powers. Significantly, no economic or business-related laws have been held unconstitutional. Even a federal criminal statute, the Racketeer Influenced and Corrupt Organization (RICO) Act was upheld, the Court finding that harm by such criminal activity had sufficient affects upon interstate commerce to allow for federal regulation. In addition, the warnings given in *Lopez* and *Morrison* have caused Congress to articulate much more clearly the purpose of its legislation and the effects on commerce when it enacts new legislation, pursuant to its Commerce Clause powers.

THE POLICE POWER

The states also have the right to enact laws and regulations concerning business, as long as such regulations are not in conflict with and preempted by federal law, as discussed earlier. States have inherent power to make laws to promote and protect the health, safety, and welfare of their citizens under the so-called **police power.** The states use this power extensively to enact laws and regulations dealing with a wide range of activities, such as schools, transportation, business regulation and licensing, health and welfare, labor and employment, fish and game, land use and community development, and many more issues. Each year every state legislature passes hundreds of laws, and all businesses are affected by the rules of many state regulatory agencies.

police power: The right of states to enact a wide range of laws to protect the health, safety, and welfare of their citizens.

However, as we have discussed, the Commerce clause of the U.S. Constitution gives the federal government the primary role in regulating Interstate commerce. Under the so-called *Dormant Commerce clause,* a state may validly enact a law which affects business and commerce as long as the state law *does not unduly burden or discriminate* against interstate commerce. However, when the state law imposes particular burdens on interstate commerce—even though it does not directly conflict with a federal law—the law may be held invalid, because it interferes with Congress' power and authority to regulate interstate commerce. For example, one state passed a law requiring trucks traveling through that state to have a different and more expensive type of mud flap ("contour" flaps) than those required by almost all other states ("straight" flaps). The Supreme Court held that this law "unduly burdened" interstate commerce.

A leading case dealing with "discrimination against" interstate commerce arose when Madison, Wisconsin, enacted an ordinance requiring that all milk sold in the city be processed and bottled within five miles from the center of Madison. The purpose of the law was said to be so that the milk could be inspected locally during processing to ensure the health and safety of residents. However, the court said the law was directly discriminatory against out-of-state businesses (much of the milk sold in Madison at that time came from Illinois) and there were many other ways to guarantee that the milk sold in Madison was safe and healthful without prohibiting out-of-state milk.

However, in the absence of evidence that the state or local regulation "discriminates against" or "unduly burdens" interstate commerce, the states still do possess the power to enact laws dealing with business, health, safety, education, transportation, communication, and other important topics. And the states do exercise the power fully.

THE TAXING AND SPENDING POWERS

Among the enumerated powers of Congress is the "power to lay and collect taxes," as well as the power "to pay the debts and provide for the common defense and general welfare of the United States" (Article I, Section 8). Clearly, the intent of the framers was to allow the federal government to use taxes to raise revenue. However, the government can use taxation to achieve social or regulatory purposes as well. Some Supreme Court cases in the early 1900s invalidated taxes, which were considered "penalties," the intent of which was to regulate business rather than to raise revenue. However, no case in the past 80 years has followed this pattern, and like the commerce power, the reach of the federal government under the taxing power is considered quite extensive today.

The spending power has not been the subject of many Supreme Court decisions, although it is controversial. Often Congress will make money available to the states and other recipients providing that certain conditions are met. For example, a few years ago, the federal government made substantial highway construction funds available to states on condition that each recipient enact a 55-mph speed limit. All states did pass such laws, but in later years the political mood changed as "states' rights" arguments became more important, and the "mandatory 55-mph limit" was removed.

In one recent case, *Sabri v. United States,* the Supreme Court addressed whether Congress had overstepped its boundaries when it made criminal certain acts of bribery by local government officials who were administering part-local and part-federal funds. Congress had cited the Spending Clause in enacting the law. Even though the specific federal program involved could not be identified for each dollar spent, the Court upheld the law, finding that the Spending power includes the power to police the integrity of the local officials' actions in using federal funds. Justice Souter wrote the Court's opinion, which stated "Congress has authority under the Spending Clause to appropriate federal monies to promote the general welfare, Art. I, §8, cl. 1, and it has corresponding authority under the Necessary and Proper Clause, Art. I, §8, cl. 18, to see to it that taxpayer dollars appropriated under that power are in fact spent for the general welfare, and not frittered away in graft or on projects undermined when funds are siphoned off or corrupt public officers are derelict about demanding value for dollars."

THE CONTRACT CLAUSE

The Constitution states that "[N]o state shall . . . pass any law impairing the obligation of contracts" (Article I, Section 10). The reason this clause was written into the Constitution was to prevent state legislators from passing laws that release debtors from their financial obligations to creditors. Some states had enacted such legislation prior to the Constitution, and the framers (most of whom were successful businessmen and farmers) wanted to avoid any repetition. While the "contract clause" succeeded in resolving this problem, the issue arose in later years as to how far this constitutional clause should be extended.

Obviously, almost every law adopted by a state has some effect on existing business relationships and contracts. It can be argued that a law (for example, a law requiring cars to have air bags) "impairs" the existing contracts between General Motors and Hertz Car Rental Company. However, in general, courts have taken a restrictive view of the contract clause, finding that if the state has a legitimate reason for the law or regulation, and the law is reasonably related to the purpose, it is not an "impairment" of private contracts just because some new duties may be required.

EMINENT DOMAIN

eminent domain: The power of government to take title to private property for a "public use," upon payment of just (fair) compensation.

Can the government take your property away from you, against your wishes? Surprisingly, the answer is clearly "yes." The power of **eminent domain,** which permits the government to take private property "for public use" in order to build or create something of benefit to the public—after payment of fair compensation to the owner, is centuries old. The U.S. Constitution recognizes this principle in the last clause of the Fifth Amendment, which states, *"Nor shall private property be taken for public use, without just compensation."*

There are thus two essential elements in a lawful eminent domain proceeding: (1) the taking of the property by the government must be for a "public use," and (2) payment of just (fair) compensation must be made to the owner. There have been many cases over the years in which individuals challenged the government's right to acquire their property because it was not for a "public use." When the government wants property for a road, school, or city park, there is little question of the public use. But in the past 35 years or so, local and state governments have used the eminent domain power to acquire private property in order to build low-income housing, to sell parcels to businesses as a "research park," to build a stadium, or to undertake other types of urban redevelopment. As a result, tougher questions have arisen regarding whether the project really is a "public use" or whether it simply is a compelled transfer of property from one private owner to another.

However, the courts have upheld governmental use of the eminent domain power in most instances, opting to defer to the state legislatures in the determination of what is a public use. Courts have often used the phrase "public purpose" interchangeably with "public use" and ruled that if the legislature has decided that the project serves a "public purpose," then the court should not interfere. The following case carried this theory to its outer limits.

KELO V. CITY OF NEW LONDON

545 U.S. 469, 125 S.Ct.2655 (2005)

FACTS

The City of New London, Connecticut has been in economic decline for many years. In 1998 the City's unemployment rate was nearly double that of the state, and its population was at its lowest level since 1920. In 2000, the City approved a development plan that was "projected to create in excess of 1,000 new jobs, to increase tax and other revenues and to revitalize an economically distressed city, including its downtown and waterfront areas."

The City and a private nonprofit agency called the New London Development Corporation created a plan to revitalize the Fort Trumball area, former home of the Naval Undersea Warfare Center, which closed in 1996. The State authorized a bond issue to support these efforts and also create Fort Trumball State Park. The large pharmaceutical company Pfizer Inc. announced that it would build a $300 million research facility on a site adjacent to Fort Trumball. Local planners hoped that Pfizer would draw new business to the area, thus serving as a catalyst for the area's rejuvenation. The plan called for the creation of development plan for the Fort Trumball peninsula, that juts into the Thames River. The area comprises approximately 115 privately owned properties and some public land. The plan calls for development of a waterfront conference hotel at the center of a "small urban village" with will have recreational and commercial uses, construction of 80 new residences, a new U.S. Coast Guard Museum, 90,000 square feet of research and development office space, a riverwalk, renovated marina, and land for office and retail space, parking and other commercial uses.

The city council approved the plan in January 2000 and designated the NLDC as the development agent in charge of implementation. The city authorized NLDC to purchase property or to acquire property by eminent domain. The NLDC did negotiate the purchase of most of the private properties needed in the 90 acre area, but failed to reach agreement with Susette Kelo and certain other landowners. Ms. Kelo has lived in the Fort Trumball area since 1997, and has made extensive improvements to her home, which she prizes for its water view. Another of the homeowners is Wilhelmina Dery, who was born in her Fort Trumball home in 1918 and has lived there all her life. There are seven other owners who are part of this lawsuit which contends that the taking of their properties would violate the "public use" restriction of the Fifth Amendment.

After a 7-day trial the lower court granted a permanent restraining order prohibiting the taking of the properties in some parts of the development. On appeal, the Connecticut Supreme Court held that all of the City's proposed takings were valid under the relevant state statute and the Federal and State Constitutions. The Court found that a legislative determination that the taking of the land as part of an economic development project was a "public use" and in the "public interest." The case was then appealed to the U.S. Supreme Court.

DECISION

In an opinion by Justice Stevens, the Supreme Court traced the history of court interpretation of the Eminent Domain clause of the Fifth Amendment. While it is perfectly clear, said

Justice Stevens, that "the sovereign may not take the property of A for the sole purpose of transferring it to another private party B . . . it is equally clear that a State may transfer property from one private party to another if future "use by the public" is the purpose of the taking." Although a future use which is available to all comers would clearly qualify as a public use, such has not been required.

While many courts in the mid-19th century endorsed actual "use by the public" as the proper test, that narrow view has steadily eroded over time. Beginning at the close of the 19th century, this Court embraced the broader and more natural interpretation of public use as "public purpose." In *Berman v. Parker* 348 U.S. 26 (1954) the Supreme Court upheld a redevelopment plan for a blighted area of Washington, DC. The plan called for a wide area of land to be condemned. Part of the land would be used for construction of new streets, schools and other public facilities, and the remainder would be leased or sold to private parties for the purpose of redevelopment, including the construction of low-income housing.

In the Berman case, the owner of a department store located in the area challenged the use of eminent domain to take his property, arguing that the creation of a "better balanced, more attractive community" was not a valid public use. However, the Supreme Court, in a unanimous opinion, upheld the condemnation, deferring to the legislative and agency judgment as to what was best for the community. The Court wrote that "the concept of the public welfare is broad and inclusive . . . it is within the power of the legislature to determine that the community should be beautiful as well as healthy, spacious as well as clean." The Court deferred to the determinations of local authorities as what was a public use or public benefit. "Congress and its authorized agencies have made determinations that take into account a wide variety of values. It is not for us to reappraise them."

The Court stated that the City had made a determination that the area was sufficiently distressed to justify a program of economic rejuvenation, and that decision "is entitled to our deference." The City has carefully formulated an economic development plan that it believes will provide appreciable benefits to the community—including such things as new jobs and increased tax revenue. To effectuate the plan the City has invoked a state statute that specifically authorizes the use of eminent domain to promote economic development. Because that plan unquestionably serves a public purpose, the takings challenged here satisfy the public use requirement of the Fifth Amendment.

Justice Stevens and the majority of the court rejected the suggestion of the landowners that economic development should not qualify as a public use. "Neither precedent nor logic supports petitioner's proposal." The Court stated that promoting economic development is a traditional and long-accepted function of government. In previous cases over many years, the Court has upheld takings that facilitated agriculture and mining, that turned a blighted area into a "well-balanced community," and helped break up a land oligopoly that interfered with the normal functioning of a State's housing market. "Clearly there is no basis for exempting economic development from our traditionally broad understanding of public purpose."

The Court also rejected the argument that using eminent domain here was improper because some private parties will benefit from the "takings." It said that any number of cases illustrate that the achievement of a public good often coincides with the immediate benefitting of private parties. Further, the Court did not agree that its ruling would lead to a situation where nothing would stop a city from transferring citizen A's property to citizen B for the sole reason that citizen B will put the property to a more productive use and thus pay more taxes. This was not the case here, and "such an unusual exercise of government power would certainly raise a suspicion that a private purpose was afoot," citing certain cases where the courts had disallowed the use of eminent domain.

Finally the Court noted that "we do not minimize the hardship that condemnations may entail, notwithstanding the payment of just compensation." And the Court emphasized that the states have the power to place further restrictions on the use of eminent domain and the takings power, and indeed many states have put in place restrictions on eminent domain and "public use" requirements that are stricter than the federal baseline.

The decision in this case was close—coming on a 5-4 majority. The Court's majority opinion was also signed by Justices Kennedy, Souter, Ginsburg, and Breyer. Justice Kennedy, although agreeing with the majority opinion, also filed a "concurring opinion," in which he wrote more about his views concerning eminent domain. Justice O'Conner filed a dissenting opinion, which was joined by Justices Rehnquist, Scalia and Thomas. And Justice Thomas filed his own dissenting opinion as well.

CONCURRING AND DISSENTING OPINIONS

Justice Kennedy emphasized that the Court's previous rulings had upheld a taking under the Public Use clause as long as it is "rationally related to a conceivable public purpose." He also said, however, that the rational basis test should not alter the fact that transfers intended to confer benefits on particular, favored private entities, and with only incidental or pretextual public benefits, are forbidden by the Public Use clause, and that he would not support the use of eminent domain in such situations. But in this case, Justice Kennedy noted, the trial court had carefully looked at whether the development was of primary benefit to the developer and private businesses, or to the city. "This taking occurred in the context of a comprehensive development plan meant to address a serious city-wide depression . . . the identities of most of the private beneficiaries were unknown at the time the city formulated its plans" . . . and the city complied with elaborate procedural requirements that allowed full review of the record and the city's purposes.

Justice O'Conner wrote a strongly-worded dissenting opinion that began with the statement "Today the Court abandons its long-held basic limitation of government power . . . To reason, as the Court does, that the incidental public benefits resulting from the subsequent ordinary use of private property render economic development takings "for public use" is to wash out any distinction

between private and public use of property—and thereby effectively to delete the words "for public use" from the Takings Clause of the Fifth Amendment." Justice O'Conner traces the line of cases cited by the majority in upholding the taking of private property under the eminent domain power. She asserts that although *Berman* and *Midkiff* did suggest that the courts should show considerable deference to the decisions of local government, in both of those cases, there was harm being caused to the public by the current conditions.

In *Berman,* the neighborhood at issue in Washington DC was severely blighted, with some 64% of the dwellings beyond repair. In *Midkiff,* we upheld a land condemnation scheme in Hawaii whereby title to real property was taken from lessors and transferred to lessees, to address the complete imbalance in ownership. At that time, the federal and state governments owned 49% of the State's land, and another 47% was owned by only 72 landowners. The state legislature had concluded that the land oligopoly was totally "skewing the State's residential market, inflating land prices and injuring the public tranquility and welfare." In both cases, the extraordinary, pre-condemnation use of the targeted property was inflicting affirmative harm on society, and the legislature had found that eliminating the existing property use was necessary to remedy the harm. That is not the case here—Susette Kelo's and Wilhelmina Dery's well-maintained homes are not the source of any social harm.

Justice O'Conner argued that under the Court's ruling "any property may now be taken for the benefit of another private party." She further stated that the beneficiaries are likely to be those citizens with disproportionate influence and power in the political process, including large corporations and development firms. "The specter of condemnation now hangs over all property. Nothing is to prevent the State from replacing any Motel 6 with a Ritz-Carlton, any home with a shopping center, or any farm with a factory." Justice O'Conner closed by saying "The Founders cannot have intended this perverse result."

CASE QUESTIONS

1. What is the standard to the use of the power of eminent domain, according to the majority opinion of the Supreme Court?
2. What is the "public benefit" which will result from the use of eminent domain in this case?
3. The Fifth Amendment talks about "taking for public use" upon payment of just compen-

sation. Should "economic development" be treated the same as a taking to build a public school or a public highway? Why or why not?
4. What is Justice O'Conner's main point of contention with the majority opinion? Do you agree with her argument that the *Berman* and *Midkiff* cases are different than *Kelo*?

"TAKING" BY INVERSE CONDEMNATION: PRIVATE PROPERTY RIGHTS

Another issue often raised is whether zoning or other government restrictions on the use of one's property can amount to a **"taking,"** requiring fair compensation from the government. In most cases, the courts have upheld the use of zoning and other types of land use restrictions under the police power of local governments, and no compensation has been required as long as the land can be used for some purposes. However, in the past 25 years, the Supreme Court has issued several decisions holding that in some cases, conditions placed upon the use of private property by governmental agencies can be so restrictive that the property has effectively been "taken" or condemned by the government, thus requiring payment of just compensation. When the private property has little value left, because of the government restrictions, courts have sometimes ordered compensation be paid to the owner. This theory is called **inverse condemnation** ("inverse" because it is the individual, not the government, who is claiming that the land has been effectively condemned).

inverse condemnation: When a significant portion of the value of one's private property is "taken" by government-imposed restrictions.

Once a court decides that the power of eminent domain has been properly used, the next issue is the "just compensation," which the owner will receive in order for the government to acquire title to the property. The governmental unit that wants the property (it may be federal, state, or local) assesses the value of the property and offers the landowner a certain sum of money for his or her property. If the owner does not think the offer represents fair market value, he or she is entitled to a due process hearing before an impartial tribunal to determine what compensation is "just." At the hearing, the owner can introduce evidence as to what his or her real estate experts or appraisers believe the property is worth. The judge or hearing officer will then make a determination as to the appropriate price.

FUNDAMENTAL RIGHTS AND PROTECTIONS

FREEDOM OF SPEECH

The First Amendment is probably the best known and perhaps the most important section of the Constitution. This 45-word sentence captures the essence of the rights and freedoms Americans hold dear and sets boundaries on the role of the government.

THE FIRST AMENDMENT

Congress shall make no law respecting an establishment of religion, or prohibiting the free exercise thereof; or abridging the freedom of speech, or of the press; or the right of the people peaceably to assemble, and to petition the government for a redress of grievances.

During the past 220 years the courts have been called upon to decide hundreds of cases in which a law, regulation, or some other governmental action may violate the First Amendment. Regarding freedom of speech, such recent controversies as laws prohibiting pornography accessible by children on the internet, flag burning, protests by anti-gay activists at military funerals, censorship of school newspapers, and limitations on cigarette and alcohol advertising have focused on interpretations of the First Amendment.

Although the amendment states that Congress may make "no law . . . abridging the freedom of speech," the courts have in fact allowed some restrictions on a person's total freedom to say anything he or she wants. Justice Oliver Wendell Holmes made a much-quoted statement in a 1919 decision that the First Amendment would not protect the right of a man to falsely shout "Fire!" in a crowded theater. The Supreme Court stated that reasonable "time, place, and manner" restrictions on speech were sometimes necessary in order to protect a compelling governmental interest. Other public safety concerns have led courts to uphold the necessity of parade permits and other types of licenses for some types of demonstrations. Protection of national security has resulted in cases refusing to allow the publication of Central Intelligence Agency (CIA) agents' names or defense intelligence secrets.

Copyright and patent laws have also been upheld as allowable legal restrictions upon certain types of speech by those who do not own the rights. In addition, laws prohibiting obscene acts and publications have sometimes been upheld, where there appears to be no artistic content and the matter in question clearly violates "community standards." However, in general, the First Amendment has been read as allowing almost all types of speech, even though the speech may be obnoxious, rude, even false. The "marketplace of ideas" theory holds that if all ideas are put forth, the public will be able to separate the worthy from the unworthy. Even some forms of actions that are done to make a statement about a political issue—such as flag burning—have been protected as "symbolic speech." One particularly controversial ruling by the U.S. Supreme Court in 2011 held that the 1st Amendment protected the right of anti-gay activists to protest the funerals of soldiers killed in the Iraq and Afghanistan wars. The court ruled 8-1 in an opinion written by Chief Justice John Roberts that freedom of speech includes even hurtful speech on public issues.

Those who have had false statements made about them may use the law of defamation (libel and slander) to recover damages from the perpetrators of the lies, but American courts are very reluctant to enter injunctions preventing the publication of the information ahead of time (**prior restraint**). Particularly with respect to social, political, and economic issues, the Constitution affords almost absolute protection for any of us to say what we want, free from government restrictions.

prior restraint: Court restrictions preventing a person from making a particular statement.

LAW IN CYBERSPACE

Concerned about pornography on the Internet and the ease with which children can access such material, Congress has enacted a number of laws. The first attempt was the Communications Decency Act (CDA) of 1996. This law [in Section 223(a)] made "knowing transmission of obscene or indecent" messages to any recipient under 18 years of age a federal crime. Another section of the law [Section 223(d)] prohibited the knowing, sending, or displaying to a person under 18 of any message "that, in context, depicts or describes, in terms patently offensive as measured by contemporary community standards, sexual or excretory activities or organs."

The law was immediately challenged as a violation of the Free Speech Clause of the First Amendment by a wide variety of groups, promoting freedom of speech. The case was titled *ACLU v. Reno*. (The ACLU was the lead plaintiff, and Attorney General Janet Reno defended the law on behalf of the government.) A three-judge federal court in Philadelphia heard the case in a thorough trial, including a detailed study of the Internet and World Wide Web, and the availability of sexually explicit material on the Internet. The court made 410 findings of fact and reached the conclusion that large portions of the law were unconstitutional and issued an injunction prohibiting its enforcement. The United State appealed the case to the U.S. Supreme Court.

The Court's opinion, written by Justice John Paul Stevens, included a detailed history of the development of the internet and world wide web. The Court then considered whether the Internet should be regulated closely, as is the case with broadcasting, or whether it should be accorded a wider range of freedom of speech, as is the case with newspapers and publications. The Court looked to some of the reasons for the extensive regulation of broadcast media—for example, the scarcity of available frequencies, and concluded there was no such problem with the internet. As to the next issue, the court found that the Internet was not as "invasive" as radio or television. As the district court had found, "communications over the internet do not 'invade' an individual's home or appear on one's computer screen unbidden. Users seldom encounter content by accident." Furthermore, "almost all sexually explicit images are preceded by warnings as to the content."

The Court noted the vagueness of certain definitions—specifically the words "indecent" and "patently offensive" were mentioned as imprecise, and undefined. Since the CDA was a content-based regulation of speech, the regulation raised special First Amendment concerns because of its obvious chilling effect on free speech. Second, the CDA was a criminal statute, threatening violators with up to two years in prison.

Although laws prohibiting "obscene" material had been upheld in the past, never had "indecent" material been legally prohibited. The definition of such material was unclear, but to the extent the law prohibited speech which was legal for adults, based on the standard of what was appropriate for children, such a law violated freedom of speech.

In conclusion, the Supreme Court found that the "breadth of the CDA's coverage was wholly unprecedented." Unlike some earlier laws the CDA was not limited to commercial speech or commercial entities. The general, undefined terms "indecent" and "patently offensive" covered large amounts of non-pornographic material with serious educational or other value. Since there was no effective way of determining the age of a user who is accessing material through e-mail, mail exploders, newsgroups, or chat rooms, the law's breadth would impact and curtail significant amounts of adult conversation on the Internet. Thus, the law must be held unconstitutional.

The Court concluded, "We agree with the District Court's conclusion that the CDA places an unacceptably heavy burden on protected speech, and that the defenses do not constitute the sort of 'narrow tailoring' that will save an otherwise patently invalid unconstitutional provision." Justice Stevens said that in a previous case (in which a law was held to violate freedom of speech), "we remarked that the speech restriction at issue there amounted to 'burning the house to roast the pig.' The CDA, casting a far darker shadow over free speech, threatens to torch a large segment of the Internet community."
Reno v. American Civil Liberties Union 521 U.S. 844 (1997)

Congress again attempted to limit access of minors to pornographic material over the internet by enacting the Child Online Protection Act (COPA) a few years later. Responding to the *Reno* decision, this law was different from the CDA in that it: (1) only applied to material displayed on the World Wide Web; (2) only covered communications made for "commercial purposes"; and (3) restricted only material "harmful to minors", rather than the broader "indecent and patently offensive" language of the CDA.

The COPA was challenged as a violation of the First Amendment and a federal district court ruled that it was unconstitutional, which was upheld by the Third Circuit. That appellate court held that the law was "overbroad" because of COPA's use of "contemporary community standards" to identify what material was "harmful to minors." This case was appealed to the U.S. Supreme Court, which in 2002 sent the case back to the lower courts for further review. The lower federal court again held the law unconstitutional and that ruling was affirmed by the Third Circuit Court of Appeals in 2008. That result became final when the Supreme Court refused to hear the appeal in 2009.

SOCIAL/ETHICAL ISSUES

Our laws make it difficult for someone to prevent another person from making a particular statement, even if that statement is false and the speaker knows it is false. Is this right? Is it ethical? Is it morally wrong to make a false statement about someone else ("Joe is a drug addict") that may cause that person significant harm and distress? If it is morally wrong, should our laws and legal system have provisions to stop the statement before it is made rather than force the injured party to sue later and prove damages? Why or why not?

commercial speech: A type of speech engaged in for business and commercial purposes.

Commercial Speech   In the domain called **commercial speech**, however, the decisions have been less clear. For many years advertising and other forms of business speech were not considered to be protected by the First Amendment. But in the mid-1970s the Supreme Court began to recognize commercial speech as a valid exercise of the "freedom of speech" clause, although it was necessary to balance the right against other important government concerns. The Supreme Court held, in several cases, that commercial speech was protected by the Constitution but might be regulated and restricted much more than noncommercial speech. The following case is the leading decision setting forth the tests a court should use in determining that balance.

CENTRAL HUDSON GAS AND ELECTRIC CORP. V. PUBLIC SERVICE COMMISSION

447 U.S. 557 (1980)

FACTS

The New York Public Service Commission decided during the "energy crisis" of 1973 that electric utilities should stop all advertising that promoted the use of electricity because the state was running short of fuel supplies to furnish additional electricity. A few years later, when the energy shortage had eased, several utilities wanted the ban lifted, but the Commission refused. Central Hudson, a large utility company, sued the Commission, alleging that its First Amendment rights had been violated. The trial and appellate courts ruled in favor of the Commission, and the plaintiff appealed to the U.S. Supreme Court.

DECISION

The U.S. Supreme Court opinion was written by Justice Powell, who noted that this case involved a "restriction on commercial speech, that is, expression related solely to the economic interests of the speaker and its audience." The First Amendment, he stated, as applied to states by the 14th Amendment, "protects commercial speech from unwarranted government

intrusion, but . . . we have rejected the view that government has complete power to suppress or regulate commercial speech. We believe that people will perceive their own best interests if they are well enough informed and the best means to that end is to open the channels of communication, rather than to close them."

The Court stated that its earlier decisions had recognized the "common sense distinction" between speech proposing a commercial transaction, which occurs in an area traditionally subject to government regulation, and other varieties of speech. "The Constitution therefore accords a lesser protection to commercial speech than to other constitutionally guaranteed expression."

Justice Powell stated that in commercial speech cases, a four-part analysis has developed to determine what level of protection is appropriate. The tests were: (1) the message must concern lawful activity and not be misleading. There is no constitutional objection to the suppression of inaccurate commercial speech; (2) the government interest or reason for regulating is "substantial;" If both of the first two inquiries yield positive answers, the court (3) must determine whether the regulation directly advances the governmental interest asserted; and (4) whether it is not "more extensive than is necessary to serve that interest."

In this case, it was not argued that the advertising was false or related to illegal activity. The Commission has established a connection between the advertising and the important public goal of energy conservation—clearly a substantial state interest, which would be advanced by the order at issue here. However, the Commission's order "reaches all promotional advertising, regardless of the impact of the touted service on overall energy use." The order would prohibit ads promoting electric services that would reduce energy use, such as heat pumps, or through diverting demand from less efficient sources. The Court found that the Commission had not shown that a more limited speech regulation would be ineffective in promoting energy conservation, and the Court could not therefore approve the "complete suppression" of Central Hudson's advertising. Thus, the decision of the lower court was reversed.

CASE QUESTIONS

1. What should the Public Service Commission do now? Is there any type of advertising ban that would be constitutional? If so, how must it be drafted?
2. Describe and discuss each of the four tests the Court says should be applied to a restriction on commercial speech.
3. Do you think that commercial messages should receive the same protection as noncommercial messages? Should a toothpaste ad be treated by the Constitution in the same way as a letter to the editor of the newspaper concerning local politics? Why or why not?
4. Suppose that the government bans all cigarette and hard liquor advertising from television. Is this fair? Is it legal? Apply the *Central Hudson* tests to this example.
5. Is a ban on tobacco and liquor advertising ethical? Is it an application of one particular standard of morality to all? There are some religions that prohibit or discourage use of these substances, and others which do not. Is the government remaining neutral or favoring one or more religions?

RELIGION AND THE CONSTITUTION

The First Amendment states that **"Congress shall make no law respecting the establishment of religion, nor prohibiting the free exercise thereof."** This 16-word sentence contains two key provisions setting forth the legal relationship between church and state in the United States—the so-called **Establishment Clause** and the **Free Exercise Clause.** There have been hundreds of cases decided by courts over the past 200 years in which the central issue involved an interpretation of these few words, as applied to particular circumstances.

The "establishment" cases have concerned situations such as school prayers, or "prayer time" in public schools, Christmas nativity displays in or on the grounds of city halls and other public buildings, and the use of public buildings by religious groups. The central legal issue usually has been whether the activity represented some governmental assistance to or promotion of (i.e., "establishment of") religion.

The Establishment Clause: The part of the First Amendment that prohibits the government from promoting or "establishing" any religion.

The Free Exercise Clause: The part of the First Amendment which prohibits the government from interfering with a person's right to "exercise" his/her religion.

In 2004 the Supreme Court heard arguments in the *Newdow* case, in which a lower court had held that it was unconstitutional for a public school to require students to recite the Pledge of Allegiance, which has included (since the 1950s) the phrase "one nation under God." Much controversy and commentary arose, and there was much speculation about what the Supreme Court would do. However, in the end the Court decided not to rule on the case, finding that the student's father, who did not have full custody of the girl, did not therefore have "standing" to make the Constitutional arguments for her. Thus the question of whether the Pledge constitutes "establishment of religion" must await another case.

The "free exercise" cases typically have involved some law or regulation that the members of one religious group contend they cannot obey because to do so would violate one of the tenets of their religion. For example, members of some religions have refused to receive or allow their children to receive medical care or blood transfusions, to attend public school, to salute the flag, or to work on Saturday or Sunday because of religious principles. These persons have argued that laws that allow them to be penalized for these practices prevent them from "freely exercising" their religion.

SOCIAL/ETHICAL ISSUES

Most of us would probably agree with the broad statements contained in the Establishment and Free Exercise Clauses of the First Amendment. We want to be able to follow our own religion without government interference, and at the same time we do not want the state or federal government to promote or mandate any religion for us. However, in everyday life, the interrelationship between religion and the law is more difficult. For example, should we have a law prohibiting liquor, dancing, or all abortions because some religions strongly believe that these activities are morally wrong? Should the supervisor of your department store have to rearrange everyone's schedule because one person cannot work on Saturday, because of her religion? Is it morally and legally acceptable for society to allow a child to die from a disease that can be treated by medication or by a blood transfusion because the parents' religion prohibits the taking of medication or the blood transfusion?

There have been a number of cases around the country recently involving the installation, or removal from government property, of monuments containing the Ten Commandments and other religious messages. While each case is different, the courts have been more tolerant of plaques and displays which have been in place for many years, than when a new monument is put in place. The "age and history" of the display as well as the intent of those who want to install new monuments does seem to make a difference in how much of an "establishment of religion" it is. One court asked "whether a reasonable observer would perceive the display as a government endorsement of religion." Try to think of other issues that have arisen recently in your community or your state that involved an interpretation of the Establishment or Free Exercise Clause. As the examples indicate, these issues tend to generate strong emotion on both sides of the question.

THE CRIMINAL PROCEDURE PROTECTIONS

Search and Seizure   The Fourth and Fifth Amendments of the Constitution demonstrate the desire of the framers to protect the public from excesses of governmental powers and intrusions. The **Fourth Amendment** provides:

> *The right of the people to be secure in their persons, houses, papers, and effects, against unreasonable searches and seizures, shall not be violated, and no Warrants shall issue, but upon probable cause, supported by Oath or affirmation, and particularly describing the place to be searched, and the persons or things to be seized.*

While you may never have studied the actual words of the Fourth Amendment, you have surely watched television shows or read newspaper accounts of cases that revolved around whether a search was "reasonable," whether there was the need for a search warrant, or whether the search warrant was properly prepared and executed.

Fourth Amendment: The Amendment to the U.S. Constitution that guarantees people the right to be secure in their homes and property against unreasonable searches and seizures and provides that no warrants shall issue except upon probable cause.

The U.S.A. Patriot Act

Following the terrorist attacks of September 11, 2001, Congress enacted a law known as The U.S.A. Patriot Act. In an effort to locate potential terrorists, this law gave government agents and police greatly expanded powers to look into various types of records and conduct extensive surveillance without the need to obtain warrants. Many persons argued that in an attempt to fight terrorism, many basic Constitutional rights of U.S. citizens were being violated.

For example, the Patriot Act allows the government access to the personal library records of an individual after obtaining approval from a secret (Foreign Intelligence Surveillance Act) court. Prior to the Patriot Act, authorities could only examine records after proving in court that there was probable cause to believe that a crime had been committed. Now the government merely needs to convince a secret court that looking at book-borrowing histories or library Internet usage is relevant to an ongoing terrorist investigation, whether or not a crime has been committed. In addition, library employees are prohibited from revealing to anyone that a patron is under suspicion.

Many librarians feel that the new law violates the right to privacy, and are resisting enforcement of the law, or posting signs that "records of books you borrow from this library may be obtained by federal agents." Courts held some sections of the law unconstitutional in 2004 and 2007. Congress was debating whether to renew certain parts of the Patriot Act when this book was going to press.

In general, in order to search a person's home or business, the government must convince a judge, before a search warrant will be issued, that there is "probable cause" that a search will disclose evidence of a crime. This burden can be met by privately showing the judge certain evidence, by the testimony of police officials or informants, or perhaps the sworn statement of someone who saw the illegal material in the subject's home or knows that it is there. The warrant, when issued, must specify where the search is to be conducted and the items for which the authorities are looking. But what if the police search without a warrant or go into places not covered by the warrant? In order to enforce the Fourth Amendment, courts have devised the so-called **exclusionary rule,** which prevents evidence from being used in court if it was seized in violation of the constitutional requirements.

Legal thinkers have hotly debated the exclusionary rule, since it does sometimes result in a "guilty" person being acquitted. For example, suppose the police search Rod's house with a warrant and find cocaine, but the warrant was issued for the house next door. Some exceptions to the exclusionary rule exist, but if none apply, the evidence found (the cocaine) cannot be used in a prosecution against Rod. In recent years, the Supreme Court has chipped away somewhat at the exclusionary rule, allowing the "good faith" of police officers to overcome minor errors in a few cases. The basic rule itself, however, is still strictly enforced by courts in most instances as a means of guaranteeing compliance with the Fourth Amendment. The framers of the Constitution were very concerned about preventing the government from conducting general searches of people's homes and businesses whenever an official chose to do so.

As with many legal rules, there are numerous exceptions to the "need for a warrant" requirement. For example, when lawfully arresting a suspect for a crime, the Supreme Court has said that a police officer may search the arrestee, as well as the area within the suspect's control. The original reason for the rule was to prevent the suspect from reaching for a weapon, or attempting to destroy incriminating evidence.

However, the rule has been extended over the years in other cases. In *New York v. Belton,* the Court ruled that a search incident to an arrest that takes place in a car may extend throughout the passenger compartment of the car (not the trunk), even though that compartment may include spaces beyond the suspect's reach and thus outside the zone from which weapons or evidence are accessible. The cases have further extended this rule to situations where the subject was no longer in the car.

Self-Incrimination   The **Fifth Amendment** provides, in part, that:

> . . . *nor shall any person be subject for the same offence to be twice put in jeopardy of life or limb; nor shall be compelled in any criminal case to be a witness against himself, nor be deprived of life, liberty, or property, without due process of law* . . . .

This amendment contains the **"double jeopardy"** clause preventing someone from being tried twice for the same crime, as well as the **"due process"** clause (about which we will have more to say later). Much attention in recent years has been given to the reach of the *"self-incrimination"* clause contained in the middle of the Fifth Amendment. Many individuals have "taken the Fifth" (that is, refused to answer any questions) when questioned by prosecutors or government officials to avoid discussing incidents that may subject them to possible criminal ramifications. In addition, the Supreme Court decided, in the

exclusionary rule: A court-made rule that prohibits evidence which was illegally seized from being used in court by the prosecutor.

Fifth Amendment: The Amendment to the Constitution that provides that no person will be compelled to be a witness against him- or herself; that no person shall be deprived of life, liberty, or property without due process of law; and that property will not be taken for public use without just compensation.

famous 1966 case, *Miranda v. Arizona,* that in order to really carry out the purpose of the Fifth Amendment, police officers were required to tell a person they had placed in custody that he or she had the right to remain silent (to say nothing), that any statements the person made could be used against him or her, and that he or she had a right to have a lawyer present during questioning. (The Sixth Amendment states that the "accused shall have the assistance of counsel for his defense.") The Supreme Court has heard many cases involving the scope of the *Miranda* case and the so-called "***Miranda* warnings.**"

In recent years, as the Supreme Court has become more conservative, some exceptions have been found to the rigid application of the *Miranda* Rule in particular cases. Nevertheless, the core principles have been sustained. For example, in 2000 the Court considered a federal law which stated that the admissibility of confessions should depend on whether they were voluntary, as determined by a judge. However, in a 7-2 decision, surprisingly written by Chief Justice Rehnquist, the Supreme Court ruled the law unconstitutional. The Court stated that *Miranda* was a constitutional decision, and that "Congress may not legislatively supersede our decisions interpreting the Constitution." Rehnquist wrote that "whether or not we would agree with *Miranda's* reasoning" the judicial principle of honoring precedent weighs heavily against overruling it now."

In 1990 the Supreme Court was faced with an interesting situation. The police suspected a man (who was in jail on some other charges) of murder. A police officer posing as an inmate, working with another inmate (the informer), got the defendant to discuss a possible escape. As the conversation progressed, the undercover officer asked the suspect if he had ever "done" anyone, at which point the suspect gave details of the murder under investigation. He was later charged with the murder, and at trial he raised the Fifth Amendment as a defense, claiming that he should have been given his *Miranda* rights before the conversation took place.

The Supreme Court denied his claim, holding that an agent posing as an inmate need not give the warnings before questioning the suspect about a crime he has not been charged with, because of the purposes of the *Miranda* rule. The reason behind the rule, stated the court, was to eliminate the risk of coercion present in an official interrogation of a defendant in custody: "The essential ingredients of a 'police-dominated atmosphere' and compulsion are not present when an incarcerated person speaks freely to someone that he believes to be a fellow inmate," wrote justice Kennedy for the Court [*Illinois v. Perkins*, 496 U.S. 292, 110 S.Ct. 2394 (1990)].

> **The Miranda rule:** The rule, issued in a famous Supreme Court case, that police officers must tell a suspect in custody, of his or her right to remain silent.

OTHER IMPORTANT CONSTITUTIONAL CONCEPTS

DUE PROCESS OF LAW

One of the most fundamental protections contained in the Bill of Rights is the statement in the Fifth Amendment that "*No person shall . . . be deprived of life, liberty, or property without due process of law*." While the Fifth Amendment applies literally to the federal government only, the 14th Amendment contains a similar **Due Process Clause** applicable to the states. What this clause

> **The Due Process Clause:** The constitutional provision that requires some type of fair hearing (process) before the government can take away anyone's life, liberty, or property.

MEMO FROM THE LEGAL DEPARTMENT

To: Students

From: Your Lawyer

The "self-incrimination clause" of the Fifth Amendment only protects individuals, not organizations. Therefore, if an individual person is charged with a crime, he or she cannot be compelled to testify or to reveal evidence that might incriminate them. But a company has no such constitutional privilege, and if charged with a crime, it cannot refuse to provide documents or physical evidence that could lead to a conviction of the firm.

Corporations and other businesses, however, are accorded freedom of speech rights and protection against illegal searches under the First and Fourth Amendments, as we have discussed.

---

means, at its simplest, is that government may indeed take away a person's life, liberty, or property, but only if that person's essential rights are not violated and some fundamentally fair way exists for the person to contest the action. Due process issues may be substantive, procedural, or both.

Substantive Due Process   Early in the 20th century the doctrine of substantive due process was successfully invoked to invalidate several laws affecting private property and business rights—such as minimum wage laws and maximum hour laws. The rationale was that such laws affected the freedom of the workers and employers to make whatever contracts they wanted. But by the 1930s and 1940s, this doctrine had lost its momentum, at least with respect to economic and social legislation, and the courts will not normally strike down a law on substantive due process grounds unless it alters a fundamental personal right, such as freedom of speech or the right to privacy.

Procedural Due Process   This aspect of due process concerns how the government goes about taking away an individual's rights. Did the individual have a fundamentally fair and impartial hearing? Did she have the chance to tell her side of the story? Essentially, the question is, "Was the procedure fair (due)?" This concept will be thoroughly discussed in Chapter 5, "Administrative Law and Regulation," because many government agencies—federal, state, and local—sometimes take away property that individuals want to retain, such as welfare benefits, business licenses, zoning permits, and so on. The "due process" question in each case is whether the government agency used a fair, impartial, just process (due process) in making its decision.

The phrase "procedural due process" merely means that a life, liberty, or property interest is at stake and that some sort of fair process is required. Exactly what type of procedure is necessary to provide "due process" depends on the seriousness of the deprivation. When someone is charged with the crime of murder, courts will demand the full range of possible procedural protections—such as notice of the charges, a full hearing, jury trial, lawyer, witnesses, impartial judge, cross-examination, full opportunity to present one's side of the case, and so on. On the other hand, if the city refuses to issue you a dog license, "due process" is still required, but probably not quite so many procedures are needed in order to afford you a fair opportunity to be heard. So the precise requirements of due process are somewhat flexible, depending on the significance of the deprivation.

Equal Protection of the Law   The 14th Amendment to the Constitution, added after the Civil War, says that *"No state shall . . . deny to any person within its jurisdiction the equal protection of the laws."* But what does this mean? Obviously, there are laws that do not affect all people the same—tax laws, welfare laws, wage and hour regulations, zoning laws, and many more. What causes a law to violate the equal protection clause? The courts have developed two different tests for deciding equal protection cases, the *rational basis test* and the *strict scrutiny* test.

Rational Basis Test In most cases, a law or regulation that charges different rates or imposes different obligations on different people will be upheld if the legislature had a *"rational basis"* for the distinction and the law bears a logical connection to a permissible government interest. In other words, if there is a good reason why some types of businesses are charged higher license fees than others or out-of-state students are charged higher tuition at a state university than in-state students, the law is valid. Courts using this approach allow the legislature to determine what is in the best interests of the population and rarely overturn such a law.

Strict Scrutiny Test When the classification involves what is called a *"suspect class,"* or a "fundamental right," however, the courts will apply *"strict scrutiny"* analysis to the law. Such a law will be held unconstitutional unless the state can prove that the classification serves a *compelling state interest.* Suspect classes are those groups of people who have experienced a history of discrimination, often based upon race and national origin. A law treating black persons differently from white persons would be presumed to violate the equal protection clause. Such laws, if subjected to strict scrutiny analysis, are most likely held illegal. Similarly, a law inhibiting a "fundamental right" (such as the freedom of association, the right to vote, and the right to travel) will likely be invalidated unless there is a compelling state interest served by the law.

OTHER BILL OF RIGHTS ISSUES

selective incorporation: Although the Bill of Rights technically applies only to the federal government, many of the important protections have been "selectively" applied to state actions by court decisions.

Many other legal questions involving the Bill of Rights affect individuals and business. One matter of importance is the doctrine of **selective incorporation.** As you have read, the Bill of Rights, by its literal terms, applies to the federal government only. Does that mean that a state government could, for example, pass a law prohibiting the publication of a certain newspaper or the practicing of a particular religion? In a series of cases over the years, the Supreme Court has held that the "due process" clause of the 14th Amendment, which specifically applies to the states, incorporates "fundamental" rights contained in the Bill of Rights. But these cases have dealt with certain rights one at a time, hence the phrase "selective incorporation." Thus, the Supreme Court has held that the important provisions of the First, Fourth, Fifth, Sixth, Eighth, and Ninth amendments *do apply to actions of the states*, but no case has held that *all* the parts of the Bill of Rights apply to the states.

THE RIGHT TO PRIVACY

Another issue of major current importance is the **"right to privacy."** If you search through the Constitution, you will not find any section specifically establishing such a right. Yet this legal right is at the heart of the controversy involving abortion, birth control information, and other issues. Where did it come from? The Constitution contains the seeds for establishing other rights in the Ninth Amendment, which provides *"The enumeration in the Constitution, of certain rights, shall not be construed to deny or disparage others retained by the people."*

Apparently, when they adopted the Bill of Rights, the framers of the Constitution were concerned that there may be some other fundamental rights that American people have but that were not specifically mentioned in the Constitution. Until 1965 no other rights were found, but in that year, in the case *Griswold v. Connecticut*, the Supreme Court found a "right to privacy." That case concerned a state law prohibiting anyone from using or providing information to anyone else about birth control devices. The Supreme Court found that the particular guarantees of the Bill of Rights have "penumbras" (fuzzy areas around the edges) that create "zones of privacy."

This zone of privacy was held to be especially important in matters affecting intimate family relations. Provisions of the First Amendment (the right of association), the Third (prohibiting the quartering of soldiers in any house), the Fourth, Fifth, and others were designed to protect "the sanctity of a man's home and the privacies of life" against government intrusion, stated the court in *Griswold*. Later, in 1973, the Supreme Court held in *Roe v. Wade* that the right to privacy "has some extension to activities relating to marriage, procreation, contraception, family relationships, and child rearing and education, and . . . is broad enough to encompass a woman's decision whether or not to terminate her pregnancy"—that is, that the government could not make that decision for her. Thus, the government could not totally prohibit all women from deciding to have an abortion.

Obviously, the *Roe v. Wade* decision has been the subject of much debate and controversy in subsequent years. In later cases, the Supreme Court has upheld some state laws that place certain restriction on abortion decisions, especially later in a woman's pregnancy. But the essential holding of *Roe* and the right to privacy have not been overruled.

NECESSITY FOR "STATE ACTION"

As we conclude our discussion of the Bill of Rights, it is important to emphasize that the Constitution, and especially the Bill of Rights, protects people from overreaching by *government* and not by other members of the public. Therefore, in order for an action to be declared unconstitutional, the plaintiff in the case must show that there is some significant **state action** involved. Obviously, if the federal government is operating the prison system you claim violates your rights or the state is using the power of eminent domain to take your property or the local city council denies your permit for a rally, there is no problem with proving "state action." But suppose your employer requires a pre-employment drug test, your neighbor puts up a sign attacking your religion, or a country club will not admit you because of your race. In order to claim violation of the Constitution, you must generally show that some branch of the government was involved in the deprivation of your rights. Private action is usually not a violation of the U.S. Constitution, although some states have passed laws making certain private actions illegal in those states.

> **state action:** The necessity that there be some governmental action in order to assert the protections of the Bill of Rights.

MEMO FROM THE LEGAL DEPARTMENT

To: Students

From: Your Lawyer

Although the U.S. Constitution does not explicitly contain a "right to privacy," several state constitutions do. Therefore, if your employer or an agency in your state is considering enacting a rule that will affect an employee's intimate personal and family relationships, reference ought to be made to the law of your state to determine if there is a "right to privacy" in the state constitution, and if so, what it covers.

Actions by state legislatures, courts, executive branch officials, and administrative agencies clearly count as state action. In addition, courts have sometimes held that actions taken by quasi-legislative bodies, like special commissions (e.g., the Governor's Commission on Higher Education), and businesses that are very closely regulated by government or receive the vast majority of their funding from government can be considered state action. Especially with respect to race discrimination, the courts have taken an expansive view of what is state action in order to eliminate instances of racism. For example, in a famous 1948 case, *Shelley v. Kraemer*, the Supreme Court held that a racially restrictive covenant in a deed ("no one but white persons may ever own this property") was unenforceable; since only the court system could enforce it, that would constitute "state action" in violation of the Constitution's equal protection clause.

SUMMARY

The Constitution is the foundation of our form of government and our legal system. This document, written in broad general terms, contains the basic outline of the relationship between the American people and their government, between the state and federal governments (called *federalism*), and between the various branches of the federal government (*separation of powers*). The fact that it has been amended relatively few times in more than 200 years and that we continue to debate on a daily basis "what does that section mean?" attests to the skill of the draftsmen.

The *Commerce Clause* has been broadly interpreted by the courts to permit federal government regulation of any activity that *affects* or is affected by interstate commerce. However, the states continue to have considerable authority to regulate within their boundaries through the *police power*. The taxing and spending powers and the Contract Clause are also important constitutional principles. Under the power of *eminent domain*, federal and state governments may take private property for a public purpose or use, upon payment of just compensation.

The *Bill of Rights* (first 10 amendments) were added to the Constitution to protect American individuals against overreaching by the federal government. The First Amendment protects freedom of speech, religion, and the press, while prohibiting the government from taking actions that "establish" religion. Other important amendments protect against unreasonable search and seizure by governmental authorities and forced self-incrimination of individuals.

The Constitution also requires that all laws and legal procedures provide due process of law to those affected by government action and that all persons be given *equal protection of the law*. Each of the many federal and state laws that will be discussed hereafter in this book can be tested (and many have been) to determine if they are constitutional, using the theories set forth in this chapter.

CHAPTER QUESTIONS

1. The City of Chicago passed an ordinance prohibiting "criminal street gang members" from loitering in public places. The law allows a police officer who observes a person he or she "reasonably believes to be a gang member"

loitering in a public place with one or more persons, to order them to disperse, with the power to arrest those who refuse the order. The law was challenged as unconstitutionally vague, and also as violating the freedom of assembly clause. What should the result be? On what basis? [*City of Chicago v. Morales*, 119 S.Ct. 1849 (1999)]

2. A police officer followed a man named Marcus Thornton, thought he was driving suspiciously, and determined that the license plates on his car did not match the registration. Thornton turned a corner, stopped his car in a parking lot and was walking away when the officer first approached him. The officer asked Mr. Thornton if he had any drugs or weapons, to which Thornton replied "no." The officer then asked if he could "pat down" Mr. Thornton, and he agreed. The "pat down" led to the discovery of 3 bags of marijuana and one bag of cocaine in Thornton's pockets. The officer then arrested Mr. Thornton, and placed him in the officer's patrol car. The officer then searched Thornton's car, and found a handgun under the seat. At no time in the sequence did the officer interact with the suspect while he was in his own vehicle. After his conviction Mr. Thornton appealed all the way to the U.S. Supreme Court, arguing that the search violated his 4th Amendment rights. What should the Supreme Court decide? *Thornton v. United States,* U.S., (124 S. Ct. 2127 (2004)).

3. In 2008, a documentary called "Hillary: The Movie," a 90-minute film of caustic political commentary and advocacy journalism, very critical of Hillary Clinton who was then campaigning for President, was produced. It was produced by Citizens United, a conservative nonprofit corporation and was released during the Democratic presidential primaries. A 2002 federal law, the Bipartisan Campaign Reform Act of 2002 (usually called the McCain-Feingold Act) banned the broadcast, cable or satellite transmission of "electioneering communications" paid for by corporations or labor unions from their general funds in the 30 days before a presidential primary and in the 60 days before the general elections. The law, as narrowed by a 2007 Supreme Court decision, applied to communications "susceptible to no reasonable interpretation other than as an appeal to vote for or against a specific candidate." Did this law violate the free speech rights of the corporation that made the movie? What are the best arguments for and against? *Citizens United v. Federal Election Commission,* 558 U.S. 50 (2010).

4. The federal Clean Air Act attempts to address sulphur dioxide pollution in several ways, including capping emission levels and allocating emission allowances to electrical utilities which reduce pollution, which can then be traded or sold to other utilities. New York State legislators were concerned about "acid rain" pollution from upwind states whose utilities and industries produce SO_2, and causes considerable environmental damage. So New York passed a statute which imposed an "air pollution mitigation offset" assessment. The "offset" law would require that any amount received by a New York utility for the sale of allowances to utilities in 14 upwind states be forfeited to the State of New York. The law was challenged by an association of energy producers that engage in federal emissions trading on preemption grounds. Should the New York law by preempted by the federal clean air act? What is the standard for determining if preemption should apply? *Clean Air Markets Group v. Pataki,* 338 F.3d 82 (2d Cir. 2003).

5. The delta smelt is a small fish, 60–70 millimeters in length, once inhabiting California's San Francisco Bay/Sacramento-San Joaquin Delta Estuary, but now its range has diminished. The United States Fish and Wildlife Service ("Service") listed the delta smelt as a threatened species under the Endangered Species Act ("ESA"). The ESA requires federal agencies to consult with the Service before undertaking any action "authorized, funded, or carried out" by the agency that might "jeopardize the continued existence of any endangered species or threatened species" or might "result in the destruction or adverse modification of habitat" used by any endangered or threatened species. After the consultation, the Service provides the agency with a written statement (a "biological opinion") describing how the proposed action will affect the endangered or threatened species. If the Service concludes that the proposed action will likely jeopardize the species, then it may suggest "reasonable and prudent alternatives" for agency action that will not result in violations of the ESA. In 2008, the Service issued a Biological Opinion to the Bureau of Reclamation ("Bureau"), concerning the Bureau's and the California Department of Water Resource's operation of the Central Valley Project and the State Water Project, two of the world's largest water diversion projects. The Biological Opinion concluded that "the coordinated operations of [the water projects], as proposed, are likely to jeopardize the continued existence of the delta smelt" and "adversely modify delta smelt habitat." The Service suggested controlling and reducing water flows during certain times of the year.

   Several large California growers sued the Service, claiming that their almond, pistachio, and walnut orchards "experienced substantially reduced water deliveries as a result of the Service's decision which caused them considerable losses. The Growers claimed that since "the delta smelt is a purely intrastate species, and because it has no commercial value, the Service's application of ESA was unconstitutional under the Commerce Clause. Is this an appropriate federal action under the Commerce Clause? What are the arguments for and against? *San Luis Delta Mendota Water Authority LLC v. Salazar,* F.3d (9th Cir. 2011).

6. The Chief Justice of the Alabama Supreme Court installed a 5,280 pound stone monument containing the Ten Commandments in the rotunda of the Supreme Court building directly across from the main entrance. Justice Moore had previously displayed a Ten Commandments monument in his courtroom in his lower court judgeship, and had campaigned for the Supreme Court post as "the Ten Commandments Judge." Does this action constitute an "establishment of religion" by state action, in violation of the First Amendment? *Glassroth v. Moore,* 335 F.3d 1282 (11th Cir. 2003).

7. In 1989 Congress passed a law making it a felony to burn the American flag. Shortly thereafter, a protester in Seattle burned a flag to test the new law and was arrested. Does the law violate the First Amendment? How so? [*U.S. v. Haggerty,* 496 U.S. 310 (1990)]

8. A Connecticut law allowed the plaintiff in an assault and battery case seeking damages to file an affidavit (sworn statement) that his claim is valid and then to obtain an immediate attachment of the defendant's real estate.

The defendant challenged this law in federal court, claiming it violated the Constitution. What part of the Constitution does this case involve? What should the decision be? [*Pinsky v. Duncan*, 898 F.2d 852 (2d Cir. 1990)]

9. The Texas legislature passed a law making it illegal to ship wine from out-of-state wineries directly to Texas residents. Texas follows the traditional three-tier liquor regulation scheme by which distillers are permitted to sell their products only to wholesalers, who can sell only to retailers, who then sell to the public consumers. However, the state has exempted in-state wineries from this system, and allows them to ship their products directly to consumers. Does this procedure violate the Commerce Clause? Why? *Dickerson v. Bailey,* 336 F.3d 388 (5th Cir. 2003).

10. A school district decided to include prayers at a public high school graduation ceremony. The school officials determined the contents of the prayers and selected a rabbi to deliver them. Does such action violate the First Amendment? Why? [*Lee v. Weisman*, 112 S.Ct. 2649 (1992)]

PRACTICAL EXERCISE

The Boston Bean Company is concerned about drug use in society and in its factory. The managers have heard stories about drug use by various employees at work or before coming to work. One of the board members remembers reading a *Time* magazine article stating that 44 percent of those entering the work force had used illegal drugs within the previous year. Robert Bright, Human Resources Director of the company, has proposed to the Board of Directors that Boston Bean initiate a pre-employment urine testing procedure to screen for drugs, as well as a policy to randomly test employees once a month. One of the board members wonders, "Is that legal?" Knowing that you have been studying law, the board asks you to write a memo describing what constitutional issues might be involved in these drug testing programs and whether you think the policy violates the Constitution.

FURTHER INFORMATION

www.law.cornell.edu/topics/constitutional.html
Cornell University.
www.usconstitution.net
Private high-tech site.
www.aclu.org
American Civil Liberties Union site.
http://epic.org
Public interest group concerned with electronic privacy issues.
www.crf-usa.org
Constitutional Rights Foundation, a nonprofit, nonpartisan group that tries to educate young people about the Constitution.

CHAPTER 5

ADMINISTRATIVE LAW AND REGULATION

After you have read this chapter, you should be able to:

1. Explain the history of administrative agencies and distinguish between the two types of agencies.

2. Describe the powers and functions of agencies, including rulemaking, enforcement, and adjudication.

3. Outline the steps of an administrative action.

4. Identify the ways in which Congress, the President, and the courts control agencies and describe the legal principles involved in adjudication of administrative cases.

5. List several laws governing agency practices.

6. Understand how to help shape administrative regulations before they become final.

CHAPTER OUTLINE

I. History and Purposes of Agencies

II. Types of Agencies

III. Powers and Functions of Agencies

IV. Control of Administrative Agencies

V. Due Process of Law

VI. Laws Governing Agency Practices

Federal administrative agencies such as the Environmental Protection Agency and the Federal Trade Commission (FTC) are well known. However, agencies at the state and local level also play a significant role in the regulation of business. The "Practical Exercise" at the end of this chapter examines a situation where a local developer wants to construct a toxic waste site on vacant land. There are several permits and approvals required, and action is required by both state and federal agencies. You are asked to play the role of the legal advisor to an environmental group that opposes the project and to give advice on a number of administrative legal issues, which are discussed in the chapter.

INTRODUCTION

Much of "the law" concerning business is really the product of administrative agencies. Almost every business is affected by regulations and policies established by government agencies on both the state and federal level. Often called the "fourth branch" of government, administrative agencies are not mentioned in the Constitution, yet their impact today on nearly every type of business decision—from the initial hiring interview to the sales and distribution of the end product—is massive. This chapter first discusses some of the history and purposes of administrative agencies and their growth and then explains the two major types of agencies. Next, the chapter delves into the powers and duties of agencies. Lastly, the chapter examines the various controls on administrative agencies and describes certain laws that apply particularly to administrative agencies.

HISTORY AND PURPOSES OF AGENCIES

As we have learned in earlier chapters, the U.S. Constitution distributed federal government power to three distinct branches. However, as American society and business became more complex, the executive branch departments (like the Justice Department, the Treasury Department, and the Labor Department) began to create subdepartments to handle particular issues and programs. For example, the Internal Revenue Service (IRS) is a part of the Treasury Department, and the Federal Housing Administration (FHA) is part of the Department of Housing and Urban Development. Beginning in the late 1800s, the nation began to face more complicated issues that were not being adequately handled by existing governmental structures. In response, Congress enacted laws providing for new rights and responsibilities and sometimes created administrative agencies to interpret, administer, and enforce these laws. The first independent administrative agency was the Interstate Commerce Commission, established in 1887 which no longer exists. Today, there are approximately 85 federal regulatory agencies.

As business practices became more sophisticated, additional agencies were created. For example, in the mid-1930s the Securities and Exchange Commission (SEC) was established. This agency saves Congress the job of formulating every rule dealing with the sale and trading of stocks and other securities, approving every public sale of securities, and bringing enforcement actions against those who violate the rules. If Congress had to spend this much time simply addressing one issue, imagine the time demands required to formulate detailed regulations concerning air and water pollution, misleading advertising, discrimination in employment, or all the other important issues brought before Congress in the form of legislation.

As an example, the SEC has been in the news often in the past 5 years in the wake of the massive scandals involving financial and accounting irregularities uncovered in Enron, WorldCom and other large corporations. These firms all had sold millions of shares of stock to the public, which shares were publicly traded, and thus they were regulated by the SEC. They were required to file numerous detailed financial reports with the agency (many of which turned out to be misleading and inaccurate). In response to the scandals, Congress passed a major new law, the Sarbanes-Oxley Act, which gave the SEC significant new duties and responsibilities.

Congress also establishes agencies for reasons of expertise. How many members of Congress do you suppose really know about the chemical and environmental effects of dioxin or mercury? How many really understand all the complex aspects of regulating the sales of stocks and bonds and mutual funds and those who sell them? Although some members of Congress are quite knowledgeable about each of these areas, it is unlikely that the same ones will have detailed knowledge about many of the other hundreds of topics in which the federal government is involved.

State governments have also established hundreds of agencies, with each one given specific tasks to perform. As we have mentioned in the previous chapter, the nature of federalism calls for some tasks to be performed at the federal level, with others left to the states. State and local agencies have taken a leading role in matters dealing with education, highways, health, police, zoning and planning, fish and game regulations, and many other issues. In addition, state agencies work closely with federal agencies in enforcing laws and administrative regulations concerning the environment; the finance, banking, and securities industries; worker safety; wage and hour matters, employment discrimination; and other issues. Although most of the discussion in this chapter concerns federal agencies, you should remember that state agencies are important to business and function in a generally similar way to federal agencies, although the agencies and functions are slightly different in each state.

The establishment of administrative agencies allows the government to employ a whole staff of persons who focus on one specific substantive area and thus develop considerable expertise. In theory at least, this should result in better rules and regulations and more speedy resolution of problems. Congress today acts more like a company board of directors, responding to public demands and enacting laws providing general rights, guidance, and policy, while delegating the day-to-day supervision of particular problem areas (air and water pollution, for example) to an administrative agency.

ENABLING LEGISLATION

enabling law: A statute passed by Congress or a state legislature, which creates an administrative agency, or which gives specific powers to an agency.

Since federal agencies are not mentioned in the Constitution, their powers come from the legislation Congress passes to establish them. These laws are called **enabling acts** for the obvious reason that the law "enables" the agency to come into existence, sets forth the purposes of the agency, and prescribes its functions and responsibilities. An agency only has the power to act within the boundaries of the responsibilities given to it by the enabling act. For example, if the Food and Drug Administration issues a regulation concerning the public sale of shares of stock in a company, the regulation will almost certainly be held invalid by a court, as beyond the power of the agency. After an agency is established, later laws will often delegate additional responsibilities to it. Please read carefully the following excerpts from a typical enabling act—the 1972 federal law creating the **Consumer Product Safety Commission.** The citation at the beginning of each section indicates where this law can be found. For example, "15 U.S.C. Sect. 2051" means the law can be found in Volume 15 of the U.S. Code at Section 2051. The U.S. Code is the set of books containing all federal statutory law.

CONSUMER PRODUCT SAFETY COMMISSION STATUTE

15 U.S.C. Sect. 2051(b). Congressional Declaration of Purpose.

The purposes of this Act are—
(1) to protect the public against unreasonable risks of injury associated with consumer products;
(2) to assist consumers in evaluating the comparative safety of consumer products;
(3) to develop uniform safety standards for consumer products and to minimize conflicting State and local regulations; and
(4) to promote research and investigation into the causes and prevention of product-related deaths, illnesses, and injuries.

15 U.S.C. Sect. 2053(a). Consumer Product Safety Commission

An independent regulatory commission is hereby established, to be known as the Consumer Product Safety Commission, consisting of five Commissioners who shall be appointed by the President, by and with the advice and consent of the Senate. The Chairman shall be appointed by the President, by and with the advice and consent of the Senate, from among the members of the Commission . . . . Any member of the Commission may be removed by the President for neglect of duty or malfeasance in office but for no other cause . . . . Each Commissioner shall be appointed for a term of seven years from the date of the expiration of the term for which his predecessor was appointed.

15 U.S.C. Sect. 2054. Product Safety Information and Research.

(a) The Commission shall—
(1) maintain an Injury Information Clearinghouse to collect, investigate, analyze, and disseminate injury data, and information, relating to the causes and prevention of death, injury, and illness associated with consumer products;
(2) conduct such continuing studies and investigations of deaths, injuries, diseases, other health impairments, and economic losses resulting from accidents involving consumer products as it deems necessary;
(b) The Commission may—
(1) conduct research, studies, and investigations on the safety of consumer products and on improving the safety of such products;
(2) test consumer products and develop product safety test methods and testing devices; and

> *(3) offer training in product safety investigation and test methods.*
>
> **15 U.S.C. Sect. 2056(a). Consumer Product Safety Standards.**
> *The commission may promulgate consumer product safety standards . . . . A consumer product safety standard shall consist of one or more of any of the following types of requirements:*
> *(1) Requirements expressed in terms of performance requirements.*
> *(2) Requirements that a consumer product be marked with or accompanied by clear and adequate warnings or instructions, or requirements respecting the form or warnings or instructions.*
> *Any requirement of such a standard shall be reasonably necessary to prevent or reduce an unreasonable risk of injury associated with such product.*
>
> **15 U.S.C. Sect. 2057. Banned Hazardous Products.**
> *Whenever the Commission finds that—*
> *(1) a consumer product is being, or will be, distributed in commerce and such consumer product presents an unreasonable risk of injury; and*
> *(2) no feasible consumer product safety standard under this Act would adequately protect the public from the unreasonable risk of injury associated with such product, the Commission may . . . promulgate a rule declaring such product a banned hazardous product.*

The paragraphs quoted in the box are only a small part of the statute establishing the Consumer Product Safety Commission, but they show how Congress goes about stating the need for and the purposes, functions, and duties of the agency it is creating. The first section quoted (Sect. 2051) indicates clearly the *purposes* for which Congress created the agency. The next section (Sect. 2053) is the "enabling" paragraph which actually creates the agency itself ("The Commission") and prescribes the selection of Commissioners. Sections 2054 and 2056 specifically *authorize the Commission to undertake certain activities*—conduct studies and research regarding injuries and deaths caused by consumer products and collect data on these issues, conduct testing of products and training of product investigation techniques, and develop standards for consumer products—that is, to write regulations dealing with consumer products. The final section quoted, Section 2057, authorizes the Commission to actually ban products that pose an "unreasonable risk of injury" where "no feasible consumer product safety standard" (as allowed by the previous sentence) would adequately protect the public . . . "

DELEGATION OF POWER

delegation of power: Congress transfers part of its legislative power to an administrative agency, by giving it the power to enact rules and regulations to implement a statute.

Article I of the Constitution provides that "All legislative powers . . . shall be vested in a Congress of the United States." When Congress creates an agency, it technically transfers some of its power to the new entity. This concept, **"delegation of power,"** has constitutional ramifications. A number of cases over the years have focused on the issue of whether the creation of agencies was a "separation of powers" problem on the grounds that Congress' delegation of power to another entity violated its duty to exercise legislative power. In all but two cases, however, the Supreme Court has held that Congress may delegate some of its power to an agency, if Congress provides some "standards" or "policy guidelines" to measure and control the boundaries of agency action. Over the years the Supreme Court has upheld a wide range of statutes by which Congress gave agencies some power to develop regulations implementing a law, as long as the statute sets forth "an intelligible principle to which the person or body authorized to act is directed to conform." Congress generally provides, as in the previous example, guidelines as to the scope of the agency's power, and since 1935 no Supreme Court case has held as unconstitutional a delegation of power to an agency In 1999, the Circuit Court of Appeals for the District of Columbia issued a surprising decision, overturning certain new air pollution standards issued by the Environmental Protection Agency (EPA). The Court, in *American Trucking Association v. EPA*, 195 F.3d 4 (D.C.Cir. 1999), said, in a 2-1 decision, the regulations were invalid because the Clean Air Act provisions giving the EPA its authority were "an unconstitutional delegation of legislative power" because the law was too nonspecific and open-ended.

This decision was later reversed by the U.S. Supreme Court in *Whitman v. American Trucking Associations, Inc.*, 531 U.S. 457 (2001). In an opinion written by Justice Scalia, the Court found that the scope of discretion allowed by the section of the Clean Air Act at issue was well within the limits of the previous court precedents dealing with delegation of authority. The Clean Air Act provision at issue in the *Whitman* case instructs the EPA to set "ambient air quality standards, the attainment . . . of which in the judgment of the Administrator, based on the criteria set forth, and allowing an adequate margin of safety, are requisite to protect the public health." Justice Scalia stated that this law requires that for a "discrete set of pollutants and based on published air quality criteria that reflect the latest scientific knowledge, EPA must establish uniform national standards at a level that is requisite to protect the public health." Further, he explained, the word "requisite" means "sufficient, but not more than necessary." These limits on EPA's discretion are "strikingly similar" to ones that the Court has approved on many other occasions. Thus the Clean Air Act did indeed contain the proper "intelligible principle" to guide EPA's exercise of authority, and the law was therefore a valid delegation of rulemaking power to the EPA.

So although the Supreme Court did uphold the legality of the delegation of rulemaking authority to a particular agency with respect to the Clean Air Act, the case sent a warning to Congress to make sure that when it enacts a law, that clear guidance is given to the agency that is authorized to write more detailed regulations.

Look back over the Consumer Product Safety Commission Act and notice how carefully Congress set forth its purposes and duties.

TYPES OF AGENCIES

On the federal level, there are two basic types of agencies: (1) executive branch agencies and (2) independent regulatory commissions. **Executive Branch Agencies** are part of the executive branch of the government—that is, under the general control of the President. Most of these agencies are headed by a single person, called an administrator, and are subparts of one of the departments of the President's cabinet. For example, the Occupational

executive branch agencies: Federal agencies which are part of the executive branch of the government, under the control of the President.

Safety and Health Administration (OSHA) is part of the Labor Department. The OSHA administrator's actual title is Assistant Secretary of Labor for Occupational Safety and Health. This person reports to the Secretary of Labor, who is a member of the President's cabinet. Many of the top officials of executive branch agencies are appointed by the President, who may remove them at any time, without any reason being given. These top officials must be confirmed by the Senate, but they are thereafter responsible primarily to the President. They are therefore called "political appointees" and are expected to offer their resignations when a new President is elected. In addition, each agency has hundreds or thousands of "career employees" who continue to work at the agency regardless of the outcome of the Presidential election. These people are the so-called "bureaucrats" who carry out most of the work of the agencies.

Independent Regulatory Commissions: Agencies established by Congress, which act independently of Congress and the President, to some degree.

The other primary type of agency, the **Independent Regulatory Commission**, is created by Congress to deal with specific problems. The Consumer Product Safety Commission, discussed earlier, is an independent regulatory commission. These agencies often were created by Congress, in part at least, to keep the executive branch from totally controlling an issue. Independent commissions typically are run by a five- or seven-member board, not a single administrator (like executive branch agencies). The Federal Trade Commission, for example, has five commissioners appointed by the President for seven-year terms. The board may have no more than three commissioners from one political party, and although the President appoints them, he cannot remove them, except for very serious misconduct (compare with Section 2053 of the Consumer Product Safety Commission statute). Once they are appointed, the commissioners are not subject to control by the President or the executive branch. They do not resign when the administration changes, but continue to serve until their terms are up. Also, the terms of the commissioners are staggered, so that the President will typically only have the chance to appoint one or two members of an independent regulatory commission during his or her four-year term.

POWERS AND FUNCTIONS OF AGENCIES

Although there are some variations among federal agencies, most possess three types of functions: rule making, enforcement, and adjudication. Each of these powers corresponds to the main function of one of the three branches of the federal government—executive, legislative, and judicial.

RULEMAKING

When people think of federal agencies, the first thought that usually comes to mind is "rules and regulations," and that is indeed an important part of the responsibility of most federal agencies. When Congress passes a law, it establishes a series of rights and responsibilities. However, federal statutes are written in broad, general terms, since they must apply to thousands of situations all over the country. In order to provide businesses and the general public with more specific guidance as to what is legal and what is not, many statutes contain a provision authorizing a particular federal agency to write "rules and regulations" indicating more precisely what conduct the law prohibits. Look back to the enabling statute for the Consumer Product Safety Commission and note Section 2056, titled "Consumer Product Safety Standards," which specifically gives the agency power to prescribe "standards" and "requirements" for consumer products. If properly issued, these regulations have the force of law unless they are overturned by a court or withdrawn by the agency. There are two primary methods of adopting regulations.

"Formal" rulemaking occurs when an agency holds one or more hearings where various witnesses testify for and against a proposed rule or whether there is a need for such a rule. The hearing must be "on the record" (someone is recording the testimony) and allow for the opportunity to cross-examine witnesses and present evidence, somewhat like a trial. Formal rulemaking is used only if the statute on which the regulation is based requires it. In other words, if Congress wants regulations developed using all possible procedural mechanisms, it can make this requirement part of the law. Since formal rulemaking is costly and lengthy, only a few laws require it.

formal rulemaking: An agency develops and issues regulations after holding at least one public hearing.

Most federal regulations are promulgated using **"informal" rulemaking,** sometimes called **"notice and comment" rulemaking**. This process begins when the agency issues a proposed rule. This usually comes after the agency's own investigation has revealed the need for a regulation and after interested parties have been consulted. The proposed rule must be published in the **Federal Register**, a daily federal publication containing all proposed and final rules and regulations of all federal agencies and departments, as well as other government notices. The actual text of the proposed rule must be published, along with a statement of the authority for the rule, the reasons for the rule, and the name and address of the appropriate person at the agency to contact regarding the rule. The Federal Register, like most federal agency information is available online at: http://www.gpoaccess.gov/fr/index.html.

informal rulemaking: An agency develops a proposed federal regulation and then publishes it in the Federal Register, so interested persons may offer comments before the regulation is final.

This first notice also will provide a period of time (usually 30–60 days) during which any person may send written comments on the rule to the agency. Every major corporation, trade association, union, and public interest group has someone who reads the *Federal Register* daily. This is so that if a regulation is proposed that affects their business or interest, they can send comments—either supportive or critical—to the agency within the time period. If the proposed regulation is controversial, the agency may receive hundreds of letters commenting on the rule. The agency must consider the comments—but does not need to bend to the majority opinion—and then will usually issue a revised rule at a later date. Sometimes, however, the rule is so heavily criticized that the agency decides to withdraw it completely. In most cases, the agency makes some modifications to the earlier proposal in an attempt to address some of the complaints, and then publishes the "final rule" in the *Federal Register*, again indicating the authority for the rule and the reasons for it. The regulation may become effective on that date or after 30 days.

The following box contains a proposed rule published in the *Federal Register* by the U.S. Fish and Wildlife Service on June 2, 2004 relating to the designation of critical habitat for certain species in Guam and the Northern Mariana Islands. The proposal asks for comments from the public, to be provided by July 19, 2004. There have been several proposed rules published previously on this topic, and also some court actions have taken place. The U.S. Fish and Wildlife Service now wants to move forward toward issuing a final rule.

[Federal Register: June 2, 2004 (Volume 69, Number 106)]
[Proposed Rules]
[Page 31073–31074]
From the Federal Register Online via GPO Access [wais.access.gpo.gov]
[DOCID:fr02jn04-28]

DEPARTMENT OF THE INTERIOR

Fish and Wildlife Service
50 CFR Part 17

Endangered and Threatened Wildlife and Plants; Determinations of Prudency of Critical Habitat Designation for Two Mammal and Four Bird Species in Guam and the Commonwealth of the Northern Mariana Islands; Designations of Critical Habitat for One Mammal and Two Bird Species in Guam and the Commonwealth of the Northern Mariana Islands

AGENCY: Fish and Wildlife Service, Interior.

ACTION: Proposed rule; reopening of comment period, notice of availability.

SUMMARY: We, the U.S. Fish and Wildlife Service (Service) announce the reopening of the public comment period for the proposed rule to designate critical habitat for the Mariana fruit bat and the Guam Micronesian kingfisher on Guam, and the Mariana crow on Guam and Rota. We have received a proposed natural resource management plan from Guam since the close of the comment period, and the comment period is reopened to allow additional time for all interested parties to consider this information and submit written comments on the Guam proposal. Comments already submitted on the proposed rule need not be resubmitted as they already have been incorporated into the public record and will be fully considered in the final determination.

DATES: The comment period for this proposal now closes on July 19, 2004. Any comments received by the closing date will be considered in the final decision on this proposal.

ADDRESSES: Written comments and information should be submitted to the Acting Field Supervisor, U.S. Fish and Wildlife Service, Pacific Islands Office, 300 Ala Moana Boulevard, Room 3-122, P.O. Box 50088, Honolulu HI 96850. Comments and materials received will be available for public inspection, by appointment, during normal business hours at the above address.

FOR FURTHER INFORMATION CONTACT: Gina Shultz, Assistant Field Supervisor, at the above address (telephone 808/792-9400; facsimile 808/792-9580).

SUPPLEMENTARY INFORMATION:

BACKGROUND:

On October 15, 2002, we proposed designating critical habitat on approximately 10,053 hectares (ha) (24,840 acres (ac)) in two units on the island of Guam for the Mariana fruit bat (Pteropus mariannus mariannus) and the Guam Micronesian kingfisher (Halcyon cinnamomina cinnamomina) (67 FR 63738). For the Mariana crow (Corvus kubaryi), we proposed designating critical habitat on approximately 9,325 ha (23,042 ac) in two units on the island of Guam and approximately 2,462 ha (6,084 ac) in one unit on the island of Rota in the Commonwealth of the Northern Mariana Islands. On Guam, the boundaries of the proposed critical habitat units for the Mariana fruit bat and Guam Micronesian kingfisher are identical, and the boundaries of the proposed critical habitat for the Mariana crow are contained within these boundaries. On Rota, critical habitat is proposed only for the Mariana crow. For locations of these proposed units and additional information, please see the proposed rule (67 FR 63738).

The original comment period for the proposed rule closed on December 16, 2002. On December 5, 2002, we published a notice in the Federal Register announcing an extension of the public comment period to January 6, 2003, and the availability of the draft economic analysis for the proposed designation of critical habitat (67 FR 72407). On January 28, 2003, we published a notice to reopen the comment period until February 18, 2003, due to hardships caused by Supertyphoon Pongsona on Guam and Rota (68 FR 4159). On May 30, 2003, the Government of Guam filed a motion to extend the court-ordered deadline for completing the critical habitat process to allow time to develop an alternative to critical habitat designation on Guam. On June 13, 2003, the Federal District Court for Guam extended the deadline for publication "indefinitely," and set a status conference for October 7, 2003. On June 23, 2003, the Plaintiffs filed a notice of appeal to the 9th Circuit from the District Court's June 13, 2003, order. On October 7, 2003, the District Court held a status conference in which the Government of Guam requested a continuance of one month. On October 16, 2003, the Guam District Court denied the request for further continuance and ruled that it would take no further action while the case was on appeal. On January 7, 2004, the U.S. Court of Appeals for the Ninth Circuit dismissed the appeal and returned the case to the District Court.

PUBLIC COMMENTS SOLICITED

Since the close of the comment period, we have received new information in the form of a proposed natural resource management plan (copy available upon request) from the Government of Guam. The comment period is reopened to allow additional time for all interested parties to consider the information and submit written comments on the proposal. In particular, we are interested in comments addressing the extent to which the proposed Guam plan would provide conservation benefits for the proposed critical habitat area, the comparative costs, or other impacts of Guam's proposal and the proposed critical habitat, and whether or not Guam's proposal would provide a basis for excluding areas from final critical habitat designation pursuant to sections 4(b)(2) or 3(5)(A) of the Endangered Species Act.

We will accept written comments and information received during this reopened comment period. If you wish to comment, you may send or hand-deliver written comments and information to the Acting Field Supervisor (see ADDRESSES section).

Comments and materials received, as well as supporting documentation used in preparation of the proposal to designate critical habitat, will be available for inspection, by appointment, during normal business hours at the Pacific Islands Fish and Wildlife Office (see ADDRESSES section). Copies of the proposed rule are available on the Internet at http://pacificislands.fws.gov or by request from the Acting Field Supervisor at the address above (see ADDRESSES section), by phone at 808/792-9400, or by facsimile at 808/792-9581.

AUTHOR

The primary author of this notice is Fred Amidon, U.S. Fish and Wildlife Service, Pacific Islands Fish and Wildlife Office (see ADDRESSES section).

Authority: The authority for this action is the Endangered Species Act of 1973 (16 U.S.C. 1531 et seq.).

Dated: May 25, 2004.
David P. Smith,
Acting Assistant Secretary for Fish and Wildlife and Parks.
[FR Doc. 04-12432 Filed 6-1-04; 8:45 am]

BILLING CODE 4310-55-P

Another federal publication, the **Code of Federal Regulations** (CFR) is published once a year, and contains all currently effective regulations of each government agency. Once an agency issues a regulation in final form, it will appear in the next annual issue of the CFR. Your college library and public library probably have copies of the Federal Register and the CFR and they can be accessed over the web as well. The URL is: http://www.gpoaccess.gov/cfr/index.html.

promulgating: The correct process for developing and issuing a regulation.

STEPS IN PROMULGATING A REGULATION

1. The statute is passed, giving the agency the power to develop regulations.
2. The agency investigates the problem and studies needs and alternatives.
3. The agency proposes the regulation and publishes it in the Federal Register.
4. There is a comment period in which the public and businesses send messages supporting and/or criticizing the proposed regulation.
5. The agency may hold a public hearing at which witnesses testify regarding the proposed regulation. (A hearing is required if formal rulemaking is followed.)
6. The agency staff analyze the comments and may make changes and revisions in the proposed regulation.
7. The agency publishes the final regulation, as amended, in the Federal Register.
8. The regulation is then effective and has the force of law.

ENFORCEMENT

Informal Agency Action   Administrative agencies carry out many tasks in connection with their responsibilities of enforcing laws and regulations in a particular area. Some of these actions result in bringing formal charges against those who allegedly have violated regulations, as discussed in the next section. But many other activities are more routine—working with businesses to improve their practices and avoid formal charges, issuing licenses for various projects, and developing better administrative techniques for regulating questionable conduct.

As we have discussed, the Consumer Product Safety Commission has been given the responsibility for regulating, and sometime recalling, unsafe products. Often the Commission can negotiate a "voluntary recall" of a product, through cooperation with the manufacturer, as it did in the situation described below.

U.S. CONSUMER PRODUCT SAFETY COMMISSION

Office of Information and Public Affairs	Washington, DC 20207
FOR IMMEDIATE RELEASE	**Firm's Hotline: (800) 841-4351**
May 27, 2004	CPSC Consumer Hotline: (800) 638-2772
Release 04-145	CPSC Media Contact: (301) 504-7908

CPSC, BACKYARD PRODUCTS ANNOUNCE RECALL OF SWINGS

WASHINGTON, D.C.—The U.S. Consumer Product Safety Commission announces the following recall in voluntary cooperation with the firm below. Consumers should stop using recalled products immediately unless otherwise instructed.

Name of product: Backyard Products Swings

Units: 47,600

Manufacturer: Backyard Products™, of Collingwood, Ontario, Canada

Hazard: Chains on the swing can detach during use and cause the child to fall to the ground and possibly suffer injuries.

Incidents/Injuries: The company has received 31 reports of chains breaking, resulting in five reports of injuries including a sore back, cut lip, and bumps and bruises.

Description: This recall involves single swings and acrobatic swings sold separately or as part of the Backyard Products wood gym set. Additional options to the gym sets include overhead ladders, slides, swings and forts. A yellow, triangular metal gusset on the gym sets con tains the brand name, "Backyard Products™" followed by "Collingwood, ON Canada." Model names and numbers are located on the assembly instructions. Contact Backyard Products or visit their Web site for model names and numbers included in the recall. Swings can be used on other gym sets.

Sold at: Department, toy and discount stores nationwide from December 2003 through April 2004 for between $300 and $1,200 for the sets. The swings were sold separately from January 2004 through April 2004 for between $12 and $16.

Manufactured in: Canada

Remedy: Consumers should not let children use the swings until they have been repaired. Backyard Products will provide consumers with a free, in-home repair kit.

Consumer Contact: Contact Backyard Products toll-free at (800) 841-4351 between 8 a.m. and 4:30 p.m. ET Monday through Friday.

Company Contact: Glenn Kilbride at (800) 323-5999 ext. 408.

http://www.cpsc.gov/cpscpub/prerel/prhtml04/04145.html

Send the link for this page to a friend! The U.S. Consumer Product Safety Commission is charged with protecting the public from unreasonable risks of serious injury or death from more than 15,000 types of consumer products under the agency's jurisdiction. Deaths, injuries and property damage from consumer product incidents cost the nation more than $700 billion annually. The CPSC is committed to protecting consumers and families from products that pose a fire, electrical, chemical, or mechanical hazard or can injure children. The CPSC's work to ensure the safety of consumer products—such as toys, cribs, power tools, cigarette lighters, and household chemicals—contributed significantly to the 30 percent decline in the rate of deaths and injuries associated with consumer products over the past 30 years.

To report a dangerous product or a product-related injury, call CPSC's hotline at (800) 638-2772 or CPSC's teletypewriter at (800) 638-8270, or visit CPSC's web site at www.cpsc.gov/talk.html. To join a CPSC email subscription list, please go to www.cpsc.gov/cpsclist.asp. Consumers can obtain this release and recall information at CPSC's Web site at www.cpsc.gov.

The Agency "Prosecutor"   Agencies typically not only have the power to make rules and regulations but also to enforce these rules and the federal law itself by bringing actions against firms and individuals who violate the law and regulations. All large federal agencies have their own legal staff, which can initiate actions seeking civil fines and penalties against violators. These actions are usually brought before an administrative law judge (ALJ) within the agency itself, as discussed in the next section. The agency's attorneys are not really "prosecutors," because they cannot bring criminal actions. If the law itself does contain possible criminal penalties, the agency staff may refer the case to the Justice Department (headed by the Attorney General) if it wants the federal government to pursue criminal action. However, the legal staff of most large federal agencies do have the power to institute civil cases, seeking fines against persons or businesses who violate an agency's rules or regulations.

Quite often the federal administrative agency files administrative charges against a company and then settles the case through an agreement. For example in June 2004, the Federal Aviation Administration reached an agreement with American Airlines to settle 50 different cases brought by the FAA over several years alleging violation of FAA rules and regulations. American agreed to pay $2.5 million and devised a plan together with the FAA to address the problems and make changes. The airline was charged with violations concerning maintenance, flight operations, training, safety and record-keeping, according to the FAA. The company did not admit to any wrongdoing, but settled the matter "to put it behind us," according to a spokeswoman.

Agencies bring many types of cases. For example, the Securities and Exchange Commission has instituted actions to recover money made by investors through illegal "insider trading." The Federal Trade Commission has brought administrative cases against companies to prohibit deceptive advertising, and the National Labor Relations Board has filed many administrative cases to penalize firms and unions that have engaged in "unfair labor practices." In each case, the legal staff of the agency files the act

THE SARBANES-OXLEY ACT AND THE S.E.C.

In 2002, following a wave of corporate accounting and financial scandals, starting with Enron Corp. and including WorldCom and several other large corporations, Congress enacted the Sarbanes-Oxley Act. This federal law imposed significant new duties and responsibilities on corporate officers, directors, board members, and those accounting and legal firms which provided services to large corporations. The Securities and Exchange Commission, a large federal agency which regulates all large public corporations, was given many additional duties in enforcing this law. For example, the law requires that the top two officers of a public corporation (one which sells stock to the public) personally sign each financial statement filed with the Securities and Exchange Commission (SEC) certifying under oath that all of the information contained in the statement was true and fully accurate to the best of their knowledge.

Search and Seizure   In connection with their duties to monitor and enforce rules and regulations, the agencies have inspectors who visit businesses to check on compliance. Even though the violations are almost always civil rather than criminal, the inspectors are still subject to the Constitution. One agency that has often caused controversy is OSHA. Established in 1970 by Congress, this agency is charged with ensuring a "safe working environment for every American man and woman." The OSHA enabling act enacted by Congress specifically gave inspectors the power to conduct surprise inspections of businesses, without a search warrant, to determine if OSHA regulations were being followed. However, many businesses were angry about the hundreds of "nit-picking" regulations issued by OSHA during the 1970s and were not happy to see the OSHA inspector appear at their door. Against this backdrop, an OSHA inspector arrived at a business in Pocatello, Idaho, in 1975. The resulting case allowed the U.S. Supreme Court to discuss the application of the Fourth Amendment to administrative searches. The Supreme Court ruling established an important precedent for all administrative agency inspections.

MARSHALL V. BARLOW'S INC.

436 U.S. 307 (1978)

FACTS

On September 11, 1975, an OSHA inspector entered the customer area of Barlow's Inc., a plumbing and electrical installation business in Pocatello, Idaho. The inspector stated that he had come to inspect the working areas of the firm for compliance with OSHA regulations. Bill Barlow, the president and manager of the firm, asked whether there had been any complaints and whether the inspector had a search warrant. The inspector said that there had not been any complaints, but that the business had simply turned up in agency files due for a random inspection. The inspector stated that he did not have a search warrant, but that he did not need one. He showed Mr. Barlow a copy of the federal OSHA statute that provided for warrantless inspections. Mr. Barlow then denied entry to the inspector, pointing to a copy of the Constitution he had hanging on the wall. Indicating the Fourth Amendment, he stated, "Well, I've got a higher law. You need a search warrant." OSHA filed an action in federal district court thereafter to seek an order compelling Barlow to admit the inspector, and Barlow also filed an action in federal court seeking an order that the part of the OSHA law allowing warrantless inspection was unconstitutional. The Idaho federal district court agreed with Mr. Barlow and issued an injunction preventing enforcement of the law, and the case was eventually appealed to the U.S. Supreme Court.

DECISION

The Supreme Court, in an opinion by Justice White, affirmed the decision. The first question in this case, according to the Court, was "whether the Fourth Amendment's protection against unreasonable searches and seizures applies to businesses as well as homes." Justice White wrote that "The Warrant Clause . . . protects commercial buildings as well as private homes. To hold otherwise would belie the origin of the Amendment." The Supreme Court noted that the Bill of Rights was closely modeled after the Virginia Bill of Rights, which specifically prohibited "general warrants" English officers had used prior to the Revolution to conduct searches of suspected places "without evidence of a fact committed." The general warrant was particularly hated by merchants whose premises were often inspected for compliance with British revenue laws. It was clear, then, that the ban on warrantless searches in the Constitution was intended to cover businesses as well as homes.

In previous cases, the Supreme Court had held that warrantless searches without proper consent were generally unreasonable. In two 1967 decisions the Court held that "The businessman, like the occupant of a residence, has a constitutional right to go about his business free from unreasonable official entries upon his private commercial property." That right is placed in jeopardy when an inspector in the field can enter and inspect without "official authority, as evidenced by a warrant." Other cases have held that this rule applies whether the investigation is civil or criminal, because the purpose of the Amendment is to "safeguard the privacy and security of individuals against arbitrary invasions by government officials."

However, later cases have established an exception for "pervasively regulated businesses" and for "closely regulated" industries "long subject to close supervision," such as the sale of liquor and firearms. OSHA sought to extend the rule to cover safety inspections. The Supreme Court, however, stated that the "exceptions" were just that—not the rule. In those specific industries, the proprietors have no reasonable expectation of privacy, given the history of government oversight. To extend that principle to all businesses involved in interstate commerce would make the exception the rule.

Therefore, when the business owner does not consent to the search, the government must obtain a search warrant. However, the Court stated that in order to get a warrant, the government will not have to show probable cause to believe that an OSHA violation has occurred. A warrant will be issued if the government can demonstrate that "reasonable administrative standards" were followed. For example, a showing that "we have set up an impartial random inspection procedure, and your name came up in our computer" ought to be sufficient to obtain a search warrant.

CASE QUESTIONS

1. Why do you think the OSHA law passed by Congress contained a provision allowing the OSHA compliance officers to inspect without a warrant? Does the Barlow case make that purpose impossible to achieve?
2. City health inspectors generally are allowed to do surprise inspections of restaurants in their jurisdiction. Under what authority is this done? Is it legal?
3. Do you think that government agency inspectors should have to meet the same "probable cause" requirements that the police do, in order to get a warrant? Why or why not?

INTERNATIONAL IMPLICATIONS

Sometimes administrative problems and issues cross national boundaries. In one recent situation, Teck Cominco Ltd., a Canadian company operated a large lead and zinc smelter on the banks of the Columbia River, in British Columbia, about 10 miles north of the United States border. For decades, waste products from the smelter have flowed down the river into the state of Washington. The U.S. Environmental Protection Agency believes that the smelter is the largest source of metals pollution in Lake Roosevelt, a national recreation area in Washington used by 1 million boaters, swimmers and fishermen each year. According to the EPA, the smelter operations have dumped an estimated 10–20 million tons of slag into the river. Slag is a smelting byproduct that contains lead, arsenic and mercury, which can cause brain and kidney damage.

The EPA has brought an enforcement action against Teck Cominco. Both the lower federal court and the 9th Circuit Court of Appeals have upheld the EPA efforts, based on the reasoning that the Canadian company's actions have had a direct effect on conditions in the United States. The EPA has been attempting to reach an agreement with the company regarding the clean up of the pollution. The company has agreed to spend $13 million on studies, but disagrees that it is under the jurisdiction of the EPA, and argues that it does need to meet all U.S. environmental standards because it is entirely located in Canada, not in the United States. The firm has raised the matter with the Canadian government, and asked that the government deal with the U.S. authorities. Teck Cominco believes that the situation should be handled through international diplomacy, pointing out there are many U.S. factories that cause pollution in Canada.

ADJUDICATION

The Administrative Law Judge Once an administrative action is filed, the case is assigned to an **administrative law judge (ALJ)** who hears that particular type of case. The business or individual charged with violating the law is given a period of time to answer the complaint, much like the process in

administrative law judge: An impartial government official who hears and decides administrative cases, involving federal rules and regulations.

a regular court case (see Chapter 3). Just as with a regular a court case, generally the agency and the defendant make an effort to settle the case. The firm charged with the violation and its attorneys talk with the agency legal staff to determine if both sides can reach an acceptable resolution. Often the case is settled with the company "neither admitting nor denying" the charges but agreeing to make some changes in its procedures and perhaps pay a fine. In return, the agency drops the charges.

If the case is not settled, however, it eventually proceeds to trial before the ALJ. This person is a career appointee who acts as a judge in cases brought by a particular agency or several agencies. Different ALJs tend to become specialists in one particular area of the law. For example, an ALJ who hears nothing but labor–management cases becomes quite expert and knowledgeable in labor law issues.

Defendants are understandably concerned, however, that the hearing officer is an ALJ from the same agency. To maintain impartiality, ALJs are hired, and decisions regarding their promotions, wages, and tenure are made by the Civil Service Commission, a separate part of the federal government. A federal statute passed in 1946, the Administrative Procedure Act (APA), puts controls on many agency practices to insure impartiality. In particular, the APA requires that the ALJs working in an agency be separate from and not subject to the supervision or control of the investigative or legal staff of the agency. Also, the ALJs are prohibited from having any outside contact with any parties to the case. Thus, although a business charged with violating an agency rule may feel like it's "going into the lion's den," when it faces a trial in front of an agency ALJ, there are important laws in place designed to provide an impartial hearing.

SOCIAL/ETHICAL ISSUES

Do you think it is possible to get a completely fair hearing before an ALJ employed by the federal government when the charges are brought by an attorney employed by a federal agency? Suppose that your company is charged by the EPA with violating regulations issued by the EPA to enforce the Clean Water Act. The ALJ, though not directly employed the EPA, hears many cases involving this agency, has considerable knowledge about EPA rules and procedures, and may have gotten to know agency personnel from earlier hearings. How would you feel if the hearing was held in the EPA building? Can you think of any suggestions for making the process more fair and/or for removing any appearance of unfairness?

The Hearing Process   The administrative trial itself is somewhat less formal than a court case (e.g., "hearsay" evidence is more likely to be allowed), but has many of the same features, such as attorneys, introduction of evidence, and direct and cross-examination of witnesses. Some time after the hearing, the ALJ will issue a written decision (there is *no jury* in administrative cases) as to whether the defendant violated the regulation and may impose a fine if there was a violation. Remember that this is not a criminal case, so no "jail time" is a possibility. In most cases, the ALJ's decision may be appealed either to an appellate body within the agency, or sometimes to the full Commission—

that is, the commissioners who actually run the agency. The decision of the commissioners is the final agency decision, which can then be appealed to the federal Circuit Court of Appeals. The procedures which apply to such an appeal are discussed in the next section.

CONTROL OF ADMINISTRATIVE AGENCIES

CONGRESSIONAL CONTROL

As mentioned earlier, agencies have been called the "fourth branch" of the government. However, they must interact with each of the three primary branches in one way or another. Each of the other three branches has ways of exerting control of administrative agencies. With respect to independent regulatory commissions, Congress has created the agency itself and can certainly amend the law to terminate or substantially change the purposes and powers of the agency. Congress sets the budget and appropriates the funding for all agencies. It also regularly holds **oversight hearings**, at which time the relevant committee calls a number of witnesses, both from the agency and outside, to review the performance of the agency. When problems arise concerning an issue within the agency's jurisdiction, the hearings can become quite heated.

oversight hearings: Hearings held by a Congressional Committee to review the performance of an agency.

Within Congress, there are numerous subcommittees, each concerned with a specific substantive area. The chairpersons, members, and committee staff of these subcommittees become quite knowledgeable in, and keep a close watch on, developments in the subject area. They can quickly call a hearing—at which the top agency personnel may be severely grilled—especially if an issue within the agency's scope of responsibility is not promptly dealt with. Also, the committees must approve key agency appointments and are the first Congressional entities to handle any amendments to laws administered by the agency.

PRESIDENTIAL CONTROL

All federal agencies are affected by the actions of the President. As previously mentioned, the top 10 or 15 officials of executive branch agencies are "political appointees" of the President and resign whenever the president asks or when he or she leaves office. These people must carry out the policies of the President, or they will be looking for new jobs. The President also appoints the commissioners of independent regulatory commissions but only when a commissioner's term runs out. Hence, a President may only have the chance to appoint one or two commissioners of an agency in a four-year term, and he or she cannot control their actions after appointment.

In the past 30 years or so, the Office of Management and Budget (OMB) has assumed an increasingly significant role in the regulatory process. This agency, part of the executive branch, has been ordered by several Presidents to review all proposed regulations of the executive branch agencies before they are published. OMB performs a cost/benefit analysis and make recommendations as to whether a proposed regulation is cost-effective. Under the Paperwork Reduction Act, the OMB has certain powers to review the regulations of all agencies. The OMB staff has grown so large that there are now OMB staff experts for each substantive area in which there is an administrative agency (e.g., occupational safety, deceptive advertising, environmental regulations).

JUDICIAL REVIEW OF ADMINISTRATIVE AGENCY ACTIONS

Rulemaking   Most agency decisions are reviewable in the courts. Unless Congress has provided specifically in the statute that the agency's decisions are not reviewable, there is the possibility of such review. For example, rules and regulations promulgated by the agency may be, and often are, challenged by parties adversely affected by them. These cases, usually filed in federal district court, may argue that the agency did not follow the Administrative Procedures Act (APA, as discussed more fully later in this chapter) procedures regarding notice and hearing, that the regulation exceeded the scope of the statute on which it was supposedly based, or that the statute was unconstitutional. If the agency has met these tests, the rule will probably be upheld by the court (which will defer to the expertise of the agency) if there is *"substantial evidence"* to support it. On the other hand, if the agency acted in an *"arbitrary and capricious"* manner in adopting the rule or in making some other determination, the court may overturn the agency decision.

Adjudication   After an ALJ has issued a decision in a case charging a violation of a regulation, an appeal may be made to the full governing board of the agency. The agency board (for example, the commissioners of the FTC) will then either affirm or reverse the decision of the ALJ. If a further appeal is taken, it usually goes to a federal Circuit Court of Appeals (although in a few cases Congress has specified that appeals go to the federal district court). Several important legal principles, listed next, affect whether the court will accept the appeal and, if so, how it will review the decisions of the agency.

exhaustion of administrative remedies: A person must use all possible methods of appeal within an administrative agency before a court will hear the case.

1. **Exhaustion of Administrative Remedies.** In order to allow administrative agencies to accomplish their purposes (one of which is to ease the burden on the court system), generally a court will refuse to hear an administrative case until the parties have "exhausted" all administrative remedies available. In other words, a party charged with a regulatory violation cannot take the case to federal court until all possible appellate procedures within the agency have been used. Only after the agency has made a "final decision" can the person appeal to the federal court of appeals. This allows the agency the opportunity to correct any errors without tying up the court system needlessly. For example, if Ace Chemical Co. is charged with illegal sales of company stock by the SEC and is assessed a fine by an ALJ, Ace must appeal to the full five-member SEC and await a decision from that Board before filing an appeal in federal court.

Occasionally, courts will make an exception and allow an individual to appeal to the court system before exhausting all agency appeals if it appears that such action would be "futile." For example, if Ace Chemical Co. is challenging a particular rule of the SEC on constitutional grounds, and the agency commissioners have consistently upheld the validity of the rule, a court might accept the case without requiring Ace to appeal to the full SEC board.

standing: A person must be directly affected by an agency action in order to challenge such action.

2. **Standing.** This topic was fully in Chapter 2 of this textbook. The same general policies apply to administrative hearings. Basically, only persons who have been directly affected or have suffered some legal injury (those who have been "aggrieved by agency action" according to the APA) may challenge agency actions. In a few cases, courts have stretched the doctrine to include those "within the zone of interests protected by the statute" upon which the regulation is based. At any rate, just as in court litigation, a person or group may have very strong feelings about a regulation or a decision of an ALJ, but unless administrative rule

or decision has some direct impact on that person or his or her economic interests, he or she probably cannot challenge the regulation or ruling in court.

   3. **Ripeness**. Another rule allowing courts to refuse to hear administrative law cases is "ripeness." Just like apples have a time when they are ripe and ready to be picked, administrative cases are not ready to be shipped (to the court system) until a certain time (when they are "ripe" for review). That moment does not arise in administrative law until the agency has taken a final action, either a final promulgation of a rule or a final adjudication in a contested case by the highest appeal board in the agency. The purpose behind this rule is to allow the agency process to work. The purpose of "notice and comment" rulemaking is defeated if someone can challenge a proposed rule in court when the agency has just published it for the first time and no comments have yet been received. The agency may totally change the rule before it becomes effective, or it may decide to drop the proposed rule completely. To permit an individual to challenge the proposed rule in court would put an unnecessary drain on the court system, as well as interfere with the agency's rulemaking process.

> **ripeness:** A court will not hear a case challenging an agency action until the action or decision is "final."

   The following case, decided in 2003 by the federal court of appeals for the District of Columbia, examines the ripeness doctrine as it applies to action by an administrative agency.

ATLANTIC STATES LEGAL FOUNDATION, INC. V. ENVIRONMENTAL PROTECTION AGENCY

325 F. 3d 281 (D.C. Cir. 2003)

Opinion by Judge Randolph

FACTS

The Environmental Protection Agency (EPA) promulgated regulations allowing electric, telephone, and natural gas utilities in New York State to accumulate hazardous waste at utility owned central collection facilities without obtaining a permit. EPA issued the regulations as part of Project XL, a program for replacing or modifying regulations in order to produce greater environmental benefits at lower costs. The New York program is in the nature of a pilot project. Three environmental organizations with members in New York claim the regulations are inconsistent with the permit requirement of the Resource Conservation and Recovery Act (a federal law), and violate the public's right to notice, contrary to law, and are "arbitrary and capricious."

   The regulations are directed at the handling of hazardous waste generated at "remote sites," which are defined as sited in New York within a utility's right of way that are not permanently staffed—which include, for example, manholes and transformer vaults. Sediment in such sites may exhibit toxicity characteristics for lead and thus be classified as a hazardous waste. Under present regulations, each remote location is considered a separate location, and must be identified. The waste is eventually sent to treatment, storage, or disposal facilities, each of which has an EPA permit. Some utilities . . . would prefer to consolidate wastes at secure central collection facilities before shipping, but present EPA regulations do not allow this. EPA claims that the new Project XL regulations would reduce the risk posed by storage of waste at remote sites and would reduce pollution and economic costs associated with transporting small loads of waste for treatment, storage or disposal.

   Before these regulations can have any effect in New York, several steps must occur. First after publication in the *State Register* and a notice and comment period, the State agency will have to promulgate the regulations in final form, or modify them, or decide not to issue them at all. If the State agency does promulgate the regulations, utilities will have to decide whether to participate in the program.

Those that do will have to notify local communities and government and all parties who have commented on the proposed rule before EPA (including the plaintiffs).

Public notice under the regulations consists of publication in a newspaper and two of the following; radio announcements, mailing to those within five miles of the site, community meetings, presentations to the local community board, placement in the nearest public library, and publication on the utility's website. The utility must compile all the comments and respond to them, and then must notify the top official of New York's Environmental Conservation Department, who will then accept, reject or place conditions on the specific proposal.

The plaintiffs claim that the collection facilities will be storage facilities under federal law and the owners must obtain permits before building them. They also argue that the regulations set up "notification . . . designed to fail" and are inconsistent with federal law.

DECISION

Although no party has raised the subject, we view the questions presented as not ripe for judicial review. Federal courts are limited by Article III of the Constitution to deciding "Cases and Controversies." . . . Issues that are ill-defined, or otherwise unfit for judicial decision at the moment, and those issues where no substantial hardship would result from postponing review are not ripe. A regulation is not ordinarily considered the type of agency action "ripe" for judicial review under the APA until the scope of the controversy has been reduced to more manageable proportions, and its factual components fleshed out, by some concrete action applying the regulation to the claimant's situation in a fashion that harms or threatens to harm him.

Among other things, the fitness of an issue for judicial decision depends on whether it is "purely legal, whether consideration of the issue would benefit from a more concrete setting, and whether the agency's action is sufficiently final." (quoting earlier case) Even purely legal issues may be unfit for review. So

here. No one can say with certainty that the New York authorities will adopt the Project XL regulations as they are now written or will modify them. Even if New York does adopt the regulations en masse, we still would not know which utilities will opt into the program or where they will locate their central collection facilities. Yet a claim is not ripe for adjudication if it "rests upon contingent future events that may not occur as anticipated, or indeed may not occur at all." (quoting earlier case)

When and if the program is implemented, it will be easy enough to determine whether the notice requirements in the regulations adequately apprised interest persons. Then too there will be evidence—none of which we have at the moment—regarding the amount of waste expected to be stored at a particular collections facility, the frequency of deliveries of waste to the facility, and other details that may assist in deciding whether the facility operates as a storage facility under Section 6925 (the federal law) and thus must obtain a permit. In short, we have the "classic institutional reason to postpone review: we need to wait for a rule to be applied to see what its effect will be." (quoting earlier case)

Another factor weighing against deciding the case at this time is the consideration of finality. EPA has finished with the regulations. But, as we have said, there is still the possibility that New York will modify the regulations after public notice and comment. This may require EPA to act again to approve any significant changes. Further, petitioners cannot show any harm from delaying judicial review. They are "not required to engage in, or to refrain from, any conduct." No collection facility is operating or even proposed at this point. With all of the further steps that must take place before a utility in New York state begins to use a central collection facility, there is no current, direct effect on the health or welfare of petitioners' members. They may protect all of their rights and claims by returning to court when the controversy ripens.

For the reasons stated the petitioners' claims for judicial review are dismissed.

CASE QUESTIONS

1. What factors were most important to the court in deciding that this case was not "ripe?"
2. What are the legal standards applied by the court in determining when a case is, or is not ripe for judicial review?
3. What public policy is behind the "ripeness" doctrine? In other words, why do you think the judicial system developed this theory?
4. Is either side of this controversy hurt by delaying judicial action and review for a while?

4. **The "Substantial Evidence" Rule.** The three previous rules effectively keep many administrative cases and disputes out of the regular court system—and accomplish two goals: (1) By forcing parties to fully use all the administrative procedures available, many disputes are resolved without involving the courts; and (2) the controversies that are not finally disposed of at the administrative level are much more fully shaped and developed by the time they reach the court system.

The APA allows Congress to enact statutes that prohibit judicial review of agency actions, and a few such laws exist. The vast majority of agency actions, however, may be reviewed by the courts, once the requirements of standing, exhaustion of administrative remedies, and ripeness have been met. When reviewing agency action, the courts follow the **substantial evidence** rule. This doctrine, based on a section of the APA, holds that a court may only set aside findings of fact made by an agency if such findings are "unsupported by substantial evidence." In other words, if there is a good deal of evidence to support the decision made by the agency, the court will support the finding made, even though the court, if it had heard the case first, might have reached a different conclusion. Findings of fact deal with "what happened."

For example, an ALJ hearing an OSHA case might determine after hearing many witnesses that the safety guards were illegally removed from 40 machines in a factory, or in an EPA case, an ALJ might rule that one business dumped sixty gallons of motor oil into the sewer system. These are "factual" matters. If the reviewing court decides that there was "substantial evidence" supporting those factual findings—even if there was also much evidence to the contrary—it will almost always refuse to overturn such conclusions. After all, the ALJ was present to view the evidence, to hear the witnesses testify, and look them in the eye, so it does not make sense for the appellate court to overturn the ALJ's determination on factual issues. Whether removal of the safety guards violated the law, on the other hand, is a *legal,* not a factual question, and the court may well overturn the final decision on legal grounds.

The "substantial evidence" theory is much easier to meet than the "preponderance of the evidence" standard used in civil court cases. In that situation, whichever side produces more (a "preponderance" of) credible evidence will win. However, the "substantial evidence" test may lead to an appellate court affirming an agency decision even if it finds less than a majority of factual evidence supporting the opinion. The question on appeal of an agency decision is merely whether there was "substantial" evidence in support. Once in a while, however, an agency makes a decision that is not supportable by the evidence cited in the decision, or it totally ignores all the evidence offered by one party. In such a case the appellate court will reverse the decision, finding there is no "substantial evidence" supporting the ruling.

substantial evidence rule: A rule followed by courts in reviewing agency decisions. The court will follow the factual findings made by the ALJ and agency as long as there is "substantial evidence" to support the findings.

Like the other rules discussed previously, the "substantial evidence" rule tends to enhance agency power and show <u>deference</u> to agency decision making. As we have said, agency decisions are generally reviewed by one of the federal Circuit Courts of Appeal, and these courts treat agency decisions much like appeals from federal district courts. In both cases there has been a trial held below, and the appellate court is mostly concerned with reviewing whether the law has been appropriately applied in the lower court or agency. The federal Courts of Appeal (the second highest court level in the country) will reverse a case when they find the law to be interpreted incorrectly, but they usually will not set aside findings of fact, as determined by agencies.

5. **Abuse of Discretion.** Once the Court of Appeals finally gets to the legal question involved in the appeal of an agency decision, there still is consideration given to and deference shown toward the agency's expertise. According to the APA, agency decisions—even as to legal matters—will not be set aside unless the agency ruling was *"arbitrary, capricious, [or] an* **abuse of discretion."** This means that if the agency has generally followed the requirements of the law, considered all appropriate matters, and operated within the boundaries of the statute in question, its action will usually be upheld. If, on the other hand, the agency made a decision or issued a regulation without considering the factors set out in the statute or based on factors not brought out at hearings or on comments from the public, then that action might be held "arbitrary" and be overturned as an "abuse of discretion." This standard particularly applies to regulations issued by an agency pursuant to the informal rulemaking procedures outlined earlier.

abuse of discretion: When an agency has not properly followed the APA rules or has acted in an "arbitrary or capricious" manner.

MEMO FROM THE LEGAL DEPARTMENT

To: Students

From: Legal Department

Regardless of the frequent political attempts to reduce the size of the federal and state government, very little reduction in the size and scope of administrative agencies has happened in the past few years. For better or worse, business is becoming increasingly complex every day. Competition is now on a global scale for many firms that previously worried only about local issues. Technology is allowing and indeed forcing more and faster decisions than ever before. At the same time—especially after the scandals and financial crises of recent years—the public is demanding higher standards of business behavior. Neither Congress nor the courts can keep up with the multi-faceted, rapidly changing, complicated new issues in business and meet the public expectations. Thus, the work of federal and state administrative and regulatory agencies is continually increasing.

As a businessperson, you will have to deal with agencies on a regular basis. They likely will be your most direct interface with the "legal environment" in which business operates. You might wish to throw up your hands and say, "There are too many agencies, I hate regulation, and I'll fight everything administrators try to do." On the other hand, you can accept administrative agencies as a fact of business life, adopt a proactive approach to work with agencies, and help them see issues from your point of view and understand your type of business.

Get to know the key administrators who prepare regulations for your industry. This can be done face-to-face on the state level, and either directly or by telephone at the federal level. Stay in tune with public discussion of issues that affect your industry, and be prepared to discuss with regulatory personnel any new rules they may decide to propose. Agency personnel must respond to new laws and to demands for action from the public. Sometimes it is possible to see an issue coming and "get ahead of the curve."

Actually, many administrative agency staff—including the top managers—have worked in the private business sector and want input from knowledgeable business officials when they are preparing regulations affecting a segment of an industry. Even career government workers know the logical and political value of receiving suggestions from the "real world" before regulations are issued. Hence, the final regulations almost certainly will better favor your point of view if you participate in the drafting and reviewing process. Also, the contacts made will likely ensure that you will be consulted early when the next regulatory issue appears on the public agenda. And if your firm or trade group later decides to challenge or criticize the regulations in public, you will be in a much stronger position, having tried to work within the system to draft reasonable rules in the first place.

DUE PROCESS OF LAW

As discussed in the previous chapter, the Fifth and 14th Amendments of the U.S. Constitution provide that no person may be deprived of "life, liberty or property without due process of law." As we have explained, this constitutional principle applies to all levels of government action. Today, the actions of local, state, and federal administrative agencies affect each individual and business in this country every day. Rules, regulations, and decisions made by administrative agencies affect significantly the air we breathe, the water we drink, the cars we drive, the schools and colleges we attend, our places of employment, the products we purchase, and many other aspects of our lives.

In many situations an individual or a business may believe that an action by a governmental agency has deprived him or her of certain property, liberty, or rights unfairly—that is, without "due process of law." The courts have heard many "due process" cases over the years involving individuals who were suspended from school, terminated from some government-sponsored training program or businesses whose operating licenses were revoked, or whose right to bid on a government contract was taken away.

As we discussed earlier, *due process* is a flexible term. The first inquiry in a case is whether the concept applies at all. As we have mentioned in the previous chapter, the Constitutional protections of the Bill of Rights only apply to governmental action, so it is important to determine if a <u>government</u> <u>agency</u> is taking away someone's life, liberty, or property. If so, the individual is entitled to due process. The second inquiry concerns the extent of the specific procedural elements necessary to afford "due process." The number of elements will vary from case to case, depending on the seriousness of the deprivation. In other words, when a person's life is at stake, the full range of possible procedures—jury trial, attorneys, judge, cross-examination of witnesses, and so on—is required in order to provide "due (fair) process". But if a lesser right is being taken away, such as suspension from school for one day, some type of due process is still required by the Constitution but may consist of fewer elements. For example, "due process" here may only require that you be given the chance to state your case to the school principal before your suspension. The following case represents the Supreme Court's most detailed analysis of the due process requirements in connection with an administrative agency's action. This case is still cited every time a court must decide whether the government used "due process" in taking away some right or license.

MATHEWS V. ELDRIDGE

424 U.S. 319 (1976)

FACTS

Under the federal Social Security Act, workers who have contributed to social security for a certain length of time are entitled to disability payments if they become disabled and are unable to work. Mr. Eldridge had been injured and had received disability payments for some time, when the Social Security Administration (SSA)—a part of the federal Department of Health, Education, and Welfare, headed by Mr. Mathews—determined that he was no longer disabled and thus not entitled to further payments. SSA notified him of its decision in a letter and stated that he could submit further medical evidence or information, if he chose to, before a final decision was made. Mr. Eldridge wrote back, protesting the determination, but sending no further information. The agency then notified him that its decision was final, and benefits were cut off. Mr. Eldridge was informed that he had the right to ask for a hearing before an ALJ, to be held at some later date. Instead, he filed suit in federal court, arguing that his rights to "due process of law" were violated by the agency procedures, which deprived him of his benefits without a prior hearing. The lower courts agreed with him, but the U.S. Supreme Court reversed the decision and upheld the agency's procedures.

DECISION

Justice Powell wrote the opinion of the Supreme Court, which began by noting that the Secretary of Health, Education, and Welfare was not contending that the due process clause was inapplicable to terminations of social security benefits. "He does argue, however, that the existing administrative procedures . . . provide all the process that is constitutionally due." Justice Powell pointed out that "The Supreme Court has consistently held that some form of hearing is required before an individual can be finally deprived of a property interest. The fundamental requirement of due process is the opportunity to be heard 'at a meaningful time and in a meaningful manner.'" Both parties in this case acknowledged that there was a right to an impartial hearing in this situation, after benefits are terminated. "This dispute centers on what type of process is due prior to termination of benefits."

"Due process, unlike some legal rules, is not a technical conception with a fixed content unrelated to time, place and circumstances . . . due process is flexible and calls for such procedural protections as the particular situation demands," stated the Court. "Our earlier decisions have established three factors which courts must analyze to determine if a certain procedure meets the requirements of due process." These factors are:

1. The private interest that will be affected by the official action in dispute;
2. The risk of an erroneous deprivation of such

interests through the procedures used, and the probable value, if any, of additional procedural safeguards; and
3. The government's interest, including the function involved and the fiscal and administrative burdens that the additional or substitute procedural requirement would entail.

The first test looks at the hardship that will be caused to the individual by the government action. In this case the current SSA rules allow a hearing after the benefits are cut off, at which time the recipient may be awarded full retroactive benefits. However, the hearing will probably not be held for about 10 or 11 months, during which time the individual will not be receiving benefits. Nevertheless, the disabled worker's need is likely to be less than that of a welfare recipient (there was another Supreme Court case a few years earlier that held that welfare recipients were entitled to a hearing prior to the termination of benefits) because there may be more private resources available, and the individual will become eligible for welfare and other benefits after social security is cut off.

As to the second test, the Supreme Court said that the decision to terminate disability benefits will normally turn upon "routine, standard and unbiased" medical reports. Although credibility of the claimant and other witnesses (which could be assessed at a pre-termination hearing) may be a factor in the decision in some cases, this is not usually true in social security disability cases. Therefore, the second test—which asks whether there is much likelihood of error in the procedures used and whether additional procedures (such as a pre-termination hearing) would make a significant difference in the result—was not applicable here.

Regarding the third test, the administrative burden on the government and on fiscal and other societal concerns would certainly be affected by a holding from the U.S. Supreme Court that, as a constitutional right, hearings were required before all disability terminations. Since benefits would continue through the hearing process, this requirement would "assure the exhaustion in most cases of this attractive option." In other words, all claimants would ask for a hearing when they were notified that their benefits were to be terminated. There would be a tremendous increase in hearings—at great cost to the government—as well as a major increase in benefits paid to ineligible recipients (which would be very difficult to recover if the later hearing resulted in a determination that the person was indeed ineligible).

Justice Powell asserted that what really was at issue here involved determining when "judicial-type procedures must be imposed upon administrative action to assure fairness." In the words of former Justice Frankfurter, the differences in the origin and function of administrative agencies "preclude wholesale transplantation of the rules of procedure, trial and review" used by courts. "Judicial procedures are neither necessary nor always the most effective method of decision making in all circumstances." Due process requires that persons facing a loss "be given notice of the case against them and an

opportunity to meet it," and procedures should be designed to ensure that they are "given a meaningful opportunity to present their case." Justice Powell concluded by stating that, "Giving weight to the good-faith judgments of the individuals charged by Congress with administering Social Security, we believe the procedures already established assure fair consideration of the claims of individual to benefits."

CASE QUESTIONS

1. Review the three tests set up by the Supreme Court to determine if a given administrative procedure satisfies "due process." Which one was the most important in the Eldridge case?
2. What does Justice Powell mean in the last sentence of his opinion, when he speaks of "good-faith judgments of individuals"?
3. What is the procedure for revocation of a driver's license in your state? Test and analyze the procedures established under the three tests required by the Eldridge case.

LAWS GOVERNING AGENCY PRACTICES

There are a number of federal laws that control, in some way, the manner in which administrative agencies function.

THE ADMINISTRATIVE PROCEDURES ACT

We have mentioned the **Administrative Procedures Act (APA)** several times in this chapter. It was enacted in 1946 in order to standardize procedures used by federal agencies in rulemaking and adjudication. The APA is the source of most of the requirements for rulemaking and adjudication procedures described in the previous pages of this chapter, such as "formal and informal rulemaking," and the procedures used at administrative hearings. It has been amended several times since 1946. The APA also sets forth practices to be followed by ALJs.

THE FREEDOM OF INFORMATION ACT

Freedom of Information Act: A federal law allowing members of the public access to information filed with administrative agencies, with some exceptions.

The federal government receives thousands of pages of information from individuals and businesses every day. Before the **Freedom of Information Act (FOIA)** was enacted in 1966, it was very difficult for individuals to obtain information held by the government. The FOIA was intended to change this situation, by specifying that most information possessed by the government—including reports, studies, photos, letters, and so on—is available to the public if a proper request is made. The request must provide a reasonable description of what is sought, and the agency then has 10 business days to comply with or reject the request.

The FOIA contains *nine categories of information* that do <u>not</u> *have to be disclosed*. These exceptions are:

1. Foreign policy or national defense matters.

2. Internal personnel practices and rules of an agency.

3. Information covered by another statute that prohibits disclosure.

4. Trade secrets and commercial or financial information that are privileged or confidential.

5. Inter-agency or intra-agency memoranda or letters.

6. Personal or medical files, which would constitute an invasion of privacy if disclosed.

7. Law enforcement investigatory records.

8. Reports of agencies responsible for regulation and supervision of financial institutions.

9. Geological and geophysical information, data, and maps concerning wells.

Although it was expected that members of the public and the press would be the most common users of the FOIA, it has been businesses that have used the law the most over the years. Many firms are interested in obtaining all information possible on their competitors, and they have employed the FOIA to gain access to various reports filed with the government regarding economic factors, environmental concerns, employment practices, health and safety issues, and other facets of competing businesses. More than 20 years ago regulations were issued requiring an agency to notify a firm if "arguably confidential" information about that firm was sought, so that the firm may object to its disclosure. An agency can still release the data, if it believes that the information does not fall under one of the exceptions, by explaining the action in writing.

THE FEDERAL PRIVACY ACT

The **Federal Privacy Act**, a 1974 law, has the opposite objective of the FOIA. The Privacy Act states that certain information possessed by the government may not be released without the prior written consent of the individual to whom it pertains. Also, the individual's name and address may not be sold to anyone without authorization from the person involved.

The Act does not prevent the agency from using appropriate personal information for agency purposes, although individuals have the right of access to government files on them and can request correction of inaccurate information. Disclosure of information is also allowed for Census Bureau use, for criminal and civil law enforcement, for use by Congress or the General Accounting Office, and for certain other statistical and governmental purposes.

Federal Privacy Act: A federal law designed to keep certain information held by agencies private.

THE GOVERNMENT IN THE SUNSHINE ACT

This law, sometimes called the "open meeting" act, was passed in 1976. Its purpose is to force the independent regulatory commissions to conduct business in open meetings ("in the sunshine"), to the maximum extent possible. There are 10 exemptions (similar to the FOIA exceptions) allowing the meeting to be closed by majority vote of the commission.

SUMMARY

Although administrative agencies are not mentioned in the U.S. Constitution, they are today considered as the "fourth branch" of government and play an important role in the legal environment in which most businesses operate. It is quite likely that an American firm will have regular interaction with both state and federal agencies in the course of its operations. This chapter has discussed the history and purposes for which agencies were created, and the functions and powers of agencies. The complexities of modern business have led to the need for the development of governmental expertise in order to regulate particular aspects of business operations and specific types of businesses for the public benefit.

On the federal level there are two main types of agencies—executive branch agencies, which are part of the president's executive branch, and Independent Regulatory Commissions, created by statutes passed by Congress. Each type of agency is controlled in part by the other branches of government. Federal agencies have three main powers—rulemaking, enforcement, and adjudication. Rulemaking is the power to write rules and regulations to more specifically describe the requirements of a law. Once regulations are properly issued, the agencies must see that they are enforced, and they may bring legal actions against individuals and firms who do not comply. These actions are "adjudicated" in administrative courts where an ALJ presides over the case.

After exhausting all possible appeals and remedies within the agency, interested parties may appeal such decisions into the federal court system. Such appeals can only be taken after the agency has completed its actions, and only by parties who have standing to raise the issues. On appeal, the federal courts often show deference to the agency decision because of its expertise in the subject matter. Agency decisions will only be overturned by courts for "abuse of discretion" or "arbitrary and capricious" action by the administrative agency.

The constitutional doctrine "due process of law" requires that agencies follow a fair and impartial procedure when deciding issues that grant or take away rights or licenses, or impose fines and penalties. Finally, the chapter explained several laws regulating agency practices, such as the APA, the FOIA, and the Federal Privacy Act.

CHAPTER QUESTIONS

1. What are the purposes of administrative agencies? Do you think that these purposes have been achieved? How could they be improved?

2. We all hear lots of complaints about government "bureaucracy" and administrative "red tape." What would be the likely consequences if all administrative agencies were abolished?

3. A married couple chose Humana as their prescription drug plan, pursuant to the federal law relating to Medicare. Although they submitted a Humana application and the premiums were deducted from their Social Security checks, they were informed a few months later that they "were not recognized as members of the Humana plan," and had to pay their own prescription drug costs. The relevant federal law—the 2003 Medicare Prescription Drug Improvement and Modernization Act—allows for judicial review of a "claim arising out of a related provision" of the Medicare Act only after the claim has been put through all levels of administrative review, at the federal Health and Human Services agency. When the couple sued Humana, the defendant filed a motion to dismiss. What is the relevant issue and how should the court rule? *Do Sung Hum v. Humana,* 79 USLW 1293, (9th Cir. 2010).

4. The federal Food, Drug and Cosmetic Act grants to the Food and Drug Administration (FDA), which is a part of the Department of Health and Human Services, the power to regulate, among other things "drugs," "food" and "devices." In 1996 the FDA issued regulations governing the promotion, labeling and accessability to children of tobacco. The FDA argued that nicotine was a "drug" and cigarettes were "devices" that delivered nicotine to the body. The tobacco industry sued, claiming that Congress had not given the FDA power to regulate tobacco and therefore the regulations were beyond its authority and were void.

   Factors considered by the courts in determining whether Congress had intended to grant the FDA the power to regulate tobacco were: (1) that Congress had passed six other laws dealing with tobacco since 1965, without mentioning the FDA; (2) that the FDA itself had long taken the position (until 1996) that it did not have the power to regulate tobacco; and (3) while "deference" should be paid to the agency's construction of an ambiguous statute, the courts should also look to other statutes to determine Congress' intent and use "common sense" to decide if Congress really meant to delegate tobacco regulation to the FDA. What should the Supreme Court decide? Why? *Food and Drug Administration v. Brown & Williamson Tobacco Corp.,* 120 U.S. 1291 (2000)

5. What specific functions has Congress given the Consumer Product Safety Commission the power to perform? Re-read the excerpt from the CPSC enabling statute and cite the sections of the law that give the Commission each function.

6. When may the Consumer Product Safety Commission actually ban a consumer product? What findings must first be made by the Commission? What section of the law gives this power?

7. A public high school in Columbus, Ohio, suspended several students for 10 days for disciplinary reasons, following a period of student unrest and protests. None of the students was given a hearing prior to the suspension. There was a provision in the Ohio law, however, allowing a student or parent

to appeal to the local board of education after the suspension had been completed. Have the students been deprived of any constitutional rights? Is the school an administrative "agency"? If so, what sort of procedures are necessary? [*Goss v. Lopez,* 419 U.S. 565, 95 S.Ct.729 (1965)]

8. The Environmental Protection Agency has the responsibility, under the Clean Air Act, to determine whether specific areas of the country meet the requirements for clean air set forth in the National Ambient Air Quality Standards (NAAQS). The law requires that EPA determine the levels of compliance and classify areas as "attainment" or "nonattainment." The designation carries with it the requirement of more stringent controls in "nonattainment" areas. However, there is an exception in the Clean Air Act for areas where the EPA finds that the nonattainment is caused by emissions coming from outside the United States. In 2001 the EPA found that the Imperial Valley of California was not in compliance with NAAQS standards for particulate matter but only failed because of emissions coming across its 80-mile border with Mexico.

   The Sierra Club filed a lawsuit challenging this decision, and claimed that the finding was "arbitrary and capricious." On appeal, the 9th Circuit Court of Appeals noted that EPA had based a large part of its decision on test results from two specific dates which found high levels of pollution at a monitoring station at Brawley, California, some 20 miles northwest of Mexicali, Mexico. Both the State of California and EPA attributed the excessive pollution to wind-blown particulate matter coming north from Mexico. However, the evidence showed that on those two dates, the winds were blowing from a westerly direction. Furthermore, a monitoring site closer to the border (south of Brawley) showed lower levels of pollution than at Brawley. Given the "substantial evidence" rule, and the "deference which should be shown to informed factual decisions of an agency," should the court uphold the EPA decision? *Sierra Club v. E.P.A.,* 346 F.3d 955 (9th Cir. 2003).

9. Milner submitted FOIA requests for explosives data and maps used by the Department of the Navy in storing munitions at a naval base in Washington State. Stating that disclosure would threaten the security of the base and surrounding community, the Navy invoked Exemption 2 of the FOIA and refused to release the data. Exemption 2 protects from disclosure material "related solely to the internal personnel rules and practices of an agency." Does the Navy have to release the information to Milner, or is it protected by Exemption 2? Why or why not? *Milner v. Department of the Navy,* U.S. (2011).

10. The Federal Communications Commission adopted several new "net neutrality" rules prohibiting internet providers from deliberately blocking or slowing Web traffic. Before the rules were formally published in the Federal Register, lawsuits were filed by Verizon Communications and MetroPCS Communications challenging the rules. The two companies argue that the FCC does not have the authority to impose or enforce rules governing traffic management on their networks. Should the federal court hear the case? Are there any principles of administrative law that might apply?

PRACTICAL EXERCISE

The Lansing, Michigan, city council is considering rezoning a large portion of land from a residential classification to a commercial/industrial designation. The land is vacant—that is, no buildings are constructed on it. The force pushing for the rezoning is Mr. Alex O'Neil, who wants to construct a large landfill/toxic waste dump on the site, for disposal of waste products from other areas of Michigan. Some of the wastes would be incinerated on the site to produce energy. Mr. O'Neil plans to donate part (a small part) of his profits to local youth programs and to build a public school on the site as a public service. The school is to be named "The Earvin Johnson School," after one of Lansing's most famous sons. The slogan for the project is "Turn Waste Into Energy—It's Magic!"

There are several federal and state laws that apply to the situation. For the purposes of this problem, assume that federal law and EPA regulations require that toxic waste facilities be located at least 1/2 mile away from any public school and that no burning of such wastes be done within city limits. Nevertheless, under public pressure, the city zoning commission approves the rezoning, and Mr. O'Neil begins construction, without obtaining EPA approval. (He did file some information about the environmental aspects of the project with EPA, but no action has been taken as yet by the agency.)

At this point, several groups begin to respond. One member of the City Council, which has the power to overturn the Zoning Commission, argues that the Council should do so and take away Mr. O'Neil's permit. The EPA director for central Michigan charges Mr. O'Neil with violation of EPA regulations. The EPA, like other federal agencies, has a two-stage administrative law hearing structure within the agency, providing for a trial before an ALJ and an appeal with an appeal board.

You are the legal advisor to the Stop Lansing Air Pollution organization (SLAP) and are asked to provide the group with information as to a number of issues, including: (1) Can SLAP file a suit tomorrow in federal court to block the project? (2) Can Mr. O'Neil file a suit in federal court seeking to prevent EPA from enforcing its rules against him? (3) Can SLAP intervene in the EPA administrative hearing against Mr. O'Neil? (4) If the City Council takes away Mr. O'Neil's permit, what legal issues does this raise? What might he argue, and how successful will he likely be? (5) Can your group obtain all information filed by Mr. O'Neil with the EPA through the FOIA? Please prepare a memo discussing these issues and explaining the basis for your opinion.

FURTHER INFORMATION

www.access.gpo.gov/hara/cfr/index.html
Code of Federal Regulations.
http://thomas.loc.gov/
Federal government's Library of Congress site "in the spirit of Thomas Jefferson."
http://uscode.house.gov/
U.S. Code (federal law) online.
www.cpsc.gov
Consumer Product Safety Commission site.

CHAPTER 6

INTERNATIONAL LEGAL ISSUES IN BUSINESS

LEARNING OBJECTIVES

After you have read this chapter, you should be able to:

1. Examine the legal issues arising in international disputes involving businesses, private parties and national governments.

2. List several international organizations and financial agencies which play important roles in international commerce.

3. Describe the history, structure and current status of the European Union.

4. Identify important restrictions and regulations concerning international trade, including U.S. import/export laws.

5. Understand the key agreements, principles and issues involving the World Trade Organization.

5. Discuss the issues that arise when domestic laws apply to actions outside the United States.

CHAPTER OUTLINE

American businesses now operate in a global arena, with production, marketing, and sales taking place in nations around the world, often including a significant affiliation with local investors and governments. One of the many ramifications of this trend is that legal problems may arise in countries far from the United States. Often it is unclear which nation's laws, and courts should handle the resolution of international business issues. In the practical exercise at the end of this chapter you are asked to analyze certain legal issues that arose from a tragic accident in India in 1984.

INTRODUCTION

The "environment" in which American businesses operate today is clearly a global one. Consider the firms that employ you or your relatives: The chances are good that those companies are directly involved in, or indirectly influenced by international methods and business.

During the past quarter century, Japanese auto manufacturers have captured a large share of the American automobile market, 80% of the toys sold in the United States—and a large percentage of many consumer product—are made in China, and our homes have become filled with electronic products, clothing, and other goods manufactured in Korea, Taiwan, Indonesia, Malaysia, and other Asian countries. Many American high tech and information technology jobs have been "outsourced" to India and other nations. The European Union (EU), which began as an effort to coordinate coal and steel policy among six nations in 1952, has now become a powerful economic, social, and political organization, spanning much of Europe. The EU has eliminated tariffs and most other nontariff trade barriers on transactions between its member nations. Clearly an economic power, the EU is now moving toward even closer political and monetary cooperation, even as it deals with serious economic problems. The EU welcomed twelve more members, mostly from Eastern Europe, in 2004 and 2006, and now has 27 member nations. This huge

Pepper...and Salt

THE WALL STREET JOURNAL

From The Wall Street Journal, October 11, 1999. Reprinted with permission of Cartoon Features Syndicate.

expansion forced the EU to reconsider the form of, and to re-structure all of its governing bodies. After more than 5 years of meetings, drafting, and voting in an attempt to write a European Union constitution (which was unsuccessful),the 27 EU nations reached agreement on the Lisbon Treaty in 2009, which has led to the re-shaping of many key EU institutions. Russia is watching these developments closely, and even this former bastion of Communism is exploring capitalism and free enterprise.

One of the most important developments in international business in recent years has been the reduction of tariffs on imported goods and the lowering of trade barriers by countries all around the world. A series of international agreements called GATT led to the formation of the World Trade Organization (WTO), which now includes most of the nations in the world. The WTO was formed to coordinate and supervise the reduction in tariffs and other barriers and thus increase trade between member nations. This "globalization" of commerce has produced many benefits and much increase in international trade, but there have been some negative effects as well. Some features of the WTO have become controversial, and its meetings have been protested by various groups.

The North American Free Trade Agreement (NAFTA) became effective in 1994. NAFTA has eliminated tariffs on almost all goods traded among Mexico, Canada, and the United States either at once or over several years. NAFTA also has opened up the markets of each country to a wide range of service and business firms located in the others. Additional Latin American nations are closely watching how NAFTA develops. Other regional organizations such as the South American organization *Mercosur* are growing in importance.

Large "multinational corporations," with operations located in countries around the world, occupy a significant position in global economic affairs. American businesses must be ready to compete in the international arena, both in the sale of goods and provision of services. Indeed, "global competitiveness" has become an important topic of political debate not only in Washington but also even in local governmental decisions regarding business development and expansion. The complexities of international trade and other international business issues involve numerous legal matters. This chapter will raise and discuss some of the most important legal aspects of the global "environment" in which American businesses now operate.

TYPES OF INTERNATIONAL TRADE AND TRANSACTIONS

INTERNATIONAL SALES CONTRACTS

The most common international business transactions occur when U.S. firms sell goods to buyers in other countries (exports) or when buyers in this country purchase goods from foreign sellers (imports). Such transactions obviously involve legal issues such as contracts, sales law, and warranties, which are discussed in other chapters. This chapter will concentrate on the particular problems and issues that arise when sales cross national borders.

One fairly fundamental issue in an international sale is how payment for the goods will be made. The most common method used is the **letter of credit,**

letter of credit: A promise or guarantee of payment by a bank.

a form of payment also used frequently for sales within the United States. The buyer arranges for a letter of credit from a bank, usually located near the buyer. This bank, called the "issuing bank," sends the letter of credit assuring the seller (or the seller's bank in another country) that funds have been set aside to be used as payment for the goods upon satisfactory performance by the seller.

The buyer and seller, as well as the issuing bank, set the terms of the letter of credit. Often the payment will be conditional on the seller producing a **bill of lading,** which is a document issued by the carrier of the goods (such as a ship or airplane), indicating that the specified goods were delivered to the carrier in good condition and indicating when, where, and how the goods were shipped. The bill of lading is then transferred to the buyer, who, in order to obtain possession of the goods upon arrival, produces that document at the receiving end. Upon receiving a proper bill of lading, the issuing bank pays the seller or perhaps the seller's bank. Sometimes, the contract between the parties requires additional documents to be produced by the seller before payment under a letter of credit, such as invoices, packing lists, certificates of inspection, or necessary import licenses.

> **bill of lading:** A shipping document that carefully describes the goods shipped and indicates the person who has the right to possession of the goods.

INTERPRETATION OF CONTRACTS

If differences or disputes arise in connection with an international contract, it is often important to determine which nation's laws will be applicable. As you may imagine, there are often significant differences in legal rules affecting contract law in different countries. The parties can, and often do, specify in the contract that the laws of a certain nation will be applied to contract interpretation. Such a clause in a contract is called a **choice of law clause**. If the buyer and seller do not so specify, the determination will be made on the basis of a series of legal principles called *conflict of laws*. These theories are complex and not always applied in a uniform fashion under various international law interpretations.

> **choice of law clause:** A provision in a contract specifying which nation's laws will apply in case of contract disputes.

Due to these uncertainties, many countries have entered into an agreement called *The United Nations Convention on Contracts for the International Sale of Goods (CISG)*. This treaty, completed in 1980 after many years of drafting by a group of international business law experts, has now been adopted by more than 76 countries, including most of the major trading nations of the world. Brazil, India, South Africa and the United Kingdom are the only major trading countries that have not yet ratified the CISG. It was signed by the United States in 1988. The CISG sets out uniform legal rules that apply to international commercial contracts involving the sale of goods between businesses in countries that have signed the agreement, unless the parties specify otherwise. The CISG does not apply to consumer transactions or to the sale of securities, vessels, aircraft, or certain other matters.

Contracts that span international boundaries require most of the same legal elements as contracts within the United States, and many of the same defenses are applicable. The essentials of a valid contract in the U.S. will be explored thoroughly in Chapter 12, but for now, we can say that a contract is a "voluntary agreement, enforceable in court if necessary." As in the United States, in order for an international agreement to be a "contract," there must be mutual assent by both parties to its terms. Similarly, if one party intentionally deceives the other regarding an important element, the defense of fraud will be successful as it is in a U.S. court.

However, the tremendous differences in language, culture, and customs among the countries of the world have resulted in many different requirements and interpretations of contracts. For example, the CISG, which is an international agreement incorporating principles from many nations, does not require "consideration" (something given in return for the other's promise—necessary in the United States) as an essential element of a contract. Most countries do not have a "statute of frauds" (as do the United States and Great Britain), which requires certain types of contracts to be written.

Americans who negotiate contracts in other parts of the world will soon learn that cultures and customs are dramatically different in each country, and a successful contractual relationship requires understanding, patience, and sensitivity to the language, gestures, and customs of the other party. U.S. businesspeople who think they can easily disregard contracts made in another country because "there is nothing in writing" may be in for an unpleasant surprise.

RESOLUTION OF INTERNATIONAL BUSINESS DISPUTES

When disputes do arise in connection with international contracts, the resolution can be problematic. As we have mentioned, a determination usually needs to be made as to which nation's laws and legal principles will be applied. Another difficult issue is selecting the proper court to hear the dispute—that is, one which has "jurisdiction" of the parties and the subject matter. Sometimes a court in one country will even apply the laws of another country to the resolution of a dispute, if the contract so requires, through a "choice of law" clause.

PRIVATE DISPUTE RESOLUTION

Earlier in this book we discussed the concept of jurisdiction with respect to U.S. courts. We learned that in order to render a decision in a case, a particular U.S. court must have jurisdiction of the parties and the subject matter. The same principles have relevance to the resolution of international disputes. It is usually permissible for a plaintiff to initiate a lawsuit in a foreign court in order to sue a company based in that country. For example, if a Mexican company wants to sue a Canadian partnership for breach of a contract between the two firms, it is normally possible for the Mexican company to sue the Canadian firm in a Canadian court. However, in general, a person is not permitted to file a case in his or her home nation and force a foreign company to come there to litigate the matter, unless there is some significant activity (like the "minimum contacts" required for long-arm jurisdiction in the United States discussed earlier) concerning the contract in that country.

forum non conveniens: A legal principle that attempts to determine the nation in which the trial would be "most convenient" or appropriate.

Where a legal matter involves more than one nation, there is an international legal principle called ***forum non conveniens***, which contains a series of tests to determine which nation's court system is the "most convenient" or most appropriate to hear the dispute. This theory is largely based on common-sense factors such as the place of performance of the contract, the location of the majority of witnesses, the principal place of business of the plaintiff and defendant, and the location where the contract was signed, among other factors. For example, the general trial courts of most nations typically have jurisdiction over contract disputes involving agreements made in their particular nation, or over contract disputes in which a major part of the contract performance has taken or will take place in their particular country.

Enforcement and collection of money judgments across national borders can create serious difficulties. Although a court in one nation will sometimes enforce a judgment lawfully entered by a court of another country, this is not always true. In one case, a U.S. firm and a Japanese company disagreed about a contract between them that was to be performed in the United States. The U.S. firm sued and won a judgment against the Japanese company in a California court. However, the Japanese business had no assets that could be seized in the United States. Therefore, the U.S. firm had to file another suit in a Japanese court to enforce the U.S. court judgment and to attach certain assets of the defendant in Japan. The Japanese court eventually did recognize and enforce part of the judgment, but it refused to enforce a large portion of the award based on "punitive damages," because Japan does not recognize this legal concept. In other cases, U.S. courts have sometimes refused to enforce foreign judgments when they were based on legal theories not known or employed in the United States.

ARBITRATION

In Chapter 3, we discussed the growing use of Alternate Dispute Resolution (ADR) and the benefits of resolving legal disputes outside of court. International legal disputes are even more complicated, and for the reasons set forth above and many others, a large number of international contracts specify that any disputes concerning the contract or performance will be submitted to arbitration. In this way the parties know in advance how and where their dispute will be settled, typically in a quicker, more private, and less costly manner than litigation. Also, international arbitration panels may have considerable experience in the subject matter of the dispute, as well as a thorough background in commercial practices.

Several international organizations have developed expertise in commercial arbitration, such as the International Chamber of Commerce in Paris, the American Arbitration Association, the International Center for the Settlement of Investment Disputes, an institution of the World Bank Group based in Washington, D.C., and the U.N. Commission of International Trade Law (UNCITRAL), which has developed rules often used by other arbitrators. In most cases, the parties have agreed that the arbitration decision is final and may be enforced in any nation's courts. However, when this stipulation is not part of the contract, one of the parties may ignore the decision and submit the dispute to a court, or may try to challenge the award for some procedural reason in a national court system.

Sometimes after signing a contract that contains a clause requiring arbitration of any disputes that may arise, one of the parties tries to file a lawsuit in a national court rather than going to arbitration. As is the case with arbitration clauses between parties in the United States, most courts will refuse to entertain the dispute if the arbitration clause appears valid and was voluntarily agreed to, without fraud or deceit of any kind. Unless one of the parties can show that enforcing the arbitration clause will cause severe deprivation of fundamental rights, courts will normally declare that the agreement is binding and order the parties to arbitrate, as they had agreed to do in the contract.

JURISDICTION OF DISPUTES INVOLVING NATIONAL GOVERNMENTS

The previous discussion concerned the jurisdiction of national courts over private parties and companies. Further legal problems exist when the government of a nation is itself involved in commercial activity or where the legal dispute involves the actions of a government.

THE ACT OF STATE DOCTRINE

sovereignty: Each nation's right to decide and determine issues within its borders without interference or control from other nations.

Every national government develops and implements its own foreign policy and engages in diplomatic efforts to benefit its national interests and those of its own citizens. Each nation is independent and expects to be able to make its own decisions free from the control of other countries. This **sovereignty** of each nation is a very important principle of international law. The power to conduct foreign policy typically resides in the executive branch of government, both in the United States and in other countries. As a means of allowing foreign governments to establish and develop their own policies and official actions, without being subjected to court review in another country, international law has developed the **Act of State Doctrine**.

Act of State Doctrine: A principle of law that holds that the courts of one nation will not judge the legality of the actions of other nations' governments.

This theory holds that the courts of one nation will not examine the validity of an action taken by a foreign government within its own territory. The Act of State Doctrine thus guarantees respect for the sovereignty of foreign nations by prohibiting U.S. courts from asserting jurisdiction over challenges to acts and actions by officials of those states. Therefore, even though an act by a foreign government might violate U.S. laws if committed here, the Act of State Doctrine prevents a U.S. court from deciding whether such an act was legal. This doctrine is recognized by many nations around the world. The theory can sometimes result in the denial of any legal remedy to an American business for harm caused by the acts of a foreign government.

THE FOREIGN SOVEREIGN IMMUNITIES ACT

Closely related to the Act of State Doctrine is the U.S. federal statute known as the Foreign Sovereign Immunities Act. This law states that in general "a foreign state shall be immune from the jurisdiction of the courts of the United States and of the states." The act contains several important exceptions, however, indicating situations when the foreign nation could be sued in the United States.

The primary exceptions include the following instances:

1. The foreign nation has waived its immunity.

2. The legal action is based on a "commercial activity" carried on in the United States, or even outside the United States if it causes a "direct effect" here.

3. Expropriation of property has taken place, allegedly in violation of international law.

4. The legal action seeks money damages against a foreign state for acts committed by officials or employees of that nation in the United States, which have caused death or injury or damage to property.

5. The legal action seeks to enforce an arbitration agreement or confirm an arbitration award.

6. The suit is brought to enforce a maritime lien against a vessel or cargo of a foreign state based on commercial activity of that state.

The following case examines the requirements of the "commercial activity" exception to a foreign nation's sovereign immunity under the Foreign Sovereign Immunities Act.

ANTARES AIRCRAFT V. FEDERAL REPUBLIC OF NIGERIA

999 F.2d 33 (2nd Cir. 1993)

FACTS

Antares Aircraft is a Delaware limited partnership with its principal place of business in New York. The partnership's sole asset is a DC-8-55 aircraft registered in Nigeria. According to Nigerian authorities, the former lessee of the plane had not paid certain airport landing and parking fees, and the airplane was thus detained at the airport in Lagos, Nigeria. The Nigerian Airports Authority (NAA) refused to release the airplane until all outstanding obligations were paid.

Antares' representatives negotiated with NAA for some time and finally sent roughly $100,000 from a New York bank, which was paid to NAA in Nigerian currency. The plane was then finally released after being held about five months. According to Antares, the plane had suffered physical damage due to exposure to the elements. Antares then filed this lawsuit against NAA and the Federal Republic of Nigeria (FRN) in federal court in New York to recover for conversion (the wrongful taking of another's property) and damages to the plane. The district court granted the defendants' motion to dismiss for lack of jurisdiction over the defendants, and the plaintiff appealed.

DECISION

The Second Circuit Court of Appeals focused its review on whether the activities at issue here fell into one of the exceptions to the Foreign Sovereign Immunities Act (FSIA). There was no dispute that both NAA and FRN were "foreign states" and were thus immune from suit in the United States unless one of the exceptions applied.

The Court then examined the "commercial activity" exception of the FSIA in detail. This exception provides that a foreign state is subject to the jurisdiction of U.S. courts in cases "in which the action is based . . . upon an act outside the territory of the United States in connection with a commercial activity of the foreign state elsewhere and that act causes a direct effect in the United States." 28 U.S.C. Sect. 1605(a)(2). The Court determined that the "act outside the territory of the U.S." was the allegedly wrongful detention of the plane in Nigeria. The court held that the alleged detention and collection of fees were also clearly "in connection with a commercial activity of the foreign state." Therefore, the final point of contention bearing on FSIA jurisdiction was whether the detention of the plane caused "a direct effect in the United States."

In *Republic of Argentina v. Weltover,* decided in 1992, the U.S. Supreme Court decided in another FSIA case that "an effect is direct" if it follows "as an immediate consequence of the defendant's activity." In that case, the government of Argentina had issued $1.3 million in bonds to various parties that were payable in New York in May 1986. When payment became due, Argentina tried to reschedule the due dates, and the other parties sued Argentina in federal court in New York. The government of Argentina asked that the case be dismissed. The Supreme Court found that there was jurisdiction in New York federal court, because the case concerned commercial activity and the "direct effect" of Argentina's rescheduling of the maturity dates would be in the United States, since New York was the contractually designated "place of performance."

However, in this case *(Antares),* the legal cause of action was a tort case rather than a breach of contract action. The Court said that in the contract case, the "legally significant act" was the breach of contract, which occurred in the United States. Reasoning by analogy, the Court analyzed what the legally significant act was in this tort case (in other words what wrongful act had constituted the "tort") and found it to be the detention of the plane, which had occurred in Nigeria.

However, the U.S. federal court might still possess jurisdiction if the tort committed in the foreign country had sufficient contacts with the United States to have a "direct effect" here. The plaintiff argued that there was such a direct effect because the money paid came from a New York bank and also that an American partnership suffered the loss. However, the Court was unpersuaded, finding that the money could have been sent from any bank, and the significant fact was that it had to be paid in Nigeria.

Rejecting plaintiff's argument that injury to a U.S. firm should give the court jurisdiction, the Second Circuit Court of Appeals stated that this fact alone could not satisfy the "direct effect" test, or it would basically eliminate the immunity of foreign nations. "Many commercial disputes, like the present one, can be pled [alleged by plaintiffs] as the torts of conversion or fraud and would, if appellant is correct, result in litigation concerning events with no connection to the United States other than the citizenship or place or incorporation of the plaintiff." The Court concluded that the mere fact that an American citizen or firm's wealth is diminished by a foreign tort does not constitute the "direct effect" necessary to eliminate the foreign governmental immunity intended by this statute.

The Court thus affirmed the decision of the lower court.

CASE QUESTIONS

1. The FSIA provides in general that foreign nations may not be sued in U.S. courts, but there are certain exceptions. What principal exception to the FSIA is involved in this case?
2. What would it have taken for the plaintiffs to show that the tort allegedly committed in Nigeria had a "direct effect" in the United States? Why is it that even though a U.S. partnership lost $100,000, this did not give the court jurisdiction?
3. Is this result fair to the U.S. partnership and investors? To the Nigerian government?
4. Does the U.S. limited partnership have any other possible course of legal action available?

INTERNATIONAL ORGANIZATIONS

THE UNITED NATIONS

Organized in 1945 following World War II, the United Nations (UN) is the largest and most well-known international organization. Most of the nations in the world now belong to the UN. With headquarters in New York City, the United Nations organization includes the legislative body called the General Assembly (with representatives from all member nations), the Economic and Social Council, which attempts to promote international welfare and progress, and the Security Council, which deals with important issues concerning threats to world peace and stability. There are 15 nations represented on the Security Council—5 "permanent representatives" (the United Kingdom, France, China, the United States, and Russia) and 10 non-permanent members representing all the other nations, who serve two-year terms each. Each country has one vote, but any of the permanent members may veto measures before the Security Council.

The United Nations has many major subdivisions, which, while they do not receive as much publicity as the Security Council or General Assembly, perform important tasks around the world. For example, the Food and Agricultural Organization (FAO) employs specialists in agriculture, fisheries, and other fields to assist the development of such projects in many countries. The World Health Organization (WHO) attempts to promote health and reduce disease around the world. The United Nations Educational, Scientific, and Cultural Organization (UNESCO) works to improve literacy, education, and science and to promote better understanding of the culture of all nations. The United Nations Commission on International Trade Law (UNCITRAL) has aided in developing uniform rules regarding international contracts, including the United Nations Convention on CISG, discussed earlier in this chapter.

THE WORLD COURT

The *International Court of Justice,* the principal judicial division of the United Nations, is better known as the **World Court**. This body, located in the Hague (in the Netherlands), adjudicates disputes between nations, applying general principles of international law, custom, and the teachings of experts on international law and interpreting treaties and other international conventions. The 15 judges on the World Court are elected for nine-year terms by the Security Council and General Assembly, voting separately. No two judges may be from the same country, and decisions are made by majority vote.

The World Court: An international court located in the Netherlands, which hears legal disputes between nations.

The World Court does not hear cases involving individuals or businesses, but only disputes between sovereign nations. In general, the court can only hear a dispute when the two nations agree that it do so. Although its decisions are expected to be binding, since the court has no power to enforce its judgments, the decisions are only carried out if the nations decide to do so.

For example, in 2001, in the *LaGrand* case, the World Court held that the United States had violated its duties under the Vienna Convention on Consular Relations (VCCR). In that case two German nationals sentenced to death in the U.S. were not informed they had the right to consult with their consulate, as is specified in the VCCR treaty. Article VI of the U.S. Constitution provides that treaties entered into by the U.S. are to be treated as the law of the land. The World Court ordered the U.S. to devise a remedy consistent with U.S. law—something more than the polite apology which was offered before the brothers were executed by Arizona. Yet in 2003, the same issue arose again when Osbaldo Torres, a Mexican national, was convicted of murder in Oklahoma and sentenced to death without being notified of his rights under the VCCR. Whether it was a knowing violation or not, it appears that the Justice Department had not taken strong actions to inform law enforcement officials of the obligations of the Treaty. The International Court of Justice ruled in 2004 that Torres' rights were violated because he had not been told about his rights guaranteed by the 1963 Vienna Convention. The governor of Oklahoma later granted Mr. Torres' petition to change his sentence to life in prison.

INTERNATIONAL FINANCIAL AGENCIES

THE INTERNATIONAL BANK FOR RECONSTRUCTION AND DEVELOPMENT

The International Bank for Reconstruction and Development (IBRD), a financial organization popularly called the "World Bank," was formed in 1945 following a multinational conference in Bretton Woods, New Hampshire, to create a means of making loans to countries when private sources were not readily available. More than 135 nations are now members. The World Bank has made many loans to developing countries for large-scale capital projects and was helpful to the nations of Western Europe in their rebuilding efforts following the end of World War II.

THE INTERNATIONAL MONETARY FUND

The International Monetary Fund (IMF) is associated with the World Bank and the UN. The IMF's primary functions are to stabilize currency and rates of foreign exchange worldwide and to promote a more flexible and fair international monetary system. Intergovernmental loans are available to members from the fund or from other members by using "special drawing rights." Because the IMF often demands that its members take strict budgetary measures to improve their economies, the IMF has often been controversial, especially in developing countries. Actions like price controls and reductions in government spending, taken in order to stabilize the national currency, are not always popular in the country in which they are imposed.

THE EUROPEAN UNION

HISTORY

The idea and dream of European unity has been in the minds of some for hundreds of years. As early as 1846 the novelist Victor Hugo was urging the governments of the main European powers to "form a fraternity of Europe." Many national leaders had advocated some type of union over the years, and it has finally come true. The organization now called the European Union (the EU) now comprised of 27 member nations, is actually the combination of three separate entities.

Shortly after the end of World War II, many Europeans sought to establish a more peaceful union between the nations of their region, which had been devastated by war twice in a 30-year period. Inspired by the ideas and writings of Frenchman Jean Monnet, Foreign Minister Robert Schuman of France proposed in 1950 that French and German coal and steel production be managed by a common authority through an institution that would be open to other European countries. The Treaty of Paris was signed in 1951, and the next year the European Coal and Steel Community (ECSC) began functioning, with France, West Germany, Italy, Belgium, the Netherlands, and Luxembourg as members.

The foreign ministers of the ECSC members met regularly, and in 1957 the same six nations signed the **Treaty of Rome**. This agreement established the

Treaty of Rome:
An important agreement among six nations in 1957 that created the European Economic Community (EEC), which has grown into the European Union.

European Economic Community (EEC), which created a more integrated economic system among the six member nations, and the European Atomic Energy Community (EURATOM), which was intended to develop a common approach to nuclear energy. The three organizations eventually combined efforts and became the European Community (EC). The United Kingdom (Great Britain), Denmark, and Ireland were admitted in 1973, Greece in 1981, and Spain and Portugal in 1986, bringing the EC membership to 12. Some nine years later, Austria, Sweden, and Finland joined in 1995, bringing the membership to 15. The name of the organization officially became the European Union in 1994. Then in 2004, another ten nations joined the EU—mostly former Communist countries from Eastern Europe, and two more joined in late 2006.

EU Members in 2011, and When They Joined

Year	Members
1952	Belgium, France, Germany, Italy, Luxembourg, Netherlands
1973	Denmark, Ireland, United Kingdom
1981	Greece
1986	Portugal, Spain
1995	Austria, Finland, Sweden
2004	Cyprus, Czech Republic, Estonia, Hungary, Latvia, Lithuania, Malta, Poland, Slovakia, Slovenia
2007	Bulgaria, Romania

The EEC (often called the Common Market in prior years) began the elimination of tariffs and duties among member states as early as 1958 and later established a common external tariff—that is, the provision that the same duty/tariff would be charged by all member nations on a given type of import (television sets, for example) from a nonmember country. As of the mid-1980s, however, so-called **nontariff barriers** (such as safety and health standards, product quality standards, and border controls) still caused considerable restrictions upon the free movement of people and trade among the members.

Then-EC Commission President Jacques Delors outlined a set of proposals in a 1985 white paper, designed to eliminate the remaining barriers, and create a true "single market." The EC debated and approved nearly 300 of these measures in the next several years. In 1987 the EC members entered into the **Single European Act (SEA)**, which contained important revisions to the earlier treaties, and was designed to eliminate all barriers to free trade within the EC. The SEA also set forth new decision-making mechanisms for the EC (providing the Parliament with more power) and gave the Community new responsibilities in the areas of social policy, research and technological development, and protection of the environment.

During the 1990s, the EU and its member nations worked toward **harmonization** of national laws to eliminate nontariff barriers. Each country took on the task of enacting legislation through its own law-making process to bring many of its laws and regulations into harmony with the legislation enacted by the EU. This effort was necessary to achieve the organization's goal of "free movement of goods, services, people, and capital between the member nations." For example if the French environmental regulations, worker safety rules, or product standards were significantly different from those in Denmark or Greece, then this would severely hamper the free movement and sale of goods and services across the EU. In theory, at least, goods can be produced much

nontariff barriers: Laws and regulations of one nation that tend to restrict the free flow of products into that country from other nations.

Single European Act (SEA): An EU treaty that led to the removal of many trade barriers.

harmonization: The process of making the laws of the 15 EU nations more similar to one another.

more cheaply in nations with significantly fewer labor or environment rules. Manufacturers in those countries can export heavily to markets in nations with higher standards (where it is assumed that goods cost more to produce), resulting in unfair competition.

At the same time that there is an effort to make national laws more similar through *harmonization,* the member nations and their citizens want to maintain their own individual *sovereignty.* When the EU has not legislated in an area, the member states may still enforce their own laws and standards, up to the point where regulation interferes with the "free movement of goods and services" essential to the single market. There is a constant tension and conflict in EU nations between the goal of making the laws of the member states more similar through *harmonization,* and retaining each nation's own *sovereignty.*

Especially with regard to public health, public security, safety, environmental, welfare, and morality matters, it has been agreed that member states are allowed to maintain some individual regulations, where no EU harmonization directive exists. The European Court of Justice (the highest court in the EU, discussed more fully later) has considered many cases in which business firms operating in one nation have argued that a particular national law effectively prevented them from competing in another EU country. The government of that nation generally argues that there is a valid, nondiscriminatory reason for the standard. The following case is one of the best-known European Court rulings in this line of decisions.

REWE-ZENTRAL AG V. BUNDESMONOPOLVERWALTUNG FUR BRANNTWEIN [CASSIS DE DIJON]

European Court of Justice (1979)

FACTS

Rewe-Zentral (a German company) attempted to import a French liqueur, called Cassis de Dijon, into West Germany. Rewe was denied permission to import the liqueur by the Bundesmonopolverwaltung (German importing authority). The reason for the refusal was a German law requiring that liqueur have an alcohol content of at least 32 percent. Cassis de Dijon had an alcohol content of only 15 percent to 20 percent.

Rewe-Zentral then filed a suit in Germany seeking to overturn the restriction, arguing that it was an illegal restraint on the free flow of goods within the EC. The German court asked the European Court of Justice for a preliminary ruling as to the validity of the law.

DECISION

At the time of this case, there were no EU regulations or directives dealing with the production and marketing of alcoholic beverages. Thus, EU law allowed the individual states to maintain laws regarding this subject, even if they resulted in some restriction on importation, if these provision related to the protection of public health, fiscal supervision, and the protection of the consumer.

The German government argued that the restrictions here did relate to both the protection of public health and the protection of the consumer against unfair commercial practices. The government asserted that fixing a minimum alcohol content served to protect public health by avoiding the proliferation of low-alcohol beverages on the market, which might more likely induce a tolerance toward alcohol than more highly alcoholic beverages. However, the Court of Justice rejected this contention, noting that the consumer can obtain an extremely wide range of weak or moderate alcohol products already on the market. In addition, many of the high-alcohol products currently sold on the German market "are actually consumed in a diluted form."

The German government also argued that setting the lowest limit of alcohol content at which certain liqueurs could be sold was designed to protect the consumer against unfair practices. This allegation was based on the fact that because of the high rate of taxation on alcohol in Germany, allowing a lower alcohol content beverage would produce an unfair competitive advantage. However, the Court noted that it would be simple to achieve the goal of providing information to the consumer by requiring the display of the amount of alcohol content on the package.

Therefore, the Court of Justice determined that the German law prohibiting the import of lower alcohol liqueurs did not serve a purpose important enough to take precedence over the principle of free movement of goods in the EU. It appears, said the court, that the principal effect of this requirement was to promote German alcoholic beverages having a high alcohol content by excluding products of other member states. This constituted an obstacle to trade, which violated the Treaty of Rome. In the absence of EU legislation, the doctrine of "mutual reciprocity" requires that products lawfully produced and sold in their home nation can generally be imported and marketed in other EU nations.

CASE QUESTIONS

1. What do you think the primary purpose of the German import restriction was—to protect public health, or something else?
2. What sort of national laws will be upheld under the rationale of the Court of Justice? Can you think of an example? What is the test?
3. Should the EU nations be allowed to set their own taxation rates on various products including food and drink? If so, in what circumstances?
4. If the EU enacts a directive regarding the allowable alcohol content of various beverages, will Germany still have the power to regulate alcohol within its borders?

The EU has adopted a number of directives regarding internal (within the EU) market matters. Each directive establishes an EU legal standard, which then must be adopted by appropriate implementing legislation in each member country. This process is designed to prevent one country from maintaining or enforcing a particular standard or regulation that effectively prohibits goods made in another country from being sold there (as we saw in the *Cassis de Dijon* case). If this does happen, the EU Commission may bring a legal action against that nation in the EU Court of Justice.

Continuing the move toward a "European Union," the heads of the EC nations signed a treaty in 1991 at Maastricht, Netherlands, which provided a timetable for moving to a full economic and monetary union. The **Maastricht Treaty** also included provisions designed to achieve more unified foreign and defense policies, and coordination of policies regarding education, environmental protection, consumer, and health legislation. In fact, changing the name of the organization to the "European Union" was part of the Maastricht Treaty. It took more than two years for all member nations to officially ratify the Treaty, but by 1993, all had done so.

Perhaps the most noteworthy move resulting from the Maastricht Treaty was the agreement for an EU monetary union. A common monetary unit, the **Euro** came into effect in 1999 for trade among businesses and nations. Actual "Euro" bills and coins replaced each nation's individual currency in 2002. England, Sweden and Denmark did not adopt the Euro, but kept their own types of money. Most of the other EU members have adopted and use the Euro,

Maastricht Treaty: An important EU treaty signed in 1991 which brought the EU closer to social, economic, and political union.

and have now eliminated their own separate forms of money. The Treaty of Amsterdam in 1997 (effective in 1999) gave the European Parliament a fully equal role in EU decision-making.

The EU has become the world's largest trading unit, accounting for more than 20 percent of world commerce. All EU members are parties to the General Agreement on Tariffs and Trade (GATT), and members of the World Trade Organization, which will be more fully discussed later in this chapter.

In 2004 the EU granted membership to ten additional countries: Estonia, the Czech Republic, Poland, Hungary, Slovakia, Lithuania, Latvia, Cyprus, Malta and Slovenia. In 2007, Romania and Bulgaria joined the EU, bringing the membership to 27 nations. The EU now has a population of 500 million people, and an economy of approximately $15 trillion, more than the United States. The new members, mostly former Soviet bloc nations, are relatively poor, compared with the older EU members. The EU has received applications from membership from Turkey, Croatia, and Macedonia, and is considering these nations for membership at some future time.

THE STRUCTURE OF THE EUROPEAN UNION

The Proposed EU Constitution, Its Rejection, and the EU Lisbon Treaty   As has been explained, the European Union has grown through a series of treaties, negotiated over the past 60 years. The major expansion of the European Union in 2004 and 2007, which increased the membership from 15 to 27 nations, forced EU and national leaders to begin working toward major structural updating of the organization. The four most essential legislative and judicial bodies of the EU, and their procedures and structure had been established many years earlier, when the EU membership was much smaller. Many influential leaders believed that it was time to update and revise portions of the EU structure to meet the needs of the organization as it existed in the 21st century.

A carefully selected group of 105 delegates, some from each of the 25 members at that time, plus some from soon-to-be member nations, chaired by former French President Valery Giscard d'Estaing, met often during a 16-month period in 2002 and 2003 to develop a plan for an improved EU structure. The group eventually produced a proposed EU Constitution, a massive document (more than 300 pages) which was intended to replace all the prior EU treaties with one comprehensive document. The proposed Constitution would have clarified the role of each EU institution, and specified areas where the EU should act, and those areas where the member nations should be the primary actors. The Constitution proposed the creation of important new positions including a President of the Council, and a Foreign Minister for the EU. The Constitution also included an EU anthem, motto, and other "unifying" symbols. It turned out that was too much "unification" and "federalism" for some Europeans, who are still fiercely proud of their individual nations, languages, and cultures.

The proposed constitution was then forwarded to each nation for review and comment, and an intense period of negotiation ensued. After some compromises and concessions on various issues, the leaders of all 25 EU nations signed the revised draft of an EU Constitution in Rome in 2004. In order to become effective, however, the Constitution needed to be ratified independently by each nation. After eight member nations had ratified the Constitution, public referenda in France and the Netherlands were held in spring 2005, and to the shock of many, the voters said "no" to the EU Constitution.

The rejection by the French and Dutch public left other EU leaders stunned. These nations were two of the six original members of the European Community and France had always been at the center of all EU developments. Since the Constitution stated that it would not come into effect unless all EU members unanimously ratified it, the process came to a halt. Other nations held off on public voting on the Constitution, and EU leaders declared a "period of reflection." For the next two years, leaders discussed privately what the next steps should be.

Then in 2007, under the leadership of German Prime Minister Angela Merkel, a series of meetings resulted in a draft of a new document, called a "Reform Treaty." This document was smaller and less comprehensive. This Treaty retained some, but not all of the proposed Constitution, and was structured as just another Treaty (amending the previous treaties) rather than a comprehensive new Constitution. One of the major differences in this approach was that as a treaty, it could be ratified by the national legislatures and parliaments, rather than by votes of the general population. In addition, the EU anthem, motto, and other "symbols" were dropped.

EU and national leaders met often to discuss certain controversial issues, and hammered out a final draft of the Treaty, which was then signed by all heads of state of the 27 EU members in December 2007 in Lisbon, Portugal, and became effective in late 2009. Now called the "Lisbon Treaty," it was ratified by all members through their own legislative process.

The Commission   The governing structure of the European Union is a complex combination of three main bodies handling legislative and executive affairs and one court system settling disputes and interpreting the various treaty provisions. Each legislative body, as it existed in 2011, will be described in more detail below. The European Commission (EC) performs many of the executive functions of the EU. Headquartered in Brussels, Belgium, the Commission consists of 27 members, with one Commissioner coming from each member nation. Once appointed, the commissioners work full-time for the EU in Brussels, act independently of their governments and represent the interest of the European Union as a whole. Each commissioner serves a five-year term and has responsibility for one of the commission's subdivisions, called **Directorates General**. In order to deal with further expansion, the Lisbon Treaty provides that from 2014 on, the number of Commissioners will equal 2/3 of the number of member-nations, working on a rotation system.

Directorates General: The cabinet sub-divisions of the EU Commission, each one having a particular area of responsibility.

The Directorates-General actually perform much of the work of the EU. Somewhat similar to the Cabinet agencies in the U.S. government, each Directorate focuses on a substantive area, such as agriculture, telecommunication, economic and financial affairs, or energy. The Directorates each have a full staff, who make recommendations to the Commission for regulations and directives, which the Commission might then formally propose to the Council of Ministers. The Commission has a staff of nearly 20,000 persons, most of who work for the Directorates-General.

The major roles of the Commission include the initial drafting and introduction of all EU legislation, oversight of the implementation of the EU treaties, and the application of community institutional decisions. The Commission can investigate and take legal action against persons, companies, or member nations that violate EU rules. As mentioned previously, the Commission also may initiate EU policy by making proposals to the Council of Ministers.

Another important responsibility of the Commission is the collection and disbursement of EU funds. The Commission may also negotiate trade agreements with nonmember states on behalf of the community as part of its authority to implement Council decisions.

The President of the Commission is appointed by the Council of Ministers, and approved by vote of the Parliament. We have mentioned that Mr. Jacques Delors of France served as President from 1985 to the end of 1994 and led the drive toward closer integration of the members and elimination of internal trade barriers. Jacques Santer of Luxembourg then served as President from 1995 to 1999.

Former Italian Prime Minister Romano Prodi was chosen as the EU Commission President in 1999. He emphasized greater accountability and better management of the Commission, and continued as president until 2004. Mr. Prodi has a law degree from the Catholic University of Milan, studied at Stanford and the London School of Economics, and has taught at several universities.

In fall 2004, Mr. Prodi completed his term, and the member nations, after much debate and discussion, selected Mr. Jose Manuel Durao Barroso, the Prime Minister of Portugal, to be the Commission president for the next five years. Mr. Barroso is a lawyer and former professor, who has held many important posts in Portugal, and has taught politics in the United States, Switzerland, Italy and Luxembourg. Mr. Barroso served as the leader of his center-right Social Democrat party and as Foreign Minister of Portugal, prior to becoming Prime Minister in 2002. He has described himself as a "moderate reformer" and worked to cut public spending and modify labor laws. He has deep European convictions, and is committed to the progressive integration of the EU, which his followers call "gradual federalism." Mr. Barroso was re-elected to a new 5-year term in 2009.

The High Representative for Foreign Affairs and Security Policy   One of the main innovations of the EU Lisbon Treaty creates another powerful position, called the High Representative for Foreign Affairs and Security Policy. The purpose of introducing such a role was to make the European Union's external action more effective and coherent, the High Representative becoming in effect the voice of the Union's **common foreign and security**

policy (CFSP). The first person chosen to hold this important post is Ms. Catherine Ashton of the United Kingdom, appointed in November 2009. Her role is to ensure that the European Union runs a coherent foreign policy using all the instruments at its disposal.

The Council of Ministers   The Council of Ministers is composed of officials representing the national governments of the member states. It is the primary legislative and decision-making body of the EU. The presidency of the Council has been rotating among the member nations, changing every six months. The president presides at meetings and speaks for the Council. The person who actually represents each nation at Council meetings may change from one meeting to the next. While each nation's foreign minister is most often its representative ("Minister") in the Council, at times other government officials, such as the ministers of finance, energy, social affairs, or environmental affairs, might serve as the minister for his or her nation, depending on the issues to be dealt with at that session.

Under the Lisbon Treaty, The Council of Ministers will, jointly with the European Parliament, exercise legislative and budgetary functions. It will also have policy-making and coordinating functions. Except where the Treaty provides otherwise, decisions of the Council of Ministers are to be taken by **qualified majority.** At present, where the treaties do not provide otherwise, the Council takes decisions by a majority of its members. This is rarely the case however, as treaties mainly make reference to unanimity or qualified majority. The Treaty is proposing to reverse this approach, with qualified majority voting becoming the general rule.

The EU has the power to enact various types of legislation. **Regulations** are directly effective in all EU countries and are enforced by the Commission. **Directives** are legislative enactments, which are binding as to the result to be achieved, but require each nation to enact legislation in order to achieve the mandated result. The directive itself is not automatically effective as a law in the member countries, but allows each nation flexibility to adopt its own national legislation through its own legislative bodies to reach the required standard. **Decisions** are orders directed at one specific person or member nation.

Although each nation has one minister at each Council meeting, the voting has not been equal. The more heavily populated EU nations have had more votes in Council matters than the smaller ones, under a process called **qualified majority** voting. The SEA created a system of "qualified majority" voting, which allowed many (but not all) measures to pass with a total of 255 votes (out of 345). A few important matters required a unanimous vote for approval. The various ministerial groups meet monthly to discuss issues within their area of responsibility. One of the most contentious items in the Lisbon Treaty negotiations was adapting this voting system to the enlargement of the EU to include the 12 new member nations. The following box indicates how the Lisbon Treaty made major changes in the qualified majority voting system.

regulations: A type of EU law that is directly effective in all member nations, as though it were a national law.

directive: A type of European Union law that establishes an EU standard but allows each member to enact a law in its own nation to implement the law.

decisions: EU legislation directed at one specific person or nation.

THE NEW QUALIFIED MAJORITY SYSTEM

The Lisbon Treaty states that the qualified majority is achieved when a decision is approved by member States, representing at least 65 percent of the population of the Union. In 2014 the formula will shift to require votes from 55% of the member states, representing 65% of the EU population. Furthermore, the "blocking minority" necessary to reject a proposal must include at least 4 member nations so that no three large countries could block action on their own.

Council of Ministers—Number of Votes per Country

Germany, France, Italy, and the United Kingdom	29
Spain and Poland	27
Romania	14
Netherlands	13
Belgium, Czech Republic, Greece, Hungary, and Portugal	12
Austria, Bulgaria, and Sweden	10
Denmark, Ireland, Lithuania, Slovakia, and Finland	7
Estonia, Cyprus, Latvia, Luxembourg, and Slovenia	4
Malta	3
Total:	345

"Qualified majority" needed for many decisions: 255 votes and a majority of member states

From 2014: 55% of the Member States with 65% of the population

The European Council   Currently, two times every six months, the heads of state of each member nation and the Commission president have been meeting as the Council. These meetings are called the **European Council** and have become major political and media events. The leaders discuss general EU internal policy, as well as political and foreign issues. The Lisbon Treaty recognizes the European Council as a formal part of the EU structure and creates a new position called the President of the European Council, who has a term of $2^{1}/_{2}$ years, with one renewal possible for a total of 5 years. The first president is Mr. Herman Van Rompuy of Belgium. He is a powerful new spokesperson for the EU.

European Council: A meeting, held every six months, attended by the head of state of each EU nation.

The European Parliament   The Parliament is a democratically elected body that directly represents European citizens and serves as a public forum to debate issues of importance to the EU. In past years the Parliament had certain limited powers to reject or amend legislation. However, the Lisbon

Treaty gives Parliament equal power with the Council in legislative and budgetary matters. The powers of the Parliament have been increasing over the years with each new EU treaty and agreement. The Parliament now plays an equal role with the Commission and Council of Ministers in enacting legislation and in budgetary matters. The Lisbon Treaty provides that Parliament will elect the President of the EU Commission, acting on a proposal from the EU Council.

Since 1979 the Parliament has been elected by universal suffrage in the member nations. The EU Parliament consists of 736 members in 2011, elected to five-year terms and grouped by political party, rather than by country. Many parties are currently represented, including Socialists, Christian Democrats, Liberals, Greens, Conservatives, Communists, and several others. Each member nation will have at least 6 seats, based on the population of each nation. Germany has the largest number of MPs with 99.

The Parliament has specialized committees on a number of substantive areas, working toward developing truly European policies on matters such as the internal market, energy, and industrial restructuring. The Parliament meets 3 weeks per month in Brussels, and one week per month in Strasbourg, France (near the German border). The Parliament members are supported by a staff of over 3,500 additional workers. The Reform Treaty calls for Parliament to be reduced to no more than 750 members.

European Union Bureaucracy   The work of the European Commission, the Directorates-General, and the other EU agencies is largely done by a large bureaucracy. More than 90 percent of the businesses in the EU employ fewer than 200 people. Small and medium-sized enterprises (called SMEs) are given considerable attention by the governing bodies of the EU. The great majority of new jobs created within the EU in recent years are with SMEs.

As in the United States, there is a large bureaucracy that administers most EU programs and projects. Many EU regulations hit small businesses particularly hard. Compliance costs are often higher than for larger businesses, due to many factors. Large firms have departments to deal with health, safety, and environmental regulations, while in small firms, the owners or partners must take the necessary steps to comply, in addition to their many other responsibilities.

Article 118A of the Treaty of Rome recognized these issues long ago, and provided that EU Directives "should avoid imposing administrative, financial and legal constraints in a way which would hold back the creation and development of small and medium-sized undertakings." A few years ago the EU created a Directorate General (DG 23) specifically aimed at helping such businesses. Some of the problems that DG 23 has worked on include cash flow difficulties caused by late payments, a lack of management skills and training, and the burdensome effect of EU regulations. The EU continues to devote significant money and energy to improving conditions for SMEs.

The European Court of Justice   The highest court within the EU is the European Court of Justice (ECJ). This Court is the final legal authority regarding the interpretation of EU laws, treaties, regulations, and directives. Meeting in Luxembourg, the Court consists of 27 justices—one from each member state plus a president—who are appointed by agreement of all member governments for six-year terms. Decisions are reached by a consensus, with no public disclosure of how each judge voted and no dissenting opinions. The Court has heard nearly 14,000 cases since it was established.

The Court hears complaints concerning treaty and rule violations brought by member states or by the Commission. In addition, member nations, EU institutions, and individuals can contest Commission and Council actions in the Court. Following the civil law tradition, the court may call witnesses or hire experts for help with its decisions. There are also eight Advocate-Generals, one of whom researches each case and then provides a memorandum and suggested decision to the Court. The decisions of the Court of Justice regarding EU law are supreme and overrule contrary decisions of national courts and inconsistent national laws in the member nations. In addition, the decisions of the Court are binding on all parties and are not subject to appeal. The Court has tended to support and strengthen EU institutions and policies.

Two legal theories employed by the ECJ have greatly enhanced its power as well as the potency of EU laws. The doctrine of **direct effects** holds that when an EU treaty provision, a regulation, or even a directive is clear and concise and establishes unconditional legal norms, it becomes immediately effective in all member nations and supersedes contrary national laws. Using this principle, the ECJ has determined that many treaty provisions, EU regulations, and even some EU directives have "direct effect."

Another significant legal procedure was created by the Treaty of Rome (Article 177), which gave the ECJ the authority to issue **preliminary rulings.** This process occurs when a case pending in a national court involves a question of EU law. Such referrals are discretionary with the lower courts but mandatory for the highest court of a member nation. The ECJ then hears and determines the meaning and interpretation of the EU legal issue and sends the case back to the national court. That court must implement the EU ruling as part of its final judgment. The *Cassis de Dijon* case earlier in this chapter was sent to the ECJ for just such a ruling.

In 1987, the Single European Act (SEA) established a second court, the Court of First Instance (CFI), essentially a lower court. This court has jurisdiction over ECSC matters, as well as matters involving competition, actions involving private companies and individuals, and actions brought by EU officials. The primary motivation behind the creation of this court was to relieve some of the caseload of the Court of Justice. Much employment and noncontractual liability litigation is now handled by the CFI. There is a right of appeal on points of law from the CFI to the Court of Justice.

Certain major changes were made to the judicial system by the **Treaty of Nice,** including a better distribution of competences between the two bodies and the possibility of setting up of judicial panels attached to the **Court of First Instance.**

direct effects doctrine: European Court of Justice doctrine that provides that when an EU law or treaty provision is very clear, it becomes immediately effective as law in all EU nations.

preliminary ruling: When a case in a national court of an EU member involves an issue of EU law, the case can be sent to the ECJ for a ruling on the EU law question, and then the case returns to the national court.

EU Court of Justice (ECJ): The highest court in the European Union, which makes final decisions concerning EU laws and regulations.

INTERNATIONAL TRADE: RESTRICTIONS, REGULATIONS, AND "FREE TRADE"

Most of us would agree that if a company in Japan or France wants to purchase 100 tons of potatoes or 100 automobiles from a U.S. firm, we should do whatever we can to eliminate any barriers hindering such a transaction. The proposition becomes somewhat more difficult, however, if we progress to the next logical step—that a U.S. firm should be able to purchase 100 tons of potatoes or 100 autos from a Japanese or French company anytime it wants to without restrictions. Suppose the Japanese or French firm is in direct competition with a U.S. company or that it receives some sort of subsidies or support from its government? What if a local company would have to eliminate 200 jobs due to a loss of business to the foreign company? What if the product being sold might help develop military power in a nation unfriendly to the United States?

Free and open trade across national boundaries is a desirable goal. But when that broad standard is applied to actual sales of particular products, the forces of competition, the possible loss of jobs in one location, the perceived unfairness due to social or economic conditions or government regulations or assistance, and national security questions lead to an extensive series of laws and regulations affecting international trade.

TARIFFS

The United States and most other countries have established detailed schedules of **tariffs** and **duties,** which are essentially taxes levied on goods at the time they are imported into a country. The general purpose of such tariffs is to protect domestic industries against lower cost imports. Goods are assessed duties (taxes) upon entry into this country according to the tariff (a percentage of their value, according to the appropriate schedule). The amount of the tariff depends on the type of goods and the country of origin. Tariffs also raise revenue for the government, of course.

tariff: A tax assessed on goods as they are imported into a country.

TRADE AGREEMENTS

Tariffs and taxes on goods have caused disputes since the early days of our country (remember the Boston Tea Party?) When the United States imposes high tariffs on goods imported from another nation, that country is likely to impose similar duties on U.S. goods shipped there, causing higher prices for consumers and sellers in both nations. Many treaties, both bilateral and multilateral, have been signed as an attempt to lower tariffs on exported goods and thus increase international trade. A few of them are discussed in the following sections.

NORTH AMERICAN FREE TRADE AGREEMENTS

The United States and Canada maintain the world's largest trading partnership. Canada is both the largest importer of U.S. goods and the second largest (after China) exporter of goods to the U.S. More than $524 billion of trade passed between the nations in 2010. In 1988 the countries signed the U.S.–Canada Free Trade Agreement, effective January 1, 1989, which provided for the elimination of all tariffs on trade between the nations over a 10-year period. The agreement also significantly reduced restrictions on foreign investment and trade in services between the two countries.

In late 1992, the United States, Canada, and Mexico signed the **North American Free Trade Agreement (NAFTA)**. This trilateral agreement created a huge free-trade area among the three nations, similar in size to the European Union. Since the United States and Canada already had entered into the free trade agreement discussed previously, most of the debate about NAFTA concerned Mexico. Mexico is now the third largest trading partner of the U.S. (after Canada and China), with a total of $393 billion in 2-way trade during 2010. NAFTA called for the elimination of all tariffs on imports between the above three nations. Many tariffs were eliminated immediately, and the rest were abolished over a 15-year period.

The debate over ratification of the agreement created considerable political controversy in the United States, and some discussion and debate in Mexico and Canada as well. The major labor unions and businessman/politician H. Ross Perot argued vigorously that the treaty would result in the loss of thousands of U.S. manufacturing jobs. They feared that many businesses would move operations to Mexico, due to lower labor costs and less stringent environmental and labor regulations there.

The United States negotiated certain "side agreements" to NAFTA with Canada and Mexico during the summer of 1993 in which the nations agreed to create two commissions to hear and decide allegations that one nation had been lax in the enforcement of its labor or environmental laws, thereby affecting NAFTA's free competition and trade provisions. The commissions were given the power to levy fines up to $20 million. If the violations continue, trade sanctions such as tariffs and quotas can be imposed on products of the offending country.

President Bill Clinton strongly supported the pact (which had been negotiated by former President George H. W. Bush during the last year of his administration), asserting that the agreement would enhance the global competitiveness of U.S. firms and would lead to the creation of many new U.S. jobs as companies expanded to serve the needs of all of North America. He also argued that United States exports to Mexico would increase, since the average Mexican tariff assessed on U.S. goods imported into Mexico (before NAFTA) was 10 percent, while U.S. tariffs on Mexican imports only averaged 4 percent. After a vigorous debate over the positive and negative aspects of free trade, the U.S. Congress approved NAFTA, and the agreement became effective in 1994.

After more than 17 years of operation, NAFTA is still controversial. Trade between the three nations has increased sharply—Canada and Mexico are now the first and second leading destination for U.S. exports. Mexican tariffs have been greatly reduced.

Many unions, employee organizations, and other groups argue that U.S. jobs have been eliminated because of NAFTA. Clearly some American companies have closed factories in the U.S. and moved operations to Mexico. However, it is also true that some American jobs have been created to handle increased imports coming from Mexico and Canada. After NAFTA began its existence, the members intended to invite other nations to join, starting with Chile. However, because of the continuing controversy over NAFTA, and

North American Free Trade Agreement (NAFTA): An agreement between Canada, Mexico, and the United States that eliminated tariffs on goods traded between the three nations over a 15-year period.

because Congress has been reluctant to enact "fast track" legislation (which allows the U.S. president to negotiate treaties without Congress having the power to attach amendments), no further negotiations about expanding NAFTA have occurred. Furthermore, other nations are beginning to take leadership roles concerning the expansion of free trade in the Western Hemisphere.

REGIONAL TRADE AGREEMENTS IN SOUTH AMERICA

Mercosur   Mercosur, the "Common Market of the South," (*Mercado Comun del Sur,* in Spanish) is the largest trading bloc in South America. Mercosur's primary interest has been eliminating obstacles to internal trade, like high tariffs, income inequalities, or conflicting technical requirements for bringing products to market.

The Mercosur trade bloc's purpose, as stated in the 1991 Treaty of Asunción, is to allow for free trade between member states, with the ultimate goal of full South American economic integration. Mercosur's full members include Argentina, Brazil, Paraguay, Uruguay, and most recently (2006), Venezuela. However, Venezuela's entry has not yet been fully ratified by Paraguay nor Brazil, and some experts wonder if Mercosur will reorient itself as a political force under the prodding of Venezuelan President Hugo Chavez. Brazil is the region's largest economy with a GDP of nearly $1.6 trillion and, together with Argentina, has been the leading force in the development of Mercosur.

The population of Mercosur countries totals more than 270 million people and members have a collective output of $2.4 trillion, accounting for over 75 percent of South America's GDP (PDF). It is now the world's fourth-largest trading bloc, after the European Union (EU), North American Free Trade Agreement (NAFTA), and the Association of South East Asian Nations (ASEAN). Mercosur advocates believe that the bloc has contributed to a significant reduction in poverty in the member countries.

Mercosur institutions include the policy-making Common Market Council and the Common Market Group, which implements policies and monitors compliance with the council's decisions. The Mercosur presidency rotates between member states every six months. A Mercosur parliament was inaugurated in December 2006, and meets in the Uruguayan capital Montevideo, where Mercosur headquarters are located.

Mercosur's five associate members—Chile, Bolivia, Colombia, Ecuador, and Peru—do not enjoy full voting rights or complete access to markets of Mercosur's full members. Of these countries, Bolivia is being considered for full membership. But the decision is complicated by Mercosur's history with Bolivia, as well as the rules for admission. Bolivian President Evo Morales has criticized Mercosur, stating that the organization was primarily a tool to benefit businessmen and wealthy people, instead of the poor people.

In December 2004 Mercosur signed a cooperation agreement with the Andean Community trade bloc (CAN) and published a joint letter of intention for future negotiations towards integrating all of South America. Mercosur has now granted associate membership to the CAN member nations.

Mercosur: The "Common Market of the South" is an organization aimed at reducing trade barriers and tariffs. Members are Brazil, Argentina, Paraguay, and Uruguay.

The Andean Community (CAN)

The Andean Community of Nations (*Comunidad Andina de Naciones* in Spanish, thus the acronym, CAN) is a trade bloc comprising the South American countries of Bolivia, Colombia, Ecuador and Peru. The trade bloc was called the Andean Pact until 1996 and came into existence with the signing of the Cartagena Agreement in 1969. Its headquarters are located in Lima, Peru. The Andean Community has 98 million inhabitants living in an area of 4,700,000 square kilometers. Chile and Venezuela were formerly members of the group, but in 1976, Augusto Pinochet withdrew Chile from the Andean Community, claiming economic incompatibilities. In 2006 President Hugo Chavez announced that Venezuela would withdraw from the Andean Community, claiming the FTA agreements signed by Colombia and Peru with the USA caused irreparable damage to the community. However, Venezuela has not yet completed the formal procedures for withdrawal, so its status is somewhat unclear.

Recently, with the new cooperation agreement with Mercosur, the Andean Community gained four new associate members: Argentina, Brazil, Paraguay and Uruguay as of 2005. This move reciprocates the actions of Mercosur, which granted associate membership to all the Andean Community nations. Chile also became an associate member of CAN in fall 2006 and may re-join as a full member in the future.

UNASUR

Discussion and negotiations are underway to combine the two South American regional trading organizations, Mercosur and the Andean Community—as part of a continuing process of South American integration. The proposed new entity would be called The **Union of South American Nations** (*Unión de Naciones Suramericanas* or UNASUR, in Spanish).

At the Third South American Summit, held in Peru in December 2004, presidents or representatives from twelve South American nations (Argentina, Bolivia, Brazil, Chile, Colombia, Ecuador, Guyana, Paraguay, Peru, Suriname, Uruguay and Venezuela) signed the *Cuzco Declaration*, a two-page statement of intent, announcing the foundation of the South American Community. The leaders announced their intention to model the new community after the European Union, including a common currency, parliament, and passport.

In November 2006, the same 12 nations waived visa requirements for tourism travel between nationals of those twelve countries, so that citizens of each nation can enter the other members by showing a national identity card. One of the objectives of UNASUR is the creation of a single market, beginning with the elimination of tariffs on some products by 2014 and all products by 2019.

The UNASUR Constitutive Treaty was signed on May 23, 2008, at the Third Summit of Heads of State, held in Brasília, Brazil. According to the Constitutive Treaty, the Union's headquarters will be located in Quito, Ecuador. The South American Parliament will be located in Cochabamba, Bolivia, while the head-quarters of its bank, the Bank of the South are located in Caracas, Venezuela.

The presidents of the member nations will have an annual meeting, which will have the superior political mandate. The first meeting was in Brasília (Brazil) in September 2005. The second meeting was in Cochabamba (Bolivia) in December 2006. The third meeting was held in Brasília on 23 May 2008.

The temporary Presidency is held for a year and rotates among the member countries between each UNASUR meeting. The ministers of foreign affairs of each country will meet once every six months. They will formulate concrete proposals of action and of executive decision. The President of the Mercosur's permanent representatives committee and the director of the Mercosur's department, and the Andean Community's general secretary, will also be present at these meetings.

On 4 May 2010, at an extraordinary heads of state summit held in Campana, near Buenos Aires, former Argentine President Néstor Kirchner was unanimously elected the first Secretary-General of UNASUR for a two-year term. This new office was conceived as a first step towards the establishment of a permanent bureaucratic body for the supranational union, eventually super-seding Mercosur and CAN political bodies. Unfortunately, President Kirchner died from a heart attack in the fall of 2010, requiring the election of a new Secretary-General.

On 1 December 2010, Uruguay became the ninth nation to ratify the UNASUR treaty, thus giving the union full legality. The Constitutive Treaty entered into force on 11 March 2011, and UNASUR became a legal entity during a meeting of Foreign Ministers in Mitad del Mundo, Ecuador, where Ecuador President Rafael Correa placed the foundation stone for the Secretariat Headquarters, which will be named after former president Kirchner. Ecuadorian Foreign Affairs Ricardo Patiño said that as UNASUR becomes effective it will help political understanding and coordination among countries of the region and integration in areas such as infrastructure, health, education, social inclusion and energy development among others.

Also at this meeting, Colombia's former Deputy Foreign Secretary Emma Mejía, an expert in International Law and Social Inclusion was chosen as Secretary-General for twelve months beginning April 2011, while Venezuela's Minister of Electricity Ari Rodriguez, an energy expert, will hold the post on the following twelve months.

Free Trade Area of America (FTAA): A proposed free trade area that would include all 34 democratic nations of South, Central, and North America.

The Free Trade Area of the Americas

In 1994 a meeting was held by the leaders of the 34 democratic nations of the Western Hemisphere to discuss the formation of an organization which would promote, reduce, or eliminate trade barriers throughout the Americas. The United States has taken a leading role in pushing for the creation of such an organization. Additional summit meetings of the 34 nations were held every two or three years thereafter, in Santiago, Chile; Quebec, Canada, and many working groups were formed. At the most recent meeting in Mar del Plata, Argentina in 2005, only 26 nations attended and no significant agreements were reached.

As with trade issues internationally, several problem areas caused negotiations to stall. The developed nations (particularly the United States) wanted expanded trade in services and increased intellectual property rights, while less developed nations (led by Brazil) sought an end to agricultural subsidies and freer trade in agricultural goods. Also the populist movements in South America, with Venezuelan President Chavez and Bolivian President Evo Morales in the lead, have strongly opposed the FTAA as nothing more than "American annexation and imperialism." It appears, in mid-2011, that the push for a FTAA has stalled, especially with the growing interest in a South American common market, such as the proposed UNASUR.

THE WORLD TRADE ORGANIZATION (WTO) AND THE GATT

A group of 50 countries met in Cuba in 1947 and reached an agreement called the General Agreement on Tariffs and Trade (GATT). The GATT has been amended several times and has become the primary multilateral treaty aimed at reducing trade barriers among nations all over the world. Since 1947 several additional "rounds" of GATT negotiations have taken place among nations (each round often lasts several years) to deal with various trade issues. For example, the "Tokyo Round" lasted from 1973 to 1979, and the "Uruguay Round" began in 1986 and was only completed in 1994. The length of each round has led one commentator to nickname GATT as "The General Agreement to Talk and Talk." At the beginning of 1995, the World Trade Organization (WTO) came into existence and took over all GATT functions and enforcement of the GATT treaties.

most favored nation (MFN): The term used to describe the rule that if one nation gives a good tariff rate to certain goods from one WTO member, it must give the same rate to all WTO members.

The two primary purposes of the WTO are the promotion of free trade and the reduction of trade barriers between nations. One major principle of GATT and the WTO is called **most favored nation** status (MFN). Under this principle, if one country grants MFN status (preferential treatment regarding tariffs) to another member nation, it must do so to all WTO members. In other words, if Spain and the United States negotiate a low tariff rate on television sets imported into Spain from the United States, Spain must use the same tariff rate on television imports from other WTO countries, without each country having to negotiate separately with Spain.

The second major GATT/WTO principle is **national treatment.** This theory prevents imported goods from being treated differently from domestic goods or being subjected to additional taxes, once they have cleared customs. For example, suppose a television set manufactured in Japan has been imported into this country and the importer has paid the required tariff. From then on, the item must not be subjected to any additional requirements not imposed on U.S. goods.

In addition to tariffs, there are a number of other obstacles to total free trade, called **nontariff barriers**. National laws and regulations often contain requirements and practices that may intentionally or unintentionally favor domestic industries over foreign firms. Laws setting product safety and labeling requirements and establishing preferences in government procurement programs for domestic products ("Buy American" acts) are but two examples of nontariff barriers.

The Tokyo Round of the GATT negotiations (1973–1979) led to several agreements directed at reducing nontariff barriers by establishing international codes related to product standards, export subsidies, and government procurement. These agreements should have applied to all GATT nations, but many countries—especially the less-developed nations—did not sign the agreements. When the nations that had agreed to the new codes decided that MFN status would be given only to those who had signed the agreements, it caused a break in the principle of applying MFN status universally.

Other problems with earlier versions of GATT, including its failure to cover such important issues as intellectual property, agriculture, services, and investment matters, have led to the creation of several regional trading blocs. We have discussed the European Union, NAFTA and Mercosur. Other regions of the world have also established organizations to further trade and cooperation, such as the Economic Community of West African States (ECOWAS), the Caribbean Community (CARICOM), and the Association of Southeast Asian Nations (ASEAN).

The 1994 GATT agreement covered a wide scope of issues and made a significant difference in the world of international commerce. It is the first global trade agreement containing provisions dealing with subjects such as commercial services, agriculture, and software. The pact allows for easier investment in foreign countries by nonnationals, provides for easier entry into one nation by those who provide commercial services, and creates more international protection for "intellectual property" subjects such as patents, copyrights (including computer software), and trademarks. Of course the 1994 agreement also established the WTO to carry out the terms of the treaty.

The WTO is now the most important world organization concerning international trade. As of April 20, 2011, there were 153 countries who were members of the WTO. China is now a full member of the WTO after complex negotiations with the U.S. and the European Union regarding the conditions of its entry. Russia has been seeking membership for more than 15 years but is still in difficult negotiations with the United States, China, and other nations over tough trade issues. The WTO establishes and enforces the rules for international trade (established by GATT and other treaties) regarding

national treatment: The GATT/WTO principle that once goods are legally imported into a nation, they must be treated the same as goods produced in that nation.

manufactured goods, services (such as banking, insurance, and more), regulations dealing with intellectual property (called T.R.I.P.s), textiles and clothing, and agricultural products.

In carrying out the GATT agreements, the WTO is the primary forum for the expansion of free trade (by removing tariffs and nontariff barriers) and for the settlement of international trade disputes. The primary governing and law making body of the WTO is the Ministerial Conference, composed of the top trade officials of all the member nations.

While only a few years ago the WTO was an organization known only to a few international business people and government officials, it has become quite a well-known and sometimes controversial organization in recent years. A major WTO Ministerial Conference meeting held in Seattle, Washington (USA) in 1999 was scheduled to consider discussions between nations over trade issues, such as unilateral trade sanctions by nations and the allowable level of government support of local business and agriculture.

However, the Seattle WTO conference was overshadowed by major demonstrations and protests from many international groups who opposed further expansion of free trade and "globalization" of business. These groups asserted that the extension of "free trade" laws had enriched the most developed nations and large multinational corporations, while causing significant injury to less developed countries and smaller local business firms. The protestors also argued that unbridled free trade had led to increased unemployment in many parts of the world and also had damaged the environment. The protests and unrest caused the Seattle conference to end without reaching agreement.

In the years since 1999, every major WTO meeting and those of other international organizations (such as the World Bank and IMF) have been met with demonstrations and vigorous protests by those opposed to further "globalization." Some of these confrontations have turned violent, with injuries and deaths resulting from interactions with police.

A major WTO meeting, the 4th Ministerial Conference in Doha, Qatar in 2001 resulted in several agreements by which the member nations promised to try to reach consensus on further development of the WTO. However, the progress on reaching such agreements has been difficult, and the next several ministerial conferences, in Cancun, Mexico, in 2003, in Hong Kong in December 2005, and the 7th Ministerial conference in Geneva in 2009, all made some progress on negotiations but failed to reach a final agreement. Negotiations are continuing but the developed and developing countries are having a difficult time agreeing on reducing subsidies for agriculture in the wealthy nations and removing tariffs and barriers to imports in the less-developed countries—and several other issues.

THE DOHA DEVELOPMENT AGENDA

PRINCIPLES FOR THE DOHA DEVELOPMENT AGENDA

The World Trade Organisation's fourth Ministerial Conference in November 2001 resulted in some far-reaching decisions on the future development of the WTO:

- Launch a new round of trade negotiations—the Doha Development Agenda (DDA)—comprising both further trade liberalisation and new rule-making, underpinned by commitments to strengthen substantially assistance to developing countries.
- Help developing countries implement the existing WTO agreements.
- Interpret the TRIPS Agreement in a manner that ensures Members' rights under TRIPS to take actions to protect public health.

WTO Dispute Settlement Procedure   One of the major features of the WTO is the establishment of a Dispute Settlement Procedure. The process is intended to resolve conflicts through a neutral arbitration system, rather than have "trade wars" erupt when nations disagree on a trade-related issue and impose unilateral sanctions.

Originally the GATT dispute resolution system included a process for arbitration of disputes, but the losing country was able to block the implementation of the decision, if it did not want to comply. The dispute settlement process has been strengthened under the WTO and one nation can no longer block the WTO panel decisions. The primary role is given to the WTO Dispute Settlement Body. The process of dispute resolution includes the following steps:

1. A party who believes another nation is violating a WTO provision can ask for consultation to seek a settlement by direct negotiation with the other country.

2. If no settlement is reached, the complaining party can request that a WTO panel be formed to hear the case.

3. A panel of three to five experts will be formed and will hear the arguments of both parties concerning the issue.

4. Other member nations with a substantial interest in the case may make written comments before the panel as well.

5. The panel will make and issue an Objective Assessment of the case and determine whether the terms of a GATT/WTO agreement have been violated.

6. The decision will be forwarded to the Dispute Settlement Body, unless one party files for appeal.

7. If one party appeals, an Appellate Body of three people will hear the appeal, and may uphold, modify, or reverse the decision. Its decision is then forwarded to the Dispute Settlement Body.

8. When the Dispute Settlement Body receives the case, it can accept the decision or vote by consensus to reject it. If the decision is accepted, the Body can recommend to the offending party some ways that it could come into compliance with the WTO rules, and the party has 30 days to respond.

9. If the offending party does not comply and the trade violation is not removed, the Body may authorize the complaining party to impose a retaliatory trade sanction against the offending party. The sanction should be imposed on the same type of goods or industry in question, be temporary, and in an amount equal to the impact of the illegal practices.

The WTO dispute resolution system has sometimes been controversial. It is clearly positive to have an international organization become involved in resolving trade disputes between nations, rather than have each nation resort to sanctions, such as increased tariffs and quotas on imports, when a controversy arises. However, the referral of the dispute to an international body takes away some of the nation's sovereignty in that it deprives the national government of the right to unilaterally impose sanctions when it feels its rights have been violated.

The United States, in particular, has praised the WTO process when it wins a panel decision but has criticized the procedure when a panel has found that a U.S. practice violated a GATT or WTO provision. Although the United States has won far more cases than it has lost, there have been calls to overhaul the WTO panel dispute settlement system after a big case is decided adversely.

U.S. LAWS CONTROLLING IMPORTS AND EXPORTS

In opposition to the movement toward reducing trade barriers between nations (exemplified by the WTO and NAFTA) is the strong domestic political pressure governments feel to protect and promote the commercial, manufacturing, and agricultural products of their own countries. To further this objective, many laws have been enacted all over the world, as well as in the United States, that allow a national government to assist domestic companies and/or to impose sanctions against foreign firms in particular circumstances. The overall purpose of such measures is either to attempt to increase domestic exports or to slow certain imports into the country. At the same time, national security concerns may dictate that some governmental controls be placed on the sale and export of sensitive military and high technology products. A closer look at certain U.S. laws restricting imports and exports is therefore in order.

LAWS REGULATING IMPORTS

A series of U.S. laws allows the federal government to impose quotas on the import of certain foreign goods or to assess duties and tariffs on goods when the exporter has engaged in unfair practices of some kind.

Section 337 of the Tariff Act of 1920 provides protection to domestic industries against "unfair methods of competition" and other unfair acts in connection with the importation of goods into the United States. The affected domestic industry must file a complaint with the International Trade Commission (ITC), a U.S. federal regulatory agency, which investigates the complaint and issues a decision. The President then reviews the agency's order and may uphold or overturn the ITC's recommendations.

Section 337 has most often been used in connection with violations of a patent and trademark infringement but may apply to a wide variety of unfair trade acts and practices. Sanctions may include cease-and-desist orders and permanent bans on certain products. For years American businesses claimed they were losing billions of dollars due to illegal use of their trademarks and patents and to other violations of intellectual property rights occurring in foreign countries. Congress strengthened the law in 1988 to eliminate the requirement that industries show economic injury due to the infringement and authorized the President to identify and name countries that were not protecting U.S. patents and intellectual property rights.

> **Section 337:** A U.S. law which permits sanctions against imports, where unfair trade acts are shown.

One portion of the Trade Act of 1974 (called **Section 201**) allows U.S. industries to seek temporary relief when they have been seriously injured by foreign imports, even if no unfair trade practices were used. The claimant must file a Section 201 petition with the ITC, which, if it determines that the domestic industry has suffered an injury, may establish quotas or higher duties on the imported products. The relief usually lasts for no more than five years, and the affected industry must show how the temporary assistance will allow the claimant to better adjust to foreign competition in the long term. The President must review the relief ordered and may affirm or overturn the order, if he finds that such relief would not serve the national economic interest.

> **Section 201:** A U.S. law which allows the temporary imposition of quotas or tariffs on certain imports, where a U.S. producer is seriously harmed.

Dumping   The practice called dumping occurs when a foreign firm sells its goods in the United States at a price lower than that charged in its home nation or sells the goods at a price below the seller's actual cost of production. Not only the United States but also some 40 other countries have antidumping laws. The GATT specifies that this practice is unfair and condemns it "if it causes or threatens material injury to an established industry in the territory of a contracting party or retards the establishment of a domestic industry." The motive for such dumping could be an attempt by a large company with many products to capture a market share for a particular product by selling below cost for a period of time.

> **dumping:** The sale of a product in a foreign country for a lower price than that charged in the home country, or below the cost of production.

In the United States, the complaining party files a petition with the ITC, which holds hearings to determine whether or not illegal dumping has occurred. The ITC may impose a duty on the imported products to raise the price of the imported goods up to the cost of production or to the sales price of the goods in the exporting country. Sometimes the proceedings are hotly contested, and become quite complicated, as the following recent case demonstrates.

In the Language of the Court

ALTX, INC. V. UNITED STATES

370 F. 3d 1108 (Fed.Cir. 2004)

Appealed from: United States Court of International Trade

Opinion by Judge Schall

FACTS

This is an anti-dumping case. The goods at issue are circular seamless stainless steel hollow products ("CSSSHPs"), of which there are two types, hot- and cold-finished. Production of either type begins with an unfinished stainless steel billet. A central cavity is formed using a hot extrusion process to drill an axial hole through the entire billet. The billet is then heated, and a die is forced through the hole to expand the cavity. The final step in the production of a hot-finished CSSSHP is to reheat the billet and force it through a die and over an internal mandrel.

Domestic, European, and Japanese producers all supply the U.S. market for CSSSHPs. U.S. subsidiaries of European companies that produce both hot- and cold-finished CSSSHPs instigated the present investigation by petitioning Commerce to review the impact of sales of Japanese CSSSHP imports ("subject imports") beginning in 1997. In conducting its part of the investigation, the International Trade Commission collected industry and shipment data for subject imports, as well as for CSSSHPs imported from non-Japanese producers ("non-subject imports"). The Commission used this data to create a statistical model that correlated the level of subject imports with the health of the domestic industry ("COMPAS"). Because many of the results predicted by the COMPAS model were contradicted by empirical data, the Commission declined to include the model in its final determination.

In August 2000, having found that the domestic CSSSHP industry was *not materially injured nor threatened with material injury* by reason of subject imports during the period covered by the investigation, the Commission announced its final negative determination.

By a 4–2 vote, the Commission found that the statutory factors for injury were not met. The Commission concluded that the volume, the price effects, and the overall economic impact of subject imports were not individually significant and did not cause material injury to the performance of the domestic CSSSHP industry.

In evaluating the volume of subject imports, the Commission was persuaded by declines in the quantity, value, and market share of subject (Japanese) imports between 1998 and 1999, and again between interim 1999 and interim 2000. Although subject import volume rose sharply between 1997 and 1998, it decreased consistently after that period. The Commission thus concluded that subject import volume was not significant during the period 1997–2000.

Next, the Commission assessed the price effects of the subject (Japanese) imports on the domestic industry, by evaluating (a) the significance of price underselling of the subject imports relative to like domestic products, and (b) the price depression and/or suppression caused by that underselling. Though underselling was prevalent, the Commission determined that corresponding price effects were minimal and could be attributed to significant declines in raw material costs and the "softening" of domestic demand, rather than to the low price of subject imports.

Finally, in measuring the impact of subject (Japanese) imports on the domestic industry, the Commission weighed a number of factors before concluding that "[d]espite the mixed overall performance of the domestic industry, its financial picture actually improved from 1997 to 1998, when subject imports registered their most significant increase, and remained above the 1997 level in 1999 as subject imports fell and nonsubject imports gained a substantial share of the domestic market." Because a negative correlation between subject imports and the financial performance of the domestic producers could not be proven, the impact of imports on the industry was deemed insignificant. In the absence of findings of significance for any of the three statutory factors required by section 1677(7)(C), the Commission reached a final negative determination of no material injury.

Altx appealed the Commission's final negative determination to the Court of International Trade, which remanded the case to the Commission for reconsideration of several factors. Finding that the Commission had impermissibly conflated the two distinct prongs of the price effects analysis (the significance of underselling and the causal connection, if any, between subject imports and price depression or suppression), the court stated that it was necessary for the Commission to reconsider "whether a lack of correlation between underselling and the condition of the domestic industry remains."

On remand, a new Commission majority reversed the initial position of the Commission and entered an affirmative determination of injury (Altx II) without holding any further hearings. Instead, the dispositive factor was the replacement of one of its members, who had initially voted against a finding of injury, with a new member, Commissioner Denis Devaney, who voted to join the original dissent. The new Commission majority concluded that, because the quantity of subject imports doubled between 1997 and 1998 and continued to exceed shipments of the domestic industry in 1999, subject import volume was significant. In the new Commission majority's view, the increase in subject import volume was the reason for the decrease in the domestic industry's U.S. shipments, notwithstanding an increase in domestic demand.

The Japanese producers appealed the affirmative First Remand Determination to the Court of International Trade, arguing that "the [new] Commission majority did not adequately address material arguments raised in . . . post-hearing briefs," Altx II. The Court of International Trade agreed, and again remanded the case with specific instructions for the Commission to consider the signif-

icance of subject import volume within the context of the conditions of competition.

An additional ground supported the Court of International Trade's remand in Altx II. The new Commission majority failed to address the possible relationship between the bankruptcy of a large domestic producer, ALTech, and the poor performance of the domestic industry. *In determining whether a domestic industry has been injured, the Commission must distinguish between harm that is caused by imports and harm that is caused by other factors;* in determining injury, it cannot attribute to imports the impact of other factors. The Japanese producers presented evidence that the ALTech bankruptcy significantly contributed to declines in domestic production.

In Altx II the court explained, the statutory directive to analyze the industry "as a whole" compels an evaluation of all material factors raised by the parties that would render a more accurate reading of the health of the industry. Therefore, if the Commission determines to discount a particular factor that bears on the relevant financial indicators, it must give substantial evidence to support its reasoning. The court finds that the Commission has failed to do so.

Thus the case was again remanded to the Commission. This time, upon remand, the Commission reinstated its original finding of no negative impact. The membership of the Commission had changed again, and the Commission addressed in greater depth the arguments made by domestic producers.

The domestic producers appealed the second negative determination to the Court of International Trade. In Altx III, the court affirmed the latest finding of the Commission, because "the Commission complied with the court's instructions in Altx I to 'address significant arguments and evidence which seriously undermines its reasoning and conclusions.'" This appeal to the Court of Appeals for the Federal Circuit followed.

THE ISSUES AND PROCEDURE

The antidumping laws protect United States industries against the domestic sale of foreign manufactured goods at prices below the fair market value of those goods in the foreign country. Under the statutory scheme established by the Tariff Act of 1930 . . . American industries may petition for relief from imports that are sold in the United States at less than fair value ('dumped'), or which benefit from subsidies provided by foreign governments. If a less than fair value sale of imported goods results in actual or threatened injury to the corresponding domestic industry, a duty may be imposed on the imported merchandise. *Micron Tech., Inc. v. United States,* 117 F.3d 1386 (Fed. Cir. 1997). The duty is "equal to the amount by which the normal value exceeds the export price . . . for the merchandise."

The Process of an Antidumping Investigation. An antidumping investigation is initiated when the domestic industry petitions the Department of Commerce ("Commerce") to investigate allegations of dumping by foreign manufacturers. After Commerce confirms that the petition "contains information . . . supporting the allegations," it makes a preliminary determination as to whether the imported merchandise is being sold, or is likely to be sold, at less than fair value. While Commerce is making its preliminary determination, the Commission makes a preliminary determination as to whether there is a "reasonable indication" that an industry in the United States is "materially injured or is threatened with material injury . . . by reason of imports of the subject merchandise [or] that imports of the subject merchandise are not negligible." If either of the Commission's preliminary determinations is in the negative, the antidumping investigation is terminated.

If the investigation is not terminated, Commerce makes its final determination "as to whether the subject merchandise is being, or is likely to be, sold in the United States at less than its fair value." At the same time, the Commission finalizes its determination as to the existence or threat of material injury. If both the injury inquiry by the Commission and the less than fair value determination by Commerce are "answered in the affirmative," Commerce issues the appropriate final

antidumping order. *Duferco Steel,* 296 F.3d at 1089; see 19 U.S.C. 1673d(c)(2) (2000).

A final determination by the Commission can be appealed to the Court of International Trade, which reviews the Commission's findings to ensure that they are not "unsupported by substantial evidence on the record, or otherwise not in accordance with law." Should the court determine that the Commission's determination is unsupported by substantial evidence or otherwise incorrect, the case will be remanded to the Commission with specific instructions. Otherwise, the Court of International Trade will affirm the Commission's findings, paving the way for an appeal to this court. Commerce's final determination also can be appealed to the Court of International Trade. There, it is reviewed under the same standard that applies to the Commission's final determination. Id. §1516a(b)(1)(B)(i); see *Yancheng Baolong Biochemical Prods. Co. v. United States,* 337 F.3d 1332, 1333 (Fed. Cir. 2003).

DECISION

Under the "substantial evidence" standard, *we must affirm a Commission determination if "it is reasonable and supported by the record as a whole, even if some evidence detracts from the Commission's conclusion." Atlantic Sugar,* 744 F.2d at 1562–64. For the reasons that follow, we agree with Japanese producers and the Commission that substantial evidence supports the views of the Commission on each of the matters raised by Altx on appeal. Accordingly, finding neither legal error nor insufficient evidence in the Commission's Second Remand Determination, we affirm the decision of the Court of International Trade.

We have closely examined the empirical data in the record and determined it to be more useful than conclusions based on the results of the COMPAS model. While COMPAS has been a tool available to the Commission, it alone is not a substitute for considering the factors specified in the statute and the data on the record. In fact, it is well settled that economic models "based on a set of assumptions, may be outweighed by real world data." In this investigation in particular, we find this to be the case.

Neither do we find persuasive Altx's arguments regarding the weight attributed to non-subject imports. The Commission is not required to determine that non-subject imports are significant in order to conclude the subject imports are not significant. *Gerald Metals, Inc. v. United States,* 132 F.3d 716, 719–20 (Fed. Cir. 1997). Non-subject import volume is just one of numerous factors the Commission may consider in its evaluation of the causal relationship between subject imports and domestic industry performance. The Commission's finding that the increase in non-subject imports may have contributed to the decline of the domestic industry permits an inference that subject imports were unlikely to have caused the decline. We review the Commission's findings only to ensure that they are without legal error and supported by substantial evidence. We find that that is the case here.

CONCLUSION

We hold that the Court of International Trade did not abuse its discretion when it remanded the First Remand Determination to the Commission. We further hold that the Second Remand Determination is supported by substantial evidence and is free of legal error. The decision of the Court of International Trade in Altx III is therefore AFFIRMED.

CASE QUESTIONS

1. Describe the complex process used to make a final determination of illegal "dumping."
2. What did Altx and the other U.S producers allege about the Japanese producers, to attempt to prove that "dumping" had occurred?
3. In Altx II, what did the Court of International Trade find wrong with the determination made by the International Trade Commission?
4. What was the main rationale for the final decision of the appellate court (Court of Appeals for the Federal Circuit) in the excerpted case?

Countervailing Duty   Another section of U.S. trade law is aimed at protecting domestic producers against unfair competition from imports that are substantially subsidized by a foreign government. The governments of most nations undertake programs designed to assist their own manufacturers in order to promote economic growth in their countries. However, subsidies such as grants and extremely low-interest or below-market-rate loans, which are available only to manufacturers of goods being exported, may distort the function of a free, competitive international market. When a U.S. industry can show that such a subsidy from a foreign nation with respect to a particular product is causing injury to a U.S. firm, a countervailing duty may be sought. Such a duty or tariff will be added to the cost of the offending goods or to other products of the same firm when they are imported into this country.

Again, the complainant files a petition with the ITC, which makes a determination whether the U.S. firm is suffering injury. Then, the International Trade Administration, a part of the Department of Commerce, can set the "countervailing duty" or added tariff on the imported products necessary, in order to achieve fair competition. The process for obtaining relief can be lengthy, since the decision is often appealed through several regulatory and legal system tribunals. Because of the many different types of government assistance (such as training programs or incentives to locate plants in certain

countervailing duty: A tax or tariff added to certain imported goods to counteract a subsidy given to the goods by the government of the nation where they were made.

areas and direct subsidies), making the determination as to whether such a plan is an unfair subsidy or not is often a difficult decision.

BOEING AND AIRBUS SUBSIDIES BOTH FOUND ILLEGAL BY WTO

The World Trade Organization ruled in April 2011 that Boeing received illegal subsidies from U.S. federal and state governments. The March 31 decision by a WTO panel was the latest in a transatlantic legal battle over government support for Boeing and its European rival Airbus. The panel said Boeing had received at least $5.3 billion in illegal subsidies, including tax breaks and research funding from NASA.

The European Commission hailed the ruling as a "clear-cut victory." But the United States said the decision vindicated its position that the Airbus had received far more support over the years, since an earlier panel found the European manufacturer had received more than $20 billion in illegal subsidies. Commentators predicted that the United States would appeal the Boeing decision to put pressure on the EU to accept the Airbus ruling, which both sides have appealed.

The WTO appellate body is expected to issue its decision in the Airbus case in late April, although it could come later. Once that ruling is issued, the United States will have a timing advantage in the dispute because the EU could soon face U.S. retaliation if it does not move quickly to eliminate any subsidies left standing by the appellate review.

However, many analysts believe the two sides will eventually negotiate a settlement, rather than hurl sanctions potentially affecting billions of dollars in trade. A deal also would bolster U.S. ties with Europe at a time when both face increased competition from major emerging economies such as China, India and Brazil. The European Union, unhappy with some aspects of the decision it won against Boeing, immediately launched an appeal that it hopes would show even more subsidies.

LAWS REGULATING EXPORTS

While most nations try to assist their own firms in exporting, certain types of exports are not favored or even allowed by governments. For reasons of national security or in furtherance of its foreign policy objectives, nations may prohibit or restrict sales of certain goods to all countries or just to some countries.

Export Administration Act of 1979: A U.S. law that allows the government to prohibit exports of certain goods from the U.S.

In the United States, the **Export Administration Act of 1979** is the most important law restricting exports. The law allows the federal government to control and limit exports in three situations: (1) where there is a short supply of such goods in the United States, (2) when protecting the U.S. national security by prohibiting the export of goods and technology that "make a significant contribution to the military potential" of other countries, and (3) where necessary to further the foreign policy of the United States.

Every export from the United States requires a license, but in most cases the license is granted without difficulty. However, the Export Administration Act and other laws limiting exports can prevent the export of various items.

The "national security" clause has led to a ban on the export of certain technological and chemical products that may have a "dual use"—that is, both military and civilian. The "foreign policy" clause has been employed by the United States to prevent most exports to Cuba, North Korea, and certain other countries as the result of specific events. Both civil and criminal penalties exist for violations of this law.

Violations of U.S. Export Law

In 2003, two top American aerospace companies, Hughes Electronics and Boeing Satellite Systems, agreed to pay a record fine of $32 million in fines to settle civil charges that they unlawfully transferred rocket and satellite data to China in the 1990s. The State Department had charged the companies with 123 violations of export laws for transferring information that was characterized as conduct which "could cause damage to the security and foreign policy of the United States." In a statement, Hughes Electronics expressed its "regret for not having obtained licenses that should have been obtained."

The Chinese had always insisted that their rocket and missile programs did not need American help. But a string of rocket failures in the 1990s ended only after American companies transferred data on guidance systems, telemetry, and aerodynamics. In 1998 a Congressional panel criticized satellite manufacturers for sometimes subordinating national security to the "bottom line" and in 1999 the U.S. stopped permitting the use of American satellites for Chinese ventures amidst concern about Chinese aid to missile programs in North Korea and Pakistan.

U.S. LAWS THAT MAY APPLY TO ACTIONS OUTSIDE THE UNITED STATES

In general, laws adopted by one country apply only within the borders of that country. As we have said, one of the difficulties with enforcing principles of international law is that there is no "Federal Statute of the World" enforceable everywhere. Each nation is considered sovereign within its borders. It would certainly restrict the sovereignty of a nation if another country's laws were applicable there. Nevertheless, certain U.S. laws have been applied to actions beyond our borders. The enforcement of these laws, not surprisingly, has created problems at home, as well as antagonism in other countries.

THE FOREIGN CORRUPT PRACTICES ACT

In the mid-1970s U.S. news media reported extensively about a series of incidents in which American companies—including some of our largest and most prestigious—admitted paying bribes to officials of foreign nations. The bribes were paid to secure major contracts with the foreign government. After considerable public outcry against this practice, Congress amended the Securities Act of 1934 by passing the Foreign Corrupt Practices Act (FCPA) in 1977.

This federal statute prohibits the payment of a sum of money to a foreign government or official for the purpose of influencing decisions or obtaining business. Even a payment made to a foreign business or agent will violate the law if the American firm knows that the payment will be used to bribe foreign officials. The FCPA contains severe civil and criminal penalties—individuals can be subject to as many as five years in prison and a $250,000 fine, and corporations can be fined up to $2,000,000.

Another feature of the FCPA requires those American firms who must register under that law to maintain stringent accounting procedures. The FCPA mandates that companies engage in careful record keeping and internal control systems, so that any questionable payments can be identified. Failure to maintain proper records will violate the act, whether or not any bribes are paid.

After complaints from American businesses that such payments were legal and expected in many countries, the law was slightly amended in 1988 to allow so-called "grease payments" to lower-level officials merely to expedite the processing of licenses and permits. Payments to higher-level officials who exercise discretionary powers are still illegal under the law, however.

During its first twenty-five years, the FCPA was not vigorously enforced, with only about four dozen cases initiated—an average of about two per year. Only seventeen different companies had been charged as of 2000, and the fines assessed typically ranged from $10,000 to $3.45 million. In one case however, Lockheed agreed to pay a fine of $21.8 million and two company officials also pleaded guilty. But overall, the Act had been lightly and sporadically enforced up to 2000.

But by 2007, as the FCPA celebrated its 30th anniversary, the U.S. Department of Justice (DOJ) and the Securities and Exchange Commission (SEC) had dramatically increased their activities and aggressiveness in prosecuting violations of the Act. The DOJ initiated four times as many prosecutions from 2002–2007 than it had over the previous five years. And the trend has continued to accelerate to the present time. The DOJ instituted 18 prosecutions in 2007, 20 in 2008, and 26 in 2009. At the same time, the SEC filed 20 cases in 2007, 13 in 2008, and 14 more in 2009.

The government has not only brought many more FCPA criminal cases, but the amounts paid as fines or settlements has grown tremendously. The largest single settlement occurred in late 2008 when Seimens, the German multinational engineering firm, agreed to pay the United States $800 million and the German government another $800 million to settle bribery charges—a total of $1.6 billion. An accountant for Siemens admitted that from 2002 to 2006 he oversaw an annual bribery budget of $50 million. And there have been several more fines and settlements of more than $100 million. In January 2010, the DOJ and FBI conducted a "sting" operation at a Las Vegas trade show and arrested 22 executives in the military and law enforcement equipment industry for engaging in a scheme to bribe the minister of defense of an African country.

In addition, the DOJ has expanded the scope of its prosecution under the FCPA to include foreign companies whose securities are publicly traded in the United States. In addition to the Siemens case, the SEC and DOJ have been aggressive in prosecuting foreign companies. In late 2010 the SEC announced it had reached a settlement with ABB Inc., a Swiss engineering company, to pay $39 million in fines (without admitting guilt) regarding charges under the FCPA. In March 2010 Daimler Corp. agreed to pay $185 million (split between the SEC and DOJ) to settle allegations that it had committed serious FCPA violations. These enforcement actions and investigations signify a stepped up effort by U.S. regulators to enforce the FCPA at the farthest reaches of its jurisdictional and territorial boundaries and should put foreign companies whose stock is traded in the United States on notice that they are no more exempt from FCPA prosecution than U.S. issuers.

IN CONSULTATION

Marvin Manager has a problem. The Vice President of International Business has asked him to expand ABC, Inc.'s operations in, Benswali, a developing country with unstable military leadership. Because Marvin has no contacts in Benswali, he hired an agent to help ABC to form the contacts necessary to enter the Benswali market. Marvin picked an agent that he thought was well connected to powerful people in the government.

The agent recently informed Marvin that in order to secure the necessary licenses and permits to expand ABC's operations in Benswali, certain payments were required. First, the agent said that the Minister of Internal Affairs insisted on a $100,000 commission for any new foreign business within Benswali's borders. The President of Benswali also mandated that any new foreign businesses make a $100,000 investment in the Benswali National Bank, which is fully government owned and run. Marvin told the agent that the payments sounded like bribes. The agent's response was simply that this was how things run in Benswali.

Marvin is afraid that the commission and investment are actually thinly disguised bribes. He approached ABC's in-house counsel to express his concerns. Here is their conversation:

Marvin:	Legal Department
1. I know bribes are illegal in the United States, but this isn't the United States. When in Rome, can't we do what the proverbial Romans do?	1. You are correct that bribing government officials is illegal in the United States. Many of our laws, however, reach our behavior even when we are outside the United States. "When in Rome" isn't a valid legal defense.
2. Even if the payments look like bribes, why can't we pay a commission and make an investment? Aren't we free to pick which companies to invest in, and if the Minister actually helps us get started, don't we owe him a commission?	2. Not necessarily. It is illegal to offer or make payments to corruptly influence a government official in order to gain business.
3. What if we were to hide the payments on our books and just call them "taxes" or "miscellaneous fees"?	3. Hiding bribes in your books is as illegal as the bribes themselves. Let me review the applicable law to see whether we can make the payments your agent has requested, and I will get back to you.

MEMO FROM THE LEGAL DEPARTMENT

To: Marvin Manager

Re: Bribery of Foreign Officials in Order to Gain Business

Dear Marvin:

A federal statute directly addresses your concerns about doing business in Benswali. According to the Foreign Corrupt Practices Act (FCPA),[1] the following behavior is illegal:

1. Payments by any company, its employees, or its agents to a foreign government official to improperly influence the government in order to obtain business abroad;

2. Making a payment to an intermediary "while knowing" that the payment is really for a bribe; and

3. Inaccurate record-keeping that disguises either the amount or purpose of a payment (or both) in order to misstate the actual purpose and recipient of the payment.

If we apply the FCPA provisions to your situation with your agent in Benswali, I suspect we would violate the law. The FCPA reaches outside the borders of the United States and prohibits U.S. companies from bribing the officials of other countries. The fact that bribes are an acceptable business practice in Benswali will not relieve ABC Inc. of liability here. The FCPA does allow so-called grease payments, which are like gratuities or small gifts to expedite routine government functions like telephone installation or mail handling. The payments your agent seeks, however, are likely too large to constitute grease payments. Also, the officials seeking the bribes are too powerful to regulate routine procedures. Although the law allows you to invest where you want and pay commissions to whom you want, you cannot do either if the purpose of the investment or commissions is to corruptly influence a foreign official.

Finally, if you make the payments and then disguise their amount or purpose on the books, you are committing a separate offense under the FCPA with its own penalties. The penalties for FCPA violations are severe. Corporations are liable for $2 million or twice their gain from the offense, along with various other penalties. Individuals are liable for up to $250,000 per offense and subject to up to five years in prison. Accordingly, I highly discourage you from making the payments your agent seeks both to protect the company and yourself from heavy liability.

[1] 15 U.S.C. § 78(a)–(LLL) (1988).

With regard to Marvin's situation, we should consider the following questions:

1. What should Marvin do now that it appears he cannot make the payments the agent says are necessary?
2. What could Marvin's company do to ensure that its employees are not in this predicament in the future?
3. Discuss the advantages and disadvantages of preventing U.S. businesses from bribing foreign officials even if that is customary in the foreign jurisdiction.

U.S. ANTITRUST LAW

As discussed more fully in Chapter 17, the United States has a series of laws dealing with the subject called "Antitrust." In general, these laws are designed to promote competition, to prohibit actions that may lessen competition (price fixing, for example), and to prevent monopolies and mergers that would negatively affect competition. The penalties for violating antitrust laws can be severe. In order to encourage such lawsuits, the U.S. antitrust laws generally allow the winning party to be awarded triple the amount of damages proved to have occurred. Many nations do not have similar laws, however, and some countries actively encourage cartels and agreements between firms in order for them to compete better internationally.

Contrary to the general rules regarding the reach of one nation's laws, U.S. courts have applied the *"intended effects doctrine"* regarding antitrust law. According to this theory, if an action taken outside the United States is intended to and does affect U.S. commerce, it is subject to U.S. antitrust law. The following case involves a refusal of some firms to participate in a U.S. antitrust case.

WESTINGHOUSE ELECTRIC CORP. V. RIO ALGAM LTD.

617 F.2d 1248 (7th Cir. 1980)

FACTS

Westinghouse sued 20 American and 9 foreign uranium producers in U.S. federal court, alleging violations of U.S. antitrust laws and asking for damages. Westinghouse claimed that the 29 companies had conspired to fix the price of uranium in the world market at meetings in France, Australia, South Africa, the Canary Islands, and England, as well as in the state of Illinois. When the 9 foreign defendants refused to answer, Westinghouse obtained default judgments against them. In the following months, the district court entered a series of injunctions prohibiting the defendants and some affiliated companies from transferring money out of the United States. Westinghouse also requested that hearings regarding damages begin against the defaulting defendants. The defendants who had answered opposed this, but the district court denied their motions, and this appeal followed.

On appeal, the governments of Australia, Canada, South Africa, and the United Kingdom filed *amicus curiae* (friend of the court) briefs supporting the defendants and protesting the exercise of jurisdiction over this controversy by the U.S. federal courts. The questions before the appellate court were (1) whether subject matter jurisdiction existed, and (2) if so, whether it should be exercised.

DECISION

The Seventh Circuit Court of Appeals, in an opinion by Judge Campbell, upheld the lower court order. Judge Campbell noted that since the *United States v. Aluminum Co. (Alcoa)* case in 1945 decided by Judge Learned Hand, U.S. courts have exercised jurisdiction over antitrust activity outside the United States where there was an "intended effect" on American commerce. In this case, according to the allegations of the complaint (uncontested as yet by the defendants), some of the meetings took place out of the United States, and some took place within this country. Therefore, the federal court had jurisdiction of this case, which was filed under the Sherman Antitrust Act.

As to whether the jurisdiction *should* have been undertaken, the court noted that the district judge considered three factors: the complexity of the multinational and multiparty litigation, the seriousness of the charges asserted, and the recalcitrant attitude of the defaulters. (One of the defendants tore up the complaint in the presence of the process server!) Although another circuit court of appeals had developed a 10-factor test in deciding whether to hear another extraterritorial antitrust case [*Mannington Mills, Inc. v. Congoleum Corp.,* 595 F.2d 1287, (3rd Cir. 1979)], this court was not bound to follow it, since the decision of one circuit court is not binding on another.

In this case (Westinghouse), the Seventh Circuit court decided that the district judge had made the appropriate decision in entering the default judgment. The court pointedly noted that in the *Mannington* case, the defendants had appeared and contested the matter, while here the alleged conspirators had "contumaciously" refused to come into court and present evidence. The Court of Appeals was "shocked" that the governments of the home countries of the defendants had served as "surrogates" for

them and had "subserviently presented their arguments" to the court. There was thus no abuse of discretion by the District Court in entering the default judgments.

CASE QUESTIONS

1. Why was the case filed in federal court? Why does the court have jurisdiction?
2. How does the U.S. court justify its jurisdiction over actions taken outside the United States by non-U.S. parties?
3. Is it fair to force a defendant to litigate a lawsuit in a foreign country, when the defendant has never been to that country? Under what circumstances would it be fair?
4. What does "contumacious" mean?

The *Westinghouse* case in particular, and others like it, have caused considerable resentment and resistance from foreign corporations and governments. Even the members of the EU, which does have laws similar to U.S. antitrust law (called "competition" law in Europe), vigorously opposed the American attempt to apply its laws to conduct outside its jurisdiction. Soon after the Westinghouse decision, eight of the nations involved enacted "blocking" laws that prevented the discovery of documents located in their countries and barred enforcement of American antitrust judgments there. Other countries have laws that prohibit companies from disclosing information to foreign courts if the request is overly intrusive.

Many nations do not have, nor do they want to follow, the "discovery" procedures allowed in American litigation (discussed earlier in this book), which permit parties to obtain substantial documentary internal information on companies and to force the depositions (under oath) of many witnesses. This is an area where substantial disagreement still exists between the United States and other nations, including Great Britain, the United States' closest ally in many legal and business matters.

U.S. CIVIL RIGHTS LAWS

The United States has the most comprehensive legislation in the world prohibiting employment discrimination. As is fully discussed in Chapter 21 of this book, most employees working in this country are protected against discrimination in employment based on race, color, national origin, sex, religion, age, disability, and certain other categories. But is an American worker in another country protected against such discrimination? Normally, as we have seen, the sovereignty of a nation means that only its laws apply within its borders, and most nations do not have employment discrimination laws similar to those in the United States. None are as extensive.

In 1991, in a case titled *Equal Employment Opportunity Commission v. Arabian American Oil Co. (Aramco)*, an American employee working for an American firm in Saudi Arabia claimed that he had been discriminated against in his employment on the basis of his race, religion, and national origin. The U.S. Supreme Court ultimately decided that Title VII of the U.S. Civil Rights Act of 1964 did not apply to his employment in Saudi Arabia, since Congress had not specifically stated that the law should so apply.

Later in 1991, Congress passed major amendments to the Civil Rights Act in an attempt to change the law resulting from the *Aramco* case and other court decisions. Congress expressly extended the application of Title VII to United States citizens working outside of the United States for a firm *"under the control" of a U.S. entity*. "Control" depends on the interrelation of operations, the commonality of management, the centralized control of labor relations, and the common ownership of financial control of the employer and the corporation. An exception was allowed (that is, the U.S. law does not apply) if compliance with Title VII would cause the employer to violate the law of the country where the workplace is located.

The United States is a multiracial, multiethnic society, composed of citizens whose ancestors came from hundreds of different nations and cultures. This mixture of backgrounds has led to many exciting developments, as well as serious problems, during our 200-year history—and the struggles are ongoing today. In many other countries, the population is much more homogenous, with respect to race or ethnic or religious background, and anti-discrimination laws have been slow to develop.

The EU, for example, has long had regulations prohibiting discrimination on the grounds of *nationality* among the members. With some exceptions, EU law prevents one nation from treating nationals of other EU members differently from their own citizens. Also, the EC long ago adopted, in Article 119 of the EEC Treaty, the principle of equal pay for men and women for equal work. Only in 2000 were directives enacted prohibiting race, religious or ethnic discrimination.

SUMMARY

It is critically important that American students look at business issues today with a global perspective. There are few types of trade, commerce, and services that are not affected in a direct way by developments around the world. The specific principles of international law are more difficult to pin down than national law, because there is no one body of statues that applies all around the world. The "law" applied to international commerce consists of a web of different laws, customs, practices, treaties, agreements, and decisions of national and international courts. Enforcement is also a problem without any one international army or police force. Much of the effectiveness of international law depends on the diplomatic and foreign relations efforts of governmental representatives.

The typical international sales transaction employs a letter of credit and bill of lading to effectively transfer title to goods and effectuate prompt payment.

Contract interpretation and dispute settlement can be considerably more complex in international business transactions than domestic sales. Interesting commercial problems arise in connection with the enforcement of national laws, while respecting the sovereignty of national governments. Several important international organizations, such as the UN and the World Bank, play important roles in shaping the rules regarding international commerce. The EU is now the world's largest trading group, and its 27 member nations are rapidly moving toward closer integration of their laws, foreign policy, and monetary systems. The EU has established a complex governing system, featuring three major agencies and its own court system as well. The adoption of the Euro as common currency has moved forward quickly.

The regulation of trade between nations includes many intricate legal issues, including the tariffs and quotas put on imports and various export and import laws and regulations. More and more nations have entered into trade agreements, such as the WTO/GATT, in an effort to remove trade barriers and to promote international trade. Regional free trade agreements, such as NAFTA and Mercosur, are growing in size and importance. The United States has a number of laws regulating exports and imports—such as those that prohibit "dumping" of products. Finally, several U.S. statutes are designed to apply to conduct outside U.S. borders, and the enforcement of these laws has caused political and legal ramifications abroad.

CHAPTER QUESTIONS

1. The primary purpose of the EU structure is to remove barriers to the trading of goods among the member nations. For hundreds of years Germany prohibited the manufacture and sale of "bier" (beer) containing additives (any substitute for malted barley). However, several other members of the EU do not have such a prohibition in their countries, and beer manufacturers in those nations wish to sell their beer in Germany. German officials defended their ban on beer containing additives on public health grounds and also stated that to allow the sale of beer containing additives would be misleading to the German public. In 1987, the Commission brought an action in the ECJ against Germany. What should be the result and why? *Commission of European Communities v. Germany*, No. 178/84, March 1987.

2. British Airways established a program whereby travel agents were to be paid a higher percentage commission for selling BA tickets after they had exceeded a target figure. This system was challenged as violating EU Competition rules by its rival Virgin Atlantic Airlines. It was alleged that this practice constituted an abuse of the dominant position of British Airways and squeezed out the smaller airlines by causing travel agents to focus their efforts on selling tickets on BA. Where will this case be heard? Who will rule on the challenge? What result?

3. Allied Chemical, an American company, entered into a contract to ship chemicals to Banylsa, a Brazilian importer. Allied delivered the goods to Lloyd, a carrier who shipped the goods by sea to Brazil. Allied received a bill of lading, which it sent to a Brazilian bank along with an invoice and with instructions

to deliver the documents on payment. However, on arrival, the goods were unloaded and put into a government warehouse. In Brazil, the law allows a buyer to obtain goods from a warehouse either with a bill of lading or with a carta declaratoria, a letter from the carrier stating that the import fees had been paid. Using such a letter, Banylsa picked up the goods without paying for them and later became insolvent. Allied sued the carrier in U.S. federal court. What should be the result and why? *Allied Chemical Co. v. Companhia de Navegacao Lloyd Brasileiro*, 775 F.2d 476 (2d Cir. 1985).

4. Zapata, a U.S. oil company, entered into a contract with Unterweser, a German firm, to tow an oil rig from Louisiana across the Atlantic Ocean to a new location near Italy. The contract included a clause stating, "Any dispute arising must be treated before the London Court of Justice." Shortly after the tug "Bremen" began towing the rig to Italy, a severe storm swept into the Gulf of Mexico, causing damage to the oil rig. At Zapata's direction, the rig was towed into port in Tampa, Florida. Zapata then started a lawsuit against Unterweser for damages in U.S. federal court. The towing company argued for dismissal, citing the "choice of forum" clause in the contract and filed a suit against Zapata in the London Court of Justice. Zapata argued that for "public policy" reasons, the U.S. court should not be "ousted" from jurisdiction of a dispute that took place near Tampa, Florida. What should be the result? Why? *M/S Bremen v. Zapata Off-Shore Co.*, 407 U.S. 1 (1972).

5. What are the primary purposes of the GATT agreements? What are the two most important principles? Describe the key parts of the WTO dispute settlement process.

6. A resident of Florida owned 11 acres of land in the Punjab region of Pakistan, which was expropriated by the Pakistani government for use as military housing and other purposes. He claimed the land was worth $10 million and brought suit in a U.S. District Court against the Government of Pakistan, the Pakistan Army, and the regional government of Punjab. Should this case be dismissed under the Foreign Sovereign Immunities Act, or does it come under the "Commercial activity" exemption? *Beg. v. Islamic Republic of Pakistan,* 353 F.3d 1323 (11th Cir. 2003).

7. A trademark owner filed an infringement action in a United States federal district court against a number of defendants, including Marquis Publications, an English corporation. Service of the complaint was sent to a post office box address in England listed in the 1997 edition of *Marquis* Magazine. Service by regular mail is permitted in England (in cases filed there) either to "the company's principal office or any place of business of the company within the jurisdiction which has a real connection with the claim." Rule 4(f) of the U.S. Federal Rules of Civil Procedure authorizes service upon individuals in a foreign country "by an internationally agreed means reasonably calculated to give notice." The British company refused to answer the complaint, arguing that it had not been properly served. Do you think the U.S. federal court has jurisdiction over the English firm? Is it fair? Why or why not? *Brockmeyer v. May,* 383 F.3d 798 (9th Cir. 2004)

8. A South Korean factory, which was a subsidiary of a U.S. corporation, closed its doors, putting many employees out of work. The union representing the workers filed suit in the United States, claiming that the action was contrary

to the labor contract with the employees, thus violating U.S. law dealing with labor–management relations. The labor law cited provided that it applies to "an industry affecting commerce . . . without regard to the citizenship of the parties." The company moved for dismissal of the case due to lack of jurisdiction, but the labor union argued that this clause gave U.S. courts jurisdiction of the matter. What should be the result? Why? *Labor Union of Pico Korea Ltd. v. Pico Products, Inc.*, 968 F.2d 191 (2nd Cir. 1992).

9. A New Jersey software provider entered into a contract to provide software and related tools to the European Space Agency (ESA), an organization formed by 18 nations that promotes peaceful space research and technology. The software provider sued the ESA in New Jersey, claiming that the ESA had distributed its software to others without permission and had failed to pay for software produced. The ESA moved for dismissal of the lawsuit on the grounds of immunity. There is a U.S. law entitled The International Organizations Immunities Act (IOIA), which provides international governmental organizations "the same immunity from suit and judicial process as is enjoyed by foreign governments." The court decided that the (IOIA) law should be interpreted as providing the same protections and exceptions as the Foreign Sovereign Immunities Act, which applies to foreign governments. Should the ESA be immune from lawsuits in the United States? Do any of the exceptions in the FSIA apply? *OSS Nokaalva Inc v. European Space Agency,* (3d Cir. 2010), 79 USLW 1292 (Sept. 14, 2010).

10. A brewer in Poland signed an agreement with an Illinois distributor regarding sales and distribution of its beer in Illinois. The agreement contained a clause providing that any disputes under the contract would be arbitrated in Poland using Polish law. When the brewer informed the distributor that it was going to start using a different distributor, the distributor filed suit in federal court in Illinois, seeking an injunction, on the grounds that the termination would violate the Illinois Beer Industry Fair Dealing Act. The brewer responded by asserting that the case should be arbitrated in Poland, according to the contract. What should the result be and why? Where should the case be heard? What law should apply? *Stawski Distributing Co., Inc. v. Browary Zywiec S.A.,* 349 F.3d 1023 (7th Cir. 2003).

PRACTICAL EXERCISE

Early in the morning of December 3, 1984, at a Union Carbide Corporation (UCC) pesticide plant in Bhopal, India, a tragic industrial accident occurred. A large storage tank of methyl isocyanate gas (MIC) malfunctioned, perhaps due to some water entering the gas chamber. When the trouble was noticed, the temperature and the pressure inside the tank were increasing dramatically. The supervisors on duty attempted to turn on the safety devices, and then, seeing a plume of gas rushing out of the stack, ran for their lives. In the next few hours, a huge quantity of gas escaped into the community, where the population was sleeping. The gas drifted silently over the small homes and huts, causing death and permanent injury to thousands. When it was over, more than 3,000 people had been killed, and some 300,000 suffered permanent or temporary injuries.

A large multinational corporation, UCC has plants, facilities, and personnel in many countries. Its headquarters are in Connecticut, and there are significant UCC business operations in New York State. The UCC facility in Bhopal was owned 51 percent by Indians and 49 percent by UCC. It is unclear whether the same safety standards were employed in the Bhopal plant as would be required at a U.S. facility.

The human tragedy led to a complex web of lawsuits and government actions in India and the United States. Within days after the accident, many U.S. lawyers flew to India, signing up victims as clients and forming partnerships with Indian attorneys. The Attorney General of Connecticut (now its U.S. senator), Joseph Lieberman, called it "the greatest ambulance chase in history. It could be the largest and most lucrative civil legal case in the history of the world." Within three months, 40 lawsuits had been filed in U.S. federal courts, 5 in U.S. state courts, and some 1,200 in Indian courts. A federal judicial panel consolidated most of the U.S. federal suits in New York City and assigned them to Judge Keenan.

About one year after the accident, American lawyer Melvin Belli (the so-called "King of Torts") filed a $15 billion class action lawsuit against UCC in a West Virginia court. Early in 1985 the government of India adopted the "Bhopal Act," establishing the authority of the government to file lawsuits representing all Indian citizens for injuries suffered at Bhopal. The government then filed suit asking for damages for all victims in district court in New York, and the case was also assigned to Judge Keenan. There were also criminal charges filed in India against UCC and against its chief executive officer Warren Anderson. Union Carbide brought a motion in the federal court to dismiss the U.S. cases on the grounds of forum non conveniens. The company also argued that the Indian courts had no jurisdiction over UCC Chairman Warren Anderson and that the criminal charges should therefore be dismissed.

India has a fully developed legal system, based on the British model. Indian tort law—like that in the United States—has developed primarily through common law, although often wrongs committed by one party against another in India are dealt with by criminal law, rather than tort law. Compensation levels for tort cases in India are generally quite minimal, compared with jury verdicts for similar cases in the United States. Nevertheless, India does recognize tort law and does have a body of common law awarding tort damages to those injured by the actions of others. The concept of "strict liability" has not developed very much in India, however, and Indian courts rarely award "punitive damages." The wages earned in India are much lower than those in the United States, which also tends to keep worker damages at a lower level.

You are a management trainee working at the UCC world headquarters in Connecticut. Since you have a good background in business law, you have been asked to work with the UCC lawyers in dealing with the legal aspects of this tragedy. First, you are to prepare a short (two- or three-page) memorandum for the crisis team dealing with the legal issues involved.

Please discuss: (1) whether the New York federal court has jurisdiction of this matter, (2) whether the Indian courts have jurisdiction of this matter, (3) how the doctrine of forum non conveniens should apply to this case, (4) whether Indian law or U.S. law should apply to this case, and (5) whether the Indian courts have jurisdiction over Union Carbide CEO Anderson for the purposes of criminal charges.

FURTHER INFORMATION

www.wto.org
   The WTO site.
www.europa.eu
   The EU site.
http://ec.europa.eu/index_en.htm
   European Commission site with many links.
www.sice.oas.org/trade/naftatce.stm
   NAFTA information.
www.americasnet.com
   Mercosur information.
www.ustr.gov
   U.S. trade representative.

CHAPTER 7

BUSINESS ETHICS AND CORPORATE SOCIAL RESPONSIBILITY

LEARNING OBJECTIVES

After you have read this chapter, you should be able to:

1. Explore the relationship between law and ethics and the tension between individual and community ethics.

2. Describe several major ethical theories and differing beliefs about the social responsibility of business.

3. Explain the concept of stakeholder relationships.

4. Discuss and analyze the facts behind some of the major business financial scandals of the past 5 years, the major ethical failures involved, and the ramifications of the actions of certain corporate insiders upon their corporation's employees, shareholders, and the investing public.

5. Apply various ethical theories to contemporary business issues.

CHAPTER OUTLINE

You are a manager in a large energy company and have been ordered by your boss to destroy certain environmental documents that have been requested by a federal agency. What do you need to know about ethics and social responsibility before deciding whether to comply with this request?

221

INTRODUCTION

Ethics is the name we give to our concern for good behavior. We feel an obligation to consider not only our own personal well-being, but also that of others and of human society as well.

—ALBERT SCHWEITZER

The majority of this book is concerned with explaining various laws, regulations, and other legal issues affecting business. As you already know, "the law" comes from a number of sources—state and federal constitutions, statutes passed by legislatures, court decisions, regulations issued by government agencies, and other sources. This chapter, however, focuses on whether business or individuals involved in business have any additional obligations—beyond simply obeying the law—due to ethical or moral reasons or to the role business plays in our society.

In the past 10 years, the business "environment" has been rocked by a series of major scandals. Beginning with the dramatic fall and bankruptcy of Enron Corp., disclosures of fraud and financial wrongdoings at a surprising number of large, prominent corporations including WorldCom, Tyco, HealthSouth, Adelphia and others, caused tremendous economic losses to shareholders, loss of thousands of jobs by employees and significant loss of pensions by retirees. In addition, public confidence about American business has fallen due to these financial scandals. Those scandals were followed by the financial crisis of 2008-2010 which caused worldwide economic problems, loss of millions of jobs, the death of prominent financial firms, and government bailouts of other banking and investment companies. Reports indicated that the crisis was caused, in part at least by risky and fraudulent mortgage practices and the bundling of sub-prime mortgages into highly speculative "derivative" investment packages.

If there ever was any doubt, it is now absolutely clear that ethics in business is central to the health of a firm and indeed the industry in which it operates. Ethical issues affect decisions at all levels and in all aspects of a business, including such "functional" areas as marketing, finance, information systems, management and accounting. If the "numbers" produced by the financial team are fraudulently inflated or altered, while there may be large profits for a time (Enron) eventually the "house of cards" will come crashing down, with severe and painful consequences for thousands of people. If honesty and fairness are not part of the management structure, and the sales and marketing program, those failings will infect the morale and attitude of all employees, to the detriment of the firm.

Prior to the recent "financial crisis" and other business scandals, certain other instances of business practices have caused public concern over the moral standards of American business. Bribes, kickbacks, insider trading, management buy-outs that seem to benefit only the managers, excessive salaries and "perks" for top executives, environmental accidents, and consumer safety cover-ups have made headlines all over the country in the past few years. Often, these incidents involve questions of whether a company or its officials have operated not only legally, but ethically or morally. In response, business ethics has become an integral component of business education. More than 2,000 corporations have drafted ethical codes for their officers and workers, and numerous universities have established ethics courses in the wake of the recent scandals.

LAW AND ETHICS

"Thou shall not steal" and "Thou shall not kill" are commands based upon ethical norms common to almost all societies, which have resulted in laws making those actions illegal as well. The "Golden Rule," which states that we should treat others as we wish to be treated, exists in some form in most major religions of the world. Much of our criminal law is also based on moral and ethical foundations. Clearly, if a person cheats, robs, or assaults another, he or she has violated both the ethical and legal rules.

Similarly, much of our common law is based, at least in theory, on what most people believe is "right." For example, if you make a promise upon which another person relies, it is only right that you should be held to that promise, at least in certain situations. This moral principle is the foundation of contract law. If you carelessly take an action that injures someone else, it is only "fair" that you compensate that person for his or her loss, and that is the basis of negligence and tort law.

Many actions, however, might be ethical but illegal, and others may be legal but unethical. The law provides a floor below which society will not tolerate certain conduct. Therefore, certain acts that fall below that standard will be punished. Simply because there is a level of conduct required by law, however, does not mean that in a given situation, a person's moral or ethical standards might not require a higher type of behavior. For example, in most states, no legal duty exists to aid a drowning person (unless you have contributed to his or her predicament in some way). However, if you are a strong swimmer and have completed a rigorous Red Cross water safety program, your own ethical, religious, or moral code may require you to rescue the drowning person.

Furthermore, in recent years many U.S. factories have been closed and the operation moved to an overseas facility where wages are significantly lower and government regulation virtually nonexistent. In connection with the financial crisis and recession of the past few years there has been much publicity about the "outsourcing" of American jobs, such as moving call centers from the U.S. to India and other Asian countries. In the process, hundreds of American employees have lost their jobs, and other community businesses have suffered. This outsourcing of jobs is legal, but some commentators have questioned the ethical consequences of such transactions.

Similarly, there are actions that are illegal, but possibly ethical. A few years ago, while a long and dangerous war raged in parts of Central America, hundreds of people living there attempted to come to the United States in order to keep their families from being killed or injured. The law imposes limits on the number of immigrants from various countries who may legally enter the United States in one year, and these limits had been reached with respect to El Salvador and Honduras. Nevertheless, many church groups in the United States, believing that they had a moral duty to save the lives of as many Central American citizens as possible, secretly smuggled illegal immigrants into this country in order to provide them sanctuary from the war. These groups who helped the immigrants into this country knew that their actions were illegal, but these groups were willing to take the chance of being prosecuted because they felt that what they were doing was "right." In their eyes, the conduct was ethical, although illegal.

Therefore, while what is legal and what is ethical often overlap, there is not a total correspondence between the two. If the law represents the floor below which conduct is illegal, ethics represents the structures erected above the floor in order to improve our lives. We all have our own standards as how far above the floor we expect one's conduct to be, and the types and degrees of "ethical structures" we believe are necessary and appropriate. Each of us, in our individual and business lives should strive to operate "above the floor" and build our own ethical structures by behaving in a manner above and beyond the minimum requirements of the law.

INDIVIDUALISM AND COMMUNITARIANISM

A starting point for any discussion of ethics necessarily concerns a discussion of values. Many students have taken value quizzes where they are asked to prioritize a series of values like love, family, peace, security, or power. Two values important in American society are individualism and communitarianism.

American society has long valued the efforts of the individual. We have celebrated the courage of the Pilgrims, the fortitude of the early settlers, and those who pushed west to populate the frontier. Today, people who have started their own businesses and achieved success are lauded as "entrepreneurs" in books and magazines. Our capitalistic economic system is based, to a large extent, on a concept sometimes called "Social Darwinism"—that is, "survival of the fittest" in business. The economic theory *laissez faire* holds that government should never, or to the minimum extent possible, interfere in economic matters and should leave individuals to succeed or fail on their own. We admire those who courageously stand up for their principles against powerful opposition, and we ardently endorse the Bill of Rights with its protection for individuals against government overreaching. Americans generally believe enthusiastically in the property rights of private individuals. In short, individualism is strongly valued in the United States.

On the other hand, our society has deeply held beliefs in equality, justice, and fairness. These values emphasize the idea that certain actions should not be taken if they would promote the interests of one individual instead of the interests of the community. Much of our Judeo-Christian religious and ethical background rests on "being your brother's keeper." Many other laws and precepts of our society are aimed at promoting conduct that benefits the larger community rather than solely one's own interests. Communitarianism is not simple majoritarianism, but rather focuses on what is good for the community, which often means protecting individual rights. As could be predicted, individualism and communitarianism often conflict.

While some people seem to clearly follow exclusively one value or the other, most of us make an effort to accommodate both values. From time to time, one value or the other becomes more prominent, and then the pendulum swings back. In the 1960s, it seemed that the community value was dominant in the United States. Congress passed more than 20 "consumer protection" laws, designed to thwart behavior that injured others, particularly those less fortunate or less educated. Following the leadership of President John F. Kennedy ("Ask not what your country can do for you, ask what you can do for your country") and Martin Luther King, Jr., a tremendous commitment was made to eliminate, or at least substantially reduce, discrimination based on race, religion, national origin, sex, or poverty. After the untimely deaths of these two leaders, many of the ideas they advocated were implemented by President Lyndon Johnson through his "Great Society" program.

By the mid-1970s, the public mood began to change. More and more focus was placed on self-development (*I'm OK, You're OK* became a very popular book), and less attention was given to the concerns of others. There was growing dissatisfaction in the United States with the expansion and proliferation of government agencies, many of them created or enlarged by legislation passed in the 1960s or early 1970s. The American public became more concerned with the tremendous cost and unclear effectiveness of such programs. By the beginning of the 1980s, many Americans were ready to embrace individualism. Riding this wave of sentiment, Ronald Reagan was elected president, stressing that "It's time to get government off the backs of the American people." Congress and the President responded to the change in mood by cutting back on regulations and lowering the budgets and staff of many agencies.

Neo-classical economics became the preeminent government theory—that is, if each person maximized his or her own welfare, the most efficient firms would succeed, and corresponding benefits would follow for society. In the late 1980s the media ran many stories about real estate developer Donald Trump and celebrated his conspicuous ambition, lifestyle, and wealth. Madonna became a music superstar, and one of her biggest hits was a semi-autobiographical song titled "Material Girl." [Both Madonna and Donald Trump have proven to be amazingly durable, as both continue to enjoy popularity and fame in the 21st century. Madonna is still a major pop star pushing the boundaries of taste and style, (and influencing younger stars such as Lady Gaga) even though she is now married with two children—and she has become involved in attempting to help poor children in Africa as well. Mr. Trump achieved new star status with his "you're fired" line on the TV show The Apprentice and various spin-offs, and as of spring 2011 was considering running for President of the U.S.].

By the 1990s, the excesses of selfishness and individual gratification had created dissatisfaction in society. The number and size of corporate mergers and takeovers reached record levels, with many companies closing facilities and, as the result, costing thousands of people their jobs. Ivan Boesky had engineered a scheme to reap enormous individual profits by buying stock of companies after learning secretly about upcoming mergers and takeover bids. He eventually was convicted, paid a $100 million fine and went to jail. Michael Milken pioneered the use of "junk bonds" (high-risk, high-yield corporate bonds) through complex transactions that allowed certain investors to make enormous profits (and Milken himself made $1.3 billion over four years). He too, however, was eventually convicted of federal law violations and sentenced to prison. His brokerage firm (Drexel Burnham Lambert) suffered large losses and filed for Chapter 11 Bankruptcy protection. Following the deregulation of the savings and loan industry during the 1980s, hundreds of savings and loans engaged in questionable lending practices and later went bankrupt, costing the taxpayers an estimated $500 billion in federal insurance payments to the depositors.

We have now completed the first decade of the 21st century, and while huge multi-national companies are becoming more dominant through globalization, and mergers and acquisitions are picking up, there is also much interest in community duty and a growing emphasis on ethics in business. The most-publicized business stories of the 2000-2010 decade were the major financial scandals of corporations like Enron, WorldCom and others. Several large corporations failed after it was found that they had built their success on fraudulent and misleading financial information. In the aftermath thousands of people lost jobs and retirement savings, and many top executives were charged with crimes.

Congress responded to these ethical lapses by enacting the Dodd-Frank Wall Street Reform and Consumer Protection Act in 2010 and the Sarbanes-Oxley Act. The Dodd-Frank Act established mechanisms to require several additional safeguards be put in place by financial institutions to prevent the type of financial crisis that happened in 2008-10, and created a new consumer watchdog position to guard against abusive practices. The Sarbanes-Oxley Act requires more honest and accurate financial information from companies, placing new duties on top corporate officers, requiring better oversight by the Board of Directors, and instituting greater government regulation of large public companies and accounting firms. The majority of large business corporations established codes of ethics. Several leading business schools have set up ethics programs, and more are adding such programs every year, including many top schools such as Harvard and Columbia. Numerous major business and news publications have featured articles on ethics in business. The passage of the Dodd-Frank Act and of Sarbanes-Oxley reflects a return to a more communitarian value system.

Understanding and identifying these and other values is important, but it is clear that values, in and of themselves, do not necessarily have ethical content. A person is not judged ethical or unethical because he or she prefers individualism over communitarianism or vice versa. For most of us, a person or a decision is either "good" or "bad" depending on our own view of what is right and wrong. Questions of right and wrong are the subject of ethics, and formal ethical reasoning (how people should think about right and wrong) is studied by many scholars.

FORMAL METHODS OF ETHICAL REASONING

In general, decisions as to what is right or wrong are made very quickly, informally, and without much thought. When asked, after the fact, why we behaved in a certain way we may give the following reasons: fear of punishment, promise of reward, adhering to a group norm, or obeying the law. For example, if Ann decides not to steal a sweater because she is afraid she will get caught, she is acting ethically only because she fears punishment. If Bobby decides not to hit Jake because his mother has promised him $50 if he does not fight, he is acting ethically only because he will receive a reward. Thirteen-year-old Kay is adhering to a group norm when she tells the truth about her age and pays an adult ticket price at the movie theater. When asked why she tells the truth she says because "in her family we always tell the truth." And when 20-year-old Adam does not drink alcohol at a fraternity party because it is against the law, he is using a legal standard to govern his behavior.

Although there is nothing inherently wrong with using these informal methods of ethical reasoning, there are more formal ways to think about right and wrong conduct. These more formal methods are the subject of ethical reasoning. The three predominant theories we are going to discuss in this text are virtue, utilitarianism, and deontology.

VIRTUE ETHICS

Take a minute to think about these questions. What does it mean to say, "He's a good person"? How do good people behave? What is a good life? What does it mean when you say you want to live a good life or that she lived a good life? What does that life look like? These questions were asked by the Greek philosopher, Aristotle, writing around 350 B.C. The answer is found in Aristotle's *Nichomachean Ethics* and is referred to as **virtue ethics**. For Aristotle, living a life of virtue was part of living a good life. Virtue does not come easily, however, and Aristotle argued that individuals only become virtuous by acting virtuously. Put another way, a person is not taught to be virtuous. Rather, individuals become virtuous by continually practicing making virtuous decisions.

Well then, just what is a virtue? First, virtues should not be confused with values, even though the popular press uses the terms almost interchangeably. Virtues are individual characteristics that make a person "good" or "bad." So while some values are also considered virtues, like honesty, a value is not a virtue if it does not say anything about a person's character. Second, Aristotle warned that it was difficult to define a virtue in exact terms because virtues can become vices if they are taken to extremes. The "golden mean" or the more modern saying "moderation in all things" is used to identify virtuous behavior. To give you an example of how the "golden mean" is used, let's take the virtue of truthfulness. On one end of the truthfulness spectrum we have lying, which is clearly not a virtue but a vice. On the other end of the spectrum, however, a person might be so truthful that he is vicious. An example would be approaching an overweight person and exclaiming, "You are very fat!" in order to make the person feel bad. This is also a vice. Therefore, the golden mean helps us remember that the virtue of truthfulness falls somewhere in between the two extremes, but it is hard to define exactly where that is without understanding the context of when the "truth" was told.

Aristotle did identify several virtues that he believed a good Athenian should possess: courage, temperance, liberality, magnificence, pride, good temper, friendliness, truthfulness, wittiness, shame, justice, and honor. Several centuries later, St. Thomas Aquinas, in *Summa Theologica,* divided virtue into the religious (theological) virtues of faith, hope, and charity and the principal intellectual virtues of prudence (wisdom), justice, temperance, and fortitude. Robert Solomon, a current philosopher, has written a book titled *Ethics and Excellence,* which is aimed at applying virtue ethics in a contemporary business setting. Solomon argues that the basic virtues applying to business relationships are honesty, fairness, trust, and toughness. He also identifies the virtues of the corporate self as friendliness, loyalty, honor, shame, caring, and compassion. As you can see, there is quite a bit of overlap between Aristotle's list of virtues and Solomon's list of virtues. Many of you probably also identified several of these virtues as you identified what it means to be a good person.

One virtue of particular importance here is justice. Justice was recognized as a virtue by Aristotle, Aquinas, and Solomon, and some have argued that justice is *the* most important virtue. There are basically two types of justice, **distributive** and **commutative.** Distributive justice is concerned with what is fair and equitable when goods and services are distributed in a society. Issues of distributive justice are very apparent in the current and continuing debate over affirmative action outlined in Chapter 21. Commutative justice looks at what is fair and equitable among individuals. One aspect of commutative justice is retribution, which deals with punishment. Much of criminal law and tort law, discussed in Chapter 11, concerns commutative justice.

As can be seen, virtue ethicists believe that the "good life" can be explained in objective terms and can be decided upon by the community. Other philosophers, however, disagree. Therefore, the good life and a sense of community are not built into the other philosophical theories we will discuss. These theories can be divided into two groups: **teleology** and **deontology**. In general, the teleologists assess whether an action is ethical by looking not only at the particular act in question, but also at the likely or actual consequences of the act. The following theories are examples of teleological philosophies.

teleology: A group of ethical theories that judge actions by their consequences.

deontology: A group of ethical theories that examine the nature of the action itself, without regard to its consequences, to determine whether it is ethical.

utilitarianism: The theory that an act is good which produces the greatest good for the greatest number of people.

TELEOLOGY

Egoism   Egoism is not a difficult theory for most of us to grasp. This doctrine basically holds that each person should decide on a course of action based upon what is best for him or her. Egoism is a form of teleology and thus includes in its ethical analysis the likely results of the contemplated action. Egoists contend that the enlightened pursuit of self-interest will lead to the full realization of each person's potential. An act is therefore "good" if it advances the self-interest of the person.

Utilitarianism   Another form of teleological ethics is **utilitarianism**, first articulated in the late 1700s by Jeremy Bentham. This theory holds that an act is good which produces the greatest good for the greatest number of people. An important part of utilitarianism lies in identifying the "good" to be maximized. For Bentham, the good was pleasure and any act that maximized pleasure was ethical. John Stuart Mill argued that happiness was the good to be maximized. Other contemporary philosophers have identified the good as knowledge or life or aesthetic beauty or liberty. Once the good is agreed on, utilitarians look at the social benefit of the action and the social harm of the action. This form of ethical analysis, with considerable modifications, constitutes the basis of the contemporary technique for assessing certain decisions called *cost-benefit analysis*, which attempts to weigh and compare the costs and savings resulting from a particular government or business decision. The good being maximized is either profit or efficiency.

Our capitalistic economic system owes much to utilitarian principles as refined by Adam Smith, the 18th century Scottish philosopher and political economist. Smith's work *The Wealth of Nations* (1776) advocated that the enlightened pursuit of self-interest by merchants and producers, through the free market, results in the most benefits for all of society (that is, "the greatest good for the greatest number"). As if by an "invisible hand," money and resources are allocated by means of free market competition to businesses that produce goods the public wants. While most business students are familiar with The Wealth of Nations, Adam Smith's earlier work, The Theory of Moral Sentiment (1759) sets forth several virtues. It is clear that Smith would not condone the lack of virtue exhibited by some corporate executives.

DEONTOLOGY

Other philosophical and religious scholars have developed deontological theories, which insist that the ethical nature of an act must be determined by examining only the act itself, without regard to its consequences. The following theories are examples of this category.

Universalization   One of the most well-known moral philosophers of all time was Immanuel Kant, a German who lived from 1724 to 1804. Kant argued that humans had duties and that those duties always had to be acted upon regardless of the consequences. These duties can be identified by using *universal law*. Put anther way, rules and actions are not ethical unless they can be made **universal**—that is, applicable to everyone. Kant argued that to test the ethical correctness of an action, one should assume that the action or decision will become a general law binding on everyone. For example, if Susan is deciding whether or not to tell a lie, she should ask whether it would be morally correct for everyone to tell lies. Kant would conclude that it is not a good moral result for everyone to tell lies, so the principle (it is all right to lie) cannot be universalized.

universal: Applicable to everyone.

Kant also asserted that it is unethical to use people as means to an end. He urged that human beings are too unique to be used as means to achieve some other goal, and instead must be treated as ends in themselves.

Judeo-Christian Principles   Although all Americans do not subscribe to any one religion and many are not religious at all, probably the most prevalent ethical force in the United States is the Judeo-Christian heritage shared by the majority of citizens. Many of the central tenets of the Jewish and Christian religions command individuals to take care of and assist one another. The ethical portions of these religions contain a strong deontological basis—that is, many actions are condemned regardless of their consequences.

The Bible, the sacred writings of Judaism and Christianity, contains a series of books accepted as scripture by both religions. The Old Testament, written by Hebrews over a period of more than a thousand years, contains 39 books and is the Jewish Bible. The Old Testament has three main sections, call the Law (the first five books, called the Torah by Jews), the Prophets, and the Writings. Christians generally accept the Old Testament, but add a second part, called the New Testament, containing 27 more books (the first four are called the Gospels), telling of Jesus Christ and other Christian leaders. The Roman Catholic and Eastern Orthodox Bibles have 73 books—46 in the Old Testament and 27 in the New. While they share much in common, each church uses the Bible somewhat differently.

Perhaps the core of the ethical teachings of the Judeo-Christian religious heritage is the Ten Commandments, which according to Exodus 20:2–17 of the Old Testament were received by Moses from God on Mt. Sinai. Whereas the first four commandments deal with man's relationship with God, the final six contain the following interpersonal duties and prohibition:

- Honor thy father and mother.
- Thou shalt not kill.
- Thou shalt not commit adultery.
- Thou shalt not steal.
- Thou shalt not bear false witness against thy neighbor.
- Thou shalt not covet. (Some versions add "thy neighbor's wife" and "thy neighbor's house.")
- Jesus summed up these commandments as "love your neighbor as yourself."

These Commandments set forth absolute ethical duties and prohibit acts, irrespective of their consequences (a deontological standard), in a manner familiar to most Americans. These six statements urge people to respect the lives, marital partners, and property of their fellow citizens, as well as their own parents, and provide an expectation of honesty and humbleness in one's actions toward others. Regardless of their religion or lack thereof, most Americans would agree that these statements provide a very basic minimum standard of ethical behavior.

CORPORATE SOCIAL RESPONSIBILITY

Did you ever expect a corporation to have a conscience, when it has no soul to be damned, and no body to be kicked?

—THE LORD CHANCELLOR OF ENGLAND, EDWARD FIRST BARON THURLOW

We have set out some of the principal ethical theories by which individuals make decisions. But what about organizations—specifically business firms? Do companies have ethical standards, social responsibility, duties, and beliefs? Can they? Should they? And if businesses do have such responsibilities, to whom are they owed?

Much has been written in the past 35 years concerning whether businesses do or ought to have ethical or moral duties. Noted economist Milton Friedman (1912–2006) effectively advocated the negative position in a 1970 *New York Times* article titled "The Social Responsibility of Business Is to Increase Its Profits." Friedman maintained that the business manager's primary moral obligation was to serve the interests of the shareholders (an argument based in part on agency theory). The shareholders, Friedman said, were interested in return on investment, and therefore, although corporations should follow "the law and ethical custom," businesses and their managers should otherwise focus on increasing their profits.

One of the most forceful advocates for greater corporate social and ethical responsibilities is Professor Christopher Stone. His 1975 book *Where the Law Ends* asserts that law alone is inadequate to keep corporations "within socially desirable bounds" because of several factors. First, there is the "time-lag problem"—that is, laws are often passed "after the fact," or after some environmental or workplace tragedy has occurred. The responsible corporate officials may have had some previous knowledge or warning of the dangers inherent in the product or procedure but were not required by the law do anything more at that time. Therefore, preventive actions were not taken, and the unfortunate results occurred. The passage of the Sarbanes-Oxley Act, following the Enron and WorldCom scandals, is a recent example of the "time-lag" problem.

Second, Stone contends that a number of limitations connected with the making of law inhibit its usefulness. Such factors include the following: (1) Corporations take an active role in shaping the law, (2) A general lack of consensus exists as to the causes and effects of various actions, and (3) Many statutes are vague. (It is often necessary to modify or "water down" a proposed law in order to gain passage.) Furthermore, Stone argued, there are limitations associated with implementing the law as well. First, there are difficulties in fashioning a remedy in complex cases when, under our legal system, one party must win and the other lose. Second, there is the inconsistency of administrative agency enforcement due to vague and over-general statutes and the considerable influence regulated businesses exert on the very agencies set up to regulate these businesses. Stone suggests that rather than force society to react to corporate actions after the fact and punish firms or individuals for violations of law, businesses should make fundamental changes in the way they receive and process information and make decisions.

STAKEHOLDER THEORY

One method of assessing and analyzing the potential social responsibilities and duties of a business is to apply the concept of **stakeholders.** Several influential business analysts have argued that each business firm has many groups or individuals, called stakeholders, who can affect or are affected by the actions of the business. This framework obviously considers a set of business relationships more encompassing than merely that between the firm and its owners— the word *stakeholder* is much broader than *shareholder*. Figure 7.1 depicts one example of the firm and the possible relationships of its stakeholders.

stakeholder: Groups or individuals who can affect or are affected by the actions of a business.

If a company accepts the stakeholder theory, it needs to devote considerable thought and energy to managing these stakeholder relationships in the most beneficial way possible. As Figure 7.1 shows, many of the stakeholders do not actually participate in the profits and losses of the business, but affect and are affected by the business in other ways. Therefore, stakeholder analysis necessarily involves consideration of corporate social and ethical duties, as well as political, competitive, and economic factors. Other writers include the natural environment as another stakeholder although its interests are represented through the advocacy of other stakeholders such as Public Interest Groups, government or members of the local community. Business scholars have coalesced around the work of Max Clarkson who developed the Clarkson principles. Those are found in Figure 7.2.

Board of Directors
Trade Associations
Media
Stockholders
Financial Interests
Competitors
Public Interest and Public Groups
Suppliers
THE FIRM
Employees
Creditors
Customers
The Community
Unions
Politicians
Local, State, and Federal Government Agencies

Figure 7.1
Model of Stakeholder Relationships

Source: Based on the work of E. R. Freeman, M. E. Porter, G. Steiner, J. Steiner, and others.

Figure 7.2

Table 1: Clarkson Principles of Stakeholder Management

Managers should acknowledge and actively monitor the concerns of all legitimate stakeholders, and should take their interests appropriately into account in decision-making and operations.

Managers should listen to and openly communicate with stakeholders about their respective concerns and contributions, and about the risks that they assume because of their involvement with the corporation.

Managers should adopt processes and modes of behavior that are sensitive to the concerns and capabilities of each stakeholder constituency.

Managers should recognize the interdependence of efforts and rewards among stakeholders, and should attempt to achieve a fair distribution of the benefits and burdens of corporate activity among them, taking into account their respective risks and vulnerabilities.

Managers should work cooperatively with other entities, both public and private, to insure that risks and harms arising from corporate activities are minimized and, where they cannot be avoided, appropriately compensated.

Managers should avoid altogether activities that might jeopardize in-alienable human rights (e.g., the right to life) or give rise to risks which, if clearly understood, would be patently unacceptable to relevant stakeholders.

Managers should acknowledge the potential conflicts between (a) their own role as corporate stakeholders, and (b) their legal and moral responsibilities for the interests of stakeholders, and should address such conflicts through open communication, appropriate reporting and incentive systems, and where necessary, third party review.

Source: Business Ethics Quarterly, Vol 12 No.2, Appendix: Principles of Stakeholder Management, page 260 (April 2002).

Stakeholder theory has also found its way into law by those states that enacted Corporate Constituency Statutes. These statutes have been adopted by over one-half of the states. They require corporate decision makers to take into account the impact their decisions have on nonshareholder constituents.

Related initiatives include the creation of "Benefit Corporations" which can pursue stakeholder and societal value creation as well as shareholder value maximization. [Archie Carroll: *Corporate charter embraces social missions,* http://www.onlineathens.com/stories/080810/bus_691758473.shtml]

Similarly, constituents in Minnesota are attempting to introduce legislation allowing a Socially Responsible Corporate Charter.

> The bill creates a new section of law for an alternative kind of corporation, the SR (socially responsible) corporation. 1. Directors will have an affirmative duty to all stakeholders, 2. Employees and representatives of the public interest will be on the Board of Directors, 3. Directors will be protected from shareholder suits when they choose to consider other stakeholders and the public interest, 4. Socially Responsible investors and consumers will know where to invest their money, and 5. Socially Responsible Companies will be protected from hostile takeover. [http://c4cr.org/]

Similar legislation has been introduced in Hawaii.

CSR in 2011

CSR today is increasingly understood as more than just philanthropy or risk management. Owing to the spectacular failures of business across the globe, trust is at an all time low. Therefore, a company that is clearly seen to be doing the right thing both ethically and in meeting broader stakeholder expectations can build a competitive advantage over its competitors. In a Harvard Business Review article by Michael Porter and Mark Kramer, emphasis is placed on seeking opportunities for "shared value" where both society (including all stakeholders other than shareholders) and the firm benefit from "CSR" initiatives.

Porter and Kramer direct firms to look for such initiatives in three ways. By examining the firm's value chain, a firm can identify ways in which its activities have either negative or positive impacts on stakeholders. Negative impacts are often referred to as externalities, actual costs or burdens resulting from the firm's activities that are not borne by the firm but are absorbed by others, e.g. pollution. A firm can increase social value by either decreasing the extent of these externalities, reducing real costs, or by increasing the extent of positive impacts. Porter and Kramer call these two opportunities "inside-out linkages." They provide opportunity to the firm in its actual cost/profit structure or in the perceived value of its brand.

The third opportunity is in the firm's "competitive context." As the firm must compete for all of the inputs required in its value chain, any initiative that improves its ability to compete provides an advantage. For instance, a firm that treats its employees well, not limited to better wages and conditions of employment, will gain in productivity, retention and reduced costs for new employees. A firm that is a good citizen in its community will be welcome when it seeks to expand there or into other communities, also reducing costs. A manager who knows how to identify such CSR opportunities and build a business case for pursuing them will be able to bring value to their firm.

SOCIAL CONTRACT THEORY

Somewhat related to stakeholder theory is social contract theory. The idea of a social contract is originally found in the works of Thomas Hobbes, the British philosopher, writing in the 17th century. Hobbes argued that morality does not depend on human nature; rather it is a practical solution for selfish individuals who want to live in a peaceful, social order. Hobbes looked at a fictitious "state of nature" or a time before humans were organized into communities. If individuals were taken back to this time, what would life be like? For Hobbes, the answer was not hopeful, and he states in *Leviathan* that in a state of nature "the life of man [is] solitary, poor, nasty, brutish, and short." Hobbes went on to argue that because of this state of nature individuals would agree to a powerful government, with laws and police. John Locke was also a social contract theorist. Using the same method, Locke arrived at a different conclusion. For Locke, humans were benevolent and kind. He believed the state of nature to be one of "perfect freedom to order their actions and dispose of their possessions and persons as they think fit, within the bounds of the law of nature, without asking leave or depending on the will of any other man." Locke, of course, argued for a limited government. Whereas these writers were concerned with the legitimacy of government, modern social contract theorists, the late Thomas Dunfee and Thomas Donaldson, have taken social contract theory into the business ethics arena.

Dunfee and Donaldson argue that a social contract between society and business does exist in the United States and in much of the industrialized world. That social contract, though unwritten and unspoken, requires that management recognize stakeholder interests. Donaldson has applied social contract theory to international business and argues that part of this social contract requires managers to "show concern for [their] employee's interests and undertake only actions that respect the bounds of rights and justice, for this is how society frames the legitimacy of the organization [they manage]." Under this theory, the international firm has three obligations: (1) to enhance the long term welfare of employees and consumers; (2) to minimize the drawbacks of industrialization; and (3) to operate in a way that acknowledges minimum standards of justice and human rights. Does the action of the EU, as set out in the next article, reflect social contract theory?

INTERNATIONAL PERSPECTIVE

Profits and Social Responsibility

A decade ago, drug makers came under fire for not making HIV/AIDS treatments widely available to poor nations in Sub-Saharan Africa, where more than two-thirds of all cases are found. Now in 2011 the industry has made broad accommodations on pricing and access to the drugs. But creating new medicines for patients in poor countries who cannot pay prices linked to the hefty cost of creating cures remains a daunting challenge. At issue is how global companies decide which treatments to work on, and how they manage operations and clinical trials in the developing world.

For drug makers, serving poor nations in Africa, Asia and Latin America calls for striking a balance between meeting public health needs and maximizing profits. Guiding the companies are codes of ethics and corporate responsibility for doing business. "There is a special duty when you are selling medicine as opposed to pantyhose or hubcaps," says Arthur Caplan, director of the Center for Bioethics at the University of Pennsylvania. When drug companies put short-term gains ahead of social responsibility, he adds, they often pay a price in bad publicity and a backlash from regulators.

Put differently, "The issue of who gets drugs developed for them is a very important ethical issue and cuts to the heart of the strength and weakness of markets," says Michael A. Santoro, a Rutgers Business School professor and co-editor of the 2005 book, *Ethics and the Pharmaceutical Industry: Business, Government, Professional and Advocacy Perspectives.*" On the one hand, we don't like it that markets are harsh and unjust," Santoro says. "But on the other hand, it's the power of the market that creates the therapies in the first place."

Efforts to deliver cures to the world's poorest regions range from new research initiatives to Big Pharma donations of medicine. Last November, the World Health Organization unveiled an alliance with six firms that pledged to donate drugs for neglected tropical diseases —the term for sick-nesses such as leprosy and dengue fever found in countries afflicted with poverty, overcrowding and a lack of good diets and hygiene. Among the con-tributions was an unlimited supply of leprosy treatments from Novartis, and up to 200 million tablets a year from Johnson & Johnson to combat intestinal worms in children.

Many such programs are modeled after alliances between drug compa-nies, governments and non-profit organizations that have expanded afford-able access to HIV/AIDS treatments in poor countries. Perhaps the most ambitious effort has been in Botswana, which in 2001 joined forces with Merck and the Bill & Melinda Gates Foundation to bring drugs to the impoverished African nation. Now 90% of Botswana's HIV/AIDS patients receive treatment, says Merck, compared with just 5% when the program began.

Such public-private partnerships promote corporate social responsibility in developing countries burdened with political and economic barriers to strong pharmaceutical markets, says Guy David, a Wharton professor of health care management. But charitable donations do not eliminate the need for companies to produce innovative new drugs for diseases that afflict the developing world, David notes. "The biggest role for pharmaceu-tical companies in terms of society is the discovery of new drugs and vac-cines," he says.

Still other moves to bring drugs to the developing world permit poor countries to produce low-cost generic alternatives to patented treatments through a process called compulsory licensing. Terms of such deals keep the generics out of the patent-holders' own major markets. Countries that have gained access to drugs in this way include Brazil and Thailand, which have licensed the production of low-cost versions of Merck's Stocrin treatment for HIV/AIDS.

Thailand also has licensed versions of Sanofi-Aventis's blockbuster blood thinner Plavix, and cancer drugs from Sanofi-Aventis, Novartis and Roche. Some drug giants are sponsoring their own initiatives. GlaxoSmithKline is sharing more than 800 of its patents with other companies working to find treatments for neglected tropical diseases. The company has also cut prices for more than a dozen drugs sold in the least developed countries — such as Rwanda, Ethiopia and Cambodia — to no more than 25% of the developed-world price. The treatments cover conditions that include asthma, malaria and hepatitis B.

Yet even if drug companies pool their efforts to cure tropical and neglected diseases, patients could be waiting 10 to 15 years for the drugs to emerge, says Stephen M. Sammut, a Wharton senior fellow in health care management and partner in the San Francisco-based venture capital firm Burrill & Co. "These are not trivial biological problems," Sammut says about the challenge of developing treatments. "There is a reason why there are not good vaccines or cures for some of these diseases. It goes beyond the fact that the clients are poor."

Excerpt from *Profits and Social Responsibility: Chastened Drug Makers Step Up Efforts to Bring Affordable Medicines to Poor Countries,* published in Knowledge@Wharton. Used with permission.

MEDIATING INSTITUTIONS

In critiquing both social contract and stakeholder theories, questions have been raised about whether large business institutions are themselves responsible for unethical behavior. Evolutionary psychologists have argued that the human brain is cognitively still primarily a hunter-gatherer brain. This implies that humans have a limited ability to interact in large groups. While these psychologists opine that the optimal size of the groups for effective interaction ranges from 30 to 150, it is clear that most businesses far exceed these numbers. In utilizing some of this research, Prof. Tim Fort has argued that businesses need to create mediating institutions if they want their employees to exhibit ethical behavior. He explains,

> mediating institutions are communities which socialize their members. "Mediating" between the individual and society as a whole, they provide a community. They require individuals to grasp their responsibilities to others, at least within their group, so that a person's very identity is developed. Mediating institutions teach individuals that they are not autonomous beings accountable only to their own wants and desires. Instead, a series of relationships comprise personhood and therefore human beings obtain their identity by becoming accountable for their relationships. In short, mediating institutions teach us that we are relational, not autonomous beings. Because we are relational beings, our very "self" is dependent upon ethical responsibilities. In mediating institutions, we develop bonds of affection that motivate individuals to treat others well.[3]

Stakeholder theory, social contract theory, and mediating institutions theory all revolve around the assumption that business can self-regulate. Recently, there has been a distrust of self-regulation and a move to use the criminal law system to reward and punish those businesses that behave unethically.

FEDERAL SENTENCING GUIDELINES

The U.S. Federal Sentencing Guidelines resulted from public frustration with corporate criminal conduct in the 1980s. There was a belief that corporations were not being adequately punished for the crimes they committed. This belief was borne out when statistics revealed that "[b]etween 1984 and 1987, only 41 publicly-traded firms were prosecuted for federal crimes nationwide. The mean fine imposed on the 288 corporations sentenced by federal courts during this period was only $48,164." Since corporate sentencing was the responsibility of the court system, there was a public consensus that stiffer penalties would reduce corporate crime. Therefore, the drafting of sentencing guidelines for organizations began in 1986 and after several proposals, these guidelines became effective November 1, 1991. The guidelines were amended in 1997. The amendments provided full restitution for victims of corporate crime and the felony assessments increased. In 2004, the United State Supreme Court in Blakely v. Washington struck down the state of Washington's sentencing guidelines as being unconstitutional.

Assuming that the guidelines will remain in force it is important to understand the four underlying principles. The first is that victims of corporate crime should be "made whole" or totally reimbursed. Second, businesses that

[3] Timothy L. Fort, "The Corporation as Mediating Institution: An Efficacious Synthesis of Stakeholder Theory and Corporate Constituency Statutes," 73 *Notre Dame Law Review* 173, 175 (1997).

are primarily criminal enterprises should be put out of business. Third, the fines for normal businesses should be based on the organization's culpability and high enough to ensure that the corporation does not ultimately profit. Fourth, options should be pursued that ensure continued and future compliance. These objectives are achieved by providing for compulsory sentencing for corporations engaged in illegal activity. Corporations can receive "bonus points," which can offset the penalties, if they have developed an ethics training program. Also, courts can order a company to institute ethics officers or boards. An example of how courts use the federal sentencing guidelines can be found in the next case, *In re Caremark*.

IN RE CAREMARK INTERNATIONAL, INC. DERIVATIVE LITIGATION

698 A.2d 959; 1996 Del. Ch. LEXIS 125

FACTS

Caremark, a large health-care provider, was involved in a series of health-care provider and referral programs. In 1989 the company had issued a "Guide to Contractual Relations" that set out policies governing contracts between the company and physicians and hospitals. All the programs were reviewed and approved by both Caremark's attorneys and accountants, although there was evidence that indicated Caremark knew the programs were questionable. In 1991 the federal government began investigating Caremark's practices to determine if they violated the Anti-Referral Payments Law, which prohibits paying physicians and hospitals for referrals of Medicare or Medicaid patients. As a result of the investigation, in 1991, Caremark's predecessor announced that it would no longer pay management fees to physicians and hospitals. It also revised its policies and required a regional president to approve all contracts between Caremark and physicians. In 1993, Caremark's Audit & Ethics Committee compiled a new employee ethics handbook that "expressly prohibit[ed] payments in exchange for referrals and requir[ed] employees to report all illegal conduct to a toll free confidential ethics hotline." Caremark's president also sent out a letter reiterating the policies and employees were required to attend training sessions on the ethics handbook. Even with all this and after an intensive investigation, a federal grand jury

issued a 47-page indictment against the company, two officers, a sales employee, and a physician. In the indictment, it was alleged that the doctor received $1.1 million, in the guise of research grants or consulting agreements, to induce him to distribute a human growth hormone drug marketed by Caremark. This allegation and others ultimately resulted in a plea agreement. Caremark agreed "to plead guilty to two counts of mail fraud, . . . pay $29 million in criminal fines, $129.9 million relating to civil claims, $3.5 million for alleged violations of the Controlled Substances Act, and $2 million, in the form of a donation, to a grant program set up by the Ryan White Comprehensive AIDS Resources Emergency Act." The plea agreement also "included several provisions in a 'Corporate Integrity Agreement' designed to enhance future compliance with law."

Several shareholder derivative actions were filed alleging "Caremark's directors breached their duty of care by failing to adequately supervise the conduct of Caremark employees, or institute corrective measures, thereby exposing Caremark to fines and liability." To resolve the consolidated derivative actions, Caremark agreed, among other things, to establish a new Compliance and Corporate Ethics Committee. This committee would contain four directors, two of whom would be non-management directors. The committee would report to the board semiannually and be responsible for monitoring compliance with anti-referral laws.

DECISION

Judge Allen wrote the opinion of the court:
The only question for the court in approving a proposed settlement in a shareholder derivative action is whether the proposal is fair and reasonable. Since the directors in this case were not involved in self-dealing or other breaches of loyalty issues, the good faith rule is applicable. Under general corporate law directors have an obligation to make "a good faith effort to advance corporate interest." Further, in looking at the federal Organizational Sentencing Guidelines, the court notes that the "Guidelines offer powerful incentives for corporations today to have in place compliance programs to detect violations of law, promptly to report violations to appropriate public officials when discovered, and to take prompt, voluntary remedial efforts." Today, a good faith effort requires that the board take into account the development of the federal Organizational Sentencing Guidelines "and the

enhanced penalties and the opportunities for reduced sanctions that it offers." This means that directors need to assure "themselves that information and reporting systems exist in the organization that are reasonably designed to provide to senior management and to the board itself timely, accurate information sufficient to allow management and the board, each within its scope, to reach informed judgments concerning both the corporation's compliance with law and its business performance." With this in mind, the court finds the proposed settlement is fair and reasonable and the derivative claims are dismissed.

CASE QUESTIONS

1. What did Caremark do that resulted in such large penalties?
2. How did the court use the criminal Organizational Sentencing Guidelines in this civil action?
3. Do you agree that the settlement was fair and reasonable or should the directors have suffered additional penalties?

Companies annually spend millions of dollars on their ethics/compliance programs. This does not include the money spent on legal fees associated with responding to accusations of legal and ethical wrongdoing. Many of these companies have adopted ethics/compliance programs because of the US Sentencing Commission requirements. Companies usually design their programs around the US Sentencing Guidelines. These programs often contain written codes of conduct, ethics officers, ethics telephone hotlines, and strict punishment for violators. Some studies have found that these types of programs did not produce ethical behavior. Below are some of the business scandals from 2001–2004. Remember that the Federal Sentencing Guidelines were in force during the time period in question and many of these companies, if not all, had written codes of ethics and ethics programs.

THE BUSINESS SCANDALS OF 2001–04

Enron
Enron Corporation began with the merger of two gas pipeline firms in the 1980s. It grew and expanded into a diversified energy company under the leadership of Mr. Kenneth Lay. By 1996 Enron was the largest combined gas and electricity company in the United States. In the latter part of the 1990s Enron moved beyond merely providing gas and electricity and aggressively entered the energy trading business. Essentially this meant that Enron would make a contract to purchase energy at a certain time and

price from one source, and then make another contract to sell energy to another company or utility firm at a specified price at some future time.

With Mr. Lay as a key proponent, natural gas and electricity were "deregulated," and the energy trading business really took off. Enron quickly took the lead, and entered into thousands of such trading contracts. By the late 1990s Enron reported huge revenues and profits, mostly from the marketing and trading in energy contracts. The company even expanded its operations beyond its traditional energy base, into online trading of telecommunication commodities like broadband services. Counting each contract as revenue, it showed massive growth in revenues which made the company a hit on Wall Street, and some years delivered shareholders a 200 percent return on investment. In early 2001 Enron was listed #5 on the "Fortune 500" list based on revenues.

The success of Enron and the rapid increase in its stock price was making millions of dollars for many brokers, analysts, bankers and others, as well as Enron executives. Enron acquired a reputation for innovation and "being ahead of the curve." Enron officers and employees also were called "aggressive" and sometimes "arrogant" for their abrasive and ultra-confidant behavior. They thought they were, as the title of a book written about Enron by a Fortune reporter described it "The Smartest People in the Room." Enron hosted extravagant social events and richly rewarded those employees who produced the highest revenues, and the investment bankers who supplied massive funding when Enron needed cash. It only became clear later that much of this profit and revenue was based upon illegal and fraudulent accounting and financial techniques.

The Enron energy trading business was run by Jeffrey Skilling, a brilliant and cocky Harvard MBA graduate, who became President of Enron. Mr. Skilling believed that older, "stodgy" energy companies would soon be eliminated by the sleek, "asset-light" Enron. "In the old days, people worked for assets," he said, but "now we've turned it around, and assets work for people." Even when Enron's share price soared above $80/share, Mr. Skilling refused to provide much financial information on how the huge numbers were calculated. When asked to provide more detail, Skilling replied, "Our business is very simple to model. People who raise questions are people who have not gone through it in detail." Apparently most of the board of directors, and the bankers, financial analysts and auditors really had no idea of how Enron was funded and the incredible level of debt it had assumed. As long as the money continued to roll in, and everyone doing business with Enron was getting rich, no one pushed hard enough to get the true answers.

Then later in 2001, Enron's stock price began to fall. By now Mr. Skilling was the CEO of Enron, with Mr. Lay as Chairman. Enron was criticized after the energy crisis in California in 2000 which resulted in shortages, brownouts and huge price increases. [Note: As this book was going to press in late 2004, news stories disclosed the contents of phone conversations between Enron traders in 2000, in which they boldly tell each other how to create and manipulate such shortages, and how to reap the greatest profits from them]. Enron, already saddled with $5 billion in debt from moneylosing projects around the world, had borrowed another $1 billion to increase it capacity to trade data transmission on fiber optic cable. In order to minimize these debts and losses, Mr. Skilling and Chief Financial Officer

Andrew Fastow began to create hundreds of off-balance sheet partnerships that did business with Enron and to which much debt could be transferred.

Mr. Fastow and his friends and family served as managers and partners of many of these "special purpose entities" (SPEs) and reaped large profits—often in the millions of dollars—from them as well as their salaries from Enron. Such off-balance sheet partnerships are legal transactions, if done properly. But many of the Enron SPEs did not have the required amount of outside investment to qualify as separate from Enron and for the transactions to be kept off the Enron books. Sometimes Enron stock was used (improperly) to fund the entities, or the "outside" party would pay using a loan from Enron and when interest on the loan was paid, it was counted (improperly) as income by Enron.

Mr. Skilling abruptly resigned as CEO in August, after less than 6 months in that post, and Mr. Lay again took the position. At this point, Enron's stock price was about $40/share, its profit margins were shrinking, and questions were being asked by outsiders. Mr. Fastow needed to raise money for Enron and was attempting to find as many assets as possible to sell. He asked Enron vice-president Sharron Watkins to find appropriate assets, but everywhere she looked, she found off-the-books arrangements that no one wanted to explain. Those who questioned Mr. Skilling or Mr. Fastow soon found themselves transferred to other positions. Ms. Watkins discovered that Enron was losing substantial money on certain projects, but the losses never showed up on the balance sheet. "It just didn't add up," she said. Meanwhile, unbeknowst to the public, Mr. Lay, Mr. Fastow and Mr. Skilling were selling millions of their Enron shares on the market.

Shortly after Skilling's resignation, Mr. Lay called an all-employees meeting to reassure them that all was well, and that the company was in fine shape. He told employees to contact him if they had any questions. Ms. Watkins did so, sending him an anonymous note and then a signed 6-page letter a few days later. She met with Mr. Lay and told him she was worried that Enron might "implode from accounting and financial problems." He promised to check on her concerns, but after he met with Enron's law firm he reported there were minor problems, but nothing serious. During this period of time, because the Enron pension plan was changing administrators, Enron employees were prohibited from selling Enron stock, which comprised the majority of the employees' 401(k) pension and retirement plans. This "black-out period" did not cover Enron executives, however.

Then in October, Mr. Lay was forced to report that Enron was taking a $35 million charge to reflect losses on the off-book partnerships, and to announce that Enron had lost $618 million in the 3rd quarter. He also reported that Enron was reducing equity by $1.2 billion, due to losses and dealings with some of the off-book partnerships. Investors and analysts began to doubt Enron's profitability claims, and suddenly its lack of financial candor became a major problem. The scope of its debt began to emerge, and as its credit rating decreased, the cost of its loans increased. Also many of the off-book deals had clauses requiring Enron to pay millions of dollars on demand if its stock price fell below a certain level.

Such news and other rumors caused the federal Securities and Exchange Commission to open an inquiry into Enron on October 31. The bad news caused Enron's trading partners to lose confidence and business went down.

Enron desperately tried to arrange new loans, or to merge with another utility trading company, but was not successful. Meanwhile, creditors closed in and on December 2, 2001, Enron filed for bankruptcy protection under Chapter 11, listing a debt of $13.1 billion, with another $18 billion debt for its affiliates. It was the largest bankruptcy in history, at that time.

In the next year or so, the true picture of the Enron financial "house of cards" became clear. Ms. Watkins' note to a colleague at the accounting firm Arthur Andersen regarding the improper off-balance sheet partnerships and other financial misdeeds was forwarded to a member of Congress, and Ms. Watkins testified at Congressional hearings about what she had found at Enron. Disclosure about the sales of stock by key executives during the decline of Enron were made public, and many Enron managers and executives, including Mr. Fastow and Mr. Skilling were charged with federal crimes. Mr. Fastow and his wife pleaded guilty to certain charges, and went to jail for different periods of time, as did several other Enron employees. Mr. Skilling pleaded "not guilty" and went to trial. Mr. Lay was not charged with any crimes until July 2004, at which time he asserted his innocence. Mr. Skilling and Mr. Lay were found guilty of many federal fraud and insider trading charges, after a 4-month trial in May 2006.

Both were sentenced to more than 20 years in prison. Mr. Lay died of a heart attack before his sentence began with the result that his conviction was vacated. Mr. Skilling is serving 24 years in prison, although he is still appealing his conviction. Mr. Skilling got some good news in 2010 when the U.S. Supreme Court limited the use of the "honest services" theory which was the basis of his conviction. For years prosecutors had used this theory to charge corporate officials with fraud based on their action in depriving shareholders of their honest services. The Court, in an appeal by Mr. Skilling and others, decided that this was too vague an interpretation of the federal fraud law, and limited such prosecutions to instances of bribes or kickbacks.

There were numerous other adverse ramifications from the Enron debacle. All shareholders (who still held Enron stock) lost essentially all of their investment. Enron stock fell from $80/share to pennies per share in value. Thousands of Enron employees were laid off as Enron shrank to a much smaller firm, and many of the employees and former employees lost all of their retirement funds, as it was mostly invested in Enron stock. Creditors and banks who loaned millions of dollars to Enron were battling within the bankruptcy court to see how much they would be able to recover. Numerous shareholders have filed suit against Enron seeking to recover some of their lost funds, claiming federal Securities law fraud, "insider trading," and other violations. The Justice Department later brought criminal charges against Enron, and several of its key lenders for violation of banking and securities laws. Ms. Watkins was named one of three "Persons of the Year" and featured in a cover story in Time Magazine.

Arthur Andersen

Arthur Andersen, LLP (Limited Liability Partnership) was Enron's auditor. This venerable international accounting powerhouse was long regarded as one of the very top auditing and accounting firms in the world. At one time it was the largest accounting firm in the world. Andersen was noted for independence in auditing its clients and its insistence on following accounting rules in a rigorous manner. However during the 1980s and 1990s, all large accounting firms developed management consulting practices, which became more and more profitable over time. The pressure on the auditing partners to approve their clients' financial reporting, in order to not lose the lucrative consulting business of the client, became tremendous.

Enron had been a client of Arthur Andersen for many years, and the relationship grew closer over time. Andersen had become much more than an outside independent auditor of Enron's financial records, and was closer to a partner. Andersen developed at Enron a system that combined the external audit role with the "internal audit"—the company's own review of its books—and combined both of those with consulting services. "Out here, we don't call audit, audit," said one Andersen auditor. Arthur Andersen even rented one whole floor of the Enron office tower in Houston for an office to house 100 of its employees, in order to be closer to Enron and serve its needs better. By 2001, Enron was one of Andersen's top three clients worldwide, with annual billings of $54 million for auditing and consulting services in 2000.

Andersen was providing constant advice to Enron regarding the keeping of records, helping create the off-book partnerships and assisting in the development of sophisticated accounting techniques needed by Enron's varied and speculative trading practices. Occasionally an Andersen partner would complain that some financial move Enron was making was not authorized by accounting rules, but that person was most often overruled, or sometimes taken off the account. On other occasions Andersen's Professional Standards Group, based at Andersen headquarters in Chicago, criticized some of the financial and accounting practices used by Enron, but apparently the advice was ignored by Andersen's Houston office which dealt directly with Enron.

As Enron began to falter and head downhill in late 2001, it was apparent that government agencies were going to probe Enron, and that private lawsuits were likely to follow. In October an Andersen attorney from the head office sent an e-mail to David Duncan, the lead partner on the Enron account, reminding him of Andersen's "document retention" policy (what to keep and what to throw away). Mr. Duncan, knowing that the SEC had started an informal investigation, held a staff meeting and told the staff about the "document retention" memo. Following the meeting, Mr. Duncan initiated a massive and wholesale shredding program. During the next two weeks the Arthur Andersen shredding machine in the Enron building was running non-stop, while "tons and tons" of Enron-related documents were shredded. Secretaries waited in a long line at the shredder with scores of trunks and boxes. Frustrated with waiting, Andersen hired a courier who shipped 20 or 30 trunks of documents to Andersen's downtown Houston office, where they were shredded. Thousands of e-mail messages were also deleted.

Only when the SEC announced the beginning of a formal investigation did the shredding stop. Meanwhile, news of the document shredding was hitting the papers and airwaves. Mr. Duncan was called to Andersen headquarters to answer questions and was later fired. Andersen officials announced that a "significant number" of documents had been destroyed, but argued that this was clearly the action of a few individuals and not the firm. However, several private lawsuits were filed by Enron creditors and investors alleging negligence and malpractice by Andersen in its audits of Enron, and the Justice Department began an investigation of criminal charges.

A few months later, the Justice Department did bring criminal charges against the firm Arthur Andersen for "obstruction of justice." The prosecutors noted that only one year earlier, the firm had entered into an agreement with the Securities and Exchange Commission related to an accounting fraud investigation of another Andersen client, Waste Management Inc. As part of the settlement in that case, Andersen had paid a $7 million fine, and had signed a consent decree promising not to commit misdeeds in the future. Now the prosecutors charged that Arthur Andersen had done it again. The Justice Department charged that Andersen did "knowingly and intentionally persuade or attempt to 'corruptly persuade' other persons (partners and employees) to withhold documents and other objects from an official proceeding." (the new SEC investigation)

After a 21-day trial in federal district court in Houston, the jury was sequestered and deliberated for 10 days. At times, the jury seemed unable to reach a verdict, but Judge Melinda Harmon sent them back to "redouble your efforts." In the end the jury did find Arthur Andersen guilty on one count of Obstruction of Justice, which is a felony—the first time any major U.S. accounting firm had been convicted of a felony. One of the jurors told the press later that decisive evidence was not the testimony of David Duncan, who had pleaded guilty himself and testified for the prosecution, but rather one e-mail message from an attorney at Andersen headquarters.

During fall 2001, as events began to unfold at Enron, Mr. Duncan had sent and received a number of e-mail messages from the Chicago office. The Professional Standards Group had sent several memos to the Houston office indicating their concern that some of Enron's off-book partnerships and the financials concerning those partnerships violated the accounting profession's "Generally Accepted Accounting Principles." Ms. Nancy Temple, a member of Andersen's legal staff, then sent out the "document retention" memo described earlier. Mr. Duncan, the Anderson partner on the Enron account, also sent Ms. Temple a draft "memo to the file" in which he described a meeting he had with Enron's accounting chief. Mr. Duncan had advised the Enron executive that a particular press release Enron was planning to issue describing a large loss as "non-recurring" was "misleading" and was the type of thing that led to SEC investigations.

Mr. Duncan recorded this conversation in his internal memo, and sent it to Ms. Temple for comment. She replied, suggesting that "to protect ourselves" he delete the part about "we concluded the press release was misleading" and also delete any reference to consultation with the Andersen headquarters legal staff and delete "my name" from the memo. Mr. Duncan did make the suggested changes in his memo before putting it in the file. The jury foreman declared that this memo from Ms. Temple was indeed the "smoking gun" that showed that Andersen knew that the SEC was coming to investigate, and that she was trying to "corruptly persuade" Mr. Duncan to alter information and keep it from the SEC.

Thus Arthur Andersen was found guilty of a federal felony, and fined $500,000. Of much more importance, after a felony conviction federal law prohibited the firm from performing audits of public companies, and in the next few months the entire Andersen firm—with 28,000 employees in the United States—was liquidated and closed. Several years later the conviction was overturned on technical legal issues by the U.S. Supreme Court—but the Andersen firm no longer existed.

WorldCom

After the spectacular fall of Enron in late 2001, and the Arthur Andersen trial and conviction in 2002, there were many calls for Congress to act to ensure better financial reporting by large companies, and force accounting firms to more accurately audit such companies and issue more detailed reports. Hearings were held, several bills were introduced and debated, and much testimony was taken. However, by summer, the momentum for major change was beginning to slow down, and Congress was dealing with other issues. Then in mid-summer 2002, the WorldCom scandal broke.

WorldCom had started out as a small Mississippi telecommunications business, but then with Mr. Bernie Ebbers as the CEO, embarked on an aggressive buying spree, purchasing numerous other companies including MCI, and turning WorldCom into a major player in the Industry. Its share price was rising, and it was reporting huge profits.

Internal auditors are charged with analyzing the financial picture of a company from the inside, with the hope of finding ways to save money and cut costs, among other duties. Ms. Cynthia Cooper was head of the internal auditing department at WorldCom and while performing her duties in 2002 she continually found numbers that she could not reconcile. She was concerned and attempted to get answers from the WorldCom's Chief Financial Officer, Scott Sullivan, but he told her it was not her business and to stop looking. However, she and her team continued to investigate, and the more they looked, the worse the situation appeared.

It turned out that a massive fraud had been going on for some time. Among other things, WorldCom had been counting charges it paid local phone companies to use phone lines as "capital expenses" rather that ordinary operating expenses, the sort of accounting principle that students learn in Accounting 101. Capital expenses (purchase of equipment, etc) can be allocated over many years, while operating expenses directly offset current income. Counting an expense as "capital" thus greatly increases current income.

Ms. Cooper estimated that hundreds of fraudulent entries had allowed WorldCom to reduce its reported expenses by $4 billion over the previous few years. Instead of making a large profit, Worldcom had actually been losing money. There were numerous other dishonest financial records as well. When Mr. Sullivan refused to listen, Ms. Cooper took her concerns to the WorldCom board of directors, who shortly thereafter fired Mr. Sullivan. A few weeks later, Mr. Ebbers resigned, and as the news of the massive fraud became public, the value of WorldCom stock plunged and the company filed for Chapter 11 Bankruptcy protection, surpassing Enron as the largest bankruptcy in history—the financial fraud is now estimated at $11 billion. In 2004, WorldCom emerged from bankruptcy and is now called MCI.

Both Mr. Sullivan and Mr. Ebbers were charged with federal crimes, including securities law violations, fraud and conspiracy. After further investigation, a WorldCom internal report in June 2003 said Mr. Ebbers fostered a poisonous corporate culture and that he was "aware, at a minimum, that WorldCom was meeting revenue expectations through financial gimmickry." Mr. Ebbers denied all charges but was found guilty and given a long prison sentence. Mr. Sullivan denied the charges at first, but in June 2004 pleaded guilty to one charge and agreed to testify against Mr. Ebbers in return for a reduced prison sentence. Several other former WorldCom officials have also pleaded guilty to various fraud charges. Ms. Cooper continued to work for

WorldCom, gave testimony to Congress, and like Ms. Watkins, was named one of the three "Persons of the Year" by Time Magazine.

Martha Stewart

Martha Stewart, the famous expert on all things concerning the home, cooking and gardening, was convicted, along with her broker, in 2004 of conspiring to lie about a stock trade. Ms. Stewart was a good friend of the CEO of Imclone Corp. and it was alleged that she had received a phone call from him alerting her to some upcoming bad news about the company. She sold her Imclone stock holdings shortly before the news was announced. Ms. Stewart and her broker claimed that her sale of stock was part of a previous arrangement with the broker to sell whenever the stock was trading at a certain price. While the government charges of insider trading were dropped, she and her broker were found guilty by a jury of lying about the nature of the trade and preparing false statements, and she served several months in prison and had to wear an "ankle" monitor for several months after her prison term ended.

Questions regarding these corporate scandals

1. While each of these instances has resulted in legal troubles for the firms, were the root causes of the difficulties really ethical issues? Discuss and argue either yes or no, giving facts to support your opinion in each case.

2. Suppose that you, as an employee in the Enron financial department, discovered that the off-book partnerships were being used improperly, in a way that gave a false impression of Enron's true financial status. If you wanted to behave ethically, and you wanted Enron to do so also, what could you have done? The power and pressure exerted by Mr. Skilling and Mr. Fastow were enormous—how could you have taken action to get Enron back on the right course?

3. Analyze the Enron and WorldCom situations using utilitarian ethical analysis. Were the actions of the corporate officers achieving "the greatest good for the greatest number?" What groups of people were affected by their actions? In what ways?

4. Ms. Watkins (Enron) and Ms. Cooper (WorldCom) were lauded by the press as "whistleblowers." While they did seek to find the truth, and refused to endorse financial and accounting practices they knew were misleading, they both stated they did not like the term "whistleblower" because they had tried to get changes made <u>within</u> the companies, rather than going to the press or government with their findings. Were their actions in the best interests of their companies?

5. The Arthur Andersen partnership had long been one of the great accounting and auditing firms in the world. When it was convicted, as a firm, for a federal crime, that caused the firm to dissolve and thousands of people lost their jobs. Was this criminal prosecution a "miscarriage of justice" as some commentators claimed, causing the death of the firm due to the bad actions of a few people? Or was it fair for Andersen to be held responsible for its actions in approving and assisting Enron in perpetuating the false and misleading financial information that eventually caused thousands of employees to lose their jobs and thousands of investors to lose millions of dollars? Discuss fully.

THE SARBANES-OXLEY ACT

In 2002, in response to the business scandals outlined above, Congress enacted the Sarbanes-Oxley Act. A full description of the numerous provisions of this major new federal statute is contained in Chapters 9 and 10 of this textbook, but a brief summary will be set forth here.

Some of the most important sections of the law required that: (1) A new federal agency was established to set rules for, and regulate accounting firms which audit public companies; (2) The chief executive officer (CEO) and chief financial officer (CFO) of public companies will be required to certify, under oath, that the financial reports of their companies truly and accurately reflect the financial status of their firms; (3) auditing firms are no longer allowed to provide most types of financial, bookkeeping, and consulting services to public companies they are auditing; (4) the lead auditor for the accounting firm which does the audit of a public company must be changed every five years; (5) the audit committee of the board of directors must be completely composed of "independent" directors, who are not employees of the company, and they must choose and supervise the auditor; (6) public corporations must have a code of ethics for their top officers or must explain why not to the SEC; (7) no officers or directors will be allowed to sell their company stock during a "blackout period" when employees cannot sell shares; (8) a company may not make loans to corporate officers or directors; (9) the top officers of a corporation may not have been employed by the firm's auditors for at least one year preceding the audit; and (10) all public company quarterly and annual financial reports must disclose any "off-balance sheet" transactions affecting the firm.

Many of these sections of the Sarbanes-Oxley Act were included because of specific instances of corporate behavior reported in the business scandals set forth above.

CONTEMPORARY ISSUES INVOLVING BUSINESS ETHICS

WHISTLE-BLOWERS

We have recounted some of the events leading to the series of ethical scandals that have hit American firms in recent years. Much of the information regarding the misleading financial information that led to the fall of Enron, WorldCom and other companies was brought to light by "whistleblowers" such as Sherron Watkins of Enron and Cynthia Cooper of WorldCom, who refused to go along with the fraud they discovered. Although neither woman felt comfortable with the term "whistleblower" because they tried to correct the problems internally within the company, rather than immediately running to the press, their courageous actions and others did lead to the public disclosure of the false and fraudulent financial schemes. In the past, there are numerous other examples of employees trying to "blow the whistle" on wrongful corporate actions before disasters occurred.

Shortly before the fateful launch of the Challenger space shuttle mission in 1986 in which all the American astronauts were killed, several engineers at Morton Thiokol Co. became concerned about the durability of the "O rings" that sealed off dangerous hot gases from the oxygen tanks on the rocket propulsion system. These experts worried that if the shuttle was launched when temperatures were below a certain level, the rings could fail and the rockets explode.

The engineers expressed their concerns to their supervisors. However, the shuttle program was behind schedule, public support for the high costs of the space program appeared to be waning, and the managers did not want Morton Thiokol to be labeled as the company that slowed down the shuttle program.

Nevertheless, the concerns were passed along to NASA, and certain meetings were convened, but there was tremendous pressure to go ahead with the launch. After all, no shuttle launch had ever resulted in an explosion, and the concerns seemed far-fetched. Unfortunately, the O Rings did fail, the rocket exploded, and the seven-member crew, including the first teacher in space, was killed.

Difficult situations arise on the job—including worker safety, waste disposal, hiring and firing employees, and financial assessment—for which difficult decisions need to be made. In a perfect world, employers would expect all employees who saw something that needed correcting either to take the necessary actions themselves or to bring it to the attention of their supervisors. This course of action would be in the best interests of the corporation, and the employees would be praised and rewarded for such conscientious and ethically proper deeds.

However, in the real world, often the employee who "blows the whistle" concerning some improper or illegal activity (such as reporting a problem to authorities) is penalized rather than praised for the action. When the **whistle-blower** reports that supplies are consistently missing from the stockroom, or that chemicals are being dumped into a nearby river, or that safety equipment has been removed from machines, or that the corporate financial records are not accurate, undoubtedly another employee or manager stands to be reprimanded or fired if the allegations are true. If the problem is serious and pervasive, many people may be involved, some of whom might be receiving significant financial rewards from the scheme. The whistle-blower's credibility will be attacked by many powerful forces, and he or she may end up being fired as the result of performing an ethical act intended to benefit the business.

> **whistle-blower:** One who reveals something covert or informs authorities about some illegal or unethical business actions.

Ernest Fitzgerald, an Air Force employee, discovered billions of dollars in excess charges and overruns billed to the federal government by Lockheed Corporation in 1968. But after he complained, he was fired. George Collier, a regional manager for MCA, noticed that several executives of the entertainment company were ordering big shipments of free records for people not entitled to them. He notified his supervisor three times of this possible kickback scheme, but instead of receiving a reward, he was fired, according to a lawsuit he has filed against the company.

Both the Dodd-Frank and Sarbanes-Oxley Acts contain "whistleblower protection" provisions. The Dodd-Frank Act even contains a section which allows whistleblowers who report financial fraud to collect 10% to 30% of the amount later extracted in fines and settlements, or at least a minimum of $100,000 for a tip that leads to penalties over $1 million. The reporting agencies are the Securities and Exchange Commission (SEC) and the Commodity Futures Trading Commission (CFTC).

Section 806 of the Sarbanes-Oxley Act protects employees of public companies who "blow the whistle" from retaliation when they report conduct that they reasonably believe constitutes a violation of federal law relating to financial, securities or shareholder fraud. The claim of retaliation must be filed with the Occupational Safety and Health Administration within 90 days of the violation occurs. A recent court decision [*Stone v. Instrumentation Laboratory Co.,* 591 F.3d 239 (4th Cir. 2009)] held that if the DOL does not issue a decision within 180 days of the complaint, the individual may file a federal court suit.

SOCIAL/ETHICAL ISSUE

Consider the following questions with regard to the treatment of whistle-blowers:

1. Studies reveal that even with the growing legal protection for whistle-blowers, many suffer demotions and ill health related to victimization. Whistleblowers are still more likely to be disciplined and ostracized than thanked. What can we do to encourage legitimate whistle-blowers to come forward when they face such risks?

2. Discuss the advantages and disadvantages of removing an employer's managerial discretion to terminate for a lack of loyalty when the lack of loyalty stems from an employee's report of illegal behavior.

EMPLOYEE PRIVACY

In an effort to more closely supervise and evaluate their employees, many companies use sophisticated technology to monitor the activities of their workers. The majority of large U.S. businesses now employ some type of drug-testing program, often before the employee is hired and sometimes on a random basis during employment. Other employers conduct searches of employee lockers or work areas, monitor employee phone calls, and videotape employees at work. One firm even installed special chairs, hooked up to computers to monitor employee wiggling while at their desks, under the belief that "wigglers aren't workers." An increasing number of firms are showing interest in off-the-job activities of workers as well, including smoking, drinking, and sexual and social activities.

In recent years there has been an explosion of the use of electronic mail and the Internet system, by which one can converse instantly with others around the world. Employers are showing concern for and more closely monitoring and controlling the amount of time these services are used by employees, as well as the content and purposes of the communications.

SWEATSHOPS AND HUMAN TRAFFICKING

For many people the "sweatshop" image conjures up photographs taken in the United States in the early 1900s showing children in coal mines and women killed in factory fires because all the doors were locked to prevent them from leaving. As a result, laws were passed aimed at preventing sweatshops. In particular, the Fair Labor Standards Act was passed, which prohibited child labor in the United States and set a federal minimum wage. (This act is discussed in more detail in Chapter 22.) The sweatshop controversy publicly resurfaced in the 1990s when it was discovered that clothes bearing the label of television personality Kathie Lee Gifford were made using child labor in overseas factories. Besides child labor, there were also allegations that Thailand makers of athletic shoes received 25 cents an hour for 18-hour days. Workers at a factory in the Dominican Republic claimed to make only 8 cents a hat for baseball caps bearing a Brown University logo.

To try to remedy the child labor problems, Ms. Gifford herself got personally involved in establishing monitoring programs for factories that produce her clothing. Also, several universities, including Brown, Notre Dame, and Duke, have passed codes of conduct aimed at monitoring factories producing college-related merchandise, including apparel. These codes of conduct range

getta **clue**

Manufacturer—orders denim and pocketing material, makes pattern and guide for cutting and sewing, and sends to a contractor for cutting.

Fabric—cotton denim, 1-1/2 yards, $6

Cutter—cuts pieces that make up the jeans. Most cutters work at an hourly rate, often not getting overtime. If the deadline is short, they may have to work 10 hours a day, 6 days a week to complete an order.

Sewer—sews together cut jeans pieces and pockets. Sewers are paid per piece. They have quotas for the number of pieces they must produce, quotas that are often set too high. Workers who can't keep up may find themselves out of a job.

Finisher—adds rivets, trims threads, sews on buttons. Some finishers get 1¢ for sewing on each button. At that rate, a worker would have to sew buttons on 20,600 pairs of jeans in a 40-hour week to make minimum wage.

Retailer—sells the product to you.

Bottom Line — How much did you pay for your last pair of blue jeans? And how much of that went to the workers who made those jeans? Think about it!

Life Cycle of a Blue Jean, Sweatshop Style

Clearly, not every garment manufacturer or contractor operates a sweatshop. Many follow the law and pay their employees legal wages, and some employers go well beyond the minimum requirements of the law. The situations above are representative of conditions found in a sweatshop. Costs of materials and labor and the production process vary from one manufacturer to the next.

"If I could convince you of one thing, it's that you **can** make a difference in this world. The decisions you make, the actions you take, how you shop can help put an end to sweatshops and make a difference in the lives of so many workers."

Alexis M. Herman
U.S. Secretary of Labor

Working Teen

Many employers in the garment industry want to do the right thing and obey the law, but some don't. Some employers operate sweatshops, where people work in unsafe environments without getting the money they have earned. Sweatshops give a whole new meaning to the phrase, "get a job." Garment workers—some of them younger than you—work to pay rent and put food on the table. They are usually paid for each piece they sew, and they don't always make minimum wage, let alone receive benefits like health insurance. For example, at 15¢ per jeans pocket, you would have to sew at least 275 pockets in 8 hours to make the minimum wage of $5.15 per hour. If you were only able to sew 200 pockets instead of 275, your hourly wage would be $3.75—less than the price of a movie ticket and less than the legal wage.

Do you know how your clothes were made?

Find out!

NO SWEAT. **U.S. Department of Labor**

Get Involved

Want to make a difference? You can help put sweatshops out of fashion and into the trash heap.

 You can ask questions where you shop about the clothes you are buying.

 You can ask where you shop whether they check on their garment manufacturers to make sure they're following the law.

 You can ask where you shop whether they support "No Sweat" clothing.

Drop into our No Sweat Website at www.dol.gov.

from requests that factories comply with local law, to provisions that workers make a living wage, to requirements that the wages match or exceed local prevailing wages or that wages meet the basic needs of workers.

Not everyone agrees that sweatshops are necessarily bad. Some utilitarians argue that sweatshops are essential to move countries to the next level of development. The claim is that sweatshops are always the first step in development and that in many countries children are better off working than being sold into slavery.

As the debate rages, it is important to note that the issue is not confined to developing countries. A U.S. Department of Labor Brochure campaign in 2000 called "Getta Clue," (see previous page) focused on some U.S. manufacturers operating sweatshops often times with illegal immigrants who are virtual "slaves," who are afraid to complain or who are unaware of their rights under U.S. law. It is estimated that 14,500 to 17,500 people, mostly girls, are smuggled into the United States each year to work in a variety of trades. This is referred to as "human trafficking" and in 2004 President George W. Bush indicated that "The American government has a particular duty, because human trafficking is an affront to the defining promise of our country." In 2004, the U.S. Department of Justice successfully prosecuted the largest human trafficking case in U.S. history, convicting the ringleader of a criminal gang that had smuggled more than 200 Vietnamese and Chinese nationals to work as slave laborers in a garment factory on American Samoa.

In 2010 the California Transparency in Supply Chains Act was passed requiring retail sellers and manufacturers doing business in California to publicly "disclose their efforts to eradicate slavery and human trafficking from their direct supply chains." It requires disclosures on the company's web site concerning the firm's efforts to evaluate and address risks of human trafficking and slavery in its supply chain, auditing of suppliers to evaluate compliance with company standards, supplier certification of compliance with standards, internal accountability procedures for failures to meet standards and training for responsible employees and management. The law takes effect on January 1 of 2012.

Human Trafficking Court Action Filed

U.S. Equal Employment Opportunity Commission filed a huge human-trafficking lawsuit against a California-based farm labor contractor in April 2011. It was called the largest case of alleged forced labor of farm workers in the United States. The EEOC accused Global Horizons Manpower Inc., based in Beverly Hills, California, and eight farms of luring more than 200 men from Thailand to work at farms in Hawaii and Washington, by promising them good jobs.

"Upon arriving to the U.S., their passports were confiscated, they were not paid for their work and they were threatened with deportation if they complained," said an EEOC attorney in announcing details of the lawsuit. It also alleges they were forced to live in cramped, dirty conditions and the workers endured screaming, threats and physical assaults by their supervisors. "In some cases bodyguards were stationed around the farms to ensure that none of the workers escaped," said the EEOC attorney.

Source: CNN.com, April 21, 2011

SUMMARY

In dealing with the problem of how to select and retain top quality employees, as well as hundreds of other issues arising every day in business, various ethical and social issues arise. At what point does a company owe its employees loyalty, trust, and responsibility? Is there a difference between what a firm can or should do to test and investigate prospective employees, as opposed to existing employees? Is there any duty to society as well as to the employees? Should a firm adopt an egoist approach (whatever is best for us) or incorporate utilitarianism (greatest good for the greatest number) or attempt to universalize the processes it undertakes? Should a business firm attempt to alter an individual's own beliefs to conform to the views of the management? These are all questions you will need to answer as you face the difficult choices inherent in any business career. The discussions in this chapter may give you some thoughts to consider when the time arrives for making decisions.

CHAPTER QUESTIONS

1. Explain the difference between individualism and communitarianism and give current examples of each. Which do you think is the more dominant theory in the United States today?

2. What is the difference between virtues and values?

3. Discuss and compare the most well-known ethical theories, as explained in the text.

4. Compare the arguments of Milton Friedman and Christopher Stone regarding the role and duty of corporations toward society. Which argument is more persuasive to you? Explain.

5. What are some other issues you believe raise ethical dilemmas for business? In your own working experience, have you been put in a situation where you had to decide whether you should do something you did not believe was right? Describe.

6. Shoplifting is a very serious problem for retail store owners, with millions of dollars of merchandise stolen each year. Obviously, some shoplifters put clothing and other items under their clothes and then attempt to leave the store. Video cameras in every bathroom and dressing room would undoubtedly reduce successful shoplifting. What ethical issues are raised by such action?

7. What are the ethical issues involved in allowing an auditing firm to provide consulting services to a firm whose financial reports they audit?

8. Many employees face problems when balancing the demands of their work and their family. Suppose that a single parent works in an office where personal phone calls are prohibited. However, this person's eight-year-old daughter is home alone for three hours every day after school. This employee receives on average two phone calls per day from her daughter as problems

arise—some days there are three or four calls, and some days one or none. If you are this person's supervisor and are aware of these calls, what would you do about it? Compare your response using different ethical theories.

9. There have been a number of lawsuits filed by former employees on the basis of libel and slander. These employees had been fired and later applied for another job, only to have their former employer provide unfavorable remarks about their performance. In response to hearing about these lawsuits, some companies refuse to disclose anything other than name and period of employment about former employees. Suppose you are a manager at the Ace Trucking Company, and you have fired a worker because he used drugs while driving and also attempted to pick up young girls for sexual purposes. Is it ethical for you to refrain from giving any of this information to another company who is thinking of hiring this person as a school bus driver? Discuss, applying different theories.

10. What were some of the underlying causes of the business scandals of the past 10 years? Why were so many false and misleading financial statements issued without anyone saying "No, that's not right"? What lessons have we learned from these scandals?

PRACTICAL EXERCISE

Albert Roberts was manager of environmental affairs for Bigtime Oil Co. The Environmental Protection Agency requires companies like Bigtime to keep various records regarding toxic wastes and discharges from facilities that may cause air and water pollution. Bigtime must also furnish the records to federal and local authorities upon request.

In May, Los Angeles environmental officials seized records from one of Bigtime's facilities. In June, Mr. Roberts' boss ordered him to remove and destroy certain environmental records from a different plant in another California location. Mr. Roberts refused to do so and ordered his staff not to participate in any such removal either. Mr. Roberts was also directed to make changes in certain internal environmental reports before they were given to the company Board of Directors, but he refused to do this as well. In August, Mr. Roberts was laid off, because, according to the company, he had "antagonized his colleagues and become an ineffective manager."

In another state, a year later, a different executive of Bigtime Oil sued the company, alleging that he was fired because he disclosed health and environmental problems associated with Bigtime products. The company denied his claim, stating that he was fired for using company assets to further his own private business.

Assuming that the claims of the fired managers were true, analyze and write a short paper discussing the ethical issues Bigtime is facing. What effect will firing the two managers have on (1) future practices concerning environmental recordkeeping, (2) environmental practices of the company, and (3) the personal ethical practices of all employees who learn of the situation? What would you do if you were now a manager of environmental affairs at a Bigtime facility and you discovered that someone in the company was improperly disposing of toxic waste? Use the ethical theories described in the chapter in reaching your conclusions.

FURTHER INFORMATION

www.ethics.ubc.ca/resources/business/
www.socialinvest.org/
www.dol.gov/dol/esa/public/nosweat/nosweat.htm

CHAPTER 8

PRINCIPAL–AGENT RELATIONSHIPS AND PARTNERSHIPS

LEARNING OBJECTIVES

After you have read this chapter, you should be able to:

1. Describe the different types of agency relationships and the duties and liabilities of agents and principals.
2. List the characteristics of the various forms of business organizations.
3. Discuss the key legal attributes of partnerships.
4. Explain the concepts of personal liability and partnership responsibility for torts and contracts.
5. Detail the special characteristics of partnerships, limited partnerships, limited liability partnerships, and limited liability limited partnerships.

CHAPTER OUTLINE

I. Creation of Agency Relationships

II. Liabilities of the Principal for Acts of the Agent

III. Sole Proprietorships

IV. Partnerships

V. Limited Partnerships

VI. Limited Liability Partnerships

VII. Limited Liability Limited Partnerships

This is first of two chapters dealing with the formation and operation of various forms of business firms. At the end of this chapter the exercise involves three friends who have decided to form a partnership to engage in the health food business. You are asked to help them put together a partnership agreement, which will reflect their contributions to the business, provide for successful operation, and anticipate changes that may occur as their operations expand.

255

INTRODUCTION

Although most students have some knowledge of corporations and partnerships, agency relationships may not be so familiar. The concept most people have of an "agent" is likely to be the person who negotiates a contract on behalf of a movie star or a baseball player. While such a person is definitely an agent, the significance of agency relationships in business is much greater. All partnerships and corporations—from the two-person accounting firm to the multibillion-dollar company—can act *only* through agents. Even corporations with 100,000 shareholders and a 20-member board of directors can only act when some person or group (an employee or the board of directors, for example) takes some action *as its agent* and on its behalf. A large firm's employees and partners will do hundreds of things every day that may or may not legally bind the firm, depending on the laws of agency. A study of the principles of agency law is thus a good place to start our examination of business organizations.

For example, a partner in an accounting firm may agree, on behalf of the firm, to do an audit for the Acme Steel Corporation at the price of $5,000. Such an action is normally within the scope of a partner's authority, and this action will therefore probably create a contract to which the partnership is bound. On the other hand, suppose that a clerk at the accounting firm goes to a bank on his lunch hour and borrows $10,000 "for the firm," without being asked to do so by anyone. It is unlikely that this action will be binding on the accounting firm because of the clerk's **lack of authority** to make such an agreement on behalf of the firm. On the other hand, the clerk might have authority to bind the firm when he goes to the office supply store and purchases $150 worth of computer disks, paper and other supplies using the firm's account. We will analyze the concept of an agent's authority thoroughly in the next few pages and then look at other aspects of the agency relationship. One of the most classic and important examples of agency law occurs with the formation and operation of partnerships. Later in the chapter, the legal aspects of the partnership form of business enterprise will be examined in detail.

CREATION OF AGENCY RELATIONSHIPS

agent: One who performs some action on behalf of another person or firm, called the principal.

principal: A person who hires another to act as an agent.

An **agent** is a person who performs some act on behalf of another person called a **principal.** The relationship may be informal, or it may involve a lengthy written contract. One important requirement is that both parties **consent** to the relationship—that is, they both must agree that one will act for and on behalf of the other. As we have mentioned, corporations and partnerships can only operate through the actions certain people (such as agents) take on their behalf. In certain situations the actions of the president of the company or a truck driver for the company may bind the organization, but in others, largely depending on the scope of their authority, the actions of agents will not bind the organization. We begin our study of agency by looking at various types of agents, as well as the duties agents and principals have to each other.

TYPES OF AGENTS

The principal has the right to specify the duties and responsibilities of the agent. The principal also has the right to control the activities of the agent even if such power is not always used. If the agent carries out a wide range of responsibilities for the principal, he or she is termed a **general agent.** If, on the other hand, the agent is hired or asked to do only one task for the principal, he or she is a **special agent.**

For example, Susan, the manager of Smith's Furniture Store, is a general agent. Susan has had many conversations with the owner of the store, and Susan has a contract of employment as well. The agreement spells out a series of specific duties, such as the method for purchasing inventory, hiring employees, and the procedure for closing up the store every night.

During the operation of the store, however, issues arise that the owner and the manager have not discussed. In general, the law assumes that owners want managers to take appropriate actions when needs arise, using their own discretion, in the course of managing. If a water pipe bursts, Susan will need to hire someone to immediately fix the pipe and may have to move and store the merchandise somewhere in order to safeguard it. The costs associated with these tasks eventually will be the responsibility of Smith's Furniture, the owner, because Susan, the general agent, had been given authority to do them.

Now assume Smith's Furniture Store has employed an attorney to represent the store in a lawsuit against Mr. and Mrs. Johnson, who have refused to pay their furniture bill. In this case, the attorney is a special agent. The lawyer has authority to represent and speak for Smith's Furniture Store in this one particular case. However, the attorney does not have authority to make any commitments for Smith's Furniture in any other legal matters unless so directed by Sally. Unlike the general agent, the special agent does not have the power to make agreements that bind the principal beyond the specific powers for which the agent is retained.

There is a type of special agent called an **independent contractor.** This person is like a special agent in that he or she has been employed by the principal to accomplish one particular task. The independent contractor also operates his or her own business and commonly is hired to do one specific job for the principal. Suppose that Jennifer has a leaky roof at her house. If she hires Joe's Roofing Service to come to her house and fix the roof, the carpenter will be an independent contractor. While Joe has the power to climb on the roof, pound nails, and do what is necessary to complete the job, he does not have the right to hire people to build a fence, work on the dishwasher at Jennifer's house, or to rent her house to someone else. And if Joe drops a hammer and hits the mail carrier, the responsibility to compensate the injured person will be his, not Jennifer's. The principal is not liable for torts committed by independent contractors. On the other hand, as we will discuss later, principals may be liable for the negligence of a general agent, in some situations, especially if that person is an employee.

The following recent case examines the tests for determining whether a person was an employee or an independent contractor.

general agent: An agent who has authority to do a wide range of actions for the principal.

special agent: An agent who is hired to do only one task for the principal.

independent contractor: A type of special agent, hired to do one type of job for the principal. The independent contractor usually is paid by the job, uses his or her own equipment, and often operates his or her own business.

In the Language of the Court

ALBERTY-VELEZ V. CORPORACION DE PUERTO RICO

361 F. 3d 1 (1st Cir. 2004)

FACTS

Judge Howard.

The plaintiff, Victoria Alberty-Velez agreed to host a new television show, "Desde Mi Pueblo," for WIPR, a Puerto Rican television station in 1993. Following the end of her employment, Ms. Alberty sued the station and its ownership for pregnancy and gender discrimination. The lower court dismissed the case, finding that the relevant law (Title VII of the federal civil rights statute) only applied to "employees" and that Ms. Alberty was an independent contractor. She has appealed the decision.

The program "Desde Mi Pueblo" profiled municipalities throughout Puerto Rico by presenting interviews with residents and interesting information about the featured community. Ms. Alberty was one of three hosts, and appeared on the program from July 1993 until November 1994. Instead of signing one overall contract to host the show, Ms. Alberty signed a new contract for each episode. Each contract obligated her to work a certain number of days (usually two) filming each show in a specific town. She was not obligated to film additional episodes beyond the one she contracted for. During her "off" time, she acted on another WIPR show, and did other jobs, such as hosting concerts and acting as master of ceremonies at graduation events. Her contracts did not permit WIPR to require her to do work other than filming "Desde Mi Pueblo."

While filming "Desde Mi Pueblo" Ms. Alberty was directed by William Denizard, the show's producer. He set the location and hours of filming and established the basic content of the program. WIPR provided the equipment for filming—lights, camera and makeup. Ms. Alberty was responsible for providing her clothing, shoes, accessories, hair styling and other services. She received a lump sum payment for each episode of the show that she filmed, ranging from $400 to $550. In order to receive payment, she presented an invoice to WIPR showing that she had performed the agreed upon work. WIPR did not withhold income or social security taxes from her checks and did not provide her with health insurance or other benefits. WIPR did not provide her with an IRS W-2 form at the end of the year. On her tax return she described her income as from professional services. After her separation from WIPR, she filed for, and did receive unemployment compensation from the Puerto Rico Department of Labor, after the agency determined she was an employee of WIPR.

DECISION

The federal anti-discrimination law known as Title VII protects employees from discrimination based upon pregnancy and gender. The statute defines an "employee" as an "individual employed by an employer" which is "completely circular and explains nothing." However, many cases have made clear that it does not cover independent contractors, but only "employees." Over the years this circuit has applied the "common law agency" test in other types of discrimination cases, and we see no reason to apply a different test under Title VII. Under the common law test, a court must consider:

> *The hiring party's right to control the manner and means by which the product is accomplished. Among other factors relevant to the inquiry are the skills required; the source of the instrumentalities and tools; the location of the work; the duration of the relationship between the parties; whether the hiring party has the right to assign additional projects to the hired party; the extent of the hired party's discretion over when and how long to work; the method of payment; the hired party's role in hiring and paying assistants; whether the work is part of the regular business of the hiring party; whether the hiring party is in*

business; the provision of employee benefits; and the tax treatment of the hired party.

There is no shorthand formula that can be applied to find the answer . . . and all incidents of the relationship must be considered. However, in most situations, the extent to which the hiring party controls "the manner and means" by which the worker completes her tasks will be the most important factor in the analysis.

Several factors favor classifying Alberty as an independent contractor. First, a television actress is a skilled position requiring talent and training not available on-the-job. In this regard, Alberty possesses a master's degree in public communication and journalism; is trained in dance, singing, and modeling; taught within the drama department at the University of Puerto Rico; and acted in several theater and television productions prior to her affiliation with "Desde Mi Pueblo."

Secondly, she provided the "tools and instrumentalities" necessary for her to perform. She provided, or obtained sponsors to provide the costumes, jewelry, and other image-related supplies and services necessary for her appearance. Ms. Alberty disputes this factor by arguing that WIPR provided the "equipment necessary to tape the show." But her argument is misplaced. The equipment necessary for Alberty to conduct *her job* as host of the show related to her appearance. Others provided equipment for filming and producing the show, but those were not the primary tools that Alberty used to perform her particular function. If we accepted her argument, independent contractors could never work on collaborative projects because other individual often provide the equipment required for different aspects of the collaboration.

Third, WIPR could not assign Alberty work in addition to filming "Desde Mi Pueblo." She was hired for her "professional services as hostess of the program Desde Mi Pueblo" and WIPR could not, and did not assign her other duties related to those tapings. Her other work for WIPR was done under separate signed contracts. Fourth, the method of payment—lump sum fee for each episode—favors independent contractor status. Fifth, WIPR did not provide her with any employee benefits, and did not deduct payroll taxes or social security benefits from her checks.

Ms. Alberty argues that she was an "employee" because WIPR controlled the manner of her work by directing her during filming, dictated the location of her work by selecting the sites for filming, and determined the hours of her work by requiring her to be on-call during filming days. While "control" over the manner, location, and hours of work is often critical to the independent contractor analysis, it must be considered in light of the work performed and the industry at issue.

A recent Eighth Circuit case, *Lerohl v. Friends of Minnesota Sinfonia,* 322 F. 3d 486 (8th Cir. 2003), considered the employment status of two "regular" musicians of the Minnesota Sinfonia. They argued that they were employees because the conductor selected the music, scheduled the rehearsals and concerts, and determined the manner in which the music was played. The court "emphatically" rejected the "control" argument, finding that "work by independent contractors is often performed to the exacting specifications of the hiring party." Musicians are necessarily subject to the control of the conductor so that the symphony performs as a single unit.

We think that a similar analysis is apt here. WIPR could only achieve its goal of producing "Desde Mi Pueblo" by having Ms. Alberty follow the instructions of the director, as to time, place, acting and location. Like the musicians in *Lerohl,* who could decline to play in future concerts, Ms. Alberty could decline to host future segments of Desde Mi Pueblo by refusing to sign additional contracts. Neither Alberty nor WIPR was under any obligation to continue working together.

Alberty asserts that the fact that the Puerto Rico Department of Labor found her qualified to receive unemployment benefits as an "employee" should be considered. However, this case involves determination of employee status under Title VII which is a federal law matter, and the Puerto Rico unemployment law determination is thus irrelevant to our issues here. Furthermore, Ms. Alberty argues that the facts that WIPR is "in business" and that her work on "Desde Mi Pueblo" was part of its business favor a finding of employee status, and we agree that these two facts do support her claim.

While no one factor is dispositive, it is clear, based on the parties' entire relationship, that she was an independent contractor. The parties structured their relationship through the use of set length contracts that permitted Alberty the freedom to pursue other opportunities and assured WIPR that it would not have to pay her for the weeks she was not filming. Further, the lack of benefits, the method of payment, and the parties' own description of the relationship all indicate independent contractor status. Alberty's "per-job" arrangement with WIPR is typical of an independent contractor, and we cannot disregard the parties'

decision simply because it deprives Alberty of Title VII protection. Accordingly, we conclude that Alberty was an independent contractor as a matter of law and therefore cannot maintain a Title VII action against WIPR.

CASE QUESTIONS

1. Why do you think Title VII only covers "employee" and not "independent contractors?"
2. What are the most important factors cited by the court in finding that Ms. Alberty was an independent contractor?
3. What factors favor her argument that she was an "employee?" What two or three different facts would have changed the result?
4. What should an employer do to make sure that people working for the firm are classified as independent contractors, rather than employees?

DUTIES OF AGENT TO PRINCIPAL

fiduciary duty:
The duty owed by the agent to the principal, which includes trust, honesty, loyalty, obedience, and full disclosure of relevant facts.

When someone agrees to act as the agent of another, the law imposes very significant responsibilities—called **fiduciary duties**—on the agent. These duties include the obligations of trust, loyalty, honesty, obedience to the principal's rules and instructions, and due care in performance of the tasks. If the agent is in a position to handle money, he or she must not "commingle" any personal funds with those of the principal and must account to the principal for every penny spent and earned. If funds get mixed up and a loss occurs, the responsibility must fall to the agent. For example, assume Carl, the agent for a bread company, receives $10,000 from a customer (a large grocery store) as a deposit toward the purchase of bread, and then Carl invests that $10,000 along with $5,000 of his own money in the stock market. If by the time Carl must account for the money to his principal the value of the stock is only $14,000, Carl must give the principal $10,000 and keep only $4,000.

The scope of the fiduciary duties prevents the agent from serving anyone but the principal while performing as agent. The agent cannot indulge in "double-dealing" or make any "side profit" in connection with his or her duties unless this other relationship is fully disclosed and approved by the principal. The agent's sole duty is to serve the interests of the principal and receive compensation from the principal.

For example, suppose the California Wine Co. is looking for a site for its new winemaking facility and hires a real estate agent, Tami, to assist in finding the right property. The company is prepared to spend $200,000 for the property. Tami finds a perfect site that can be purchased for $100,000. Tami buys the property herself and then sells it to the company for $150,000, without disclosing to the company her profit. Even though the company might be happy with the price paid, Tami has clearly violated her fiduciary duty. Tami's job was to find the best property at the best price for the company—she was being trusted and compensated to do so. Tami violated her obligation to the principal by making a personal profit on the deal rather than buying the property for the company at the $100,000 price. If the company learns the true facts and sues Tami, any profit she made will be awarded to the company. In addition, other damages and penalties might be assessed against her.

SOCIAL/ETHICAL ISSUES

Many of the disclosures that have come to public notice in the wake of the Enron, Arthur Andersen, WorldCom and other scandals, appear to involve clear violations of fiduciary duty. For example, the fact that Mr. Fastow, the Chief Financial Officer for Enron was also forming and serving as general partner for many off-book partnerships which did millions of dollars of business with Enron, seems a clear case of an agent working for two principals at the same time. How could he effectively represent the best interests of Enron, while making deals with a partnership he controlled, and at the same time use millions of Enron dollars to compensate him, his wife, and various friends, for their roles in the partnerships? How could key officers of Enron, who controlled the billions of dollars in the employees' pension funds, sell their own shares of Enron (knowing that bad days were ahead) while continuing to advise employees to keep their funds in Enron stock? What were the pressures that led key partners of Arthur Andersen to apparently forget about their ethical duties to strictly follow the rules set by the national accounting standards board when they were auditing and approving Enron's financial reports?

DUTIES OF PRINCIPAL TO AGENT

In contrast to the strict obligations of the agent set out previously, the principal does not owe the agent nearly the same duties. No fiduciary duty flows from the principal to the agent. Instead, the principal merely has the duty to pay the agent whatever compensation was agreed upon (and many agencies involve no compensation) and to reimburse the agent for expenses reasonably incurred in carrying out the duties of the agency. In other words, if the agent had to spend $50 on gasoline and $75 on repairs while on the road selling the principal's goods, the principal should reimburse the agent for these expenses unless an agreement exists to the contrary. The principal should also refrain from doing anything to hinder the agent's performance of the assigned tasks.

LIABILITIES OF THE PRINCIPAL FOR ACTS OF THE AGENT

LIABILITY FOR TORTS OF THE AGENT

Whenever a person commits a tort (a wrongful act which creates civil liability), he or she is liable for the consequences of that action. For example, if Harry drives his car negligently and injures Joe, then Harry will be liable. Often the tougher question, however, is whether someone else may also be liable. For example, suppose Harry was not driving his car when he had the accident but was driving a Federal Express van, delivering a package, when the accident occurred. Should Federal Express be liable along with Harry?

The answer to this question depends on several factors. One issue is whether Harry was an *independent contractor or* an *employee.* As we briefly discussed earlier, an independent contractor is a person who is hired or retained to do a particular job, like the carpenter in the example used earlier in the chapter. Independent contractors are usually hired to accomplish a specific result, often have their own business and tools, work for many different people or companies, and are paid by the job. The principal wants them to accomplish particular results and does not directly supervise the physical aspects of their work.

On the other hand, an **employee** (sometimes called a "**servant**" under older legal terminology) generally is paid by the hour or by the week, normally uses the tools and equipment owned by the principal, and is under the control of the employer (sometimes called the "*master*") regarding the physical performance of his or her job. Thus, while the carpenter who comes to your house for a one-time roof repair would probably be an independent contractor, a carpenter who works for General Motors Corporation (GM) every day for two years, uses GM tools, reports to a specific GM carpentry shop every day for work, and is paid $500/week by GM would probably be considered an employee.

In general, principals are not liable for torts committed by independent contractors. As mentioned earlier, a homeowner would probably not be liable for a hammer dropped by the carpenter on the mail carrier. However, under the legal theory ***respondeat superior*** (which means "let the master respond"), principals are liable for **torts committed by employees** if the tort was done **"while acting within the scope of employment."** Therefore, in the Federal Express example, if Harry were driving the company van to deliver packages, the company (in addition to Harry) would likely be liable to the person he injured through his negligent driving. The "public policy" behind the rule is that those who hire employees should bear some responsibility for what they do to others while on the job. Another rationale for the rule is that imposing some liability on employers will encourage them to hire, train, and supervise their employees more carefully. An example of what is sometimes called the "vicarious liability" of principals under *respondeat superior* is shown in the following case.

employee or servant: An agent whose actions are under the control of the principal/employer. The employee is usually paid by the hour or week, uses the tools of the employer, is directly supervised by the employer, and may work for several different principals at the same time.

respondeat superior: The legal theory that holds that an employer/principal can be held liable for torts committed by employees within the scope of employment.

LANGE V. NATIONAL BISCUIT COMPANY

211 N.W. 2D 783 (MINN. 1973)

FACTS

Ronnell Lynch was a cookie salesman for National Biscuit Company (Nabisco). His duties included selling Nabisco's products to grocery stores and actually placing previously delivered merchandise on the shelves of the stores in his area. Mr. Lynch was first assigned his own territory on March 1, 1969, and by the end of his first two months, Nabisco had already received numerous complaints from grocers that he was overly aggressive and was taking the shelf space reserved for competing cookie companies.

On May 1, 1969, Mr. Lynch arrived at the small grocery store managed by Jerome Lange to place previously delivered merchandise on the shelves. An argument developed between the two men concerning Lynch's activities, and Lynch became very angry and started swearing. Lange told Lynch to stop swearing or to leave the store, as children were present. Lynch then became angrier, shouting, "I ought to break your neck!" He went behind the counter and dared Lange to fight. Following Lange's refusal of this offer, Lynch viciously attacked him, threw merchandise around the store, and left. Lange brought a lawsuit against Nabisco, but the trial court entered judgment for the defendant, and Lange appealed to the Minnesota Supreme Court.

DECISION

The court stated that according to the requirements of *respondeat superior*, in order to impose liability on the principal-employer for torts of the agent-employee, the employee must have been acting within the scope of his employment when the actions that caused the lawsuit took place. Some previous Minnesota cases had required that, in addition, the employee's acts must have been motivated by a desire to "further the employer's business." And that is the rule followed in some other states, through their court decisions.

The Minnesota court refused to follow this theory, finding that the majority of jurisdictions did not agree with it. Justice Todd, writing for the court, quoted an old Mississippi case that had held, "The fallacy of this reasoning was that it made a certain mental condition of the servant the test by which to determine whether he was acting about his master's business or not. It clothed the master with immunity if the act was right, because it was right, and if it was wrong, it clothed him with like immunity because it was wrong." The public might be left totally without redress for intentional injuries inflicted by the agents of a business.

The public policy underlying the theory of *respondeat superior* or vicarious liability is that the employer, knowing that he can be held liable for the torts of his servants, can and should consider this liability as a cost of doing business. He will be more careful in hiring employees and can pass some or all of the cost along to his customers through his prices. "In this way, losses are spread and the shock of the accident is dispersed."

The court stated that the proper rule was "an employer is liable for an assault by his employee when the source of the attack is related to the duties of the employee and the assault occurs within work-related limits of time and place." Applying those factors to this case, the court held that (1) the assault occurred at a work-related place, since it took place in a grocery store where the employee was working; (2) it occurred during normal working hours, so the "time" requirement was met; and (3) the cause of the argument and subsequent assault was a dispute about Lynch's working conduct, that is, where his cookies were to be placed on the shelves. Therefore, the employee was acting within the scope of employment at the time of the aggression, and the employer is liable for his torts under the doctrine of *respondeat superior*. The lower court decision was reversed.

CASE QUESTIONS

1. Assuming that Nabisco had a rule prohibiting its salespeople from slugging store managers while on duty, does it make sense to hold the employer liable for the assault of the salesman here? Is it fair to the company?
2. Is the salesman liable here, too? Why do you think Mr. Lange did not sue him? Could he recover two judgments if he did?
3. What was wrong with the "motivation" test that had been the standard for employer liability in Minnesota until this case?
4. Would the company be liable if the assault had taken place at a bar where the two men were drinking later that evening?

frolic: When an employee deviates significantly from the scope of employment.

detour: When an employee deviates slightly from the scope of employment. The employer-principal is still liable (along with the employee) for torts committed on a detour.

Although the employer will generally be liable for torts committed by the employee "in the scope of employment," as the *National Biscuit* case demonstrates, in some cases the employee's actions are so far from the employment that only the agent-employee is responsible. The courts have developed a theory called **frolic and detour** to analyze situations where the boss should not bear responsibility for an employee's torts. For example, if Heather's job requires her to take a shipment of computers from San Francisco to Dallas, and she decides to visit her sister in Seattle on the way (and has an accident there), it is likely that a court would find her on a "**frolic**" and thus solely responsible, since it was clearly not on the way to Dallas. A "**detour**" is a slight deviation from work duties or rules but which is not so far afield that the employer is released from liability for the tort committed by the employee. For example, an employee driving in the course of employment but exceeding the speed limit in violation of company rules would still be within the general scope of employment if he or she negligently causes an accident.

The law has also developed a "going and coming" to work rule that holds generally that the principal is not responsible for torts committed by employees who are on their way to work or on the way home. However, if the employee is taking care of business while on route or is on call 24 hours a day, and really does get called sometimes, then this rule might be relaxed. Therefore, employers have sometimes been held liable for employee torts committed on the way to and from work in those situations.

LIABILITY FOR CONTRACTS MADE BY THE AGENT

third party: Someone with whom the agent interacts, on behalf of the principal.

Actual Authority   As agents go about representing the interests of the principal, they often do things that create contracts between the principal and someone with whom the agent has dealt, called the **third party**. The key ingredient in determining this contractual liability is whether the agent was acting *within the scope of authority* given by the principal. In many situations, the principal clearly intends that a contract be created. For example, if Jason is a salesman for IBM Corporation, his job is to travel around his region, persuading customers to purchase IBM computers and other products. He and his company (the principal) hope that his efforts will lead to contracts between the customers and IBM.

When Jason and a customer reach agreement on the purchase of a computer system, they prepare and sign a written contract containing the details of their agreement. Let us assume that Jason has been given authority from IBM to enter into contracts on behalf of IBM, at specified prices and terms, up to a maximum of $10,000. Therefore, when Jason and the customer sign the contract for the purchase of a computer system for $6,000 (Jason signs as "Jason, agent of IBM"), the contract is really between the customer and IBM, because Jason has **actual authority** to enter into such a contract on behalf of his principal.

actual authority: An agent's actions that are within the power given by the principal. The principal is bound to contracts made by the agent within the agent's actual authority.

The actual authority of an agent to enter into contracts that bind the principal may be *express* or *implied*. In the preceding example, Jason's authority was express, or clearly spelled out or expressed. However, in the situation we discussed earlier, Susan, the manager of Smith's Furniture

Store, had the authority to hire a plumber when a pipe burst in the store although the authority was not expressed. Smith's Furniture, the principal, would be bound to pay for the repair because, although Susan was never expressly told to make repairs, such authority can be implied from her role as manager of the store.

In the IBM example above, suppose that Jason signed the contract with the computer customer as "Jason Hamilton, agent of IBM Corporation." This is an example of what is called a **disclosed principal.** Jason has made perfectly clear the identity of the business he was representing. Therefore, Jason should not be a party to and should not be liable for the contract.

In two other situations the identity of the principal is not made so clear. If Jason had told the customer, "I am representing a large computer company, but I can't tell you which," this is an example of a **partially disclosed principal.** In this situation, the customer can hold Jason responsible on the contract. When the customer (the third party) learns the true identity of the principal, he or she can elect to hold *either* the agent or the principal liable but not both.

Furthermore, if Jason signs the contract "Jason Hamilton" without mentioning that he is working for IBM or anyone else, the principal is **undisclosed.** In this case, Jason is liable on the contract. If and when the identity of the principal is disclosed, however, the customer can elect which party he or she wants to hold responsible.

> **disclosed principal:** Where the agent clearly informs the third party whom he/she is working for.

> **partially disclosed principal:** Where the agent indicates that he/she is representing a principal, but does not disclose the identity.

> **undisclosed principal:** A type of agency in which neither the existence nor the identity of the agent is disclosed to the third party.

MEMO FROM THE LEGAL DEPARTMENT

To: Students

From: The Legal Department

The use of an undisclosed agency occurs frequently when a developer wants to purchase a large tract of land, perhaps for a shopping center. The desired properties may be owned by many people. Often the developer will engage the services of several different agents to purchase various parcels. All agents have agreed to sell all properties purchased to the developer. If the developer went to each property owner individually and disclosed his identity, the price of the real estate would climb sharply after the first few purchases.

In the following case the court examines the question of whether the firm hired to handle security at a concert was a general agent or an independent contractor.

FACTS

On November 1, 2003, Alicia West attended a concert at Reliant Arena in Houston, TX, featuring two bands, "A Perfect Circle" and "The Icarus Line." When The Icarus Line was on stage, the crowd booed the band. Band members retaliated by spitting on the crowd and throwing water bottles into the audience. One of those bottles struck West on the side of the head, causing her to fall to the concrete floor and suffer injuries.

SMG operated Reliant Arena for Harris County, Texas. In turn, SMG licensed the arena to Pace Concerts for the November concert. SMG required Pace to use CSC for concert security.

In November, 2005, West filed a lawsuit against SMG, Pace Concerts, and CSC (among others), claiming that she was permanently disabled as a result of the incident and was unable to work, drive, go to school, or otherwise care for herself. SMG filed a motion for summary judgment, which the trial court granted. West appealed the summary judgment decision.

DECISION

The court first discussed the duty of premises owners to protect guests from assaults by third parties. In Texas, a person who owns or controls property has a duty to protect guests on the property from the risk of criminal activity only when that risk is both unreasonable and foreseeable. In this case, the court held that West failed to produce any evidence which would indicate that the band's criminal actions were foreseeable, thus imposing a duty upon SMG to take extra security precautions.

Second, the court considered West's claim that CSC was SMG's agent, rather than an independent contractor, making SMG vicariously liable for CSC's actions. West argued that the contract between SMG and Pace required Pace to hire CSC, which was evidence that SMG exercised control over the details through which Pace provided security for the concert. Accordingly, West argued that this level of control made CSC a general agent rather than an independent contractor.

Analyzing this claim, the court first noted the general rule that an entity who hires an independent contractor will not be liable for the independent contractor's negligence. However, the court noted that "when the hiring entity retains control over the specific details and methods by which the task is to be accomplished, the independent contractor acts as an agent, and the individual or entity that hired the contractor can be held to be vicariously liable for the torts or negligent acts of the agent. By contrast, when one has the right to control the end sought to be accomplished, but not the means and details of how it should be accomplished, the person employed acts as an independent contractor, and not as an agent, and the person or entity that hired the contractor is not liable for the contractor's negligent acts." Here, the court determined that simply because SMG required Pace to hire CSC, that did not mean that SMG had exclusive control over the details of the security CSC provided at the concert. Despite the fact that the CSC employee manual instructed CSC employees that they were to look to either CSC or SMG management for help with unruly guests, the court held that this was not evidence that SMG "actually" exercised control over guests, much less control over CSC.

West also introduced evidence that SMG would meet with CSC in advance of events at the arena and tell CSC specifically how many ticket-takers, ushers, and on-staff security should be hired. In fact, SMG had such a meeting with CSC before the concert at which West was injured. Again, the court focused on the fact that the evidence West produced did not show that SMG actually controlled the details of security *during* the performance. Therefore, the court held that CSC was not SMG's agent, such that SMG was not liable for CSC's actions in allegedly failing to provide proper security. The court affirmed the trial court's decision to grant SMG's motion for summary judgment.

CASE QUESTIONS

1. What factors did the court find particularly important in reaching its decision? Does the court's distinction between control during the event vs. control before it make sense? Were there any factors which may have indicated that SMG *did* have control over the security at the concert?
2. Is it fair to Ms. West to prevent her from suing SMG? Why do you think SMG was an important defendant in Ms. West's quest to recover her damages?
3. Who won the case? Is there a chance Ms. West might still prevail against one of the other defendants?

Apparent Authority The previous discussion concerned situations in which the agent had actual authority—either express or implied—to enter into contracts on behalf of the principal. It is sometimes possible, however, for an agent to bind a principal to a contract even when the agent did not have *any* authority to do so. How can this be? In some cases, it would be unfair to the third party to allow the principal to escape responsibility.

Suppose the Chicago Toy Company manufactures this year's hottest new toy—a soft bean bag variation on the G.I. Joe line called "Beanie Commando." Assume that Brenda has been a member of the sales staff at Chicago Toy for 10 years and has represented that company in many dealings with retailers in the Midwest. For 10 years, whenever a store made a contract with Chicago Toy, Brenda did the negotiations and signed the papers. All deposits made to Brenda always reached Chicago Toy. Later, Brenda and Chicago Toy have a disagreement over the ethical implications of the toy. After failing to resolve the dispute, Brenda is fired, effective immediately.

Brenda, however, decides to make one last visit to her five best customers. When visiting these customers, she fails to tell them she has been fired and receives $15,000 in deposits to be applied to orders of Beanie Commando from Chicago Toy. Several months later, after no shipments of the

apparent authority: A situation where an agent acting without authority can sometimes enter contracts binding on the principal. This theory requires that some action *of the principal* leads the third party to believe that the agent has the authority he or she claims to have.

actual notice: Directly telling the other party about a legal matter either in person or by a letter.

constructive notice: An indirect type of notice, such as putting a notice in the newspaper.

ratification: When a principal who would not be bound to a contract made by an agent (beyond authority) nevertheless accepts the benefits of the contract, then the principal may be bound to honor it.

toy have arrived, one of the retailers calls the company and only then learns that Brenda was not employed by the company when the order was taken and the deposit paid.

Chicago Toy states that "she was no longer our agent when she took your money and made the contract." In fact, Chicago Toy never received any money, only a postcard from Brenda in Tahiti saying, "Having a wonderful time; give my regards to Commando." In this situation, the concept of **apparent authority** would probably bind Chicago Toy to the contract. When the *actions of the principal* (not just the agent) lead a third party to the reasonable belief that an agent does have authority to bind the principal, it is possible to hold a principal to a contract even when the agent exceeded his or her authority.

In our scenario, the actions of the principal in accepting and performing all contracts made by Brenda on its behalf for ten years created the reasonable belief that a contract made with her would be honored by the company. The only way for the principal (Chicago Toy) to avoid the liability by apparent authority would have been to give **actual notice** to all its customers that Brenda was no longer with the company. Actual notice means directly telling the other party about the change either by letter or in person. Another type of notice, **constructive notice** (such as putting a notice in the newspaper), would work with retailers and other third parties with whom the agent had not directly dealt before.

Ratification   Sometimes it is even possible for a principal to be bound to contracts made in his or her behalf by an agent who clearly acts without any type of authority. This situation could arise when the principal, although not bound to do so, acts in a way to indicate that he or she feels bound to or wishes to enforce the agreement made by the agent. For example, if the agent is sent to an office supply store to purchase paper and pencils for the business but instead goes to a car dealership and purchases on credit an automobile for the firm, the principal would not be bound to the contract because the agent was acting outside the scope of his authority and there was no "apparent authority" upon which the third party relied. But if the principal keeps the car for several weeks, drives it regularly on business matters, and says nothing about returning it, the principal will be bound to the contract with the third party by the doctrine of **ratification**, even though the agent acted without authority. By his/her later actions, the principal has "ratified" the contract, to which he/she would not have been bound before, due to the lack of authority of the agent.

TERMINATION OF AGENCY

Since the agency relationship is based on consent, when either the principal or agent decides to end the relationship, the agency is generally terminated. In other words, either party usually has the **power** to terminate the agency at any time. But what if they had a contract? Can the principal still fire the agent? Yes, in almost all situations. Courts have often distinguished between the *power* to terminate the agency and the *right* to do so.

For example, let us look at the baseball career of the late Billy Martin. Over a period of 10 years, Martin was hired approximately seven times to manage the New York Yankees. Each time he was hired, he and the team owner entered into a contract that detailed his salary and the term of his duties. But, on each occasion, he was fired by the principal owner of the team (George Steinbrenner) before his contract had been completed. When Steinbrenner would call Martin and say, "You're fired," that did in fact terminate the agency relationship. Martin could not put on the uniform, make out the lineup for the game, or sit in the dugout—he was no longer the manager. His authority to act on behalf of the owner/principal was over.

In this case, the principal had the **power to terminate** the agency. However, because a contract existed, Steinbrenner did not have the **right to terminate** the agency and therefore had to continue to pay Martin on the contract. Similarly, Martin would have had the *power*, but not the *right*, to quit at any time. In other words, Martin could effectively quit when he wanted, but he might have to pay damages if his breach of contract cost the club money.

One type of agency does exist where the principal fails to have the power to terminate the relationship at his or her option, and this is an **agency coupled with an interest.** In this situation, which is fairly rare, the agent has an actual legal interest (part ownership or a mortgage or security interest) in the property that is the subject of the agency, and it would be unfair to allow the principal to cancel the agency without compensation. For example, suppose Leslie takes a ring to a pawnshop and leaves it as collateral for a loan she receives. She gives the shop owner the power, as an agent for her, to sell the ring if she does not pay the loan in a certain time. It is unfair to allow Leslie simply to notify the pawnshop before she had paid back the loan and say, "I'm canceling the agency." Why? The owner will lose his legal interest in the ring. This agency coupled with an interest cannot be terminated without the consent of the agent.

agency coupled with an interest: An unusual type of agency in which the agent has a legal interest in the property of the agency. Such an agent cannot be terminated "at will," unlike a normal agency.

IN CONSULTATION

Marvin Manager has a problem. He recently terminated Andy, one of his account managers, for failure to meet sales goals. Andy was furious and told Marvin that he would steal all of ABC, Inc.'s clients. Despite Andy's threats, Marvin did not insist that Andy give back his company identification, his company cards, or company letterhead. Marvin did not notify any of Andy's accounts that Andy was no longer with ABC— Marvin did not want to embarrass Andy or hinder him from obtaining future employment. He simply reassigned Andy's clients to another account manager.

A month later, Marvin received an angry phone call from one of Andy's former accounts. The client stated he ordered 1,000 widgets from ABC almost three weeks ago and paid a deposit but did not receive his order. Marvin showed no record of the order and asked with whom the client placed his bid. The client replied that he placed his bid with Andy, of course, since Andy is his account manager. Marvin contacted the rest of Andy's former accounts and discovered that many of them had also placed orders and paid deposits to Andy after his termination.

Marvin wants to know whether ABC is responsible for filling the orders and/or refunding the deposits since the orders were placed with Andy after he was terminated. He contacted Laura Lawyer, in-house counsel, for her advice on what ABC's liability is. Here is their conversation:

Marvin:

1. If I fired Andy, how can ABC be responsible for his post-termination actions?
2. Aren't we protected by the fact that we assigned a new account manager to each of Andy's clients?
3. Even if the clients didn't know, Andy knew he wasn't our employee anymore. Doesn't that make a difference?

Legal Dept:

1. Simply firing an employee does not terminate your responsibility for his or her actions. More steps are required to protect third parties that may do business with your agent.
2. Not necessarily. The clients may not have known about the new manager.
3. It makes a difference if we want to sue Andy, but it may not matter for Andy's clients. **Let me review the applicable law to see what our potential liability is, and I will get back to you.**

MEMO FROM THE LEGAL DEPARTMENT

To: Marvin Manager

Re: Liability of Company for Acts of Former Employee

Dear Marvin:

Your scenario raises the issue of company liability for agent's actions and the company's responsibility to its innocent clients. Employees are agents who can create liability for their employer, the principal. Statements, promises, and contracts made by an employee/agent will bind the company that they represent as long as the agent is acting within their authority. Authority can mean something as simple as the specific duties delegated to an agent. Authority, however, can be much broader. It may include any power a reasonable third party thinks that agent has. When you terminated Andy, you removed his actual authority to act on behalf of ABC. On the surface, Andy's termination would end any liability ABC may have for Andy's actions.

Unfortunately, terminating Andy was not enough when you dig beneath the surface and explore what Andy's clients were thinking. The law protects innocent third parties who reasonably believe that an agent has authority to act on behalf of a principal. If third parties like Andy's customers reasonably believed that Andy had authority, then the law gives Andy what is known as apparent authority. Apparent authority is the authority that is "apparent" from the innocent third party's perspective. When Andy left ABC, he did so with all of the materials that identified him as an ABC employee. You never directly notified his accounts that Andy no longer managed them, nor did you tell Andy's clients that someone new would now handle their orders. Andy's clients were probably reasonable in thinking that Andy had authority to act on behalf of ABC. ABC would, therefore, likely be liable to Andy's customers for the deposits and for fulfilling the orders.

A possible exception to ABC's liability to Andy's former accounts would exist for any customers who had been contacted by the new account manager you assigned. If a customer heard from a new manager, he or she is likely to think that the new manager is the person to whom he or she should direct business, pay deposits, and send orders. Customers who are aware that they have a new manager may have "constructive notice" that Andy is no longer their account manager, and they may not be reasonable in thinking that Andy still had authority to represent ABC.

You are correct that Andy knew he was no longer our agent. ABC, as the principal, can terminate our agency relationship with Andy at any time. By firing Andy, we ended our employment and agency relationship. Without giving notice to third parties, we still have a legal liability to Andy's former accounts. The termination, however, may allow us to seek reimbursement for that liability from Andy. The law will protect the innocent third party—but Andy is not innocent. He represented, either expressly or implicitly, to his former accounts that he had the authority to act on behalf of ABC. He knew he had no authority, which makes him liable to ABC for his behavior.

With regard to Andy's behavior and ABC's resulting liability, consider the following questions:

1. What should Marvin have done differently when he terminated Andy?
2. What sort of policy could ABC put in place to eliminate this type of liability in the future?
3. Discuss why you think the law protects innocent third parties like Andy's accounts but does not protect ABC. Do you think the protection third parties receive is appropriate?

SOLE PROPRIETORSHIPS

Now that we have examined the concepts of agency and analyzed the legal principles governing the common situation where an individual acts on behalf of another person or business firm, it is time to take a closer look at the various legal structures under which businesses are organized. The legal principles of agency have significant impact on all forms of business organizations.

The simplest and most common type of business formation is the **sole proprietorship.** This type of business is very easy to form—one person simply begins to offer some services or products for sale. No written document, formal organization, or filing of papers with the state are necessary (although, depending on the type of business, a license or permit may be required). The owner has sole power to make decisions and sole liability and responsibility for all business debts. If the business earns a profit, the owner must pay taxes on the income as part of his or her own personal income—there is no separate taxation on the business. Legally, this type of business is not a separate entity from the owner. There are more sole proprietorships than any other form of business, but since there is no separation between the owner and the entity, there is no legal status attached to this form of business. We will now move on to examine some forms of business entity that are more complex.

> **sole proprietorship:** A business owned by one person, who has full control and full responsibility.

PARTNERSHIPS

partnership:
An association of
two or more per-
sons, as co-owners,
to carry on a busi-
ness for profit.

With a partnership, at least to some extent, a business entity is formed that is
separate and different from the owners. A **partnership** is defined as *an association of two or more persons, as co-owners, to carry on a business for profit*.
This definition is contained in the Uniform Partnership Act (UPA), a model
law drafted by a group of businesspeople and legal experts that has been
adopted in almost all the states.

FORMATION AND CHARACTERISTICS

A partnership contains several separate requirements, each of which may be
important in determining whether a partnership exists. First, there must be at
least two people involved. There is no such thing as a "sole partnership."
Although many partnerships have two or three partners, some nationwide and
worldwide accounting and law firms have over 1,000 partners. Second, these
persons must be co-owners—that is, they must, in some manner, share in the
ownership aspects of a business, as will be discussed subsequently. Finally, the
partners must be engaged in a business enterprise in which they are trying to
make a profit—simply being co-owners of property is not enough to constitute
a partnership.

Every year thousands of small businesses are started—all with high hopes
of great success. Some succeed, and the owners have profits to share; others do
not, and the owners have substantial losses and debts to pay. In either event, if
the business is a partnership, the partners share the profits and losses personally (and equally, if nothing else is agreed upon).

Partnerships are easy to form—so easy, in fact, that people often do not
realize they are partners. If Paul and Donna, currently juniors in business
school, cut lawns in the summer and remove snow in the winter for 10 businesses, sharing expenses and profits, they probably are partners. No written
partnership agreement is required by law. Partnership status does require an
agreement, but courts have found that the agreement may be *implied* by the
actions of the parties. Since the consequences of being a partner may be very
significant, you should *never* begin a business with another person without
putting your agreement down in writing. Make sure that if you are a partner,
you begin your partnership with an *express agreement*, usually called the **articles of partnership**.

**articles of part-
nership:** A written
document contain-
ing the names of
the partnership and
the partners, which
sets forth the agree-
ments of the part-
ners, including such
items as the organi-
zational structure,
purposes, owner-
ship percentages,
capital contribu-
tions, sharing
of profits and
losses, and other
agreements.

What can happen without an express agreement? Suppose that after three
years of running the lawn service and snow removal business, Paul and Donna
have built a business worth $100,000 and now have 200 clients paying a total
of $300,000 per year. After debts, Paul and Donna are finally turning a small
profit, with the future prospects bright. At this point, Paul wants to expand the
business considerably, while Donna, who has graduated from business school
with an accounting degree, wants to leave the business in order to develop her
accounting practice. Paul has put $30,000 into the business—some of it bor-
rowed from his father—and Donna has invested only $5,000 but has worked
many more hours on the business. What problems will arise when Donna and
Paul attempt to divide the shares of the business and determine and pay the
departing partner (Donna) her share?

Partnerships almost always undergo significant changes—people change their minds, they move, they divorce and marry, and their business interests shift. The *only* time it is really feasible to put together a solid partnership agreement is in the very beginning of the enterprise, when the partners are friendly, optimistic, and without substantial assets or debts.

MEMO FROM THE LEGAL DEPARTMENT

To: Students

As you begin a business enterprise with a friend, if you hear yourself saying, "We don't need a written agreement; a handshake will do," STOP! Instead, say "Let's prepare a simple agreement, so we'll all know where we stand if anything happens or our plans change." The best course of action is to consult a local lawyer to have a partnership agreement drafted that is tailored to your business. The few hundred dollars it will cost is well worth it. If you cannot or will not take that step, draft a simple agreement yourself.

Among other points, you should specify the following:

- Percentage of ownership
- Division of responsibilities and authority
- Salary and distribution of profits
- Buy-in and buy-out provisions
- Death, disability, and retirement contingencies
- Dispute resolution

Many partnership agreement forms can be found in libraries, bookstores, and on the internet. The following is one fairly simple form.

PARTNERSHIP AGREEMENT

This agreement of co-partnership, is made and entered into on this _____ day of _____, 2010, by and among *John Smith* of *Cleveland, Ohio, Rhonda Jones* of *Provo, Utah*, and *Thomas Anderson* of *Tulsa, Oklahoma*.

WHEREAS, it is the desire of the parties hereto to form a partnership on terms and conditions as set forth below, the parties having mutual confidence in each other, do hereby agree as follows.

1. *PURPOSE*. The parties do hereby form a partnership to conduct a real estate investment and management business, including, but not limited to, the buying, selling, leasing, renting, managing, and otherwise dealing in real estate of any and all kinds and to engage in all other lawful activities that the partners shall, from time to time, deem appropriate.

2. *NAME AND PRINCIPAL OFFICE*. The partnership shall operate under the name and style of *JRT Associates*. The partnership shall maintain offices for the conduct of partnership affairs at *Cleveland, Ohio*, or at such other place or places as the parties may later agree.

3. *PARTNERSHIP ASSETS*. There have been created, and shall be, three partnership interests, and all partnership assets shall be owned in the following proportions: John—50%, Rhonda—25%, and Thomas—25%.

4. *NET PROFITS AND LOSSES*. All net profits and losses of the partnership will be divided among the partners in accordance with the respective percentage interests set forth in Article 3.

5. *PARTNERSHIP AUTHORITY*. No one of the partners shall, without the consent of one other partner, endorse any notes or act as a surety for any persons. All decisions, other than day-to-day operations, shall be made by a majority vote of the partners. Without such consent, no partner shall, on behalf of the partnership, borrow or lend money, make or accept any commercial paper, execute any mortgage, purchase or contract to purchase or sell any property for or of the partnership.

   No partner shall, except with the advance written consent of all partners, assign, mortgage or sell his/her share in the partnership or its capital assets, or do any acts detrimental to the best interests of the partnership.

   New partners shall only be admitted upon unanimous vote of the partners.

6. *TIME DEVOTED TO PARTNERSHIP*. It is not contemplated that any of the partners will devote full time to the partnership affairs but that John will manage much of the day-to-day business and supervise the Cleveland office. The partners may from time to time allocate additional duties to each partner, as situations may require.

7. *TERM AND TERMINATION*. The partnership shall continue for an indefinite time period during the pleasure of the partners.
   a. *In the event of termination of the partnership because of the mental incapacity or death of a partner*, the remaining partners and the heir or representative of the deceased or incapacitated partner shall jointly determine the market value of the partnership and its assets. In the event they are unable to reach agreement, they will mutually select two appraisers who will attempt to reach an accurate valuation of the partnership. If the two appraisers cannot agree, they will select a third appraiser, whose determination of the value of the partnership will be final.

   After the value determination, the remaining partners will have the right to purchase the former partner's interest by paying to the heirs or representative the departing partner's proportionate share of the valuation. The purchase price shall be paid as follows: 25% within 30 days, and the balance within one year, at 8% interest. If the remaining partners do not choose to purchase the share of the incapacitated or deceased partner, all partnership assets shall be sold, and after payment of debts, the proceeds shall be distributed to the partners and the heirs or representatives of the departing partner.

b. *In the event of termination of the partnership because of the voluntary withdrawal of one of the partners*, the withdrawing partner shall make a written offer to the other partners, indicating the terms and conditions of which he/she is willing to sell his/her interest. The other partners shall have 30 days in which to reach agreement on the purchase of the departing partner's share. If no agreement is reached, the remaining partners may continue the business under the partnership name and initiate the valuation procedure set forth in paragraph 7a, or they may elect to terminate the partnership and distribute the assets according to paragraph 7a.

c. *Termination by sale and / or distribution of assets*. It is agreed that in the event of the sale and/or distribution of all or a majority of the assets of the partnership, then this partnership shall terminate, and each partner shall receive his/her appropriate share of assets and proceeds as set forth previously.

8. *BOOKS AND RECORDS*. The partnership shall maintain full and accurate books of account that shall be kept at the partnership office. Each partner shall cause to be entered in such books all transactions relating to the partnership or its business, and each partner shall at all times have access to and the right to inspect and copy such books and all partnership records.

9. *ACCOUNTING YEAR*. The accounting year of this partnership shall run from January 1 to December 31 of each year, and the books and records shall be maintained on this basis.

10. *PARTNERSHIP ACCOUNTS*. At the end of each year, a full and accurate account shall be made in writing of all of the assets and liabilities of the partnership; all its receipts and disbursements; and the assets, liabilities, and income shall be ascertained; and the accounts of each partner shall be credited or debited accordingly, with his/her share of such net profit or loss. Any partner may demand that the financial statement be audited and certified by a certified public accountant, but in the absence of such a demand, such certification is not required.

IN WITNESS WHEREOF, the parties have executed these documents this _____ day of _____, 2010, at Cleveland, Ohio.

In the presence of:

_____   _____
                                                            John Smith

_____   _____
                                                            Rhonda Jones

_____   _____
                                                            Thomas Anderson

DOES A PARTNERSHIP EXIST?

The courts often must decide if a partnership exists when a business without a partnership agreement is breaking up, when an owner wants to leave the business or has died, or when the business owes a large liability. The two most important tests are (1) whether there has been a sharing of profits and/or losses and (2) whether there has been a sharing of the right of management and control. The courts also use other tests, such as whether the partners have purchased property together, used funds earned by the business to purchase property, or filed a partnership tax return.

The most significant indication that a partnership exists is if the owners have *shared the profits* earned by the business. Normally, one owner does not split his or her hard-earned profits with someone else without a reason. Courts look closely to determine if such sharing is in the nature of wages for specific jobs performed or payment on a specific debt—which would tend to negate the existence of a partnership. However, if after all debts are paid the owners divide up what is left, that creates the appearance of a partnership. Remember that *profits* are different than *gross income*.

The management/control test examines whether the business owners appear to accept the fact that they all have the right to participate in decision making. When an issue needs to be decided, does one person unilaterally make the decision or do the several owners decide together? If several decide together, this creates the appearance of a partnership.

RELATIONS AMONG PARTNERS

The partnership is a unique form of interdependent business relationship in which a group of individuals join together to create a commercial unit, never totally separate from the individuals. Partners are considered to have high *fiduciary* duties to each other, with all the responsibilities discussed in the preceding section on agency law. They are both agents and principals of each other. The partnership is, for some purposes, a separate **entity** apart from the partners, and for other purposes is merely an **aggregate** of individuals. For example, although the partnership may maintain profit and loss records as an entity, it does not pay income tax. Instead, each partner pays tax on his or her share of the profit. Although the partnership can buy and own property in its own name, in many states the partnership cannot sue or be sued unless each partner is named individually.

As we will learn, individual partners can be held personally liable for things other partners do. Therefore, the decision regarding who becomes a partner is critically important and generally must be made by a unanimous vote of the partners. Other partnership decisions addressing normal business matters, however, are made by simple majority vote of the partners. Each partner has one vote, regardless of how much money each put into the business. In many partnerships, the partners will select a "managing partner" or an "executive committee" of partners to make everyday business decisions, subject to reversal by a majority vote of the other partners. In the absence of such a process, all partners have an equal right in decision making.

Due to their fiduciary relationship, partners have the right to expect complete loyalty, honesty, and good faith from each other. Any partner who acts for personal benefit or profit at the expense of the partnership will be liable to the partnership. Also, each partner has the right to inspect the partnership books and records and to ask for an **accounting**—a detailed statement of all income, expenses, and assets—from the partnership.

The following case concerns whether a partnership existed, and if so, whether one of the partners breached her fiduciary duty to the others by withdrawing and starting her own business.

> **accounting:** A detailed statement of all income, expenses, and assets of the partnership.

BECK V. CLARKSON

387 S.E. 2d 681 (S.C. App.1989)

FACTS

In January 1985 Allen Beck, Sheelah Clarkson, and Gerrye Clegg agreed to form a partnership to be known as CBC Investments. The purpose of the partnership was to build and develop a warehouse in Cherokee County, South Carolina, to be leased to Spring City Knitting Co. Over the next few months the partners (especially Clarkson and Beck) researched the information necessary and made contacts with Spring City. Beck's wife, a real estate agent, procured plats and contacted all property owners near Spring City's plant to ascertain their interest in selling property. The parties obtained building proposals from several contractors and discussed financing. A written proposal was sent to Spring City by Clarkson in March, signed "Sheelah Clarkson, CBC Investments," listing Beck, Clarkson, and Clegg underneath CBC Investments. A follow-up proposal was sent by Clarkson in June.

In July, however, Clarkson notified Beck that she was withdrawing from the partnership and that she planned to develop the Spring City project with her brothers and sisters. In September, Clarkson, now acting for a family partnership known as "Clarkson Associates" entered into a contract to purchase the land for the warehouse facility and completed the purchase in November. On January 20, 1986, Clarkson Associates entered into a lease agreement with Spring City. The warehouse was built at a cost of about $1,879,000

and leased for $25,800 per month. By the time of the trial, the warehouse was estimated to be worth over $3 million.

Beck sued Clarkson, alleging breach of fiduciary duty, and asking that Clarkson account for all profits from the venture and pay to Beck his rightful share. The trial judge entered a directed verdict in favor of Clarkson, and Beck appealed to the South Carolina Court of Appeals.

DECISION

The court had to decide if Beck, Clarkson, and Clegg formed a partnership. They did not have a written partnership agreement, so the court looked at the events that had occurred. Beck testified that they had agreed to "share profits and losses." Beck's wife testified that Clarkson had told her that Beck, Clarkson, and Clegg were one-third partners. In addition, the parties testified that various documents bore the letterhead "CBC Investments" and the proposals to Spring City had been signed "CBC Investments."

The court cited the UPA definition that "A partnership is an association of two or more persons to carry on as co-owners a business for profit" and pointed out that a partnership does not need to be in writing but may be implied by the conduct of the parties. "If the partners intend to and do enter into such a contract as in the eyes of the law constitutes a partnership, they thereby become partners whether they are designated as such or not . . . ."

Here there was ample evidence that the parties did form a partnership known as CBC Investments.

Clarkson then argued that even if there had been a partnership, it was a "partnership at will," which could be terminated by one of the partners whenever he or she wished, as she (Clarkson) had done. The court agreed that since no term was specified by the partners, it probably would have been a partnership at will except for the fact that the partnership was formed for a "definite undertaking" (the building and leasing of a warehouse to Spring City). Given this fact, it was quite possible, said the court, that a jury hearing this case may conclude that the partnership term could not be rightfully terminated by one partner until the completion of the project.

Although the act of one partner in leaving the partnership acts as a dissolution of the partnership, that does not necessarily terminate the fiduciary duties owed by one partner to another. South Carolina law provides that every partner must "account to the partnership for any benefit and hold as trustee for the partnership any profits derived from him" through any transaction connected with the partnership. The court noted with approval the holding of an Oregon court in a similar case:

When a partner wrongfully snatches a seed of opportunity from the granary of his firm, he cannot, thereafter, excuse himself from sharing with his co-partners the fruits of its planting, *even though the harvest occurs after they have terminated their association.*

A formal disassociation of one partner from the partnership does not allow that partner to exploit a partnership opportunity for his or her own benefit to the exclusion of the copartners.

The court concluded that there was strong evidence that the partnership was not "at will" and that Clarkson had violated her fiduciary duties to her former partners, which should have been decided by the jury. If the jury finds for Beck, "there must be an accounting of any profits" obtained by Clarkson from seizing the "seed of opportunity" connected with the project initiated by CBC Investments. The decision was therefore reversed and remanded back to the lower court for a new trial.

CASE QUESTIONS

1. Why is it that Clarkson could not withdraw from the partnership whenever she wanted to? Why do you suppose she did withdraw?
2. Could a written partnership agreement have made this dispute easier to solve or perhaps prevented it?
3. How long after a partnership terminates do you think a partner should be bound by fiduciary duties owed to copartners?
4. Would a "noncompetition clause" (a contract clause prohibiting one of the business owners from opening a competing business) have prevented this dispute from reaching the courts?

LIABILITIES OF PARTNERS

Personal Liability Partners can be *personally liable* for partnership debts. In other words, the partners' personal bank accounts, cars, homes, and so on can be attached (seized and sold through a judicial process) if the partnership assets are insufficient to pay partnership debts. This potential liability is a very important factor underlying the need to choose partners carefully and draft a partnership agreement before beginning business with someone else.

Liability for Torts As we have discussed earlier, a *tort* is the name for a wide variety of wrongful actions taken by one person which may harm another (such as negligence, battery, or slander). Torts are fully explored in Chapter 11. As we learned earlier in this chapter, employee-agents have the power to create liability on the part of the principal for torts they commit "in the ordinary course of business." Since partners are all agents of the partnership, if they or other agents or employees of the partnership commit torts within the course of business, such actions may bring about liability for the partnership and for the partners as individuals (UPA Section 13). For example, if Kenneth drives negligently and causes someone to be injured while delivering a jade plant from the partnership floral shop, he, the partnership, and the other partners are all liable for the damages caused.

Liability for Contracts   As we have learned, according to agency law, the principal is responsible for contracts entered into by an agent on behalf of the principal when the agent is acting within his or her authority. Therefore, the partnership is held to contracts entered into by any partner with a third party when the partner was acting with express, implied, or apparent authority. According to the UPA, partners have implied authority to enter into agreements for the "carrying on of the partnership business in the usual way." This means that if, in the particular business in which the partnership is engaged, it is normal to borrow money, hire employees, or enter into contracts to sell goods and services, one partner has the power to make contracts that are binding on the partnership even if the other partners do not know about or approve such particular contracts.

SOCIAL/ETHICAL ISSUES

Is it fair to impose personal liability on partners for torts committed by other partners or employees of the partnership? This, in effect, allows the personal assets of one partner, such as one's home, bank account, or automobile, to be seized and sold to pay damages for a negligent act by another person. Is this ethical? What about personal responsibility? Even if the person who committed the wrongful act is also liable, does it seem fair to impose joint liability on an innocent partner?

Is it more or less fair or ethical to impose legal contractual liability upon a partner when another partner makes a contract on behalf of the partnership without consulting the partnership? Who is helped and who is hurt by such a principle of law? Does it benefit society?

PARTNERSHIP PROPERTY AND PARTNERSHIP INTERESTS

A partnership is an entity consisting of a distinctive combination of individuals who have chosen to go into business together. Since substantial trust and loyalty (fiduciary duties) are expected of all partners, it is not surprising that all partners have equal rights to use and possess all partnership property. Suppose that the ABC partnership (consisting of Alan, Beth, and Cynthia) owns three vehicles, three desks, and three computers. If Alan always uses the red car, the brown desk, and the Apple computer, and the other two partners always use the other cars, desks, and computers, does Alan have a greater claim on any of the items if the partnership breaks up? No. Can he obtain a personal loan, pledging his interest in the car, desk, and computer as collateral? No. Alan does not have any ownership interest in the items owned by the

partnership, called **partnership property.** The partners each have equal
rights in all such property.

Partners, however, may have merely loaned or rented certain property to
the partnership (such as desks or computers) and retained title in the items
themselves. The partnership agreement should specify any such items, and
any rental agreements should be put in writing. When a partnership is being
dissolved, the partners (and their creditors!) all want their shares to be as
large as possible, and memories may be dim about which property was given to
the partnership rather than loaned or rented. Although it is probably easy to
remember who owns cars and trucks, decisions about other items often become
more perplexing.

Suppose two accountants leave successful private practices to join a partnership, each purchasing part of their interest in the partnership by assigning
to the partnership their "accounts receivable" (money owed to the accountant
from clients) and their 1/5 interest in a real estate joint venture. If the partnership dissolves 10 years later due to serious disagreements between the
partners, it may be difficult to remember, calculate, and allocate each partner's
contributions unless they have been carefully documented earlier.

Although partners do not have any ownership interest in specific property
owned by the partnership, they each have an interest in the partnership itself,
a percentage of ownership of the total net worth of the partnership, called the
partnership interest. A partner can assign this interest to a creditor or use
it as collateral for a loan. When a partner withdraws from the partnership, she
(or her heirs if she dies) is entitled to be paid the net value of her partnership
interest, as is discussed in the next section. This partnership interest can also
be attached by creditors of the individual partner. In other words, creditors of
a withdrawing partner may be able to put a hold on payment of the partner's
interest, to be applied to their debts.

TERMINATION OF PARTNERSHIPS

Partnerships only last as long as the partners want them to last. The articles
of partnership may specify that the partnership will only exist for a certain
period of time or until a certain task is achieved, and its existence will terminate when these events occur. Many partnerships are "at will", which means
that they last until one partner decides to withdraw. Or the partnership can be
ended by what is called "operation of law" if the business of the partnership
becomes illegal or a partner dies or goes bankrupt.

The most common way for partnership to end, however, is through the
withdrawal of one or more partners. Since partnership is a special relationship
among a certain group of individuals, when any one of them dies or withdraws,
that causes the **dissolution** of the partnership. The partnership is not finally
terminated, however, until all the assets and liabilities are calculated and the
partners' shares determined and paid. This process, called the **winding-up,**
takes place after dissolution, and when completed, the partnership is said to
be **terminated.**

A significant revision of the model Uniform Partnership Act was completed
a few years ago. One of the key provisions changed was to replace the word
"dissolution" with a new word "**dissociation.**" The reason behind this change
was to modify the harsh rule that a partnership must come to an end if one

partner left the partnership (dissolution). The new UPA provision changes the default position to one that assumes that, in most cases, the partnership will continue after one partner "dissociates" himself from the partnership. Of course, the Partnership must still pay the departing partner or her family the value of that partner's share within a reasonable time. Many of the states have adopted this new version of the UPA.

Many partnership agreements allow for the continuation of the "business" by the remaining partners even if the particular partnership entity is dissolved. For example, suppose that Sheila, Amanda, and Mary have operated SAM's Coffee Shop for 10 years as partners, and now Sheila decides to leave the business. Sheila's withdrawal causes the *dissolution* of the partnership under the original UPA. The partnership they formed will now end, and Sheila is entitled to receive her share of the net assets of the partnership business. The partners will have to make a financial determination of the assets and liabilities of the partnership (winding up) and compute the net worth of the partnership, and upon payment to Sheila, the former partnership will be terminated. However, Amanda and Mary may decide to continue the business—the coffee shop—under a new partnership arrangement. Or they all may decide to close down the business, sell their property and divide the net assets.

Large law and accounting firms have some partners joining and leaving the partnership nearly every year. Their carefully drafted agreements call for an immediate transfer of all assets and liabilities of the business from the old partnership to the new one that begins operations at once. Nevertheless, the old partnership entity does end, and the departing partners or their heirs must be paid the value of their partnership interest within a reasonable time.

During the **winding-up period,** the assets are sold, and the debts of the partnership paid (if the business is not going to be continued). The partnership can finish projects underway at this time but cannot begin new ones—there is no partnership entity. Regarding the payment of debts, creditors of the partnership have first claim on partnership assets. If these creditors are not fully paid, they may go after the individual assets of the partners, because the partners still have individual liability for partnership debts incurred while they were partners.

In addition, the partners may have considerable individual debts as well. The creditors of the individual partners have first claim on each partner's individual assets. If these individual creditors are not satisfied, they can seek a **charging order**, which is a court order allowing them to attach the partner's partnership interest (his or her share of the partnership).

Once all debts have been paid, and any remaining surplus divided among the partners, the partnership is said to be **terminated**.

charging order:
A court order allowing creditors of a partner to "attach" and receive the proceeds of the partner's share of a partnership.

LIMITED PARTNERSHIPS

FORMATION AND CHARACTERISTICS

A special type of partnership combines some of the features of partnerships with some of the features of corporations—the **limited partnership.** This type of business entity cannot be formed by accident—it takes a specific intent to do so. A limited partnership requires a written agreement (often quite long and detailed). The agreement, usually called the articles of limited

limited partner:
The partner in a limited partnership who does not have any personal liability for partnership debts.

partnership, must then be filed with and approved by the appropriate official of the state in which the partnership is located. Sometimes a separate certificate must be filed as well. Each state has a law spelling out the requirements for limited partnerships, and the articles of limited partnership must comply with the law in order for the state to certify the creation and existence of the limited partnership.

As is the case with general partnerships, a group of business law experts (the National Conference of Commissioners on Uniform State Laws) has drafted a model law adopted by almost all the states, called the **Uniform Limited Partnership Act (ULPA)**. This law stipulates the primary legal principles applicable to the creation, operation, management, and termination of limited partnerships. The first ULPA was drafted in 1916 and has been updated several times, including a major revision called the Revised Uniform Limited Partnership Act (RULPA) in 1976, which was designed to replace the original ULPA. In 1985, however, the Commissioners wrote a separate new ULPA and later combined its provisions with the RULPA. One of the main stipulations of the revised version was to remove the requirement that the names and addresses of limited partners be listed on the certificate filed with the state. Several states have enacted the newest revisions of the RULPA, often with changes in some provisions, while most states have enacted some form of the older ULPA.

uniform limited partnership act (ULPA): A model statute setting forth principles governing limited partnerships, which has been adopted by many states.

DIFFERENCES FROM GENERAL PARTNERSHIPS

The primary difference between general and limited partnerships is the **limitation on the liability** of the partners—hence the name "limited partnership." In each limited partnership, there must be at least one **general partner**, who has unlimited personal liability, like partners in a regular (general) partnership. The general partner has the duty of managing the business and making almost all business decisions. There must also be at least one **limited partner** (and generally are several). The limited partners do not have any personal liability. If the limited partnership incurs a large debt or loss, the limited partners may lose the money they paid to purchase a share of the partnership, but their personal assets will not be at risk for partnership debts.

general partner: The managing partner in a limited partnership who has unlimited personal liability.

Investors in various types of business ventures, particularly real estate developments, are often limited partners. They purchase shares with the hope that the value of the business increases, and they can sell their share for a profit later. Equally important is the opportunity to receive various tax benefits, such as taking a share of the depreciation allowance on the real estate, although this benefit has been limited by tax revision legislation. Profits and losses of the partnership "pass through" to the partners, as discussed below.

Management of the business is the responsibility of the general partner or partners. As long as the limited partners do not participate in the management of the enterprise or allow their names to be publicly used in connection with the enterprise, they do not have personal liability for the partnership debt. If the limited partners do get involved in management, however, they may lose their preferred status and find themselves as individual defendants in a lawsuit. The removal (in the latest revision of RULPA) of the requirement that the names and addresses of all limited partners be listed on the certificate filed with the state is intended to confirm that the partnership agreement is the controlling document of a limited partnership. The tax revisions mentioned earlier and the creation of limited liability companies (discussed in the next chapter) have dramatically reduced the value of limited partnerships as a form of business ownership.

TAXATION

One key aspect of both general and limited partnerships is that they are not taxed as an entity. In other words, the partnership does not pay income tax, as a firm, on its profits. Instead, each partner (whether limited or general) pays income tax on his or her share of the profit and can deduct his or her share of the losses as well.

Thus the income tax liability is said to "pass through" the firm, directly to the partners. This tax liability is different from corporations, as we will see in the next chapter. In general, corporations are taxed as an entity, separate from the owners (shareholders). Then, if the corporation distributes some of its profit to shareholders as dividends, those distributions are taxed again as income of the shareholders.

LIMITED LIABILITY PARTNERSHIPS

A new and improved (from the partners' point of view) form of partnership has been created by statutes recently passed in many states, called the **limited liability partnership** (LLP). These organizations have important legal differences from both a general partnership and a limited partnership.

As we have discussed, one of the scariest aspects of the general partnership form of entity is that each partner has unlimited personal liability for debts of the partnership, including negligence and other torts done by other partners and employees. The LLP entity allows all partners to participate fully in the management of the business, but without facing that unlimited personal liability for the actions of others. The LLP laws protect one partner from personal liability for the torts of the other partners. Some of the state LLP laws offer partners limited liability (no personal liability) for other types of partnership debts (such as contracts) as well. Partners do remain personally liable for their own torts.

Most law and accounting firms, which have traditionally been formed as general partnerships, are quickly changing to the new LLP form, for obvious reasons (liability). As with other limited liability entities, proper written documents must be filed with the appropriate state officials to formally establish an LLP. But changing the partnership agreement to an LLP form, and filing some papers with the state is not a difficult task, and the benefits to the partners are huge.

limited liability: When investors, such as limited partners, only risk losing their investment in the business, not their personal assets.

limited liability partnership: A relatively new form of business entity, which permits the partners to take an active role in management, while protecting them from personal liability.

LIMITED LIABILITY LIMITED PARTNERSHIPS

As with partnerships, in recent years many state legislatures have enacted laws designed to make limited partnerships safer investments. As you will recall, in a Limited Partnership, the limited partners have limited liability, but the general partner has unlimited personal liability for partnership debts. There is now a new, improved version of Limited Partnership called a Limited Liability Limited Partnership (LLLP) which allows even the general partner of a Limited Partnership to enjoy limited liability. Obviously, this change pleases those individuals and businesses who wish to serve as the general partner of a limited partnership.

SUMMARY

Many of the important principles controlling the liability of business organizations are based on the law of agency. Organizations can act only through the deeds of people. When one person (principal) asks or hires someone else (an agent) to act for him or her, it creates several significant legal duties and relationships. Agents owe the highest degree of loyalty and trust to their principals—called fiduciary duty. Agents often have the power to make contracts binding on the principal, depending on the scope of their authority. Also, principals sometimes find that they are liable for torts (wrongful actions) committed by employee-agents in the scope of employment.

A sole proprietorship is a business that legally is merely the extension of one owner—who makes all business decisions, is responsible for all debts, and can keep all profits. The business does not have a legal existence separate from the owner. Partnerships are a popular type of business organization, in which the business has an existence somewhat, but not totally, separate from the owners. Partnerships are easy to form, are flexible in structure, and can be used in many categories of ventures. The partners directly control and manage the operation of the business, and partnerships do not pay taxes as an entity—the partners each pay taxes on their shares of the profits. However, partnerships involve significant personal liability risks for the partners. A written partnership agreement and adequate business insurance are extremely important for any partner, in order to protect, as much as possible, his or her personal assets. A new form of business entity, the Limited Liability Partnership (LLP), is being adopted by many law and accounting firms, which allows general partnerships to elect to protect the partners from liability for the acts of other partners.

Limited partnerships serve as an investment vehicle for persons who do not want to be actively involved in the management of the business or to put their personal assets at risk in a business venture. And there is a newer form of limited partnership called the Limited Liability Limited Partnership, which allows the general partner, as well as the limited partners to enjoy limited liability. All forms of business are significantly affected by the principles of agency law in determining the liabilities of the various members of the business to each other and to outside parties.

CHAPTER QUESTIONS

1. What is the usual rule about the termination of an agency relationship? What must the principal or agent do? What is an "agency coupled with an interest"?

2. Explain the legal theory *respondeat superior.* What is the policy behind such a rule? What effect does this rule have on business organizations?

3. Jane, Edward, and Terry form the JET Partnership to perform accounting and financial planning services. They do not discuss how to share profits or losses. Jane contributes $6,000, Edward $3,000, and Terry $9,000. At the end of the first year, the partnership has a loss of $6,000. How should this be shared? The next year JET makes a profit of $54,000. How should this be allocated?

4. A magazine publisher entered into a contract with a professional photographer to arrange a photo shoot illustrating a particular scene. The contract specified that the photographer was an independent contractor. The magazine told the photographer exactly what type of resulting photo it needed for its next issue, but did not send anyone to supervise the session. The photographer obtained the services of a model to appear in the photo. Unfortunately during the shoot, the model fell while riding a bicycle in one of the shots and was injured. The model sued the magazine as well as the photographer. Was the photographer an independent contractor or an agent of the magazine? *Raben v. Conde Nast Publications, Inc.,* 767 N.Y.S. 2d 440 (N.Y.A.D. 2003).

5. What is the "apparent authority" theory? What is the reason for and public policy behind this rule?

6. In the 1970s, Louis Trombetta and his wife Marion began operating an adult bookstore, Carnival Books, in Brooklawn, New Jersey. At the rear of the premises, behind the bookstore, Anthony Trombetta, the brother of Louis, and Richard Basciano, operated a "live and machine entertainment" business. According to Louis, he and Marion began running the bookstore because the "peep shows and dancing girls" business at the rear of the building was not doing well. He and Marion kept all the proceeds from the bookstore and, according to an alleged oral agreement between Louis and Anthony, Louis received one-third of the net profits from the live entertainment business. The parties operated the two businesses under these terms for over 30 years. After Anthony began to change the terms of the agreement, allegedly saying to Louis, "This is my place, I own everything, you don't own nothing," Louis filed a lawsuit alleging that his brother Anthony had violated the terms of their partnership agreement. At trial Anthony claimed that *he* offered the bookstore to his brother and Marion because of their financial difficulties. He also claimed that the business was operated under a franchise agreement and was not a partnership. What is the difference between a franchise and a partnership agreement? Does this agreement meet the definition of a partnership? [See *Trombetta v. Trombetta,* 2008 WL 246011 (N.J.Super.A.D.).]

7. An owner of a firm asked an employee to travel to the post office 4 blocks away to refill the postage meter. After doing so, the employee passed her office, and continued 18 blocks further to cash her payroll check at her bank. While nearing the bank, she had an auto accident, causing injuries to another person. Can the injured person sue the employer? What is the issue? What will be the key test? *Timmons v. Silman,* 761 So. 2d 507 (La. 2000).

8. International Paper Co. employee Vanessa McGrogan was talking on her company cell phone while driving on Interstate 16 in Georgia. She had set her cruise control speed at 77 mph; the speed limit on the interstate was 70 mph. She rear-ended a vehicle driven by Debra Ford, a widowed mother of four children. The collision pushed Ford's car into a nearby ditch, rolling it with the driver's side down and Ford's left arm pinned between the door and the asphalt. After multiple unsuccessful surgeries and skin grafts, Ford's arm was amputated just below the shoulder. McGrogan's testimony and cell phone call records indicated that she was not on the phone at the time of the accident, but a truck driver on the interstate at the time testified that he saw McGrogan with her phone to her ear immediately before the collision. Ford filed a lawsuit against International Paper, claiming that she was entitled to both compensatory and punitive damages for her injuries based on McGrogan's "intentional negligence." In its defense, International Paper argued, among other things, that Ford's arm failed to heal properly because she was a smoker, which impacted her vascular system. What is "intentional negligence?" Should the jury award Ford compensatory damages? Punitive damages? What do you think of International Paper's defense regarding Ford's smoking habits?

9. The owner of a gas station that also rented Avis cars was sued as the result of a tragic traffic accident. One Sunday afternoon, when the gas station was closed, a 16-year-old boy (Robert Bruno) was on duty for the sole purpose of renting Avis cars. Later that afternoon another young employee arrived to work on his own car. Although the owner had told the employees not to use Avis cars for personal errands, Bruno (with his girlfriend) took an Avis car to get a pizza for lunch for the two young men. Apparently, despite the rule, it was quite common for employees to use rental cars for personal business, and no one had been fired for this practice. On the way back to the station, Bruno negligently collided with another car, killing two people. The families sued the owner of the gas station as well as Bruno. The owner's defense was that Bruno was on a "frolic" at the time of the accident, and he (the owner) should not be liable. How should the court decide? [*O'Boyle v. Avis Rent-A-Car System, Inc.*, 435 N.Y.S. 2d 296 (1981)]

10. A local minister also had served for eight years as an unpaid voluntary chaplain with the county sheriff's office. He provided various types of counseling and support services to crime victims and officers, performed various ceremonies, and was on 24-hour call. The Department provided him with a car equipped with a sheriff's radio and pager. Early one evening while on a personal errand at Wal-Mart, the chaplain ran over the foot of a 16-year old part-time Wal-Mart employee who was collecting shopping carts in the parking lot. The injured man sued the chaplain, the county and the sheriff's department.

Most of the chaplain's duties came as the result of request from the department—to come to a crime scene, or to perform weddings, to give counseling to deputies and their families, or giving invocations and benedictions. The court wrestled with how to apply the "right to control" test to professional duties. Furthermore, the New Mexico statute regarding claims for damages against governmental employees uses the phrase "'scope of duties" which may be larger than the "scope of employment" test for private employees. The department "requested, required or authorized" use of the official vehicle to travel between home and work. But clearly the stop at Wal-Mart represented a personal errand by the chaplain, and he could not recall what he had been doing just prior to the accident.

The county and the department moved for dismissal which was granted by the lower court. Issues in the case included (1) was the chaplain an employee or independent contractor; and (2) was he within the scope of employment? What do you think are the key issues in each question? What should the court decide? *Celaya v.Hull,* 85 P.3d 239 (N. Mex. 2004).

PRACTICAL EXERCISE

Robert, Kathleen, and Seth are recent graduates of State College. Seth, who has a science and technical background, has been experimenting with ways to use sagebrush as a healthful, high-fiber, dietary food source. Kathleen is a business graduate, well-schooled in the latest management, finance, accounting, marketing, economic, and statistics practices. Robert, a liberal arts graduate, knows a lot about the world and comes from a family of some wealth. These three graduates have decided to embark on a venture together to open a health food store that they hope will expand over the next few years. The project will attempt to develop Seth's sagebrush ideas into a marketable product (perhaps a breakfast cereal called "Sage Loops") and sell a wide variety of other health food items.

Robert has taken a job as a teacher for next year but would be willing to invest $50,000 in the project in return for a substantial share of ownership. Kathleen is excited about the project and would be willing to work full-time on it, at least for a year. Seth can devote part of his time to developing the sagebrush food supplement while he takes some courses in grad school. He can invest $10,000 in the venture and will use various scientific tools and materials of his own in his work (but wants to retain ownership of these items). Kathleen has no money to invest at this point but would like to earn a salary while managing the business.The three entrepreneurs believe that it will take about $75,000 to start and stock their business for the first year and somewhat less during the second year. They hope to earn a profit by the end of year two. Obviously, if their business expands, they will need substantially more capital. Robert, Kathleen, and Seth have decided to form a general partnership. Prepare a brief (three to five pages) partnership agreement that sets forth the basics of the organizational structure and anticipates and avoids some of the problems they may face later. You may use the form contained in the chapter as a starting point, but it will be necessary to alter it to fit the particular needs of the parties. Some of the provisions will not be necessary.

FURTHER INFORMATION

www.dol.gov
U.S. Department of Labor.

www.sbaonline.sba.gov
Small Business Administration.

www.law.cornell.edu/topics/partnership.html
Cornell Legal Information Institute.

CHAPTER 9

CORPORATIONS AND OTHER BUSINESS ENTITIES

After reading this chapter, you should be able to:

1. Understand the steps involved in establishing a corporation.

2. Explain the legal structure of a corporation and the responsibilities and liabilities of the owners.

3. Describe the roles and duties of the various groups governing the corporation, including shareholders, the board of directors, and the corporate officers.

4. Detail the process of capital formation.

5. List the ways in which corporations can be terminated.

6. Describe the characteristics of special types of corporations.

7. Understand the requirements and attributes of a limited liability company.

CHAPTER OUTLINE

I. Establishing a Corporation

II. Corporate Structure

III. Corporate Governance

IV. Capital Formation

V. Termination of Corporations

VI. Other Types of Corporations and Companies

The three friends we met at the end of the previous chapter who wanted to start a health food business have met with some success. They now want to expand their business by opening more stores and selling their cereal nationwide. Therefore, they are now considering changing their business entity to a corporation. You are asked to help them prepare articles of incorporation for their business in the "Practical Exercise" at the end of this chapter.

INTRODUCTION

Corporations are the most important form of business organization in the world today. The legal structure of the corporation is significantly different from partnerships and sole proprietorships. The most important distinction is that the corporation is a completely separate **legal entity** that exists independently from any individual person involved in the business. As we discovered in the last chapter, partnerships are partially separate entities from the owners (for example, they can own property and sue and be sued) but are not totally separate (the partners have personal liability for partnership debts, and the entity usually dissolves when a partner leaves).

Corporations however, are considered as fully separate *legal persons*. Thus, a corporation can own property in its own name and file and defend lawsuits; however, the corporation must file a tax return and pay income taxes on the profits it earns, much like an individual. Unlike partnerships, though, the owners of the corporation do not normally have personal liability for debts of the business. And when one of the owners (called shareholders) of the corporation dies or wishes to leave the business, that person's shares are simply inherited by or sold to someone else, and the corporation continues its existence.

Although the corporation itself has a separate existence, it is an intangible entity and can only act through agents—individuals who perform various services on behalf of the corporation. Thus, the principles of agency law we examined in the preceding chapter are centrally important to determining the liability of corporations for all types of torts and contracts. Large companies have thousands of employees and shareholders as well as many officers and directors—all may be agents of some type for the corporation. Each group has different tasks and responsibilities—the "scope of authority" or "scope of employment" within which an individual's action may become the action of the corporation. We begin by examining how corporations are formed and then discuss the roles and legal responsibilities of the board of directors and shareholders and other important corporate issues.

legal entity: A corporation has an existence separate from, and independent of, any individual shareholder or director.

ESTABLISHING A CORPORATION

Unlike general partnerships, a corporation cannot come into existence informally or by accident. Corporations are artificial entities that can be created only through full compliance with the law of the state in which they are incorporated (like limited partnerships). Each state has its own **statutory corporate law** that specifies what must be done to form a corporation, the activities that corporations may undertake, the formalities required of corporations on an annual basis to maintain their status, the capital structure necessary, the manner and requirements for dissolving (terminating) corporations, and other matters.

As with partnerships and limited partnerships, an organization of legal and business experts (The National Commission on Uniform State Laws) has drafted a model law regarding corporations that most states have adopted in whole or in part. This statute, the **Model Business Corporation Act (MBCA)**, sets forth suggested provisions regarding all aspects of corporate formation, operation, and termination. Most of the material reviewed in this chapter is consistent with the principles of the MBCA as revised. The fact that

state corporation law: Corporations are formed by following the law of the state where they choose to be incorporated.

Model Business Corporation Act (MBCA): A model state law dealing with corporations, drafted by an organization of business lawyers, which has been enacted by many states.

many states have adopted the MBCA promotes uniformity of law from state to state, which is important to the many corporations with operations in several states. Again, we should emphasize that corporations are chartered by states, not the federal government, and each corporation, in order to begin its existence and to operate in a legal manner during its life, must comply with the laws of the state in which it is incorporated.

The powers of corporations are established not only by the relevant state law but also by the corporation's **articles of incorporation.** Every state requires corporations to prepare such a written document, setting forth the name, address, and purposes of the corporation, the key people involved in its creation (the *incorporators*), and its capital structure and internal organization. Often called a **charter**, this document must be filed and approved by the appropriate state official before the corporation can legally exist. In some states, the secretary of state actually issues the charter to the corporation if its paperwork is all in order. In other states, the responsible state official stamps "Approved" on the corporation's articles of incorporation and returns the document to the corporation if it is in compliance with the law.

As a practical matter, someone needs to come up with the idea for starting a corporation. That person determines the need or opportunity for the business, raises the necessary funds, obtains commitment from other investors and lenders, finds office space, deals with potential suppliers, obtains any required licenses, and does the other things necessary prior to the beginning of the corporation's legal existence. These persons, called **promoters,** are personally liable for all actions they take before the corporation is formed (since there is no principal at that time). Once the corporation has filed the appropriate documents with the state, and the first board of directors has adopted its articles of incorporation, the promoters will no doubt seek to have the corporation adopt, on its behalf, all contracts and actions the promoters have entered into up to that point.

When the corporation accepts responsibility for the contracts, this may relieve the promoter from personal liability, as long as the other party to the contract is willing to substitute the corporation for the promoter. As we said in the previous chapter, when an agent makes a contract on behalf of a partially disclosed principal (for example, a corporation that does not yet fully exist), the contract is between the agent and the third party until the identity of the principal is known. At that time, the third party must choose whether to hold the agent (promoter) or principal (the corporation) liable. The promoters are quite interested, therefore, in seeing that all requirements for incorporation are properly met. When this is accomplished, it is said that a **de jure corporation** (a corporation of law) exists.

Once the corporation has correctly established its separate entity, its existence cannot be successfully challenged by the state or creditors. Until the corporation has properly completed all the required steps for incorporation, the promoters will still have primary personal liability for contracts they have made (they will be treated as partners). However, if the promoters have taken almost all necessary steps toward incorporation in good faith but some matter was not completely accomplished, courts may term the corporation a **de facto corporation** (a corporation in fact). For example, one of the promoters may not have signed the articles of incorporation filed with the state. If the corporation is considered *de facto,* the individual shareholders will not be personally liable

articles of incorporation: A written document prepared by founders (incorporators) of a corporation, which sets out its name, purposes, number of authorized shares, official address, and other information.

charter: Another name for the articles of incorporation, establishing a corporation.

promoters: The people who organize and start the corporation. They may be liable for contracts they make before the corporation is incorporated.

de jure corporation: A corporation which has been properly established and has met all incorporation requirements in its state of incorporation.

de facto corporation: A corporation which has been properly established except for minor details, which the incorporators intend to promptly correct.

as long as they promptly correct the problem. The state may challenge the existence of a de facto corporation, but creditors may not. This rule protects the promoters from personal liability. On the other hand, if there is a significant failure to follow state law or if the promoters acted in bad faith, the corporation will not be considered *de facto* or *de jure*, and the promoters (as agents for a nonexistent principal) will be individually liable for any actions taken.

CORPORATE STRUCTURE

There are three important groups of people involved in the legal structure of a corporation—the shareholders, the board of directors, and the officers. One aspect of a corporation that differs from partnerships and sole proprietorships is that often ownership and management of the organization remain separate. The **shareholders** are the owners of the company, and each one has invested money or something else of value in return for a part ownership of the company. The shareholders then elect a group of people called the **board of directors** to manage the business. The number of directors and how they are elected will usually be set forth in the articles of incorporation. Although members of the board are usually shareholders, this is not technically necessary. Some corporations have only one or two directors, while others have 20 or more.

Once elected, the board will often hire certain people to run the day-to-day operations of the company. Called **officers**, these persons (such as the president, vice-president, and treasurer) may or may not be shareholders or directors as well. They are technically employees of the company and carry out the tasks given them by the board of directors. In smaller corporations, the same people may serve as shareholders, directors, and officers; in larger corporations, however, this will not be the case. Thus, in larger companies a real separation exists between control and management of the corporation (by the officers and board of directors) and the ownership (thousands of shareholders, only a few of whom serve as directors).

Many important differences exist between the legal structure of partnerships and corporations and the responsibilities and liabilities of the owners. The next few sections highlight and explain some of these characteristics.

LIMITED LIABILITY

limited liability: Where the investors' liability for business debts is limited to the loss of their investment.

Perhaps the single most significant legal distinction, at least for the business owners, between a partnership and a corporation is that shareholders of a corporation enjoy **limited liability**. These investors purchase an ownership interest in the corporation, and whatever they have contributed to the company (money or property, for example) becomes part of the corporate assets. For example, if George purchases $1,000 worth of shares in the ABC Company and the corporation does not pay a debt it owes, the creditors may be able to attach (seize) the corporate assets, including the capital contributed by George. But in most situations, George cannot be personally sued by the creditors of the corporation for corporate debts. In other words, the liability of George, the shareholder, is *limited* to the loss of his investment in the company and is not extended to his personal assets.

As with many legal concepts, there is an exception to the general rule of limited liability for corporate shareholders. Occasionally, one or two individuals may be held personally liable for a corporate debt, usually when the organization has not acted like a corporation. Courts apply this concept, called **piercing the corporate veil**, to prevent unfairness when it appears that someone is trying to realize the benefits of incorporation (limited liability) without properly conforming with the requirements. This theory allows a court to overcome the corporate liability shield (i.e., to "pierce" it) and hold a dominant individual shareholder personally responsible to creditors.

piercing the corporate veil: The normal rule that shareholders do not have personal liability for debts of the corporation may be overcome where a dominant shareholder has disregarded the corporate form and operated the firm like it was a sole proprietorship, or a mere "alter ego" of that person.

MEMO FROM THE LEGAL DEPARTMENT

To: Students

From: Your Lawyer

Many of you will start businesses or work in small firms. The corporate form offers significant advantages, such as limited liability for shareholders. However, if the business owners want the benefits of the corporate form, they must make sure that the organization behaves like a corporation whether it has two shareholders or 2,000. This means that it must elect a board of directors, hold meetings and keep minutes (in a "corporate book" along with the articles of incorporation, preferably), ensure that the corporate money and financial records are kept separate from any one individual's money, file all necessary state corporate reports, prepare and pay corporate taxes, and perform other acts as a corporation.

Another factor courts consider when "piercing the corporate veil" is whether the corporation is grossly undercapitalized for its own needs. For example, if a manufacturing corporation has only $400 in its treasury and the primary shareholder simply puts money into the corporation as needed, it would appear that the corporate firm is being used merely as a device to avoid personal responsibility by the primary owner. However, it is certainly possible for a corporation with only one or two shareholders to maintain a separate existence and to preserve limited liability if proper procedures are followed.

Sometimes a person who has gone to the expense and effort of organizing a corporation under the appropriate state law operates it like a sole proprietorship, either intentionally or unintentionally. Suppose Heather has created the HRC Company, of which she is the president and sole shareholder (this is legal in most states and is allowed by the MBCA), and has properly followed state law in establishing its legal existence and has properly obtained her charter from the state corporations office. However, Heather makes all decisions by herself, never holds board of director meetings, mixes her own money with corporate funds, and uses the corporate property (cars and computers, for example) for her own purposes whenever she chooses.

Suppose also that Larry has supplied $20,000 worth of office equipment to HRC Corporation. Now HRC Corporation says that it cannot pay Larry and that it has only $500 in assets. Larry would like to sue Heather directly, but since it is a debt of the corporation, Heather claims that she is not personally liable. If Larry sues Heather, as well as HRC Corporation, the court might decide that she has made the corporation her *alter ego* (merely a manifestation of herself) and allow the creditor (Larry) to pierce the corporate veil.

The following case represents an example of what can happen to an individual who seeks the benefits of the corporate legal structure but does not take the necessary steps to maintain the corporation's separate existence.

CARPENTER PAPER CO. V. LAKIN MEAT PROCESSORS, INC.

231 Neb. 93, 435 N.W. 2d 179 (1989)

FACTS

Lakin Meat Processors, Inc., was incorporated in 1975. Throughout its existence, Charles Lakin was the president and either the sole shareholder or the majority shareholder. Although the corporation's capitalization was stated as $100,000, at no time was more than $75,000 paid. During the course of the operation of the business (purchasing, slicing, packaging, and selling beef livers to retail outlets), Mr. Lakin made personal loans to the corporation on a regular basis. The loan balances reached as high as $1 million at times, and the loans were covered at all times by a security interest in favor of Mr. Lakin in all the tangible and intangible personal property of Lakin Meat, including furniture, machinery and equipment, inventory, accounts receivable, and notes. In other words, Mr. Lakin loaned the cor-

poration considerable money, and the corporation put up as collateral all of its furniture, machinery, and equipment (which could then be seized by Mr. Lakin if the loans were not paid back).

Mr. Lakin was also involved in various other businesses and corporations. He had a checking account in his name at the American National Bank in Omaha that he used as a "sweep account." As checks were received by some of Lakin's various businesses, the checks were deposited into the account. For every business except Lakin Meat Processors, the exact amount of deposited money would then be transferred out of this account into the correct business account within a few days. For Lakin Meat, however, the funds remained in the American National Bank account until someone from Lakin Meat called and requested a transfer to its bank, Emerson State Bank in Emerson, Iowa. The transfers were always made in round numbers, not the exact amounts deposited earlier.

Lakin Meat did have its own place of business, its own employees, and a separate office within the Lakin Building for accounting and bookkeeping work. It also had its own phone, its own letterhead, and used its own invoices. Lakin Meat kept a corporate minutes book, filed its own tax returns, and kept its books and records separate from Lakin's other businesses.

In March 1981, Lakin Meat Processors, Inc., sold substantially all of its assets to Prime Meat Processors, for which Prime Meat paid $450,000 for fixed assets and $196,709 for inventory. At the time of the sale, Lakin Meat owed Mr. Lakin more than $1 million as the result of the loans discussed earlier. Mr. Lakin received the sale proceeds personally, and after the sale, he loaned another $271,000 to Lakin Meat and received loan payments from Lakin Meat of more than $1.2 million, leaving a balance due Mr. Lakin of $37,000.

Carpenter Paper Co. was one of Lakin Meat's creditors and had been a regular supplier for years. However, a dispute had arisen over five invoices in 1979 and 1980 concerning late payments and a shipment of printed liver film by Carpenter that Lakin said was defective. At the time of the sale of the business, the amount in dispute was about $5,900. Carpenter Paper obtained a default judgment against Lakin Meat in July 1982, but there were no assets to attach, so the firm sought to collect from Charles Lakin individually, that is, to pierce the corporate veil. The lower court dismissed the case, and the plaintiff appealed to the Nebraska Supreme Court.

DECISION

The Nebraska Supreme Court started its discussion of the legal issues with the general statement that "When a corporation is or becomes the mere alter ego or business conduit, of a person, it may be disregarded."

Looking to the holding of a previous case, the court stated that some of the factors relevant in determining whether to disregard the corporate entity were:

1. Grossly inadequate capitalization;
2. Insolvency of the debtor corporation at the time the debt is incurred;
3. Diversion by the shareholder or shareholders of corporate funds or assets to their own or other improper uses; and
4. The fact that the corporation is a mere facade for the personal dealings of the shareholder and that the operations of the corporation are carried on by the shareholder in disregard of the corporate entity.

The court then applied these tests to the facts of the Lakin Meat case. It found that Lakin Meat had gross receipts of $5 million in 1980 and paid dividends of as much as $200,000 to Lakin in one year, although its capitalization never rose beyond $75,000. Expert witnesses at the trial testified that using various "debt-to-net worth" and other tests, Lakin Meat was "grossly inadequately capitalized," especially since it ran an overdraft of $100,000 in the bank for six years.

Concerning insolvency, Lakin Meat apparently did pay all of its creditors on a regular basis but since it owed Mr. Lakin somewhere between $214,000 to $1 million during most of its operation, its debts greatly outweighed its assets, making it insolvent in the bankruptcy sense at all times. Concerning "diversion of assets for improper uses," there was nothing other than the dividends of over $300,000 paid to Mr. Lakin and the final loan payoff of over $1 million.

The final point was the most telling. The court stated that in spite of the separate bank accounts and bookkeeping, "Lakin Meat was Charles E. Lakin. He controlled the corporation's every move. He ran it as he saw fit." The complicated series of books and accounts did not obscure the fact that "there was a unity of interest as far as Mr. Lakin and Lakin Meat were concerned." The court found that Lakin's manipulations of the business permitted him to, and he did, "terminate the corporation for his own financial well-being to the prejudice of the corporation's creditors." The lower court decision was therefore reversed.

CASE QUESTIONS

1. What was the most important factor the court used in deciding to pierce the corporate veil in this case? What factors supported Mr. Lakin's argument that only the corporation should be liable?

2. What should Mr. Lakin have done differently to avoid personal liability for the debts of the corporation?

3. Does the result in the case seem fair to you? Does it seem that justice was done in this case? Why?

SEPARATE ENTITY

Legally, corporations, much like individuals, are considered separate entities, distinct and apart from one another. Although certain persons play very important roles in every company, the corporation itself is made up of a combination of all the parts—the board, the officers, the shareholders, and, of course, the employees. Even if the sole shareholder dies or the top officers quit, the corporation would continue to exist. The share ownership would transfer after the death of the sole shareholder, and the board would select new officers to replace those who resigned. The corporation itself, however, would neither die nor resign. It is often said that corporations have perpetual existence because they do not depend on any one person, legally at least, for their existence.

TAXATION

Since corporations are considered separate entities, they not only enjoy the benefits of individuals, but they also share certain individual responsibilities—one of which is paying taxes. Unlike partnerships, corporations must pay income taxes on their net profit each year. The tax rates are not the same as those for individuals, but the payment of federal income tax (and generally state income tax, too) is a major corporate responsibility.

In addition, if after the corporation pays its income taxes it still shows a profit for the year, some of that profit will probably be paid to its shareholders as a *dividend*. The individual shareholders then must pay tax on these dividends as income on their own tax returns, a practice that has been called **"double taxation."**

CORPORATE GOVERNANCE

The actions of shareholders, members of the board of directors, officers, and employees are all important to the proper functioning of corporations. Each group has an important legal position in the process of governing corporate affairs, as discussed in the following sections. The corporate scandals in recent years, and the tremendous public outcry which followed, led Congress to pass a significant new law, which placed substantial additional duties on corporate officers, directors and the company auditors. This law will have a major effect on the rules regarding corporate governance.

THE SARBANES-OXLEY ACT

In July 2002, Congress enacted and President George Bush signed into law the Sarbanes-Oxley Act. The passage of this sweeping law followed the massive corporate accounting and financial scandals—including Enron, WorldCom, Adelphia, Tyco, HealthSouth and more—which dominated the business news in 2002 and 2003. The Sarbanes-Oxley Act (SOA) is a major federal statute that imposes significant new duties on corporate officers, directors, and other corporate personnel as well as the accountants, auditors and attorneys who advise them. The SOA is designed to create numerous additional safeguards for public investors by ensuring that the financial statements and reports issued by public companies are reliable and truthful. It also attempts to decrease potential conflicts of interest in the preparation of financial statements and audits of company records.

In the previous 20 years, all the large international accounting firms had established consulting practices, which gradually became more profitable to the firms than providing accounting and auditing services. The Enron and WorldCom scandals disclosed that the companies' accounting and auditing firms had become very closely involved with financial, recordkeeping, management, taxation, and human resources issues and other business decisions made by their corporate clients. Such a situation seemed likely to compromise the independence and rigor of the audits performed on their clients' financial records. Sarbanes-Oxley included several sections to address this issue.

Some of the more important features of the Sarbanes-Oxley Act are:

1. Establishment of a new body, the Public Company Accounting Oversight Board (PCAOB) to supervise and regulate auditing of public companies;

2. The PCAOB must: (1) register public accounting firms; (2) establish, or adopt, by rule, "auditing, quality control, ethics, independence, and other standards relating to the preparation of audit reports for issuers;" (3) conduct inspections of accounting firms; (4) enforce compliance with the Act, the rules of the Board, professional standards, and the securities laws;

3. Prohibiting a registered public accounting firm from providing a wide range of non-audit services to an issuer which it also audits, including such services as: (1) bookkeeping or other services related to the accounting records; (2) financial information systems design and implementation; (3) appraisal or valuation services; (4) actuarial services; (5) internal audit outsourcing services; and (6) management functions or human resources;

4. A "conflict of interest" section stating that the CEO, Controller, CFO, Chief Accounting Officer or person in an equivalent position in a public company cannot have been employed by the company's audit firm during the 1-year period preceding the audit. (Many of the top accounting and financial people in Enron had previously worked for Arthur Andersen.)

5. The new law places extra responsibility on a public company's audit committee (one of the sub-committees of a company's board of directors) by requiring that it "shall be directly responsible for the appointment, compensation, and oversight" of the work of any registered public accounting firm employed by that issuer. Furthermore, the law requires that each member of the audit committee be an "independent" member of the board of directors—that is, one who does not receive, other than for service on the board, any consulting, advisory, or other compensatory fee from the issuer.

6. The CEO and CFO must prepare a statement to accompany the audit report and personally certify the "appropriateness of the financial statements and disclosures contained in the periodic report, and that those financial statements and disclosures fairly present, in all material respects, the operations and financial condition of the issuer."

7. Section 306 of the SOA now generally prohibits the purchase or sale of stock by officers and directors and other insiders during blackout periods. (One of the more frustrating aspects of the Enron scandal was that Mr. Lay and Mr. Skilling and other insiders sold millions of dollars of Enron stock during a "blackout" period when employees were unable to sell their shares (and that which was in their 401(k) plans), and the value of Enron stock was falling rapidly.)

8. The SOA requires each annual and quarterly financial report to disclose all material off-balance sheet transactions" and "other relationships" with "unconsolidated entities" that may have a material current or future effect on the financial condition of the issuer.

9. Under the SOA it is now generally unlawful for a public company to extend credit or make loans to any director or executive officer. (There were reports of multi-million dollar loans made by Tyco and other companies to key officers)

10. Each annual report must contain an "internal control report," which shall: (1) state the responsibility of management for establishing and maintaining an adequate internal control structure and procedures for financial reporting; and (2) contain an assessment, as of the end of the issuer's fiscal year, of the effectiveness of the internal control structure and procedures of the issuer for financial reporting.

11. A public company will be required to disclose annually whether the company has adopted a code of ethics for the company's principal executive officer, principal financial officer, principal accounting officer or controller, or persons performing similar functions, and if it has not, to explain why it has not

12. The SOA prohibits knowingly "altering, destroying, or concealing records with the intent to impede, obstruct, or influence and investigation or proper administration of any matter within the federal government's jurisdiction."

close corporations: Corporations with a small number of shareholders, often family members.

THE ROLE OF THE SHAREHOLDERS

A corporation consists of many different groups of people with different responsibilities—all contributing to the whole. The shareholders are the owners of the corporation, and many corporations consist of only a few shareholders. These companies, often called **close corporations**, may be owned primarily by family members with no shares being sold to the general public. And, of course, there are multibillion dollar corporations with thousands or millions of shareholders all over the world. In each type of corporation, however, the legal structure is essentially the same. The shareholders—whether there are three or 300,000—are the owners.

Even though they own the company, the shareholders do not manage the business. In a corporate structure, that role falls to the board of directors and the officers. The shareholders' main power is to elect the members of the board. Therefore, when people battle for control of a corporation or an outsider attempts to mount a takeover of a corporation, each side seeks to secure enough votes from the shareholders to elect the people they want to the board.

Expanding Engagement Between Shareholders and Corporations

> Institutional Shareholder Services ("ISS"), which often works with shareholder groups, released a report in 2011 on engagement between investors and public corporations in the United States that included the finding that this "engagement is expanding beyond financial and strategic issues and 'traditional' governance topics to include more environmental and social issues." The report was based on a survey of 355 issuers of stock and 161 investors.
>
> While much press coverage focuses on the filing of shareholder resolutions, engagement between shareholders and companies often begins with letters and phone calls. Asset managers reach out to investor relations departments, corporate secretaries, and other senior executives, to initiate dialogue about issues of shareholder concern. The report notes that:
>
>> Asset managers with an ESG (environmental, social, and governance) or SRI (socially responsible investment) orientation often contact an issuer's CSR (corporate social responsibility) or sustainability office, and one such asset manager noted that "the most effective engagements tend to be with the people actually working on the issue.
>
> Notably, the report found that both investors and issuers believe that "constructive dialogue" is indicative of a successful engagement, but investors were, of course, much more likely to be satisfied with concrete corporate actions. Both sides felt that a withdrawn shareholder proposal was as much a sign of accomplishment as a proposal with high support votes. A withdrawn proposal is often a sign of productive discussions where the company is willing to make changes.
>
> In the 2011 proxy season, members of the Interfaith Center on Corporate Responsibility have filed a number of resolutions raising human rights concerns including: resolutions asking for the adoption or amendment of human rights policies (e.g., Carnival Corporation, Caterpillar); resolutions asking for the identification of gaps in existing human rights policies (e.g., General Dynamics, KBR); and resolutions asking for companies to adopt policies articulating respect for the human right to water (e.g., Johnson & Johnson, Green Mountain Coffee Roasters).
>
> Resolutions like the ones noted above likely reflect unsuccessful attempts at constructive dialogue. The study suggested that it is important to ask what needs to happen, on both sides, for these resolutions to lead to the types of discussions, and/or actions, that each side can view as successful.

The shareholders are investors, not managers, and if they become dissatisfied with the way the corporation is going, they can always sell their shares. This is especially true in large companies, where there is a ready market for the shares on either a national stock exchange or the over-the-counter market. Furthermore, the likelihood of one investor being able to have an effect on the corporate policies is small.

The following cartoon is a humorous look at the sometimes contentious relationship between shareholders and managers.

From *The Wall Street Journal*, January 12, 1995. Reprinted with permission of Cartoon Features Syndicate.

"There's a shareholder here to see you, sir."

SHAREHOLDER VOTING

Shareholders do have the right to vote on certain matters of great importance to the company, such as a merger or dissolution, amendment of the articles of incorporation, or adoption of measures restricting the free transfer of shares (e.g., a resolution prohibiting the sale of shares to outsiders without first offering the shares to the corporation). But most business decisions are made by the board of directors, not the shareholders.

In voting shares, generally each shareholder has as many votes as shares. Thus, large shareholders have a better chance of electing their choices to the board. Many corporations, however, have adopted a method of voting called **cumulative voting**, which increases the chance that those owning smaller amounts of shares can elect someone of their choice to the board. In cumulative voting, each shareholder gets as many votes as his or her number of shares multiplied by the number of directors to be elected. If Nancy owns 50 shares and there are five director spots to be filled, she has 250 votes, which she can vote entirely for one person if she chooses. Thus, a shareholder owning 51 percent of the shares in the company cannot be sure of electing *all* the directors—which she could do under regular voting.

In a small company or close corporation, most of the shareholders may also be members of the board and/or officers of the company (and often are employees as well). In this situation, one shareholder may actually be able to change the direction of the company. Also, the shareholder, without a stock market in

cumulative voting: When the shareholders are allowed to vote their shares multiplied by the number of directors to be elected. A shareholder can cast all of these votes for one person.

which to trade, will probably have more difficulty selling his or her shares. But battles for control of small companies do occur. They are often decided by determining whose directors are elected to the board, which is based on share ownership.

In a battle for control of a larger corporation, the two competing sides will attempt to solicit support from the shareholders by mailing them letters explaining the benefits of their position and asking for *proxies* (the right to vote the shareholders' shares) at the meeting. Obviously, access to the shareholder list is critical to this effort, and the management of the corporation is not generally eager to assist its opponents. Although shareholders do have certain rights to obtain a copy of the list of corporate shareholders in order to wage a "proxy battle," that right is not unlimited, as the following case demonstrates.

PILLSBURY V. HONEYWELL, INC.

191 N.W. 2d 406 (Minn. 1971)

FACTS

Mr. Pillsbury was a member of a group of people opposed to American involvement in the Vietnam War. Members of the group learned that Honeywell, Inc., was a major producer of munitions for the Defense Department and embarked on an effort, called the "Honeywell Project," to get Honeywell to stop producing arms, particularly "fragmentation bombs." Pillsbury purchased some Honeywell shares and then requested a copy of the shareholder list and an opportunity to inspect the corporate books and records dealing with weapons and munitions manufacture. The request was denied by Honeywell management, and Pillsbury filed suit. The lower court denied his request, and the case was appealed to the Minnesota Supreme Court.

DECISION

The Court noted that several other courts had agreed with Pillsbury's contention that a shareholder's desire to communicate with other shareholders and to elect directors who shared his views gave him the right to obtain a list of corporate shareholders. However, the court stated, "We believe that a better rule would allow inspections only if the shareholder has a proper purpose for such communication. . . ."

The court took note of the burden that would be placed on large corporations if all shareholders could "roam at will" through the corporate books and records. In addition, it was apparent to the court that Pillsbury had no interest in the affairs of Honeywell other than its production of weapons. He had purchased a very small number of shares and "had made no attempt to determine whether Honeywell was a good investment." In the court's view, he did not have a "proper purpose" for obtaining corporate records.

In determining what was a proper purpose, the court looked primarily at economic factors. "We do not mean to imply that a shareholder with a bona fide investment interest could not bring this suit if motivated by concern with the long- or short-term economic effects on Honeywell resulting from the production of war munitions" (or, noted the court, the economic effects of abstaining from profitable war contracts).

In this case, however, the shareholder's concerns were not for the well-being of Honeywell or for the value of his own investment, but "his sole purpose was to persuade the company to adopt his social and political concerns." While normally an attempt to elect one's slate of directors would be a proper purpose, the court said that "here the purpose was not germane" to either Pillsbury's or

Honeywell's economic interests and was therefore not "proper." Therefore, the lower court decision was affirmed.

CASE QUESTIONS

1. How could Pillsbury have rephrased his request so that he would have had the right to look at the corporate records?

2. Do you think that a shareholder should have the right to obtain a list of all shareholders for any and all reasons? Why or why not?

3. What other reasons, other than "economic interest," might qualify as a proper purpose for shareholder access to corporate books and the shareholder list?

THE ROLE OF THE BOARD OF DIRECTORS

board of directors: This group of people, elected by the shareholders, has the legal duty of managing the corporation.

Following their election by the shareholders, the **board of directors** has the legal right and duty to manage the regular business affairs of the company. A large number of decisions must be made by the board, as set forth in the following sections.

Regular Business Decisions   Regardless of how many executive officers are hired or how often the board meets, it cannot escape the duties and responsibilities of governing the corporation. The Board is charged, for example, with deciding if the company should open a new plant, manufacture a different product, adopt a certain personnel policy, issue new stock, pay dividends, and many other business decisions. As mentioned previously, only extraordinary matters, such as a merger or dissolution of the corporation, need the approval of the shareholders; all other decisions are for the board to make.

How Board Decisions Are Made   One important aspect of the board's role is that the directors may only take action as a board—that is, one or two directors acting independently have no power. A majority action of the board, however, taken at a duly scheduled meeting, upon proper notice, is an act of the corporation. The essence of the legal structure of a corporation is that the shareholders' best interests are served when all the board members meet together, share ideas, debate various courses of action, and then take a majority vote. In many cases courts have overturned board actions when there was no proper notice of the meeting given to all directors, or actions were taken without a meeting. Most states and the MBCA do allow directors to act in some cases without a meeting if they all have agreed to waive prior notice of the meeting. This might occur if there is a need for immediate action and the directors are fully informed of the situation and approve of the action. It will not be upheld if some of the directors decide to hold a meeting without proper notice and do not inform and obtain written consent from all the directors. What kind of people are members of the board at large corporations? The following box gives information on the Board of Directors of Hewlett Packard Co. in April 2011.

Board of Directors of Hewlett Packard Corp. in April 2011

Marc L. Andreessen, Director since 2009

Mr. Andreessen is co-founder and a general partner of Andreessen Horowitz, a venture capital firm founded in July 2009, and co-founder and Chairman of Ning, Inc., an online platform founded in 2004 for people to create their own social networks. Mr. Andreessen co-founded Netscape Communications Corporation, a software company, and served in various positions, including Chief Technology Officer and Executive Vice President of Products from 1994 to 1999.

Léo Apotheker, Director since 2010

Mr. Apotheker has served as HP's President and Chief Executive Officer and as a member of the Board since November 2010. Mr. Apotheker served as Chief Executive Officer of SAP AG, a software company, from June 2009 until February 2010 after having served as co-Chief Executive Officer of SAP from April 2008 to May 2009.

Lawrence T. Babbio, Jr., Director since 2002

Mr. Babbio has served as a Senior Advisor to Warburg Pincus, a private equity firm, since June 2007. Previously, Mr. Babbio served as Vice Chairman and President of Verizon Communications, Inc., a telecommunications company, from 2000 until his retirement in April 2007.

Sari M. Baldauf, Director since 2006

Ms. Baldauf served as Executive Vice President and General Manager of the Networks business group of Nokia Corporation, a communications company, from 1998 until February 2005.

Shumeet Banerji, Director since 2011

Mr. Banerji has served as Chief Executive Officer of Booz & Company, a consulting company, since July 2008. Previously, Mr. Banerji served in multiple roles at Booz Allen Hamilton, a consulting company and predecessor to Booz & Company, while based in offices in North America, Asia and Europe.

Rajiv L. Gupta, Director since January 2009

Mr. Gupta has served as Chairman of Avantor Performance Materials, a manufacturer of chemistries and materials, since August 2010 and as Senior Advisor to New Mountain Capital, LLC, a private equity firm, since July 2009. Previously, Mr. Gupta served as Chairman and Chief Executive Officer of Rohm and Haas Company, a worldwide producer of specialty materials, from 1999 to April 2009.

John H. Hammergren, Director since 2005
Mr. Hammergren has served as Chairman of McKesson Corporation, a healthcare services and information technology company, since 2002 and as President and Chief Executive Officer of McKesson since 2001.

Raymond J. Lane, Director since 2010
Mr. Lane has served as HP's non-executive Chairman since November 2010. Mr. Lane has served as Managing Partner of Kleiner Perkins Caufield & Byers, a private equity firm, since 2000. Prior to joining Kleiner Perkins, Mr. Lane was President and Chief Operating Officer and a director of Oracle Corporation, a software company.

Gary M. Reiner, Director since 2011
Mr. Reiner has served as Special Advisor at General Atlantic, a private equity firm, since September 2010. Previously, Mr. Reiner served as the Senior Vice President and Chief Information Officer at General Electric Company, a technology, media and financial services company, from 1996 until March 2010.

Patricia F. Russo, Director since 2011
Ms. Russo served as Chief Executive Officer of Alcatel-Lucent, a communications company, from December 2006 to September 2008. Previously, she served as Chairman of Lucent Technologies Inc., a communications company, from 2003 to November 2006 and Chief Executive Officer and President of Lucent from 2002 to November 2006.

Dominique Senequier, Director since 2011
Ms. Senequier has served as Chairman and Chief Executive Officer of AXA Private Equity, a private equity firm, since founding the firm and joining AXA Investment Managers in 1996. Earlier in her career, she worked at the Commission Francaise des Assurances and at the French insurance group GAN.

G. Kennedy Thompson, Director since 2006
Mr. Thompson has served as Senior Advisor to Aquiline Capital Partners LLC, a private equity firm, since May 2009. Previously, Mr. Thompson served as Chairman of Wachovia Corporation, a financial services company, from 2003 until June 2008, and was CEO of Wachovia before that time.

Margaret C. Whitman, Director since 2011
Ms. Whitman served as President and Chief Executive Officer of eBay Inc., an ecommerce and payments company, from 1998 to March 2008. Prior to joining eBay, Ms. Whitman held executive level positions at Hasbro Inc., a toy company, FTD, Inc., a floral products company.

Source: HP website

Payment of Dividends   Not surprisingly, the payment of dividends is a matter of considerable interest to the shareholders. After all, receipt of dividends is one of the reasons why they invested in the company. However, as with most other corporate decisions, determination regarding payment of dividends rests with the board. It may be in the interests of the corporation to retain a larger surplus for some debt or liability contingency or for future construction projects in a particular year rather than to pay most of it out in dividends. As long as the board does not "abuse its discretion" in making the decision (i.e., deciding not to pay dividends for some fraudulent or improper reason), the questions of whether or not to pay dividends or how much of a dividend to pay are strictly for the board. In a very few cases, courts have ordered boards to declare dividends where profits are excessive and no reason exists for refusing to award dividends. The dividends can *only* be paid *out of surplus,* however, and cannot be paid if to do so would render the corporation insolvent.

Corporate Officers   The board of directors will, in most cases, appoint certain persons to serve as officers of the corporation. These people, such as the president, vice-president, treasurer, and so on, serve at the pleasure of the board. In other words, they work for the board and can be fired if their performance does not satisfy the board. Some officers do enter into written contracts with the corporation (through the board) and then can be fired only for good cause. In large corporations, the officers are well paid for their services, while in close corporations, they are usually unpaid. Often, certain officers are elected to serve on the board as well. The officers are in charge of the day-to-day operations of the company, making all normal business decisions. Then, every few months, the board meets, listens to reports, and asks questions of the corporate officers. The board still legally has the responsibility for managing the corporation.

Unfortunately sometimes the board does not keep a close enough eye on the officers of the corporation, with catastrophic results. As we have mentioned earlier, in the past 10 years there have been numerous scandals involving false and misleading financial information and reporting by major corporations. Among the many ramifications of these business scandals was the enactment of the Sarbanes-Oxley Act (discussed earlier in this chapter), which significantly increased and clarified the duties of a corporation's board of directors.

WHO REALLY GOVERNS THE CORPORATION?

Despite the formal legal structure depicted in the preceding section, in which officers answer to the board, which must then answer to the shareholders, for large corporations the actual practice may be just the opposite. A number of commentators have observed that many corporations are actually run by powerful officers who make almost all the decisions. These decisions, then, are later ratified by the board, which may be filled with friends and business associates of the top officers. Directors who are also employees or officers of the corporation are called **inside directors**, and those not so employed are called **outside directors**. The outside directors may be officers of other companies and have only a few hours a month to study the affairs of this corporation. They may rely heavily on information given them by the corporate officers.

Even the election of directors may be actually controlled by the officers through the use of *proxies* (described earlier). In large corporations, relatively few

inside directors: Members of the board of directors who are also officers and/or employees of the corporation.

outside directors: Members of the board who are not officers or employees of the corporation.

shareholders attend the annual meeting where directors are elected. Along with the notice of the annual meeting, the management typically mails out to the shareholders a request to authorize the top management to vote the shareholder's shares. This form, called a **proxy**, if signed and returned by most of the shareholders (as is common), allows the management to vote large numbers of shares for the slate of directors proposed by the board. Management may vote the shares on any other matters that come before the annual meeting as well. Along with the proxy, the management must send the shareholders a *proxy statement*, which describes the main items of business expected to come up at the annual meeting, as well as the total salaries and compensation paid to the top five corporate officials and other interesting information. The following memo describes some of the information that can be learned from reading proxy statements.

proxy: A written document by which one shareholder authorizes someone else (often management) to vote his or her shares at the annual meeting.

MEMO FROM THE LEGAL DEPARTMENT

To: Students
From: The Legal Department

WHY YOU SHOULD READ PROXY STATEMENTS

As explained in the text, when management is requesting proxies from its shareholders prior to the annual meeting, it is also required to send "proxy statements." Although the statements are lengthy and filled with numbers and legalistic jargon, there is much useful and interesting information contained in them, which may help shareholders decide on selling or holding their stock.

Proxy statements must explain proposals which will come before the annual meeting, including routine matters such as the appointment of the auditing firm. Proxy statements also contain much more, such as how much the top management is paid, what stock options were granted, lawsuits pending against the company, and any special deals between the corporation and its management and directors.

Some of the specific items which must be disclosed in proxy statements, according to the rules of the Securities and Exchange Commission are:

Stock Options. Shareholders can compute how much of the corporation's stock is being given to key management, and what part of their total compensation is in stock options. The shareholders, after all, should have final word on how much of their company they want to give to the management.

Lawsuits. The proxy statement must list and describe all significant lawsuits filed by or against the company, and give a short status report on the litigation. Often a shareholder can detect a disturbing pattern of problems, or a major threat to the company which may not have been clearly explained to shareholders by the management. (Who likes to give out bad news?)

Directors. Proxy statements disclose who the directors are, and who is standing for election this year. Shareholders should look at the background and experience of each person who has been nominated to serve on the board of directors. (The board is nominated by a small sub-committee of existing directors in most cases.) Shareholders should also find out the occupations of the proposed directors and how many of the nominees are "outside" directors. Most shareholder groups believe that having more outside directors (not company management) is good for a company. Too many "good buddies" of the CEO sitting on the board of directors may not be in the best interest of the organization as a whole.

Related Transactions. Many corporate directors have extensive outside business interests. Shareholders should find out if one of the directors is the president of their company's main supplier or customer. Shareholders can learn if their company's officers and directors are benefiting from such "sweetheart" deals between the officers' and directors' other firms and the shareholders' corporation. Does a director own the land or building on which the shareholder's company is located? Does a director own a plane that is leased to the company?

Compensation for Top Management. The proxy statement must list the annual compensation, for the last year, of the five most highly paid executives in the company. It is often interesting and instructive to compare the salary and bonuses and stock benefits paid to the top executives with the overall performance of the corporation, its profit and loss, and the stock price.

Sources: The Wall Street Journal, Business Week, CNN, and others.

In recent years, under the name of "corporate democracy," several proposals have been made to increase the powers of shareholders and to dilute the power of the incumbent officers and board. Some of the ideas include requiring more outside directors, requiring the selection of board members who represent consumer and environmental organizations, changing the law to allow shareholders to more easily propose resolutions to the annual meeting, and various reforms to the proxy system. While only a few of these proposals have been enacted into law as yet, many corporations have made changes in their procedures in response to public discussion of these issues.

New Rights for Shareholders

Two recent trends are giving shareholders more power to affect corporate decisions. The Securities and Exchange Commission has adopted a rule allowing large investors to nominate their own candidates for the Board of Directors, while using the company's proxy ballots. Traditionally, shareholders who wanted to elect directors not selected by the Board nominating committee had to pay for the costs of sending their own proxies, which might cost millions of dollars in large companies.

The new SEC rule will greatly reduce that cost by allowing investors with at least a 3% ownership for two years to propose their own slate of directors, which will be listed in the company's proxy next to the company's selections. Shareholder groups see the new rule as an important new tool to improve underperforming boards, such as those that have rejected corporate governance changes approved by shareholders, or rewarded top executives despite poor results.

In 2010, Michael Dell, the CEO and largest shareholder of Dell Corp. got a rude surprise when 25% of the shareholders opposed his re-election to the board. Two labor groups had campaigned against him, citing a recent SEC suit alleging accounting manipulations. Mr. Dell continues as CEO and a board member, but Dell Corp. paid a fine of $100 million and Mr. Dell himself paid a $4 million fine without admitting guilt.

Another growing trend is for corporations to have all directors elected annually, replacing the more traditional staggered board terms where 1/3 of the board is elected each year to terms of 3 years. Advocates of annual elections say it boosts a board's accountability to shareholders on key issues like acquisitions and executive pay. One shareholder group withdrew half of the 28 resolutions it had filed seeking yearly board elections at different corporations, when the big companies they had targeted agreed to make the changes.

So-called "classified boards" whose members have staggered three-year terms, discourage hostile takeovers since it is hard for outsiders to alter a board's composition if only 1/3 of the directors are elected each year. But the use of staggered boards began to feel investor pressure some 10 years ago, as part of an effort to reform corporate governance. The number of Standard & Poor's 500 companies with staggered boards has fallen from 303 in 1998 to 139 in 2011, according to one study. Eaton Corp. agreed to move to yearly board elections in 2014, stating in its proxy statement that "A classified board may contribute to diminished director accountability . . . and many investors believe that the election of directors is the primary means for shareholders to influence policies."

SOCIAL/ETHICAL ISSUES

There has been criticism directed at corporations where the members of the board become "rubber stamps" who approve the policies of the chief executive officer (CEO) and other top officers. As we have discussed, although board members are technically elected by the shareholders, actually they are often chosen by a committee of the board (which may include the CEO or another key inside director). Then the board selects a group of persons who will "run" for election. The management sends out proxies to all shareholders, and most shareholders sign them. Only a small percentage actually attend the annual meeting. Therefore, by the beginning of the meeting, the board-nominated group usually has more than enough votes to be elected.

Some changes are occurring. Many large corporations now have established rules that call for the board to select a "lead director" who will call at least three meetings a year of the outside directors; also that the outside directors will make a formal evaluation of the CEO each year; and the outside directors will make decisions regarding corporate governance issues.

What do you think about the need for the board to be independent of management? Should outside directors have more power or different rules than inside directors? What is wrong with having close friends of the CEO on the board?

FIDUCIARY DUTIES OF OFFICERS AND DIRECTORS

The officers and directors of a corporation, like agents and partners, have fiduciary duties to the corporation. The shareholders have put them in a position of considerable trust and responsibility, and they must act accordingly. Two primary legal responsibilities are incumbent upon them: the duty of care and the duty of loyalty.

The Duty of Care.   Shareholders have the right to expect the directors to exercise their responsibilities thoroughly and carefully. The board, after all, is managing the corporation in which the shareholders have invested their money. The law recognizes and enforces these expectations, and directors are held to the **standard of due care** with respect to their performance.

standard of due care: Board members owe to the shareholders the duty to act with care and to diligently carry out their responsibilities in a non-negligent manner.

The standard of due care is essentially based on *negligence theory*. The legal principle of negligence is based on comparing the actions taken by a person in a particular situation with the level of conduct a reasonably careful person would have used in the same situation. In the corporate setting, if a director carries out the duties of the position in a reasonable and competent manner, he or she will not be liable to the shareholders if the business loses money or encounters trouble. If, on the other hand, a director is negligent in managing the corporation, he or she may be sued by shareholders if the business incurs substantial debts or goes into bankruptcy and the shareholders lose their investment.

The Business Judgment Rule.   To handle such situations, the legal system has developed a theory called **the business judgment rule**. The rule provides that if the board has made decisions after exercising careful business judgment, the board members will be immune from liability even if the decision turns out to be a bad one for the company. For example, if the board of directors of the Bronco Golf Co. decides to manufacture a line of blue and orange striped golf balls after careful market study, cost analysis, and product testing, the board will probably avoid liability to the shareholders if the project is a failure. However, if the decision was made to go ahead with the project simply and solely because the company president "just loves stripes," then the board might be liable to the shareholders for the project's failure (double bogey).

In other words, the business judgment rule protects directors by allowing them to make mistakes as long as they go about making the decision in a thorough way. Shareholders cannot expect that the board will never make a bad decision, but they have the right to expect that all decisions will be fully researched and carefully made. Board members of all corporations—big and small—must be prepared to attend meetings regularly, read reports given them by officers, ask questions when something is not clear, and generally act without negligence in order to properly carry out the duties entrusted to them by the shareholders. There is no such thing as a "silent director." If a board member does not have the time or the ability to actively serve as a director, he or she should resign from the board.

During the past twenty years a large number of corporate mergers and takeovers took place. While some were handled in a friendly manner, others were **hostile takeovers** in which an outside investor attempted to purchase all or a majority of stock in the company, against the wishes of the corporate management. This type of bid is called a **tender offer** when it is directed to the shareholders of a company. In the face of an unwanted tender offer from an outsider, generally at a high price, corporate directors were often called on to make difficult decisions, under considerable time pressure, about what was in the best interests of the company and the shareholders. Tender offers will be discussed in more depth in Chapter 10.

A colorful new vocabulary evolved as corporations tried to repel unwanted takeovers. Many companies enacted **poison pill plans**, triggering new shareholder rights whenever a corporate raider acquired a certain percentage of the corporation's stock. Such plans allow the existing shareholders to receive large amounts of stock at a very low price, making the takeover exceedingly expensive for the raider. As the nickname "poison pill" suggests, the corporation's strategy was to tell prospective raiders, "If you swallow our company against our wishes, you will become very ill."

the business judgment rule: If the directors have made a decision after careful consideration, they will not be liable to the shareholders even if the decision has bad consequences for the company.

hostile takeover: A takeover in which an outside investor attempts to purchase all or a majority of stock in a company against the wishes of corporate management.

tender offer: An investor attempts to take control of a corporation by buying a majority of the shares from existing shareholders.

poison pill plan: A defensive tactic used by a company facing an unwanted takeover bid that makes the purchase of its stock very costly.

During the battle for control of a company, sometimes the existing management enlists the aid of a third company, with whom a merger would be acceptable, in order to thwart a takeover by an unwanted suitor. This acceptable third company has been termed a *white knight*. One big worry for top company management is that if the company is taken over by another company, after a hostile battle the first thing that the new board of directors will do is fire the former company's management and elect a totally new board of directors. In response to this concern, a number of company boards adopted **golden parachute** plans, guaranteeing their key executives a handsome severance package if they should be terminated following a takeover.

In the following important case, the Delaware court interpreted the business judgment rule in a situation in which a corporation's board voted to approve rather than reject a merger.

> **golden parachute:** The nickname for a generous severance package provided to a corporate executive terminated in a takeover.

SMITH V. VAN GORKOM

488 A.2d 858 (Del. 1985)

FACTS

As he approached retirement, the chairman and chief executive officer (CEO) of Trans Union Corporation, Jerome Van Gorkom, concluded that he wanted to sell the company. Mr. Van Gorkom—a lawyer and certified public accountant—had been CEO of the company for 17 years, during which time he had participated in many acquisitions. He analyzed the value of Trans Union on his own (with the aid and knowledge of only one other Trans Union employee) and determined what he considered a fair buyout figure per share.

Mr. Van Gorkom then took his proposal to Jay Pritzker, a well-known takeover specialist and acquaintance of Mr. Van Gorkom's, at Mr. Pritzker's home. At this point Mr. Van Gorkom had not told any Trans Union board members or officers about his idea. Mr. Pritzker was interested, and he and Mr. Van Gorkom then met several times over the next few days (with a few corporate officers present some of the time). Mr. Pritzker decided he wanted to go forward and do a "cash-out merger" (merging Trans Union completely into one of Mr. Pritzker's companies). Mr. Pritzker also demanded that the deal be completed in three days, or he would withdraw his offer.

Trans Union Corp. had, of course, many shareholders and a board of directors. Mr. Van Gorkom hurriedly called an emergency meeting of senior management and a board meeting for the next day without giving the reason for the meetings. After hearing Mr. Van Gorkom's presentation calling for the hasty sale of the company, the top management officials of Trans Union reacted quite negatively. Nevertheless, Mr. Van Gorkom proceeded with the board meeting one hour later. He made a 20-minute presentation, followed by short remarks from the president and chief financial officer (who stated that the proposed share price was "at the low end" of the acceptable range). During this two-hour meeting, the board, at Mr. Van Gorkom's urging, nevertheless approved the merger, despite the absence of any relevant documents, legal opinions, or financial analysis or materials of any kind. Later that evening Mr. Van Gorkom signed a merger agreement at a formal social event he hosted for the Chicago Lyric Opera (attended by Mr. Pritzker). Again, no one else from Trans Union (nor any of its legal or investment advisors) had seen or reviewed the merger document.

Two weeks later, as dissent to the sale mounted within the company, the board met again and heard further details of the agreement and approved some amendments to the merger (although the actual written amendments later put in the contract were not quite the same as Mr. Van Gorkom told the board they would be). The board still did not ask any significant questions or request more time. The board also failed to seek outside advice from any attorneys or the company's investment banker, Salomon Brothers. A few months later the shareholders formally approved the merger. However, several shareholders filed suit against Mr. Van Gorkom and the board of directors, arguing that they had violated their duty of care by approving the sale so quickly. In doing so, they argued, the board had not exercised prudent business judgment. Had the board acted more carefully and thoroughly and considered other buyers, the shareholders argued, they could have gotten considerably more for their shares.

DECISION

The Delaware Supreme Court noted that:

1. The directors based their decision almost entirely on Mr. Van Gorkom's short oral presentation and analysis of the transaction.
2. They did not know that he had actually suggested the price to the buyer.
3. They failed to ask relevant questions about the terms of the merger agreement and approved it in one two-hour meeting.
4. No consultations were made or requested with management or independent advisers (such as the company's investment banker) regarding the "intrinsic value" of the company or the fairness of the transaction.
5. The directors did not request or review copies of any major documents, nor did they seek the advice of their attorneys.

The directors argued that their later meeting, at which further material was provided, along with the subsequent approval of the shareholders, had cured the problems created by the short initial meeting. The Court disagreed, however, finding that the corporation was effectively bound to the agreement after the first meeting, and the shareholder vote was meaningless because the shareholders were not informed fully of the facts behind the board's decision.

The Delaware Supreme Court cited a case it had decided only one year earlier (*Aronson v. Lewis*) concerning the business judgment rule, where the court had written that directors must "inform themselves, prior to making a business decision, of all material information reasonably available to them," in order to come within the protections of the rule. The court held that the directors in *Van Gorkom* had breached their duties of care by approving, in a most hasty manner, the very sale of the corporation—perhaps the most significant decision they would ever be asked to make. The actions of the board members in this instance amounted to "gross negligence" in the performance of their duties.

The case was remanded to the lower court for the purpose of holding hearings on the fair value of the stock of the corporation, with the directors being personally liable for the difference between what was paid for the stock and its fair market value. (The case was later settled, with the individual directors and the company's insurance company paying a large settlement to the shareholders.)

CASE QUESTIONS

1. What should the directors have done differently? Why is it that they did not do more when they had the chance?
2. Why did the directors not have the right to trust and believe the president when he, the CEO of the company, told them the price was fair?
3. Because they want their company to continue as is—with them as directors—a targeted company's board may take action to block a takeover, including the adoption of poison pill resolutions. At what point does this type of activity violate the board members' duty to the shareholders?

SOCIAL/ETHICAL ISSUES

The Boards of Directors of American companies are often criticized by commentators for being composed primarily of white males, who may include friends and business associates of the CEO. Things are changing slowly, with boards becoming somewhat more diverse and including more outside directors who are not tied to the CEO or top management, due to pressure from shareholder activist groups.

Other nations have different historical and cultural factors that affect the composition and duties of the board of directors. In Germany most companies have two different boards, one of which is largely composed of employee representatives and "public" members.

The Duty of Loyalty   Shareholders have the right to expect their officers and directors not only to do their best to make good business decisions after careful consideration but also to execute their duties based on what is best for the corporation, not on what is best for them as individuals. In many cases, of course, those goals are similar—if the corporation makes a good profit, the directors and officers will benefit as well as the shareholders.

But suppose the corporation is seeking a site to build a new factory and is willing to pay $100,000 for such a piece of property. One of the directors, Art, is involved in real estate and learns of a suitable location. However, before telling the appropriate corporate official about it, Art purchases it himself for $60,000, has the title put in the name of his sister-in-law, and then notifies the company about the land. When the corporation later purchases it for $100,000 (a fair market price), has Art done anything wrong? The answer is definitely yes, because under the **corporate opportunity rule**, officers and directors cannot benefit personally from an opportunity in which the corporation might have been interested. These people are fiduciaries, after all, and they should be thinking about how they can save money or otherwise aid the corporation they have been entrusted to manage. If Art had been thinking about his fiduciary duty to the corporation instead of how he could benefit himself, the corporation could have bought the property for $60,000.

> **corporate opportunity rule:** If a director learns of a business opportunity that the corporation might want to pursue, he or she must bring the idea to the board for consideration, before taking advantage of it personally.

SOCIAL/ETHICAL ISSUES

Is there really anything ethically wrong with the actions of Art, the director set forth previously? who was hurt by his action? After all, the corporation got the land it needed at a fair price. Would it have been ethically proper if Art had not put the property in his in-law's name but had told the company that he owned the land? What if he did not disclose that he had just purchased it or the price of the purchase? May a director ever be involved in another business enterprise that does business with the director's corporation?

CLOSE CORPORATIONS

The fiduciary duties of the officers and majority shareholders of "close corporations" are greater than those of public corporation officers. Since such corporations are composed of fewer shareholders, often family members, with no public sales of stock, it makes sense that it would be highly improper for the few people controlling the company to take advantage of the other shareholders, in order to enrich themselves. Courts have been particularly sensitive to the rights of minority shareholders of close corporations, as the following recent case shows.

In the Language of the Court

LAWTON V. NYMAN

327 F. 3d 30 (1st Cir. 2003)

FACTS

Nyman Manufacturing Company was a closely held, fourth-generation family-owned company in Rhode Island that manufactured paper and plastic dinnerware. Robert Nyman, the President and CEO of the company, and his brother Kenneth, the Vice-President of Manufacturing, had worked in the business their entire adult lives. There were two classes of company stock: Class A shares, which were non-voting, and Class B shares, which were voting stock. Traditionally, one or two family members owned all of the Class B stock, while the Class A shares were dispersed throughout the family. No dividends were ever paid on either class of stock. Robert and Kenneth Nyman had each inherited 375 shares of the Class B voting stock from their uncle; this was the entirety of the issued Class B stock. Because they were the controlling shareholders, we refer to them as the majority shareholders of the company.

In the beginning of 1995, all of the Class A stock was owned by various family members—the two sisters of Robert and Kenneth and their children—and by two trusts held by estates. The company teetered on the verge of bankruptcy in the late 1980s. In 1991, the company's performance again began to suffer. In 1994, after three consecutive years of losses, the company hired Keith Johnson, a specialist in turning around and then selling companies, as a consultant. Johnson was made the Chief Financial Officer and Treasurer in August 1994 and he was promised an equity share of the company if he could revive the company's flagging profits.

By the spring of 1995, it appeared that the fortunes of the ailing company were being reversed. Earlier, in the fiscal year ending March 25, 1995, the company reported a profit of nearly $1.6 million, in vivid contrast with its past losses. On April 3, 1995, the company granted Johnson 1,000 options to buy Class A stock at $145.36 a share. No effort was made to ascertain the actual market value of the stock, as required by the bylaws. In the words of the district court, at this time "the prospect of a future sale of the company to a strategic buyer was, at most, nothing more than a remote possibility."

In July 1995, after a series of discussions, the company offered to redeem 2,256 Class A shares from the Magda Burt Estate (a family trust) and did so in November for $145.36 per share. That price represented eighty percent of the $180 book value of the stock in April 1995, not the higher November 1995 book value of $312.02 a share. The Board, which now consisted of Johnson, Robert, and Kenneth, then issued options to themselves to buy the same number of shares as those redeemed, at the same price, $145.36 a share. Robert received 1,128 options, while Kenneth and Johnson received 564 options each. The company then offered to redeem the shares held by the other trust (by this time, the book value had risen to $318.59 a share), but the offer was refused by one of the beneficiaries of the trust, Beverly Kiepler (sister of Robert and Kenneth).

The company's fiscal year ended on March 29, 1996. The unaudited financials showed a profit of $3.5 million and a quadrupling of shareholder equity. Robert, Kenneth, and Johnson, sitting as the Board, also adopted deferred compensation plans for themselves, which had a total value of $2 million, and decided to hire a consultant to help them sell the company. The letter hiring the consultant included duties such as performing services related to assessing the long term value of the firm, maximizing Nyman's position in the eyes of a potential acquirer, and the specific dynamics of the merger and acquisition market. *None of this information was disclosed to the minority shareholders.*

In April 1996, Johnson, on behalf of the company, offered to purchase 700 shares of Class A stock directly from Ms. Kiepler (Robert and Kenneth's sister) and her daughter for $145.36 a share. By that point, shareholder equity had risen to $576.40 per share. Johnson put Kiepler under a false deadline, saying that the bank waivers which would permit the purchase would expire on May 1, 1996. *This was untrue: no waivers had yet been secured. Kiepler declined the offer, based on the low price.*

On May 8, 1996, the company, over Johnson's signature, sent letters to all Class A shareholders (except Robert and Kenneth, their spouses, and the Walfred Nyman Trust), offering to redeem their shares for $200 per share. The letter said the following:

> I would like to report to you some information about Nyman Mfg. and a limited term opportunity that you now have as a Nyman shareholder with shares of Class A Non-Voting Stock. As you know, the Company has had major "ups and downs" over the past 10 years including 5 years in which significant losses were

experienced. In the two most recent years, the Company's financial condition has improved and its lending banks have agreed that limited amounts of its common stock may be re-purchased. This is an opportunity for shareholders who are interested in achieving liquidity now.

> Last November, the Company was able to re-purchase certain shares of stock held by Rhode Island Hospital Trust Bank as co-executor of Marge Burt's estate at a price of $145.36 per share. Since that time, the Company has received several inquiries from other minority shareholders concerning their desire to sell their shares of Nyman Mfg. Co. stock. In response to these inquiries, the Company has negotiated with its lending banks to allow it to offer to purchase additional shares of Nyman stock at this time.

> Given favorable economic factors and current estimates of operating results, the Company is offering to purchase all of your shares at a price of $200 per share. Since the Company cannot provide you with any advice as to whether the sale of the stock by you is in your best financial interest, we suggest that you discuss this matter with your financial advisor.

> Please indicate on the enclosed form your interest in selling your shares back to the Company at the offer price of $200.00 per share. This offer will expire on May 22, 1996. The Company is planning to complete this transaction with you within two weeks after the receipt of your written acceptance of this offer along with the receipt of your stock certificates.

Several statements in the letter were not accurate. The impetus to redeem the shares came from the company, and it was not true that the company made the offer in response to several inquiries from other minority shareholders concerning their desire to sell their stock. The record also shows that there was no bank-imposed deadline of May 22, as the letter implied. This phony deadline of May 22 meant that the minority shareholders had to decide whether to sell before the company made its next audited financial statements available.

The very next day, on May 9, 1996, Johnson reported to Heller Financial, Inc. that Nyman's fiscal year-end profit was estimated to be $3.533 million, and he included a copy of Nyman's unaudited FY 1996 financial statement. *The unaudited financials were not disclosed to plaintiffs, nor was the decision to retain a consultant, nor was the fact that the defendants were in May engaged in discussions to acquire other companies.* The letter also implied that the $200 a share price was based on "favorable economic factors and current estimates of operating results," but did not disclose what was meant by this. In fact, the stock price of $200 a share was based on neither current market value nor book value. Defendants did not seek to have an appraisal done.

On May 10, Robert called his sister Judith Lawton to ensure that she had received the letter. *He described the offer as a "once in a lifetime" opportunity.* He gave no further financial information about the company's recent upturn or its plans. Most of the Lawtons met on the evening of May 10 and, after ruminating over the weekend, all of the Lawtons who held stock in Nyman Manufacturing Co. agreed to sell their shares. Judith, her husband Thomas, and seven of their children sold all of their combined 952 shares back to the company on May 30, 1996 for $200 a share; the children of Robert and Kenneth Nyman also sold their 140 shares back to the company at $200 a share. Because this stock was redeemed by the company, the redemption increased defendants' share of the outstanding Class A stock.

On June 25, 1996, the company awarded Robert, Kenneth, and Johnson options to purchase a total of 1,092 Class A shares, which was the entire number of shares redeemed by the company on May 30. The officers also purchased all Class A and B shares in the company treasury on June 25 and signed promissory notes totaling $973,000 that called for interest payments to be made commencing on June 30, 1997. *Again, there*

was no appraisal of shares. By making these moves, Robert, Kenneth and Johnson had acquired ownership of almost all outstanding shares in the company.

By June 1996, the book value of the shares was $527.50. Defendants' expert, William Piccerelli, testified that the fair market value of the company's stock was approximately $303 a share. Johnson at some point in fall 1996 discovered that the Van Leer Corporation, a Dutch company whose subsidiary, Chinet, was a competitor of Nyman Manufacturing, had funds available to acquire other companies. Discussions began regarding the possibility of a strategic acquisition by Van Leer. In March 1997, Johnson met with representatives of Van Leer to discuss a sale. Van Leer offered to purchase the company, and it signed a letter of intent on June 25, 1997. The sale closed on September 29, 1997.

Van Leer purchased all of Nyman Manufacturing's stock for $28,164,735.00. After deducting closing costs of $980,383.00, and an escrow amount of $1,423,331.00, set aside to satisfy a potential liability of the company, the net amount paid to shareholders was $25,761,021.00. Almost all of the shares were now held by Robert and Kenneth Nyman and Keith Johnson and they received virtually all the proceeds.

Once they learned of the sale of the company for more than $28 million, Judith and Thomas Lawton and seven of their eight children filed suit against Robert and Kenneth Nyman, Keith Johnson, and Nyman Manufacturing in the United States District Court for the District of Rhode Island on May 22, 1998. They alleged that the defendants were in breach of their fiduciary duties and had committed securities and common-law fraud. The plaintiffs asserted that the redemption price they were paid for their stock was less than the true value, that the defendants knew that the company might be sold, and that they misrepresented and failed to disclose material facts regarding the sale of the company and the value of the stock.

The court found that the company's purchase of the Lawtons' shares was a breach of common-law fiduciary duty and the defendants appealed.

DECISION

Defendants here stand in three intertwined capacities: as directors, as officers, and, for Robert and Kenneth Nyman, as majority shareholders of a closely held corporation. We consider these capacities as a group for purposes of the analysis. For more than a century, Rhode Island law has viewed directors of companies as owing a fiduciary duty to the shareholders of the company. It has analogized the duties corporate officers owe to stockholders to those of trustees.

Such a relationship is one of trust and confidence and imposes the duty on the fiduciary to act with the utmost good faith. That good faith requirement forbids action on the part of a fiduciary without the knowledge and consent of his cestui que trust [trustees] when he has an individual interest in the subject matter or when his interest is in conflict with that of the person for whom he acts.

In *A. Teixeira & Co. v. Teixeira,* 699 A.2d 1383 (R.I. 1997), the court reiterated that corporate officers stand in a fiduciary capacity and are liable if they take corporate opportunities.

The Rhode Island Supreme Court has held in earlier cases that "shareholders in a close held family corporation *may* have a fiduciary duty toward one another." The court noted that "the existence of such a fiduciary duty is a fact-intensive inquiry" and that shareholders could show by evidence, such as a stockholder's agreement, that no such duty had been undertaken.

The fiduciary duties of corporate directors, officers and majority owners encompass a variety of different situations. Still, defendants have essentially conceded that Rhode Island law would recognize a fiduciary duty among shareholders in a closely held family corporation and that it would be a heightened duty. We too think that the Rhode Island Supreme Court would recognize such a duty, at least in the absence of an express shareholder agreement to the contrary.

We hold, therefore, that it is a violation of a fiduciary duty for an officer or director of a close corporation to purchase the stock of minority shareholders without disclosing material facts affecting the value of the stock, known to the purchasing officer or director by virtue of his position but not known to the selling shareholder. Again, defendants agree that under Rhode Island law there is a duty to disclose material information to minority shareholders faced with an offer by the close corporation, controlled by majority shareholders, to purchase their shares.

The district court defined the standard for determining *materiality* as follows: "When directors of a closely held corporation are purchasing a minority stockholder's shares, fiduciary duty imposes an obligation of 'complete candor' to disclose 'all information in their possession "germane" to the transaction.' " That is a generally accepted standard and its use was appropriate. The court found that under state law, negotiations for a sale need not be underway for there to be a duty to disclose; the duty "also encompasses transactions that the directors anticipate are reasonably likely to occur or that are something more than remote possibilities." The district court, in its finding that the defendants were in breach of their fiduciary duties, focused on the company's repurchase of the plaintiffs' stock for $200 a share in May 1996, when the defendants, as it found, had a realistic expectation that Nyman Manufacturing might be sold. The defendants argue that when a company is considering the possibility of sale, the standard for materiality, even under state law, requires something much more definite.

Rhode Island law would, we think, recognize a heightened duty of disclosure in a close corporation setting by officers who are majority shareholders with undisclosed information, who are purchasing minority shares or causing the corporation to do so. Materiality depends on all the circumstances. Here there were only two possible types of buyers for plaintiffs' shares—the defendants (either directly or by causing redemption of the shares) or an outside buyer looking to acquire the company. *Here the defendants did not disclose their decision to work toward selling the company, their decision to hire a consultant, or their acquisition talks in May with other companies.* Each is pertinent to the question of whether there was an outside buyer for the shares.

The mere causing of a closely held corporation to offer an inadequate price by majority shareholders to minority shareholders is not itself sufficient to establish a breach. It may be evidence, though, as to breach of other duties. And if a majority shareholder violates his duties of disclosure and the minority shareholder sells at an inadequate price, the minority shareholder can seek damages based on the difference between the offered price and the fair value of the stock.

If the finding of breach of fiduciary duty turned purely on the definiteness of the plan to sell, this would be a difficult liability issue. However, the case does not turn on that isolated proposition, but instead on an *interrelated series of non-disclosures and misrepresentations. There is ample evidence to support the district court's finding of breach of fiduciary duty.*

As the district court also held, *"Additional indications of the defendants' suddenly strong and, otherwise, inexplicable interest in acquiring more shares may be found in the urgency with which they sought to redeem the Lawton and Kiepler shares as shown by the artificial deadlines established for responses to the redemption offers."*

The evidence supports the plaintiffs' theory that these defendants engaged in a concerted, accelerating effort to buy up the minority shareholders' stock, thus increasing the defendants' ownership of the company, in anticipation of a sale of the company. We understand the district court to have concluded that the non-disclosure of the possibility of a sale was material, even at this early stage, because it motivated the defendants' actions and was information which would aid and be important to the plaintiffs in evaluating the offer made.

There is more than adequate supporting evidence. The district court found the corporation had from 1995 embarked on a program to "re-purchase shares of the Company in order to eliminate any shareholders who are not active in day-to-day operations of the Company." The district court found that the defendants made the decision to redeem the minority shares even though the company had a pressing need for cash and was laying off workers to conserve funds. The district court reasonably concluded that the explanation was that "on May 8, 1996, when the defendants offered to buy back all of the plaintiffs' shares, they anticipated that the company soon could be sold for much more than the amounts that they paid for those shares."

Of course, with the May 1996 redemption offer the plaintiffs knew that defendants (and their families) were attempting to get sole ownership of the company. This might have led a reasonable investor to ask why and to seek further information. Still, this is not enough to render immaterial as a matter of law the undisclosed and misrepresented information. In all events, the district court's factfinding that there was a violation of fiduciary duty is supportable.

Thus, the evidence reasonably can be interpreted to show a scheme by defendants to obtain total ownership of the company for less than fair value through a variety of devices, anticipating a future sale. The devices fall into two general categories: first, the failure to disclose that management had decided to try to sell the company and, second, the withholding of other material information as to the redemption and misrepresentation of other information. For example, while defendants on May 9 thought it was material to Nyman's lenders that they have the company's unaudited financials, the defendants failed to disclose that information to the plaintiffs when they offered to buy their shares.

To effectuate this scheme, defendants pressured plaintiffs to sell by imposing false deadlines, telling Judith Lawton this was a "once in a lifetime opportunity," failing to disclose financial information which would call into question the adequacy of the price offered, and timing the offer so that plaintiffs would not have the audited financial results while defendants simultaneously disclosed financial results to lenders. We find no clear error in the conclusion that this totality of information would be germane and material to a selling minority shareholder and we uphold the liability finding. The lower court ruling is therefore affirmed.

CASE QUESTIONS

1. What duties, in general, are owed by majority shareholders and officers of a close corporation to the minority shareholders?
2. What "material" information was withheld by the defendants and not disclosed to the plaintiffs?
3. What is the significance of the court's statement that, "Additional indications of the defendants' suddenly strong and, otherwise, inexplicable interest in acquiring more shares may be found in the urgency with which they sought to redeem the Lawton and Kiepler shares as shown by the artificial deadlines established for responses to the redemption offers."
4. What were the key arguments of the defendants, regarding the breach of fiduciary duties?

CORPORATE LAWSUITS

In almost all cases, decisions concerning whether the corporation should initiate a lawsuit against someone or how, when, and in what manner the corporation should defend a lawsuit are board decisions, as part of its responsibility for management of the company. An individual shareholder or a group of shareholders normally has no role in corporate litigation. However, occasionally a shareholder may file what is called a *derivative action*. This type of lawsuit is brought to remedy situations in which the directors or officers have acted outside the scope of their duties, performed in a fraudulent manner or have engaged in self-dealing (creating benefits for themselves through the corporation) in violation of their fiduciary duties.

A **derivative suit** is brought by a shareholder "on behalf of the corporation," and any recovery obtained goes to the corporation, not to the shareholder who brought the suit. Generally, in order to initiate such a suit, the shareholder must have owned stock in the corporation at the time the wrongful act occurred, requested that the board take action, and been turned down. Also, some state laws require the shareholder to post a bond or security to cover the corporate expenses should the lawsuit be decided in favor of the corporation.

derivative lawsuit: A lawsuit brought by one or more shareholders on behalf of a corporation, where the board of directors has refused to act.

(The corporation, through its board of directors, will no doubt be on the other side of the case, vigorously opposing the lawsuit.) Sometimes a group of shareholders or a successor (a government body that takes over the corporation) will be given extra time to sue the directors because no suits could be brought while the company was under the "adverse domination" of the old board. Derivative actions serve a useful purpose in allowing shareholders to punish misconduct by directors and officers, but they also offer the possibility for misuse by dissident shareholders unhappy with the way the Board is running the company. Therefore, they are subject to careful control by the courts and are only available in certain situations in which the directors clearly are not acting in the best interests of the corporation.

CORPORATE COMPLIANCE PROGRAMS

corporate compliance program: A program undertaken by the management of a corporation to ensure that all relevant laws are being followed.

Even before The Sarbanes-Oxley Act, it had become increasingly important for corporations to implement and maintain **corporate compliance programs**, in order to detect and punish wrongdoing internally. Such programs, instituted by the board of directors and management, started becoming popular 10–15 years ago as a way of limiting a company's criminal liability for acts of employees, as well as its civil and regulatory responsibility in a wide range of situations from sexual harassment to workplace safety.

The development of compliance programs is a good example of how the board of directors' duty of care changes and expands with changes in society. The development of the Federal Sentencing Guidelines (as discussed in Chapter 7) gave corporations strong incentive to implement compliance programs (criminal sentences would be reduced). The courts also began to look at a company's internal practices when enforcing criminal law and setting damages in civil cases. Delaware Chancery Judge William Allen wrote, in a case involving Caremark International (which we studied in Chapter 7), "Senior managers and directors must make a good faith effort to ensure that the company has an adequate system to internally detect illegal activity in a timely manner."

So it has now become quite common for large corporations to have a formal plan, involving all job levels and phases of operation, to prevent, detect, and punish illegal actions and other wrongful acts. Corporate counsel and experienced business attorneys argue that large companies cannot afford *not* to have compliance plans in place before Federal Bureau of Investigation agents or regulatory officials show up. "If the first time you talk to the government about your compliance program is when you're filling out a presentence report (after a conviction) you've got a problem," said the general counsel for International Paper Co.

Companies that find a problem and promptly report it to authorities are much less likely to be charged with criminal violations and, even if convicted, will face lower penalties. However, the firm is expected to cooperate with government inspectors and prosecutors and furnish reports of its internal investigation. In addition to avoiding criminal liability, a compliance program that is vigorously practiced can reduce punitive and other damages in a civil case and may result in lower insurance premiums as well—and perhaps most important of all, will catch and hopefully prevent wrongdoing before it becomes so serious that criminal charges are filed.

Prosecutors and corporate lawyers agree that getting the board of directors and high-level managers on board is key to creating a "compliance culture," which leads to a successful program. The best programs are ones in which the management leads by example. The most effective plans stress company values and positive behavior, rather than focusing only on criminal violations and punishment.

CAPITAL FORMATION

EQUITY AND DEBT SECURITIES

Corporations are the type of business organization most capable of raising large amounts of capital. When corporations are formed, they normally authorize the sale of corporate shares in the form of stock. No real limitation exists on how many shares of stock a corporation can sell, with each share representing a small percentage of ownership of the company. Such shares are called **equity securities.** Over the life of a corporation, there may be only one or two shareholders or several hundred thousand, each owning a number of shares.

When a corporation finds itself needing money for expansion or some other purpose, it can issue new shares, thereby raising money for the corporation and adding many new shareholders. The laws regulating the issuance and trading of shares of stock are an important aspect of the "legal environment of business" and will be thoroughly discussed in the next chapter. Of course, this sale of thousands or millions of new shares would dilute the percentage of ownership of each existing shareholder. To deal with this problem, many corporations have adopted a policy called **preemptive rights.** This policy allows existing shareholders the option of purchasing the same percentage of the new shares as their current ownership percentage. For example, if Juanita currently owns 5 percent of the outstanding shares in ABC Corporation, she will have the option to purchase 5 percent of any new shares offered. Current shareholders, therefore, will continue to have the opportunity to continue to own the same percentage of the corporation.

Most shares of stock are **common stock,** which means that when the board of directors of the corporation declares a dividend, all shareholders are paid the same amount per share of ownership. Each shareholder has one vote for each share of stock owned. Owners of **preferred stock** are generally entitled to receive dividends before the common stockholders do. This stock often specifies dividends of a certain amount and normally does not carry voting rights.

Corporations may also raise money by issuing **debt securities,** such as **bonds.** These instruments actually represent a type of loan by an individual or firm to the corporation that the company promises to pay back at a certain rate of interest. The bondholders do not become stockholders through the purchase of these debt securities.

One other type of stock is called **treasury stock.** This is stock that a corporation issues and sells, but then repurchases. While owned by the corporation, this stock does not carry voting rights and does not receive dividends. The corporation can use this stock for bonuses to key employees or for other purposes, or it may decide to resell this stock later.

---

equity securities: Shares of stock representing ownership interests in a corporation.

preemptive rights: The right of shareholders to purchase the same percentage of new shares, as they hold in existing shares.

common stock: The most typical type of equity (stock) ownership by shareholders in a corporation.

preferred stock: A type of equity (stock) ownership which provides the owners certain preferences over common stockholders.

debt securities: A loan made to the corporation, such as a bond, that does not carry an ownership interest.

treasury stock: Shares of stock that have been issued and sold by a corporation, and then later repurchased by the corporation.

TERMINATION OF CORPORATIONS

MERGER

The period between 1995 and 2000 saw several of the largest mergers in the history of the United States. Some were voluntary, in which two corporations decided to become one (as in *Smith v. Van Gorkom*) and others were hostile takeovers, as discussed earlier. During the early part of the 21st century mergers declined due to poor economic conditions, but picked up again in 2004–2007. Then after little activity during the "Great Recession" of 2008–2010, big deals began to be made again in 2011, such as Texas Instruments' $6.5 billion purchase of National Semiconductor. In order for two corporations to legally merge, the action must be agreed to by a majority of the Board of Directors of both companies, then usually must be approved by both companies' shareholders (many states and the MBCA require a two-thirds majority). The resulting corporation acquires all the assets and liabilities of both corporations.

Generally, in a true **merger,** shareholders of the corporation that has been absorbed are given shares, in a predetermined amount, in the surviving corporation. The other corporation ceases to exist. There is also a type of merger called a **consolidation** in which the two companies both cease to exist, and a totally new company comes into existence. If some shareholders do not wish to merge or become shareholders in the new company, they can **dissent** in writing from the merger and have the right to be paid the fair market value of their old shares.

dissent: The right of a shareholder to object to a merger and to be paid the fair market value for the shares owned.

dissolution: The termination of the existence of a corporation.

DISSOLUTION

We said earlier that while corporations may have a perpetual existence, sometimes their existence is terminated, which is called **dissolution.** It may be voluntary as when a merger occurs or when the articles of incorporation specify a predetermined life span of, say, 10 years. Or the dissolution may be involuntary, as when, for example, the corporation has failed to file necessary papers with the state or pay state taxes for several years, or when the corporate charter was obtained by fraud. In these cases, the state has the power to dissolve the corporation. Also, if the shareholders are equally divided and unalterably opposed on every issue, one may seek a court order dissolving the corporation. When the corporation is dissolved, the assets are sold, the creditors paid off, and the balance distributed to the corporate shareholders.

TRANSFER OF A FAMILY BUSINESS

Many small businesses were started by one person who through hard work has built a successful enterprise that now employs many family members. Focused on building their business, these founders typically have not thought about what would happen to the business if they died. The consequences can be disastrous, however, if the primary owner dies and a family feud ensues for control of the business. The *Nyman Corporation* case examined earlier in this chapter demonstrates how a family business can end up in very serious disputes.

A business succession plan can be integrated into an overall plan for the distribution of one's estate. Experts are continually surprised by the number of family business owners who do not have a will that provides for how the owner's shares will be distributed so that the business survives. They advise the creation of a succession plan as the business grows, long before the founder is ready to retire.

The simplest way to transfer business assets is for the founder to make gifts of stock to his or her children—as of 2011 up to $13,000 per child can be given per year tax-free. This plan reduces the owner's taxes and transfers ownership at the same time. Another smart idea is a "buy-sell agreement," by which the corporation or the remaining stockholders are obligated to buy the departing or deceased owner's stock. The value and payment terms of the purchase should be determined in advance. Often the company or each of the major shareholders purchases life insurance covering the key owners, so there is an amount of money available to fund the buyout upon a principal owner's death.

Trusts can also be useful in business succession. Stock can be transferred into a child's trust account, with estate tax savings as described previously. Certain types of trusts can allow the primary owner time to address the issue of who will eventually control the business, especially if the children are young or undecided about joining the business.

THE PRITZKER FAMILY

The *Van Gorkom* case involved the purchase of a company by Mr. Jay Pritzker, the scion of Chicago's wealthiest and leading philanthropic family. It now appears that, although he tried, even Mr. Pritzker was unable to transfer his businesses as he wished to his family after his death.

Mr. Pritzker was an immigrant from the Jewish ghetto near Kiev Russia, who taught himself English by reading the *Chicago Tribune*, then became a lawyer, and then a businessman who owned more than 60 companies in a $15 billion empire. In 1995, he called a family meeting and distributed a memorandum outlining how the money should be shared among the whole family, and appointed a triumvirate to replace him at the helm.

However, after his death in 1999, a nasty squabble ensued among the triumvirate and the other cousins, and a new secret plan was later hammered out by 11 family members, to carve up the empire, including the likely sale of the Hyatt hotel chain. However, some cousins left out of that pact brought a lawsuit. The cousins alleged that their trust funds (set up when they were young) had been emptied to benefit others. One family member said reading the lawsuit "made me sick." Another person close to the family said "most people are upset by this and sorry to see it."

The family has long been known for closeness, for keeping their affairs out of the media, and for making major contributions to civic and social organizations. Pritzkers sit on the boards of nearly every major cultural institution in Chicago, and their foundation has made nearly 100 charitable gifts to local groups every year. For example, the Illinois Institute of Technology has received nearly $60 million, the University of Chicago $48 million, and the City was given $15 million to construct the Frank Gehry-designed bandshell in Millenium Park.

Longtime family associates agreed that the negotiations and problems would never have happened during Jay Pritzker's lifetime. "Jay was the ringmaster, everything revolved around him—he was the sun," said one friend. "Now all the binds that hold have disappeared."

OTHER TYPES OF CORPORATIONS AND COMPANIES

The traditional type of corporation we have discussed up to this point is a "for-profit corporation" (called a "C corporation"). Such corporations hope to make a profit and distribute dividends to shareholders as previously discussed. However, there are several other important types of corporations.

S CORPORATIONS

S corporation: A type of corporation in which the shareholders have limited liability.

Under a section (Subchapter S) of the Internal Revenue Service Code, it is possible to form a corporation that is taxed like a partnership (not taxed as an entity), thereby avoiding double taxation. So-called **S corporations** cannot have more than 100 shareholders and must obtain 75 percent of their gross revenues from active operations rather than "passive" sources, like receipt of dividends or investment income. All shareholders must agree to the S corporation status, and there can be only one class of common stock. Shareholders must be U.S. citizens or residents, and must be natural persons, so corporate shareholders and partnerships are generally excluded. However, certain trusts, estates, and tax-exempt corporations, notably 501(c)(3) corporations, are permitted to be shareholders. If an S corporation is successfully created, each shareholder will be treated as receiving (and be taxed on) his or her proportionate share of the corporation's income or loss in a year (whether distributed or not) just as if the organization were a partnership. At the same time, as shareholders of a corporation, the investors enjoy limited liability.

The chart on the next page compares some of the key features of the different forms of business organizations.

LIMITED LIABILITY COMPANIES

limited liability company: A type of unincorporated business entity which provides limited liability to the owners.

In recent years, the hottest new form of business entity has been the **limited liability company** (LLC). Starting with the passage of the first LLC law in Wyoming in 1977, all states have now enacted laws permitting the formation of LLCs. Nearly one in every six new business registrations in the early 2000s was an LLC, and the number has increased since then.

The LLC as a business form combines both the limited liability features of the corporate form, with the "pass-through" tax benefits of a partnership. That is, the investors risk only their investment in the business and are not held personally liable for LLC debts. But the entity is not taxed on profits, and each owner pays tax on his or her proportionate share of LLC income. While these features make an LLC similar to an S corporation, the LLC offers some additional advantages. First, unlike an S corporation, the LLC has no restrictions on the number and type of investors (called *members* in an LLC). Thus, members of an LLC can include an unlimited number of corporations, partnerships, trusts, pension plans, and even charitable organizations.

Second, the LLC offers flexibility in management. Most state laws allow an LLC to choose either (1) management directly by all members or (2) management by one or more managers appointed by the members. Third, LLCs are not subject to the "passive income" limitations of S corporations. Fourth, S corporations can only have one class of stockholder, whereas LLCs may have different classes of ownership. Fifth, there are certain tax advantages to LLCs. For example, if an LLC member transfers appreciated property (assets that

Characteristics of Business Organizations

	Sole Proprietorship	Partnership	Limited Partnership	Corporation	S Corporation	Limited Liability Companies
Ease of formation	Easy—no requirements.	Easy—written articles not required, but strongly recommended.	Written articles required—comply with state law.	Written articles required—comply with state law.	Written article required—comply with state law and IRS rule.	Written articles of organization, filed with state.
Liability of owners	Total personal liability.	Personal liability for partnership debts.	Limited partners have limited liability. General partners have personal liability.	Shareholders have limited liability.	Shareholders have limited liability.	Members have limited liability.
Management	Total control by owner.	Partners control—majority vote.	General partner manages limited partnership.	Shareholders elect board of directors. Board may hire officers.	Shareholders elect board of directors. Board may hire officers.	Members may manage or hire manager.
Transfer of ownership	Owner can sell business.	"Entity" dissolves as a partner leaves—new partners can be admitted by unanimous vote.	Limited partners can sell shares, but it may be difficult to do.	Easy—shareholders can sell shares.	Shareholders can sell shares—may be less market for small corporation shareholders.	Other members must consent to transfer.
Continuity of existence	Difficult—need to find new owner.	Articles can provide for continuation of business—under new partnership—otherwise, may be difficult.	Ends when general partner withdraws.	Continues to exist as shareholders come and go.	Continues to exist as shareholders change—usually less change than C corporation.	Dissolved if member leaves, unless all others decide to continue business.
Taxation	Owner taxed on profit.	Partners each taxed on share of profits.	Partners each taxed on share of profits.	Corporation taxed on profits—shareholders then pay tax on dividends.	Corporation is not taxed. Shareholders are taxed like partners.	LLC is not taxed; members are taxed on their share of income.

have increased in value) to an LLC, there is no tax paid on the gain, whereas there would be tax assessed on the gain if those assets were transferred to an S corporation by a shareholder. Sixth, an LLC can provide that income, gain, and losses can be allocated to members in percentages different from their shares of ownership, which is generally not true of S Corporations.

LLCs are created by preparing and filing *articles of organization* with the appropriate state office (usually the secretary of state). The articles should include the name of the LLC, its registered address, and the name and address of the manager or one of the members. Then the LLC needs to prepare an *operating agreement*, which sets forth the management structure and governs the rights and duties of the members. Similar to corporate bylaws, such things as allocation of profits and losses of members, restrictions on transfer of membership, and provisions for termination of the LLC are often covered in the operating agreement.

So as not to be taxed as corporations, LLCs cannot have perpetual life or free transferability of shares. Typically, the LLC will dissolve upon the expiration of a period fixed in the articles of organization, by the consent of the members, or upon the disassociation of any member through causes such as death, resignation, bankruptcy, or expulsion, unless there is an agreement by all other members to continue the business.

NONPROFIT CORPORATIONS

nonprofit corporations: Corporations formed under another state law, which are not established to earn a profit, but rather to provide a service. There are no shareholders and no dividends.

While most corporations are formed with the hope of earning profits for the investors, an increasingly important category of corporations, called **nonprofit corporations**, or **not-for-profit corporations**, are formed for other reasons. These businesses may be as small and local as your neighborhood Parent-Teacher Association, or they may be as large and powerful as Stanford University, the UAW-CIO labor union, or Blue Cross Health Insurance corporation, large hospitals, and educational and religious associations.

Nonprofit corporations have many similarities to for-profit corporations. They have boards of directors and officers; they must file nonprofit articles of incorporation with the state of incorporation, stating their purposes and structure, and make annual reports to the state; they must hold meetings periodically and maintain appropriate corporate books; and perhaps most importantly, they can shield their officers and directors from personal liability for torts and contracts of the corporation.

On the other hand, nonprofit corporations are not in business to make a profit, and if there is an excess of income over expenses at the end of the year, it is not distributed to the members. They have no shareholders, as such, but often have members who must pay a fee to join the organization. It is not illegal for the corporation to have a modest surplus at the end of the year (after all, if there was a deficit for very long, the organization would cease to exist), but the surplus must be retained and used for corporation purposes and not divided up and distributed to members. Nonprofit corporations do not pay income taxes, and some may not have to pay other types of taxes (such as property tax) as well. Some, but not all, nonprofit corporations qualify under IRS Code 501(c)(3) as a charitable, educational or scientific organization, so that contributions to them can be deducted from one's income for tax purposes.

Board members are selected in a number of ways. Many corporations use a nominating committee to choose certain people to stand for election at a general meeting, similar to the process used by for-profit corporations. Smaller groups may reserve a certain number of spots on the board for persons to be appointed by particular organizations with whom the nonprofit entity works.

For example, one of the authors of this textbook was once the director of a legal services organization (providing free legal assistance to low-income persons) with a 15-member board of directors. Ten members were lawyers appointed by the local bar association; five members were "representatives of the poor," appointed by certain organized groups of low-income persons; and two were law school professors, appointed by the local law school dean. It was an interesting group. Although all members were generally in favor of an effective program of legal assistance for poor people, there was sometimes strong disagreement between the local lawyers and the low-income representatives about how aggressive the program should be in bringing lawsuits against government agencies, landlords, and businesses and about the types of cases that should be accepted and rejected. On the other hand, at times the local attorneys and law school professors were among the most forceful members of the board in insisting on vigorous representation of our clients.

SUMMARY

There is no one "right" legal form of business organization for all purposes. When a person decides to go into business, the choice of form needs to be made as carefully as all other business decisions. Factors such as liability, cost of formation, number of persons involved in the business, management and control of business decisions, the need for raising capital, taxation, continuity, ease of share or ownership transfer, and many other issues should be considered when deciding whether to form a partnership, limited partnership, LLC, corporation or to simply go with a sole proprietorship.

A corporation is a legal entity, separate from any of the owners, that can offer limited personal liability to its shareholders. Certain steps must be carefully taken in order to form a corporation in accordance with the appropriate state law, and there are a number of important legal principles that regulate corporate operation.

In the structure of a corporation, shareholders invest funds in the business but refrain from taking an active role in management. Instead, the shareholders elect a board of directors whose duty it is to make the business decisions necessary to govern the operations of the company. Directors have the legal responsibility to fulfill their duties with care, and they owe fiduciary duties to the shareholders and the corporation as well. The directors hire officers such as a president, treasurer, and others to handle the day-to-day operations of the business. In "close" corporations, the same people are shareholders, officers and directors.

Other important aspects of corporations are that they have perpetual existence—that is, they do not cease to exist as shareholders come and go—and they have the ability to raise significant amounts of capital for the business. When corporations require funds for business purposes, they can issue and sell more stock to the public, unlike the other forms of organizations, which are more dependent upon the assets and borrowing power of the owners.

Three other special types of companies exist—the S corporation, the LLC, and the nonprofit corporation. A nonprofit corporation has no shareholders/investors, pays no dividends, and is normally formed for some socially beneficial purpose, whereas the S corporation and the LLC are for-profit companies that offer limited personal liability as well as special taxation and other benefits to shareholders.

CHAPTER QUESTIONS

1. Jack was the president of the Arizona Bicycle Co. (ABC), which manufactures bikes and related equipment. He also owned 75 percent of the stock in the company. Although the company was properly incorporated and there was a board of directors (composed of Jack, his wife, and a close friend), he made most of the decisions. When he needed money, Jack borrowed it from the company account and then paid it back later. For the past five years Jack has hired all employees of the company, and he has entered into whatever contracts he felt were necessary without interference from the board. In fact, the board has not met at all for the past five

years. A consumer who had purchased an ABC bike was injured when the frame of the bike fell apart. The company has few assets at present, and the consumer has now sued Jack personally. Can the consumer prevail against Jack? Under what theory? What will the consumer have to prove? Can the other board members be held liable if the company is insolvent?

2. The CEO of a publicly-held Maryland corporation informed the Board of Directors that he intended to make an offer to purchase Laureate, at which time the Board created a Special Committee composed of three independent directors, who retained a law firm and financial advisors. The board recommended approval of the offer. Several shareholders filed suit, claiming violation of fiduciary duties, but the case was dismissed. About one month later, the board announced that it had accepted an increased offer from Investors to acquire the company by way of a tender offer and second-step merger. The Special Committee's financial advisors again concluded the offer as financially fair, although several of Laureate's institutional shareholders disagreed, and the Board approved the transaction. Shareholders filed a second complaint alleging that the Board breached its fiduciary duties owed to them, and that shareholders received too low a value for their shares in a cash-out merger and could have received a better price. The Circuit Court again dismissed the claims. The Court held that Maryland law bars all direct shareholder claims and that any claims by shareholders against directors for breach of fiduciary duties must be brought as a derivative action on behalf of the corporation. Are the shareholders limited to derivative actions in such a situation or may they file direct suits alleging violation of fiduciary duty? What should be the result on appeal? *Shenker v. Laureate Education, Inc.,* 2009 Md. LEXIS 837 (Court of Appeals, November 12, 2009)

3. Szymanski was the sole shareholder, director, and officer of several construction corporations, which included Delmarva Concrete, Del Concrete, and David Concrete, among others. The general contractor for the construction of an elementary school subcontracted the concrete work for this project to Delmarva Concrete Corp. A dispute arose between the two companies during the construction. Fletcher took the dispute to arbitration, and Fletcher was awarded the sum of $313,179.52 plus fees. Szymanski however, continued to do concrete work with his other companies. When Delmarva Concrete Corp. ceased operations and filed for bankruptcy, Fletcher sought recovery directly from Szymanski. At trial Syzmanski testified that he was the sole shareholder, of several corporations that were all located in the same office and shared the same computer system. Szymanski either did not keep proper financial records, or purposely withheld relevant documents during discovery, or both. Szymanski claimed he could not produce several relevant financial records, but the documents Szymanski did provide showed that he would loan Delmarva money, through his personal money market account, when the company needed money to operate, as the company was undercapitalized. The lower court dismissed the case, stating that Fletcher had failed to prove fraud. Should Fletcher be able to "pierce the corporate veil" and obtain a judgment against Syzmanski personally? What does he need to show? *Fletcher-Harlee Corp. v. Szymanski,* 936 A.2d 87 (Pa. Super 2007)

4. What are some of the advantages of a general partnership over a corporation as a form of business organization? Why might some people choose to start a partnership rather than a corporation? What are some of the

advantages of a corporation over a partnership? Why might some people choose to start a corporation instead of a partnership? If a partnership is chosen, is there a particular type that the partners should choose?

5. Facing an unwanted tender offer, a corporation's board of directors adopted a new form of poison pill takeover defense, called a "dead hand" provision. This resolution would prevent the members of any new board of directors nominated by the hostile bidder from redeeming rights under the company's shareholder rights plan for a six-month period in order to facilitate a merger. Certain shareholders challenged the provision as a violation of Delaware law, which gives a corporation's board of directors the power to manage the company. What should the Delaware Supreme Court decide? Why? [*Quickturn Design Systems, Inc. v. Shapiro*, 721 A. 2d 1281 (Del. 1998)]

6. An Idaho ranch was owned as the only asset of a close corporation consisting of two families. The stock was owned 50 percent by one family and 50 percent by the other. For many years, the arrangement worked well, with duties and profits equally divided. Then, one of the founders died. Several years later, one family has no interest in ranching and wants to sell the land, and the other wants to continue ranching. The votes are evenly split, and no directors have been elected, nor has any business been conducted for the past three years. One family files a court action seeking dissolution of the corporation. What should the court do? [*Gillingham v. Swan Falls Land & Cattle Co.*, 106 Id. 859, 683 P.2d 895 (Ct. App. 1984)]

7. While acting as officers, directors, and shareholders of a company called Bio-Lab Inc., Mr. Morad and Mr. Thomson started and incorporated a competing business in a nearby town called Med-Lab Inc. They believed that Bio-Lab did not have the funds to undertake the project, so Morad and Thomson incorporated Med-Lab on their own. The only other shareholder, Mr. Coupounas, had not been told about this venture. When he found out about it, he filed a derivative lawsuit, on behalf of Bio-Lab, against Morad and Thomson, asking the court to declare that Med-Lab was an asset of Bio-Lab. What is the issue in this case, and what should be the result? [*Morad v. Coupounas*, 361 So.2d 6 (Ala. 1978)]

8. The board of directors of a California banking corporation made a variety of decisions regarding loans, expenses, and other financial issues, shortly before the bank became insolvent. The directors obtained advice from a number of outside consultants before making their decisions and tried in good faith to do what they believed was in the best interest of the corporation, but their efforts were not successful and the bank failed. The directors were later sued for negligence by the federal agency that took over the bank. What will their defense be? Should the directors win the case? [*FDIC v. Castetter*, 184 F.3d 1040 (9th Cir. 1999)]

9. An Oregon corporation was owned by three brothers who were the directors and equal shareholders. The three brothers, as members of the board, voted 2-1 to declare a dividend of $12,000 to each shareholder and retain $144,000 to ease the cash flow problems the business was experiencing. The other brother sued, alleging breach of fiduciary duty, since he felt a much larger dividend should have been declared. What should be the result? Why? [*Iwasaki v. Iwasaki Bros. Inc.*, 58 Or. App. 543, 649 P.2d 598 (1982)]

10. A 20% shareholder and former employee of a close corporation made a formal request to inspect and copy financial records of the company. The

individual had been fired as an employee and he had filed a separate lawsuit regarding his termination. The company denied his request to see the corporate records and he filed suit. The Connecticut law (following the Model Business Corporation Act) requires that a shareholder's demand to inspect and to copy the records must be made in good faith and for a proper purpose. The shareholder testified that he was interested in valuing his shares, for possible sale, but did not have any documents in his possession that would have permitted him to determine the value of his shares. He requested "all annual and quarterly financial statements for the time he was a shareholder, all state and federal tax returns of the company and all accounting records including ledgers, balance sheets profit/loss statements and other records." Is the shareholder entitled to view and copy the corporate records? What are the best arguments for and against? Discuss the legal issues. *Pagett v. Westport Precision, Inc.*, 845 A.2d 455 (Conn. App. 2004)

PRACTICAL EXERCISE

Robert, Kathleen, and Seth have now operated their business as a partnership for three years (recall Chapter 8). Their store is now earning a good, solid profit, and they are ready to open four more stores around the state. In addition, Seth has developed his experimental "Sage Loops" into a great-tasting, crunchy, high fiber cereal that the group wants to market nationwide. Kathleen, remembering what she learned in her legal environment class, has persuaded the other two that they need to form a corporation. Your task is to prepare articles of incorporation for the business. The articles should include paragraphs detailing the following:

1. The purpose of the business;
2. The name of the corporation;
3. The officers and directors;
4. The address and principal place of business;
5. The authorization to issue a certain amount of stock;
6. The provision for amendment of the articles;
7. The provision for duration of the corporation and circumstances that might result in dissolution;
8. Whether cumulative or straight voting by shareholders will be used; and
9. Whether there will be restrictions placed on the shareholders' right to sell their stock to anyone they choose;

Your instructor may ask you to look up the corporation laws in your state to determine if there are other subjects that should be included in order to make the corporation legal.

FURTHER INFORMATION

www.sba.gov
   Much government information and services for business.
www.lectlaw.com
   The " 'Lectric Law Library" at the University of Nevada. A wacky, irreverent, yet informative legal information site. A "must see."
www.ilrg.com
   Large legal site with information on many legal issues; also corporate forms and filing information.

CHAPTER 10

SECURITIES LAW AND PROTECTION OF INVESTORS

After reading this chapter, you should be able to:

1. Describe a security.
2. Detail the legal consequences of buying and selling securities.
3. Explain the various exemptions.
4. Explain insider trading and the consequences of engaging in insider trading.

CHAPTER OUTLINE

I. History and Purpose

II. What Is a Security?

III. The Registration Process

IV. Liability Under the 1933 Act

V. 1934 Securities Exchange Act

VI. State Blue Sky Laws

Robert, Kathleen, and Seth want to raise money to expand their existing business selling Sage Loops. What do they need to know about securities laws before approaching people to invest?

INTRODUCTION

capital: Accumulated assets (as money) invested or available for investment.

In Chapters 8 and 9 we learned about the different legal structures people can use to conduct business. Regardless of the structure chosen, all businesses need money to operate. In technical terms, money is referred to as **capital**. Raising capital can be perplexing and frustrating. Business capital can be obtained from a number of sources, including personal funds, family and friends, financial institutions, or unknown persons. If the money comes from personal funds, few laws come into effect. Several laws apply, however, if the money is borrowed from family, friends, or a financial institution, as will be discussed in Chapter 18. The business may also raise capital by selling its **equity** (ownership interest) to investors or by selling its debt to **bondholders**. When a business sells its equity (or a share of its business) to an investor, the business has sold **securities**.

equity: The ownership interests of shareholders in a company.

Securities regulation is a highly technical area of the law, and all securities questions should be referred to a competent lawyer. Some lawyers even specialize solely in securities matters. As we will discuss later, violations of the securities laws could lead to stiff financial penalties and jail sentences. In fact, over the past couple of years, several prominent business executives have been criminally charged with violating various securities laws.

bondholder: The person or company that holds a certificate of debt issued by a company or government and payable on a specified date.

HISTORY AND PURPOSE

securities: Term applied to a wide variety of investment vehicles.

England had forms of securities regulation as early as 1285. These early English regulations were primarily aimed at registering those who sold securities. In the United States, however, securities regulation (known as **blue sky laws**) began at the state, rather than federal, level when Kansas adopted a comprehensive licensing statute in 1911. This statute, the first to use the term "blue sky," was aimed at those individuals who would sell worthless investments—in other words, who would try to sell pieces of the "blue sky." Blue sky laws spread rapidly, and virtually every state had adopted them before the stock market crash of 1929. Primarily because of the failure of the stock market, the first federal law, the *1933 Securities Act*, was enacted with two objectives: (1) to provide investors with financial information about an investment and (2) to prohibit misrepresentation, deceit, and fraudulent acts and practices.

blue sky laws: State statutes designed to protect the public from the sale of worthless stocks and bonds.

The second federal law enacted was the *1934 Securities Exchange Act*, which established the *Securities and Exchange Commission (SEC)*. The SEC, an independent regulatory agency, has five members who are appointed by the President with the advice and consent of the Senate. The SEC is also a bipartisan administrative agency, which means that no more than three of the five members may be from one political party at any one time. Thus, a Democratic president, for example, must appoint a Republican commissioner if three Democratic commissioners already serve, and vice versa. The President does get to select the chair of the commission. Each commissioner's five-year term is staggered so that only one member's term expires each year. The SEC also employs attorneys, accountants, examiners, and analysts.

Over the past several years, the SEC has faced a number of significant challenges. During the 1990s, and with the advent of the Internet, the SEC was required to address the ease with which individuals traded stocks without using a stockbroker. The Internet has also made it easier for companies, especially smaller companies, to seek investors using a *direct public offering* (DPO), also called *Internet Securities Offering* (ISO). Further, *electronic communication networks* (ECNs) have been established to facilitate Internet stock transactions. Unfortunately, the Internet has also provided unscrupulous investors with the opportunity to engage in online securities fraud.

The SEC's current major challenge is addressing corporate wrong-doing and public confidence in the stock markets, in the wake of corporate scandals such as those that occured within Enron, WorldCom, and the infamous case involving the Bernard Madoff ponzi scheme in which thousands of investors lost billions of dollars in investments. Further, Martha Stewart and other business celebrities have been investigated and/or charged with insider trading. The cumulative effect of this negative news has caused the SEC to reevaluate its role in the securities process. Congress has also responded by passing legislation, such as the comprehensive Dodd-Frank Wall Street Reform and Consumer Protection Act of 2010, which will be discussed in more detail later in this chapter. This background should give you the context in which to understand current laws regarding securities.

SOCIAL/ETHICAL ISSUES

Cheryl Eckard was a quality assurance manager at GlaxoSmithKline, a pharmaceutical company. As part of her job, she learned of some serious manufacturing problems involving drug mix-ups and mislabeling occurring in one of the company's plants in Puerto Rico. The company had received many complaints, including one regarding a 10-year-old boy who received twice the recommended dosage of Paxil, a strong anti-depressant drug. However, the company ignored her recommendation that it immediately stop shipping pharmaceutical products from the plant until the problems were resolved. Eckard filed a lawsuit with the FDA, which ultimately resulted in a $750 million settlement between Glaxo and the Justice Department. Eckard was also awarded $96 million as a whistleblower under the False Claims Act. The recently enacted Dodd-Frank financial reform law provides for similar awards to people who report securities or accounting fraud to the SEC. Many in the securities industry are opposed to such whistle-blower laws, claiming that they undermine the internal fraud-monitoring requirements imposed on companies by the Sarbanes-Oxley Act. These critics argue that whistle-blower laws such as these give employees incentives to go straight to the SEC with evidence of wrong-doing rather than first work within the internal structures companies have spent years implementing. What do you think about these whistle-blower laws? Should whistle-blowers be required to work within their companies to solve ethical lapses before turning to government regulators?

WHAT IS A SECURITY?

Usually, the term *securities* refers to stocks and bonds issued by a corporation. Other financing schemes may also be considered securities, however, if the investor relies on another's efforts to achieve success. For example, assume that Sam gives Dana $100 to invest in Dana's business. Sam does not work for the business, nor is Sam involved in any business decisions. If Dana's business is successful, Sam will receive $150. If the business is unsuccessful, Sam will receive nothing. Because Sam does nothing personally to earn this money, this investment can be considered a security. Sam is relying on Dana's efforts to achieve success. Courts have held that limited partnerships, closely held corporations, and other business arrangements can be securities if the person who invests is hoping to profit without expending personal effort. For instance, the case of *SEC v. Howey* involved contracts for the sale of property in Florida cultivated with citrus trees. Purchasers entered into a land sales contract with the Howey Company, granting the company total control over the cultivating, harvesting, and marketing of the citrus. The purchasers did not have the right to enter the property without the consent of Howey Company. The U.S. Supreme Court held that this investment was a security because the scheme involved "an investment of money in a common enterprise with profits to come solely from the efforts of others." However, the following case, *SEC v. Koscot Interplanetary,* shows that "solely" does not necessarily mean solely.

SEC V. KOSCOT INTERPLANETARY, INC.

497 F.2d 473 (5th Cir. 1974)

FACTS

Koscot Interplanetary was engaged in a multi-level network of independent distributors who sold cosmetics. The first level in the network was "beauty advisor." A beauty advisor's sole income came from the retail sale of cosmetics. The second level was "supervisor or retail manager." Supervisors paid Koscot $1,000. In return, supervisors received cosmetics discounted from the retail price. These cosmetics could be sold at retail or directly to the beauty advisor. Furthermore, supervisors bringing others into the supervisor level received $600 out of the $1,000 paid to Koscot. The third level was "distributor." Distributors invested $5,000 with Koscot. This enabled distributors to purchase cosmetics at a greater discount. Furthermore, distributors received $600 for every supervisor and $3,000 for every distributor brought in to the Koscot program.

To attract additional investors, current Koscot investors would bring prospects to an "opportunity meeting" or a "go-tour." These events reflected an evangelical atmosphere. Investors read from a preordained script, drove Cadillacs, dressed expensively, and flaunted money. At the end of these events, prospective investors would sign into the network. Koscot had not registered with the SEC. The SEC filed suit against Koscot, claiming that the pyramid scheme Koscot operated involved the sale of a security, which required registration before being sold.

DECISION

Judge Gewin wrote the opinion of the Court of Appeals. The 1933 and 1934 Acts should be read broadly, since they are designed to protect investors, not to test the creativity of lawyers. The correct test is "whether the efforts made by those other than the investor are the undeniably significant ones, those essential managerial efforts which affect the failure or success of the enterprise." In this case, the luring effect of the opportunity meetings was the critical aspect that determined whether the scheme would succeed. Once the prospects arrived at the meeting, everything else was devised by Koscot. The investor's sole contribution was in "following the script." The promoters had immediate control over all of the scheme's essential management. The investor could not realize any profits without tying it to the promotional scheme. The scheme was not a conventional franchise arrangement. The "solely" requirement set out in the Supreme Court's decision in *SEC v. Howey* is "whether the scheme involves an investment of money in a common enterprise with profits to come solely from the efforts of others." Solely, however, does not necessarily mean solely. The fact that the investor has to expend some efforts to make money does not mean that the securities regulations do not apply. This scheme falls under securities regulation and must be registered with the SEC.

CASE QUESTIONS

1. What distinguishes the Koscot scheme from other multilevel networks?
2. What efforts did the investors expend?
3. Why wasn't the investor's effort enough to take the scheme out of securities regulation?

In light of cases such as *Howey* and *Koscot,* businesspeople should use caution and obtain the advice of a competent attorney when contemplating such transactions. If an investment is held to be a security, then the seller must comply with all SEC regulations. In the next case, *SEC v. Edwards,* the U.S. Supreme Court considered whether an investment which offers investors a fixed rate of return was a security.

SEC V. EDWARDS

540 U.S. 389 (2004)

FACTS

Charles Edwards was the sole shareholder and CEO of ETS Payphones, Inc., which sold payphones through independent distributors and then leased the phones back from purchasers. Purchasers were typically paid $7000 for a leaseback and management agreement, in which they received $82 per month and a 14% annual return, but did not manage the payphones they owned nor were they involved in the installation and maintenance of the phones. Owners were entitled to a return of the full purchase price at the end of the lease or within 180 days of a request for a refund. ETS marketed its business as an exciting opportunity with "potential for ongoing revenue generation" due to deregulation of the telephone industry. ETS did not register the sale of this investment with the SEC, who subsequently filed a lawsuit against ETS, alleging violation of the 1933 Securities Act.

DECISION

Justice O'Connor delivered the Court's opinion. The Court noted at the outset that its decision in *SEC v. Howey* set forth the test for determining whether an investment scheme was a security. The so-called *Howey* tests looks at whether "the scheme involves an investment of money in a common enterprise with profits to come solely from the efforts of others." The earlier Court of Appeals decision in this case had held that the ETS scheme was not a security because it offered a fixed rate of return, rather than participation in the company's earnings. The Supreme Court disagreed. The profits referred to in the *Howey* test are those profits sought by the investors who had invested money in the scheme, *not* the profits of the scheme in which they invest. In other words, the profit in question is not the company's profits, but the amount of money paid to the investor. Thus, it makes no difference whether the investment contract promised investors a fixed rate of return or a variable return because in either case "the investing public is attracted by presentations of investment income." In fact, investments guaranteeing a fixed rate of return are particularly attractive to "more vulnerable" individuals. If the Court of Appeals interpretation of the definition of security became law, that decision would provide incentive to "unscrupulous marketers of investments [who] could evade the securities

laws by picking a rate of return to promise." The Court declined to uphold such an outcome. The ETS scheme should have been registered. The Supreme Court reversed the Court of Appeals decision.

CASE QUESTIONS

1. Do you see any differences between the independent distributor scheme in this case compared to the multilevel distributorship scheme in *Koscot*? If so, what are they? Are they significant to a determination of whether the scheme meets the definition of a security?
2. Why might Edwards not have wanted to register the sale of this scheme with the SEC?
3. Can you think of any actions a company who wants to raise money might take to avoid the registration requirement?

THE REGISTRATION PROCESS

underwriter: Purchases or participates in original offering of securities.

dealer: Buys securities from underwriter to resell to general public or for its own account.

broker: Buys securities from underwriter for accounts of others.

issuer: Controlling person, individual, or business offering to sell its own securities.

A major purpose of the SEC is to help investors decide for themselves whether to make a certain investment decision. Therefore, the SEC does not concern itself with whether an investment is good or bad. In order to perform its function, the SEC requires companies to fully disclose material information about securities they wish to issue to the public. The SEC, however, is powerless to rule on the merits of any particular security. The 1933 Act is purely a disclosure statute. It is not meant to guarantee that the security is a safe investment. In fact, some securities are required to disclose that "these securities involve a high degree of risk and substantial dilution. Potential purchasers should not invest in these securities unless they can afford the risk of losing their entire investment." This statement allows the purchaser to decide whether to invest.

The 1933 Act's registration rules only apply to the *original issuance* of securities (when securities are first sold by the issuing company), or the initial public offering (IPO). Traditional IPOs use **underwriters**, **dealers**, and **brokers**, although a DPO on the Internet may not. Once securities are in the hands of an investor, the securities are generally freely transferable in the market, and the 1933 Act no longer applies.

Most securities offerings must be registered with the SEC. The SEC breaks the registration process into three periods. The first period is the prefiling period, when the securities are being prepared for sale but before the actual registration takes place. During prefiling, the securities cannot be offered for sale or advertised, nor may the promoters or **issuer** try to create excitement or interest in the upcoming offering, a technique called *conditioning* the market.

The next period, the waiting period, starts on the day a registration statement is filed with the SEC and proceeds for the next 20 days. The registration statement must contain the name of the issuer, a balance sheet, year-to-date profit and loss statements, and profit and loss statements for the preceding five years. It also must contain both hard (financial) and soft (e.g., market reports) material information. If the SEC believes that the registration statement does not adequately disclose material information, the issuer will be required to amend the statement, and the 20-day waiting period is extended. During the waiting period, the issuer may provide prospective investors with a preliminary prospectus. A *prospectus* is defined as "a notice, circular, advertisement, letter, or other communication published or transmitted to any person after a registration statement has been filed." The preliminary prospectus must contain the following so-called *red herring* language (set out in red ink in the margin). This language informs potential purchasers that the registration statement may be changed:

> A registration statement relating to these securities has been filed with the Securities and Exchange Commission but has not yet become effective. Information contained herein is subject to completion or amendment. These securities may not be sold nor may offers to buy be accepted prior to the time the registration statement becomes effective. This prospectus shall not constitute an offer to sell or the solicitation of an offer to buy nor shall there be any sale of these securities in any State in which such offer, solicitation or sale would be unlawful; prior to registration or qualification under the securities laws of any such State.

Oral offers for the sale of securities may occur during the waiting period.

Lastly, the post-effective period begins once the SEC approves the registration statement. At this point, the securities may be advertised and sold. The sales contract must be in writing to be enforceable, since the sale of securities falls under the Statute of Frauds (which we will cover in more detail in Chapter 12). All final sales of securities must be accompanied by a final prospectus.

Securities must be advertised using a "tombstone advertisement," so named because it contains a minimum of information and is printed in plain black and white. As can be seen in Figure 10.1, this advertisement identifies the security, states the price and the number of shares offered, and indicates from whom the orders can be executed. These advertisements are found in financial presses like *The Wall Street Journal* and *New York Times*. They are also increasingly being found on the Internet. In some cases companies are choosing to use "virtual road shows" to promote their stock. These road shows take place on the Internet and include the final prospectus and may even have the chief executive officer of the issuer answering questions by e-mail or conducting a chat session.

Because registration statements are prepared by attorneys, accountants, and other professionals, it is very expensive to register securities with the SEC. Therefore, regulations provide that some types of securities are exempt from registration with the SEC, although they may still need to be registered with a state securities commission. The exemptions are mostly designed to allow unregistered securities to be sold to those who are presumed to have the ability to protect themselves in a securities offering. Exempt securities include intrastate offerings, offerings by businesses whose total sales do not

Figure 10.1
Tombstone Ad

This announcement is neither an offer to sell nor a solicitation of offers to buy any of these securities. The offering is made only by the Prospectus, copies of which may be obtained in any State or jurisdiction in which this announcement is circulated only from such of the underwriters as may legally offer these securities in such State or jurisdiction.

NEW ISSUE

February 10, 2000

$92,000,000

Lante

Lante Corporation

4,600,000 Shares
Common Stock

NASDAQ Symbol: "LNTE"

Price $20 Per Share

Prior to the offering there had been no public market for these securities. Lante Corporation is an Internet services company that develops sophisticated technology-based solutions for electronic markets. These markets, which the Company refers to as e-markets, are Internet based networks through which multiple buyers and sellers efficiently conduct business online.

Credit Suisse First Boston

Deutsche Banc Alex. Brown

Thomas Weisel Partners LLC

Friedman Billings Ramsey

Adams, Harkness & Hill, Inc.

Barrington Research Associates, Inc.

Donaldson, Lufkin & Jenrette

E*Offering

First Union Securities, Inc.

Invemed Associates

Lehman Brothers

SG Cowen

Stifel, Nicolaus & Company
Incorporated

TD Securities

Wit SoundView

CREDIT SUISSE | FIRST BOSTON

exceed certain specified dollar limits, and private offerings. Exempt securities usually contain restrictions that prohibit their resale for a limited amount of time.

INTRASTATE OFFERINGS

To qualify for an intrastate exemption (SEC Rule 147), all shareholders and the business must be residents of the same state. This means that the issuing company either is incorporated in the state or does a substantial amount of its business (at least 80 percent) in the state in which all buyers of the securities are residents. The securities cannot "come to rest" with any nonresident of the state for at least nine months. If any nonresident owns the securities within this time frame, the entire exemption is invalidated. The courts have even held that the offering does not qualify for an intrastate exemption if the proceeds from the offering will be used out of the state.

REGULATION A

SEC Regulation A allows a company to raise up to $5 million in a one-year period with no resale restrictions or limit on the number of investors or investor sophistication requirements. An issuing company is required to make a *low-level registration* with the SEC and provide an offering circular and disclosure document. Since the offering circular and disclosure document closely resemble a preliminary prospectus and therefore contain much of the information required for a full-blown registration, the costs for preparing a Regulation A offering are similar to costs required for a full registration. Once the low-level registration document is registered, after a 10-day waiting period the securities can be sold, with no restrictions on resale.

REGULATION D

Under SEC Regulation D, rules 504, 505, and 506, securities may be sold without registration to sophisticated investors. Sophisticated investors are divided into two categories: *accredited* and *nonaccredited* investors. Accredited investors (1) have $1 million in net worth; or (2) have incomes exceeding $200,000 over the past two years and reasonably expect a $200,000 income this year; or (3) are directors, executive officers, or general partners of the issuing company; or (4) are institutions, like banks and insurance companies with total net assets of over $5 million. Nonaccredited investors are those who do not meet the accredited investor criteria but who are "capable alone, or with the assistance of a representative, of evaluating the merits and risks of the investment." Investors fill out signed, witnessed forms indicating how they qualify as accredited investors. These forms are kept by the issuing company. Regulation D does not allow any general advertising of the securities. The Dodd-Frank Wall Street Reform and Consumer Protection Act (CFPA), passed in 2010, prohibits certain people convicted of felonies in connection with the sale or purchase of a security from selling securities under Regulation D. The CFPA will be discussed in more detail later in this chapter.

Rules 504 and 505   SEC Rule 504 lets a company raise up to $1 million within a 12-month period of time without registration and without any limit on the number of accredited and nonaccredited investors. Resale is not restricted. Under SEC Rule 505, a company can raise up to $5 million, in a 12-month period, without registration. There is a limit of 35 nonaccredited investors but no limit on accredited investors. Under Rule 505, the issuing company must disclose all material information to each investor, including past financial statements and a summary of the business operation. Resale is restricted and can only occur after registration or if the transaction qualifies under another exemption.

Rule 506   SEC Rule 506 allows for a private placement exemption. To qualify for a private placement, a company can have no more than 35 nonaccredited investors but any number of accredited investors. Each investor buying in a private placement offering must sign an investment letter stating that the securities are being bought for investment purposes and will not be resold for at least two years.

Rule 144   SEC Rule 144 governs the resale of restricted securities. Restricted securities can be resold after two years if there is adequate public information about the issuer, a limited volume of sales, and the SEC is notified. If a person is not affiliated with the issuer, the securities can be resold in three years without restriction.

Facebook Sets Stage for IPO Next Year

Facebook Inc., one of the world's hottest technology companies, gave the clearest sign yet that it is preparing to take itself public sometime next year, as it revealed new details in a 100-page document sent to a select group of potential investors.

Facebook, of Palo Alto, Calif., said it plans to increase its number of shareholders above 500 this year, according to the private-placement document, forcing the social-networking company to begin disclosing reams of financial information or go public by April 2012.

Facebook Chief Executive Mark Zuckerberg has said he is in no rush to go public, but those intentions have been hotly contested since the company launched an equity offering of as much as $1.5 billion through Goldman Sachs Group Inc. earlier this week.

Frenzied investor interest in the deal, offered solely to Goldman partners and handpicked clients of the securities firm, has put a stamp of approval on the $50 billion valuation of Facebook implied by its agreement with Goldman and Digital Sky Technologies for a $500 million infusion from the two companies.

The strong demand and sharp increase in Facebook's value from $10 billion in mid-2009 give Mr. Zuckerberg, other Facebook executives, and its relatively small circle of investors a potentially irresistible incentive to take the fast-growing company public, despite the downside of doing so. As a private company, Facebook isn't required to report its revenue, profits or losses, and executive compensation, as publicly traded companies must do.

A Facebook spokesman declined to comment. Goldman declined to comment.

The social-networking company had fewer than 500 investors as of the end of last year, said a person familiar with the company, including current and former employees, venture-capital firms, and private investors. In 2008, Facebook told the Securities and Exchange Commission that the company had fewer than 499 holders in each of five classes of stock.

The number of investors is crucial because of the SEC's 47-year-old rules governing private companies. The rules require firms with 500 or more shareholders of record in a given type of stock to publicly disclose certain financial information. The requirement is designed to protect investors from unduly risking their money.

Crossing the threshold triggers the SEC's filing requirements, even if a company's shares don't trade publicly. Such companies must register as a reporting company within 120 days after the end of year in which the limit is breached. At that point, companies typically conclude that they might as well go public, listing their shares on an exchange and cashing in if the offering succeeds.

Facebook's current fiscal year ends on Dec. 31, making its disclosure deadline the end of April 2012. People familiar with the matter have said Facebook sought a benchmark valuation from a leading investment bank in preparation for a potential initial public offering next year and was keen on a "round-number" valuation of $50 billion.

"When they do go public, the valuation could be much higher or lower, but it probably did them no harm to get people talking $50 billion now," said Lise Buyer, founder of the Class V Group, who has advised on IPOs of Google Inc. and other technology companies. "Getting it out there should get some people off their case."

The investment world has been so eager for a Facebook IPO, it has spurred active trading in shares of Facebook's still-private stock in secondary markets.

The 100-page document that includes the potential timetable for a Facebook public offering is being circulated to would-be investors in the $1.5 billion "special-purpose vehicle" created by Goldman.

Goldman sent copies of the private-placement memo throughout the day Thursday, often by messenger instead of email to prevent leaks. In some cases, even spouses of the document's recipients were asked to sign a confidentiality agreement.

The document contains much more financial information about Facebook than previously known outside the company. For example, in the first nine months of 2010, Facebook had net income of $355 million on revenue of about $1.2 billion, said one person who reviewed the results.

Fourth-quarter results weren't disclosed to potential investors, but one person familiar with the company said Facebook likely had 2010 revenue of $1.9 billion to $2 billion. Analysts have said the company's revenue last year could be as high as $2 billion, fueled by advertising growth.

Because of huge demand to get a piece of Facebook, Goldman had planned to close the deal as soon as Thursday, according to people familiar with the situation. But a deadline hasn't been officially set. Clients of the firm still were clamoring to get into the private offering as of late Thursday, these people said.

The Facebook deal is "very reminiscent of the Internet bubble," says one Goldman client who received information about the offering but planned to spend little time reviewing it, partly because the deal is being assembled so fast. Still, he was leaning toward buying Facebook shares. "You'd like to be part of it," he says.

Other technology firms and investment banks are racing to raise capital and hatch potential IPOs because of the sky-high valuation Facebook is establishing with its private share offering and infusion from Goldman and DST.

It isn't clear why Facebook decided to tell potential investors that it intends to breach the 500-shareholder limit. But executives have been uncomfortable about the secondary market that has sprung up to buy shares from current and former Facebook employees because such sales have led to inconsistent valuations of the company that are based on small numbers of shares changing hands.

The investment vehicle being created by Goldman is intended to pool investors' money to create the legal effect of a single new shareholder in Facebook, since each special-purpose vehicle counts as one shareholder of record.

Companies may exceed that limit during their financial year but still avoid reporting requirements, as long as the total declines to 499 or fewer at the end of the company's fiscal year.

Source: "Facebook Sets Stage for IPO Next Year" by Anupretta Das, Geoffrey Fowler, and Liz Rappaport, *Wall Street Journal*, Jan. 6, 2011.

LIABILITY UNDER THE 1933 ACT

The 1933 Act provides significant civil and criminal penalties for violating its regulations. Under Section 11, investors harmed by the registration statement may, within two years of the effective date of the registration statement, bring a civil lawsuit for the damages suffered. To show harm under the 1933 Act, investors must prove only that the registration statement contains material omissions or misstatements. Section 11 creates almost absolute liability. Investors, if they still own the securities, may recover the money paid for securities, plus interest. If the securities have been sold, investors may recover the damages they incurred. In addition, criminal penalties of $10,000 are possible, as well as up to five years in jail, if the violations were willful.

All of the following people can be held liable for any misstatements or misinformation found in the registration statement: those who sign the registration statement, for example, an attorney; those who prepare the certified report, for example, an accountant or engineer; directors or those who were slated to be directors; and underwriters (the company that agreed to sell the stock for the issuer or to buy the shares not sold). Preparers of the registration statement or preparers of portions of the registration statement may have a *due diligence defense*, which requires a showing that the preparer made a reasonable investigation of the offering and had reasonable grounds to believe, and did believe, that the registration statement was accurate. Experts, like accountants and engineers, are only liable for the portions of the registration statement that they actually prepared. Directors, officers, and underwriters (nonexperts) are liable for any misstatements or omissions contained in the entire registration statement. Nonexperts can prove due diligence as to the portions prepared by experts if they show that they made a reasonable investigation and reasonably believed that the experts' portions were accurate.

In addition to provisions of Section 11, the 1933 Act also allows the SEC, under Section 17, to obtain an injunction prohibiting the sale of *any* security by the following means: (1) any device, scheme, or artifice to defraud; (2) untrue statements or material omissions; or (3) a fraudulent business. Only negligence is required to prove subsections 2 and 3. The courts, however, require *scienter*—the intent to deceive—in proving subsection 1. Scienter is, of course, more difficult to prove than mere negligence.

1934 SECURITIES EXCHANGE ACT

The 1934 Securities Exchange Act covers corporate reporting, proxy solicitation, public tender offers, insider trading, and fraud. All publicly traded corporations with over 500 shareholders and $10 million in assets are required to be registered with the SEC and to file reports. Each company must file with the SEC a form 10-K (the annual report), a form 10-Q (the quarterly report), and a form 8-K (the monthly report) required during the time material events are occurring. These forms become public records and allow interested parties to research publicly traded companies. Also, anyone holding at least five percent of a registered company must file a report with the SEC disclosing the amount of stock owned.

SARBANES-OXLEY ACT OF 2002 AND DODD-FRANK WALL STREET REFORM AND CONSUMER PROTECTION ACT OF 2010

The onset of several prominent business scandals prompted Congress to amend the 1934 Securities Exchange Act. This Act, known as Sarbanes-Oxley, has changed the way public companies report to the SEC. Sarbanes-Oxley applies to all public companies. It requires that each financial report filed with the SEC be accompanied by a personal certification from the Chief Executive Office (CEO) or Chief Financial Officer (CFO). This certification must state that the report accurately and fairly presents the financial conditions of the company. New rules issued in 2010 also require detailed information about the qualifications of nominees for the board of directors, as well as information concerning board member compensation. Also, the CFPA amended the Sarbanes-Oxley Act to require a report to be filed within 10 days by any person gaining the position of director, officer, or shareholder owning over 10% of the company's stock. Officers and attorneys are required to report any internal fraud and all officers are responsible for ensuring that internal control deficiencies are reported to company audit committees. The penalty for submitting a report knowing it does not comply with the Act is $1 million and/or 10 years imprisonment for any officer. If it is a willful violation, the penalty is $20 million and/or up to twenty years in jail. Sarbanes-Oxley also prohibits companies from making personal loans to executive officers and directors. The goal of the Act is to create an environment where senior management provides more financial oversight and better accountability to shareholders.

The U.S. financial crisis which began in 2007 prompted Congress to reevaluate U.S. law regulating the financial industry. In July 2010, Congress passed a sweeping financial reform bill, the *Dodd-Frank Wall Street Reform and Consumer Protection Act,* often referred to as either the Dodd-Frank Act or the CFPA. Many consider Dodd-Frank to be the most comprehensive financial reform bill since the Great Depression. It greatly expanded the SEC's enforcement and regulatory power. It provided for new regulation of hedge funds and other risky investments. It created new agencies, including a new, independent consumer bureau, the Bureau of Consumer Financial Protection (which will be discussed in more detail in later chapters). As discussed previously, it expanded the Sarbanes-Oxley Act reporting requirements. It grants a monetary award to whistleblowers who provide the SEC with information leading to a successful enforcement action of anywhere between 10% to 30% of the total penalty collected. Implementation of Dodd-Frank will take years to complete.

PROXY SOLICITATION

As we saw in Chapter 9, *proxies* allow someone other than the shareholder to vote shares of stock. The 1934 Act also governs proxy solicitation. When management is planning to solicit proxies, it must file a preliminary copy of the proposed proxy statement with the SEC. The proxy statement must identify those who are soliciting proxies, the means that will be used (usually the U.S. mail), those who will pay for the solicitation, the amount that has already been spent on the solicitation, and an estimate of the amounts that will be spent. Detailed information must also appear about those running for the board of directors and their backgrounds. Management almost always solicits its own proxies. In 2007, the SEC began allowing proxy materials to be posted on the Internet. However, shareholders may still request paper or email copies.

disgruntled shareholders:
Those shareholders who disagree with the current management of the company.

Sometimes **disgruntled shareholders** may want to solicit their own proxies and run their own slate of candidates for the board of directors. This is called a *proxy contest.* Anyone may solicit proxies from 10 or fewer persons without complying with the 1934 Act. **Beneficial owners** may also solicit proxies without complying with the federal rules. However, if the disgruntled shareholders want to solicit proxies from more than 10 persons, then they too have to comply with the registration requirements. If management is soliciting proxies, then it must give the disgruntled shareholders either the shareholder list or include the disgruntled shareholders' material with management's material.

beneficial owner:
Brokerage firms holding securities in their own name.

Information in the proxy materials is governed by a materiality test. If a misrepresentation or omission of a material fact (one that influences the decision) occurs, then those who prepared the statement can be liable to shareholders.

Proxy contests can be very expensive, and management can be reimbursed for the expenses it incurs in a proxy contest if the expenses were reasonable and the contest occurred because of a difference in corporate policy. Management cannot be reimbursed if officers engaged in the proxy contest in order to keep their jobs with the company. The disgruntled shareholders can be reimbursed if they win, the contest benefited the corporation, and the shareholders ratify the reimbursement.

TENDER OFFERS

A proxy contest is one way to take control of a company. During the 1980s a more popular way was to initiate a **public tender offer**, a public request that shareholders sell their stock to a particular person or company. Before 1968, no federal law specifically regulating tender offers existed. In 1968, the 1934 Act was amended by the Williams Act with the intent of protecting investors from the complexities of tender offers. The Williams Act requires that upon commencement of a tender offer, the *bidder* (in some adverse circumstances, the bidder is called the "raider") must notify the target company's management, all target company shareholders, and the SEC that a public tender offer is taking place. The statement must include the bidder's terms, background, past dealings with the target company, and whether the bidder intends to control the company. A public tender offer must be open to all shareholders, although the bidder may specify that it will only buy a certain percentage of the shares. For example, the bidder may only want to buy 50 percent of the outstanding shares in the belief that 50 percent is enough to exercise control. If more shares are tendered (offered) than the bidder specified, then each tendering shareholder takes pro rata. If there are 1,000 outstanding shares and 800 are tendered, the bidder is only responsible for buying 400, or 50 percent of the total shares tendered. Each shareholder would then sell only 50 percent of her shares to the bidder. Further, all shareholders must be paid the same for each share. If the shares have not been purchased, any stockholder who tenders shares may withdraw them during the first 15 days of the offer or anytime after 60 days. The offer has to remain open for at least 20 days. If the price per share is increased during the offer, then all tendering shareholders receive the benefit of the increased price.

> **tender offer:**
> A public offer to purchase stock at a specified price per share.

If someone has access to information that suggests a tender offer will take place and that person trades stock based on that information but before the announcement is public, he or she could make a lot of money. The SEC has also enacted Rule 14e-3, which prohibits any person from trading on nonpublic tender offer information.

During the 1980s, so many firms merged that the decade is often referred to as "merger mania." Many of these takeovers were considered hostile. This means the target company's board of directors did not approve of the merger and set out to fight the takeover attempt. Management's attempts to thwart the takeover took on terms like "scorched earth," "poison pill," and "selling the crown jewels." Management's payment to the raider to stop the takeover attempt was known as "greenmail." There was also a "pacman" defense, where management would make a reverse tender offer on the raider's company.

Since the 1980s, many states have passed antitakeover statutes to protect local businesses from out-of-state control. Most of the statutes are specifically aimed at increasing the amount of time it takes to complete a takeover of a corporation. In 1987, the Supreme Court upheld an Indiana antitakeover statute. Since then, a majority of the states have passed some form of antitakeover statute. Most of these statutes require that any merger be postponed for several years unless there was prior approval of the merger by the target company's board of directors.

SHAREHOLDER RESOLUTION

Sometimes shareholders do not wish to take over the company; rather, they want existing management to change certain policy decisions. One way to get management to change policy is through a shareholder proposal or resolution. A shareholder resolution is voted on by shareholders at the company's annual meeting. If management opposes the resolution, the shareholders may propose a 200-word statement to be voted on by the shareholders. The proposal must be presented if the action requested does not violate the law, relates to the company's business, relates to a business policy issue, does not relate to the payment of a specific amount of dividends, and if no similar proposal has been presented within the past five years and defeated within the past three years.

FRAUD

Section 10(b) of the 1934 Act and the SEC's Rule 10b-5 make it "unlawful and illegal to willfully engage in any practice intending to defraud or to willfully state an untrue material fact in connection with the sale of securities." Unlike Section 12 of the 1933 Act, which only applies to sales, Section 10(b) and **Rule 10b-5** apply to both purchasers and sellers as well as to securities that are exempt from registration. As with Section 17 of the 1933 Act, scienter is required to prove a Section 10(b) and Rule 10b-5 violation. In order to violate 10(b) and 10b-5, the statement must be **material**. Materiality, addressed by the Supreme Court in a 1988 case, *Basic v. Levinson*, is not judged by financial criteria but by whether the reasonable shareholder would consider the information in making an investment decision. Injured parties can bring a civil action demanding an injunction and/or damages under section 10(b). The SEC may bring civil actions against violators, who may be fined up to three times the amount of illegal profit. Willful violations can result in criminal penalties of up to five million dollars and up to 20 years in jail. Corporations may be fined up to $25 million. Section 10(b) has also been used to prevent insider trading.

INSIDER TRADING

short swing profits: Profits made by an insider through sale or disposition of the corporate stock within six months after purchase.

Insider trading occurs in two circumstances. The first is when a traditional insider, officer, director, or shareholder owning 10 percent or more of the company's stock trades in the securities of his company. It is assumed that these individuals always possess inside information (information that is not public). Therefore, another section of the 1934 Act, section 16(b), prohibits **short swing profits**, which are any profits made by a traditional insider through the purchase and sale of securities in any six-month period. Short swing profits must be returned to the company. For example, if June, the president of AC Corp., bought 20 shares of AC stock for $10 a share on January 1 and then sold 20 shares of AC stock on April 1 for $12 a share, she has made a profit of $40. Under section 16(b) June cannot make a profit on the shares for six months, in this case until July. Under the short swing profit rule, she would have to return her profit to the company. In fact, a television reporter was required to pay her company over $53,000 when, unbeknownst to her, her husband violated the short-swing rule when he tried to sell a few shares of stock only one month after the IPO of the Internet company she started with former U.S. Surgeon General C. Everett Koop.

Sometimes traditional insiders buy several shares of stock over several different time periods. In determining whether the insider is liable for short swing profits, the courts generally use the *lowest in/highest out* rule. This means that the court matches the number of securities bought and sold. Assume that Carlos, the president of BC Corporation, bought 6 shares on July 1 at $1 per share, 10 shares on July 15 at $2 per share, and 8 shares on July 30 at $3 per share. If Carlos then sells 6 shares on January 14 for $4 per share, the court will rule that all the shares cost $2 per share, because the lowest price in was the July 15 purchase at $2 per share. The July 1 purchase, at $1 per share, has exceeded the six-month time frame. Carlos owes the company $2 per share for 6 shares, or $12. The short swing profit rule is a strict liability rule, meaning that if traditional insiders engage in short swing trading, they are liable.

The other circumstance where inside trading occurs is when someone with access to nonpublic information trades on the information. As the case on the following page shows, certain persons must disclose material information to the public before trading on the stock.

SEC V. TEXAS GULF SULFUR
401 F.2d 833 (2d Cir. 1968)

FACTS

Texas Gulf Sulfur (TGS) was engaged in mineral exploration in Canada. Its geologists discovered what they believed to be a large copper and minable ore find in Canada. Drilling was halted for about five months while the visual estimates were confirmed through a chemical assay. During these five months TGS's president and vice-president and several geologists executed trades on the company's stock. When drilling resumed, it became clear that a major find existed. Each hole reflected substantial copper mineralization. Several newspapers reported rumors about a "rich strike" in Canada. To combat the rumors, TGS issued a press release indicating that the results of its drilling were "inconclusive." This announcement was false in that TGS had already discovered 6.2 to 8.3 million tons of ore with a value of between $26 to $29 per ton. Three days later, a public announcement was issued stating that TGS had a strike of at least 25 million tons of ore. Some of the defendants also traded shares immediately before the public announcement became widespread.

DECISION

Judge Waterman wrote the opinion of the Court of Appeals. Rule 10b-5 is based on the principle that in the securities market, all investors should have equal access to information. Information can only be kept private if it is used for corporate purposes. The information cannot be kept private and then used for the personal benefit of an individual. Anyone possessing material inside information must either disclose it to the public or abstain from trading and/or recommending the securities to anyone while the information is secret.

In this case, the major mineral discovery was material information. Therefore, all stock transactions in TGS stock by individuals who knew of the drilling results violated Rule 10b-5. Those individuals were not eligible to trade until the official public announcement had been disseminated. Those individuals who traded on the stock in anticipation of the public announcement were responsible for ensuring that the information was available to the investing public. "[A]ll insider activity must await dissemination of the promised official announcement."

CASE QUESTIONS

1. Does the Court's rule extend to secretaries, janitors, and other employees who may have learned of the mineral find?
2. When can individuals with inside information trade on that information?
3. Do you think that the insider trading prohibitions are good or bad for the market? Why?

fiduciary: A relationship that creates a duty to exercise a high degree of care and to not be involved in conflicts of interest. Employees have a fiduciary relationship with their employers.

The rule announced in *Texas Gulf Sulfur* is known as the *disclose or refrain rule*. After *Texas Gulf Sulfur*, several cases have been decided that further refined the limits on who is prohibited from trading on nonpublic information. The first insider trading case to reach the Supreme Court was *Chiarella v. SEC*. Chiarella was a printer and had traded on information he had obtained, through his own efforts as a financial printer, about some public tender offers. The Supreme Court held that he was not guilty of insider trading because he did not have a **fiduciary** relationship to the companies in which he was trading and he did not receive his information from any company insiders. Years after *Chiarella* was decided, however, the U.S. Supreme Court expanded the reach of insider trading laws in *U.S. v. O'Hagen*.

In the Language of the Court

U.S. V. O'HAGAN

521 U.S. 642 (1997)

Justice Ginsburg delivered the opinion of the Court.

FACTS

Respondent James Herman O'Hagan was a partner in the law firm of Dorsey & Whitney in Minneapolis, Minnesota. In July 1988, Grand Metropolitan PLC (Grand Met), a company based in London, England, retained Dorsey & Whitney as local counsel to represent Grand Met regarding a potential tender offer for the common stock of the Pillsbury Company, headquartered in Minneapolis. Both Grand Met and Dorsey & Whitney took precautions to protect the confidentiality of Grand Met's tender offer plans. O'Hagan did no work on the Grand Met representation. Dorsey & Whitney withdrew from representing Grand Met on September 9, 1988. Less than a month later, on October 4, 1988, Grand Met publicly announced its tender offer for Pillsbury stock.

On August 18, 1988, while Dorsey & Whitney was still representing Grand Met,

O'Hagan began purchasing call options for Pillsbury stock. Each option gave him the right to purchase 100 shares of Pillsbury stock by a specified date in September 1988. Later in August and in September, O'Hagan made additional purchases of Pillsbury call options. By the end of September, he owned 2,500 unexpired Pillsbury options, apparently more than any other individual investor. O'Hagan also purchased, in September 1988, some 5,000 shares of Pillsbury common stock, at a price just under $ 39 per share. When Grand Met announced its tender offer in October, the price of Pillsbury stock rose to nearly $ 60 per share. O'Hagan then sold his Pillsbury call options and common stock, making a profit of more than $ 4.3 million.

O'Hagan was charged with 20 counts of mail fraud, 17 counts of securities fraud, in violation of 10(b) and Rule 10b-5 of the Securities Exchange Act of 1934 and 3 counts of violating federal money laundering statutes, A jury convicted O'Hagan on all 57 counts, and he was sentenced to a 41-month term of imprisonment.

A divided panel of the Court of Appeals for the Eighth Circuit reversed all of O'Hagan's convictions. We address first the Court of Appeals' reversal of O'Hagan's convictions under §10(b) and Rule 10b-5.

DECISION

Twice before we have been presented with the question whether criminal liability for violation of §10(b) may be based on a misappropriation theory. In *Chiarella* v. *United States,* the jury had received no misappropriation theory instructions, so we declined to address the question. In *Carpenter* v. *United States,* the Court divided evenly on whether, under the circumstances of that case, convictions resting on the misappropriation theory should be affirmed.

. . .

Under the "traditional" or "classical theory" of insider trading liability, §10(b) and Rule 10b-5 are violated when a corporate insider trades in the securities of his corporation on the basis of material, nonpublic information. Trading on such information qualifies as a "deceptive device" under §10(b), we have affirmed, because

"a relationship of trust and confidence [exists] between the shareholders of a corporation and those insiders who have obtained confidential information by reason of their position with that corporation." That relationship, we recognized, "gives rise to a duty to disclose [or to abstain from trading] because of the 'necessity of preventing a corporate insider from . . . taking unfair advantage of . . . uninformed . . . stockholders.'" The classical theory applies not only to officers, directors, and other permanent insiders of a corporation, but also to attorneys, accountants, consultants, and others who temporarily become fiduciaries of a corporation.

The "misappropriation theory" holds that a person commits fraud "in connection with" a securities transaction, and thereby violates §10(b) and Rule 10b-5, when he misappropriates confidential information for securities trading purposes, in breach of a duty owed to the source of the information. Under this theory, a fiduciary's undisclosed, self-serving use of a principal's information to purchase or sell securities, in breach of a duty of loyalty and confidentiality, defrauds the principal of the exclusive use of that information. In lieu of premising liability on a fiduciary relationship between company insider and purchaser or seller of the company's stock, the misappropriation theory premises liability on a fiduciary-turned-trader's deception of those who entrusted him with access to confidential information.

The two theories are complementary, each addressing efforts to capitalize on nonpublic information through the purchase or sale of securities. The classical theory targets a corporate insider's breach of duty to shareholders with whom the insider transacts; the misappropriation theory outlaws trading on the basis of nonpublic information by a corporate "outsider" in breach of a duty owed not to a trading party, but to the source of the information. The misappropriation theory is thus designed to "protect the integrity of the securities markets against abuses by 'outsiders' to a corporation who have access to confidential information that will affect the corporation's security price when revealed, but who owe no fiduciary or other duty to that corporation's shareholders."

In this case, the indictment alleged that O'Hagan, in breach of a duty of trust and confidence he owed to his law firm, Dorsey & Whitney, and to its client, Grand Met, traded on the basis of nonpublic information regarding Grand Met's planned tender offer for Pillsbury common stock. This conduct, the Government charged, constituted a fraudulent device in connection with the purchase and sale of securities.

We agree with the Government that misappropriation, as just defined, satisfies §10(b)'s requirement that chargeable conduct involve a "deceptive device or contrivance" used "in connection with" the purchase or sale of securities. We observe, first, that misappropriators, as the Government describes them, deal in deception. A fiduciary who "[pretends] loyalty to the principal while secretly converting the principal's information for personal gain. . . .

In sum, the misappropriation theory, as we have examined and explained it in this opinion, is both consistent with the statute and with our precedent. Vital to our decision that criminal liability may be sustained under the misappropriation theory, we emphasize, are two sturdy safeguards Congress has provided regarding scienter. To establish a criminal violation of Rule 10b-5, the Government must prove that a person "willfully" violated the provision. Furthermore, a defendant may not be imprisoned for violating Rule 10b-5 if he proves that he had no knowledge of the rule. O'Hagan's charge that the misappropriation theory is too indefinite to permit the imposition of criminal liability, thus fails not only because the theory is limited to those who breach a recognized duty. In addition, the statute's "requirement of the presence of culpable intent as a necessary element of the offense does much to destroy any force in the argument that application of the [statute]" in circumstances such as O'Hagan's is unjust.

The judgment of the Court of Appeals for the Eighth Circuit is reversed, and the case is remanded for further proceedings consistent with this opinion.

CASE QUESTIONS

1. Why did the court say O'Hagan did not have a fiduciary relationship with Pillsbury?
2. Why did the Court have to adopt a new theory to convict O'Hagan of securities fraud?
3. What is the policy reason for the adoption of the misappropriation theory?

TIPPER/TIPPEE LIABILITY

One other type of liability for insider trading is tipper/tippee liability. In tipper/tippee liability, the court views the *tippee* as stepping into the shoes of the insider who breached his or her fiduciary duty to the company. The tippee ends up with the same liability as the insider. Assume your uncle calls and tells you that his company has just discovered an oil well and that the discovery will be announced tomorrow. Should you buy the company's stock today? If you do, you will be guilty of insider trading. Why? You are a tippee and as such will be required to **disgorge** your profits. If you trade, the *tipper*, your uncle, is also liable.

disgorge: To give up illegally gained profits by court order to prevent unjust enrichment.

RECENT INSIDER TRADING ISSUES

Insider trading has been a concern of Congress since the 1980s. To try to prevent insider trading, Congress passed legislation aimed at increasing the penalties. In 1984, the Insider Trading Sanctions Act (ITSA) was passed. ITSA provides for criminal penalties of five million dollars, civil penalties of three times the profit (treble damages), and a jail term of up to 20 years for anyone convicted of insider trading in companies engaged in a takeover attempt. Congress also passed the Insider Trading Liability Sanctions Act (ITLSA), which penalizes any person who controls a person trading on inside information.

However, even with these laws, insider trading continues to be a concern. For example, in 2003, Samuel Waksel, CEO of ImClone Systems and friend of Martha Stewart, plead guilty to insider trading and was sentenced to 7 years in jail. Martha Stewart's selling of ImClone stock which occurred almost simultaneously with the sale of Waksel stock, set into motion the investigation which resulted in her conviction for making false statements to federal investigators.

Another example involves infamous financial investor Bernard Madoff. Over a period of at least 30 years, Madoff engaged in a complex **ponzi scheme,** bilking thousands of investors out of billions of dollars. Although the SEC investigated Madoff's business practices, it failed to uncover the fraud until 2008 when Madoff, aware that his scheme was about to collapse, informed his sons of the fraud. They in turn provided SEC investigators with information leading to his arrest. Madoff pled guilty to all charges and was sentenced to the maximum of 150 years in prison.

A more recent insider trading case, still ongoing as of the date of this publication, is considered by many to be the biggest insider trading scandal in the country's history. In October 2009 the Justice Department arrested six defendants allegedly involved in an insider trading ring linked to hedge fund manager Raj Rajaratnam and the Galleon Group, the hedge fund management firm he founded. The Justice Department relied on wiretaps and investigation methods not typically used to combat insider trading to gather enough evidence to justify the arrests.

ponzi scheme: A type of fraudulent investment in which investors are not paid with returns from an actual investment, but instead are paid from the proceeds given to the advisor from subsequent investors.

SOCIAL/ETHICAL ISSUES

In January 2011, Reuters released a legal analysis which indicates that people found guilty of insider trading often escape harsh sentences. The report, which analyzed sentences imposed in 15 insider trading cases in 2009 and 2010, determined that 87% of the sentences imposed were lighter than what the U.S. Sentencing Guidelines recommend. Seven of the sentences did not impose prison time at all. As the report indicated, this rate is 30% above the rate in other cases in which New York federal judges imposed sentences of less than the guidelines recommended in 57% of non-insider trading cases. Theories about the cause of this discrepancy range from location, to the character references insider trading defendants often provide judges, to the lack of insider trading victims presenting victim-impact statements to judges before sentencing. Is this discrepancy in sentencing fair? Do you agree with the rationale for why insider trading defendants generally receive less harsh sentences? Do you think people who engage in insider trading harm society more or less than other criminals?

Online securities fraud is a new and challenging problem facing the SEC. Online fraud can occur through a variety of tactics. For instance, SPAM email sent to thousands of email addresses may provide false claims of insider tips as a ploy to gain access to investors' funds. Fictitious websites may claim to provide investors with investing services, only to later disappear with investors' money. Illegitimate community bulletin boards and chat rooms are also common methods of online investment fraud.

Insider Trading: Why We Can't Help Ourselves

Say it ain't so, Warren.

Investors were shocked to learn this week that David Sokol, a trusted lieutenant to Berkshire Hathaway Chairman Warren Buffett, had bought nearly $10 million worth of stock in Lubrizol just over a week before he suggested to Mr. Buffett that Berkshire should acquire the company.

Leave aside the obvious point that Mr. Sokol might not have lived up to Berkshire's high ethical standards. Focus instead on this: If even Mr. Buffett can fail to appreciate a potential conflict of interest under his very nose, then ordinary investors need to realize just how pervasive and insidious conflicts are throughout the financial world.

In the past few weeks alone, a chemist at the Food and Drug Administration was charged with trading on confidential information about drug approvals; a former Goldman Sachs Group director has been accused of leaking secrets to hedge-fund manager Raj Rajaratnam; and Mr. Rajaratnam has gone on trial for allegedly masterminding an insider-trading ring. The director and the hedge-fund manager maintain their innocence; the chemist hasn't yet been arraigned.

But how could Mr. Buffett, universally regarded as a beacon of integrity, have let Mr. Sokol's unusual trading occur unchecked?

Although Mr. Sokol resigned on March 28, both he and Mr. Buffett have insisted that he did nothing unlawful; Mr. Sokol has stressed that his resignation had nothing to do with his Lubrizol trades.

"Dave's purchases were made before he had discussed Lubrizol with me and with no knowledge of how I might react to his idea," Mr. Buffett said in a news release on Wednesday. "Furthermore, he knew he would have no voice in Berkshire's decision once he suggested the idea."

Mr. Buffett said in the news release: "In our first talk about Lubrizol, Dave mentioned that he owned stock in the company. It was a passing remark and I did not ask him about the date of his purchase or the extent of his holdings."

Mr. Buffett told me on Friday that "everything in [the news release] is accurate." All he would add is that "I don't know of anything even remotely material that was omitted from the release."

Mr. Sokol's trading falls under what Stephen Bainbridge, an expert on securities at the UCLA School of Law, calls "an enormously gray area of the law." It also is a reminder that a basic principle of securities law—disclosure cures conflicts—is nonsense.

"Even assuming that [Mr. Sokol] did nothing illegal, [his action] is typical of the kinds of conflicts of interest permitted by our financial system that undermine the integrity of markets," says Max Bazerman, an ethicist at Harvard Business School and co-author of the new book "Blind Spots."

Most people have what Mr. Bazerman calls an ethical blind spot. Faced with a potential conflict of interest, you automatically conclude that it couldn't possibly offer any temptation to someone of superior character—like you or those closest to you.

One study among doctors, for example, found that 53% felt it was ethical to accept a high-paying consultancy from a pharmaceutical firm. Only 36% felt it might skew their judgments about which medications to prescribe. Yet 62% felt that other doctors' decisions might be tainted by the same arrangement.

Likewise, a survey of nearly 1,000 Wall Street analysts found that two-thirds have accepted favors from the companies they follow—everything from career advice to reference letters for admissions into private clubs. Analysts who accept such favors generally deny that their integrity has been compromised—yet are twice as likely to maintain their rating after an earnings shortfall by a company that provided them with favors.

Or think of student-loan officers steering borrowers to lenders that secretly offered kickbacks or junkets; credit-rating agencies being paid by the firms they rate; financial advisers accepting trinkets like tote bags and T-shirts from fund companies; auditors examining the books of companies to whom their firms provide consulting services; mutual-fund traders who used to accept gifts from brokers like casino outings and stays at ski resorts. All have maintained that they aren't conflicted.

In testimony to Congress in 1991, Mr. Buffett said he expected all his employees "to ask themselves whether they are willing to have any contemplated act appear the next day on the front page of their local paper, to be read by their spouses, children and friends, with the reporting done by an informed and critical reporter. If they follow this test, they need not fear my other message to them: Lose money for the firm and I will be understanding; lose a shred of reputation for the firm and I will be ruthless."

Those are words to live by. But living by them isn't easy for anybody.

Source: "Insider Trading: Why We Can't Help Ourselves," by Jason Zweig, *Wall Street Journal*, April 2, 2011.

STATE BLUE SKY LAWS

Besides complying with the federal securities laws, state blue sky laws are still in effect and apply even when the federal laws do not. State blue sky laws may require companies to register the sale of securities that are exempt from federal registration. Some blue sky laws are patterned after the federal laws and require the filing of extensive registration statements. Others require the payment of a fee and a notification statement that is filed with the state's securities regulatory commission. The notification statement contains basic information about the issuer, like name, address, business form, general character, and a description of the type and price of the security.

Most state blue sky laws do not require that a tombstone ad be used. The laws do, however, require that the regulatory commission receive a copy of any advertisement. In 1998, Congress passed the Securities Litigation Uniform Standard Act, which preempts state securities class action suits.

SUMMARY

Securities regulation is a complex area of the law. The primary rules are found in the 1933 Act and the 1934 Act, which aim to provide investors with complete information and to prevent fraud in the securities market. Because of the expense of registration, however, several exemptions exist. More recently, Congress has enacted specific legislation aimed at ensuring that senior management take greater financial oversight responsibilities. States, too, are interested in regulating securities, and state Blue Sky Laws apply to securities that are exempted from federal registration requirements. There has been an explosion of changes due to the advent of the Internet. The states and SEC are still in the process of determining how best to regulate this new approach to raising capital.

CHAPTER QUESTIONS

1. An investment banker passes information concerning pending mergers and acquisitions to a stockbroker. The stockbroker, along with two friends, trades on the information, reaping substantial gains when the takeover information is made public. What should the court do? [*United States v. Newman*, 664 F.2d 12 (2d Cir. 1981)]

2. A patron at a restaurant innocently overhears two individuals at the next table talking about a hot stock tip. The patron immediately calls a friend who calls his stockbroker and both of them trade on the information. Is anyone guilty of insider trading? Why or why not? [See *SEC v. Switzer*, 590 F. Supp. 756 (W.D. Okla. 1984)]

3. Are all multilevel marketing schemes securities? What determines whether the scheme needs to be registered? [See *In the Matter of Amway Corporation*, 93 F.T.C. 618 (1979).]

4. Alpha was in the business of selling, installing and maintaining pay telephones and business systems. After several years Alpha not only sold the pay telephones but also entered into service agreements with buyers. There were four levels of service agreements but most individuals selected the highest level. This level allowed the buyers an opportunity for a buyback option. If they chose the buyback option then Alpha received 70% share of any revenue and the investor received the balance. A base amount was set and if the base amount was not met then Alpha agreed to waive its share in order to meet the base amount. The business was not profitable even though the sales materials stated that pay telephones made substantial profits. Is there any violation of the securities laws? [See *S.E.C. v. Rubera*, 350 F.3d 1084 (9th Cir. 2003).]

5. Mark Cuban, who owned the Dallas Mavericks and Landmark theaters, was a large minority shareholder in Mamma.com, a Canadian search engine company. In 2004, Cuban learned through the company's CEO that the company was intending to raise capital through a private investment

of public equity (PIPE) offering. Before offering Cuban the information, the CEO asked him to agree to keep the information confidential. Cuban agreed, but became upset after learning of the company's intention because he believed it would dilute the value of his stock. At the end of the conversation, Cuban allegedly stated, "Well, now I'm screwed. I can't sell." Nonetheless, Cuban did sell his shares before Mamma.com publicly announced the PIPE offering, avoiding over $750,000 in losses. Under the misappropriation theory, did Cuban violate Rule 10b-5? [See *SEC v. Cuban*, 620 F.3d 551 (2010).]

6. The Corel Corporation through its CEO and CFO made several public statements about its 1999 fourth quarter and its 2000 first quarter. These statements, made in several articles as well as on TV, reflected an optimistic view concerning its new Linux and Windows products. These statements were very optimistic and claimed that Corel's financial troubles were over and that the company had returned to profitability. Its publicly traded stock price rose during this time period. In fact the company was still in financial difficulty and had suffered losses.Is it illegal to be overly optimistic? [See *In re Corel Corporation*, 293 F. Supp. 484 (2003).]

7. Raymond Dirks provided investment advice, for a fee, to a number of institutions and individual investors. In the course of his work, Dirks was contacted about employee fraud in Equity Funding. During the course of his investigation several Equity employees substantiated the claims. Dirks discussed his findings with several of his clients who then sold their Equity stock and it plunged in value. Did Dirks violate insider trading prohibitions? Why or why not? [See *Dirks v. SEC*, 463 U.S. 646 (1983).]

8. A junior accountant with a large publicly traded company, suspects that the financial statements of the company are not fairly represented. What should the accountant do?

9. A publicly traded company has several liabilities and transactions that are not included in its annual report. Many of these liabilities were actually incurred by a wholly owned subsidiary. Is there any problem with leaving these transactions off the annual report?

10. Patricia Rocklage was married to Scott Rocklage, the CEO of Cubist Pharmaceuticals, a publicly traded company. In late 2001, Mr. Rocklage learned that one of the company's newly developed drugs had failed its clinical trial. He phoned his wife with the news, instructing her to keep it confidential. However, Mrs. Rocklage had an understanding with her brother, William Beaver, that she would inform him of information such as this from her husband's company with "a wink and a nod." When she told her husband that she intended to inform her brother of this information before the company's public disclosure, he encouraged her not to do so. Nonetheless, she called Beaver and told him about the failed drug trial. Beaver then sold his stock before the company announced the news, avoiding a $99,500 loss. He also tipped off a friend, David Jones, who also sold before the disclosure, avoiding a loss of $133,200. Which of these three are guilty of insider trading? Why? Under what theory? [See *SEC v. Rocklage*, 470 F.3d 1 (2006)].

PRACTICAL EXERCISE

Robert, Kathleen, and Seth want to open a new store in an adjoining state (recall Chapter 9). However, they have exhausted the amount of money they can borrow from friends, family, and financial institutions. They now want to get money from rich individuals to open the new store and provide capital to advertise and market "Sage Loops." They currently have a Web page and are thinking about putting a "request for investors" section on the existing page. You are asked to advise Kathleen, Robert, and Seth on their alternatives. Your task is to decide (1) whether they should sell part of the business to several rich individuals, (2) whether bringing in new investors is selling securities, (3) whether they need to file a registration statement with the SEC and/or the state, (4) what types of exemptions are available, (5) the best exemption available for their situation, and (6) whether they can use the Internet to solicit investors. Your instructor may want you to research your own state securities laws to determine what you need to do to comply in your state.

FURTHER INFORMATION

http://securities.stanford.edu/
www.ace-net.org
www.direct-stock-market.com
www.sec.gov/

CHAPTER 11

BUSINESS TORTS AND CRIMES

This chapter examines business torts (wrongful actions that lead to civil lawsuits) and crimes. The scenario at the end of the chapter takes place outside a health club after a big snowstorm. Various actions by club employees may result in tort liability or criminal charges against the club, where you have just begun work as manager. After reading this chapter, you will have a clearer understanding of tort law, and how you can better protect your company from liability.

INTRODUCTION

In the course of business operations, it is inevitable that operations will not always go perfectly. From time to time in any organization, employees will take actions that are negligent or careless, and they may occasionally commit crimes as well. A worker or manager, for example, may cause damages by driving a vehicle or performing an audit negligently, by making false statements about a competitor, or by cutting corners on workplace safety or environmental protections. As we examined in Chapter 8, such actions by an agent quite frequently create liability not only for the employee but for the business firm as well.

Sometimes, employees, partners, or corporate officers or directors actually engage in work-related criminal activity. Business crimes often involve such financial offenses as embezzlement, forgery, or bribery; today, an increasing number of business crimes involve environmental, antitrust, and worker safety violations. Although it is less likely that one employee's conduct will create corporate criminal liability than create civil liability, the number of corporate criminal prosecutions is increasing. Certainly the business financial scandals of the past few years, and the resulting criminal cases against top executives of Enron, WorldCom, Tyco, Alelphia, HealthSouth, and even Martha Stewart have shown that corporate crime is still an important part of the "legal environment of business." This chapter explores the different types of civil and criminal liability encountered by business firms.

DISTINGUISHING TORTS AND CRIMES

tort: A wrongful action done by one person which causes damage or injury to another, and which results in liability for the injured person's damages.

Essentially, a **tort** is a wrongful action (or failure to act) that violates a noncontractual duty one person owes another, which action causes injury—physical or economic—to a person or property. The many types of torts range from long-established concepts like negligence and battery to newer, still-evolving torts such as infringement of trade secrets, invasion of privacy, and computer tampering. Torts are a "common law" subject in that the applicable legal principles have developed almost entirely from court cases rather than from statutes. Generally, when one person commits a tort that causes some type of physical, economic, or emotional injury or loss to another, the injured

THE WIZARD OF ID   Brant parker and Johnny hart

By permission of Johnny Hart and Creators Syndicate, Inc.

person may file a tort lawsuit seeking money damages. New types of torts will be recognized as new forms of wrongful actions, such as those involving computers and the Internet, evolve.

Even though some particular acts will constitute both a tort and a crime, it is important to understand the differences between the two. A criminal action is instituted by a federal, state, or local prosecutor, on behalf of the people of that jurisdiction, to enforce a specific criminal statute. The thrust of a criminal prosecution is to punish an individual who has transgressed the laws of behavior established by society. The penalty upon conviction is generally imprisonment or a fine payable to the appropriate government. Sometimes, as part of the penalty, the defendant is ordered to pay an amount of money as restitution to the victim, but this is secondary in importance to punishing the criminal.

A *tort action* (a civil case), however, does not usually depend on any particular statute. The primary goal is *compensation of the victim* for the consequences of someone else's wrongful (not necessarily criminal) actions. The local, state, and federal prosecutors are not involved. The burden is on the plaintiff to show that the actions of the defendant breached a common law duty to the plaintiff, directly causing some particular harm, and then to show how much money is needed to compensate the injured party.

PURPOSE OF TORT LAW

Criminal law serves the interests of society by setting minimum standards of conduct and providing punishment for those who violate the rules. Tort law, on the other hand, concerns one person's *duty* toward others and involves determining what one's obligations *ought* to be toward one or more specific persons and *providing compensation to the injured person* when another's conduct falls below the expected level. Most often, no contract exists between the parties, nor is any criminal statute involved. In many cases, like auto accidents, the parties do not even know each other prior to the commission of the tort.

For example, Denise is driving her car and runs into Kim's vehicle at an intersection. Has a tort been committed? This decision depends on whether the judge and jury feel that Denise's actions were those of a "reasonable person" at the moment she took the action she did. In other words, the judge and jury will measure Denise's conduct (in driving her car) against that of a mythical person who would have acted in a careful and prudent manner at the same time in the same situation. If the jury believes that Denise should have been more careful in driving her car then they may find her negligent, which is a tort.

Although there are certain well-known types of torts, such as libel, slander, battery, and negligence, tort law is flexible enough to allow courts to find new torts when someone has acted wrongfully toward another. The most well-known writer on tort law, Dean William Prosser, once stated to this effect:

> Changing social conditions lead constantly to the recognition of new duties. No better general statement can be made than that the courts will find a duty where, in general, reasonable men would recognize and agree that it exists.

In recent years, for example, courts have found torts to be committed through the use of computers, video recorders, and other tools of modern technology, which have been used in ways that interfere with the privacy of, or cause economic damage to, others.

INTENTIONAL TORTS

Some torts are intentional, whereas others are unintentional or accidental. Intentional torts are the result of one or more persons taking some deliberate action that causes personal or economic injury to another. Even though the person taking the action may not have intended the eventual result (for example, a serious injury), if he or she deliberately took the action that caused the injury, it will be classified as an intentional tort. In other words, the "intent" required to commit an intentional tort is intent to take the action that results in harm, not intent to cause harm.

ASSAULT AND BATTERY

assault: A condition that occurs when one person's actions put another in fear of bodily harm.

Although assault and battery are two torts often combined on television crime shows, each really is a separate act. **Assault** is intentionally putting another person in reasonable apprehension of immediate physical injury. If Rudy points a gun at Sebastian and says, "I'm going to shoot you," that would probably constitute an assault. However, if Sebastian knew that the gun was a toy, there would not be the same reasonable apprehension and would likely not be held as an assault. In addition, the victim must know about the threat in order to have the required apprehension. Thus, if Sebastian were asleep when Rudy pointed a gun at him, there would not have been an assault.

battery: The intentional, offensive, unwanted physical touching of another.

Battery is the intentional, offensive, unwanted physical touching of another. Some batteries are preceded by an assault, and some are not. Battery often results from one person hitting or beating another, but unwanted caressing, kissing, or touching can also constitute a battery.

MEMO FROM THE LEGAL DEPARTMENT

To: Students

From: Legal Department

One increasingly common form of battery lawsuit today results from sexual harassment in the workplace. Persons who are the victims of unwanted touching, pinching, or sexual contact need to file a tort lawsuit (battery) against the wrong-doer to collect damages. If a manager is the offender, or if the employee complains to management but no action is taken to correct the situation, the employer may also be liable. To protect their employees and to reduce their own liability, employers should adopt policies to prevent workplace sexual harassment as well as other types of harassment and should promptly investigate and punish such conduct.

One of the main defenses to the tort of battery is "consent." Defendants often argue that the person who was touched or hit had voluntarily engaged in the fight or invited the overly friendly contact which led to the battery allegation. Another common argument by a defendant is "self-defense"—that is, the person accused of battery was defending against an attack. The law does recognize such a defense but only to the extent necessary to defend against the attack. If Monica and Georgia are having a discussion, and Georgia slaps Monica's face, she cannot shoot Georgia and then claim self-defense from the tort of battery.

The following case involves a tort lawsuit for battery that resulted from a hockey game.

OVERALL V. KADELLA

361 N.W. 2d 352 (Mich. App. 1984)

FACTS

At the conclusion of a hockey game between the Waterford Lakers and the Clarkston Flyers, two amateur teams, a fight broke out between Mr. Kadella, who played for the Flyers, and a Lakers player. The fight soon became general, with players from both teams "leaving the bench to join the melee." Mr. Overall was a member of the opposing team but remained on the bench during the fight. Nevertheless, during the altercation Kadella skated over to the bench and hit Overall, knocking him unconscious and fracturing the bones around his right eye. Overall sued Kadella for battery. Overall was awarded $21,000 by the trial court for out-of-pocket expenses and pain and suffering and $25,000 as punitive damages because defendant's act had been "intentional and malicious."

DECISION

On appeal Kadella argued that the trial court's findings of fact were erroneous. Kadella pointed out that his three witnesses had testified that although Overall was seated on the bench, he had poked Kadella with his stick before Kadella retaliated. (Overall and his witnesses denied this.) One of the referees at the game also testified that he saw Overall poke Kadella with his stick before Kadella attacked

him. The referee also stated that Kadella had been involved in three separate fights after the game and had been given three "game misconduct" penalties (a very serious penalty in hockey). The Appeals Court decided that the trial judge had the right to decide which witnesses to believe and obviously felt that Overall's witnesses had more credibility.

Kadella's other main argument on appeal was that Overall could not sue for battery because of consent—that he was voluntarily participating in a hockey game. This argument is expressed in the phrase *volenti non fit injuria*, or "he who consents cannot receive an injury."

The court noted that participation in a game does involve consent to those bodily contacts that are permitted by the rules of the game. "However, there is general agreement that an intentional act causing injury, which goes beyond what is ordinarily permissible, is an assault and battery for which recovery may be had."

Looking back at a number of decisions from earlier cases, the court particularly mentioned a 1975 Illinois case in which a soccer player had kicked the opposing goalkeeper in the head while he was holding the ball, causing serious injury. The Illinois court had rejected the argument that there was tort immunity for any injury that might occur during the course of a game. "It is our opinion that a player is liable for injury in a tort action if his conduct is such that it is either deliberate, wilful, or with a reckless disregard for the safety of the other player so as to cause injury to that player, the same being a question of fact to be decided by a jury." *Nabozny v. Barnhill,* 31 Ill. App. 3d 212, 215, 334 N.E. 2d 258, 260 (1975).

In this case the defendant's own witnesses agreed that the Michigan Amateur Hockey Association rules, in order to stop violence, specifically prohibit fighting. Furthermore, arguably the battery did not occur during the game at all, but after the game. Whatever consent to physical contact there was during the game did not apply after the game was over. The Appeals Court therefore affirmed the decision of the lower court.

CASE QUESTIONS

1. The jury heard conflicting evidence about whether Overall poked Kadella with his stick before the attack. If you believe the poking did occur, should this change the outcome? What if Overall called Kadella a dirty name?
2. If Overall had skated out and joined the free-for-all on the ice, instead of remaining on the bench, would the result be different?
3. Amateur hockey may be different, but in professional hockey, fighting is quite common even though it is against the rules. How can we fairly determine the point at which the penalty for fighting should be punished by hockey rules (5 or 10 minutes in the penalty box) and when it should be the subject of legal action in the court system? Write out what your standard would be.

Not only can physical injuries incurred in a hockey game result in tort actions, but in criminal cases as well. During the 2003–04 NHL hockey season, one player (Todd Bertuzzi of Vancouver) skated up behind another and punched him and then violently pushed him down head first onto the ice. The second player suffered serious injuries and criminal battery charges were brought against Mr. Bertuzzi.

DEFAMATION

defamation: The communication of damaging, false information about a person to at least one other person.

libel: Written defamation.

slander: Oral or verbal defamation.

Defamation, the communication of damaging, false information about someone to at least one other person, includes two subparts, *libel* and *slander*. If the statement is published (communicated) in written form, the tort is called **libel**; if it is published in oral form, the tort is called **slander**. The purpose of these torts is to protect one's reputation in the community and to impose liability on those who falsely damage another's character.

To prove defamation, the plaintiff must establish each element of the tort. The statement must be: (1) untrue, (2) of the type that will cause hurt and injury to the plaintiff or lower others' opinion of the plaintiff, (3) an intentional communication to at least one person other than the plaintiff, and (4) injurious (usually economically) to the plaintiff. For example, Michael can write a news article stating that Lee is a thief, as long as that is true. In addition, he can accuse Lee of theft, in private, even if it is untrue, and there is no defamation. But if he accuses Lee of theft in a staff meeting, and it is untrue, Lee may be able to sue for slander. Since Michael's statement would be false, of the type that would cause harm to Lee, and would be communicated to others, this would probably create a valid tort cause of action for defamation.

Certain types of statements can be made without fear of a defamation lawsuit. Statements made in court by the judge, attorneys, and witnesses are covered by an **absolute privilege.** This means that someone about whom a slanderous statement was made during the trial would not be able to sue for defamation. The same privilege applies to statements made by legislators during legislative proceedings. Why? Absolute privilege encourages the fullest possible expression of opinion and debate in certain limited circumstances. Within the legislature or the courtroom, a senator or attorney or witness can speak freely without fear of being sued if something said turns out not to be true. If the same statement was made just outside the courthouse or statehouse, however, the individual slandered could sue the speaker for defamation.

In a California case a few years ago, *Soliz v. Williams,* an appellate court refused to dismiss part of a libel action against a judge relating to his comments to a plaintiff in a pending case. Apparently Judge Alexander Williams III became angry at the settlement demands of plaintiff Robert Soliz and screamed at him in a settlement conference in a hallway outside the courtroom. The judge yelled at Mr. Soliz that if he thought there was money in the case, he "had sh.. for brains." Several days later the judge was interviewed by a news reporter and certain comments of his regarding Mr. Soliz were published in the *Los Angeles Daily Journal.*

Mr. Soliz sued Judge Williams for libel, but the lower court dismissed the case, based on the absolute privilege of a judge. The court of appeal upheld the dismissal for Judge Williams' comments in the hallway, finding that he was acting as a judge at that time. However, the appellate court allowed the libel case to go forward as to the comments in the newspaper. "Speaking to a reporter about a pending lawsuit is not a normal judicial function," and thus is not conduct protected by the privilege, ruled the court.

Other types of false or erroneous statements are protected by what is called a **qualified privilege.** This means that the person who made the statement may be protected in some situations but not in others. The usual requirement is that the person must have made the statement in good faith rather than with malice or with knowledge that what he said was false. The most common instance of qualified privilege occurs with regard to defamation suits by *public figures.* These are people who are in the public eye on a regular basis and have to expect that there will be many things said and written about them that may be untrue. For people such as politicians, sports stars, and entertainment figures to win defamation suits, they must prove all the regular elements of the case as described previously. They must also show that the defendant published the statement *with malicious intent* or *knowledge that what was said was false* at the time the statement was made. This rule recognizes the public interest in information (yes, even gossip) about well-known people and makes it more difficult for them to win defamation suits.

However, sometimes even television stars can win cases where the defamation is particularly outrageous. For example, in a well-known 1983 decision, actress Carol Burnett won a judgment against the *National Enquirer.* The news tabloid had published an article stating that she was drunk and boisterous in a Washington, D.C., restaurant and had engaged in a loud argument with Henry Kissinger. However, she proved that neither of these statements were true. The *Enquirer* never bothered to check the accuracy of a report from a freelance tipster and, in addition, editors embellished the report without any factual basis whatsoever. [*See Burnett v. National Enquirer, Inc.,* 144 Cal. App. 3d 991 (1983).]

absolute privilege: Protection from liability for slander or libel given under certain circumstances regardless of the fact that the statements are false or maliciously made.

qualified privilege: Protection from liability for defamatory statements only if the defendant uttered them without actual malice or had a good reason for doing so.

The growth of Internet blogging and social media, such as Twitter and Facebook, has resulted in a series of recent cases involving online defamation. The following article considers the pitfalls of posting comments on Twitter, in which the speaker is limited to only 140 characters within which to make a statement.

Libel by Twitter? The Suit Against Kim Kardashian Over the "Cookie Diet"

Twitter's famous 140-character limit for "tweets"—that is, posted comments—has a number of advantages, such as allowing readers to access succinct updates about people and events they are following, in something close to real time.

But the limit may also have a serious—and probably unanticipated—downside: It may make Twitter a trap for the unwary when it comes to libel suits.

In this column, I'll consider the suit that was recently filed against Kim Kardashian, based on her negative comments about the COOKIE DIET®, as a possible example of that trap.

The Lawsuit, and the Statements at Issue

On December 28, Dr. Sanford Siegal filed a defamation complaint against Kardashian in state court in Florida, on behalf of himself and the company through which he distributes his COOKIE DIET® products.

The choice of Florida isn't surprising: Siegal resides in Florida, and most defamation suits are brought where the plaintiff resides—on the ground that his or her reputation is centered there. Moreover, Siegal's company is a Florida corporation.

Readers may wonder if it's fair for California resident Kardashian to be forced to go to Florida to litigate. But case law suggests that it does not violate constitutional due process to require a resident of another state to come to Florida for a lawsuit, when the suit's allegation is that she directed a tortious comment toward a plaintiff known to reside in Florida.

The basic idea is that if you target someone in Florida, you can be required to resolve that dispute in Florida. (The problem with this idea, though, is that if the comment turns out not to be libelous, then the defendant still has had to bear the cost and inconvenience of the Florida forum, for no good reason.)

The beginning of the complaint against Kardashian chronicles what seems to have been a misunderstanding: A third party claimed, in an online article, that Kardashian had been on Siegal's diet. Siegal's site then linked to the third party's article.

Then, the use of the link led Kardashian to post the following two tweets:

"Dr. Siegal's Cookie Diet is falsely promoting that I'm on this diet. NOT TRUE! I would never do this unhealthy diet! I do Quick Trim!"

"If this Dr. Siegal is lying about me being on this diet, what else are they lying about? Not cool!"

If Kardashian had not claimed that the diet was "unhealthy," it seems likely that an agreed-upon joint statement could have resolved this dispute. Apparently, Siegal and his company made an honest mistake in relying on (and linking to) third-party statements claiming Kardashian was on the diet. Then, it seems that Kardashian, in turn, made an honest mistake in taking Siegal's honest mistake to be an outright lie.

Thus, a brief joint statement noting that everyone involved agrees that Kardashian has never been on Siegal's diet, and that no one did anything wrong, might have been the end of the matter.

But there's little chance of a joint statement now—for the "unhealthy" claim opened another can of worms, as I will explain.

Is Calling a Product "Unhealthy" a Statement of Fact, or of Opinion?
Most of us toss around words like "unhealthy" every day without thinking much about it. But when it comes to libel law, such words can be bombshells that trigger liability.

That's because such words tread the boundary between statements of opinion—which generally cannot be the basis for a libel suit—and statements of fact, which can trigger high-dollar liability.

Was Kardashian's comment a First-Amendment-protected statement of opinion, or a liability-risking statement of fact? It's hard to say.

Imagine a diet that simply counseled dieters to substitute almonds for their daily snack of potato chips or the like. Calling that diet "unhealthy" would, I believe, be a false statement of fact. That's because it is pretty much universally believed that almonds are healthier than potato chips. It's a no-brainer.

Now, imagine a diet that counseled dieters to replace one meal a day with a protein shake. Calling that diet "unhealthy" would, I believe, be a statement of opinion, since reasonable minds can differ on whether a protein shake is a sufficient replacement for a regular meal.

In turn, I believe that the question whether Dr. Siegal's diet is healthy is closer to the protein shake example, than to the almonds/potato chips example. Dr. Siegal may well be right that his diet is healthy, but the answer to that question is not a complete no-brainer—an issue as to which reasonable persons could not differ. Instead, it takes some analysis and evidence to get to the conclusion.

For that reason, I think Kardashian is apt to win the lawsuit, on the grounds that when she used the word "unhealthy," she was stating an opinion, not a fact. Indeed, a Google search reveals a range of opinion, pro and con, as to whether the cookie diet is unhealthy.

However, I could also see a court saying that healthfulness is a practical fact: Either the diet, over time, has improved the health of those who used it, or it hasn't. If it has, the judge might say, then it's healthful.

The complexity here comes from the fact that the diet's cookies might not be as healthy as, say, fresh vegetables, but if eating the cookies ends obesity for some dieters, then the diet's overall effect could still be termed healthful.

Overall, I think a court is more likely to see healthfulness as a matter of opinion, not a matter of fact (except at the extremes). Still, Kardashian would have been better-protected, from a libel standpoint, if she had cited some true facts regarding Dr. Siegal's diet as the basis for her opinion.

Doing so would have meant that her comments would have fit into a special, ironclad libel-law privilege for "opinion based on disclosed fact."

The idea behind the privilege is that if the facts stated are true, then the reader can decide for himself or herself whether the opinion that is stated really follows from them or not.

The classic example goes like this: "John had three drinks at lunch today. He did the same yesterday. Thus, I believe he is an alcoholic."

It's easy to see why a lawsuit based on these comments should fail: The listener can independently judge whether he agrees with the conclusion that John is an alcoholic—and can draw his or her own conclusions, perhaps commenting "John may have a problem, but his behavior at two lunches isn't enough to conclude he's an addict."

The Danger of Twitter: Little Space to Reveal the Facts Behind a Statement of Opinion in a Single Tweet

That point brings us to the danger of Twitter: One hundred and forty characters, the limit for a tweet, simply isn't enough to spell out the facts behind an opinion. Granted, a follow-up tweet might be provided as a clarification—but will courts allow a succession of tweets to come under the privilege for "opinion based on disclosed fact"? I wouldn't bet on it.

On one hand, any Twitter follower will have access to all the tweets that have been sent by a given sender. On the other hand, there's no guarantee that the follower will read the relevant tweets all together—or will read all of them. Instead, some followers may check in periodically, reading whatever comment is most current on the feed. As a result, courts may find that later tweets may mitigate damages—reducing what losing defendants must pay—or constitute retractions, but are unlikely to see later tweets as a reason to dismiss the suit.

The bottom line, then, is that no one—celebrity or not—is well-advised to have a fight on Twitter in which potentially or borderline libelous comments are made. And for deep-pocketed celebrities like Kardashian, that advice goes double. Defending an opinion is much easier when it is coupled with a series of strong, true supporting facts, but Twitter may not allow enough space to effectively provide them.

Julie Hilden, who graduated from Yale Law School, practiced First Amendment law at the D.C. law firm of Williams & Connolly from 1996–99 and has been writing about First Amendment issues for a decade. Hilden's article "A Contractarian View of Animal Rights: Insuring Against the Possibility of Being a Non-Human Animal" appeared in the journal *Animal Law* and can be found on her website.

Source: Julie Hilden, http://writ.1pfindlaw.com/hilden/20100104.html. January 4, 2010.

> **INTERNATIONAL VIEW**
>
> Legal concepts often differ significantly from one country to another. After an argument over a parking space, a court in Trieste, Italy ruled in 2004 that a driver who told a parking attendant "You are nobody" had committed slander, and imposed a fine of 300 Euros ($370). The court ruled that the phrase means precisely that "you are a nonentity" and to state such a thing is offensive and damaging to the dignity of that person. In another case in Italy a court ruled that the phrase "bail breaker" was not slander because although rude, it is an expression "now in common use."

Source: FindLaw.com, July 9, 2004.

Defamation cases often arise in business in connection with the giving of job references and recommendations. For example, when Rebecca applies for a job, she will usually be asked for the names of her previous supervisors. Some of her previous employment experiences may not have gone as well as she would have liked (after all, she is looking for a new job!). Suppose that a former boss tells the prospective employer some unfavorable things about Rebecca, perhaps magnifying the actions that caused her dismissal or confusing Rebecca with another employee who left about the same time after failing a drug test. Assuming that Rebecca does not get the new job, what sort of liability for defamation does the former employer have? Are any defenses available to the employer? Generally, employers have a qualified privilege regarding defamatory statements about a current or former employee made to a person who has a legitimate interest in the information, such as a prospective employer. However, most courts have held that the statement must be made without malice, i.e., without knowledge that it is false, for the employer to escape liability.

FALSE IMPRISONMENT

As one court put it, "false imprisonment is the intentional, unlawful, and unconsented restraint by one person of the physical liberty of another." In order for this tort to occur, the defendant must intentionally restrain the plaintiff, who must realize that his or her freedom has been impaired. Many false imprisonment cases have resulted when retail stores have detained suspected shoplifters. Shoplifting is a major concern, and retail stores have developed various ways to combat this problem, including one-way mirrors, secret cameras, and plain-clothed store security personnel. When a person is suspected of shoplifting, the store will generally try to apprehend the customer, conduct questioning, and examine the questionable items in a private room somewhere on the premises.

false imprisonment: The intentional, unlawful, and unconsented restraint by one person of the physical liberty of another.

This situation—where a person is apprehended and held against his or her will by the store—can obviously lead to a lawsuit for false imprisonment when the accused person is innocent. To avoid some litigation and provide retailers with some latitude in fighting shoplifting, many states have passed statutes giving merchants the legal right to detain suspected individuals for a reasonable time and in a reasonable manner. For example, read the Iowa law set out below.

> **IOWA CODE ANNOTATED**
>
> **Section 808.12 Detention and Search in Theft of Library Materials and Shoplifting**
>
> 1. Persons concealing property . . . may be detained and searched by a peace officer, person employed in a facility containing library materials, merchant, or merchant's employee, provided that the detention is for a reasonable length of time and that the search is conducted in a reasonable manner by a person of the same sex and according to subsection 2 of this section.
>
> 2. No search of the person under this section shall be conducted by any person other than someone acting under the direction of a peace officer except where permission of the one to be searched has first been obtained.
>
> 3. The detention or search under this section by a peace officer, person employed in a facility containing library materials, merchant, or merchant's employee does not render the person liable, in a criminal or civil action, for false arrest or false imprisonment, provided the person conducting the search had reasonable grounds to believe the person detained or searched had concealed or was attempting to conceal property as set forth in section 714.5 [which defines shoplifting].

Therefore, in most states, statutes allow merchants to detain suspected shoplifters for a "reasonable period of time" if the detention is handled "in a reasonable manner." Furthermore, there must have been "reasonable grounds to believe" that the person had concealed the item, in order for the later detention to be valid. If the store observes all these "reasonable" precautions, it should not be liable even if the accused person is innocent. The normal process is to question the individual for a short period of time in private and allow him or her to produce a receipt or other indication that the item was not shoplifted. If there is no such proof, the police will be called promptly and charges filed. However, if the merchant's employees treat the shopper roughly, hold the person a long time without calling the police or asking the accused to prove his or her innocence, or if they have no good basis for stopping the suspect in the first place, the merchant may be liable for the tort of false imprisonment.

NEGLIGENCE—AN UNINTENTIONAL TORT

negligence: The most common type of tort. It involves a person causing injury to another, by doing some action with less than the amount of care expected of a "reasonable person."

Negligence is the most important type of unintentional tort, and it is no doubt the most significant category of tort suit in our court system. Negligence law has had a major effect on business. The legal principles concerning what actions constitute negligent conduct have developed through numerous court decisions, involving every type of situation imaginable. Negligence is the epitome of the common law legal process. The essence of negligence is "fault"—that is, that someone did something without exercising reasonable care or failed to do something that we would have expected a reasonable person to do in that exact situation, with the direct result being an injury to another person.

ELEMENTS OF NEGLIGENCE

Four elements must be present to hold a defendant liable for negligence: (1) duty, (2) breach of that duty, (3) actual and proximate cause, and (4) injury to another. *Duty* means that the defendant owed some type of legal obligation to the plaintiff. If the defendant did not meet his or her duty to act reasonably, this is called *breach*. If the failure to meet the standard resulted directly in foreseeable *injury* to someone else, this is *actual and proximate cause* of the *injury*. Let us examine each element in more detail.

DUTY OF CARE AND BREACH OF DUTY

The legal duty involved in negligence cases need not flow from any previous relationship between the parties (although sometimes that is the case). Hundreds of court decisions have established the general principle that everyone must take reasonable care in all actions so as not to injure another person. Each of us has the duty to act as a jury feels a mythical "reasonable person" would act in any given situation. This is called the *reasonable person* standard. Hence, if Rachel is riding her bicycle across campus, she has the duty (whether she knows it or not) to operate her bike in a reasonably careful manner in order not to injure others. She owes this duty of care to everyone she might encounter on her ride.

If Rachel does not meet this standard—if, for example, she steers with her feet while looking sideways—a court probably will find that she breached (fell below) her duty to operate her bike in a reasonably careful manner in accordance with the standards of the mythical "reasonable person."

PROXIMATE CAUSE AND INJURY

Even though Rachel may have failed to meet the appropriate standard of care, she will not face a negligence suit unless the other two elements are present. Fortunately for all of us, most of the time no one is injured when we are negligent or careless. But when our failure to meet the standard of care of a "reasonable person" does *actually* and *proximately* cause an *injury* to another person, then all the elements of negligence have been established.

The negligence must directly cause the injury. This is sometimes referred to as *causation in fact*. For example, if Rachel's careless bicycle riding caused her to smash into and break the leg of an older business law professor who was slowly walking across campus, she might well be found liable of negligence. Many cases apply the "but for" test to determine actual cause—that is, whether the injury would have occurred "but for" the negligence of the defendant.

proximate cause:
One of the key elements of a negligence case is that the plantiff's injury was a "foreseeable" result of the defendant's lack of care.

The second part of the causation requirement, **proximate cause,** hinges on a question of *foreseeability*. Negligence cases often are won or lost on the determination of proximate cause questions. Suppose in the preceding example that Rachel had recently had her bike repaired at a cycle shop and while riding across campus, one of the wheels came off. As she began falling to the ground, the books she was carrying were thrown toward the sidewalk, right in front of Dwayne, who was riding a skateboard. Dwayne swerved to miss the books, running into Tom, who screamed, "Look out!" Some 20 yards away, the professor, startled by the scream, tripped on the steps of the Business Building, breaking his leg. What is the proximate cause of the accident? Can the cycle shop be held liable for its negligence? In resolving such questions, courts often apply a *foreseeability* test—that is, "was the injury that occurred within the range of harm that should have been foreseeable to the person who is being charged with negligence?"

Suppose that a negligence suit by the professor against the cycle shop arises from the facts set forth previously. Whether Rachel or any of the other players in this drama are liable to the professor depends upon an analysis of the elements of negligence—first, whether they were negligent, and then, if so, whether that negligence was an actual and proximate cause of the professor's injuries. The professor argues that the failure to properly tighten the wheel was a breach of the duty of care, since a reasonably careful bicycle shop would have made sure that the wheels were in good order before turning the bike over to Rachel. The professor also claims that "but for" the shop's failure to tighten the wheel properly after repairing the bike, the accident would not have occurred. Furthermore, the professor argues that his injuries were a foreseeable and proximate result of this negligence. It is quite possible, however, that the court will conclude that the series of events were too remote and "unforeseeable" to make the bike shop liable for the professor's injuries—in other words, that its negligence was not the "proximate cause" of the injuries.

Sometimes the owners or managers of property have been sued for negligence due to the criminal acts of third persons. It is not unusual for a landlord to face a negligence suit after a tenant is injured by the assault of a criminal. The general allegation made in these cases is that because of some negligent act that the landlord took or did not take (such as failing to repair broken locks on the building or not replacing lights that had burned out in the entryway or parking lot), the landlord had not met the standard of care expected of a reasonable building owner and was at least partly the direct cause of the injury to the tenant.

Supermarkets and large stores such as K-Mart and Wal-Mart have been sued for negligence as the result of robberies, assaults, and murders that have taken place in their parking lots on occasion. Sometimes the victims win if it is shown that the store management knew or should have known that crimes had taken place in their parking lots earlier, and they had done nothing to try to prevent such crimes from occurring in the future. Most of the time, the stores win because the courts find that the "proximate cause" of the damages was actually the criminal act. But the case result can turn on the amount of knowledge possessed by the store and whether the actions it took were "reasonable." It is possible for there to be two "proximate causes" of the accident. Issues such as this have have been the subject of many recent tort lawsuits.

Often a negligence case involves the question of whether a restaurant or other retail establishment met its "duty of care" to customers who enter the store to shop. Thousands of so-called "slip and fall" cases have been filed against all types of stores in all states. Sometimes the store wins, and sometimes the customer does, depending on the facts of the case. These are classic negligence cases, with the result turning on the analysis by the court and the jury of the exact duty of the store to its customers, whether the duty was met, and if not, whether the "fault" of the store was the proximate cause of the plaintiff's injuries. Also important is the question of whether the plaintiff was also negligent, and if so, if that negligence contributed to the accident. The following case is an example of a typical "slip and fall" case.

AGUSTA COUNTRY CLUB, INC. V. BLAKE

634 SE 2nd 812 (2006)

FACTS

One morning in November 2000, on a "beautiful windless day," Linda Blake was visiting the Augusta Country Club for the first time to participate in a tennis match. Walking toward the tennis court down a bricked path, she passed under a magnolia tree. She was walking with friends and focused on the tennis courts ahead, not looking down at the pathway as she walked. Stopping briefly at the top of two steps, she noticed magnolia seeds on the pathway, but she did not see any on the steps before her. She specifically did not see a pod lying at the base of the second step because it was obstructed from her view. Proceeding ahead, her right foot stepped directly onto the pod on the second step, causing her to fall and suffer serious injury.

Blake filed a negligence suit against the Augusta Country Club, alleging that the club had negligently failed to maintain a safe walkway. After all evidence had been introduced, Augusta moved for a directed verdict in its favor, which the judge denied. The jury then returned a verdict in favor of Blake, awarding her $78,000 in compensatory damages. Augusta appealed to the George Court of Appeals.

DECISION

The appellate court first reviewed the law regarding the duty of landowners to invitees. "The owner/occupier is not required to warrant the safety of all persons from all things, but to exercise the diligence toward making the premises safe that a good business person is accustomed to use in such matters. This includes inspecting the premises to discover possible dangerous conditions of which the owner/occupier does not have actual knowledge, and taking reasonable precautions to protect invitees from dangers foreseeable from the arrangement or use of the premises."

The court also noted that landowners may have "constructive knowledge" of a hazard in certain circumstances. "Constructive knowledge of a hazard may be shown in at least two ways. First, where evidence shows that the hazard was on the walkway for a sufficient length of time that it would have been discovered and removed had the owner exercised reasonable care in inspecting the premises, constructive knowledge may be inferred when there is evidence that the owner lacked a reasonable inspection procedure. Second, even if the owner had a reasonable inspection procedure, constructive knowledge may be inferred in these circumstances if evidence shows that the owner failed to follow that inspection procedure."

Analyzing this issue, the Court of Appeals noted that the Club was aware that the magnolia pods were a "huge maintenance problem." The Club's tennis director had previously instructed employees to blow off the walkway between 7:00 am and 9:00 am each day. The director was also supposed to inspect the walkway each morning when he arrived. However, the court noted that the evidence showed that in reality, these duties were done only occasionally, and not every day.

On the morning of Ms. Blake's injury, no inspection had been done. The tennis director did not come to the club at all, but instead relied upon his assistant supervisor to do the inspection. However, the assistant supervisor arrived at the Club at 8:30 and went directly to the tennis shop without inspecting the walkway. Although the employee who had the responsibility for blowing off the walkways testified in court that he had blown off the walkway on this particular morning, and that he had told the assistant supervisor when he was finished, all other evidence contradicted his testimony. The assistant supervisor testified that she did not hear from this employee that he had blown off the walkway, nor did she see the walkway being cleared after she arrived at 8:30 am. Moreover, on the morning of the accident, the employee had been preoccupied with other maintenance personnel repairing a burst water pipe. Finally, several other Club patrons who were at the Club on that morning testified that the walkway under the magnolia trees was covered with debris, including branches, leaves, and seed pods covering the area.

Based upon this evidence, the Court held that the jury could easily have concluded that the Club did not maintain a reasonable inspection procedure, and that even if it had, that procedure had not been followed on the morning Ms. Clark was injured.

The Club also argued that it had no duty to remove the magnolia pods because they "accu-mulated on the property as a naturally occurring condition." However, the court noted that even naturally occurring conditions require a landowner to exercise ordinary care in inspecting the premises.

Finally, the Club argued that Ms. Blake contributed to her own injuries by failing to exercise ordinary care for her personal safety. However, the court held that in such cases, the plaintiff must have knowledge of the specific hazard which causes a fall, not merely knowledge of the general hazardous conditions. "Blake presented evidence that she did not see the particular seed pod that caused her fall inasmuch as it lay at the base of the second step in an area not visible to her from her standing perspective because of the lip of the second step. In addition to being unfamiliar with fallings from magnolia trees, she also denied knowing of the presence of the debris generally other than viewing a few seed pods on the patio as she was descending the steps." The Court thus affirmed the jury's verdict in favor of Ms. Blake.

CASE QUESTIONS

1. What was the "duty of care" that the Club had to its customers? What exactly did the Club do, or not do, that breached its duty?
2. Did the assistant supervisor or anyone else at the Club actually know that there was a magnolia pod on the second step leading down from the walkway? Why did the Club have "constructive knowledge" of the magnolia pod?
3. Suppose there had been proof that the magnolia pod had only been on the step for five minutes before Ms. Blake fell. Would the Club still have been negligent? Why or why not?
4. Do you agree that Ms. Blake did not contribute to her own injury?
5. Does the legal rule imposing a duty of care on commercial establishments such as the Augusta Country Club serve a public purpose? Discuss.

As we learned in Chapter 8, often business firms are held liable for the actions of their employees. In the past few years there have been an increasing number of cases which concerned possible negligence on the part of drivers who were using cell phones. Do you think that driving a car while talking on a cell phone meets the standard of conduct of the "reasonably prudent" driver?

CELL PHONES CAN LEAD TO LIABILITY

The increasing use of cell phones while driving has led to many negligence lawsuits. How many times recently have you seen a person driving a car while holding a cell phone in one hand and talking? Does that action breach the "duty of care" of a reasonably careful driver? Several cases have held that to be the case, while others have required more proof of negligence. To date, several states, such as Connecticut, California, and Minnesota, have passed statutes which prohibit cell phone use, including text messaging, while driving. Additionally, as you learned in Chapter 8, sometimes a company can be held liable under the theory of *respondeat superior* for harm caused by an employee's negligence. Several recent courts have extended this to cases involving employee cell phone use.

DEFENSES TO NEGLIGENCE

Three main legal theories have been used to defend against negligence cases. One traditional defense is called **contributory negligence.** To claim this defense, the party charged with negligence argues that the accident or injury was at least partially caused by the negligence of the plaintiff. In other words, the negligence of the plaintiff "contributed to" the injury. This doctrine developed through the common law during the 1800s and served to protect the interests of businesses against suits by workers and others. Under the strict application of this rule, *any* negligence by the plaintiff (even if small) that contributed to the accident completely barred the plaintiff from recovery against the defendant. This was true even if the defendant was clearly negligent.

For example, suppose Richard is driving down Broadway Avenue in his 1999 Ford. He knows that his brakes are bad but has not had time to get them fixed. In addition, his windshield is covered with ice, but he is in a hurry and has not cleaned it off. After a "rolling stop" at the corner of Broadway and Longmont Streets in her 2002 Porsche, Mary Lou pulls out onto Broadway several hundred feet in front of Richard. He fails to see her at first. When he does, his brakes fail, and he runs into Mary Lou, causing damage to her car. In a lawsuit by Mary Lou against Richard, the jury might find that Richard's negligence was 80 percent of the cause of the accident and Mary Lou's was 20 percent. However, if that state follows the contributory negligence rule, Mary Lou's case will be dismissed, and she will get nothing.

contributory negligence: A defense to negligence that asserts that the plaintiff was also negligent. If applied, this defense results in dismissal of the case.

comparative negligence: A defense to negligence that calls for the jury to assess ("compare") the negligence of the plaintiff and the defendant, and adjust the damages to reflect the percentage of negligence of the plaintiff.

Because of the harshness of this rule, during the past 25 years most states have enacted statutes replacing contributory negligence with a similar principle called **comparative negligence.** Using this doctrine, a jury compares the negligence of the plaintiff and the defendant and awards the plaintiff a recovery reduced by the amount of his or her negligence. In the previously described situation, for example, if Mary Lou had established damages of $10,000, the jury would award her a judgment of $8,000 under a comparative negligence standard. In other words, the jury would reduce the amount of her recovery by the percentage she was at fault (20 percent in our example).

Most state statutes follow a *modified comparative negligence* rule which allows the plaintiff to recover damages until his or her negligence reaches 50 percent of the cause. When the plaintiff is at least equally at fault with the defendant, modified comparative negligence statutes would cut off his right to recover anything. A few states, however, have adopted a *pure comparative negligence* rule and allow the plaintiff to recover damages if the defendant is negligent at all, reduced by the appropriate percentage of the plaintiff's negligence. (That is, if the defendant was 25 percent negligent and the plaintiff 75 percent, the plaintiff could still recover 25 percent of the damages.)

SOCIAL/ETHICAL ISSUES

Which of the two defenses—contributory or comparative negligence—do you think is more socially and ethically correct? Is it fair or just to completely deprive a person of any recovery against a negligent person, just because he or she was a little bit negligent himself? Or is it more fair or just to allow a person to sue and win a damage award against another even if his or her negligence was a 30 percent cause of the accident? Which theory better accommodates business? Which one is better for society?

assumption of the risk: A defense to negligence that asserts that the plaintiff voluntarily and knowingly accepted the risks of the activity causing the injury.

Another long-recognized defense to a negligence lawsuit is called **assumption of the risk.** This theory holds that if a person *voluntarily* undertakes an activity *knowing* exactly what risks are involved, he or she cannot sue later for injuries incurred. To successfully use the defense, however, the defendant must show that the plaintiff actually knew and understood the risk. When you attend a major league baseball game, for example, you probably assume the risk that a ball may be hit into the stands. However, you do not assume the risk that the walkway leading to your seat will be negligently constructed and maintained and will collapse when stepped on. In some states assumption of the risk is just one of the factors to be considered in allocating the comparative negligence percentages.

The following case involves the legal issue of whether the assumption of risk doctrine should apply to injuries suffered by a young man as the result of a collision between two Sea-Doo personal watercraft. The California Court of Appeals analyzes the facts of the accident in detail and fully discusses the rationale behind the assumption of the risk doctrine. The Court mentions briefly that there are two types of assumption of risk in California, but mainly focuses on what it calls "primary assumption of risk," which is in fact what most courts simply call "assumption of risk."

In the Language of the Court

PEART V. FERRO

13 Col. Rptr. 3d 885 (Cal.App. 2004)

Opinion written by Judge MCGUINESS

FACTS

The accident at issue in this case involved the use of two Sea-Doo personal watercraft. A Sea-Doo is similar to a jet ski in its operation, differing only in that it is equipped with a seat similar to that of a motorcycle upon which the operator generally sits rather than stands. Defendant Ferro owned a model XP Sea-Doo; his mother, respondent Julie Ferro, owned a model GTI Sea-Doo. The model XP was a two-person vehicle, had approximately 110 horse-power, and could go 60 to 65 miles per hour. The model GTI was larger, could seat three people, and had a smaller engine with 90 horsepower that could go 50 to 55 miles per hour. The Ferros kept the two Sea-Doos at their vacation residence at Clear Lake in Lake County. Ferro himself had "[q]uite frequently" instructed guests in how to operate the Sea-Doos.

On July 10, 2000, appellant Adam Peart and his cousin Jason, were visiting at Ferro's Clear Lake residence. At the time, Peart and Jason were 16 and 13 years old, respectively. Peart told Ferro that although he had never operated a sit-down Sea-Doo before, he had previously used stand-up jet skis by himself, and therefore had experience with that kind of personal watercraft. Jason told Ferro he had ridden on a sit-down Sea-Doo before, and had taken a boating class through Boy or Cub scouts. Ferro did not ask Jason if he had ever operated a Sea-Doo by himself.

Peart and Jason wanted to ride the Sea-Doos. When Jason asked his mother if he could, she told him to ask Ferro. According to Jason, Ferro said: "They are not toys; they are just to have fun on, not to fool around on." He agreed that the two boys could ride, and explained to them how to operate the Sea-Doos. Among other things, Ferro told Peart to wear the key on a bracelet, how to use the key to start the Sea-

Doo, and how to make turns. He also told Peart and Jason always to wear safety jackets. Aside from telling the boys about the 5-miles-per-hour zone extending approximately 100 feet from the dock to the buoys, Ferro did not discuss the speed at which they should travel on the lake, the route to follow, or how long to stay out.

Ferro knew that an individual had to be at least 16 years of age in order legally to operate a Sea-Doo alone, and minors 12 years and older were only permitted to operate a Sea-Doo when accompanied by an adult. Consequently, he allowed Peart to operate one of the two Sea-Doos, and volunteered to accompany Jason on the other. Ferro, Peart and Jason were all wearing life vests.

At approximately 3:00 p.m., Peart departed from the dock on one of the Sea-Doos. Ferro observed that Peart was going under 5 miles per hour up until he reached the buoys. Within a minute, Ferro and Jason left the dock on the other Sea-Doo, with Jason driving and Ferro behind him as passenger. At first, Jason followed the same direction that Peart had taken. Once they passed the limits of the 5-miles-per-hour zone, Jason accelerated to approximately 35 miles per hour.

For a while, Peart drove his Sea-Doo around the lake, accelerating and making turns. Jason and Ferro simply maintained a straight course without turning. After a while, Peart began to cut back and forth across the wake of the Sea-Doo driven by Jason and Ferro, coming less than 100 feet behind them. Feeling that Peart was "cutting it a little close," Ferro tried to signal to Peart to "push off a little further" from them. Peart maneuvered his Sea-Doo about 200 feet away and alongside Ferro and Jason. Then, as Jason and Ferro maintained a speed of approximately 30 miles per hour, Peart accelerated to approximately 45 to 50 miles per hour and pulled directly in front of them, again about 200 feet away. Ferro saw Peart start to make a complete turn, first moving to the right and then veering sharply to the left and directly across their path. Peart "sort of disappeared behind [a] wall of water" caused by the 180 degree turn. When Peart reappeared almost immediately thereafter, he was directly in front of them and only 75 feet away. Ferro told Jason to "[t]urn." Less than 2 seconds later, the Sea-Doo they were riding collided with Peart's Sea-Doo.

In deposition testimony, Peart said he had decided to make a U-turn and go back to the dock. As he slowed down and started to make his turn, the Sea-Doo he was operating stalled or "shut off." Peart tried unsuccessfully to restart the engine. The next thing he knew, he was waking up in the hospital.

The Peart family filed this lawsuit against defendants Ferro, Julie Ferro, his cousin Jason, and the Ferro Family Trust, alleging that Peart had been seriously and permanently injured, and had incurred substantial and ongoing costs and expenses for medical care and treatment, "[a]s a direct and legal result of the carelessness and negligence" of respondents "and each of them."

All of the defendants filed answers, asserting among other things the affirmative defense of assumption of risk. All the respondents filed a motion for summary judgment on the ground that the affirmative defense of assumption of risk acted as a complete bar to all of appellants' claims. The Plaintiff-Appellants filed opposition to the motion for summary judgment, arguing among other things that riding a Sea-Doo in a public venue was not an activity subject to the doctrine of assumption of risk; and there were material disputed issues of fact with regard to whether respondent Ferro was subject to an additional duty not to increase the risk of harm to appellant Peart because he was instructing minor Jason in the operation of the Sea-Doo.

The trial court entered an order granting respondents' motion for summary judgment ". . . on the basis of undisputed evidence showing that appellants' action was barred in its entirety and as a matter of law by the doctrine of primary assumption of risk." The trial court found that Sea-Doo riding was a "sport" within the meaning of that doctrine, because it was an activity akin to water skiing or inner tubing performed "for enjoyment or thrill, [that] requires physical exertion as well as elements of skill, and involves a challenge containing a potential risk of injury." The trial court specifically found that "[t]he existence of obstacles in the environment, such as spraying water, wakes to be crossed and other watercraft to be passed, [were] part of the thrill of the sport," and that Peart "was not using the Sea-Doo merely as a means of transportation." Noting that appellants had "offered no evidence that [respondents'] behavior was intentional or reckless, or increased the risks to [Peart] over and above those inherent in the sport," the trial court concluded that "collisions between sea-doo riders are such a risk."

Because of the sporting nature of the activity, the doctrine of assumption of risk was applicable, making immaterial any factual issue as to whether respondents were careless or negligent in operating or supervising the operation of the Sea-Doo. The trial court also found that the statutes cited by appellants manifested no intent to supersede the existing doctrine of primary assumption of risk as applied to sporting activities such as those at issue. On April 30, 2002, the trial court entered summary judgment in favor of respondents and against appellants. This appeal was timely and properly filed.

DECISION

In this case, the trial court granted respondents' motion for summary judgment on the basis of its finding that respondents had met their burden of establishing that appellants' complaint was completely barred as a matter of law by the defense of primary assumption of risk. Appellants' central contention is that the trial court erred in applying the doctrine of primary assumption of risk to this case, because respondents failed to bear their burden of establishing that the doctrine of primary assumption of risk applies to the recreational activity at issue in this case.

Under general principles of negligence law, "persons have a duty to use due care to avoid injury to others, and may be held liable if their careless conduct injures another person." Nevertheless, in certain cases of injury resulting from participation in a given activity, the doctrine of assumption of risk may operate as a complete bar to recovery "where, by virtue of the nature of the activity and the parties' relationship to the activity, the defendant owes no legal duty to protect the plaintiff from the particular risk of harm that caused the injury."

The term "assumption of risk" has been used in connection with two classes of cases: those in which the issue is whether the defendant actually owed the plaintiff a duty of care (primary assumption of risk); and those in which it has been determined that the defendant breached a duty of care, and the remaining issue is whether the plaintiff chose to face the risk of harm created by the defendant's breach of duty (secondary assumption of risk). In the latter class of cases, the plaintiff's knowing and voluntary acceptance of the risk functions as a form of contributory negligence which does not operate as a complete bar to recovery, but may be resolved by applying principles of comparative fault. In the former class (primary assumption of risk) on the other hand, the plaintiff's claim is completely barred as a matter of law because of a legal determination that the defendant did not owe any duty to protect the plaintiff from the particular risk of harm involved in the claim. In short, the doctrine of primary assumption of risk "embodies a legal conclusion that there is 'no duty' on the part of the defendant to protect the plaintiff from a particular risk."

As relevant to this case, the common law doctrine of primary assumption of risk has been used as a complete defense in personal injury lawsuits arising from any particular sports activity that "is done for enjoyment or thrill, requires physical exertion as well as elements of skill, and involves a challenge containing a potential risk of injury." The overriding consideration in the application of primary assumption of risk is to avoid imposing a duty which might chill vigorous participation in the implicated activity and thereby alter its fundamental nature.' [Citation] Thus, the doctrine has been

applied specifically to sports and sport-related activities involving physical skill and challenges posing significant risk of injury to participants in such activities, and as to which the absence of such a defense would chill vigorous participation in the sporting activity and have a deleterious effect on the nature of the sport as a whole.

As the [California] Supreme Court has emphasized, application of the primary assumption of risk doctrine is "a legal determination that the defendant did not owe a duty to protect the plaintiff from the particular risk of harm involved in the claim." Whether a given defendant owed a legal duty to protect a plaintiff from a particular risk of harm, or whether instead the primary assumption of risk doctrine is to be applied, is a question of law that "depends on the nature of the sport or activity in question and on the parties' general relationship to the activity."

In making this determination, a court looks first at the nature of the sporting activity at issue to determine what conditions, conduct or risks that might be viewed as dangerous in other contexts are so integral to or inherent in the activity itself that imposing a duty of care would either require that an essential aspect of the sport abandoned, or else discourage vigorous participation therein. In such cases, defendants generally do not have a duty to protect a plaintiff from the inherent risks of the sport, or to eliminate all risk from the sport. On the other hand, defendants do have a duty not to increase the risk of harm beyond what is inherent in the sport through intentional or reckless behavior that is completely outside the range of the ordinary activity in the sport.

In addition to examining the inherent nature of the sport, a court must consider the relationship of the parties themselves to the sporting activity. Duties with respect to the same risk may vary depending on what role was played in the sporting activity by a particular defendant, whether that role be as co-participant, passive observer, instructor, coach, owner of the venue in which the sport is played, or supplier of the equipment used in the sport. Accordingly, the general duty of due care to avoid injury to others does not apply to co-participants in sporting activities with respect to conditions and conduct that might otherwise be viewed as dangerous but upon examination are seen to be an integral part of the sport itself.

In the recent case of *Whelihan,* the California court of appeal was presented with the question whether the personal use of jet skis was an active sport to which the primary assumption of risk doctrine was applicable. Noting that previous cases had determined that the doctrine of primary assumption of risk applied to several similar personal, noncompetitive water sports such as (1) water skiing and (2) "tubing" while being pulled by a motor boat, the court determined that "as a matter of common knowledge, jet skiing is an active sport involving physical skill and challenges that pose a significant risk of injury, particularly when it is done—as it often is—together with other jet skiers in order to add to the exhilaration of the sport by racing, jumping the wakes of the other jet skis or nearby boats, or in other respects making the sporting activity more challenging and entertaining. Consequently, it is the type of sporting activity that meets the criteria governing application of the doctrine of primary assumption of risk."

We are not persuaded by appellants' assertions that *Whelihan* was wrongly decided. Contrary to appellants' assertion, the court of appeal in *Whelihan* analyzed both the nature of the specific conditions, conduct or risks involved in jet skiing, and the particular role of the defendant in the activity and in relation to the plaintiff. The *Whelihan* court observed that—just as in the case of other sports to which it was very similar, particularly when engaged in as a group activity—jet skiing involves certain significant inherent risks and challenges. The court specifically rejected assertions that the doctrine can be applied only to contestants in competitive events or spectator sports, noting that the Supreme Court has repeatedly found assumption of risk applicable to any active sport, whether competitive or noncompetitive [citations].

The *Whelihan* court also addressed the relationship of the defendant to the plaintiff and to the activity, noting that the parties were

co-participants who had both purchased jet skis just two days before the incident, and that the plaintiff " 'was a novice jet skier, having a total of only six (6) hours of actual operating time . . . [and] no experience or familiarity with such "thrilling" maneuvers' " as those executed by the defendant. The decision in *Whelihan* is clearly on point with the case before us. As set out in the parties' separate statements of material facts, it is undisputed that the only significant difference between a jet ski and a Sea-Doo is that instead of having to stand up, as one does on a jet ski, a person using a Sea-Doo can sit down on a "motorcycle type" seat. For our purposes, there is no legally material difference.

We agree with *Whelihan's* analysis of jet skiing as "an active sport involving physical skill and challenges that pose a significant risk of injury to participants in the sport," a description which applies equally to the recreational activity of riding a Sea-Doo." There is nothing in the record concerning the recreational activity of using Sea-Doos that would distinguish it in any way from other similar activities found by the courts of this state to constitute sports to which the doctrine of primary assumption of risk is applicable. We conclude that, in the absence of other considerations, the doctrine of primary assumption of risk applies generally to the recreational activity of using a Sea-Doo, just as it does to other similar sports such as water skiing, "tubing" behind a motorboat *(Record v. Reason),* jet skiing *(Whelihan),* snow skiing, "off-roading" with a motorcycle or "dune buggy", skateboarding, figure ice skating, river rafting, and long-distance group bicycle riding [citations of cases omitted]

Appellants contend that *Whelihan* is distinguishable from this case because the roles and relationships of the parties to this incident—Ferro, Jason and Peart—differed in significant respects from those of the individuals before the court in *Whelihan.* Specifically, they assert that, unlike *Whelihan,* this case involves two minors, one of whom (respondent Jason) was a 13-year old novice operating a Sea-Doo for the first time while respondent Ferro sat behind him to supervise. We conclude that, to the extent they exist, the factual distinctions cited by appellants do not affect the applicability of the doctrine of primary assumption of risk in this case.

The ages of the parties in *Whelihan* are in fact never mentioned. On the other hand, the court did note that the plaintiff was a "novice" jet skier. Other cases involving comparably youth-oriented sports have either failed to mention the age of the participants at all [in the skateboarding and tubing cases] or essentially treated the ages of the co-participants as irrelevant *(Bjork v. Mason)*. Appellants have cited no case law holding that the applicability of the doctrine of primary assumption of risk to a sporting injury turns on the age of the participants.

Neither does the fact Ferro was riding on the same Sea-Doo as Jason in order to supervise the minor's operation of the watercraft affect the applicability of the assumption of risk doctrine to this case. The evidence shows that despite his supervisory role, Ferro was also a co-participant in the activity with Peart and Jason. Unlike the defendant swim coach in *Kahn,* Ferro was neither a coach nor a sports instructor.

Here, appellants failed to allege recklessness in their complaint. Neither have they adduced any specific evidence of intentional or reckless actions on the part of Ferro—or any other respondent—that actually increased the risks inherent in operating a Sea-Doo sufficient to demonstrate a triable issue of material fact as to the applicability of the primary assumption of risk doctrine to this case.

To the contrary, the undisputed evidence shows that Ferro's actions in supervising Jason were prudent and well within the boundaries of normal Sea-Doo riding conduct. The record shows Ferro adequately explained the basics of operating a Sea-Doo to both minors, required them to wear life jackets, and accompanied them when they went out. Jason and Ferro then simply drove their Sea-Doo in a straight line and at a moderate rate of speed without acceleration. It was in fact appellant Peart who engaged in the riskier activities of accelerating, executing turns, and cutting back and forth across the wake of respondents' Sea-Doo. Ferro did not encourage either Jason or Peart to take risks beyond their experience or ability.

Contrary to the argument in appellants' brief, the circumstances of this case are utterly unlike those addressed by the California Supreme Court in *Kahn*. There, the record showed that the defendant swimming coach not only encouraged the novice plaintiff to take extraordinary risks beyond her ability, but actually threatened to drop her from the team if she failed to execute a dangerous dive for which he knew she was completely unprepared and of which "she had expressed a mortal fear," and that he had in fact previously promised she would not be required to undertake. It was this arguably intentional and reckless behavior that the *Kahn* court concluded took the case outside the range of ordinary risk inherent in the sport at issue, making the doctrine of primary assumption of risk inapplicable. Nothing in the record of this case approaches the degree of intentionally reckless behavior at issue in *Kahn.*

In sum, we conclude that the trial court did not err in finding that the recreational Sea-Doo activity of the parties in this case constituted a sport as a matter of law, thereby making the defensive doctrine of primary assumption of risk applicable to respondents. The dismissal of the case is therefore affirmed.

CASE QUESTIONS

1. What were the key factual issues in the case that led the court to apply the "assumption of the risk" doctrine?
2. What is the definition used by the Court to describe the type of sports activity to which the theory "assumption of risk" applies? (Not examples of sports, but the definition of the standard).
3. What is the legal effect of applying the assumption of risk doctrine, according to the Court?
4. Is there any way for an injured plaintiff to get around the application of the doctrine? In other words, what did the plaintiff here try to prove?
5. How does the court use the *Whelihan* case, decided one year earlier, as precedent for this decision? Do you agree with the court's rationale, or are the facts of the case different enough to change the legal result? What about the *Kahn* case?

The "assumption of the risk" theory was strictly applied in the 1800s, making it very difficult for workers to sue employers for injuries that occurred on the job since they "assumed the risks" of employment. For example, if Shawna worked in an automobile factory, she would know that there was a chance of getting her arm caught in machinery. If such an accident happened, courts often held that she had "assumed" that risk, and they refused to hold the company liable, even if there was some evidence of negligence. (Perhaps the company had never inspected the machine, for example.) One response to the harsh results of strict application of this rule was the development of *workers compensation* laws in all states. Workers compensation statutes expressly prohibit the defenses of contributory negligence and assumption of the risk from being raised in connection with a claim for compensation. These statutes also eliminate the so-called *fellow-servant rule*. This defense formerly allowed the employer to escape liability not only if the employee him- or herself was negligent but also if the injury was caused by the negligence of another employee (the fellow servant). Workers compensation is discussed more fully in Chapter 22.

PRESUMED NEGLIGENCE

negligence per se: A category of negligence in which the defendant has violated a statute intended to protect the public from such conduct.

In most cases, negligence must be proved, as set forth previously, by showing that the defendant did not meet the standard of care of the mythical "reasonable person." In a few instances, however, the jury is permitted to presume that the defendant was negligent. One such situation is called **negligence per se,** or "negligence in itself." This might occur if the defendant has violated a statute designed to protect the public, such as a speed limit. If the plaintiff can show that the defendant violated a statute and that the plaintiff was within the class of people the law was designed to protect, the jury may be instructed that the defendant was negligent (but the plaintiff will still have to prove proximate cause and damages to win the case).

res ipsa loquitur: A situation in which the injury-causing incident could not have happened without negligence, and the defendant was in control of the event or premises where the accident occurred.

Another instance in which negligence can be presumed involves the doctrine called **res ipsa loquitur,** or "the thing speaks for itself." In some cases, the particular accident is so unlikely to happen without negligence, that once the facts are established, the burden of proof shifts to the defendant to show that there was no negligence. For example, if a pedestrian on the sidewalk is hit by a piano falling from a second story window, common sense tells us that someone up there on the second floor was negligent.

Two elements are necessary to invoke *res ipsa loquitur.* First, the incident must be one that does not normally occur without negligence. Second, the defendant must have had exclusive control of the precipitating events (he or she occupied or rented the second floor). A case often cited for the principle of *res ipsa loquitur* arose some years ago when a California man sat down on a chair upon his arrival in a cocktail lounge (before he had anything to drink). The chair collapsed, causing injuries to the customer. The court found both elements of the doctrine to be present and upheld a verdict for the plaintiff.

BUSINESS TORTS

In addition to torts that take place between individuals, and between individuals and businesses, a number of torts normally occur only in business situations. Several of them are related to actions taken by one business that cause injury to a competing business.

DISPARAGEMENT

Disparagement is a type of defamation directed at the product or service of another business, usually a competitor. The same elements necessary to establish defamation—an untrue statement, communicated to at least one other party, relating to a specific business, causing injury—will constitute disparagement. For example, if the Miller Brewing Co. began running ads stating that Budweiser beer was made with contaminated water, that would be considered disparagement, assuming that the statement was untrue. In a series of sharp competing ads in 2004, Miller made fun of Budweiser's claim to be "King of Beers," stating that we do not have a "king" in the United States, and that Miller was running for "president." Budweiser responded with ads in which two frogs (Budweiser characters) commented that Miller had been disqualified for president because it was not American, but was owned by a South African brewery.

> **disparagement:** Defamation of a business or product.

INTERFERENCE WITH CONTRACTS

Our market system favors and promotes competition. To obtain new contracts for and sales of their products, businesses are encouraged to streamline operations, cut costs, improve services, and try to do a better job than the competition. However, once two firms have entered into a contract, it is considered a tort for a third firm to take actions that interfere with that contract or seek to get either company to breach its contract. Even interference with unsigned contracts has been held as a tort in some states if the parties were reasonably certain to enter into one.

The elements necessary for this tort are (1) the plaintiff has a contract with a third party; (2) the defendant knew about the contract; (3) the defendant intentionally interfered with that contract or did something to prevent performance; and (4) the defendant caused harm to the plaintiff by its actions. The following case is one of the best-known business cases involving an **interference with contract** dispute between two large companies, Texaco and Pennzoil.

> **interference with contract:** One person intentionally interferes with a contract between two other people (or businesses).

TEXACO, INC. V. PENNZOIL CO.

729 S.W. 2d 768 (Texas 1987)

FACTS

Late in 1983, Pennzoil Co. was closely watching the growing conflict between the board of directors of Getty Oil Co. and Gordon Getty, a director who controlled (as trustee for the Sarah C. Getty Trust) 40.2 percent of the shares of Getty Oil. In late December, Pennzoil tendered an offer of $100 per share for 43 percent of Getty Oil.

Pennzoil soon contacted Gordon Getty and an agent of the J. Paul Getty Museum (holder of 11.8 percent of the Getty Oil shares) to discuss the offer and possible purchase of Getty Oil. During the first few days of January 1984, intensive discussions between these parties resulted in a written memorandum of agreement (an agreement in principle) for the purchase of a majority of Getty Oil (the Trust and Museum shares) at $110 per share plus a $3 per share bonus. The agreement was then submitted to the Getty board, which voted 15-1 to accept Pennzoil's offer if the bonus share was raised to $5.

On January 3, Pennzoil (and the Museum and the Trust) agreed to the modification proposed by the Getty board. Later that day, a press release was drafted by Getty Oil staff and lawyers announcing that an agreement in principle had been reached based on the memorandum of agreement. This press release and a similar one from Pennzoil were issued the next day, January 4. On January 6, *The Wall Street Journal* reported that an agreement had been reached.

While these events were transpiring, Getty Oil's investment banker continued trying to find a better offer for Getty and spoke with Texaco. On January 5, 1984, Texaco's board of directors decided to make an offer of $125 per share for 100 percent of Getty Oil. Texaco representatives met with Gordon Getty that evening to inform him that the Museum had agreed to sell its shares to Texaco. Getty had previously been advised that if Texaco purchased the museum shares and enough public shares to exceed 50 percent ownership of Getty Oil, the Trust could be put in a minority position. Consequently, Gordon Getty accepted Texaco's offer and signed a letter of intent to sell the Trust shares to Texaco.

On January 6, the Getty Oil board met and unanimously decided to "withdraw" its previous agreement or understanding with Pennzoil and to accept Texaco's offer. Immediately, Texaco issued a press release stating that Texaco and Getty Oil would merge [which did occur].

Shortly thereafter, Pennzoil sued Texaco, charging that Texaco had committed the tort of intentional interference with contractual relations. Following trial, the jury found for Pennzoil, and awarded it $7.53 billion in compensatory damages and $3 billion in punitive damages. Texaco appealed to the Texas Supreme Court.

DECISION

Writing for the court, Justice Warren made the following statement: "The main question for our determination is whether the evidence supports the jury's finding that there was a binding contract between the Getty entities and Pennzoil, and that Texaco knowingly induced a breach of such contract."

The first issue addressed was whether Pennzoil had proved that Texaco actually had known that a contract existed between Pennzoil and Getty. According to law it was required that Texaco know "of the existence of contractual rights as an element of inducing a breach of the contract." But it was not necessary that Texaco have "full knowledge of all the detailed terms of the contract" to be held liable.

Testimony by Texaco's chairman indicated that he was alerted to problems by several facts, including the following: (1) the Museum and the Trust both demanded that Texaco assume any legal liability they had toward Pennzoil, (2) the Getty Museum and Trust both refused to guarantee that the sale to Texaco would not violate the memorandum of agreement, and (3) they required that Pennzoil's offer price be guaranteed even if the sale to Texaco fell through.

The Museum and the Trust refused to sell to Texaco without these conditions being met. Although Texaco presented other testimony that it was informed many times by top executives and representatives of Getty Oil that no binding contract with Pennzoil existed, the fact that the Trust and the Museum made their demands was sufficient evidence to the jury to conclude that Texaco did know of the existence of an obligation to Pennzoil.

Another issue on appeal was whether the evidence was "legally and factually sufficient to show that Texaco actively induced breach of the alleged Pennzoil/Getty contract." In other words, Texaco argued that it was not enough for Pennzoil to show that Texaco knew about the contract and still entered into its own contract with Getty. The burden was on Pennzoil to show that Texaco actively influenced Getty Oil to break its contract with Pennzoil.

Texaco argued that it was merely responding to a "campaign of active solicitation" by representatives of Getty Oil who wanted a better offer. However, Texaco was strongly motivated to acquire Getty's oil reserves because of its own dwindling reserves and the high costs of locating new ones. Evidence at trial also indicated that Texaco had held extended meetings and procured expert advice on the best tactics to acquire Getty. These facts contradicted Texaco's claim that it simply accepted terms advanced by Getty Oil, and this supported the jury's verdict.

Therefore, the Texas Supreme Court upheld the compensatory damages award of $7.53 billion. The court found that the punitive damages award of $3 billion was excessive and reduced that figure to $1 billion.

CASE QUESTIONS

1. What should Texaco have done differently? Getty? Pennzoil?
2. What public purpose is served by this type of decision?
3. Do you think that Pennzoil and Getty had a binding agreement at the time Texaco entered the picture?
4. Could Pennzoil have sued Getty? What for? Why might it have chosen to sue Texaco instead?

MISAPPROPRIATION

Trade secrets are business assets such as formulas, devices, customer lists, or other nonpublic information. Such information often becomes the subject of **misappropriation** cases when the material comes into the hands of a competitor. Sometimes a company uses an idea or invention of an author or inventor without compensating the person who thought of it or who has the right to use it. The required elements of a misappropriation case are the following: (1) the existence of an idea or secret that is not available to the public; (2) information that is novel, concrete, and useful; (3) some type of wrongful taking of that information, such as by theft or by breach of confidentiality; and (4) the use of the information by the second party. For example, a series of cases have been brought against the large automobile manufacturers by a man who claims to have invented the technology for intermittent auto windshield wipers. He claimed that he had demonstrated his invention to them before the companies went ahead and produced millions of cars with such devices. He received no compensation. As a result, courts have awarded him several million dollars. (This story was the subject of a 2008 movie, *Flash of Genius,* starring Greg Kinnear.)

misappropriation: The wrongful taking of a nonpublic business secret or asset from one firm and its use by another firm.

 SOCIAL/ETHICAL ISSUES

Do the torts of misappropriation, interference with contract, and disparagement have an ethical basis? Is it not good business to try to determine what your competition is planning or to run ads showing how your product is superior to the competition? Is it appropriate to hire one of your chief competitor's key employees, who has much knowledge of the other firm's financial situation and marketing strategy, and may bring with her some trade secrets? What is the dividing line between good hard competition and wrongful action?

All of the tort theories discussed so far are based on actions that were either intentionally taken or were taken unintentionally but without the degree of care expected of a reasonable person. The next section of this chapter examines a rapidly growing theory that extends liability to the manufacturers of products and others even though they exercised reasonable care and did not intend to injure anyone.

STRICT LIABILITY

strict liability:
Liability without
proof of negligence
or fault.

The theory of law called **strict liability** originated many years ago in response to situations in which one person created a hazardous condition (without being negligent) that caused injury to another. For example, suppose that Gary uses explosives to tear down a building on his property. Although he is as careful as the mythical "reasonable person," several rocks are nevertheless propelled onto Bart's property, breaking windows in his house. Under negligence theory Bart would have to prove the required elements (duty, breach, proximate cause, and damages). In this situation he would lose the lawsuit, since Gary had observed the safety precautions of the normally careful person.

**ultrahazardous
activity:** One
which is inherently
dangerous.

Such a result (Bart would get nothing) seems unfair; thus the doctrine of strict liability has evolved. It provides that if one person engages in **ultrahazardous activities** (such as the use of explosives), and these actions cause injury to another, the one who caused the problem should be liable for the injuries whether or not he or she acted reasonably. Why? Courts and legislatures have begun to believe that public policy was better served by putting the liability on the one who created the risk (even though he or she may not have been negligent) rather than on the innocent person who was injured. If Marlin keeps a lion as a pet and it escapes, or if Martha builds a reservoir on her property to store a toxic liquid and the reservoir breaks, the theory of strict liability would impose the risk of the damage caused by these activities on Marlin and Martha, regardless of whether they were negligent and how careful they were.

In the past 20 or 30 years, the theory of strict liability has come to be widely used as a legal theory allowing recovery of damages by persons injured by defective products. For example, when a machine does not work correctly and someone is injured as a result, public policy in most states now favors placing the liability for the injuries on those who manufacture and sell the products rather than on the innocent consumers. When applied to manufactured products, strict liability is called "product liability." The many aspects and ramifications of this development are more thoroughly discussed in Chapter 13.

TORT REFORM

Considerable debate has arisen in recent years about the need for reform of the tort system. *Newsweek* magazine published an eleven-page cover story in December, 2003 entitled "Lawsuit Hell: How the Fear of Litigation is Paralyzing Our Professions." The article was part of a series called "Civil Wars" which *Newsweek* produced with NBC and MSNBC which included television and internet stories on the tort system. What the *Newsweek* series demonstrated is that "tort reform" has become a popular, and very political, issue. To oversimplify—the Republican party, corporate groups, and medical associations support the statistics reported by, and the types of reforms advocated by the American Tort Reform Association. On the other hand, Democrats, citizen groups, and consumer organizations support the statistics and studies done by the American Association for Justice (formerly the American Trial Lawyer's Association). But within the groups there is considerable variation on different issues and suggested reforms.

Certainly there are many multimillion dollar verdicts against companies every year based on tort and strict liability principles. Some reported verdicts do appear to be quite high, given the situation. But clearly many individuals suffer from defective products or malpractice by doctors, lawyers and others, and do not sue. Business associations have strenuously argued that jury verdicts in tort cases against business have reached "crisis" levels, to the serious detriment of American firms. The legal systems in other countries have generally not been as generous with awards to plaintiffs as have U.S. courts. However, a few years ago the European Union did adopt a "strict product liability" standard that is quite similar to the U.S. doctrine, so damage awards against companies in Europe based on strict liability may increase in the future.

Organizations allied with business and insurance interests on one side and attorney and consumer groups on the other have conducted studies in recent years concerning whether there actually has been a major increase in the number and size of verdicts, and if so, whether it is justified. The conclusions on both sides, as one would guess, have been vastly different. Where one side sees a "tort crisis" the other side sees no significant increase in cases filed, or damage awards in recent years, and no crisis at all.

For example, a study done in 2004 by the Institute for Legal Reform (ILR), an affiliate of the U.S. Chamber of Commerce, reported that the cost of the tort system to American business was $129 billion per year, with some 68% of the cost borne by small businesses (less than $10 million in annual revenues). The ILR called on Congress to reform the tort system. "America's small businesses are paying the price of our legal crisis in lost business opportunities," stated the group president. Small businesses have argued that after healthcare, the most important problem for small businesses is the cost and availability of liability insurance.

The Consumer Federation of America criticized the ILR study as "grossly overstating" the amount of tort costs, and for including insurance costs in the total, which number included many non-litigation expenses. Moreover, in 2011, the American Association for Justice (AAJ) website argues that the number of tort cases filed declined over 25% from 1998 to 2008, and accounted for just over 4 percent of all civil cases filed in 2008. The AAJ also relies upon statistics to support its argument that medical malpractice litigation is not the cause of increasing health costs, and that litigation does not have a negative impact on small business.

Statistics can be looked at and used in many ways, to support either side of the argument. For example, one "neutral source" used in the *Newsweek* series was Jury Verdict Research (JVR), a private company that reports on jury verdicts across the country. The JVR web site states that the company does not report its results in terms of *average* awards. Instead they report *median* verdicts for different types of torts. The difference is dramatic. In 2001, according to JVR, the average personal injury award in the the U.S. was $1.2 million, while the median award was only $51,000. A few very large awards skew the "average."

In the past several years, almost all of the states have enacted some type of **"tort reform"** laws. These statutes typically place monetary limits on *noneconomic damages* (such as "pain and suffering" awards), **punitive damages** (extra damages awarded to punish a defendant for malicious or intentional acts), and *attorney fees*. Also many of these laws establish strict *statutes of limitation* (a time limit within which the plaintiff must sue), and eliminate the concept of *joint and several liability* (by which a winning plaintiff can collect the entire award from any one of several defendants).

punitive damages: Damages, in excess of those required to compensate the plaintiff for the wrong done, that are imposed in order to punish the defendant because of the particularly wanton or willful character of the wrongdoing.

DEPARTMENT OF JUSTICE STUDY ON CIVIL CASE DAMAGE AWARDS

One "neutral study" is the "Civil Justice Survey of State Courts" (CJSSC) report done by the U.S. Department of Justice Bureau of Justice Statistics. The most recent iteration of the report released in 2005 examined "general civil trials concluded in a nationally representative sample of urban, suburban, and rural jurisdictions." Previous versions of the report (issued in 1992, 1996, and 2001) focused on general civil trial litigation in the nation's 75 most populous counties.

From 1992 to 2005, the total number of civil trials declined by over 50% in the nation's 75 most populous counties. The overall median jury awards declined by 40% from 1992 to 2005.

According to the report, in 2005 the median award to successful plaintiffs in all civil suits was $28,000. Less than 5% of all civil trials resulted in damage awards of over $1 million. Individuals, rather than businesses, made up 81% of the plaintiffs in civil trials. Over 40% of all winning cases were motor vehicle accident cases. Forty percent of these cases that were successful involved less than $10,000, with the median award being $15,000.

Plaintiffs sought punitive damages in only 13% of the more than 14,000 general civil trials, and were awarded punitive damages in only 5% of those cases. The overall median punitive damage award was $64,000. Twenty-seven percent of punitive damages awards in 2005 were over $250,000, and 13% were $1 million or more.

The debate over tort reform is likely to continue being a topic of controversy in coming years. For instance, in February 2010 the Illinois Supreme Court ruled that the state's medical malpractice law was unconstitutional because it violated the separation of powers clause by imposing decisions that must be made by judges and juries. In Washington DC, tort reform was a major focus in the debate over health care reform that took place soon after President Obama took office. In his 2011 State of the Union address to the nation, President Obama gave some hope to supporters of continued tort reform by stating that he would be open to "medical malpractice reform to reign in frivolous lawsuits."

Although companies must be concerned about facing tort lawsuits related to the products they produce as well as the activities of their employees and other agents, there is another serious type of legal liability that causes concern. In recent years, federal and state prosecutors have increasingly brought criminal charges against U.S. business firms for violations of a wide array of laws.

CRIMINAL LAW AND BUSINESS

In the past several years, the business news has been dominated by a continuing and wide-ranging series of scandals involving the disclosure of false and misleading financial information and schemes used by many large companies, including Enron, WorldCom, Adelphia, HealthSouth and more. As we have discussed earlier, these financial "tricks" and "misstatements" gave an untrue picture of the financial situation of these companies. Enron and WorldCom filed for bankruptcy protection (two of the largest bankruptcy cases in history) and thousands of employees lost their jobs while company share values plunged and thousands more investors lost millions of dollars in shareholder value and pension savings.

In addition, several brokerage companies, accounting and law firms, and investment bankers have faced lawsuits and criminal charges for their role in assisting the companies in creating and maintaining a false financial picture. Also certain mutual fund companies have paid multi-million dollar fines for engaging in after-hours trading and other unlawful actions. Criminal charges were brought against many top and middle-level executives of many of these firms, and several convictions resulted in significant jail time.

Some years ago, long before the Enron scandal, a study was done to determine what types of legal issues are most often reported in *The Wall Street Journal*, the nation's leading daily business newspaper.[1] The expectation of the study was that the most-reported issues would concern torts, business contract disputes, or perhaps environmental or toxic waste problems. Surprisingly, more news stories addressed criminal prosecutions of business firms and managers than any other category. A casual look at the news today seems to indicate that this is still true.

Perhaps these events only prove the old adage that "bad news sells newspapers." While newspapers and television newscasts may give an exaggerated impression as to the number of crimes, arrests, and criminal investigations that occur, one cannot ignore that many leading corporations, as well as hundreds of smaller ones, have been charged with and convicted of serious crimes in recent years. As is discussed more fully subsequently, if a criminal action was somehow authorized or knowingly permitted by managers or other top officials of a business firm, criminal liability may be imposed on the firm as well as the individual. Although a corporation cannot be physically put in prison, it most certainly can be sentenced to pay a high fine, and a criminal conviction may also mean the loss of important business licenses. As we have discussed, the prominent worldwide accounting firm Arthur Andersen was forced to dissolve after being convicted of the federal crime "obstruction of justice." It could no longer conduct audits of public companies and closed its doors.

Typically, the types of crime most associated with business have been the so-called white collar crimes involving financial misdealings, such as embezzlement, fraud, bribery, and conspiracy. In recent years, however, we have also seen prosecutions for environmental and other nonfinancial workplace crimes, perhaps reflecting greater public concern with business conduct in these areas. (Chapter 15 describes environmental prosecutions in more detail.)

Another area where criminal charges have occurred concerns occupational safety. In recent years many criminal cases have been instituted by local prosecutors following the death or serious injury of a worker. Most often, criminal actions have been brought when a subsequent investigation reveals that key officials in the business knew about an unsafe, dangerous condition posing a serious threat to employees but failed to take action to correct the problem. Sometimes these conditions have even been the subject of violation notices from the federal Occupational Safety and Health Administration (OSHA), as discussed in Chapter 22. Although OSHA has the power to refer a case to the

---

[1] Bixby, "Coverage of Legal Events in *The Wall Street Journal*," *Journal of Legal Studies in Education* 8 (Fall 1989/Spring 1990), 127.

Justice Department (headed by the U.S. Attorney General) for criminal charges when a violation of law leads to a worker's death, it has rarely done so, preferring to emphasize civil fines. However, certain local and state prosecutors in a few large cities have brought criminal charges against firms and individuals in recent years—most often for "negligent homicide"—when a known and uncorrected hazardous condition causes the death of a worker.

Although most criminal activities undertaken by employees and managers subject only those individuals to criminal liability, occasionally the employer (the corporation) is also charged with a crime. This situation may occur if the company board of directors or other high managerial personnel authorize the action or if those persons have knowledge of the activity and do nothing to discourage it. For example, if Jason is a truck driver for the Brown Company and he stops to rob a gas station while on duty, he has committed a crime. The Brown Company, however, probably has not committed a crime, assuming no manager suggested that he rob the gas station. On the other hand, if the president or the environmental manager of the Brown Company tells employees to dump toxic chemicals in the river, or knows that they are doing it and does nothing to stop the practice, the criminal charges might be brought not only against the manager but also against the company, since the official is in a position to act "for the company."

Partly in response to a public perception that business organizations and officials were not being penalized as severely as other defendants convicted of similar crimes, the U.S. Sentencing Commission, an arm of the federal court system, issued a tough set of **Corporate Sentencing Guidelines** in late 1991 (as more fully discussed in Chapter 7). These standards called for substantially larger fines for companies and more use of jail time for managers convicted of crime. The guidelines suggest that judges give sentences within a range of penalties for each type of crime, with considerable variance allowed, depending on the corporation's past and present activities.

For example, the normal fine against a company for a criminal environmental violation would increase substantially if, in previous years, the company had failed to take action against those employees or officers responsible for earlier crimes committed, the company had reduced spending for environmental control equipment, or the crimes committed had caused significant harm to the public. Conversely, the penalties would be reduced from the norm if the firm had set up an active program to monitor and prevent corporate criminal actions and had swiftly and firmly disciplined employees found guilty of criminal activity or violation of company policies. One of the reasons given by the Justice Department for prosecuting Arthur Andersen was that the firm had been accused of financial wrongdoing shortly before the Enron scandal, and had reached a settlement with the government, which included a promise not to violate the law again. The Sarbanes-Oxley Act, enacted in 2002 as a response to scandals such as Enron, also established tough criminal penalties for violations of its provisions, as discussed earlier.

One significant addition to the criminal laws affecting business is the **Racketeer Influenced and Corrupt Organization Act (RICO).** This federal law was enacted with the purpose of penalizing businesses that engaged in organized crime activity. RICO provides for both criminal and civil lawsuits against those businesses that have engaged in a "pattern of racketeering activity."

Racketeer Influenced and Corrupt Organization Act (RICO): A federal law allowing a prosecutor to charge a business firm with racketeering if the firm has engaged in two or more prohibited acts within a 10-year period. The law contains very serious penalties and can also be used in civil suits.

To constitute a "pattern of racketeering activity," however, it is only necessary for a firm to have engaged in two prohibited acts within a 10-year period. Such "racketeering acts" include gambling, arson, robbery, bribery, pornography, embezzlement, and fraud. It is not unusual for large corporations with thousands of employees to have at least two such convictions in one year, much less 10 years, and thus be subject to RICO. Some of the best-known U.S. firms have faced RICO suits, even though they clearly are not involved in organized crime.

In addition to severe criminal penalties for RICO violations, the law permits prosecutors to freeze the assets of the defendant while the charges are pending. When the Justice Department takes this step, the defendant faces harsh consequences and is almost forced to consider a quick settlement of any RICO charges. In a civil RICO case brought by a competitor, a successful plaintiff may win treble (three times) the actual damages proved, plus court costs and attorney fees. Individuals can be prosecuted for RICO violations as well if they have allegedly "conducted or participated directly or indirectly in the conduct of such enterprise's affairs through a pattern of racketeering activity." A case decided by the U.S. Supreme Court in 1993 against a large accounting firm held that in order for an individual to be prosecuted for a RICO crime, it must be shown that "he took some part in directing the enterprise's affairs."

Most civil cases have involved allegations of bribery, securities fraud, and mail or wire fraud. Because of the harshness of both civil and criminal RICO penalties, and because the defendants have often been legitimate businesses rather than organized crime organizations, Congress has considered amending the statute. No major changes have been passed as yet, however.

CRIMINAL PROCEDURE

After an event occurs that may constitute a crime, the state or local police or sheriff's office, or the FBI, investigates the matter and makes a recommendation to the appropriate prosecutor (often called a "Prosecuting Attorney" or "District Attorney" at the county level and an "Attorney General" at the state level). The prosecutor questions the officers and then makes a decision as to whether a crime has been committed and whether one or more specific people have committed it. If so, charges (somewhat like a complaint in a civil case) are filed in court, and papers are served on the defendant.

Depending on the seriousness of the matter, the defendant may already be in custody or may know nothing about the case. At any rate, the defendant is served with the papers and ordered to appear in court, where the judge will formally announce the crime charged, ask the defendant if he or she understands the charges and wishes to have an attorney, and set the amount of bail. Next, a hearing called an **arraignment** will be held. At this time the defendant, accompanied by an attorney, is asked to plead either guilty or not guilty (legally, there is no such plea as "innocent") to the charges. Depending on the plea, a future date is set either for sentencing or for a preliminary hearing.

The **preliminary hearing** is a procedure designed to protect those accused of crime from erroneous or wrongful prosecutions. At the preliminary hearing, the prosecutor is required to produce enough evidence to convince the judge that reason exists to believe that the defendant committed the crime charged. The defendant generally does not offer any evidence or call any witnesses but listens to and cross-examines the prosecutor's witnesses. If the

arraignment: A court hearing at which the defendant is asked to respond to the criminal charge by stating "guilty" or "not guilty."

preliminary hearing: A court hearing in a criminal case, at which the prosecutor must produce sufficient evidence to show that a crime has been committed and that there is good cause to believe that the defendant committed it.

prosecutor has a very weak case or is charging the wrong person, the judge will dismiss the case at the preliminary hearing, thus ending the case. But most of the time, sufficient evidence exists to allow the case to go forward and the defendant is "bound over" to stand trial.

Because criminal cases have less discovery than civil cases and the Sixth Amendment to the Constitution guarantees the right to a speedy trial in criminal cases, the proceedings move along fairly quickly to the trial. Most criminal cases (estimates of 85 percent to 90 percent are common) are settled before the date of the trial, usually by the defendant's agreement to plead guilty to a less serious charge in return for dismissal of the pending charge—a process called **plea-bargaining.** This procedure has been controversial, with citizens complaining that defendants are "getting off easy" by pleading to a lesser charge. Prosecutors have countered that plea bargaining does guarantee a conviction, whereas if a trial was held, the defendant could be found not guilty and set free.

The U.S. judicial system, based on the protections afforded by the U.S. Constitution, defends the rights of individuals against the powers of the government. Defendants in criminal cases in U.S. courts carry a **"presumption of innocence,"** which means that although they are accused of a crime, they should not be found guilty until the prosecution has **proved beyond a reasonable doubt** all necessary elements of the crime. In other words, if any members of the jury have doubts about whether all the elements of the crime have been proved with respect to a particular defendant, they must render a finding of *not guilty*. Since in many cases the defendant has a strong argument that he or she did not commit the crime, was somewhere else at the time, or lacked the intent necessary for conviction, plea bargaining (which does result in a conviction) sometimes makes sense for both the prosecutor and the defendant. The prosecutor must carefully evaluate each case to make sure that society's interests are being protected.

plea-bargain:
The settlement of a criminal case, whereby the prosecutor dismisses one charge if the defendant pleads guilty to another charge.

CONSTITUTIONAL PROTECTIONS

As we have mentioned, our justice system carries significant protections for individuals accused of crimes. Hundreds of television shows and movies, along with such books as Scott Turow's *Presumed Innocent* and *The Burden of Proof* and John Grisham's *The Firm, The Runaway Jury, Streetlawyer*, and *A Time to Kill*, have brought this point home. We often read in the newspaper that a person accused of a crime has been acquitted on a "technicality." What is not usually spelled out, however, is that the *technicality* is often based on one of the provisions in the *Bill of Rights in the Constitution*. The Bill of Rights, as we learned in Chapter 4, contain the fundamental protections Americans have against the intrusive powers of the government—hardly a "technicality." It is therefore important to take a closer look at some important constitutional protections.

Freedom from Unreasonable Searches and Seizures   The Fourth Amendment provides that *"The right of the people to be secure in their persons, houses, papers, and effects, against unreasonable searches and seizures, shall not be violated."* It further provides that *"no warrants shall issue, but upon probable cause . . . particularly describing the place to be searched, and the persons or things to be seized."*

This powerful statement of protection from government intrusion has led to hundreds of cases concerning what is *"unreasonable,"* what is *"probable cause,"* and other like issues. It is clear that in most cases, however, the police need a search warrant to enter someone's house or business unless permission for the search is obtained. Many cases, such as *Marshall v. Barlow's Inc.,* discussed in Chapter 5 (in which OSHA conducted a surprise inspection of a plumbing supply company without a warrant), have reaffirmed that this constitutional protection applies to businesses as well as to individuals in their homes. Thus, a police officer or other government official generally needs to obtain a warrant to search a business, unless the consent of the business proprietor is obtained.

Certain exceptions have been carved out for various situations, such as when a police officer sees a crime committed, or is in "hot pursuit" of a criminal. But in most cases the Fourth Amendment requires that before a search is conducted, the officer appear before a judge and justify the need for a warrant.

Protection Against Self-Incrimination The Fifth Amendment of the Constitution provides that *"No person . . . shall be compelled in any criminal case to be a witness against himself."* This important clause has been interpreted broadly and affords criminal defendants the right not only to refuse to testify at their own trial but also to remain silent when questioned by police. The familiar *Miranda* warnings that police are required to give to persons whom they take into custody were formulated by the U.S. Supreme Court in the case *Miranda v. Arizona* to make the Fifth Amendment protection against self-incrimination effective, since many people did not know of their Fifth Amendment rights.

Over the years courts have analyzed a number of law enforcement practices in deciding how to fully enforce the Fifth Amendment. One important fact to note is that the privilege against self-incrimination has been held to apply *only to individuals not to business firms*. Therefore, while a company treasurer may be able to assert the privilege and refuse to testify or disclose damaging financial records or other information in his own trial, the same rights are not accorded to a corporation if it is charged with a crime.

Right to an Attorney The Sixth Amendment states that *"In all criminal prosecutions, the accused shall have the right . . . to have the assistance of counsel for his defense."* This provision has been interpreted as requiring not only that a defendant be allowed to have an attorney but that a person accused of any crime that may result in a jail sentence be provided an attorney at public expense if he or she cannot personally afford one.

SUMMARY

A business firm may have one employee or thousands. In either event, the organization acts only through the deeds of people, such as employees, officers, directors, partners, and agents. Sometimes in connection with their duties, these representatives commit torts—intentionally or unintentionally—that cause injury to others. Occasionally business managers or employees engage in criminal actions. This chapter has examined the legal consequences of several types of such actions, beginning with intentional torts, in which an action taken deliberately, such as assault, battery, false imprisonment, or defamation, causes economic or physical injury to another person. The most important unintentional tort—negligence—occurs when someone performs an action without using the degree of care expected of a "reasonable person." There are also a series of torts that are normally only committed by businesses, such as disparagement of competition and interference with contract.

An extension of tort theory, called strict liability, sometimes holds liable those who perform very dangerous activities and those who manufacture defective products for injuries caused by their actions and products, without the necessity of proving any intentional or negligent acts. Partly in response to numerous large jury verdicts against companies based on torts or strict liability, there has been a vigorous debate in recent years concerning the need for reforms in the way the U.S. legal system treats tort cases. Many states have enacted tort reform laws.

Finally, situations exist in which corporations and/or their representatives may be held criminally liable for certain actions. Such situations include "white collar" crimes like embezzlement, fraud, bribery, and conspiracy, as well as crimes involving the workplace and the environment. The Sarbanes-Oxley Act, enacted after the Enron and WorldCom scandals, created a new set of crimes, involving the creation and authorization of fraudulent and misleading financial information by public companies and their officers. The federal RICO law has powerful criminal penalties. The chapter concludes with a short discussion of criminal procedure and the rights of defendants in criminal cases.

CHAPTER QUESTIONS

1. A woman had worked as an employee of a grocery store for more than 20 years, and for the last 12 years had been manager of the bakery section. She began receiving flowers and cards from an anonymous source, often signed "Neena." The cards stated that Neena wanted to get to know the employee better, and were often signed "love." The employee became increasingly upset, and had complained several times to her manager. She finally sought counseling to deal with her depression and anxiety. It finally turned out that the manager himself had been sending the cards and flowers. She sued for the tort called "extreme and outrageous conduct," an intentional tort, like the ones discussed in the chapter. What will she have to show, to survive a motion to dismiss the case? *Riske v. King Soopers,* 366 F. 3d 1085 (10th Cir. 2004).

2. In June 2007, Sam Ives, an 11-year-old boy, was killed by a bear while camping with his mother, stepfather, and brother in American Fork, Utah. The night before Sam was killed, another camper had been attacked by a bear in the area. Sam's parents filed a wrongful death lawsuit against the U.S. Forest Service (USFS), alleging it had been negligent by failing to provide visitors with an adequate warning of the risk of a bear attack. At trial, the USFS defended itself by arguing that it had no duty to warn visitors of "unforeseeable" events and, additionally, it had acted reasonably by posting general signs and by pursuing the bear allegedly involved in the earlier attack. USFS also alleged that Sam's mother may have been contributorily negligent because she had drunk beer the night Sam was killed, and that they assumed the risk by knowingly camping in the area. [As of the date of publication, the judge had not reached a conclusion in this case.] Do you think USFS was negligent? Are its defenses of contrib-

utory negligence and assumption of the risk justifiable? How should the judge decide this case?

3. In March 2009, clothing designer Dawn Simorangkir sued rock singer Courtney Love for defamation based upon a series of "tweets" Love posted about Simorangkir. Previously, Love had hired Simorangkir to create some clothing for her, but objected to the invoice Simorangkir sent for the cost of the clothing. Among the tweets in question were, "She [Simorangkir] has received a VAST amount of money from me over 40,000 dollars and I do not make people famous and get raped TOO!" Another claimed that the designer was an "a**wipe nasty lying hosebag thief." Are these statements defamatory? Are "tweets" more or less likely to be defamation? Why?

4. A 70-year-old man (Mr. Coblyn) went into a department store in Boston and, after some shopping, purchased a sport coat. After leaving it for alterations, he put back on his hat and topcoat and began to exit the store. At the doorway, he put an ascot around his neck (which he had brought into the store with him) that was in his pocket. Just outside the door he was immediately and roughly stopped by a store employee who demanded to know "Where did you get that scarf?" He was ordered in a loud voice (heard by several other customers) to go back into the store and "See the manager." On the way to the manager's office, the salesman who had sold Mr. Coblyn the sport coat saw him and assured the other store employee that the ascot belonged to Mr. Coblyn. At that point, Mr. Coblyn experienced chest pains and was hospitalized for a heart attack. He subsequently sued the store for false imprisonment. Will he likely win? Why? [*Coblyn v. Kennedy's, Inc.,* 268 N.E.2d 860 (Mass. 1971)]

5. A company located near Chicago developed a process of recovering silver from used photographic and x-ray film. Most of the employees were Mexican and Polish immigrants, whose English was poor or nonexistent. They cut the film into pieces and dumped them into open vats of sodium cyanide. After the silver separated, the workers removed plates at the bottom of the tanks to which the silver had attached and scraped off the deposits. Many workers experienced dizziness, nausea, and vomiting on a regular basis, but no additional health or safety procedures were taken. The employees' safety equipment consisted of paper masks and cotton gloves. According to one report, "the air was thick with the odor of cyanide and a yellowish haze of cyanide fumes hung inside the plant." The workers were not told much about the hazards of cyanide, and there was some evidence that managers had scraped the "skull and crossbones" symbols off the cyanide containers. Although an antidote for cyanide poisoning was widely available, none was kept at the plant. One day a 61-year-old worker collapsed on the plant floor and died soon thereafter. The company president, safety director, and foreman (all of whom worked in the same building as the workers, but in a different area) were charged with murder. The applicable Illinois law provided that one may be charged with murder where he or she performs certain acts knowing "that such acts create a strong probability of death or great bodily harm," and someone does die from such acts. Should the managers be convicted of this crime? [*People v. Film Recovery Systems, Inc.,* (Cook County Cir. Ct. 1985), rev'd 194 Ill. App. 3d 79, 550 N.E.2d 1090 (1990)]

6. At a Christmas party, employees of an auto dealership discovered that an electric automobile condenser could deliver an electric shock. The company

president got into the fun and chased one of the employees around, shocking him several times on the neck. The employee suffered serious headaches later, passed out numerous times in the next few months, and eventually required nerve surgery. He sued the president and the company for damages. The defendants' arguments were (1) it was not a battery but just "horseplay" and (2) if it was battery, workers compensation was the employee's only remedy. What should be the result? Why? [*Caudle v. Betts,* 512 So. 2d 389 (Louisiana 1987)]

7. A store in Kansas leased its gasoline pumping area to an oil company, which then set up and maintained gas pumps for public use. One day a gasoline spill occurred near the pumps. A store employee noticed the spill and alerted the store manager, warned a customer of the store to avoid the spill and shut off the pump. However, before any further safety measures could be taken, the customer walked through the spill to retrieve her purse and fell, suffering an injury. Will the customer succeed in a negligence case against the store? Why or why not? *Crowe v. True's IGA, LLP,* 85 P. 3d 1261 (Kan. App. 2004)

8. A gunman walked into a San Francisco law firm in 1993 armed with two TEC-DC9 semiautomatic assault weapons and a semiautomatic pistol and began shooting, eventually killing eight people and wounding six others. Families of those killed and wounded later sued the maker of the weapons for negligence and strict liability. Evidence was introduced that the gun manufacturer's advertising was "targeted to certain types of persons attracted to or associated with violence," featuring its "military combat style," and that these guns were the "weapons of choice" used in gang shootings and other criminal activities. The case was dismissed by the trial court, but the plaintiffs appealed to the California Court of Appeal. What would the plaintiffs have to show to establish a case (and get to a jury trial) with regard to the elements of negligence, as discussed in this chapter? How could they show "duty," "breach of duty," and "causation"? [*Merrill v. Navegar, Inc.,* 89 Cal. Rptr. 2d 146 (Cal. App. 1999)]

9. At an apartment building in West Hollywood, California, two neighbor families did not get along. Ms. Marcia Rand (who had several health problems) and her adult son Michael lived in one unit, and complained loudly and often about various actions of Mr. Steven Kesmodel and his wife and young son who lived nearby. The Kesmodels suggested use of a neighborhood dispute resolution program and scheduled a hearing, but the Rands failed to attend. Then after more arguments took place concerning use of a water spigot on the back of the apartments, Ms. Rand and her son called the police. Ms. Rand was shouting, became "hysterical," and when the police arrived, she and Michael signed a form for a "citizens arrest" claiming that Mr. Kesmodel had been "peeping into" Ms. Rand's bedroom while he was using the water spigot to wash the sidewalk, where his son had spilled Popsicle juice.

The police did then arrest Mr. Kesmodel and took him to jail, where he was released 12 hours later. Fearing that a confrontation was about to occur, Steven had asked his wife to videotape his use of the water spigot. She did videotape the entire incident, which clearly showed that Steven had not even looked in the direction of the Rand apartment at any time while using the water. The criminal case was dismissed and the Kesmodels sued Ms. Rand and her son for false imprisonment. The jury awarded the Kesmodels over $30,000 in damages. Should the award be upheld? What are the elements of false imprisonment? Were the elements met in this case? If so, describe. *Kesmodel v. Rand,* 15 Cal. Rptr. 3d 118 (Cal.App-2004)

10. An individual was convicted of bribery and conspiracy violations under RICO because of actions he took in connection with his job at a business firm. The judge's instructions to the jury stated that the defendant could be convicted of participating directly or indirectly in the affairs of the business—and thus be guilty of a RICO crime—even if he "played no part in the management and control of the enterprise." Was that a correct statement of the law, or should the conviction be reversed on appeal? Why? [*U.S. v. Viola,* 35 F.3d 37 (2d Cir. 1994)]

PRACTICAL EXERCISE

Pump Iron, Inc., operates 450 fitness centers around the United States, with many types of weight machines, aerobic walkers, stair climbers, and other equipment in each facility. In addition, Pump Iron features racquetball courts, swimming pools, and exercise classes in many of the centers. You have graduated from business school and have just been appointed as the manager of the local Pump Iron club.

One cold day in January, a snowstorm hits town early in the morning. When you arrive at the facility, the walks and driveway are snow-covered and slippery. Shortly after entering your office, the phone rings, and two of your employees call to tell you they cannot get to work. Desperately seeking help, you call Rocky, a part-time employee, who is a football player on the local college team, and he arrives at work about 10 A.M.

You are trying to keep the center open and have not had time to shovel the walk, even though a city ordinance requires that snow be cleared from the sidewalks of all commercial establishments within two hours of any snowstorm. Brenda Smith, a Pump Iron member, comes to work out at 11 A.M. Unfortunately, she slips on some snow and ice and falls on your walkway, breaking her arm. You ask Rocky to take Brenda to the hospital, and he agrees. Unbeknownst to you, his driver's license has been suspended. On the way to the hospital, Rocky negligently runs into another car, causing damage to Jon Summers, the driver, as well as further injuries to Brenda.

While a police officer is investigating the accident, Rocky gets into an argument with him, which ends with Rocky punching the officer and knocking out two of his teeth. Rocky is arrested on criminal battery charges, and Brenda is finally taken to the hospital. The police are considering criminal charges against the club as well.

The Pump Iron regional director, Ms. Patricia Kelly, has asked you to describe, in memo form, the various liability claims the club may face, both criminal and civil, from Ms. Smith, Mr. Summers, and the police as the result of the events described here. Please prepare such a memo, discussing the club's possible responsibility for the torts and crimes committed.

FURTHER INFORMATION

www.rand.org
RAND "think tank" site.
www.aaabiz.com/ATRA
American Tort Reform Association.
www.ATLA.org
American Trial Lawyers Association.
www.findlaw.com/01topics/22tort/sites.html
FindLaw sites with links to tort cases, laws, articles, and Web sites.

CHAPTER 12

PRINCIPLES OF CONTRACT LAW

LEARNING OBJECTIVES

After reading this chapter, you should be able to:

1. Explain when you are required to keep your promise.
2. Determine when the Uniform Commercial Code applies to a contract.
3. Identify the remedies available for breach of contract.
4. Discuss why an understanding of contract law is important for businesspersons.

CHAPTER OUTLINE

While surfing the Internet, you found a business that you were interested in buying. What do you need to know about the law of contracts before seizing this "once-in-a-lifetime" opportunity? The "Practical Exercise" at the end of the chapter will explore this issue in more detail.

INTRODUCTION

Almost every transaction a businessperson enters into involves a contract. For example, a contract is made when leasing a building. Hiring an employee creates another contract. Obtaining a loan from your bank involves a contract. Ordering merchandise from a manufacturer and then selling it to a customer creates two different contracts. As you saw in Chapter 10, even convincing a friend to invest in your business creates a contract. Because contracts are such an important part of doing business, it is necessary to discuss in some detail how contracts are formed and enforced.

A contract is a legal document, and as such, the parties to the contract agree to allow a court to enforce the agreement. Note, however, that contracts are not just paper and words: they also involve relationships between people. Contracts can be very formal or very informal. As you will soon discover, most contracts do not even need to be in writing.

The United States has a long history of enforcing the terms of contracts. When you enter into a contract in the United States, you can expect that under most circumstances, you will be required to do exactly what the words in the contract say you will do. In some other countries businesspeople do not view contracts as rigidly. In the heterogeneous culture of the United States, however, contracts are one way to ensure that each party understands exactly what is expected.

THE UNIFORM COMMERCIAL CODE

Historically, all contracts were governed by the common law. As you will remember from Chapter 1, the common law is found in case law and can differ from state to state. The **Restatement of Contracts** sets out what legal scholars believe the common law rules are that govern contracts. But like other areas of common law, judges can modify those rules. Even though the common law of contracts is similar in all states, as business transactions expanded across state boundaries, it became imperative that *commercial law* (the law governing commerce) be uniform, or the same, in all 50 states. The Uniform Commercial Code (UCC) was drafted with this goal in mind. Besides uniformity, the UCC also reflects legal realism jurisprudence, discussed in Chapter 1, in that the UCC attempts to draft laws governing contracts that reflect the way businesspeople really behave.

> **Restatement of Contracts:** One of several volumes produced by the American Law Institute and authored by legal scholars that sets forth statements on the law of contracts. It is widely referred to but not binding.

Several legal scholars, initially selected by Professor Karl N. Llewellyn of Columbia Law School, drafted the UCC. Currently, legal scholars make up the Permanent Editorial Board. These scholars are chosen on the basis of their skill and knowledge of commercial law by the American Law Institute and the National Conference of Commissioners on Uniform State Laws. The UCC itself is not law, however, until the state legislature in each state chooses to adopt it. The UCC has several articles on various commercial law aspects. Every state has adopted some form of the UCC. Louisiana, however, has not adopted Article 2, and several states have not adopted Article 2A. So while the UCC's goal is to be uniform, in reality, the state legislatures can change the draft legislation if they want. The UCC continues to be revised to reflect current changes in the way business is conducted. In fact, the Internet has provided many challenges to existing contract law. Congress and some states have passed laws to counter these challenges. The *Uniform Electronics Act (UETA)* and the *Electronic Signatures in Global and National Commerce Act (E-SIGN)* are two such pieces of legislation. They will be discussed later in this chapter.

There are three basic kinds of contracts: (1) contracts for the sale or lease of goods, (2) contracts for service or employment, and (3) contracts for the sale or lease of real property. Distinguishing among these types of contracts because the UCC, Article 2, only applies to the sale of goods and Article 2A only applies to the lease of goods. The other types of contracts are governed by the common law, discussed in Chapter 1. In some circumstances, the UCC and the common law may differ. To determine what law applies, look at the subject matter of the contract. Goods are tangible, personal property; that is, they can be touched, and they are not land or anything attached to the land. Examples of goods are cars, computers, food (as long as it is not currently growing on the land), books, clothes, and golf clubs.

Sometimes it is hard to distinguish between a contract for the sale of goods, which is governed by Article 2, and a service contract, which is governed by the common law. For example, when you go to the doctor for a flu shot, have you entered into a contract for the sale of goods (the flu vaccine) or have you contracted for the doctor's services (injection of the flu vaccine)? In this type of case, in which you have both a sale and service aspect to the contract, the court looks at the *main purpose* of the contract. If the main purpose of the contract is to buy the goods, then the UCC controls it. If the main purpose is to receive the service, then the common law rules control it. In regard to the flu shot, the main purpose is to receive the service of the doctor, so the UCC does not control it. Assume, however, that the doctor is purchasing the flu vaccine from the manufacturer, who provides a sales representative to explain the research behind the vaccine. Is this a goods contract or a service contract? Because the main purpose of the contract is to buy the vaccine, the doctor has entered into a goods contract with the manufacturer. The information provided by the sales representative is ancillary.

Why does it matter whether it is a contract for goods or some other type of contract? The answer lies in the differences between the UCC and the common law of contracts. For example, how a contract can be formed, whether a contract needs to be in writing, the **remedies** available, and how an offer can be accepted all depend on whether the UCC or common law applies. As we proceed to explain contract law, it is important for you to recognize those differences.

remedy: Money or performance awarded by a court.

GENERAL CONTRACT TERMS

consideration: The promise or performance that the promisor demands as the price of the promise in a contract.

Creating any contract requires an *offer*, *acceptance*, and **consideration**. The contract also has to be legal, and the parties need to exercise free will and have *legal capacity*. We will consider each of these elements separately. First, understanding some basic contractual terms is important.

When all terms of the contract have been spelled out, the contract is called an *express contract*. As you will see by the following article, many lawyers have learned to be creative regarding the express terms of a contract, so that the contract governs as many possible scenarios as possible.

Sometimes individuals agree to contract but do not spell out all of the terms. If the intent of the parties can be determined by their conduct, the contract is *implied in fact*. When the parties have not agreed to contract or have not fulfilled the legal requirements necessary to form a contract, the court may still find an **implied in law contract**. Implied in law contracts are not legal contracts; rather, the court implies a contract in order to avoid **unjust enrichment**, or harm to an innocent party. These contracts are sometimes referred to as **quasi-contracts**.

> ### Lawyerese Goes Galactic as Contracts Try to Master the Universe
>
> #### From Stage to Pickle Shop, These Terms Cover All Rights for All Time in All Worlds
>
> By Dionne Searcey and James R. Hagerty
>
> Decked out in sequined black and gold dresses, Anne Harrison and the other women in her Bulgarian folk-singing group were lined up to try out for NBC's "America's Got Talent" TV show when they noticed peculiar wording in the release papers they were asked to sign.
>
> Any of their actions that day last February, the contract said, could be "edited, in all media, throughout the universe, in perpetuity."
>
> She and the other singers, many of whom are librarians in the Washington, D.C., area, briefly contemplated whether they should give away the rights to hurtling their images and voices across the galaxies forever. Then, like thousands of other contestants, they signed their names.
>
> Ms. Harrison figured the lawyers for the show were trying to hammer home the point that contestants have no rights to their performances, "but I think they're just lazy and don't want to write a real contract," she says.
>
> Lawyers for years have added language to some contracts that stretches beyond the Earth's atmosphere. But more and more people are encountering such everywhere-and-forever language as entertainment companies tap into amateur talent and try to anticipate every possible future stream of revenue.
>
> Experts in contract drafting say lawyers are trying to ensure that with the proliferation of new outlets—including mobile-phone screens, Twitter, online video sites and the like—they cover all possible venues from which their clients can derive income, even those in outer space. FremantleMedia, one of the producers of NBC's "America's Got Talent," declined to comment on its contracts.
>
> The terms of use listed on Starwars.com, where people can post to message boards among other things, tell users that they give up the rights to any content submissions "throughout the universe and/or to incorporate it in other works in any form, media or technology now known or hereafter developed."
>
> Lucasfilm Ltd., *Star Wars* creator George Lucas's entertainment company that runs the site, said the language is standard in Hollywood. "But, to be honest with you, we have had very few cases of people trying to exploit rights on other planets," says Lynne Hale, a Lucasfilm spokeswoman.

implied in law contract: A contract expressed by conduct or implied or deduced from the facts.

unjust enrichment: A benefit received by chance, mistake or at someone else's expense.

quasi-contract: An obligation that is not created by a contract but is imposed by law to prevent unjust enrichment of one party from the acts of another party.

In a May 15, 2008, "expedition agreement" between JWM Productions LLC, a film-production company, and Odyssey Marine Exploration Inc., a shipwreck-exploration outfit, JWM seeks the rights to footage from an Odyssey expedition. The contract covers rights "in any media, whether now known or hereafter devised, or in any form whether now known or hereafter devised, an unlimited number of times throughout the universe and forever, including, but not limited to, interactive television, CD-ROMs, computer services and the Internet."

Odyssey said the wording was standard entertainment-law contract language. Jason Williams, JWM's president, said he feels a bit strange when his lawyers start using "cosmic language," but it's prudent. "These days there is an enormous amount of concern about how rights get appropriated," he said. "Paranoia is paramount."

The space and time continuum has extended to other realms outside the arts, including pickles. A 189-word sentence in a September agreement between Denver-based Spicy Pickle Franchising Inc. and investment bank Midtown Partners & Co.—which has helped raise capital for the sandwich and pickle shops dotted across the region—unconditionally releases Spicy Pickle from all claims "from the beginning of time" until the date of the agreement. "We're trying to figure out how to cover every possible base as quickly as possible," says Marc Geman, chief executive officer of Spicy Pickle. "When you start at the beginning of time, that is pretty clear."

As for the wordy language, he says, "the length of the paragraph is only limited by the creativity of the attorney."

Midtown Partners CEO John Clarke didn't realize the wording was in the contract until it was pointed out and said it "probably is a little extreme." Had he drafted the contract, he says he may have suggesting substituting "dating back to the birth date of the oldest party involved."

James O'Toole, politics editor of the Pittsburgh Post-Gazette, recently signed a release form for WQED, a PBS TV station in Pittsburgh, before he appeared on a news talk show. The contract allows the TV station to make use of "any incidents" of his life and reproduce his image or voice "throughout the universe in perpetuity, in any and all media now known or hereinafter devised."

Mr. O'Toole, who says he didn't bother to read the release before signing it, took the news calmly. "I'm very popular in some of the far reaches of the Milky Way," he says. Even so, he says, "I don't think I've missed out on a lot of potential income."

Jacquelyn Thomas, general counsel for WQED, says the company has "never gotten any pushback" on this language. "I don't mean to sound like a science-fiction nut . . . but it's not inconceivable that media will move beyond planet Earth," Ms. Thomas says.

Some legal experts rail against such language as imprecise and unnecessary. Ken Adams, a Garden City, N.Y., attorney and lecturer at the University of Pennsylvania Law School who advocates for clarity in contract language, says references to outer space and the end time are silly. That kind of language could even be a way of drumming up business, he says. "It adds an aura of magic—you're dabbling in the occult and you of course need a lawyer to guide you through the mysteries."

But Eric Goldman, an associate professor at the Santa Clara University School of Law who specializes in intellectual-property and Internet law, says the language could be "a stroke of brilliant foresight." Referring to geographical limits loosely can be dangerous, he says. For instance, "the United States is an ambiguous term . . . American Samoa, yes or no?"

"Throughout the world" would be one alternative, but that excludes possible future markets, he says. Some day, Mr. Goldman adds, people might ask, "What were they thinking? Why didn't they get the Mars rights?"

Promissory estoppel is an equitable doctrine that is used to enforce a promise even though for some technical reason a contract has not been formed. Promissory estoppel requires that a promise be made with the expectation that it would be relied on, and it is justifiably relied upon to the detriment of the other party. Since one party will be unjustly enriched, the court may say that promissory estoppel applies, and the other party is stopped from denying that a promise was made.

promissory estoppel: A situation in which one party's reliance on a promise prevents the promisor from denying the existence of a contract.

REQUIREMENTS FOR PROMISSORY ESTOPPEL

- Defendant makes a promise
- Defendant expected that the promise would be relied on
- Plaintiff justifiably relies on the promise
- Plaintiff suffers detriment
- Defendant is unjustly enriched

MUTUAL ASSENT

Contracts usually require that two parties mutually agree to all the contract's terms. A **bilateral contract** is formed when one party makes an offer and the other party accepts the offer with a promise. For example, Larry offers to sell Ann his car for $1,000. Ann agrees to buy Larry's car for $1,000. When Ann makes the return promise to buy the car, a bilateral contract has been formed. Larry cannot withdraw his offer.

A **unilateral contract** occurs when performance is required to accept the offer rather than a return promise. A unilateral contract still has mutual assent even though neither party is bound until performance is complete. For example, Sue agrees to pay Alan $2,000 if Alan paints her house. Alan does not agree to do anything. Sue can withdraw her offer at any time before Alan's performance is completed; however, a unilateral contract is formed when Alan finishes painting Sue's house. In some states, unilateral contracts are accepted by beginning performance.

Other contract terms you should know are *executory*, *partially executed*, and *executed*. When Larry and Ann enter into the car contract it is called an *executory* contract because the contract has been entered into but neither party has performed their obligations under the contract. When Ann pays

bilateral contract: A contract in which each party makes a promise to the other.

unilateral contract: A contract in which one party makes a promise offering some benefit if another party performs a specified act (rather than making a return promise).

Larry $1,000, the contract is *partially executed* because one party, Ann, has performed her obligations. When Larry delivers the car to Ann, the contract is considered *executed* since both parties have performed their obligations.

ENFORCEABILITY

Contracts may also be *void*, *voidable*, or *unenforceable*. Neither party to a contract can enforce a void contract (in fact, technically it never was a "contract" to begin with). Void contracts usually are illegal. For example, gambling contracts are illegal in Utah. Assume that Joe and Jerry are skiing in Utah in December. On the ski lift Joe bets Jerry $20 that Notre Dame will beat UCLA in that night's bowl game. Notre Dame wins, and Joe tries to collect the $20 from Jerry. Jerry refuses to pay. No Utah court will enforce the contract because the contract was illegal and is therefore *void*.

A **voidable contract** is enforceable by only one party to the contract. As you will soon discover, contracts with a minor are voidable. Jessica, who is 21 years old, agrees to sell her computer to Amy, who is 16, for $400. Amy agrees to buy the computer. Two days later Amy changes her mind and refuses to give Jessica the $400. Jessica will not be able to enforce the contract because Amy is a minor, and minors' contracts are voidable. But if Jessica had been the one to change her mind, Amy would have been able to enforce the contract, since minors' contracts are enforceable at their option.

An **unenforceable contract** is a contract that the law will no longer allow the courts to enforce. For example, in January 1999, Betty enters into a contract with Bill to pay Bill $700 for his canoe. However, Betty only pays $550 and indicates that she will pay the additional $150 in a month. Betty never pays Bill the remaining amount. Later, in January 2004, Bill hears that Betty won the lottery. Since Bill never received the $150, he decides to sue Betty. However, since the statute of limitations for the sale of goods is four years and expired in 2003, the contract between Bill and Betty is now unenforceable.

voidable contract: A contract in which one party has the option to disaffirm the bargain or back out.

unenforceable contract: A contract for which the law gives no court remedy.

ELEMENTS OF A CONTRACT

OFFER

Before a contract is formed, one party needs to make an *offer*. The offer must: (1) be explicit, (2) set forth the applicable terms, and (3) be communicated to the offeree (the party receiving the offer). An offer typically can be withdrawn at any time before it is accepted. One exception to this is the **option contract**. An option contract is a contract to hold an offer open for a period of time. Like most other contracts, an option contract needs *consideration* (a mutual exchange of something valuable) to be binding. For example, James is interested in buying Sally's home for $100,000. He is unsure, however, if he can raise the financing. Sally agrees in writing to give James until October 1 to raise the money. James gives Sally $1,000 to hold the offer open. This is an option contract. Sally cannot sell the home to anyone else until after October 1. If James does not raise the

option contract: A preliminary contract in which value is given to the offeror in exchange for keeping the offer open for a specified time.

money by October 1, Sally is free to keep the $1,000 and sell the home to another buyer.

Under the UCC §2-205, a written **firm offer** for the sale of a good by a **merchant** is enforceable for a reasonable time or for the time period stated, not to exceed three months, if, by its terms, the offer gives the assurance it will be held open. A firm offer does not need consideration. For example, Abigail walks into her local car dealership and asks for the price of a new model sports car. Janet, the salesperson, writes down that she will sell Abigail a new model sports car for $40,000 and that the price will be valid for five days. Abigail decides to think about it and leaves the store. Three days later she returns. Can Abigail enforce the offer? Yes, this is a firm offer by a merchant (someone in the business of selling that particular merchandise) and it is in writing. Therefore, it is enforceable even though there was no consideration.

> **firm offer:** An offer to sell goods that cannot be revoked, withdrawn, or amended for the time stated.

> **merchant:** Person who deals with goods of the kind sold in his or her business.

ENFORCEABLE FIRM OFFERS BY MERCHANTS
(U.C.C. §2-205)
- The offer is made by a merchant
- The offer is in writing
- The offer is signed by a merchant
- The offer states it will be held open for a certain or reasonable amount of time
- The offer involves a sale of goods

ACCEPTANCE

Once an offer is made, the offeree can accept the offer, reject the offer, or make a counteroffer. Under the common law, both the offer and acceptance have to be identical or *mirror* each other. This is called the **mirror image rule**. For example, Cathy offers to sell Joe her horse for $1800. Joe says that for $1800 he also wants Cathy to "throw in" a saddle. So far, there is no contract. Rather, Cathy made an offer, and Joe has made a counteroffer. Cathy tells Joe she will sell the horse and saddle for $1850. Joe agrees. Now, the offer and acceptance are the same, and when put to writing a contract is formed.

An exception to the mirror image rule is found in §2-207 of the UCC. Merchants often exchange forms detailing the particulars of their transactions. After all, merchants are those who are in the business of conducting business. These forms are drafted by each merchant's lawyer and are inevitably different in that they do not mirror each other. For example, one form may say that interest will accumulate at 10 percent per annum on unpaid bills, and another may not mention anything about interest. Section 2-207 says that when merchants are dealing with each other and there is a written confirmation, additional terms contained in the acceptance form become part of the contract unless the terms materially change the offer or the other party objects within a reasonable time. Many terms are considered "material," including the price or the quantity. A change in these terms reflects that the parties have not reached mutual assent. Other terms, however, may be made part of the contract if a party does not object. The box, "Acceptance and Offer Do Not Need to Mirror Each Other,"

> **mirror image rule:** A rule that states that in order for an acceptance to exist, the response must be a mirror image of the offer and cannot add new terms.

summarizes the conditions under which an acceptance and an offer need not mirror one another. This means that it is very important for merchants to read their mail and pay attention to the terms found in other merchants' forms.

ACCEPTANCE AND OFFER DO NOT NEED TO MIRROR EACH OTHER
(UCC §2-207)

- The contract is for sale of goods
- The contract is between merchants
- The changes in acceptance are minor
- The response includes a clear expression of acceptance
- The acceptance is not made conditional on assent by the offeror to different terms
- Additional terms become part of the contract unless:
  - The offeror limits acceptance to the terms of the offer; or
  - The new terms materially alter the offer; or
  - The offeror notifies the offeree within a reasonable amount of time concerning any objections

---

mailbox rule:
Making an offer or acceptance valid when it is deposited in the mail.

When the parties are not dealing with each other face to face, a problem may arise as to when acceptance has occurred. In general, the **mailbox rule** applies here. An offer is accepted at the time the acceptance is placed in the mail. For example, on November 1, Troy sends Tana an offer to sell his computer for $800. On November 5, Tana sends Troy a counteroffer to buy the computer and desk for $800. On November 10, Troy sends his offer to sell the computer and desk for $850. Tana receives the offer on November 12 and mails her acceptance on November 13. Troy calls Tana and *rescinds* (withdraws) the offer on November 14. He receives her acceptance on November 15. Under the mailbox rule, Tana accepted on November 13, and Troy's rescission one day later is ineffective. He is bound to the contract. The person making the offer is master of the offer. If Troy wants Tana's acceptance to be effective when he receives it, then he needs to make that term part of the original offer.

Under the common law, if the offeree accepts the offer using an *unauthorized method* (one not specified by the offer), the acceptance is effective only when received. For example, if rather than putting the acceptance in the mail, Ann sends her acceptance with Aunt Betty who is traveling cross-country, then the acceptance is only effective when Aunt Betty delivers it. Accepting the offer by the same means as the offer was received is considered, by the common law, to be an implied authorization. Under the UCC an acceptance can be sent by any reasonable method and is effective when sent, unless the offer itself specifically states otherwise.

Under the common law, silence does not constitute an acceptance—if the other party does not respond, no contract exists. The UCC, however, provides an exception for merchants. Under §2-201(2) of the UCC, if a merchant does not respond to a written confirmation within 10 days, the merchant has accepted the offer. Once again, merchants are responsible for reading and responding to their mail.

Generally, once a contract is accepted the parties must perform. Under §2-608 of the UCC, however, an acceptance of the goods can be revoked under some circumstances. For example, if the goods are *nonconforming* (do not meet the specific terms of the contract) and the nonconformity substantially impairs the value of the contract, then the contract can be revoked. The purchaser must have had to accept the goods unaware of the nonconformity or, if aware, assured that the nonconformity would be *cured* (fixed). **Revocation** must occur within a reasonable time. The following case demonstrates how the law applies to these types of contracts.

> **revocation:** Withdrawing an offer before it is accepted, or a mutual agreement to cancel contract.

DURFEE V. ROD BAXTER IMPORTS, INC.

262 N.W.2d 349 (Minn. 1977)

FACTS

John Durfee purchased a Saab automobile from Rod Baxter Imports. After the purchase, Durfee started to drive home. Within a few blocks several warning lights came on. Durfee returned to the dealership where the warning lights were stopped. Durfee then continued on home; however, on the way, the knob on the shift lever came off, a rattle in the dash began, and another warning light came on. He immediately called the dealership and was told to either bring the car back for repairs or wait until the 1,000-mile inspection. Durfee decided to wait for the 1,000-mile inspection. At the 1,000-mile inspection, Durfee also complained about the windshield-wiper system and air vents. The car was returned to repair the defroster, a continuing rattle, a sticking accelerator, and a brake squeal and choke. The front passenger seat was also removed in an attempt to fix the warning system lights.

After the 6,000-mile inspection, the problems became more pronounced. The car began to stall and was towed several times to the dealer lot. When the car had 6,300 miles on it, Durfee wrote a letter revoking acceptance and canceled the contract. He listed the following as defects: (1) the passenger seat had not been reinstalled; (2) the automobile continued to stall; (3) the seatbelt warning system continued to activate without apparent cause; (4) the "ungodly" rattle persisted; (5) the temperature gauge registered "hot"; and (6) shortly after starting the motor, the heating unit malfunctioned.

The trial court found for Durfee but only awarded him $600 in damages for breach of a warranty. Durfee appealed, claiming that the acceptance should be revoked and the contract should be canceled.

DECISION

The Supreme Court of Minnesota felt that the governing law in this case was §2-608 of the UCC. Section 2-608 allows for revocation when (1) a nonconformity exists that substantially impairs the value of the contract; (2) the nonconformity was not discoverable; and (3) the revocation occurs within a reasonable time. Saab-Scandia, the codefendant, argued that the defects did not substantially impair the contract "because they had already been repaired or were easily repairable." The court found, however, that Durfee "was plagued by a series of annoying difficulties with the Saab (the recurrent rattle and seatbelt buzz among them) as well as difficulty that directly interfered with the Saab's operation (the repeated stalling, which began five months after purchase and which, despite several attempted repairs, was never remedied)." The combination of minor defects and frequent stalling creates substantial impairment. Further, the defendants had numerous opportunities to repair the automobile. The court found revocation appropriate in this case and ordered that Durfee may recover the purchase price and $116.30 in incidental damages.

CASE QUESTIONS

1. Was Durfee justified in revoking his contract?
2. How many times must a consumer have a vehicle repaired before a contract should be allowed to be revoked?
3. Many states have enacted "lemon laws." What is the status of lemon laws in your state?

Click on agreement: An online contract in which the buyer indicates agreement to the terms by clicking on a box indicating "I agree" or "I accept."

shrink-wrap agreement: Terms of a contract which are expressed outside a box or container in which goods are located. Generally, the buyer is considered to have agreed to the terms by opening the container and keeping the goods. Not all courts will enforce shrink-wrap agreements.

Offer and acceptance can be difficult to ascertain when buyers and sellers are doing business online. A **click-on agreement** is one in which one party accepts an online offer by clicking a box that indicates language such as "I agree" or "I accept." Generally, courts have held that this is enough to indicate agreement to the terms contained in the offer. A **shrink-wrap agreement** is one in which the terms are expressed inside the box or container in which the goods are located. The outside of the box tells the buyer that he or she will agree to terms which are contained inside of it by keeping and using the product. Although some courts have refused to enforce the terms of a shrink-wrap agreement because the buyer did not expressly agree to them, others have found them to be enforceable.

CONSIDERATION

Besides having an offer and acceptance, a contract must also have legal consideration. The law does not bind people to all promises they make. For example, if Laura promises to love David forever and then later changes her mind, the law will not enforce her promise! *Consideration* means that each party to the contract gave up something that has value. Usually each party will give up money or property. Once in a while, though, an individual will give up a legal right rather than money or property. Imagine that Ned, 21 years old, promises his uncle that he will not drink any alcoholic beverage for five years. In return, his uncle promises that he will pay Ned $10,000 if he successfully lives up to his promise. After five years, Ned is entitled to $10,000 because he gave up his legal right to drink alcoholic beverages. On the other hand, assume Ned's uncle promises to give Ned $10,000 in five years without extracting any promise from him in return. But just before the five years expires, Ned's uncle dies. Is the uncle's estate liable to Ned for $10,000? The answer is no. If Ned's uncle had lived, he would not be legally liable to give Ned the $10,000 because no mutual consideration occurred. Ned did not give up anything of value. In other words, the promise of a gift is not enforceable. A gift is only enforceable when it has actually been delivered.

The promise to perform a new contract without additional consideration is also not sufficient consideration. For example, suppose Randy agrees to build Gary a home for $120,000. Halfway into the construction, Randy decides that it will really cost $150,000 to build the home and demands that Gary pay the higher price. Gary, having just sold his old home and currently living in his car, agrees to pay $150,000 rather than the contract price of $120,000. The new $150,000 contract, however, does not have consideration because Randy did not agree to do any additional work or give up any additional value. Since there was no new consideration, Gary will only have to pay $120,000.

Under the UCC, a *written modification* of an existing contract need not have new consideration to be effective. For example, Randy agrees to sell Gary his sports car for $60,000 and then changes his mind and refuses to sell the car unless Gary pays $70,000. If Gary agrees, in writing, to the $70,000 modification, he will be bound to the contract.

While consideration is very important to contracts, a distinction also exists between mutual consideration and adequacy of consideration. *Mutual consideration* means that consideration underlies the contract and is essential to forming a contract. *Adequacy of consideration* asks whether each party is receiving a fair bargain. The general rule is that courts do not care whether someone entered into a bad bargain. For example, if Zoe sold her $100,000 home to Roe for $5,000, a court would probably not disturb the contract for lack of adequacy. Courts sometimes do look at adequacy, however, to determine whether there was voluntary consent.

One type of problem arises when someone pays less than the amount due on a debt and writes on the check *payment in full*. In most circumstances, paying less than the amount owed does not result in a release from paying the full amount. In these circumstances, the parties are satisfying a **liquidated debt**, and the parties do not dispute how much is owed. However, an exception exists for **disputed** or **unliquidated debts**. In these cases, the parties legitimately disagree as to how much is owed, and the question then becomes whether there has been an *accord* and *satisfaction*. An accord and satisfaction occurs when the parties have agreed to a lesser amount on a disputed debt (the accord) and the amount has been paid and accepted (the satisfaction). For example, Gary discovers problems with the cabinetry throughout the house Randy built for him. Gary writes Randy a check for $115,000, rather than the $120,000 he originally promised to pay, and writes "payment in full" on the check. If Randy cashes the check, he has agreed that the lesser amount will satisfy the debt he is owed.

> **liquidated debt:** A debt not in dispute.

> **unliquidated debt:** A debt that is disputed.

VOLUNTARY CONSENT

As discussed, generally a valid contract has an offer, acceptance, and consideration. However, what if the person entering the contract was threatened or lied to: Does a contract still exist? The answer is no. Before a valid contract is formed, both parties have to agree freely to be bound. If the contract is not freely entered into, it is usually considered voidable, although sometimes it may be void.

Duress **Duress** is the threat of physical intimidation or coercion aimed at forcing individuals to enter into contracts against their will. The individual has to reasonably believe that the threat can be carried through, and the threat has to be the reason the individual enters into the contract. If he or she would have entered into the contract anyway, the defense of duress is not available. Entering into a contract because of severe financial constraints or the fear of embarrassment is not usually considered duress if the other party did not create the circumstances.

Contracts entered into under duress are voidable. In other words, simply because the one party enters into a contract under duress does not always mean the contract is automatically invalid. Rather, the party may end or void the contract at any time; until he or she does, however, the contract is valid. If, on entering into the contract, the person was subject to physical duress—actually getting beat up—as opposed to the threat of duress, the contract is void.

> **duress:** The threat of physical intimidation or coercion aimed at forcing individuals to enter into contracts against their will.

Undue Influence **Undue influence** may also invalidate a contract. Undue influence occurs when the parties have a special relationship with each other and one party uses that relationship to influence the other party to enter into a contract. Undue influence is not the same as duress. Undue influence concerns whether one person used a superior position to take unfair advantage of the other person. Typical contracts that raise suspicions are those involving a child and a parent, a physician and patient, a priest and a penitent, a husband and a wife, and an attorney and a client. These types of relationships can result in inequalities and are fraught with emotion. Dominant individuals have the

> **undue influence:** A situation in which a dominant person, or a person in a position of trust and confidence, takes advantage of another person.

opportunity to use the relationship to entice weaker individuals to enter into unfair contracts. A court looks at whether the parties acted freely and with full knowledge. A party can contract with someone with whom he or she shares a special relationship, but the contract is scrutinized much more carefully. The following case describes a typical situation involving undue influence.

IN THE MATTER OF THE WILL OF LEYLA K. BAIT-SCHORA V. ABAYHAN

700 S.E. 2d 50 (2010)

FACTS

Leyla Bait-Schora was 76 years old and lived in an apartment in New York City with her son, Martin Totorgul. Totorgul had been living with his mother for over a year, caring for her while she underwent cancer treatment. One evening in May 2007, Bait-Schora and Totorgul got into an argument. Bait-Schora asked her son to return her keys and leave the apartment, which he did. Bait-Schora later met with her financial advisor and changed the beneficiary designation on two of her brokerage accounts and an annuity from her son to her nephew, Ismail Abayhan, and his sisters, Ursula and Zubayda, in equal shares.

Shortly after she made these changes, Bait-Schora was admitted to the hospital and hospitalized. Upon her release, Abayhan packed her possessions and moved her to his home in North Carolina. Once she arrived at his home, Abayhan set about having her New York accounts transferred to North Carolina. Although she was "frail and weak," he took her to the bank to open two brokerage and/or IRA accounts, which she funded from accounts in New York, naming Abayhan and his sisters as beneficiaries.

On May 31, she was again admitted to the hospital. On June 4, while she was still in the hospital, Abayhan made arrangements with an attorney to prepare Bait-Schora's will and a power-of-attorney document designating him as her attorney-in-fact. He told the attorney's office that he would be the sole recipient of Bait-Schora's property under the will.

Bait-Schora was released from the hospital for a brief time on June 7, but was re-admitted to the emergency room on June 11.

While she was being readmitted, Abayhan made arrangements for the attorney to meet with Bait-Schora in the hospital to discuss her will and have her sign the power-of-attorney document. After the attorney left the hospital, Abayhan phoned the attorney three times within the next day and a half to find out when the will would be ready. Bait-Schora finally signed her will on June 12. Several hours later, a "Do Not Resuscitate Order" was issued for her. Bait-Schora was released from the hospital on the morning of June 13 "in order to go home and die." She did indeed die on June 22, in Abayhan's home.

Under the terms of her will, Abayhan was to be the sole beneficiary of all of Bait-Schora's cash and savings and checking accounts, with the residuary being left to his sisters. Before Bait-Schora died, between June 11 and June 18, Abayhan moved approximately $224,000 into the accounts he was to inherit solely, liquidating her IRA funds and other accounts that would have been part of residuary estate left to the sisters. This effectively meant that Abayhan inherited $243,260 under the will and his sisters inherited nothing. Bait-Schora's "non-probate assets," her brokerage accounts, remained equally divided between him and his sisters. Bait-Schora's son, Martin Totorgul, was left nothing.

In August, Totorgul filed an action to contest the probate of his mother's will, arguing that she had been unduly influenced by Abayhan. At trial, the jury agreed that the will had been procured by undue influence. The trial court set the will aside and granted Totorgul's request for attorney fees in the amount of $68,678. Abayhan appealed.

DECISION

Judge Hunter delivered the court's opinion. Four elements must be met to prove undue influence. First, the person in question must be subject to influence. Second, there must be an opportunity to exert influence. Third, there must be a disposition to exert influence. Finally, the result must indicate that undue influence occurred. In this case, the court held that the jury's finding of undue influence was strongly supported by the evidence. The court stated:

> At the time of the execution of the will, [Bait-Schora] was of advanced age, seventy-six years old, and suffering in Duke University Hospital from terminal uterine sarcoma. According to her medical records, the cancer had metastasized into her lungs and liver; and at the time the will was signed, [she] appeared sickly, feeble, and in poor physical condition. During this time, [Bait-Schora] was also dependent upon [Abayhan] to sign medical releases at the hospital. [Totorgul] testified that his phone calls to speak to his mother went unreturned. The attorney who drafted the will was procured by [Abayhan], and [Abayhan] was present during the interview with the paralegal who prepared the will. [Abayhan] made transfers of sums of cash from his aunt's accounts prior to her death, which had the effect of maximizing his post-death inheritance to the exclusion of his sisters when [Bait-Schora] had specifically included the sisters in beneficiary designations. There was extensive evidence demonstrating [Abayhan's] impatience in connection with the execution of the will and the power of attorney, and the rapid pace that [Abayhan] moved money and accounts as soon as he had the ability to do so. These events occurred within the immediate time frame of the execution of the will, and specifically concern indicia our appellate courts have held to be highly probative on the issue of undue influence.

The court affirmed the jury's finding of undue influence and award of attorney fees.

CASE QUESTIONS

1. How did the court reach its decision?
2. Do you agree with the jury that Abayhan unduly influenced his aunt regarding her will? Is this a fair outcome?
3. Situations such as this have been referred to as "elder abuse." Are they common? What can elderly people and their families do to avoid being taken advantage of?

Fraud   A contract can be voided if its formation was based on fraudulent representations. There are two types of fraud: *fraud in the execution* and *fraud in the inducement*. Fraud in the execution occurs when one party does not intend to contract. For example, say Sara approaches her blind grandmother and asks that she sign a piece of paper enabling Sara to rent for her grandmother some novels on tape. In fact, the paper is a contract for the sale of Grandma's new condominium. This is fraud in the execution, and the contract is void. Grandma did not intend to contract.

Fraud in the inducement occurs when one party lies to the other party about a material fact. But for the lie, the contract would not have been formed. Suppose Sara approaches her blind grandmother and asks if she wants to buy Sara's three-bedroom luxury condominium in Florida where Sara has lived the past three years. Her grandmother, tired of the cold winter, agrees to buy the condominium. She discovers later that the condominium does not have three bedrooms, is not luxurious, and is literally falling apart. Under these circumstances, there is fraud in the inducement. Sara intentionally lied to her grandmother about material facts. The grandmother reasonably relied on those misrepresentations, much to her detriment, but she intended to contract. The contract is voidable.

Mistakes   Sometimes contracts can be voided because a mistake was made. There are three types of mistakes: *unilateral*, *ambiguous*, and *bilateral*. A unilateral mistake occurs when one party is mistaken under the contract and the other party did not know the party was mistaken. For example, Roger submits a bid to install the lights for a new office building. In compiling his bid, he makes a mathematical error. Roger's bid is accepted. Unless the owners of the office building knew or should have known that Roger made an error, the mistake is unilateral and Roger is bound.

Sometimes terms in the contract are ambiguous, and neither party understands what the other party intended. In the classic example, a contract was formed that stated that goods are to be sent on the ship *Peerless*. The seller believed that the goods would be sent on the *Peerless* that left Bombay, India, in December. The buyer believed that the goods would be sent on a different *Peerless* that left Bombay in October. The court held the term Peerless was ambiguous in this situation and that the parties did not have a "meeting of the minds."[1] When the contract was first entered into, both parties believed they understood its terms. When the contract was to be fulfilled, however, it became clear that neither party had actually understood that each believed Peerless to be a different ship. Ambiguous contracts are voidable at either party's option.

The third type of mistake is a mutual, or bilateral, mistake. In this type of case, both parties are mistaken. The question then turns on whether the parties are mistaken as to the subject matter of the contract or if they are mistaken as to the value of the contract. If the mistake is over subject matter, the contract is voidable. The contract is not voidable, however, if the mistake is over value. For example, Ted agrees to buy Tana's Rembrandt painting for $6,000,000. Unknown to either Ted or Tana, the Rembrandt is really a forgery. This is a mutual mistake about the subject matter of the contract and the contract is voidable. On the other hand, assume the Rembrandt is authentic but when Ted tries to resell it, the piece turns out to be worth only $3,000,000. This is a mistake as to the value of the contract, and the contract is not voidable.

CAPACITY

The law presumes that certain individuals, such as minors and incompetents, cannot protect themselves. As a result, the law steps in to protect them when they enter into a contract. These individuals do not have legal *capacity* to enter into contracts.

minor: An individual under the legal age to contract.

Minors   A **minor** is an individual under the legal age to contract. In most states, that age is 18 years. If a contract is entered into with a minor, the contract is voidable, at the minor's option, anytime until the minor reaches

---

[1] Raffles v. Wichelhaus, 159 Eng. Rep. 375 (Court of Exchequer, 1864).

majority. When the minor reaches majority, the minor can either **disaffirm** the contract or **ratify** the contract. Minors disaffirming contracts are entitled to be returned to the position in which they began; that is, they get their money back. They are responsible for returning anything they received under the contract, if they still have it. Note that, since the law is aimed at protecting minors from themselves, in most states it makes no difference if minors misrepresent their age—the contract is still voidable.

Incompetency   Some people suffer from mental illnesses that might impair their ability to contract. If a court judges a person mentally incompetent, any contract he or she formed is void. If a person is mentally incompetent but not judged so by a court, the question turns on whether the mental illness results in the inability to adequately protect his or her interest. For example, suppose Jan suffers from schizophrenia and believes that demons are following her around town. She stops at Joe's Jewelry Store and insists on buying a large diamond cross necklace costing $5,000 to protect her from the demons. In this case, the mental illness has affected her ability to contract, and the contract is voidable. On the other hand, if Jan stops in the store to buy a gift for her mother's birthday and her mental illness does not affect her ability to understand the contract, she is bound to the contract.

Sometimes intoxication or drug use can impair a person's ability to contract. The question, however, is not merely whether a person had been drinking alcohol (many business contracts could not pass that test!) or under the influence of drugs. Rather, the question is whether there was a *genuineness of assent*. To put it another way, did the individual know that a contract was being formed. If the intoxication or drug use did not impair the ability to understand the contract, incompetency is not a defense.

Necessities   Both minors and persons who are found mentally incompetent are still bound to contracts for necessities. Courts reason that incompetent individuals still need the items necessary to sustain life. Necessities are food, clothing, and shelter not otherwise provided.

LEGALITY

As stated earlier, contracts must be *legal*, which means they cannot violate public policy. Some contracts are illegal because the legislature makes them illegal. In most states, a contract for prostitution is illegal by state statute. Contracts that are not illegal but that violate public policy, however, are more difficult. One such contract is an antenuptial contract, which is a contract entered into before a marriage. Early case law considered these a violation of public policy. That rule is changing and now these contracts are often enforced.

In order to be legal, contracts also have to contain legal subject matter. Therefore, for example, a contract to sell heroin is illegal. Illegal contracts are void. However, questions of legality often are not so clear-cut. For example, is a contract between a couple who cannot have children and a woman who agrees to bear a child for the couple legal? The New Jersey Supreme Court, in the so-called *Baby M* case, ruled that such contracts are illegal and therefore invalid. "While we recognize the depth of yearning of infertile couples to have their

disaffirm: A decision not to be bound to a contract.

ratify: To adopt the act even if it was not approved beforehand; to agree to be bound to a contract.

own children," wrote Chief Justice Robert Wilentz, "we find the payment of money to a 'surrogate' mother illegal, perhaps criminal, and potentially degrading to women." However, other states, like California, have enforced surrogacy contracts. In recent years, as more same-sex couples have sought to adopt children, issues regarding surrogacy contracts have become more complex, as the next article explains.

Hudson County, N.J., Trial Judge Declares Gestational Surrogacy Contract Involving Gay Male Couple Unenforceable

A New Jersey Superior Court Judge ruled on December 23, 2009, that a gestational surrogate who has no genetic relationship to the twin girls she bore by agreement with a gay male couple is the legal mother of the children. The case illustrates the complications that may ensue when same-sex couples seek to have children by involving third parties. We first heard about this case last month through press reports, but have just come into possession of a copy of the court's unpublished decision in *A.G.R. v. D.R.H. & S.H.*, Docket # FD-09-001838-07 (N.J. Superior Ct., Hudson County, Dec. 23, 2009).

The opinion by Superior Court Judge Francis B. Schultz is vague about some of the dates, so reconstructing the factual history requires some guesswork.

It seems that D.R. and S.H., a gay male couple who reside in New Jersey, registered as domestic partners in that state under the Domestic Partnership Act. They sought to have a child, and D.R.'s sister, A.G.R., volunteered to be a surrogate for them. When it turned out that her own eggs were not suitable for the procedure, eggs were obtained from an anonymous woman. S.H. was the sperm donor. A doctor performed the insemination. A.G.R., D.R., and S.H. entered into written agreements spelling out the rights and obligations of the parties, under which A.G.R. agreed to consent to the termination of any parental rights and the adoption of the child by D.R.

The court also states that D.R. and S.H. were married in California, but does not mention a date, so it seems likely that they were married subsequent to the main events in this case, as same-sex marriage did not become available in California until the spring of 2008. The New Jersey Attorney General's Office during the Corzine Administration (which ended January 19) took the position that same-sex couples validly married in other states would be treated as civil union partners for purposes of New Jersey law. However, apart from reciting that the men married in California and registered as domestic partners in New Jersey, Judge Schultz never mentions their legal status as partners again in the opinion and apparently placed no weight on that factor in reaching his conclusions.

Twin girls were born on October 4, 2006. A.G.R. visited the girls in the hospital and after they were released to the custody of D.R. and S.H. until January 2007, when their dispute arose. After A.G.R. filed suit seeking a declaration of her legal status as parent of the twins, the court ordered that visitation resume. Since September 2007, A.G.R. has had three full days of parenting time with the twins every week, and D.R. and S.H. have had the twins the other four days.

In her lawsuit, A.G.R. claimed that as birth mother of the twins she was entitled to the legal status of a parent. D.R. and S.H. pointed to the various agreements that were executed, under which A.G.R. had agreed in advance to allow the twins to be adopted by her brother, which necessarily terminated her parental rights. A.G.R. countered that the agreement to give up the twins for adoption was not valid under New Jersey law because of the New Jersey Supreme Court's 1988 decision *In the Matter of Baby M.*, 109 N.J. 396. In that case, the dispute was between a surrogate (who was also the egg donor, and thus genetically related to the child she bore) and the different-sex married couple who contracted with her to produce a child for them, using the husband's sperm. The surrogate was compensated financially. The New Jersey Supreme Court found the element of compensation objectionable, tantamount to baby-selling prohibited by N.J. law, and also objected to a biological mother consenting to adoption in advance of the birth of the child. Thus, the court held that the surrogacy agreement was invalid and unenforceable as a matter of public policy, and that the child's legal parents were the surrogate mother and the genetic father, giving the surrogate mother the right of visitation after concluding that it was in the best interest of the child to live with its genetic father and his wife.

D.R. and S.H. sought to distinguish *Baby M.*, because A.G.R. is not the genetic parent of the twins. They also argued that A.G.R. was a volunteer, not a paid surrogate. Judge Schultz rejected these distinctions as being legally insignificant. The judge pointed out that the court in the *Baby M* case did not focus on the surrogate's genetic tie to the child, and had relied on various factors apart from compensation in reaching its determination that surrogacy agreements were contrary to public policy in New Jersey.

"It was pointed out in *Baby M* that the Parentage Act was silent as to acknowledging surrogacy agreements and that Court suggested that the silence of the Legislature suggested that the Legislature chose not to recognize surrogacy. If that interpretation of the Legislature's silence is correct, the additional twenty-one years of silence as to surrogacy agreements speaks even louder," wrote Judge Schultz.

"It also was the position of the Court that surrogacy as a whole is bad for women even if in any one particular case the surrogacy agreement is entirely satisfactory to all parties involved. *Baby M* did not find a constitutional right for a surrogate mother to the companionship of her child only because that issue was moot since the surrogacy contract was invalid, and the parental rights were not properly terminated. The Parentage Act gave both the birth mother, because she gave birth to the child, the status of parent as well as the man who contributed the genetic link. This is because 'the natural mother, may be established by proof of her having given birth to the child,' NJSA 9:17-41(a), and 'the natural father may be established . . . on a blood test or genetic test,' NJSA 9:17-41(b)."

"Essentially," the judge continued, "the Supreme Court had no difficulty with surrogacy agreements so long as there was no payment and so long as the surrogate mother is given the right to change her mind. While the *Baby M* decision did not distinguish between 'gestational' carriers and 'surrogate' mothers, the Court was well aware of the preservation of sperm and eggs and embryo implantation," procedures which are mentioned in passing in the *Baby M* opinion. In *Baby M,* the New Jersey Supreme Court had also stressed psychological issues, particularly the bonding between a pregnant woman and her expected child, as a factor that counseled against enforcing agreements to terminate parental rights for adoption that were made before the child is born.

Judge Schultz disagreed with the defendants' argument that the lack of a genetic tie between A.G.R. and the twins made the case distinguishable from *Baby M.* "The public policy considerations enumerated above from *Baby M* are far reaching and unrelated to a strict genetic connection," Schultz insisted. "The lack of plaintiff's genetic link to the twins is, under the circumstances, a distinction without a difference significant enough to take the instant matter out of *Baby M."*

Schultz also rejected the significance of California cases holding that the intent of the parties upon entering into a surrogacy arrangement would later be binding when a surrogate changed her mind and sought parental status. Schultz pointed out that California has a different statutory framework and has embraced different public policies from New Jersey. "If the underlying principles in California were consistent with the principles in New Jersey, then the reasoning in the California case upholding the gestational carrier agreement might have been tempting," Schultz wrote. "However, New Jersey's law as expressed in *Baby M* and the California case had so many conflicting underpinnings that this judge sees no reason to follow the California law or that of other jurisdictions for the same reason."

"The parties' intent in voluntarily entering into the surrogacy agreement was of no significance under *Baby M,"* wrote Schultz. "This clearly suggests that arguments derived from intent such as detrimental reliance and estoppel would be of no significance either."

Thus, Schultz concluded that A.G.R. was entitled to summary judgment on her claim to be a legal parent of the twins. Schultz declared that the surrogacy agreement was void and could not serve as a basis for terminating A.G.R.'s parental rights or implementing her consent to having the children adopted by her brother. At the same time, Schultz found that S.H. "is the legal father of the twins."

This ruling on the motion does not end matters, since the declaration that A.G.R. and S.H. are the legal parents of the twins leaves open questions of custody. When legal parents are not living together and cannot work out an amicable agreement on custody and visitation, a court will decide these issues based on its determination of what would be in the best interest of the child. Having been declared a legal parent of the twins, A.G.R. is now in an equal position with their legal father, S.H., to contend for custody. The opinion does not indicate whether A.G.R. was seeking to be a custodial parent, or merely seeking to assert parental rights to visitation and a decisional role in the upbringing of the children.

A.G.R. is represented by Harold J. Cassidy. D.R.H. and S.H., the fathers, are represented by Alan S. Modlinger. Daniel A. D'Allessandro served as Law Guardian appointed by the Court to represent the interest of the twins in this lawsuit.

Source: Taken from Leonard Link Blog at: newyorklawschool.typepad.com/leonardlink. Accessed June 21, 2011.

Sometimes contracts are not illegal but take unfair advantage of a person—usually a poor, disadvantaged consumer. If the contract is so one-sided that a reasonable person would not have agreed to it, a court may find that it is **unconscionable** and refuse to enforce it. Often it is consumers who do not understand the terms of the contract, and the enforcement of those contractual terms puts these consumers at a serious disadvantage. These contracts are signed by consumers and contain technical legal language. **Adhesion contracts** may fall into this category. Adhesion contracts are standardized forms that are offered on a "take-it-or-leave-it" proposition. The consumer lacks "meaningful choice." Unconscionability is rarely found in contracts between businesspeople, because the court generally assumes that businesspeople have equal bargaining power and the ability to protect themselves. An unconscionable contract is voidable.

> **unconscionable contract:** A contract so unfair that no reasonable person would enter into it.

> **adhesion contracts:** Standardized contract forms offered to consumers of goods and services on a "take-it-or-leave it" basis.

 SOCIAL/ETHICAL ISSUES

Contract law assumes that most individuals can protect themselves when it comes to entering into contracts. It assumes that most of the time everyone has equal bargaining power. Can you think of contracts that you have entered into in which you might not have had equal bargaining power? For example, think about your employment contract, your housing contract, or the warranty contract on your automobile. Did you have equal bargaining power when you entered into those contracts? Should the law continue to assume equal bargaining power?

CONTRACTS IN WRITING

Up until this point we have assumed that contracts can be either oral or in writing. As a practical matter, however, contracts should be in writing because it is more difficult to prove the terms of an oral contract.

STATUTE OF FRAUDS

Some contracts have to be in writing to be enforceable. These contracts fall under the **Statute of Frauds**. All contracts for the sale of real property, for instance, must be in writing, as well as all contracts that cannot possibly be performed within one year. Contracts by executors of estates to personally pay a decedent's debts must be in writing. A contract to guarantee another's debt must also be in writing to be enforced, as does a contract in which marriage is the consideration. Under the UCC, all contracts for the sale of goods over $500 must also be in writing. The UCC rule does exclude contracts in which the goods have been specially manufactured, there has been part performance or part delivery, or the parties admit, in court, that a contract exists.

> **Statute of Frauds:** A state law modeled on the English Statute of Frauds, which requires that certain contracts must be in writing to be enforceable.

> ### CONTRACTS THAT NEED TO BE IN WRITING
>
> - Sale of goods over $500
> - Sale of real property
> - Cannot possibly be performed in one year
> - Executor agreement to personally pay the debt of the deceased
> - Guarantee to pay the debt of another
> - Marriage is the consideration

PAROL EVIDENCE

parol evidence: Oral testimony in court about the terms of a written contract.

Parol evidence is oral testimony in court about the terms of a written contract. Parol evidence only applies to evidence of prior oral agreements, not subsequent ones. Even though most contracts do not have to be in writing to be enforced, it is, of course, very good practice to enter into written contracts. A written contract helps all parties understand exactly what is expected of each. To be enforceable, a written contract needs to be signed by the party who is being sued. If there is a written contract, courts generally do not allow the parties to testify as to what the contract means. The assumption is that the contract contains all the parties' intentions, the contract is **integrated**, and the court can read the contract to determine what it means. This is especially true if the contract contains a **merger clause** that specifically says all previous agreements are merged into the final contract, which is to be the complete statement of the parties' agreement.

integrated: The contract contains all of each party's understanding.

Sometimes a contract is said to be *partially integrated*, which means that the parties have not put all of their agreement in writing. For example, if Wayne sells his house to Wanda and includes in the contract a provision for selling his lawn mower and boat, the contract is fully integrated with regard to real and personal property that are to be sold. If Wanda then wants to testify that Wayne also agreed to sell her his lawn furniture, a court probably will not allow the testimony. On the other hand, if the contract did not say anything about the personal property, Wanda can argue that the contract is only partially integrated and that she should be allowed to testify about the sale of personal property. Note that Wanda may only argue this if the amount in question is under $500, since contracts of over $500 for the sale of goods must be in writing—and lawn furniture is a good. Also, if the terms of the contract are ambiguous or a subsequent agreement has taken place, the parties are allowed to testify.

merger clause: A clause in a contract stating that the contract is a complete statement of the agreement and supersedes any prior terms, representations, or agreements whether made orally or in writing.

If there is a written contract, the court first looks at the express meaning of the words. If the express meaning does not help in deciding what the contract means, the court next looks at the parties' course of performance (how they dealt with each other on this particular contract). If the court still cannot tell what the contract means, it then looks to course of dealing (how the parties acted on previous contracts). If the court is still undecided, it looks at usage of trade or trade practice (how others in the industry act). If the contract is too ambiguous, the court ultimately may decide that there was no meeting of the minds and, therefore, that the contract does not exist.

Traditionally, contracts are signed by each party but in fact only need to be signed by the person against whom the contract is being enforced. This has become problematic for fax and internet contracts. Currently, most courts will enforce a faxed signature. To answer questions concerning electronic signatures, Congress passed the Electronic Signatures in Global and National Commerce Act (E-SIGN). E-SIGN makes it clear that electronic signatures are as valid as written signatures. Also, electronic documents can create a valid contract if the contract would be valid if it were in writing.

In addition to E-SIGN, most states have adopted some form of the Uniform Electronic Transactions Act (UETA), which was first proposed in 1999. The UETA establishes rules which govern electronic writings and signatures relating to business, commercial, or governmental transactions. Under UETA, electronic records, signatures, and contracts are to have the same legal effect as paper versions of similar documents. E-SIGN and UETA are generally compatible, but to the extent that any given state's adoption of UETA conflicts with E-SIGN, E-SIGN will prevail because it is federal law.

THIRD-PARTY BENEFICIARY AND ASSIGNMENT CONTRACTS

Once a contract has been formed, the contract is enforceable against either party to the contract. Usually someone who is not a party to the contract cannot sue for its enforcement. However, exceptions do exist for **third-party beneficiary** and **assignment** contracts. In a third-party beneficiary contract, another person (the third party) benefits from the contract. This third party may either be an *intended beneficiary* or an **incidental beneficiary**. Intended beneficiaries are named in the contract itself. They may be **donee beneficiaries**, which means they received the benefits as a gift. An example is a beneficiary of a life insurance policy. When the policy holder dies, the beneficiary can sue to enforce the policy. Intended beneficiaries may also be **creditor beneficiaries**. A creditor beneficiary is someone who is owed benefits from another contract. For example, suppose Beth owes Al $200. Beth contracts to sell Cass $200 worth of beans, and Cass agrees in the contract to pay the $200 to Al. Al is a creditor beneficiary under the contract and can sue to enforce it.

An incidental beneficiary benefits from a contract (although not named in it) but cannot sue to enforce it. For example, Ellen agrees to pay Dave $5,000 for accounting services. Dave performs the services, but Ellen only pays $1,000. Frank, Dave's 20-year-old son, was planning to receive the $5,000 from his dad to pay for tuition. Although Frank suffers from Ellen's failure to satisfy the contract, Frank is an incidental beneficiary and cannot sue. Only Dave can sue to enforce the contract.

Third parties are also involved when a contract is **assigned**. Contracts have both *rights* and *duties*. A party to a contract may have the right to receive money or the right to receive performance under the contract. Moreover, these rights and duties can be assigned to third parties. For example, Grant has a contract with Harry in which Harry agrees to pay Grant $300 and, in return, Grant agrees to provide Harry with a purebred English springer spaniel. Grant sells his right to receive Harry's $300 to Ingrid for $250. Once Harry receives notice that the contract has been assigned, Harry must pay Ingrid and not Grant. If Harry does not pay Ingrid, Ingrid can sue to enforce the contract. Generally, *rights* can be assigned unless assignment is expressly prohibited in the contract. The right to receive money can always be assigned. Under the UCC, the right to assign damages for breach of contract also can be assigned. A contract cannot prohibit assigning these rights.

third-party beneficiary: A person or entity that is not a party to but has rights under a contract made by two other parties.

incidental beneficiary: A third-party beneficiary to a contract whom the parties to the contract did not intend to benefit.

donee beneficiary: A direct beneficiary whom the party paying for the other party's performance intends to benefit as a gift or donation.

creditor beneficiary: A direct beneficiary whom the party paying for the other party's performance intends to benefit as payment for a debt or obligation.

assignment: A present transfer of property or rights.

Contractual *duties* may be delegated. If the duty is ministerial (something anyone can do), then the duties are freely delegable. If, however, the duties are unique to that particular person, then they cannot be delegated. For example, Jerry hires Kate to paint his portrait. Kate gets too busy and wants to delegate that duty to her assistant Lee. Since an artist's talents are uniquely personal, Jerry would not have to accept the delegation.

PERFORMANCE, DISCHARGE, AND BREACH

discharge: To release from an obligation.

After a contract is formed, it is important that it be performed. Both parties, of course, anticipate that each will fully perform the contract. Otherwise, they would never have entered into the contract in the first place. When a contract is fully performed, each party is **discharged**, which means they have no more obligations under the contract. Discharge can also occur when (1) the contract has a condition that has not been met, (2) the parties agree to discharge, (3) the law allows for a discharge, or (4) one party breaches the contract.

condition precedent: A condition that must be fulfilled before performance under a contract can become due or a right can become effective.

All contracts are conditional by nature. For example, Harry agrees to buy Paula's car for $5,000, and Paula agrees to sell her car for $5,000. Harry need not pay the $5,000 until he receives the car, and Paula need not give Harry the car until she receives the $5,000. This is referred to as *simultaneous conditions*. As a practical matter, one party will perform before the other, but the conditions are still considered simultaneous. Another type of condition is a **condition precedent**. This is a condition that has to occur before any party has performance obligations. For example, Harry agrees to buy Paula's car for $5,000 if the interest rate on automobile loans drops to 6 percent in the next month. If automobile loan interest rates do not drop to 6 percent within the month, neither Harry nor Paula is required to perform the contract. The last type of condition is referred to as a condition subsequent. This is a rare condition that is imposed after a *breach* (default) has occurred. For example, it is not unusual for insurance companies to require that they be notified of impending lawsuits within one year of when the accident occurred. This is a **condition subsequent** in that it is a condition that has to be complied with after the insurance company has failed to pay the amount the policy holder believed was due.

condition subsequent: A condition whose fulfillment defeats or modifies a right already in effect or discharges an already existing duty under a contract.

Furthermore, the parties can mutually agree to discharge obligations under a contract. A material change in a contract can discharge the nonagreeing party. Bankruptcy (Chapter 18) and the running of the statute of limitations will also discharge the performance obligations. *Impossibility* and *commercial impracticability* may discharge a party. Impossibility occurs when the subject matter of the contract is destroyed and the contract cannot be performed. For example, Bryan contracts to buy Barbara's house for $100,000. The very next day, Barbara's house burns to the ground. The contract is now impossible to perform, since the subject matter has been destroyed (through no fault of either of the parties). Neither party has to perform under the contract. Other incidents that create impossibility include death of one of the parties in a personal service contract and a change in the law that makes performance illegal.

Sometimes courts release individuals from their performance obligations if performance is commercially impracticable or if the *purpose of the contract is frustrated*. Commercial impracticability refers to situations in which, although possible to perform, such performance will be extremely costly. For example, AJ

Airways agrees to a contract with JB Petroleum whereby AJ Airways will buy gasoline from JB Petroleum at $2 a gallon for the next year. Within three months of signing the contract, war breaks out in the Middle East, raising gas prices to over $6 a gallon. In this case, since the war maybe viewed as *unforeseeable* and the price per gallon rose *exceedingly high*, some courts would invoke the doctrine of commercial impracticability and release JB Petroleum from its performance obligations. Frustration of purpose occurs when the parties intended one event when the contract was signed and the event did not occur. If the purpose of the contract is frustrated, the parties may not need to perform. Courts are skeptical, however, about invoking either frustration of purpose or commercial impracticability. Therefore, it is only the most extreme circumstances that generally qualify for discharges under these legal doctrines.

SOCIAL/ETHICAL ISSUES

One of the international complaints about U.S. business practices is that contracts are viewed too formally. U.S. businesspeople expect that others will perform a contract even when conditions have changed. Should contracts be more flexible and not so formalistic? Should they be viewed as absolute agreements to perform or should the underlying value of the relationship be more important?

As was stated earlier, each party to the contract can expect full performance from the other party. If full performance does not occur, then the breaching or defaulting party can be sued for damages. The time for performance is generally considered to be a reasonable time. If the parties to a contract want performance to occur at a specific time, they need to include the words "time is of the essence" to ensure that the contract will be performed on a specific day; otherwise, reasonableness is the standard.

Generally, a party is not in breach until performance is due. For example, Sam agrees to deliver a refrigerator to Martha on December 1. Technically, Sam has until December 1 to deliver the goods. If Martha calls Sam on November 15 to make sure that he will be able to deliver the refrigerator and Sam tells Martha that he has sold all of his refrigerators and will not be able to deliver Martha's, Sam has created an immediate breach, referred to as an **anticipatory breach**. If Sam only expressed doubt that he would be able to perform, then under the UCC Martha can demand *adequate assurances* from Sam that he will be able to perform. This is a *written* statement that Sam will be able to deliver the refrigerator on December 1. If Martha does not receive adequate assurances, she can wait until December 1, she can retract her own performance, or she can *cover*, which means she can try to get another person to provide her with a refrigerator. Regardless, Martha is still entitled to damages.

When there has been a breach of contract, under the common law, whether the nonbreaching party has to perform on the contract depends on whether there was *substantial performance*, *partial performance*, or *nonperformance*. Of course, if there is complete performance, then the other party is required to completely perform. Suppose Simpson hires Chancy to build him a house, and as part of the contract, Chancy is to paint Simpson's door brown. Instead of

anticipatory breach: The repudiation by a promisor of the contract prior to the time that the performance is required when such repudiation is accepted by the promisee as a breach of the contract.

painting the door brown, Simpson paints it white. Clearly the main purpose of the contract has been performed, but it has not been performed completely; therefore, Chancy is in breach. Under this circumstance, the contract has been substantially performed, and Simpson must pay Chancy the agreed-upon price. Simpson is entitled to damages from Chancy, which is the price of having the door repainted. But if Simpson has hired Chancy only to paint the door brown and Chancy painted the door white, Chancy would have only partially performed the contract. The main purpose of the contract is to paint the door brown. Since this purpose was not performed, Simpson is relieved of his performance obligation *under the contract*. This is not the end of the story, however, since Simpson does have a newly painted door. The court will apply the equitable doctrine of ***quantum meruit***. Simpson will not have to pay the contract price, but he will have to pay the reasonable value of Chancy's services minus the damages that he will incur having the door repainted. As the following case indicates, it can sometimes be difficult to prove whether one party has fully performed a contract.

quantum meruit:
"As much as he deserved."

In the Language of the Court

YOUNG V. FACEBOOK 2010

WL 4269304 N.D.Cal.

Judge Fogel delivered the court's opinion.

On July 30, 2010, Plaintiff Karen Beth Young filed a complaint in the Superior Court of California against Defendant Facebook, Inc., alleging claims, pursuant to 42 U.S.C. § 1983, for . . . state law claims for breach of contract [and] breach of the implied covenant of good faith and fair dealing. . . . Facebook removed the action to this Court on August 13, 2010, and thereafter brought the instant motion to dismiss. For the reasons set forth below, Facebook's motion will be granted, and Young's complaint will be dismissed with leave to amend.

I. BACKGROUND

In February 2010, Young opened a personal account on Facebook. She subsequently created additional Facebook pages for the " Cancer Forum," "Cartesian Plane For The Cure," "Karen Beth Young-Public Figure," and "Join Karen Petition Facebook Say No to 5000 Friends." Young sent "friendvites" to others she believed were interested in cancer-related issues and developed "genuine and heartfelt" relationships with those she met online. Young's personal page grew to include approximately 4,300 "friends."

While engaged in social networking on Facebook, Young came across a page titled "DEAR LORD, THIS YEAR YOU TOOK MY FAVORITE ACTOR, PATRICK SWAYZIE. YOU TOOK MY FAVORITE ACTRESS, FARAH FAWCETT. YOU TOOK MY FAVORITE SINGER, MICHAEL JACKSON. I JUST WANTED TO LET YOU KNOW, MY FAVORITE PRESIDENT IS BARACK OBAMA. AMEN" ("Prayer for Death" page). Young spoke out against the page and was subjected to "hatred, violence, discrimination, threats, pornography, . . . and personal attacks" as a result. In particular, her profile picture—a photo of her holding a baby with her sister in church—was reposted "with the baby as a giant penis shooting sperm" in her sister's face. Young joined a petition requesting that Facebook remove the Prayer for Death page. Young alleges that her account was modified to prevent her from accessing the petition to remove the Prayer for Death page.

In June 2010, Young's Facebook account was deactivated for the first time. According to an email from Facebook, Young's account was disabled for behavior identified as harassing or threatening to other people on Facebook, including sending friend requests to people she did not know, regularly contacting strangers, and soliciting others for dating or business purposes. She was told that the decision was final and could not be appealed. Young made numerous email and telephone inquiries regarding the deactivation, but she did not receive any "human interaction" regarding her account. Young then drove from her home in Maryland to Facebook headquarters in Santa Clara, California. At Facebook headquarters she was told by a receptionist that no one could meet with her in person or by telephone, although she was allowed to fill out a form requesting assistance.

Two days later, Young received an email stating that her account had been disabled because Facebook security systems determined that she had been sending friend requests too quickly or that her friend requests were being ignored at a high rate. She was told that her account would be reactivated, but she was warned that sending friend requests to people she did not know or other violations of Facebook's Statement of Rights and Responsibilities, would result in her account being disabled permanently. Young responded to the email requesting clarification and a personal meeting. Receiving no response, she returned to Maryland, where after two days her account was deactivated again. She received another email informing her that her account had been disabled permanently for violating the Statement of Rights and Responsibilities, that it would not be reactivated for any reason, and that she would not be provided further information about her violation or an opportunity to appeal. Young then drove to California a second time, where she commenced the instant proceedings.

II. STANDARD OF REVIEW

Under Fed.R.Civ.P. Rule 8(a), a plaintiff must plead her claim with sufficient specificity to "give the defendant fair notice of what the . . . claim is and the grounds upon which it rests." Dismissal for failure to state a claim under Rule 12(b)(6) "is appropriate only where the complaint lacks a cognizable legal theory or sufficient facts to support a cognizable legal theory." The pleading of a *pro se* litigant is held to a less stringent standard than a pleading drafted by an attorney, and is afforded the benefit of any doubt. Further, a *pro se* litigant must be given leave to amend unless it is absolutely clear that the deficiencies of the complaint cannot be cured by amendment.

Young has not stated a claim for breach of contract.

Under California law, "when a contract has been reduced to writing, a court must ascertain the parties' intent from the writing alone, if possible." In an action for breach of a written contract, a plaintiff must allege the specific provisions in the contract creating the obligation the defendant is said to have breached.

Young alleges generally that Facebook violated its Statement of Rights and Responsibilities, its advertised Facebook Principles, and its Privacy Policy. However, Young has not identified with any particularity how Facebook breached any obligation owed to her. She states that her claims "are based on user content, page content, poor business practices and poor business procedures." She points to Facebook's failure to enforce provisions of its Statement of Rights and Responsibilities that call for users not to engage in bullying, intimidating, or harassing other users or posting content that is "hateful, threatening, or pornographic; incites violence; or contains nudity." However, while these provisions place restrictions on users' behavior, they do not create affirmative obligations.

Indeed, the Statement of Rights and Responsibilities includes an express disclaimer: "WE DO NOT GUARANTEE THAT FACEBOOK WILL BE SAFE OR SECURE. FACEBOOK IS NOT RESPONSIBLE FOR THE ACTIONS, CONTENT, INFORMATION, OR DATA OF THIRD PARTIES."

III. DISCUSSION

Young has not stated a claim for breach of the implied covenant of good faith and fair dealing.

Under California law, "there is implied in every contract a covenant by each party not to do anything which will deprive the other parties thereto of the benefits of the contract." The "implied covenant of good faith is read into contracts in order to protect the express covenants or promises in the contract, not to protect some general public policy interest not directly tied to the contract's purpose." To state a claim for breach of the implied covenant, a plaintiff must show "that the conduct of the defendant, whether or not it also constitutes a breach of a consensual contract term, demonstrates a failure or refusal to discharge contractual responsibilities." The implied covenant will not apply where "no express term exists on which to hinge an implied duty, and where there has been compliance with the contract's express terms." In other words, a party must take on an obligation, either expressly or impliedly, before it can be said to have acted in bad faith by not carrying it out.

Young alleges that Facebook breached the implied covenant of good faith and fair dealing by (1) failing to provide the safety services it advertised and (2) violating the spirit of its terms of service in handling the termination of her account. Young's first contention is without merit because, as noted above, Facebook expressly disclaimed any duty to protect users' online safety. The Statement of Rights and Responsibilities notes that, "We do our best to keep Facebook safe, but we cannot guarantee it." Because Facebook did not assume the duty alleged by Young, it could not have acted in bad faith by breaching such a duty.

Young's second contention is not so easily put aside. Facebook acknowledges that its Statement of Rights and Responsibilities is an operative contract. As with all contracts, Facebook has an implied duty not to frustrate the other party's right to receive the benefits of the agreement actually made. The agreement in this case is to provide users access to Facebook's services subject to certain terms and conditions. While users do not pay for the services directly, Facebook benefits from user activity through the sale of advertising. Facebook expressly reserves the right to terminate the accounts of users who "violate the letter or the spirit of this Statement, or otherwise create risk or possible legal exposure" for Facebook, but it does not expressly reserve the right to terminate an account for any reason, and indicates in its Statement of Principles that users "should not have their presence on the Facebook Service removed for reasons other than those described in Facebook's Statement of Rights and Responsibilities." It is at least conceivable that arbitrary or bad faith termination of user accounts, or even termination of user accounts with no explanation at all, could implicate the implied covenant of good faith and fair dealing.

However, Young's current complaint does not allege that the termination of her account was undertaken in bad faith or violated Facebook's contractual obligations. Instead, she alleges that she was deprived of human interaction the process surrounding the termination of her account. The termination provision of the Statement of Rights and Responsibilities provides that when a user account is terminated, Facebook "will notify you by email or at the next time you attempt to access your account." Given the express language, Facebook could not have an implied obligation to provide a different termination process.

ORDER

Accordingly, IT IS HEREBY ORDERED that Facebook's motion to dismiss is GRANTED, with leave to amend. Any amended complaint must be filed within thirty (30) days.

IT IS SO ORDERED.

CASE QUESTIONS

1. Why did the court reach this holding? Do you agree with it?

2. Was Facebook justified in terminating Young's user privileges? What do you think about Facebook's attempts to communicate with her?

3. Do you think Facebook's Statement of Rights and Responsibilities is enough to give users notice that their accounts may be terminated?

REMEDIES

When there is not complete performance, the nonbreaching party is entitled to a legal remedy. What that remedy may be depends on the type of contract at issue and what remedy the nonbreaching party wishes to elect. While the non-breaching party may be able to mix and match forms of relief, there can be only one recovery and the nonbreaching party will be required to elect one of the following remedies.

DAMAGES

Damages are the difference between the contract as promised and the contract as performed. To ask for damages is to ask for a *legal* remedy. For example, Gary promises Dave that he will deliver 500 dogs on March 1, and that time is of the essence. Dave agrees to pay $10 per dog. They also agree that in the event that either party defaults (breaches) the contract, the damage amount will be $50,000. Unknown to Gary, Dave plans to use the dogs in a dog commercial. On March 1, Gary only delivers 250 dogs. Dave calls another supplier, who ships him 250 dogs at a price of $20 per dog. The film crew has to be paid $1,000 for the lost day of filming. The phone calls and shipping prices amount to $200.

Gary owes Dave $2,500 for the dogs that were delivered by the other supplier. This is the price difference that Dave was forced to pay at the last minute. Gary was required to try to reduce Dave's liability under a doctrine of *mitigation of damages*. Mitigation requires that the nonbreaching party try to prevent the breaching party's loss. A person does not have to be successful at mitigating the loss; he or she just has to try. All costs incurred as a result of mitigation are recoverable as **incidental damages**. Dave incurred $200 worth of incidental damages, and Gary must pay this amount. Incidental damages are also recoverable under the UCC in breach of contract cases for losses that include expenses incurred in handling and caring for goods which were the subject of the contract, reasonable expenses incurred in obtaining cover, and any other reasonable expenses resulting from the breach that do not fall into any other category.

incidental damages: Damages recoverable as a result of the non-breaching party's obligation to mitigate damages.

compensatory damages: Actual damages.

consequential or special damages: Damages awarded in an amount deemed to compensate for losses that arise not as a natural result of an injury but because of some particular circumstance of the injured party.

Compensatory damages (damages that compensate or make the nonbreaching person whole) are also recoverable and can be calculated in two ways. The first is to figure the difference between what was promised and what was received. For example, Sue agrees with Sally to buy a 1964 Corvair, and Sally delivers a 1968 Corvair. Sue's damage is the difference in price between a 1964 and a 1968 Corvair. In the contract between Gary and Dave, however, Dave had to pay $5,000 in order to receive the additional dogs. Since he owes Gary $2,500 and his total contract price with Gary was $5,000, Dave is entitled to $2,500 in compensatory damages.

Dave also had to pay the film company $1,000 for the lost day of filming. These are damages that are suffered as a *consequence* of the breach. **Consequential** or **special damages** are only recoverable if they were *foreseeable* to the breaching party. In the previous case, Gary had no idea that the dogs were being used in a dog commercial, so he is not liable for the lost day of filming. If instead of using the dogs in a dog commercial, what if Dave had planned on reselling the dogs for $15 a dog? Dave still could not recover. *Lost profits* are not recoverable because they, too, are considered consequential damages. An exception exists for *volume sellers* (those in the business of reselling goods). If Dave owned a pet shop, he would be a volume seller and could recover his lost profits.

liquidated damages: Damages whose amount is agreed upon by the parties to a contract as adequately compensating for loss in the event of a breach.

The contract between Dave and Gary also had a clause stating that, in the event of a breach, the breaching party would pay the nonbreaching party $50,000. This is called a **liquidated damage clause**. Such a clause agrees to a damage amount before the breach has occurred. A court will not enforce a liquidated damage clause if the amount penalizes rather than compensates the person for breaching the contract. In this case, $50,000 is far in excess of the actual damage suffered and, therefore, is nonenforceable. Courts will enforce liquidated damage clauses if the damages are speculative and hard to calculate after the breach. Failure to complete a construction contract is one such contract in which liquidated damage clauses are common. Also, if the amount is close to the actual damage suffered, the clause will be enforced. Generally, punitive damages are not allowed in breach of contract cases, although in particularly egregious breach of contract cases involving bad faith, punitive damages may be awarded.

SPECIFIC PERFORMANCE

specific performance: A court order which requires a seller to perform a contract as agreed.

Specific performance is only available for certain types of contracts. In **specific performance** the nonbreaching party asks that the breaching party be required to perform the contract. Specific performance is an *equitable remedy* and is available when damages will not make the nonbreaching person whole. For example, specific performance is available for nonperformance on a contract for the sale of real property. Since real property is *unique*, courts will force a person to sell the property if there is a valid contract. The same is true for contracts to sell *unique* personal property, like the original Mona Lisa. Once again, that exact property cannot be found anywhere else. On the other hand, although a personal service contract is unique, specific performance is not allowed because the 13th Amendment to the U.S. Constitution prohibits involuntary servitude or slavery. For example, Chris, a basketball player, has a seven-year contract to play basketball. After five years, Chris decides he wants to make more money. Chris tells his coach that he will not play unless his contract is renegotiated. However, the coach informs Chris that the team will not renegotiate the contract. The team cannot force Chris to play basketball; however, his seven-year contract probably contained a *negative covenant*, a clause prohibiting Chris from playing basketball for another team. Negative covenants are usually enforced.

RESCISSION

Once in a while, nonbreaching parties want to be put back into the position they were in before the contract was formed. For example, Dane contracted to sell her barren property to Zoe for $50,000. Zoe paid $25,000 but failed to pay the remaining amount. Meanwhile, oil is discovered on Dane's property. Dane does not want damages; rather, Dane wants **rescission** and **restitution.** Restitution means that you give up what you received under the contract. Dane gives Zoe $25,000 back, and Zoe relinquishes the property.

> **rescind:** To take back and make void.

> **restitution:** To return what was received under the contract.

SUMMARY

Because almost all aspects of a business involve contracts, they are very important for businesspeople. Forming a contract requires an offer, acceptance, consideration, legality, free will, and capacity. While contracts should be in writing, most contracts can be oral. The UCC applies to contracts for the sale of goods. Under the UCC, some rules differ from the common law rules of contracts. These differences include the statute of frauds and rules governing when consideration is necessary. If a contract is breached, the nonbreaching party is entitled to damages. Since the damages can be extensive, it is important for individuals to understand what contracts require before they are negotiated.

CHAPTER QUESTIONS

1. DBI, a manufacturer of metal and steel processing equipment, contracted with Wysong for the purchase of two mechanical trimming shears. In September, DBI contacted Wysong concerning the shears. Wysong's sales manager sent DBI's sales manager a price quote and a list of specifications. This quotation was silent on knife length and minimum knife opening. DBI's manager of purchasing faxed back a list of design specifications and asked Wysong to quote a price "most similar to accompanying specifications." DBI's list included the length and minimum knife opening specifications. In response, Wysong faxed to DBI a statement that it could not produce a shear with "kick-out rolls," but the fax was silent as to the other features. Two more faxes concerning the price of the knives changed hands. The price was ultimately agreed upon. On December 9, 1996, in response to Wysong's counterproposal price, Harris sent DBI's purchase order to Wysong for two Wysong Mechanical Trim Shears, price $119,680. The purchase order

contained a merger clause. When the shears arrived, DBI discovered the shears were too narrow for the intended purpose and demanded that Wysong ship conforming goods or return the purchase price. Is there a contract? [See *Delta Brands, Inc., v. Wysong & Miles*, N.D. Tex. 1998 LEXIS 14768, 1998 WL 641810]

2. Several nations and a prominent philanthropist have promised the pay the United Nations several billion dollars. To date, the actual contributions have fallen far below the promised amount. Does the United Nations have any legal recourse?

3. Jackson taught horseback riding lessons to Kittye Mason's daughter, Lydia. Ms. Mason asked Ms. Jackson to find a suitable 10-year-old gelding, trained as a hunter-jumper, for her daughter. Ms. Mason orally agreed to pay Ms. Jackson $500 if Ms. Jackson could find such a horse for $10,000. Ms. Mason heard of an 11-year-old horse, named Norway, for sale in Florida for $11,500. Both Ms. Mason and Ms. Jackson flew to Florida to look at Norway and some other horses. Norway was owned by Coral Hill Farm, and an employee, Carolyn Tanner, told Ms. Mason and Ms. Jackson that Norway was 11 years old. After watching Norway perform at a horse show, Ms. Mason decided to purchase the horse, and the "barn vet" of Coral Hill Farm certified the horse to be 11 years old. Ms. Mason agreed to purchase the horse and have him sent to Arkansas.

   When Norway arrived he was ill and suffered from bouts of colic. About two and a half years after his purchase, Ms. Mason asked another veterinarian to examine Norway. This veterinarian determined Norway to be over 20 years old. Ms. Mason brought a lawsuit alleging breach of contract. Does the U.C.C. apply? Was the contract breached? [*Kittye Mason v. Jody Jackson,* 323 Ark. 252; 914 S.W. 2d 728 (1996)

4. In 1998, Leonard and Celin decided to marry. Before the marriage, they entered into an ante-nuptial agreement. Both parties were represented by attorneys as they negotiated and drafted the document. At the time it was signed, Leonard had approximately $2.4 million in assets, while Celin had only $4500. The parties also had one three-year old child, and Celin was eight months pregnant with their second child. Eight years later, Celin filed an action for divorce. Leonard argued that the ante-nuptial agreement they signed before marriage determined their rights upon divorce. Celin argued that the agreement was unconscionable because she was pregnant and in a "heightened emotional state" when she signed it, and also because it would leave her with no funds to support herself after the divorce. Is this contract unconscionable? How should the court decide this case? [See *Reizfeld v. Reizfeld,* 2011 WL 4600 (Conn.App.).]

5. In March, 2004, Brenda Borah entered into a contract with Dana McCandless, who operated a business called The Great Snake River Log Home Company, to purchase logs she intended to use to build a cabin on her property in Camas County, Idaho. The total purchase price of the logs was approximately $27,000. In June, Borah gave McCandless a deposit of approximately $17,000. McCandless indicated that he would deliver the logs in early August, 2004, but possibly sooner. McCandless made three deliveries in September and October, but they were short of the total logs he had promised to deliver. Brenda was unable to complete her cabin before winter began, so

she was forced to pay for winterizing the logs McCandless had already delivered. In November, McCandless promised to deliver the remaining logs by May 15, 2005, but again the logs were not delivered by the specified date. After further negotiations with McCandless fell through, Borah entered into a contract with a different company to deliver the remaining logs necessary to complete her cabin. She then filed a breach of contract lawsuit against McCandless. At trial, McCandless argued that because he had not signed the contract until September 2004, his failure to deliver the logs until the following summer was not a breach of contract. He also argued that he should not have been ordered to pay damages for equipment rental and winterization. Did McCandless materially breach this contract? What damages should Borah have been awarded? [See *Borah v. McCandless,* 147 Idaho 73, 205 P.3d 1209 (2009).]

6. Cynthia Hines purchased a vacuum cleaner online from Overstock.com. When she later returned the item, Overstock.com charged her a $30 restocking fee pursuant to its "Terms and Conditions" policy set forth on the company's website. Overstock.com's purchase process did not require buyers to scroll down and specifically "agree" to its terms and conditions. Cynthia filed a class action lawsuit against Overstock, who then moved to dismiss her complaint, claiming that its Terms and Conditions page also provides that all disputes will be subject to arbitration. Can Overstock.com enforce the $30 restocking fee and the arbitration clause? If Cynthia did not specifically agree to Overstock.com's terms and conditions, is she bound to them? [See *Hines v. Overstock.com Inc.,* 2009 U.S. Dist. LEXIS 81204 (E.D. N.Y. Sept. 4, 2009).]

7. In 2000, Gateway celebrated its 10th anniversary by offering significant savings on several models of its computers. In response to an ad in a computer magazine, the Hills ordered a computer. When the computer arrived, the box contained a standard terms and condition agreement. This "agreement" including a warranty, an arbitration provision and a provision limiting return to 30 days. The Hills were unaware of this agreement until the computer arrived at their home. The Hills sued Gateway and Gateway sought to enforce the arbitration agreement. Is there a contract? Why or why not? See *Hill* v. *Gateway 2000, Inc.*, 105 F. 3d 1147 (7th Cir. 1997).

8. 16-year-old Brian Monahan agreed to buy a car from Mr. Friedrick and paid $1750. Brian then drove the auto to and from work and for recreation for several months. After mechanical problems occurred with the car, Brian wanted to return the car and recover the purchase price. What result? *Monahan* v. *Friederick,* 155 Wis 2d 468 (Wis. App. 1990).

9. Alyeska Pipeline Services found it necessary to look for a wildlife rehabilitation facility for use in case of an oil spill. Sea Hawk Seafoods wanted to sell its plant and approached Valdez Fisheries about the possible sale. Valdez was looking at leasing Sea Hawk's facilities to Alyeska. Alyeska told Sea Hawk that Valdez would be the successful bidder. It also told Sea Hawk that if it did not contract with Valdez, it would contract directly with Sea Hawk. Alyeska and Valdez entered into an agreement which stated that its enforcement was contingent on Valdez receipt of the Alyeska contract. Subsequently, Alyeska did inform Valdez that it was the "successful bidder" and began negotiating the terms of the contract. Valdez and Sea Hawk performed on their contract.

When difficulties with some of the contract terms occurred, Alyeska decided to break off its negotiations with Valdez. Can Valdez and/or Sea Hawk enforce Alyeska's promises? *Valdez Fisheries Development Ass'n* v. *Alyeska Pipeline Service Co.*, 45 P.3d 657 (Alaska 2002).

10. The law allows people to break their promises if they are willing to financially reimburse those whom they have harmed. Should all promises be performed? Is it ethical to break a promise?

PRACTICAL EXERCISE

You have always wanted to own your own business. When surfing the Internet for business opportunities you have discovered that the Castle Health Spa, in your area, is for sale. You e-mail the owner, who tells you that Castle is in its third year of a five-year lease. The spa owns, free and clear, all the exercise equipment. There are currently five employees, two clerks and three instructors. The selling price is $150,000. You have decided to draft your own contract before running it through your attorney.

1. Before buying this business, what other facts do you need to know?
2. Draft a sales contract that includes all the appropriate clauses.
3. What do you need to consider before pursuing a business opportunity found on the Internet?

FURTHER INFORMATION

www.law.cornell.edu/ucc/ucc.table.html
cisgw3.law.pace.edu/
www.cclaw.net/
www.jus.uio.no/lm/eu.contract.principles.part1.1995/index.html

CHAPTER 13

WARRANTY AND LIABILITY ISSUES IN THE SALE OF PRODUCTS

LEARNING OBJECTIVES

After reading this chapter, you should be able to:

1. Describe the different kinds of warranties and distinguish between express and implied warranties.

2. List the provisions of the Magnuson-Moss Warranty Act.

3. Understand and discuss negligence and strict product liability as they apply to the sale of products.

4. Detail the rights and remedies of buyers and sellers.

CHAPTER OUTLINE

I. Warranties

II. Negligence

III. Strict Product Liability

IV. Other Legal Issues in the Sale of Goods

Your friend Larry has purchased several expensive works of art from a gallery after being assured that they were "original lithographs" done by Salvador Dali. Now Larry suspects that the works may not be genuine. The Practical Exercise asks you to consider whether Larry has any legal rights based on express or implied warranties.

INTRODUCTION

In Chapters 11 and 12, we discussed the basic principles of tort and contract law. When two parties voluntarily agree that one will perform some action in return for a promise or payment or performance by the other, a contract may be formed. Also, when one person or business takes some action negligently or intentionally that injures another person, this is likely to be considered a tort. In this chapter we examine how each of these theories has developed with respect to a very common situation—the sale of products.

Remember that sales transactions are governed by Article 2 of the Uniform Commercial Code (UCC), a model law that has been adopted in 49 states. Most of the common law principles of contract law examined in Chapter 12 have been adopted by the UCC and therefore apply to the sale of goods. In this chapter we discuss **warranties**—a subject that originates in contract law but is not part of common law. We will also examine the basis for, and important legal aspects of the theory used most often in lawsuits involving people who are injured by products—from automobiles to power tools to hot coffee—the theory called "strict product liability."

> **warranty:** A promise that the goods are of the quality indicated.

WARRANTIES

Most of us are familiar with the word "*warranty.*" We have all purchased consumer products that include a card or piece of paper with a pretty border around it, titled "Warranty." This warranty usually contains certain statements about the goods and may include promises to repair or replace the item if it does not function properly. Later, we will examine an example of a typical warranty.

Warranties are essentially "promises" regarding the goods sold and create something like a contract. However, warranty issues often involve elements of both contract and tort law. That is why we have placed the discussion of warranties in this chapter—right after you have learned about contracts and torts. A warranty may be expressly given by the seller or manufacturer of a product, or it may arise automatically because of the type of transaction that has taken

"We had a great Christmas—I just mailed 43 warranty cards."

From *The Wall Street Journal*, February 14, 1995. Reprinted with permission of Cartoon Features Syndicate.

place. In contrast to traditional contract principles, in which only the two parties to the contract are bound, the warranty given to the buyer by the seller may (and usually does) extend back to the manufacturer and forward not only to the buyer but also to other members of his or her family and perhaps to subsequent purchasers.

EXPRESS WARRANTIES

Like an express agency (discussed in Chapter 8), an **express warranty** is one that is clearly stated ("expressed") Generally, such a warranty is written, but it is also possible to create an express warranty in other ways. In the last chapter, we learned about the UCC, a uniform law adopted in 49 states, which establishes legal principles involving the sale of goods. Section 2-313 of the UCC provides that an express warranty may be created by a seller in three ways: (1) through "an affirmation of fact or a promise" relating to the goods, (2) by a "description of the goods," or (3) by the use of a "sample or model" in connection with the sale of the goods.

> **express warranty:** A warranty that is expressed in written or verbal form, or by use of a sample or model.

Therefore, if the seller provides a written warranty that states, "This product is 100 percent cotton" (affirmation of fact) or "The manufacturer will replace this item if it becomes defective within 90 days" (promise), these are certainly express warranties. But an express warranty is also created if the shoe salesperson demonstrates a pair of cross-training shoes to the buyer and indicates that a different pair of shoes that the buyer is purchasing is "just like these," or a verbal statement is made by the sales clerk that "these shoes will not ever rip or tear."

As explained in our earlier discussion of fraud and misrepresentation, it is important to distinguish between affirmations of fact and **puffing** (mild bragging) or opinion. When the seller states that a wooden table is "made of oak," that statement is an "affirmation of fact." This statement is either true or false and will create an express warranty if the sale is completed. If the table the buyer gets is not oak, the buyer has important legal rights. But the statement "this is the strongest table you can buy" is likely to be held as puffing and will not create an express warranty that this is in fact the strongest table for sale anywhere. Similarly, the seller's remark "this table is an excellent value at $400" would probably be held as mere *opinion,* rather than as an express warranty.

> **puffing:** Mild bragging about an item, not specific enough to create a warranty.

An additional requirement for creating an express warranty is that the statement, promise, description, or use of sample must become part of the **basis of the bargain**. In other words, the affirmation, promise, description, or use of model must be important (the UCC uses the word *"material"*) to the buyer—it must be a significant factor in the decision to purchase the item. A statement made in a brochure, advertisement, or the contract itself, or by the sales clerk at the time of sale, may become part of the basis of the bargain, if it is important and relied on by the buyer.

IMPLIED WARRANTIES

When a consumer purchases a new television set from an appliance store, he or she makes certain assumptions about the product regardless of whether the item carries any express warranties. If the television set develops a serious defect within the first few weeks of use, most of us would agree "there ought to be a law" allowing the consumer to take the set back for repairs or replacement. Fortunately for consumers, *there is such a law*. The UCC establishes two types of *implied warranties* that apply to sales of goods in certain situations and give purchasers important rights. The two warranties are **the "implied warranty of merchantability"** and the **"implied warranty of fitness for a particular purpose."**

merchantability: The implied warranty given to a purchaser by a merchant—that the item is fit for its ordinary use.

Implied Warranty of Merchantability   The implied warranty of **merchantability**, set forth in UCC §2-314, provides that if the goods are purchased from a **merchant** (one who normally sells goods of this type), the goods must (1) be fit for the ordinary purposes for which such goods are used, (2) be adequately contained and packaged, (3) be of "fair average quality," and (4) pass without objection in the trade. There are other factors listed in §2-314 as well, but the thrust of the warranty is that if a consumer buys an item from a manufacturer, a store, or other seller who normally sells such items, the consumer can expect the item to work properly, for its ordinary purposes, for a reasonable time.

This warranty is "implied," since it *arises automatically* from the purchase and does not require any specific promises or statements by the seller. Suppose that Katy, a business student, purchases a textbook at the bookstore. When she opens it for the first time, however, the cover falls off. She purchased the book from a merchant and thus may take it back for replacement or a full refund. Clearly, if the cover falls off the first time the book is opened, the book is not "fit for ordinary purposes." If, on the other hand, Katy had purchased the book from a classmate, the implied warranty of merchantability does not apply. Why? The seller was not a merchant. Similarly, if Katy bought a hammer from a hardware store, an implied warranty of merchantability would apply. However, if she bought a used car from the owner of the hardware store (his car), the warranty of merchantability would not apply as long as the store did not sell autos.

The following case concerned the purchase of a used automobile from a dealer. The consumer was very disappointed by certain information he learned about the car shortly after the sale and brought a lawsuit claiming breach of warranties.

B. J. CURRIER V. ROD SPENCER

772 S.W.2d 309 (Ark. 1989)

FACTS

B. J. Currier placed an advertisement in an Arkansas newspaper in 1986 offering to sell a "one-owner 1984 Datsun 300ZX" for $8,750. Rod Spencer saw the ad and later purchased the car for $8,250 (by giving Currier $5,000 in cash and a $3,250 check). Before his check had cleared, the car began to give Spencer problems. He took it to a repair shop, where he learned that the car had been previously wrecked and the rear one-third of the car had been replaced with the body of another Datsun 300ZX that had been welded onto the front two-thirds of the original auto. The entire car had been repainted.

Spencer stopped payment on the check and tried to return the car, but Currier refused. Spencer stored the vehicle for awhile but was later able to sell it for $6,750. Currier filed suit to recover the balance of the purchase price (the $3,250 check which had not been paid), and Spencer counterclaimed for damages due to breach of express and implied warranties, misrepresentation, and other grounds. The lower court dismissed Currier's claim and instead awarded Spencer $1,500 (the difference between what he had agreed to pay for the car and its true worth). The court then doubled the award because of Currier's misrepresentation and his violation of other laws. Currier appealed.

DECISION

The Arkansas Supreme Court discussed both express and implied warranties under the UCC. "Any affirmation of fact by the seller to the buyer which relates to the goods and becomes part of the basis of the bargain creates an express warranty." Currier had stated that the car was a one-owner 1984 Datsun. The court said, "What Spencer purchased was two-thirds of one car and one-third of another," which clearly violated the warranty given. Obviously, there had been at least two previous owners of this car as it now existed, since it was the combination of two separate cars.

Currier claimed that the implied warranty of merchantability should not apply because he was not a merchant. The Court rejected this argument, noting that since 1985 he had been licensed by the state as a car dealer and had sold 12–15 used cars in the preceding year.

Finding that the auto was not "fit for the ordinary purposes for which such goods are used" and could not "pass without objection in the trade" (UCC §2-314), the Court held that the warranty of merchantability had been breached.

Since the standard measure of damages for either breach of warranty or misrepresentation is the difference in value between the product as warranted and its actual value, the Supreme Court of Arkansas affirmed the lower court's decision and award to Mr. Spencer. One justice dissented, arguing that "something is out of whack when the purchaser of a car pays $5,000 for a vehicle, sells it for $6,750 and then collects another $3,000 from the seller."

CASE QUESTIONS

1. What did the seller say (affirmation of fact) that became part of the "basis of the bargain" necessary to create an express warranty?
2. Why did the auto not meet the implied warranty of merchantability? Was the warranty breached simply because Currier did not tell the whole truth?
3. Do you think that Mr. Currier's ethics had a bearing on the court decision? Do you agree with the dissenting justice that the purchaser is getting more of a recovery than he is entitled to? If something is "out of whack" here, what is it?

The warranty of merchantability also applies to "the serving for value of food and drink," whether it is purchased at a restaurant or at a grocery store. People who have had the unpleasant experience of discovering various unexpected objects in their food or drink such as mice or pieces of glass, have brought cases against the producer, seller, or manufacturer. The traditional rule was that the warranty of merchantability was breached by "foreign" objects found in food, such as nails or glass, but not for "natural" objects, such as bones in chicken and pits in olives. However, over time most state courts have modified this rule and employed a "reasonable expectation" test that considers whether the consumer should reasonably have expected the item to be in the food. This test tends to place higher duties on those who sell food and results in more judgments for consumers. For example, everyone knows that chickens have bones, but when Adam purchases a chicken sandwich at Wendy's he really does not have a *reasonable expectation* of biting into a large chicken bone in the sandwich. So Wendy's would be liable under the second test, but perhaps not under the older "foreign/natural" rule.

FEDERAL COURT DISMISSES OBESITY LAWSUITS AGAINST MCDONALD'S

Despite the strong consumer protections afforded by the warranty of merchantability, some consumer claims are rejected. In a much-publicized case, two minors (through their parents) sued McDonald's restaurants claiming that their consumption of fast food had caused them to become obese, and suffer other health problems. The federal district court in New York dismissed the case once, allowing the plaintiffs to amend their complaint, but after the amendment, the case was finally dismissed again. The court found that the plaintiffs had not sufficiently alleged a causal connection between their consumption of food, McDonald's advertising, and their health problems.

Implied Warranty of Fitness for a Particular Purpose   The other important implied warranty does not require that the seller be a merchant. The implied warranty of **fitness for a particular purpose** is set forth in UCC §2-315, which reads as follows:

> Where the seller at the time of contracting has reason to know any particular purpose for which the goods are required and that the buyer is relying on the seller's skill or judgment to select or furnish suitable goods, there is unless excluded or modified . . . an implied warranty that the goods shall be fit for such purpose.

fitness for a particular purpose:
The implied warranty given when the buyer needs the item for some particular (not regular) purpose and relies on the seller to furnish such an item.

This warranty, like merchantability, is *implied*—that is, it arises because of the transaction itself, without any express promise or written document from the seller. The warranty of fitness, however, only exists when the buyer has some *particular purpose* for the goods, and both parties realize that the buyer is relying on the seller's knowledge and experience to provide goods that will work satisfactorily for the exact purpose of the buyer.

For example, if Teresa goes to a furniture store and purchases a chair, she will, by implication, receive a warranty of merchantability that the chair will be suitable for ordinary purposes—that is, a normal amount of being sat upon. Suppose, however, that she actually is buying it for the waiting room of the local bus station, and it falls apart after two months due to heavy use. Since the chair was purchased from a merchant, Teresa received an implied warranty of merchantability. However, if the chair *was fit for ordinary purposes,* this warranty was not breached. But if Teresa had told the furniture store salesperson about her *particular needs* and both she and the sales associate knew that she was relying on the salesperson to sell her a heavy-duty chair that would withstand the type of use she had described, the implied warranty of fitness for particular purpose might have been breached when the chair fell apart. The following case involves the purchase of a horse, to be used by the buyer for breeding purposes.

In the Language of the Court

WHITEHOUSE V. LANGE

128 Idaho 131, 910 P.2d 801 (1996)

Judge Karen Lansing wrote the Court's opinion.

FACTS

Dennis and Carol Lange owned and operated a horse ranch and had been "in the Morgan horse business" since 1978. In the spring of 1990, Alan and Sandy Whitehouse decided to enter the Morgan horse breeding business. They became interested in perpetuating the bloodlines of horses then owned by the Langes, including a mare named Revelation Prophecy. An agreement was reached for the Whitehouses to purchase Revelation Prophecy for $15,000 and to purchase also a stallion, and also a mare that was the offspring of the stallion and Revelation Prophecy. Alan Whitehouse explained to Lange that the Whitehouses were purchasing these horses for breeding purposes and intended to start a horse breeding business, although they had no prior experience in horse breeding.

At the time of the contract, both parties thought that Revelation Prophecy was with foal. When the horses were delivered, the Whitehouses engaged a veterinarian to examine the mare. The doctor determined that the mare was not pregnant. Consequently, the parties renegotiated the price of Revelation Prophecy down to $10,000.

The Whitehouses thereafter attempted to breed the mare, but she did not conceive. A subsequent examination of the mare revealed that she had a susceptibility to a uterine infection that prevents conception and is precipitated by exposure to bacteria in a stallion's ejaculate. The Whitehouses twice gave the Langes notice of revocation of their acceptance of Revelation Prophecy, but the Langes refused to refund the purchase price. Consequently, the Whitehouses filed a complaint seeking rescission of the contract, or in the alternative, damages for breach of warranty.

After the case was tried to the district court, the judge at first entered findings of fact and conclusions of law in which he found that the Langes had made no express warranties, and that the warranty of fitness for particular purpose had not been breached. The Whitehouses moved for reconsideration, and after another hearing, the court altered its decision and found that although there was no breach of express warranty, that both the implied warranty of fitness for a particular purpose and the implied warranty of merchantability had been breached. The court entered judgment in favor of the Whitehouses, for the difference between the value of the mare as warranted and her actual value, together with incidental damages for breeding and veterinary expenses. The Langes appealed.

DECISION

The circumstances under which an implied warranty of fitness for particular purpose will arise are specified in Idaho Code Section 28-2-315:

> *Where the seller at the time of contracting has reason to know any particular purpose for which the goods are required and that the buyer is relying on the seller's skill or judgment to select or furnish suitable goods, there is unless excluded . . . an implied warranty that the goods shall be fit for such purpose.*

Although the Whitehouses' complaint neither cites this statute nor uses the term "implied warranty" . . . such an omission is not fatal if the facts underlying such a cause of action are adequately pleaded. The Whitehouses' complaint alleges in part:

> *Revelation Prophecy was purchased for the express and only purpose of breeding . . . .Defendants were informed and knew that plaintiffs were purchasing the animal for such purpose . . . Defendants represented, warranted, and promised plaintiffs that the animal was a good breeder and sure foal getter . . . Relying on the . . . warranties, plaintiffs purchased Revelation Prophecy.*

These allegations are sufficient to present a claim for breach of the implied warranty of fitness for a particular purpose.

By the terms of Section 2-315, an implied warranty of fitness will not arise unless the buyer "is relying on the seller's skill or judgment to *select or furnish* suitable goods." (emphasis added). The trial court found that the plaintiffs had not proved that they had relied on the Langes to select the actual horse purchased. However, they did prove that they relied on Dennis Lange to *furnish* a mare suitable for breeding, and therefore the implied warranty was breached when a mare not suitable for breeding was furnished.

The trial court was correct in recognizing that buyers may rely upon a seller to "furnish" goods suitable for a particular purpose even though the individual unit purchased is "selected' by the buyer. As one commentator explains:

> The seller must have reason to know two things: First, the particular purpose for which the buyer requires the goods; and second, that the buyer is relying on the seller's skill or judgment to select or to furnish suitable goods. The two requirements are connected by an "and"; both must exist before the warranty will be implied. Robert J. Nordstrom, *HANDBOOK OF THE LAW OF SALES*, Section 78 (1970)

A California case addressed this issue in a case involving the sale of a hereford bull as a herd sire. *Willig v. Brethauer*, 127 Cal. App. 2d 650 (1954). In that case, the bull proved to be temperamentally and physiologically unfit for breeding. The court found that the implied warranty of fitness for particular purpose had been breached even though the buyer had actually selected the bull from the seller's herd. The court stated:

> Appellant was engaged in the business of furnishing herd sires for the propagation of purebred Hereford cattle and he knew that the respondent wanted an animal solely for that purpose . . . Appellant says

> there was no reliance on the skill and knowledge of the seller, and points to testimony that respondent went to appellant's ranch, examined a number of animals, and selected one. But is is not likely . . . that a visual examination could have detected any existing unfitness, unless the physical attributes of the animal might have given warning . . . The fact that the animal was inspected and selected affords no reason to say that the trial court could not still infer that respondent relied upon the seller to deliver to him a fit and qualified animal.

We agree with the California court's analysis. The fact that the Whitehouses selected the horse they wanted based upon bloodline considerations does not preclude reliance on Lange to furnish a horse suitable for breeding. It is evident that the Whitehouses' interest in Revelation Prophecy's genetic characteristics would not have led them to purchase that mare if they had known she was unable to reproduce. Therefore, we perceive no inconsistency in the district court's finding that the Whitehouses did not rely upon Lange to select the specific horse, but did rely upon him to furnish a mare suitable for the particular purpose of breeding.

Lange next argues that even if an implied warranty of fitness arose, the court erred in finding that the warranty was breached because the evidence was insufficient to show that Revelation Prophecy was unfit as a broodmare at the time of delivery. Therefore, we examine the evidence to determine whether it supports the conclusion that the horse's susceptibility to uterine infections, which made her unsuitable for breeding purposes, existed at the time of her delivery to the Whitehouses.

Dr. Richard Silvestor, a veterinarian who examined Revelation Prophecy after the Whitehouses' purchase, reviewed the mare's medical records. He testified that the records indicated that the mare had been bred in 1989 but had not conceived, and that the veterinarian who examined her at that time detected an enlargement of the uterus, which could be a symptom of uterine infection. The evidence also showed that Revelation Prophecy had not produced a foal for the three years prior to her sale to the Whitehouses. Based on the mare's medical records and history, Dr. Silvestor testified that in his opinion she had reproductive problems at the time of the purchase. Therefore we will uphold the trial court's findings.

The judgment of the trial court awarding damages for breach of the implied warranty of fitness for particular purpose is **affirmed.** Consequently we need not address the decision regarding the implied warranty of merchantability.

CASE QUESTIONS

1. What facts show that the Whitehouses were relying on the seller to furnish a horse suitable for their breeding purposes?

2. What is the difference between "selecting" and "furnishing" particular goods?
3. Do you agree with the court's decision, under the UCC implied warranty section? Do you think the decision is fair to the seller?
4. What were the most important legal authorities cited by the court? What part of the rationale was based on each authority?
5. If the court had needed to decide whether the implied warranty of merchantability was breached, what would the decision have been? Why?

WARRANTY OF TITLE

Another assumption most of us probably make when purchasing goods is that the seller has good title to the items and the right to sell them. This expectation is confirmed and reinforced by another UCC provision, §2-312, which establishes an implied warranty of title. The warranty also provides that the goods are delivered free of any security interest or lien unless the buyer is informed of it. Although many warranties can be disclaimed (excluded), as we see in the next section, this warranty is difficult to exclude and can be disclaimed only by clear notification to the buyer that the seller does not claim title.

DISCLAIMERS

Although the UCC establishes the implied warranties described previously, which are of significant benefit to consumers, it also allows sellers to **disclaim** or cancel such warranties quite easily. UCC §2-316 provides that implied warranties may be eliminated by the use of written statements containing phrases like *"as is"* or *"with all faults."* In addition, the warranty of merchantability may be excluded by specifically mentioning "merchantability" (and if the disclaimer is in writing, it must also be *"conspicuous"*). The warranty of fitness for particular purpose may be disclaimed by a "conspicuous written statement." If you look at a warranty you have received with your purchase of a consumer product, you will likely find that some of the implied warranties have been at least partially disclaimed, probably in capital letters or bold lettering (in order to be "conspicuous").

disclaimer: A statement in a warranty that limits or eliminates implied warranties.

SOCIAL/ETHICAL ISSUES

Are implied warranties of merchantability and fitness for particular purpose based on ethical principles? Do they appear to conform with what most people would think of as "right" or "fair"? If so, is the rule allowing these warranties to be easily disclaimed (simply using the phrase "as is," for example) an ethical one? Do most consumers really read the text of their product warranties and hence understand that they have no implied warranties?

THE MAGNUSON-MOSS WARRANTY ACT

In the 1970s, Congress held a number of hearings concerning warranties. The ease with which warranties could be eliminated was just one of the serious problems consumers faced in connection with warranties. At the hearings, numerous individuals testified regarding the great difficulties they had in obtaining warranty service and repairs and determining what parts of their products were covered by warranties. Others were concerned with the high cost of obtaining repairs and the general "illusory" nature of warranties (the warranties the customers thought they had received had been disclaimed by the manufacturers and were no longer in effect). As a congressional report stated, "Too often, what the large print giveth, the fine print taketh away."

Magnuson-Moss Warranty Act:
A federal law that requires certain disclosures and provides certain rights to consumers, where written warranties are provided.

To help with these problems Congress enacted the first federal law dealing with warranties, the **Magnuson-Moss Warranty Act**, effective in 1975. This law *did not require any seller or manufacturer to provide warranties*, but when a seller did choose to give a written warranty, the law imposed several new duties. The Magnuson-Moss Act did not replace the UCC warranty provisions that are part of the law in 49 states but *supplemented these provisions* by imposing new requirements on all **written warranties.**

When a written warranty is provided, the Magnuson-Moss Act requires the warrantor to *disclose certain information*. The warranty must state clearly (1) what parts of the product are covered by the warranty, (2) how and where the consumer can obtain repairs covered by the warranty, (3) how long the warranty lasts, and (4) whether the warranty extends to a person other than the first purchaser of the product. The warranty must also tell consumers that they may have additional rights under their state laws (such as the UCC implied warranties) and provide other information. The act also provides that the seller must make warranty information available to the buyer prior to the sale, in one of several ways.

The Magnuson-Moss Act states that when a seller gives a written warranty on a consumer product that costs at least $10, the warranty must be entitled either a **"full" or "limited" warranty.** A full warranty means that the seller must repair the product free of charge, replace the product, or refund the purchase price if the product cannot be fixed after reasonable efforts. The act does not specify exactly how many times a consumer must try to have the item repaired before he or she can demand money back. Most states have enacted **"lemon laws"** that indicate precisely how many attempts to fix the same defect in a new car are required to constitute "reasonable efforts." A limited warranty does not require such relief.

Another important Magnuson-Moss Act provision concerns *disclaimers*. As we have mentioned, the UCC allows warrantors to disclaim implied warranties fairly easily. However, Magnuson-Moss puts new limitations on such disclaimers. In a _full warranty_, *there can be no disclaimer of implied warranties*. In other words, if you receive a written warranty titled "full," you will be able to fully enforce any implied warranties of merchantability or fitness for a particular purpose. If the _warranty is limited_, it still may not totally disclaim implied warranties but may *limit them to the duration of the express warranty*. Therefore, most written warranties today are "limited warranties" which contain a clause that limits the length of time the implied warranties exist to the same time period provided for the written express warranty.

One of the most important parts of the Magnuson-Moss Act allows consumers to sue for warranty violations and to collect not only their damages but their attorneys' fees as well. Prior to this enactment, few consumers sued to enforce their UCC rights under express and implied warranties, because the costs of the lawsuit were more than the amount at stake in the warranty claim. Remember that under the so-called American rule, each side of the lawsuit must normally pay its own legal fees, win or lose. However, Magnuson-Moss allows consumers to recover actual attorneys' fees, if they win. Also, both the UCC §2-719(3) and the Magnuson-Moss Act provide that consumers may not be prevented from suing for *consequential damages* due to *personal injuries* caused by defective products. Note, however, that there are different interpretations of this section with regard to other types of consequential damages in various states. The following box displays an example of a limited warranty. Look closely at the warranty to see how its provisions comply with the Magnuson-Moss Act.

LIMITED 90-DAY WARRANTY—FOR HEWLETT-PACKARD PERSONAL COMPUTER MAINFRAMES AND PERIPHERALS

What We Do

In the U.S.A. and Canada this unit is warranted by Hewlett-Packard against defects in materials and workmanship for 90 days from date of original purchase.* If you transfer ownership, this warranty is automatically transferred to the new owner and remains in effect for the original 90-day period.

During the warranty period we will repair or, at our option, replace at no charge any unit that proves to be defective, provided it is returned, shipping prepaid, to an identified Hewlett-Packard repair facility. You are responsible for all customs duties in connection with the return of the unit.

What Is Not Covered

This warranty does not apply if the product has been damaged by accident or misuse, or as a result of service or modification by other than an authorized

*In other countries, contact your local authorized HP dealer or your local Hewlett-Packard Sales and Service facility to determine warranty terms. (For addresses, please see the list on the following page or consult your owner's manual.)

HP Repair Facility, or by hardware, software, interfacing or peripherals not provided by Hewlett-Packard. Hewlett-Packard shall have no obligation to modify or update products once manufactured. This warranty does not apply to HP Software Products.

No other expressed warranty is given. The repair or replacement of a product is your exclusive remedy. **Any implied warranty of merchantability or fitness is limited to the 90-day duration of this written warranty**. Some states or provinces do not allow limitations on how long an implied warranty lasts, so the above limitation or exclusion may not apply to you. **In no event shall Hewlett-Packard Company be liable for consequential damages**. Some states or provinces do not allow the exclusion or limitation of incidental or consequential damages, so that above limitation or exclusion may not apply to you.

This warranty gives you specific legal rights, and you may also have other rights which vary from state to state, or from province to province.

This is your warranty. Please retain for your records.

How To Obtain Service for Your Equipment

During the warranty period: If after you follow the maintenance procedures outlined in the owner's manual, you determine that a repair is required, you can help assure efficient servicing by following these guidelines:

- Fill in the attached Repair Information Form and include it with your equipment. Return your equipment to your nearest HP Dealer Repair Center or Field Repair Center.
- Provide a copy of your sales invoice or other documentary proof-of-purchase date to establish warranty coverage period.
- If you need to ship your unit, be sure to ship it in a protective package and insure it. We recommend that you save the original shipping materials for this purpose.
- Note: Your warranty will be upgraded from return-to-HP to on-site service free of charge if you purchase a 12-month On-Site Maintenance Agreement within ten days of equipment delivery.
- After the Warranty Period: Maintenance is available at your location, at HP Dealer Repair Centers, or at HP Field Repair Centers. You can purchase service at an annual fixed price or on a per-incident basis.
- Under a Field Repair Center Maintenance Agreement, you ship the product to an HP Field Repair Center, where it is repaired within three working days.
- On-Site Maintenance Agreements are available with various levels of response time and coverage, to allow you to select the level of support that fits your needs.
- If you prefer, service on site or at a Field Repair Center is also available on a per-incident, rather than contract, basis.
- Many authorized HP Dealers offer hardware servicing. To locate your nearest Dealer Repair Center consult your yellow pages or call 800-547-3400. In Oregon, Alaska, or Hawaii, call 503-758-1010. TTY users with hearing or speech impairments, please dial 503-758-5566.

Hewlett-Packard Field Repair Centers

The HP Field Repair Centers listed below provide return-to-HP repair for HP computing equipment—both during and after the warranty period.

If there is no Field Repair Center in your country, contact your authorized HP Series 80 Dealer or your HP Sales and Service Office for shipping instructions.

To find the location of one of the 240 Hewlett-Packard offices serving you worldwide, check your local telephone directory, or contact one of the HP Sales and Service offices listed below.

UNITED STATES
Illinois
Hewlett-Packard Company
5201 Tollview Drive
Rolling Meadows, IL 60008
(312) 255-9800

California
Hewlett-Packard Company
5400 West Rosecrans Avenue
Lawndale, CA 90260
(213) 970-7500

Hewlett-Packard Company
3003 Scott Boulevard
Santa Clara, CA 95050
(408) 988-7000

Georgia
Hewlett-Packard Company
2000 South Park Place
Atlanta, GA 30339
(404) 955-1500

Massachusetts
Hewlett-Packard Company
32 Hartwell Avenue
Lexington, MA 02173
(617) 861-8960

Texas
Hewlett-Packard Company
930 East Campbell Rd.
Richardson, TX 75081
(214) 231-6101

New Jersey
Hewlett-Packard Company
W. 120 Century Road
Paramus, NJ 07652
(201) 265-5000

CANADA
Hewlett-Packard Company
6877 Goreway Dr.
Mississaugua, Ontario LV4 1M8
(415) 678-2350

EUROPE
Hewlett-Packard, S.A.
7 Rue du Bois-du-Lan,
P.O. Box
CH-1217 Meyrin 2
Geneva, Switzerland

OTHER INTERNATIONAL
LOCATIONS
Hewlett-Packard Intercontinental
3495 Deer Creek Road
Palo Alto, CA 94304 U.S.A.

MEMO FROM THE LEGAL DEPARTMENT

To: Students

From: Your Lawyer

Most of us have a drawer or shelf at home in which we put all the written warranties that come in the boxes of products we purchase. While you are studying warranties, it might be a good time to take a closer look at the warranties on the more expensive items you own. Do the items carry full or limited warranties? How and where do you obtain warranty service? What parts of the products are covered and for how long? Have the warranties of merchantability and fitness for a particular purpose been limited? In the Hewlett-Packard warranty just shown, can you tell what express warranties were given, and if there were are any implied warranties or disclaimers?

WHO MAY ENFORCE WARRANTIES?

privity: When two parties have contract with each other. This concept is no longer very important in warranty cases.

The general rule in contract cases is that only those parties who are **in privity of contract** with each other may enforce the contract. Privity means that the parties have a direct contract relationship with each other. In warranty situations, however, the privity rule is not strictly followed. For example, if Adam buys a car manufactured by Ford Motor Co. from Barbara's Auto Sales, he does not have a direct contract with Ford, although he receives a warranty from Ford. Adam is "in privity" of contract with Barbara's Auto Sales, but not Ford. Despite the lack of privity, Adam will be able to hold Ford to the terms of its warranty, because Ford was expecting (and hoping) that the car would not remain in Barbara's hands but would be sold to a consumer like Adam.

Another privity problem arises at the other end of the transaction. Adam allows his wife Jen to drive his new car. If a defective part causes an accident, injuring Adam's wife, both Ford and Barbara might argue that they have no privity with Adam's wife because they only dealt with Adam. However, the UCC injects a commonsense rule here that states that persons other than the buyer may be covered by the existing warranties. The drafters of the UCC set forth three alternative clauses (A, B, and C) for §2-318, thus allowing each state to decide how far the warranties should be extended at the consumer end of the deal. Alternative A extended the warranty to "any natural person in the family or household of the buyer, or who is a guest in his home." Alternative B extended the warranty even further to "any natural person who may reasonably be expected to use, consume, or be affected by the goods." Alternative C adopts the language of Alternative B but substitutes "any person" for "any natural person," allowing corporations and partnerships to be covered as well as natural persons.

NEGLIGENCE

Chapter 11 discussed fully the concept of the tort of **negligence**. As you recall, the elements necessary to establish a negligence case are the following: (1) the existence of a duty of reasonable care by one person toward another, (2) the defendant's breach of this duty, (3) proof that this breach of duty was the proximate cause of an injury to the plaintiff, and (4) damages suffered by the plaintiff.

> **negligence:** The most common type of tort—discussed in Chapter 11—that involves an injury caused by another's lack of due care.

Negligence theory has often formed the basis of personal product injury lawsuits where the injuries were caused by manufactured products. In order to show that the manufacturer had breached its duty of care (was negligent), consumers who have suffered injuries due to defective products have alleged such failings as follows: (1) negligent product design; (2) negligent product assembly, manufacture, and packaging; and (3) the failure to warn product users of dangers known to the product manufacturer.

In order to prevail in negligence cases, of course, plaintiffs need to prove the other essential elements as well, such as the defendant was "at fault"—that some action the defendant took or did not take failed to meet the standards expected of the mythical "reasonable" manufacturer. Also, in a "design" case, plaintiffs must show that the product was designed without proper care or in a way that made the product dangerous. For example, a company might have hired designers without experience, failed to follow industry standards, or failed to test the design as sufficiently as a reasonably careful producer should have done. To show negligence in assembly or packaging, plaintiffs must prove that the manner of assembly was not carefully done, did not meet normal industry standards, or that the product was packaged in a way that was hazardous to likely users.

Also, many "failure to warn" negligence cases have been brought against manufacturers and retailers. In these cases, plaintiffs must show that the manufacturer knew or should have known that the product was dangerous to certain potential users and that these users were unlikely to realize the danger, but the manufacturer had not warned them of their peril. The now-familiar warnings seen on many products, from hair dryers to stepladders to skis, are an attempt by manufacturers to limit their liability for negligence because of a failure to warn of product hazards.

Of course, the defenses of contributory negligence, comparative negligence, and assumption of the risk may be raised by the defendant in a product negligence lawsuit, just as in any other type of negligence case, as was explained in the Torts chapter. Therefore, even though in many cases plaintiffs can establish that the product manufacturer was negligent, they will lose a negligence case or have the damages reduced if they were personally negligent or knowingly assumed the risk of injury when using the product.

MEMO FROM THE LEGAL DEPARTMENT

To: Students

From: Your Lawyer

Companies and organizations often attempt to limit their liability for negligence through notices printed on the packaging containing a consumer product or through signs warning customers of hazards. These signs and notices do have some legal effect, and it makes good business sense to use them where appropriate. At the very least, they have a deterrent effect—that is, many people may refrain from suing because of a sign on a package or in a store stating, "We are not responsible for any injuries from the use of this product," for example.

     However, these warnings are not always binding in court, especially if the result would offend public policy. For example, if the consumer is injured by a defective product while using the item in a relatively normal fashion, no disclaimer of responsibility is likely to be upheld in court.

STRICT PRODUCT LIABILITY

Consumers injured by products have often encountered difficulties in recovering damages from sellers and manufacturers under warranty and negligence theories. As we have seen, warranties are often given only for a limited time period and may be limited or disclaimed fairly easily. In order to win negligence lawsuits, plaintiffs must prove that the manufacturer or seller was "at fault" somehow in the manufacture, design, packaging, or labeling of the product. In addition, defenses of contributory or comparative negligence may prevent or diminish recovery if plaintiffs were at fault in any way.

As our society has become more technologically complex, it also has become more difficult for consumers to prove exactly what a manufacturer did that was negligent in designing or constructing a product, or exactly what part of the product was defective. Most of us do not have a comprehensive understanding of all the parts of an automobile or a piece of machinery, or how each one is manufactured. It is hard for an individual to show, for example, that an auto manufacturer did not meet the standard of a reasonably prudent car builder in the manufacture of one particular part of a complex steering mechanism. Yet, in order to prevail in a negligence suit, if the power steering wheel on an automobile suddenly jerked to the left causing the car to crash, the consumer would have to prove not only that there was a defect and an injury, but also that the manufacturer was "at fault" in some specific way in the manufacture or design of the steering mechanism—that is, that "due care" was lacking.

In response to this problem, many courts in the past forty years or so have adopted a new theory called **strict product liability**. As discussed in Chapter 11, this theory originally developed to create liability for those who engage in "ultrahazardous" activity, without requiring the plaintiff to prove negligence or fault. For example, if The Jackson Company was performing dynamite operations to clear a site for construction and the blasting caused injury to a neighboring business, Jackson would be liable no matter how much care it exercised.

In recent years, the strict liability doctrine has been increasingly applied not only to those engaging in ultrahazardous actions but to all those who manufacture and distribute products. Today, in most states, if a consumer is injured by a defective product that he or she is using in a normal way, the consumer can prevail without proving negligence. The liability is called *"strict"* because the *plaintiff does not have to show fault* on the part of the defendant.

This doctrine imposes considerably greater duties upon merchants and manufacturers than does negligence theory. Among the justifications set forth in support of the rule are the following:

1. Manufacturers are better able to bear the economic losses caused by defective products than are individual consumers, since they have greater assets and can purchase insurance to protect themselves against liability.

2. Merchants and manufacturers can "pass along" the increased costs of lawsuits by injured customers to all of society through higher prices, rather than forcing an injured consumer to bear the entire cost of an injury.

3. Companies that manufacture and sell products will have an incentive to take preventive measures to design and build safer products if they are held responsible for injuries caused by defects.

Manufacturers, on the other hand, have argued against strict liability because it greatly increases their costs of doing business. They claim that the increase in lawsuits and judgments against the makers of products of many types, have caused insurance costs to rise dramatically in some industries. Business groups have asserted that some firms have gone out of business because of lawsuits and insurance costs, and new product innovations have been delayed or canceled because of fears of liability. The much-discussed "liability crisis" or "tort crisis" of recent years has arisen in large part from the development and ramifications of the strict product liability doctrine.

One of the first cases to explicitly adopt and explain carefully the rationale for the strict liability theory was the California Supreme Court's decision in *Greenman v. Yuba Power Products*, which is presented next.

> **strict product liability:** A legal theory that allows a person injured by a defective product to win a lawsuit against the manufacturer without proving "fault" or lack of due care.

GREENMAN V. YUBA POWER PRODUCTS, INC.

377 P.2d 897 (Calif. 1963)

Opinion written by Justice Roger Traynor

FACTS

Yuba Power Products, Inc., manufactured the Shopsmith, a combination power tool that could be used as a saw, drill, and wood lathe. After seeing the Shopsmith demonstrated and reading a manufacturer's brochure, Mr. Greenman decided he wanted one. His wife purchased a Shopsmith for him for Christmas in 1955. Some two years later he was using the tool as a lathe, when a piece of wood flew out of the machine and struck him on the forehead, causing serious permanent injuries to Mr. Greenman.

Mr. Greenman later sued both the manufacturer and the retailer of the Shopsmith, claiming breach of express and implied warranties and negligence. The lower court judge refused to allow the jury to consider some of the theories, and the jury later entered a verdict against the manufacturer alone for $65,000. It was not clear whether the verdict was based on negligence or on warranty theory. Both Mr. Greenman and Yuba Power Products appealed.

DECISION

The California Supreme Court has often been a trendsetter in the adoption of new legal theories. Justice Roger Traynor, a respected leader of the court for many years, wrote the appellate decision in this case, in which the court upheld the lower court decision but based its decision on the theory of strict product liability.

The defendants argued on appeal that the plaintiff should not have been allowed to pursue his warranty claims because he did not give notice of the product defects to the manufacturer within the appropriate time period specified by a California law. Justice Traynor rejected this allegation, finding that although the notice requirement was "a sound commercial rule" in contract cases between two parties in privity, it was "not an appropriate one" for the court to adopt in actions by injured consumers against manufac-

turers with whom they have not dealt and thus would simply be "a boobytrap for the unwary."

Mr. Greenman had introduced evidence that his injuries were caused by the Shopsmith's defective design and manufacture. His expert witnesses testified that the set screws used to hold key parts of the machine together were inadequate. The vibration that occurred when the machine operated caused certain parts to loosen, which allowed the piece of wood to fly out. The experts stated that there were alternative ways of designing and constructing the machine that would have prevented the accident.

The California Supreme Court refused to decide the case on the basis of warranty or negligence theory, as the trial court had done. Instead, the court held that regardless of the existence of an express warranty, "a manufacturer is strictly liable in tort when an article he places on the market, knowing that it is to be used without inspection for defects, proves to have a defect that causes injury to a human being." Justice Traynor wrote that the warranty rules (and notice requirements) previously developed to meet the needs of commercial transactions could not properly be used to limit a manufacturer's liability to consumers for defective products.

The purpose of strict liability, stated the court, was to ensure that the costs of injuries resulting from defective products were borne by the manufacturers that put such products on the market rather than by the injured persons who were powerless to protect themselves. Since this was not a contracts case, the question of whether or not Mr. Greenman carefully read the brochure (as he had done here) should not control the result, nor should the details of the sales agreements between the manufacturer, retailer, and Mrs. Greenman. "The remedies of injured consumers ought not to be made to depend upon the intricacies of the law of sales."

The Supreme Court therefore affirmed the lower court award, basing the decision solely on the doctrine of strict liability.

CASE QUESTIONS

1. In the *Greenman* case, what problems did the plaintiff have in proving his case under warranty theory?
2. What benefits, from a plaintiff's standpoint, does the strict liability theory have over (a) warranty theory and (b) negligence theory?
3. Does the strict liability doctrine reflect a public policy of corporate social responsibility? Discuss.

Following the Greenman case, many other courts across the nation adopted the doctrine of strict liability for cases involving defective products in one form or another—not all the same. Probably the clearest statement of the **principles of strict product liability** is contained in the **Restatement of Torts (2d),** a multivolume treatise on tort law prepared by a group of legal scholars. The Restatement is a summary and compilation of common law principles based on court decisions around the country, first published in 1965 and updated on a regular basis ever since. It is essentially a statement of what the law is or how it is evolving, concerning various types of torts. Although it is not a statute and has no binding authority, the Restatement has often been cited by courts in deciding cases involving common law tort cases. The Restatement tracked the development of the strict liability doctrine as it spread throughout the country.

> **elements of strict liability:** 1. Product was defective. 2. Product was unreasonably dangerous. 3. Seller was "in business" of selling these products. 4. Product reached the consumer without alteration in the distribution chain.

Section 402A of the Restatement states the following:

1. *One who sells any product in a defective condition unreasonably dangerous to the user or consumer or to his property is subject to liability for physical harm caused to the ultimate consumer or to his property; if*
   a. *the seller is engaged in the business of selling such a product, and*
   b. *it is expected to and does reach the user or consumer without substantial change in the condition in which it is sold.*

2. *The rule stated in Subsection (1) applies although*
   a. *the seller has exercised all possible care in the preparation and sale of his product, and*
   b. *the user or consumer has not bought the product from or entered into any contractual relation with the seller.*

The outline of strict liability contained in the Restatement definition shows that certain elements are necessary before a court will impose strict liability on a seller or manufacturer. First, the theory applies only to products sold in a **defective condition.** Thus, in order to recover any damages, the consumer has to establish, by actual or circumstantial evidence, that the item was defective when sold. Although this can prove difficult for purchasers, the standard is much easier to show than the "fault" required in a negligence case. If the brakes on a new car fail, causing an accident, the consumer will likely be able to convince a jury that there was a "defect" (for strict liability purposes) much more easily than to show that the manufacturer's procedure in designing, constructing, or testing the brakes was below the standards of other auto manufacturers (for negligence purposes).

Second, the theory requires that the defect make the product **unreasonably dangerous** to the user. The problem must be such that it creates a danger "beyond that which would be contemplated by the ordinary consumer" who purchases the product with the "ordinary knowledge common to the community as to its characteristics." Certain plaintiffs who are injured by persons using handguns or by drunkards have tried to sue the specific gun or alcohol manufacturer. In most cases, though, the courts have ruled against those claims, finding that the guns and alcohol are not defective in that they contain no mechanical flaws or hidden ingredients not known to the ordinary consumer. However, if in a specific case the alcohol contained a hazardous chemical or the gun had a defective mechanism that caused injury to the shooter and those standing behind him, strict liability might apply.

Note that this theory only applies to those *engaged in the business of selling such products*. Much like the warranty of merchantability, discussed earlier, the rationale for this rule is that merchants and manufacturers are better able than consumers to take steps to prevent defects in the first place, to assume the financial risk of defective products, and to pass along the cost of defective products as part of their sales price in the future.

A third requirement of strict liability is that the product *is expected to and does reach the user or consumer* **without substantial change in the condition in which it is sold.** The manufacturer should not bear the responsibility for products that have been altered or contaminated after leaving the manufacturer. If, for example, a hardware store removes the safety guards on all its lawn mowers in order to display them better, the manufacturer should not be liable for a consumer's injury that the guard would have prevented, although the retailer might be liable. Similarly, the maker of Tylenol was not held liable for the deaths of two people who took Tylenol tablets that had been injected with cyanide while on a grocer's shelf.

The American Law Institute, the group of lawyers and scholars who issued the *Restatement (2d)*, published a new *Restatement of Torts (3d): Product Liability*, a few years ago. In it, the authors attempt to "restate" the law of strict product liability, after many different definitions of terms such as *"defective"* and *"unreasonably dangerous"* had appeared in different state court decisions.

In the new *Restatement*, the experts find that there have been three main ways in which products have been found defective: (1) manufacturing defects, (2) design defects, and (3) defective warnings or instructions. The New *Restatement: Product Liability (3d)* describes *manufacturing defects* as occurring "when the product departs from its intended design, even though all possible care was exercised in the preparation and marketing of the product." This definition is not a significant change from the earlier version.

Probably the most controversial section of the third edition is the definition of *design defects*. Rejecting the view of some courts and consumer advocates, the *Restatement (3d)* does not focus on "consumer expectations" in defining *design defects*. Instead, the authors have moved in the direction of certain courts, which had adopted a so-called "risk utility" test. This test weighs the utility of the product's design against the risks of the design.

The language of the *Restatement (3d)* states:

> A product is defective in design when the foreseeable risks of harm posed by the product could have been reduced or avoided by the adoption of a reasonable alternative design by the seller . . . and the omission of the alternative design renders the product not reasonably safe.

This version of the Restatement basically suggests that courts around the country adopt, through case decisions, a more strict standard for design defects. The new standard would require the plaintiff in a product liability case to demonstrate to the court a "reasonable alternative design" in order to get a jury trial on the design defect issue—a considerably tougher standard than now exists in many states.

As to *"lack of warning"* defects, the *Restatement (3d)* also uses the "risk utility" and "reasonableness" tests. A product is defective because of inadequate warnings when "the foreseeable risks of harm posed by the product could have been reduced or avoided by the provision of reasonable instructions or warnings by the seller." The authors also note that consumers bear some responsibility for preventing harm. They should be expected to read warnings and to observe risks that are obvious or generally known to users.

This new *Restatement* consists more of a statement as to the direction the authors think the law "ought to go" rather than recapping what the decisions have been. So far, many state court decisions (based on common law case decisions—remember the *Restatement* is not a statute) have chosen not to adopt the suggested new standards for "design defects" and "failure to warn" liability. It remains to be seen if the *Product Liability Restatement (3d)* will be as widely followed by state courts as the previous *Torts Restatement.*

THE "CRASHWORTHINESS" DOCTRINE

One controversial variation on strict liability theory is the so-called **crashworthiness** doctrine. Under this rule, a vehicle manufacturer may be liable in negligence or strict liability for injuries suffered in a motor vehicle accident in which the design of the vehicle was not the cause of the accident but nevertheless *enhanced the injuries suffered.* This theory, first recognized in the landmark case *Larsen v. General Motors Corp* [391 F.2d 495 (8th Cir. 1968)], holds that the manufacturer's duty to produce a product reasonably safe for its intended use and not unreasonably dangerous must take into consideration the fact that injury-producing collisions are a regular, foreseeable, and statistically expectable result of such normal use. Therefore, an automobile manufacturer must use reasonable care in designing and manufacturing cars, trucks, and motorcycles, so that its vehicles minimize, rather than increase, the injuries caused when they become involved in collisions.

> **crashworthiness:** The duty of vehicle manufacturers to build cars, trucks, and motorcycles that do not enhance or worsen the injuries of persons when involved in accidents.

In the *Larsen* case, for example, the motorist suffered serious head injuries, not in the initial collision, but when his vehicle rolled over and the roof collapsed on him. As one court noted, the crashworthiness doctrine does not require a manufacturer to provide absolute safety, but it does require the manufacturers to take into account in all phases of the design and manufacturing process the known fact that many vehicles are involved in accidents. The manufacturer must provide some measure of reasonable, cost-effective safety features for the foreseeable use of the product, which includes the very real possibility of collisions and accidents.

For example, following is a photo of Prof. Bixby's (co-author of this textbook) vehicle after being struck by a driver running a red light—and then again by a car in another lane—in spring 2011. Thank goodness for air bags and seat belts! The vehicle was totalled, but the professor was not seriously injured; the vehicle was definitely crashworthy.

DEFENSES TO STRICT LIABILITY

assumption of risk: A common law defense against a personal injury claim that states that when an employee knows an activity is dangerous but continues, he or she cannot collect damages.

While businesses face considerable hurdles in defeating a strict liability claim, certain defenses are available. First, the doctrine of **assumption of risk** is still available. When plaintiffs fully realize the risks of injury in using a product, they cannot sue when one of the known risks causes injury. For example, skiers must realize that, despite purchasing high-class equipment, they may fall and even break bones sometimes while skiing. Susan will not win a lawsuit against the manufacturer of her skis if she takes a tumble while skiing and breaks her leg, unless she can show that some unknown defect in the skis caused her to fall.

On the other hand, where consumers do not realize the hazards inherent in the products they purchase, strict liability can be used against both sellers and manufacturers. In one of the most publicized and controversial cases in recent years, a 79-year-old woman spilled coffee when opening the cup to put in cream and sugar. At the time, she was sitting in the McDonald's parking lot, in the passenger seat of her nephew's car. She was originally awarded $2.9 million by a jury (later reduced to $480,000 by the judge). Although the case was the subject of many jokes on television, the actual facts were not very funny. Ms. Liebeck suffered extremely painful 3rd degree burns to her groin and thighs, was in the hospital for seven days, and underwent multiple surgical skin grafts. Her medical bills were almost $200,000.

Evidence at trial showed that McDonald's intentionally heated its coffee to 190 degrees even though other restaurants generally heated coffee only to about 160 degrees. Ms. Liebeck had originally just asked McDonald's to pay her medical expenses, but the company had refused to pay anything. Witnesses testified at the trial that McDonald's had received hundreds of complaints about its coffee being too hot, and more than 700 people had been burned, but company headquarters had stubbornly refused to lower the temperature. The jury decided that McDonald's coffee was so much hotter than other fast-food and restaurant coffee that therefore it was "unreasonably dangerous."

Probably the most effective defense manufacturers have to a strict liability lawsuit is to show **misuse** of the product by the consumer. In order to constitute "misuse," the product must be used in a way that was not foreseeable to the reasonable seller. Suppose that Susan is not using her skis for skiing but instead as a bookshelf. If the one hundred books she has piled on the skis cause them to crack and the books fall down and hit her, breaking her arm, she will probably not succeed in recovering damages from the ski company due to her misuse of the product. The classic example of misuse is the case in which a consumer was using his lawn mower as a hedge trimmer. As a result, the mower jumped and injured his leg. In this situation, the jury denied recovery, finding that the manufacturer had no responsibility for anticipating this type of use or for taking steps to prevent injuries in such an obvious misuse of the product.

The *Van Duzer v. Shoshone Coca-Cola Bottling Co.* case which follows discusses the critical elements of strict product liability and the misuse defense.

> **misuse:** When someone uses a product in a way that the manufacturer could not have reasonably foreseen.

VAN DUZER V. SHOSHONE COCA-COLA BOTTLING CO.

103 Nev. 383, 741 P.2d 811 (1987)

FACTS

Shelley Van Duzer was working as a cashier at Raley's Supermarket in Reno, Nevada, when a customer wheeled a shopping cart full of groceries into the checkout aisle. As Van Duzer began to remove a bag of potato chips from the cart, a bottle of Canada Dry Seltzer exploded, causing severe injuries to her eye. Her injury required surgery and eventually a cornea transplant. Under strict liability, she sued Owens-Illinois, Inc., the manufacturer of the bottle, and Shoshone Coca-Cola Bottling Co., which bottled the product and placed it on the shelves of the store. The jury rendered a verdict for the defendants, and Van Duzer appealed.

DECISION

The Nevada Supreme Court reiterated that the doctrine of strict liability had long been recognized in Nevada for defects in products that cause injuries. The judge had properly instructed the jury that a "product is defective when it fails to perform in the manner reasonably to be expected in light of its nature and intended function."

The customer had testified at trial that the bottle had exploded while in the shopping cart,

without being dropped or mishandled. Van Duzer did not even touch the bottle. The court stated that "a product container that cannot withstand the rigors of normal shopping practices is unreasonably dangerous and, by definition, defective."

The defendants argued that the bottle had shattered after colliding with one of the other glass containers in the cart. They asserted that a "sharp external blow to the bottle" constituted misuse, relieving them of liability. However, the court stated that even if this theory were true, it is of no importance if the external blow happened as the result of normal handling. "Use of a product in a manner which should be reasonably anticipated is not misuse or abuse."

The court found that it was normal for a bottled product to be placed in a shopping cart with other items, some of which may be glass containers. "Some jostling can be anticipated as the items are wheeled around the store." The cart was at a stop at the checkout counter when the accident occurred, and none of the witnesses testified to any unusual impact. As the court stated, "this was not a case where one object was hurled across a speeding cart at another object."

According to the facts of this case (even as stated by the defendants), the bottle shattered because it came into contact with another bottle in the cart. This susceptibility to breakage on impact with other bottles ordinarily found in shopping carts "rendered the bottle dangerous and defective." Because the evidence showed that this defect was inherent in the bottle and present when it left the control of the manufacturer and when it was sold by the distributor, both are liable under the doctrine of strict liability.

Since the jury could only have reached its verdict by disregarding the judge's instructions on strict liability, the decision of the lower court was reversed, and the case was remanded for a new trial.

CASE QUESTIONS

1. Whose "fault" was it that the bottle exploded? Does it make a difference in the outcome of this case? What must be proved in order for a plaintiff to win a strict liability case?
2. What did the defendants attempt to establish as a defense? Why did this argument not work to protect them from liability?
3. It is often said that strict product liability represents a public policy decision involving risk allocation. Is it fair to place the risk of injuries from defective products on the sellers and manufacturers of products even if they "exercised all possible care" in the manufacture of the product? Is it ethical?

LIMITATIONS ON THE USE OF STRICT LIABILITY

The theory of strict product liability shifts much of the burden of defective products to the manufacturers and sellers of all types of goods. Not only is there significant liability exposure for those who make defective products, but the cost of insurance for businesses of all kinds has increased in recent years regardless of whether a firm has sold any defective goods. In addition, businesses have had to increase spending for various preventive measures, such as increased research and testing, before a product can be marketed. Many firms and trade groups have argued that the frequent use of the strict liability theory has not only led to an excess of lawsuits against businesses—often for frivolous claims—but has stifled innovation and new product development by manufacturing companies afraid of lawsuits. It is often argued that U.S. manufacturers' competitive position in world markets is hurt by how U.S. courts use strict liability. Ironically, a few years ago the European Union adopted a product safety standard quite similar to the U.S. concept of strict liability.

In the past 20 years business trade groups have pushed for the passage of legislation by state legislatures and Congress to alleviate the so-called "tort crisis" created by the strict liability doctrine. Almost all of the states have enacted laws that, in one way or another, attempt to put some limits on the manufacturer's potential liability. Also, perhaps in response to the success of companies' and insurance firms' publicity campaign to make the public aware of the excesses of some jury verdicts, it appears that plaintiffs are losing more product liability cases than was true a few years ago. One study of jury verdicts in product defect cases showed that individuals suing companies won 54 percent of the cases in 1987 but won only 41 percent by the mid-1990s.

All states have **statutes of limitation** for various types of legal claims. These laws limit the time period during which a plaintiff may file a case raising a certain argument. Various types of cases call for different time periods. A typical statute of limitation for a product liability claim is four years from the time the defect is discovered, or should have been discovered, by the consumer.

For example, the statute of limitations on the exploding soda bottle would begin to run the day after the explosion. If the consumer waits longer than the statutory period to sue, the court case will be dismissed.

Sometimes a product user will be injured by a malfunction in a machine or other product that is 20 or 30 years old. The statute of limitations would not bar the suit if the consumer sued within four years after discovering the defect (when the malfunction occurred). Under strict liability (unlike warranties) no automatic expiration of the manufacturer's responsibility exists. To address the problem of a lawsuit being filed twenty years or more after the product was made, a number of states have passed **statutes of repose.** These laws put an outer limit, in some cases 10 or 15 years, on how long a manufacturer would face possible liability for defects in a product no matter when the problem was discovered by the user or consumer. In 1994 Congress established an 18-year statute of repose for lawsuits against manufacturers of private aircraft.

Some states have enacted laws imposing a "statute of repose" in certain situations. For example, Oregon enacted an amendment to a previous law, which now requires that a product liability suit must be brought within 8 years after the product was purchased (in wrongful death cases) or 10 years (personal injury or property damage cases). Oregon also has a Statute of Limitations which requires that product liability actions be brought within 2 years (personal injuries) or 3 years (deaths) of the time the plaintiff discovers, or reasonably should have discovered, the causal relationship between the injury and the product defect.

In recent years, manufacturers and business groups have advocated legislation that would make substantial changes in product liability laws and enact federal standards to preempt many state laws and common law principles. Table 13.1 describes some of the changes proposed in some of the legislation. These measures would put limits on noneconomic damages and would limit punitive damages. As of spring 2011, these proposed federal laws had not been enacted. But many states have enacted measures incorporating some of the reforms discussed below.

One provision advocated by business groups is the **state of the art defense.** This theory, adopted in some form by many states, allows a manufacturer to defend a product liability lawsuit by proving that at the time the product was made, the company used the best technology, design, and methods then available. Remember that the prevailing law regarding strict liability holds that the manufacturer of a defective product is liable for injuries caused "even though the seller has exercised all possible care in the preparation and sale" of the product. The state of the art defense, then, would bring strict liability theory back closer to negligence law, with which the plaintiff must show some sort of "fault" to prevail.

Another liability reform measure business backs is the elimination of **joint and several liability.** The general rule in the United States is that if the plaintiff in a liability case proves that two or more defendants each were partially responsible for the plaintiff's injuries, they will be held "jointly and severally" liable. In other words, each defendant is liable for the *whole judgment*—that is, the plaintiff can collect the whole amount awarded from any one defendant. Obviously, this theory allows (indeed encourages) the plaintiff to attempt to collect the entire judgment from the wealthiest defendant, rather than go after a percentage share from each one. This procedure, with the plaintiff looking for the "deep pocket," seems unfair to large companies that were only partly responsible for a consumer's injuries.

statute of repose: An outer limit on how many years after a product was manufactured that the maker could be held liable for a defect.

state of the art defense: A defense to liability recognized in some states, if the product was made using the best methods then available.

joint and several liability: When two or more defendants are found liable, the plaintiff can collect the entire award from any one defendant.

Table 13.1
Current and Proposed Product Liability Standards

PROPOSED FEDERAL LEGISLATION: PRODUCT LIABILITY

Subject	Current Law	Proposed Federal Law
Standards for personal injury and product liability lawsuits	No uniform federal laws exist. Variations based on common law from state to state.	Would establish uniform federal laws and standards.
State of the art defense	Some states allow the manufacturer to show that the latest and best technology was used, as a defense to liability.	Would establish a national standard allowing the state of the art defense in product liability cases.
Punitive damages	Plaintiff must prove that manufacturer was "flagrantly indifferent to consumer safety." No national caps on damages, but some states have caps.	Would cap punitive damages at three times compensatory damages. Would require "clear and convincing evidence" of intentional or flagrant action by defendant.
Joint and several liability	Many states provide for this type of liability, which means that the winning plaintiff can collect the whole award from any one of the defendants.	Would require the court or jury to specify the amount of damages for which each defendant is responsible.
Statute of repose	Many states have statutes of repose, no longer than 15 years.	Would establish a federal statute of repose of 18 years for products, with some exceptions.

Suppose, for example, that Toyota Corporation produces and sells a "Camry" vehicle to Nick. While driving down a residential street, the accelerator sticks, and Nick crashes into a tree, causing injuries to himself. The accelerator mechanism was actually made by the Ace Machine Co. and supplied to Toyota, where it was installed in the Camry. If Nick sues Toyota and Ace, he might win a judgment with joint and several liability imposed on both defendants, even though Ace was really much more responsible for the defect. Nick would be able to collect the $200,000 judgment from either one or both, in whatever proportion he can; probably, though, Nick will try to collect the whole amount first from Toyota, the larger and wealthier company. Toyota could then seek reimbursement from Ace Machine.

More than 30 states have enacted laws that have eliminated or modified joint and several liability. In these states, the jury must apportion the percentage of liability of each defendant. Say, for example, the jury decides that Toyota was 20 percent responsible and Ace was 80 percent responsible for Nick's injuries. Thus, if Nick is awarded $200,000, he can only receive $40,000 from Toyota, and the remainder, $160,000, will come from Ace. This plan appears to be more equitable for manufacturers, but consumer advocates and personal injury attorneys generally oppose the elimination of joint and several liability, arguing that it imposes significant additional burdens on the injured consumer. They assert that in many cases, the plaintiff who has been awarded monetary damages by the jury will be unable to collect from the smaller firms and there-fore will not actually receive the full amount of damages awarded by the jury.

Strict liability cases are often brought as **class actions.** As we have dis-cussed earlier, this form of lawsuit allows a few plaintiffs to represent a very large group of consumers who have purchased similar items or have suffered similar types of harm due to exposure to harmful or defective products. In recent years, thousands of persons have alleged harm from such products as asbestos, breast implants, the Dalkon Shield, and other products. Numerous class-action lawsuits have been filed in each of these cases as well as hundreds of individual cases. However, the determination as to whether a class action case is appropriate is vigorously fought by the large companies being sued, and in each case the court must decide if a class action is appropriate.

In 2003, the U.S. Supreme Court refused to hear a federal appeals court rul-ing that a nationwide class action would be inappropriate in a massive lawsuit against Firestone and Ford Motor Co. alleging that defective tires and design had caused numerous rollovers. The claims in this proposed class action did not involve any injuries or deaths, but were for "diminished value" of vehicles due to the possibility of rollovers, for tires that could lose tread, and for being put at risk of death or injury. Lawyers for the plaintiffs were proposing to represent the interest of more than 3 million owners of Ford Explorers made between 1991 and 2001 equipped with Firestone tires. However, the federal appellate court found that the case would be "unmanageable" due to the several different state laws applied and the great number of products sold over a long period of time. That decision became final when the Supreme Court declined certiorari.

SOCIAL/ETHICAL ISSUES

The strict liability theory is controversial. Is it ethical for a business firm to be required to pay damages to an individual injured by a defective product when the firm used the latest techniques and best method of design and manufacture in producing its product? If the business is forced to pay damages and carry additional insurance, it may have to lay off some employees as a result. What ethical issues are involved?

On the other hand, if a consumer is injured by a defective product, under negligence theory the manufacturer may escape liability to the individual simply by showing that the firm was careful in designing, making, and packaging the product. Is it fair to place the burden on consumers to inspect complex products and to tell persons who were injured while using the products correctly that they must suffer their own losses without compensation simply because they did not uncover the defect? Who eventually pays for the costs of the injuries? What ethical issues are involved here?

How can we fashion a rule that is fair to all sides? How safe should products be?

PREEMPTION

One other defense raised by manufacturers is **preemption**. The argument is that if a product must meet federal standards in order to be sold, the manufac-turer should not face product liability lawsuits in state courts based on state common law negligence or product liability principles which would likely be somewhat different in each state, based on court decisions.

preemption doc-trine: The theory that when a federal law and a state law govern the same subject and are con-flicting, the federal law may displace or cancel the state law.

This theory has not always been applied the same way in the courts. The results depend on the exact language used in the federal statute. In a case decided about 15 years ago, the U.S. Supreme Court refused to apply preemption to block a lawsuit in a state court against the maker of a pacemaker that malfunctioned. Although the medical device had been approved for sale by the Food and Drug Administration (FDA), it had not gone through much regulatory evaluation, and the FDA had not really focused on the safety of that particular device [*Medtronic, Inc. v. Lohr*, 518 U.S. 470 (1996)].

However, in 2008 the U.S. Supreme Court heard another case against Medtronic—this time involving a balloon catheter inserted into a patient during an angioplasty. The catheter ruptured, causing serious health injuries to the patient. But the Supreme Court found that in this case there had been much more rigorous testing and "premarket approval" of the medical device than in the Lohr case, and ruled that the state law negligence and product liability claims were preempted by the federal regulatory scheme here. *Riegel v. Medtronic Inc.,* 128 S. Ct. 999 (2008)

PUNITIVE DAMAGES

As we have discussed briefly in Chapter 11 (Torts), one of the most controversial issues involved in lawsuits regarding liability for defective products is the awarding of punitive damages. For more than a century, American courts have permitted, in a few cases, the awarding of so-called punitive damages to winning plaintiffs. American and English courts are alone in recognizing this type of damage award. As its name indicates, these monetary damages are intended to *punish* a defendant for some sort of particularly outrageous or malicious or intentional behavior. Sometimes called "*exemplary*" damages, the award is made to "set an example," at the discretion of the jury, but only when the judge rules that the jury may consider such damages.

Although the number of cases in which punitive damages are awarded is relatively small, when such damages are awarded, the amount tends to be large, since the purpose is to punish the defendant. When a company engages in some sort of really reckless conduct, or continues to manufacture and sell a product after it has knowledge that the product is dangerous or harmful to the public, juries occasionally award punitive damages. In order to "send a message" to a large corporation, the amount of money awarded must be substantial, often several million dollars. In Alaska, a jury awarded punitive damages of several billion dollars after the *Exxon Valdez* oil spill.

Among the more controversial aspects of punitive damages are the following: (1) the plaintiff receives the entire punitive damages award in addition to the compensatory and consequential damages based on the actual losses proved by the plaintiff; (2) the jury has complete discretion to determine the amount of damages it finds appropriate to punish the defendant; (3) the manufacturer of one product may be hit with several punitive damage awards in different lawsuits around the country, each one intended to "send a message"; (4) lawyers have incentive to seek punitive damages, since product liability cases are usually taken on a contingency fee, with the lawyers' compensation based on a percentage of the total award; and (5) the jury may base its decision on passion or sympathy, rather than hard evidence.

Consumer groups and plaintiffs' lawyers have argued in support of the continuation of punitive damages. They assert that when a large company deliberately continues to sell a product with known defects, such as the Dalkon Shield or asbestos, a few relatively modest compensatory damage awards can easily be absorbed by the firm as a business expense—a cost of doing business. The possibility of a large award of punitive damages, assessed by a jury of ordinary citizens, is necessary to focus the attention of some large firms on the effect of their products and actions of the public.

In recent years, businesses have intensified their attempts to have the U.S. Supreme Court review the legality of punitive damages, or at least to define the standards to be used in such awards. Since most punitive damages occur in tort and product liability cases, they are based on state laws and state common law decisions, rather than federal standards. Some states have developed much more generous policies than others, based on case decisions. Business firms have argued that the "due process" clause of the U.S. Constitution requires some fair standards be employed in the determination and awarding of punitive damages.

In 1991 the U. S. Supreme Court ruled in *Pacific Mutual Life Insurance v. Haslip* that punitive damages were a long-accepted part of American common law and were not, as a matter of law, unconstitutional. However, the Court stated that in a given case such damages might violate the due process clause if there was not sufficient guidance from the trial court to the jury, and some standards provided on which to base the award.

The *Haslip* case concerned a situation in which an insurance agent fraudulently pocketed premiums from clients, which resulted in the lapse of their health insurance policies, causing considerable financial losses. The jury awarded $210,000 in compensatory damages, and $840,000 in punitive damages. In *Haslip* the Supreme Court mentioned seven factors that the Alabama Supreme Court had established regarding the appropriateness of punitive damages in that state. The jury had been instructed on some of the factors and on the nature of such damages (retribution and deterrence). The court held that trial courts should give juries "adequate guidance" and that appellate courts should have the power to review punitive awards based on standards established in their states. Finding that these "general concerns of reasonableness" had been met, the Supreme Court upheld the award in *Haslip*.

In 1994, in *Honda Motor Co. v. Oberg,* the U.S. Supreme Court reversed a punitive damages award of $5 million entered against Honda as the result of an injury suffered on a three-wheel all-terrain vehicle. However, the basis for the reversal was not the size of the damages, but the fact that the Oregon legal system did not provide for any judicial review of punitive damages, a principle apparently unique to Oregon. Justice Stevens found that the absence of appellate review based on previously established standards did violate the due process clause of the Constitution.

The next opportunity the Supreme Court had to consider punitive damages was in the 1996 case *BMW of North America v. Gore*. In that case, which came from Alabama, Dr. Gore had purchased a new BMW automobile. Some time later, he learned that the car had suffered some scratch and paint damage in shipping and that a portion of the car had been repainted before its sale as "new" to Dr. Gore. Apparently it was the national policy of BMW not to disclose fairly minor damage to new car buyers. At trial, the court determined compensatory damages were $4,000 but awarded Gore $2 million to "send a message" to BMW that its policy was deceptive. On appeal, the U.S. Supreme Court found the award (a 500-to-1 ratio between the compensatory and punitive damages) "grossly excessive" and reversed the decision. In the years after the *BMW* case, lower courts in various states had interpreted the decision in many different ways, both affirming and reversing punitive damage awards of more and less than a 500-to-1 ratio.

In 2003, the Supreme Court again examined punitive damages, and held in *Campbell v. State Farm,* that a punitive damages award that was 145 times greater than the actual, compensatory damages was "excessive" and violated constitutional "due process" guarantees. Justice Anthony Kennedy wrote the court opinion which stated by a 6-3 vote that "courts must ensure that the measure of punishment is both reasonable and proportionate to the amount of harm to the plaintiff." The case arose after Curtis Campbell, a State Farm policyholder had been involved in an accident that killed one driver and left another disabled. Mr. Campbell had been sued, and State Farm refused a $50,000 settlement offer on his behalf. Later the case went to trial, and Campbell was ordered to pay $186,000 in damages. He then sued State Farm, alleging a bad-faith failure to settle. Mr. Campbell's lawyers introduced evidence that State Farm (America's largest insurance company) had a nationwide policy of instructing agents to minimize the claims they agreed to pay. A jury awarded him $2.6 million in compensatory damages and $145 million in punitive damages.

The U.S. Supreme Court, after reviewing the earlier punitive damages cases, found that the "guideposts" set by the 1966 *BMW v. Gore* case led to a clear result here. While refusing to set a rigid formula for calculating how much higher punitive damages could be than compensatory damages—and still be Constitutional—the Court stated as a "guidepost" that **few awards where punitive damages were more than 9 times compensatory damages would be upheld.** Imposed indiscriminately, punitive damages "have a devastating potential for harm," wrote Justice Kennedy. In 2008, the U.S. Supreme Court reduced the punitive damages award in the Exxon Valdez oil spill case from $2.5 billion to $500 million, based in part on the *State Farm* case decision, as well as some precedents from maritime cases.

IN CONSULTATION

Marvin Manager has a problem. His team recently designed a cutting-edge new product that has been named the Jetson 2011. The Jetson is the first product of its kind and is expected to sweep the market before ABC, Inc.'s competitors know what hit them. The research and development supporting the Jetson is extensive—ABC has evaluated the Jetson for quality, ease of use, and most importantly, safety. As each group of Jetsons comes off the production line, a safety inspector pulls random samples and runs them through a series of tests. The Jetson has passed every test—except one.

Ivan Inspector recently reported to Marvin that while he conducted the standard tests on one of the Jetsons, he accidentally spilled a little oil and a small fire erupted. Marvin and Ivan agreed that the risk of such a spill occurring again was very small, but they did not want to take any chances. They convened the Jetson's design team to a meeting where they discussed adding a safety shield. The engineers described two possible alternatives. The first shield was permanently welded onto the Jetson and removed any risk of a fire. The second was bolted on but, with enough effort, could be removed, leaving open the risk of burn injuries. The first shield added $25 to the cost of each Jetson, and the second added only $8. The marketing manager adamantly opposed the welded shield because all of the Jetson's market analysis was based on keeping the price low. Ivan Inspector thought either would be fine since the possibility of a spill was small.

Marvin decided that the shield selection should be based on more than market share and guesses as to the likelihood of a spill. He consulted his in-house counsel, to see if the two shields presented differing levels of potential liability. Here is their conversation:

Marvin:

1. Given how safe the Jetson is, do we have to use a shield in the first place?
2. Doesn't the Jetson's safety record at least justify the less-expensive shield?
3. What if we use the cheaper shield and add a warning?

Counsel:

1. Probably. It would only take one accident to create significant product liability for ABC.
2. Not necessarily. Our obligation is to make the product as safe as we can. We do not have to make the product perfectly safe at the expense of our market. We do not, however, relish explaining to an injured customer that we could have made the product safer but it was too expensive to do so.
3. Adding a warning helps, but it may not be enough. **Let me review the applicable law to see what our obligation and potential liability is. I'll get back to you.**

MEMO FROM THE LEGAL DEPARTMENT

To: Marvin Manager

Re: Product Liability for Jetson 2011

Dear Marvin:

Product liability law is designed to protect consumers. The law is designed to ensure that innocent product users who suffer injuries can recover their loss. We risk liability if any of our products hurt a purchaser, user, or even bystander. Product liability law allows an injured user to recover if he or she can prove intentional acts, negligence, defective product, or failure to warn of a known danger. If the Jetson causes injury, the court is likely to look at whether we knew the product was unsafe, whether we did everything we could to make it safer, and whether we warned users of potential risks.

Our awareness that there is a risk of fire is the very reason we do safety tests in the first place. Why do safety tests if we do not intend to learn from the results and make the products safer? Now that we know the Jetson could burn someone, we protect our customers and ourselves from liability if we make the Jetson safer. If we do not use a shield at all, we have knowingly placed a product into the marketplace that is unsafe. That constitutes at least negligence and possibly even an intentional act. Our liability for any injuries would be very high. The question, then, is which shield we should use.

An unsafe product is a defective product. Since defective products create liability, our goal, then, is to make the Jetson as safe as possible. If making a product as safe as possible merely raises costs, then we have a duty to make the product safer. Every manufacturer wants to make its product in as cost-effective a manner as possible—but cost-effectiveness cannot occur at the expense of safety. In this case, we need to balance the cost of the welded shield against the benefits of the safety it brings to the Jetson. We do not want to lose the profit we are likely to make from the Jetson in a lawsuit with an injured user.

> In the alternative, we could use the less expensive, removable bolted shield and then provide a warning. Warning users of a product's potential dangers is an effective defense in a product liability suit. Our best defense, however, is to never injure anyone in the first place. From a legal perspective, our safest course of action is to use the welded shield. We then remove the danger of a fire altogether and thereby remove the defect. If this option continues to distress the marketing manager, I will need very detailed information so that I can prove that raising the cost by $25 will make the product virtually impossible to sell. Then ABC can defend against a product liability lawsuit.

Consider the following questions with regard to product liability:
1. Do you agree with the company lawyer, or would you have chosen to add the removable shield and place a warning? What are the risks of following this course of action?
2. Do you think manufacturers should have to go to such lengths to make their products safer when it raises the costs of products that will never injure most of us?
3. Can you propose an alternative way for the law to ensure product safety and yet allow manufacturers to bring costs down and continue to place new products in the marketplace?

OTHER LEGAL ISSUES IN THE SALE OF GOODS

Many other important legal issues frequently arise in connection with the sale of products. As goods move in commerce from manufacturers, to wholesalers, to retailers, and finally to consumers, the various parties create numerous contracts and expectations among one another. When a seller and a buyer make a contract for the purchase of some product, whether it is a shipment of one million pounds of potatoes or one airplane, each is expecting the other to fully perform all obligations, and happily, this is often the case. But what if it does not work out that way? Sometimes either the buyer or seller does not fulfill the obligations he or she promised to perform. What are the rights of the buyer and seller?

Each state has enacted laws dealing with the rights of buyers and sellers of goods. In addition to the provisions we have already discussed dealing with warranties and disclaimers, the **UCC** (the "sales law" section has been adopted by all states but Louisiana) also contains many provisions concerning the rights of the parties involved in the sale of products, as will be discussed in the following sections.

uniform commercial code (UCC): A model law dealing with the sale of goods, adopted by 49 states, that specifies contract rights and remedies of buyers and sellers (and other issues).

BUYER'S RIGHTS AND REMEDIES

UCC §2-711 provides that where the seller fails to make delivery or repudiates the contract (states that he or she will not honor the contract), or the buyer rightfully rejects the goods delivered (usually because they do not conform to the contract), the buyer may cancel the contract. The buyer may also do one or more of the following: (1) "cover" (purchase substitute goods), (2) recover damages for nondelivery, (3) recover certain goods still held by the seller, and/or (4) possibly obtain specific performance.

At the time of delivery, the buyer has the right to inspect the goods to determine if they meet the contract specifications. If they do not, the buyer can

reject the goods. Sometimes the buyer can even *revoke acceptance* of the goods at a later time, even though he or she did not reject them initially (UCC §2-608). For example, a buyer who did not reject the goods upon delivery because of a reasonable assumption that the problem would be cured or because the nonconformity was difficult to discover may revoke acceptance if this assumption proves false. When the buyer later discovers that the goods are nonconforming, the seller must be notified promptly and before "any substantial change in the condition of the goods" has occurred.

When the buyer rejects or revokes acceptance of the goods or the seller simply does not deliver them, quite often this puts the buyer in a real bind. The buyer may need the goods for his or her business or may have a contract to sell the products to someone else. Therefore, the buyer often decides to **cover**, that is, to purchase substitute goods to meet his or her needs (UCC §2-712). In many cases, the substitute goods will cost more than the contract price, and in such situations, the buyer is permitted to recover the difference along with any incidental damages (such as shipping, storage, and other costs) from the seller who has breached the contract.

The buyer does not have to cover, however. He or she may have already accepted the goods when the defects become apparent or have decided to keep the goods even though they were not quite right because of an urgent need to use them in a commercial project. In this case the buyer can deduct his or her damages from the price due the seller. The buyer (and perhaps a court eventually) will have to determine how much less the goods as delivered were worth.

Sometimes the buyer does not want money damages but would rather get the actual goods, as promised. The UCC provides for this remedy in §2-716 by allowing a buyer to seek *specific performance* where "the goods are unique or in other proper circumstances." For example, when the buyer really cannot purchase substitute goods anywhere else or when the goods were specifically made to fit the buyer's requirements, the buyer may be able to force the seller to deliver the actual products that were the subject of the contract.

SELLER'S RIGHTS AND REMEDIES

What if the breach of the sales contract is made by the buyer rather than the seller? Suppose that by contract James promises to deliver 100 custom-made leather jackets to Paula on September 1, 2011. James delivers the 100 jackets to Paula on the correct date, but at that time she tells James that she no longer needs the jackets. She refuses to accept or pay for them. What can James do?

The usual and preferred remedy is for James to **resell** the jackets and then sue Paula for any damages he suffers, such as receiving a lower price for the jackets, and any extra costs incurred, such as storage, advertising, or transportation. James must notify Paula of his intention to resell and must sell the goods in good faith and in a "commercially reasonable" manner, according to UCC §2-706. The objective is to put the seller in as good a position as if the contract had been performed. In some cases the seller may claim, under UCC §2-708, the profit he would have made.

In some situations, the goods may be specially manufactured for the buyer or are for some other reason unusual and unique. If the seller is unable to

---

rejection: The buyer inspects the goods and says, "These are not the correct items."

cover: The buyer's right to purchase substitute goods if the seller fails to deliver the correct goods.

resell: If the buyer wrongfully refuses to accept the goods, the seller can sell the goods and then sue the buyer for any loss.

resell the goods after reasonable efforts, it may be possible to sue for the *full price* of the products. This is an exception, however, and can only be employed when the goods are essentially worthless to the seller or anyone else. Why? It normally would be unfair to allow the seller to keep the products and receive full payment as well. Suppose that James had made 15 leather jackets individually to fit the members of Paula's professional basketball team, with each person's name and team logo on the jacket. Assuming that the players were all quite large people, it might be impossible for James to sell the jackets elsewhere. Thus, if Paula breached the contract without a good reason, James might be able to recover the price in a legal action.

cure: The seller who delivers nonconforming goods to the buyer can correct the deficiency if the contract time limit has not expired.

Interestingly, the seller also has the right to **cure** an instance of nonperformance. If the seller has delivered goods that the buyer refuses to accept because they do not conform to the contract, the seller, whenever possible, is given the right to "cure" the nonperformance. UCC §2-508 provides that "where any tender or delivery by the seller is rejected because it is nonconforming [it does not meet the contract requirements] and the time for performance has not yet expired, the seller may reasonably notify the buyer of his intention to cure and may then within the contract time make a conforming delivery." Thus, if James has delivered one month before the end of the contract period jackets that are not quite right and Paula rejects them, James can redo the jackets to meet the contract specifications if he does so in time.

James may even have the right to cure nonperformance after the "contract time" if he had reasonable grounds for believing that the performance would be acceptable. For example, in one case, a seller delivered a newer model of a hearing aid ordered previously by a customer, but the customer refused to accept it and attempted to cancel the contract. The seller was permitted to cure by obtaining the exact (older) model ordered and delivering it to the buyer.

SUMMARY

The purchase of manufactured products, an everyday occurrence, involves a series of legal issues of importance to business and consumers. Many sellers provide written *express warranties* with their products that guarantee the item will work properly for a certain time and that the seller will repair it during that same time if a problem develops. The sale of products may also carry *implied warranties*, created by provisions in the UCC, which give consumers certain rights based on their probable expectations at the time of the sale. Both the express and implied warranties may be *disclaimed* to some extent, however, by particular language in the written warranty. The federal Magnuson-Moss Warranty Act establishes requirements for all written warranties, restricts the seller's right to completely disclaim implied warranties, and guarantees the right of consumers to sue for warranty violations.

When individuals are injured due to product defects, lawsuits may be brought based on the legal theories of both negligence and *strict liability*. In a negligence action, the plaintiff must show that the manufacturer did not meet the standards expected of a reasonably careful manufacturer in some aspect of the design, production, or sale of the product, and that this negligence was the cause of the injury.

The strict liability theory, which has been increasingly used by the courts in recent years, is based on the philosophy that those who manufacture defective products should bear the costs of resulting injuries, whether or not the manufacturer was negligent. Thus, in a strict liability case, the plaintiff need prove only that the product was *defective*, was unreasonably dangerous, and caused the injury. The increase in number and size of product liability judgments based on strict liability has led many state legislatures to put restrictions on the total freedom of juries to award damages in such cases. Legislation has been introduced in Congress that would establish a uniform set of federal product liability standards and that would make other major changes in the tort liability system.

Other important legal issues arise in connection with the sale of products, such as the rights and responsibilities of buyers and sellers when one side fails or refuses to perform in accordance with the contract. The UCC contains a series of rules for dealing with the breach of sales contracts. The buyer has the *right to reject* goods that do not conform to the contract and may also have the right to *cover* (purchase substitute goods) in the event of improper performance by the seller. On the other hand, if the buyer refuses to pay for the goods, the seller can *resell the goods* and sue the buyer for his or her losses or, in some cases, for the whole price. If the seller delivers goods that do not conform to the contract and there is still some time left before final performance is due, the seller can often *cure* that nonperformance by promptly delivering the proper goods. In most situations, the UCC's remedy is designed to place the parties, as nearly as possible, in the position they would have occupied had the contract been fully performed.

CHAPTER QUESTIONS

1. Johnny was riding his new bicycle when the front wheel came off, and he was injured. His family sued the store where the bike was purchased for violation of the warranty of fitness for a particular purpose, arguing that the store knew that the bike was to be used for pleasure riding by a young boy. Does this warranty apply? What about the warranty of merchantability? What should be the result? Why? [*Crump v. Times Square Stores,* 157 AD 2d 768, 550 NYS 2d 373 (1990)]

2. A car dealership sold a used car to a consumer, and the retail contract stated in bold capital letters, that there were no express or implied warranties, and that the car was sold "as is" and "with all faults." The purchaser later had problems with the car and brought an action against the seller. He argued that the express warranties had not been properly disclaimed. Since the seller had written a note to the buyer stating that the vehicle was still covered by the manufacturer's warranty, the buyer asserted that the seller had given a written warranty and thus could not disclaim the implied warranties because of the Magnuson-Moss Act. What should be the result and why? Was there an express warranty? Were the implied warranties properly disclaimed? [*Haight v. Dale's Used Cars, Inc.,* 87 P.3d 962 (Id. App. 2003).]

3. A man was working for a general contractor using an elevated platform at a construction site when the lift fell over. He suffered serious and permanent injuries. He sued the owner of the platform and the company which manufactured the platform. It was shown at trial that the "kill switch" had been removed from the platform's control box sometime after the platform was sold. The purpose of the "kill switch" was to deactivate the platform and prevent inadvertent operation. Does this fact affect the product liability claim against the manufacturer? Why? *Seibel v. JLG Industries, Inc.,* 362 F.3d 480 (8th Cir. 2004).

4. During a July 4 fireworks show at the Western Washington State Fairgrounds in Puyallup, one of the mortars was knocked into a horizontal position. A rocket inside then ignited and flew 500 feet parallel to the ground where it discharged, causing injury to several spectators. The exact cause of the malfunction could not be determined. The plaintiffs sued under strict liability, arguing that fireworks displays are an "ultrahazardous activity" and the operators of the fireworks show should be strictly liable without a showing of negligence or fault. What should be the result? Why? [*Klein v. Pyrodyne Corp.*, 117 Wash.2d 1, 810 P.2d 917 (1991)]

5. A man named Harmon lit a cigarette with a BIC lighter, and then put the lighter back in his shirt pocket and resumed working. He claimed that a few minutes later, when leaning over his computer, he saw flames coming from his shirt, causing burns to his chest and arm. Mr. Harmon sued BIC, alleging product liability defects. BIC presented detailed illustrations and testing data showing that the BIC lighter he was using was not the cause of the accident. The plaintiff claimed he had used the lighter only 12 times prior to the accident, but BIC's experts said that the lighter he introduced in evidence had been used thousands of times, and in testing it extinguished properly each time it was tested. Also Mr. Harmon claimed that although he was alone at the time of the accident, he gave the lighter to two other workers to look at later, but at trial they both denied ever seeing the lighter. Should Mr. Harmon or BIC win the case? Why? [*Harmon v. BIC Corporation,* 16 A.D.3d 953, 792 N.Y.S.2d 656 (2005)]

6. Jaime Camacho was operating his two-month-old Honda motorcycle when he collided with an automobile and suffered serious leg injuries. He sued not only the other motorist but also Honda under a strict liability theory, claiming that the motorcycle was defectively designed and therefore unreasonably dangerous. Camacho argued that the motorcycle was not equipped with "crash bars" (steel bars connected to the frame), which would have protected his legs in the event of a collision. The trial court dismissed this claim, and Camacho appealed. What should be the result if Colorado follows the "crashworthiness" doctrine? [*Camacho v. Honda Motor Co.,* 741 P.2d 1240 (Colo. 1987)]

7. What ethical obligation should a manufacturing firm have toward consumers with respect to its products? If a product has been approved by federal regulators but the company's own in-house testing shows that there are some problems, what should the company do? Should it have ethical obligations to its wholesalers and retailers? Do all of these entities have ethical duties to the consumers?

8. A California lower court had entered a judgment of $5 million compensatory damages and $290 million punitive damages against Ford Motor Co. in a product liability case in 2002 and the award was affirmed on appeal. But after the U.S. Supreme Court's *State Farm* decision, the case was remanded to the California Court of Appeals for re-consideration of the punitive damages award. Should the Court reduce the amount of punitive damages? Why? [*Romo v. Ford Motor Co.* 6 Cal.Rptr. 3d 793 (Cal.App. 2003)].

9. A California family was involved in a bad highway accident, which resulted in the death of one family member, who was riding in the rear aisle seat of a minivan. The family brought a product liability lawsuit against Mazda, claiming that the seat in which the family member was sitting, was defective and unsafe because it had only a lap belt, instead of lap and shoulder belts. At that time the relevant federal safety standards required auto manufacturers to install lap and shoulder belts on rear seats next to a vehicle's doors and frames, but they may install either those belts or simple lap belts on rear inner seats (those next to a minivan's aisle). Should the lawsuit be preempted by the federal regulation? What are the arguments for and against preemption? *Williamson v. Mazda Motor of America, Inc,* ___U.S.___ (2011)

10. A company in Pennsylvania purchased an expensive router from a manufacturer. The buyer had ample time to inspect the router for defects, but several weeks later, the router did not function as well as expected when attached to various electronic systems made by another company. It was not proved that the router was defective in any way. Could the buyer "revoke acceptance" of the router, or does the buyer owe the contract price? Why? [*SCM Group, USA, Inc. v. Custom Designs & Mfg. Co. Inc.,* 89 Fed. Appx. (3d Cir. 2004)]

PRACTICAL EXERCISE

Your friend Larry visited Hawaii several years ago. While there, he and his wife, Lucille, visited an art gallery several times, and eventually purchased two expensive pieces of artwork (original lithographs), supposedly done and hand-signed by the famed surrealist artist Salvador Dali. In the years since, the gallery has solicited Larry and Lucille several times, offering them more Dali works of art, and they have purchased three more lithographs and two wall sculptures. To date, Larry and Lucille have spent more than $35,000 purchasing Dali pieces from this gallery. At the time of each purchase, the gallery assured Larry that the work was done by Dali, and furnished him with a written "Certificate of Authenticity" and an appraisal stating that the piece was of equal or greater value than the purchase price.

Recently Larry and Lucille found out that many complaints had been made against the gallery for selling forged artwork and that the Hawaii Attorney General had filed a complaint against the gallery. Knowing that you are studying law, Larry has asked you to comment on his rights as the purchaser of artwork. "Aren't there some kind of warranty laws that I could use if the art is not genuine?" he asks you. Prepare a memo for Larry and Lucille describing express warranties and implied warranties, the seller's defenses, and the Magnuson-Moss Warranty Act. Also, advise them on their chances of winning a lawsuit using any of these theories. You need to discuss, among other issues, the "basis of the bargain" concept necessary to create an express warranty, as well as the seller's likely defense that UCC §2-313(2) states that "any affirmation merely of the value of the goods or a statement purporting to be merely the seller's opinion" regarding the goods does not create a warranty.

FURTHER INFORMATION

www.cpsc.gov
Consumer Product Safety Commission.
http://atra.org
American Tort Reform Association site.
http://www.cbo.gov/doc.cfm?index=5549&type=0&sequence=1
The Effects of Tort Reform: Evidence from the States

CHAPTER 14

REAL AND PERSONAL PROPERTY: OWNERSHIP, TRANSFER AND LAND USE CONTROLS

LEARNING OBJECTIVES

After you have read this chapter, you should be able to:

1. Define real property and describe the different kinds of estates and ownership of property.
2. Discuss the process of acquiring ownership of real property, including financing and recording.
3. List the ways in which public and private laws restrict and control the use of real property.
4. Define and give examples of personal property and bailments.
5. Discuss how property owners can control the transfer of property through wills and trusts.

CHAPTER OUTLINE

I. Real Property

II. Personal Property

III. Wills, Probate, and Trusts

INTRODUCTION

The right to own property and to prevent other persons from using, abusing, or interfering with one's property rights is basic to the free enterprise system. Almost every business will need to rent or own real and personal property of some kind. In this chapter, we examine the different legal concepts pertinent to real property (real estate) and personal property and discuss the methods of acquiring, maintaining, and transferring ownership of each type of property.

Real property includes land and everything permanently attached to it, as well as the airspace above it and minerals beneath its surface. The legal principles that apply to real property in the United States today are based on common law doctrines, many of which originated in feudal times in Europe. Personal property, on the other hand, generally includes all property that is not real property. Personal property may be tangible (such as chairs, computers, and automobiles) or intangible (such as patents, accounts receivable, and stock).

The chapter will also look into several important issues concerning regulation of land use—both governmental and private—which are becoming significant legal matters for local governments and developers. Finally we will examine the methods of transferring property rights upon an owner's death, through wills, trusts, and the probate process.

REAL PROPERTY

As we have noted, much of the law regarding real property can be traced back to English decisions from the Middle Ages. In medieval England, the ownership of land determined one's position in society. The legal principles that developed protected the lord of the manor and his crops, animals, and houses, and sustained his wealth and his position of power. Over hundreds of years the rules relating to ownership, use, and inheritance of property developed into important common law legal doctrines. The other primary "common law" topics—contracts and torts—began to develop only as offshoots of property-related transactions and problems. Legal theories concerning such matters as contracts for the sale of land and "trespass" and "nuisance" torts affecting the rights of land owners evolved in this way, especially after the industrial revolution as changes occurred to the mercantile society.

The rights of private property owners have always been accorded a very high priority in the United States. The early American legal doctrines were based on the English principles but were modified after reaching this country. Some, but not all, of the numerous detailed rules regarding property were discarded over time. Spanish and French legal theories also had some influence on the development of American common law relating to real property.

freehold estate: An ownership interest lasting at least for one's life.

Historically, an estate (ownership interest) in land could be categorized as "freehold" or "nonfreehold." **Freehold estates** were those that were compatible with a free man, in that they lasted for at least the length of a person's life. Nonfreehold estates, conversely, lasted for a set period of time (whether 30 days or 30 years); therefore, someone like a tenant acquires not ownership but the legal right to possession.

TYPES OF OWNERSHIP

fee simple absolute: The most complete ownership of real property.

Fee Simple Absolute   The most complete type of "freehold" ownership possible is called the **fee simple absolute**. The word "fee" denotes an ownership interest. The owner of a fee simple absolute (often just called "fee simple") can use or abuse the land; can sell, lease, or mortgage it; and can leave it to his or her heirs upon death. Because of zoning, environmental issues, and other restrictions to be discussed later, it is not quite accurate to say the owner can do "anything" with the land. However, when you purchase property for your home or business, you will almost certainly want to own it in fee simple.

Fee Simple Determinable   Let us suppose that Jill is selling some land to Thomas. Sometimes the **grantor** (the person selling or giving the land—Jill in this example) will put a clause in the deed, such as "To Thomas, so long as this property is never used as a tavern." Although Thomas will have a fee simple ownership, if the land is ever used as a tavern, the title will automatically revert back to Jill (the grantor) or her heirs. Since Thomas has only those rights to the land which he was given, when he sells the land to Teresa, she will be subject to the same condition. Thomas cannot increase the amount of ownership beyond what he was given. If Teresa ever allows the property to be used as a tavern, the title of the land goes back to Jill, or her heirs if she has died by that time. This type of deed is often used by those who donate land to cities for parks or schools to guarantee that the land will always be used in that particular fashion. If a city school district used, for non-school purposes, land given to it under a **fee simple determinable** ("so long as this property is used as a public school"), the title to the land would automatically revert to the grantor or his or her heirs, even if this happened 50 or 90 years after the deed.

Fee Simple on a Condition Subsequent   A fee simple on a condition subsequent is similar to the fee simple determinable, except that the title does not revert automatically. If the deed says, "To Thomas except that if the land is ever used as a tavern, the grantor has the right to retake possession and ownership," it is a fee simple on a condition subsequent. Thomas's title to the land will not be extinguished (even if he operates a tavern) until the grantor (Jill) takes action to repossess the land.

Life Estate   The **life estate** is a type of freehold estate that exists for as long as a particular person lives. If the deed from Jill states, "To Sarah for life and then to Ryan," Sarah has a life estate. It is a freehold interest in that she has the exclusive right to possess the land, use it, lease it, and maybe even sell it (her life interest). When she dies, however, the land will belong to Ryan. If Sarah should sell the land to Brittney, she (Brittney) will own the land but her ownership will end when Sarah dies. The owner of a life estate has the rights of all other freehold owners, except that she cannot "waste" the property—that is, do something that destroys its value.

Although Ryan or his heirs will certainly own the land some day, he does not have any legal rights of entry or possession of the property now. Ryan has what is called a **future interest** in the real estate. He has a legal interest in the property; but for now, this interest is not a right to possession or ownership. He can only take legal action if he believes Sarah is "wasting" the property. Although he may be very concerned with the use of the land and with Sarah's health ("How are you doing? Don't you feel kind of sick?"), he must await her death before he can become the owner.

Jill, the grantor in the earlier examples, also has a future interest in the property if it is a fee simple determinable or fee simple on a condition subsequent. Her future interest is "contingent" because Jill may or may not reacquire

grantor: the person who is conveying (giving up) an interest in real property.

fee simple determinable: A fee simple ownership that may be lost if the property is used in certain ways.

life estate: A type of ownership that lasts only for the life of the owner and cannot be extended.

future interest: A legal right in real property, which will or may become full ownership in the future.

ownership of the property; she does have, however, a present legal interest in it that may possibly become possessory in the future.

nonfreehold estate: A legal right to possession, but not ownership, of real property, such as a lease.

Nonfreehold Estates   The most common type of **nonfreehold estate** is the landlord–tenant relationship. In this case, the fee simple owner makes an agreement to transfer possession (but not ownership) to another person for a period of time. Whether the property is rented for one month or 40 years, the tenant acquires the legal right to possession but does not become the owner.

The landlord (lessor) retains the ownership of the land during the term of the lease. The tenant (lessee) acquires an interest depending on the type of lease. In an *estate for years*, the tenant has the right of possession for a definite period, often one or more years, but it may be for any specific time. In a **periodic tenancy** the property is rented for a certain period, often one month at a time. This type of tenancy can generally be ended when either party gives the other one month's notice. An *estate at will* is not based on any formal rental period but may exist as long as both parties allow it to. This type of tenancy is often created when a tenant "holds over"—holds on to the premises after the lease expires. The landlord can either accept rent and the tenant becomes "at will," or he can begin eviction procedures.

periodic tenancy: A tenancy lasting for a certain time.

Concurrent Ownership   At any one time two or more persons may own together any of the various types of real estate interests, except the life estate described previously. The most frequent type of joint ownership is the tenancy in common. (Note that even though the word "*tenancy*" is used, this can either be a freehold (ownership) or nonfreehold estate.)

In a **tenancy in common,** two or more persons own together an "undivided" interest in the property. "*Undivided*" means that although the persons each own a certain percentage of the total property rights, no one owns any particular area within the property. The ownership interests do not have to be the same percentage and do not have to arise at the same time. When one co-owner dies, she can leave her percentage of ownership to her heirs. In other words, if Stacey, Bill, and Jessica own a piece of property as tenants in common, it is possible for Stacey to own 50 percent, Bill to own 30 percent, and Jessica 20 percent of the total. No one of them has any greater rights to any particular area within the property, since the ownership is undivided. If the property is sold, each owner will receive his or her proportionate share of the proceeds. If Stacey decides to sell her interest to Bruce, he would then become a tenant in common with Bill and Jessica. If Bill dies, his share of ownership will pass to his heirs.

tenancy in common: Ownership of property by two or more persons. Each can sell his or her share or leave to heirs. Shares do not have to be equal.

In a **joint tenancy,** some aspects of ownership are different. All ownership interests must be equal, no matter how many joint tenants there are. Joint tenancy interests must be created at the same time and carry the right of **survivorship.** Thus, if Stacey, Bill, and Jessica own a property in joint tenancy, they each must own a one-third interest that was created by the same deed to the three of them. If Bill dies, his interest will automatically be redistributed to Stacey and Jessica, not to his heirs. Stacey and Jessica will then be joint tenants, each owning a one-half interest in the property. Even if Bill had drafted a will leaving his share of the property to his sister, Connie, she will receive nothing if the property was owned in joint tenancy. Because this is an unusual condition, the courts will rule that a tenancy in common exists if there is any

joint tenancy: Ownership of property by two or more persons. When one dies, his or her share is automatically distributed to the co-owners who **survive**. Joint tenants cannot leave their share to their heirs. Shares must be equal.

doubt about the type of ownership or any confusion arises about whether a joint tenancy or tenancy in common was intended.

One of the joint tenants can convey his or her portion of the estate to someone else without permission of the others, however. If, for example, Stacey sells her one-third interest to Shaun, he will then have a one-third interest in the property. But he will not be a joint tenant with Bill and Jessica, since he did not acquire his interest at the same time as they did. He will be a tenant in common with the other two, while Bill and Jessica will remain as joint tenants to each other.

Between husband and wife, a special form of joint tenancy exists called the **tenancy by the entireties.** This estate is similar to a joint tenancy, except it only exists for persons married to each other. The law presumes that a married person who buys property with his spouse would want her to automatically become the sole owner in case of his death. If this is not what both spouses want, then they should not purchase property together. Unlike a regular joint tenancy, one spouse cannot convey any interest in property owned in tenancy by the entireties without the signature of the other. Divorce, however, usually converts this tenancy into a tenancy in common; in this case, either party can convey his or her interest. Tenancy by the entireties is used in more than one-half of the United States. (Many of the western states, for example, do not use this form of joint tenancy.)

Property acquired during marriage by married couples in nine states—Arizona, California, Idaho, Louisiana, Nevada, New Mexico, Texas, Washington, and Wisconsin—is owned **as community property.** This concept, originated in Spanish law, means that all property bought or acquired during marriage is presumed to be part of the "marital community," owned equally by both spouses. Such property cannot be conveyed without the

> **tenancy by the entireties:** A type of joint tenancy for married couples.

> **community property:** A type of property ownership for married couples recognized in nine states.

MEMO FROM THE LEGAL DEPARTMENT

To: Students

From: Legal Department

If you desire to purchase property with others as joint tenants, you need to make sure that the deed is drafted properly. The deed must clearly convey the property to "A, B, and C as joint tenants, with rights of survivorship." If there is any ambiguity, the courts will construe the ownership as tenancy in common, since that is a much more typical type of concurrent ownership. In a tenancy in common, of course, when a property owner dies, his or her share is passed on to that person's heirs.

signature of both spouses. When one spouse dies, the ownership of community property passes to the surviving spouse. It is sometimes possible, although difficult, for one spouse to maintain as "separate property," sole ownership in property owned by that person prior to marriage or inherited during marriage. Only individual funds can be used to maintain the property, and receipts from and expenses related to the property must not be commingled with the community property of the couple (such as a joint bank account) or the asset will become community property. Many divorce cases in these nine states have been characterized by nasty fights over property that one spouse tried to keep "separate" and out of the marital community.

ACQUIRING OWNERSHIP OF REAL PROPERTY

deed: A written document used to transfer ownership in real property.

Deeds   The primary method of transferring ownership in real property is through the sale by one owner to another confirmed by proper execution of a **deed**. A deed is a formally drafted document that conveys ownership from one or more persons to another individual or group. The deed must meet the following requirements:

- It must be written.
- It must name the grantor(s), which is the person or persons giving up ownership, and the grantee(s), which is the person or persons acquiring ownership.
- It needs to be signed by the grantor(s).
- It has to provide the legal description of the property.
- It must contain certain words indicating that the property is being conveyed.
- It must be witnessed by two or three persons (depending on the state law).

warranty deed: A deed that "warrants" that the buyer is receiving good, clear title to the property.

quitclaim deed: A deed that merely conveys what ownership the grantor has without any warranties.

There are several types of deeds. The most common type of deed—and the best from a purchaser's standpoint—is the **warranty deed.** This instrument contains a "warranty" or promise from the seller to the buyer that he or she is getting good title (a clear title with no defects or problems). Another common type of deed is called a **quitclaim deed.** This document, generally used only to clear up title problems, contains no promises or warranties of any kind. All the seller is stating is that "I am giving you whatever interest I have in this property" (in other words, "I am quitting whatever claim I had to this property"). If you are purchasing real estate for your home or business, you want to make sure you receive a warranty deed for the property.

Defects and Problems with Real Estate   There have been many cases in recent years brought by purchasers of homes who discovered problems, defects and other problems after the purchase. These cases can be difficult, expensive and sometimes very distressing for the new homebuyer, as well as for the seller who thought she was finished with this transaction. "There is nothing more unpleasant—not only unpleasant but unsatisfying—than suing a seller who's long gone for some problem with the physical condition of the property," says a Minneapolis real estate lawyer. It is important for the buyer to get a full disclosure from the seller of all known defects. Some state laws now require disclosure forms to be signed by the seller, and perhaps the real estate agent, listing physical defects and environmental hazards. "Yes, get the disclosures, but really more important—get a good inspector," says the lawyer.

Obtaining a good and thorough home inspection before the purchase is final can save thousands of dollars and many headaches. The inspection should be done by a professional and cover, at the least, the major systems, such as plumbing, heating, electrical and structural. But today there are many other less obvious hazards which have caused legal problems, such a radon (a colorless and odorless gas that is found in basements), mold caused by water infiltration, insect or termite infestation, foundation problems, lead-based paint, asbestos and other hazards.

While the buyer may be able to recover on a warranty theory from contractors who installed new goods into new construction, it is more difficult with existing houses. In addition to whatever warranties and disclosures were made by the seller, several courts have ruled, in common law case decisions, that there is a *"warranty of habitability"* in that state, which means that a homebuyer should receive a house that is fit to live in upon purchase. Somewhat like the warranty of merchantability discussed in Chapter 13, the warranty of habitability would provide that the house should be "fit for ordinary purposes"—which means at the very least that the major systems function well, the roof does not leak, and sewage does not back up in the basement. Also, homeowner's insurance may cover some problems, but policies differ greatly on what is covered, particularly for mold and environmental hazards.

MEMO FROM THE LEGAL DEPARTMENT

Buying a house is the largest single purchase most of us make. It is very important to go about the selection and purchase of a house (or commercial property) carefully. Some advice to consider:

1. use a reputable real estate agent who is knowledgeable about the type of property you are seeking and the area.

2. Look at and compare several houses before making an offer on one.

3. Insist on the right to have the house inspected, perhaps by 2 or 3 different inspectors before reaching the final agreement, or put a clause into the contract providing for an inspection, with the owner required to make the needed repairs before closing.

4. Discuss clearly with the seller, or the seller's agent, any concerns you have about the house prior to the contract, and don't be afraid to insist that any oral promises which are made (the roof will be fixed, or the gutters cleaned, or that the chandelier is staying) be put in writing in the final contract.

5. If any problems do arise, carefully document them in writing, along with any steps taken to solve them, as well as any communication with the seller, agent or insurance company. And it is sometimes important to give notice (written) to your insurance company within a set number of days after a problem occurs, in order to claim coverage.

Inheritance   Often the ownership of real estate is acquired by inheritance. In many cases, this happens when an owner of property dies, leaving a will (discussed later in this chapter). The will might state, for example, that "I leave my real property in Washington County called 'Blackacre' to my niece, Heather." After the court concludes the probate process (legal procedures for disposing of the assets of the deceased person), Heather will be declared the owner of the property in fee simple.

For those who die without a will, any real estate they own will, following the probate process, become the property of their nearest heir as specified by the laws of that state.

Adverse Possession   It is also possible for someone to gain ownership of property through the doctrine of **"adverse possession."** In this case, the property is clearly owned by one person, but another person begins to use part of the land without permission. After a certain period of years passes (which may vary from 5 to 20 years, depending on the state), the adverse possessor can become the owner of the property. This doctrine appeared in English common law as far back as the reign of Henry I (1100 A.D.) when land ownership or "seizin" was based upon possession. Possession and title to property were not separated, as they are today (as we discussed in connection with life estates and landlord–tenant matters). When an owner lost possession of land, he (and it was always "he" in those days) lost ownership as well. During the reign of Henry VIII, a statute was passed prohibiting persons from bringing actions to regain possession of land after three score (60) years. Later, while James I was king, the time for these and certain other suits to be filed was changed to 20 years, which became the "common law" rule regarding adverse possession upon the founding of the United States.

One of the reasons the adverse possession rule survived in the United States was that it forced property owners to look after their land. In order to

adverse possession: One person obtains title to real property by actually "possessing" a portion of the property, for a number of years, without the permission of the owner.

acquire ownership by adverse possession, the use of the land has to be "open and notorious." If the true owner looks at the land, he should readily see that another is using it. The possession must also be "adverse," that is, hostile to the owner and without his permission. Quietly sneaking on the land once in a while at night to build a campfire will not work. One court said that in order to start the clock ticking, the adverse possessor must basically "unfurl his flag" there. The use must also be continuous, with no significant breaks in usage for the required time period. Some states require the adverse user to "farm it or fence it" to let the true owner know that ownership is being claimed. Many states also require that the adverse possessor pay the taxes on the property in order to claim adverse possession. However, for adjoining landowners, if you pay the taxes you were assessed, that is usually sufficient. Also it should be noted that one cannot acquire ownership of government land by adverse possession—the doctrine does not apply to such land.

SOCIAL/ETHICAL ISSUES

What do you think of the doctrine of adverse possession? Do you think a legal theory that allows one person to acquire ownership of another's property simply by using it—without permission—makes sense in today's world? Does this encourage responsible property ownership or does it encourage trespassing?

Although some adverse possession cases do occur when one person intentionally begins using land owned by another, others result from fences being improperly placed or rivers changing course. In these situations, if the fence is mistakenly put in the wrong place and the land is actively used by the apparent owner for the required period of time, it is possible that the legal boundary has been changed by the theory of adverse possession. In many western states, for example, the period is only five years, so it behooves owners of property to double-check fence lines, to examine their land "back in the hills" every so often to make sure no one else is using it, and to take action to evict all who are using it. The following case describes an adverse possession dispute that occurred in rural Alaska.

NOME 2000 V. FAGERSTROM

799 P.2d 304 (Alaska 1990)

FACTS

Charles Fagerstrom recalls that his family used a piece of land overlooking the Nome River in Alaska in the 1940s, while he was still a child, for subsistence and recreation purposes. In 1966 he and his wife brought a small quantity of building materials onto the property. In 1970 or 1971 the Fagerstroms placed four cornerposts on the property to stake off a rectangular portion. They also built a picnic area on one end of the parcel, including a gravel pit, beachwood blocks as chairs, firewood and a 50-gallon barrel for use as a stove.

In July 1974 they placed a camper trailer on the north end of the parcel until September, and they repeated this action every summer until 1978. At about the same time, they build an outhouse and a fish rack on the north end of the parcel and planted some spruce trees.

In the summer of 1977 the Fagerstroms built a reindeer shelter on the north end of the parcel, about 8 feet by 8 feet and tall enough for Charles to stand up in it. They also built a pen, about 75 feet in diameter, around the shelter, and housed a reindeer for about six weeks in the summer of 1978. They testified that they were present on the parcel from 1974 through 1978 "every other weekend or so" and "a couple of times during the week if the weather was good." They did, however, allow other people to occasionally come onto the land to pick berries and to fish. In the summer of 1978, the Fagerstroms built a cabin on the property and used the property more extensively after that. However, the record title to the property was held by a firm called Nome 2000. In July 1987, Nome 2000 filed an action to eject the Fagerstroms from the land. Mr. and Mrs. Fagerstrom counterclaimed, arguing that they had acquired title by adverse possession. The trial court, after a jury trial, ruled in favor of the Fagerstroms, and Nome 2000 appealed to the Alaska Supreme Court.

DECISION

Alaska law provides that title to property could be acquired by adverse possession following a 10-year period. Quoting from an older case, the court stated that in order to win, the claimant must show that for the statutory period, "his use of the land was continuous, open and notorious, exclusive and hostile to the true owner." Nome 2000 argued that the Fagerstroms had not met these tests in part because they did not make "significant physical improvements" or show "substantial activity" on the land. Nome admitted that when they constructed the cabin, the Fagerstroms

started to be adverse possessors, but that prior to that, their use was insufficient. Nome filed suit in 1987.

The Alaska Supreme Court, in an opinion by Chief Justice Matthews, rejected the arguments of Nome 2000. Stating that nothing in the law requires "significant improvements," the Court ruled that the type of acts necessary for adverse possession depends on the character of the land in question. Where, as here, the land is rural, a lesser degree of dominion and control may be sufficient. With regard to the necessary elements of continuity and exclusivity of possession, the court stated that the question was whether the land was used as an average owner of similar property would use it.

Finding that the disputed parcel was located in a rural area suitable as a seasonal homesite for subsistence and recreational activities, the Court held that this was exactly how the Fagerstroms had used it. Since Nome 2000 admitted the Fagerstroms' adverse possession from 1978 to 1987, the Court focused its inquiry on activities from the summer of 1977 to summer 1978. It found that the Fagerstroms' conduct went well beyond "mere casual and occasional trespasses" and instead "evidenced a purpose to exercise exclusive dominion over the property." Justice Matthews noted that they had placed certain structures such as an outhouse, a fish rack, and a large reindeer pen on the premises for the entire year. During the warmer season the Fagerstroms also placed a camper trailer on blocks on the disputed parcel. The fact that they allowed others to pick berries and fish was consistent with the conduct of "a hospitable landowner" and did nothing to undermine their continuity or exclusivity of ownership.

As to the notoriety requirement, the court found that "a quick investigation of the premises, especially during the season which it was best suited for use, would have been sufficient to place a reasonably diligent landowner on notice that someone may have been exercising dominion and control over at least the northern portion of the property." Further inquiry would have shown that the members of the community regarded the Fagerstroms as the owners. Thus, the notoriety test had been met.

Nome 2000 also argued that the Fagerstroms' adverse possession claim should be denied because they may not have really intended to claim ownership during the time of their possession. An expert witness for Nome 2000 testified that the Fagerstroms' use of the property was consistent with traditional Native American land use, which does not recognize exclusive ownership, but is more in the nature of stewardship. "That is, other members of the claimant's social group may share in the resources of the land without obtaining permission, so long as the resources are not abused or destroyed." However, the Court rejected this argument as well, stating that what the Fagerstroms believed or intended has nothing to do with the legal question of whether their possession was hostile. "Hostility is determined by application of an objective test which simply asks whether the possessor 'acted toward the land as if he owned it,' " stated the Court.

Therefore, the Supreme Court upheld the decision of the trial court that the Fagerstroms had acquired title to the land by adverse pos-session for the required period of time. The court did, however, only award them title to the northern portion of the property, where the structures were located. The trial court had included the southern portion, where the Fagerstroms had merely used preexisting trails for recreation and had occasionally picked up litter. The Supreme Court held that these actions did not show exercise of dominion and control and thus did not lead to title by adverse. The case was remanded to the lower court for further hearings on the exact bound-aries of each portion of the land.

CASE QUESTIONS

1. What were the most important facts support-ing the Fagerstroms' case for adverse posses-sion? Do you agree that the Fagerstroms exercised dominion and control over the property?
2. Do you agree with the Court's decision? What purpose is served here by taking the title to the property away from the true record owner? What ethical principles are involved?
3. If this property had been a residential lot within a city, would the Fagerstroms' actions have been enough to acquire title by adverse possession?

Financing of Real Estate Transactions Most of us do not have enough funds in the bank to pay cash when we purchase a house or commercial prop-erty. Therefore, a complex system of financing real estate transactions has arisen. Usually when purchasing a home or other real property, the buyer will make a downpayment (maybe 10% or more of the price) and then will arrange for a loan from a bank or other lender for the rest of the purchase price. The buyer will then sign a "mortgage note" that is a written promise to pay the loan back on a specific schedule, often over a period as long as 30 years.

When the lender advances such a substantial sum of money, it wants some security for its loan—in other words, it wants to be a "secured lender." Before making the loan, the lender will almost certainly want to take a **security inter-est** in the real property being conveyed. The security interest is a legal interest (but not ownership) that one person or firm has in certain property owned by someone else. For example, Peter purchases a house for $90,000. He pays $10,000 down, and borrows $80,000 in the form of a "mortgage loan" from Friendly Bank

security interest: The legal interest in property owned by another that allows a creditor to repossess and resell collateral and to apply the proceeds to pay off the owner's loan.

mortgage: An agreement to give a lender a legal right in real property owned by another person.

to pay the rest. When Peter receives the money (which is then immediately transferred to the seller of the house), he signs a document called a **mortgage.** This legal instrument gives Friendly Bank a security interest in the real property. If Peter does not make his loan payments, Friendly Bank has the legal right to enforce its security interest by taking action to foreclose on the mortgage. Some states also use a somewhat similar document called a "deed of trust."

foreclosure: The process by which the holder of the mortgage exercises the legal right to force the sale of the property.

Each state has a statute governing **foreclosure** of mortgages, and there are some differences among the laws. However, in general, a lender must notify the owner that he or she is in "default" on the mortgage loan obligations. If the owner does not quickly comply, the lender can begin the process of foreclosure. This usually involves a certain number of publications in the newspaper (the not so easy-to-read "Legal Notices" section), followed by a public sale of the property.

Although anyone can attend and bid on the property at the foreclosure sale, often the lender is the only bidder and purchases the property for the amount of the outstanding mortgage plus costs. The lender (bank or mortgage company) then resells the property to someone else later. The proceeds are applied to the former owner's loan obligation; if that still does not pay off the balance (after adding the costs of the foreclosure sale) the former owner will still be liable and may be sued for the "deficiency."

redemption period: A period of time during which a foreclosed owner can re-acquire the property.

As a means of affording compassion to homeowners who lose their property, most state statutes allow the foreclosed owner a **redemption period** after the sale. During this time, which might be as long as six months, the foreclosed owner can "redeem" (reacquire ownership of) the property by paying the entire sale price plus expenses to whomever (usually the lender) purchased the property at the sale. That step (redemption) is usually only possible if the individual obtains another new mortgage loan or wins the lottery, and this does not occur often. After all, if the homeowner had the money, he or she would have paid the loan in the first place. After the redemption period expires, the buyer at foreclosure can sell the property to someone else.

Recording   The proper execution of the mortgage and the mortgage loan documents establish the rights between the lender and the borrower in a real estate transaction. However, in order to safeguard the buyer and lender against other legal interests in the property, the documents should be **recorded**. In each county there is an office, often called the "County Recorder" or "Register of Deeds," that maintains official records of all real estate transactions.

recording: Filing a deed or mortgage in a public records office to give notice to others of the legal interests in the real property.

When Peter purchases property from Nina, he will no doubt receive a warranty deed and will probably execute a mortgage in favor of a lender like Friendly Bank. Peter and Friendly Bank will "record" these documents in the appropriate offices to protect their ownership and security interests, respectively. "Recording" means to place documents on public record in an appropriate way, at the proper office. By filing these documents with the county official, they will be giving *notice of their rights* in the property to anyone who might consider taking a legal interest in that property in the future.

Sometimes through dishonesty or mistake, two parties claim interest in the same real property, and it will be necessary to decide who has the primary claim. These disputes are often settled by deciding who recorded first. For example, suppose Peter purchases a home from Nina on June 10 for $90,000 but does not record his deed. Nina is in urgent need of cash and short on honesty, so on June 20 she sells the home (again) to Lois for $85,000. Let us assume that Peter has not moved in as yet and Lois knows nothing about the sale to Peter. When Peter and Lois both claim ownership of the house, who wins? (By this time, Nina has disappeared and is enjoying life somewhere in the Caribbean.)

In the majority of states, where there are two *bona fide purchasers* (those who buy in good faith, without knowledge of any fraud), the *first one to* record his or her instrument will have a superior claim. Why? Between two innocent purchasers, the law disfavors the one who could have done something to prevent the harm. In this example, if Peter had recorded his deed, that would have provided notice to the world (including Lois) of his interest, and the problem may not have occurred. In most states, then, if Lois were to record her deed before Peter recorded his, she would be considered the rightful owner of the property. Of course, Peter could sue Nina if he ever can find her; between the two innocent purchasers, however, generally the one who records first has greater rights to ownership of the property.

LIABILITIES OF PROPERTY OWNERS TO VISITORS

There are hundreds of common law court cases, decided over a long period of time, that discuss the duties and liabilities of property owners to those persons who come upon their land. In the Torts chapter we examined the duty of a grocery store owner or manager to maintain the property in a non-negligent way. In one case we saw that when the store management did not have a procedure for checking the aisles of the store every hour, or for promptly cleaning up spills that occur, the store could be found negligent and held liable to a customer who slipped on something that had been spilled on the floor some time earlier and had not been not cleaned up.

Over the years a set of common law rules developed imposing varying degrees of care upon landowners depending on the status of the person who came onto the land and was injured. The lowest level of duty is, not surprisingly, owed to **trespassers,** who enter the land without any permission. In general the owner owes no duty to trespassers. But some courts have stated that the owner has a minimum duty—to refrain from taking actions that intentionally cause injury to the trespasser. The owner cannot create very dangerous hazards on the property, just to keep trespassers off. If the owner knows that numerous trespassers are coming on the land she has a duty not to injure them and protect them from non-obvious dangers.

One well-known case, which was part of many law school property courses, involved the owner of an uninhabited cabin back in the woods in Iowa. The owner became frustrated when people kept breaking into and using the cabin, so he set up a "spring gun" inside which was aimed at the door, and was triggered by a string attached to the door. In fact, a hunter did enter the cabin one fall, and the gun went off, causing him quite serious injuries. He sued the owner and the court ruled in his favor, finding that "using life-threatening force" to defend property against damage was excessive and violated his duty to the trespasser.

Trespassing children have been accorded greater rights. Since children often do not know where land boundaries are, and do not perceive dangers as clearly as adults, the courts have developed a doctrine called **attractive nuisance.**

Under this theory, if children are attracted to, and go upon someone's property as trespassers due to some "artificial" condition on the land, the owner has a duty to them. The owner may have liability if: such children are injured by an encounter with an artificial condition on the land (such as a swimming pool, water slide, or a pile of building materials) which the owner should know involved the risk of injury to children; the landowner knew or should have known that children were coming on to the property or were likely to trespass; the children did not appreciate the risks; and where the burden on the owner of eliminating the risk is small compared to the risk to the children.

A slightly higher level of duty is owed to a group of people called **licensees.** These are people who have some right to enter the land of another—perhaps they are postal employees or water meter readers. The largest category of licensees is "social guests"—friends whom you have invited over to your house. The duty owed by the landowner is to use reasonable care—that is, to keep the property free of hazards that the licensees are unlikely to perceive, and to repair those that the owner knows about on the property.

The highest legal duty is owed to people called **"invitees,"** who are people who come upon the owner's land for a purpose which benefits the owner. The largest group of invitees is "customers" who come to a property location to engage in business with the owner, thereby conferring a benefit on the owner. The landowner owes invitees the duty to maintain the property as a reasonably careful person would (the negligence standard) and to protect invitees against hazards that the owner knows about, or should know about if he was exercising reasonable care. The "slip and fall" case in the grocery store we studied earlier is a common type of case involving "invitees" and the duty of care owed to them.

Owner's Liability for Criminal Acts by Others It might seem harsh, but sometimes property owners have been held liable to persons injured or killed by criminal actions that occur on the property. This type of situation arises when the owner knows or should know of some type of hazard that endangers customers (invitees) but does nothing to decrease the danger, or fix the problem. Certain cases have involved landlords who owned rental property in a high crime area, yet allowed security in their apartments to lapse—perhaps failing to fix broken door locks, or repairing lights in parking lots or entry areas. If a rape or robbery occurs, it may be the "foreseeable" result of the landowner's negligence, along with the criminal act. You will recall that we learned in the Torts chapter that there could be two "proximate causes" of a particular tort injury—in this case both the criminal and the landlord might be liable.

If you analyze these situations in terms of negligence, you can see how the elements of (1) duty of care—the duty of the landlord or owner to maintain the property as a "reasonably prudent" owner would; and (2) breach of duty—the owner did not take the steps that a "reasonably prudent" owner would have taken—could create negligence tort liability when a customer or tenant is injured. In the cases where property owners were found liable the owner had some sort of previous knowledge of the hazard and an opportunity to redress the problem before this liability will exist. In one case several other convenience stores in the area had been robbed and all but this one now employed security guards. Or there may be liability if this particular store or apartment had been the subject of robberies or break-ins, and the management had made no changes to increase security. Certainly the property owner is not held liable every time someone gets shot by a criminal in a store, or every time a tenant is robbed in her apartment. There must be some knowledge of facts or circumstances giving rise to an increased "duty" which was not met with any prudent or corrective action by the owner.

For example, in a California case, a woman was sexually assaulted in a commercial parking garage beneath the office building where she worked. She had paid to park in the garage, and sued the owner of the garage for failure to take appropriate safety measures in the garage. The California Supreme Court held that indeed a commercial landlord did have a duty to take reasonable steps to secure common areas against foreseeable criminal acts of third parties that are likely to occur in the absence of greater safety measures. However, in this case the Court found that there had been no criminal incidents in the garage for at least ten years, and thus "absent other indications of a reasonably foreseeable risk of criminal acts" the landlord had not violated any duty of care to people using the parking garage by failing to install further security measures. *Sharon P. v. Arman, Ltd.*, 989 P. 2d 121 (Cal. 1999)

RESTRICTIONS ON THE USE OF REAL PROPERTY

As we mentioned previously, regardless of the type of ownership one has, usually owners are not permitted to do "anything they want" with their property. Such legal restrictions as zoning laws, land use planning requirements, restrictive covenants, easements, and environmental regulations often put limits on what the landowner can do with the property. First, we will discuss a venerable common law theory that may be used when one person's legal use of his or her property causes problems for the neighbors.

Nuisance   The common law principle called **nuisance** holds that there is a right of action for a landowner whose use and enjoyment of his or her property is adversely affected by another's use of his or her property. Most of us would quickly agree with the proposition that "you should be able to use your land in any *legal* way." However, if Jim lives in a nice residential area and his next-door neighbor Brian decides to open a cattle feedlot or a toxic waste dump on his property, Jim might not embrace this theory so completely. Brian's use of his property as a feedlot would no doubt significantly interfere with Jim's backyard barbecues and volleyball games.

In hundreds of cases over the years, nuisance theory has been employed to a wide variety of lawful actions, including animal feed lots; industrial factories that produce smoke, dust, and noise; even churches that have lighted baseball fields on which night games are played. In recent years, many cases have raised issues regarding the right of homeowners to have unrestricted sunlight when neighbors build structures on their land that interfere with such light. Sometimes a "nuisance" occurs when one neighbor constructs something that intentionally interferes with his neighbors' view or access to light and air. Other conflicts have occurred when subdivisions move out into rural areas and encounter common farm land use customs (involving manure, other fertilization practices, and noise) that conflict with suburban homeowner expectations.

nuisance: A common law theory that allows one owner a right to sue a neighbor if that person's use of his or her land interferes with the first owner's use and enjoyment of his or her property.

Zoning Starting more than 80 years ago, communities began to develop zoning regulations in order to prevent some of these land use conflicts. City planners reasoned that rather than having one neighbor sue another whenever a new use of land was undertaken, it makes better sense to control, in advance, the use of land. As a result, cities and counties began to specify that certain areas of their jurisdiction be reserved for single-family homes, apartments, heavy industrial manufacturing, commercial use, and so on. This practice is called **zoning**—that is, dividing the city into zones in which different land uses are allowed.

Zoning maps are usually drawn and decisions made—with the assistance of professional staff—by a citizen's panel. Once the first zoning plan is established, it must be constantly revised as new areas undergo development and land use patterns change. All over the country, subdivisions are being developed in areas that used to be farmland.

Zoning classifications do restrict what an owner can do with his or her land. For example, if Letitia owns some property that is zoned for single-family residential housing, she will not be able to open a shoe store or build a shopping mall there. She may go to the zoning board and attempt to have the classification of her property changed; however, if all the land around her is residential, she will have a difficult time persuading the zoning board to make the change. Still, as the population expands, land use patterns may change, and zoning boards do change classifications from time to time to reflect physical and social changes. In other cases, a landowner can sometimes get the board to allow a **variance,** which basically is a permit allowing one person an exception from the zoning laws for a particularly good reason, without changing the overall zoning classification of the neighborhood.

Sometimes a particular use of property was once legal, but the zoning has been changed, and the use is now illegal. In certain cases, the city may allow the use (a hair salon, now part of a neighborhood zoned for single-family use, for example) to continue as a **nonconforming use.** The city might order the nonconforming use to be eliminated within a certain time, or allow it to continue until there is a change of ownership. Generally, the city will not issue a building permit allowing a nonconforming use to be enlarged or modified.

Not only do cities and counties have authority to regulate property use under their inherent "police powers" (a subject discussed in Chapter 4), but many other quasi-governmental entities, such as irrigation districts, flood control authorities, and historical preservation authorities, also have the power to enact regulations affecting building and development on the land.

The "Taking" of Property and Eminent Domain As was discussed in Chapter 4 (in connection with constitutional issues), government has the power under the Fifth Amendment to actually take title to private property for some public use through the power of **eminent domain.** However, when this is done, the landowner must be paid "just compensation," in other words the fair market value of the land **taken.** In recent years property owners have often protested that zoning, building restrictions, and other extensive land use regulations have significantly diminished the value of their property and have thus effectively taken away part of their property, for which they should be compensated. In most cases, these arguments are rejected because, since a

zoning: A plan developed by a city or county that regulates the uses of land in different "zones" of the city or county.

variance: Permission from a zoning board to use land in a way not allowed by the zoning classification.

eminent domain: The power of a state, local, or federal government agency to acquire ownership of property from a private owner for some "public use," after paying fair compensation.

taking: When some government action deprives an owner of significant property rights without compensation.

Supreme Court decision in 1926, the governmental power to regulate land use for the greater benefit of the whole community has been well recognized.

But the U.S. Supreme Court has held that where the restrictions are particularly extensive, do not substantially advance legitimate state interests, deprive the owner of most of the value of the land, or force the owner to give up part of the land in return for some governmental approval, landowners have sometimes succeeded in forcing compensation from government agencies. When the lawsuit is brought by the landowner claiming that part or all of her property has been "taken," rather than instituted by the government seeking to use eminent domain, this theory is often called "inverse condemnation."

The following case is a good example of these arguments in a case decided by the Supreme Court in the mid-1990s.

DOLAN V. CITY OF TIGARD

512 U.S. 374 (1994)

FACTS

Florence Dolan owned a 71,500-square-foot lot on Main Street in Tigard, Oregon, on which she operated a retail electrical and plumbing supply store. Pursuant to Oregon law, the city had adopted various land use regulations, including a Community Development Code (CDC) and a Master Drainage Plan (MDP). The CDC established certain landscaping and open space requirements that applied to property in the central business district. These regulations also required new developments to dedicate land for pedestrian/bicycle pathways to help alleviate traffic congestion. The MDP noted that flooding had occurred in several areas in the past and called for certain drainage improvements to particular waterways, including a creek that ran across part of Ms. Dolan's property.

In 1991 Ms. Dolan asked the city for a permit to tear down the store and replace it with a much larger building. The city responded by conditioning the granting of a permit upon Ms. Dolan's giving the city about 7,000 square feet of her property. The City Planning Commission required her to dedicate the portion of her property within the creek floodplain for drainage improvements and an additional 15-foot strip for a pedestrian/bicycle pathway.

The city of Tigard did not propose to pay for the part of the Dolan property it would receive, since it would benefit the entire public.

Ms. Dolan claimed that the land transfer would amount to an uncompensated taking of her property, in violation of the Fifth Amendment. Dolan challenged the city's action before the Oregon Land Use Board of Appeals but lost. She then appealed to the Oregon Court of Appeals and the Oregon Supreme Court, without success. Finally, the U.S. Supreme Court agreed to hear the case.

DECISION

In a 5-4 decision, written by Chief Justice Rehnquist, the Supreme Court reversed the lower court decisions. The Supreme Court stated that it was clearly legal, in general, for governments to place various conditions on the granting of permits when the goal is to avoid traffic congestion and other potential problems linked to development. Justice Rehnquist stated that Tigard's goals (flood and traffic control) were legitimate and noted that "cities have long engaged in the commendable task of land use planning, made necessary by increasing urbanization."

However, when the permits are conditioned on the owner giving up ownership of part of her land, the Court held that government planners must produce "specific justifications" that relate to the land in question. Planners had not adequately explained why it was necessary for the 7,000 square feet strip of land to become public property. For example, why not let the owner keep title to the land but be prohibited from building on it? In a key section of the opinion, the Court said that the city, in order to legally impose the conditions it wanted, had to show a "rough proportionality" between the necessity for the owner to give up title to the land and the potential harm of the proposed development.

As to the land in the floodplain, the Court stated that the city must state more clearly why it needed to acquire title to that part of the Dolan property (rather than just an easement) in order to make the drainage project a success. Justice Rehnquist pointed out that the "difference to petitioner (Dolan), of course, is the loss of her ability to exclude others . . . one of the most essential sticks in the bundle of rights that are commonly characterized as property."

Similarly, the majority opinion suggested that Tigard could have offered adequate justification for the pedestrian/bicycle walkway if it had more definitely shown that it would relieve congestion caused by Dolan's larger store. The city had said only that the path "could" offset some of the additional traffic. "No precise mathematical calculation is required, but the city must make some sort of individualized determination that the required dedica-tion is related both in nature and extent to the impact of the proposed development."

In conclusion, while the Court stated that the city's goals for improving the community were laudable, there were "outer limits" on how it could be done. "A strong public desire to improve the public condition [will not] warrant achieving the desire by a shorter cut than the constitutional way of paying for the change." Thus the decision of the Oregon Supreme Court was reversed.

CASE QUESTIONS

1. If the city of Tigard had only conditioned the granting of the building permit upon Ms. Dolan's giving an easement across her land for a bicycle path, would the result of the case have been the same? Why or why not?
2. What sort of "specific justification" could the city have provided that would have satisfied the Supreme Court's test?
3. What does the Court mean when it says there must be a "rough proportionality" between the need for the owner to give up title to the property and the harm caused by the desired project?
4. Can the city acquire title to the land if it decides to do so, even though Ms. Dolan does not want to sell? If so, how would this work?

---

restrictive covenant: A restriction on the use of real property, contained in a deed. Such covenants are common in subdivision developments.

Restrictive Covenants   An owner's use of land may also be restricted by a **restrictive covenant.** This restriction is not imposed by government, but by a previous private owner of the property. For example, when a seller of property puts in the deed a clause such as "no fences higher than six feet shall be constructed on this property," that restriction binds the new owner and probably all future owners as well. This type of deed restriction is particularly common in newer housing developments created by one developer. When the lots and houses are sold to individual owners, commonly all the deeds will contain restrictions such as "no basketball hoops may be installed on garages" or "there shall be no television antennas on roofs." These restrictions are intended to enhance the appearance of the neighborhood, and are binding on the homeowners and on future buyers. It is said that they "run with the land."

Restrictive covenants are usually stricter than the zoning regulations enacted by the local government. Therefore, a homeowner may be restrained by a covenant from doing something on the property that is perfectly legal under the zoning laws. Often, a neighborhood association may take legal action against a property owner who violates a covenant. If, on the other hand, many owners violate a covenant for several years and the governing body takes no action against them, the court might decide that the covenant is no longer valid and refuse to enforce it. Generally the city zoning board has no involvement in enforcing restrictive covenants—these are private agreements.

Easements   Although a person might own property in "fee simple," chances are good that there are other individuals and businesses that have some legal rights in the property. We have already mentioned mortgages, in which a lender has a security interest in the property. An **easement** is another type of legal interest held by one person or company in another's real property. An easement is a legal right one person has to use, for a limited purpose, part of the land owned by another.

> **easement:** A legal right to use a portion of real property owned by someone else for a specific purpose.

Common types of easements are roads, paths, or utility lines over and under one's property. Most residential properties are subject to easements owned by phone, electric, water, and cable television companies, which give them the legal right to place wires or pipes over or under the surface of one's property. These rights (easements) are usually written down in legal documents and recorded in the county office prior to the first sale of the property to a homeowner. Although easements do not give the holder an ownership in any of the land, they do establish the legal right of the holder to use a specific portion of the land for the stated purpose.

There is a type of easement, called a **prescriptive easement,** that is established by adverse possession. Much like acquiring ownership by adverse possession, the person or business that claims the easement over someone else's property (without documentation or permission) must show that there has been an open, notorious, continuous, adverse use of the easement (such as a road, or power lines or an irrigation ditch) for the required period of time. But here if the easement is established in this way, it does not give ownership of the land, but only use of the easement, just as in a normal easement.

MEMO FROM THE LEGAL DEPARTMENT

To: Students

Most of the planned residential developments in the United States contain restrictive covenants, placed on the property by the developer, that control many aspects of the use of the property. When you purchase residential real estate, you should certainly ask the seller or real estate agent if there are any restrictive covenants on the property. You may be perfectly happy with the covenants, since they are intended to enhance the value of property in the neighborhood. But it is better to know in advance if you cannot build a certain type of fence or install certain types of shrubs, trees, or utility sheds, than to find out later when a dispute arises with the neighborhood association.

The easement, once granted, continues to exist on the land even as owner-ship of the dominant and subservient parcels changes. But it the owner of the easement "abandons" it by lack of use for a significant period of time, or by announcing the intention to abandon it, then the easement rights may disappear, as was the issue in the following case.

In the Language of the Court

TOEWS V. UNITED STATES

376 F. 3d 1371 (Fed Cir. 2004)

Opinion written by Senior Circuit Judge Plager.

FACTS

Plaintiffs in this case own property in fee simple located in the City of Clovis in Fresno County, California. In 1891, the San Joaquin Valley Railroad Company acquired rights of way for the purpose of operating a rail line, known as the Clovis Branch, between the City of Clovis and the City of Fresno. The owner at that time, Charles H. Bouchey, executed an "Agreement for Right of Way" containing the following pertinent language:

> *I do hereby grant bargain sell and convey unto the said San Joaquin Valley Railroad Company the Right of Way for its proposed Railroad over West line of [land parcel] owned by me in the County of Fresno in said State of California along the line of said proposed Railroad, and for its side tracks, turn tables depots water tanks and other appurtenances where the same may be located by said Company to the extent of 50 feet on said West line in width along and across said lands as now located by the Engineer of the Company . . . Provided, however, that if said Railroad Company shall permanently discontinue the use of said railroad the land and Rights of Way shall at once revert to the undersigned.*

In 1951 Menno and Evelyn Toews purchased land that had been part of the property once owned by Bouchey. The railroad right of way lies within the western edge of their property and is 50 feet wide and approximately 384 feet long.

The San Joaquin Valley Railroad Company began construction on the Clovis Branch in July 1891 and commenced freight service in October of that year. Not long after, the Southern Pacific Railroad purchased all interests in the rail line and operated it for nearly a century. In 1992, at a time when nearly all service on the rail line had terminated, Southern Pacific leased its interests in the line to a new and different San Joaquin Valley Railroad Company ("SJVR").

In May 1994, SJVR filed with the Interstate Commerce Commission ("ICC") a petition for an "abandonment exemption," seeking the right to discontinue operations on a 4.5-mile segment of the Clovis Branch. The ICC granted the petition in April 1995. The City of Clovis, which as early as 1993 had begun planning for future uses of the railroad right of way, sent a May 1995 letter to the ICC requesting that the ICC impose a public-use condition for interim trail use on abandonment of the 4.5-mile segment of the rail line.

In October 1995 the ICC issued a Notice of Interim Trail Use or Abandonment ("NITU") for the 4.5-mile segment, which authorized the implementation of interim trail use and rail-banking if the City of Clovis could reach an interim-use agreement with SJVR and Southern Pacific, which still owned the right of way.

In February 1996, the City of Clovis, along with the City of Fresno and the County of Fresno, executed a Memorandum of Understanding regarding the abandonment of area rail lines, including the Clovis Branch. The parties agreed that in the near term, the rail corridor would be "developed with pedestrian, equestrian and bike paths." In the long term, the agreement provided, the corridor "may also accommodate transit in addition to pedestrian and bike paths. Transit is understood to mean local rail, light rail, or other transit modes."

After the City acquired the railroads' interests in 1997, the City entered the first development phase by establishing the Clovis Old Town Trail, which consists of a twelve-foot wide paved path along the former railroad right of way. Today the trail is lined with trees planted on both sides and amenities common to recreational trails, such as park benches, water fountains, and bicycle racks. Commercial billboards have been placed along the trail. The City of Clovis allows a variety of activities on and alongside the trail, including bicycling, walking, jogging, skateboarding, rollerblading, playing ball, picnicking, and other activities that would be lawful in a public space.

Plaintiffs allege that when the subject corridor was a functioning railroad line, they could use the land so long as the use was not inconsistent with the railroad's use. That is no longer the case. Since the City of Clovis acquired the former railroad interests, the City has erected a fence to separate the portion of the right of way on the Toews property from the remainder of their property and has planted trees on the right of way. The City also required their tenants, who had farmed the property, to remove their fruit stand from the railroad corridor; the tenants subsequently terminated their lease.

Plaintiffs filed complaints in the Court of Federal Claims seeking just compensation under the Fifth Amendment for the alleged taking of their property. The trial court con-

cluded that the Government's regulatory actions effected takings. The court concluded that, as a matter of California law, the interim trail use by the City of Clovis is not within the scope of the easements granted by the owners to the railroad. The court also determined that, under California law, the SJVR had abandoned the easements, although the court noted that this conclusion was not necessary to the result in the case.

The parties thereafter entered into a joint stipulation as to the amount of just compensation, and the trial court entered final judgment for the plaintiffs. The Government has now appealed.

DECISION

We address first the question of whether there was an abandonment of these easements for railroad purposes by the railroad, either on its own initiative or in response to the federal actions. The trial court concluded that, as a factual matter, the railroad's management had acted in an unequivocal and decisive manner clearly showing an intention to abandon that section of the line.

The defining issue in this case is the question of the scope of the easements originally granted to the railroad. The grants that created these easements stated that what was sold to the San Joaquin Valley Railroad Company was a "Right of Way for its proposed Railroad." The grants expressly included authorization for side tracks, turntables, depots, and other railroad uses (limited to the width of the granted right of way).

There was a provision in the grants that if the Railroad Company permanently discontinued the use of the railroad, the land and rights of way "shall at once revert to the undersigned" landowner. After evaluating the entire deeds of grant, the trial court held that these grants constituted easements and not fee simple transfers. This is undoubtedly correct, and on appeal neither party has challenged that holding. We note in passing that as a matter of traditional property law terminology, a termination of the easements would not cause anything to "revert" to the landowner. Rather, the burden of the easement would simply be extinguished, and the landowner's property would be held free and clear of any such burden.

It is elementary law that if the Government uses (or authorizes the use of—a point to be considered later) an existing railroad easement for purposes and in a manner not allowed by the terms of the grant of the easement, the Government has taken the landowner's property for the new use. The consent of the railroad to the new use does not change the equation—the railroad cannot give what it does not have.

It appears without doubt that use of these easements for a recreational trail—for walking, hiking, biking, picnicking, frisbee playing, with newly-added tarmac pavement, park benches, occasional billboards, and fences to enclose the trailway—is not the same use made by a railroad, involving tracks, depots, and the running of trains. The different uses create different burdens. In the one case there was an occasional train passing through. In the other, individuals or groups use the property, some passing along the trail, others pausing to engage in activities for short or long periods of time. In the one case, the landowner could make such uses of the property as were not inconsistent with the railroad's use, crossing over the tracks, putting a fruit stand on one edge of the property, or whatever. In the other, the government fenced the trail in such a way as to deny that access.

Some might think it better to have people strolling on one's property than to have a freight train rumbling through. But that is not the point. The landowner's grant authorized one set of uses, not the other. Under the law, it is the landowner's intention as expressed in the grant that defines the burden to which the land will be subject. The Government does not dispute this proposition—the Government agrees that, consistent with the state's law, the landowner's grant defines the burden with which the land is burdened.

But, argues the Government, California law reads into the original grant the kind of change in a granted railroad easement seen here. The argument goes this way: a railroad easement is a "public" right of way for transportation; California law permits changes in public transportation uses, citing in particular the California case of *Faus v. City of Los Angeles,* 431 P.2d 849 (Cal. 1967), thus the change to interim trail use involved here thus is consistent with the original grants, and thus as a matter of law cannot be considered to impose a greater burden than that imposed by railroad use.

The plaintiff landowners respond that use of these rights of way as a recreational trail and linear park is fundamentally different in kind than a railroad use; such use does not comply with the purposes of the grantors; the burden imposed by such a use is different in degree and nature, citing *Preseault v. United States,* 100 F.3d 1525, 1542–43 (Fed. Cir. 1995) (en banc); and thus the use constitutes a new easement under California law, not a continuation of an existing one.

In *Faus v. City of Los Angeles,* the question was whether public motor coach service could be substituted for public electric railway service over rights of way that were granted for an electric railway. It appears that the grants were for easements for an electric railway or streetcar, and that the streetcars were to provide local and express service from the residential communities involved into downtown Los Angeles. Various conditions were included in the grants to ensure that regular service was provided, and several of the deeds explicitly provided that if railway service ceased for six months there would be a "reversion" of the land.

In the course of time, and with the consent of the railroad company and in some cases the adjacent homeowners, the City of Los Angeles paved longitudinal strips in the easement alongside the tracks for use as local streets. Finally, in 1955, an arrangement was made under which the railroad company ceased train service and the City substituted motor coach service along the same routes. The City then took title to the underlying land by condemnation, paved over the areas where the tracks had been and combined them with the adjoining road network. Plaintiff Faus located the heirs of the original grantors, acquired whatever rights they had, and, alleging that the City's use of the property violated the conditions contained in the original grants, sued the City for the heirs' damages for the taking. The trial court gave judgment for Faus.

Faus had won three previous cases on similar situations, but the California Supreme Court apparently thought that three was enough, and reversed the lower court. The essential holding of the California Supreme Court was that the original grantors' purpose was to ensure that the inhabitants of the properties which the grantors wished to subdivide would enjoy the best means of interurban public transport which was feasible, and that over time technological change produced a situation in which motor buses won public preference because of their greater flexibility of route and schedule.

In the court's view, public transport, whether by rail or bus, was within the intention and purpose of the original grantors, and had they been able to conceive of the changed circumstances they would have provided for it.

What can we gather from these cases? The rule applied in these cases is quite limited, and in that sense unremarkable. *Faus* holds that an easement for a streetcar that runs on a track can include a motor bus running on a pavement. The bus performs the same function in essentially the same way with the same result. The grantors' purpose is thus protected and carried forward, despite the change in mechanical technique; the easement for local transportation remains fulfilled.

We find in these cases when put in their proper context a consistent and appropriately narrow theme: a right of way for public transportation uses, initially defined in terms of a specific form of public transport (railroad trains or boats) may, under proper circumstances, be taken to include other mechanical methods for public transport (buses or cars), so long as the change is consistent with the grantor's purpose and general intention.

Applying that narrow theme to the case before us, it is clear that under the rule as it is applied in California a public transportation easement defined as one for railroad purposes is not stretchable into an easement for a recreational trail and linear park for skateboarders and picnickers, however desirable such uses may be for these linear strips of land. The Government has the legal power and is thus free to impose such new uses upon the fee interests held by the adjacent landowners. But the private property interests taken are not free; the Government must pay the just compensation mandated by the Constitution.

In the case before us . . . the terms of the deed of grant are explicit, and phrased in traditional railroad right of way terms. The trial court properly found the grant to constitute an easement, and that is neither in doubt nor challenged. The Government's reading of that law is not supported by the California cases.

In Sum. We have concluded that the trial court correctly found the scope of the easement not to encompass the new use as a recreational trail. As a result of the imposition of the recreational trail and linear park, the easement for railroad purposes was converted into a new and different easement . . . There is a reality test in takings law. It is clear from the record that for the foreseeable future these lands will be used for the recreational trail project.

Whether there ever will be a light rail system or other railroad service over these paved routes in Clovis is a matter of speculation about the distant future, based on uncertain economic and social change, and a change in government policy by managers not yet known or perhaps even born. Such speculation does not provide a basis for denying protection to existing property rights under the Constitution.

CONCLUSION

The trial court did not err in its judgment, which is AFFIRMED.

CASE QUESTIONS

1. How was it proved that the railroad had abandoned the railway line?
2. Why did the court decide that what had been granted over 100 years ago was an easement, not a fee simple interest in a strip of land?
3. What was the rationale used by the court for deciding that the easement could not be continued in a slightly different form? What is the "shifting use doctrine?" What sort of use do you think would have been allowed by the court as a natural extension of the railway easement?
4. Do you agree with the court that the *Faus* case is "distinguishable" and different from this one, so that the same conclusion should not be reached? Why? Explain.

PERSONAL PROPERTY

tangible personal property: Property, other than real estate, that has a physical existence.

Property that is not real property is *personal property* and may be of two types: *tangible* or *intangible* personal property. **Tangible personal property** has a physical existence, and includes items we can see and touch, like a car, a book, a shirt, or a television set. **Intangible** personal property may be quite valuable yet have no physical existence, such as a bank account, a shareholder's ownership interest in a corporation, a debt owed to another, or a patent on a product. A patent is an example of an increasingly important type of intangible personal property known as intellectual property; it is discussed in more detail later in this textbook.

It is possible for personal property to be owned in joint tenancy or tenancy in common (like real property), although it is more typical for personal property to be owned by one person or by a married couple. Perhaps when you were younger you were fortunate enough to have a joint bank account with a parent or grandparent. Usually the deposits are made by the grandparent, and the withdrawals made by the grandchild. Upon the death of either (it was expected that the parent or grandparent would pass away first), the entire balance of the account belonged to the survivor if it was owned in joint tenancy with the right of survivorship.

gift: the transfer of ownership of personal property. It requires: (1) intent and (2) delivery.

There are various ways in which one may acquire ownership of personal property. The most common way is through a purchase or gift. A deed is only used in connection with real property. Instead, when Ted buys a car or television set, he may receive a bill of sale to provide proof of his ownership.

In order to effectively transfer ownership of personal property through a gift, the person making the gift (the donor) must have the *intent* to make the gift, and the item must actually be *delivered* to the new owner (the donee). Both elements must exist to make the gift valid. For example, when Patty announces that she is going to make a gift to another person ("I am going to give you this valuable painting for your birthday next year") but does not actually deliver the item, the donee does not acquire ownership until delivery. Patty may change her mind, or may have passed away in the interim, and the transfer of ownership has not occurred. Sometimes, however, delivery of a *symbolic* part of the gift (for example, the keys and title to the car but not the car) may be enough to show that the donor intended to part with ownership of the item.

Ownership of personal property can also be acquired when the property is *abandoned* by the former owner. In order to be considered abandoned, there must be some indication that the owner really did desire to give up ownership—such as by putting a television set out with the trash by the curb. The first person to take possession of abandoned property becomes the owner, since the former owner intended to give up his or her rights.

When a person finds personal property that has only been *lost* or *mislaid* by the owner, however, the finder does not acquire ownership. If, for example, Alyssa accidentally drops an expensive fountain pen somewhere in the street, she has *lost* the property, but has not intended to transfer ownership. Felix, the finder of the pen *(lost property)* is entitled to *possession* of the pen in relation to everyone except the true owner (Alyssa) but *does not become the owner* simply by finding the pen. Many states have passed a law that provides that if the owner does not claim the property within a certain number of years, the finder can become the owner.

Property is considered *mislaid* if the owner intentionally put it somewhere and then forgot it. For example, if Alvaro stays in a motel, hides $500 under the mattress in the bed, and then leaves the next morning without retrieving the money, it is *mislaid property*. In this case the owner of the place where the property is found (the motel) has a right to possession of the property that is superior to anyone's right except that of the true owner. Why? Most likely, when Alvaro discovers that his property is missing, he will contact the owner of the premises where the property was left. As with lost property, most states have a statutory law that provides that after a certain number of years the owner of the real estate becomes the owner of the mislaid items.

BAILMENTS

When the owner of personal property delivers possession of the item to another person to be held, stored or delivered, this is called a **bailment.** This situation happens quite commonly, as we hire a moving company to take our furniture to a new house, hand our coat to an coatroom attendant in a restaurant to be checked, pay to store some belongings in a warehouse, or give a package to UPS or Federal Express for delivery. The owner who parts with his/her property is the **bailor,** and the person or business holding the property is the **bailee.**

Bailment only involves personal property. The **requirements** for a bailment are that the bailor must intend to deliver possession of the property, the bailee must knowingly accept the possession and have exclusive control of the personal property. The creation of the bailment does not require any formal contract, but many bailments—certainly most commercial bailments—do have contracts.

For example, suppose that Richard is going on a long trip and asks Carolyn if he can store his car in her garage. If she agrees, a bailment is created when he parks the car in her garage. This type of bailment, for the benefit of the bailor without charge, is called a **gratuitous bailment.** In this situation, Carolyn's duty is merely not to be grossly negligent in caring for the car.

Most bailments are commercial—giving the coat to the attendant or storing goods in a warehouse—and are for the **mutual benefit** of bailee and bailor. The bailor wants someone else to take care of or deliver the goods, and the bailee is charging a fee for the service. The bailee in these situations has the *duty of reasonable care* to protect and safeguard the goods, and *return them in the same condition as they were when received*. If the goods are lost, stolen or damaged, there is a presumption that the bailee has been negligent, and will owe money damages to the bailor. However, the bailee is entitled to attempt to show that the loss was not caused by negligence.

During the bailment the bailee has the right of possession of the goods, but not the ownership of the property. In some situations, depending on the agreement of the parties, the bailee may have the right to use the property. (Maybe Richard asks Carolyn to drive his car once or twice a week while he is gone) The bailor has the right to receive the goods back, at the time specified in the agreement. Generally either bailor or bailee can terminate a gratuitous bailment at any time without liability.

WILLS, PROBATE, AND TRUSTS

Ownership of all types of property—real, personal, and intellectual—can also pass through the death of the property owner. There are several ways for the property owner to control who becomes the owner of property after his or her death; these include wills and trusts.

WILLS

will: A document that states how a person wishes his or her property distributed after death.

When an individual dies, his or her real and personal property is distributed to others. Who is entitled to the property depends on whether the deceased person (the decedent) left a will or not. A **will** is a written document, prepared by a person of "sound mind" (who understands what he or she is doing at the time he or she signs the will), that designates how property is to be distributed following his or her death. Although most states allow handwritten wills (*holographic wills*) in certain cases, the best procedure is for the person making the will (the **testator**) to prepare a typewritten will, with the assistance of an attorney, and sign it in the presence of witnesses (most states require two or three), who then also sign the will.

The original copy of the will should be kept in a safe place, where it will be easily found after the person's death. Until the testator dies, the will has no legal effect and can be changed, amended, or totally canceled by the testator at any time. The people named in someone's will as beneficiaries have absolutely no rights to any of the testator's property until his or her death (the will may be totally changed before then). If the will is amended or material is added (called a **codicil**), or a new will is prepared, the same formalities must be followed as in the original will.

codicil: An amendment to an existing will.

PROBATE COURT

After the testator's death, the will can be filed in the local probate court, and the court will take jurisdiction of the distribution of the decedent's (the person who died) assets. Usually the will is filed in court by the **executor,** the person named in the will to represent the testator and carry out the testator's wishes regarding the distribution of his or her estate.

Sometimes one of the decedent's heirs (who probably has been left little or nothing by the will) challenges the will, and the court has to decide if the person was *of sound mind* when the will was made. The witnesses may be called to testify about the testator's state of mind on the date he or she signed the will. Also, someone may argue that the will being offered to the probate court is not the last one prepared by the testator. Some people make changes in their wills every few years, and this can cause confusion (as well as anger in those left out or cut out by the later wills—"I hereby leave everything to my kind nurse"). The last valid will made by a testator will be the one certified by the court, and battles often take place about whether the last one found has been prepared correctly or is in fact the most recent one. When preparing a new will, it is a good idea for a person to actually destroy all earlier wills made so that this confusion can be avoided.

If a person dies without leaving a will, he or she is said to have died **intestate**. In this event, every state has a law that specifies how his or her property will be distributed. Although each state law is slightly different from the others, in general the property will be distributed to the person's closest heirs, starting with the spouse and children, then parents, and so on. Only if the decedent dies without any heirs at all will the property go to the state, through the doctrine of *escheat*.

executor: The person named in the will to carry out the decedent's requests and pay bills and expenses.

intestate: When a person dies without leaving a will, the property is distributed according to state law.

MEMO FROM THE LEGAL DEPARTMENT

To: Students

From: The Legal Department

There have been many nasty disputes among family members after the death of a father or mother. When it has not been made clear who is to inherit what, or in situations where the parent has changed his/her will a number of times, grief and sorrow among family members after the death of a loved one can end up as distrust and anger. It is a good idea for all adults to have a will, and for each person to periodically review the contents of his/her will, and inform the children and heirs of that person's wishes and intent. Throughout life a person's situation, assets and the needs of family members are bound to change, and the will should be modified from time to time.

When a person decides to change his will, either by adding a "codicil" or by preparing a completely new will, it is a good idea to destroy all older wills which no longer apply. Generally when one prepares a will, some family members are given copies, and those "old" wills sometimes resurface and cause problems when a newer one has been executed which changes the distribution of the deceased person's estate.

TRUSTS

trust: A legal mechanism by which one person transfers ownership of property to a **trustee**, who holds, uses, or invests the property for the benefit of another person (the **beneficiary**).

A **trust** is a legal mechanism whereby a person (Jerry, for example) transfers ownership of and title to certain property to someone called a **trustee** (First Bank, for example), usually according to a written document that specifies how the trustee is to hold and use the property. The document normally provides that the trustee is to invest or manage the property in a way so that benefits can be paid to someone else (e.g., Jerry's mother), called a **beneficiary.** Trusts can have tax benefits and also facilitate the transfer of property at one's death without the use of a will or the probate court.

For example, Jerry creates a *testamentary trust* as part of his will. This trust states that on his death, if he is not survived by his wife, all assets will automatically transfer to First Bank. Under the trust agreement, First Bank will hold the assets in trust and invest them in certain ways with the income paid to his two children. Furthermore, Jerry may have provided in the trust document that the trust will terminate when the youngest child reaches 21 years of age, with the entire balance of the trust funds distributed equally to his children at that time.

In general, this sort of document ensures that money left by the parents will be safeguarded for the children, that the interest will be used for their benefit, and the balance will be transferred to them in full when they become adults.

SUMMARY

The legal topic of property includes some of the oldest legal principles and some of the newest. Theories regarding real estate ownership, deeds, possession, use, and restrictions date back hundreds of years, and are still important today to large and small businesses. Courts are dealing with newer issues as well, such as eminent domain, "taking" by government action, and restrictive covenants in planned use development. The ownership and transfer of personal property is based on traditional legal principles such as sale, delivery, and intent.

CHAPTER QUESTIONS

1. Marion Allaire purchased a residential lot in Kansas in 1966. There was a chicken/hog wire fence dividing her back yard from her neighbor's back yard. Ms. Allaire believed that all the property on her side of the fence was hers, and she acted accordingly. She continuously used and maintained her portion, up to the fence. A woman named Akers purchased the property in 1976. Neither she nor the previous owner did anything to indicate that the fence was not the property line until a survey was done in 1987. It was then discovered that the fence was approximately 10 feet across the true boundary line and effectively took 10 feet of Akers' land. The required time period for adverse possession in Kansas is 15 years. Who owns the 10 feet of land? Why? *Akers v. Allaire,* 17 Kan. App. 2d 556, 840 P.2d 547 (1992)

2. Dowdell's home is on a hillside overlooking the Atlantic Ocean. Bloomquist lives on a lot below, and petitioned the zoning board to grant him a variance so he could build a second story addition to his home, which would block Dowdell's view. Dowdell opposed the variance request, and it was denied. Bloomquist then planted a row of forty-foot trees on his property which blocked Dowdell's ocean view. Dowdell sued, claiming the trees were a nuisance and an intentional "spite fence." Bloomquist claimed the trees were a privacy hedge, and he had the right to put trees on his property. What should be the result of the case? Nuisance or property right? Why? *Dowdell v. Bloomquist,* 847 A.2d 827 (Rhode Is., 2004).

3. A South Carolina man purchased two lots on the ocean in an area called the Isle of Palms near Charleston. He planned to build a house on one and sell the other. After his purchase, in order to protect the beachfront, state and local regulations were enacted barring the construction of any permanent structures on property in the area. He sued, claiming that the government had essentially "taken" his property and that he should be compensated. What should be the result? *Lucas v. South Carolina Coastal Council,* 112 S. Ct. 2886, 120 L.Ed. 2d 798 (1992)

4. Atlanta, Georgia, enacted a zoning ordinance that required surface parking lots with more than 30 parking spaces to install a certain number of

trees, barrier curbs, and other landscaping measures. The city declared the purposes of the law to be the promotion of aesthetic appeal, the improvement of water runoff and other environmental concerns, and the reduction of crime. No owner was required to donate any property to the city, nor could any owner be required to reduce the number of parking spaces by more than 3 percent. Several parking lot owners sued the city, claiming that a "taking" of their property had occurred, relying on *Dolan v. Tigard*. What should be the result and why? *Parking Association of Georgia v. Atlanta, Ga.,* 450 SE 2d 200 (Ga. 1994), cert. den. 115 S. Ct. 2268 (1995)

5. Montana Power Company (MPC) installed an overhead power line in 1964 and an underground power line in 1978 on property owned by the Taylors. No easement was ever recorded for these lines on any property documents. In 2000 the Taylors sued MPC for trespass and unjust enrichment due to the power lines. MPC contended that it had long ago acquired a "prescriptive easement" for the lines. The law in Montana requires 5 years of "open, notorious, continuous, adverse use" to establish a prescriptive easement. Who should win and why? *Taylor v. Montana Power Co.,* 312 Mont. 134 (Sup. Ct., Montana, 2002)

6. Eight states and the City of New York sued the nation's five largest coal-burning electric power companies, alleging that the discharge of greenhouse gases from their plants had created a public nuisance by contributing to global warming. Does this allegation meet the tests for a nuisance? Why or why not? *Connecticut v. American Electric Power Co.,* 582 F.3d 309 (2d Cir. 2009).

7. Over a period of time, including some wet and some dry years, a river changed its course. Essentially, a bend in the river was eliminated, creating several new acres of land on the west bank. The owner of the property adjoining the new land began to allow his animals to graze on the land. He effectively used the land from the former riverbed up to the new river course. After a period of 10 years, the landowner on the east bank (where the river had cut into his land) brought an action seeking to evict the other owner from using his land. If the state law on advese possession is 5 years, who wins and why?

8. Two women parked in a public parking lot behind the Bottlecaps Bar. They were going to hear a band that was playing there and had heard an advertisement saying that parking was available behind the bar. When they parked, an unknown assailant shot and killed one of the women. Her estate (family) sued the bar, alleging that it had a duty to either warn or protect the victim. The evidence showed that the bar owner knew that some crimes had occurred in the parking lot, but he did not own or control the parking lot. Should the owner be held liable? Was there a duty that was breached? *Rhudy v. Bottlecaps Inc.,* 830 A. 2d 402 (Sup. Ct., Delaware, 2003).

9. All the property lots in one Missouri subdivision were covered by restrictive covenants, which said that "none of the lots shall be improved, used, nor occupied for other than private residence purposes." A church which owned several lots in the subdivision announced that it was going to construct parking spaces on the lots for church use. The homeowners associa-

tion filed suit to block construction, pointing out that all the lots were covered by the restrictive covenant. There were no other commercial uses of neighborhood property. The church argued that use for church parking was to be expected in a residential neighborhood and the covenant should not be enforced. What should the court decide about enforcing the restrictive covenant? Why? *Country Club Dist. Homes Assn. v. Country Club Christian Church,* 118 SW 3d 185 (Ct. App. Mo. 2003).

10. A home in Ohio included a swimming pool, which was unfenced. Children frequently trespassed into the yard and went into the pool without the permission of the homeowner. One day a neighbor child fell into the pool and his mother jumped in to try and save him, but both drowned. The family of the deceased persons brought suit against the homeowner under the attractive nuisance doctrine. Can and should that theory be applied here? What are the requirements of the theory and how do they apply to this case? *Bennett v. Stanley,* 748 N.E. 2d 41 (Sup. Ct., Ohio, 2001)

PRACTICAL EXERCISE

Mr. Jann Wenner hired Anderson to build a driveway on his ranch near Sun Valley, Idaho. While Mr. Anderson and his employee Corliss were excavating soil for the driveway they uncovered a jar containing 96 gold pieces which were dated from 1857 to 1914. Anderson and Corliss agreed at first to split the proceeds but later got into an argument. Anderson fired Corliss and then turned the coins over to Wenner, the property owner (who is also the co-founder and publisher of the music and politics biweekly *Rolling Stone,* as well as the owner of *Men's Journal* and *Us Weekly* magazines). Corliss filed a lawsuit contending that the coins belonged to him as finders.

Some states have followed the "finders keepers" rule of treasure trove (which originated hundreds of year ago to deal with buried Roman treasures discovered in feudal times), and under this principle, Corliss and Anderson would be the owners. Other states have followed rules concerning "lost" and "mislaid" property, as described in this chapter, which would lead to other results. Write a one-page memo outlining the possible benefits to society, and to landowners of each rule. Which do you think is the better rule for today's world, and why? Based on *Corliss v. Wenner,* 136 Id. 417, 34 P.3d 1100 (Id.App. 2001)

FURTHER INFORMATION

www.nolo.com
Nolo Press, publisher of many books about legal issues for nonlawyers.

CHAPTER 15

ENVIRONMENTAL LAW AND REGULATION

One of your friends was the president of a small company that picked up and disposed of oil waste from various businesses. The disposal site was located on land owned by another person. In the Practical Exercise at the end of this chapter, you are asked to advise your friend and the landowner about their liability if the EPA finds that the tanks holding the oil were leaking.

INTRODUCTION

One of the most significant public policy developments of the last 35–40 years has been the increase in concern for environmental issues. Some years ago, people carelessly threw soda pop cans and pop tops out of car windows, tossed paper on the ground, and dumped various toxic substances into rivers and lakes. Today these actions are universally condemned. Words and phrases little known 40 years ago—*wetlands, acid rain, recycling, effluents, open space, global warming, greenhouse gases, sustainability, solar and wind power, toxic waste*—are now commonly used in conversation.

For years, the environment was viewed as a free resource for business. As industry grew and the nature and operations of business became increasingly complex, it became clear that commercial and industrial activities were causing considerable harm to the environment. Today, the public generally accepts that air, water, and other natural resources belong to society, and a business that causes depletion or pollution of these common natural elements should pay for the loss, just as if the firm had cut down a tree on someone else's land. However, because of the economic crisis of the past several years, whether or not this trend will continue is uncertain. Increasingly, state and federal governments and elected officials and politicians have taken a hard look at some of the more stringent regulations in an effort to assess the costs and benefits of various requirements under all environmental laws. "Will this environmental rule cause the loss of jobs?" is a question being asked more frequently today.

The law often develops in an organic manner. Doctrines that originated hundreds of years ago sometimes generate new theories as the times change, as legal solutions are needed to address new issues. In Chapter 14, we looked at property law and specifically examined several legal theories relating to real property some of which developed a long time ago. In the past 30 years, the general public has become concerned with the harm caused to the environment by business and industrial activity. Some of the ancient doctrines of property law have engendered new laws and regulations aimed at controlling actions taken by industrial firms that may cause contamination of land, water, and air. This chapter examines a series of federal laws establishing controls on the discharge of various substances into the public air and water, as well as the production, transportation, use, and disposal of chemicals and other hazardous substances on private property. Although many states also have laws dealing with the environment, they differ from one state to another, while the federal laws apply uniformly across the country. We will thus examine a series of important federal laws including the Clean Air Act, the Clean Water Act, the National Environmental Policy Act, and several federal laws dealing with hazardous and toxic waste.

THE NATIONAL ENVIRONMENTAL POLICY ACT

The individual states had made some efforts to combat pollution in the years prior to 1969 but without a great deal of success. Many citizens groups formed during the 1960s and 1970s which pressured Congress to pass environmental laws at the federal level. The so-called "environmental movement" was an important public policy effort during those years. Federal involvement in environmental regulation began with the passage of the National Environmental Policy Act of 1970 (NEPA). Congress stated the purposes of NEPA to be as follows:

> To declare a national policy which will encourage productive and enjoyable harmony between man and his environment; to promote efforts which will prevent or eliminate damage to the environment and biosphere and stimulate the health and welfare of man; to enrich the understanding of the ecological systems and natural resources important to the Nation; and to establish a Council on Environmental Quality.

NEPA does not require that any particular measures be taken to prevent water, air, or other types of pollution, but responding to the considerable public demand, Congress passed NEPA to establish a federal government policy that environmental issues were of the highest concern. This policy was intended to permeate all activities of the federal government. Congress explicitly recognized "the profound impact of man's activity on the interrelations of all components of the natural environment." The act required that the federal government (in cooperation with state governments and other organizations) "use all practicable means and measures" to protect environmental values and to "create and maintain conditions under which man and nature can exist in productive harmony."

The most important actual legal mandate of NEPA was the requirement that an **Environmental Impact Statement** (EIS) be prepared for each "major federal action significantly affecting the quality of the human environment." Another important section of NEPA established the *Council on Environmental Quality*.

ENVIRONMENTAL IMPACT STATEMENTS

The preparation and filing of an EIS requires substantial time and effort. The "major federal action" section of NEPA has been interpreted broadly, so that not only does the federal agency actually constructing a project need to prepare an EIS, but also any agency sponsoring, supervising, or perhaps only approving or licensing a project for some action that may significantly affect the environment. The EI Statements themselves often are well over 100 pages long. NEPA requires the statement to analyze and describe a number of factors, including the following:

(1) the environmental impact of the proposed action;

(2) any adverse environmental effects of the project that cannot be avoided;

(3) alternatives to the proposed action;

(4) the relationship between short-term uses of the environment and the maintenance of long-term productivity; and

(5) any irreversible and irretrievable commitments of resources that would be involved.

As agencies prepare to embark on a project, a draft EIS is circulated to interested parties and government officials for comment. Once finalized, the EIS is provided to other federal agencies, state agencies, the Council on Environmental Quality, and the public. The EIS is primarily intended to *provide information* to anyone who is interested in the environmental effects of the project and to explain the rationale behind the choices made by the proposing agency. The law does not require that the courts review every EIS, nor are they asked to determine whether the environment will be harmed. Rather, the EIS is intended to inform other agencies and the public about the environmental consequences of a proposed project; with this information, then, any group unhappy with the tentative decisions made by the agency can bring public and internal pressure to force the proposing agency to make changes before the project is begun.

A number of cases, however, have held that a court may review an EIS to determine whether an agency has complied with the requirements of the NEPA. Did the agency actually consider the 5 issues set out above? Did the agency ignore other alternatives? Courts have also held that they can order an agency to prepare a new EIS or issue an injunction to stop a project if the requirements of NEPA have not been met. Some courts have gone even farther and looked into the "substantive" aspects of the agency's decision—that is, whether the agency legally could have made the decision it did if all the aspects of the project had really been evaluated in accordance with NEPA. If the decision proved "arbitrary and capricious," some courts have enjoined the project until a new EIS was done. The following case, decided by the federal district court in Hawaii, shows how the EIS requirement can be applied.

BLUE OCEAN PRESERVATION SOCIETY V. U.S. DEPARTMENT OF ENERGY

767 F.Supp. 1518 (D. Haw. 1991)

FACTS

For several years, the state of Hawaii and the federal government have been working cooperatively on a venture to develop geothermal power as an alternative energy source. The project is called the Hawaii Geothermal Energy Project, and it is located on the slopes of the active volcano Kilauea, on the "big island" of Hawaii. Phases I and II of the project, involving the building of a small plant for research and a study of the feasibility of transporting power to other islands via underground cable, have been completed. (No EIS was prepared.)

Phase III, which involved the drilling of 25 commercial-scale exploration wells throughout the Kilauea East Rift Zone, had started at the time of the lawsuit. If the geothermal resource was "verified" after testing, Phase IV would consist of constructing up to 20 separate geothermal power plants of about 25 megawatts each. The plants would each need 8–10 working wells, and all of the plants would then be connected by roads, plumbing, and power lines. Finally, considerable overland and underwater cable would need to be laid to carry power to the islands of Maui and Oahu.

Although the final project was to be privately built, Congress had contributed $34.7 million to Phases I and II (over 80 percent of the total funding of those phases) and had appropriated $5 million toward Phase III. The Blue Ocean Society, a citizens' group, along with the Sierra Club and other plaintiffs, then filed suit, requesting that all work on the project be halted until an EIS was done.

The Department of Energy (DOE) denied that an EIS was necessary, arguing that this was largely a "research" project, not a "major federal action significantly affecting the human environment." During the course of the lawsuit, the DOE tried unsuccessfully to have the $5 million appropriation "reprogrammed" to another project by Congress. As the lawsuit neared a decision, the DOE finally agreed to prepare an EIS and then argued that the case was "moot"—that is, there was no reason for the court to act. The plaintiffs disagreed, asserting that without a court order, DOE officials could easily change their minds again regarding the EIS and that there were other unresolved issues remaining in the lawsuit.

DECISION

District Judge David Ezra first considered whether the case was moot. Judge Ezra found that it would be quite possible for the government to alter its position on preparing the EIS and denied the DOE claim. The court cited previous cases holding that a lawsuit challenging an action is moot only when it has been "fully and irrevocably carried out." As the judge noted, "This is not a case in which the government has already prepared an EIS, or even commenced such preparation." Judge Ezra wrote that "Not only is the EIS process not completed here, it has not begun."

In an earlier hearing, the court had ruled that Phases III and IV of the project had to be considered together as part of the same project and that clearly this was a "major federal action," based on the $5 million appropriation and the other federal involvement. Thus, the only remaining question was whether the action was one "significantly affecting the quality of the human environment."

The DOE argued that the project would not significantly affect the environment and that an EIS was thus unnecessary. The DOE claimed that the plaintiffs must prove "significant environmental effects" in order to force the preparation of an EIS. The court, however, noted that the very reason for the EIS requirement is to study and reveal the effects of a project on the environment prior to the time it is undertaken, so the initial decision on whether to do an EIS will always be based on incomplete information. Therefore, stated Judge Ezra, the burden on the plaintiffs is only to *"raise substantial questions"* regarding whether the proposed action *may* have a significant effect upon the human environment. If such questions are raised, "a decision not to prepare an EIS is unreasonable."

The court noted that the project contemplated a network of geothermal plants, wells, power lines, roads, and pipes over 26,000 acres in an area that had once been designated as a Natural Area Reserve. A U.S. Fish and Wildlife employee testified in court that the forest was a "unique dynamic ecosystem, valuable for both research on and management of the lowland rain forest habitat on the island of Hawaii," that would be adversely affected by the geothermal development. In addition, three other experts—an ornithologist, a geneticist, and a botanist—submitted affidavits to the court expressing grave concern for the environmental effects of the proposed project. The judge stated that this information "easily raises" the "substantial questions" of possible environmental impact sufficient to require the preparation of an EIS.

Therefore, the court ordered the federal government to commence the preparation of an EIS in compliance with the NEPA, which would address the serious concerns raised regarding the geothermal project. Also, an injunction was issued preventing all defendants from any further participation in the project (other than the funding and preparation of the EIS) until the EIS was completed.

CASE QUESTIONS

1. What is the key legal issue in this case? What legal issue is it that the court must decide?
2. What standard did the plaintiffs have to meet in order to trigger the preparation of an EIS?
3. In this case, the court was unwilling to defer to the decision of the federal agency that an EIS was unnecessary. Why?
4. What is the purpose of the section of NEPA that requires the preparation of an EIS in certain cases? Was that purpose fulfilled by the decision in this case? Explain.

SOCIAL/ETHICAL ISSUES

Regardless of the legal issues in the previous case, is it ethically proper to allow a private company to drill 160 to 200 wells on the slopes of the Kilauea volcano—one of the most active in the world? How can anyone know for sure what the environmental effects of these actions will be in the future? How would you feel if you lived in a village a short distance below? Would it affect your decision if your power rates would be reduced 30 percent as the result?

Like many lawsuits, the controversy over the Hawaiian Geothermal Project involved many more issues than just the interpretation of the meaning of one section of federal law (NEPA). The following reading describes some of the social and cultural issues raised by the project.

THE PELE DEFENSE FUND

Named for Hawaii's volcano goddess and sworn to protect the islands, the Pele Defense Fund is a fiery, grass-roots organization with impact as mighty as its namesake. It has thwarted the Aloha State's effort to tap a live volcano and harness its steam in a $4 billion, federally funded experiment in a rain forest on the "Big Island" of Hawaii, the largest tropical island in the Pacific.

Pele (pay-lay) is the legendary Hawaiian fire goddess who causes volcanoes to erupt. Despite 170 years of Christianity, many Hawaiians not only believe in Pele's power, they still worship her—and for good reason.

Since January 3, 1983, Madame Pele, as she is known, has thrown up enough hot lava, it is estimated, to build a four-foot wide, four-inch deep sidewalk from Honolulu to New York every two days. The eruptions, still in progress, began soon after the first drills pierced the east rift zone of the 13,679-foot Mauna Loa; one eruption inundated 10,000 acres of the original site with lava. Madame Pele was angry, Hawaiians said.

A dozen outraged islanders first took up Madame Pele's defense in 1982 only to be dismissed as pot-smoking hippies by the local media. "Nobody took us seriously at first," said Ralph Palikapu Dedman, the founding president. Their cause was not immediately understood even in Hawaii, where fewer than 20 percent of the population is Hawaiian, because it recalled arcane Hawaiian religious rites many thought abandoned. "We worship nature gods, like Pele," Dedman said.

This native Hawaiian belief, Dedman claims, has been "ongoing for thousands of years"—much like rites of native American Indians who find spirituality in nature. "The forest is to us like a cathedral to Christians," he said. "To poke holes in Pele is sacrilegious."

In 1988, the Pele Defense Fund brought its cause to national attention in full-page ads in the *San Francisco Chronicle* and the *New York Times*. Claiming Hawaii would become an "industrial slum," the ads stressed the importance of native religious rites and deplored the geothermal plant in the 27,000-acre Wao Kele O Puna rain forest as "Ugly, Toxic, Costly & Sacrilegious." An illustration showed a "new" Hawaii jammed by high rise hotels, its landscape marred by thousands of 10-story electrical towers; a geothermal plant pumps out volcanic steam to chill Waikiki's 50,000 air-conditioned tourist hotel rooms 150 miles away.

Their mouse roar focused media attention on the struggle in the rain forest between native Hawaiians who worship a fire goddess and wildcat drillers from Wyoming trying to plumb the world's most active volcano for steam. "It really changed the awareness," Dedman said. "We are five thousand strong now. People from all over the world support our cause."

Ecology groups like the Sierra Club, Greenpeace, EarthFirst, and the Rainforest Action Network took up the defense of the Wao Kele O Puna (it means "green forest"), which is home to endangered Hawaiian birds, insects, plants—and on occasion humans. "As native Hawaiians, we are part of the ecosystem of these islands," Dedman said. "If we are as important as an endangered tree, environmental groups should chain themselves to us as much as they would a tree." For Pele worshippers the battle was to save what the *New York Times* called "the last big tropical rain forest in the United States . . . ."

An advocate of geothermal for oil-starved Hawaii, the governor lost political face again when his own state health director called geothermal "the stupidest thing we could possibly be doing . . . in the forest." Later that summer, a test well exploded and sent people fleeing noxious gases; the hazardous conditions forced the state to shut down operations. It was another setback for the haunted geothermal project. Or was it—as Dedman and other native Hawaiians believe—only Madame Pele voicing her displeasure once again?

After considerable controversy (including the arrest of 400 protesters who were taken away in handcuffs at one point) the large original plans were dropped and a much smaller geothermal plant was built near Kilauea, which has operated for several years. However, in Spring 2011, another group began to seek public support for a new geothermal facility. Innovations Development Group, which claims to specialize in "socially responsible development," held a forum which included presentations by six native Hawaiian leaders who offered their views on how development of geothermal energy can be done in a way that protects cultural and resources.

Patricia Brandt, IDG's chief executive officer, said it is important that the native Hawaiian and local community has a say in future geothermal projects. "The people of the land need to be real partners in any geothermal development, and we have the expertise to make that happen," she said. Only time will tell if those plans and the supposedly newer and better geothermal technology will be accepted by the local population.

Madame Pele meets Prof. Bixby near Kilauea volcano.

THE COUNCIL ON ENVIRONMENTAL QUALITY

The NEPA also established the **Council on Environmental Quality (CEQ)**, which calls for a three-member council, appointed by the President and approved by the Senate. The CEQ and its staff advise the President on environmental matters. Also, the CEQ attempts to coordinate programs of the various federal agencies that influence the environment and to mediate disputes between federal agencies over environmental issues. The CEQ receives and comments on EISs filed with it and issues guidelines to agencies concerning the preparation of an EIS. In recent years, the role of the CEQ has diminished somewhat.

CEQ: A three-member agency which advises the President on environmental matters.

THE ENVIRONMENTAL PROTECTION AGENCY

The Environmental Protection Agency (EPA) was created in 1970 through a reorganization of several federal agencies by President Richard Nixon. By combining some 15 departments from five agencies—all of which had some responsibilities for environmental issues—the President created the EPA, which immediately became the primary federal regulatory body addressing environmental issues.

The EPA is an independent agency within the executive branch of government, headed by an administrator appointed by, and serving at the pleasure of, the President. As the scope of environmental issues has grown and the public's interest in environmental issues has increased, the EPA has expanded significantly and is now one of the largest federal agencies. Unlike the CEQ, which has remained a fairly small advisory body, the EPA is a powerful agency with a huge staff. Most of the major environmental laws that Congress has enacted since 1970 have given rulemaking and enforcement responsibilities to the EPA.

We will now turn our attention to the specific federal laws that are designed to prevent and decrease various forms of environmental pollution.

AIR POLLUTION—THE CLEAN AIR ACT

The Clean Air Act is the primary federal statute aimed at preventing air pollution. The Act as we know it today combines more than 10 separate laws passed by Congress, beginning with the Air Pollution Control Act of 1955. The first version of the Clean Air Act was enacted in 1963, with Congress adding major amendments in 1966, 1967 (the Air Quality Act), 1970, 1977, and 1990. The act requires the EPA to establish standards for certain substances that cause air pollution. These standards, called the **National Ambient Air Quality Standards (NAAQS),** set forth the maximum allowable amount of each pollutant that the air may legally contain, that "allowing an adequate margin of safety, are requisite to protect the public health." There is no requirement in the law that the EPA consider the economic costs involved, when setting the standards. These pollutants are as follows: particulates, sulfur oxide, carbon monoxide, nitrogen dioxide, ozone, hydrocarbons, and lead. The EPA has established both *primary* standards, which must be met in order to protect human health, and *secondary* standards, which are necessary to protect the "public welfare" (soil, water, vegetation, weather, property, animals, and other aspects of the human environment).

National Ambient Air Quality Standards (NAAQS): Maximum allowable amounts of seven types of pollutants.

The structure of the Clean Air Act calls for each state to draft its own **State Implementation Plan (SIP)** to provide for "implementation, maintenance, and enforcement" of the ambient air quality standards in that particular state. This provision furthers the goal of federalism by allowing each state to decide how best to reach the required standards in its own jurisdiction and then to enforce the law and regulations. If state rules or enforcement are lacking, the EPA can require revisions or can impose other sanctions, such as banning new pollution sources (new factories, for example).

As the result of the Clean Air Act, manufacturing, agriculture, and other types of businesses must often spend millions of dollars to meet the NAAQS. Although expensive, the purchase and installation of complex equipment and procedures may be necessary in order to reduce emissions of certain hazardous substances to allowable levels.

The Clean Air Act requires that before major new sources of emissions can be constructed in areas that have met or surpassed the NAAQS (which are called "Prevention of Significant Deterioration" or PSD areas) a permit must be obtained. In order to issue a permit, the EPA or the appropriate state environmental agency must determine on a case-by-case method that the **best available control technology (BACT)** is going to be employed by the facility. The following decision of the U.S. Supreme Court discusses the PSD program, the requirements for obtaining a permit, the role of the state and federal government agencies, how the economic costs of installing appropriate equipment might be considered, and what is required under the BACT standards.

In the Language of the Court

ALASKA DEPARTMENT OF ENVIRONMENTAL CONSERVATION V. EPA

U.S. Supreme Court
540 U.S. 461, 124 S.Ct. 983 (2004)

Justice Ginsburg wrote the opinion of the Court (decided by a 5-4 majority).

FACTS

This case concerns the authority of the Environmental Protection Agency (EPA or Agency) to enforce the provisions of the Clean Air Act's (CAA or Act) Prevention of Significant Deterioration (PSD) program. Under that program, no major air pollutant emitting facility may be constructed unless the facility is equipped with "the best available control technology" (BACT). BACT, as defined in the CAA, means, for any major air pollutant emitting facility, an emission limitation based on the maximum degree of [pollutant] reduction . . . which the permitting authority, on a case-by-case basis, taking into account energy, environmental, and economic impacts and other costs, determines is achievable for [the] facility."

Teck Cominco Alaska, Inc. (Cominco), operates a zinc concentrate mine, the Red Dog Mine, in northwest Alaska approximately 100 miles north of the Arctic Circle and close to the native Alaskan villages of Kivalina and Noatak. The mine is the region's largest private employer. In 1988, Cominco obtained authorization to operate the mine, a "major emitting facility" under the Clean Air Act and Alaska's SIP. The mine's PSD permit authorized five 5,000 kilowatt Wartsila diesel electric generators, MG-1 through MG-5, subject to operating restrictions; later the Alaska Department of Environmental Conservation (ADEC) issued a second PSD permit in 1994 allowing addition of a sixth full-time generator (MG-6),

In 1996, Cominco initiated a project, with funding from the State, to expand zinc production by 40%. Anticipating that the project would increase nitrogen oxide emissions by more than 40 tons per year, Cominco applied to

ADEC for a PSD permit to allow increased electricity generation by its standby generator, MG-5. On March 3, 1999, ADEC preliminarily proposed as BACT for MG-5 the emission control technology known as selective catalytic reduction (SCR), which reduces nitrogen oxide emissions by 90%. In response, Cominco amended its application to add a seventh generator, MG-17, and to propose as BACT an alternative control technology—Low NOx—that achieves a 30% reduction in nitrogen oxide pollutants.

On May 4, 1999, ADEC, in conjunction with Cominco's representative, issued a first draft PSD permit and preliminary technical analysis report that concluded Low NOx was BACT for MG-5 and MG-17. To determine BACT, ADEC employed EPA's recommended top-down methodology:

> *"In brief, the top-down process provides that all available control technologies be ranked in descending order of control effectiveness. The PSD applicant first examines the most stringent—or 'top'—alternative. That alternative is established as BACT unless the applicant demonstrates, and the permitting authority in its informed judgment agrees, that technical considerations, or energy, environmental, or economic impacts justify a conclusion that the most stringent technology is not 'achievable' in that case. If the most stringent technology is eliminated in this fashion, then the next most stringent alternative is considered, and so on." EPA, New Source Review Workshop Manual*

Applying top-down methodology, ADEC first homed in on SCR as BACT for MG-5, and the new generator, MG-17. "[W]ith an estimated reduction of 90%," ADEC stated, SCR "is the most stringent" technology. Finding SCR "technically and economically feasible," ADEC characterized as "overstated" Cominco's cost estimate of $5,643 per ton of nitrogen oxide removed by SCR. Using Cominco's data, ADEC reached a cost estimate running between $1,586 and $2,279 per ton. Costs in that range, ADEC observed, "are well within what ADEC

and EPA conside[r] economically feasible." Responding to Cominco's comments on the preliminary permit, engineering staff in ADEC's Air Permits Program pointed out that, according to information Cominco provided to ADEC, "SCR has been installed on similar diesel-fired engines throughout the world."

Despite its staff's clear view "that SCR (the most effective individual technology) [was] technologically, environmentally, and economically feasible for the Red Dog power plant engines," ADEC endorsed the alternative proffered by Cominco. To achieve nitrogen oxide emission reductions commensurate with SCR's 90% impact, Cominco proposed fitting the new generator MG-17 and the six existing generators with Low NOx.

Cominco asserted that it could lower net emissions by 396 tons per year if it fitted all seven generators with Low NOx rather than fitting two (MG-5 and MG-17) with SCR and choosing one of them as the standby unit. Cominco's proposal hinged on the "assumption . . . that under typical operating conditions one or more engines will not be running due to maintenance of standby-generation capacity." If all seven generators ran continuously, however, Cominco's alternative would increase emissions by 79 tons per year. Accepting Cominco's submission, ADEC stated that Cominco's Low NOx solution "achieve[d] a similar maximum NOx reduction as the most stringent controls; [could] potentially result in a greater NOx reduction; and is logistically and economically less onerous to Cominco."

EPA wrote to ADEC on July 29, 1999, commenting:

> *"Although ADEC states in its analysis that [SCR], the most stringent level of control, is economically and technologically feasible, ADEC did not propose to require SCR . . . . [O]nce it is determined that an emission unit is subject to BACT, the PSD program does not allow the imposition of a limit that is less stringent than BACT." New emissions could be offset only against reduced emissions from sources covered by the same BACT authorization.*

After receiving EPA comments, ADEC issued a second draft PSD permit and technical analysis report on September 1, 1999, again finding Low NOx to be BACT for MG-17. Contradicting its May 1999 conclusion that SCR was "technically and economically feasible," ADEC found in September 1999 that SCR imposed "a disproportionate cost" on the mine. ADEC concluded, on a "cursory review," that requiring SCR for a rural Alaska utility would lead to a 20% price increase, and that in comparison with other BACT technologies, SCR came at a "significantly higher" cost.

EPA protested the revised permit. In a September 15, 1999, letter, the Agency stated: "Cominco has not adequately demonstrated any site-specific factors to support their claim that the installation of [SCR] is economically infeasible at the Red Dog Mine. On December 10, 1999, ADEC issued the final permit, once again, approving Low NOx as BACT for MG-17. The same day, EPA issued an order to ADEC, prohibiting ADEC from issuing a PSD permit to Cominco" unless ADEC satisfactorily documents why SCR is not BACT for the Wartsila diesel generator [MG-17]. In the letter accompanying the order, the Agency stated that "ADEC's own analysis supports the determination that BACT is [SCR], and that ADEC's decision in the proposed permit therefore is both arbitrary and erroneous." On February 8, 2000, EPA, again invoking its authority under the Clean Air Act, issued a second order, this time prohibiting Cominco from beginning "construction or modification activities" at the Red Dog mine.

ADEC and Cominco petitioned the Court of Appeals for the Ninth Circuit for review of EPA's orders. The Court of Appeals resolved the merits in a judgment released July 30, 2002. [298 F. 3d 814 (CA9)]. It held that EPA had authority to issue the contested orders, and that the Agency had properly exercised its discretion in doing so. The Ninth Circuit found that EPA had properly exercised its discretion in issuing the three orders, because (1) Cominco failed to "demonstrat[e] that SCR was economi-

cally infeasible," and (2) "ADEC failed to provide a reasoned justification for its elimination of SCR as a control option." We granted certiorari to resolve an important question of federal law, i.e., the scope of EPA's authority, and now affirm the Ninth Circuit's judgment.

DECISION

Relevant Provisions of the Clean Air Act

Regarding EPA oversight, the Act authorizes EPA, when it finds that a State is not complying with a CAA requirement governing construction of a pollutant source, to issue an order prohibiting construction, to prescribe an administrative penalty, or to commence a civil action for injunctive relief. Directed specifically to the PSD program, CAA §167 instructs EPA to "take such measures, including issuance of an order, or seeking injunctive relief, as necessary to prevent the construction" of a major pollutant emitting facility that does not conform to the PSD requirements of the Act.

The question presented in this case is what role EPA has with respect to ADEC's BACT determinations. Specifically, may EPA act to block construction of a new major pollutant emitting facility permitted by ADEC when EPA finds ADEC's BACT determination unreasonable in light of the guides that the Clean Air Act prescribes? We hold that the Act confers that checking authority on EPA.

Congress enacted the Clean Air Amendments of 1970 in response to "dissatisfaction with the progress of existing air pollution programs." The amendments aimed "to guarantee the prompt attainment and maintenance of specified air quality standards." The 1970 amendments require EPA to publish lists of emissions that "cause or contribute to air pollution which may reasonably be anticipated to endanger public health or welfare," and to promulgate primary and secondary national ambient air quality standards (NAAQS) for such pollutants.

NAAQS "define [the] levels of air quality that must be achieved to protect public health and welfare."

Under §110 of the Act, also added in 1970, each State must submit for EPA approval "a plan which provides for implementation, maintenance, and enforcement of [NAAQS]." Relevant to this case, EPA has approved Alaska's implementation plan. To gain EPA approval, a "state implementation plan" (SIP) must "include enforceable emission limitations and other control measures, means, or techniques . . . as may be necessary or appropriate to meet the applicable [CAA] requirements." While States have "wide discretion" in formulating their plans, SIPs must include certain measures Congress specified "to assure that national ambient air quality standards are achieved."

The PSD permit requirements "are designed to ensure that the air quality in attainment areas or areas that are already 'clean' will not degrade. [The] purpose of the PSD program is to "protect public health and welfare from any actual or potential adverse effect which in [EPA's] judgment may reasonably be anticipate[d] to occur from air pollution.

An attainment area is one in which the air "meets the national primary or secondary ambient air quality standard for [a regulated pollutant]. Northwest Alaska, the region this case concerns, is classified as an attainment or unclassifiable area for nitrogen dioxide, therefore, the PSD program applies to emissions of that pollutant in the region.

A permit is required for any "major emitting facility," defined to include any source emitting more than 250 tons of nitrogen oxides per year.

No such facility may be constructed or modified unless a permit prescribing emission limitations has been issued for the facility. Modifications to major emitting facilities that increase nitrogen oxide emissions in excess of 40 tons per year require a PSD permit.

Under the Clean Air Act no PSD permit may issue unless "the proposed facility is subject to the *best available control technology* for each pollutant subject to [CAA] regulation . . . emitted from . . . [the] facility."

Alaska defines BACT as "the emission limitation that represents the maximum reduction achievable for each regulated air contaminant, taking into account energy, environmental and economic impacts, and other costs." CAA also provides that a PSD permit may issue only if a source "will not cause, or contribute to, air pollution in excess of any . . . maximum allowable increase or maximum allowable concentration for any pollutant" or any NAAQS.

Centrally at issue in this case is the question whether EPA's oversight role, described by Congress in the CAA, extends to ensuring that a state permitting authority's BACT determination is reasonable in light of the statutory guides. Congress armed EPA with authority to issue orders stopping construction when "a State is not acting in compliance with any [CAA] requirement or prohibition . . . relating to the construction of new sources or the modification of existing sources," when "construction or modification of a major emitting facility . . . does not conform to the requirements of [the PSD program]."

The federal Act enumerates several "[p]reconstruction requirements" for the PSD program. Absent these, "[n]o major emitting facility . . . may be constructed." One express preconstruction requirement is inclusion of a BACT determination in a facility's PSD permit. The permitting authority, ADEC here, exercises primary or initial responsibility for identifying BACT in line with the Act's definition of that term.

All parties agree that one of the "many requirements in the PSD provisions that the EPA may enforce" is "that a [PSD] permit contain a BACT limitation. It is therefore undisputed that the Agency may issue an order to stop a facility's construction if a PSD permit contains no BACT designation."

EPA stresses that Congress' reason for enacting the PSD program was to prevent significant deterioration of air quality in clean-air areas within a State and in neighboring States. That aim, EPA urges, is unlikely to be realized absent an EPA surveillance role that extends to BACT determinations. The Agency notes in this regard a House Report observation:

> Without national guidelines for the prevention of significant deterioration a State deciding to protect its clean air resources will face a double threat. The prospect is very real that such a State would lose existing industrial plants to more permissive States. But additionally the State will likely become the target of "economic-environmental blackmail" from new industrial plants that will play one State off against another with threats to locate in whichever State adopts the most permissive pollution controls. H. R. Rep. No. 95-294, p. 134 (1977).

ADEC argues that the statutory definition of BACT, unambiguously assigns to "the permitting authority" alone determination of the control technology qualifying as "best available." Because the Act places responsibility for determining BACT with "the permitting authority," ADEC urges, CAA excludes federal Agency surveillance reaching the substance of the BACT decision. EPA's enforcement role, ADEC maintains, is restricted to the requirement "that the permit contain a BACT limitation."

Congress vested EPA with explicit and sweeping authority to enforce CAA "requirements" relating to the construction and modification of sources under the PSD program, including BACT. We fail to see why Congress, having expressly endorsed an expansive surveillance role for EPA in two independent CAA provisions, would then implicitly preclude the Agency from verifying substantive compliance with the BACT provisions and, instead, limit EPA's superintendence to the insubstantial question whether the state permitting authority had uttered the key words "BACT."

In sum, EPA interprets the Act to allow substantive federal Agency surveillance of state permitting authorities' BACT determinations subject to federal court review. We credit EPA's longstanding construction of the Act and confirm EPA's authority, to rule on the reasonableness of BACT decisions by state permitting authorities.

Applying the Legal Principles to this Case

We turn finally, and more particularly, to the reasons why we conclude that EPA properly exercised its statutory authority in this case. ADEC urges that, even if the Act allows the Agency to issue stop-construction orders when a state permitting authority unreasonably determines BACT, EPA acted impermissibly in this instance. Because the Act itself does not specify a standard for judicial review in this instance, we apply the familiar default standard of the Administrative Procedure Act and ask whether the Agency's action was "arbitrary, capricious, an abuse of discretion, or otherwise not in accordance with law."

In the two draft permits and the final permit, ADEC formally followed the EPA-recommended top-down methodology to determine BACT, and first concluded that SCR was the most stringent emission-control technology that was both "technically and economically feasible." That technology should have been designated BACT absent "technical considerations, or energy, environmental, or economic impacts justif[ying] a conclusion that [SCR was] not 'achievable' in [this] case." ADEC nevertheless selected Low NOx as BACT, in May 1999 based at first on Cominco's suggestion that fitting all Red Dog Mine generators with Low NOx would reduce aggregate emissions.

In September and December 1999, ADEC again rejected SCR as BACT but this time candidly stated that it aimed "[t]o support

Cominco's Red Dog Mine Production Rate Increase Project, and its contributions to the region." In these second and third rounds, ADEC rested its selection of Low NOx squarely and solely on SCR's "disproportionate cost."

EPA concluded that ADEC's switch from finding SCR economically feasible in May 1999 to finding SCR economically infeasible in September 1999 had no factual basis in the record.

ADEC, indeed, forthrightly explained why it could not reach any judgment on whether implementation of SCR would adversely affect the mine's operation or profitability: Cominco had declined to provide the relevant financial data, disputing the need for such information and citing "confidentiality" concerns. Therefore there is no evidence in the record to suggest that the mine, were it to use SCR for its new generator, would be obliged to cut personnel, or raise zinc prices. Absent evidence of that order, ADEC lacked cause for selecting Low NOx as BACT based on the more stringent control's impact on the mine's operation or competitiveness.

ADEC's basis for selecting Low NOx thus reduces to a readiness "[t]o support Cominco's Red Dog Mine Production Rate Increase Project, and its contributions to the region." This justification, however, hardly meets ADEC's own standard of a "source-specific . . . economic impac[t] which demonstrate[s] [SCR] to be inappropriate as BACT." In short, as the Ninth Circuit determined, EPA validly issued stop orders because ADEC's BACT designation simply did not qualify as reasonable in light of the statutory guides.

We emphasize that today's disposition does not impede ADEC from revisiting the BACT determination in question. In letters and orders throughout the permitting process, EPA repeatedly commented that it was open to ADEC to prepare "an appropriate record" supporting its selection of Low NOx as BACT. (See an EPA letter to ADEC, stating "an analysis of whether requiring Cominco to install and operate [SCR] would have any adverse economic impacts upon Cominco specifically" might demonstrate SCR's economic infeasibility). Even at the oral argument in this appeal, counsel for EPA reaffirmed that, "absolutely," ADEC could reconsider the matter and, on an "appropriate record," endeavor to support Low NOx as BACT. We see no reason not to take EPA at its word.

In sum, we conclude that EPA has supervisory authority over the reasonableness of state permitting authorities' BACT determinations and may issue a stop construction order, under the Clean Air Act, if a BACT selection is not reasonable. We further conclude that, in exercising that authority, the Agency did not act arbitrarily or capriciously in finding that ADEC's BACT decision in this instance lacked evidentiary support. EPA's orders, therefore, were neither arbitrary nor capricious. The judgment of the Court of Appeals is accordingly Affirmed.

CASE QUESTIONS

1. The Clean Air Act is administered jointly by the states and the federal EPA. Concerning the approval of new construction that will have effects on air quality, what is the role of the state? The role of the EPA?
2. What is a PSD area? What is the applicable standard for approval of new construction in a PSD area? Describe the BACT standard.
3. What was the key two legal issues in this case? What was the Supreme Court' basis for deciding that the EPA had acted correctly? What standard of conduct was the State of Alaska supposed to meet? Why did the state fail to do so?
4. Four justices dissented from the court opinion. What do you think their arguments were? What would be your arguments, if you represented Alaska or Cominco?

When the Clean Air Act was amended in 1977, Congress placed several requirements on areas that had not achieved the national air quality standards established earlier by the EPA. The 1977 amendments required those *"nonattainment"* areas to create a permit program regulating new plants or major modifications of existing stationary sources of air pollution. In order to obtain a permit in these areas, the state or federal agency must determine that the source will use the lowest achievable emission rate. (LAER) This standard is called "technology forcing" because the word "achievable" may require the use or invention of new technology to reach the standards. The EPA regulations later issued to implement this statute allowed the states to adopt a plantwide definition of the term *stationary source* (pollution that emanates from one particular fixed point rather than mobile sources, such as automobiles).

bubble policy: An EPA rule that allows a company to expand and emit more pollution from one source of the plant, if it reduces pollution from another source. The plant is said to be under an imaginary "bubble."

These EPA regulations thus allowed businesses some flexibility in complying with the Clean Air Act under what has become known as the **bubble policy.** Under this concept, a large manufacturing plant with several different emission points may treat its facilities as though they are all under an imaginary bubble. Therefore, if the company wants to expand operations in one section of the facility (and thus increase one type of air pollution), it can legally do so as long as it reduces the discharge of that particular type of pollutant somewhere else within its facility (within the "bubble"). If a company reduces pollution without adding a new source, it receives a "credit" from EPA, which can be used later, sold, or traded to another company that wants to expand its operations in a manner that will increase the emission of that type of substance.

The U.S. Supreme Court considered the legality of the bubble policy in the following case.

CHEVRON V. NATURAL RESOURCES DEFENSE COUNCIL, INC.

467 U.S. 837 (1984)

FACTS

After the EPA adopted its regulation allowing for use of the "bubble" policy in nonattainment areas, the Natural Resources Defense Council (NRDC), an environmental group, challenged the rule. The NRDC argued that this policy was not authorized by the Clean Air Act and in fact would not achieve a reduction in the pollution levels of areas that were already out of compliance with clean air standards. The Court of Appeals agreed and set aside the EPA rule. Chevron had a large industrial plant that was going to be adversely affected if the rule was not upheld, and it appealed to the U.S. Supreme Court.

DECISION

In an opinion by Justice Stevens, the Supreme Court reversed the Court of Appeals and upheld the "bubble rule" issued by the EPA. The Court set forth a two-step procedure for reviewing a regulation of an agency. First, the Court must determine whether Congress has directly spoken with regard to the issue, and if so, the matter ends. If, however, the statute is silent as to the precise point at issue, the Court must ask whether the agency's policy is based on a permissible and reasonable construction of the law.

The 1977 Amendments did not specifically refer to or create a bubble policy. The Amendments did provide that permits were required "for the construction and operation of new or modified major stationary sources" in nonattainment areas. The earlier Clean Air Act defined "stationary source" as "any building, structure, facility, or installation which emits or may emit any air pollutant." Therefore, the real legal question here is whether the term "stationary source" can be interpreted as applying to an entire plant, containing several chimneys and stacks, rather than to each stack separately.

The EPA had articulated several reasons for the bubble policy when it was promulgated. The agency argued that the rule would encourage replacement of "older, dirtier processes and pieces of equipment with new, cleaner ones . . ." and would aid in accommodating the conflict between economic and environmental concerns.

The Supreme Court decided that in interpreting an agency's construction of a statutory provision, the court's role is not to assess the "wisdom" of the policy but only to assess if it is a reasonable choice within the gap left by Congress. The responsibility of resolving the struggle between competing views of the public interest is a policy decision best left to those in the political arena, who have constituencies.

In this case, the Court found that the administrator's interpretation represented a reasonable accommodation of manifestly competing interests and was entitled to deference, the regulatory scheme was technical and complex, the agency had considered the matter in a detailed and reasoned fashion, and the decision involved reconciling conflicting policies. In conclusion, the Court stated, "We hold that the EPA's definition of the 'source' is a permissible construction of the statute which seeks to accommodate progress in reducing air pollution with economic growth."

CASE QUESTIONS

1. Do you believe the Court's holding here will lead to a reduction in air pollution? Is the ruling good for business?
2. What would the plaintiffs have had to prove to win this case? What was the precise legal issue?
3. Is it ethical or socially responsible for a company to add a new wing to a manufacturing plant (in an area that already is in violation of federal air pollution standards), which will increase the amount of pollution, as long as the company reduces the pollution somewhere else in its facility?

It will probably not surprise you to learn that the largest source of air pollution from nonstationary sources comes from automobiles. A number of the amendments to the Clean Air Act over the years have concerned emissions of lead, nitrogen oxide, and carbon monoxide pollution from automobile exhaust. The problems are particularly acute in large cities, where auto exhaust combines with other substances in the air to form smog. The amendments to the Clean Air Act have mandated the use, in most instances, of unleaded gasoline, have required catalytic converters in new cars, and have established fuel economy standards that must be met by manufacturers in order to sell new vehicles in the United States.

The 1990 Clean Air Amendments passed by Congress called for substantial reductions in auto tailpipe emissions by 1998, and further reduction in future years. The law also required greater use of alternative fuel vehicles by companies that have fleets of vehicles. Car manufacturers were required to install new pollution control devices to reduce emissions of hydrocarbons and nitrogen oxides, and the equipment will have to last for 10 years (twice as long as previously required). Cleaner blends of gasoline ("reformulated" gasoline), including more use of methanol and ethanol additives, were required by 1995 in the nine smoggiest cities in order to reduce carbon monoxide emissions. A pilot program in California requires auto companies to produce 300,000 clean-fueled vehicles a year. Cars in California will have to get better gas mileage, and some electric cars will be produced as well.

Acid rain is a type of pollution caused when sulfur dioxide and nitrogen oxide, emitted largely from coal-burning utility plants, combine with oxygen and moisture at high elevations in the atmosphere to form solutions of nitric and sulfuric acids. When this moisture falls to the ground in the form of rain, drizzle, or snow, it causes serious damage to vegetation, lakes, fish, and other wildlife. Many of the coal-burning utility plants are in the Midwest, where the prevailing winds blow much of the pollution into the Northeastern states and Canada, although many other areas are affected as well.

The production of acid rain can be reduced by using coal with a lower sulfur content and by installing "scrubbers" in the utility plants. Not only are these measures quite expensive to implement, they have political implications as well. Although residents of the Northeast suffer the most from acid rain, corrective measures may mean the loss of industrial jobs in the Midwest and coal-mining jobs in Kentucky and West Virginia (which produce mainly high-sulfur coal). On the other hand, more mining jobs might be created in the West (which has large amounts of low-sulfur coal). In enacting the Clean Air Act of 1990, after many years of negotiations, Congress reached a compromise that requires significant reductions in emissions of nitrogen oxide and sulfur dioxide from electric and manufacturing plants.

acid rain: Pollution caused by certain gases mixed with rain, which then becomes acidic and causes damage to plants and animals.

EPA REGULATIONS AND ENFORCEMENT

Regulations issued by the EPA in 1992 called for electric utilities to cut sulfur dioxide emissions in half, at a cost to industry estimated at $3 billion per year. These rules also include provisions permitting utilities to choose how to reduce their emissions and creating a market-based trading system that allows utilities to earn *emission allowances and credits* (which can be sold or traded to other companies) for making greater reductions than necessary.

Properly called **emission allowances**, these credits allow companies with "dirty" power plants to either install new equipment to cut emissions or buy the right to exceed federal air-pollution limits from other energy companies that have reduced their emissions below what is required. This innovative concept, included in the Clean Air Act Amendments of 1990, allows market forces to help achieve reductions in pollution, rather than the "command and control" approach of many federal regulations.

Originally the EPA apportioned air pollution allowances among the 445 largest U.S. power plants and some large factories. Then, as the facilities reduced air pollution, they received additional allowances. The allowances are traded by brokerage companies across the nation, and billions of dollars of allowances have been traded. Companies that sell allowances often use the proceeds to buy state-of-the-art pollution reducing equipment. A group of brokerage firms specializing in pollution credits has emerged, and even energy companies that do not need pollution allowances have formed trading operations and buy and sell credits to increase their profits.

emission allowances: The amount of reduction in emissions of a polluting substance, which results in a "credit" granted by the EPA.

The program has been quite successful. According to the EPA, electric utilities emissions have decreased some 25 percent since 1980, while 41 percent more electricity was produced. The government's General Accounting Office estimates that the trading program saves utilities $3 billion per year over previous pollution-enforcement approaches. The main criticism of the program is that in some regions of the country, most utilities purchase credits and keep on polluting the air, after buying allowances from energy firms far away that have achieved reductions.

The United States had suggested that the concept be expanded to international trading of emissions credits. An international treaty to reduce global warming was signed by more than 80 countries in Kyoto, Japan, in 1997 calling for "greenhouse gas" (primarily carbon dioxide) emissions to be cut to below 1990 levels by 2012 but the emissions trading program was not part of the treaty. Negotiations to gain sufficient signatures for the Treaty and implement the program have been difficult, as the topics, industries, national governments, and international issues are much more complicated in a world-wide setting. The Bush administration announced in 2003 that for many reasons, the United States would not join the Kyoto Treaty and the Obama administration has agreed with this view.

The EPA has also issued regulations requiring substantial reductions in nitrogen oxide emissions. The rules are in two parts. The first required coal-fired utilities to cut emissions at a cost estimated at $300 million per year. The second part of the rule, which took effect in 1995, regulates both utility and nonutility boilers in urban areas with high smog levels and is expected to cost an estimated $500 million a year, although polluters can ask for extensions and exceptions.

The EPA believes that the new rules have cut nitrogen oxide emissions more than 2 million tons per year (from about 19 million tons 10 years ago). Utility and business groups argued that the rules are overly stringent and require costly retrofitting in many power plants and industrial boilers used for refining, manufacturing, and processing. In contrast, environmental groups have accused the EPA of being too lenient by failing to require certain technology that would have resulted in deeper cuts in nitrogen oxide (to meet the standards set by Congress) and by setting the stage for the approval of exceptions when the standards are not met.

GREENHOUSE GASES

One of the most important and hotly debated environmental issues of today concerns global warming and greenhouse gases. Many scientists argue that human activity is clearly creating a much warmer earth, which will have many undesirable consequences for people, plants, and animals due to climate changes, polar ice melting, and other effects. Politicians in several countries and political parties, however, remain unconvinced of the seriousness or cause or the reality of global warming. Since the "cure," if there is any, would require significant reduction in pollution by many industries at great expense to businesses and governments, this is a key political issue.

One of the leading causes of global warming (if one believes the scientists) is emission of "greenhouse gases" such as carbon dioxide. Since it is a controversial political issue, the EPA has received considerable pressure both to regulate, and not to regulate such gases. In 2005, twelve states and several cities in the U.S. brought a lawsuit against the EPA to force that agency to begin setting standards for carbon dioxide and other greenhouse gases. Several other states and industrial firms, as well as the EPA, opposed the lawsuit.

The law at issue was Section 202(a)(1) of the <u>Clean Air Act</u>, which requires the EPA administrator to set standards for "the emission of any air pollutant from any class or classes of new motor vehicles or new motor vehicle engines, which in his judgment cause, or contribute to, air pollution which may reasonably be anticipated to endanger public health or welfare." The Clean Air Act defines "air pollutant" as "any air pollution agent or combination of such agents, including any physical, chemical, biological, radioactive . . . substance or matter which is emitted into or otherwise enters the ambient air."

The Plaintiffs argued that the definition in the CAA was so broad that carbon dioxide must be counted as an air pollutant and that the question was controlled by the words of the statute. They filed substantial scientific evidence that the toxicity of carbon dioxide results from high concentrations and that alleged causation of global warming transforms the gas into a pollutant.

The Plaintiffs asserted that the EPA Administrator's decision not to regulate carbon dioxide and other greenhouse gases violated the terms of the CAA. If the statutory definition of the CAA included carbon dioxide, as they asserted, then the Federal courts would have no discretion to reach any other conclusion.

The EPA argued that the Administrator has the discretion under the CAA to decide not to regulate. The Administrator argued that other actions were already being taken to increase fuel efficiency of automobiles and that (as of 2003) scientific investigation was still under way. Thus, the EPA Administrator decided not to regulate *"at this time."* One of several reasons that the EPA Administrator declined to regulate carbon dioxide was uncertainty about whether man-made carbon dioxide emissions did actually cause global warming.

In 2007 the Supreme Court issued its decision in *Massachusetts v. Environmental Protection Agency*, 549 U.S. 497 (2007). Justice John Paul Stevens wrote the majority opinion in which the Court held that the Clean Air Act did give the EPA the authority to regulate tailpipe emissions of greenhouse gases. The majority opinion (which was 5-4) commented that " greenhouse gases fit well within the Clean Air Act's definition of air pollutant."

The Court remanded the case to the EPA, requiring the agency to review its contention that it has discretion in regulating carbon dioxide and other greenhouse gas emissions. The Court found the current rationale for not regulating to be inadequate and required the agency to articulate a reasonable basis in order to avoid regulation.

Chief Justice Roberts authored a dissenting opinion. He argued first that Massachusetts had no standing to present the issues. Then Roberts stated that the alleged injury (*i.e.*, Massachusetts' loss of land because of rising sea levels) was too speculative and without adequate scientific support. According to Roberts, there was not a traceable causal connection between the EPA's refusal to enforce emission standards and petitioners' injuries. He also maintained that redressing the alleged injuries was even more problematic given that countries such as India and China are responsible for a large amount of greenhouse-gas emissions.

On remand, the EPA found that six greenhouse gases "in the atmosphere may reasonably be anticipated both to endanger public health and to endanger public welfare" and thus should be regulated. However, the states of Alabama, Texas, and Virginia sought judicial review of EPA's determination in the United States Court of Appeals for the DC Circuit, so the issue is still being debated.

EPA SUES SEVEN UTILITIES FOR AIR POLLUTION VIOLATIONS

In late 1999, in one of the largest environmental enforcement actions in U.S. history, the EPA sued seven giant electric companies in the Midwest and South, alleging that they had violated the Clean Air Act. Even the federally owned Tennessee Valley Authority, the nation's largest wholesaler of electricity, was targeted for administrative action. The charges involved 32 older power plants, which comprise 30 percent of the nation's capacity of coal-fired plants. If proved, the allegations could result in hundreds of millions of dollars in fines and penalties, the installation of pollution controls costing billions, and higher utility rates for millions of consumers.

The heart of the charges was that the utility companies had made major modifications to their generating plants without modernizing pollution controls as required by the Clean Air Act. The older plants had been "grandfathered" when the 1990 amendments were enacted so they would not have to immediately comply and could make minor improvements without obtaining federal permits and meeting the new standards. However, the law required that if the plants made "major renovations" they must get permits, and install equipment that would bring them into compliance with the new standards.

Since the cases were filed, many have been settled, with the utilities agreeing to make substantial changes. In 2002 the Bush Administration EPA issued proposed new rules dealing with "New Source Reviews" which would have had the effect of allowing coal-fired utilities and others plants to make certain improvements to their facilities (that increased emissions) without triggering the BACT requirements. The changes in rules would increase the scope of the exceptions granted for "routine maintenance, repair and replacement."

Shortly after the rules were put into effect, twelve states—including California and New York—filed suit to block the rules. The lawsuits contended that the changes amounted to a significant weakening of the Clean Air Act by making it easier for some industrial polluters to avoid installing modern pollution controls. The New Source Review would only be triggered if the owner spent more than 20 percent of the cost of replacing a plant's essential production equipment Critics contended that the new rules would allow thousands of older power plants, oil refineries and industrial units to make extensive upgrades without having to install new anti-pollution devices. These changes would allow them to emit thousands of tons of pollutants and save them millions of dollars, even if emissions increased. In December 2003, a federal appeals court judge issued an injunction preventing the rules from taking effect until the lawsuit could go to trial and be decided.

The cases discussed above, brought by the EPA in 1999 have continued—some tried and some settled. In 2007, in the largest environmental settlement in Justice Department history, American Electric Power agreed to install $4.6 billion in equipment to sharply reduce emissions at coal-fired power plants in five states, sources said.

AEP, one of the nation's largest power producers, owns coal-fired plants in the Ohio River Valley. The record settlement came eight years after the Justice Department, headed by then-Attorney General Janet Reno, filed suit alleging AEP and six other power companies had "illegally released massive amounts of air pollutants for years."

SOCIAL/ETHICAL ISSUES

The EPA defines "Environmental justice" as the fair treatment and meaningful involvement of all people regardless of race, color, national origin, or income with respect to the development, implementation, and enforcement of environmental laws. While the prevention and elimination of pollution is an issue that concerns most U.S. citizens, it is clear that the worst environmental hazards are faced by minorities and the poor. A comprehensive statistical study done 15 years ago found that communities in which commercial waste facilities were located had about twice the percentage of minorities in their population as those communities without such facilities.

Some 15 studies over the past 25 years have shown that distribution of pollution was unequally concentrated based on race and in some cases, income. For example, from 1920 to 1970 in the city of Houston, all of the city-owned municipal landfills and six of the eight garbage incinerators were located in African-American neighborhoods.

One study in the Detroit area concluded that minority residents in the greater metropolitan area were four times more likely than white residents to live within one mile of a commercial hazardous waste facility. Other studies have shown that Hispanics, Native Americans, and other minorities have also borne more than their share of toxic waste facilities, polluted air, and other environmental hazards. The EPA has stated that "environmental justice is the goal to be achieved for all communities and persons across this Nation." Toward this end the EPA has set up a National Environmental Justice Advisory Council that meets and provides independent advice and consultation and recommendations to the EPA Administrator. Starting in 2003, each major program and regional EPA office was required to submit a plan detailing their efforts to integrate environmental justice into the policies, programs and activities, and give a progress report later on the accomplishments toward meeting the goal. And the EPA has other grants and activities to further its environmental justice efforts. See the EPA webpage on Environmental Justice at: www.epa.gov/compliance/environmentaljustice/index.html.

What do you think government and/or business should do about this problem? What can the public do? Is it fair that many toxic and hazardous waste facilities are located in poor and minority neighborhoods? Certainly the more well-to-do areas do not want such facilities near them. Can you suggest some solutions?

WATER POLLUTION—THE CLEAN WATER ACT

The federal government began to take a role in combating water pollution with the enactment of the *Rivers and Harbors Act* in 1899, which banned ships and manufacturing firms from discharging refuse into any navigable waterway or tributary. But significant federal involvement did not occur until 1948 with the *Federal Water Pollution Control Act*, which was substantially amended in 1972 and 1977 (*Clean Water Act*), and by the *Water Quality Act* of 1987. The combined law, as it now stands, is commonly called the *Clean Water Act* (CWA).

One aspect of the Clean Water Act requires the states to designate the uses of significant bodies of water in their jurisdictions and to establish water quality standards to reduce pollution to appropriate levels. Another important feature of the Clean Water Act is the establishment of the **National Pollutant Discharge Elimination System (NPDES),** which imposes tough standards on the discharge of pollutants from **point sources** into navigable waterways and public sewage systems. A point source is a "discernible, discrete conveyance" such as a pipe, ship, or ditch. Any person or business wishing to make a discharge from a point source must obtain a permit from the EPA. The following case, for example, involved a determination of whether the runoff from a cattle feedlot was a point source.

National Pollutant Discharge Elimination System (NPDES): The system by which those who discharge (from a point source) effluent into streams or lakes are to obtain a state or federal permit.

point source: An identifiable point where liquid waste is discharged.

CARR V. ALTA VERDE INDUSTRIES, INC.

931 F.2d 1055 (5th Cir. 1991)

FACTS

Alta Verde Industries operates a cattle feedlot on 230 acres of land in Texas, generally feeding between 20,000 and 30,000 cattle. Not surprisingly, this feedlot produces considerable waste, primarily cow manure, which drains into a wastewater disposal system of six holding ponds. Alta Verde then uses this water to irrigate and fertilize three adjacent fields.

In the spring of 1987, a series of heavy rains caused the holding ponds to exceed their capacity. In early June, Alta Verde cut a spillway out of the embankment of one pond and discharged wastewater into an unnamed tributary of Rosita Creek. Other discharges may also have resulted at that time. Two citizens filed suit, claiming that Alta Verde did not have a NPDES permit, and therefore the discharges violated the Clean Water Act. The citizens sought damages of $600,000 and an injunction prohibiting Alta Verde from any further discharges in violation of the Act. The federal district court in Texas dismissed the case, and the plaintiffs appealed.

DECISION

The Fifth Circuit Court of Appeals, in an opinion by Circuit Judge King, thoroughly analyzed various sections of the Clean Water Act. The court first addressed Alta Verde's contention that it did not need an NPDES permit for its discharges.

"The Clean Water Act [actually the Federal Water Pollution Control Amendments of 1972] was enacted with the stated purpose of restoring and maintaining the integrity of the nation's waters," wrote the court. "In order for any person lawfully to discharge any pollutant from a point source into navigable waters of the United States, that person must obtain an NPDES permit and comply with its terms." The court explained that, in general, any other discharge would be unlawful.

An NPDES permit must incorporate effluent (discharge) limitations for point sources based on guidelines "promulgated by EPA on an industry-by-industry basis." [33 U.S.C. §1311(b)] requires the EPA to establish effluent limitations guidelines for existing point sources . . . based on the application of the "best available technology economically achievable" (BAT).

Alta Verde claimed, however, that it qualified for an exemption under the EPA regulations dealing with animal feedlots. The Clean Water Act specifically defined point source as including "concentrated animal feeding operations" [33 U.S.C. §1362]. An EPA regulation offered more detail:

A concentrated animal feeding operation [exists] if . . . more than 300 slaughter or feeder cattle [are contained] and pollutants are discharged into navigable waters. . . .

Provided, however, that no animal feeding operation is a concentrated feeding operation as defined above if such animal feeding operation discharges only in the event of a 25-year, 24-hour storm event. 40 C.F.R. §122, App. B (1988).

Therefore, if a feeding operation met the tests set forth in the second paragraph of this regulation, it was not treated as a concentrated feeding operation, was not considered a "point source," and did not need an NPDES permit. Alta Verde admitted that it was a feeding operation with more than 300 cattle but argued that it should be exempted under the second paragraph. Why? Its wastewater system could contain effluent pollution except for a 25-year storm, stated Alta Verde.

A "25-year, 24-hour" storm is defined as one that has a probability of occurring only once every 25 years. Experts testified at the trial that in the Eagle Pass area (where Alta Verde was located), such a storm would mean total rainfall of 7.1 inches in 24 hours. However, this level was not reached in the storm that led to the Alta Verde discharge. The lower court determined that the accidental discharge was caused not only by one storm but by the combined rainfall that had occurred during the spring, which exceeded Alta Verde's disposal system capacity.

The district court had found that the Alta Verde facility probably could have met the EPA effluent guidelines at the time of the accident and certainly by the time of the trial. However, the facts as determined by the trial court (there was no jury), showed that the Alta Verde facility *did discharge wastewater*, without the occurrence of a 25-year storm, regardless of the technical capacity of the system. Since an exemption from the permit requirements only applies to operations that discharge "only" in the event of a 25-year, 24-hour storm, clearly Alta Verde did not qualify. Thus, the EPA effluent guidelines quoted previously did not provide an exception to the NPDES requirement, as argued by Alta Verde.

Alta Verde also argued that the plaintiffs lacked "standing" to challenge its operations. According to a recent U.S. Supreme Court decision (Gwaltney), in order to bring a citizen suit under the Clean Water Act, the plaintiffs must show that they are seeking to "enjoin or otherwise abate an ongoing violation." To do so, they must make a "good faith allegation of continuous or intermittent violations" by the defendant.

Standing is usually determined at the time the case is filed, and since at that time Alta Verde had no NPDES permit, there was a violation of the law. Because no permit had since been obtained by Alta Verde, there was a "continuing violation" of the act, stated the Court. Although Alta Verde had improved its wastewater disposal system since the discharge, the lower court found that it still might not be sufficient to hold discharges from a "catastrophic or chronic rainfall" (much less a 25-year storm). Therefore, the "trier of fact" (the lower court) could conclude that there was "a likelihood of a recurrence of intermittent or sporadic violations," which would violate the act. The plaintiffs thus had standing to challenge the actions of the defendant Alta Verde. The decision of the lower court was reversed and remanded for further proceedings.

CASE QUESTONS

1. What was the point of discharge in this case? What is the definition of a point source discharge?
2. Why did Alta Verde think that an NPDES permit was not needed in this case?
3. When is an NPDES permit required? What is the purpose of such a permit?
4. Alta Verde Industries was a large commercial operation. The owners felt, in 1987, that their wastewater disposal system was sufficient to contain the discharge of cow manure effluent from their operations, even in a 25-year storm. After the accident in 1987, further improvements were made to the system. Is it fair, or just, to subject the company to another trial for damages over the 1987 discharges into the creek? Is society served by this procedure?
5. What is the public policy basis for allowing other private citizens (not just the EPA) to bring legal actions to enforce statutes passed by Congress?

The previous case includes terms such as **effluents** and BAT. The EPA has issued increasingly tough standards regarding any substances (called effluents) discharged into waterways. In order to obtain permits, industrial sources originally were required to meet standards based on the **"best practicable technology currently available" (BPT).** However, as the Alta Verde case demonstrated, new sources of pollution and all other point sources were required to meet higher standards—**"the best available technology economically achievable" (BAT).** These standards have been called *"technology-forcing,"* because they may require an industrial firm to develop new measures of treating effluent discharges in order to obtain a permit rather than use the technology that is "currently available," as they can under the BPT standards. The BAT standards speak of the "maximum use of technology within the economic capability of the owner or operator," which will result in "reasonable further progress toward eliminating the discharge of all pollutants." Thus, a firm may have to expend the maximum economic resources possible in order to obtain a permit under the BAT standards. Toxic wastes are covered by BAT rules.

In *Environmental Protection Agency v. National Crushed Stone Association,* the U.S. Supreme Court held that, although the law allowed the EPA to grant businesses variances from the tougher BAT guidelines where the firm had spent all that it was economically possible for it to do, no variances were possible under the less-stringent BPT standards. The court stated that the EPA administrator was empowered to make the determination, when a BPT regulation was established, that the benefits of effluent reduction were worth the costs imposed on the industry.

Thus, to grant a variance (exception) to an individual firm because it cannot bear the normal costs of the technological requirements is inconsistent with Congress's intent. Stated the court, "The 1977 limitations were intended to reduce the total pollution produced by an industry, [which] . . . necessarily imposed additional costs on the segment of the industry with the least effective technology." The Supreme Court noted pointedly that "if the statutory goal is to be achieved, these costs must be borne or the point source eliminated," even if that meant some plants must close. As to the tougher, technology-forcing BAT standards, however, the court ruling did permit variances on some occasions.

The Clean Water Act has been applied to wetlands where the water in the wetland flows into a navigable waterway. As mentioned the CWA requires a permit for pollutant discharges, and a "discharge" is defined as "any addition" of "any pollutant" to the navigable waters of the United States from any "point source." Sometimes the CWA can be applied to actions such as farming, mining, or excavating that destroy or alter wetlands, even though no outside pollutant has been added to the water. Courts have ruled on occasion that significant disturbance to the soil of land adjoining wetlands which is adjacent to navigable waters requires a permit before action can be taken.

In an important decision in 2004, the U.S. Supreme Court had to consider a situation involving the rapidly urbanizing Broward County in Florida, and the neighboring Florida Everglades. In *South Florida Water Management District v. Miccosukee Tribe,* a water district (SFWMD) had installed a massive diesel-powered pump which propelled water uphill from a drainage canal containing Broward County's run-off into a 915 square mile section of the Everglades conservation area. No NPDES permit had been obtained.

effluent: Liquid substances discharged into waterways.

BPT standard: Best practicable control technology currently available; the average of the best existing technology of industrial plants of various sizes.

BAT standard: The best available technology—that is, control and treatment—that now exists or is capable of being achieved.

Without the pump, western Broward County would flood within days. But the run-off is highly polluted, containing levels of phosphorous up to 10 times higher than the applicable water quality standard. The elevated phosphorous is noxious to fish and native flora, such as sawgrass that provide critical habitat for endangered species. The conservation land in the Everglades was leased to the Miccosukee Tribe, which brought an action to have the pumping stopped under the Clean Water Act, for lack of a permit.

The SFWMD first claimed that the pump was not a "point source" and the pumped water was not "an addition" of pollutants because the pump was just moving water from one place to another. The Supreme Court rejected this argument. "Point source" is defined in the CWA as "any discernible, confined and discrete conveyance . . . from which pollutants are or may be discharged," 33 U.S.C. δ 1362 (14) and as such it need not be the original source of pollutant, but need only convey it to navigable waters. Justice O'Conner wrote the Supreme Court opinion, stating that the pump was a "conveyance" covered by the CWA, just as a pipe, ditch, channel or tunnel . . . which do not themselves generate pollutants but merely transport them."

However, the Supreme Court did not fully enter judgment for the Tribe. All the parties agreed that the Clean Water Act does not prevent the movement of pollution within the same body of water, because there is no "addition" of pollutants. Justice O'Conner analogized "if one takes a ladle of soup from a pot, lifts it above the pot, and pours it back into the pot, one has not added soup or anything else to the pot." The water district argued, in essence, that the Everglades was all one body of water, and the pump was merely moving water from one part to another.

The Supreme Court remanded the case back to the lower court for further fact-finding on this issue. The ramifications of a decision that the Everglades and the Broward County run-off were the same body of water could be catastrophic. While the court noted that there were some groundwater connections between the two, and some "seepage" across the levies, (to be fully considered on remand) it does seem that they are distinct types of water. As one commentator noted, "it is preposterous for the SFWMD to contend that a man-made canal that drains run-off from suburbs, gas stations, and shopping malls is somehow the same body of water as the "River of Grass" in the Tribe's conservation area." If the court rules for the SFWMD it would have the ripple effect of "allowing continued unregulated pollution of rivers, lakes, and streams across the country." [Noah Sachs, "*Muddy Waters: Why Both Sides are Declaring a Victory After a Supreme Court Clean Water Act Decision*," FindLaw.com, April 1, 2004.]

Another section of the Clean Water Act deals with the perils posed by the transport of petroleum products by oil tankers. Unfortunately, incidents of such oil spills are not uncommon. Perhaps the most publicized accident happened in 1989, when the tanker *Exxon Valdez* ran aground in Prince William Sound, Alaska, spilling an estimated 11 million gallons of crude oil. The oil spread for 700 miles, causing serious pollution damage to Alaskan waters and shoreline and killing thousands of fish. In addition, more than 36,000 birds died, including at least 100 bald eagles. As the result of that accident, Exxon was charged with two felonies and three misdemeanors by the federal government and was sued by the United States, the state of Alaska, and more than

1,000 other individuals in civil cases. A jury in Alaska ordered Exxon to pay more than $5 billion to these parties, although that amount was later reduced to $500 million by the U.S. Supreme Court. Exxon also spent more than $2 billion on its own in cleanup costs.

In April 2010, a huge explosion occurred at the British Petroleum (BP) oil rig Deepwater Horizon, some 50 miles off the Louisiana coast, killing workers and creating an immense oil spill. Oil gushed from the well for 87 days, but by the time it was capped, more than 5 million barrels of oil had escaped into the Gulf. This disaster caused tremendous damage to the Gulf waters, affecting many whose livelihoods depended on fishing, shrimp, or tourism. BP has set up a $20 billion fund to pay those injured as well as state and local governments for cleanup costs. As of April 2011 the fund had paid out $4 billion in claims to 200,000 people. Many lawsuits have been filed against BP, Transocean, and others involved in building and maintaining the oil rig.

WETLANDS

Areas saturated or inundated by surface or groundwater are considered **wetlands** and are covered by the Clean Water Act. It has been recognized in recent years that these areas are an important part of the ecosystem, supporting a wide variety of plant and animal species. The EPA has therefore taken steps to protect such areas as swamps, marshes, and bogs from destruction by developers and others.

In order to make any change in an area designated as a wetland, a permit must be obtained from the Army Corps of Engineers. The EPA may block the issuance of a permit under the Clean Water Act, to prevent environmental damage. Nevertheless, some 10,000 permits are granted each year allowing dredging or filling in wetlands. There have been criminal charges brought, and severe fines and penalties assessed for violating this law.

> **wetlands:** Areas saturated or inundated by surface or groundwater.

NON–POINT SOURCES OF POLLUTION

The focus of EPA enforcement efforts under the CWA in the past has been directed at the discharge of effluent from identifiable point sources, as we have discussed. However, the EPA has issued a series of proposed regulations that would begin to regulate pollution from *non–point sources*, such as the runoff from farms, logging operations, parking lots, mining and other large sites. These operations do not have a readily ascertainable pipe or ditch that carries liquid material, but estimates are that as much as 50 percent of water pollution comes from such sources.

The proposed EPA regulations would require the states to submit plans for controlling such pollution and cleaning up waterways that fail to meet water quality standards for fishing, drinking, and swimming, depending on the category in which the waterway is placed. Large hog and poultry farms, cattle feedlots, and dairy operations produce vast amounts of waste, which flows into lakes and streams. Currently less than 2,000 livestock operations are covered by EPA regulations (because of the exceptions discussed in the *Alta Verde* case), and the new regulations would require another 18,000 such operations to obtain permits.

The manure produced on these huge "factory farms," is often used as fertilizer on many other farms as well. The runoffs from thousands of farms and other agricultural facilities after a rainstorm are rich in nutrients like nitrogen and phosphorous, deprive lakes and streams of oxygen essential to maintaining viable fisheries, and may also cause dangerous toxic microorganisms, which have caused fish kills in Maryland and the Carolinas. Loggers would be affected as well and might have to place buffers along streams to control runoff from their operations.

THE ENDANGERED SPECIES ACT

Endangered Species Act: A federal law enacted to protect plant and animal species from extinction.

In the past few years, the **Endangered Species Act** has become one of the more controversial environmental laws. This statute, enacted in 1973, requires the Secretary of the Interior to list those animal and plant species that are either **"endangered"** (in danger of becoming extinct) or **"threatened"** (slightly less serious) and to define the critical habitat of these species.

The Act then states that each federal agency shall, in consultation with the Secretary, "insure that any action authorized, funded, or carried out by such agency . . . is not likely to jeopardize the continued existence of any endangered species or threatened species or result in the destruction or adverse modification of habitat of such species . . . ."

Several prominent cases have involved situations in which a business firm was prevented from undertaking some activity, often mining or logging, because such action would cause adverse effects to an endangered species. One much-publicized case concerned the adverse effects that extensive logging in Oregon was having on the northern spotted owl. In the aftermath of that court decision, the Forest Service put into effect substantial restrictions on logging in federal forests. These reductions in the allowable timber harvest caused job losses and layoffs in the timber industry, and numerous protesters argued that "people should be more important than owls."

Congress has been taking a hard look at modifications to the Endangered Species Act to determine if the benefits of preserving a species and its habitat should always outweigh the adverse economic costs to the surrounding community or if some balancing test should be required. In the Pacific Northwest, a vigorous debate has been taking place over the rapidly decreasing numbers of salmon returning from the ocean to their native steams to spawn and whether the removal of several dams on major rivers such as the Snake and Columbia would help their survival. The fish have a hard time climbing the 100–200 foot walls of these dams, as they try to return to the rivers where they were born. "Fish ladders" have been built along the sides of many of the dams, and some fish do make it upriver, but the number of salmon returning to the rivers of their origin has dropped considerably from their former levels, although 2010 saw an increase in the number of salmon returning to mountain rivers in Idaho and Washington. On the other hand, the dams provide a steady supply of relatively cheap electric power to the northwest, as well as irrigation and flood control, and are strongly supported by farming, ranching and industrial users.

During the past 20 years or so, federal agencies have built and operated several large fish hatcheries in the Northwest to raise millions of salmon smolts which are then put into streams where they try to make their way to the Pacific. Some of the juvenile salmon are put in barges to carry them around the dams on their migration to the sea, and also the water flow is increased over dam spillways and fish ladders to help the fish in their downstream journey. But the reduced flow of water increases the need for power companies to purchase more expensive power elsewhere to meet users' needs. In a case decided in 2004, a federal judge in Portland ordered the Bonneville Power Administration (which supplies electricity to the region) not to reduce the amount of water to be spilled over 4 dams on the Snake and Columbia Rivers to assist the salmon migration, as the agency had planned to do. The judge stated that "I don't want anyone to walk out of here thinking I ignored the public interest in ratepayer dollars . . . It's a difficult case, but my job is to consider the Endangered Species Act and the fate of juvenile salmon," said the judge, calling the summer spill cut plan "arbitrary and capricious." This case is still pending and the government has submitted several plans for how best to protect the salmon without "breaching" (tearing down) the dams, as some environmental groups have urged. Another major hearing is set for Summer 2011.

HAZARDOUS AND TOXIC WASTE

The disposal of the millions of tons of waste generated by agriculture, business, and individuals is one of our major environmental problems today. Congress has attempted to control all aspects of the use and disposal of various toxic and hazardous water materials by enacting a series of important statutes in the past 35 years, several of which are discussed in the following sections.

THE RESOURCE CONSERVATION AND RECOVERY ACT

The **Resource Conservation and Recovery Act** (RCRA) was passed in 1976 as an attempt to control substances defined as **hazardous waste** from the "cradle to the grave." The EPA has defined "hazardous waste" to include any solid waste or combination of solid wastes that, when improperly treated, stored, transported, or disposed of, may pose a substantial hazard to human health or the environment. RCRA instituted a **manifest system** to track and control such wastes from the time they are generated, through their transportation, storage, and use, to their ultimate disposal. A permit must be obtained when the wastes are created and must be updated (and accompany the materials) at each subsequent waste management stage.

The intent of RCRA is to prohibit the previously common practice of simply dumping hazardous materials either on land or in the water. Operators of hazardous waste facilities are now required to obtain permits and to comply with tough standards regarding the construction and operation of their businesses, as well as to maintain a certain level of insurance and provide financial assurances. Although the law exempts municipal resource recovery facilities that receive and burn only household waste, companies and individuals who improperly dispose of hazardous waste or are involved with illegal disposal practices by someone else (e.g., a hazardous waste facility) also have significant liability under RCRA.

Resource Conservation and Recovery Act (RCRA): A federal law requiring that certain hazardous wastes be documented and tracked from the time they come into existence until proper disposal.

hazardous waste: Solid waste that poses a substantial hazard to human health.

manifest system: A series of documents designed to track hazardous waste.

In 1984, Congress passed the *Hazardous and Solid Waste Amendments Act*, which added several new programs to RCRA. Regulations were added concerning underground storage tanks, tighter control of small quantity generators, "corrective action" to clean up facilities, and other provisions. The 1984 amendments also required generators of hazardous waste to report to the EPA on their plans for reducing the amount and toxicity of their wastes. This law also added increased penalties for violations, significantly toughened criminal provisions, and authorized private citizens to bring suits when the EPA fails to act.

THE TOXIC SUBSTANCES CONTROL ACT

Toxic Substances Control Act (TSCA): A federal law that requires the notification to, and approval of, the EPA before chemicals can be made or imported.

The **Toxic Substances Control Act (TSCA)**, passed in 1976, requires the EPA to develop a complete inventory of all existing chemicals, along with the characteristics and hazards of each. Americans have now discovered that the thousands of new chemicals developed in recent years to make our lives easier often have long-range negative effects on humans and our environment that were not intended or known when the substances were produced.

In addition to the inventory of existing chemicals, TSCA requires manufacturers to notify the EPA 90 days before manufacturing or importing any new chemicals. The EPA may require testing and analysis of such chemicals before they can be used. The EPA also may prevent use of the substance entirely or require labeling or restrictions on certain uses, and may mandate the reporting of any adverse reactions that occur. The EPA has, for example, totally banned further production of polychlorinated biphenyls (PCBs). Congress did, however, establish a cost/benefit test for TSCA regulations. The law requires that EPA demonstrate a "reasonable basis" for its rules and show that the regulations adopted were the "least burdensome" necessary to achieve a level of "minimum reasonable risk."

THE COMPREHENSIVE ENVIRONMENTAL RESPONSE, COMPENSATION, AND LIABILITY ACT OF 1980 (CERCLA) AND THE "SUPERFUND"

Comprehensive Environmental Response, Compensation, and Liability Act (CERCLA) ("Superfund") Law: A federal law that provides funding for the cleaning up of contaminated areas and imposes strict liability on "owners or operators."

The main purpose of the two laws described previously (RCRA and TSCA) is to **prevent** environmental damage from occurring through a detailed series of controls on the production, treatment, handling, and disposal of hazardous substances. Similarly, the primary purpose of the Clean Air Act and Clean Water Act is to prevent air and water pollution before it occurs. In contrast, the **Comprehensive Environmental Response, Compensation, and Liability Act (CERCLA)** is primarily concerned with providing funding and appropriate legal mechanisms for *cleaning up* sites where improper use and disposal of hazardous waste has caused serious environmental damage.

A number of environmental disasters in the 1970s caused Congress to consider how to redress serious environmental contamination after it had occurred. Perhaps the most-publicized incident took place in the Love Canal area in New York state. Here, a canal originally dug many years earlier to connect Lake Ontario with the Niagara River had been used as a dumpsite for more than 80 deadly chemicals during the 1940s and 1950s. Eventually, a residential subdivision and school were built on the site. In following years, many of the residents experienced serious health problems. As a result, the site was abandoned, and the government purchased all the homes. Legal actions involving Love Canal are still winding their way through the courts.

When Congress enacted CERCLA in 1980, the goal was to provide funds for cleaning up contaminated areas and to impose legal and financial responsibility on those who owned or operated such property, those who transported or arranged for disposal of the waste, and on those who caused the harm. The words *compensation* and *liability* are at the heart of CERCLA and are not found in the other environmental laws. In order to implement the law, the EPA publishes annually a list of the most seriously contaminated sites in the United States called the "Superfund List." The EPA can then either start cleaning up the site or attempt to require others to do it.

When it enacted CERCLA, Congress set up a huge fund to pay for the cleanup of contaminated sites. Over the years, more than $15 billion has been put into this cleanup fund, which has become known as the **"Superfund."** Part of the money came from Congressional appropriations and part from a tax assessed on crude oil and certain chemicals and other large corporations. However the tax part of the law expired in 1995 and has not been renewed. The EPA asked for $150 million in cleanup funds in recent years, but received only $23 million from Congress. The Superfund budget is now lower than any time since 1988.

Work on a number of important Superfund sites was being slowed down due to a shortage of funds. The residents of the contaminated areas are not happy. One resident of Tar Creek, Oklahoma where mining companies left pilings of lead and zinc reaching 200 feet high says that while the government has spent $132 million restoring residents' yards and playgrounds with uncontaminated soil "we still have a creek that runs orange" and "our people are sicker. We want things better; to clean up all the waste so it won't continue to harm us for the next four or five generations."

When the EPA identifies the Superfund sites that need to be cleaned up, it looks **for potentially responsible parties (PRPs)** to hold responsible. Under the CERCLA as amended, PRPs include (1) the current owner or operator of the site; (2) the owner or operator at the time the hazardous wastes were put on the property; (3) any person who arranged for the treatment or disposal of the hazardous substances at the facility; or (4) any person who transported hazardous substances to and/or selected the facility.

The EPA has vigorously enforced CERCLA against various individual and corporate parties who have owned or operated sites where wastes have been deposited, as well as those who actually deposited the wastes. CERCLA is a *strict liability law*, which means that parties may be found liable for cleanup costs, even though they were not "at fault." For example, the current owner of the property, or a previous owner who leased the land to a business tenant, may have had no role in causing the pollution problem but still may be held responsible for the costs of the cleanup. Some estimate the average cost of a Superfund site cleanup at $25 million and the costs are rising each year. And because the doctrine of *joint and several liability* is used in CERCLA cases, one of the defendants may end up paying the whole cost of the remediation and then have to try to recover a share by suing other defendants. Often the party who actually contaminated the site is not in business any longer or has filed for bankruptcy. Therefore the government can seek compensation from one or a few defendants and then that defendant may institute actions to obtain reimbursement for part of its expenses from other responsible parties.

Another important issue for business is whether a parent corporation can be held liable under CERCLA for cleanup expenses due to the actions of a subsidiary [a parent corporation owns most or all of the stock of the subsidiary corporation]. Often the parent corporation has considerably more financial assets, and the government or one of the other parties held responsible for CERCLA expenses will be seeking to recover significant costs. Lower court decisions in a number of cases had established different tests for determining when a parent corporation should be held liable for actions of a subsidiary. In 1998 the U.S. Supreme Court considered such an issue and rendered an important decision in the following case.

UNITED STATES V. BESTFOODS

118 S. Ct. 1876 (1998)

FACTS

This case concerned an action by the federal government (EPA) to recover the costs of cleaning up contamination created by a Michigan chemical plant that had been operated by a subsidiary of CPC International, Inc. from 1965 to 1972. [There were several defendants in this case, including Bestfoods, CPC, Cordova Chemical Company (the current owner), and other owners and operators of the property.] The issue on appeal primarily concerned the liability of CPC for the actions of its subsidiary.

During the early 1960s, while the property was owned by a chemical manufacturer, the groundwater under the site became contaminated. Then in 1965 the land was purchased by Ott Chemical Co., a subsidiary of CPC International. Over the next seven years, the disposal of chemical waste in unlined lagoons and overflows of chemicals from a storage basin caused additional pollution of the soil, surface water, and groundwater. The property was later owned by several other parties before the EPA became involved in cleaning up the site in 1981. Later the government sued five former and present owners and operators for liability under CERCLA, and all private owners were held liable by the district court. On appeal, the Sixth Circuit Court of Appeals reversed the liability of CPC, holding that there was no basis for piercing the corporate veil and holding it liable for the actions of its subsidiary, either as an owner or operator. The United States then appealed to the U.S. Supreme Court.

DECISION

The Supreme Court carefully reviewed the language of CERCLA, and the general principle that parent corporations are not liable for the acts of their subsidiaries. Under CERCLA rules liability attaches to (1) the present "owner or operator" of a contaminated facility, and (2) any prior "owner or operator" whose ownership coincided with the contamination of the property. In this instance, since CPC was not the current owner, its only liability would be if it was found to be an "owner or operator" at the time of the disposal of hazardous waste. CPC never did own the property in its own name, and therefore its liability, if any, must be premised on (1) the fact that CPC was an "owner" because of its subsidiary's ownership or (2) the fact that CPC was directly liable as an "operator."

The Supreme Court, in a unanimous opinion written by Justice Souter, vacated and remanded the case for additional evidence. First, the Court looked at CERCLA and determined that the law did not attempt to change the general rule that a corporation is generally not liable for acts of its subsidiaries. However, under fundamental principles of corporate law (as explained in Chapter 9) the corporate veil may be pierced when the corporate form has been misused to accomplish wrongful purposes, most notably fraud of some type. Then, one or more shareholders (in this case, the parent company, which owned most of the stock of the subsidiary) can be held individually liable. The Court called this "derivative" liability.

The district court had held CPC liable largely because CPC had selected Ott's board of directors and filled Ott's executive ranks with CPC officials, and another CPC official had played a significant role in shaping Ott's environmental policy. The Sixth Circuit reversed, finding that whether the parent corporation has derivative liability depends on an analysis of state law principles on piercing the corporate veil, not merely on the fact that the boards of directors of the two companies are quite similar. The Supreme Court agreed with this analysis, and further criticized certain lower court opinions that had imposed vicarious (derivative) liability on corporations because of interlocking boards of directors with the subsidiary.

The Supreme Court stated that a finding of "operator" liability under CERCLA must focus on the parent corporation's relationship with the *facility* at issue, not its relationship with its *subsidiary*. In other words, the parent corporation would only be liable if it actually played a significant part in *operating the facility*, not just having a large role in the management of the subsidiary corporation. The plain language of CERCLA defines *operator* as "any person . . . operating" a facility. Looking further into the meaning of *operator* the Court held that it means:

Manages, directs, or conducts operations specifically related to pollution, that is, operations having to do with the leakage or disposal of hazardous waste, or decisions about compliance with environmental regulations.

Applying this definition to the facts of the case, Justice Souter wrote that activities that are normal for a parent corporation to do in monitoring the activities of its subsidiary, such as reviewing finances, looking at budgetary matters, and setting general policies, do not give rise to liability as an "operator." Nor did interlocking directors (the same people sitting on the boards of the parent and the subsidiary) create operator

liability. It is a well-established norm of corporate law for directors and officers of a parent and a subsidiary to hold positions with both.

Finding that CPC did not have derivative liability, the Court turned to the question of whether it had direct liability as an operator. Here, the Supreme Court did not agree with the Sixth Circuit's narrow application of the test for direct liability. Although the existence of interlocking directorates would not be enough for the parent to be held directly liable as an operator, other facts needed to be analyzed. For example, a parent's decision to send an employee of its own to direct disposal and compliance activities of the facility might create direct liability on the part of the parent.

In fact, noted the Court, there was some evidence here that an agent of CPC alone engaged in activities at Ott's plant that were "eccentric" under accepted norms of parental oversight of a subsidiary's facility. Careful examination of the facts of each case is necessary to "distinguish a parental officer's oversight of a subsidiary from his control over the operation of the subsidiary's facility." Here, the District Court's opinion speaks of an agent who played a conspicuous part in dealing with the toxic risks emanating from the plant's operation. This is enough to raise an issue of fact regarding CPC's possible operation of the facility. The case thus must be remanded to the trial court for further hearings and evidence in order to resolve that issue.

CASE QUESTIONS

1. What actions would a parent corporation have to take to be held vicariously liable (on a derivative basis) for the acts of its subsidiary, according to the Court? What actions of a parent are considered "normal" supervision of a subsidiary, and thus do not create liability as an "operator"?
2. When is a parent corporation held liable as an operator of a facility? What actions are considered those of an operator?
3. What advice would you give to managers, officers, and directors of companies, in view of the Bestfoods decision?

innocent landowner: One who carefully researches the history of a property prior to purchase and has no knowledge of any improper disposal of hazardous wastes.

In response to considerable commentary about the unfairness of possibly imposing significant liability on anyone who ever owned the land, Congress has added the **"innocent landowner" defense** to CERCLA. To benefit from this defense, an owner must show that the party ("third party") who contaminated the site was not an employee or in any contractual relation with the owner. If the owner purchased the property from a third party, the current owner must demonstrate that he or she exercised "due diligence" before purchasing the property and that he or she had no knowledge nor any reason to know that hazardous substances were disposed of on the land. To establish such knowledge, the amended CERCLA law provides that the innocent owner must show that it made "all appropriate inquiry into the previous ownership and uses of the property consistent with good commercial or customary practice in an effort to minimize liability."

MEMO FROM THE LEGAL DEPARTMENT

To: Students

From: Legal Department

Although the EPA has attempted to clarify and limit the liability of "innocent" parties, the potential consequences of being named a Superfund defendant are enormous. It is foolish for any business to purchase, use, or take a security interest in commercial property, or make any substantial commitment of funds regarding such property, without making a thorough assessment of all environmental issues. All prudent lending institutions now require a detailed "environmental assessment," prepared by scientific consultants, on properties the lenders are considering taking a security interest in, and other businesses should do no less.

In addition to the potential Superfund liability of creditors for the cost of cleaning up environmental contamination, other cases have involved the liability of parent and subsidiary corporations, joint venture partners, and corporate officers and managers, who were somehow involved with the property. A number of company officials have gone to jail as the result of environmental misdeeds.

Any well-run business must have a clear corporate policy, coming from the top, stating that (1) environmental concerns are a high priority, (2) internal compliance efforts must be continuous and serious, (3) problems that do occur are promptly and effectively corrected (not covered up), (4) violators are punished, and (5) continuous improvement in environmental practices of the firm is a top corporate goal and strategy.

In addition, it is important to use care in choosing one's business associates. Why? The law imposes significant liability, and it is not unusual for poorly run firms to improperly dispose of hazardous wastes and have serious financial difficulties and/or go out of business. The result is that society will look for another firm to hold responsible for cleaning up the damage. The joint and several liability allowed by CERCLA often means that a financially sound company will end up paying the full cost of a CERCLA cleanup because the company that dumped the waste is no longer in existence.

LENDER LIABILITY UNDER CERCLA

Lending institutions have had great concern about potential liability under CERCLA as well. Typically, when a bank makes a mortgage loan to enable a person or company to purchase real property, the lender will take a mortgage on the land. But if the land should later show indications of contamination, does the lender really want to foreclose the mortgage? Suddenly it is the "owner" of the property, and therefore a potentially responsible party under CERCLA (and a PRP with a lot of money, or so it would seem!).

An appellate case decided in 1990 reinforced the fears of the lending community. In *U.S. v. Fleet Factors Corp,* 901 F.2d 1550 (11th Cir. 1990), the lender's motion to be dismissed from a CERCLA case involving property on which it held a mortgage was denied. The court found that liability was possible if the creditor participated in management to a degree indicating a capacity to influence the corporation's treatment of hazardous waste—that is, if the creditor "could affect hazardous waste disposal decisions if it so chose." This case opened the door for tremendous liability exposure for lenders who become actively involved in trying to assist a struggling business owner with contamination issues.

In 1996, Congress amended the CERCLA law by enacting the Asset Conservation, Lender Liability, and Deposit Insurance Protection Act. This law excluded from the "owner or operator" definition in CERCLA a lender who did not participate in the management of a facility prior to foreclosure. The law defined *participate in management* as "actually participating in the management or operational affairs of the facility." Such a definition should eliminate the possibility of holding the lender liable merely because it had "the capacity" to influence management. But lenders need to be careful because when a commercial business starts to fall substantially behind in its mortgage loan payments to a bank, there is a temptation on the part of the bank to get involved in helping the business firm solve its problems, which may involve on-site assistance. That could be dangerous to the bank.

Therefore, lenders today should be exempt from CERCLA liability as owners or operators as long as they stay in their role as creditor and do not become active in managing the facility. Nevertheless, it has become standard, prudent practice in the lending industry to make no loans on real property without doing a careful, thorough "environmental assessment" of the property. Such an assessment should include not only a careful review of the title history (to see who owned the property) but an actual on-site investigation, perhaps taking soil and water samples, if the property has ever been used in an industrial or commercial way.

SOCIAL/ETHICAL ISSUES

In one case decided under CERCLA, the owner of the property, Ashland Oil, was held solely liable for $10 million in order to clean up contamination on property it owned but had leased to another business. Ashland argued that this was unjust and unfair. "We are saddled with liability, just because we are the landlord," said Ashland. The lending institution, Ashland continued, "ought to contribute because it was responsible for the business." Ashland argued that the lender should have looked at to whom they were lending. What do you think? Is it right to make Ashland pay all or part of the cost? Should the financial institution that financed the business share in the cleanup cost?

CIVIL AND CRIMINAL ENFORCEMENT

All of the laws mentioned in this chapter are enforced by the EPA. Most of them also allow one landowner to sue a person or company whose actions cause damage to the landowner's property. Some also allow "citizen" suits, where an individual (and often an environmental or community organization) is suing to enforce the provisions of an environmental law, as in *Alta Verde*.

The vast majority of actions brought by the EPA are regulatory in nature. That is, the actions are brought first within the administrative law system as outlined in Chapter 5, and then many are appealed through the federal court system. These actions generally seek civil fines and enforcement orders due to alleged violations of one of the environmental laws examined in this chapter (or one of the many others we did not have space to mention).

When the EPA feels that a particularly serious or intentional violation has occurred, it refers the case to the Department of Justice, which has the power to initiate criminal charges. The EPA has an Enforcement Investigations Center with a staff of more than 200 (including 50 special agents trained as criminal investigators) who work closely with the Justice Department's Environmental Crimes Unit in initiating criminal charges for environmental violations. While a relatively small part of the total enforcement of environmental laws, criminal enforcement is taken seriously. These cases take more time to handle and are typically more complex. Business groups sometimes argue that the EPA should stick to bringing only civil, administrative charges. Environmental groups, however, believe that criminal charges are important. An attorney with one group stated, "I think it is very important to set an example by bringing some criminal charges. There is nothing more chilling than sending someone from the boardroom to the jailhouse."

For example, a chemical company salesman from Ohio was convicted for illegally transporting hazardous waste from Ohio and disposing of it in Georgia in violation of the RCRA. The salesman was also ordered to pay almost $150,000 in restitution to the owner of the land in Georgia on which he had abandoned 317 tons of hazardous waste (*U.S. v. Cunningham*, (11th Cir. 1999).

Company officials and individuals have also been found criminally responsible for environmental actions under state law. For example, the president of one chemical storage company was sentenced to 14 years in prison for dumping chlorinated solvents onto the water table. Richard Newman, president and chief executive officer (CEO) of Thoro Products of Arvada, Colorado, was convicted of violating Colorado's hazardous waste laws and of committing criminal mischief. Mr. Newman was found to have been directly involved in his firm's "repeated, intentional, and reckless" dumping of hazardous wastes over a 13-year period, which caused a "toxic plume" one-half mile wide and one and one-half miles long.

SUMMARY

Environmental issues are among the most important and controversial public policy issues of our time. We all value clean air and water, open spaces, and wilderness, and we treasure our rich variety of birds, fish, and wildlife. Yet the American public is also concerned about jobs and employment. We want our businesses to be able to continue to grow and prosper, and to be able to expand to meet new global competition. When a manufacturing facility seeks to expand, it often causes a conflict between environmental regulations and the desire for increased employment opportunities. Those of you who will be business managers in the next few years will face many complex decisions in balancing the need for growth with protection of the environment.

The primary federal environmental laws explored in this chapter include the Clean Air Act, which seeks to cut air pollution by establishing federal standards which are enforced and interpreted by the states, and the Clean Water Act, which requires permits be obtained prior to the discharge of effluent material into all navigable waterways in the United States. Regulation of chemical substances and toxic material is the priority of the TSCA and the

RCRA. Once an area has been contaminated, the CERCLA allows the EPA to use its "Superfund" to clean up the site and then seek damages from a wide circle of "owners" and "operators" of the property.

These laws have all been enacted within the past 35 years, and will surely undergo some modification in the future. Government will learn to regulate more effectively, businesses will learn how to manufacture with less pollution, to treat their waste more carefully, and to better control the discharge of hazardous substances. We will all learn more about the short- and long-term effects of various air and water pollution, acid rain, and toxic waste material. The challenge of protecting our environment while promoting business growth is one of the key issues of the 21st century.

CHAPTER QUESTIONS

1. The Sky Harbor Airport in Phoenix has experienced considerable growth in the number of flights arriving and departing. The Federal Aviation Administration decided to improve the management and safety of air traffic there by changing the structure of flight plans at the airport. The proposed change in flight patterns was controversial, and some cities and residents affected by the changes filed suit claiming that an Environmental Impact Statement should have been done by the FAA. The agency decided that the changes it was making did not require an EIS. What should the court decide, and why? *Town of Cave Creek v. Federal Aviation Admin.,* 325 F.3d 320 (D.C. Cir. 2003).

2. A truck manufacturer sought an exemption from the state implementation plan (SIP) regarding the limits on emissions of volatile organic compounds released into the air by its manufacturing and assembly plant. What would the company have to show to get an exemption? [*Navistar International Transportation Corp. v. EPA,* 941 F.2d 1339 (6th Cir.1991)]

3. A mercury processing plant was operated for many years at a site in New Jersey. The process used prime virgin mercury (PVM) and then converted "dirty" mercury into intermediate compounds for some of its customers. The plant released harmful waste into the environment for decades. Several different companies owned the site at different times, and the plant was closed in 1974. Morton Thiokol (now Morton) is the current owner, and has been held jointly and severally liable for discharge of pollutants over a long period of time by its predecessor companies. The site is now listed on the national priorities site for the Superfund, under the CERCLA law and Morton faces huge liability for cleanup costs. Morton brought an action against Tennessee Gas Pipeline Co. (Tenneco) and others seeking contribution toward the cleanup, because of Tenneco's role as an "arranger" under CERCLA. Morton argues that Tenneco is liable as an "arranger" because it owned the PVM at the time it was treated, shipped its "dirty mercury" to Morton's plant for treatment, and that Tenneco had knowledge that the release of hazardous waste was an inherent aspect of mercury processing. Tenneco denies all these allegations. If Morton's claims are correct, can Tenneco

be held liable as an "arranger?" Describe the purposes of the CERCLA law, and the section which holds "arrangers" jointly and severally liable. What should the standard be for deciding that someone is an "arranger?" What result and why? *Morton Intern. Inc. v. A.E. Staley Mfg. Co.,* 343 F. 3d 669 (3rd Cir. 2003).

4. The president and CEO of a chemical blending and distribution company in Washington state was charged with criminal violations of the CWA. The company shipped its products in drums, which were then returned to be cleaned and reused by the company. The cleaning process generated a wastewater regulated by the CWA, but the company never obtained a discharge permit and resorted to various illegal disposal methods. The president did not actually dump any of the wastes himself, but was closely involved and informed about the disposal activities. Can he be held personally responsible in a criminal action? [*U.S. v. Iverson* 162 F.3d 1015 (9th Cir. 1998)]

5. When Congress passed the Clean Air Act, the EPA was delegated the authority to set ambient air quality standards that "allowed an adequate margin of safety, and are requisite to protect the public health." This delegation of authority was challenged by an industry group, on the basis that it was unconstitutional, because it was too broad, and did not contain adequate standards to guide the EPA action. The group also wanted the EPA to give greater consideration to economic effects, in setting NAAQS. What should the result be and why? *Whitman v. American Trucking Assn.,* 121 S. Ct. 903 (2001)

6. The California delta smelt is a small fish that lives only in California. It was once harvested commercially as bait, but has no present commercial value. Its range has diminished considerably in recent years, and was first listed as "threatened" and later "endangered" by the U.S. Fish and Wildlife Service, under the Endangered Species Act. The Service issued a Biological Opinion to the Bureau of Reclamation suggesting that it reduce water flows from two huge California water diversion projects in order to prevent "jeopardizing the continued existence and habitat of the delta smelt." Three large agricultural businesses filed suit claiming that their almond, pistachio, and walnut orchards would suffer serious harm as the result of the reduced water flows. The growers further argued that the order was unconstitutional under the Commerce Clause because the delta smelt is a purely intrastate species and has no commercial value. What should the court decide and why? *San Luis & Delta Mendota Water Authority v. Salazar,* ___F. 3d ___ (9th Cir. 2011)

7. A company foreman and a supervisor who directed the discharge of hazardous waste from an industrial firm into a trench, which then emptied into a creek, were charged with a criminal violation of RCRA. The firm did not have an EPA permit for such discharges. The two men argued that the law only contained punishment for "owners and operators" and that, therefore, they could not be held criminally responsible as individuals. What should be the result? Why? [*U.S. v. Johnson & Towers, Inc.,* 741 F.2d 662 (3d Cir. 1984)]

8. A real estate developer purchased a ranch that he intended to turn into vineyard and orchard parcels for sale. The land had a deep layer of soil, called a "restrictive layer" that prevented surface water from penetrating deeply, thus resulting in several wetland areas on the property. The developer began a process called "deep ripping" to convert the property to use as a vineyard. Deep ripping involves dragging four to seven-foot-long metal prongs through the earth to rip up the soil. This caused the water that was trapped to drain out, creating a discharge, which ran into a navigable waterway. The Army Corps of Engineers charged him with violating the Clean Water Act. Did he? What is the test for a violation? Explain. *Borden Ranch Partnership v. U.S. Army Corps of Engineers,* 537 U.S. 99 (2002).

9. A photo etching company and its president were convicted of violating RCRA because they improperly stored and disposed of hazardous waste without a permit. The defendants claimed on appeal that they could not be convicted of the crime because they did not know they needed a permit and thus had no "criminal intent." Are they right? Why? [*U.S. v. Wagner,* 29 F.3d 264 (7th Cir. 1994)]

10. When it rains in Los Angeles, billions of gallons of water pour into the Los Angeles County storm drains, which then carry bacteria, pathogens, animal waste, metals, oils, and other pollutants as the water flows untreated into the Pacific Ocean and onto nearby beaches. Two environmental groups filed suit for violations of a 2001 Clean Water Act permit issued by California's Regional Water Quality Control Board. The plaintiffs alleged that Los Angeles County, through its Flood Control District, has been illegally discharging polluted water into the Los Angeles and San Gabriel Rivers since 2003. Is this type of discharge covered by the Clean Water Act? Why or why not? *NDRC v. Los Angeles,* _____ F. 3d___(9th Cir. 2011).

PRACTICAL EXERCISE

Irene is the president of a small company, Oil Industries Limited (OIL), which collects waste oil products from other firms, hauls it away, and disposes of it. For more than 10 years, she and her company have picked up waste oil from several customers and have taken it to a disposal site on a farm owned by Bruce. Irene (through OIL) leased 10 acres from Bruce for $5000 per year and installed four tanks on the property to hold the waste oil.

After a few years Bruce noticed that one of the tanks was leaking and ordered Irene to pump all the oil out of that tank. He also asked Irene to remove the tanks, but she refused, since her lease still had two years to run. Some six years later, when Irene and OIL were no longer in the oil hauling business, the EPA investigated the site and found that several of the tanks had developed serious leaks, and oil containing PCBs (a very hazardous chemical) had contaminated the ground on the site. The EPA then hired another firm to clean up the site, at a cost in excess of $10 million, and has notified Irene, Bruce, and OIL that they are PRPs. Irene and OIL deny liability, claiming that they never knew that any oil they handled contained PCBs. Bruce denies that he is liable because he was not involved in the business in any way.

Knowing that you are studying "legal stuff," your good friend Irene has asked you to prepare a memo discussing the relevant laws; potential liability of herself, Bruce, and OIL for the contamination; and any defenses that any party might have. Also, she wonders whether Bruce has any rights against her and OIL (which has now been merged into a larger company), in case he has to pay damages. Prepare such a memo discussing these issues thoroughly.

FURTHER INFORMATION

www.epa.gov
  U.S. Environmental Protection Agency.
www.doi.gov
  U.S. Department of the Interior.
www.usace.army.mil
  U.S. Army Corps of Engineers.
www.edf.org
  Environmental Defense Fund.
www.nrdc.org
  Natural Resources Defense Council.
www.sierraclub.org
  Sierra Club.

CHAPTER 16

CYBERLAW AND INTELLECTUAL PROPERTY

1. Understand the legal basis for, and requirements of patents, copyrights, trademarks and trade secrets.

2. Determine which type of intellectual property your firm has, and the best way to protect such property.

3. Discuss the changes which are occurring in traditional legal concepts such as contract, torts and business organizations due to "cyberlaw" developments.

4. Assess the current and future developments in such "cutting edge" topics as the downloading of music and movies, legal issues involved with the use of social media, protection of domain names, legal aspects of E-commerce, the Digital Millenium Copyright Act, control of pornography over the internet, and criminal law developments in cyberspace.

Two of your friends from college have started a business providing software and other services to local hospitals and doctors, but they have recently received a letter from another company alleging that they have violated the other firm's patents, trademarks and trade secrets. They have asked you for some advice concerning these intellectual property issues.

INTRODUCTION

In an earlier chapter we examined certain types of property, such as personal property and real property as well as various types of wills and trusts used to transfer ownership of property. Today, for many businesses, the most important form of property is something called Intellectual Property—so named because it is a type of property created through the efforts of a person's mind. Such critically important assets as copyrights, patents, trademarks and trade secrets are intellectual property, and they are often worth more than the total value of a corporation's physical property. Certainly many of the most profitable firms in the United States, such as Microsoft, Time-Warner, Disney, Facebook, and the recording industry have the vast majority of their value invested in intellectual property, but companies making all types of products—from cars to computers to soft drinks—have a tremendous investment in intellectual property.

When an individual or company invents a product or an innovative process, or creates works of literature, art, music, movies, computer programs, or markets goods using its trademarks or trade names such as "Nike" shoes, or develops and maintains trade secrets such as customer lists and the Coca Cola formula—such subjects are "intellectual property" that has considerable value. These types of intellectual property have long been protected by various federal and state laws, as will be fully discussed in this chapter, and the law is adapting to new uses and issues every day.

In recent years, a remarkable new technology—the Internet—has developed, which allows us to communicate with each other easily and at a high rate of speed, at relatively little or no cost to the individual. At the same time, the creation and development of the World Wide Web allows us to easily access all types of information—art, music, literature, business, news, entertainment, historical, or humorous—with the click of a "mouse" on our computers. This new technology allows us to "surf the web" to obtain information, purchase airline tickets and all sorts of merchandise, visit famous art museums and libraries, listen to and download music and movies, and conduct a wide variety of business transactions directly from our computers.

From a legal standpoint, the development of the internet and world wide web have created many new legal issues, and put a new "spin" on most of the traditional legal subjects already examined in this textbook. For example, we now routinely enter into contracts by clicking our computer mouse, with the cursor in a box labeled "I agree" on a page of text. Our businesses regularly advertise and sell products to consumers located all over the country (and world) using the internet and Web. It is quite possible to commit the tort of defamation by posting a derogatory and false statement about someone else on a blog or bulletin board which can be accessed by thousands or millions of people instantly. This new field of law (and new twists on traditional subjects) is sometimes called "Cyberlaw." Some scholars believe that cyberlaw is a totally new legal topic, and should be treated in a unique way, while others argue that it merely represents a new development of traditional subjects like contracts, torts and copyright law.

It is now quite possible and easy to distribute copyrighted and patented "intellectual property" to the whole world with the click of a finger. The federal copyright, patent, and trademark laws, which have existed for centuries, are being tested everyday by the ease of transfer of information using the internet and Web. Cases involving the "downloading" of music and movies have made national headlines, and software companies have issued press releases claiming the loss of hundreds of millions of dollars annually due to the "pirating" of their programs.

We will now begin our examination of the different types of intellectual property in more detail, and look at the developments in Cyberlaw.

INTELLECTUAL PROPERTY

intellectual property: The legal rights covering such topics as patents, copyrights, trademarks, and trade secrets.

PATENTS

A business can gain a competitive edge over its competitors through technological improvement and innovation. Many companies spend millions of dollars on research and development, seeking to develop new and better products and processes. If someone creates a new type of plastic compound, or invents a machine capable of novel functions, patent law allows the inventor to obtain exclusive rights to the invention.

Patent protection is specifically mentioned in the U.S. Constitution, which in Article I grants Congress the power to "promote the progress of science and the useful arts, by securing for limited times to . . . authors and inventors . . . the exclusive right to their discoveries." Congress has enacted a number of federal laws regarding patents since that time.

patent: A legal right of the creator or inventor of a product, process, or invention. The patent holder has the exclusive right to use, develop, and license the subject of the patent for 20 years.

Specifically, a patent is a legal right, issued by the U.S. government, pertaining to an invention, product, or process. There are three types of patents—utility patents, design patents, and plant patents. The *utility patent* is by far the most common. In order to obtain a utility patent, the applicant must show that the process or invention is **"novel, useful, and nonobvious."** To be "novel," an invention must be new—that is, it cannot be previously known or used by others in the United States. If the invention has been publicly used or sold or described in a printed publication more than one year prior to the patent application, it will not be granted a U.S. patent. In most other countries, the patent application must be filed even *before* any public disclosure or use.

Upon issuance of the patent, the holder has the exclusive right to make, use, or sell the process, product, or invention in the United States. Even if another person independently develops such a product, he or she will be unable to sell it legally if it is covered by an earlier patent. Other countries also issue patents to control the manufacture, use, and sale of products and inventions within their jurisdictions. Several major treaties exist, signed by the United States and other countries, by which each country agrees to respect patents issued by other member nations, or at least give the applicant a "grace period" after applying for a U.S. patent, during which time they (and only they) can apply for a patent in that nation. However, there is no such thing as an "international patent," so a patent application needs to be filed in each country where an inventor or business firm wants to obtain a patent.

In the United States, patent protection now lasts for a period of 20 years from date the application for patent was filed. After that time, any member of the public can use the invention or produce the product. The process of applying for, and obtaining a patent is long and complicated, often taking two to three years. Detailed drawings and descriptions of the invention must be forwarded to the U.S. Patent and Trademark Office (PTO), and the inventor must compare this item or process with similar patented items (called **"prior art"**) and demonstrate how this invention is different and unique ("novel").

The patent application must include "specifications" which describe the invention in a way that a person skilled in the field could make and use it. The patent application must also include detailed "drawings" of the item or process on which the patent is sought. The real heart of the application is the **"claims"**—a precise description of exactly what elements of this invention or process or item are "novel, useful and nonobvious." It is only these "claims" that will be protected against use by another if the patent is granted.

Often the holders of earlier patents on similar devices challenge the issuance of a new patent. It is usually necessary and wise to retain the services of an attorney specializing in intellectual property to successfully process a patent application. Some 95% of patent applications are initially rejected by the Patent Office, but the inventor is entitled to make amendments to the application, adding necessary information and specificity to the "claims," and apply again. In recent years, patent lawyers (who often have an engineering or science background) have become very high profile and much sought-after attorneys by all leading law firms and many companies.

In the past 20 years the PTO has allowed the issuance of patents on software programs if they perform useful and unique functions, and thousands of such patents have been issued to U.S. and foreign companies. Also, in a somewhat controversial move, the Patent Office began issuing **"business method patents"** about 10 years ago, where such processes represent a unique, nonobvious useful way of doing business. This development was spurred by a decision of the Court of Appeals for the Federal Circuit in *State Street Bank v. Signature Financial Group* (149 F.3d 1368) in 1998.

In the *State Street Bank* case, Signature Financial Group had obtained a patent on its computerized system for managing mutual fund investments. The system used a "hub and spoke" process whereby individual funds pooled their assets into an investment portfolio which is organized as a partnership. The system worked well with Signature's business as administrator and accounting agent for mutual funds. State Street Bank sought a license to use the system from Signature, but was refused and filed a court action to have the patent invalidated. The appellate court ruled that three categories of subject matter were not patentable—laws of nature, natural phenomena, and abstract ideas. While mathematical formulas and algorithms are abstract, the transformation of data through a series of mathematical formulas into a final share price was a "practical application" and thus patentable. The court concluded that "business method patents" were not necessarily illegal, as some previous cases had determined.

In 2010 the U.S. Supreme Court decided an important patent case, *Bilski v. Kappos.* Many commentators had predicted that the Court would use this case to overturn or cut back on the patentability of business methods. However, the decision turned out to be somewhat unclear as far as providing tests for future patent cases.

While all nine justices concurred that the Federal Circuit was right in affirming the denial of Bilski's application to patent a method of hedging risk

prior art: earlier invention or processes which already have patents

claims: an important part of a patent application which specifies what elements of this invention are new and should be protected.

in commodities trading, Justice Kennedy, in an opinion for the Court joined by Justices Roberts, Thomas, and Alito, wrote that the "machine-or-transformation test" was best suited for evaluating the patentability of processes similar to those in the Industrial Age (i.e., inventions grounded in a physical or other tangible form), but with regard to emerging technologies, including expressly advanced diagnostic medicine techniques, it may not make sense to require courts to confine themselves to asking the questions posed by the machine-or-transformation test—that is, the process was not tied to a particular machine or did not change a particular article into a different state or thing. In Justice Kennedy's words, "Section 101's terms suggest new technologies may call for new inquiries." No five justices agreed on how much importance should be attached to the "machine-or-transformation test" in deciding the patentability of processes or methods in future cases.

Justice Stevens wrote a lengthy concurrence joined by Justices Ginsburg, Breyer, and Sotomayor, which, while conceding that the machine-or-transformation test was not the exclusive test for determining whether a process was patentable under § 101, endorsed a different, less flexible approach to deciding the patentability of process claims. It is clear that Justice Stevens and the three other justices who joined his concurrence would have adopted a black letter rule holding that a business method is not a "process" under § 101. Stevens' opinion further hints that patenting methods of doing business may exceed the constitutional grant of authority to Congress to exercise its patent power to promote innovation. While *Bilski* does not preclude the patentability of all business methods in the future, the decision does seem to indicate that most business methods are unlikely to be eligible for patent protection. While the justices all agreed that the claims at issue were unpatentable "abstract ideas," *Bilski* offers no signposts for deciding what claims are drawn to abstract ideas, rules of nature, or natural phenomena. So we will have to await future decisions to determine the full impact of the *Bilski* case.

infringement:
Unauthorized use of copyrighted or patented material.

When someone else uses, manufactures, or sells an invention or process that is patented, without permission from the patent holder, this is called **infringement.** The patent holder can bring suit against the alleged infringer and seek damages and/or an injunction prohibiting use of the infringing product. The court will conduct an independent analysis of the validity of the patent. (The PTO's previous determination is only one factor that is considered.) Many patents previously issued by the PTO have been held invalid at later trial. There is also a theory called the **doctrine of equivalents,** which holds that even if a second invention or device does not use exactly every element of the first patented item, if it is essentially the same product, and works in the same way to accomplish the same result, the court may find infringement. Again the exact words used in the "claims" section of the patent application are important to determine exactly what is protected by the patent.

INTERNATIONAL PERSPECTIVE

Business is now conducted on a global basis, and patent protection around the world is important. Most nations do have patent laws, and have a process for filing for patent protection, although they are not exactly the same everywhere. Several important international treaties attempt to achieve coordination regarding intellectual property. The Paris Convention has been signed by 173 countries (including the United States) and provides that each nation will establish a "grace period" for persons after they have filed for a patent in their home country. During that time—6 months for trademarks and one year for patents—the applicant will have the sole right to file the necessary applications to obtain patent protection in the other signatory nations. The applicant will, of course, have to properly meet the requirements in the second nation in order to obtain a patent.

Another treaty, the Patent Cooperation Treaty (PCT) allows a patent applicant to file one application and seek an international patent. The application can be filed in the home country or with the World Intellectual Property Organization (WIPO), which had 184 member nations in 2011. The application will be considered as a patent application in all member nations "designated" by the applicant. The application then will be carefully examined by the International Searching Authority, whose experts will study all "prior art," evaluate the likelihood of obtaining a patent in nations "designated" by the applicant, which will be useful if the applicant does go forward to formally seek a patent in any of the member countries (which would involve some extra paperwork and payment of fees).

The international patent application is not published for 18 months, which gives the applicant the opportunity to either withdraw the application or go forward and apply for national patents, before any publication. There were 142 members of the PCT in 2011, according to the WIPO web site. [www.wipo.int].

There is also a European Patent Organization which has established a centralized patent grant system administered by the European Patent Office on behalf of all contracting states, It was established by the Convention on the Grant of European Patents (EPC) signed in 1973.

A *European patent* can be obtained by filing a single application in one of the official languages of the European Patent Office (English, French or German) in a unitary procedure before the EPO and is valid in as many of the contracting states as the applicant cares to designate. A *European patent* affords the same rights in the designated contracting states as a national patent granted in any of these states. There were 38 members of the EPO when the website http://www.european-patent-office.org/index.en.php was accessed on April 27, 2011.

IN CONSULTATION

Marvin Manager has a problem. His company recently began selling sporting goods on-line. To increase the appeal of its Web site, ABC, Inc. developed one-click access so customers could simply key in a user name and immediately begin shopping. The one-click technology only requires customers to fill out registration and shipping forms the first time they visit the site. Repeat customers can buy merchandise by just clicking on a single button. ABC's market research shows that customers are much more likely to buy via a Web site if they do not have to enter a lot of information.

Othercorp, one of ABC's primary competitors, actually began selling on-line first. It also uses one-click access on its Web site. ABC became aware of one-click technology after Othercorp began using it. ABC did not, however, copy Othercorp's actual program. Instead, ABC simply developed its own one-click algorithm.

Othercorp filed suit against ABC, challenging that ABC infringed upon Othercorp's patented one-click software. Othercorp stated in its complaint that not only did ABC copy the technology, but it engaged in unfair competition.

Marvin approached his company's in-house corporate counsel, to determine whether Othercorp's allegations have any chance of succeeding. He asked the lawyer about ABC's potential liability to Othercorp. Here is their conversation.

Marvin:

1. Just because we came up with software that accomplishes the same one-click access, are we infringing upon Othercorp's patent?
2. What is unfair competition anyway? Isn't all fair in love and war—and business is war?
3. Is the Internet even covered by all of these old laws? I thought that the law did not yet address e-commerce, allowing us to basically do what we want on the Web.

Legal Counsel

1. Patenting software is a new phenomenon. The courts are unsettled as to what sorts of software can be patented and what constitutes infringement.
2. Unfair competitive practices usually include actual violations of the law. The answer to your question depends upon whether ABC infringed as Othercorp alleges.
3. Courts have been challenged by the new technology and the difficulty in applying old law to the Internet. The Internet is, nonetheless, subject to certain rules, including rules that prohibit patent infringement. Let me research the applicable law to see whether Othercorp's claim is viable, and I'll get back to you.

MEMO FROM THE LEGAL DEPARTMENT

To: Marvin Manager

Re: Liability for Patent Infringement on the Internet

Dear Marvin:

Protecting software via intellectual property is difficult. Software and computer programs are text, so copyrights were the original protection of choice. Copyrights are limited, however, because if the software designer simply uses different text, he or she can evade another designer's copyright. Not surprisingly, a push toward patents for software has emerged. Patents are a superior form of protection because they allow the patent holder to exclude others from making, using, or selling your invention. A patent holder can increase its profits by licensing its technology in a way a copyright holder cannot.

Patenting software is controversial because not everyone agrees that software is an invention or process. Others assert that software is essentially a machine that performs a function, thereby deserving patent protection. The Patent and Trademark Office has been issuing patents on software in recent years, but many believe that those patents will be challenged in the courts.

The controversy over patenting software affects our case in a couple of ways. First, ABC may be able to prove that Othercorp did not deserve a patent on its one-click software. We would need evidence that either someone else had developed a similar process in the past (i.e., prior art) or that the software is not novel.

Second, even if Othercorp can prove that it deserved a patent, we can defend that we did not infringe on that patent. We developed our own technology that merely accomplishes the same goal as Othercorp's—one-click access. We did not copy Othercorp's code or process and, instead, used our own creative resources to establish one-click access on our Web site. In support of our defense, we can show that many other retailers and wholesalers use some form of one-click access. If it is becoming an industry norm, Othercorp will be hard-pressed to show that the entire sales industry is infringing. If we did not infringe, then we also cannot be accused of unfair competition.

With regard to Othercorp's patent infringement claim, consider the following:
1. Do you think software should be patented? Give arguments against and in support of using patents to protect software development.
2. Do you think Marvin or ABC could have done something differently to prevent Othercorp from having any substance to its claim in the first place?
3. Do you think the United States' current intellectual property system is compatible with the Internet? Describe what you see as the main gaps in the current system and the evolving e-commerce marketplace.

COPYRIGHTS

A copyright is a legal right that protects the creative output of authors, songwriters, artists, and others who create and produce original works. Under U.S. federal law, copyright protection is available for **"original works of authorship fixed in a tangible medium of expression."** Such "expression" may be contained in literary, dramatic, musical, artistic, and certain other intellectual works. This protection is available to both published and unpublished works and covers books, journals, movies, sound recordings, computer programs, photographs, sculptures and other creative works. The copyright covers the **"expression"** of an idea, not the idea itself. In other words, copyright protects against the "copying" or certain uses by another, without permission, of the actual *expression* of the work except in certain circumstances. The **ideas** embodied in a book or in a work of art can be discussed and debated—and

copyright: The legal right of an author, composer, or artist to prevent others from copying or reproducing his or her work.

authors and artists hope that they are—but the actual sentences, pages, music, photos, or replicas usually cannot be photocopied or reproduced or duplicated without the permission of the author or artist.

Section 106 of the 1976 Copyright Act generally gives the owner of copyright the *exclusive* right to do and to authorize others to do the following:

- *To reproduce* the work in copies or phonorecords;
- To prepare *derivative works* based upon the work;
- *To distribute copies or phonorecords* of the work to the public by sale or other transfer of ownership, or by rental, lease, or lending;
- *To perform the work publicly,* in the case of literary, musical, dramatic, and choreographic works, pantomimes, and motion pictures and other audiovisual works;
- *To display the copyrighted work publicly,* in the case of literary, musical, dramatic, and choreographic works, pantomimes, and pictorial, graphic, or sculptural works, including the individual images of a motion picture or other audiovisual work; and
- In the case of *sound recordings, to perform the work publicly* by means of a *digital audio transmission.*

Copyright law first developed from common law case decisions—but has been part of U.S. statutory law for two centuries. The U.S. copyright law has been amended several times since early 1800. Currently the copyright comes into existence and belongs to the author *immediately and automatically* upon producing the work, even without any notice of copyright or any filing with the Copyright Office. Although registration is not now required in order to create a copyright, the author must register the copyright with the U.S. government Copyright Office [http://www.copyright.gov/] before bringing a lawsuit for infringement, so it makes good sense to register any copyrightable works.

THE LENGTH OF COPYRIGHT PROTECTION

Congress has amended the copyright law many times in the past 200 years, generally extending the life of copyright to a longer period. In 1998 the *Sonny Bono Copyright Term Extension Act* (CTEA) extended the length of the basic copyright term from "life of the author plus 50 years" to "*life plus 70 years.*" In other words, copyright protection for all works created after January 1, 1978, now lasts for the author's life plus an additional 70 years (the person's heirs acquire the rights after the author's death). In the case of a joint work, the term lasts for 70 years after the last surviving author's death. For anonymous and pseudonymous works and "works made for hire," the term will be 95 years from the year of first publication or 120 years from the year of creation, whichever expires first; the terms of copyright were generally extended for an additional 20 years.

The "Sonny Bono" CTEA act was controversial, as the term extension was pressed hard by the major movie studios and other media groups. It seemed that several of the copyrights on early "Mickey Mouse" stories, cartoons, etc. were about to expire, some 50 years after Walt Disney's death, and the Disney company did not want those works to go into the public domain. Another reason for the amendment was to bring the length of U.S. copyright law into conformance with European Union laws. The new law extending the copyright term was challenged by a group of scholars who used and wanted to promote greater use of "public domain" works. They felt that Congress had gone too far—that the Constitution allowed Congress to pass statutes providing copyright protection "for limited times", and this law exceeded that standard. But the U.S. Supreme Court upheld the law in 2003 in the case *Eldred v.Ashcroft*.

The Court in an opinion by Justice Ginsburg, stated "Guided by text, history, and precedent, this Court cannot agree with petitioners that extending the duration of existing copyrights is categorically beyond Congress' Copyright Clause authority. Although conceding that the CTEA's baseline term of life plus 70 years qualifies as a "limited Tim[e]" as applied to future copyrights, petitioners contended that existing copyrights extended to endure for that same term were not "limited." The Court stated that the word "limited," however, does not convey a meaning so constricted. At the time of the Framing, "limited" meant what it means today: confined within certain bounds, restrained, or circumscribed. Thus understood, a time span appropriately "limited" as applied to future copyrights does not automatically cease to be "limited" when applied to existing copyrights.

The Supreme Court thus concluded that the Copyright Term Extension Act was legal and constitutional.

COPYRIGHT REGISTRATION AND COVERAGE

The federal "registration" process merely requires authors to send copies of their work to the U.S. Copyright Office (part of the Library of Congress), accompanied by a modest fee (generally only $35–$65) and a short form claiming copyright. In contrast to patents, the Copyright Office does not compare similar works, or look for "prior art" and does not certify that the owner has the exclusive right to the work—it is merely a "registration." The Copyright Office does not bring enforcement actions. Any author or artist who believes that his or her work has been copied must personally bring a lawsuit against the alleged copier.

Prior to 1989, it was also necessary to place a copyright notice (including the word Copyright or © , along with the date and author's name) on the first page of all copyrightable works, in order to protect the copyright, but this is no longer a requirement. Today, when one creates a work that meets the tests for copyrightability, the copyright *exists automatically*. However, it is still a very good idea to place such a notice on any materials leaving the author's hands; this lets others know that a copyright is claimed and that such works cannot be used without permission.

When one person copies, reproduces, performs, or displays a work that is copyrighted by someone else, this is called **infringement** (as in patent law). The copyright owner may bring a lawsuit against the alleged infringer seeking money damages and/or an injunction prohibiting the person from continuing such activities. There may also be a criminal law violation for intentional copyright infringement of significant amounts of material. To be successful, the copyright owner must prove that the infringer "copied" the owner's work. It is the **copying** that is wrong. Unlike patents, it is not infringement if one person independently creates a work that just happens to read like, look like, or sound like an existing work. Remember, copyright protects the particular

expression of the idea, not the **idea** itself. It is only infringement if the earlier work was copied.

For example, the best-selling book a few years ago was *The DaVinci Code,* written by Dan Brown. In this exciting novel, the leading characters strongly advocate that there is much historical, religious and philosophical evidence that the significant contributions of women, and the role of Mary Magdalene in particular, have been suppressed for centuries by conservative elements of the Roman Catholic church. The author probably hopes that many people discuss whether they believe these allegations are true and vigorously debate whether the evidence supports those views (**the "idea"**). However, no one but the author can legally photocopy, reproduce, digitally or directly copy in any manner more than a very small portion of the exact sentences used in the book. To do otherwise will infringe the copyright of the author (by copying **the "expression"**). For example, the authors of this textbook could probably quote a few sentences of the novel to illustrate some point (under the "fair use" doctrine, discussed below), but beyond that any lengthy direct reproduction of Dan Brown's exact words would be copyright infringement. Dan Brown himself was actually sued by two other authors who claimed that he had used characters and text from their earlier works, but Mr. Brown won the case.

Many recent cases involving popular songs, where one person claims that the melody or lyrics of a song that became a hit record were copied from his or her previously copyrighted song. One key issue in cases where the first song is not well-known is "access"—that is, whether the second song writer actually had a copy of or a record containing the first song. A second issue in many copyright cases is whether there is "substantial similarity" between the two songs.

DOWNLOADING AND COPYING OF MUSIC IN CYBERSPACE

Listening to music is a favorite activity for many people. The manufacturers of electronic equipment advertise various means of capturing the exact sounds of a popular song. Certainly one of the most-publicized copyright issues in recent years has been the massive "downloading" of music, without the permission of the owners of the music copyrights. Since music is now produced digitally and is available for purchase on compact discs, the owner of the disc has the right to listen to it as often as he/she wants.

Furthermore, the internet and computers have made it quite possible for the owner of a music CD to load an exact copy of the song onto his/her computer, and then "share" the recorded (and copyrighted) song with any number of other persons (thousands or more) who log onto a "peer to peer" (P2P) network on the Web and "download" the song. These same digital sounds can also be transferred to various types of portable players (MP3, Rio, I-Pod, etc.) so the music can be played whenever and wherever the user chooses. Millions of people can thus acquire the exact same musical performance for free—and listen to it over and over. Perhaps even some of you students reading this text have downloaded a few songs over the internet.

SOCIAL/ETHICAL ISSUES

But what about the copyright? Someone wrote the lyrics and composed the tune, and owns the copyright in the song (and there is likely another copyright on the particular performance by this artist on this disc) so that any reproduction or exact copying of the "expression" is copyright infringement. The recording industry has argued vigorously that this massive "infringement" is destroying their industry, and denying musicians and composers millions of dollars in royalties, which would have been earned if music consumers had purchased the CDs and cassettes containing the recorded songs, rather than downloading them for free.

While members of the authors' generation grew up buying records and cassettes of songs and albums they wanted to hear, millions of college students (like most of you reading this book) and many other consumers have become quite accustomed in recent years to being able to acquire, for free, any recorded songs they want.

The recording industry has insisted that copyright law still exists, despite the ease of circumventing it and should be enforced. The industry has pressed its copyright claims, and has filed suit against several hundred individual consumers, who have been identified as large-scale abusers. Apparently these lawsuits have had some effect, and the number of downloaded songs has decreased. Yet, many millions of consumers continue to download for free, ignoring copyright law, or believing that whatever can be accessed on the internet should be free. As the son of one of the textbook authors told him recently, "Dad, it's a new age and your old copyright law is out of date."

The movie industry has been watching this struggle closely, as the increasing speed and power of computers is making movie downloading easy as well, since movies are now digitally produced and sold on DVDs. Clearly the act of making a perfect copy of an entire copyrighted sound recording or motion picture is, in effect, the direct copying of the "expression" of the copyrighted work, without the permission of the copyright owner. Such actions do undoubtedly detract from the sales of videotapes, DVDs, and CDs by the producers and copyright holders. Yet it is so easy to do, should it be unlawful?

What do you think? Should the copyright law be changed? Is it still relevant to the digital electronic world of today? Should we care about the rights of authors, composers and inventors? Would you feel differently if you had spent 100 hours writing a software program for your own business firm and then someone got hold of it and put it on the internet for anyone to use for free? Should manufacturers be allowed to sell products that enable and encourage others to violate copyright laws? What about regulation of the Internet? Can or should anything be done?

The most well-known case involving the issues raised above was the *Napster* case. The Ninth Circuit Court of Appeals decision is set forth below, in the language of the court. Although the plaintiff is simply listed as "A & M Records" you should remember that when cases are put in court reports and casebooks only the first plaintiff is named. Actually almost all the major record companies, including Geffen Records, Interscope Records, Sony Music

Entertainment, MCA Records, Atlantic Recording Corp., Island Records, Motown Record Co., and Capitol Records were also plaintiffs in the case. Other major record companies including Universal and Warner, had also filed different suits against Napster, which were joined in this one.

In the Language of the Court

A & M RECORDS V. NAPSTER, INC.

239 F.3d 1004 (9th Cir. 2001)

FACTS

BEEZER, Circuit Judge:

Plaintiffs are engaged in the commercial recording, distribution and sale of copyrighted musical compositions and sound recordings. The complaint alleges that Napster, Inc. ("Napster") is a contributory and vicarious copyright infringer. On July 26, 2000, the district court preliminarily enjoined Napster "from engaging in, or facilitating others in copying, downloading, uploading, transmitting, or distributing plaintiffs' copyrighted musical compositions and sound recordings, protected by either federal or state law, without express permission of the rights owner."

Napster has designed and operates a system which permits the transmission and retention of sound recordings employing digital technology. In 1987, a standard file format for the storage of audio recordings in a digital format was established, called MPEG-3, abbreviated as "MP3." Digital MP3 files are created through a process colloquially called "ripping." Ripping software allows a computer owner to copy an audio compact disk ("audio CD") directly onto a computer's hard drive by compressing the audio information on the CD into the MP3 format. The MP3's compressed format allows for rapid transmission of digital audio files from one computer to another by electronic mail or any other file transfer protocol.

Napster facilitates the transmission of MP3 files between and among its users. Through a process commonly called "peer-to-peer" file sharing, Napster allows its users to: (1) make MP3 music files stored on individual computer hard drives available for copying by other Napster users; (2) search for MP3 music files stored on other users' computers; and (3) transfer exact copies of the contents of other users' MP3 files from one computer to another via the Internet. These functions are made possible by Napster's MusicShare software, available free of charge from Napster's Internet site, and Napster's network servers and server-side software. Napster provides technical support for the indexing and searching of MP3 files, as well as for its other functions, including a "chat room," where users can meet to discuss music, and a directory where participating artists can provide information about their music.

A. Accessing the System

In order to copy MP3 files through the Napster system, a user must first access Napster's Internet site and download the MusicShare software to his individual computer. Once the software is installed, the user can access the Napster system. A first-time user is required to register with the Napster system by creating a "user name" and password.

B. Listing Available Files

If a registered user wants to list available files stored in his computer's hard drive on Napster for others to access, he must first create a "user library" directory on his computer's hard drive. The user then saves his MP3 files in the library directory, using self-designated file names. He next must log into the Napster system using his user name and password. His MusicShare software then searches his user library and verifies that the available files are properly formatted. If in the correct MP3 format, the names of the MP3 files will be uploaded from the user's computer to the Napster servers. The content of the MP3 files remains stored in the user's computer.

Once uploaded to the Napster servers, the user's MP3 file names are stored in a server-side "library" under the user's name and become part of a "collective directory" of files available for transfer during the time the user is logged onto the Napster system. The collective directory is fluid; it tracks users who are connected in real time, displaying only file names that are immediately accessible.

C. Searching For Available Files

Napster allows a user to locate other users' MP3 files in two ways: through Napster's search function and through its "hotlist" function. Software located on the Napster servers maintains a "search index" of Napster's collective directory. To search the files available from Napster users currently connected to the network servers, the individual user accesses a form in the MusicShare software stored in his computer and enters either the name of a song or an artist as the object of the search. The form is then transmitted to a Napster server and automatically compared to the MP3 file names listed in the server's search index. Napster's server compiles a list of all MP3 file names pulled from the search index which include the same search terms entered on the search form and transmits the list to the searching user.

To use the "hotlist" function, the Napster user creates a list of other users' names from whom he has obtained MP3 files in the past. When logged onto Napster's servers, the system alerts the user if any user on his list (a "hotlisted user") is also logged onto the system. If so, the user can access an index of all MP3 file names in a particular hotlisted user's library and request a file in the library by selecting the file name. The contents of the hotlisted user's MP3 file are not stored on the Napster system.

D. Transferring Copies of an MP3 file

To transfer a copy of the contents of a requested MP3 file, the Napster server software obtains the Internet address of the requesting user and the Internet address of the "host user" (the user with the available files). The Napster servers then communicate the host user's Internet address to the requesting user. The requesting user's computer uses this information to establish a connection with the host user and downloads a copy of the contents of the MP3 file from one computer to the other over the Internet, "peer-to-peer." A downloaded MP3 file can be played directly from the user's hard drive using Napster's MusicShare program or other software.

Plaintiffs claim Napster users are engaged in the wholesale reproduction and distribution of copyrighted works, all constituting direct infringement, and that Napster itself has committed both contributory and vicarious copyright infringement. The district court agreed. We now review the preliminary injunction and the tests for copyright infringement.

DECISION

Plaintiffs must satisfy two requirements to present a prima facie case of direct infringement: (1) they must show ownership of the allegedly infringed material and (2) they must demonstrate that the alleged infringers violate at least one exclusive right granted to copyright holders under 17 U.S.C. S 106. Plaintiffs have sufficiently demonstrated ownership. The record supports the district court's determination that "as much as eighty-seven percent of the files available on Napster may be copyrighted and more than seventy percent may be owned or administered by plaintiffs."

The district court further determined that plaintiffs' exclusive rights under §106 were violated: "here the evidence establishes that a majority of Napster users use the service to download and upload copyrighted music. . . . And by doing that, it constitutes—the uses constitute—direct infringement of plaintiffs' musical compositions, recordings." The district court also noted that "it is pretty much acknowledged . . . by Napster that this is infringement." We agree that plaintiffs have shown that Napster users infringe at least two of the copyright holders' exclusive rights: the rights of reproduction, §106(1); and distribution, §106(3). Napster users who upload file names to the search index for others to copy violate plaintiffs' distribution rights. Napster users who download files containing copyrighted music violate plaintiffs' reproduction rights.

[Ed. note: The court next discussed in detail Napster's argument that it and its users were engaging in "fair use" of the copyrighted material, and after analyzing each of the "four factors," concluded that this was not "fair use."]

Accordingly, we next address whether Napster is secondarily liable for the direct infringement under two doctrines of copyright law: contributory copyright infringement and vicarious copyright infringement.

Contributory Copyright Infringement.

We first address plaintiffs' claim that Napster is liable for contributory copyright infringement. Traditionally, "one who, with knowledge of the infringing activity, induces, causes or materially contributes to the infringing conduct of another, may be held liable as a 'contributory' infringer." Put differently, liability exists if the defendant engages in "personal conduct that encourages or assists the infringement."

Contributory liability requires that the secondary infringer "know or have reason to know" of direct infringement.

It is apparent from the record that Napster has knowledge, both actual and constructive, of direct infringement. Napster claims that it is nevertheless protected from contributory liability by the teaching of *Sony Corp. v. Universal City Studios, Inc.,* 464 U.S. 417 (1984). We disagree. We observe that Napster's actual, specific knowledge of direct infringement renders *Sony's* holding of limited assistance to Napster. We are compelled to make a clear distinction between the architecture of the Napster system and Napster's conduct in relation to the operational capacity of the system.

The *Sony* Court refused to hold the manufacturer and retailers of video tape recorders liable for contributory infringement despite evidence that such machines could be and were used to infringe plaintiffs' copyrighted television shows. *Sony* stated that if liability "is to be imposed on petitioners in this case, it must rest on the fact that they have sold equipment with constructive knowledge of the fact that their customers may use that equipment to make unauthorized copies of copyrighted material."

The *Sony* Court declined to impute the requisite level of knowledge where the defendants made and sold equipment capable of both infringing and "substantial noninfringing uses." We are bound to follow *Sony,* and will not impute the requisite level of knowledge to Napster merely because peer-to-peer file sharing technology may be used to infringe plaintiffs' copyrights.

However, if a computer system operator learns of specific infringing material available on his system and fails to purge such material from the system, the operator knows of and contributes to direct infringement. Plaintiff[s] . . . demonstrated that defendant had actual notice of direct infringement because the RIAA informed it of more than 12,000 infringing files. We conclude that sufficient knowledge exists to impose contributory liability when linked to demonstrated infringing use of the Napster system.

The record supports the district court's finding that Napster has actual knowledge that specific infringing material is available using its system, that it could block access to the system by suppliers of the infringing material, and that it failed to remove the material. Under the facts as found by the district court, Napster materially contributes to the infringing activity. The district court concluded that "[w]ithout the support services defendant provides, Napster users could not find and download the music they want with the ease of which defendant boasts."

We agree that Napster provides "the site and facilities" for direct infringement. The district court properly found that Napster materially contributes to direct infringement. We affirm the district court's conclusion that plaintiffs have demonstrated a likelihood of success on the merits of the contributory copyright infringement claim.

Vicarious Copyright Infringement

We turn to the question whether Napster engages in vicarious copyright infringement. Vicarious copyright liability is an "outgrowth" of *respondeat superior.* In the context of copyright law, vicarious liability extends beyond an employer/employee relationship to cases in which a defendant "has the right and ability to supervise the infringing activity and also has a direct financial interest in such activities."

A. Financial Benefit

The district court determined that plaintiffs had demonstrated they would likely succeed in establishing that Napster has a direct financial interest in the infringing activity. We agree. Financial benefit exists where the availability of infringing material "acts as a 'draw' for customers." Ample evidence supports the district court's finding that Napster's future revenue is directly dependent upon "increases in userbase." More users register with the Napster system as the "quality and quantity of available music increases."

B. Supervision

The district court determined that Napster has the right and ability to supervise its users' conduct. (finding that Napster's representations to the court regarding "its improved methods of blocking users about whom rights holders complain . . . is tantamount to an admission that defendant can, and sometimes does, police its service"). We agree in part.

The ability to block infringers' access to a particular environment for any reason whatsoever is evidence of the right and ability to supervise.

Here, plaintiffs have demonstrated that Napster retains the right to control access to its system. Napster has an express reservation of rights policy, stating on its website that it expressly reserves the "right to refuse service and terminate accounts in [its] discretion, including, but not limited to, if Napster believes that user conduct violates applicable law . . . or for any reason in Napster's sole discretion, with or without cause."

To escape imposition of vicarious liability, the reserved right to police must be exercised to its fullest extent. Turning a blind eye to detectable acts of infringement for the sake of profit gives rise to liability. The district court correctly determined that Napster had the right and ability to police its system and failed to exercise that right to prevent the exchange of copyrighted material.

Napster, however, has the ability to locate infringing material listed on its search indices, and the right to terminate users' access to the system. The file name indices, therefore, are within the "premises" that Napster has the ability to police. We recognize that the files are user-named and may not match copyrighted material exactly (for example, the artist or song could be spelled wrong). For Napster to function effectively, however, file names must reasonably or roughly correspond to the material contained in the files, otherwise no user could ever locate any desired music. As a practical matter, Napster, its users and the record company plaintiffs have equal access to infringing material by employing Napster's "search function."

Napster's failure to police the system's "premises," combined with a showing that Napster financially benefits from the continuing availability of infringing files on its system, leads to the imposition of vicarious liability.

ORDER

The district court correctly recognized that a preliminary injunction against Napster's participation in copyright infringement is not only warranted but required. However, the scope of the injunction needs modification in light of our opinion. Specifically, we reiterate that contributory liability may potentially be imposed only to the extent that Napster: (1) receives reasonable knowledge of specific infringing files with copyrighted musical compositions and sound recordings; (2) knows or should know that such files are available on the Napster system; and (3) fails to act to prevent viral distribution of the works.

We thus place the burden on plaintiffs to provide notice to Napster of copyrighted works and files containing such works available on the Napster system before Napster has the duty to disable access to the offending content. Napster, however, also bears the burden of policing the system within the limits of the system. We order a partial remand of this case on the date of the filing of this opinion for the limited purpose of permitting the district court to proceed with the settlement and entry of the modified preliminary injunction.

CASE QUESTIONS

1. What are the essential requirements of "contributory copyright infringement? How did the court determine that Napster had committed this infringement?
2. What are the essential requirements of "vicarious copyright infringement? What factors led the court to find the Napster had done this?
3. What is required of the plaintiff record companies by the court's order? What is required of Napster?

4. Soon after this appellate decision, the lower court issued a revised injunction in accord with the court opinion, and the record companies then gave Napster a long list of all copyrighted music which they believed was being made available on Napster. After a few months, the record companies went back to court and argued that although much of the music had been blocked, there was still a significant number of copyrighted songs still contained in the user files being shared on Napster. What do you suppose the result was then?

Napster was a fairly easy target for the music industry because it was a company located in a specific place in California, whose computers were directly used to facilitate the exchange of music. However, many other "free' web sites such as Kazaa, eDonkey, Gnutella, Grokster and others, allowing peer-to-peer sharing which do not have any fixed location, and are dispersed among hundred of computers. Some even base their operations out of the country. It is much more difficult for the music industry to sue and close down these services. This is one reason that the industry has taken to bringing individual copyright suits—more than 3000 lawsuits so far—against the largest downloaders. Also it is less clear legally that these sites are "contributory infringers" when they don't download any music on their computers, as one lower court said in refusing to find the site Grokster liable for contributory infringement— although that decision was reversed on appeal, based on the fact that Grokster had publicly promoted its site as a great site for downloading music. However, in another case, the music site Aimster was found liable.

There are now several "for-pay" online music services, such as "iTunes" established by Apple. Even Napster itself has revived, under new ownership, and now offers a version which permits users to sample tunes briefly and make purchases. The following story shows that developments involving the music industry and music downloading are occurring rapidly (and more will have happened by the time you read this).

BILLBOARD WILL MONITOR SONGS ALL OVER

In the past, appearing on the pages of *Billboard* magazine was a powerful symbol for musical artists. Today the publication famous for its music-sales charts (such as "The Billboard 200") is developing new technologies to regain its place and relevance in the industry. *Billboard* has launched a new ranking for undiscovered artists and a subscription service to help them get noticed by managers, promoters and labels.

Billboard has teamed up with MySpace Music (a joint venture of the 4 major music labels) which will allow, for about $100, unsigned artists to upload their music to the Web and track exposure on a range of outlets, from Twitter and music blogs to radio airplay and sales. These factors will be used to create a new ranking called the "Dreamseekers" chart, which will appear regularly in *Billboard* magazine and on its website.

The new venture comes at a time when the standard measures of musical success are struggling to account for all the new channels through which music is consumed. "Everybody has to modernize," said Richard Beckman, CEO of E5 Global Media, which owns *Billboard*. "We want to be the catalytic force to help the industry monetize itself."

Downloading of music is not just an American issue, as the following story demonstrates.

INTERNATIONAL PERSPECTIVE

French Internet service providers have agreed to cooperate in a crackdown against Web surfers who illegally download music online. In a government-backed agreement also signed by record labels and musicians' groups, France's leading Internet companies agreed to pull the plug on pirates and step up cooperation with copyright prosecutions. The agreement was signed by representatives of Internet service providers Free, Noos, Club-Internet, Wanadoo and Tiscali France.

The French Internet companies agreed to use "termination or suspension clauses" to cancel the subscriptions of pirates caught in the act. They also pledged to send warning messages to individual customers upon request from rights holders and to "act immediately" on court orders to identify clients or cut them off. The companies and societies that collect their royalties all agreed to speed up the development of legitimate download sites with "clear and competitive pricing."

The signatories also agreed to study music industry suggestions that Internet service providers offer "peer-to-peer filters" to users, allowing them to block their own—or their children's—access to file-sharing sites like Kazaa and eDonkey.

THE "FAIR USE" DOCTRINE

The copyright law allows a few exceptions to the exclusive rights of the copyright owner. The most important of these exceptions is the "fair use" doctrine. Napster tried to use the "fair use" theory as a defense, but did not succeed. "Fair use" began as common law doctrine hundreds of years earlier, and it was made part of the federal law when the Copyright Act was amended in 1976.

The Copyright Act states in §107 [17 U.S.C. 107]:

Notwithstanding the provisions of Sections 106 and 106A [dealing with the exclusive rights of the copyright owner], the fair use of a copyrighted work, including such use by reproduction in copies or phonorecords or by any other means specified by that section, for purposes such as criticism, comment, news reporting, teaching (including multiple copies for classroom use), scholarship, or research, is not an infringement of copyright. In determining whether the use made of a work in any particular case is a fair use the factors to be considered shall include—

1. the purpose and character of the use, including whether such use is of a commercial nature or is for nonprofit educational purposes;
2. the nature of the copyrighted work;
3. the amount and substantiality of the portion used in relation to the copyrighted work as a whole; and
4. the effect of the use upon the potential market for or value of the copyrighted work.

"fair use" doctrine: A legal principle, an exception to a copyright owner's exclusive rights, that allows another to make some limited ("fair") use of the copyrighted work without permission.

Key Fair Use Factors:
1. The purpose and character of the use.
2. The nature of the copyrighted work.
3. The amount and substantiality of the amount taken.
4. The economic effect of the second use on the copyright owner.

Therefore, the fair use doctrine holds that, despite the copyright owner's exclusive rights, other persons can use a limited portion of the copyrighted work without the author's permission for certain purposes. As one court said, "the fair use doctrine offers a means of balancing the exclusive rights of copyright holders with the public's interest in dissemination of information affecting areas of universal concern, such as art, science, and industry."

The scope of allowable fair use has been the subject of many court decisions. The four factors set out in the statute had already been used and interpreted in many common law cases. In fact, when Congress enacted this section, the Judiciary Committee report accompanying the bill stated that it "intended to restate the present judicial doctrine of fair use, not to change, narrow or enlarge it in any way." Nevertheless, these four factors have been reinterpreted frequently since the 1976 statute.

In order to help understand how these factors might affect an analysis of fair use, let us assume that Henry has written a 30-page article about zoning laws for an academic journal. At some later time, Jason, without permission from Henry, uses much of the article (including six pages verbatim) in a book he writes. Jason's book is sold by his publisher in bookstores across the nation. The first fair use factor considers *the purpose and character of the use* that is being made by the second user. In this case Jason's use is commercial—he hopes to earn some royalties from the sales of his book. If the user had been a nonprofit public school, it would have had somewhat greater rights; but his use, to make a profit for himself, is not favorable. However, the court would still have to analyze all the factors before deciding on fair use.

The second factor examines the *nature of the copyrighted work*—in our example, Henry's article. With regard to some scientific, legal, or medical works, courts have generally agreed that, in order to advance science or art, identical words or phrases may be used by later authors. On the other hand, a "student study guide" or some similar work is clearly intended to be sold for profit and does not contain any scientific knowledge that could be used without infringement by other authors in their works. Professors who write for academic journals do not do so for money, and they usually hope that people read their articles. Thus, the "nature of the use" may protect Jason somewhat.

The third factor relates to the *amount or substantiality of the copyrighted work that is used* by the second person. Courts have sometimes actually counted words or pages in determining the amount of the original work that was copied. Clearly, if 10–20 percent or more of the original is copied, it is likely to be held infringement. However, even if a fairly small part of the original work is used verbatim, it may still be "substantial" if the part taken is a "key or essential" portion. Jason's use here is fairly large, and if the part taken is important, this test will hurt his fair use argument.

Although each factor is important, the last point, the *economic effect* on the copyright holder—has often been treated as the most critical. The public benefits from the discussion of books, plays, musical compositions, and so on; such discussions, however, do not harm the market and potential economic value of the work—as long as the amount of the original reproduced is fairly small. Indeed, a favorable book review or a description on a news show may well increase the market and the profits for the author. But when the material taken from the copyrighted work begins to cut into the author or artist's potential market, the purposes of the copyright law are violated and fair use will not apply.

The following well-known case involves an analysis of several of the fair use factors.

BASIC BOOKS, INC. V. KINKO'S GRAPHICS CORP.

758 F. Supp. 1522 (N.Y. 1991)

FACTS

Kinko's Graphics Corp., a national chain of photocopy shops, was sued by a group of publishers for copyright infringement. The publishers held copyrights on a number of books from which Kinko's had photocopied portions for "course packets" that were sold to students taking certain classes at New York University. The publishers introduced at the trial five course packets sold by Kinko's in connection with college courses. Each one included several portions of photocopied material from other copyrighted books. In many cases, entire chapters of books were copied, and in one case, three chapters of a book were copied and included in the packet. Kinko's had not sought permission for any of the copying, relying on the fair use doctrine and the clauses in the copyright law about "educational use" and "multiple copies for classroom use."

Kinko's markets its services directly to university students and professors. Several brochures introduced at trial showed that Kinko's openly solicits from professors lists of readings that they plan to use in their courses and then copies excerpts and sells them in bound form to students. Kinko's had net revenue of $42 million in 1988 and $54 million in 1989, with net profits of $300,000 and $3 million, respectively. The publishers sought statutory damages, attorneys' fees, an injunction against further copying without permission, and payment of royalties.

DECISION

Kinko's did not deny that it had photocopied material from copyrighted books and journals; instead, it argued that it was protected by the doctrine of fair use. The federal district court thus was required to carefully analyze the four factors that determine whether a use is "fair."

With regard to the "purpose and character of the use," the court noted that Kinko's was a commercial enterprise and sought to make a profit from its photocopying. Although Kinko's argued that its use was educational, Judge Motley commented that the use of the course packets "in the hands of the students, was no doubt educational." "However," Motley continued, "the use in the hands of Kinko's employees is commercial." In other words, the use of the material by Kinko's was not for commentary, criticism, or other scholarly purpose but for profit.

The second test, "the nature of the copyrighted work," worked in favor of Kinko's. Generally, the scope of fair use is greater with respect to factual than nonfactual works. Fictional works, largely based on an author's subjective impressions, require more protection than biographies, criticism, and commentary. The materials copied here were factual, containing information of public interest, and thus receive somewhat less protection.

The third factor, "the amount and substantiality of the portion used," weighed heavily against Kinko's. Many cases have held that even fairly small amounts of copying can be "substantial" when they are the "heart" of the material. Here, Kinko's copied passages ranging from 14 to 110 pages, representing between 5.2 percent and 25.1 percent of the works. In many instances entire chapters were copied. The court had no trouble finding that the portions copied were both quantitatively substantial and qualitatively significant. Judge Motley pointedly noted that in one case, Kinko's had copied 110 pages of someone's work and sold it to 132 students, a practice "grossly out of line with accepted fair use principles."

The fourth factor, "the effect of the use on potential markets for or value of the copyrighted work," is usually critical, as was true here. Kinko's operates some 200 stores nationwide in close proximity to hundreds of colleges and universities. Thus, stated the court, the potential for widespread copyright infringement is great. The fact that several chapters of other books were copied and included in the packets clearly obviates the need for students to purchase those books, causing loss of income to publishers and authors. The loss is felt even more by authors of out-of-print books, for whom permissions fees constitute a significant source of income. This factor counted heavily against Kinko's.

Kinko's final argument was that a section of the copyright law specifically mentioned that fair use might apply to "multiple copies for classroom use." Part of the legislative history of the 1976 amendments to the Copyright Act included an agreement between groups representing publishers, authors, and educational institutions, titled "Agreement on Guidelines for Classroom Copying in Not-for-Profit Educational Institutions." Although not actually law, this statement has been used in assessing the fairness of certain educational practices. The Guidelines provide a "safe harbor" for classroom use (up to one copy per student) if such copying meets the other fair use tests, if each copy includes a notice of copyright, and if such copying meets the tests of "brevity, spontaneity, and cumulative effect."

In this case, not only did the copying fail the "four factors" tests for fair use, it failed to meet the Guidelines tests as well. First, none of the copies included copyright notices. *Brevity* is defined in the Guidelines to be "an excerpt of not more than 1,000 words or 10% of the work,

whichever is less." The copying here vastly exceeded this standard. *Spontaneity* requires that the decision to use the work and the moment of its use be so close that request for permission is unreasonable. The court found this not to be the case here. Finally, *cumulative effect* prohibits any more than nine instances of multiple copying for one course during one term, and to no more than one piece of work per author. Both of these standards were violated here.

In conclusion, the federal court found that Kinko's had clearly violated the Copyright Act and had infringed the copyrights of the various publishers on 12 occasions. Judge Motley issued an injunction prohibiting Kinko's from future "anthologizing" and copying of plaintiffs' works without permission, and assessed statutory damages of $510,000 against Kinko's.

CASE QUESTIONS

1. Does this case mean that it is no longer possible for professors to put together a course packet of readings for use in a course? Does the fair use doctrine still have effect as it applies to education?
2. How much copying from another source can a professor or a copy shop legally do under the fair use doctrine? What must be done to avoid infringement?
3. Would the result have been the same if the copying had been done by the university or the professor? What if the packets had been given, not sold, to the students?

INTERNATIONAL PERSPECTIVES

INTERNATIONAL COPYRIGHT PROTECTION

The U.S. Copyright office states on its web page that there is no such thing as an "international copyright" that will automatically protect an author's writings throughout the entire world. Protection against unauthorized use in a particular country depends, basically, on the national laws of that country. However, most countries do offer protection to foreign works under certain conditions, and these conditions have been greatly simplified by international copyright treaties and conventions.

One of the major international treaties concerning copyright is the Berne Convention. This agreement has been signed by 164 nations, including the United States, and assures that nationals of all signing countries will be treated equally in the copyright process with home country citizens. The Berne Convention included a provision that all nations would extend the terms of copyright protection to "life plus 70 years," as the U.S. did in the Copyright Extension Act. The Berne Convention also contained a clause by which all nations agreed that the author of a work has the exclusive right to translate, reproduce, perform, or adapt protected works.

COMPUTER PROGRAMS

Numerous cases filed in recent years have dealt with copyright issues involving computers and computer programs. In the early days of computer programs, some courts refused to accord copyright status to such forms as the software program for a computer game or other software products. Courts were unsure whether a series of symbols was a type of literary or artistic creation that qualified for copyright protection. However, after several important court cases and an amendment to the Copyright Law, it is now clear that computer programs can be copyrighted. Such programs can qualify as a creative work that has been reduced to a "tangible means of expression"—the object code and source code have been expressed in words and symbols in a certain order.

The next wave of computer litigation concerned the so-called "look and feel" cases. This situation arose when one software product became successful, and other developers attempted to produce a similar product. They could not simply copy the underlying code of the first program because that would clearly be copyright infringement. Thus, developers would independently devise a new program that looked and acted very much like the first product—that is, one that had the same "look and feel." Although the graphics and the user interface (such things as menu screens, icons, symbols, and key strokes required of the user) would look and feel very much like the earlier copyrighted program, the actual underlying computer code (the "expression") was not the same.

Those who favor strict application of copyright laws argue that it is unfair for developers to reap profits based on their mimicking a program produced through the considerable research effort, time, and expense of someone else. Such experts assert that it is bad public policy to allow software companies to simply "clone" successful products without incurring research expenses, because this discourages innovative and time-consuming efforts.

On the other hand, many software and computer industry veterans argue that public policy should encourage developers to build onto the advances of others, and that standardized icons and menu screens help consumers and the software industry move forward. If basic icons and "looks" are tied up by patents and copyrights, so each program must interface differently with the user, it will make computer use more difficult for the public.

The results of the many "look and feel" cases varied, depending on a number of factors, including how similar the programs appeared; how original the graphic elements, menu screens, and words used in the first program were; whether the second programmer had "access" to the first program; and whether the second program took earlier ideas and expanded on them or merely misappropriated another's ideas. Courts have held that it would clearly be improper for anyone to claim exclusive use of such terms as "file" or "edit" or

look and feel cases: Where someone has created a computer program or user interface that "looks" and acts ("feels") like another copyrighted program, but the second author did not copy the actual code of the first program.

to prohibit one company from using a graphic of a trash can just because someone else used a garbage can to depict "trash."

Obviously, today's advanced computer technology and the Internet and World Wide Web make it possible to browse museums, libraries and other sites all over the world and to actually copy (download) onto one's own computer books, articles, photographs, music, artwork, and other forms of creative expression covered by copyright. The problems associated with protection of the copyright owner's rights and potential methods are becoming increasingly complex.

Jury Rules in Favor of Bratz Dolls

The sassy, billion-dollar Bratz dolls appear poised to confront Barbie on toy shelves again after a jury in April 2011 rejected Mattel Inc.'s claims that rival MGA Entertainment stole the idea for the wildly popular fashion toy. Instead the jury slapped Mattel with more than $88 million in economic damages in a stunning rebuke of the toy giant's claims.

Mattel had filed the original lawsuit in 2005, claiming that it owned the copyright on the Bratz dolls since the dolls' designer, Carter Bryant, was working for Mattel when he did the initial concept sketches for the provocative, hip hop-inspired dolls with large eyes, heads, lips and feet, and tiny noses. The Bratz doll, introduced in 2001, was a blockbuster hit with "tweens," as Barbie sales declined.

Bryant asserted that he had not worked on the idea while with Mattel and that his ideas were developed before and after his contract with Mattel. In 2008 an earlier jury trial had resulted in an award of $100 million to Mattel, and the judge had ordered the copyright and Bratz name be given to Mattel and all remaining Bratz products be destroyed. However that order was vacated as "Draconian," and the jury verdict was overturned in 2010 by the 9th Circuit Court of Appeals.

In addition to denying the copyright infringement claims, MGA had also countersued Mattel for misappropriation of trade secrets for engaging in corporate espionage at toy fairs and conspiring to keep Bratz products off retail shelves. Jurors found that Mattel stole 26 of the 114 trade secrets MGA listed, resulting in the $88.4 million in damages awarded to MGA.

Hundreds of millions of dollars in potential damages and the rights to the fashion doll were at stake in the acrimonious case, which was tremendously costly for both sides. MGA's Chief Executive Officer, Isaac Larian, said he had spent as much as $170 million on legal fees, while analysts estimate Mattel's expenses at $400 million thus far. The doll line has been in limbo since the first trial and retailers have been hesitant to stock it because of uncertainty about its fate, Larian said.

Source: Based in part on the news story, *Jury Rejects Mattel's Bratz Doll Copyright claim*, Friday, April 22, 2011, by Gillian Flaccus, Associated Press, accessed at FindLaw.com

TRADEMARKS

Trademarks, like patents and copyrights, can be and are protected by federal law. A **trademark** is a word, phrase, symbol, or design that identifies and distinguishes the source of the goods and services of one party from those of someone else. A trademark may be created in the United States either by (1) actual use of the mark or symbol or (2) the filing of an application to register the mark with the U.S. Patent and Trademark Office (PTO), stating that the owner has a bona fide intent to use the mark in commerce. (The owner must then begin to actually *use* the trademark within 8 months.) So, as with copyrights, one can acquire a trademark simply by use, but it makes good sense to register the mark with the PTO. Such registration gives notice to others and provides greater rights in any lawsuit.

Unlike patents and copyrights, trademark rights can last for an indefinite time period if the owner continues to use the mark to identify goods or service, and renews the registration periodically. Whereas early trademark cases were based on common law protection, most trademark issues today are based upon the **Lanham Act,** a federal statute enacted in 1946 and amended several times since. Under this law, federal trademark protection lasts for 10 years but can be continuously renewed.

An individual may file his or her own trademark application with the PTO, with or without an attorney. The application must include a drawing of the mark. When the application is received, an examining attorney with the PTO will compare the mark with other previous registrations and determine if the mark may be registered. If there is a "likelihood of confusion" between the applicant's mark and a registered mark, the applicant will be denied a trademark.

Also, if the term or mark is "descriptive"—that is it merely describes the goods or services, the trademark request will be refused. Descriptive terms are those that identify a characteristic or quality of the article, such as color, function, or ingredients. Thus, the phrases "blue chair" or "high chair" could not receive trademark protection. Sometimes, however, a descriptive word can acquire "secondary meaning" through advertising and use—such as "Apple Computers." When the term acquires a secondary meaning it can be protected by trademark law.

In addition, an attempt to trademark a generic term like "table" or "car" will be denied. **Generic** terms identify a class of products, like "ballpoint pens" or "stereos." However, sometimes a registered trademark term comes, through usage over time, to identify the entire class of similar products and thus becomes generic. The result then is that the owner of the trademark loses the right to exclusive use of the term. Words like "cellophane" and "aspirin" started out as trademarks, but have since become generic. Xerox Corporation, for example, uses a portion of its advertising budget each year to produce ads which state that "Xerox is a registered trademark, so please use the term only when referring to our products, not as a substitute for the noun 'photocopiers' or for the verb 'to photocopy.'"

The mere fact that one company is allowed to register a trademark with the PTO does not prevent another firm to suing for infringement. As is true

trademark: A word, phrase, or symbol that identifies and distinguishes a product.

generic term: A word or phrase that is synonymous with a whole class of products and cannot receive trademark protection.

with the PTO, when the owner of one trademark sues a second business for using a somewhat similar trademark, the basic standard adopted by the courts is the **"likelihood of confusion"** by consumers. In other words is the average consumer likely to be confused about the origin of the second product, and might it be confusing to determine which company actually made the product. There have been many big lawsuits between companies, often featuring the testimony of several marketing experts who have done surveys of consumers to determine whether they are confused about the product origins.

It is not necessary for the first firm to prove that the second one "intended" to infringe, only that consumers will likely be confused. For example, a few years ago, a man named Robert Corr had been making beer at home for several years, when his friends persuaded him to go into business. He started to make beer in larger quantities and sold it as "Corr's Beer." Not long after he began, Mr. Corr received a letter from the attorney for Coors, one of the largest beer manufacturers in the United States, demanding that he cease selling "Corr's Beer" because there was a strong likelihood of confusion in the public mind as to the origin of the beer. After some skirmishing, Mr. Corr did change the name of his beer, despite the fact that he was simply using his own name.

In an unusual case decided a few years ago, the U.S. Supreme Court ruled in a unanimous decision that in some cases, the particular *color of a product* may even be protected by trademark. In *Qualitex Co. v. Jacobson Products Co. Inc.,* 514 U.S. 159 (1995), the issue concerned commercial dry cleaning press pads. For more than 30 years Qualitex had manufactured "Sun Glow" press pads, which came in a distinctive greenish-gold color. Qualitex had spent some $1.6 million to promote them. When competitor Jacobson began making press pads of the same color, Qualitex sued for unfair competition and trademark infringement.

The color was a "symbol" of the product and had developed a **"secondary meaning"** that "identified and distinguished" that particular brand, wrote Justice Stephen Breyer. The Court noted that trademarks had been upheld previously for the shape of a Coca-Cola bottle, the sound of NBC's three chimes, and the scent of plumeria blossoms on sewing thread. "If a descriptive word, and a 'shape,' a sound and a fragrance can act as symbols," ruled Breyer, "why can't a color do the same?" The Court held that there had been a trademark infringement.

Another trademark issue is **"trademark dilution."** In 1995 Congress amended the federal Trademark Act, to provide a remedy for the "dilution of famous marks." The amendment, known as the Federal Trademark Dilution Act (FTDA), describes the factors that determine whether a mark is "distinctive and famous," and defines the term "dilution" as "the lessening of the capacity of a famous mark to identify and distinguish goods or services."

Domain Names   Another significant new type of trademark issue concerns domain names, the "URL" set of letters and numbers used to access a site on the World Wide Web. Companies naturally want their domain names to be as close as possible to their corporate name, so consumers can easily access their Web site.

For many years, one company, Network Solutions, Inc. (NSI), controlled the allocation of all commercial Web sites—those that end with ".com." Today such registrations are handled by a corporation named ICANN which was selected by the U.S. Commerce Department to oversee domain names and other aspects of cyberspace in 1998. Not surprisingly, various entrepreneurs saw a business opportunity—they would register a domain name (e.g., "www.mci.com") and then sell the rights to the name to the "real" MCI when it wanted use of the name for its Web site. Such so-called **cybersquatters** caused considerable anger from companies who felt that their trademark registration should cover the domain name issue, and that they should not have to pay a premium just to obtain what should have been theirs—the right to use their name on the Web.

Several cases have been filed by holders of trademarked names against cybersquatters and other businesses that have obtained domain names using symbols, names, and phrases associated with other companies and products. Where it has been shown that the first firm did have a legal trademark and that use of its name by a second firm would cause "dilution" of the trademark's value and likelihood of confusion to consumers, courts have entered injunctions and/or ordered the transfer of the domain name.

In 1999 a new federal law called The Anticybersquatting Consumer Protection Act was enacted. This law added a section to the Lanham Act prohibiting the bad faith registration or use of an Internet domain name that infringes on a trademark or famous mark. This law should prevent cybersquatters from tying up domain names, even if the trademark owner does not immediately object. The law allows proof of actual damages or statutory damages of between $1,000 and $300,000. This provision is important, said one industry lawyer, because "most of these outfits kidnapping domain names are Mom-and-Pop shops or kids sitting in the basement." The first suit to enforce the provisions of the law was filed a few days later by actor Brad Pitt, who successfully sued two California men who had obtained the domain name "bradpitt.com" and then tried to sell it to Mr. Pitt for as much as $50,000.

TRADE SECRETS

The preceding three types of intellectual property—patents, copyrights, and trademarks—all involve "rights" that are granted by (patents) or are registered with (copyrights and trademarks) the federal government. The fourth main type of intellectual property, trade secrets, does not share this trait.

Trade secrets consist of important information created or developed by a business that is not filed in any government office but instead kept secret and confidential by the business. For example, the formula for Coca-Cola has never been patented but is carefully maintained as a corporate secret. Only a very few Coca-Cola employees and officers know the formula at one time, and they are strictly bound to secrecy and the formula kept in a locked vault. The same is true for the mix of ingredients making up the basic Kentucky Fried Chicken sauce. Other types of important business secrets may include the strategic financial or marketing plan of a firm, a customer list, or a specific method of doing business. In each case, in order to qualify as a trade secret, the firm must consider the information confidential and must take steps to keep it confidential. Most medium-sized and large businesses today have all their key employees sign **confidentiality agreements,** also called non-disclosure agreements (NDAs), by which the employees promise not to disclose trade secrets or other confidential information.

In addition, many companies require employees to sign **non-compete agreements,** or **covenants not to compete,** by which the employee promises not to open a competing business within a certain area for a certain

trade secrets: Intellectual property assets of a business, such as a formula or a customer list, which are kept secret.

non-compete agreement: An agreement between a firm and an employee, by which the employee promises not to open a competing business within a certain area, after leaving the firm.

period of time after leaving the first employer. These agreements usually include a clause barring use of any confidential information gained from the first employer. Such agreements are generally enforced by courts if they are reasonable in scope and length of time.

What is a trade secret?   Trade secret legal principles have developed as a common law subject—that is, they have been established and developed by many court decisions involving a company and an ex-employee, who have different views about what the former employee knows and should be able to do with the information. Concepts such as "fairness," "equity," "economic injury," and the "terms of the contract" signed by the parties—factors typically involved in common law cases—determine the outcome of cases and development of the law.

The *Restatement of Torts* in 1939 stated:

> Definition of Trade Secret. A trade secret may consist of any formula, pattern, device or compilation of information which is used in one's business, and which gives him an opportunity to obtain an advantage over competitors who do not know or use it. It may be a formula for a chemical compound, a process of manufacturing, treating or preserving materials, a pattern for a machine or other device, or a list of customers . . . .Generally it relates to the production of goods, as for example, a machine or formula for the production of an article. It may, however, relate to the sale of goods or other operations in the business, such as a code for determining discounts, rebates or other concessions in a price list or catalogue, or a list of specialized customers, or a method of bookkeeping or other office management.

The *Restatement* also noted that while an exact definition was not possible, important factors in determining the existence of a trade secret included; (1) the extent to which the information is known outside the business; (2) the extent to which it is known by the business' own employees; (3) the extent of the measures taken to guard the secrecy of the information; (4) the value of the information; (5) the amount of money and effort expended to protect the secret; (6) the ease or difficulty with which the information could be properly acquired or duplicated by others.

The concepts discussed in the *Restatement* were widely accepted and were included in court decisions (common law) during the next 40 years and still today. However, as with many common law doctrines, the decisions varied considerably in scope and application from state to state. In 1979 the National Conference of Commissioners on Uniform State Laws approved the **Uniform Trade Secrets Act** (UTSA) which has now been adopted in some form by forty-four states and the District of Columbia.

Under the UTSA, a trade secret is:

> Information, including a formula, pattern, compilation, program, device, method, technique, or process, that: (1) derives independent economic value, actual or potential, from not being generally known to, and not being readily ascertainable by the proper means by, other persons who can obtain economic value from its disclosure or use, and (2) is the subject of efforts that are reasonable under the circumstances to maintain its secrecy.

The Uniform Trade Secrets Act (UTSA): A model law defining and protecting trade secrets which has been enacted in 44 states.

The UTSA provides protection against actual and also "threatened" misappropriation of a trade secret. Like the *Restatement of Torts* definition, the essentials of a trade secret under the UTSA are that the information must not be generally known, must have economic value, and must be kept confidential to maintain secrecy. Comments to the UTSA indicate that "proper means" to obtain information might include reverse engineering, observation in public use, independent discovery—any of which might defeat a trade secret claim.

Meanwhile, "improper means" of obtaining a trade secret under the UTSA include "theft, bribery, misrepresentation, breach of duty or inducement of a breach of duty to maintain secrecy or espionage through electronic means." The UTSA updated some of the principles of the *Restatement* to include confidential information related to a single event or information that had a short life span, such as a marketing plan, and also protected negative information—that which showed what type of action would not work. However, in general, the UTSA was not radically different from the *Restatement,* and many courts have continued to rely on the principles of, and cases decided under, the *Restatement of Torts* for guidance in interpreting and applying the UTSA.

The experts that compile case decisions and writes the *Restatements* periodically update their research. When the *Restatement (Second) of Torts* was published in 1979, the subject of trade secrets was not included. However, trade secret principles were examined and expanded in 1995, when the American Law Institute issued the *Restatement (Third) of Unfair Competition.* This treatise defined trade secrets as "any information that can be used in the operation of a business or other enterprise and that is sufficiently valuable and secret to afford an actual or potential economic advantage over others." The drafters of the new Restatement believed that trade secret law had evolved over the years from a simple articulation of a standard of commercial morality into an important tool for encouraging investment in research and development. Changes in business required that confidential information be disseminated to a broader group of employees, agents, and licensees who could assist in exploiting the information.

Misappropriation of trade secrets became a criminal act when the federal government enacted the **Economic Espionage Act of 1996 (EEA)** in an attempt to protect trade secrets in a more broad and uniform way. Congress believed that state civil remedies were sometimes insufficient because companies lacked the time and resources to investigate and bring suits in all cases, and some defendants had no assets. The EEA creates a new federal crime for: (1) the theft of trade secrets with the intent to benefit a foreign government, and also for (2) the theft or misappropriation of trade secrets by "anyone other than the owner." Congress wanted to create a "comprehensive and systematic" solution that would "put some teeth into the punishment" for trade secret theft and other forms of industrial espionage.

Although some criminal cases have been brought by federal prosecutors, most trade secret cases are still civil cases initiated by one company when a key employee leaves and starts to work for a competing firm. The courts have had to determine the line, on a case by case basis, between the twin goals of (1) allowing an individual to freely engage in employment in the field in which he/she has expertise and experience; and (2) protecting valuable information that one company has spent time and money to create and has attempted to keep confidential.

In trade secret cases, a court must first determine if in fact there is some information or process or formula that qualifies as a trade secret—using some of the definitions set out above, based on previous court decisions. The court needs to determine whether the information is primarily "general knowledge and skill" that any good employee would acquire in the course of employment, or is it valuable, confidential, important and unknown information that would significantly aid a competing firm? If the answer is "trade secret" the court must move to the next question—whether the trade secret has been or is about to be "misappropriated." Has the information been acquired by "proper means" or by theft, trickery or stealing away a key employee from the main competitor?

The Inevitable Disclosure Doctrine. As mentioned the UTSA addresses three circumstances that must be present for an owner to obtain relief. One of the essentials is that the trade secret has been actually misappropriated or is "threatened" to be misappropriated. As in actual misappropriation, the threatened misappropriation must benefit the person not authorized to use the secret, or harm the trade secret's owner—which harm can be shown whether the information was taken in tangible or intangible form (such as an employee's memory). This intangible form of trade secret loss has led some courts to adopt the doctrine called **"inevitable disclosure"** to protect the trade secret owner.

This theory holds that in some cases, the job that an employee held with company #1 is so similar to the job he/she has accepted with company #2 that it is "inevitable" that trade secrets of company #1 will be used in the new position. The cases which have adopted this theory may apply it even in the absence of a signed non-disclosure or non-compete agreement. The leading case applying this theory in recent years is set forth below.

PEPSICO. V. REDMOND

54 F. 3d 1262 (7th Cir. 1995)

FACTS

In late 1994 William E. Redmond was one of PepsiCo's high-level managers, having recently been named general manager of the California business unit (that was responsible for 20 percent of PepsiCo North America's profits in the United States). His senior position had given him access to a large volume of competitively sensitive information, including overall strategic plans for marketing, manufacturing, production, packaging, distribution, promotional event planning and pricing. PepsiCo and Quaker Oats were engaged in fierce competition with respect to their sports drinks (PepsiCo's All Sport vs. Quaker's Gatorade) and other drinks such as PepsiCo's Lipton tea and Ocean Spray vs. Quaker's Snapple beverages.

Redmond had worked for PepsiCo for ten years when he was hired by Quaker as Vice President of Field Operations for its Gatorade division. Redmond had kept his dealings with Quaker secret until he had accepted the offer, and even after his acceptance he misled PepsiCo officials and colleagues about the nature of his new position.

PepsiCo filed suit immediately in federal court in Illinois, asking for temporary and permanent injunctive relief (under the Illinois Trade Secrets Act, which mostly followed the UTSA) prohibiting Redmond from disclosing PepsiCo's trade secrets, as well as a temporary injunction prohibiting him from assuming his duties at Quaker. PepsiCo argued that its innovative selling and delivery systems, and its "Strategic Plan" and "Annual Operating Plan" (outlining PepsiCo's financial goals, marketing and promotional plans), which Redmond had helped prepare, were trade secrets and confidential material.

Quaker defended by pointing out the differences between the Quaker and Pepsi distribution systems, and the fact that Redmond had signed a confidentiality agreement with PepsiCo. Quaker also argued that it had policies in place that would prevent Redmond from disclosing a competitor's trade secrets.

Federal District Judge Lindberg considered Redmond's familiarity with PepsiCo's trade secrets, the similarity between his duties for PepsiCo and his planned responsibilities with Quaker, as well as his lack of candor about his job, and ruled that it was "inevitable" that Redmond would use or disclose PepsiCo's trade secrets in his new position. The court took note of Mr. Redmond's "lack of forthrightness," both in his dealings with PepsiCo and his testimony before the court and enjoined Redmond from assuming his proposed new position at Quaker for six months and from using or disclosing any PepsiCo trade secrets or confidential information.

DECISION

Quaker appealed the decision to the Seventh Circuit where the lower court order was affirmed. In a unanimous opinion by Judge Flaum, the Court concluded that "a plaintiff may prove a claim of trade secret misappropriation by demonstrating that a defendant's new employment will inevitably lead him to rely on plaintiff's trade secrets." Although the court noted that *PepsiCo* was not a traditional trade secret case where the former employee has "knowledge of a special manufacturing process or customer list that can give the competitor an unfair advantage by transferring the technology or the customers to the new employer," the case still fell within the boundaries of trade secret protection. The court reasoned that "PepsiCo finds itself in the position of a coach, one of whose players has left, playbook in hand, to join the opposing team before the big game."

In reaching its conclusion, the 7th Circuit devoted considerable attention to the question of when disclosure of trade secrets is "inevitable" so as to justify the imposition of an injunction prohibiting competitive employment. The court acknowledged that lawsuits which allege only a threatened misappropriation of trade secrets heighten the tension between the conflicting goals of protecting a

firm's intellectual property and a worker's right to pursue a livelihood. However, the court ultimately concluded that prohibiting a party from undertaking a new endeavor for a reasonable period of time is proper if: (1) the employee has knowledge of the employer's trade secrets; (2) the new employment involves the same, or substantially similar, duties or technology as the former employment; and (3) the employee cannot be trusted to avoid using these trade secrets in his or her new job.

Like the lower court the appellate court made particular note of Mr. Redmond's lack of candor and truthfulness toward his associates at PepsiCo. He had denied any interest in another job while he was negotiating with Quaker, had delayed his resignation a few days after accepting the new job, and he and Quaker had submitted affidavits early in the case concerning his new position and duties that were later undermined and contradicted by testimony at the preliminary injunction hearing. The 7th Circuit stated that Redmond's "lack of forthrightness on some occasions and out and out lies on others . . . led the court to conclude that defendant Redmond could not be trusted to act with the necessary sensitivity and good faith under the circumstances."

CASE QUESTIONS

1. What facts in this case did the court find were most important in weighing and reaching its decision? Do you agree that it would be "inevitable" that Mr. Redmond would use PepsiCo trade secrets in his new job?
2. What are the "pros" and "cons" of the inevitable disclosure doctrine? What are the competing "public policy" reasons for supporting and opposing the rule?
3. Please draft in one or two sentences, in your own words, a rule that makes sense for determining when an employee should be barred from new employment under the "inevitable disclosure" rule.
4. Should Mr. Redmond be prohibited from ever going to work for Quaker, or only for some period of time? How should a court determine how long to bar him from taking the position with the competitor? What rule should be developed for future cases?

Many courts have considered the inevitable disclosure doctrine since its "rebirth" in the *PepsiCo* case, and it has received mixed reviews. Courts have granted injunctions in cases where a party used confidential information for purposes other than those for which it was disclosed, when an employee stockpiled confidential information immediately prior to leaving a job, or when a party's undertaking could not be accomplished without using another's confidential information. On the other hand, courts have refused to grant injunctions where the employee's subsequent activities did not involve the subject matter of the confidential information, where the information had lost its value as a secret, and where the grant of an injunction would effectively preclude the person from employment. Some forty-one states have considered the inevitable disclosure doctrine in certain circumstances and about half of them have accepted the theory, while half have rejected it.

CYBERLAW—THE INTERNET, THE WEB, AND THE LAW

One of the most dramatic changes in daily life and business practice in the past few years has been the incredible growth of the Internet and World Wide Web. Most of us exchange numerous e-mail messages and visit several "Web sites" every day—a practice unknown a few years ago. Today we are constantly connected to each other and to every possible source of information through our smartphones, Facebook pages, Twitter, and other electronic means. Almost every legal issue discussed in this textbook is now being raised in new ways, through cases involving the Internet and the Web—so-called **cyberspace.** Many other legal issues are arising in new formats or are made more complex by the Internet and the Web. There are legal and professional journals devoted to reporting the latest issues in computer law, **cyberlaw** and internet-related legal developments. Some advocates believe that a whole new set of legal principles should be applied to the internet, and others, part of the so-called "freenet" movement, have pushed for an internet free of any regulation at all.

On the other hand, many legal scholars think that "cyberlaw" is not a new subject at all, but just a natural development of the law—with the internet and web shaping and being shaped by traditional theories governing contracts, torts, employment, property, patents and copyrights. Many experts believe that the internet and world wide web, while an exciting new technologies, do not require their own law, but should fit in with existing legal principles. There is no question, however, that issues involving the internet and the Web are influencing nearly every legal theory discussed so far in this textbook.

For example, one of the cases examined early in this book involved the issue of whether a court in California had jurisdiction over the outdoor retail giant, L.L. Bean, based in Maine, due to the fact that the company had a Web site that was accessible in California and all states. This "jurisdiction" issue will be discussed more fully later in this chapter. Several other cases have challenged the legality or terms of contracts entered into over the Web, when a person using his or her computer clicks a box on the screen with his or her mouse. If you click on a box that says "I agree" have you entered into a contract just as binding as if you signed a 7-page written contract in an office? New forms of torts are created and recognized by courts when one person invades another's privacy, through the use of computer data or searches, or when a software program uses "cookies" to capture information about consumers who visit its Web site and then sell that information. New types of crimes can now be committed using the web and the internet to embezzle and defraud. And there are many more such emerging issues. One involves the tort of defamation using the Internet.

Social Media

In the past few years Social Media has become a part of almost everyone's lives. It is estimated that Facebook now has more than 500 million users, all around the world, who average some 90 posts each month. Many Facebook users have hundreds of "friends" who get to receive messages whenever one of their other "friends" has something to say or share or photos to show. It is either a tremendous way to always keep in touch with others, or a "terrible waste of time," as Betty White and others have suggested.

Not only has Facebook (and to a lesser extent, other sites such as MySpace, Linkedin and Twitter) has changed the way people communicate and relate to one another, social media has spawned several interesting legal issues. While many social media users know how to set privacy settings that limit somewhat the number of people who can access their posts, many others do not place limits on access. This means that one's privacy is totally eliminated, as almost anyone can look at the photos of you, your friends, family and anyone else whom you "tag." Even when a social media user limits access to her so-called "friends," some of the hundreds of users who really don't know you that well, may forward your posts and photos to many others who you do not know at all.

Those "funny" photos of you drinking or partying or acting goofy may well end up on the computer of a professor, or a present or possible future employer—who may not find them very humorous. Similarly when a person expresses his/her views very strongly on some issue where there are strongly held opinions, such as abortion, gay rights, political or religious matters, that Facebook user may find that those statements are forwarded far beyond what was expected, and may have unwanted results.

It is clear that employers now routinely look at the Facebook pages of job applicants before making hiring decisions. Is that ethical? Legal? Or perhaps it is negligent on their part if they do not look, when the information on a person and his/her hobbies, activities, friends, is so readily available. Many other legal issues are arising from social media, such as if employers look at an applicant's Facebook page, they may learn things about the applicant that they should not ask or use in hiring decisions, such as the person's age, national origin, race, religion—which might be used against them if the applicant or employee claims discrimination.

Should banks check a person's Facebook page before deciding to make a loan? Should landlords check Facebook and Linkedin before deciding to rent an apartment? If a person develops a fictitious persona for fun on Facebook, does that raise any legal issues—fraud? Misrepresentation? And what if the fictitious persona makes outrageous or defamatory statements? There are new legal issues arising each day as social media usage continues to explode, all around the world.

DEFAMATION IN CYBERSPACE

In Chapter 11 we discussed the tort of defamation, where one person makes a false and damaging statement about another person. Most of us access Facebook, Linkedin, and other internet sites for several hours a day, and sometimes we write and send messages without carefully thinking about what we say. Our message will reach at least one person, and may be sent on to hundreds of others throughout the "social media" networks as well. Bulletin boards, blogs, "listserves," and internet chatrooms provide instant audiences of hundreds for everyone's commentary. The possibilities for defamation in cyberspace are limitless, and many lawsuits have been brought against the speaker.

One other interesting aspect of this legal issue is whether the internet service provider (ISP) which enabled the remark to be made and sent through "cyberspace" faces liability for defamation. Prior to the Internet, it would have been difficult to send more than a few hundred such false messages, and there would have been added costs for photocopying, envelopes, postage, and more. Such is no longer true. In Chapter 1 of this book, one of the first cases we studied, *Zeran v. America Online* on p. 16, involved the possible liability of an online service provider for libel, due to a nasty, untrue "prank" posting on America Online, celebrating the horrible Oklahoma City bombing. Congress had previously heard from many internet service providers, expressing their fears about unlimited liability for messages traveling across their computers, and the case deals with the interpretation of a federal law, protecting internet service providers. Ken Zeran, the victim of the prank sued America Online, claiming the ISP was liable for allowing the posting, and then not removing it quickly after he complained. The court ruled against him on the basis of federal law.

The *Zeran* case shows that many legal issues take on new dimensions and have new ramifications due to the Internet and Web. For example, in the Zeran case, the person who posted the false notice was able to send out his or her message to millions of other people with the click of a mouse.

The federal law in the *Zeran* case generally grants immunity to Internet service providers for false postings on their services, unless the provider is aware of or has been involved in creating the posting. This statute was the primary reason that America Online won the *Zeran* case. However, there have been other cases in which one person has used the Internet to send messages containing false and hurtful information about someone else. As in non-cyberspace defamation, if the sender can be identified, and the statements are proved false and damaging, there should be liability. Although a lawsuit someday against the perpetrator might somewhat compensate the victim, the speed and scope of the Web allows millions of people to learn of the falsehood in an instant. Most of them will not learn of the later lawsuit or retraction, and most of the time the perpetrator will not be forced to pay sufficient damages to compensate the defamed person.

THE DIGITAL MILLENIUM COPYRIGHT ACT

In 1998, the U.S. Congress passed the Digital Millennium Copyright Act. This law was designed to implement two treaties signed in December 1996 at the World Intellectual Property Organization (WIPO) Geneva conference, but also contains additional provisions addressing related matters. The DMCA was enacted as an amendment to the Copyright Act and was designed, in part, to provide copyright protection for music, books, software, movies and other creative works transmitted in digital form over the Internet.

The law prohibits the manufacture, sale or distribution of devices used to illegally copy software and makes it a crime to circumvent the antipiracy measures that are contained in most commercial software. The bill was proposed and supported by the software and entertainment industries, and opposed by scientists, librarians, and academics, many of whom felt that their rights to access and use digital information were being limited. This part of the law has been used against those who have published programs such as the DeCSS code on web sites, as discussed below.

The law also provides that Internet Service Providers (ISPs) are immune from copyright infringement "by reason of the storage at the direction of a user of material that resides on a system or network controlled or operated by . . . the internet service provider." Therefore the DMCA provides immunity to ISPs from copyright infringement for the temporary and automatic storage of material that occurs during the internet message forwarding process. It reinforces and expands the protections discussed in the *Zeran* case.

In order to fully enjoy its immunity from liability under this provision, the ISP must not have actual knowledge that the material infringes a copyrighted work, and must not be aware of facts and circumstances from which infringing activity is apparent. Furthermore, upon receiving such knowledge or awareness (such as hearing from a copyright owner), the ISP must act "expeditiously to remove, or disable access to, the material that is claimed to be infringing or to be the subject of infringing activity."

Other Highlights of the DMCA include provisions which:

- Outlaw the manufacture, sale, or distribution of code-cracking devices used to illegally copy software.

- Permit the cracking of copyright protection devices, however, to conduct encryption research, assess product interoperability, and test computer security systems.

- Provide exemptions from anti-circumvention provisions for nonprofit libraries, archives, and educational institutions under certain circumstances.

- Limit liability of nonprofit institutions of higher education—when they serve as online service providers and under certain circumstances—for copyright infringement by faculty members or graduate students.

- Require that "webcasters" pay licensing fees to record companies.

- Require that the Register of Copyrights, after consultation with relevant parties, submit to Congress recommendations regarding how to promote distance education through digital technologies while "maintaining an appropriate balance between the rights of copyright owners and the needs of users."

- State explicitly that "[n]othing in this section shall affect rights, remedies, limitations, or defenses to copyright infringement, including fair use . . . " (this section was added after many complaints from educators and libraries about the loss of the "fair use" doctrine.)

FREE SPEECH AND WEB PORNOGRAPHY

It is often said that sexually explicit sites are among the most visited places on the Web. Parents are obviously concerned that their children will visit sites that are inappropriate and harmful to them, out of error or curiosity. Legislators, in response to the wishes of their constituents, have attempted to regulate sexually oriented Internet sites. Congress has passed several laws in an effort to control on-line pornography. However, as we discussed in Chapter 4, the United States has a strong tradition of protecting freedom of speech, and the reach of the First Amendment is wide and powerful. In 1996 Congress enacted the federal Communications Decency Act (CDA), in its first attempt to protect children from sexually explicit Web sites.

The Communications Decency Act of 1996.   The CDA banned, and in fact made it a felony criminal offense, to use a telecommunications device to transmit "obscene or indecent" material, knowing that the recipient is under age 18 years. Another key provision outlawed the use of a "computer interactive service"—such as the Internet or a computer bulletin board—to send or display "patently offensive" material. The law was immediately challenged by a wide variety of groups and corporations as a violation of the First Amendment's free speech clause.

In June 1996, a three-judge panel unanimously struck down the CDA, finding the restrictions in it "profoundly repugnant" to the First Amendment. Borrowing language from an earlier free speech case, Judge Dalzell wrote that "the internet may be fairly regarded as a never-ending world wide conversation. The government may not [through the CDA] interrupt that conversation." Judge Dalzell continued with the strong assertion that "As the most participatory form of mass speech yet developed, the Internet deserves the highest protection from government intrusion."

The U.S. Supreme Court affirmed the lower court, ruling 7-2 that the CDA was overly broad, in violation of the First Amendment. In *Reno v. American Civil Liberties Union,* 521 U.S. 844 (1997) the Court looked at three earlier cases cited by the government, which had each upheld some restrictions on sex-related material or conduct. However, each case was distinguishable from this one. In one case a New York law banning the commercial sale of "obscene" material to minors was upheld. That law used and carefully defined the word "obscene" which had been the subject or earlier Supreme Court cases, while the CDA used (without definition) the word "indecent" which had not been construed in previous cases. Also the CDA applied to both commercial and non-commercial actions, and prohibited "patently offensive material" but defined the term differently than previous cases.

In another case cited by the Supreme Court, one of the issues was whether radio broadcasting should be afforded the same level of constitutional protection for speech as print media (which had received broad First Amendment support and freedom from government restriction in earlier cases). Finding that radio messages come easily into the home, and are quite often heard by children, the Court permitted more restrictions on such speech than it had on print media (newspaper, magazines), where the reader had to seek out the message in order to view it.

The Supreme Court decided that the internet was more like print media, in that the Internet was more like a public square, where freedom of speech is accorded significant protection. Justice Stevens stated that although sexually explicit material on the Internet and Web "is widely available, users seldom encounter such content accidentally." He wrote, "The receipt of information on the Internet requires a series of affirmative steps more deliberate and directed than turning a dial." And since the Internet appeared to offer an infinite number of Web sites, unlike radio frequencies, the government role in supervision should be much less here.

The Court found that the nature of cyberspace made the defenses built into the CDA basically ineffective. That is, restricting access by minors and verifying user ages were, as a practical matter, impossible. Similarly, verification with credit cards was not a workable solution, because many sites were noncommercial and many adults did not own credit cards.

In conclusion, the Supreme Court found that the CDA was overly broad, in that it placed an unacceptably heavy burden on protected speech—such as the broad categories of "indecent" and "patently offensive" material—which adults were constitutionally allowed to view. The Court recognized the government's legitimate interest in protecting children from harmful material but found that the Constitution prohibited "an unnecessarily broad suppression of speech addressed to adults. . . . As we have explained, the Government may not reduce the adult population . . . to . . . only what is fit for children."

OTHER FEDERAL ATTEMPTS TO REGULATE PORNOGRAPHY ON THE WEB

The Children's Internet Protection Act.   In subsequent years, Congress has attempted several more times to pass laws, more specific than the CDA, to regulate sexually explicit material on the internet and web and limit content that can be accessed by children. These laws have all been challenged as violations of the First Amendment and have been interpreted differently by lower courts and the U.S. Supreme Court.

In 2003 the Supreme Court ruled in *United States v. American Library Association,* that the Children's Internet Protection Act (CIPA) was legal. That law required public libraries to make it harder for internet surfers to look at pornography, or lose government funding. The Court held that the federal government can withhold money from libraries that fail to install blocking devices to prevent minors from accessing pornography. The law had been challenged by many libraries on the basis of the freedom of speech clause. The libraries argued that the technology available blocks a vast amount of valuable information about science, medicine and other topics, along with dirty pictures. Libraries face the choice of installing the filters, or losing federal funds (which some have elected to do).

The Supreme Court ruled 6-3 in upholding the law, with 4 justices finding it constitutional, and another 2 saying it was allowable as long as the filters could be disabled for those adults who ask. Librarians complained that the risk of embarrassment will keep patrons from making such a request, but

Chief Justice Rehnquist stated that the Constitution "does not guarantee the right to acquire information at a public library without any risk of embarrassment." Rep. Ernest Istook of Oklahoma, a main drafter of the law, said the ruling will "mean libraries can continue to fulfill their mission because parents won't need to be reluctant about dropping off their children for an afternoon at the library." Justice David Souter dissented from the ruling, stating that the use of filters is like "buying an encyclopedia and then cutting out pages with anything thought to be unsuitable for all adults."

The Child Online Protection Act.   In 2004 the Supreme Court considered the federal Child Online Protection Act (COPA) which, among other things, makes it a federal crime, with a possible $50,000 fine and 6 months in prison for the knowing posting, for "commercial purposes," of World Wide Web content that is "harmful to minors." COPA provided an affirmative defense to commercial Web speakers who restrict access to prohibited materials by "requiring use of a credit card" or "any other reasonable measures that are feasible under available technology." The federal district court had entered an injunction against enforcement of the law, and the 3rd Circuit Court of Appeals affirmed, finding that COPA was not the "least restrictive means" available for the Government to serve the interest of preventing minors from using the Internet to gain access to harmful materials.

In June 2004 the U.S. Supreme Court affirmed the injunction entered by the lower court, in *Ashcroft v. American Civil Liberties Union*. The court noted that the plaintiffs had argued that blocking and filtering software was a less restrictive alternative than a criminal ban on freedom of speech, and the Government had not shown it would be likely to disprove the contention at trial. Writing for the Court in a 5-4 decision, Justice Kennedy said that, "When plaintiffs challenge a content-based speech restriction, the Government has the burden to prove that the proposed alternatives will not be as effective as the challenged statute . . . The purpose of the test is to ensure that speech is restricted no further than is necessary to accomplish Congress' goal." And in this case the government had not met its burden of proof.

The Court said that filters imposed selective restrictions on speech at the receiving end, not universal restrictions at the source. "Under a filtering regime, childless adults may gain access to speech they have a right to see without having to identify themselves or provide their credit card information, and adults with children can access material they have a right to see by turning off the filter."

Justice Kennedy stated that promoting filter use had several advantages: it did not condemn as criminal any category of speech, and so the potential chilling effect was eliminated, or at least much diminished. Also, filters, moreover, may well be more effective than COPA. First, the record demonstrates that a filter can prevent minors from seeing all pornography from around the world, not just pornography posted to the Web from America. Since COPA does not prevent minors from accessing foreign harmful materials, this alone makes it possible that filtering software might be more effective in serving Congress' goals. COPA's effectiveness is further diminished because providers of the materials covered by the statute simply can move their operations overseas.

FREE SPEECH VS. TRADE SECRETS: DVDS AND THE DECSS PROGRAM

Another interesting "cyberlaw" conflict has worked its way through the courts in the past few years. The movie studios place encryption technology called the

Content Scrambling System (CSS) on DVDs that are distributed to the public, in an effort to keep them from being copied, accessed and distributed over the internet and web. Apparently the studios use different encryption codes for DVDs sold in different countries. However, a few years ago a Norwegian teenager, Jon Johansen and a few of his internet "hacker" friends, were able to crack the CSS code, through reverse engineering. He then wrote a program called DeCSS that decrypts the codes of movies stored on DVDs and enables users to copy and distribute these movies. Johansen then posted his DeCSS program on the internet.

Johansen's work was quickly sent around the world, via the internet, and was even published in several magazines and web sites which advocate freedom of information on the internet. In California, Andrew Bunner, a computer programmer, published the DeCSS code on his web site. The DVD Copy Control Association, an arm of the movie studios, sued Bunner, arguing that the computer code for CSS was a "trade secret," that it had not been disclosed, that considerable effort had been made to keep it secret, and that is was of considerable value to the movie industry. The DeCSS program "embodies, uses, and is a substantial derivation of the confidential proprietary information found in CSS," said the plaintiffs. The lower court had agreed, and entered an injunction, but a California appellate court reversed, finding that the injunction violated Bunner's free speech rights.

However, the California Supreme Court reversed the appellate court and held in a unanimous decision that certain trade secrets can be protected without violating the First Amendment. In an opinion by Justice Janice Rogers Brown, the Court emphasized the public policy bases for the Uniform Trade Secrets Act—incentive for invention and the encouragement of corporate ethics. The Court stated that "the trial court's preliminary injunction burdens no more speech than necessary to serve these important interests . . . The protection of trade secrets depends on the judiciary's power to enjoin disclosures by those who know or have reason to know of their misappropriation." *DVD Copy Control Association v. Bunner,* 4 Cal. Rptr. 3d 69 (Cal.2003) The Court did agree that software code like the DeCSS should be afforded some strong First Amendment rights, even if the trade secret rights were greater in this case.

Jurisdiction in Cyberspace   As we learned early in this book, courts in one state generally do not have "personal jurisdiction" in civil cases over defendants who reside in another state. But there are some exceptions to this rule. In Chapter 3 of this textbook we studied a case in which the nationwide retailer, L.L. Bean (based in Maine), was sued in a California court, based on its marketing and sales efforts over the internet and Web.

"Jurisdiction" is a traditional legal concept, which is basically concerned with "due process" and "fairness." Many cases over the years have considered when is it fair to force a defendant in a civil case to defend a lawsuit in a location chosen by the plaintiff, which may be far from the defendant's home or business. To summarize a complex area, the general rule is that the court will only have jurisdiction if that defendant has engaged in at least "minimum contacts" (such as engaging in business there, or becoming involved in an accident there) with the forum state (where the court is located).

But now in the Internet age, most all companies have web sites that can easily be accessed anywhere in the nation and around the world. Today, the presence of out-of-state business firms in our homes, via our computers, is a regular part of our day, and we call this "e-commerce." Millions of shoppers and businesses regularly purchase goods from out-of-state firms without leaving their homes. Suppose that something goes wrong, and a lawsuit is needed. Can you sue the out-of-state firm in your home state court system? Courts, as in the *L.L. Bean* case, have had to interpret and adapt the traditional rules on jurisdiction to apply to contracts made over the internet or web.

Most courts that have heard such cases so far have adopted some form of an "interactive-passive" test. Generally courts have allowed personal jurisdiction in cases in which "interactive" uses of the Internet have taken place within the state. A Web site can be characterized as interactive if business transactions can be conducted over the Internet or if information can be exchanged with users for the purpose of soliciting business.

The greater the commercial nature and level of interactivity associated with the site, the more likely the court will find that it has engaged in "minimum contacts" with the forum state for the purposes of jurisdiction. For example, in one case the court said there was personal jurisdiction in one state because the nonresident defendant sold software over the Internet to 12 people in the forum state.

On the other hand, where an operator maintains a passive Web site that merely makes information available for browsing, courts have been reluctant to allow the owner of the Web site to be sued in any state where someone may merely access the site. It does not seem "fair" in that situation. Unlike interactive sites, which foster business transactions, "passive" Web sites merely allow users to gain information about products or services or facts about a firm. Such passive sites generally do not subject a firm to jurisdiction in states where it has no offices or business operations.

INTERNATIONAL PERSPECTIVE

Jurisdiction becomes more complicated as internet questions expand on a global basis. In 2000 France ordered internet giant Yahoo to prevent people in France from accessing its sites which advertised the sale of Nazi memorabilia. It is illegal in France to exhibit or sell objects with racist overtones. After first arguing that such action could not be done, Yahoo was able to severely restrict such advertisements over its French site. However, French surfers, like all others, can switch to Yahoo.com with the click of a mouse. A U.S. court later ruled that Yahoo was not bound to comply with French laws governing content on U.S.-based sites.

In 2004, a French criminal court said it would charge Yahoo and its CEO Timothy Koogle with criminal violations. The court said that French law still applied to English-language sites, and it would hear allegations that Yahoo was inciting racial hatred by allowing French surfers to buy Nazi books, daggers, uniforms and SS badges on its Yahoo.com service.

Privacy   The nature of the Internet, Web, and E-commerce, and the fact that we all use computers, smartphones, and on-line services daily, gives rise to the potential loss of privacy. The director of the Electronic Privacy Information Center (EPIC; *www.epic.com*) has stated that "online consumers are more at risk today than they ever were." The group researched whether popular on-line stores used profile-based advertising or used "cookies" (a device that tracks user on-line browsing and shopping habits).

The survey found that 18 of the leading shopping sites did not post any privacy policy, while 35 of the sites had profile-based advertisers operating on their pages, and 87 of the leading e-commerce sites used "cookies." The president of a private advocacy firm noted "the stated policies of most big shopping sites run the gamut from bad to atrocious. People should have the right to buy without being tracked and without having their personal information sold."

An article in the *Wall Street Journal* on September 20, 2010, titled "Cookies Cause Bitter Backlash," reported on a new wave of lawsuits against websites and companies that create advertising technology, accusing them of installing online-tracking tools that are so surreptitious that they essentially hack into users' machines without their knowledge. Although some court cases years ago upheld the use of "cookies," the new tracking tools are much more sophisticated. One suit accuses Fox Entertainment group and the American-idol.com website of using a new kind of cookie—known as a "Flash cookie"— that can "re-spawn" tracking files that users have deleted, without the users' knowledge.

Privacy in the Workplace. Privacy in the workplace is another issue of increasing importance. As is discussed more fully later in this book, many employers are using technology to monitor the actions of employees. A survey done recently by the American Management Association found that nearly 80 percent of major U.S. firms engage in some electronic monitoring of employee communications and activities. Sales of employee software surveillance programs are estimated at $140 million per year. Some programs allow surreptitious "screen shots" of employees' computers at selected intervals for employers to view. Others programs monitor an employee's keystrokes and can determine what the employee typed on the computer, even if the document was not saved.

Employers are concerned not only about the general level of employee performance, but also about such actions as using e-mail to sexually or racially harass other employees, giving away company information, engaging in illegal activities, or conducting personal business on work time. Most employers notify their employees that they will be monitored, and the cases generally support employers who do so against the privacy claims of employees, as long as the surveillance is done in a reasonable manner, and private information is not disclosed to others. See Chapter 20 for further information on this topic.

The American Management Association sent an advisory to its 10,000 member companies, urging that policies and practices in electronic monitoring and surveillance should be posted and issued so that "employees are aware that their actions and communications are subject to recording and review." The highest level of electronic monitoring was in the financial services sector, including banking, brokerage, insurance, and real estate industries.

European Union Laws. The nations of the European Union (EU) are more concerned about privacy issues than the United States. In 1998, the EU enacted a Directive on Data Privacy, which guarantees European citizens absolute control over data concerning them. If a company wants to obtain personal information, it must get that person's permission and explain what the information will be used for. It must also promise not to use it for anything else without the citizen's consent. A company would not be allowed to sell its mailing list to another firm that wanted to solicit its customers.

EU citizens have the right to know where information about them came from, to demand to see it, to correct it if wrong, and to delete it if objectionable. And they have the right to file suits against any person or company they feel is misusing their data.

Furthermore, Article 29 of the Data Protection law requires that foreign governments provide data protections as rigorous as Europe's or risk having data flows cut off. This means that the EU Commission has the power to prosecute companies and block Web sites that fail to live up to the EU data privacy standards. As the global leader in on-line business, the United States, with its relatively lax rules on privacy, is of particular concern to EU officials.

Europeans do not appreciate the American practice of planting "cookies" that hook into a name, then track the Web sites the person has explored and send back consumer profiles. They are outraged that U.S. governments and firms use the Web to learn facts that people would rather keep to themselves. At the root of the battle is a major philosophical difference. One businessman in Europe says "In Europe, people don't trust companies, they trust government." In the United States, he says, "It's the opposite way around—Americans feel citizens must be protected from actions of the government."

American firms are concerned about the EU data privacy rules, and some agreements have been worked out regarding how global firms can comply with necessary rules so that information can be sent back and forth between Europe and the USA. Meanwhile software makers and high-technology companies are developing programs to meet privacy needs, while preserving producers' rights to ask questions of consumers.

Piracy   As we have examined earlier in this chapter, the primary purpose of intellectual property protection is to give authors, inventors, and trademark holders the "exclusive rights" to sell or license others to sell products using the books, songs, computer programs, processes, or goods covered by the intellectual property rights. However, both in the United States and very definitely in other parts of the world, many goods are made and sold without permission or approval of the owner of the intellectual property rights. In some parts of the world, most of the Microsoft software products in use are not made or licensed by Microsoft, but are illegally copied, a practice called "piracy."

One global music rights organization stated a few years ago that pirated CDs accounted for 1/3 of all CDs sold in the world and the percentage is probably higher today. The International Federation of the Phonographic Industry, representing 1,500 record companies in 70 countries, gave the estimated value of pirated CDs at $4.6 billion per year. The agency said that 50 million pirated discs were seized in the past year, mostly in Southeast Asia. The IFPI employs 250 investigators and analysts, largely ex-law enforcement personnel, including former American FBI and Russian KGB officers.

Right on the street in many cities in Asia and around the world, it is easy to buy the latest popular music CDs and copies of the latest movies on DVDs. However these products were not made or produced under a license from the copyright holder, but were illegally copied from an original CD or from the internet. No authorization was given, and no royalties will be paid to the artists or producers of these songs or movies. The photo below shows a typical street scene in Shanghai, China, where pirated copies of the latest DVDs can be easily purchased—for about $1 each.

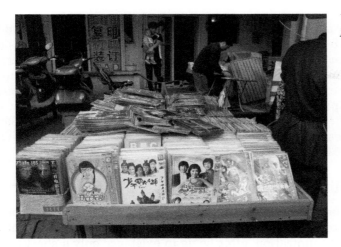

Want to Buy a DVD?

Producers of movies and software have complained loudly in recent years that the vast majority of video tapes and software products sold in China, India, Brazil, and many other countries are pirated copies, made illegally— which has cost the owners of the intellectual property rights billions of dollars in lost royalties. Many actions have been taken in foreign nations to seek out and close down manufacturers and producers of pirated compact discs and software. However, despite such actions, many consumers around the world and in the United States continue to see copying of copyrighted software, videos, and music as a necessary evil. As one Chinese student told one of the authors of this book recently, "We have to use the [pirated] copies—we can't afford to buy Windows at the prices charged by Microsoft. We can buy the program for $2 in the street, or pay $100 in a store—what would you do?"

INTERNATIONAL PERSPECTIVE

Even in China, things are changing. While the Chinese have not traditionally followed Western views on intellectual property, and for centuries the Chinese cultural tradition has considered that, to some extent, copying someone's art is a sincere form of flattery, the law in China is changing. With its entry into the World Trade Organization in 2001, China has had to learn to play by international rules regarding IP, established by the United States and European nations. Also, the Chinese are starting to see themselves as owners and creators of intellectual property which needs protection.

In summer 2004, during his first visit to Europe since taking office, Chinese Premier Wen Jiabao pledged to increase protection of intellectual property in China. Wen said that Vice Premier Wu Yi would coordinate the effort to promote awareness about the need to respect patents, licenses and copyrights. China's own state Council has estimated the market value of counterfeit goods produced in China to be around $19 billion to $24 billion per year.

Some Chinese courts are even beginning to enter judgments in favor of the owners of intellectual property rights, claim some Western lawyers. In a case in 2003, the Beijing High People's Court (roughly equivalent to a U.S. federal court of appeals) ruled against a Chinese firm and upheld a judgment in favor of Lego, the Danish toy firm, confirming copyright legal protection for the industrial design of a special type of Lego blocks.

American lawyers say there are many such judgments issued by courts in China, but that the system for indexing and reporting cases is difficult to decipher and use. In the fall of 2010 China reported a sharp increase in the number of intellectual property cases heard by its court system. During the first 6 months of 2010, local courts in China accepted 20,357 civil complaints concerning intellectual property (mostly copyright cases), an increase of 45% over the first 6 months of 2009. Some 583 of these cases were foreign-related IP suits. (InternationalLawOffice.com, Oct. 10, 2010)

E-MAIL ISSUES

Most of us send many e-mails every day, to friends, family and business associates across town and around the world. E-Mail has become one of the primary means of communication, after being in existence only a short time. When we sit at our keyboard and type and send a message, few of us wonder (1) where it goes, or (2) how private the contents of the message are. A very general answer is (1) "though many computers and internet service providers" and (2) "not very private."

Perhaps surprisingly, despite typing in our own "user ID" and "password" every time we log on, our e-mail is not very private, under the law—especially when we are at work. Courts have allowed employers to monitor their employees' e-mail and look at their web usage, in a number of court cases (described more fully in the Employment chapter) where the employer has paid for and installed the system—which is usually the case.

And of course someone (certainly the Information Tech (IT) supervisor and perhaps others) has access to all employee passwords, and can even look directly at every employee's computer screen from the IT office in many instances. If the boss says "I am worried about the loss of trade secrets. I want to see all messages that Jeremy has sent and received in the last month" can the IT supervisor realistically say no? Even the employee's work telephone can be monitored under the so-called "business use exception" to the Electronic Communications Privacy Act, which generally prohibits wiretapping without a court order. Listening in on an extension of an existing business phone line is not considered "wiretapping." The same sort of analysis is being followed in e-mail cases.

Although it would seem that a message (either sent or received) should be deleted from the user's computer after the "delete" key is hit, this is not necessarily true. It is quite technically possible to recover most deleted messages, as several corporate executives, even including Bill Gates (Microsoft Chairman), have discovered to their distress, in various court cases where e-mail records have been subpoenaed by the opposing side. In addition, some services, such as AOL hold deleted messages in a special folder for several days, so that customers can undelete them if they so choose.

In one case, the First Circuit Court of Appeals upheld the dismissal of criminal charges against an executive of an online bookstore who had surreptitiously looked at e-mail messages sent to customers by rival Amazon.com Inc. The court noted that e-mails were briefly stored in various computers while they hopped across the internet, so the wiretap laws did not apply—the messages were not "intercepted." This decision makes it easier for third parties to access one's e-mail, as court orders are much easier to obtain in court than authorization to wiretap. Some privacy advocates believe that this appellate ruling will open the door to much more intrusion upon consumer e-mail, from marketers to lawyers. It also increases the effectiveness of subpoenas served on internet service providers and operators of computer networks that pass traffic along the network.

SPAM AND UNSOLICITED ELECTRONIC MAIL

Often our computers and e-mail inboxes are filled with unsolicited e-mail from various commercial enterprises—called "spam." While a few years ago it seemed that ridiculous advertisements for penis or breast enlargement comprised much of our "spam," today it is more likely to be offers to participate in financial deals or to join a black market for pharmaceuticals and software. "Spam is now much more likely to be used as a channel for malicious and illegal activity," says the technical director of the BBC News Service. Financial (39%) and healthcare (30.6%) spam now make up the majority of spam. Spam pornography has been significantly reduced due to improved filtering technology. We are much more likely to be offered the chance to try Viagra today.

The unfortunate secret of spam is that it works. Even a hit rate of one in 40,000 counts as a success in the spam world where the cost of sending those messages is small. Although spam is annoying, the most dangerous spam messages are those that try to steal information from you, like your Social Security and credit card numbers. If a user clicks on some messages, disguised to look like legitimate sites, one's personal data can be stolen, a practice called **"phishing."**

A law passed by Congress a few years ago is called the "Controlling the Assault of Non-Solicited Pornography and Marketing Act" **(the CAN-SPAM Act).** The Act imposes certain requirements on anyone who initiates the "transmission of a commercial electronic mail message." Businesses who send such messages must: (1) make a clear identification that the message is an advertisement; (2) provide a clear and conspicuous e-mail address that the recipient can use to request that no further e-mail be sent by the sender; and (3) provide the sender's valid physical postal address.

If the recipient requests not to receive future e-mail messages, neither the business nor anyone acting on its behalf may send further messages. It is also unlawful for a business entity to promote its business in a fraudulent commercial e-mail message. Although the CAN-SPAM Act does not give individuals the right to sue for violations, it may be enforced by the FTC or any state attorney general. Remedies can include damages, cancellation of contracts, refunds of money expended and injunctions. In intentionally deceptive instances, criminal charges are possible.

In early 2004, several large internet service providers including America Online, Microsoft, EarthLink and Yahoo filed suit against several defendants charging that they had sent hundreds of millions of messages over their services using deceptive techniques, through third-party computers to disguise their actual point of origin. The FTC has set up an e-mail address to receive complaints about spam. It is: spam@uce.gov. The Massachusetts attorney general filed the first case under the law brought at the state level.

SUMMARY

Copyright law began in an age when monks were copying works of art and literature by hand. In the 20th century copyright cases concerned issues such as copying with a photocopy machine, and then using video tape recorders. In the 21st century, computers, smartphones, iPads, the internet, and the Web allow one to easily make an exact copy of a musical or literary work, or movie or software program, and distribute the work to millions of others with one keystroke or click of a mouse. The same sort of challenges face owners of patents on inventions, products, and processes and the manufacturers of products protected by a trademark. Likewise a trade secret carefully safeguarded by a company for 50 years can be lost when a disgruntled employee decides to distribute it to all his friends by posting the secret on the Web.

"Cyberlaw" includes the many new intellectual property issues which are arising, as well as the older legal issues which are being reexamined due to the possibilities for infringement brought on by the Internet and Web, as well as the globalization of business. The legal issues raised in cyberspace promise to be challenging for all businesses in the next millennium.

CHAPTER QUESTIONS

1. Douglas invented OBX as an abbreviation for the "Outer Banks" of North Carolina. His company, OBX-Stock, obtained a trademark registration for OBX and sold oval stickers for cars to indicate that they had visited the Outer Banks. OBX-Stock also used OBX on other souvenirs sold in Outer Banks stores. However, "OBX" has been widely used for years by many Outer Banks businesses to advertise their location. A firm named Bicast began to sell stickers printed with "OB Xtreme" and was sued by OBX-Stock for trademark infringement. Did OBX-Stock have a valid trademark? Was there infringement? *OBX-Stock Inc. v. Bicast, Inc.,* 558 F. 3d 334 (4th Cir. 2009).

2. Well-Made Toy Co. makes and sells a 20-inch rag doll ("Sweetie Mine") on which it has a registered U.S. copyright, and also a 48-inch rag doll, which it has not registered with the Copyright Office. The larger doll was not substantially similar to the smaller doll. Well-Made sued Goffa Corp. for copyright infringement after Goffa introduced a 48" rag doll, which competed with the Well-Made doll. Goffa claimed that the court did not have jurisdiction over any possible infringement action because Well-Made had never registered the larger doll with the Copyright Office. Is Goffa correct? Why? *Well-Made Toy Co. v. Goffa International Corp.,* 354 F. 3d 112 (2d Cir. 2003)

3. Since the early 1900s, two Swiss firms, Victorinox Cutlery Co. and Wenger, S.A., have been the sole manufacturers of multifunction pocket knives for the Swiss Armed Forces. Their knives have earned a reputation for durability and quality and have been sold around the world as "Swiss Army" knives. However, the companies have never filed for trademark protection on that phrase. In 1992, an American company began selling in the United States what the court called an "inexpensive and shoddy" red pocketknife made in China with the words "Swiss Army" on the side. Can Victorinox obtain protection for the phrase "Swiss Army" on the basis of geographic origin, or has the phrase become generic? *Forschner Group, Inc. v. Arrow Trading Co.,* 833 F. Supp. 385 (SDNY 1994)

4. A Texaco scientist commonly photocopied articles of interest from various journals, without permission of the copyright owners. He kept copies of the articles for later use by himself and other Texaco employees. The publisher of one journal (from which the scientist had admitted copying eight articles) sued Texaco for copyright infringement. Texaco argued that the "fair use" doctrine should protect such photocopying, but its argument was rejected by the New York court. Explain briefly what Texaco's fair use argument was, and what reasons the court might have had for refusing to apply the rule in this case. [*American Geophysical Union v. Texaco, Inc.,* 37 F.3d 881 (2d Cir. 1994)]

5. Harvey Barnett founded Infant Swimming Research (ISR) in 1966. ISR developed a "scientific, behavioral approach to pediatric drowning prevention" which used a method containing nearly 2,000 specific "prompts and procedures" for teaching infants how to survive in water. ISR trained and certified many instructors who then taught the skills to infants in 10 minute lessons, five days a week for several weeks. The methods were not publicly disclosed and the employees had signed nondisclosure agreements. Several former ISR instructors started a competing firm that used the ISR methods. Mr. Barnett sued the former employees for misappropriation of trade secrets. Are trade secrets involved here? What result and why? *Harvey Barnett Inc. v. Shidler,* 338 F. 3d 1125 (10th Cir. 2003)

6. A firm called Virtual Works registered the domain name "vw.net" with Network Solutions, which at that time was the registrar of domain names. The partners of Virtual Works knew that some internet users might think "vw.net" was affiliated with Volkswagen. One of the partners called Volkswagen's trademark department and stated that unless Volkswagen bought the "vw.net" domain name within 24 hours, they would sell it to the highest bidder. Instead Volkswagen sued Virtual Works seeking damages for trademark infringement, trademark dilution, and cybersquatting, and asked for assignment of the domain name. Does this conduct violate the Anti-Cybersquatting Consumer Protection Act? Why or why not? *Virtual Works, Inc. v. Volkswagen of America, Inc.,* 238 F. 3d 264 (4th Cir. 2001).

7. Hamidi was an employee of Intel Corp. but was fired. He later obtained Intel's e-mail address list and sent e-mails strongly complaining about the company to between 8,000 and 35,000 employees. Intel demanded that Mr. Hamidi stop sending such e-mails, but he continued and sent his mass mailings out six times. Intel sued Hamidi, arguing that he had committed the tort called "trespass to chattels," which is a very old form of tort. Intel asked for an injunction barring further e-mails by Mr. Hamidi. The essence of the "trespass to chattels" tort is that one is trespassing against another's personal property by interfering with the owner's use of his property, thereby causing loss to the property owner. Can this "arcane" tort be used to apply to this type of misuse of company property in a cyberspace setting? Discuss whether this theory should be used here or not, and why. *Intel Corporation v. Hamidi,* 1 Cal. Rptr. 3d 32 (Cal. 2003)

8. Mr. Konrad had received three patents concerning how a computer user accesses and searches databases in remote computers. Prior to filing for the patents, he demonstrated his inventions to various university computing personnel, without imposing any requirement of confidentiality upon them. Later he became involved in a dispute with Netscape, Microsoft and

AOL regarding infringement. The companies claimed that his patent was invalid because of "public use" prior to the filing of the patent claim. Who is correct and why? *Netscape Communications v. Konrad,* 295 F.3d 1315 (Fed. Cir. 2002).

9. Certain freelance authors sold articles to newspapers and magazine publishers for use in collective works (magazines containing a number of different articles). Under the Copyright Law, the authors retained the copyrights in their own articles, while the publisher of the collective work had the copyright to that collective work and "revisions" of that work. When the publisher provided the individual articles to electronic databases such as NEXIS, without the permission of the authors or payment of royalties, the authors sued for infringement. What should the result be? Why? *Tasini v. New York Times Co.*, 533 U.S. 483 (2001)

10. A man named Grottanelli had operated a motorcycle repair shop called "The Hog Farm" since 1969. During the 1980s Harley-Davidson Co. began to use the word "hog" to apply to its motorcycles and registered the trademark in 1987. Harley claimed that it now has control of the word as it is used in the motorcycle business, and brought an action seeking to prohibit Grotanelli from using the term further. Evidence at trial showed that the term "hog" was in public use prior to 1980 in reference to large motorcycles. Now that Harley-Davidson has the trademark, can it prevent others from using the term "hog" in their businesses? What should the court decide and why? *Harley-Davidson, Inc. v. Grottanelli,* 164 F. 3d 806 (2d Cir. 1999).

PRACTICAL EXERCISE

Kristin and George are both graduating from college this year. While in school they have become friends and have had many talks about starting different businesses. George has been working full-time during his last two years of college at the software development firm TechStart. While there he has been closely involved with developing software which enables hospitals and other large medical providers to coordinate their account management and billing procedures in an efficient, cost-effective way. TechStart has developed and has obtained a patent on its software product called "PatientServe." In addition TechStart has filed for and obtained federal trademark protection for both the names "TechStart" and "PatientServe." Sales of PatientServe have been over $1 million in each of the past two years, and considerably more has been earned by TechStart through installation and service on the systems.

Kristin has been studying business, and she and George want to start a business, building on her financial and management skills and his technical expertise. They rent some office space and begin to work on various software and hardware products, as well as trying to build a management and information tech consulting practice. George has a good memory of all the hospital and medical people that he and others dealt with while he worked at TechStart. Although he did not actually keep a copy of the customer list, there were only five hospitals and three HMOs in his city, and he knows the key IT and credit and billing people at each one. He is very familiar with the process by which PatientServe was developed, and the marketing techniques and planning of TechSmart.

George and Kristin develop a software package that, although building on the PatientServe product, goes even farther, using some new mathematical formulas and updated techniques, that they believe will be perfect for small hospitals and doctors' offices, both large and small. It offers software which assists in client management, billing and staff and human resources management. They form an LLC and decide to call their business "TechSmart." The two begin calling on hospitals and doctors to market their new system called "PatientFirst." Kristin secures a few clients and several doctors purchase PatientFirst. Soon thereafter, George receives a letter from a lawyer representing TechStart, alleging that his actions violate both patent and trademark law, and that legal action will be brought if he and Kristin do not "cease and desist from using the names TechSmart and PatientFirst, and cease using the patented process underlying PatientServe. The letter also mentions something about using "trade secrets" belonging to TechStart. Since you are studying "legal things" they ask you to write a memo (about 2 pages) outlining the patent, trademark and trade secret issues involved, what the tests are for infringement, and how strong a case can be made by TechStart. Please do so.

FURTHER INFORMATION

http://www.copyright.gov/
   U.S. Copyright Office.
www.eff.org
   Electronic Frontier Foundation, an organization focusing on privacy issues.
www.wipo.org
   World Intellectual Property Organization
www.findlaw.com/legal/news/scitech/tech/
   FindLaw is a large legal web site, with many topics covered and cases reported

PART 4:
LEGAL ISSUES INVOLVING CONSUMERS,
COMPETITORS, AND SUPPLIERS

CHAPTER 17

ANTITRUST LAW: THE REGULATION OF CORPORATE BEHAVIOR AND STRUCTURE

LEARNING OBJECTIVES

After you have read this chapter, you should be able to:

1. Describe the development of antitrust laws and explain how they are enforced.

2. Contrast the economic, social, and political viewpoints of antitrust policy.

3. Define the rule of reason and the per se rule.

4. Explain the structural provisions of the antitrust laws addressing monopoly, oligopoly, and mergers.

5. Describe the behavioral antitrust provisions dealing with horizontal and vertical restrictions.

6. List the antitrust provisions of the Robinson-Patman Act and Federal Trade Commission Act.

CHAPTER OUTLINE

I. Federal Antitrust Legislation

II. Judicial Analysis

III. Structural and Behavioral Antitrust

IV. Price Discrimination

V. Section 5 of the Federal Trade Commission Act

VI. Exemptions from Antitrust

The largest online search firm seeks to acquire the firm that has developed the leading online search engine software used by online travel sites. Other online search firms that offer travel searches and services are concerned about what the proposed merger would mean for their business. After studying this chapter, you should be able to determine whether the merger would violate any antitrust laws.

INTRODUCTION

The competitive behavior and the structure of firms are regulated by antitrust laws. The purpose of antitrust law is to ensure that, by enforcing the rules of the market and eliminating threats to competition, the marketplace in which business operates remains free. Antitrust law in the United States consists of both federal and state statutes. Federal antitrust laws apply to all business activity that qualifies as interstate commerce; in some cases, these laws also apply to wholly intrastate activity that affects interstate commerce. State laws, on the other hand, apply to activity that is wholly intrastate and that does not affect interstate commerce. Because state laws vary, we will focus primarily on federal antitrust law.

FEDERAL ANTITRUST LEGISLATION

The first federal antitrust statute was the *Sherman Act*, passed by Congress in 1890. Section 1 of the Act prohibits any contract, combination, or conspiracy in restraint of trade. Section 2 prescribes monopolizing trade or commerce. The Sherman Act was aimed at eliminating the concentrations of economic power that had developed in the railroads and major industries through the use of cartels and voting trusts and the predatory practices such concentration made possible. A **voting trust** was a device that allowed a few individuals to control the stock of the major firms in the industry. The term *antitrust* is derived from the law's attack on the voting trusts. The Sherman Act initially was only criminal legislation—it made violations of its provisions criminal offenses and imposed penalties of fines and/or imprisonment.

voting trust: Legal device by which a few persons could control leading firms in an industry through voting rights of the firms' stock.

Despite its intentions, the Sherman Act was not very effective due to several problems with enforcement. Because the act was criminal legislation, penalties were usually imposed after the harm to competition had already occurred; moreover, the criminal penalties did nothing to restore the competition that had been eliminated. The fines that were imposed generally were greatly exceeded by the financial gains resulting from the anticompetitive activity. In addition, several early court decisions held that manufacturing was not "commerce" within the meaning of the Sherman Act, so anticompetitive conduct by manufacturers was beyond the reach of the law. (Those decisions have long since been overruled.)

In response to the problems of enforcing the Sherman Act, Congress passed the *Clayton Act* in 1914. The Clayton Act prohibits specific kinds of conduct that injure competition and provides for civil, rather than criminal, penalties. The Clayton Act also allows for civil remedies under the Sherman Act. The civil nature of the Clayton Act allows for more flexible and effective enforcement—injunctions prohibiting conduct likely to injure competition can be granted by the courts before actual harm to competition occurs. The Clayton Act applies only to activities that are actually in interstate commerce, in contrast to the Sherman Act's coverage of conduct *in or affecting* interstate commerce.

The Clayton Act also allows for private remedies—persons or firms injured as a result of a violation of the act can sue the violator for triple damages (three times the amount of the actual harm suffered). In addition, §4 of the Clayton Act extends the availability of triple damage suits to violations of the Sherman Act as well. These suits may only be brought by parties directly affected by violations, such as competitors or customers who purchase directly from the violator. Indirect purchasers—those who purchase from the customers of a violator—may not bring triple damage suits, and the federal government is also precluded from bringing such suits against antitrust violators. Foreign firms injured by U.S. firms engaging in anticompetitive conduct abroad may not sue those firms in the U.S. courts, *F. Hoffman-La Roche Ltd. v. Empagran S.A.*, 542 U.S. 155 (2004).

The Clayton Act has been amended several times: the *Robinson-Patman Act* of 1936 strengthened the §2 prohibitions on price discrimination; the *Celler-Kefauver Act* of 1950 amended the §7 prohibition of mergers that injure competition; and the *Hart-Scott-Rodino Act* of 1976 imposed premerger notification requirements under §7.

The Federal Trade Commission Act was also passed in 1914. It created the Federal Trade Commission (FTC) to administer and enforce the antitrust laws, in addition to the enforcement efforts of the Justice Department. Congress wanted the FTC to operate as an independent enforcement agency, free from the political pressure that could be brought to bear on the Justice Department.

ENFORCEMENT OF THE ANTITRUST LAWS

Federal antitrust laws are enforced by both the U.S. Justice Department and the FTC. The Antitrust Division of the Justice Department is responsible for the enforcement of the criminal provisions of the Sherman Act, which now provides for fines of up to $10 million for corporations and fines of up to $350,000 and jail terms of up to three years for individuals. The Antitrust Division can file civil or criminal suits in the federal courts; it also enforces the merger provisions of §7 of the Clayton Act. The FTC has no criminal enforcement jurisdiction. It is responsible for enforcement of the Clayton Act and §5 of the Federal Trade Commission Act.

divestiture orders: Court orders requiring firms to separate—to "undo" the merger.

dissolution orders: Court orders requiring a monopolist firm to split up into several firms.

consent decrees or **consent orders:** Settlement agreements allowing firms to cease allegedly anticompetitive conduct without admitting to a violation of the law.

Both the FTC and the Antitrust Division can bring civil enforcement actions. Possible remedies in civil actions include injunctions, **divestiture orders** (court orders requiring merged firms to separate), and **dissolution orders** (court orders requiring single firms to split into separate firms). Other remedies, such as orders to make patents available to competitors or orders prohibiting firms from entering certain fields of business, are also available through civil actions. The FTC can initiate administrative hearings on alleged violations. Both the FTC and the Antitrust Division are making increasing use of pretrial (or prehearing) settlements with firms alleged to have violated the law. These settlements, known as **consent decrees** or **consent orders**, allow a firm to agree to cease challenged conduct without admitting guilt or liability under the laws. These settlements enable the enforcement agencies to stop alleged anticompetitive practices without having to resort to trials, which are both time-consuming and expensive.

In addition to enforcement actions by the government, private antitrust suits by firms or individuals seeking triple damages (under §4 of the Clayton Act) for injuries caused by alleged violations have also become an important enforcement mechanism of the antitrust laws. For example, the price-fixing convictions of manufacturers of electrical equipment in the 1960s resulted in some 2,300 civil suits being filed against the companies involved. The damages awarded in those suits amounted to over $400 million. In recent years, the antitrust enforcement agencies concentrated on concerted activity—price-fixing and collusion by competitors—rather than pursuing merger or monopoly cases. Apart from the U.S. suit against Microsoft, most of the recent cases involving merger or monopoly claims have involved private suits rather than government enforcement actions.

GOALS OF ANTITRUST POLICY

The basic purpose of antitrust laws is to ensure the free operation of the marketplace. The policies behind the enforcement and interpretation of these laws reflect conflicting interests, however, because antitrust policy is based on a mixture of social, political, and economic theories.

The economic goal of antitrust is to promote efficiency through free competition in the market. When competition is free, though, some firms may compete more effectively than others. According to the economic viewpoint concept (also known as the "Chicago School," after the views of economists associated with the University of Chicago), antitrust law should not penalize firms that become dominant in a market because they have competed successfully; the size of firms should be irrelevant as long as the firms' activities promote efficiency. In contrast, according to the social and political goals of antitrust policy (also known as the "Harvard School," after the views of economists associated with Harvard University), antitrust law should emphasize concern for protecting competing firms as well as promoting competition. From this viewpoint, small individual competitors should be protected to preserve economic freedom of choice; thus antitrust law should strive to avoid the concentration of economic power and political influence in the hands of a few giant firms. This concern for protecting competitors may mean that the size of a firm may determine the legality of its conduct and that protection of competitors should be pursued despite its cost in terms of efficiency. For the Reagan and both Bush Administrations, antitrust enforcement was not a major priority; with their emphasis on freeing the market from government regulation, they favored the Chicago School's approach. The Clinton Administration reflected more of a balance between the two schools of thought, and antitrust enforcement actions increased significantly during the years of President Clinton's administration.

Judicial interpretations and government enforcement of the antitrust laws have reflected the tensions between these competing goals of antitrust law. The famous decision in the case of *U.S. v. Aluminum Co. of America*, 148 F.2d 416 (2nd Cir. 1945) and decisions in merger cases in the 1960s emphasized the social and political goals of antitrust. More recent decisions and the enforcement policy of recent administrations reflect an emphasis on the economic goal of antitrust. The courts and enforcement agencies are now more aware of the global character of economic competition and realize that domestic firms should not be unduly hampered in competing against international competitors.

NEW TECHNOLOGY AND NEW THEORIES GIVE ANTITRUST ENFORCERS MORE EFFECTIVE TOOLS

Technology and new economic theories have supported the enforcement efforts of the Justice Department and the FTC. The development of more powerful computers has allowed economists to develop and analyze increasingly complex models of competitive behavior of firms. Such sophisticated econometric analysis allows antitrust enforcers to predict whether a merger would likely result in higher prices for consumers by reducing competition in the relevant market, rather than simply looking to the increased market share that the merged firm will enjoy. The use of checkout scanner data allows antitrust enforcers to monitor actual price behavior of firms in various geographic markets, and when coupled with the sophisticated econometric analysis, provides support for predictions of a merger's likely effect on prices. For example, in 1997, the office supply retailer Staples sought to merge with its rival, Office Depot. The firms argued that because literally thousands of retail outlets sell office supplies, the merger of the two "superstore" chains would not significantly reduce competition. However, FTC economists, using actual scanner data for all items sold by both chains, discovered that Staples charged lower prices in cities where Office Depot also had a store, but could charge higher prices for the same items in cities where there was no Office Depot store. That evidence provided strong support for the argument that the merger would allow Staples to raise prices and would reduce competition in the office supply market; a federal court for the District of Columbia blocked the merger [*F.T.C. v. Staples, Inc.*, 970 F. Supp. 1066 (D.D.C. 1997)].

In addition to technological improvements, developments in economic theory have also aided antitrust enforcers. The Chicago School economists focused on competitive markets and assumed that the workings of the market would quickly erode any market power a firm might temporarily gain through anticompetitive practices. As a result, Chicago School economists were not overly concerned with predatory conduct. But using more sophisticated economic "game theory" and models of strategic competition, economists can more realistically predict the effects of barriers to entry into markets and of predatory behavior of dominant firms. When two leading aerospace companies, Lockheed-Martin and Northrop Grumman, sought to merge in 1997, the Justice Department argued that the firms' role as leading component suppliers to other aerospace and defense contractors could allow the resulting firm to raise prices to competitors, who would have few other alternative suppliers. After the Justice Department filed suit to stop the merger, the firms abandoned the merger and pledged to compete vigorously in the supply of components to the defense industry.

With the powerful new tools and theories at their disposal, antitrust enforcers can more effectively target firms whose market dominance or predatory practices allow them to exercise power to set prices above the level that would result from competition.

Sources: "The Trustbusters' New Tools," *The Economist* (May 2, 1998); "The Law Is an Ass," *The Economist* (August 29, 1998).

rule of reason:
Judicial approach to antitrust law that holds certain conduct illegal only if it unreasonably restricts competition.

***per se* rule:**
Judicial approach to antitrust law that holds certain conduct to be illegal regardless of its actual effect on competition.

JUDICIAL ANALYSIS

When the legality of a firm's conduct is challenged under the antitrust laws, a court must consider the impact of that conduct on competition. The courts have developed two different approaches for analyzing that impact—the **rule of reason** and the ***per se* rule**.

The rule of reason stems from the Supreme Court's decision in *Standard Oil Co. v. U.S.*, 221 U.S. 1 (1911), in which the Court held that some forms of conduct are illegal only if they unreasonably restrict competition. The rule of reason is applied today when the conduct in question has a legitimate business purpose despite its anticompetitive effects. Under the rule of reason, the actual effects of the conduct on competition must be considered; when the effects result in an unreasonable or undue lessening of competition, the court will prohibit the conduct.

The *per se* rule is derived from the rule of reason; it states that some forms of conduct are considered to be so inherently anticompetitive that they are deemed to be illegal regardless of their actual effects on competition. When the court applies the *per se* rule, it will refuse to consider any justification for the anticompetitive conduct or any evidence of the impact of the conduct on competition. The *per se* rule is generally applied to conduct that has no legitimate business justification. An example of such conduct, sometimes called "a naked restraint of trade" by the courts, is price-fixing. The courts have adopted the *per se* rule in such cases because price-fixing is blatantly anticompetitive; the *per se* rule eliminates the need to show actual harm to competition from the price-fixing. The *per se* rule provides a clear standard for predicting the legality of proposed business conduct. (The *per se* rule will be discussed more fully later in this chapter.)

STRUCTURAL AND BEHAVIORAL ANTITRUST

One way to categorize antitrust law provisions is to decide whether they are structural or behavioral in their focus. Structural provisions are concerned primarily with the competitive structural organization of an industry—monopoly, oligopoly, or workable competition—and with whether such activities as mergers are likely to affect structural organization. Structural antitrust provisions generally involve the application of the rule of reason—particular conduct or activities will be prohibited only if they are likely to have an unreasonable effect on competition in any industry. Behavioral provisions are concerned with anticompetitive practices by firms—price-fixing, group boycotts, price discrimination, or the imposition of restrictive terms as a condition of doing business. Behavioral provisions may involve the application of either the rule of reason or the *per se* rule: Some behavior, such as price-fixing, may be illegal, regardless of its effect on competition, whereas the legality of other practices, such as price discrimination, may depend on their effects on competition.

STRUCTURAL ANTITRUST PROVISIONS

The legislative provisions involved in structural antitrust policy are §2 of the Sherman Act, which deals with monopolies and oligopolies, and §7 of the Clayton Act, which deals with mergers.

Monopoly From an economic standpoint, the concept of **monopoly** refers to a single firm that is the sole supplier of a unique product—one for which no substitutes exist. Buyers are forced to deal with the monopolist or with no one, and the monopolist has the power to set price and output. The economic harm that results from monopoly is the restriction of output (too little of the product is produced) and the distortion of price (it is higher than it would be if the market were competitive). The social harm resulting from monopoly is the maldistribution of income—from the customers of the monopoly to its owners

monopoly: A single firm that is the sole supplier of a product; a firm that has power over price and output.

or shareholders—and the increasing concentration of economic power in a single firm. Monopoly also creates the potential for undue political influence by the monopolist.

Monopoly and the Sherman Act   Monopoly power is the power to set prices or to exclude competitors. Pure "single firm" monopoly is rare, but the possession of some monopoly power by the dominant firm in an industry is a cause for concern. Antitrust policy seeks to prevent any firm from gaining the power to set prices or to exclude competitors. A firm may become dominant in an industry through its superior products, research, and strategy; that may spur other firms to compete more aggressively, which may actually increase competition in the industry. On the other hand, a dominant firm may seek to use its power to prevent other competitors from challenging it, which could lessen competition in the industry. Because of the need to look at the effects upon competition rather than simply consider the existence of monopoly power, the courts use the rule of reason, rather than the *per se* rule, when considering a charge under §2. The use of monopoly power to destroy or restrict competition may result in the imposition of sanctions under §2 of the Sherman Act, which states:

> Every person who shall monopolize, or attempt to monopolize, or conspire or combine with any other person . . . to monopolize any part of the trade or commerce among the several states . . . shall be deemed guilty of a felony. . . .

Notice that §2 outlaws the act of monopolizing, not the monopoly itself. Any firm that introduces a new product, or that has a patent for such a product, has a monopoly of that product. However, such a monopoly will only be in violation of §2 when the firm uses its power to restrict or to attempt to restrict competition unreasonably.

Judicial Analysis in Monopoly Cases   In analyzing a charge of monopolizing under §2, the court must first consider whether the firm charged actually possesses monopoly power. The first step in this process is to identify the product and the geographic market in which the firm operates.

product market: All the reasonably interchangeable products that may be substituted for a particular product.

The courts have defined the **product market** as including all "commodities reasonably interchangeable by consumers for the same purposes." If substitutes for the product in question are available, then the firm producing the product in question may not be able to set the price and determine output independently; consumers will turn to substitutes if the product is too expensive or is unavailable. Thus, the firm producing the product faces competition from the substitutes and therefore does not possess monopoly power. For example, if a firm producing cellophane for food packaging raises its prices, its customers may decide to use foil, kraft paper (brown "butcher paper"), or other wrapping alternatives instead. If the customers seek other packaging materials as substitutes rather than being forced to pay the higher prices for cellophane, then the appropriate product market in which to consider the power of the cellophane firm is the packaging materials market rather than just focusing on cellophane alone.

The definition of the product market is crucial to the determination of whether or not monopoly power exists. The more narrowly the product market is defined, the less likely it is that substitutes will be available and the more likely that the firm producing the product will be held to have monopoly power.

The **geographic market** is that area of the country in which a firm exercises its market power or where the effects of that power are felt. The definition of the geographic market depends upon how far the consumers will go to obtain substitutes. If substitute products are available only at great distances from the consumer, the consumer may choose to deal with the monopolist rather than undergo the difficulty and expense of obtaining the substitutes. If the consumer is willing to go a long way for substitutes, the geographic market will be broadly defined, and the market power of the alleged monopolist is likely to be diminished. Conversely, if the consumer is unwilling to go very far in the search for substitutes, the geographic market will be narrowly defined, and the market power of the alleged monopolist is likely to be enhanced. For example, liquid bleach is a relatively low cost item; the chemical composition of the product is the same regardless of which firm produces it. Because of the product's weight, the cost of transporting it more than a few hundred miles is greater than the value of the product itself. Consumers are likely to purchase bleach produced nearby rather than paying the extra shipping costs for bleach from distant producers. Therefore, the geographic market for considering the market power of a bleach producer would be the geographic area in which its product is marketed rather than the nation as a whole.

> **geographic market:** The area of the country in which a firm exercises market power.

After defining the relevant markets, the court must determine the market share held by the firm charged; that is, the court must consider whether the firm has a dominant position in that market. A dominant firm may be able to set the pricing and production conditions against which the other firms in the industry must compete. The nature of competition in the market must also be considered, because the number and sizes of the other firms in the market will determine the extent to which the alleged monopolist can control pricing and production conditions. If the market is populated by many small firms, a market share of 35 percent may be sufficient to find dominance; in a market populated by a few large firms, dominance requires a much larger market share. If the technology of the industry is rapidly changing, then today's dominant firm may not be so dominant in the future, and its ability to exercise market power may be greatly reduced. For example, IBM was dominant in the computer industry when most computers were large mainframes; the development of the personal computer, however, has greatly reduced the reliance on mainframes, and IBM is no longer dominant in the computer industry as a whole.

Intent to Monopolize If the court finds that a firm possesses a substantial share of the relevant market, it must then determine whether the firm has monopolized or attempted to monopolize that market before the firm can be found in violation of §2. The activity of the firm must be examined to determine whether the firm's behavior displays the intent to maintain or to extend its dominant position. According to the decision in *U.S. v. Aluminum Company of America, (Alcoa)*, 148 F.2d 416 (2nd Cir. 1945), the evidence need only display the firm's general intent to maintain its dominant position; that is, there need not be specific evidence of an intention to exclude competitors or to restrict competition. In Alcoa, the court held that apparently normal practices—such as stimulating demand, increasing capacity to meet that anticipated demand, and controlling supplies of raw materials—constituted evidence of general intent to monopolize when engaged in by a dominant firm.

The emphasis on a firm's size in determining the legality of its actions (reflecting the Harvard School's concern about the social and economic power of huge corporations) has been rejected in more recent decisions. Courts (emphasizing the Chicago School approach) now consider whether the activities engaged in by the alleged monopolist are normal business practices available to any firm; only if the activities are "predatory" in intent—that is, only if they are designed to exclude competitors or to restrict competition—will they be considered evidence of an intent to monopolize.

MICROSOFT AND MONOPOLY UNDER §2 THE SHERMAN ACT

The U.S. Department of Justice and eighteen states filed complaints against Microsoft, alleging that Microsoft had illegally monopolized the market for Intel-compatible PC operating systems, had attempted to gain a monopoly for Internet browsers, in violation of § 2 of the Sherman Act, and illegally tied two purportedly separate products, Windows and Internet Explorer (IE), in violation of § 1 of the Sherman Act. The suit alleged that Microsoft violated both §1 and §2 of the Sherman Act by attempting to use its dominance in the computer operating systems market (through its Windows products) to force computer manufacturers to include Microsoft's Internet browser (Internet Explorer or IE) rather than browsers from rivals such as Netscape. The Justice Department alleged that operating systems and Internet browsers were two separate product markets, and that Microsoft sought to exploit its market power over operating systems to increase its market share of the browser market by "bundling" Internet Explorer with Windows, and by forcing computer manufacturing firms (OEMs) such as Gateway or Dell that "preinstall" Windows products on their computers to include Internet Explorer, thereby restricting user access to rival browsers. Microsoft argued that the operating systems and browsers were a single product, and that by bundling them together, Microsoft was benefiting consumers by offering additional program features at reduced prices.

The trial on the suit began October 19, 1998, and lasted through June 24, 1999. The Justice Department offered extensive evidence to support its charges, including numerous e-mail messages between Microsoft executives and executives of computer manufacturers. The following are two examples of the Justice Department's evidence:

Government Exhibit /#295
[Source: http://www.justice.gov/atr/cases/ms_exhibits.htm]

Erik Stevenson (LCA)

From: Bill Gates [billg]
Sent: Friday, January 05, 1996 2.18 PM
To: Joachim Kempin
Cc: Brad Silverberg, Brad Chase, John Ludwig, Steve Ballmer, Cameron Myhrvold, Russell Siegelman, Nathan Myhrvold, Pete Higgins, Paul Mantz
Subject: OEMs and the Internet

Winning Internet browser share is a very very important goal for us.

Apparently a lot of OEMs are bundling non-Microsoft browsers and coming up with offerings together with Internet Service providers that get displayed on their machines in a FAR more prominent way than MSN or our Internet browser.

I would like to see an analysis of the top OEMs of what they are doing with browsers.

I would like to understand what we need to do to convince OEMS to focus on our browser. Is our problem proving our technology and its capability? Is our problem that they are getting bounty fees by having Internet service providers pay them a sum or a royalty on the business they get? Is a 3 1 browser a key issue for them?

If their problem is getting an easy way for customers to click and get to their home page we can provide that as a feature of Internet explorer and make it very easy to set up in the OPK.

We really need you to explain to use OEM thinking about browsers and what we need to do. Sometime in the next few weeks I would like to see some analysis.

Promoting our Internet 2.0 browser to Oems and helping them see our commitment to leadership is very important.

Ideally we would also get them to exploit our browser on their web sites. Maybe we could incent them by having a page in the Windows95 free that reference licensees home pages if they are enhanced for IE.

MSV 0009445 A
CONFIDENTIAL

Government Exhibit /#308
[Source: http://www.justice.gov/atr/cases/ms_exhibits.htm]

CONFIDENTIAL

To:	Ted Waitt, Rick Snyder, Jim Von Holle, Jim Collas, Bill Elliott
From:	Kathy Skidmore @ GW2KUSA
Cc:	
Bcc:	
Subject:	Microsoft / Concerns
Attachment:	
Date:	2/28/97 5:30 PM

GATEWAY 2000 CONFIDENTIAL INFORMATION

I just got off the phone with Brian Fujiwara, our new MS account rep. Brian is young and only a 15 month employee with MS. He doesn't "think" before he speaks. The below comments definately crosses the line of "what is legal".

- - -

Brian asked my help in determining if there was any hope for MS that GW changed our mind and not use Netscape on our Intranet.

Brian wanted me to find out what our objects were and make sure that MS has an opportunity to address those objections to their software. They want to know if it was a technical issue or something else.

Brian said that this is a HUGE issue with MS. He said MS want to get back to doing co-marketing and sales campaigns with GW, but they won't if they see GW is anything but pro Microsoft.

He said and I quote, "Dell turned Netscape down because they did not want to hurt their relationship with Microsoft. Therefore, they (Dell) get special things because of it".

Brian is meeting with Joachim on Tuesday, 3/4/96 and wants to let him know where GW stands. He said that this has Ballmer's attention as well.

* * *

More than five months after the close of the trial, U.S. District Judge Thomas Penfield Jackson issued his 207-page findings of fact, *U.S. v. Microsoft* [85 F.Supp.2d 9 (D.D.C. 1999)]. Judge Jackson defined the relevant product market as the market for "licensing of all Intel-compatible PC operating systems world-wide," and held that Microsoft, with more than 95 percent of that market, is clearly a monopolist and enjoys market power in the relevant market. New entrants to the operating systems market must face high barriers to entry, and PC users lack commercially viable alternatives to Windows. Judge Jackson stated that Microsoft's corporate policy toward firms such as Apple, Netscape, Intel, and Sun Microsystems, whose products (such as Java) might pose a threat to the Windows monopoly, was to pressure those other firms to stop development of software that either competes with Windows or might make it easier for other firms to compete with Microsoft. Microsoft's conduct, especially that regarding Netscape and its browser, Navigator, made sense only when viewed as an attempt to maintain high barriers to entry to the relevant market, and to protect the Windows' entrenched dominance. Microsoft used restrictive licensing agreements, pricing policies, and other tactics to make sure that OEMs installed only Internet Explorer on new personal computers; such restrictions closed off a major channel of distribution from Netscape and forced Netscape to use more expensive, less efficient distribution channels. Microsoft used the enormous profits it made from licensing Windows to OEMs to subsidize the losses from giving away Internet Explorer in order to build market share. Netscape, in order to compete with Microsoft in the browser market, was forced to give away Navigator, but Netscape lacked other sources of profit to make up for the resulting loss of revenue. Microsoft bundled Internet Explorer with Windows 98 in such a way to make it extremely difficult for consumers to use a different browser, or no browser at all. That increased customer support costs for OEMs, and made OEMs much less likely to install browsers other than Internet Explorer.

Judge Jackson specifically concluded that Microsoft had harmed consumers in three ways: (1) Windows 98, while allowing the use of a "default" browser, still required the use of Internet Explorer in certain situations, causing consumer confusion; (2) consumers who wish to use Windows 98 without a browser are forced to put up with reduced system performance and wasted hard drive space because of the inclusion of Internet Explorer; and (3) for users of Windows 98 with Internet Explorer, a browser "crash" is likely to affect the entire system, and the bundling of Internet Explorer in Windows makes the system more vulnerable to viruses transmitted through Internet Explorer. Judge Jackson held that there was no technical justification for Microsoft's refusal to license Windows 95 and then Windows 98 without including Internet Explorer —"No consumer benefit can be ascribed, however, to Microsoft's refusal to offer a version of Windows 95 or Windows 98 without Internet Explorer, or Microsoft's refusal to provide a method for uninstalling Internet Explorer from Windows 98."

Judge Jackson delayed issuing of his conclusions of law, including whether Microsoft has violated any antitrust laws, to allow the parties time to file additional briefs. Following the release of the findings of fact, Microsoft and the Justice Department entered into negotiations on a possible settlement to the case; Justice Jackson appointed U.S. Court of Appeals Judge Richard Posner, an expert on antitrust law, to act as a mediator in those negotiations. Negotiations for a settlement broke down, and on April 13, 2000, Judge Jackson ruled that Microsoft had illegally used its market power in the operating systems market to attempt to monopolize the Web browser market. As a remedy for the violations, the District Court proposed plan of divestiture, with Microsoft to be split into an operating systems business and an applications business.

Microsoft then appealed the decision to the U.S. Court of Appeals for the D.C. Circuit. The following is an edited excerpt from the D.C. Circuit's 64-page decision:

In the Language of the Court

UNITED STATES V. MICROSOFT CORPORATION

253 F.3d 34 (D.C. Cir. 2001)
Per Curiam:

• • •

II. MONOPOLIZATION

Section 2 of the Sherman Act makes it unlawful for a firm to "monopolize." 15 U.S.C. §2. The offense of monopolization has two elements: "(1) the possession of monopoly power in the relevant market and (2) the willful acquisition or maintenance of that power as distinguished from growth or development as a consequence of a superior product, business acumen, or historic accident." The District Court applied this test and found that Microsoft possesses monopoly power in the market for Intel-compatible PC operating systems. Focusing primarily on Microsoft's efforts to suppress

Netscape Navigator's threat to its operating system monopoly, the court also found that Microsoft maintained its power not through competition on the merits, but through unlawful means. Microsoft challenges both conclusions. We defer to the District Court's findings of fact, setting them aside only if clearly erroneous. . . .

A. Monopoly Power

While merely possessing monopoly power is not itself an antitrust violation, it is a necessary element of a monopolization charge. The Supreme Court defines monopoly power as "the power to control prices or exclude competition." *United States v. E.I. du Pont de Nemours & Co.,* 351 U.S. 377, 391, 76 S.Ct. 994, 100 L.Ed. 1264 (1956). More precisely, a firm is a monopolist if it can profitably raise prices substantially above the competitive level. Where evidence indicates that a firm has in fact profitably done so, the existence of monopoly power is clear. Because such direct proof is only rarely available, courts more typically examine market structure in search of circumstantial evidence of monopoly power. Under this structural approach, monopoly power may be inferred from a firm's possession of a dominant share of a relevant market that is protected by entry barriers. . . . "Entry barriers" are factors (such as certain regulatory requirements) that prevent new rivals from timely responding to an increase in price above the competitive level. The District Court considered these structural factors and concluded that Microsoft possesses monopoly power in a relevant market. Defining the market as Intel-compatible PC operating systems, the District Court found that Microsoft has a greater than 95% share. It also found the company's market position protected by a substantial entry barrier.

Microsoft argues that the District Court incorrectly defined the relevant market. It also claims that there is no barrier to entry in that market. Alternatively, Microsoft argues that because the software industry is uniquely dynamic, direct proof, rather than circumstantial evidence, more appropriately indicates whether it possesses monopoly power. Rejecting

each argument, we uphold the District Court's finding of monopoly power in its entirety.

1. MARKET STRUCTURE

a. Market definition

"Because the ability of consumers to turn to other suppliers restrains a firm from raising prices above the competitive level," the relevant market must include all products "reasonably interchangeable by consumers for the same purposes." In this case, the District Court defined the market as "the licensing of all Intel-compatible PC operating systems worldwide," finding that there are "currently no products—and . . . there are not likely to be any in the near future—that a significant percentage of computer users worldwide could substitute for [these operating systems] without incurring substantial costs. . . ."

b. Market power

Having thus properly defined the relevant market, the District Court found that Windows accounts for a greater than 95% share. The court also found that even if Mac OS were included, Microsoft's share would exceed 80%. Microsoft challenges neither finding, nor does it argue that such a market share is not predominant.

Instead, Microsoft claims that even a predominant market share does not by itself indicate monopoly power. Although the "existence of [monopoly] power ordinarily may be inferred from the predominant share of the market," we agree with Microsoft that because of the possibility of competition from new entrants, looking to current market share alone can be "misleading." In this case, however, the District Court was not misled. Considering the possibility of new rivals, the court focused not only on Microsoft's present market share, but also on the structural barrier that protects the company's future position. That barrier—the "applications barrier to entry"—stems from two characteristics of the software market: (1) most consumers prefer operating systems for which a large number of applications have already been written; and (2) most developers prefer to write for operating systems that already have a substantial consumer base. This "chicken-and-egg" situation ensures that applications will continue to be written for the already dominant Windows, which in turn ensures that consumers will continue to prefer it over other operating systems....

B. Anticompetitive Conduct

As discussed above, having a monopoly does not by itself violate §2. A firm violates §2 only when it acquires or maintains, or attempts to acquire or maintain, a monopoly by engaging in exclusionary conduct "as distinguished from growth or development as a consequence of a superior product, business acumen, or historic accident."

In this case, after concluding that Microsoft had monopoly power, the District Court held that Microsoft had violated §2 by engaging in a variety of exclusionary acts (not including predatory pricing), to maintain its monopoly by preventing the effective distribution and use of products that might threaten that monopoly. Specifically, the District Court held Microsoft liable for: (1) the way in which it integrated IE into Windows; (2) its various dealings with Original Equipment Manufacturers ("OEMs"), Internet Access Providers ("IAPs"), Internet Content Providers ("ICPs"), Independent Software Vendors ("ISVs"), and Apple Computer; (3) its efforts to contain and to subvert Java technologies; and (4) its course of conduct as a whole. Upon appeal, Microsoft argues that it did not engage in any exclusionary conduct.

Whether any particular act of a monopolist is exclusionary, rather than merely a form of vigorous competition, can be difficult to discern: the means of illicit exclusion, like the means of legitimate competition, are myriad. The challenge for an antitrust court lies in stating a general rule for distinguishing between exclusionary acts, which reduce social welfare, and competitive acts, which increase it.

From a century of case law on monopolization under §2, however, several principles do emerge. First, to be condemned as exclusionary, a monopolist's act must have an "anticompetitive effect." That is, it must harm the competitive *process* and thereby harm consumers. In contrast, harm to one or more

competitors will not suffice. "The [Sherman Act] directs itself not against conduct which is competitive, even severely so, but against conduct which unfairly tends to destroy competition itself." ...

Second, the plaintiff, on whom the burden of proof of course rests, must demonstrate that the monopolist's conduct indeed has the requisite anticompetitive effect.... Third, if a plaintiff successfully establishes a *prima facie* case under §2 by demonstrating anticompetitive effect, then the monopolist may proffer a "procompetitive justification" for its conduct. If the monopolist asserts a procompetitive justification—a nonpretextual claim that its conduct is indeed a form of competition on the merits because it involves, for example, greater efficiency or enhanced consumer appeal ... then the plaintiff must demonstrate that the anticompetitive harm of the conduct outweighs the procompetitive benefit.... Finally, in considering whether the monopolist's conduct on balance harms competition and is therefore condemned as exclusionary for purposes of §2, our focus is upon the effect of that conduct, not upon the intent behind it. Evidence of the intent behind the conduct of a monopolist is relevant only to the extent it helps us understand the likely effect of the monopolist's conduct. With these principles in mind, we now consider Microsoft's objections to the District Court's holding that Microsoft violated §2 of the Sherman Act in a variety of ways.

1. LICENSES ISSUED TO ORIGINAL EQUIPMENT MANUFACTURERS

The District Court condemned a number of provisions in Microsoft's agreements licensing Windows to OEMs, because it found that Microsoft's imposition of those provisions (like many of Microsoft's other actions at issue in this case) serves to reduce usage share of Netscape's browser and, hence, protect Microsoft's operating system monopoly.... If a consumer could have access to the applications he desired—regardless of the operating system he uses—simply by installing a particular browser on his computer, then he would no longer feel compelled to select Windows in order to have access to those applications; he could select an operating system other than Windows based solely upon its quality and price. In other words, the market for operating systems would be competitive.

. . . In evaluating the §2 monopoly maintenance claim, however, our immediate concern is with the anticompetitive effect of Microsoft's conduct in preserving its monopoly in the operating system market. . . .

a. Anticompetitive effect of the license restrictions

The restrictions Microsoft places upon Original Equipment Manufacturers are of particular importance in determining browser usage share because having an OEM pre-install a browser on a computer is one of the two most cost-effective methods by far of distributing browsing software. (The other is bundling the browser with internet access software distributed by an IAP.) The District Court found that the restrictions Microsoft imposed in licensing Windows to OEMs prevented many OEMs from distributing browsers other than IE. In particular, the District Court condemned the license provisions prohibiting the OEMs from: (1) removing any desktop icons, folders, or "Start" menu entries; (2) altering the initial boot sequence; and (3) otherwise altering the appearance of the Windows desktop.

The District Court concluded that the first license restriction—the prohibition upon the removal of desktop icons, folders, and Start menu entries—thwarts the distribution of a rival browser by preventing OEMs from removing visible means of user access to IE. The OEMs cannot practically install a second browser in addition to IE, the court found, in part because "[p]reinstalling more than one product in a given category . . . can significantly increase an OEM's support costs, for the redundancy can lead to confusion among novice users." That is, a certain number of novice computer users, seeing two browser icons, will wonder which to use when and will call the OEM's support line. Support calls are extremely expensive and, in the highly competitive original equipment market, firms have a strong incentive to minimize costs. . . .

As noted above, the OEM channel is one of the two primary channels for distribution of browsers. By preventing OEMs from removing visible means of user access to IE, the license restriction prevents many OEMs from pre-installing a rival browser and, therefore, protects Microsoft's monopoly from the competition that middleware might otherwise present. Therefore, we conclude that the license restriction at issue is anticompetitive. . . .

The second license provision at issue prohibits OEMs from modifying the initial boot sequence—the process that occurs the first time a consumer turns on the computer. Prior to the imposition of that restriction, "among the programs that many OEMs inserted into the boot sequence were Internet sign-up procedures that encouraged users to choose from a list of IAPs assembled by the OEM." Microsoft's prohibition on any alteration of the boot sequence thus prevents OEMs from using that process to promote the services of IAPs, many of which—at least at the time Microsoft imposed the restriction—used Navigator rather than IE in their internet access software. Microsoft does not deny that the prohibition on modifying the boot sequence has the effect of decreasing competition against IE by preventing OEMs from promoting rivals' browsers. Because this prohibition has a substantial effect in protecting Microsoft's market power, and does so through a means other than competition on the merits, it is anticompetitive. . . .

Finally, Microsoft imposes several additional provisions that, like the prohibition on removal of icons, prevent OEMs from making various alterations to the desktop: Microsoft prohibits OEMs from causing any user interface other than the Windows desktop to launch automatically, from adding icons or folders different in size or shape from those supplied by Microsoft, and from using the "Active Desktop" feature to promote third-party brands. These restrictions impose significant costs upon the OEMs; prior to Microsoft's prohibiting the practice, many OEMs would change the appearance of the desktop in ways they found beneficial. . . .

The anticompetitive effect of the license restrictions is, as Microsoft itself recognizes, that OEMs are not able to promote rival browsers, which keeps developers focused upon the IAPs in Windows. . . . This kind of promotion is not a zero-sum game; but for the restrictions in their licenses to use Windows, OEMs could promote multiple IAPs and browsers. By preventing the OEMs from doing so, this type of license restriction, like the first two restrictions, is anticompetitive: Microsoft reduced rival browsers' usage share not by improving its own product but, rather, by preventing OEMs from taking actions that could increase rivals' share of usage.

. . . we hold that with the exception of the one restriction prohibiting automatically launched alternative interfaces, all the OEM license restrictions at issue represent uses of Microsoft's market power to protect its monopoly, unredeemed by any legitimate justification. The restrictions therefore violate §2 of the Sherman Act.

2. INTEGRATION OF IE AND WINDOWS

. . . the District Court found that "Microsoft's executives believed . . . its contractual restrictions placed on OEMs would not be sufficient in themselves to reverse the direction of Navigator's usage share. Consequently, in late 1995 or early 1996, Microsoft set out to bind [Internet Explorer or IE] more tightly to Windows 95 as a technical matter."

Technologically binding IE to Windows, the District Court found, both prevented OEMs from pre-installing other browsers and deterred consumers from using them. In particular, having the IE software code as an irremovable part of Windows meant that pre-installing a second browser would "increase an OEM's product testing costs," because an OEM must test and train its support staff to answer calls related to every software product preinstalled on the machine; moreover, pre-installing a browser in addition to IE would to many OEMs be "a questionable use of the scarce and valuable space on a PC's hard drive."

Although the District Court, in its Conclusions of Law, broadly condemned Microsoft's decision to bind "Internet Explorer to Windows with . . . technological shackles," its findings of fact in support of that conclusion center upon three specific actions Microsoft took to weld IE to Windows: excluding IE from the "Add/Remove Programs" utility; designing Windows so as in certain circumstances to override the user's choice of a default browser other than IE; and commingling code related to browsing and other code in the same files, so that any attempt to delete the files containing IE would, at the same time, cripple the operating system. . . .

a. Anticompetitive effect of integration

As a general rule, courts are properly very skeptical about claims that competition has been harmed by a dominant firm's product design changes. In a competitive market, firms routinely innovate in the hope of appealing to consumers, sometimes in the process making their products incompatible with those of rivals; the imposition of liability when a monopolist does the same thing will inevitably deter a certain amount of innovation. This is all the more true in a market, such as this one, in which the product itself is rapidly changing. Judicial deference to product innovation, however, does not mean that a monopolist's product design decisions are *per se* lawful.

. . . Microsoft had included IE in the Add/Remove Programs utility in Windows 95, but when it modified Windows 95 to produce Windows 98, it took IE out of the Add/Remove Programs utility. This change reduces the usage share of rival browsers not by making Microsoft's own browser more attractive to consumers but, rather, by discouraging OEMs from distributing rival products. Because Microsoft's conduct, through something other than competition on the merits, has the effect of significantly reducing usage of rivals' products and hence protecting its own operating system monopoly, it is anticompetitive. . . .

Second, the District Court found that Microsoft designed Windows 98 "so that using

Navigator on Windows 98 would have unpleasant consequences for users" by, in some circumstances, overriding the user's choice of a browser other than IE as his or her default browser. Plaintiffs argue that this override harms the competitive process by deterring consumers from using a browser other than IE even though they might prefer to do so, thereby reducing rival browsers' usage share and, hence, the ability of rival browsers to draw developer attention away from the APIs exposed by Windows. . . . Because the override reduces rivals' usage share and protects Microsoft's monopoly, it too is anticompetitive.

Finally, the District Court condemned Microsoft's decision to bind IE to Windows 98 "by placing code specific to Web browsing in the same files as code that provided operating system functions." Putting code supplying browsing functionality into a file with code supplying operating system functionality "ensure[s] that the deletion of any file containing browsing-specific routines would also delete vital operating system routines and thus cripple Windows. . . ." As noted above, preventing an OEM from removing IE deters it from installing a second browser because doing so increases the OEM's product testing and support costs; by contrast, had OEMs been able to remove IE, they might have chosen to pre-install Navigator alone. . . . we conclude that such commingling has an anticompetitive effect; as noted above, the commingling deters OEMs from pre-installing rival browsers, thereby reducing the rivals' usage share and, hence, developers' interest in rivals' IAPs as an alternative to the IAP set exposed by Microsoft's operating system. . . . Accordingly, we hold that Microsoft's exclusion of IE from the Add/Remove Programs utility and its commingling of browser and operating system code constitute exclusionary conduct, in violation of §2. . . .

3. AGREEMENTS WITH INTERNET ACCESS PROVIDERS

The District Court also condemned as exclusionary Microsoft's agreements with various IAPs. The IAPs include both Internet Service Providers, which offer consumers internet access, and Online Services ("OLSs") such as America Online ("AOL"), which offer proprietary content in addition to internet access and other services. . . .

The District Court condemned Microsoft's actions in . . . agree[ing] to provide easy access to IAPs' services from the Windows desktop in return for the IAPs' agreement to promote IE exclusively and to keep shipments of internet access software using Navigator under a specific percentage, typically 25%. . . . We turn now to Microsoft's deals with IAPs concerning desktop placement. Microsoft concluded these exclusive agreements with all "the leading IAPs," including the major OLSs. The most significant of the OLS deals is with AOL, which, when the deal was reached, "accounted for a substantial portion of all existing Internet access subscriptions and . . . attracted a very large percentage of new IAP subscribers." Under that agreement Microsoft puts the AOL icon in the OLS folder on the Windows desktop and AOL does not promote any non-Microsoft browser, nor provide software using any non-Microsoft browser except at the customer's request, and even then AOL will not supply more than 15% of its subscribers with a browser other than IE. . . .

. . . the [District] court stated: ". . . [A]ll of Microsoft's agreements, including the non-exclusive ones, severely restricted Netscape's access to those distribution channels leading most efficiently to the acquisition of browser usage share." . . .

In this case, plaintiffs allege that, by closing to rivals a substantial percentage of the available opportunities for browser distribution, Microsoft managed to preserve its monopoly in the market for operating systems. The IAPs constitute one of the two major channels by which browsers can be distributed. Microsoft has exclusive deals with "fourteen of the top fifteen access providers in North America[, which] account for a large majority of all Internet access subscriptions in this part of the world." By ensuring that the "majority" of all IAP subscribers are offered IE either as the default browser or as the only browser, Microsoft's deals with the IAPs clearly have a significant effect in preserving its monopoly; they help keep usage of Navigator below the critical level necessary for Navigator or any other rival to pose a real threat to Microsoft's monopoly. Microsoft's only explanation for its exclusive dealing is that it wants to keep developers focused upon its IAPs—which is to say, it wants to preserve its power in the operating system market. That is not an unlawful end, but neither is it a procompetitive justification for the specific means here in question, namely exclusive dealing contracts with IAPs. Accordingly, we affirm the District Court's decision holding that Microsoft's exclusive contracts with IAPs are exclusionary devices, in violation of §2 of the Sherman Act.

4. DEALINGS WITH INTERNET CONTENT PROVIDERS, INDEPENDENT SOFTWARE VENDORS, AND APPLE COMPUTER

The District Court held that Microsoft engages in exclusionary conduct in its dealings with . . . ISVs, which develop software; and Apple, which is both an OEM and a software developer. The District Court condemned Microsoft's deals with ICPs and ISVs, stating: "By granting . . . ISVs free licenses to bundle [IE] with their offerings, and by exchanging other valuable inducements for their agreement to distribute, promote[,] and rely on [IE] rather than Navigator, Microsoft directly induced developers to focus on its own APIs rather than ones exposed by Navigator." . . .

The District Court described Microsoft's deals with ISVs as follows:

> In dozens of "First Wave" agreements signed between the fall of 1997 and the spring of 1998, Microsoft has promised to give preferential support, in the form of early Windows 98 and Windows NT betas, other technical information, and the right to use certain Microsoft seals of approval, to important ISVs that agree to certain conditions. One of these conditions is that the ISVs use Internet Explorer as the default browsing software for any software they develop with a hypertext-based user interface. Another condition is that the ISVs use Microsoft's "HTML Help," which is accessible only with Internet Explorer, to implement their applications' help systems.

The District Court further found that the effect of these deals is to "ensure [ ] that many of the most popular Web-centric applications will rely on browsing technologies found only in Windows," and that Microsoft's deals with ISVs therefore "increase [ ] the likelihood that the millions of consumers using [applications designed by ISVs that entered into agreements with Microsoft] will use Internet Explorer rather than Navigator."

. . . Although the ISVs are a relatively small channel for browser distribution, they take on greater significance because, as discussed above, Microsoft had largely foreclosed the two primary channels to its rivals. In that light, one can tell from the record that by affecting the applications used by "millions" of consumers, Microsoft's exclusive deals with the ISVs had a substantial effect in further foreclosing rival browsers from the market. Because, by keeping rival browsers from gaining widespread distribution (and potentially attracting the attention of developers away from the APIs in Windows), the deals have a substantial effect in preserving Microsoft's monopoly, we hold that plaintiffs have made a *prima facie* showing that the deals have an anticompetitive effect. . . . Microsoft having offered no procompetitive justification for its exclusive dealing arrangements with the ISVs, we hold that those arrangements violate §2 of the Sherman Act.

Finally, the District Court held that Microsoft's dealings with Apple violated the Sherman Act. Apple is vertically integrated: it makes both software (including an operating system, Mac OS), and hardware (the Macintosh line of computers). . . . Microsoft recognized the importance to Apple of its continued support of Mac Office. (quoting internal Microsoft e-mail) ("[We] need a way to push these guys[, *i.e.*, Apple] and [threatening to cancel Mac Office] is the only one that seems to make them move."); ("[Microsoft Chairman Bill] Gates asked whether Microsoft could conceal from Apple in the coming month the fact that Microsoft was almost finished developing Mac Office 97."); ("I think . . . Apple should be using [IE] everywhere and if they don't do it, then we can use Office as a club.").

In June 1997 Microsoft Chairman Bill Gates determined that the company's negotiations with Apple "'have not been going well at all. . . . Apple let us down on the browser by making Netscape the standard install.' Gates then reported that he had already called Apple's CEO. . . to ask 'how we should announce the cancellation of Mac Office. . . .'" The District Court further found that, within a month of Gates' call, Apple and Microsoft had reached an agreement pursuant to which

> Microsoft's primary obligation is to continue releasing up-to-date versions of Mac Office for at least five years . . . . [and] Apple has agreed . . . to "bundle the most current version of [IE] . . . with [Mac OS]" . . . [and to] "make [IE] the default [browser]" . . . . Navigator is not installed on the computer hard drive during the default installation, which is the type of installation most users elect to employ. . . . [The] Agreement further provides that . . . Apple may not position icons for nonMicrosoft browsing software on the desktop of new Macintosh PC systems or Mac OS upgrades.

The agreement also prohibits Apple from encouraging users to substitute another browser for IE, and states that Apple will "encourage its employees to use [IE]."

This exclusive deal between Microsoft and Apple has a substantial effect upon the distribution of rival browsers. If a browser developer ports its product to a second operating system, such as the Mac OS, it can continue to display a common set of APIs. Thus, usage share, not the underlying operating system, is the primary determinant of the platform challenge a browser may pose. Pre-installation of a browser (which can be accomplished either by including the browser with the operating system or by the OEM installing the browser) is one of the two most important methods of browser distribution, and Apple had a not insignificant share of worldwide sales of operating systems. (Microsoft has

95% of the market not counting Apple and "well above" 80% with Apple included in the relevant market). Because Microsoft's exclusive contract with Apple has a substantial effect in restricting distribution of rival browsers, and because (as we have described several times above) reducing usage share of rival browsers serves to protect Microsoft's monopoly, its deal with Apple must be regarded as anticompetitive. . . . Accordingly, we hold that the exclusive deal with Apple is exclusionary, in violation of §2 of the Sherman Act.

. . .

5. JAVA

. . .

Microsoft's conduct related to its Java developer tools served to protect its monopoly of the operating system in a manner not attributable either to the superiority of the operating system or to the acumen of its makers, and therefore was anticompetitive. Unsurprisingly, Microsoft offers no procompetitive explanation for its campaign to deceive developers. Accordingly, we conclude this conduct is exclusionary, in violation of §2 of the Sherman Act. . . .

Microsoft does not deny the facts found by the District Court, nor does it offer any procompetitive justification for pressuring Intel not to support cross-platform Java. Microsoft lamely characterizes its threat to Intel as "advice." The District Court, however, found that Microsoft's "advice" to Intel to stop aiding cross-platform Java was backed by the threat of retaliation, and this conclusion is supported by the evidence cited above. Therefore we affirm the conclusion that Microsoft's threats to Intel were exclusionary, in violation of §2 of the Sherman Act.

. . .

III. ATTEMPTED MONOPOLIZATION

. . . Plaintiffs did not devote the same resources to the attempted monopolization claim as they did to the monopoly maintenance claim. But both claims require evidentiary and theoretical rigor. Because plaintiffs failed to make their case on attempted monopolization both in the District Court and before this court, there is no reason to give them a second chance to flesh out a claim that should have been fleshed out the first time around. Accordingly, we reverse the District Court's determination of §2 liability for attempted monopolization.

. . .

IV. TRIAL PROCEEDINGS AND REMEDY

. . . we vacate the District Court's remedies decree for three reasons. First, the District Court failed to hold an evidentiary hearing despite the presence of remedies-specific factual disputes. Second, the court did not provide adequate reasons for its decreed remedies. Finally, we have drastically altered the scope of Microsoft's liability, and it is for the District Court in the first instance to determine the propriety of a specific remedy for the limited ground of liability which we have upheld.

. . .

VII. CONCLUSION

The judgment of the District Court is affirmed in part, reversed in part, and remanded in part. We vacate in full the Final Judgment embodying the remedial order, and remand the case to the District Court for reassignment to a different trial judge for further proceedings consistent with this opinion.

CASE QUESTIONS

1. How did the trial court define the product market in this case? Did the Court of Appeals agree with that definition?
2. What was Microsoft's share of the product market? Was that share sufficient to establish that Microsoft had monopoly power in the product market?
3. Apart from a dominant market share, what was necessary to find that Microsoft was guilty of monopolizing and attempted monopolization in violation of §2 of the Sherman Act? What specific conduct by Microsoft did the Court of Appeals look to as evidence?
4. Did the Court of Appeals propose a remedy for Microsoft's violations? Why or why not?

AFTERMATH OF THE MICROSOFT CASE: THE MICROSOFT SETTLEMENT

After the U.S. Court of Appeals for the D.C. Circuit remanded the Microsoft monopoly case to the district court, the Justice Department and Microsoft began negotiations to settle the case. The Bush Administration and Microsoft agreed to a consent decree that was subsequently approved by the U.S. Court of Appeals for the District of Columbia, *Commonwealth of Massachusetts v. Microsoft Corp.*, 373 F. 3d 1199 (D.C. Cir. 2004). The settlement agreement required Microsoft to share technical information with its industry rivals. Microsoft agreed to license 112 previously secret communications protocols to third party software venders in order to improve interoperability of the vender's software with Microsoft's Windows operating system. Microsoft also agreed to make Windows available to original equipment manufacturers [OEMs] at a uniform price and to publish its applications programming interfaces [APIs] and communications protocols. The agreement also requires that Microsoft allow OEMs to ship non-Microsoft applications such as Internet browsers or media players with their systems. The consent decree will last for five years, and requires Microsoft to appoint a three-member committee of its corporate board to ensure that the company carries out the terms of the settlement. Nine of the eighteen states who joined in the suit against Microsoft also agreed to the settlement. However, the remaining nine states (California, Connecticut, Florida, Iowa, Kansas, Massachusetts, Minnesota, Utah, West Virginia and the District of Columbia) argued for more strict sanctions to be applied to Microsoft. Those objections were effectively overruled when the D.C. Circuit approved the consent decree. [As discussed later in this chapter, Microsoft was also subject to an antitrust suit for violating the antitrust laws of the European Union, and ultimately agreed to comply with an order by the E.U. Commission to offer consumers a version of Windows that does not include the Media Player, and to make its software code available to other software developers for a one-time license fee.]

Sources: NY Times Nov. 9, 2002, "Microsoft Names Committee to Oversee Orders by Court," Steve Lohr, p. C-3; Global News Wire—CMPnetAsis.com, "US Court Approves Microsoft Anti-trust Settlement," Rick Merritt, Nov. 5, 2002; Global News Wire—CMPnetAsis.com, "Rivals Challenge Microsoft on Anti-trust Compliance," Paula Rooney, Nov. 7, 2002; AFX European Focus, "Microsoft Wins Antitrust Settlement, Sets Stage for Rally in Shares," Nov. 2, 2002; *The Dallas Morning News,* "S. District Judge Approves Settlement between Microsoft, Justice Department," Alan Goldstein, Nov. 2, 2002; Associated Press, "Key Dates in the Antitrust Case against Microsoft," Nov. 1, 2002; Computer Reseller News, "Analysis—Microsoft Hammers Home Victory in Antitrust Case," Paula Rooney, Nov. 11, 2002.

oligopoly: Industry dominated by a few large firms.

conscious parallelism: Firms acting independently, but similarly to their rivals.

concerted activity: Firms acting together, or collectively.

Oligopoly The structure of competition in an industry is considered to be an **oligopoly** when a few large firms dominate the industry. When this is the case, the firms are likely to be able to anticipate the reaction of the other firms to any competitive action, and the competitive decisions of the firms are likely to be similar. For example, if Ford announces that it will raise new car prices by an average of 5 percent for the next model year, Chrysler and General Motors may decide to raise their prices a similar amount. Such conduct, where the firms act independently but similarly, is known as **conscious parallelism** and is beyond the reach of the antitrust laws as long as each firm reaches its decisions independently—no agreement or understanding among the firms exists. If, however, the firms act pursuant to a common understanding or agreement, their conduct is in violation of §1 of the Sherman Act, which prohibits **concerted activity** (collective activity among competitors). The existence of oligopoly may make it easier for the firms to engage in concerted activity or collusion. In the absence of concerted activity, oligopoly itself is legal.

The economic effects of oligopoly may be the same as those of monopoly, as a result of the lack of competition. Nevertheless, oligopoly is not subject to attack under §2 of the Sherman Act because no single firm possesses monopoly power. The legal approach to oligopoly is therefore purely behavioral—did the firms act pursuant to a common arrangement, agreement, or understanding? Behavioral antitrust provisions are discussed in more detail later in this chapter.

Various attempts to pass legislation allowing for a structural attack on oligopoly have been unsuccessful. The FTC at one time attempted to attack oligopolies as "shared monopolies" under §5 of the FTC act, but it subsequently abandoned those efforts. As a result, legal challenges to oligopolies require the courts to search for some sort of concerted behavior—collusion or agreement, either explicit or implicit—among the firms involved. In the absence of an agreement or understanding, even identical behavior by competing firms is legal. For example, Continental Airlines may decide to offer discount rates on popular routes, to try to gain a competitive advantage; if, in response, the other competing airlines offer similar discounts, competition on those routes remains the same. If the airlines each independently decide to offer discounts, their parallel behavior is legal; but if the decision to offer discounts results from an agreement or understanding among the firms, the decision violates the antitrust laws.

Mergers The last few years of the 20th century and the first few years of the 21st century have witnessed an explosive wave of mergers, dwarfing the merger waves of previous decades: Disney's purchase of ABC, Viacom's acquisition of CBS, Chrysler merging with Daimler-Benz, Ford purchasing Volvo, General Motors acquiring Saab, Exxon merging with Mobil Oil Corp., Time-Warner merging with AOL, Boeing's merger with McDonnell Douglas are just a few examples. Firms in developing industries such as the Internet or telecommunications merged to keep pace with rapidly changing technology that requires innovation and "one stop shopping" (being able to offer consumers complementary products such as cable and Internet service). Firms in "mature" industries such as defense, oil, or automobiles merge in order to compete more efficiently in the global market, and to react more effectively to the changing nature of the market. The increasing globalization of trade means that firms face increasing competition from "foreign" firms, even in their home market; firms may see mergers as the way to counter such threats, or as the key to opening up new markets abroad. A soaring stock market provides firms with enormous amounts of capital to use for such "buying sprees."

Although the legislation dealing with mergers and the general judicial analysis to the legality of mergers have not changed, the attitudes of antitrust enforcement officials have changed. Antitrust enforcers recognize that firms now compete globally and that the nature of competition in industries is changing. They are more willing to allow mergers between huge competitors such as Exxon and Mobil if they result in a large domestic firm able to compete more effectively with foreign "giants" such as Royal Dutch Shell Oil Co. Mergers such as that between Boeing and McDonnell Douglas will be allowed in order to allow firms to rationalize productive capacity in the dwindling government defense and aerospace industry. Even the changed outlook of the antitrust enforcement officials, however, will not stop them from challenging mergers that create dominant firms with power over prices, or that substantially lessen competition in a given industry.

Section 7 of the Clayton Act prohibits mergers of firms in interstate commerce when the effects of the merger are likely to result in a substantial lessening of competition. Mergers are acquisitions or takeovers of another firm; Section 7 applies to mergers in which one firm purchases either the assets or the stock of another firm. Mergers are only illegal if they are likely to have a detrimental effect on competition; hence, the courts apply the rule of reason in merger cases. The effects of a merger on competition depend on the competitive relationship between the merging firms and the conditions in the industry or industries in which the firms operate. (While most merger cases are brought under §7 of the Clayton Act, mergers can also be challenged under the Sherman Act as an unreasonable restraint of trade or an attempt to monopolize.)

The judicial approach to merger cases under §7 involves the identification of the product market and the geographic market affected by the merger. As in monopoly cases, the product market is defined according to the principles of substitutability; the geographic market is the area or areas of the country likely to be affected by the merger. As in monopoly cases, the definitions of the markets are crucial. The more narrowly the markets are defined, the more likely it is that a merger will substantially affect competition in those markets. After defining the relevant markets, the court must assess the probable effects of the merger on competition in those markets. Note that the court does not have to find any actual lessening of competition—it need only concern itself with the probable results of the merger. If the court finds that the probable result of the merger is a substantial reduction of competition, then the merger is in violation of §7. The court may prohibit the merger or order that it be dissolved.

The assessment of the probable effects of a merger on competition involves consideration of both structural and behavioral factors. The relative importance of those factors depends upon the relationship between the merging firms. Mergers are classified as **horizontal mergers**, involving firms that are competitors; **vertical mergers**, involving firms that are involved in production–supply relationships; or **conglomerate mergers**, involving firms that are neither competitors nor have a production-supply relationship. A merger between large firms may have aspects of all three types of mergers.

Horizontal Mergers When the merging firms are competitors in the same market, the merger is a horizontal merger and is likely to have a direct effect upon competition in that market. In this case, the court will consider whether the resulting firm will be dominant in the market. If the merger results in a firm that has a dominant share of a market, in which there are few competitors or in which the competitors are significantly smaller, the merger will probably be held to violate §7. When two small firms merge in order to compete more effectively with a larger rival, the merger is likely to be allowed.

Until the mid-1970s, the courts in most horizontal merger cases placed heavy emphasis upon the size of the resulting firm. When the new firm would have a significant market share in a concentrated industry, the merger would be held to be illegal. As a result, large firms generally avoided acquiring competitors and instead sought to expand through diversification. More recently, the courts have considered the nature of competition in the industry as well as the merged firm's position in that industry. The courts have also been more willing to recognize that competition is now international in character—foreign firms may pose a competitive threat to the merged firm—in determining the probable effects of a merger on competition. As a result, mergers that create firms that are dominant in the domestic market, in order to compete more effectively with international rivals, are more likely to be permitted by the courts today than in the early 1970s. [The Justice Department's horizontal merger guidelines can be found at http://www.justice.gov/atr/public/guidelines/hmg-2010.html.]

Vertical Mergers Mergers between firms at different levels of the production chain are called vertical mergers. Examples of such a merger would be the acquisition of a petroleum refining company by a firm that produces petrochemicals or the purchase of a chain of gas stations by a petroleum refining company. In the first example, the acquired firm produces the raw materials for the product of the acquiring firm; in the second example, the acquired firm distributes (or retails) the product of the acquiring firm.

Because the merging firms in a vertical merger do not compete directly with each other, the size of the resulting firm is not significant in determining the probable effects upon competition. The court will consider the size of each firm and its relative position in its market: Does either firm occupy such a

horizontal mergers: Mergers among firms that compete with each other.

vertical mergers: Mergers involving firms that are suppliers or customers of each other.

conglomerate mergers: Mergers that are neither horizontal nor vertical.

significant position in its market that the merger will foreclose a major source of supplies or a major distribution outlet from other competitors? For example, if a chain of gas stations previously carried the products of a number of refiners, the court will consider whether the acquisition of the chain by one refiner will deny the other refiners access to the chain's sales outlets. If so, and if the chain represents a significant share of the retail gasoline sales market, then the acquisition could violate §7 by substantially lessening competition in the distribution and retail sale of gasoline.

In addition to considering the size and relative position of each firm in its own market, the court will determine whether the merger will enable the resulting firm to engage in anticompetitive behavior in either market. When a merger creates significant opportunities for anticompetitive conduct, it can be held to violate §7.

As was the case with horizontal mergers, the courts in the early vertical merger decisions emphasized the relative size of the merging firms in determining the merger's probable effect on competition. The courts also took the position that the size of all of the firms was directly related to the creation of opportunities for predatory conduct; that is, the larger the firms were, the more likely it was that such opportunities would be significant. More recent judicial analysis takes the view that the sizes of the firms are not directly relevant to the creation of opportunities for predatory conduct. Rather, the courts now focus on whether the firm is dominant or possesses monopoly power in its respective market. Much less emphasis is placed on the mere potential for anticompetitive behavior. [The Department of Justice guidelines for non-horizontal mergers can be found at http://www.justice.gov/atr/public/guidelines/hmg-2010.html]

Conglomerate Mergers   Most recently, corporate mergers have involved conglomerate mergers—in which the merging firms are not competitors and are not involved in a production-supply relationship. Because the firms are not directly related, their sizes are not relevant to the merger's effect on competition. The court must therefore consider whether the combination of the firms will create significant opportunities for anticompetitive behavior.

A court must determine whether the assets of the acquiring firm will enable the acquired firm to engage in predatory pricing or improve an already dominant position. The court must also consider whether the acquiring firm had contemplated entering the market in which the acquired firm operates; if so, the merger precludes that potential entry into the market and prevents an increase in competition in that market. The difficulty in proving that the probable effects of a potential merger will be the creation of significant opportunities for anticompetitive practices makes a legal challenge to a conglomerate merger a formidable task. The antitrust enforcement agencies have not seriously challenged conglomerate mergers in recent years; the last successful government challenge to a conglomerate merger was in the mid 1970s. Conglomerate mergers are no longer as common as they were in the 1970s. Firms have largely abandoned the claims that "synergy" would result from the combination of unrelated businesses; most of the mergers since the 1990s have been horizontal or vertical mergers, as firms focus on core businesses and key products.

The following case involves a private suit challenging a proposed merger of competitors. The case raises the issue of whether the merger provisions of §7 of the Clayton Act protect competitors or competition: What kind of harm to competition must a plaintiff allege in order to challenge a merger successfully?

CARGILL, INC. V. MONFORT OF COLORADO, INC.

479 U.S. 104 (1986)

FACTS

The meatpacking industry is highly competitive, and profit margins of the major beef packers are low. The industry is characterized by two distinct markets—the input market, involving the supply of feed cattle for slaughter, and the output market, involving cut and trimmed beef products ("fabricated beef"). Excel Co., a subsidiary of Cargill, Inc., is the second largest meat packer in the United States; it operates five integrated plants (with both slaughtering and meat fabrication) and one fabrication plant. Cargill, Excel's corporate parent, is a large privately owned corporation with more than 150 subsidiaries in at least 35 countries. Excel agreed to buy Spencer Beef, the third largest meat packer in the United States, which operates two integrated plants and one slaughtering plant.

Monfort is the fifth-largest meat packer in the United States, operating three integrated plants. Monfort's share of the input market was 5.5 percent, and its share of the output market was 5.7 percent. Excel's share of those markets, before the purchase of Spencer, was 13.3 percent and 14.1 percent; after the purchase, Excel's shares would be 20.4 percent and 20.4 percent, respectively. The country's largest meat packer is IBP, Inc.; its market shares are 24.4 percent of the input market and 27.3 percent of the output market.

Monfort filed suit under §7 of the Clayton Act, arguing that the merger of Excel and Spencer would substantially lessen competition and increase concentration of economic power in the input and output markets in the fabricated beef industry. Monfort argued that the increased concentration in the input market would increase the cost of cattle to Monfort and would severely narrow Monfort's profit margin. The trial court held that the merger would cause "antitrust injury" (injury that the antitrust laws were designed to prevent) to Monfort and therefore violated §7 of the Clayton Act; the court issued an injunction prohibiting the merger under §16 of the Act.

Excel appealed, arguing that any harm Monfort would suffer from the merger was simply losses resulting from vigorous competition and was not antitrust injury. The court of appeals affirmed the trial court decision; Excel then appealed to the U.S. Supreme Court. The question before the Supreme Court was whether a private plaintiff seeking to prevent a merger under the Clayton Act must show a threat of antitrust injury to get an injunction under §16 of the Act.

DECISION

The Supreme Court held that a private plaintiff suing under §4 (for triple damages) or §16 (for an injunction) of the Clayton Act must prove that the merger would cause antitrust injury to them. In the case of *Brunswick Corp. v. Pueblo Bowl-O-Mat, Inc.,* 429 U.S. 477 (1977), the Court held that losses due to continuing competition were not antitrust injuries and that the antitrust laws were intended to protect competition, not to protect competitors. Monfort claimed that, after the merger, Excel would be able to lower its prices to a level at, or just slightly above, its cost in order to gain market share. Cargill, Excel's parent, had the financial resources to enable Excel to pursue the price-cutting strategy. Monfort, in response, would have to lower its prices and would suffer a loss in profits as a result. The Supreme Court held that the injury that Monfort would allegedly suffer as a result of the merger was injury resulting from increased competition for market share, which was not antitrust injury. "To hold that the antitrust laws protect competitors from the loss of profits due to such price competition would, in effect, render illegal any decision by a firm to cut prices in order to increase market share." The Court also stated that it "is in the interest of competition to permit dominant firms to engage in vigorous competition, including price competition."

Monfort had only demonstrated that any losses it would suffer because of the proposed merger would result from increased competition; Monfort did not show that the merger threatened the company with antitrust injury. Monfort had failed to prove that the merger would result in harm to competition; therefore, the merger would not violate §7 of the Clayton Act. The judgment of the court of appeals was reversed, and the merger was allowed to proceed.

CASE QUESTIONS

1. What kind of merger is involved here—horizontal, vertical, or conglomerate?
2. What kind of harm does Monfort allege will result from the merger? Who will suffer the alleged harm?
3. Is harm to competitors the same as harm to competition? What kind of harm, according to the Supreme Court, were the antitrust laws intended to prevent?
4. Does this decision emphasize the social or the economic approach to enforcing the antitrust laws?

Premerger Notification Requirements   The 1979 amendments to §7 of the Clayton Act, added by the Hart-Scott-Rodino Act, instituted a premerger requirement for mergers involving firms of a certain size. The legislation added §7A, which sets premerger reporting requirements; the revised guidelines require that both the Antitrust Division of the Justice Department and the FTC be notified prior to any merger involving the acquisition of assets exceeding $56.7 million and total assets for one of the parties exceeds $113.4 million and the other party exceeds $11.3 million. The notice must be given at least 15 days prior to the merger if it involves a cash purchase of the acquired firm; for mergers that involve an exchange of securities, the notice period is 30 days.

The purpose of the premerger notification requirement is to give the enforcement authorities an opportunity to analyze the probable effects of the proposed merger before it takes place. The notification requirement does not constitute a formal approval system; the merging firms need not get the permission of the enforcement authorities in order to consummate the merger. In practice, the requirement has allowed the authorities to raise legal concerns prior to some mergers. In most cases in which such concerns have been raised, the firms either abandoned the proposed merger or agreed to sell off operations of the firms that raised competitive concerns.

For example, the FTC approved the Exxon and Mobil merger in 1999 only after the firms agreed to sell off 2,431 gas stations in the Northeast, California, and Texas, where both firms had significant market shares, and Exxon agreed to sell a refinery in California, terminals, and a pipeline.

THE IMPACT OF E.U. ANTITRUST LAW ON AMERICAN FIRMS

The United States has long taken the position that actions of foreign firms that have a negative effect on competition within the United States are subject to U.S. antitrust law—even if the merging firms have no offices, plants, or operations in the United States. As they begin to operate globally, U.S. firms become subject to the laws and regulations of countries around the world. Increasingly, the antitrust policies of the European Union are being applied to the behavior and actions of U.S. firms. The E.U. maintains that its antitrust laws and competition policy apply to the U.S. firms whose actions affect competition within the E.U.

The main provisions of the E.U. antitrust policy are Articles 81 and 82 of the Treaty Establishing the European Community (as renumbered by the Treaty of Amsterdam). Article 81 is similar in concept to Section 1 of the Sherman Act; it prohibits all agreements restricting competition within the common market. Article 82, similar to Section 2 of the Sherman Act, prohibits firms from abusing a dominant position within the common market. Penalties under the E.U. provisions include the power to impose fines of up to 10% of the offending firm's annual business revenue. In recent years the E.U. antitrust policies have been applied to mergers of U.S. firms and to allegedly anticompetitive conduct by U.S. firms that have dominant positions with regard to particular products.

Mergers. Generally, when a merger of U.S. firms is approved by U.S. authorities, the E.U. competition authorities also grant approval. (The U.S. Justice Department and the FTC executed an agreement with the E.U. competition authorities on antitrust enforcement in 1991, and a supplemental agreement in 1998.) However, in more recent cases, the E.U. authorities have objected to mergers that had been approved by U.S. antitrust authorities.

Boeing–McDonnell Douglas. When Boeing announced plans to merge with McDonnell Douglas in 1997, the E.U. insisted upon subjecting the merger to E.U. law because Boeing accounts for a significant volume of business in Europe. The FTC approved the merger, but the E.U.'s competition commissioner announced that the E.U. would seek to block the merger because it would significantly reduce competition in Europe. Boeing, the world's leading manufacturer of civilian aircraft, sought to acquire McDonnell Douglas, the number three manufacturer of civilian aircraft and a leading supplier of military aircraft, primarily as part of a consolidation of the U.S. defense industry. The E.U. authorities opposed the merger because it would leave European airlines with a choice between Boeing and Airbus, a European firm; the merger would increase Boeing's share of the world market from 64 percent to 70 percent, whereas Airbus had about 30 percent of that market. Boeing and Airbus were dominant in the market for large civilian airliners; Boeing had about 70 percent of the market (based on recent aircraft orders) and accounted for about 80 percent of existing airliner fleets. Boeing also had signed exclusive 20-year supply contracts with several airlines—American Airlines, Continental, and Delta (accounting for 11 percent of the world market)—by which the airlines agreed to buy all new airliners from Boeing. The E.U. commissioner for competition claimed that such contracts would have the effect of shutting out the only other competitor, Airbus, from a large segment of the U.S. market. Lastly, the E.U. officials were concerned that McDonnell Douglas's research for defense contracts would "spill over" into the civilian airliner market and give Boeing a technological advantage over Airbus. If Boeing and McDonnell Douglas went ahead with the merger, and the E.U. declared it illegal, the E.U. could impose fines against Boeing of up to almost $4 billion. The E.U. could also fine any European airline that purchased Boeing aircraft, could impound any new Boeing aircraft landing in Europe, and would effectively cut Boeing off from the European large air-liner market, about 26 percent of the world market. Rather than face such consequences, Boeing ultimately agreed to accept certain conditions imposed by E.U. authorities in return for E.U. approval of the merger. Boeing agreed to license to competitors (such as Airbus) any patents that result from its defense work, agreed not to enter into any new exclusive supply contracts for 10 years, and agreed not to enforce its existing exclusive supply contracts. The E.U. approval then cleared the way for the merger to proceed.

General Electric–Honeywell. General Electric proposed a $40 billion merger with Honeywell in October 2000; the U.S. antitrust authorities approved the merger. The E.U. competition commissioner objected to the merger on grounds that it would reduce competition in the market for jet engines for aircraft. G.E. was a leading producer of jet engines, and Honeywell was strong in avionics (electronic flight controls). By combining, G.E. allegedly would gain a significant advantage through offering aircraft customers bundled engines and avionics at prices lower than such products could be offered separately. The E.U. also claimed that G.E. Capital, G.E.'s financial services operation, was a leader in the aircraft leasing market, and it specifically requires that any aircraft it finances use G.E. jet engines. The E.U. would approve the merger if G.E. would sell off the avionics business or reduce the percentage of its ownership of G.E. Capital's aircraft leasing business. G.E. refused to agree to such conditions, and the proposed merger was abandoned in 2001.

Google–DoubleClick. In November 2007, the E.U. Commission announced an investigation into Google's plan to buy the online advertising firm DoubleClick for $3.1 billion. The E.U. Commission expressed concern that the purchase of DoubleClick, which is the world's largest broker of online banner advertising, by Google, which controls more than 70% of the paid-search advertising market, would raise competitive concerns in the online advertising market. The E.U. Commission was responding to complaints from Microsoft and Yahoo, rivals of Google; other organizations have argued that the proposed acquisition would also pose threats to privacy rights and could limit Internet content.

Microsoft. As the U.S. antitrust authorities were negotiating a settlement in the Microsoft monopoly case, the E.U. competition commissioner was conducting an investigation into alleged anticompetitive practices by Microsoft. The E.U. ultimately filed a complaint against Microsoft for abusing its dominant position in the operating systems market for personal computers. Through the various versions of its Windows operating system, Microsoft has an overwhelmingly dominant position in the market for personal computer operating systems. The E.U. alleged that Microsoft sought to extend (or "leverage") that dominance into the market for low-end servers by refusing to share Microsoft Windows code with other firms, such as IBM and Sun Microsystems, who also produce servers. The refusal to share code or data about Windows put the other producers at a marked competitive disadvantage. The E.U. also argued that Microsoft's inclusion (or "bundling") of the Windows Media Player in the Windows operating system reduced competition in the market for audiovisual software, stifled product innovation and ultimately reduced consumer choice.

In March 2004, the E.U. Commission proposed to fine Microsoft €497 million (approximately $612 million), and proposed requiring Microsoft to share its Windows code with other firms in the "low-end server market" and that it offer a version of Windows without the Media Player, or agree to allow inclusion of rival media players with its Windows operating system. Microsoft filed objections to the proposed penalty and appealed the E.U. Commission's decision to the E.U. Court of First Instance, which upheld the E.U. decision and fine (which, given exchange rate changes, had risen to approximately $690 million as of late 2007) in September 2007. In October 2007, Microsoft announced that it would drop any further appeal and accept the E.U. Commission's decision. Microsoft also agreed to license its software code to other software developers for a one-time license fee of €10,000 (approximately $ 15,000) and to make its code available to open-source developers. Microsoft had already been selling a version of Windows that did not include its Media Player.

Intel. In July 2007, after a six-year investigation, the E.U. Commission filed a formal complaint against Intel Corp., alleging that the world's largest chip maker had abused its dominant position in the computer chip market. The E.U. charged that Intel, with an 80% share of the $33 billion market for personal-computer chips, had been offering illegal rebates to computer makers to maintain a competitive advantage over rival chip maker AMD. In a related matter, in 2005 Intel had agreed to obey an antitrust recommendation by Japan's Fair Trade Commission to stop offering rebates to computer makers who agreed to limit their use of competitors' computer chips. Korean antitrust authorities are also investigating Intel's practices.

The actions against Microsoft and the Intel investigation reflect an aggressive attitude on the part of the E.U. and other foreign antitrust enforcement authorities against firms perceived to be dominant in particular markets.

Microsoft Goes on the Offensive. Software giant Microsoft filed a formal antitrust complaint with EU antitrust authorities, alleging that Google is using its dominance of the Internet search markets to adversely affect other tech firms. Microsoft's complaint is somewhat ironic in light of the fact that it has been subject to antitrust actions in both the U.S. and Europe for the past twenty years. Microsoft's complaint follows a broad inquiry into Google's practices by EU antitrust regulators that was launched in November 2010. Microsoft's own search engine, Bing, competes with Google; Google has approximately 95% of the search market in Europe, which is less competitive than the U.S. search market. One of the allegations made by Microsoft is than Google limited the ability of other search engines to examine and index information controlled by Google, such as YouTube videos, and that makes it difficult for the search firms to display search results properly. Google has also allegedly blocked smartphones that run Microsoft's Windows software from operating properly with YouTube, and has limited the ability of advertisers with Google to access the data given to Google, which limits their ability to serve ads through other search competitors. Advertising revenue accounts for most of Google's $30 billion annual revenue, and internet searches are central to such revenue. If Google is found to have violated EU antitrust law, it could be subject to a fine of up to 10% of the firm's annual revenue. Joaquin Almunia, the EU antitrust chief, indicated that Google will likely be subject to other complaints, and stated that the EU regulators were interested in the elimination of barriers that may prevent rival firms from competing with Google.

Sources: "E.U. to Probe Google-DoubleClick Plan," The Hollywood Reporter.Com (November 14, 2007); "Microsoft Says 'Uncle' in Its Battle with E.U.," *Los Angeles Times* (October 23, 2007); "Antitrust Charges Filed against Intel," *San Jose Mercury News* (July 27, 2007); "Antitrust Ruling against Microsoft Upheld in E.U.," *The Atlanta Journal-Constitution* (September 18, 2007); "The Borders of Competition," *The Economist* (July 4, 1998); "Brussels v. Boeing," *The Economist* (July 19, 1997); "Peace in our time: Boeing v. Airbus," *The Economist* (July 26, 1997); "Turbulence," *The Economist* (May 10, 2001); "Welch Squelched," *The Economist* (June 21, 2001); "The Next Battleground," *The Economist* (November 8, 2001); "Monti Braves the Catcalls," *The Economist* (December 13, 2001); "Engine Failure," *The Economist* (July 5, 2001); "A Bundle of Trouble," *The Economist* (July 5, 2001); "Monti's Double Whammy," *The Economist* (October 25, 2002); "Reform's Last Gasp," *The Economist* (May 22, 2003); "A Stone Hurled from Across the Pond," Washingtonpost.com (August 6, 2003); "E.U. Officials Accuse Microsoft of Monopoly," Associated Press (August 6, 2003); "Windows a la Carte," *The Economist* (March 25, 2004); "Regulators, Rivals React," Washingtonpost.com (March 25, 2004); "Can Microsoft Be Tamed?", *The Economist* (March 25, 2004); "Intel Probe Highlights E.U.-U.S. Regulation Tussle," *The New York Times* (June 8, 2004). Jai Lynn Yang, "Microsoft Turns to Europe for Help in Antitrust Fight Against Google," *The Washington Post,* April 1, 2011; Jim Puzzanghera, "Microsoft Plans Antitrust Filing," *Los Angeles Times,* April 1, 2011; "Microsoft Accuses Google," *The Irish Times,* April 1, 2011; "Microsoft Files Antitrust Complaint Against Google," *Techweb,* March 31, 2011; "Google Will Face More EU Antitrust Complaints, Almunia Says," *Business: Washington Post Business Page,* April 8, 2011; James Kanster and Steve Lohr, "Claim Against Google Puts Microsoft in Unusual Spot," *The International Herald Tribune,* April 1, 2011; Steve Lohr, "Microsoft Takes Its Fight with Google to Europe," *The International Herald Tribune,* April 1, 2011; Steve Lohr, "Antitrust Cry from Microsoft," *The New York Times,* March 31, 2011; "Google May Face U.S. Antitrust Probe," *Techweb,* April 5, 2011.

BEHAVIORAL ANTITRUST PROVISIONS

Behavioral antitrust provisions focus on arrangements or agreements among firms and upon firms' pricing policies. Section 1 of the Sherman Act, which prohibits every " . . . contract, combination . . . or conspiracy in restraint of trade or commerce," is the main provision of behavioral antitrust provisions.

In determining the legality of an arrangement, it is usually necessary to determine whether the arrangement is horizontal or vertical. The judicial analysis of the legality of such arrangements generally differs for horizontal and vertical arrangements. It is also important to consider whether the arrangement involves prices or relates only to nonprice matters.

Horizontal Concerted Activity   Horizontal arrangements, or concerted activities, involve competing firms. Such arrangements may be pursuant to explicit contracts or to tacit understandings, and they may involve pricing or nonprice competition. Any agreement among competitors is likely to have an adverse effect on competition; therefore, the antitrust laws deal harshly with horizontal arrangements. Any concerted activity among competitors that restricts competition or that is intended to restrict competition is illegal *per se*. Thus, the conduct is illegal, regardless of its actual effect on competition. (Note that horizontal concerted activity that has little effect on competition rarely ever occurs.)

Per Se Rule   The *per se* rule is the usual judicial approach to horizontal concerted activity. The impact of the *per se* rule is mainly evidentiary—the court will not consider any justification for the concerted behavior. For example, the fact that an agreement to set prices maintains them at a reasonable level or only specifies a ceiling price is irrelevant to the legality of the agreement. The *per se* approach, under §1 of the Sherman Act, applies to a variety of horizontal concerted activities. Examples of such activity include territorial market divisions, agreements to restrict output or production, agreements not to deal with certain firms or customers, group boycotts, and agreements not to advertise prices. Because concerted activity intended to restrict competition is illegal *per se*, it is illegal regardless of the actual effects on competition and regardless of the motives behind the activity. Firms acting independently may choose not to deal with certain customers or in certain areas or to charge certain prices. When such decisions are made in conjunction with competing firms, however, they are illegal. The crucial factor for determining the legality of particular behavior is whether the firms involved are acting jointly or independently.

Because of the *per se* rule, the judicial approach to cases of alleged horizontal activity involves only the determination of whether the conduct was concerted rather than independent and whether the arrangement was indeed horizontal. If both questions are answered affirmatively, a court will refuse to consider any justification for the activity.

The following case illustrates the application of the *per se* rule to alleged horizontal concerted activity.

UNITED STATES V. TOPCO ASSOCIATES, INC.

405 U.S. 596 (1972)

FACTS

Topco Associates is a cooperative association of small, regional supermarket chains. Topco's main function is to serve as a purchasing agent for its member chains; it procures and distributes more than 1,000 products that are marketed under the Topco brand name. By 1967, Topco members had combined retail sales of more than $2.3 billion—a figure exceeded only by three national grocery chains. The member supermarket chains operate independently; there is no pooling of profits or advertising efforts, and no grocers do business under the Topco name. The member supermarkets control all of Topco's stock and voting rights, and Topco's board of directors is made up of executives from the various member chains. As a result, the member chains have complete control over Topco's operations.

When a chain applies for membership in Topco, it first has to be approved by the Topco board of directors and then by an affirmative vote of at least 75 percent of the members. However, if the member whose operations are closest to the applicant or members with operations within 100 miles of the applicant vote against the applicant, then an affirmative vote of 85 percent of the members is required for admission. The Topco members generally cooperate in accommodating the wishes of other members, so that in actual practice, the members have a veto against the admission of actual or potential competitors in the territories in which they operate. Following admission, each new member signs an agreement designating the territory in which it may sell Topco brand products; the member may not sell outside the designated territory. Combined with the veto that members have over competitors, the result of the arrangement is effectively to insulate members from competition in Topco brand products.

The grocery industry is very competitive; profit margins from grocery firms of 1 percent to 2 percent are common. The Topco member grocery chains argued that their membership in Topco allows them to compete more effectively with the national grocery chains. Because the members do not face any competition for the Topco brand items within their territories, those items are very profitable; the profits from Topco items allow the members to reduce prices on items to compete with the national grocery chains.

The U.S. government claimed that the arrangement constituted a market division agreement among the supermarket chains (competitors) that operated to prohibit competition in Topco brand products among the retail grocery chains and was in violation of §1 of the Sherman Act. The trial court held that the arrangement was legal, and the U.S. government appealed directly to the U.S. Supreme Court. Topco argued that restricting competition in Topco brand products actually increased competition by enabling its members to compete successfully against the larger chains.

DECISION

The Supreme Court noted that the evidence indicated that the Topco members were frequently strong competitors in their respective areas, largely due to the success of the Topco brand products. The profits on the Topco brand products were substantial, and their existence had improved the competitive potential of the Topco members against other large grocery chains. But the Court held that the trial court had erred in holding that restricting competition in Topco brand products was legal because it increased competition among grocery chains; the Sherman Act does not grant Topco authority to determine the "respective values of competition in the various sectors of the economy." The Court held that each member chain must decide for itself "whether or not competition with other supermarket chains is more desirable than competition in the sale of Topco-brand products." If any decision to sacrifice competition in one portion of the economy for increased competition in another portion is to be made, stated the Court, it must be made by Congress, and not by private parties or in the courts. In the absence of any congressional directive to the contrary, the arenas in which the Topco members choose to compete must be left to their independent, unfettered choice. The Supreme Court therefore reversed the judgment of the trial court and held that the Topco arrangement was a combination or conspiracy in restraint of trade in violation of §1 of the Sherman Act.

CASE QUESTIONS

1. What was the purpose of Topco's restriction upon the sales areas of its members?
2. What were the effects of Topco's restrictions on competition among large grocery chains? What were the effects on competition among sellers of Topco brand products?
3. Did the trial court characterize the Topco restrictions as horizontal or vertical? Why did the trial court find the restrictions to be legal?
4. Did the Supreme Court characterize the Topco restrictions as horizontal or vertical? Why? Why did the Supreme Court refuse to consider the purpose of the restrictions in considering their legality?
5. If the chains that were members of Topco chose to merge into a single firm in order to compete with the national chains, would their conduct have been held to be illegal?

DEPARTMENT OF JUSTICE

FOR IMMEDIATE RELEASE   AT
MONDAY, NOVEMBER 1, 2010   (202) 514-2007
www.justice.gov   TDD (202) 514-1888

ALL NIPPON AIRWAYS CO. LTD. AGREES TO PLEAD GUILTY TO PRICE FIXING ON AIR CARGO AND AIR PASSENGER SERVICES
Company Agrees to Pay $73 Million Criminal Fine

WASHINGTON—All Nippon Airways Co. Ltd. (ANA) has agreed to plead guilty and to pay a $73 million criminal fine for its role in two separate conspiracies to fix prices in the air transportation industry, the Department of Justice announced today.

According to a two-count felony charge filed today in U.S. District Court for the District of Columbia, Japan-based ANA engaged in a conspiracy to fix one or more components of cargo rates charged for international air cargo shipments from at least as early as April 1, 2000, until at least Feb. 14, 2006. ANA is also charged with engaging in a conspiracy to fix unpublished passenger fares on tickets purchased in the United States from at least as early as April 1, 2000, until at least April 1, 2004. Under the plea agreement, which is subject to court approval, ANA has also agreed to cooperate with the department's ongoing antitrust investigation.

ANA transports a variety of cargo shipments, such as heavy equipment, perishable commodities and consumer goods, on scheduled international flights, including to and from the United States. ANA also transports passengers on scheduled flights within Japan and internationally, including to and from the United States. ANA typically offered unpublished passenger fares to travel agents for purchase by certain consumers.

According to the charges, ANA carried out the conspiracies by agreeing during meetings and other communications on certain components of the cargo rates to be charged for shipments on routes between the United States and Japan, and on unpublished passenger fares to be charged on tickets purchased in the United States. As part of the conspiracies, ANA levied cargo rates and unpublished passenger fares in accordance with the agreements reached, and monitored and enforced adherence to the agreed-upon cargo rates and unpublished passenger fares.

ANA is charged with two counts of price fixing in violation of the Sherman Act, which carries a maximum fine for corporations of $100 million for each violation committed after June 22, 2004, and $10 million for violations committed before that date. The maximum fine for each count may be increased to twice the gain derived from the crime or twice the loss suffered by the victims of the crime, if either of those amounts is greater than the statutory maximum fine.

Including today's charge, as a result of this investigation, a total of 19 airlines and 14 executives have been charged in the Justice Department's ongoing investigation into price fixing in the air transportation industry. To date, more than $1.6 billion in criminal fines have been obtained and four executives have been sentenced to serve prison time. Charges are pending against the remaining 10 executives.

Today's charge is the result of a joint investigation into the air transportation industry being conducted by the Antitrust Division's National Criminal Enforcement Section, the FBI's Washington Field Office, the Department of Transportation's Office of Inspector General and the U.S. Postal Service's Office of Inspector General. Anyone with information concerning price fixing or other anticompetitive conduct in the air transportation industry is urged to call the Antitrust Division's National Criminal Enforcement Section at 202-307-6694 or visit www.justice.gov/atr/contact/newcase.htm, or call the FBI's Washington Field Office at 202-278-2000.

10-1236 [available at http://www.justice.gov/atr/public/press_releases/2010/263643.htm]

Horizontal Concerted Activity and Trade Associations   Business executives and firms generally participate in a trade association or industry promotion council, organizations formed by the firms in a particular industry to promote their interests with the government and consumers. The associations may also collect and publish information about economic and competitive conditions in the industry. Because the member firms of such organizations are competitors, their activities may arouse interest from antitrust enforcement agencies. Joint lobbying and promotional activities are unlikely to pose legal problems, but collecting and distributing information about industry conditions present the potential for concerted activity based on such information. The associations and their member firms must therefore exercise great caution in gathering and publishing production and pricing information. Collecting and publishing aggregate information, with no individual firms or customers identified, is legal; however, it is illegal to distribute current prices offered to specific customers when the effect of such information may be to stabilize prices in an industry. Even informal exchanges of current price information, when the firms involved have agreed to adhere to the prices quoted, have been held to violate §1 of the Sherman Act. Groups whose membership is not restricted to the firms of a single industry, such as the Chamber of Commerce or the Business Roundtable, are less likely to pose antitrust problems by their activities.

Horizontal Concerted Activity and the Rule of Reason   Although the courts generally apply the *per se* rule to horizontal concerted activity, occasional instances arise when the courts may choose to apply the rule of reason. These include situations in which the alleged concerted activity has legitimate justifications or the concerted restrictions are necessary to allow the product to be provided to the public. The case of *N.C.A.A. v. Board of Regents of the University of Oklahoma*, 468 U.S. 85 (1984), involved a challenge to the restrictions placed on college football games involving members of the National Collegiate Athletic Association (NCAA). The restrictions on televising games limited the number of times that a particular team could appear on television in a particular season. Other NCAA restrictions limited the number of athletic scholarships that a school could give, limited the number of games that could be played each season, and ensured that the players remained amateurs. The Supreme Court noted in the following passage that some of the NCAA restrictions were necessary to ensure the availability of college football at all:

> What the NCAA and its member institutions market in this case is competition itself—contests between competing institutions. Of course, this would be completely ineffective if there were no rules on which the competitors agreed to create and define the competition to be marketed. A myriad of rules affecting such matters as the size of the field, the number of players on a team, and the extent to which physical violence is to be encouraged or proscribed, all must be agreed upon, and all restrain the manner in which institutions compete. Moreover, the NCAA seeks to market a particular brand of football—college football. The identification of the 'product' with an academic tradition differentiates college football from and makes it more popular than professional sports to which it might otherwise be comparable, such as, for example, minor league baseball. In order to preserve the character and quality of the 'product,' athletes must not be paid, must be required to attend class, and the like. And the integrity of the 'product' cannot be preserved except by mutual agreement; if an institution adopted such restrictions unilaterally, its effectiveness as a competitor on the playing field might soon be destroyed. Thus, the NCAA plays a vital role in enabling college football to preserve its character, and as a result enables a product to be marketed which might otherwise be unavailable. In performing this role, its actions widen consumer choice—not only the choices available to sports fans but also those available to athletes—and hence can be viewed as procompetitive.

The court therefore held that the rule of reason, rather than the *per se* rule, should be applied to the NCAA restrictions regarding the rules of the game and player eligibility. Those restrictions were held to be legal; however, the restrictions on the televising of games of NCAA members had the effect of restricting output of the product and raising the price that the networks had to pay for the rights to televise them, restricting competition unreasonably, and were therefore illegal under §1 of the Sherman Act.

The following reading involves the application of the rule of reason to other horizontal concerted activity among universities.

ANTITRUST AND THE IVY LEAGUE

In 1991, the U.S. government filed an antitrust suit against the Ivy League schools—Brown, Columbia, Cornell, Dartmouth, Harvard, Princeton, Yale, and the University of Pennsylvania—as well as the Massachusetts Institute of Technology (M.I.T.), alleging that the nine schools joined together to fix salaries and establish common levels of financial aid for needy students. This system, called "overlapping," began in the late 1950s in an attempt to avoid the need for each school to spend considerable amounts of time and money outbidding the others for students and faculty.

The Ivy League schools quickly settled with the Justice Department, agreeing to act in accordance with a consent decree that prohibits the schools from meeting to fix salaries and set tuition and scholarship levels. The Justice Department, however, did permit the schools to meet to exchange data on "general principles" governing such aid.

M.I.T. at first refused to settle with the Justice Department, instead choosing to argue its case in federal court. M.I.T. insisted that its actions had not constituted an antitrust violation because the school should be governed by laws concerning charitable organizations rather than those which concern businesses. In particular, M.I.T. argued that the practice had the effect of keeping tuition prices down, thus allowing more poor and minority students to attend the university.

The federal district court refused to accept M.I.T.'s argument; however, the federal court of appeals reversed the lower court's ruling and sent the case back to the district court for a fuller hearing of M.I.T.'s position. Despite this success, M.I.T. agreed a few months later to settle with the Justice Department. In the settlement, M.I.T. agreed to follow the 1991 consent decree that the other Ivy League schools had signed. M.I.T. President Charles M. Vest stated that the settlement offered two particular benefits:

First, the Justice Department will dismiss all claims against M.I.T. Second, the settlement establishes guidelines under which colleges and universities can coordinate their financial aid practices to ensure that their limited financial aid funds are awarded to qualified students solely on the basis of need.

Sources: "Court Gives M.I.T. Another Chance in a Federal Price-Fixing Case," *The New York Times* (18 September 1993), 6; Jackson, Robert L., "MIT Agrees to Settle Antitrust Suit, U.S. Says," *The Los Angeles Times* (23 December 1993), A-14.

Vertical Restrictions   Restrictions imposed by a manufacturer or supplier of a product or service upon firms that distribute or retail that product are known as **vertical restrictions**. Such restrictions may involve territorial limits on sales or agreements not to deal with competitors of the supplier. Vertical restrictions are subject to §1 of the Sherman Act or §3 of the Clayton Act. The judicial approach to such restrictions varies with the nature of the restriction. Factors that the courts consider include whether a restriction pertains to pricing or to nonprice issues and whether it is a **tying arrangement** (which requires the purchaser of a product to take other products of the supplier as well) or an **exclusive dealing agreement** (which prohibits a dealer from dealing with other suppliers).

Vertical Price Restrictions   Attempts by suppliers or manufacturers to control the price at which their products are sold by a retailer or distributor may be illegal under §1 of the Sherman Act. Although a supplier may set the price for its products by retail outlets that it owns, should it be able to control the price at which independent outlets resell the product? The supplier is free to choose the retailers with which it will deal and to set the prices at which it will sell products to those retailers.

Some commentators have questioned the application of the *per se* rule to vertical price restrictions. Those commentators argue that such restrictions only affect **intrabrand competition** (competition among the sellers of the supplier's products, such as competition among Toyota dealers) and not **interbrand**

vertical restrictions: Restrictions imposed by a manufacturer or supplier on firms that distribute the product.

tying arrangement: Vertical restriction that conditions the sale of one product upon the sale of a different product.

exclusive dealing arrangement: Agreement prohibiting a firm from dealing with other suppliers of a particular product.

intrabrand competition: Competition among the dealers of a particular brand of a product—such as all the Starbucks Coffee Shops.

interbrand competition: Competition among all the dealers of a product—such as competition among all the coffee shops.

competition (competition among the products of various suppliers such as competition among all the auto dealers in an area).

It is clear that vertical price restrictions setting a particular price, or setting a minimum price below which the product cannot be sold, may have anticompetitive effects—they may substantially limit or totally eliminate intrabrand competition on price—but they may also have pro-competitive effects by promoting interbrand competition. Eliminating intrabrand competition may encourage retailers of a product to invest in service or promotional efforts that aid a manufacturer in competing against rival manufacturers. Consumers may then have a choice between higher-priced, high-service brands and lower-priced, low-service brands. However, if interbrand competition is dominated by a large manufacturer, the use of vertical price restrictions by that dominant manufacturer may result in monopoly profits and reduced consumer choice. Vertical price restrictions may also be used to facilitate price collusion among the retailers of a particular brand, or to create a cartel among the manufacturers and the retailers of a particular product.

The legal approach used by the courts to analyze the legality of vertical price restrictions has been changing over time. In *Dr. Miles Medical Co. v. John D. Park & Sons Co.,* 220 U.S. 373 (1911) the Supreme Court held that a vertical price agreement between a manufacturer and a retailer to set minimum resale prices was subject to the *per se* rule under §1 of the Sherman Act. In *Monsanto Co. v. Spray-Rite Service Corp.,* 465 U.S. 752 (1984), the Supreme Court held that vertical price arrangements were illegal when "the manufacturer and others had a conscious commitment to a common scheme designed to achieve an unlawful objective." The court's approach to vertical price restrictions did not differentiate between minimum and maximum price restrictions. Maximum price restrictions do not prevent price competition, because they allow retailers to sell the product at whatever price they choose, as long as it is below the maximum or ceiling price. Sellers are thus free to compete on price, although there may be a tendency for them to sell at the maximum price. If that is the case, then the ceiling price becomes the set price, and the effect of the maximum price restriction is the same as an agreement to set a particular price, thus eliminating price competition. In *Albrect v. Herald Co.,* 390 U.S. 145 (1968) the Supreme Court held that vertical maximum price restrictions were subject to the *per se* rule—that is, they were inherently anticompetitive and were automatically illegal. But in recent years, the Supreme Court has reconsidered the issue of whether vertical maximum price restrictions should be subject to the *per se* rule or the rule of reason. In *State Oil v. Khan,* 522 U.S. 3 (1997) the Court overruled *Albrecht v. Herald Co.,* and held that vertical maximum price restrictions were subject to the rule of reason. That means the legality of vertical maximum price restrictions depends upon their effects on competition—if they unreasonably affect or restrain competition, they will be illegal under the rule of reason.

If vertical maximum price restrictions are now subject to the rule of reason rather than the per se rule, should the same approach be used for vertical minimum price restrictions? The Supreme Court considered that question in the following case.

LEEGIN CREATIVE LEATHER PRODUCTS, INC. V. PSKS, INC., DBA KAY'S KLOSET . . . KAY'S SHOES.

127 S.Ct. 2705 (2007)

FACTS

Leegin Creative Leather Products, Inc. (Leegin), designs, manufactures, and distributes leather fashion goods and accessories for women. The Leegin products are sold under the "Brighton" brand name, and are sold in the U.S. by 5,000 retail establishments, mostly independent, small boutiques and specialty stores. Leegin's president, Jerry Kohl, believes that small retailers treat customers better and provide more services than larger, often impersonal retailers. PSKS, Inc. operates Kay's Kloset, a women's apparel store in Lewisville, Texas. Kay's Kloset first started purchasing Brighton goods from Leegin in 1995; it would promote Brighton by running Brighton advertisements and holding Brighton days in the store. Kay's Kloset became the destination retailer in the area to buy Brighton products. Brighton was the store's most important brand and once accounted for 40 to 50 percent of its profits. In 1997, Leegin instituted the "Brighton Retail Pricing and Promotion Policy." Under the policy, Leegin refused to sell to retailers that discounted Brighton goods below suggested prices. Leegin adopted the policy to give its retailers sufficient margins to provide customers the service central to its distribution strategy. It also expressed concern that discounting harmed Brighton's brand image and reputation. A year later Leegin introduced a marketing strategy known as the "Heart Store Program." It offered retailers incentives to become Heart Stores, and, in exchange, retailers pledged, among other things, to sell at Leegin's suggested prices. Kay's Kloset became a Heart Store soon after Leegin created the program. After a Leegin employee visited the store and found it unattractive, the parties appear to have agreed that Kay's Kloset would not be a Heart Store beyond 1998; despite losing Heart Store status, Kay's Kloset continued to increase its Brighton sales. In December 2002, Leegin discovered Kay's Kloset had been selling Brighton's entire line at a 20 percent discount. Kay's Kloset stated that it discounted Brighton products to compete with nearby retailers who also were undercutting Leegin's suggested prices.

Leegin, nonetheless, requested that Kay's Kloset stop the discounting, and when Kay's Kloset refused, Leegin stopped selling to the store. Losing the Brighton brand significantly reduced the store's revenue from sales. PSKS sued Leegin in the United States District Court for the Eastern District of Texas, alleging that Leegin had violated the antitrust laws by entering into agreements with retailers requiring them to charge the prices fixed by Leegin. In its defense, Leegin attempted to introduce expert testimony describing the procompetitive effects of its pricing policy. The District Court, however, held that vertical price restrictions were subject to the *per se* rule established in *Dr. Miles*, and excluded the testimony. The jury agreed with PSKS and awarded it $1.2 million; the District Court trebled the damages and awarded PSKS attorney's fees and costs. It entered judgment against Leegin in the amount of $3,975,000.80. Leegin appealed to the U.S. Court of Appeals for the Fifth Circuit. On appeal, Leegin did not dispute that it had entered into vertical price-fixing agreements with its retailers. Instead, it argued that the rule of reason, rather than the *per se* rule, should apply to those agreements. The Court of Appeals rejected this argument and affirmed the trial court decision. Leegin then appealed to the U.S. Supreme Court; the Court agreed to hear the appeal to determine whether vertical minimum resale price maintenance agreements should continue to be subject to the *per se* rule, or should be under the rule of reason.

DECISION

Justice Kennedy, writing for the majority, noted that *Dr. Miles* treated vertical agreements a manufacturer makes with its distributors as analogous to a horizontal combination among competing distributors. In more recent cases, however, the Court rejected the idea of applying the *per se* approach governing horizontal restraints when considering the legality of vertical restraints. Those recent cases formulate antitrust principles in accordance with the appreciated differences in economic effect between vertical and horizontal agreements. In light of those cases, the court held that it was necessary to examine the economic effects of vertical agreements to fix minimum resale prices, and to determine whether applying the *per se* rule to vertical restraints is appropriate.

The protection of competition is the primary purpose of the antitrust laws. The justifications for vertical price restraints are similar to those for other vertical restrictions: minimum resale price maintenance can stimulate interbrand competition—the competition among manufacturers selling different brands of the same type of product—by reducing intrabrand competition—the competition among retailers selling the same brand. A single manufacturer's use of vertical price restraints tends to eliminate intrabrand price competition; this in turn may encourage retailers to invest in tangible or intangible services or promotional efforts that aid the promotion of the manufacturer's product against those of rival manufacturers. Resale price maintenance also has the potential to give consumers more options so that they can choose among low-price, low-service brands; high-price, high-service brands; and brands that fall in between.

Without vertical price restraints, retailers may not provide the retail services that enhance interbrand competition because discounting retailers can free ride on the efforts of retailers who furnish such services, and then capture some of the increased demand those services generate. Consumers might learn, for example, about the benefits of a manufacturer's product from a retailer that invests in fine showrooms, offers product demonstrations, or hires and trains knowledgeable employees. Or consumers might decide to buy the product because they see it in a retail establishment that has a reputation for selling high-quality merchandise. If the consumer can then buy the product from a retailer that discounts the price because it does not provide services, the high-service retailer will lose sales to the discounter, and may be forced to cut back its services to a level lower than consumers would otherwise prefer. Minimum resale price maintenance prevents the discounter from undercutting the service provider. With price competition decreased, the manufacturer's retailers may then compete among themselves over services. New products and new brands are essential to a

dynamic economy, and if resale price maintenance can increase interbrand competition by facilitating the entry of new firms and brands in the market, then it has a procompetitive effect. Resale price maintenance can also increase interbrand competition by encouraging retailers to provide services that would not be provided otherwise; offering the retailers a guaranteed margin (and threatening termination if they do not meet expectations) may be an efficient way to induce retailers to provide such services, and may also expand the manufacturer's market share.

In addition to having procompetitive justifications, vertical price restraints may also have anticompetitive effects in some circumstances; and unlawful price fixing, designed solely to obtain monopoly profits, is an ever present temptation. Resale price maintenance may be used to facilitate a cartel among manufacturers and could aid the cartel in identifying manufacturers that undercut the cartel's fixed prices. Resale price maintenance could also discourage a manufacturer from cutting prices to retailers, thus denying consumers the benefit of lower prices. Vertical price restraints could also be used to organize cartels at the retailer level: a group of retailers might collude to fix sales prices and then compel a manufacturer to aid the unlawful arrangement with resale price maintenance. In such a case the vertical price restraints would be intended to give inefficient retailers higher profits rather than encourage the provision of services or promote a brand. Because of the cartel agreement, more efficient retailers with better distribution systems and lower cost structures would be prevented from charging lower prices. Such a horizontal cartel among competing manufacturers or competing retailers that decreases output or reduces competition in order to increase price is *per se* unlawful. To the extent a vertical agreement setting minimum resale prices is entered upon to facilitate either type of cartel, it, too, would need to be held unlawful under the rule of reason. Resale price restrictions can be abused by a dominant manufacturer or retailer; for example, a dominant retailer might request resale price maintenance to forestall innovation in distribution that would decrease costs. Manufacturers may feel that they have little choice but to accommodate the dominant retailer's demands for vertical price restraints because they believe they need access to the retailer's distribution network. A manufacturer with market power, by comparison, might use resale price maintenance to induce retailers not to sell the products of smaller rivals or new entrants. As should be evident, the potential anticompetitive consequences of vertical price restraints must not be ignored or underestimated.

Despite the risks of such unlawful conduct, it cannot be stated conclusively that resale price maintenance always or almost always tends to restrict competition and decrease output. Vertical agreements establishing minimum resale prices can have either procompetitive or anticompetitive effects, depending upon the circumstances in which they are formed. Because applying the *per se* rule would proscribe a significant amount of procompetitive conduct, these agreements should not be held illegal *per se*.

Vertical price restraints may entail some economic dangers; applying the rule of reason to them would require courts to be diligent in eliminating their anticompetitive uses from the market. In order to do so, the court would need to consider a number of relevant factors. For example, the number of manufacturers that use the practice in a given industry is an important consideration: if only a few manufacturers lacking market power adopt the practice, there is little likelihood of facilitating a manufacturers' cartel, because such a cartel could be undercut by rival manufacturers. Similarly, a retailers' cartel is unlikely if only a single manufacturer in a competitive market uses resale price maintenance. Healthy interbrand competition would provide consumers with lower priced substitutes and thus would eliminate any gains to retailers from a price-fixing agreement over a single brand. However, if many competing manufacturers adopt resale price maintenance, the practice should be scrutinized more carefully. Another important factor is the source of the restraint: if retailers were the impetus for a vertical price restraint, there is a greater likelihood that the restraint could facilitate a cartel among retailers or support a dominant, inefficient retailer. If, however, a manufacturer adopted the policy independent of retailer pressure, the restraint is less likely to promote anticompetitive conduct. A manufacturer also has an incentive to protest inefficient retailer-induced price

restraints because they can harm its competitive position. A dominant manufacturer or retailer can not abuse resale price maintenance for anticompetitive purposes unless that manufacturer or retailer has market power: if a retailer lacks market power, manufacturers can sell their goods through rival retailers; and if a manufacturer lacks market power, there is less likelihood it can use the practice to keep competitors away from retail distribution outlets.

The rule of reason is intended to eliminate anticompetitive transactions from the market; this rationale also applies to vertical price restraints. A party alleging injury from a vertical agreement setting minimum resale prices will have, as a general matter, the information and resources available to show the existence of the agreement and its scope of operation. Courts considering the effects of such restraints by applying the rule of reason can ensure that the rule operates to eliminate anticompetitive restraints from the market and to promote procompetitive ones.

The Court's majority therefore held that *Dr. Miles Medical Co. v. John D. Park & Sons Co.* is overruled, and that the legality of vertical price restraints is to be judged under the rule of reason. It reversed the decision of the Court of Appeals and remanded the case for reconsideration in light of the Supreme Court's decision. Justices Breyer, Stevens, Justice Souter and Ginsberg dissented, arguing that vertical price restrictions should remain *per se* illegal.

CASE QUESTIONS

1. How does a vertical price restriction or agreement differ from a horizontal price restriction or agreement?
2. How can a vertical price agreement serve to promote competition? How could such an agreement harm competition?
3. What is the rationale for the *per se* rule? Why should the *per se* rule be applied to horizontal price agreements? Did the Supreme Court hold that vertical price restrictions should be subject to the *per se* rule or the rule of reason?
4. What factors should a court consider when determining the legality of vertical price restrictions?

Vertical Nonprice Restrictions

Restrictions on Sales Efforts   Vertical nonprice restrictions generally pertain to the right of a retailer or distributor to sell in particular areas or to particular customers. These restrictions usually involve the designation of certain retailers as the exclusive supplier of a given product in a particular geographic area. These restrictions benefit the retailer by giving it market power in the particular product market through its status as a sole supplier. The manufacturer or distributor benefits by ensuring that all its retailers will not compete with each other.

Vertical nonprice restrictions affect both interbrand and intrabrand competition. The restrictions generally limit the source of supply for the manufacturer's product in a given area, and they reduce or eliminate intrabrand competition. However, when a number of other firms manufacture and sell similar products, the restrictions may actually enhance interbrand competition. (Recall that this was also the justification for the restrictions on the members in the *Topco* case.) On the other hand, where only one or two firms manufacture and sell the product, any restrictions on intrabrand competition may also reduce interbrand competition.

Because the effects of vertical nonprice restrictions depend on the conditions in the particular industry, a court determining the legality of such restrictions must consider their actual effects on competition in that industry. In *Continental T.V., Inc. v. GTE Sylvania,* 433 U.S. 36 (1977), and *Business Electronics Corp. v. Sharp Electronics Corp.,* 485 U.S. 717 (1988), the Supreme Court ruled that vertical nonprice restrictions were subject to the rule of reason. As a result, a court must now consider the actual effects that intrabrand restrictions have upon interbrand competition.

Exclusive Dealing Requirements   Vertical nonprice restrictions can also take the form of exclusive dealing contracts or requirements contracts. These agreements require that a retailer deal only with a certain manufacturer or require a customer to purchase its supply of a particular product from a particular manufacturer or supplier. Exclusive dealing or requirement contracts benefit the retailer by ensuring a stable source of supply of a product; the manufacturer benefits because it has a guaranteed market for its product, and it can be certain that the retailer will devote its efforts to selling the manufacturer's product rather than that of a competitor.

Exclusive dealing or requirement contracts are subject to §1 of the Sherman Act and §3 of the Clayton Act if they involve goods or commodities. When such contracts only involve a service, such as maintenance work or advertising, they are subject only to §1 of the Sherman Act. Section 1 of the Sherman Act prohibits contracts, combinations, or conspiracies in restraint of trade; it applies to any exclusive dealing requirement in or *affecting commerce* when actual harm to competition can be shown. Section 3 of the Clayton Act, on the other hand, applies only to sales, leases, or contracts of sale involving goods or commodities *actually in interstate commerce*. Section 3 also provides that such arrangements are illegal if their effect may be to lessen competition substantially. Thus, a showing of probable harm to competition, as opposed to having to show actual harm, suffices to invalidate such arrangements.

In determining the legality of exclusive dealing or requirements contracts, a court must consider their effect upon competition, requiring a definition of both the relevant product market and the geographic market. The approach is similar to that involving a vertical merger under §7 of the Clayton Act because the degree of control over the customer acquired by the seller through such contracts has an effect on competition similar to that resulting from a vertical merger.

Because the judicial analysis of exclusive dealing or requirements contracts involves consideration of the effect of the arrangement upon competition, courts use the rule of reason approach. Early court decisions based on §3 of the Clayton Act held that such arrangements were illegal when they involved a substantial volume of commerce, regardless of their actual or probable effects on competition. However, in *Tampa Electric v. Nashville Coal,* 365 U.S. 320 (1961), the Supreme Court held that the effect of the arrangement on competition in the relevant market must be considered along with the volume of commerce affected. Today, such arrangements are illegal only if they foreclose competition in a substantial share of the relevant market. For example, if a customer accounting for 30 percent of the purchases of specialized machine tools agreed to use only the products of a leading machine tool manufacturer having 50 percent of the market, other manufacturers would be denied access to a substantial share of the market for machine tools and would be less able to compete with the dominant firm. Because the exclusive dealing arrangement between the customer and the dominant firm substantially reduces competition in the machine tool market, it would likely be illegal.

Tying Arrangements   The supplier of a particular product or service may condition the sale of that product upon the purchaser taking a different product as well. For example, the supplier of a fax machine may require that its customers agree to use only its brand of paper in the fax machine. Such agreements "tie" the sale of one product (the fax machine) to the sale of another product (the paper) and, hence, are known as *tying arrangements*. A manufacturer's requirement that customers use only its own products for maintenance and servicing would also be a tying arrangement. The sale of products that are normally sold together or used together, such as the sale of both a left shoe and a right shoe in a pair or the sale of an engine and a set of tires as part of an automobile, are not considered by the courts to be tying arrangements.

Tying arrangements are only practical when one of the supplier's products is highly desirable or when the supplier has some market power with regard to that product. If no one wishes to buy the fax machine, then tying the purchase of paper to the purchase of the fax machine is irrelevant. However, if the supplier of the machine is the sole supplier or the machine is superior to others, then a customer desiring to purchase the fax machine will probably agree to purchase the paper as well, even though the paper may be inferior or overpriced compared with other brands. Tying arrangements often reflect an attempt by the supplier to extend its market power with respect to one product (the *tying product*—the fax machine) to another product in which it does not have such market power (the *tied product*—the paper).

In *U.S. v. Microsoft*, the U.S. Justice Department alleged that Microsoft was trying to use its market dominance in operating systems (through its Windows products) to help its Internet browser (Internet Explorer) gain market share against Netscape's Navigator. Microsoft required that personal computer (PC) manufacturers who wished to install Windows on the PCs they sold must also install Internet Explorer and must not feature any other program icon on the same screens as Microsoft Windows and Internet Explorer. Because the PC manufacturers wanted to include Windows, they were forced to take Internet Explorer over Navigator, even if Navigator may have been a superior product. (Recall that Microsoft was charged with violations of §1 and §2 of the Sherman Act—restraining competition and monopolizing.)

Tying arrangements are an attempt to give the tied product an advantage that is unrelated to the qualities of that product itself. A court determining the legality of such an arrangement must consider the effects of the arrangement upon competition in the market for the tied product. Both §1 of the Sherman Act and §3 of the Clayton Act apply when the arrangement involves goods or commodities; however, only §1 of the Sherman Act applies when the arrangement involves services. If the supplier is dominant in the tying product market or possesses a legal monopoly over that product because of a patent or copyright, the use of a tying arrangement could also be challenged under §2 of the Sherman Act as an attempt to extend monopoly power into the tied product market, as in the Microsoft case.

Section 3 of the Clayton Act requires that the tying arrangement involve the sale or lease of goods or commodities involved and that the transaction actually be involved in interstate commerce. Section 1 of the Sherman Act applies to any contract in restraint of trade or affecting interstate commerce. Whereas §1 requires that actual harm to competition result from the restrictive arrangement, §3 only requires the showing of probable substantial lessening of competition. Despite these differences in the statutory provisions, the judicial approach to tying arrangements is similar under either provision.

Court decisions involving tying arrangements have found such arrangements to be illegal *per se* when the supplier has sufficient power in the tying product market to restrain competition in the tied product market appreciably and the amount of commerce involved is "not insubstantial." However, the application of the *per se* rule to tying arrangements is not like its application in other situations because it does require the court to consider the effects of the arrangement upon competition in the tied product market. Because of this requirement, the judicial approach to tying arrangements really resembles the rule of reason approach, despite its judicial characterization as a *per se* approach. Tying arrangements are not automatically illegal; they will be held illegal only if they substantially restrict competition in the tied product market.

A court considering the legality of a tying arrangement must first determine whether two separate and distinct products—the tying product and the tied product—are involved. If so, then the court must consider whether the supplier possesses market power in the tying product market. This market power may be due to the supplier's dominance in the market, to the possession of exclusive rights because of a patent or copyright, or to the uniqueness of the product offered. If the supplier is found to have market power in the tying product market, the court must then determine whether linking that market power to the tied product has the effect of substantially lessening or restricting competition in the tied product market. When the effect is to reduce competition substantially, the tying arrangement is illegal if it involves a "not insubstantial" amount of commerce.

Because patents, copyrights, and trademarks create legal monopolies, they confer substantial market power to the firm holding the patent or copyright. Any attempt to tie the sale of a different product to the sale of the patented, copyrighted, or trademarked product in a tying arrangement will likely be illegal because the arrangement will probably substantially lessen competition in the tied product market.

A number of tying arrangement cases have involved franchise agreements. The company granting the franchise—the franchisor—agrees to allow the franchisee to use its particular system of doing business, to market products under the franchisor's well-recognized trademark and to benefit from the franchisor's promotional efforts in return for the payment of a franchise fee. As a condition for being granted the franchise, the franchisee may also be required to purchase supplies from the franchisor. As a general rule, the courts have allowed such arrangements when the supplies tied to the franchise are reasonably related to the identity or the quality of the franchise's characteristic products. For example, a fried chicken company's franchisee may be required to purchase from the franchisor the special blend of "herbs and spices," used in cooking the chicken. By the same token, a Baskin-Robbins ice cream franchisee can be required to purchase its ice cream from Baskin-Robbins. However, when the tied product is not so related, such as paper napkins or drinking straws, then tying the purchase of those items to the sale of the franchise may be illegal.

In the case of *Jefferson Parish Hospital Dist. No. 2 v. Hyde*, 466 U.S. 2 (1984), the Supreme Court considered the legality of a hospital's requirement that patients undergoing surgery at the hospital use a particular group of anesthesiologists. The Court held that the requirement was a tying arrangement. As to its legality under §1 of the Sherman Act, the Court stated:

> Tying arrangements need only be condemned if they restrain competition on the merits by forcing purchases that would not otherwise be made. . . . It is safe to assume that every patient undergoing a surgical operation needs the services of an anesthesiologist; at least this record contains no evidence that the hospital "forced" any such services on unwilling patients. . . . Petitioners' [the hospital's] closed policy may raise questions of medical ethics, and may have inconvenienced some patients who would prefer to have their anesthesia administered by someone other than a member of [the required group] . . . , but it does not have the obviously unreasonable impact on purchasers that has characterized the tying arrangements that this court has branded unlawful. There is no evidence that the price, the quality, or the supply or demand for either the "tying product" or the "tied product" involved in this case has been adversely affected . . . by the hospital's requirement . . .

In *Illinois Tool Works v. Independent Ink, Inc.*, 547 U.S. 28 (2006), the Supreme Court held that the mere fact that a tying product is patented does not support a presumption of market power in a patented product, and in all cases involving a tying arrangement, the plaintiff must prove that the defendant has market power in the tying product.

PRICE DISCRIMINATION

Price discrimination is simply the charging of different prices to different customers for the same product. When price discrimination occurs in interstate commerce and its effects are "substantially to lessen competition or tend to create a monopoly . . . or to injure, destroy, or prevent competition," it is illegal under the Robinson-Patman Act. The Robinson-Patman Act is actually §2 of the Clayton Act, although most commentators refer to the prohibitions against price discrimination as the Robinson-Patman Act rather than §2 of the Clayton Act. It was passed in 1936 to strengthen the Clayton Act prohibitions against price discrimination.

The Robinson-Patman Act, passed during the Great Depression, reflects a concern that large retail chains could use the leverage of their purchasing power to extract price concessions from their suppliers. With those price concessions, the chains would have a significant competitive advantage over smaller, independent retailers and could eventually drive them out of business. Congress therefore sought to prohibit sellers from discriminating in price among customers when the effect of such discrimination would be detrimental to competition.

The Robinson-Patman Act reflects a strong emphasis on the social and political concerns of antitrust law rather than on the economic concerns—the act's primary purpose appears to be the protection of competitors rather than the protection of competition. Because the act's focus conflicts with the current emphasis on economic concerns, the antitrust enforcement authorities have not actively enforced the price discrimination provisions since the late 1960s; the courts, reflecting the economic and political climate, have also become less concerned about protecting competitors and have focused more on protecting competition. Most cases brought under the Robinson-Patman Act recently have been private civil actions by competitors of the price discounters. For example, the owners of small, independent pharmacies in Arkansas sued Wal-Mart, alleging that Wal-Mart's high discounts on prescription drugs substantially lessened competition; the trial court upheld their complaint as valid, but it was dismissed on appeal, *Wal-Mart Stores, Inc. v. American Drugs, Inc.*, 319 Ark. 214, 891 S.W.2d 30 (Ark. Sup. Ct. 1995). In *Brooke Group Ltd., v. Brown & Williamson Tobacco Corp.,* 509 U.S. 209 (1993), the Supreme Court held that a tobacco company's practice of granting discriminatory price rebates based on volume of purchases of generic brand cigarettes did discriminate against some customers but did not injure competition and therefore did not violate the Robinson-Patman Act.

PRICE DISCRIMINATION UNDER THE ROBINSON-PATMAN ACT

Section 2(a) of the Robinson-Patman Act prohibits:

> discrimination in price between purchasers of commodities of like grade and quality, where either or any purchasers involved in such discrimination are in commerce . . . where the effect of such discrimination may be to substantially lessen competition or tend to create a monopoly in any line of commerce, or to injure, destroy, or prevent competition with any person who either grants or receives the benefit of such discrimination, or with the customers of either. . . .

From the wording of §2(a), we can see that the protection of the act extends not only to firms in competition with the firm granting the discriminatory price (referred to as primary competitive effects), but also to firms in competition with customers who receive the discriminatory price (secondary competitive effects), and even to firms in competition with the customers of the firms that receive the discriminatory price (tertiary competitive effects). For example, if a pharmaceutical manufacturer grants substantial price discounts to a few wholesalers, it may affect competition with other drug manufacturers who do not offer such discounts (primary competition). The drug wholesaler that receives the discounts may have a competitive advantage over other wholesalers that do not receive discounts (secondary competition); and if the wholesaler receiving the discounts passes them along to its pharmacy customers, other pharmacies that compete with those customers may also be at a competitive disadvantage (tertiary competition). When the price discrimination has the effect of substantially lessening any one of these forms of competition, it may be illegal.

Defenses to Price Discrimination   Price discrimination may not be illegal if it falls under any of the defenses provided in §2(a) and (b) of the act. When the price differences apply to perishable or obsolete items or when they reflect actual differences in cost due to different methods of manufacture or delivery or because of the volume purchase, they are legal under §2(a). When a discriminatory price is offered by a seller in a good-faith attempt to meet the price of a competitor, it is legal under §2(b). If the price discrimination is only temporary and has no significant effect on competition, it is also legal under the Act.

OTHER PROVISIONS OF THE ROBINSON-PATMAN ACT

Sections 2(c), (d), and (e) of the Robinson-Patman Act prohibit other potential abuses by large retail chains. Section 2(c) prohibits granting any allowance or discount as a commission or other compensation for promotional or brokerage services in connection with the sale of a product unless the services are actually performed by the firm receiving the allowance or discount. For example, a small company that manufactures toys may sell its products through a broker, who arranges the sale of the products to retailers and promotes and distributes the product for the manufacturer. In return for these services, the manufacturer pays the broker a commission on sales. If the manufacturer decides to bypass the broker and sell directly to a large retail chain ("eliminate the middleman"), the manufacturer saves the cost of the broker's commission. In this situation, the manufacturer may grant the retail chain a discount reflecting its savings on the broker's commission only if the retail chain performs the distribution and promotion services normally performed by the broker. To grant the retail chain a discount when it does not actually perform those services would violate §2(c).

Sections 2(d) and (e) prohibit paying promotional fees or allowances or furnishing promotional facilities or services only to some customers. Such fees, allowances, facilities, or services must be provided to all customers on proportionately equal terms. For example, if a food processing company pays a large supermarket chain for advertising the processor's products but does not pay for advertising by small, independent grocers, the food processor violates §2(d).

Similarly, when a company making sewing patterns provides free display racks and cabinets to large department stores but requires small fabric stores to purchase the equipment, it violates §2(e).

Violations of §§2(c), (d), and (e) are *per se* offenses, which make the defenses under §§2(a) and (b) unavailable. In other words, when allowances, facilities, or services furnished to some customers are not available to all customers on a proportionate basis, or when allowances are granted for services not actually performed, the Act is violated, and no defenses are available. In contrast, §2(a) can only be violated when the effect of the price discrimination is to lessen competition substantially, which is a rule of reason approach.

Section 2(f) of the Act makes it a violation for a firm to "knowingly induce or receive" a discriminatory price that is prohibited by §2. Unlike the other provisions of the Act, which are directed against the firm engaging in price discrimination, §2(f) is aimed at the customer who receives the discriminatory price. In the case of *Great Atlantic & Pacific Tea Company, Inc. v. Federal Trade Commission,* 440 U.S. 69 (1979), the Supreme Court held that a customer who knowingly receives a discriminatory price that was granted by a supplier who was under the mistaken impression that the price was necessary to meet competition did not violate §2(f). The supplier had a good faith belief that the price was necessary to meet competition, so granting the discriminatory price was protected under §2(b). Because granting the price did not violate §2(a), the customer receiving the price was not in violation of §2(f).

WALMART AND LOW, LOW PRICES

Wal-Mart is the largest retailer in the U.S.; last year it had $345 billion in sales, which accounted for about 10% of all retail sales in the U.S. One of the keys to Wal-Mart's success is its pricing policy—it constantly strives to reduce prices by pressuring its suppliers to reduce prices for the products they sell to Wal-Mart. Wal-Mart then passes those prices on to the consumer. Wal-Mart uses the huge size of its orders as leverage against its suppliers, and as a result it enjoys a cost advantage over smaller retail firms. When Wal-Mart opens a store in an area, small, independent retailers in the surrounding area generally suffer and may ultimately be forced out of business. In order to meet the lower costs required by Wal-Mart, suppliers are forced to reduce labor and production costs; for many suppliers, that means re-locating their production to China. In 2004, Wal-Mart accounted for almost 10% of all U.S. imports from China and approximately 80% of all Wal-Mart suppliers are in China.

Wal-Mart's policies are controversial—critics charge that Wal-Mart's policies result in the loss of locally owned businesses, particularly in small towns. Critics also argue that Wal-Mart's pricing policies are causing the loss of American manufacturing jobs because they forcing suppliers to produce overseas. Wal-Mart argues that it is simply striving to become ever more efficient, and that its pricing policies pass the savings from such efficiency on to its customers.

Are Wal-Mart's policies socially responsible? Are they ethical? Explain your views.

SECTION 5 OF THE FEDERAL TRADE COMMISSION ACT

In addition to the primary antitrust provisions of the Sherman Act and Clayton Act, §5 of the Federal Trade Commission Act has also been used to attack anticompetitive business practices. Section 5 provides that "unfair methods of competition in or affecting commerce and unfair or deceptive acts or practices in or affecting commerce, are hereby declared unlawful." The Federal Trade Commission Act does not define the terms "unfair methods of competition" or "unfair or deceptive acts or practices." Congress wanted to avoid listing specific practices because such a list would have to be updated continually to include new practices as they appeared; Congress therefore empowered the FTC to determine which practices violated §5. The FTC, through its expertise, can adapt §5 to changing business practices.

Given the general wording of §5, its potential reach is very broad. The FTC has generally used §5 to attack deceptive advertising or high-pressure sales practices. The Supreme Court held, in *Federal Trade Commission v. Cement Institute,* 333 U.S. 683 (1948), that §5 could be applied to conduct that the FTC has determined to be injurious to competition even though the conduct does not violate other antitrust laws.

EXEMPTIONS FROM ANTITRUST

The federal antitrust laws extend to all activities in or affecting interstate commerce; however, several exceptions have been legislatively or judicially created.

Agricultural marketing cooperatives are exempted from the antitrust laws by the Capper-Volstead Act, and the Webb-Pomerene Act allows U.S. firms to join together for the purpose of export trade. The results of such joint export activity must not, however, restrict trade within the United States or injure U.S. firms that do not join the concerted export activity. The Foreign Trade Antitrust Improvements Act grants federal courts jurisdiction over anticompetitive export conduct only when such conduct has a direct, substantial, and reasonably foreseeable effect on trade or commerce within the United States or on import trade or commerce; anticompetitive conduct abroad that is independent of any domestic anticompetitive conduct is not subject to the U.S. antitrust laws, *F. Hoffman-LaRoche Ltd. v. Empagran S.A,* 542 U.S. 155 (2004). The National Cooperative Research Act of 1984, amended in 1991, provides that contracts among firms to carry out joint research activities are not *per se* illegal, and in suits involving such contracts, no triple damages can be recovered against the joint research ventures. The Local Government Antitrust Act of 1984 provides municipalities with immunity from any antitrust damage liability for "any official action directed by a local government, or official or employee thereof acting in an official capacity."

Bona fide labor union activities are also exempted from antitrust sanctions. Section 6 of the Clayton Act, which states that labor is not an article of commerce, was an early legislative attempt to exempt labor activities from the antitrust laws. It was not until the Supreme Court decision in *U.S. v. Hutcheson,* 312 U.S. 219 (1941), however, that conventional labor activity by a labor organization acting alone was held to be immune from antitrust law. The Supreme Court has held that a union may make agreements with a group of employers as long as the subject matter of the agreement is directly related to terms or conditions of employment and the agreement occurs within the context of a bona fide collective bargaining relationship. On the other hand, if unions join employers' groups in agreements about nonlabor matters, such as prices, or if unions make agreements with one set of employers to demand concessions from a different set of employers, such agreements are not protected by the labor exemption. The Supreme Court has also consistently held that professional baseball is not "commerce" within the meaning of the antitrust laws and is therefore exempted from them (although the recent baseball strike resulted in legislation eliminating baseball's exemption as it applies to labor relations matters); other professional sports do not enjoy baseball's antitrust immunity.

state action doctrine: An exemption from the antitrust laws when government regulation requires the conduct in question.

Perhaps the broadest area of exemption falls under the **state action doctrine**, which deals with the anticompetitive effects of government regulation. Regulatory schemes may require some businesses to engage in conduct that is anticompetitive. For example, agricultural marketing regulations may limit the size of farmers' crops and may set the prices at which those crops can be sold. Such an arrangement, created by the farmers on their own, could violate §1 of the Sherman Act; however, in *Parker v. Brown,* 317 U.S. 341 (1943), the Supreme Court held that such conduct is exempt from the antitrust laws when it is pursuant to a valid government regulatory scheme. Subsequent decisions have narrowed and more clearly defined the state action doctrine exemption: the government (whether state, local, or federal) must play an active role in the regulatory scheme, and the anticompetitive conduct must be required by the regulatory scheme in order to be exempt from the antitrust laws.

PATENTS, COPYRIGHTS, AND ANTITRUST

Patents and copyrights are legally granted monopolies for a limited period for the production, reproduction, distribution, or use of the patented or copyrighted item. They give the developing inventors or artists protection from competition, for a limited time, so they can reap the benefits of their efforts. By encouraging invention and artistic creation, patents and copyrights promote the public interest. Therefore, the limited monopoly status that they grant is acceptable even though it may seem inconsistent with the antitrust policy of promoting competition.

Firms or persons that hold patents or copyrights may license others to produce, use, or distribute the protected item. A patent owner may grant a price-restrictive license (which imposes a minimum resale price requirement) only to one other firm; imposing restrictions through licenses on two or more firms creates a concerted price-fixing arrangement and is illegal. Patent licenses may also be used to impose reasonable territorial restrictions upon the licensee's use or distribution of the protected product. However, such restrictions are illegal when their primary purpose is to create a horizontal division of markets among competitors. Firms owning patent rights may not combine their rights or patents with those of competing firms in order to create a "patent pool" cartel, in which the competitors share the patents to the exclusion of all other firms. In addition, In *Illinois Tool Works v. Independent Ink, Inc.,* 547 U.S. 28 (2006), the Supreme Court stated that merely because a tying product is patented does not automatically support a presumption of market power in a patented product; as in all tying cases, the plaintiff must prove that the defendant has market power in the tying product.

SUMMARY

Although the antitrust laws are intended to protect and promote competition, the policy behind enforcement efforts has shifted in emphasis from social considerations to economic factors over the years. Courts are less likely to be concerned with protecting competitors and are more likely to analyze the nature of competition in a given industry or market. In monopoly and merger cases, the emphasis on the size of the firms involved (or resulting from the merger) has lessened while the focus on whether they have engaged in, or are likely to engage in, predatory or exclusionary conduct has increased. Horizontal concerted activity such as price fixing, market division, and price restrictions are illegal *per se*. Vertical price restrictions and other vertical, nonprice restrictions, such as tying arrangements, territorial restrictions and exclusive dealing requirements are subject to the rule of reason and are illegal only when they have an unreasonable effect on competition. Price discrimination is illegal only when it has the effect of substantially lessening competition. Legislative exemptions to the antitrust laws allow U.S. firms to act collectively in order to compete more effectively in the international market, but concerted actions affecting competition within the United States are still prohibited.

In addition to government enforcement efforts, firms must also be concerned about the threat of private antitrust actions filed by competitors. It is therefore vital that business managers and executives have an understanding of the antitrust laws and their effect on business. Managers must also be aware of the impact of foreign antitrust laws, particularly those of the European Union, on the operations of their firm.

CHAPTER QUESTIONS

1. The Telecommunications Act of 1996 required local dominant telephone companies to share their local phone networks with competing phone companies; the phone companies are also required to provide access to the operations support systems that are necessary to service customers and to maintain the quality of telephone services. Verizon, Inc., is the dominant local telephone service provider in the New York City area. Other telephone companies that desire to make connections to Verizon's local network must send orders for interconnection to an electronic interface system set up by Verizon. After Verizon completes certain steps to allow interconnection, it sends confirmation to the other telephone company through the interface. Interconnections cannot be made until Verizon completes the various steps. Other local telephone companies have complained that Verizon was slow to fill orders for interconnection, which prevented the other companies from offering phone service to local customers. Several customers of the other local telephone companies filed suit against Verizon under §2 of the Sherman Act, alleging that Verizon deliberately discriminates against, and delays fulfilling, orders from the competing telephone companies for interconnection. The customers claim that Verizon does so in order to maintain its dominant position in the local telephone market, by discouraging customers from switching from Verizon to the competing telephone companies, or from remaining customers of the competing telephone companies. Does Verizon's conduct violate §2? Must a dominant firm cooperate with its

rivals? Explain your answers. [*Aspen Skiing Co. v. Aspen Highlands Skiing Corp.*, 472 U.S. 585 (1985); and *Verizon Communications, Inc. v. Law Offices of Curtis V. Trinko*, 540 U.S. 398]

2. The Kansas City Star Publishing Company publishes the only two major daily newspapers in the Kansas City area, the morning Star and the afternoon Times. The papers are distributed at the retail level by a group of independent distributors to whom Star Publishing awards exclusive distribution routes under one-year contracts. The distributors purchase the papers at wholesale prices from Star Publishing and are free to set their own retail prices. Star Publishing decides to distribute the paper through its own distribution network in order to improve circulation and enhance advertising revenues. Star Publishing announces that it will not renew any distributor contracts when they expire, and it will not sell the papers at wholesale prices anymore. If the distributors, who stand to lose their businesses, file a suit under §2 of the Sherman Act challenging Star Publishing's new policy, who will win the case? Explain. [*Paschall v. Kansas City Star Co.*, 727 F.2d 692 (8th Cir. 1984)]

3. R.J. Reynolds Tobacco Holdings, Inc. is the second largest tobacco company in the U.S. and has about 25% of the domestic market for cigarettes. Reynolds' brands include four of the top ten brands in the U.S.: Camel, Winston, Salem, and Doral. Brown & Williamson Tobacco Corp. is the third largest U.S. tobacco firm, with about 10% of the U.S. market; it is wholly-owned by British-American Tobacco, an international firm. Brown & Williamson's leading brands are Kool, Pall Mall, Lucky Strike, and Misty. The leading tobacco firm in the U.S. is Philip Morris, which accounts for about half of all cigarettes sold in the U.S. Philip Morris's leading brand is Marlboro, which by itself has about 40% of the U.S. market. The remainder of the U.S. cigarette market is made up of smaller firms, and producers of generic, discount brands. Reynolds and Philip Morris compete vigorously for smokers under 30, who generally smoke the premium brands; smokers older than 30 tend to stay with their preferred brand, or else switch to discount or generic brands. Brown & Williamson's brands are not premium brands, and are more affected by competition from the discount and generic brands. In recent years, because of health concerns about smoking, there has been a sharp decline in the sale of cigarettes in the U.S. Both Reynolds and Brown & Williamson have lost market share in recent years, while the generic brands have increased their share. In addition to declining sales, the tobacco industry is required to pay out $246 billion over twenty years to state governments as a result of the 1988 settlement to a class action suit against them. Reynolds and Brown & Williamson have proposed a merger—creating a new firm, to be called Reynolds American. Reynolds would control 58% of the new firm, with British-American controlling 42%. The new firm would have about 35% of the U.S. cigarette market and would be able to compete more effectively with Philip Morris and with the generic discount firms. After the merger, Philip Morris and Reynolds American together would account for about 80% of the U.S. market. Is the merger likely to be approved by the U.S. Department of Justice and the Federal Trade Commission? Why or why not?

4. Canco is the nation's second largest producer of metal containers, producing 33 percent of all metal containers sold in the United States. The largest can producer has 38 percent of the market, and the third largest producer accounts for 5 percent of the market. The remaining 24 percent of the market is shared among 75 firms. Cans are used for packaging foods, beverages (primarily soda and beer), and other liquids such as motor oil products. Glassco manufactures glass containers and produces 9.6 percent of all the glass containers sold in the United States. It ranks third in the glass container industry. The two largest producers account for 34.2 and 11.6 percent of the market, respectively. Glass containers are used for foods, sauces, baby food, toiletries, and beverages. They have become increasingly popular as nonreturnable packaging for soda and beer. Canco has considered developing its own glass container division, but it decided to acquire Glassco instead. If the government brings a legal action challenging the Canco-Glassco merger under §7 of the Clayton Act, who will win the case? Explain. [*U.S. v. Continental Can Corp.*, 378 U.S. 441 (1968)]

5. General Motors (GM) is a producer of automobiles in the United States. The domestic car manufacturers experience stiff competition from a number of foreign producers, some of whom have set up their own manufacturing operations in the U.S. The U.S. manufacturers dominate the large car market (luxury and SUV models); the foreign producers are superior in the production and sale of fuel-efficient compact and subcompact models. Nippon Auto is the largest car producer in Japan. It accounts for the largest segment of the U.S. compact and subcompact car sales. Some Japanese producers, such as Honda and Mazda, are establishing plants in the United States. Rather than set up its own plant, Nippon agreed with GM to create a jointly owned firm to produce subcompact models in the United States. The newly created firm, General Nippon, Inc., is controlled entirely by the two parent firms, each owning 50 percent of the stock. If the government brings a legal action challenging this joint venture under §7 of the Clayton Act, who will win the case? Explain. [*U.S. v. Penn-Olin Chemical Corp.*, 378 U.S. 158 (1964)]

6. Wilson Corporation is the largest firm selling a general line of sporting goods equipment in the United States. Wilson sells golf clubs; football, basketball, and baseball equipment; sports uniforms; and gym mats. Wilson has annual sales of almost $150 million, and it has 18 percent of the general sporting goods market. Wilson has been seeking to broaden its product line by expanding into other markets such as fishing and gymnastics equipment. Nissen Company is the largest producer of gymnastics equipment in the United States. It has annual sales of $45 million, which account for 26 percent of the gymnastics equipment sold in the United States. There are eight other firms producing gymnastics equipment in the United States, but the top four firms account for 70 percent of all sales. The remaining five firms are small and sell regionally rather than nationally. Wilson had considered starting its own gymnastics division, but it decides to acquire Nissen instead. If the government brings a legal action challenging the merger, who will win the case? Explain. [*U.S. v. Wilson Sporting Goods Co.*, 288 F. Supp. 543 (N.D.Ill. 1968)]

7. Holiday Motels International (HMI) is a firm that grants franchises to persons wishing to operate Holiday Motels. At present, there are four Holiday Motels operating in the Fort Wayne area, but HMI feels that the area could probably support another franchise. After discussing the new franchise with the four existing franchisees, HMI agreed to award it only if none of the existing franchisees objected. They also agreed to give the existing franchisees priority if any of them wished to operate the new franchise. Smith, who is not presently a franchisee, wishes to operate the new franchise. However, one of the existing franchisees has objected, and no franchise has been awarded. If Smith sues under §1 of the Sherman Act, is his suit challenging the refusal to award the franchise likely to be successful? Explain. [*American Motor Inn, Inc. v. Holiday Inns, Inc.*, 521 F.2d 1230 (3rd Cir. 1975)]

8. The Local Standard is a daily newspaper published in Syracuse, New York, by Local Publishing Company. The paper is sold by numerous retail outlets and is delivered to homes by paper distributors. The small independent businesses are billed weekly by Local for the papers they deliver. The prices Local charges the distributors are wholesale prices. The distributors charge their customers the "suggested retail price," which is printed on the front page of each paper.

   a. Is the pricing arrangement between Local and the distributors in violation of §1 of the Sherman Act? Why or why not?
   b. Local assigns each distributor a delivery route—a geographic area in which the distributor is the exclusive home-delivery outlet for the Local Standard. Is this territorial arrangement legal? Explain your answer.
   c. Local prohibits the distributors from charging a price greater than the suggested retail price, although distributors are free to charge less than the suggested retail price. Distributors who violate this policy have their routes taken away. Is this policy legal under §1? Explain your answer.

9. Local Publishing Company publishes both the Local Standard, a morning daily paper, and the Post Herald, a Sunday paper. Local requires advertisers wishing to place ads in either paper to purchase advertising space in both. Shaw's Shape-Up, a physical fitness club, wants to advertise in the Local Standard, because it reaches a bigger audience than the Post Herald. Shaw's feels that ads in the Sunday paper are not cost-effective. Local will only accept Shaw's ad if it appears in both papers. Shaw's files suit challenging Local's advertising policy.

   a. Which provision of the antitrust laws is applicable to the advertising policy? Explain.
   b. What arguments will Local use to support the policy? What arguments will Shaw's use to attack it?
   c. Who will win the case? Explain. [*Times Picayune v. U.S.*, 345 U.S. 594 (1953)]

10. Balkan Burgers, Inc. licenses franchisees to operate Balkan Burger fast-food restaurants. In addition to agreeing to rent the restaurant building from Balkan Burger, Inc., franchisees are required to purchase all kitchen equipment, paper products, packaging materials, and food products from Balkan Burgers. Balkan Burgers maintains that this requirement is necessary to ensure the quality of the products to preserve Balkan Burgers' reputation and corporate image. Balkan Burgers also prohibits the fran-

chisee from operating any fast-food restaurant other than those licensed by Balkan Burgers. Several franchisees have complained that the prices charged by Balkan Burgers for kitchen equipment and food products are higher than those charged by other suppliers and that Balkan's products are of low quality. These franchises would also like to operate other franchised fast-food restaurants. If they bring a legal action challenging Balkan Burgers' policies, who will win the case? Explain. [*Siegal v. Chicken Delight, Inc.*, 448 F.2d 43 (9th Cir. 1971)]

11. Posner Paving is a small paving contractor that bids on municipal paving jobs in and around Chicago. Its operations are entirely within the state of Illinois. Posner is supplied with asphalt and other paving materials by Bork Products. Bork is a large building materials supply firm that operates throughout the Midwest. Posner has discovered that Bork has been supplying asphalt to the large contractors who work on the interstate highway system in Indiana and Illinois at $300 per truckload while it charges Posner $370 per truckload. Bork sells only in minimum units of at least one truckload, and the costs of delivery per truckload are constant. If Posner brings legal action challenging Bork's pricing policy under the Robinson-Patman Act, is the challenge likely to be successful? Explain. [*Gulf Oil Co. v. Copp Paving Corp.*, 419 U.S. 186 (1974)]

12. The Sullivans desired to purchase a house in Arlington, Virginia. They contacted several lawyers about performing a title search. Each lawyer they contacted informed them that the fee for the search would be the fee set by the minimum-fee schedule of the Virginia State Bar Association. The minimum-fee schedule suggests the minimum fee that Virginia lawyers should charge for various kinds of legal services. Lawyers who wish to practice law in Virginia are required by law to join the Virginia State Bar Association and to abide by the association's Ethical Rules. The Ethical Rules include a prohibition on "habitually charging fees less than those in the minimum-fee schedule." No state laws require adherence to the fee schedule, and the state does not review or approve the fee schedule. The Sullivans have brought a legal action suit against the Virginia State Bar Association, alleging that the minimum fee schedule is illegal under §1 of the Sherman Act. What arguments can each party make to support its case? Who will win? Explain. [*Goldfarb v. Virginia State Bar*, 421 U.S. 773 (1975)]

PRACTICAL EXERCISE

Google, Inc., the leading internet search firm, entered into an agreement to acquire ITA Software, Inc. for $700 million. ITA develops and licenses a product called QPX, which is used by airlines, online travel agents and online travel sites to provide complex and customized flight search services; QPX has unique capabilities that allow it to act as a mini-search engine [known as a price and shopping system, or P&S] for travel sites. Google intends to offer an online travel search product that will compete with existing travel search sites that allow users to search for airfares across a range of airlines that use QPX; those travel websites are referred to as Online Travel Intermediaries [OTIs]. Google has approximately 65% of the online search market in the United States; while Microsoft and Yahoo! Inc. combined have about 30% of the market. In 2009, Google earned over $23 billion in revenue, most of which came from online search advertising. Its only significant online search competitor is Microsoft's Bing, which has a much smaller share of search inquiries and advertising revenue. Bing presently offers a travel site that uses QPX to provide comparative flight search services. If Google acquires ITA, it might have an incentive to limit or deny other comparative flight search competitors such as Bing and other OTIs to QPX; that would potentially diminish competition in the comparative flight search industry.

You are an analyst working for the Antitrust Division of the U.S. Department of Justice; your boss has asked you to prepare a memo analyzing the competitive effects of Google's proposed acquisition of ITA. In your memo, address the following questions:

1. Is the proposed acquisition a horizontal or a vertical merger?
2. What is the relevant product market?
3. What is the relevant geographic market?
4. How will the proposed merger affect competition in the relevant markets?
5. How will the proposed merger affect consumers?
6. If you recommend that the Justice Department challenge the merger, what legislation could be used for the challenge?
7. Would it be possible to allow the merger but impose certain conditions on Google to protect competition in the relevant market?

Be sure to explain your opinions and conclusions and support them with references to cases, legislation and other materials from the text wherever possible.

CHAPTER 18

LEGAL RIGHTS OF CONSUMERS, DEBTORS, AND CREDITORS

After you have read this chapter, you should be able to:

1. Explain the various laws that protect consumers.
2. Describe how to perfect a security interest.
3. Understand the differences among Chapter 7, Chapter 11, and Chapter 13 bankruptcy.
4. Determine how to collect on a bad debt.

Your business sells merchandise on credit and is now having problems collecting the money that is owed. What do you need to know about debtor/creditor law in order to collect on the debt? This chapter will explore this issue in more detail.

INTRODUCTION

Under the common law, consumers were responsible to watch out for their own interests. In general, laws did not protect consumers. The prevailing rule was caveat emptor, "let the buyer beware." Why did such a rule exist? This rule originated in an agrarian society in which buyers and sellers knew each other—they were probably neighbors—and products were few and simple. Further, since most products were bought with cash or bartered for, buyers had little need for borrowing money.

The industrial age introduced complex products, processes, and the need for borrowed capital. Manufacturers, far removed from consumers and often located in other countries, now build products that wholesalers and retailers sell. Today, consumers rarely buy products directly from manufacturers. Moreover, consumers commonly borrow money to pay for products.

The stark differences between a commercial transaction in an agrarian society and a commercial transaction in an industrial society gave impetus to the consumer's movement in the 1960s and 1970s, which resulted in the passage of several pieces of federal legislation aimed at protecting consumers from unscrupulous or unfair business practices. These pieces of legislation were also aimed at giving the consumer enough information to make an informed buying decision.

First, in 1968 Congress passed the *Consumer Credit Protection Act*. This Act is very comprehensive and includes the *Equal Credit Opportunity Act*, *Truth in Lending Act*, *Fair Credit Billing Act*, *Fair Debt Collection Practices Act*, *Fair Credit Reporting Act*, and the *Consumer Leasing Act*. Next, in 1972, Congress passed the Consumer Product Safety Act, which created the *Consumer Product Safety Commission (CPSC)*. This commission regulates product safety by recalling unsafe products and banning hazardous products. The CPSC will be discussed in more detail in Chapter 19.

In response to the recession which began in the United States in 2008, Congress has passed several sweeping legislative reforms intended to protect consumers from unscrupulous acts. These acts include the *Credit Card Accountability, Responsibility, and Disclosure Act* and the *Dodd-Frank Wall Street Reform and Consumer Protection Act*. The Dodd-Frank Act created a new *Bureau of Consumer Financial Protection* which is intended to regulate consumer financial products and services.

collateral: Property used by the debtor to protect a creditor's interest in case of default.

In addition to these federal consumer protection laws, state laws also detail how collateral can be used to secure a loan. **Collateral** is the property that a debtor agrees to give the creditor if the debtor fails to pay the debt in full.

Finally, even the best of intentions can go awry when it comes to debtor/creditor relations. To avoid the debtors' prisons of the past, Congress has established federal bankruptcy laws. To understand how these laws affect business, one must look at the rights of consumers as well as the rights of business. This chapter will take the reader through the consumer credit process, starting with applying for credit and ending with bankruptcy.

CONSUMER-RELATED ISSUES

Compiling a credit history is very important. However, as you may know, a typical reason for the denial of credit is the lack of a credit history. Indeed, establishing credit for the first time can be difficult.

Applying for credit (borrowing) usually requires filling out a credit application. Credit applications ask a number of questions about the applicant's financial history, including where the applicant works, how much the applicant earns, what type of property the applicant owns, and how much the applicant owes to others. The Equal Credit Opportunity Act (ECOA) prohibits creditors from discriminating based on sex, marital status, race, color, religion, national origin, and age, although these types of questions are sometimes asked on the application form. The ECOA also prohibits discrimination against persons who receive public assistance or those who exercise their rights under the ECOA. If a person intends to use a spouse's income to qualify for the loan, the creditor can request the spouse's financial information.

After filling out the credit application, a creditor will often do a *credit check*. Instead of personally checking all the public records, the creditor will usually request a credit report from a **credit bureau** or a *credit reporting bureau*. *Credit bureaus* compile many types of information, often using public documents like bankruptcies, lawsuits, and judgments to assess a person's creditworthiness. The information kept by credit bureaus is generally confined to financial information. A credit reporting bureau prepares reports at the request of individuals like landlords, insurance companies, employers, and, to a lesser extent, creditors. The credit reporting bureau conducts an investigation and talks to family, friends, and acquaintances. If an account has been turned over to a collection agency, it is usually noted on the credit history.

credit bureau: A private business that compiles information on consumers' creditworthiness and provides this information to lenders.

Several problems are associated with credit reports. For example, sometimes they contain inaccurate, misleading, or irrelevant information. Also, people may obtain the report who do not have a legitimate interest in the information.

Before 1971, consumers did not have the right to look at their credit histories. In 1971 the Fair Credit Reporting Act (FCRA) was added to the Consumer Credit Protection Act. The FCRA requires credit bureaus to maintain accurate information. Adverse information can only be used for seven years; after seven years, it must be purged. Bankruptcy information can only remain on the record for 10 years. Investigative reports must purge the information on a person's character, living arrangements, and other personal attributes every three months unless it is reverified. Reports can only be furnished for credit, insurance, employment, the gaining of a government license or benefit, or any legitimate business need. A consumer must be notified, in advance, if an investigative report has been ordered. A creditor is required to furnish the name and address of the credit bureau if a credit report is used in rejecting credit or insurance.

In 1997, the FCRA was amended to give consumers better rights when a consumer report was ordered in connection with some type of employment decision. Now, if an employer wants to order a credit report, the employee (or applicant) must receive notice of the request and give permission, in writing. Before pulling the report, the employer must also tell employees that if they are not hired or are terminated based on what is contained in the report, they have a right to see the report. The employer also needs to provide employees with a copy of the Federal Trade Commission's (FTC's) summary of rights under the FCRA. If an adverse decision is made because of the report, the employer must provide employees with the name and address of the credit bureau providing the report and inform them of their right to dispute information in the report. If the employer does not follow these rules, the employer may be liable for damages.

In other cases, a consumer does not have a right to see his or her actual credit report. However, the consumer is entitled to receive, free of charge and within 30 days of the rejection, a summary of the nature of the report, which includes the nature and substance of the information and source and names of those who have used the report over the past six months. He or she may also, upon payment of a small fee, see a summary of the file at any time. If the information is inaccurate or unverified, the consumer has a right to have it removed from the report. If the credit bureau and consumer dispute the information, the consumer is entitled to file a 100-word rebuttal statement to be included in the credit report.

Since consumers are entitled to have correct information in their credit reports, credit agencies are responsible for investigating and correcting a consumer's file if the report is erroneous. As the next case indicates, sometimes this correction does not occur quickly.

DIXON-ROLLINS V. EXPERIAN INFORMATION SOLUTIONS, INC., ET AL.

753 F.Supp.2d 452 (E.D.Pa., 2010)

FACTS

In June, 2004, Carmen Dixon-Rollins got into a dispute with her landlord and vacated her apartment without paying the last month's rent. The landlord referred the debt to a collection agency, Associate Credit and Collection Bureau (ACCB), for collection. ACCB in turn reported the outstanding debt to the defendant Trans-Union (TU), a credit reporting agency, which listed it on Dixon-Rollins' credit report. She ultimately reached a settlement with her landlord, but the landlord failed to inform ACCB that the debt had been paid. The debt remained a negative entry on Dixon-Rollins' credit rating.

In 2005, on four separate occasions, Dixon-Rollins attempted to dispute the continued entry of this settled debt on her credit report with TU. Each time, TU sent ACCB an automated customer dispute verification form, and each time ACCB verified that the debt was outstanding. Neither ACCB nor TU attempted to obtain any outside verification that the debt had been paid, despite Dixon-Rollins continued insistence that it had been. Dixon-Rollins then filed a lawsuit against TU alleging violation of the Fair Credit Reporting Act (FCRA) due to its failure to reinvestigate the inaccurate information in her credit report. The jury found in her favor and awarded her $30,000 in actual damages and $500,000 in punitive damages. TU appealed.

DECISION

Judge Savage wrote the court's opinion. The question before the court was whether TU neg-

ligently and willfully violated the FCRA by failing to reinvestigate and then delete inaccurate information contained in Dixon-Rollins' credit report. The FCRA requires that credit agencies reinvestigate the accuracy of information contained in a consumer's credit report when a consumer disputes the completeness or accuracy of the information. If the information is inaccurate or cannot be verified, it must be deleted. Reinvestigation may require the agency to go beyond the original source of the information, depending upon (1) whether the consumer has alerted the agency that the original source may be unreliable; (2) whether the agency knows or should know that the original source is unreliable; and (3) the cost of verifying the accuracy of the original source vs. the potential harm the inaccurate information may cause the consumer.

In this case, TU argued that it fulfilled its duty to reinvestigate because it verified the information from ACCB, the original source of the information. It also argued that Dixon-Rollins did not provide any evidence that a reinvestigation would have produced a different result. The court disagreed with both arguments, holding that the law does require investigation beyond the original source under certain circumstances, which were present in this case. For instance, Dixon-Rollins' provided TU with a letter verifying that the debt had been settled together with a receipt of the money order used to settle the debt and contact information for the landlord and others who were familiar with the settlement.

TU failed to investigate this additional information. The court held that this failure was a violation of the clear requirements of the FCRA and affirmed the award of compensatory damages. However, the court reduced the punitive damages award from $500,000 to $270,000. The court held that punitive damages were warranted in this case, but the amount the jury awarded was excessive since Dixon-Rollins had not suffered any physical injury nor did TU behave with intentional malice or deceit.

CASE QUESTIONS

1. Do you agree that TU did not adequately reinvestigate Dixon-Rollins' claim that the information contained in her credit report was inaccurate?

2. What is the purpose of punitive damages? Were they justified in this case? Do you agree with the court's decision to reduce the punitive damages award?

3. Do you think that TU's actions were ethical?

Someone who knowingly and willfully obtains information from a credit agency under false pretenses can be subject to one year in jail and a $5,000 fine. A credit bureau will pay civil damages for failure to provide reasonable procedures to gain access to accurate and complete information.

On December 4, 2003, the **Fair and Accurate Credit Transactions Act** of 2003 (FACT) was signed into law. FACT amends the FCRA "to prevent identity theft, improve resolution of consumer disputes, improve the accuracy of consumer records, make improvements in the use of, and consumer access to, credit information, and for other purposes." FACT has a number of provisions aimed at addressing the growing problem of identity theft and the growth of technology related problems. The Act allows consumers to direct consumer reporting agencies to put a "fraud alert" on each consumer report issued by the agency if they suspect that their identities have been stolen. It also has provisions which allow notification that the consumer is currently on active military duty. In 2010, the U.S. Federal Reserve released an online consumers' guide to credit scores and credit reports. In light of the Dodd-Frank Act and other consumer protection reforms, this guide is intended to give consumers basic information so that they can better understand the new information lenders are now required to give them.

DISCLOSING CREDIT COSTS

Another problem associated with obtaining credit is the determination of its exact cost. For example, Jim may want to buy a television but cannot afford the $800 price. A store may offer to allow Jim to pay $100 a month until the television is "paid off." The store inevitably will charge Jim interest on the $800 debt until the debt is paid in full. Depending on which interest rate is chosen and how it is calculated, Jim may pay well over three or four times the amount of the original $800 price. To protect consumers, some states prohibit charging interest over a certain maximum rate. These statutes are known as usury laws. **Usury laws** only apply in a very few states, and exceptions exist even in those states. Usury laws are still important, however, in those states in which they are retained.

Other states have abandoned the notion of protecting consumers from themselves and replaced it with a full-disclosure policy. In these states most usury laws have been repealed and have been replaced by the **Uniform Consumer Credit Code (UCCC)**. The National Conference of Commissioners on Uniform

usury laws: Laws regulating interest rates.

Uniform Consumer Credit Code: Uniform law adopted by states governing the amount of interest and charges that can be assessed on consumer loans.

finance charge:
Amount of money added to a loan payment when payment is late.

State Laws drafted the UCCC, and the American Bar Association approved it. Ironically, while the UCCC was written to make the laws uniform throughout the states, in fact, states have altered the UCCC provisions and fewer than 20 states have adopted it. In general, the UCCC applies to "all credit offered or extended by a creditor to an individual person primarily for personal, family, or household purposes" under $50,000. Its aim is to require full disclosure of credit terms. It also limits the amount that can be charged on unpaid accounts (**finance charges**). These amounts vary from state to state. Since the UCCC's major goal is disclosure rather than protection, interest rate charges can be very high, unlike usury statutes, which keep interest rates relatively low. Some states adopting the UCCC, however, place a maximum interest rate of 36 percent. The UCCC also allows a person to cancel a contract made at a person's home by door-to-door sales that falls under its provisions within three business days of when the contract is made. This three-day period is known as the **cooling-off period**. We will discuss cooling-off periods in Chapter 19.

cooling-off period:
A period of time to allow further consideration.

SOCIAL/ETHICAL ISSUES

Historically, some religions prohibited making money on money itself. This is one reason why there were prohibitions on the amount of interest that could be charged on debts. Is there any ethical justification for limiting the amount of interest that can be charged? Is there such a thing as a fair price?

CREDIT CARD LEGISLATION

In 2009, Congress amended the Truth in Lending Act by passing the Credit Card Accountability, Responsibility, and Disclosure Act (CARD), which is also known as the "Credit Card Bill of Rights." CARD regulates credit card companies regarding, among other things, their ability to impose or raise interest rates and fees, issue credit cards to students under the age of 21, and change billing dates. For instance, cardholders are entitled to be given advance notice of interest rate increases and changes in terms, to set limits on the amount of credit that may be extended, and to be free from due date gimmicks and misleading terms.

annual percentage rate (APR):
The periodic rate (the monthly effective interest rate) times the number of periods in a year.

The Fair Credit and Charge Card Disclosure Act requires disclosure of all charges associated with credit cards. These include the **annual percentage rate (APR)**, membership fees, etc. It also provides that a credit card holder is only liable for up to $50 for unauthorized charges resulting from loss or theft.

TRUTH IN LENDING AND CONSUMER LEASING

Federal legislation aims to provide full disclosure to consumers so they can protect themselves when applying for a loan. In 1968 Congress passed the *Truth in Lending Act*. Like the UCCC, the purpose of Truth in Lending is to give consumers full disclosure of credit terms and to encourage consumers to shop around for credit. Truth in Lending does not limit or fix interest rates on credit. Rather, it requires that all interest rates be stated in terms of an APR. The creditor must also disclose all finance charges, direct or indirect, in a dollar amount. If a buyer uses a home as collateral for consumer borrowing, the buyer has a right to cancel the credit within three days of the purchase. This particular rule does not apply to first mortgages on homes.

The Truth in Lending Simplification and Reform Act of 1980 made several changes in the Truth in Lending Act. Most of these changes reduced the amount of paperwork a creditor must file. Further, all agricultural transactions were removed from its coverage.

The *Consumer Leasing Act* applies when a consumer leases personal property for more than four months. Currently, many people enter into long-term leases of cars, furniture, appliances, and computers. The Consumer Leasing Act applies to these transactions. It requires that the consumer receive a written statement about the amount of monthly payments and other costs, like insurance, security deposits, registrations, taxes, and maintenance. Consumers either enter into *open-ended* or *closed-ended* leases. Closed-ended leases generally have higher monthly payments but no **balloon payment** at the end of the lease. Open-ended leases have lower monthly payments, but they may also contain balloon payments based on the value of the leased property when the lease expires. Assume that Clair leases a new automobile for three years at $300 per month. The leasing company assumes that the automobile will be worth $5,000 at the end of three years. At the end of the lease period, the leasing company decides that the car's condition makes it only worth $4,200 and requires that Clair pay an additional $800. This is an open-ended lease with a balloon payment. Clair may think that the car is worth more than $4,200. Under the act she is entitled to have an independent appraisal of the property value of the car, and the balloon must be limited to three times the monthly payment. In this case, if the leased car is appraised at $4,200, she will have to pay the additional $800, since it is less than the $900 allowed under the act.

> **balloon payment:** A large payment due at the end of the contract term.

FAIR CREDIT BILLING ACT

The *Fair Credit Billing Act (FCBA)* became effective in 1975. This Act only applies to **open-ended credit**, which occurs when the parties contemplate repeated transactions; the use of credit cards or an open account at a department store are examples. **Closed-ended credit**, on the other hand, usually involves the sale of a home or automobile. Under the FCBA, if the consumer suspects an error has been made on a billing statement, he or she has 60 days to notify the creditor of the error. The creditor then has 30 days to respond and another 90 days to correct the mistake or to explain why it will not be corrected. During the investigation, the consumer is not responsible for the disputed amount. If the consumer turns out to be wrong, the creditor is entitled to prior finance charges and prompt payment. If the creditor and consumer disagree, the creditor must notify credit bureaus of the disagreement and notify credit bureaus of any settlement. The FCBA can be very useful when goods are ordered but not delivered or when goods turn out to be defective and the seller refuses to correct the problem.

> **open-ended credit:** Credit that can be used again and again until a certain prearranged borrowing limit is reached.

> **closed-ended credit:** Credit in which there is a set number of payments over a set period of time.

The act requires that consumers receive a billing statement each billing period. The act also allows a credit card user to refuse to pay for unsatisfactory goods or services that are over $50 if they were purchased in the consumer's home state or within 100 miles of his or her mailing address. Finally, the Act requires the billing agency to notify consumers concerning the proper procedure for disputing a statement.

FAIR DEBT COLLECTION PRACTICES ACT

The *Fair Debt Collection Practices Act (FDCPA)* was passed in 1978. Before FDCPA was passed, bill collectors were allowed to call debtors early in the morning, late at night, and at work. FDCPA's goal was to stop bill collectors from using harassing, intimidating, or abusive methods to obtain payment. Originally, attorneys were exempted from the FDCPA if they were acting as debt collectors. In 1986, however, attorneys lost their exemption and must now comply with the act.

GALLAGHER V. GURSTEL, STALOCH & CHARGO, P.A.

645 F.Supp.2d 795 (2009)

FACTS

Kiara Gallagher owed $4338 to a client of the law firm of Gurstel, Staloch & Chargo. In May 2005 the parties agreed to settle the case for $4000, with Gallagher paying $2000 up front and then $200 per month for 10 months. They agreed that if Gallagher defaulted on any of the agreed-upon payments, Gurstel would be entitled to seek a default judgment against her for the entire $4338 plus interest, less any amount she had already paid. Gallagher paid all but the last $200 payment because she erroneously believed she had made all the required payments. This was the first of four major errors leading to this lawsuit.

Gurstel then filed for a default judgment against Gallagher. His affidavit in support of the judgment correctly stated that Gallagher had paid $3800 of the total, but it mistakenly requested judgment in the amount of $5215, the full amount of the debt plus interest. This was the second of four major errors leading to this lawsuit.

Gallagher either did not receive or ignored the paperwork regarding Gurstel's application for a default judgment. The default judgment Gurstel received was in the amount of $2139, which was far more than Gallagher actually owed. Gurstel then sent two garnishment summons, each relating to the same debt, to Wells Fargo Bank where Gallagher had an account. The first garnishment summons was for the amount of the default judgment, $2139. Inexplicably, the second garnishment summons was for $1909. This was the third of four major errors leading to this lawsuit.

Wells Fargo treated each summons as though it were a separate debt and garnished each from Gallagher's account for a total of $4153. This amount placed a hold on all of the money in Gallagher's account and equaled approximately twice the actual amount of Gurstel's judgment against her, which in itself was not the total she actually owed. Gallagher complained to Wells Fargo, who referred her to Gurstel. When she phoned Gurstel's office asking that the money in her account be released, she claimed she was laughed at "cruelly." However, based upon her call, Gurstel's office phoned Wells Fargo to verify the amount that had been garnished. Wells Fargo incorrectly stated that only $2354 was being withheld from Gallagher's account. Thus, Gurstel believed that Gallagher was lying about the garnishment. This was the fourth of four major errors leading to this lawsuit.

Gallagher called Gurstel again a few days later to ask that the hold on her account be released. Gurstel refused, still believing that only $2354 had been garnished. A few weeks later, Gallagher filed a motion to quash the original default judgment. Upon receiving her motion, Gurstel contacted Wells Fargo again and learned that the second garnishment had indeed frozen an additional $1725 in funds as Gallagher had claimed. Gurstel immediately released those excess funds and offered to repay Gallagher for any overdraft fees she may have incurred as a result of the second incorrect garnishment. Gallagher then filed this lawsuit claiming that Gurstel had violated the Fair Debt Collect Practices Act by treating her abusively, filing an erroneous affidavit in support of the default judgment, and garnishing more from her account than he was entitled to. This case was brought pursuant to the defendant's motion for summary judgment.

DECISION

Judge Schiltz wrote the court's opinion. Regarding the first claim of abusive conduct, the FDCPA prohibits bill collectors from harassing, oppressive, or abusive behavior. In this case, Gallagher alleged that the one phone conversation in which she was laughed at violated this provision of the FDCPA. The court disagreed, noting that one "laugh is not remotely comparable to the type of conduct that has been found to give rise to liability under [FDCPA.]" Therefore, the court granted Gurstel's motion for summary judgment with regard to this claim.

Regarding Gallagher's second claim that the affidavit was erroneous, the FDCPA prohibits debt collectors from using "any false, deceptive, or misleading representation or means in connection with the collection of any debt." The court held that a reasonable jury could easily find that the affidavit was false and misleading. "Even a sophisticated consumer would have understood Gurstel's demand for $5215.38 to be a representation that Gallagher owed that amount, and there is no dispute that Gallagher did not, in fact, owe that amount." Thus, the court denied the motion for summary judgment with regard to this claim.

Finally, regarding Gallagher's third claim that the two garnishments were illegal, the FDCPA prohibits debt collectors from collecting more than the amount that the debtor owes. However, the FDCPA provides for an exception for unintentional violations resulting from a "bona fide error," *i.e.,* one that is reasonable and plausible. Here again, the court ruled that there was a genuine issue of fact regarding whether Gurstel's error in serving Wells Fargo with two garnishment summons rather than one was a bona fide error. Thus, the court denied the motion for summary judgment.

CASE QUESTIONS

1. What is the result of the court's holding in this case? What happens when a motion for summary judgment is denied? [You may want to refer back to Chapter 3 to help you answer this question.]
2. Do you think Gurstel is entitled to rely upon the "bona fide error" defense in this case? Was his filing of the two separate garnishment summons reasonable?
3. What do you think about Gallagher's responsibility in this case? As a debtor, does she have an obligation to keep track of her payments? Does she have an obligation to look at court documents when they are sent to her?

For the most part, creditors collecting their own debts are exempt. If the consumer, in writing, refuses to pay the debt or has notified the collector that an attorney has been retained or has written a letter requesting freedom from harassment, the collector cannot contact the consumer again except to inform the consumer of action that the collector is taking. Violators of FDCPA are liable for up to $1,000 without any proof of actual damage. Creditors, of course, are entitled to be paid for any legitimate debts

Debt collection is often a difficult process. Debt collectors rely on sophisticated technology to reach debtors and persuade them to pay their debts. For instance, collectors use predictive auto-dialers, also referred to as robo-dialers, which call several debtors at the same time. Those who answer the call are routed to a large call center which may employ as many as 600 workers. Often these centers are located outside of the United States. Monitor screens automatically provide the employee with the debtor's background and debt information. "Talking scripts" collection agencies use to convince debtors to pay are specialized for individual debtors and confidential. Moreover, debt collectors often rely upon *skip tracing* to investigate consumers who have "skipped out" on their debts. Callers will often "spoof" their telephone numbers to fool debtors into thinking they are receiving a local call. The FDCPA imposes liability on collection agencies that use automated robo-dialers to call consumers or leave pre-recorded messages on debtors' cell phones without consent. As the following article makes clear, some consumers are quite knowledgeable about the requirements of the FDCPA and use it to their advantage.

Better Off Deadbeat: Craig Cunningham Has a Simple Solution for Getting Bill Collectors Off His Back. He Sues Them.

Unlike his neighbors' homes, Craig Cunningham's house in Northeast Dallas looks abandoned. The grass is dried out. The concrete slab under the front door is lopsided and cracked. The green exterior has faded to a toxic-looking shade. Yellow Pages pile up near the front door, and the black mailbox is stuffed full. Maybe the home has been foreclosed on. That wouldn't be a surprise in this economy.

Craig Cunningham says no one offered hurting small-time investors like him a government bailout when he landed deep in debt. That made him mad, so he decided to get even.

Steven Katz, author of a book on fighting bill collectors, says the idea that consumers have a moral obligation to pay their creditors is a myth created by lenders.

But no, that's not the case. Inside, the 29-year-old Cunningham hunkers his 6-foot-2-inch frame on a dumpy couch. His heavy arms extend from his sides, palms up, so two Chihuahuas, Angel and Chuay, can curl under them. Although it's 10 A.M. on a weekday, he's wearing slippers.

He leans forward to lift some paperwork out of a plastic tub on the coffee table. The phone rings, and he answers with a soft voice. It's just a friend, and soon he hangs up. He's waiting for a particular type of phone call—one from a representative of a debt collection agency or a credit card company, whom he'll try to ensnare like a Venus fly trap. It's not unlikely that Cunningham's next call will be from a bill collector, since he's between jobs—except for being in the Army Reserve—and owes $100,000 in debts.

While most Americans with unpaid bills dread the collector's call, Cunningham sees them as lucrative opportunities. Many collection and credit card companies, intentionally or not, violate little-known consumer rights laws, and Cunningham's favorite pastime is catching them doing so and then suing them. In fact, it's a profitable side job.

Call it ironic, but the only house on the block that appears to be the foreclosed end to some sad financial story is in fact the home of one of the debt collection industry's emerging and persistent threats. Cunningham calls himself a private attorney general—someone who files private lawsuits in the public interest. Debt collectors call him a credit terrorist.

Patrick Lunsford, who edits *InsideARM*, a trade magazine for the debt collection industry, knows the term. "There is a sub-group out there that does actually advise people on how to bait [collectors]," he says. "That's something that really gets under the skin of, well, obviously, collectors."

Cunningham beats the debt collectors at their own game. He turns their money-making practice into a financial liability. He is a regular guy who has become a radical enemy of the banking system.

In 2005, two foreclosures pushed Cunningham near financial ruin. Like many Americans, he fell enchanted by the siren's song of easy credit and borrowed more than $100,000 to bet on risky, high-yielding investments, such as stock in the now vilified sub-prime mortgage industry.

Then, while stationed with the Army in El Paso, he attempted to become an absentee landlord and got zero-percent-down sub-prime mortgages to buy low-income four-plexes in Houston and Dallas. With the interest earned on his high-yielding stocks he was paying back his low-interest credit card debt; now, he was using the mortgages to borrow even more.

Then the bottom fell out. Investors like Cunningham fell the fastest. He sold his Houston homes, but his Dallas properties were foreclosed on. The collection calls started. He was running scared.

Desperation took him online in a search of anything that could save him from his own $100,000 in bad choices. One afternoon while sitting on his couch in his El Paso home, he found a way to fight back. He stumbled across hundreds of other distraught consumers like himself on credit message boards, each with some different version of the same story of bad choices and greed. And, he found a new way to deal with his debt: He could hide behind the law.

His new online friends pointed him to a number of federal and state statutes protecting consumers like him against overly aggressive and abusive debt collectors and a credit system stacked against the little guy. If you knew your rights, he learned on the message boards, you were very likely to catch a collector violating them. Then you could sue.

Cunningham armed himself with this knowledge, and the next time a debt collector called, the trap was set.

It didn't take long. Cunningham had canceled a home alarm service with ADT Security after two months, and the company had billed him a $450 early termination fee, which he disputed. ADT sent his account to Equinox Financial Management Solutions, a third-party debt collector. The collection agency sent him a letter asking that he call back immediately. He dialed, armed with a voice recorder.

"Can you garnish my wages if I don't pay?" he asked.

"Yes," the voice on the other end of the line said.

"Can you put a lien on my house?"

"Yes."

Wrong answers. Turns out, Texas consumer rights laws are some of the most consumer-friendly in the country. And according to a federal consumer protection law, the Fair Debt Collection Practices Act (FDCPA), debt collectors are prohibited from threatening legal action that would violate state laws. In this case, garnishing wages or putting a lien on Cunningham's house would violate the Texas Debt Collection Act.

Cunningham knew he had a good enough case to file a lawsuit against the debt collection agency, and for his first lawsuit, he decided to enlist the help of a lawyer. Two months later, he had a check in his hand for $1,000.

"It's like discovering fire," says Cunningham, thumbing through the stack of lawsuit papers on his table.

"It's their system. I didn't make the rules. I'm just learning what the rules are."

He immediately started devouring as much information as he could about the three chief federal laws that protect consumers from collectors: the *Fair Debt Collection Practices Act, the Fair Credit Reporting Act (FCRA)* and the *Telephone Consumer Protection Act (TCPA)*. In the next four years, Cunningham accused debt collectors of misrepresenting the amount he owed (an FDCPA violation that entitles a consumer to collect up to $1,000). He sued over prerecorded and auto-dialed calls to his cellular phone (a TCPA violation worth up to $1,500 per call). He also filed complaints that agencies failed to investigate his claims that his credit file contains inaccurate information, a breach of the Fair Credit Reporting Act worth up to $1,000 per violation. All told, he filed 15 other lawsuits in federal court without the help of a lawyer, earning himself settlements totaling more than $20,000.

"Most people hear about the abuses that debt collectors do, but you just didn't hear about the second part of it, where people sue the collectors," he says.

Cunningham is one of thousands of hounded debtors who are trading in their paralyzing fears and learning to stand up for themselves. Americans as a whole owe some $2.5 trillion in consumer debt, according to the Federal Reserve, a figure that doesn't include home mortgages. Nearly four in five Americans have credit cards and half carry a balance, according to the Obama administration.

In 2008, the Federal Trade Commission, the nation's consumer protection agency, received more than 78,000 complaints against third-party debt collectors, 8,000 more than in 2007, and early numbers for 2009 indicate the growth will double. While the FTC gets the bulk of consumer complaints, today more consumers are fighting back with their own lawsuits than ever before. In 2009, nearly 10,000 cases under FDCPA, FCRA, or TCPA statutes were filed around the country, mostly in federal courts. That's a 50 percent increase from 2008, and an 83 percent growth from 2007.

A cottage industry has sprung up to counter the flood of cases. Two new companies now offer the credit and collection industries databases of repeat plaintiffs filing under the FDCPA. The companies, FDCPA Case Listing Service LLC and WebRecon, offer something akin to a background check for collection agencies. For example, if an agency received a delinquent account belonging to Cunningham, it could run his name through a database and learn he's a repeat litigant; then the agency could either close his account or sue him first.

Back in his dim living room, Cunningham returns to the pile of paperwork on the table. His soft voice gets bolder when he recounts his war stories with the collection industry. His 15 lawsuits include one filed in federal court against Alliance One, a third-party agency collecting on behalf of Verizon. Alliance One added a $50 collection fee and misrepresented the debt he owed Verizon, he says, which is an unfair practice under FDCPA. Another lawsuit was over the collection of an outstanding bill from Time Warner. The collection agency, Advantage Cable Services, failed to post a surety bond required by the state of Texas in order to collect debts here. Plus, after telling them to stop calling his cellular phone with automated calls, they continued, so he sued and won around $3,500, the industry standard for many consumer rights violations. (Collection agencies frequently settle such lawsuits because that's cheaper than taking them to trial.)

His debt with Time Warner hasn't gone away, and he's in the middle of his biggest FDCPA violation lawsuit ever, demanding upward of $200,000 from the current collection agency.

Debtors, either because they feel morally obligated or because they don't know their options, get backed into a corner by their creditors and believe they *have* to repay their debts, he says. Not so with Cunningham. "I don't have to do anything but stay black and die," he says, a small, smug smile on his lips.

Cunningham wasn't always such a stickler.

As a kid growing up in Detroit, family time meant gathering around the living room table to play stock market board games. His mother was a registered nurse, and his father worked for 25 years as a computer engineer for Ford. When he was 15, Cunningham met his "first millionaire," as he tells it, still wide-eyed. This high school teacher grew wealthy off the then-booming real estate market of the mid-90s. "He accomplished it through business and not sports," he says. "For me, that was where the light first went on."

Cunningham, a high school athlete, dreamed of making millions playing pro football, but he was accepted to U.S. Military Academy at West Point, where a degree would give him a more grounded back-up plan. The economics major also sought out an additional perk unique to West Point: stipends and absurdly low-interest loans. In his junior year, in 2002, Cunningham took out the maximum amount for a loan and dumped the $25,000 into the booming stock market. "Everybody was making easy money," he recalls, and the young cadet wanted a shot at making even more. He spent hours on his dial-up Internet connection learning money-making strategies that capitalized on the cheap and easy credit of the times. By Googling "credit help" or "increase credit score," he landed on message boards on which posters shared how-to tips to boost his credit score and dupe major banks and credit card companies into giving him cards with credit limits around $10,000 and $20,000 at low interest rates. He'd borrow from the cards, invest the money in stocks with payouts higher than his interest rate and pay back the debt with the profits.

Cunningham learned on these boards that the credit card companies, banks and the credit bureaus worked together to determine not only your credit score but how much credit to extend you and at what interest rate.

Cunningham had no problem spending all the money anyone would loan him, but he needed to pay off some of the accrued debt to maintain his credit score. He knew his military loan did not get reported to any of the three major credit bureaus, Equifax, Experian and TransUnion. So, by paying off his credit card debt with money from that loan, he artificially maintained his credit score and continued to be approved for high credit. Sounds fishy, but Cunningham didn't feel that he was taking advantage of the system, at least not anymore than the next guy or the brokers and bankers at the time.

Cunningham now had more than $100,000 in credit card debt, but he had a lot of money coming in as well. He was a big-time shareholder in one sub-prime lending company, Nova Star Financial, and for three years in a row he saw dividends as high as 20 percent for his investment.

Any money he was making went right back into the system. Those good times, of course, wouldn't last.

Not wanting to miss out on the easy money in real estate buying and selling, he bought two low-income four-plexes in Dallas in 2005, using a mortgage company for the loan. He put no money down, but the interest rate was high.

Then he got burned. The four-plex's seller wasn't completely honest about the occupancy of the properties. Cunningham's scheme disintegrated within six months. He was scrambling to make the mortgage payments at the high interest rate without any tenants. He knew it wouldn't be long until he couldn't make the payments and he would be foreclosed on. Somehow, he didn't despair.

"I remember one day I just got pissed," Cunningham says. "I'm running around trying to keep the ship afloat, and the banks don't care."

Cunningham had called the bank as well as the FBI to report the mortgage fraud committed by the seller, but nobody pursued his case.

"The regulators, the FBI, they don't care. So, why should I care?" he says.

The Dallas properties were foreclosed, and his obsessively maintained credit score seemed wrecked. Cunningham returned to the online credit board for help. This time, however, he wasn't looking to add an artificial shine to his credit score, he was looking for a way out of the ashes. Cunningham discovered a whole other world of consumer-generated knowledge. This was a rogue group of disgruntled consumers who were trying to save themselves and their credit by filing lawsuits when the collection industry screwed up the mechanics of debt reporting and collection. What he found was an instrument not of repair or reconciliation, but of vengeance.

"All the conventional wisdom, all the right people say, 'Pay your bills on time and work with your creditors,'" Cunningham says, recalling his thoughts at the time. Yet he had discovered a new set of people who posted their credit reports on line and their successful lawsuits, showing how much money they won in settlements that simultaneously removed a bad debt from their credit report. "I said, 'Maybe there's another way.' Again, just revolution. I never even thought about it."

The knowledge on these boards originated from consumers testing the boundaries of the credit system through their own experiences. The nature of this information, from the beginning, was a mixture of anarchistic tendencies, vengeance and greed. Now the wisdom of the boards has been distilled into an e-book published in January. *Debtsmanship* was written by Steven Katz, a former New York debt collector turned consumer advocate, who now lives in Phoenix. In 2005, Katz founded a message board called "Debtorboards," with the slogan "Sue your creditor and win!"

Katz doesn't believe that people are morally obligated to pay back their debts. That notion was invented by debt collectors as a way to beat people into submission, he says. "Bill collectors would love for you to send them a check and then explain to your kids because you have the moral obligation to pay your debt they're not eating this week," he says. "But they don't see the moral obligation to feed your children or yourself.

"People are brainwashed to think that paying a credit card is more important than paying for the necessities of life," Katz says. "If you're in a position where you have to make a choice, my argument is food, clothing and shelter come first . . . Nobody ever went to hell for not paying a debt."

"Fight back" is the take-away message from a visit to Debtorboards, which is intended to help consumers who wish to file lawsuits without the help of lawyers. Debtorboards outlines steps consumers can take to deal with bothersome debt collectors. For example, if a debt collector is only bothering you, you could send them a letter or sue them. However, if you're so far in debt that you see no way out but bankruptcy, then you can check out the board's "frustrating the skip tracer" technique. There, you'll find tips on how to run and hide from a collector.

Another Debtorboards user is 29-year-old Daniel Smith, who lives with his fiancé outside of Seattle, Washington. Early in 2009, he tried to obtain financing for a home, but was turned down by Bank of America. He soon discovered that an old girlfriend had put his name on her bank account before she fell into massive debt. He wrote angry letters to the bank, but nothing changed. He sat down at his computer and typed in "Bank of America" and "Fair Debt Collection Act" and soon landed on Debtorboards. "I spent hours upon hours upon hours on there," Smith says. "The big epiphany is I'm a little guy but I've got a voice and I'm going to use it."

Like Cunningham, Smith now armed himself with voice recorders and began keeping meticulous financial files. His file cabinet grew quickly. "I mean there's nothing I don't document now and that's probably the best thing a consumer can do."

Smith is an Army vet, an EMT, and a project manager for a construction company. He doesn't advocate stiffing the original creditor on the bill. In fact, Smith will often pay the original creditor, but still go after the violating collection agency.

"The standard line from collection agencies is always, 'Oh, gosh, no, we never violate.' . . . For the most part, the reality of it is you can sit down and find violation in almost every collection attempt made in America."

Cunningham insists that the court system ignores lawsuits over frivolous violations. His cases, he claims, are built on true screw-ups. Cunningham won his first lawsuit, after all, after a collection company threatened to garnish his wages and put a lien on his house, both violations of Texas law.

Although that first lawsuit was filed with the help of a consumer rights lawyer, Cunningham has been filing on his own since then. Once he saw that the entire amount of the original settlement was upward of $3,500, and he only got $1,000, while his lawyer pocketed the rest as payment, Cunningham was motivated to go pro se.

"I remember seeing the $3,500 and thinking shoot that's a lot of money, and I'm only getting a grand, so maybe I can do a little better than that if there is a next time."

Cunningham made sure there'd be a next time. A company was trying to collect on an outstanding utility bill. They threatened to send this debt to the credit bureaus and wreck his credit score. He ended up paying the utility company the money he owed, but sued the collection company because of how they threatened and harassed him for the debt. The case earned him close to $3,500.

He was fast becoming one of the most hated debtors in Dallas, and part of an especially loathed minority of debtors in the country.

Cunningham returned to Texas from a year of active duty with the Army in late 2007, and moved to Dallas. He continued filing lawsuits against debt collection agencies, and he became ever more active on the message boards, holding long conversations about the state of the country with his online pals. In the meantime, he noticed that Debtorboards founder Steven Katz had created a new thread titled "The list you want to be on." Here, Katz reported that a new company had appeared that was dedicated to aiding collection companies scrub their database against repeat FDCPA litigants, like Cunningham.

Cunningham toyed with the idea of suing them. After all, he thought, if they were working with the collection industry and the credit bureaus (FDCPA Case Listing Service partnered with TransUnion in 2009), then the companies sounded like credit reporting agencies to Cunningham, which would mean they would have to abide by certain credit reporting laws. Cunningham wrote to FDCPA Case Listing Service asking for a copy of his credit report (by law, a credit reporting agency must provide a consumer report if asked for one). Instead of a report, however, Cunningham found a lawsuit against him in his mailbox filed in May 2008 in Atlanta federal court. It alleged: "The defendant subscribes to and makes postings to a Web site in which consumers share information and promote litigation against the collection industry . . . The defendant has now conspired with others on the internet to incite civil litigation against plaintiff for the exclusive purpose of extorting money from the plaintiff."

FDCPA Case Listing Service asked the court to declare that they are not a consumer reporting agency and not subject to the Fair Credit Reporting Act. To Cunningham, this was a clear attempt to silence him. Cunningham filed a motion to dismiss the case. For one thing, filing the suit in Atlanta was improper venue, Cunningham wrote. They should have sued him in Texas. Furthermore, since Cunningham hadn't actually sued the company, the company had no valid reason to sue him. The court sided with Cunningham

WebRecon offers a similar but expanded service to FDCPA Case Listing Service. Rather than only track FDCPA cases, WebRecon makes an effort to track FCRA, TCPA, and state and local cases, as well. WebRecon is headed by Jack Gordon out of Michigan. Gordon ran his own third-party collection agency for years until a spate of FDCPA lawsuits in 2008 forced him out of business. He is familiar with Cunningham's type.

"This is definitely, if I can use a really strong word, a cesspool," Gordon says. "The overwhelming majority of these suits are not pro se. Now when you're focusing exclusively on pro se, I think you're getting into a little bit of a different area. I've spent time personally on some of the Web sites that a lot of pro se litigants frequent . . . I would have to say they are far more radicalized element of society, and there's certainly I think reason for concern.

"You're dealing with somebody who's looking for an opportunity. They revel in either getting opportunities or making opportunities to try out everything they're learning online. That's hardly an exaggeration," he says, laughing. "It's really an experience spending time there!"

Gordon may have a personal vendetta against Cunningham types, but so do others who represent the collection industry.

ACA International is the largest trade group representing third-party debt collection agencies. Tom Morgan is the Texas executive director for ACA International and he believes that FDCPA lawsuits will continue to rise as more and more people in this economy can't pay their debts. He views the agencies as a kind of indirect victim in the rising tide of consumer fury and desperation.

"While our members do get filed on from time to time, the FDCPA is so highly technical there are quote, technical, violations that can occur," Morgan says. "You know, somebody makes a mistake. But there's no intent, OK, to defraud people or to violate the law.

"Usually it's settled because the agency says, 'Uh, we didn't intend to do that. Our collector said the wrong thing and we fess up and say, 'I didn't mean to do it but I did it . . .'

"And this is where some of our members feel aggrieved in that because there's a hyper-technical opportunity for a plaintiff's attorney to come in, it is cheaper to settle than to fight it. And sometimes they'd really like to fight it because they don't believe they are guilty, but it's so costly, so they settle it."

Thomas Stockton is on the executive committee of ACA International and also the founder and chief executive of a local collection agency, CMI.

(Cunningham is in the midst of an ongoing legal dispute with CMI, which picked up his outstanding Time Warner debt.)

"In my opinion there are two reasons why there are more suits being filed today," Stockton says. "You've got the Internet sites . . . And, it's easy to file suit. You can do it on your own. You don't have to have an attorney."

Stockton says, however, that the better question is how many of the suits are successful.

The answer depends on how you define success. Debt collectors point to all the settlements they are forced to make because it's cheaper than fighting a frivolous suit. To Cunningham and other pro se litigants, any payment is a victory.

"Does if make sense to spend $10,000 to win this suit or pay the litigant $500 to settle?" says Stockton. "Depending on the situation, it becomes a business decision at some point."

Cunningham filed his lawsuit against Credit Management, L.P. (CMI) in August 2009, claiming violations in the amount of around $200,000—by far his gutsiest lawsuit yet. The original bill for Time Warner was for $79.84 back while he was living in El Paso. Cunningham admits he may have missed the last payment for the Time Warner bill. Time Warner, rather than validate the bill, sent his account to a collection agency. That was ACS, which Cunningham sued for violating his Texas rights, as well as federal law. ACS closed his account, but the debt wasn't forgiven. Instead, CMI picked it up.

CMI started calling Cunningham's cell phone with an auto-dialer, leaving prerecorded messages to please call them immediately regarding an outstanding bill. Cunningham told them to stop calling his cell phone on the auto-dialer, but they continued, each call a violation of TCPA. As Cunningham disputed the bill, CMI by law is also expected to cease collection efforts. So every call was another violation of FDCPA. Plus, to this day, CMI has not provided Cunningham with anything from Time Warner, he says, either a bill or a letter, verifying that he in fact owes anything, another violation of the law. "I don't really know if I owe it," Cunningham says. "If I do, send me a bill. If they don't want to send me a bill, I don't think I need to pay 'em."

CMI has countersued Cunningham, and even asked the court for a protective order from Cunningham: "Plaintiff Craig Cunningham (herein "Plaintiff") has filed suit against a business, Credit Management, LP (herein "CMI"), and twenty-seven (27) of its employees in their individual capacities," reads the motion for a protective order filed in Northern District of Texas in December 2009. "Defendants move for a protective order to protect Defendants from the annoyance, oppression, undue burden and expense of objecting and responding to improper, repetitive and irrelevant discovery requests."

In December, Cunningham was called in for a six-hour deposition, the longest he's ever sat through, at which the lawyers printed out pages of his online comments to accuse him of acting like a lawyer. Plus, CMI insists that they didn't violate any laws and that Cunningham is acting in bad faith. Although the company already offered Cunningham money to settle the case, Cunningham refused, asking for much more than the "industry standard," as Cunningham calls it, of $3,500.

"If they don't pay a bunch of money, if they don't feel pain, they will not change," he says.

A big win in his case against CMI could go a long way toward clearing Cunningham's debts—if he ever chose to pay them, that is.

confession of judgment: Acknowledgment by a debtor of a claim and consent that a judgment may be entered without notice or hearing for the amount of the claim when it is due and unpaid.

wage assignment: An assignment by an employee by which an amount of his or her wages is transferred to a creditor before the wages are paid to the employee.

prejudgment garnishment: A remedial device whereby a creditor attaches the property of a debtor to pay the debt owed to the creditor before a court has issued a judgment in the creditor's favor.

supplementary proceeding: Court proceeding occurring after a judgment has been entered, aimed at determining the extent and whereabouts of the judgment debtor's money and property.

execution sale: A sale carried out to execute a judgment under authority of a judicial officer.

"I took outsize risks, and I got burned," he says. "When myself and some other fellow small investors were losing their assets, nobody cared."

Up until now, everything was about making easy money for Cunningham. Now, it's about justice—or at least what he sees as justice.

"When you or I make a mistake, they say, 'Hey, tough nuts, be smarter next time, you know, bad luck, didn't work out for ya,'" he says. "When the fat cats on Wall Street make a mistake, they say, 'Oh, national emergency! We've got to bail these guys out.'"

Since nobody has showed up to bail Cunningham out, he's decided some of the $100,000 debt he once amassed will never get paid back.

"I already paid them off," he says. "The government took my money without asking me and gave it to the banks. And since I owe the banks money, but they already got my money from the government, I say we're even."

Source: Kimberly Thorpe, *The Dallas Observer News,* http://www.dallasobserver.com/2010-01-21/news/better-off-deadbeat-craig-cunningham-has-a-simple-solution-for-getting-bill-collectors-off-his-back-he-sues-them/. January 21, 2010.

If debt collection efforts fail, and the debt is unsecured, then the creditor must file a lawsuit against the debtor. The creditor must receive a judgment, as described in Chapter 2, before the debt can be collected. **Confession of judgment** is a provision in a document permitting the creditor to obtain an entry of judgment by a court. This document is signed by the debtor before any default has even occurred. Confessions of judgment are generally prohibited by state statutes. Wage assignments are also prohibited in most states. **Wage assignments** occur when the debtor signs over a percentage of his or her wage to the creditor.

Prejudgment garnishment is also prohibited. Garnishment occurs when a creditor takes a debtor's property to pay for a debt; such garnishment is prejudgment if it occurs before the creditor has received a court judgment that the creditor is owed money on a debt. Historically, some creditors repossessed collateral before they received a judgment. In *Fuentes v. Shevin* [407 U.S. 67 (1972)], the U.S. Supreme Court held that this activity violated the due process clause of the U.S. Constitution.

AFTER-JUDGMENT REMEDIES

Once a creditor receives a judgment, however, there are several methods that can be used to receive payment. Usually, the debtor will be required to attend a **supplementary proceeding** which allows the creditor to question the debtor about the debtor's sources of income as well as any property he or she may own. This property may be *attached* (taken) and sold. An **execution sale** occurs when the court orders the sale of the debtor's property to satisfy the debts. The sale is conducted by the sheriff, and the money is turned over to the creditor. The debtor will receive any surplus monies. Some items are exempt from execution. For example, most states have a *homestead exemption*, in which the debtor retains some of the equity in a home. Other exemptions can include appliances, furniture, and other household essentials. The exemption lists are very specific as to what can and cannot be sold. All property that is not exempt can be sold at auction to satisfy the debt.

Another method of debt collection is to garnish the debtor's wages. Wage garnishment occurs after the creditor receives a judgment. In order to garnish wages, creditors must file a garnishment request with the court and with the debtor's employer, requesting that the employer pay a percentage of the debtor's wage to the creditor. Most states require that the statement be filed by the creditor every pay period. The FTC's Credit Practice Rules do not allow more money to be garnished than the lesser of 25 percent of take home pay (per pay period) or an amount that exceeds 40 times the federal minimum wage. Most states have similar restrictions.

Creditors are not allowed to engage in *unconscionable practices*. Unconscionable practices are practices that are so unfair to a consumer that a court will refuse to enforce that action. Unconscionable contracts are discussed in Chapter 12.

One of the best ways for a creditor to be protected when a debtor defaults on a loan is to use **collateral** for a loan. If money is given to buy a home or other piece of real property, the creditor almost always uses the real property as collateral. If the debtor then defaults on the debt, the creditor can take the property back and resell it to someone else to satisfy the debt. To use real property as collateral, the creditor must have the debtor sign a mortgage or trust deed. Some states also allow the use of a land sales contract. These devices are discussed in Chapter 14.

SECURED TRANSACTIONS

A creditor may also take personal property as collateral for a loan. Personal property is any property that is not real property. (The differences were discussed in detail in Chapter 14.) If a creditor takes personal property as collateral for a loan, in most states the creditor must comply with *Article 9* of the *Uniform Commercial Code (UCC)*. Taking personal property as collateral is referred to as **secured transactions**. In 2001, *Article 9* underwent significant revisions in order to make it applicable to the 21st century. It was updated to take into account technology advances as well as global organizations. This section will discuss the rules associated with Revised Article 9.

To use personal property as collateral, a debtor and creditor must create a *security interest*. The collateral used to create the security interest is divided into two categories, tangible and intangible. Tangible collateral includes items like *consumer goods* (e.g., televisions, stereos), *equipment* (e.g., cash registers), *inventory* (items that will be resold to the consumer), and *farm products* (e.g., milk, chicken, beef). The same item can be categorized differently, depending on the debtor's use of the product. For example, a microwave oven is a consumer good if it is bought by the consumer for personal use. The same microwave oven is inventory if the debtor is a retailer. Further, the same microwave oven becomes equipment if it is used by a restaurant. Intangible collateral are items that cannot be touched but whose value is represented by a paper instrument. Intangible collateral include software, payment intangibles, **accounts receivable**, **chattel paper**, instruments, documents of title, trademarks, and money.

secured transactions: A credit sale of goods or a secured loan that provides special protection for the creditor in the form of acquiring some legal rights in the goods or property.

accounts receivable: A balance due a creditor from a debtor on a current account.

chattel paper: A paper that sets out the buyer's obligation to pay and the lender's security interest in the goods.

CREATING THE SECURITY INTEREST

To create a security interest, the parties must have a *security agreement*. The security agreement must specifically grant a security interest in the collateral and must be in writing or be a record stored in electronic or other medium retrievable in a tangible form (a printout). The agreement must also describe the collateral and be signed by the debtor. The **secured party** or creditor also has to give up something of value. It is not a requirement that the debtor own the collateral, but he or she must have an interest in the collateral. For example, Jane, a debtor, cannot use her neighbor's truck as collateral for a loan if she does not have a legal interest in the truck. Sometimes the security agreement can be oral if the collateral is in the possession of the secured party. If a debtor promises to turn an item over to the possession of the secured party, this is called a pledge. Some items must be in possession of the secured party before a security interest can be created, such as tangible chattel paper, instruments and negotiable goods. Items like stock and money are easily transferred, and therefore the secured party must hold possession of the collateral in order to retain the security interest. Written or an electronic record of security agreements is required to secure intangible collateral, since there is no way it can be possessed. Once this process occurs, the security interest becomes enforceable against the debtor, or in UCC terminology, it **attaches**, as shown in Figure 18.1. Attachment means that the security interest remains attached to the collateral until the debt is paid, no matter who owns the collateral (assuming that the security interest is also perfected, as explained later).

One major problem with security interests occurs when several people have a security interest in the same item. For example, assume Don borrows $1,000 from First National Bank to set up a retail store. He gives the bank a security interest in all of his equipment, inventory, and accounts receivable. Don then negotiates with Carla's Clothes to provide him with a line of coats to sell in the store. Carla sends the coats to Don and expects payment in 30 days. Carla also takes a security interest in the coats. (She actually obtains a written document indicating that she has a security interest in the coats.) If Don fails to pay both Carla and the bank, who is entitled to recover the coats? This is a question of *perfection and priority*.

secured party: A party holding a security interest in another's property.

attach: To create a security interest in property thereby acquiring the right to foreclose on or otherwise deal with property for payment of debt.

Figure 18.1
Attachment

A Security Interest Attaches When the Debtor
Has Rights in the Collateral

AND A

- Written security agreement:
  - granting a security interest
  - describing the collateral
  - signed by the debtor

OR

- Oral security agreement:
  - granting a security interest and
  - secured party possesses the collateral

PERFECTION

To enforce its security interest in the collateral, a creditor must perfect its interest. **Perfection** of a security interest occurs when the security interest has attached to the collateral and the creditor has taken the necessary steps to complete perfection. *Perfected security interests* take priority over *unperfected security interests*. The manner in which a creditor perfects a security interest depends on what type of collateral he or she is using. Most security interests are perfected on the date the creditor either takes possession of the collateral or files a *financing statement* with the appropriate state office. The filing must occur in the state where the debtor is located. Corporations or limited liability companies are located in the state in which they are organized. Remember, creating a security interest in some items requires that the creditor take possession of the collateral. A financing statement contains the debtor's name, the name of the secured party and a general description of the collateral covered. Once the financing statement is filed, the security interest is said to be perfected. Filing the financing statement allows other potential creditors the opportunity to check to see if the debtor is using collateral that another party already has secured. Checking for financing statements can be done through electronic search engines. Since perfected security interests take preference over junior security interests or interests that are perfected later, those junior interests may turn out to be worthless. All the items necessary to perfect a security interest are shown in Figure 18.2.

> **Perfection:** The process through which a creditor creates an enforceable security interest in collateral.

- Security agreement (written agreement required for intangible collateral)
- Attachment (See Figure 18.1)
- File financing statement (required for intangible collateral)
  - in state office (or required office in the case of fixtures)
  - lists name and address of debtor
  - lists name and address of secured party
  - describes collateral
  - signed by debtor

OR

- Take possession of collateral (required for money and stock)

Figure 18.2
Perfection of Security Interest

One last type of filing is a *fixture filing*. As you will remember from Chapter 14, fixtures are personal property that have become real property. For example, when a furnace is purchased, it is personal property; but when it is installed in a home, it becomes part of the real property. To obtain a perfected security interest in the fixture, the filing must be made in the office where the mortgage on the real property is filed, usually the county recorder's office.

Consumer goods, or goods sold to a consumer for personal or household use on credit (except automobiles), are *automatically perfected*. Thus, the creditor does not need to take possession of the property or file a financing statement to obtain the best claim on the collateral. For example, if Ann goes to Don's Store, purchases a coat, and agrees to pay Don $30 a month until the coat is paid off, Don does not need to do anything more to perfect his security interest. However, Don's security interest is only attached to the collateral (the coat) so long as Ann stays in possession of the coat. If Ann turns around and sells the coat to Steve in a garage sale, Don will not be able to recover the coat from Steve if Ann defaults on the loan and Don has not filed a financing statement. Even though Don's security interest was automatically perfected, because he had not filed a financing statement, that perfection does not apply to other purchasers of the collateral.

Returning to the original scenario in which Don borrowed $1,000 to start a retail store, National Bank has taken a security interest in Don's inventory. In the event of default, if the Bank had filed a financing statement and Carla's Clothes had not, then the bank may recover the coats, and Carla may only sue Don on the underlying debt. Carla would not be able to recover the coats. A perfected security interest will always take precedence over an unperfected security interest. Therefore, since the bank had the only perfected security interest, the bank has the best right to the coats. Assume, though, that Carla had taken a good legal environment course and knew better than to be unperfected. Therefore, she too had filed a financing statement. Now both creditors are perfected. Who wins?

PRIORITY

This is a question of *priority*. If more than one perfected security interest exists, the creditor who perfected the security interest first may repossess the collateral. The creditor who filed second will only collect from the sale of the collateral if the collateral is worth more than the first creditor's debt.

PURCHASE MONEY SECURITY INTEREST

purchase money security interest: A security interest in which the debtor uses the credit extended by the creditor to purchase the collateral which is being used to secure the loan.

The priority rule seems straightforward except that it does not take into account the **purchase money security interest (PMSI)**. A PMSI is a security interest in which the debtor uses the credit extended by the creditor to purchase the actual collateral being used as security. In other words, a PMSI is created when the creditor gives value for the goods the debtor is financing. To see how a PMSI works, assume Ed goes to Bank 1 and borrows $1,000 for a trip to Europe. Bank 1 takes Ed's boat as collateral for the loan. This transaction does not create a PMSI because Ed did not use the loan proceeds to buy the collateral (the boat). On the other hand, if Ed goes to Bank 1 to borrow $1,000 for the purchase of a boat, and the bank takes that specific boat as collateral, this creates a PMSI. A PMSI is *automatically perfected* for 10 days. This means that if Ed obtains the loan on August 1, no other creditor can obtain a higher priority until August 11. Let us assume, then, that Ed goes to Bank 2 and borrows $1,000 to take his trip to Europe and uses his recently purchased boat, which is secured by Bank 1, as collateral. Bank 2 checks the public record on August 3 and determines that no other security interests exist on the boat, loans Ed $1,000 and files a financing statement on August 4. Bank 1 files its financing statement on August 5. If Ed defaults on both loans, who is entitled to repossess the boat? Bank 1 still has priority, because it has a PMSI that was automatically perfected for 10 days. Bank 1 did not need to file a financing statement for 10 days; therefore, it does not matter that Bank 2 checked the records on August 3 and found no financing statement.

What could Bank 2 have done differently? It should have filed a financing statement on August 4 and then waited 10 days before giving Ed any money. After the 10-day period, Bank 2 would have discovered Bank 1's financing statement by checking the public record. If Bank 1 had failed to file its financing statement and no other financing statements secured the boat, Bank 1 could loan the money safely.

INVENTORY FINANCING

Besides those rules governing a PMSI, special rules also exist for inventory financing. A PMSI in inventory takes priority over other secured parties if the PMSI holder notifies, in writing, other secured parties before the inventory is delivered. The PMSI must be perfected *before* delivery. Remember our earlier example in which Don has borrowed $1,000 from National Bank to set up a retail business, and the bank has taken a security interest in all of Don's equipment, inventory, and accounts receivable. Later, Don ordered coats on open account from Carla's Clothes. Carla's, in this case, has a security interest in inventory. In order for Carla to obtain priority over National Bank, Carla will need to send written notification to National Bank that she has taken a purchase money security interest in the coats she is selling on credit. Moreover, she will need to file a financing statement with the appropriate public office before any of the coats are delivered to Don. If Carla does this, she will be able to repossess the coats to satisfy her debt. If she does not follow the proper procedures, National Bank will be able to repossess the coats to satisfy its debt.

Once a security interest is perfected, as explained previously, it becomes attached to the collateral, which means that all later or subsequent buyers of the collateral take subject to the security interest until the debt is paid in full. Thus, subsequent buyers may have to relinquish the collateral to the original secured party or pay the original secured party the price of the collateral if the collateral is no longer in their possession. For example, assume that Don no longer needs his cash register and offers to sell it to Joan. Since National Bank has a security interest in Don's equipment, Joan buys the cash register with the possibility that the Bank can repossess it from her if Don defaults on his loan. Therefore, if Joan buys the cash register, and Don defaults on National Bank's loan, National Bank can repossess the cash register from Joan. Joan's only remedy would be to sue Don.

An exception to this rule occurs if Joan is a *buyer in the ordinary course of business*, a person who buys goods from someone in the business of selling those types of goods. If Joan goes into Don's store and buys a coat, neither National Bank nor Carla's can repossess the coat from Joan in the event of Don's default, even though (1) they both have perfected security interests in the inventory and (2) Joan may know of the existence of the security interest. The reason for this rule is clear. When shopping in retail stores, consumers do not want to check the public records to ensure that no security interests exist on the goods they buy. To require consumers to do this would thwart the very purpose of retail shopping. The UCC, then, takes this into account and does not make buyers in the ordinary course of business responsible for checking for security interests. Figure 18.3 summarizes the rules for priority in secured transactions.

Figure 18.3
Priority of Secured Transactions

**The First Party to Perfect the Security
Interest Has Priority Unless**:

1) The goods are purchased in the ordinary course of business;

2) One party has a purchase money security interest (PMSI) with the following characteristics:

    a) The debtor used the credit extended to purchase the collateral of the security interest; and

    b) A financing statement is filed within ten days (a PMSI is automatically perfected for 10 days).

3) One party has a perfected security interest in inventory with the following characteristics:

    a) The holder has notified the other secured parties;

    b) This notification is in writing; and

    c) This perfection and notification occur before delivery.

REPOSSESSION

Of course, none of these rules matter if the debtor pays on time. The problem occurs when the debtor defaults on the loan. A creditor who possesses a security interest has two options if the debtor defaults: first, the creditor may repossess the collateral and sell it; or second, the creditor may repossess the collateral and keep it in full satisfaction of the debt. Private parties are allowed to **repossess** collateral if repossession can be done without breaching the peace (i.e., without causing a fight or breaking the law).

> **repossess:** To take possession of collateral by judicial process or self-help when a debtor defaults on a debt.

    Once collateral is repossessed, the creditor may sell it at a private or public sale. If this is done, the creditor must send written notification of the sale to the debtor, all other secured parties and any guarantors. Also, the sale must be *commercially reasonable* which means that the time, place, manner, and terms of the sale must be reasonable. If the collateral is sold for more than the debt plus costs and attorneys' fees, the debtor is entitled to the surplus. If the collateral is sold for less, the debtor is liable for any deficiency.

    A secured party may choose to keep the collateral in full satisfaction of the debt. However, the secured party must notify the debtor and other secured parties of that intention. The recipient of this notice has a certain number of days to object (in most states it is 21 days). If a written objection is received, the secured party must sell the collateral. Most states have special rules for consumer goods. These rules may allow the secured party to keep the goods in full satisfaction of the debt only if less than 60 percent of the debt has been paid. In this case, the creditor must obtain a written statement from the debtor allowing the creditor to keep the goods. As you can see, perfecting security interests is very important in everyday commercial transactions. Security interests are also very important when a debtor declares bankruptcy.

BANKRUPTCY

Part of the risk associated with a free market economy is the risk of failure. Given the statistics on how many new businesses fail, it is almost surprising that anyone would want to borrow money and start a business. Of course, it is essential for the economy that people continue to start businesses and risk losing their money. Most people would be unwilling to accept this risk if failure meant spending time in debtor's prison or suffering crushing debt from which they would never recover. Thus, the federal bankruptcy laws are intended to strike a balance between **debtor** and **creditor** rights while encouraging people to take financial risks.

Another reason for bankruptcy laws is to give the debtor's creditors a fair way to split what is left of the debtor's property. Without bankruptcy laws, some creditors could receive everything while other creditors receive nothing. The bankruptcy rules set up a hierarchy for receiving payment.

The U.S. Constitution gives Congress the power to establish bankruptcy laws. (As a result, no state bankruptcy system exists.) Congress passed the first bankruptcy law in 1800 and repealed it in 1803. Congress then passed and repealed several bankruptcy laws until creating the Bankruptcy Act of 1898. This Act was amended in 1938 and then stayed virtually the same until 1978. In 1978, the bankruptcy courts were completely overhauled with the passage of the *Bankruptcy Reform Act of 1978*. The 1978 Act sets forth several chapters by which individuals or businesses can file for protection under the bankruptcy statutes. For example, Chapter 7 is known as a *liquidation*, Chapter 11 is known as a *reorganization*, and Chapter 13 applies to persons with a regular income.

In 1982, the U.S. Supreme Court ruled in *Northern Pipeline Co. v. Marathon Pipe Line Co.* [458 U.S. 50 (1982)] that portions of the 1978 Act were unconstitutional because they gave bankruptcy court judges more power than they could constitutionally possess. Congress then amended the act with the *Bankruptcy Amendments Act of 1984* which clarifies the role of bankruptcy judges. Bankruptcy judges work under federal district court judges and hear everything concerning the bankruptcy laws. This is called the **core proceeding**. State courts also retain jurisdiction over lawsuits involving the debtor, other than the bankruptcy proceedings, such as personal injury lawsuits. The 1984 Act also changes the bankruptcy court's jurisdiction and requires that the federal district court enter all final rules unless the parties agree otherwise.

In 2005, Congress passed the *Bankruptcy Abuse Prevention and Consumer Protection Act,* (sometimes referred to as the *Bankruptcy Reform Act*), a sweeping reform of federal bankruptcy law. The Act was intended to make it more difficult for consumers to file for bankruptcy, particularly Chapter 7. It increased the waiting period during which debtors cannot file another petition for bankruptcy from six to eight years. It requires all Chapter 7 petitioners to undergo consumer credit counseling within 180 days of filing a petition for bankruptcy. It also imposed additional paperwork and filing fees and limited the previous homestead and other exemptions.

bankruptcy debtor: An individual or business that owes money to a creditor and who has filed for bankruptcy protection.

bankruptcy creditor: An individual or business that has a claim against the debtor before the bankruptcy petition is filed.

core proceeding: A proceeding that is integral to the adminstration of a bankruptcy estate and so falls under the jurisdiction of the bankruptcy court.

INTERNATIONAL ISSUES

Not all countries allow for debts to be discharged. For example, it was not until February 2004 that Finnish Law provided that debts could only be enforced for up to 20 years. Up until that time persons with heavy debts carried the debts throughout their lives.

CHAPTER 7 OF THE BANKRUPTCY ACT

All parties except railroads, banks, insurance companies, and so on can file a Chapter 7 bankruptcy. If a Chapter 7 bankruptcy is filed, the court appoints a **trustee** who has the responsibility to accumulate the assets and pay the debts with whatever funds are available. The trustee will return collateral to secured creditors and will sell the rest of the debtor's nonexempt property (which will be discussed later in this chapter). Priority claims, also discussed later in the chapter, are then paid and if there is anything left, unsecured creditors will be paid **pro rata**. For example, unsecured creditors may receive 10 cents for each dollar they are owed. More often in a Chapter 7 bankruptcy, unsecured creditors do not receive anything.

The 2005 Bankruptcy Reform Act amended Chapter 7 by requiring a "means test" to be applied to any debtors claiming bankruptcy whose income is above the median income in the debtor's state. These debtors are often forced to file for Chapter 13 bankruptcy rather than Chapter 7 because their projected future disposable income is determined to be high enough that they are capable of paying off some of their debt. Because the means test is based upon state median income figures, the means test figures change as median incomes change, which means that qualifications for Chapter 7 bankruptcy are not static but will change over time.

CHAPTER 11 OF THE BANKRUPTCY ACT

Most businesses and some individuals decide that rather than liquidate, they want to **reorganize** their debts. This is possible with a Chapter 11 bankruptcy. Usually the debtor continues to operate the business and is referred to as the **debtor in possession**. Sometimes the court appoints a trustee to run the business if the court believes that the debtor is unable to continue running the business. The debtor has 120 days from the date the petition is filed to present a reorganization plan. Reorganization plans divide debts into certain *classes*. Each class of debt is then paid differently. For example, Class A debt may be the amount owed to Bank 1, Class B debt is the amount owed to Bank 2, and Class C debt may be the amount owed to unsecured creditors. After the plan is presented, the creditors vote whether to accept or reject the plan. Each class of creditors must accept the plan to ensure that the creditors themselves believe they are being treated fairly under the circumstances. For a plan to be accepted, the debtor must receive the positive vote of creditors representing two-thirds the total dollar amount and one-half the number of creditors in each class. If secured creditors will receive as much from the plan as they would receive in a Chapter 7 bankruptcy, unsecured creditors can force the

---

trustee: One trusted to administer something.

pro rata: In proportion to the calculated debt.

reorganization: The rehabilitation of the finances of a business according to a plan approved by a bankruptcy court.

debtor in possession: A debtor who remains in possession of an estate during bankruptcy and has the same duties as a trustee in bankruptcy.

secured creditors to accept the plan. This tactic is known as a "cram down." A creditors' committee is organized by the Court and includes the seven unsecured creditors with the largest claims that are willing to serve on the committee. Often with the help of its own attorney, the creditors' committee can formulate its own reorganization plan if the debtor fails to get a plan accepted within 120 days. The creditors' committee can seek to have a trustee appointed if it believes the debtor has committed fraud, is dishonest, or is guilty of gross mismanagement. The creditors' committee can also move to dismiss the case or to convert the case to a Chapter 7 bankruptcy. Plans for small businesses with less than $2,343,300 in debt may proceed without a creditors' committee, and there are simpler procedures for voting on the plan.

Recent events, such as the September 11th terrorist attacks, the war in Iraq, and the financial crisis beginning in 2008, have financially stressed even large businesses. In September, 2008, in the wake of financial crisis involving many large U.S. banks and financial firms, Lehman Brothers filed the largest bankruptcy petition to date. Other large companies who have recently filed for Chapter 11 bankruptcy protection include MGM Studios, the A&P grocery store chain, and Blockbuster. As the next article suggests, Chapter 11 bankruptcies are increasingly hard on unsecured creditors.

Blockbuster and the Pushback by Unsecured Creditors

Blockbuster's fight to stay in Chapter 11 may represent another round in the pushback against aggressive secured lenders and the increasing use of quick 363 sale in place of traditional Chapter 11 plans.

A while ago I noted some signs that the bankruptcy courts were pushing back against the senior lenders, and today we see the efforts of unsecured creditors to do the same. And they managed to get the United States Trustee—the government watchdog for bankruptcy—on their side.

The current plan outline in Blockbuster calls for the senior noteholders to finance operations until a sale, after which the lenders will become owners and the pre-bankruptcy unsecured creditors will get bupkis. (That's the technical bankruptcy term, of course.) And there is a substantial amount of pre-bankruptcy unsecured debt outstanding: almost $300 million in subordinated bonds and more than $57 million owed to trade creditors.

But the present dispute involves something more: Blockbuster's obligations to trade creditors who have continued to supply the debtor's operations pending a sale. The creditors' committee sees many of its constituents taking a further hit if these post-bankruptcy claims are left unpaid, and, perhaps more worryingly, the creation of a large group of priority creditors who will have first claim on the few scraps left after the sale.

The senior note-holders respond that it is their cash that has kept Blockbuster alive to date. That may be so, but there is a real question of whether trade creditors are being asked to make an involuntary contribution to Blockbuster's survival. The note-holders are in this for the risk and return; the trade creditors are unlikely to want to go along for that ride.

> The larger issue looming here is when is it appropriate for bankruptcy courts to facilitate a sale that benefits nobody except the senior lenders.
>
> More broadly, there are important policy considerations embedded in the decision to allow a corporate reorganization scheme to transform into a kind of supercharged foreclosure mechanism, particularly if secured lenders are able to avoid incurring costs that they would normally absorb in a state debt collection action. That question becomes especially problematic when the bankruptcy code allows the debtor to run up further exposure to trade creditors, while limiting the ability of those creditors to terminate their relationship with the debtor.
>
> As the automotive cases showed, quick 363 sales are the current status quo in Chapter 11. To date, the senior lenders have largely run this show. We are just seeing the beginnings of a response. Blockbuster stays in Chapter 11 for now, and the senior lenders still get to try to do their thing, but maybe, just maybe, they have awakened the unsecured creditors.

Source: Stephen J. Lubben, *NY Times,* http://dealbook.nytimes.com/2011/03/11blockbuster-and-the-pushback-by-unsecured-creditors/

CHAPTER 13 OF THE BANKRUPTCY ACT

Chapter 13 of the Bankruptcy Code can be used by a debtor with a regular source of income (i.e., a regular job). Sole proprietors are also eligible if debt requirements are met. The debtor must have unsecured debt of less than $360,475 and secured debt of less than $1,081,400. A Chapter 13 bankruptcy includes the following two types of debt: (1) debt that is incurred before bankruptcy was filed (*prepetition debt*) and (2) debt that was incurred after the bankruptcy was filed (*post-petition debt*). Once a Chapter 13 bankruptcy is filed, the bankruptcy court names a trustee who has the responsibility to ensure that all post-petition debt is paid on time. The trustee, with the debtor's help, also proposes a plan to pay the prepetition debt. The plan should pay the prepetition debt in three years, although the court can extend the payment period to five years. Creditors must vote on the plan. The unsecured creditors must accept the plan if they receive as much as they would have received in a Chapter 7 bankruptcy. Secured creditors must accept the plan if the plan makes a good faith effort to pay the debts.

SOCIAL/ETHICAL ISSUES

Bankruptcy protection was originally intended to provide a "safety net" to consumers in financial dire straits. However, the changes to bankruptcy law imposed by the 2005 Bankruptcy Reform Act have made it harder for many individuals to file for bankruptcy. One rationale for the reform is that bankruptcy had become a "lifestyle choice" for a large group of consumers who wished to continue overspending. However, a recent study done by the Harvard Medical School indicates that over 60% of all bankruptcies are caused by crushing debt due to medical bills rather than irresponsible consumer spending. Moreover, given the high unemployment rates the United States has suffered in recent years, the number of Chapter 7 bankruptcies filed is likely to reach all-time highs. Do you think the Bankruptcy Reform Act is fair? Is it good public policy to prevent more people from getting the "fresh start" that bankruptcy laws were supposed to give them?

A Chapter 13 bankruptcy is not a good solution for those whose debts exceed their income; however, it is a good solution for those who have incurred debts as the result of a job layoff or illness and have now recovered and have income that exceeds debts.

DECLARING BANKRUPTCY

A person may declare bankruptcy without being insolvent. Some very large companies have filed for bankruptcy protection before they were insolvent. For example, Johns Manville Corporation, an asbestos manufacturer, and A.H. Robbins, the manufacturer of the Dalkon shield used the bankruptcy laws in this manner after losing several product liability lawsuits. Some small gun manufacturers have also recently declared bankruptcy in anticipation of the filing of several gun liability lawsuits.

Before filing a bankruptcy petition, the debtor needs to decide under which chapter to file. If the debtor files under Chapter 7, the debtor is admitting that the situation is hopeless and agrees to liquidate the estate. If a debtor files under Chapter 11, the debtor attempts to reorganize the debts. If the debtor files under Chapter 13, the debtor asks the court to reorganize some debts and pay other debts as they become due. In 1986 Congress passed Chapter 12 to help family farmers restructure their debts. Regardless of the type of bankruptcy the debtor uses, all chapters have some common concepts. The 2005 Bankruptcy Reform Act requires all individual petitioners to receive credit counseling within 180 days before filing a bankruptcy petition.

To file for bankruptcy relief, a *bankruptcy petition* must be filed with the bankruptcy court. The petition lists the debtor's assets and debts categorized in various schedules. The *schedules* list all of the creditors, the amounts they are owed, and their addresses. Creditors not listed in the schedules are not subject to the final order.

Once the petition is filed, an **automatic stay** occurs. An automatic stay prohibits all creditors from contacting the debtor; from initiating any collection procedures, including lawsuits; and from continuing lawsuits. Secured creditors are entitled to *adequate protection*, or they can request that their collateral be returned. Adequate protection means the collateral will not depreciate, in effect making the creditor unsecured. For example, in 1995, Bank 1 loaned Francis $50,000, taking a brand new machine worth $60,000 as collateral. Each year, the machine depreciates. By 1996, the machine is worth $50,000, and by 1997 it is worth $40,000. Meanwhile, Francis has paid down the loan to $40,000 before the bankruptcy petition is filed. If Francis declares bankruptcy in 1997 and does not pay on the debt, before very long the machine will be worth much less than the loan amount. To prevent this from happening, Bank 1 may ask the bankruptcy court to give it more collateral for its loan or ask that Francis pay an amount equivalent to the amount of depreciation. This is known as providing adequate protection. Once again, it is only available to secured creditors.

If it is the debtor's decision to file a bankruptcy petition, the bankruptcy is said to be *voluntary*. Creditors can also force a debtor into a Chapter 7 or Chapter 11 bankruptcy by filing an *involuntary* petition. Twelve or more creditors can file an involuntary petition if any three or more of those creditors together hold a debt of $11,625. If there are fewer than 12 creditors, anyone holding a debt can file. These amounts are adjusted periodically according to

automatic stay: A stay that comes into operation upon the filing of a bankruptcy petition in accordance with bankruptcy law that prevents creditors from attempting to collect from the debtor for debts incurred before the filing.

the Consumer Price Index. Creditors may choose to file an involuntary petition for a variety of reasons. One of the most common is the fear that the debtor is preferring some creditors over others and, by filing the involuntary petition, the debtor will have to pay the creditors in the order set out by the Bankruptcy Code. Farmers and charitable corporations cannot be forced into bankruptcy.

FIRST MEETING OF THE CREDITORS

Each creditor listed in the schedules is notified by the bankruptcy court that a petition has been filed. The creditors are then invited to a first meeting of the creditors in which they have the opportunity to question the debtor. The questions usually concern the location of collateral and whether the debtor intends to pay the debt.

PROOF OF CLAIM

Since the petition schedules list all the creditors, each creditor receives a notice of the filing. The notice asks each creditor to file a *proof of claim*, which states the amount of the debt that is due. It also states whether the debt is an unsecured, secured, or a priority. If it is secured, the creditor has to file documentation of the security interest.

PRIORITY DEBTS

Some debts are labeled *priority* debts which are paid before any other debts. The bankruptcy code lists the following order for payment of priority debts: (1) administrative expenses (like court costs); (2) GAP creditors (these are unsecured creditors whose debt arises in the ordinary course of doing business after the involuntary commencement of a petition and before the appointment of a trustee; usually GAP creditors are utility companies, like power, water, and telephone); (3) wages, salaries, and commissions owed to employees up to $4,650 per employee and occurring within 90 days before the petition is filed or cessation of the debtor's business; (4) some payments to benefit plans; (5) money owed to grain producers and fishing professionals up to $4,650; (6) consumer goods that were ordered and paid for but were not delivered, up to $2,100 (7) alimony, maintenance, and child support; and (8) some tax claims. Secured creditors are entitled to a return of their collateral. All other debts are unsecured.

THE BANKRUPTCY ESTATE

The bankruptcy estate includes all of the debtor's assets that exist on the date the petition is filed. It also includes anything the debtor acquires within 180 days after the petition is filed and any item that was in the estate 90 days before the petition was filed. Anything transferred out of the estate within 90 days before the petition is filed is known as a *preferential transfer* and may have to be returned to the estate by the person to whom the transfer was made. Anything transferred to a creditor classified as an insider within one year of filing bankruptcy is also considered preferential and is included in the estate. Fraudulent transfers are also preferential. For example, Sue transfers the title to her house to her daughter, Kay, on August 1 and files a bankruptcy petition on December 1. Since Kay is Sue's daughter, the transfer is preferential, and the house is included in the bankruptcy estate since the transfer occurred within the one-year time frame.

Some transfers are not considered preferential even though they occur within the 90-day period. The first is referred to as *contemporaneous exchange for new value*. For example, on January 2, Jeff goes into Fred's Store and purchases an overcoat for $300. On January 15, Fred's files a bankruptcy petition. Jeff does not need to return the overcoat since he bought the overcoat and paid for it at the same time. It is assumed that the money paid is now part of the estate. The second exception is for payment of accounts in the ordinary course of business. Fred's paid its light bill 15 days before the petition was filed. The utility company will not have to return the money since the debt was incurred in the ordinary course of business. The third exception is the PMSI discussed previously, as long as it is perfected within 10 days. Perfected security interests for new value, as well as transfers of less than $600 on consumer debts, are also exempted from the preferential transfer rule. A court recently ruled that contributions made to a church (i.e., tithe) within the 90-day period were considered preferential and had to be returned to the estate.

EXEMPTIONS

Several items are exempt from the bankruptcy estate. Federal exemptions exist, or each state can choose to use its own exemptions. A majority of the states have chosen to have their own exemptions, although most are similar to the federal exemption. If an item is exempt from the bankruptcy proceeding, it is not included as part of the bankruptcy estate. The federal exemptions include the following:

1. Up to $21,625 of equity in a home (homestead exemption) and burial plot.
2. Up to $3,450 equity in an automobile.
3. Up to $550 for each item of ordinary household furnishings and clothing. The total value cannot exceed $11,525.
4. Up to $1,450 in jewelry.
5. Up to $2,175 in books and tools used in the debtor's trade.
6. Any other property up to $1,150, plus up to $10,825 of any unused amount in the homestead exception, not including the house.
7. Unmatured life insurance contract owned by debtor.
8. Certain rights in pension, profit sharing, and annuity plans, including Social Security, veterans, disability benefits, and alimony and child support.
9. Tax exempt retirement funds.
10. Up to $21,625 in payments from an award in a personal injury lawsuit.

DISCHARGE

Once the court issues its final order, the debtor is **discharged** from paying the debts. Discharges are only available to individuals; businesses must liquidate or reorganize. Also, certain debts are not dischargeable. For example, a

discharge: To release a debtor in bankruptcy from liability for his or her debt.

discharge is not allowed if fraud is present, the debt was incurred because the debtor willfully injured someone (an intentional tort, discussed in Chapter 11), or there has been an earlier discharge within six years. Government-secured student loans cannot be discharged, absent hardship, nor can alimony and child support payments. Certain tax and custom duties cannot be discharged, nor can debts that are not listed with the bankruptcy court. Further, a debtor cannot load up. Loading up occurs when the debtor buys, on credit, luxury goods over $600 from one creditor within 90 days of filing the petition or takes over a $875 cash advance within 70 days of filing the petition. These debts are also nondischargeable. Also, a discharge can be revoked if it is later discovered that the debtor committed fraud during the bankruptcy proceedings. As the next case suggests, questions about discharging debts continue to arise.

In the Language of the Court

IN THE MATTER OF: JONATHON R. GERHARDT

348 F.3d 89 (5th Cir. 2003)

OPINION:

Circuit Judge Edith H. Jones delivered the court's opinion.

Over a period of years, Jonathon Gerhardt obtained over $77,000 in government-insured student loans to finance his education at the University of Southern California, the Eastman School of Music, the University of Rochester, and the New England Conservatory of Music. Gerhardt is a professional cellist. He subsequently defaulted on each loan owed to the United States Government.

In 1999, Gerhardt filed for Chapter 7 bankruptcy and thereafter filed an adversary proceeding seeking discharge of his student loans pursuant to 11 U.S.C. §523(a)(8). The bankruptcy court discharged Gerhardt's student loans as causing undue hardship. On appeal, the district court reversed, holding that it would not be an undue hardship for Gerhardt to repay his student loans. Finding no error, we affirm the district court's judgment.

I. STANDARD OF REVIEW

We review the decision of a district court, sitting as an appellate court, by applying the same standards of review to the bankruptcy court's findings of fact and conclusions of law

as applied by the district court. Generally, a bankruptcy court's findings of fact are reviewed for clear error and conclusions of law are reviewed de novo.

Whether courts review the "undue hardship" determination de novo is a matter of first impression in this circuit. A number of our sister circuits have confronted this precise issue, determining that the dischargeability decision is a question of law subject to de novo review. Similarly, this court has held that determining dischargeability of a debt arising from a willful and malicious injury under 11 U.S.C. §523(a)(6) is a question of law subject to de novo review. The decision to discharge Gerhardt's debts represents a conclusion regarding the legal effect of the bankruptcy court's factual findings as to his circumstances. Thus, the district court correctly applied de novo review to the bankruptcy court's dischargeability holding, and this court applies the same standard on appeal.

II. UNDUE HARDSHIP TEST

This circuit has not explicitly articulated the appropriate test with which to evaluate the undue hardship determination. The Second Circuit in *Brunner* crafted the most widely-adopted test. To justify discharging the debtor's student loans, the *Brunner* test requires a three-part showing:

> (1) that the debtor cannot maintain, based on current income and expenses, a "minimal" standard of living for [himself] and [his] dependents if forced to repay the loans; (2) that additional circumstances exist indicating that this state of affairs is likely to persist for a significant portion of the repayment period of the student loans; and (3) that the debtor has made good faith efforts to repay the loans.

Because the Second Circuit presented a workable approach to evaluating the "undue hardship" determination, this court expressly adopts the *Brunner* test for purposes of evaluating a Section 523(a)(8) decision.

A. Minimal Standard of Living

Under the first prong of the *Brunner* test, the bankruptcy court determined that Gerhardt could not maintain a minimal standard of living if forced to repay his student loans. Evidence was produced at trial that Gerhardt earned $1,680.47 per month as the principal cellist for the Louisiana Philharmonic Orchestra ("LPO"), including a small amount of supplemental income earned as a cello teacher for Tulane University. His monthly expenses, which included a health club membership and internet access, averaged $1,829.39. The bankruptcy court's factual findings are not clearly erroneous. Consequently, we agree with the bankruptcy court's conclusion of law, which we review de novo, that flows from these factual findings. Given that Gerhardt's monthly expenses exceed his monthly income, he has no ability at the present time to maintain a minimal standard of living if forced to repay his loans.

B. Persisting State of Affairs

The second prong of the *Brunner* test asks if "additional circumstances exist indicating that this state of affairs is likely to persist [for a significant period of time]." "Additional circumstances" encompass "circumstances that impacted on the debtor's future earning potential but which [were] either not present when the debtor[] applied for the loans or [have] since been exacerbated. This second aspect of the test is meant to be "a demanding requirement." Thus, proving that the debtor is "currently in financial straits" is not enough. Instead, the debtor must specifically prove "a total incapacity . . . in the future to pay [his] debts for reasons not within [his] control."

Under the second prong of the test, the district court correctly concluded that Gerhardt has not established persistent undue hardship entitling him to discharge his student loans. Gerhardt holds a masters degree in music from the New England Conservatory of Music. He is about 43 years old, healthy, well-educated, and has no dependents, yet has repaid only $ 755 of his over $77,000 debt. During the LPO's off-seasons, Gerhardt has collected unemployment, but he has somehow managed to attend the Colorado Music Festival. Although trial testimony tended to show that Gerhardt would likely not obtain a position at a higher-paying orchestra, he could obtain additional steady employment in a number of different arenas. For instance, he could attempt to teach full-time, obtain night-school teaching jobs, or even work as a music store clerk. Thus, no reasons out of Gerhardt's control exist that perpetuate his inability to repay his student loans.

In addition, nothing in the Bankruptcy Code suggests that a debtor may choose to work only in the field in which he was trained, obtain a low-paying job, and then claim that it would be an undue hardship to repay his student loans. Under the facts presented by Gerhardt, it is difficult to imagine a professional orchestra musician who would not qualify for an undue hardship discharge. Accordingly, Gerhardt "has failed to demonstrate the type of exceptional circumstances that are necessary in order to meet [his] burden under the second prong" of

Brunner. Finding no error, the judgment of the district court is **AFFIRMED.**

CASE QUESTIONS

1. Under what circumstances could you imagine the undue hardship defense being accepted by a bankruptcy court?
2. Why should some debts be dischargeable and others not dischargeable?
3. Do you agree with the Court in this case?

SUMMARY

As you can see, the process of borrowing and lending money is complicated. The rights of debtors and creditors are the subject of several pieces of legislation both at the state and federal level. Consumers are protected against discrimination in the Equal Credit Opportunity Act. They are protected against unscrupulous business practices with the FCRA, UCCC, FCBA, FDCPA, and Truth in Lending Act.

Creditors who use collateral for their loans are able to repossess the collateral in the event of default using the law of mortgages or the law of secured transactions. Finally, the bankruptcy laws attempt to balance the rights of both creditors and debtors when the debtor gets into financial trouble.

CHAPTER QUESTIONS

1. Mr. and Mrs. Gutierrez watched a TV infomercial proclaiming the advantages of automobile leasing which included no down payment and low monthly rates. Based on the infomercial, the Gutierrez' leased an automobilie. The down payment and monthly payments turned out to be substantially higher than the infomercial indicated. Further, on the back of the lease agreement and in small print (which neither Gutierrez read) was a mandatory arbitration clause. The clause required lessees to pay an administrative fee in order to use arbitration. The Guiteirz did not have the financial resources to pay the fee. Is the contract unconscionable? Why or why not? [See *Guitierrez v. Autowest*, 114 Cal. App. 4th 77 (2003).]

2. Michelle entered into an employment agreement with Jack, who obtained a credit report on her from Acxiom Information Security Services, Inc., without her written consent. Jack relied upon the credit report, which contained inaccurate information indicating that she had been convicted of a crime of dishonesty, to terminate Michelle's employment. Michelle filed a lawsuit against Jack, claiming violation of the Fair Credit Reporting Act. How should the court rule? [See *Lagrassa v. Gaughen, LLC.*, 2011 WL 1257384 (M.D.Pa.).]

3. Wollenberg agreed to sell his business to Mays. As part of the sale of the business, Wollenberg took a promissory note and security agreement in lieu of full payment. The security agreement gave Wollenberg a security interest in the company's accounts receivable. Mays told Wollenberg that he was going to immediately transfer the business into his corporate entity, Sunrise Security. Wollenberg filed a financing statement naming only Mays as the debtor. Later, Phoenix Leasing agreed to loan Sunrise Security $150,000 and took a security interest in Sunrise Security's accounts receivable. Phoenix checked the state filings and did not find a prior financing statement on Sunrise Security. It was unaware of the security agreement with Wollenberg. Sunrise defaulted on both the Wollenberg and Phoenix Leasing Loans. Who has priority? [See *Wollenberg and Wollenberg v. Phoenix Leasing*, 182 Ariz. 4; 893 P.2d 4; 1994 Ariz. App. LEXIS 180 (1994).]

4. Andy is a guitarist. He buys a guitar from MusicVille on January 10. The cost of the guitar is $1,000. Andy agrees to pay $150 a month. MusicVille receives a security interest and files its financing statement on January 17. Meanwhile, Andy borrows $1,000 from Equity Security on January 11. He gives Equity Security a security interest in the same guitar and Equity Security files a financing statement on January 12. On January 16, Andy also borrows $1,000 from his friend Beth. Beth receives a security interest in Andy's guitar and takes possession of it on the same day. Andy defaults on every loan. Discuss the legal ramifications.

5. Martha, age 60, and Jay, age 62, are married and want to buy a new home. They want to use a 30-year mortgage to finance the purchase. Both are gainfully employed and can easily afford the monthly payments. Can the lending institution deny the loan?

6. Commonwealth was a debt collection agency that sent automated form letters when a consumer "bounced" a check at a retail establishment. The form letter included a threat that Commonwealth would bring a lawsuit against the debtor. Some letters even included a sample complaint. In fact, Commonwealth never intended to sue any consumers for the bounced checks. Is this letter legal? [See *Irwin et al. v. Commonwealth Equity Adjustments*, 370 F.3d 924 (9th Cir. 2004).]

7. Jonathan LeBahn had an ownership interest in a figure eight race car built from a late 1970s or early 1980s Chevy. Other debtors also worked on the race car and had an interest in the race car. The race car was located in LeBahn's garage when he filed the bankruptcy petition but it did not have all of its parts. Neither the car nor the parts were listed on the bankruptcy schedule. LeBahn received a discharge. Creditors found out about the race car and sought to have the discharge revoked. What result? [See *U.S. Trustee v. LeBahn*, 2004 Bankr. Lexis 363.]

8. Malcolm filed a Chapter 7 bankruptcy petition but did not include a $70,000 residence that he shared with his wife. Is the residence part of the bankruptcy estate? You may want to go back to Chapter 14 and determine if the manner in which the property is owned changes the outcome. [See *In re: Bonnie May Soears, In re: Michael J. Sedgwick., In re: Ronnie Lynn Gillis, In re: Roger Alan Brehm*, 308 B.R. 793; 2004 Bankr. LEXIS 558.

9. Edward Cohen owned several rental properties in New Jersey that were subject to rent control. He violated the rent control provisions and was found liable under New Jersey law for fraudulently obtaining $31,382.50 in rent payments. Under New Jersey law he was also liable for treble damages and attorneys' fees. He subsequently filed for Chapter 7 relief and asked that the debt be discharged. The tenants filed an action in bankruptcy court arguing that the debt payments owed to them were "obtained by actual fraud." Can the debt be discharged in Bankruptcy Court? [See *Cohen v. De La Cruz*, 1998 U.S. Lexis 2119]

10. Attorney Michael Margelefsky operated two separate businesses, a law practice and a debt collection agency. In January 2005, Amanda Kistner received a collection letter printed on the letterhead of "The Law Offices of Michael Margelefsky." The letter stated that "This communication is from a debt collector" and instructed Kistner to pay the amount she owed in a check made out to Michael P. Margelefsky and to mail it to his law office address. It was signed "account representative." Kistner filed a lawsuit against Margelefsky, claiming that the letter violated the Fair Debt Collection Practices Act which prohibits debt collectors from creating "[t]he false representation or implication that any individual is an attorney or that any communication is from an attorney." Margelefsky argued that he had no personal involvement in sending the letter, and that the phrase "account representative" should have led Kistner to believe that the letter was sent by a debt collector rather than an attorney. Did the letter violate the FDCPA? [See *Kistner v. Law Offices of Michael P. Margelefsky, LLC*, 518 F.3d 433 (6th Cir. 2008).]

PRACTICAL EXERCISE

Zinna is a new business involved in manufacturing and selling golf clubs to large retail stores as well as to small golf shops. However, Zinna has been having trouble getting customers to pay for its clubs before they are delivered. Most of Zinna's sales are now made on open account, and the customer is given 30 days to pay for the delivered golf clubs. Zinna wants to be able to repossess the golf clubs if its customers fail to pay the account in 30 days.

1. What type of questions can and should Zinna ask on a credit application before it allows customers to use an open account? Draft a credit application that could also be used as a security agreement and still comply with Truth in Lending.

2. What steps can Zinna take in order to ensure that its customers are good credit risks?

3. What steps does Zinna need to take to ensure that it can repossess the golf clubs in the event a customer defaults?

4. Draft additional appropriate documents necessary to create a perfected security interest.

5. Obtain from a local merchant a copy of a security agreement. Interview the manager to determine how important such filings are to the business' sale volume. Summarize the interview.

Your instructor may want you to check your local state law to determine what interest rate you can charge on past due accounts, what finance charges you can use on past due accounts, and what documents are necessary to perfect a security interest in golf clubs in your state.

FURTHER INFORMATION

www.abiworld.org/
www.creditpage.com/
www.pueblo.gsa.gov/money.htm
www.law.cornell.edu/ucc/ucc.table.html

CHAPTER 19

UNFAIR AND DECEPTIVE TRADE PRACTICES AND ADVERTISING

After you have read this chapter, you should be able to:

1. Describe how the Federal Trade Commission (FTC) operates.
2. Identify several types of deceptive trade practices.
3. Explain the difference between federal and common law protections.
4. Discuss the regulations affecting advertising.

Phil wants to open a business to help individuals lose weight. He wants to advertise his "weight loss" plan on the Internet as well as solicit potential customers by telephone. What does Phil need to know about deceptive advertising before he begins?

INTRODUCTION

Consumers are constantly bombarded with marketing ploys aimed at convincing them to purchase one product over another. Marketing means more than simply advertising a product for sale. One need only watch college football bowl games, underwritten by corporate sponsors totally unrelated to collegiate athletics, to understand how multifaceted marketing has become.

In a market economy, marketing is a fact of doing business. It is the process by which consumers are introduced to businesses and their products. Even though marketing has become commonplace, it is not without its critics. Popular opinion polls reflect the fact that the general public does not hold business, especially big business, in high esteem. Much of this perception results from highly publicized events in which some businesses have been less than honest in their advertising. One need only look at the profusion of "cure-alls," "special potions," "magic pills," con artists, and swindlers to understand why consumers may be skeptical. Unfortunately, legitimate businesses have also been known to deceive customers. When consumers are deceived, they often have very little real power as individuals against large business organizations that simply can ignore their complaints.

FEDERAL TRADE COMMISSION

During the Progressive Period (1880–1920) in U.S. history, and at the urging of President Woodrow Wilson, Congress in 1914 passed the *Federal Trade Commission Act*. Its main goal was to shore up the remedies provided under earlier antitrust legislation, most notably the Sherman and Clayton Acts discussed in Chapter 17. Under the Federal Trade Commission Act, Congress established the *Federal Trade Commission (FTC)* in 1915. The FTC is an independent, bipartisan agency governed by five members called *commissioners*. (Independent agencies are discussed in Chapter 5.) The President appoints the members to the Commission, the Senate confirms them, and each member serves a term of seven years. No more than three members of the commission may be members of the same political party. The Federal Trade Commission Act gives the FTC several powers, including, under §5, the authority to issue rules that define unfair methods of competition, as well as additional authority established by subsequent legislation.

In 1938, the *Wheeler-Lea Act* amended the 1914 Act. Wheeler-Lea prohibited deceptive trade practices as well as unfair methods of competition. In 1973, the *Alaska Pipeline Act* amended the FTC Act by increasing the penalties for violating FTC-issued **cease and desist orders**. A cease and desist order, like an injunction, prohibits a company from continuing a deceptive act or practice. If the FTC finds that a violation has occurred, a cease and desist order requires that the violator completely stop the unlawful activity. The FTC can impose a fine of $25,000 for each day that a cease and desist order is violated. The Act also allows for injunctive relief, and the FTC can impose fines of up to $10,000 per violation. The FTC can require that the violator pay damages to anyone whom the deceptive act has harmed, and that the violator rescind a contract that violates the Act. The *FTC Improvement Act*, another amendment to the FTC Act passed in 1975,

> **cease and desist order:** An order from an administrative agency to stop engaging in a particular activity.

gives the FTC even more power. For example, it allows the FTC to impose fines for violating trade rules.

The FTC issues *trade practices*, which are industry-specific guides. They set out, in ordinary language, what acts and practices of a particular industry are deceptive or unfair. For example, in the jewelry industry a specific rule provides for when the term *pearl* may be used. The trade practice rule states:

> It is unfair or deceptive to use the word "pearl" to describe, identify, or refer to a cultured pearl unless it is immediately preceded, with equal conspicuousness, by the word "cultured" or "cultivated," or by some other word or phrase of like meaning, so as to indicate definitely and clearly that the product is not a pearl. 16 C.F.R. sec. 23.19(b).

The FTC also has the power to issue *trade regulation rules*. These rules define and interpret specific acts the FTC determines to be unfair competition and deceptive trade practices. The difference between trade practice rules and trade regulation rules lies in what burden of proof is necessary to prove a violation. If a company is charged with violating a trade regulation rule, the FTC need only show that the rule was violated. On the other hand, a violation of a trade practice rule requires a showing that the committed act itself was unfair or deceptive. Although the distinction is technical, the result is that it is easier for the FTC to prove violations of trade regulation rules than it is to show violations of trade practice rules.

Under the Federal Trade Commission Act, the FTC has the authority to investigate actions that it believes are violations. The FTC may receive a complaint by a competitor, another government agency, or a consumer. The FTC may or may not decide to investigate the complaint to determine if a violation has occurred. The Federal Trade Commission Act does not allow an individual to bring a private lawsuit against a violator, nor does it require the FTC to independently initiate an investigation. Rather, if someone believes that the Act has been violated, he or she must file a complaint with the FTC. The FTC determines an act is deceptive if it has the "potential to **mislead**" a reasonable consumer, and the deception would likely affect the consumer's decision. The fact that a single consumer is deceived may not mean the action is **deceptive**. Rather, the FTC looks at consumer research data and economic analysis to determine whether "reasonable consumers" were deceived. Some states allows a consumer to bring an action in state court if he or she has been deceived.

misleading: Possessing the capacity or tendency to create a mistaken impression.

deceptive: Tending to or having the capacity to cause to accept as true something that is false.

SOCIAL/ETHICAL ISSUES

Since the Federal Trade Commission Act does not allow an injured person, either consumer or creditor, to file a lawsuit against a violator, some have argued that no real penalty exists for running deceptive advertising, especially if the company is small and local. There is little likelihood that the FTC would use its limited resources to go against anyone other than very large businesses. Do you agree with this argument? Should enforcement depend on the size of the company being sued?

One of the FTC's major weapons is the authority to require a violator to run corrective advertising. The FTC can require that a violator spend up to 25 percent of its budget on corrective advertising, although the actual dollar amount imposed varies.

NOVARTIS V. F.T.C.

223 F.3d 783 (2000)

FACTS

Novartis manufactures the over-the-counter back pain product known as Doan's Pills. Doan's Pills have been marketed for ninety years. Novartis conducted a marketing study which found, "Doan's has a weak image in comparison to the leading brands of analgesics and would benefit from positioning itself as a more effective product that is strong enough for the types of backaches sufferers usually get." Based on the study, Novartis engaged in an aggressive advertising campaign from May 1988 to June 1996. The television and newspaper advertisements suggested that Doan's had a special ingredient not found in other back pain medicines and was therefore more effective. The FTC filed a complaint alleging that the ad contained unsubstantiated claims. The ALJ found that Novartis's advertisements of its Doan's back pain remedies were deceptive because the claims were unsubstantiated, but rejected the FTC's request for corrective advertising, finding the remedy to be too "drastic." The Commission upheld the finding of deceptiveness but reversed the corrective advertising directive, concluding that it was warranted because the ads created a misbelief about the effectiveness of the product that was likely to continue. Novartis appealed both the finding of deception and the Commission's order of corrective advertising.

DECISION

The Court found that the information presented in the advertisements was false.

Several studies show that efficacy is important to consumers in making decisions about pain relief. Claims about superior efficacy were found to be highly material. On the issue of whether corrective advertising was an appropriate remedy, the Court looked at the test in *Warner-Lambert Co. v. FTC,* 183 U.S. App. D.C. 230 (D.C. Cir. 1977) (the Listerine case). According to the court, there are two questions that need to be answered, "(1) did [respondent's] advertisements play a substantial role in creating or reinforcing in the public's mind a false belief about the product? and (2) would this belief linger on after the false advertising ceases?" As to the first question, two studies found that Doan users and nonusers believed that Doan's was more effective for back pain relief than other over-the-counter drugs. The Court also found that these beliefs were likely to linger since a study conducted six months after the advertisements ended showed a disproportionately high percentage of consumers still believed the claims. The Court upheld the Commission's decision and reversed the decision of the ALJ on the corrective advertising issue.

CASE QUESTIONS

1. Novartis also claimed that corrective advertising violated the First Amendment. How should the court respond to this claim?
2. Should the FTC order a time limit on running ads or order a dollar amount? Why?
3. Do you believe the claims made in advertisements? Why or why not?

COMMON LAW PROTECTIONS

Since the FTC does not allow for a private right of action, some injured parties choose to file civil lawsuits to collect money damages. Consumers injured by deceptive acts and practices can file lawsuits based on the tort claims of fraud by misrepresentation, using the same *prima facie* case as discussed in Chapter 11. Injured competitors can file common law tort claims based on trade disparagement, trade defamation, and trademark infringement. *Trade disparagement* occurs when untrue statements are made about a product and the competitor suffers financial loss. A competitor claiming *trade defamation* need not show financial loss but does need to show that a false statement was made that was damaging to its business reputation in general rather than damaging to one of its products in particular. *Trademark infringement* is also known as *passing* or *palming off*. This occurs when a competitor can show that the consumer is likely to be confused as to who is sponsoring the product. For example, "Enjoy Coca-Cola" was transposed on a poster to read "Enjoy Cocaine." The court held that the poster manufacturer was passing off, since consumers may believe that Coca-Cola was engaged in an advertising gimmick. On the other hand, when the scout motto "Be Prepared" was placed on a picture of a pregnant girl in a girl scout uniform, that court held that the consumer would not be misled into thinking that the "wholesome" Girl Scout organization would sponsor such a poster.

NATIONAL ADVERTISING DIVISION

Another entity addressing deceptive advertising is a self-policing entity known as the *National Advertising Division (NAD)*, the advertising industry's self-regulatory body. It was formed by the American Association of Advertising Agencies, American Advertising Federation, Association of National Advertisers, and the Council for Better Business Bureaus. Consumers, competitors, and consumer groups can file complaints with NAD. If an advertiser disagrees with a NAD decision, the advertiser can appeal the decision to the *National Advertising Review Board (NARB)*. If an ad is found to be deceptive, NAD generally requires the ad to be substantiated, modified, or discontinued. Advertisements that are modified or discontinued are reported to the public. NAD's decisions are not legally binding, and a complainant cannot receive financial compensation. However, advertisers participating in NAD investigations tend to abide by the NAD decision.

LABELING

Never before has the need to properly label a product been so important. Early legislation, such as the *Wool Products Labeling Act*, the *Textile Fiber Products Identification Act*, the *Fur Products Labeling Act*, and the *Flammable Fabrics Act,* required certain products to be properly labeled. The FTC, under the 1966 *Fair Packaging and Labeling Act*, now has the power to issue labeling regulations in all areas. Further, the *Food and Drug Administration (FDA)* and the U.S. Department of Agriculture are charged with overhauling food labeling and promotion under the *1990 Nutrition Labeling and Education Act*. As a result of this act, almost all products are now required to contain nutritional labeling. The Act exempts fresh meat, which is regulated by the U.S. Department of Agriculture, but cheese, peanut butter, and other foods high in fat must comply. All regulated products must now have nutrition labels that indicate the amount of cholesterol, sodium, and grams of fat contained in each serving size. Further, new labeling guidelines require packages to indicate true serving sizes. For example, is a 12-ounce can of soda really two servings? Is a true serving of potato chips 10 chips? These and other serving claims come under the scrutiny of the FDA. Also, the FDA looks at the use of terms like "healthy," "cholesterol free," and "lite" as those that might be considered deceptive. In 2009, the Act was amended to require labels on fresh meat and vegetables to indicate where the food originated.

The following article describes a recent case regarding food labeling which many claimed was an example of a frivolous lawsuit.

McDonald's Obesity Suit Tossed

U.S. judge says complaint fails to prove chain is responsible for kids' weight gain.

NEW YORK (CNN)—A lawsuit alleging food from McDonald's restaurants is responsible for making people obese got thrown out by a federal judge Wednesday.

The landmark legal action was the first of its kind against a fast-food chain to make its way into a U.S. courtroom.

McDonald's spokesman Walt Riker said that common sense had prevailed in the suit. "We said from the beginning that this was a frivolous lawsuit. Today's ruling confirms that fact."

Although he dismissed the suit, Judge Robert Sweet granted the plaintiffs the option of filing an amended complaint within 30 days addressing the problems that Sweet found in the plaintiffs' original arguments.

Sweet said some of the arguments could be compelling if addressed in more depth, including the allegation that the processing of McDonald's food makes it more dangerous than a customer would have reason to expect.

"If plaintiffs were able to flesh out this argument in an amended complaint, it may establish that the dangers of McDonald's products were not commonly well known and thus that McDonald's had a duty towards its customers," Sweet wrote.

In the current suit, he said, no such hidden dangers are shown.

"Where should the line be drawn between an individual's own responsibility to take care of herself and society's responsibility to ensure others shield her? The complaint fails to allege the McDonald's products consumed by the plaintiffs were dangerous in any way other than that which was open and obvious to a reasonable consumer," Sweet said in his ruling.

Samuel Hirsch, the plaintiff's attorney, remained defiant. In a written statement his law firm said, "the plaintiffs are very pleased with the decision and have every intention of amending their complaint and refiling it in the federal court in the next 30 days."

"Contrary to what many may think," said Hirsch in a telephone interview with CNN, "we are not looking to get rich from a large money settlement. We are proposing a fund that will educate children about the nutritional facts and contents of McDonald's food."

McDonald's (MCD: Research, Estimates) attorneys warned that if this case were allowed to proceed "it would lead to an avalanche of litigation."

"Every responsible person understands what is in products such as hamburgers and fries, as well as the consequence to one's waistline, and potentially to one's health, of excessively eating those foods over a prolonged period of time," said the food chain's lawyers.

In August, a suit filed by the parents of two girls claimed that McDonald's and two of its restaurants in the Bronx failed to disclose clearly and conspicuously the ingredients and effects of its food, much of which is high in fat, salt, sugar and cholesterol.

The plaintiffs argued that McDonald's should therefore be held accountable for the girls' obesity, heart disease, diabetes, high blood pressure, and elevated cholesterol.

The girls are Jazlyn Bradley and Ashley Pelman. Bradley, 19, is 5 feet, 6 inches tall, and weighs 270 pounds. Pelman, 14, is 4-foot-10 and 170 pounds.

Bradley said that a McMuffin for breakfast and a Big Mac meal for dinner was her regular diet. Pelman preferred the Happy Meals and used to eat at McDonald's three or four times a week.

Bradley's father, Israel, said he never saw anything in the Bronx restaurants that informed him of the food's ingredients. "I always believed McDonald's was healthy for my children," he said in an affidavit.

Samuel Hirsch, the lawyer bringing the case, called McDonald's food "physically or psychologically addictive." Hirsch accused the company of deliberately withholding information and targeting children. The effects of its food on people's health were "a very insipid, toxic kind of thing," Hirsch said.

Hirsch also was critical of McDonald's billion-dollar advertising campaign. "Young individuals are not in a position to make a choice after the onslaught of advertising and promotions," Hirsch contended.

McDonald's lawyers added it would be impossible to establish whether eating at McDonald's was a major cause of the girls' ailments. Genetics, medical conditions and sedentary lifestyles could also be factors, they said.

Judge Sweet's ruling dampens the hopes of fellow New Yorker Caesar Barber. Barber, 56, filed a suit in July against McDonald's, Wendy's, Kentucky Fried Chicken and Burger King. The 272-pound Bronx resident alleged that their food caused his obesity, two heart attacks and diabetes.

A McDonald's spokesman in the United States told CNN in a telephone interview that "this is one person's opinion. Eating McDonald's food can easily fit into a balanced diet. I eat its food every day and I'm perfectly healthy."

Source: Jonathan Wald, CNN Money.com http://money.cnn.com/2003/01/22/news/companies/mcdonalds/. February 17, 2003.

Food labeling has also become an international issue.

> ## INTERNATIONAL ISSUES
>
> The European Union requires that all bioengineered food be labeled. In particular, foods made with corn and soybean are especially at risk since most strands have been modified to make them more disease resistant. Even though genetically modified foods have not been shown to pose any health risk, European countries, reeled by 'mad cow' disease, are not taking any chances. Whether this trend will move to the United States and other countries have yet to be seen. What do you think? Should we require bioengineered food to be labeled in the United States?

DECEPTIVE ACTS AND PRACTICES

Although all deceptive acts and practices are illegal, some practices have been specifically identified as inherently deceptive.

PYRAMID SALES SCHEMES

A **pyramid sales scheme** is a type of sales pitch that promises that once a person buys an item, that person gets paid for each additional buyer he or she finds for the company. It is also called multilevel distributorship, chain referral plan, or referral sales plan. The FTC has determined that many forms of pyramid schemes are deceptive acts and practices and are therefore illegal. One of the reasons that such schemes are usually deceptive is that the plan's promoters do not reveal the nature of the plan. Often, the plan is sold as a way to make a lot of money without actually working. In a true pyramid scheme, a person makes money by bringing other individuals into the plan, and that person receives money when those that he or she brought in brings others into the plan. For example, Patty approaches you with a great deal. You pay her $50, and then you recruit two other people into the plan, who each pay you $50. Sounds great! What makes it deceptive, however (besides the question of why pay Patty $50, when you can just ask for $50 from two other unsuspecting "friends"), is that, mathematically, it is impossible for very many people to make money. For example, if there are 7 promoters of the plan and each of the 7 promoters bring in 7 investors, and then those 49 investors each bring in 7 investors, it brings the number of investors to 343. If the pattern continues, eventually the total number exceeds over 2 billion people. By the 12th level you need more people than are alive in the world to continue to make money. The difference between legal and illegal pyramid schemes is sometimes difficult to determine. The key fact is a determination as to what is actually being sold. If it is the "scheme" that is being sold and an individual is rewarded based on the number of recruits brought into the scheme, then the pyramid is illegal. If the individual is rewarded by product sales and the sales goals are not unrealistic, then the pyramid may be legal. This difficulty is discussed in the next FTC case.

pyramid sales scheme: A scheme in which participants give money or other valuables in exchange for the opportunity to receive payment for recruiting others to participate in the scheme.

IN THE MATTER OF AMWAY CORPORATION, INC. ET AL.

93 F.T.C. 618 (1979)

FACTS

Amway manufactures over 150 products including soaps, detergents, polishes, cleaning supplies, and pharmaceutical preparations. Amway is relatively small when compared with other industry giants. Without large advertising budgets, it is almost impossible to enter this field. "Amway skirted these near-insurmountable barriers and interjected a vigorous new competitive presence into this highly concentrated market by developing what is known as a 'direct selling' distribution network."

Amway sells its products through 360,000 independent distributors, who work through Amway's multilevel distributor system. Under the Amway Plan, a select few distributors, known as direct distributors, purchase products at wholesale directly from Amway and resell the products both at retail to consumers and at wholesale to the distributors they personally "sponsored." Each second-level distributor resells the products both at retail to consumers and at wholesale to the distributors he or she personally sponsored. The third-level distributors perform the same two functions. This multilevel wholesaling network ends with those distributors who have not sponsored any new distributors and who make purchases from their sponsors solely for their own use or for resale to consumers. Distributors earn money by making retail sales themselves and/or by receiving a percentage of their business volume. This computes in the following manner. The direct distributor is paid 25 cents by Amway on each dollar of business volume but only pays 15 cents to second-level distributors on each dollar of the respective business volumes. The direct distributor would net a 25-cent bonus

on each dollar of business volume representing retail sales made by him or her to consumers and a 10-cent bonus on each dollar of business volume representing wholesale sales made by the sponsored distributors. Second-level distributors do the same to third-level distributors and so forth down the line. A person can become a direct distributor by being a very high-volume performer.

In 1975, the FTC charged Amway Corporation with violating §5 of the Federal Trade Commission Act, alleging that Amway's method of conducting business was an illegal pyramid scheme. All of the violations involved Amway's distribution network. The Administrative Law Judge (ALJ) found that Amway "had engaged in illegal resale price maintenance but had failed to establish that respondents had committed other violations of §5."

DECISION

The Commission has defined an illegal pyramid scheme as the "payment of money to the company in return for which they receive (1) the right to sell a product and (2) the right to receive in return for recruiting other participants into the program rewards which are unrelated to sale of the product to ultimate users." "The Amway plan does not contain [these] essential features . . . and therefore, it is not a scheme which is inherently false, misleading, or deceptive."

Amway has several rules that encourage retail sales: (1) a new distributor is required to spend $15.60 for a sales kit, and the purchase price can be refunded if the person decides to leave; (2) a " buy-back" rule requires sponsoring distributors to buy back any unused merchandise from a sponsoring distributor who is leaving the organization; (3) before a distributor receives the performance bonus, the 70-percent rule (requiring distributors to sell at wholesale or retail 70 percent of the products bought during the month) and the 10-customer rule (the distributor must sell products to 10 different customers during the month) must be satisfied. All of these rules make "retail selling an essential part of being a distributor." "Specifically, the Amway Plan is not a plan where participants purchase the right to earn profits by recruiting other participants, who themselves are interested in recruitment fees rather than the sale of products."

Finally, Amway was charged with making misrepresentations and omissions concerning unrealistic earnings or sales claims. The first category of claims can fall under the heading of "non-earning." These claims consist of "vague references to the achievement of one's dreams, having everything one always wanted, and so on," are phrased in terms of "opportunity," "possibility," or "chance" and are surrounded by warnings that hard work is required. Moreover, these claims are primarily inspirational and motivational, and amount to puffing.

Statements that contain specific references as to how much one is likely to make, however, are deceptive. Recruiting manuals leave the distinct impression that individuals can make $200 per month as an Amway distributor. "[T]he record shows that in 1969–70 the average monthly Business Volume of Amway distributors was about $20, and in 1973–74 it was about $33." Less than 1 percent of Amway distributors make thousands of dollars. "Therefore, these statements constitute illegal misrepresentations under §5."

CASE QUESTIONS

1. What could an Amway distributor say to potential distributors to make the proposition attractive but still comply with the law?
2. What specifically distinguishes Amway's marketing scheme from illegal pyramid schemes?
3. What kinds of statements constitute puffery in this case? What kinds of statements constitute misrepresentations?

LITERAL TRUTH

As the Amway case suggests, **puffery** is not illegal. Puffery occurs where no reasonable person would believe the statement. For example, if a seller tells a buyer that "this car is the best little car in the world," the statement is obviously puffery.

Misrepresentations, on the other hand, are illegal under §5 of the Federal Trade Commission Act if they have the capacity to deceive. Usually, the difference between puffery and misrepresentation lies in how close to factual the statement sounds. For example, "This car has 100,000 miles on it" is a factual statement. It is either true or false. Absolute truth, however, may not be a defense in some cases. If a statement is literally true but the total impression given by the advertisement is such that the consumer is deceived, there may be a violation, as the following case demonstrates.

puffery or puffing: The practice of making exaggerated comments especially for promotional purposes.

KRAFT V. FTC

970 F.2d 311 (7th Cir. 1992)

FACTS

In the 1980s, Kraft began losing market share in the individually wrapped process cheese market. In response, Kraft ran a series of advertisements indicating that Kraft Singles were made with five ounces of milk and implying that the Singles contained the equivalent amount of calcium. The advertisements were focused on growing consumer interest in increasing amounts of calcium in the daily diet. In the individually wrapped process cheese slices market, there are three types of "cheese": process, imitation, and substitute. The FTC requires that products cannot be labeled "process cheese slices," unless they have at least 51 percent natural cheese. Imitation cheese slices, on the other hand, contain little or no cheese and are mostly water, vegetable oil, flavoring, and fortifying agents. Imitation cheese is considered nutritionally inferior to process cheese and must carry the "imitation" label. Substitute cheese falls in between process cheese and imitation cheese.

There were two sets of advertisements at issue. The "Skimp" television advertisements contained the following:

Woman (voice-over): I admit it. I thought of skimping. Could you look into those blue eyes and skimp on her? So I buy Kraft Singles. Imitation slices use hardly any milk. But Kraft has five ounces per slice. Five ounces. So her little bones get calcium they need to grow. No, she doesn't know what that big Kraft means. Good thing I do.

Singers: Kraft Singles. More milk makes 'em. . . more milk makes 'em good.

Woman (voice-over): Skimp on her? No way.

The second television advertisement depicts a group of school children having their class picture taken.

Announcer (voice-over): Can you see what is missing in this picture? Well, a government study says that half the school kids in America don't get all the calcium recommended for growing kids. That's why Kraft Singles are important. Kraft is made from five ounces of milk per slice. So they're concentrated with calcium. Calcium the government recommends for strong bones and healthy teeth!

Photographer: Say Cheese!

Kids: Cheese!

Announcer (voice-over): Say Kraft Singles. 'Cause kids love Kraft Singles, right down to their bones.

The FTC filed a complaint against Kraft, alleging that these ads misrepresented the calcium content contained in an individually wrapped Kraft Single. The Commission agreed, finding that the implied claims in Kraft's ads were that a slice of Kraft processed cheese had the same amount of calcium as five ounces of milk, and that Kraft Singles contained more calcium than imitation cheese. The Commission issued a cease-and-desist order against Kraft. Kraft appealed the decision.

DECISION

Judge Flaum wrote the opinion of the Seventh Circuit Court of Appeals. Kraft argued that the FTC was wrong in not requiring proof of actual consumer deception. Since there was no proof of actual deception, the FTC's order chills commercial speech. Further, Kraft claimed there is no evidence that the advertisement's claims were material to the consumer.

To determine if an advertisement is deceptive, a court first views it. If it cannot be determined whether the advertisement is deceptive after the viewing, then the fact-finding body turns to scientific evidence, such as consumer testimony, expert opinion, and copy tests of the advertisement. The Court found this approach to be appropriate, finding that the FTC was entitled to use its subjective judgment and does not need extrinsic evidence to find an advertisement false or deceptive.

Further, the Court also held that the First Amendment protection of commercial speech is not harmed by this approach. Commercial speech is not protected as heavily as other forms of speech, and consumer surveys are not required for proof of deception when the alleged deception is conspicuous even though the deceptive claim is implied. Although Kraft argued that its statements were literally true, literally true statements can be deceptive. The court noted that "the average consumer is not likely to know that much of the calcium in five ounces of milk (30%) is lost in processing, which leaves consumers with a misleading impression about calcium content. The critical fact is not that reasonable consumers might believe that a 3/4 ounce slice of cheese actually contains five ounces of milk, but that reasonable consumers might believe that a 3/4 ounce slice actually contains the calcium of five ounces of *milk*."

In looking at whether the calcium claims were material to the consumer, the court noted that Kraft was warned by ABC television, the California Attorney General, and its own advertising agency in a legal memorandum that the claims were potentially misleading and needed to be substantiated. Instead, a high-level executive argued against altering the advertisement copy, stating, "Singles business is growing for the first time in four years due in large part to the ad copy." This indicated to the court that Kraft thought the claims were material to consumers. Further, the expert who testified at trial and Kraft's own consumer surveys indicated that the calcium content of cheese was important to consumers. The Seventh Circuit agreed with the FTC that the advertisements were deceptive and that the claims made in the advertisements were material to the consumer. The FTC's cease and desist order was upheld.

CASE QUESTIONS

1. Do you find Kraft's advertisements to be deceptive? Why or why not?
2. Does Kraft's disclaimer change your opinion about whether the advertisement is deceptive? Why or why not?
3. Is a cease and desist order an effective remedy against deceptive advertising? Explain.

MISLEADING CLAIMS

Several types of specific claims are also considered to be deceptive. For example, businesses that advertise a "Going Out of Business Sale" or a "Total Liquidation Sale" are engaging in deceptive acts if, in fact, they are not going out of business. Some stores make claims that a product is being sold below its original price or is on sale when, in fact, it is the same price as always. These marketing tactics are considered to be deceptive. Advertising a sales price means that the product must be sold for less than what it actually sold for in the past.

Other claims that are misleading occur when products are sold together. For example, claims that a consumer will receive three bars of soap for the price of two bars of soap must be read literally. If the consumer can only buy the soap in three-bar packages, then the claim is deceptive. Weight-loss claims must run **disclaimers** that reflect the fact that weight loss rates and amounts vary from individual to individual and are usually the result of exercise and diet rather than the advertised "miracle" device. In the following case, the court considered whether a series of ads making a claim of rapid weight loss was misleading.

disclaimer: A denial of responsibility or a limitation of a statement or impression.

In the Language of the Court

FTC v. BRONSON

564 F.Supp.2d 119

FACTS

The Federal Trade Commission ("FTC") brought this enforcement action challenging as false advertising the claims that the defendants, Bronson Partners, LLC ("Bronson"), Martin Howard, H & H Marketing, LLC, and Sandra Howard (collectively "defendants"), made in their advertisements for two products: Chinese Diet Tea and the Bio Slim Patch. The exemplar advertisement for Chinese Diet Tea touts the tea almost exclusively as a weight-loss product, and, when read objectively and in context, virtually guarantees the user that, by drinking the tea, the user will lose large quantities of weight in a relatively short period of time without dieting or exercising. The defendants also advertised the Bio Slim Patch as an effective weight loss product.

The FTC seeks a permanent injunction and damages, and has moved for summary judgment on all claims. For reasons that follow, the FTC's motion is granted with respect to liability.

I. BACKGROUND

Chinese Diet Tea is not materially different from any other green tea product on the market. The defendants' exemplar one-page advertisement for Chinese Diet Tea is entitled, "Powerful Green Diet Tea, **SHEDS POUND AFTER POUND OF FAT—FAST!**" It includes a picture of a slim Asian woman on a scale wearing what appears to be a bathing suit or tight-fitting tank top. The advertisement states:

> You eat your favorite foods—but STILL lose weight!
> Eliminates an amazing 91% of absorbed sugars.
> Prevents 83% of fat absorption.
> Doubles your metabolic rate to burn calories fast.
> Powerful herbal formula helps you stop snacking.

> Let this powerful Chinese Green Diet Tea help you to lose those unwanted pounds. Can you

imagine losing weight by simply drinking a cup of refreshing tea? Well, that is all you now have to do to lose weight with one of the "easiest" and most effective diets ever discovered. Chinese Green Diet Tea is a 2000 year old secret remedy now available in the U.S. Obesity is a big problem in Western societies but is almost unheard of in China. That is because millions of Chinese men and women regularly drink herbal tea after every meal. Clinical trials have shown that by drinking a cup of Chinese Green Diet Tea your body will absorb less sugar and animal fats. Participants on Chinese Green Diet Tea clinical trials carried on eating a normal healthy measure of sugar and fats—but they still lost weight. Just make sure you drink one cup of Chinese Green Diet Tea after each meal to neutralize the absorption of fattening foods. You'll get the satisfaction and flavor of eating a balanced diet but without any fattening effects.

The advertisement continues to assure the reader that Chinese Diet Tea is:

> **GUARANTEED!** Chinese Green Diet Tea has been clinically trialed on 163 patients. All participants lost between 18 lbs and 75 lbs over the 12-week trial period. If you do not lose similar amounts of weight we guarantee to refund your purchase price in full (less s/h). **REMEMBER,** the more Chinese Green Diet Tea you drink, the more weight you may lose!

It also asserts that "[r]esearchers found that those who drank Chinese Diet Green Tea burned an additional 500 calories per week, with no change in diet or physical activity," and that:

> Chinese Green Diet Tea's secret herbal ingredients act in four ways to help you lose weight:

> 1) Reduces sugar absorption by an amazing 91%. This means you can eat sweet buns and chocolate without putting on so much weight. But be careful—drinking Chinese Green Diet Tea is not a license to gorge yourself.
> 2) Reduces the absorption of animal fats and dairy products by as much as 83%. This controls the fattening effects of butter, cheese, pate, sausages and fatty meats.

3) Doubles the digestion of food in the intestine. This prevents food laying in your stomach for 24 hours or more and contributing to that "pot belly" look. The faster digestion of food means fewer calories are absorbed into the body.

4) Acts as an effective appetite suppressant to reduce snacking.

The FTC filed a four-count complaint pursuant to Section 13(b) of the Federal Trade Commission Act ("FTC Act", 15 U.S.C. § 53(b) , to secure a permanent injunction against and disgorgement of allegedly ill-gotten gains from the defendants. The FTC alleges that the defendants violated Sections 5(a) and 12 of the FTC Act, 15 U.S.C. §§ 45(a) and 52 , by making false and unsubstantiated claims with respect to Chinese Diet Tea (counts one and two), and by making false and unsubstantiated claims with respect to the Bio-Slim Patch (counts three and four). They now move for summary judgment on all counts.

DECISION

Liability Under the FTC Act

The FTC Act, 15 U.S.C. § 52(a), provides that "[i]t shall be unlawful for any person, partnership, or corporation to disseminate, or cause to be disseminated, any false advertisement . . . for the purpose of inducing, or which is likely to induce, directly or indirectly, the purchase in or having an effect upon commerce of food, drugs, devices, services, or cosmetics." Section 52(b) of the FTC Act continues that the "dissemination or the causing to be disseminated of any false advertisement within the provisions of subsection (a) of this section shall be an unfair or deceptive act or practice in or affecting commerce within the meaning of section 5." Section 5 of the FTC Act provides that "[u]nfair methods of competition in or affecting commerce, and unfair or deceptive acts or practices in or affecting commerce, are hereby declared unlawful," and that the FTC "is hereby empowered and directed to prevent persons, partnerships, or corporations . . . from using unfair methods of competition in or affecting commerce and unfair or deceptive acts or practices in or affecting commerce."

The Act defines "false advertisement" as follows:

The term "false advertisement" means an advertisement, other than labeling, which is misleading in a material respect; and in determining whether any advertisement is misleading, there shall be taken into account (among other things) not only representations made or suggested by statement, word, design, device, sound, or any combination thereof, but also the extent to which the advertisement fails to reveal facts material in the light of such representations or material with respect to consequences which may result from the use of the commodity to which the advertisement relates under the conditions prescribed in said advertisement, or under such conditions as are customary or usual.

Two types of false advertising are actionable: "(1) advertising which makes claims which are literally false on their face, and (2) advertising which, although literally true on its face, is perceived by a significant proportion of the relevant market as making 'subliminal' or 'implicit' claims which are provably false. With regard to the second type of false advertising, the courts sometimes say that the advertising has a tendency to mislead, confuse or deceive."

To prove a violation of Section 5, the FTC must show three elements; (1) the existence of "a representation, omission, or practice," that is (2) "likely to mislead consumers acting reasonably under the circumstances," and (3) "the representation, omission, or practice is material." "To be actionable under section 5, these misrepresentations or practices need not be made with an intent to deceive. Indeed, an advertiser's good faith does not immunize it from responsibility for its misrepresentations. Moreover, the omission of material information, even if an advertisement does not contain falsehoods, may cause the advertisement to violate section 5."

A. Does the Advertisement for Chinese Diet Tea Make the Alleged Claims?

In the complaint, the FTC alleges that the Chinese Diet Tea advertisement makes the following claims:

(a) Chinese Diet Tea causes rapid and substantial weight loss without the need to reduce caloric intake or increase physical activity;

(b) Chinese Diet Tea enables users to lose as much as six pounds per week over multiple weeks and months without the need to reduce caloric intake or increase physical activity;

(c) Chinese Diet Tea enables users to lose substantial weight while enjoying their favorite foods, including foods high in sugar and animal fat;

(d) Chinese Diet Tea blocks the absorption of fat and calories thereby enabling users to lose substantial weight;

(e) Chinese Diet Tea causes substantial weight loss for all users; and

(f) Chinese Diet Tea is clinically proven to cause rapid and substantial weight loss without the need to reduce caloric intake or increase physical activity.

• • •

I can conclude from the face of the advertisement that the advertisement makes the alleged claims. The advertisement is not subtle. It does not employ innuendo, subliminal messages or hints to convey its message. It does not contain conflicting messages that are reasonably susceptible to different interpretations. It makes no meaningful qualifications. Instead, it is clear, stark and dramatic. Only four words in the entire advertisement do not relate to weight loss in some way: "makes great iced tea." Defendants attempt to torture the language in the advertisement to create an ambiguity where none exists. For example, they point out that the advertisement does not use the specific terms alleged in the complaint. For one, that is not true of all claims. And to the extent it is true of other claims, the advertisement's statements are so clear, repetitive, and unambiguous that they constitute the functional equivalent of express claims.

In conclusion, I hold that the advertisement expressly makes the alleged claims, or at least so strongly and unambiguously implies those claims that the claims are the functional equivalent of express claims.

B. Are the Alleged Claims Made in the Chinese Diet Tea Advertisement False and Misleading?

Simply stated, the claims the advertisement makes are either false or unsupported. Given the complete lack of support for the specific claims made in the advertisement, and given [the FTC's] credible report that the claims in the advertisement are both unsupported and beyond the realm of scientific plausibility, I hold that the advertisement's claims are false and misleading.

C. Are the Advertisement's Claims "Materially" False or Misleading?

"A 'material' misrepresentation is one that involves information that is important to consumers, and that is therefore likely to affect a consumer's choice of or conduct regarding a product. Proof of actual consumer injury is not required." In considering false advertising claims, the FTC presumes several types of claims to be material, including any express claim, or "implied claims where there is evidence that the seller intended to make the claim." The underlying rationale for finding a claim to be presumptively material in both instances is "the assumption that the willingness of a business to promote its products reflects a belief that the consumers are interested in the advertising."

In this case, I have held that the subject advertisement made all six of the alleged claims either expressly, or by such strong implication that they are the functional equivalent of an express claim. As such, those claims are presumed to be material.

Even if I had found the advertisement made the claims only implicitly, the statements in the advertisement were so unambiguous and repetitive that they were clearly intended by the advertiser to make the alleged claims, and as such, can be presumed material.

Finally, even if the claims were not intended by the advertiser, no reasonable juror could find, after reading the advertisement, that the claims were not "important to consumers" and thus "likely to affect a consumer's choice of conduct regarding a product." The advertisement is almost entirely a weight loss advertisement. Therefore, consumers who purchase Chinese Diet Tea because of the advertisement are thus purchasing Chinese Diet Tea because it would have the advertised effect on weight loss. As such, I hold that the alleged claims are material.

CASE QUESTIONS

1. According to the court, what types of false advertising are actionable?

2. Is the advertisement in this case one that is likely to deceive a "reasonable" consumer? Would you believe the claims in this ad?

3. Do you agree with the decision? Why or why not?

MISLEADING PICTORIALS AND DEMONSTRATIONS

Not only can statements be misleading, but the pictures used in advertising can also be deceptive. For example, the makers of Volvo ran a television advertisement that depicted a "monster truck" trying to unsuccessfully crunch a Volvo car. An investigation revealed that the roof of the car used in the advertisement had been reinforced with steel. Volvo agreed to withdraw the promotion and ran corrective advertisements. The corrective advertisement indicated that two of the three cars used in the ad were reinforced. The advertising company that produced the original advertisement was fired.

SOCIAL/ETHICAL ISSUES

Many beer commercials show upscale party scenes with young, attractive men and women having a very good time. Some cigarette advertisements have used cartoon characters as the primary focus. Fast food commercials never show individuals who are overweight. These types of advertisements have been attacked for various ethical reasons. What might these reasons be? Should advertisers be allowed to advertise products that are dangerous to people's health? Should they be required to run disclaimers or other types of warnings?

ENVIRONMENTAL CLAIMS

Some products are advertised as "earth friendly," "recyclable," or "green" and large markets have arisen for environmentally friendly products. The implication of such labeling is that the product offers a general environmental benefit. In 1998, the FTC modified its guidelines, which are referred to as "Guides for the Use of Environmental Marketing Claims." They apply to all logos, advertisements, promotional material, packaging and labeling. As in all advertising, the FTC requires that environmental claims must also be substantiated. For example, if a company claims the product is biodegradable, then the product needs to biodegrade in a reasonable time frame. If a product is claimed to be made from 50% recyclable material, then in fact it needs to be made from 50% recyclable material.

FREE CLAIMS

Everyone likes to receive free items. The claim "Buy One, Get One Free" can be misleading if, in fact, the item is not free. According to FTC regulations, "free" must indeed mean "free." If the consumer has to pay anything for the product, then the product is not free. Under FTC regulations, the "regular price" of a product is the lowest price at which the product sold during the previous 30 days. Engaging in a pizza promotional campaign and advertising "free pizza delivery," when, in fact, there had not been a charge for pizza delivery over the past 30 days might be construed to be misleading. Also, no free offer should extend for longer than six months. If there are requirements for receiving the free offer, these requirements must be stated clearly and conspicuously in the promotion. If the free offer is not available in all locations, that fact must be stated. To comply with this rule, it is not unusual to see the phrase "subject to local dealer participation" in promotional literature.

BAIT AND SWITCH

bait and switch:
A fraudulent or deceptive sales practice in which a purchaser is attracted by advertisement of a low-priced item but then is encouraged to purchase a higher priced one.

Another act that the FTC has deemed deceptive is known as **bait and switch**. Bait and switch occurs when a business advertises a product at a very low price (the bait). When the consumer tries to buy the product, the business either does not have the product available and refuses to order the item, or disparages (says bad things about) the product and tries to convince the consumer to buy a higher-priced product (the switch). For example, Sharon reads in the newspaper that Swindler's Store has a boom box for sale at $69. Sharon goes to Swindler's to buy the $69 boom box. Once in the store the sales clerk tells Sharon that the $69 boom box is "a piece of junk." But, luckily for Sharon, the store has a $249 boom box that will be perfect. This is classic bait and switch and is considered to be deceptive.

Refusing to demonstrate the advertised product, demonstrating a defective product with the intent to sell the more expensive product, and failure to have enough of the advertised product in inventory can also be bait and switch practices. Compensating sales clerks in a manner that encourages bait and switch is also considered deceptive.

PRODUCT COMPARISONS

Advertising one's product by comparing it with another product is known as *comparative advertising*. At one time, comparative advertising was rare. Comparative advertising was not used because advertisers feared that the public would feel sorry for the competing product or that the competitor would receive more publicity. In 1972, the FTC began informally to encourage comparative advertising. In 1978, the FTC stated that comparative advertising was not illegal if the advertising was not deceptive. Comparative advertising is now encouraged by the FTC but is watched carefully to ensure that the advertising is truthful. Individuals and companies engaged in comparative advertising must keep records that will substantiate their claims. For example, in an advertisement which claims that four out of five people prefer cola A over cola B, cola A needs records that will detail the research methods that were used to arrive at those numbers. If the claim cannot be substantiated, then the FTC may order the advertisement withdrawn.

Some competitors have not relied on the FTC to bring a lawsuit when they believe that comparative advertising is deceptive. Rather, they have initiated private lawsuits under the federal *Lanham Act of 1946*. The Lanham Act is more commonly known for its protection of trademarks through registration and misuse, as discussed in Chapter 14. However, competitors have used the Act when deceptive and misleading comparative advertising is the issue. Section 43(a) of the Lanham Act states:

> [A]ny person who, on or in connection with any goods or services, or any container for goods, uses in commerce any word, term, name, symbol, or device, or any combination thereof, with a false designation of origin, false or misleading description of fact, or false or misleading representation of fact, which . . . is likely to cause confusion, or to cause mistake, or to deceive . . . shall be liable in a civil action by any person who believes that he or she is or is likely to be damaged by such act [15 U.S.C. 1125a].

If a competitor is successful in a Lanham Act lawsuit, the competitor can receive monetary damages, punitive damages (up to three times the amount of monetary damages), and attorneys' fees. In the 1980s, U-Haul was the target of a misleading comparative advertising campaign. At trial, the jury granted U-Haul $20 million in lost profits, $20 million in punitive damages, $13.6 million it spent on advertising to combat the misleading claims, and $2.5 million in attorneys' fees. The trial judge doubled the damages under the Lanham Act. The decision was upheld on appeal.

Suits filed under the Lanham Act are entitled to preliminary injunctions in appropriate cases. For example, a series of cases arose between 1978 and 1988 involving the manufacturers of Tylenol, Advil, and Anacin. These manufacturers alleged that each other's nonaspirin pain reliever advertisements were deceptive. For instance, a statement that Maximum Strength Anacin contained "more of the pain reliever doctors recommend most" was held to be misleading because the advertisements seemed to indicate that Maximum Strength Anacin was stronger than Extra-Strength Tylenol. This was untrue. In another interesting case brought by the makers of Advil against the makers of Tylenol, a judge ruled that both Tylenol and Advil's advertising contained misleading statements and issued injunctions on statements made by both companies.

Product comparisons continue to be a national issue, as the following article makes clear.

AT&T, Verizon Face Off in TV Ads

Companies attacking each other's wireless networks

NEW YORK—What would the holidays be without bickering between siblings? AT&T and Verizon are swamping TV with ads attacking facets of each other's wireless networks. While the ads stick fairly close to the truth, there's a lot they don't say.

AT&T Inc. has been running ads with actor Luke Wilson checking off points in AT&T's favor over Verizon Wireless. It's the continuation of a spat that started a month ago, when Verizon started airing cheeky commercials that highlighted how its fast, third-generation ("3G") network has wider coverage than AT&T's 3G system.

Verizon's ad used the slogan "There's a map for that," a play off Apple Inc.'s ads for the iPhone, which tout the diversity of third-party applications for the phone with the line "There's an app for that."

AT&T sued Verizon Wireless over the "map" ads, not because the maps were incorrect, but because AT&T felt there was a danger that viewers could get the impression that AT&T had no coverage at all where it doesn't have 3G. Last week, a judge declined to force Verizon to pull the ads.

AT&T and Verizon, two offspring of Ma Bell, are getting more aggressive in their marketing, though it's not clear how much they are spending. Verizon and AT&T are both pulling away from their smaller rivals, so instead of competing with Sprint Nextel Corp. and T-Mobile USA, they're increasingly focused on each other. Verizon Wireless has more subscribers than AT&T—89 million versus 81.6 million. But AT&T added more wireless subscribers in the latest quarter—2 million versus 1.2 million at Verizon, which is a joint venture of Verizon Communications Inc. and Vodafone Group PLC of Britain.

Here is a look at some of the arguments being raised in the ads:

- Coverage: It's incontrovertible that Verizon's 3G network has broader coverage than AT&T's, which is why the federal judge in Atlanta wouldn't stop the "There's a map for that" ads. Verizon's network reaches 280 million Americans, compared to AT&T's 233 million. By area, the difference is even greater—Verizon covers cities and vast, thinly populated areas of the Midwest and West, while AT&T's 3G coverage hews closer to cities and highways. However, AT&T's older, slower "EDGE" data network covers 301 million people and is adequate for e-mail access and many other smart phone functions.

- Speed: Luke Wilson's top point is that AT&T has "the nation's fastest 3G network." The ad doesn't cite any sources or figures. AT&T spokesman Mark Siegel said the claim is based on "extensive testing by outside research firms." The company isn't providing the studies. The claim "hasn't been formally challenged by a competitor," Siegel said.

Speed tests are tricky. Wireless speeds vary depending on how many other people in the neighborhood are trying to access the network at the same time. While all U.S. 3G networks have similar theoretical top speeds, AT&T had a relatively poor showing in tests conducted this year by PC World and ARCchart, a British company. AT&T customers also frequently complain about 3G being unavailable. AT&T is likely a victim of its own success here: Millions of iPhone users are getting in each other's way, clogging the network.

- Talk and surf: Wilson fronts an AT&T ad that points out that it's possible to talk on a smart phone and surf on AT&T's 3G network at the same time, which isn't possible on Verizon. Apple has jumped into the fray with its own ad, echoing that message and demonstrating how convenient it is to be able to look up show times while chatting with your friend about which movie to see.

It's true that Verizon phones can't handle simultaneous voice and 3G data connections. However, the ones that have Wi-Fi capability, such as the new Motorola Droid, can be used to surf and talk at the same time if the phone is connected to a Wi-Fi hot spot. Also, the AT&T ads don't mention that the EDGE network does not support simultaneous voice and data. AT&T's ads focus on the coverage of the EDGE network while touting the capabilities of the 3G network.

- Best phones: Wilson says AT&T has the "most popular smart phones." It's true that AT&T sells more smart phones than Verizon, largely because it is the exclusive U.S. carrier of the iPhone.
- Most applications: Wilson checks a box that says "Access to over 100,000 apps" in AT&T's favor. He doesn't mention that the vast majority of those applications are accessible only to iPhone users. It's true that the iPhone has a large lead over other smart phone platforms in the number of third-party programs that are available. There are less than 20,000 available for Verizon's Droid phone, for example.

Source: www.msnbc.com/id/34154174/ns/business-us business/print/1/displaymode/1098. November 27, 2009.

ENDORSEMENTS

Celebrities and experts also sell a variety of products. Lance Armstrong sells automobiles for Subaru, actress Halle Barry endorses Revlon cosmetics, and Tiger Woods (despite his infidelity scandal) still advertises for Nike. Because endorsements such as these, either implicit or explicit, have the capacity to deceive the public, the FTC has issued rules governing the use of celebrity endorsements. The first of these states that the celebrity must actually use the product. If a gymnast indicates that she wears a certain brand of leotard, then she actually must wear that brand. If the celebrity or expert claims to give an expert opinion, then in fact the person must be qualified to give such an opinion. The celebrity may also be responsible for the opinions of others. In one interesting case, Pat Boone, a popular singer, endorsed an acne product, "Acne-Statin." In the ad, he claimed that the product would result in skin free of acne blemishes, and that his daughters had used it successfully. These allegations proved to be false. In this case, the FTC held that endorsers must verify claims before they appear in advertisements. Further, if the endorser is not an expert, then the endorser must make a reasonable investigation as to the claim's truthfulness. Failure to make an independent evaluation can result in personal liability for the endorser. Some advertisements must also include a statement that the endorser is being paid for providing the endorsement. In 2009, the FTC revised its guidelines regarding product endorsements to cover endorsements made through social media sites and celebrity endorsements. Any "material" connection between the endorser and the product, such as payment or the receipt of free products, must be disclosed to consumers. Also, celebrity endorsers may be liable for false claims made in endorsements or for failure to disclose a material connection with the company whose product is being advertised.

ADVERTISING TO CHILDREN

Since advertising is a major part of American society, most adults are adept at distinguishing puffery from fact. Children, however, given their age and inexperience, are more likely to be deceived by advertising than adults. Therefore, the FTC has issued several rules regarding advertising to children.

The FTC is concerned with premium advertising and considers exclusive premium advertising (advertising the trinket rather than the product) to be an unfair trade practice. Another area of concern for the FTC is advertising that may potentially harm children. For example, a commercial showing a child jumping from a roof with a superhero cape would probably be pulled for fear that children may actually try to imitate the commercial. Advertisers are also prohibited from portraying the use of their products in an unsafe manner. A commercial showing a child using a child's oven around a swimming pool probably would be banned for fear that a child may be electrocuted by using the oven in the same way.

Using hero figures to sell products can create problems for advertisers. Children exhibit a trust relationship with hero figures, and they are used to sell everything from cereal to bed sheets. However, not all products may use hero figures in their advertisements. For example, the FTC has ordered manufacturers of vitamins to stop using hero figures to sell vitamins due to concern that children would take too many vitamins and that children would believe that vitamins would help them exhibit "superhero" characteristics. Once again, these regulations are aimed at protecting children who frequently do not have the ability to separate fantasy from reality. Some consumer and parent groups would like the FTC to ban children's advertising altogether.

NAD has also issued voluntary guidelines advertisers are asked to follow regarding children's advertising. Further, NAD has a unit, *Children's Advertising Review Unit (CARU)*, that specifically reviews compliance with the NAD guidelines. Some of those guidelines address advertisements that focus on *premiums*, which are those items used to induce a child to buy a product. The clearest examples are toys that are found in cereal boxes and toys that are given with fast-food purchases. Anyone who has been around small children knows how quickly they know the premium that comes with a special kid's meal at the local fast-food restaurant. CARU specifically requires the advertisement to emphasize the product rather than the premium. One frequent violation occurs when advertisements focus almost exclusively on the premium rather than on the product. Another guideline limits the amount of commercials that can occur during children's programming. New NAD guidelines limit advertising to children during children's programming to 10 1/2 minutes per hour during weekdays and 12 minutes per hour during the weekend.

UNFAIR TRADE PRACTICES

COOLING-OFF PERIODS

Door-to-door sales can sometimes cause problems for consumers. Many products are sold door to door, including magazines, cosmetics, and vacuums. Once a salesperson is allowed into your home, it may be difficult to get the salesperson to leave, especially if he or she has just poured dirt on your rug and is attempting to vacuum it up. Because of these problems, the FTC requires a three-day **cooling-off period** for door-to-door sales. Consumers have three days from the date of the sale or from the date that they are notified of the three-day cooling-off period to cancel the sale. If the transaction was made in Spanish, then the cancellation notice must also be done in Spanish. Many states also have statutes providing for cooling-off periods. If the state statute is more protective for the consumer than the federal provision, then the state statute controls.

cooling-off period: A period of time to allow further consideration for the consumer to change his or her mind.

UNSOLICITED MAIL

Consumers occasionally receive merchandise through the mail that they did not order. When they do not pay for the merchandise, usually they are then sent a series of threatening bills. In 1970, Congress passed the *Postal Reorganization Act* which included a prohibition against unsolicited mail merchandise and the subsequent threatening bills. This practice is known as *dunning*. Under current law, any unsolicited merchandise that is received through the mail may be kept as a gift and need not be returned.

SWEEPSTAKES AND CONTESTS

A *sweepstakes* is a promotion in which consumers win a prize just by being entered in the sweepstakes. On the other hand, *contests* require that a consumer perform some act to win. For example, the consumer may need to provide the winning jingle or guess the number of jelly beans in a jar to win a contest. The food, retailing, and gasoline industries often use "games of chance" for promotional purposes. The FTC issued special regulations dealing with those contests, but those rules were repealed in 1996. As the article below suggests, sweepstakes continue to be regulated and enforced by the states.

Delaware Settles with Reader's Digest

Delaware Attorney General Jane Brady entered into an AVC with the Reader's Digest Association, Inc., resolving allegations its sweepstakes **contest was deceptive and misleading**. According to Attorney General Brady, Reader's Digest misled consumers about their chances of winning and the effect of a purchase on those chances. The settlement requires Reader's Digest to: 1) include in its advertising "sweepstakes facts," such as "buying won't help you win," "entry is free," and "you have not yet won," as well as a statement of the odds of winning the contest; 2) identify "high activity customers" who have spent substantial amounts of money in response to Reader's Digest solicitations and advertising for restitution purposes; 3) pay $18,731 in restitution to a special Consumer Protection Fund; and 4) pay $75,000 in costs and attorneys' fees.

Source: "Delaware Settles with Reader's Digest" by Lori Sitler, *National Association of Attorneys General Consumer Protection Report*, July 2003.

Sometimes sweepstakes or contests do not work out as they planned. Kraft had one sweepstakes in which a consumer could win a van if he or she bought a box of macaroni and cheese that contained the proper game piece. Due to a manufacturing mistake, thousands of boxes had the winning game piece. Kraft canceled the sweepstakes as soon as the mistake was discovered, but not before several consumers believed they had won vans. Sometimes individuals figure how to "beat" contests. Also, in many states, games of chance are considered to be **illegal lotteries**, and promoters can be subject to criminal prosecutions. Therefore, promoters need to be very careful when using contests and sweepstakes.

NEGATIVE OPTION PLANS

Book-of-the-Month, CD-of-the-Month, and Doll-of-the-Month clubs all have something in common. They are likely to be **negative option plans**. A negative option plan arises where a consumer receives an item (e.g., a book) and agrees to pay for the item unless he or she specifically requests otherwise each time period. Negative option plans are considered unfair and deceptive trade practices unless they are conducted in line with FTC regulations. The FTC requires that all promotional material for the plan conspicuously state the terms and provide for a method whereby the consumer may reject the item. Consumers are entitled to a 10-day period during which they decide whether to accept the item (by doing nothing) or reject the item (by sending a statement indicating rejection). When consumers cancel their memberships in such plans, they will be required to pay for the next item shipped. If items are shipped after the cancellation period, the consumer may keep the items as a gift. It is wise, however, for the consumer to keep records of when the membership was canceled.

MAIL ORDER MERCHANDISE

Merchandise can be ordered and purchased through the mail, by fax or on the Internet. In fact, more and more people are using the convenience of the Internet as a replacement for shopping expeditions. Ordering through the mail or on the Internet can be very satisfying, but it can also be frustrating. For instance, the length of time it takes between ordering the merchandise and shipping the merchandise may be unreasonable. To address this problem, the FTC enacted the *Mail and Telephone Order Merchandise Rule* which applies to all mail, fax or Internet ordering. The rule requires the merchandise to be shipped within 30 days after receiving the order. If a merchant cannot ship within 30 days, the original advertisement must state when the product can be shipped. If for some reason the merchandise cannot be shipped within the specified time-frame, the consumer is required to be notified as to the new shipping date. If the consumer is silent, the merchant may assume that the consumer agrees to the new shipping date. The consumer must consent to subsequent delays. If the consumer does not consent or wants to cancel the order, the merchant must provide the consumer with a prompt and full refund.

---

illegal lottery versus sweepstakes: An illegal lottery has three elements: a prize, chance, and consideration. If one of these is missing, it is a sweepstakes.

negative option plan: A plan where the seller periodically sends the buyer announcements that describe a current selection or new offering. If the buyer wants the selection it will be shipped automatically. If the buyer does not want the selection then a card rejecting the selection needs to be sent to the seller by a certain date.

TELEPHONE, FAX, AND INTERNET SOLICITATIONS

Several consumer protection acts have been passed in response to the abuses in the telephone solicitation business. The *Telephone Consumer Protection Act of 1991* outlaws autodialing to fax machines, pagers, and cellular phones and pre-recorded calls to a residence without the person's consent. The Act is enforced by the *Federal Communications Commission (FCC)*. In 1999, several Texas companies agreed to pay $400,000 to 11 businesses that received unwanted fax advertisements. The FCC also requires telemarketers to keep a list of persons requesting that they not be called and sets calling times from 8 A.M. to 9 P.M. State laws are often more restrictive than the federal law. Some states allow cooling-off periods for products bought during a telephone solicitation.

The second act, the *Telemarketing and Consumer Fraud and Abuse Prevention Act* ("Telemarketing Act"), is designed to prohibit deceptive telemarketing acts or practices. It specifically limits the use of automated dialing equipment, artificial and prerecorded voices and unsolicited fax advertisements. The *Do Not Call Implementation Act* amended the Telemarketing Act. It allows consumers to register with the FTC and theoretically be free from unwanted telephone solicitations. The Act contains a number of exceptions, including exceptions for those with whom consumers already have a business relationship, charitable organizations, and those with whom the telemarketer has a written agreement allowing the call.

The FTC has made it clear that current laws also apply to internet advertising. The FTC publication "Dot Com Disclosures" reminds businesses that prohibitions on unfair and deceptive acts and practices do not change because of the internet. For example, all disclaimers and disclosures must be on the same screen as the claim, rules using the term "written" also apply to visual text, and direct mail solicitation rules apply to email solicitations. The major rules require that a disclaimer and disclosure be obvious and labeled, and that the consumer's attention be drawn to it.

CONSUMER PRODUCT SAFETY COMMISSION

Besides the FTC, the *Consumer Product Safety Commission (CPSC)* also governs some consumer issues. The CPSC was formed in 1972 under the *Consumer Product Safety Act (CPSA)*, and is an independent regulatory commission with five commissioners serving seven-year appointments. The CPSC issues safety rules for dangerous or hazardous products. The CPSC also can issue outright bans on products if it finds that there is an "imminent or substantial" hazard, and can recall products. In 1976, Congress passed the *Consumer Product Safety Commission Improvement Act*, which allows consumers to sue the CPSC when it fails to keep a hazardous product off the market. The CPSC is also responsible for implementing the *Refrigerator Safety Act*, aimed at preventing children from getting trapped in refrigerators; the *Poison Prevention Packaging Act*, requiring child-resistant safety caps; the *Flammable Fabrics Act*, requiring flammability standards for fabrics, especially for children's clothes; and the *Federal Hazardous Substances Act*, which looks at children's toys and other hazardous products.

Although the CPSC was intended to make consumer items safer, its record is mixed. Thousands of dangerous products have been recalled and/or banned, but other dangerous products have been allowed to stay on the market or were only recalled after several consumers were seriously injured.

SUMMARY

Unfair and deceptive trade practices are prohibited by the Federal Trade Commission Act, state deceptive practices acts, and common law torts. Further, self-regulating entities in the advertising community also issue advertising guidelines. The FTC has issued industry-specific regulations prohibiting deceptive practices. It also brings complaints against businesses that are engaged in several types of unfair and deceptive practices. These practices include misleading pictorials and claims, free claims, product comparisons, cooling-off periods, and bait and switch practices. The FTC also regulates labeling as well as endorsements, unsolicited mail, and negative option plans. Telephone solicitation, the Internet, and faxes have recently been more heavily regulated. In some instances consumers or competitors may bring a direct civil action against an unscrupulous business for deceptive practices. In most instances, however, only the FTC has the power to proceed.

The Consumer Product Safety Commission is responsible for ensuring that dangerous and hazardous products are properly labeled or banned.

CHAPTER QUESTIONS

1. Warner-Lambert Company manufactures the mouthwash Listerine. Listerine has been marketed since 1879 with no change in its original formula. During all this time, Listerine has been advertised as helping prevent, cure, and alleviate symptoms of the common cold and sore throats. In an extensive hearing, the FTC found that each of these claims was false. What types of remedies can the FTC seek? [See *Warner-Lambert Company v. Federal Trade Commission*, 562 F.2d 749 (D.C.Cir. 1977).

2. A private company doing business as "U.S.A. Immigration Services" set up Spanish websites suggesting that the company could help individuals obtain a permanent visa, or green card. The websites indicated, that for a fee, they could help consumers register for the State Department's Diversity Visa (DV) lottery. This lottery gives individuals an opportunity to apply for a permanent visa. Is the website misleading? Why or why not?

3. In May, 2009, Sara Lee, Inc., which owns Ball Park Franks, sued Oscar Mayer, alleging that Oscar Mayer's claim that its hot dogs were "100 percent pure beef" was false and hurt Ball Park Franks' reputation. In its complaint, Sara Lee claimed that Oscar Mayer was "well aware of the chemical and other non-beef contents" of its hot dogs. Sara Lee also challenged Oscar Mayer's statements that its hot dogs outperformed Ball Park Franks in taste tests. What do you think about comparative advertisements such as this? Is Sara Lee wise to challenge Oscar Mayer in court? How do you think this case should be resolved?

4. Brian and Rita filed a class action lawsuit against several cigarette manufacturers, alleging that the defendants' advertisement for Marlboro Light cigarettes, which claimed that the cigarettes were "low tar," "light," or

"ultra light," were deceptive because they lead consumers to conclude incorrectly that Marlboro Lights are safer than regular cigarettes, when in fact they are not. How should the court decide this case? [See Cleary v. Philip Morris USA, Inc., et al., 683 F.Supp.2d 730).]

5. Attorneys Farrin, Lewis, and Daggett contracted with a marketing company, Market Masters, to produce and run ads in their respective markets. The ads in question depicted a "strategy session" held by a fictional insurance company. During the meeting, actors playing insurance adjusters discussed a claim involving plaintiffs represented by the attorneys. Upon learning the name of the attorney representing the fictional client, a loud gong rang, and the actor playing the senior adjuster displayed an alarmed face. The ads in question contained small disclaimers that the scene was a dramatization and that "no specific result" was implied. Other attorneys in the area objected to the ads and filed an ethics complaint with the state bar, which ruled that the ads violated the code of ethics governing attorney conduct. Should attorneys be allowed to advertise in this way? How should the court decide this case? [See *Farrin v. Thigpen*, 173 F.Supp.2d 427 (2001).]

6. US Sales Corporation's television and radio advertising used the following copy: "Thinking of buying a red hot car? Did you know that you can find cars and trucks and vans, right now for hot prices . . . as little as . . . $100. That's right . . . red hot cars in good condition, right now for as little as $100. . . . These hot cars were confiscated by drug seizures, used by government agents, or repossessed by banks . . . and they're practically giving them away!" Showroom quality sports cars were shown during the television commercials, and consumers were given a 900 number to call. The advertisement informed consumers that the call was $2. Callers who stayed on the 900 line until the end of the recorded message were charged $24 and were given another toll-free number to call. If consumers called the toll-free number they were solicited to buy a lifetime membership in US Sales for $99.95. Although 40 out of 42 cars sold at auction by the Department of Defense sold for under $500, 41 were deemed unserviceable. In what ways is the advertisement misleading? [See *FTC v. US Sales Corp.*, 1992 U.S. Dist. LEXIS 1078.]

7. The FTC has recently challenged two separate claims made by Kellogg Co. regarding Rice Krispies and Frosted Mini-Wheats cereals. In 2010, Kellogg claimed on Rice Krispies boxes that the cereal helped children's immunity with "25% daily value of antioxidants and nutrients—vitamins A, B, C and E." Rice Krispies boxes also stated that the cereal "has been improved to include antioxidants and nutrients that your family needs to help them stay healthy." In 2009, the FTC challenged the company's claim that Frosted Mini-Wheats improved children's attentiveness by nearly 20%. In both cases, the FTC found that the claims were unsubstantiated and therefore misleading. In a similar case, General Mills, another cereal manufacturer, came under scrutiny by the FDA, who claimed that the company's claims that Cheerios was "clinically proven to help lower cholesterol" was a serious violation of federal law because the claim was not substantiated. Do you agree that claims such as these are misleading? If so, is it enough that the FTC simply demand that companies stop the misleading ads? Or should the FTC impose fines and/or counter-advertising requirements?

8. Some telemarketers, posing as representatives of major credit card companies, tell consumers they could be liable for unauthorized charges that

appear on their credit cards. They then try to sell the consumer additional fraud protection insurance costing between $200 and $400. Federal law already protects consumers from unauthorized charges to their credit cards that exceed $50 and most credit card companies have a zero liability policy if the unauthorized charge is reported immediately. Have the telemarketers violated any laws?

9. A local electronics store advertised a "new" brand-name personal computer, PC, for a very low price. The PC was not assembled by the brand manufacturer, but rather the store reconfigured the PC with a variety of parts. Only the motherboard and computer casing were from the brand-name manufacturer. The same store also heavily advertised low-end computers. When consumers inquired about the advertised computer, the sales staff would try to convince the customer to buy a higher-end computer. Are these actions legal?

10. Given mathematical improbabilities, are multilevel marketing schemes ethical? Why or why not?

PRACTICAL EXERCISE

Phil has just lost 100 pounds by reducing fat in his diet and by exercising. Phil now wants to open a business where customers, for a large fee, would buy prepared food under the label "Phil's Fat-Free Food." Customers would also have access to exercise classes (at the current time, this means a low-impact aerobic class once a day and two stationary bicycles) and "Phil's Famous Counselors" (who at this time includes only Phil himself). Phil has come to you to design a marketing plan that will entice customers to pay for this service in what is a highly competitive market.

Your task is to develop a marketing plan that will comply with both federal and state regulations (use your own state regulations). Your instructor may also want you to compile a list of current advertisements in the weight-loss field and discuss whether they are deceptive.

FURTHER INFORMATION

www.ftc.gov/opa/1996/9602/scam.htm
www.bbb.org/advertising/nadproc.html
www.ama.org/
www.asa.org.uk/

CHAPTER 20

CONTEMPORARY LEGAL ISSUES IN EMPLOYMENT

LEARNING OBJECTIVES

After you have read this chapter, you should be able to:

1. Describe the concept of employment at will and the primary exceptions to it.
2. Discuss guidelines for avoiding defamation of former employees.
3. Discuss and analyze the legal and managerial issues involved with drug testing of employees.
4. Describe the limits of the legal protection for employees' use of e-mail and the Internet on the job.

CHAPTER OUTLINE

I. Employment at Will

II. Defamation of Former Employees

III. Drug Testing of Employees

IV. Other Privacy Issues

An employer concerned that his employees are falsely filing claims for workers' compensation decides to check up on one of those employees. How far can the employer go to investigate the employee? What actions can the employer take against the employee? What claims could the employee bring against the employer because of the investigation?

705

INTRODUCTION

No area within the legal environment of business is undergoing change faster than the law concerning the employment relationship. Significant social changes in the U.S. workforce, the globalization of business and increasing competitiveness affecting all aspects of business, and heightened public concern for fair treatment of workers have contributed to the creation of new legal rights and responsibilities for employers and employees. Many of these rights are extensions of earlier legal theories and are developing through the common law on a case-by-case basis.

Employee dishonesty and theft, the loss of productivity, and the rising medical and safety expenses caused by drug and alcohol abuse cost U.S. business billions of dollars a year. These concerns have driven many employers to institute drug or alcohol testing of employees, to conduct extensive background checks on prospective employees, to subject employees to increased surveillance on the job, or even to adopt rules prohibiting certain off-the-job conduct, such as dating coworkers. All of these actions have significant legal and ethical implications.

This chapter explores several of the most challenging contemporary issues affecting the employment environment, involving job security, and employee privacy.

EMPLOYMENT AT WILL

The relationship between employer and employee is governed by contract—the contract of employment. The employment contract may be written or implied, and it may be for a definite period of time, or it may be an "at will" contract. Some employees, such as professional athletes and high-level executives, are hired under written contracts for a specified term or period of time. If the employee is discharged, or fired, before that set period is up, then the employee may bring suit for breach of contract; likewise, if the employee leaves before the contract expires, the employer may pursue breach of contract action against the employee. Most employees, however, work under contracts of employment that are not of a specified length. Such contracts are said to be *at will contracts*—either the employer or the employee can terminate the employment relationship at his or her discretion.

This legal principle, originally borrowed from the English law of master and servant, was an extension of agency theory (as discussed in Chapter 8) in that the employment relationship was said to last only as long as the employee and employer both consented that it continue (in other words, had the "will" to continue). Therefore, if either one wanted to end the relationship, he or she could do so merely by saying, "I quit," or "You're fired." The effect of this concept in practice was that an employer could terminate an employee for, as one court said, "any reason or no reason." Similarly, an employee could quit at any time without reason.

Although the rule no longer holds force in England, courts in the United States have continued to follow it. This has tremendous significance for U.S. workers because the majority—perhaps as many as 70 percent—are "employees at will." Subsequent state and federal legislation, however, has narrowed the broad scope of the at will doctrine. For example, the National Labor

Relations Act forbids firing employees because they join a union or engage in union activities; Title VII of the Civil Rights Act of 1964 prohibits discharge because of an employee's race, color, sex, religion, or national origin; the Age Discrimination in Employment prohibits discharging older workers because of their age; and the Occupational Safety and Health Act forbids discharging an employee in retaliation for filing a safety complaint. State law may also limit an employer's right to fire—most states forbid firing an employee who has filed a workers' compensation claim for a work-related injury, and a number of states have also adopted "whistle-blower" laws, which prohibit discharging employees who have publicly disclosed employer wrongdoing. Montana has adopted legislation that requires an employer to have "good cause" for firing employees.

The at will rule, and any nonlegislative exceptions to it, are creatures of the common law; that is, they are judicially created. In the United States, common law doctrine is generally a matter of state jurisdiction—thus, the courts of each state determine to what extent the at will rule applies in their state.

Although on its face, the rule appears to treat employers and employees equally, in fact its application is usually harder on employees. When a worker is abruptly fired for no reason by a firm where he or she has worked for many years, the effect on the worker and his or her family is likely to be much more damaging than the effect on the company caused by one worker quitting a job. The company can typically hire someone else or eliminate the position, whereas the employee's family may be without income while he or she searches for another job.

Many commentators have argued that it is unethical and unfair to allow a business firm with numerous workers and considerable financial resources to simply terminate an employee without any good reason, thereby cutting off his or her sole source of income.

As the result of public pressure and numerous lawsuits initiated by fired employees over the past 10–20 years, three major nonstatutory exceptions to the employment at will rule have emerged (described in the following sections). Although no states have totally eliminated the rule, the growth of those exceptions has permitted many employees to challenge successfully their terminations. The cases usually arise when the fired employee brings a tort or contract lawsuit against the former employer under the theory of **wrongful discharge**.

VIOLATION OF PUBLIC POLICY

Most of us would be outraged if a friend of ours was fired from a job simply because he or she refused to perform an illegal act. Even though the employee may not have an employment contract for a definite term, this type of termination causes serious ethical concerns. Many would question the wisdom of our legal system if, for example, it permitted or encouraged the firing of a distributor who refused to pay a bribe to a customer, a lab technician who refused to certify false test results in a government safety report, or a salesperson who refused to participate in a price-fixing scheme.

Courts in several states have recognized this position by establishing the *public policy* exception to the employment at will rule. This doctrine generally holds that it is unlawful to terminate an employee for doing something that the official public policy of the state supports or promotes, such as refusing to break the law. It is sometimes difficult to determine exactly what "public policy" is; at the very least, however, this policy is established at the state level by the laws enacted by the legislature, the executive orders of the governor and top officials, and the major court decisions of the state. Some state courts are willing to construe statutory provisions very liberally in order to find a public policy that has been violated by a discharge. Other states are less willing to stretch conceptions of public policy; for example, the California Supreme Court, in *Foley v. Interactive Data Corp.* [47 Cal. 3d 654 (1988)], held that the employee alleging a discharge in violation of public policy must show that the policy or duty involved exists for the benefit of the public at large, not just the particular employer or employee. If the employee relies upon a statute to define the public policy, and that statute provides for remedies in the event of violation, the courts generally require that the employee pursue those statutory remedies rather than pursue a claim for wrongful discharge in violation of public policy. The following case discusses whether a plaintiff can rely upon federal, rather than state, legislation to define a public policy sufficient to allow a claim for wrongful discharge in violation of public policy:

In the Language of the Courts

FAULKNER V. UNITED TECHNOLOGIES CORPORATION, SIKORSKY AIRCRAFT DIVISION

240 Conn. 576, 693 A.2d 293 (Conn. Supreme Ct. 1997)

CALLAHAN, Chief Justice.

The plaintiff, John Faulkner, appeals from the judgment of the trial court . . . rendered in favor of the named defendant, United Technologies Corporation, Sikorsky Aircraft Division . . . . The plaintiff claims that his discharge for refusing to participate in the scheme violated public policy against government contract fraud as expressed in the Major Frauds Act. 18 U.S.C. §1031. He argues that the trial court improperly struck the first count of his . . . complaint on the ground that it failed to allege a connection between the public policy expressed in the federal statute and the public policy of the state of Connecticut . . . .

. . . The plaintiff worked for the defendant as a supplier quality assurance representative from October 2, 1978, until April 29, 1991, when he was discharged by the defendant. The plaintiff's job involved inspecting helicopter parts provided by various suppliers to ensure that the parts met with the defendant's engineering specifications. As part of his job, he was required to inspect parts supplied by subcontractors that were to be used in constructing United States Army Blackhawk helicopters

that the defendant was producing pursuant to contracts with the federal government. On numerous occasions, the plaintiff rejected substandard and defective parts provided by suppliers despite pressure from the suppliers and from his superiors to accept the parts. The plaintiff reported the existence of the defective parts to his superiors, who did nothing constructive in response, but instead warned the plaintiff that he might be disciplined in the future for rejecting parts he deemed defective. Thereafter, the allegedly defective parts were used in the construction of various Blackhawk helicopters.

On April 29, 1991, the defendant discharged the plaintiff on the ground that he had engaged in misconduct. In his complaint, the plaintiff alleged that the defendant actually discharged him because he refused to accept the substandard and defective helicopter parts supplied by the defendant's subcontractors on the Blackhawk helicopter project. He alleged further that the defendant discharged him because he refused to participate in allowing the use of the defective parts in producing helicopters under the government contract. He claimed that the defendant's action constituted a breach of the covenant of good faith and fair dealing existing between the parties because the discharge violated public policy against government contract fraud as expressed in the Major Frauds Act. 18 U.S.C. §1031(a).

The trial court construed the first count of the plaintiff's . . . complaint as alleging a wrongful discharge claim pursuant to the public policy limitation on the at-will employment doctrine, as enunciated in *Sheets v. Teddy's Frosted Foods, Inc.,* 179 Conn. 471, 427 A.2d 385 (1980), and its progeny. The court determined that, when a plaintiff brings such a claim charging a violation of public policy as expressed in a federal statute, the plaintiff must allege in his complaint that that violation of federal public policy also interfered with an important state interest. The court stated: "[T]here must be a substantial connection between the federal law that is violated and the state's own public policies. The federal law must protect an interest that has a substantial impact on state concerns." Because the plaintiff had failed to include in his complaint an allegation that his discharge implicated state public policy concerns, the trial court granted the defendant's motion to strike. . . .

In *Sheets v. Teddy's Frosted Foods, Inc., supra,* 179 Conn. at 480, 427 A.2d 385, in an effort to balance the competing interests of employers and employees, we recognized a public policy limitation on the traditional employment at-will doctrine. In *Sheets,* we sanctioned a common law cause of action for wrongful discharge in situations in which the reason for the discharge involved "impropriety . . . derived from some important violation of public policy." In *Morris v. Hartford Courant Co.,* 200 Conn. 676, 679, 513 A.2d 66 (1986), we recognized the "inherent vagueness of the concept of public policy" and the difficulty encountered when attempting to define precisely the contours of the public policy exception. In evaluating claims, "[w]e look to see whether the plaintiff has . . . alleged that his discharge violated any explicit statutory or constitutional provision . . . or whether he alleged that his dismissal contravened any judicially conceived notion of public policy."

The plaintiff . . . alleged that the defendant discharged him in violation of the public policy against government contract fraud expressed in the Major Frauds Act. 18 U.S.C. §1031. The Major Frauds Act "criminalizes the knowing execution or attempted execution of a scheme or artifice in order to defraud the [United States]." The act "targets schemes to defraud the United States in connection with procurement contracts executed by (1) prime contractors with the United States, or (2) subcontractors or suppliers on contracts in which there is a prime contract with the United States," if the value of the contract upon which the fraud is based is $1,000,000 or more. The act provides for the imposition of fines up to a maximum of $10,000,000 and for imprisonment up to a maximum of ten years. Congress enacted the Major Frauds Act "to curtail the ubiquitous and rampant fraud in the defense procurement area . . . The Joint Committee on the Judiciary asserted that procurement fraud was the most costly type of fraud being perpetrated against the federal government. The committee also noted the evils associated with the practice of "product substitution"—in which contractors provide defective products to the federal government—asserting that defense contractors that engage in "product substitution" endanger the lives of American soldiers and threaten national security. . . .

The complaint alleged that the defendant was producing the helicopters under a government contract, and that the defendant knew that it was using defective parts in the construction of the helicopters. As alleged in the complaint, the defendant's actions appear to constitute precisely the type of conduct that Congress intended to deter and punish by enacting the Major Frauds Act. In addition, the complaint alleged that the defendant discharged the plaintiff because he refused to approve the use of the defective parts. In sum, the complaint alleged that the defendant discharged the plaintiff because he refused to participate in violating 18 U.S.C. §1031.

In *Sheets,* we stated that "an employee should not be put to an election whether to risk criminal sanction or to jeopardize his continued employment." This appeal requires us to determine whether that proposition applies in a situation in which the source of the criminal sanction is federal, rather than state, law. In *Sheets,* the plaintiff alleged he had been discharged for reporting to his superiors repeated violations by his employer of the Connecticut Uniform Food, Drug and Cosmetic Act. We noted that the plaintiff's position as quality control director and operations manager exposed him to the possibility of criminal prosecution under the act. In allowing the plaintiff's wrongful discharge claim to proceed, we stated: "We need not decide whether violation of a state statute is invariably a prerequisite to the conclusion that a challenged discharge violates public policy. Certainly when there is a relevant state statute we should not ignore the statement of public policy that it represents." We did not, however, preclude the use of a federal statute to demonstrate that a discharge violated public policy. We perceive no difference between a situation in which an employee is forced to engage in conduct that may expose him to federal criminal sanctions and a situation in which an employee is forced to engage in conduct that may expose him to state criminal sanctions. The effect on the employee of being forced to choose between violating the law or facing discharge by his employer is the same regardless of which sovereign criminalizes the conduct. The plaintiff in the present case, like the plaintiff in *Sheets,* held a position requiring him to ensure the quality of the defendant employer's products. If he had followed his superiors' orders, and had approved the use of helicopter parts that he knew to be substandard and defective, he might have exposed himself to potential criminal sanction pursuant to 18 U.S.C. §1031. We conclude, therefore, that the plaintiff's substitute complaint, in which he alleged that his employer discharged him because he refused to violate a federal criminal statute, and specifically cited the statute, adequately stated a cause of action for wrongful discharge pursuant to *Sheets* and its progeny.

The defendant argues that a wrongful discharge claim pursuant to the public policy limitation on the at-will employment doctrine cannot be predicated solely on a violation of federal law . . .

First, we do not agree with the defendant that *Sheets* requires a violation of *state* public policy in order for a plaintiff to state a cause of action. Rather, *Sheets* and its progeny refer generally to violations of public policy as expressed in explicit statutory or constitutional provisions, or judicial decisions. In situations such as the present case, in which the plaintiff alleged that his employer discharged him because he refused to violate a federal criminal statute, and specifically cited the federal statute in his complaint, we do not find it necessary for the plaintiff also to allege an explicit connection between the federal statute and the policy of the state. We find support for our conclusion in the decisions of the courts of many other jurisdictions that have determined that claims brought pursuant to the public policy limitation on the at-will employment doctrine can be predicated on the violation of public policy expressed in a federal statute. . . .

Moreover, it is not necessary that the plaintiff specifically allege that his discharge violated the public policy, expressed in *Sheets,* against employers forcing employees to commit criminal acts. The question of whether a challenged discharge violates public policy, state or federal, by forcing the commission of criminal acts, or otherwise, is a question of law to be decided by the court, not a question of fact that a plaintiff must allege in his complaint . . . .

Finally, we do not believe that our decision today impermissibly tips the balance between the interests of employer and employee, or creates any more uncertainty for employers than that generated by *Sheets.* The very nature of our decision in *Sheets* requires a case-by-case analysis of employee claims, which necessarily creates a certain degree of uncertainty in the law. . . . It is clear from the record that the plaintiff's . . . complaint sufficiently alerted the defendant, as well as the trial court, that the plaintiff's claim was a claim for wrongful discharge pursuant to the public policy limitation set forth in *Sheets.*

"We are mindful that courts should not lightly intervene to impair the exercise of managerial discretion or to foment unwarranted litigation. We are, however, equally mindful that the myriad of employees without the bargaining power to command employment contracts for a definite term are entitled to a modicum of judicial protection when their conduct as good citizens is punished by their employers." *Sheets v. Teddy's Frosted Foods, Inc.,* supra, 179 Conn. at 477, 427 A.2d 385. Our decision today falls squarely within the analytical framework enunciated in *Sheets* and its progeny.

The judgment is reversed and the case is remanded with direction to deny the defendant's motion to strike, and for further proceedings according to law.

CASE QUESTIONS

1. What public policy did Faulkner rely upon to support his claim of wrongful discharge? What was the source of that policy?
2. Does Connecticut recognize the public policy exception to the at will doctrine? Why did the trial court refuse to recognize Faulkner's claim?
3. Explain the rationale behind the public policy exception to the at will doctrine.
4. Should it matter that an employee bases a claim of public policy on federal law rather than state law? How does the Connecticut Supreme Court decide that question? Why?

EXPRESS OR IMPLIED CONTRACTS OF EMPLOYMENT

Some states have also recognized other exceptions to the at will doctrine. If a company provides its employees with a personnel handbook that says that employees will only be fired for certain enumerated offenses or that the company will follow certain procedures in disciplining employees, some state courts hold that the manual forms part of the contract of employment, binding the employer to follow its terms. Employers can avoid that result by including a disclaimer in the handbook stating that it does not constitute part of the contract or create a binding obligation on the employer to follow its terms.

In other cases, fired employees have been able to convince a court that employers intended employees to rely on certain conduct, promises, or statements made by the employer. Where those actions have created an impression or reasonable belief in the employee's mind that the employing firm will live up to its promises, courts have sometimes held that those promises became part of an "implied contract" with the employee. The courts have held that the conduct of the employer, in light of the statements or procedures, serves to create a contract that amends the employee's at will employment relationship.

In one leading case in this area of the law, Charles Toussaint, a manager for Michigan Blue Cross/Blue Shield, was fired for no stated reason after working there for five years. Blue Cross argued that he was hired for an indefinite time and thus was an employee at will. Mr. Toussaint stated that, when he was hired, he was told that he would be retained as long as he did his job properly. For proof, Mr. Toussaint pointed to the company personnel manual, which stated that the firm would release employees "for just cause only." The Michigan Supreme Court found that even though there was no actual contract, "when the employer chooses, presumably in its own interest, to create an environment in which the employee believes that . . . the personal policies and practices . . . are established and official at any given time, purport to be fair, and are applied consistently and uniformly," the employer is bound to honor that promise as part of the "implied contract" with its employees. [See *Toussaint v. Blue Cross and Blue Shield of Michigan*, 408 Mich. 579 (1980).] However, the court decisions from a number of other states make it much more difficult to establish such an implied contract for at-will employees, as in *Lobosco v. NY Telephone Co.,* 96 N.Y.2d 312, 751 N.E.2d 462 (N.Y. 2001).

COVENANT OF GOOD FAITH AND FAIR DEALING

implied covenant of good faith and fair dealing: Obligation, implied by law, that the employer cannot terminate an employee in bad faith.

Perhaps the broadest exception to the employment at will rule is the **implied covenant of good faith and fair dealing**. This doctrine, only adopted in approximately 10 states so far, is based on the concepts of ethics and fairness and is enforced through the judicial power of equity—the ability of courts to reform contracts, create implied trusts, and take other actions to avoid an unjust result. The cases recognizing this implied "covenant" (a word often used in connection with religious or ethical concepts) represent instances in which one party, usually a company, has terminated an employee for a reason or in a manner that simply cannot be allowed. In such cases, the court holds that the law requires the employer must treat the employee in good faith when exercising aspects of the employment relationship. A number of states, such as New York and Pennsylvania, have refused to adopt this exception to the at will doctrine; the courts in those states hold that implying a covenant of good faith and fair dealing is inconsistent with the at will nature of the employment relationship.

In one example, an employer terminated an employee, after many years of good service, just a few days before the worker would have qualified for a company pension. In another example, a court sided with an employee who had been fired after 25 years without any good cause, apparently so the firm could avoid paying him $46,000 in sales commissions. These covenant of fair dealing cases often involve situations in which the first two exceptions cannot be used, that is, the employee cannot prove the existence of any implied contract term, or he or she cannot show that the firing was due to a refusal to violate a state law.

The following case discusses the implied contract and the covenant of good faith and fair dealing exceptions to the employment at will rule.

E.I. DUPONT DE NEMOURS AND CO. V. PRESSMAN

679 A.2d 436 (Del. Sup. Ct. 1996)

FACTS

Pressman, a biomedical engineer at DuPont, was hired to develop the company's medical imaging technology. During his time at DuPont, Pressman received raises and positive evaluations from his managers, including Pensak, his immediate supervisor. In January 1988, Pressman met with Pensak to discuss a possible conflict of interest created by Pensak's involvement as a paid technical advisor with a competing medical imaging technology company, Genesis. Pensak had arranged for Pressman to meet with representatives of Genesis to discuss Pressman's knowledge of medical imaging technology. When Pressman told Pensak that the relationship with Genesis was a conflict of interest, Pensak became livid and told Pressman to mind his own business.

Shortly thereafter, Pensak ordered Pressman "grounded"—restricting his travel and requiring Pensak's permission to meet with any visitors. Pensak also began to raise questions about Pressman's work performance with company personnel officials. Pensak placed an "anonymous unsigned" negative evaluation in Pressman's file. Pressman's performance rating was lowered to "satisfactory," and then "marginal." Pressman was terminated by Pensak on April 12, 1989. Pressmen sued DuPont and Pensak for wrongful dismissal in breach of an implied contract and for breach of the implied covenant of good faith and fair dealing. The trial jury held that Pensak misrepresented Pressman's responsibilities to make it appear that Pressman did not complete assigned tasks, edited progress reports to superiors to understate Pressman's accomplishments, and failed to pass along reports showing Pressman's significant accomplishments during the time period in which Pressman's termination was decided. For DuPont's breach of the implied covenant of good faith and fair dealing, the trial jury awarded Pressman $422,700 in compensatory damages for lost wages. The jury also awarded Pressman $25,000 for emotional distress and interest, and $75,000 in punitive damages on the breach of the covenant claim. The court held for DuPont on the breach of implied contract claim. DuPont appealed; the appeals court reversed the trial court verdict, holding for DuPont on all claims. Pressman appealed to the Delaware Supreme Court.

DECISION

Where an employee does not have a contract of employment for a specified term, there is a strong legal presumption that the contract for employment is at will. However, courts have recognized exceptions to the at will doctrine in which the employer acts in violation of public policy, in violation of an implied contract, or in bad faith, fraud, or deceit in violation of an implied covenant of good faith and fair dealing.

Pressman's claim does not fit within the public policy category since he has not identified a clear statement of public policy that was violated prior to his termination. He alleges that DuPont fired him in retaliation for questioning the propriety of Pensak's business practices. This fact, standing alone, does not rise to the level of a recognized claim under the public policy exception.

Another recognized exception to the at will doctrine involves an implied contract—in which the employee reasonably relies upon employer's promises of job security statements, as created by the employer's actions, promises, or documents such as a handbook. Here Pressman did not establish that there was any promise of secure employment.

Some courts have held that an employee has a claim for wrongful termination in breach of an implied covenant of good faith and fair dealing where the discharge was based on an employer's desire to avoid the payment of benefits already earned by the employee, such as the sales commissions [as in *Fortune v. National Cash Register*, 373 Mass. 96, 364 N.E. 2d 1251 (Mass. Sup. Ct. 1977)] or sick leave benefits [as in *Metcalf v. Intermountain Gas Co.*, 116 Idaho 622, 778 P. 2d 744 (Idaho Sup. Ct. 1989)]. But Pressman has not stated a claim under that line of cases because he has not identified any benefit to which he was entitled, such as earned commissions.

Other courts have held that the implied covenant of good faith and fair dealing allows an employee to sue when an employer or its agent induces another to enter into an employment contract through actions, words, or the withholding of information, which is intentionally deceptive in some material way to the contract, or manufactures materially false grounds to cause an employee's dismissal. In Pressman's case, the application of the implied covenant of good faith and fair dealing relates solely to the acts of the employer manifesting bad faith and unfair dealing through deceit or misrepresentation in falsifying or manipulating Pressman's employment record to create false grounds to terminate him. Because Pressman was an at will employee, he can not sue over the termination itself; rather his legal claim arises from Pensak's creation of false grounds and manufacturing a fictitious record as a basis for termination. The evidence shows that Pensak set out on a campaign to discredit Pressman by creating fictitious negative information about Pressman's work and hiding positive information. Based on the distorted record he created, Pensak went to his superiors and caused Pressman to be terminated. If Pensak did these acts, and did them intentionally, that amounted to a breach of the implied covenant of good faith and fair dealing.

But the trial court erred when it stated that DuPont breached the implied covenant of good faith and fair dealing if it discharged Pressman as a result of hatred, ill will, or intent to injure. Dislike or hatred as the sole basis for termination of an at-will employee does not violate the implied covenant; but fraud, deceit, and misrepresentation, either in the inducement to enter a contract or in intentionally fictionalizing the employee's performance to cause dismissal, may be actionable as a breach of the implied covenant. The legal harm to Pressman, and the breach of the implied covenant of good faith and fair dealing, come from Pensak's creation of false and fraudulent grounds for the discharge; such maliciously employed deceit and subterfuge constitutes bad faith prohibited by the implied covenant. DuPont was made aware of this course of events after the fact and ratified Pensak's actions. Thus, DuPont can be held liable to Pressman on the claim of breach of the implied covenant of good faith and fair dealing.

But even though Pressman has established that he was discharged in breach of the implied covenant, he cannot recover damages for emotional distress or punitive damages; according to *Foley v. Interactive Data Corp.* [47 Cal.3d 654, 254 Cal. Rptr. 211, 765 P. 2d 373 (Cal. Sup. Ct. 1988)], only contractual damages, that is, lost wages and employment benefits, are available as damages for the wrongful termination of an at-will employee in breach of the implied covenant of good faith and fair dealing.

The decision of the court of appeals was reversed and the trial court decision for Pressman on the breach of the implied covenant of good faith and fair dealing was affirmed; the court remanded the case for the calculation of damages in accordance with its opinion.

CASE QUESTIONS

1. Why did the courts state that Pressman's firing was not in violation of public policy? Did Pressman establish that there was an implied contract not to discharge him except for good cause?
2. What does the implied covenant of good faith and fair dealing require of an employer? Could Pressman have been legally fired for refusing to follow his supervisor's orders?
3. Why does the court state that the legal harm to Pressman comes not from his discharge but from the manner in which Pensak caused it? Explain.
4. What remedies are available for an employee discharged in breach of the implied covenant of good faith and fair dealing?

WHISTLE-BLOWERS

Many wrongful discharge cases involve employees who were terminated after they reported to the press or to governmental authorities some illegal or unethical actions that had occurred in the company. These people are often called *whistle-blowers* because they "blew the whistle" (like a referee in a game) on some activity they thought was improper.

Whistle-blowers who are fired because they disclose employer wrongdoing may be able to challenge their discharge under the exceptions to the at will doctrine. Such whistle-blower claims usually raise a claim that the discharge was in violation of public policy, especially where the employee was fired for refusing to violate a law. A number of states have passed whistle-blower laws to protect employees who act to report employer wrongdoing that poses a threat to public safety or health, and federal legislation such as the Occupational Safety and Health Act and Energy Reorganization Act (applying to employees of nuclear facilities) protect employees from retaliation for reporting employer violations of the law. The Sarbanes-Oxley Act, passed in the wake of the Enron and Worldcom corporate scandals, prohibits employers from discharging, demoting, suspending, harassing or threatening employees who provide information regarding the possible commission of any federal offense to law enforcement authorities. Sarbanes-Oxley provides for both civil and criminal penalties against employers who violate the whistle-blower protection provisions.

The whistle-blower laws are clear statements of public policy to protect employees who blow the whistle, as required by the courts to establish a claim under the public policy exception to the at will doctrine. However, where the whistle-blower laws provide for specific remedies for employees terminated in violation of such laws, the courts generally require that the fired employee seek the statutory remedies under the whistle-blower laws rather than sue under the common law exceptions to the at will doctrine. Where the whistle-blowing employee, for whatever reason, does not come under the coverage of the whistle-blower law, courts may allow the employee to sue under the common law public policy exception and will still look to the whistle-blower law as the expression of public policy, as in *Kulch v. Structural Fibers*, Inc. [78 Ohio St.3d 134, 677 N.E. 2d 208 (Ohio Sup. Ct. 1997)].

DEFAMATION OF FORMER EMPLOYEES

Increasingly, employers who fire employees are facing defamation suits by those former employees. This may occur, for example, when the former employer gives an unfavorable reference regarding the employee to a potential future employer. One recent national study estimated that one-third of all defamation actions filed in recent years were suits brought by former employees. As was discussed in Chapter 11, the tort of defamation can result when one person makes a false statement about another that is "published" (communicated to one or more third parties). The statement must not only be false but also cause harm to the employee—for example, by damaging his or her reputation or hurting his or her future job prospects. The defamation will be called *libel* if it is written and *slander* if it is verbal. Juries are often sympathetic to the claims of fired employees. During the 1980s employees won 72 percent of employment defamation cases tried in California, with an average award of $582,000[1].

JOB REFERENCES

Most employee/employer defamation cases have resulted from statements made by employers regarding job references for ex-employees. Employment applications typically ask for a list of an applicant's previous employers. If an employee has been terminated for poor performance on the job, the former employer is likely to make negative comments about the worker when contacted by a prospective employer. Of course, in order to be defamatory, the statements made must be false. If the comments are accurate, then there is no defamation. But if the former employer reports, for example, that the employee was fired for theft, habitual lateness, or poor work habits, such information will adversely affect the individual's employment opportunities. If the information is not true, or if the documentation of the poor performance is so incomplete that it is unclear whether the statements are true, the employee may succeed in a defamation lawsuit.

[1] Yulish and Heshizer, "Defamation in the Workplace," Labor Law Journal (June 1989), p. 355.

qualified privilege: Protection from liability for good faith actions by employers providing references to prospective employers.

compelled self-publication: The doctrine holding an employer liable for an employee's reporting of the reason for the employee's dismissal to a prospective employer.

Employers who, in good faith, mistakenly furnish inaccurate information to prospective employers are afforded some protection, however, by the legal principle called **qualified privilege**. This theory holds that if a good reason exists why the employer made the statement, the statement is made in good faith, and it is limited to the response to the inquiry, then the employer is not liable even though the statement made is inaccurate—in other words, the statement is "privileged."

The doctrine of qualified privilege is especially applicable where the ex-employee has asked for a reference—there will be no liability for an innocent misrepresentation. On the other hand, if the former employer intentionally or maliciously gives false information, or if the information is disseminated to a wider circle than necessary, such communication is not covered by the privilege.

In light of these theories, many firms have refused to provide any information on former employees. However, employers who believed that a "no comment" policy would totally protect them have occasionally still been held liable for defamation under the doctrine of **compelled self-publication**. This theory provides that if the employer can "foresee" that an employee will have to repeat to a prospective employer the false reason given for his dismissal, the former employer may be held liable. This developing doctrine has only been adopted in a few states but represents a threatening trend to management. To protect employers against defamation claims arising out of references, several states, such as California, Illinois, Georgia, Oklahoma, and West Virginia, have passed laws that provide immunity for employers providing references. Most such legislation simply restates the common law qualified privilege doctrine as it applies to employers communicating information regarding current or former employee job performance to prospective employers; however, the Oklahoma law also requires that the affected employee consent to the employer's communication to the prospective employer.

DRUG TESTING OF EMPLOYEES

One of society's most difficult problems today is the abuse of drugs by persons at all economic levels. According to one report, 68 percent of drug users are employed. Without doubt, some of this drug use occurs on the job, as well as off. Studies have shown that workers under the influence of drugs have more accidents, contribute disproportionately to other safety problems, have higher rates of absenteeism and turnover, raise health insurance and liability costs, and produce less, at a lower quality level, than other employees. One study put the cost of drug use to U.S. business at $60 billion per year. By 1996, more than 81 percent of U.S. companies had instituted some sort of program to test potential and/or current employees for drugs, and many more test today. Firms have also developed drug awareness, education, and counseling programs. Companies often have decided to begin pre-employment drug testing programs, mainly to avoid a rush of drug-using applicants who cannot get jobs elsewhere.

BRITISH EMPLOYERS PLAN TO BEGIN DRUG TESTING

Workplace drug testing appears to be another American trend that is being adopted in England. A report issued by the Independent Inquiry into Drug Testing at Work, funded by the Joseph Rowntree Foundation, and the Network of European Foundations, predicted that there will be a huge increase in the number of firms testing employees for drug use. According to the report, approximately 4% of British employers presently tested employees, but an additional 9% indicated that they were likely to begin such testing within the next year. The report also stated that the evidence of the impact of drug testing on employee performance and safety is inconclusive. A public opinion poll connected with the report found that 8 out of 10 employers would consider implementing drug testing if they believed that drug or alcohol use were affecting staff productivity. Employers raised concerns that drug testing could pose privacy and legal issues, and could cause morale problems; most employers viewed excessive drinking as a greater problem than drug abuse. The report urged the government to set clear guidelines for drug testing of employees.

Sources: "Big Brother Fear as Employers Plan to Triple Drug Tests," *The Times* (London), June 29, 2004; "Employers Want Clearer Guidelines on Drug Testing," *The Daily Telegraph*, June 28, 2004; "Testing Times for Drug Takers?," *Nottingham Evening Post*, June 29, 2004.

Although surveys have shown that a large majority of the population favors drug testing in connection with employment, technical, ethical, and legal problems abound. Testing procedures normally involve taking a sample of urine, hair or blood from an individual. Nonspecific, "broad spectrum" tests, such as radio immunoassay (RIA) and Enzyme-Multiplied Immunoassay Technique (EMIT), have not proven to be particularly reliable. These tests only identify a broad class of organic chemicals rather than a particular chemical. A person who has eaten a poppyseed bagel, or taken over-the-counter medication like Advil or Nuprin, can produce positive results under these tests.

Other more comprehensive, "narrow spectrum" tests, such as Gas Chromatography (GC) and the Gas Chromatography/Mass Spectrometry Test (GC/MS), are much more accurate—and more expensive. The latter tests cost $200 to $300, compared with $20 to $30 for the broad spectrum tests. Many companies use the cheaper tests first and then follow up with a second narrow spectrum test when the individual's first result is positive. Another technical problem is that the tests cannot show exactly when the person used the drug, only that it is present in the body fluids at the time of the test.

Drug testing can create ethical problems for companies as well, depending on how the tests are conducted. Ethical issues associated with drug testing are discussed in Chapter 7.

On the legal front, the National Labor Relations Board has held that unionized employers must bargain with their respective unions before implementing drug testing programs for employees, since such tests represent a "substantial change in working conditions." Blood and urine tests have been legally challenged as a violation of the right to privacy. A valid urine test requires that an individual urinate into a container in the presence of another person—normally a very private act. The need for actual observation has been demonstrated because some potential employees have actually hidden a bag containing "clean" urine in their clothes when they went for their pre-employment drug test.

A number of legal issues concerning the right to perform drug testing in employment apply somewhat differently for public and private employees.

PUBLIC EMPLOYEES

Public employees have greater rights to "privacy" and against illegal search and seizure because the Constitution protects persons against actions *by the government*. The Constitution does not protect individual citizens against acts by other private parties (such as private businesses). Public sector employers are subject to the requirements of the Fourth (for federal employers) and the Fourteenth (for state and local employers) Amendments of the U.S. Constitution, which prohibit unreasonable searches and seizures. Drug testing is considered to be a search; therefore, in order to conduct legal drug tests, government agencies must show that a strong public interest is involved to overcome the individual's rights under the Constitution.

Drug use in the workplace can have devastating consequences. Several well-publicized railroad accidents have occurred in recent years, and some were apparently caused by employees who were acting under the influence of drugs. A particularly tragic accident happened in 1987 when a Conrail engineer, driving a string of locomotives, ran a stopswitch and collided with an oncoming Amtrak passenger train. Sixteen people were killed and 176 injured. The engineer later admitted to smoking a marijuana joint shortly before the crash. The following case involves drug testing requirements in the railroad industry.

SKINNER V. RAILWAY LABOR EXECUTIVES' ASSOCIATION

489 U.S. 602 (1989)

FACTS

The Secretary of Transportation of the United States is authorized by a federal statute to issue rules and regulations addressing railroad safety. Evidence indicates that alcohol and drug abuse by railroad employees has contributed to several train accidents. As a result, the Secretary issued regulations prohibiting crew members and certain other railroad employees from using drugs or alcohol while on duty or while subject to being called for duty. The federal regulations required railroads to perform blood and urine tests on all those employees after accidents, even though there was no indication of previous or current drug use by those persons. Several labor organizations representing employees of private railroads challenged the regulations on the grounds that they violated the Fourth Amendment of the Constitution.

DECISION

In an opinion written by Justice Kennedy, the U.S. Supreme Court noted first that although the drug tests were carried out by privately owned railroad corporations, the actions were required by regulations of the federal government. Although the acts of private businesses are not usually covered by the Constitution, where the private party acts as an instrument or agent of the Government, the protection of the Fourth Amendment was held to apply to the procedure in question.

As to whether the blood and urine tests were considered a "search," the Court stated that "a compelled intrusion into the body for blood to be analyzed for alcohol content" has been recognized, in many previous cases, to be a search. Similarly, the collection and testing of urine intrudes upon an expectation of privacy long recognized by society. Therefore, the Fourth Amendment will apply to these actions to prevent unreasonable searches and seizures.

The Constitution does not prohibit all searches, only those that are not "reasonable" and are not made pursuant to a warrant issued by a judicial officer. The permissibility of the search is determined by balancing "its intrusion on the individual's Fourth Amendment interests against its promotion of legitimate governmental interests." Clearly, the government has a strong interest in regulating the conduct of railroad employees to ensure "the safety of the traveling public and of the employees themselves."

The Court considered whether a warrant, based upon "probable cause," should be required before such a search could be conducted. Finding that the warrant requirement was designed in large part to protect citizens from random or arbitrary searches, the Court noted that the law and regulations at issue here set limits and specify when such a test can be performed. Furthermore, since the evidence of drugs will disappear quickly, any testing must be done soon after the accident to have meaning. The government, therefore, has a strong interest in performing the tests without delay.

Justice Kennedy also pointed out that employees in safety-sensitive railroad positions have a diminished expectation of privacy because they are employed in an industry pervasively regulated by the government. Further, the regulations will promote the public and governmental interest by deterring employees from using drugs or alcohol in the first place. Since they realize that they will be discovered if an accident occurs, employees will be less likely to use drugs and alcohol, and accidents will be prevented.

Overall, the Court found that the concerns for public safety, the limited nature and scope of the tests, and the lessened privacy expectations of the railroad employees, more than balanced their individual privacy rights. Thus, the Court upheld the drug testing program of the Department of Transportation.

CASE QUESTIONS

1. Did the employees to be tested work for the federal government or private business? Why were the testing procedures subject to the requirements of the Fourth Amendment?
2. Are public or private employees given more Constitutional protection related to searches and privacy issues? Why?
3. What are the interests that are balanced by the Supreme Court in reaching its decision? Do you agree with the decision?

As the Supreme Court held in *Skinner*, the government may subject employees to random drug testing when the testing supports an important government interest, such as public safety. In *National Treasury Employees Union v. Von Raab* [489 U.S. 656 (1989)], decided the same day as *Skinner*, the Supreme Court also upheld drug testing for U.S. Customs Service employees who were involved in combating drug smuggling, who carried guns, or who had access to classified material. In general, such "focused" drug testing requirements are more likely than "blanket" testing programs to pass constitutional requirements, because it is easier to demonstrate that the focused programs promote a compelling government purpose or public interest. However, the Supreme Court did uphold a mandatory drug testing program for all high school varsity athletes in *Vernonia School District v. Acton* [515 U.S. 646 (1995)], and testing for all students participating in extra-curricular activities, *Board of Ed. Of Indpt. School Dist. No 92 of Pottawatomie County* v. *Earls* [536 U.S. 822 (2002)]; and refused to hear an appeal of a U.S. Court of Appeals decision allowing a school district to subject all employees to random testing for drugs and alcohol to promote and protect public safety [*Knox County Education Association v. Knox County Board of Education*, 158 F.3d 361 (6th Cir. 1998), cert. denied, 528 U.S. 812 (1999)]. The Supreme Court did strike down a Georgia law that required all candidates for state political offices to certify that they passed a drug test, because the state officials had not shown that there was a drug problem among public officials, and the political offices did not involve high-risk or safety-sensitive positions [*Chandler v. Miller*, 520 U.S. 305 (1997)].

PRIVATE EMPLOYEES

In 1988, Congress enacted the Drug-Free Workplace Act. This law established a federal policy that federal contractors must maintain a work environment free of illegal drugs. All contractors who receive federal funds must certify that they will abide by this rule and must inform employees of their written policy. Employers doing more that $25,000 of business per year with the federal government must have a written drug-free workplace policy and establish a drug-free awareness program.

In addition to the Drug-Free Workplace Act, other federal regulations require drug testing of employees in particular industries, such as transportation. (Recall that regulations requiring testing of all members of train crews involved in accidents were discussed in the *Skinner v. Railway Labor Executives' Association* case.) Although the U.S. Constitution does not afford protection to employees in the private sector, some state constitutions do extend rights to private sector employees. Several states, such as Alaska, Arizona, California, Illinois, Florida, Louisiana, Hawaii, Massachusetts, Montana, Rhode Island, and South Carolina, have an express right to privacy in their state constitutions. Other states have constitutional provisions that recognize some specific aspects of privacy rights or have established the right to privacy as part of their common law, allowing persons whose privacy is violated to sue in tort. West Virginia courts have held that drug testing, in the absence of reasonable suspicion, is an invasion of privacy (except for employees in safety-sensitive positions or subject to federal testing regulations). Laws in Connecticut and Iowa restrict drug testing of employees to those employees in safety-sensitive positions, to employees subject to federal testing regulations, or when the employer has reasonable grounds to suspect an employee is using drugs. These legal provisions offer private sector employees some protection against unreasonable drug testing—testing that is overly intrusive or that violates the reasonable expectations of privacy of employees.

Although the states are taking some steps to protect employees from unreasonable drug testing requirements, they are also taking steps to discourage employees from abusing drugs and to encourage employers to test employees. A number of states have drug-testing laws; such legislation generally sets out procedural requirements to be followed by employers testing their employees or applicants for drugs. Those requirements usually include giving employees and applicants written notice of the employer's drug testing policy, strict requirements for handling and storing of testing samples, confidentiality requirements, and the right of employees who test positive for drug use to demand a confirmatory test at their own expense. In a number of states, employers that establish drug testing programs for employees receive reductions in their insurance premiums for the state workers' compensation programs. Many states also deny unemployment benefits to employees fired for failing, or refusing to take, a drug test, and also deny workers' compensation benefits to employees injured on the job while under the influence of drugs.

OTHER PRIVACY ISSUES IN EMPLOYMENT

POLYGRAPH AND HONESTY TESTING

Many other types of tests are used to screen prospective employees today. Polygraph tests effectively measure the sweat in a person's palm or a rise in blood pressure when someone is subjected to stressful questioning on sensitive matters; the reliability of such testing is questionable and polygraph results are not admissible in court cases. The federal Employee Polygraph Protection Act of 1988 [EPPA] made polygraph (lie detector) testing by most private sector employers illegal; the act does not cover public sector employers. The EPPA prohibits employers from administering polygraph tests, and from disciplining or discharging employees for refusing to take a polygraph test. There are four exceptions under the act; employers are allowed to administer polygraph tests to: 1) employees working as consultants to, or employees of, firms that are contractors to federal national security intelligence operations; 2) employees engaged in providing private security services, armored car services, and installing or maintaining security alarm systems; 3) employers whose business involves manufacture, sale, or distribution of certain drugs may test employees who have direct access to the drugs; and 4) employers who have a reasonable basis to suspect that employees may have been involved in an incident that resulted in economic loss to the employer may request that those employees take polygraph tests. The act sets strict conditions for any polygraph tests permitted under the act: 1) the tests must be administered by a licensed polygraph examiner; 2) the employer must provide employees to be tested with a written statement describing the incident being investigated, and specifically identifying the economic loss and the reason for testing those employees; 3) the employees must be given a written notice of the date, time, and location of the test; 4) the employees must read and sign a written notice that they can not be required to submit to the test as a condition of employment; and 5) the employees have the right to review all questions that will be asked during the test and the right to terminate the test at any time. The EPPA also specifically prohibits the polygraph operator from asking questions relating to the religious beliefs, political beliefs or affiliations, beliefs or opinions on racial matters, questions relating to sexual behavior, and questions relating to affiliation with, opinions regarding, or the participation in activities of, labor unions. After the test has been administered, the employer is required to provide the employee with a written copy of the examiner's conclusions about the test, a copy of the questions asked, and of the responses of the employee. The testing examiner can only disclose information acquired through the test to the employer requesting the test and the employees subjected to the tests. Employers may not discharge or discipline the employees, or refuse to hire applicants, solely on the basis of the polygraph test results.

Violations of the EPPA are subject to penalties of up to $10,000; individual employees or applicants who are affected by such violations can sue for damages, reinstatement, back pay and legal fees.

Most states also have legislative prohibitions on the use of polygraph tests. As a result, employers are increasingly turning to psychological tests and exhaustive database searchs.

Paper-and-pencil tests, designed to measure an employee's or applicant's honesty and integrity, have become commonplace since polygraph testing was outlawed. Such tests may include "honesty tests" or psychological profile tests; honesty tests generally seek to measure various counterproductive workplace behaviors such as untruthfulness, perceptions about the pervasiveness of employee theft, illegal drug use, and admissions of theft. The validity of the honesty tests is a matter of controversy—a 1990 study by the federal Office of Technology and Assessment found research on the effectiveness of such tests to be inconclusive, but a 1991 study by the American Psychological Association is much more positive and favorable to honesty testing. Psychological profile tests are generally not intended to be used as an employment screening device, but some employers may use them in the hiring process. Honesty testing is not prohibited by the federal EPPA but is restricted in several states. Massachusetts specifically prohibits employers from using honesty tests; Rhode Island bars using honesty tests as the primary basis of employment decisions, and Wisconsin also limits the use of honesty tests by employers.

Psychological tests may include questions regarding religious beliefs, sexual behavior, or even bathroom habits—such testing may be viewed by employees (or applicants) as overly intrusive. Using psychological profile tests as an employee selection device may raise issues under the Americans with Disabilities Act or state antidiscrimination legislation; those laws will be discussed in Chapter 22. Employers desiring to use psychological profile tests should have a legitimate, work-related rationale for such testing and should not use psychological tests as a screening device for employment.

ON-THE-JOB SURVEILLANCE

Traditionally, employees have had little legal protection from various forms of spying, eavesdropping, and surveillance by their bosses. Many employers believe that electronically monitoring employee actions provides important data related to product quality and customer satisfaction. In recent years, technological advances have made it possible for companies to monitor workers using computers, cameras, and sophisticated audio and video recording equipment. Companies have installed tiny, fish-eye lenses in walls to watch employees suspected of crimes, as well as computers that can track which airline employees write the most reservations. One even used special chairs to measure employee wiggling ("wigglers aren't working"). In response to this increased use of new technology, employee groups have pushed for creation of additional state and federal statutory and common law protections regarding a right to privacy for employees. Connecticut law prohibits employers from using any electronic surveillance in workplace areas "designed for their health or personal comfort", such as rest rooms, locker rooms or lounges; employers who use any form of electronic monitoring of other areas of the workplace must give employees written notice of the monitoring, and must post the notice in a conspicuous place.

In general, federal and state laws allow employers to intercept phone and electronic communications with a court order or with the consent of at least one party to the call. The employer owns the telephones and can normally give the required consent. Secret tape recording of such phone conversations, particularly those of an employee's personal conversations, and later disclosure of the contents of private conversations, however, are beyond the provisions of the law and may subject the employer to substantial criminal and tort liability.

Employers contend that such methods improve efficiency, honesty, and guarantee that customer calls will be handled quickly and politely. Employee groups argue, however, that the surveillance creates an atmosphere so full of stress and fear that productivity and quality actually decline. They point to a series of studies suggesting that workers who are secretly monitored suffer significantly higher stress levels, including depression, anxiety, and exhaustion. Some employers have reduced use of monitoring of employees because of concerns about employee morale and privacy.

Some workers have turned the tables by secretly recording conversations with their bosses. Federal law allows secret taping, as long as one of the people being recorded knows about it. At least 12 states (including New York) have similar state laws, while about 14 other states (including California) prohibit such secret taping. Maryland law prohibits secret taping of telephone conversations. Whether legal or not, employees who feel they are being set up for termination are increasingly more likely to hide tape recorders in their purses or jackets when they meet with their bosses.

In the modern workplace, many employees are encouraged or told to use e-mail to send messages to fellow workers and other business contacts. Although each employee has a different code that he or she enters to access the appropriate electronic menu, such codes are commonly known and, in fact, increasingly published in directories. Employees are human beings, and there is no doubt that many e-mail messages sent and received on company computers are of a personal nature. The employee may believe that such messages are private and cannot or will not be monitored by other employees of the company, but this is not true.

E-mail and the Internet make it possible for employees to communicate instantaneously with coworkers and clients halfway across the world and let employees access up-to-the-minute news or financial information. Employees can also visit on-line with friends, circulate dirty jokes or chain letters to thousands of people, shop on-line, play the stock market, bid on items for auction, or download hard-core pornography from their desk—instead of working on their employer's business. Employers—both public and private sector—are increasingly becoming concerned about how employees use the company's computer network and are attempting to control that use. Business firms that invest substantial sums of money to establish e-mail systems intend that they be used for business purposes. Moreover, it is not difficult to write programs allowing managerial employees to access all e-mail files. There are even some commercial software programs available for purchase to achieve this goal. Hence, many firms monitor employees' messages regularly or occasionally.

Employees who are fired as a result of using their systems for personal purposes have sometimes sued their employers for invasion of privacy. The Electronic Communications Privacy Act of 1986 [ECPA], 18 U.S.C. 2510 *et seq.,* directly prohibits accessing or disclosing the contents of e-mail without proper consent. The ECPA is an amendment to Title III of the Omnibus Crime Control and Safe Streets Act of 1968, also known as the "wiretap law." The ECPA does not directly address employer rights but offers three exceptions that allow employers to monitor workplace e-mail. E-mail may be monitored if (a) one party consents, (b) the employer provides the e-mail service, and (c) the monitoring is done in the ordinary course of business. Courts have interpreted the ECPA to allow employers to monitor e-mail if the employee has consented, the employer provides the e-mail service, or if the employer is monitoring e-mail for business content and use. Delaware law requires employers who monitor or intercept employee telephone communications, e-mail or Internet access or usage must provide written or electronic notice of such monitoring to the employees.

Most suits filed by employees fired for misusing e-mail have been decided in favor of the companies, on the grounds that they own the systems, and ought to be able to monitor them, similar to telephone calls. In *Smyth v. The Pillsbury Co.,* 914 F.Supp. 97 (E.D. Pa. 1996), the court upheld the firing of an employee for sending "inappropriate and unprofessional" comments (including threats to "kill the backstabbing bastards") over the company e-mail system. The court stated: "Once [the] plaintiff communicated the alleged unprofessional comments to a second person (his supervisor) over an e-mail system which was apparently utilized by the entire company, any reasonable expectation of privacy was lost . . . . plaintiff voluntarily communicated the alleged unprofessional comments over the company e-mail system. We find no privacy interests in such communications . . . . Moreover, the company's interest in preventing inappropriate and unprofessional comments or even illegal activity over its e-mail system outweigh any privacy interests the employee may have in those comments." In *Bohach v. City of Reno,* 932 F.Supp. 1232 (D.Nev. 1996), the court held that police officers had no reasonable expectation of privacy for messages sent over the police department's computerized paging system; the city, as provider of the system, was free to access messages stored in the system as it saw fit. The ECPA, §2701(c)(1), specifically allows employers to access or seize e-mail stored on the employer's computer system, according to *Fraser v. Nationwide Mutual Insurance Co.,* 352 F.3d 107 (3rd Cir. 2004).

However, when an employer goes beyond monitoring to publish and publicly humiliate an employee as the result of some personal message, the employer may be held liable.

CONNECTICUT GENERAL STATUTES ANNOTATED

§31-48b. Use of electronic surveillance devices by employers limited.
(a) For purposes of this section, "employer" means the owner or owners in the case of an unincorporated business, the partners in the case of a partnership, the officers in the case of a corporation or in the case of the state, any town, city or borough, or district, local or regional board of education, or housing authority or district department of health, the chief executive officer thereof.

(b) No employer or agent or representative of an employer shall operate any electronic surveillance device or system, including but not limited to the recording of sound or voice or a closed circuit television system, or any combination thereof, for the purpose of recording or monitoring the activities of his employees in areas designed for the health or personal comfort of the employees or for safeguarding of their possessions, such as rest rooms, locker rooms or lounges.

(c) Any employer, who violates any provision of subsection (b) of this section shall, for the first offense, be fined five hundred dollars, for the second offense be fined one thousand dollars and for the third and any subsequent offense be imprisoned thirty days.

* * *

§31-48d. Employers engaged in electronic monitoring required to give prior notice to employees. Exceptions. Civil penalty

(a) As used in this section:

(1) "Employer" means any person, firm or corporation, including the state and any political subdivision of the state which has employees;

(2) "Employee" means any person who performs services for an employer in a business of the employer, if the employer has the right to control and direct the person as to (A) the result to be accomplished by the services, and (B) the details and means by which such result is accomplished; and

(3) "Electronic monitoring" means the collection of information on an employer's premises concerning employees' activities or communications by any means other than direct observation, including the use of a computer, telephone, wire, radio, camera, electromagnetic, photoelectronic or photo-optical systems, but not including the collection of information (A) for security purposes in common areas of the employer's premises which are held out for use by the public, or (B) which is prohibited under state or federal law.

(b) (1) Except as provided in subdivision (2) of this subsection, each employer who engages in any type of electronic monitoring shall give prior written notice to all employees who may be affected, informing them of the types of monitoring which may occur. Each employer shall post, in a conspicuous place which is readily available for viewing by its employees, a notice concerning the types of electronic monitoring which the employer may engage in. Such posting shall constitute such prior written notice.

(2) When (A) an employer has reasonable grounds to believe that employees are engaged in conduct which (i) violates the law, (ii) violates the legal rights of the employer or the employer's employees, or (iii) creates a hostile workplace environment, and (B) electronic monitoring may produce evidence of this misconduct, the employer may conduct monitoring without giving prior written notice.

(c) The Labor Commissioner may levy a civil penalty against any person that the commissioner finds to be in violation of subsection (b) of this section, after a hearing conducted in accordance with sections 4-176e to 4-184, inclusive. The maximum civil penalty shall be five hundred dollars for the first offense, one thousand dollars for the second offense and three thousand dollars for the third and each subsequent offense.

(d) The provisions of this section shall not apply to a criminal investigation. Any information obtained in the course of a criminal investigation through the use of electronic monitoring may be used in a disciplinary proceeding against an employee

DELAWARE CODE ANNOTATED, TITLE 19

§705 Notice of monitoring of telephone transmissions, electronic mail and Internet usage.

(a) As used in this section, "employer" includes any individual, corporation, partnership, firm or association with a place of business in Delaware and the State of Delaware or any agency or political subdivision thereof.

(b) No employer, nor any agent or any representative of any employer, shall monitor or otherwise intercept any telephone conversation or transmission, electronic mail or transmission, or Internet access or usage of or by a Delaware employee unless the employer either:

(1) Provides an electronic notice of such monitoring or intercepting policies or activities to the employee at least once during each day the employee accesses the employer-provided e-mail or Internet access services; or

(2) Has first given a 1-time notice to the employee of such monitoring or intercepting activity or policies. The notice required by this paragraph shall be in writing, in an electronic record, or in another electronic form and acknowledged by the employee either in writing or electronically.

The notice required by this subsection shall not apply to activities of any law enforcement officer acting under the order of a court issued pursuant to Chapter 24 of Title 11.

(c) Whoever violates this section shall be subject to a civil penalty of $100 for each such violation. A civil penalty claim may be filed in any court of competent jurisdiction.

(d) The provisions of this section shall not be deemed to be an exclusive remedy and shall not otherwise limit or bar any person from pursuing any other remedies available under any other law, state or federal statute, or the common law. The violations of this section by an employer shall not be admitted into evidence for the purpose of, or used as, a defense to criminal liability of any person in any Court in this State.

(e) The provisions of this section shall not apply to processes that are designed to manage the type or volume of incoming or outgoing electronic mail or telephone voice mail or Internet usage, that are not targeted to monitor or intercept the electronic mail or telephone voice mail or Internet usage of a particular individual, and that are performed solely for the purpose of computer system maintenance and/or protection.

OFF-THE-JOB ACTIVITIES

Not only do some employers occasionally monitor their employees' actions at work, but others take an interest in what their workers do away from the job. With health care costs rising about 9 percent each year, some companies have instituted programs that charge higher health care premiums to those employees who engage in activities that cause health problems, such as smoking. Some firms simply will not hire smokers at all. Texas Instruments found, through an in-house study, that smokers' health costs at the company were 50 percent higher than nonsmokers; the company began charging smokers an additional $10 per month.

Although the negative health implications of smoking are quite well-established, there is concern about the future implications of employer monitoring of off-the-job actions. "When they tell you that you can't smoke on your own time, the next thing you know they'll tell you that you can't have sex but once a week, and if you have sex twice a week you're fired," declared Oklahoma State Senator Carl Franklin. "What about the health implications of the guy who eats fried chicken 20 times a month?" asked one company executive.

A few companies have allowed employees to reduce their health-care premiums if they achieve certain levels of weight loss or cholesterol standards, or if they quit smoking. In response to employer actions against smokers, some 29 states have passed laws prohibiting discrimination against people who smoke off the job. These efforts are often supported by the tobacco companies.

LOVE, SEX, AND DATING: WHAT CAN THE EMPLOYER SAY?

Whenever men and women work together, the potential for dating and workplace romance arises. Office romances raise several concerns for employers. Employers worry that employees' morale and productivity will suffer if and when the romance sours and the employees must work in close proximity. Fellow employees who must work with the lovers may feel resentment and jealously. The prospect for sexual harassment claims resulting from one employee's unrequited attempts to date a coworker are also major concerns for employers. As a result, some employers have adopted work rules prohibiting dating among coworkers. The following case involves a suit by a manager who was fired because he was involved in a romantic relationship with a subordinate.

BARBEE V. HOUSEHOLD AUTOMOTIVE FINANCE CORPORATION

6 Cal.Rptr.3d 406, 113 Cal.App.4th 525 (Cal. Ct. of App. 2003)

FACTS

Robert Barbee was the national sales manager for HAFC and was responsible for leading HAFC's entire sales force. He began dating Melanie Tomita, a member of HAFC's sales force, in October 2000. The chief executive officer of HAFC, John Vella, became aware of rumors that Barbee was dating someone within the sales force. During December 2000, Vella informed Barbee that "intercompany dating was a bad idea." HAFC had a conflict of interest policy that provides in relevant part: "Situations of relationships between employees may . . . cause a conflict of interest. If a consensual intimate relationship between a supervisor and any employee within that supervisor's direct or indirect area of responsibility is desired, it is the supervisor's responsibility to bring this to management's attention for appropriate action (i.e., possible reassignment to avoid a conflict of interest)." In March 2001, Barbee met with Vella and Pat Boney, HAFC's national director of human resources. Barbee was asked about the nature of his relationship with Tomita. Barbee replied that he had a "special relationship" with her and that they were very good friends. Boney told Barbee that such a relationship created a potential conflict of interest and that Barbee would have to end the relationship or, in the alternative, either Barbee or Tomita could resign. Boney said that he would let Barbee consider his options over the weekend. The following Monday Barbee informed Vella and Boney that both he and Tomita wanted to stay with HAFC. Barbee conceded that based on this conversation, Vella and Boney "probably assumed" he was agreeing to end his relationship with Tomita. Not long after that meeting, an HAFC customer called Barbee and offered him tickets to the National Collegiate Athletic Association regional semi-final and final basketball games. Barbee asked Tomita's fellow sales representative, who was at the customer's office at the time, to pick up the tickets for him. Barbee attended the games with Tomita. Boney and Vella later asked Barbee whether he had attended the games with Tomita, and Barbee admitted that he had. Soon thereafter, Vella and Boney fired Barbee. Barbee filed a suit against HAFC, alleging, among other claims, invasion of privacy. HAFC moved for summary judgment and the trial court granted HAFC's motion for summary judgment and entered judgment in favor of HAFC. Barbee then appealed to the California Court of Appeals.

DECISION

Barbee claimed that HAFC's termination of his employment based on his relationship with Tomita violated his right to privacy under article I, section 1 of the California Constitution, which provides: "All people are by nature free and independent and have inalienable rights. Among these are enjoying and defending life and liberty, acquiring, possessing, and protecting property, and pursuing and obtaining safety, happiness, and *privacy*." (Italics added.) Article I, section 1 of the California Constitution creates a right of action against private action as well as government. Plaintiffs alleging an invasion of privacy in violation of the state constitutional right to privacy must establish each of the following: (1) they had a legally protected privacy interest; (2) they had a reasonable expectation of privacy in the circumstances; and (3) that conduct by the defendant constituted a serious invasion of privacy.

1. A Legally Protected Privacy Interest

Barbee argues that he has a legally protected privacy interest in pursuing an "intimate relationship." By using the phrase intimate relationship, and arguing that his right to privacy under article I, section 1 of the California Constitution, Barbee claims that section 1 protects the "sexual lives of the unmarried"; and appears to contend that he has a legally protected privacy interest in pursuing a sexual relationship with Tomita. Barbee has not cited, and we have not found, any California cases that have directly addressed whether a person has a privacy interest in pursuing an intimate relationship under the state constitutional right to privacy. The cases on which Barbee relies involve primarily the right to be free from intrusive questioning regarding one's sexual activities. None stand for the proposition that individuals have a legally protected privacy interest in pursuing sexual relationships pursuant to the state constitutional right to privacy.

In *Lawrence v. Texas* (2003), 539 U.S. 558, 123 S.Ct. 2472, 156 L.Ed.2d 508 (*Lawrence*), the United States Supreme Court held that a statute that prohibited sodomy between persons of the same sex violated the due process clause of the United States Constitution. The court also stated that a prohibition on sodomy that applied to both same-sex and different sex participants would also be invalid. The *Lawrence* court also wrote that the statute at issue in that case was unconstitutional because, "the State cannot demean [the petitioners'] existence or control their destiny by making their private sexual conduct a crime." In reaching its holding, the *Lawrence* court stated: "[I]ndividual decisions by married persons, concerning the intimacies of their physical relationship, even when not intended to produce offspring, are a form of 'liberty' protected by the Due Process Clause of the Fourteenth Amendment. Moreover, this protection extends to intimate choices by unmarried as well as married persons."

The California state constitutional right to privacy provides protection that is distinct from, and in some respects greater than, that provided by the federal Constitution. Accordingly, in the wake of *Lawrence,* Barbee may have a legally protected privacy interest in pursuing an intimate or sexual relationship, guaranteed by article I, section 1 of the California Constitution. However, although we make this assumption for purposes of the analysis of this case, we need not resolve this issue because, as discussed below, Barbee cannot establish the second necessary element of his invasion of privacy claim that he had a reasonable expectation of privacy in the circumstances of this case.

2. A Reasonable Expectation of Privacy in the Circumstances

Barbee argued that he had a "reasonable expectation of privacy in his relationship with Tomita."However, the court noted that the extent of a privacy interest is not independent of the circumstances. Even when a legally cognizable privacy interest is present, other factors may affect a person's reasonable expectation of privacy. For example, customs, practices, and physical settings surrounding particular activities may create or inhibit reasonable expectations of privacy. A 'reasonable' expectation of privacy is an objective entitlement founded on broadly based and widely accepted community norms. HAFC has cited numerous cases in which courts have approved of restrictions on intimate relationships between employees of an organization or entity where such relationships presented potential conflicts of interest within the organization. The fact that courts have recognized that employers have legitimate interests in "avoiding conflicts of interest between work-related and family-related obligations; reducing favoritism or even the appearance of favoritism; [and] preventing family conflicts

from affecting the workplace," strongly suggests that a supervisor has no reasonable expectation of privacy in pursuing an intimate relationship with a subordinate. Courts have also recognized that managerial-subordinate relationships present issues of potential sexual harassment. These cases indicate that "customs, practices, and physical settings," weigh heavily against finding a "broadly based and widely accepted community norm" that supervisors have a privacy right to engage in intimate relationships with their subordinates. In addition, HAFC had an express policy requiring that any supervisor who wanted to maintain an intimate relationship with a subordinate bring the matter to the attention of management to allow management the opportunity to take appropriate action to avoid the potential conflict of interest. Further, Vella expressly told Barbee that "intercompany dating was a bad idea." Thus, Barbee had "advance notice" that HAFC believed his conducting an intimate relationship with a subordinate would present a potential conflict of interest. This notice further diminished any expectation of privacy Barbee otherwise may have had in pursuing an intimate relationship with Tomita.

The court concluded that Barbee did not have a reasonable expectation of privacy in pursuing an intimate relationship with Tomita and therefore was unable to establish a necessary element of his invasion of privacy claim. Therefore, the grant of summary judgment for HAFC on Barbee's privacy claim was proper. The court affirmed the judgment of the trial court.

CASE QUESTIONS

1. Why would an employer have a policy prohibiting managers from dating employees under their supervision?
2. Was Barbee aware of HAFC's policy? How did Barbee's supervisors react to his relationship with Tomita?
3. Was Barbee able to establish that he had a privacy interest protected under the California Constitution? Why or why not? Explain.

4. Would the court have decided the case differently if Barbee had been dating an employee not under his supervision? In Rulon-Miller v. IBM, 162 Cal. App. 3d 241 (1984), the California Court of Appeals held IBM liable for tort damages for firing an employee because she was dating an employee of a competing company. Is that decision inconsistent with this case? Explain.

OFF-DUTY CONDUCT

At least six states have passed laws that prohibit firms from discriminating against employees for any off-the-job actions that are legal in that state. This type of law prohibits discrimination against those workers who smoke or drink alcohol or eat fried chicken away from work, but also possibly those employees who date other employees in violation of company policy or commit other violations of company regulations. Note that the determination of just what conduct is protected by such laws is open to judicial interpretation.

Section 201-d of the New York State Labor Law protects employees from discrimination in terms or conditions of employment because of their "legal recreational activities," their political activities, and their "legal use of consumable products" off the job. The courts are split over the question of whether the New York legislation protects an employee from being fired because of a personal relationship: the Appellate Division of the New York Supreme Court, in *New York v. Wal-Mart Stores, Inc., 207 A.D.2d 150 (1995)*, held that it did not protect an employee from termination for violation of Wal-Mart's "no fraternization" but the U.S. District Court for the Southern District of New York held that an employee could not be fired because she lived with a former employee [*Pasch v. Katz Media Corp.*, 10 I.E.R. Cases 1574, 1995 WL 469710 (Aug. 8, 1995)]; the U.S. Court of Appeals for the Second Circuit followed the Wal-Mart decision in allowing the employer to fire an employee who was having an affair with a co-worker, *McCavitt v. Swiss Reinsurance Amer. Corp.*, 237 F.3d 166 (2001). Other courts have also upheld employer "no dating coworkers" policies: *Patton v. J.C. Penney Co.*, 301 Or. 117, 719 P.2d 854 (1986), and *Federated Rural Ins. Co. v. Kessler*, 131 Wis.2d 189, 338 N.W.2d 553 (1986); but *Slohoda v. U.P.S., Inc.*, 193 N.J.Super. 586, 475 A.2d 618 (1984) held that UPS's "non-fraternization" policy violated New Jersey law.

Employers may go beyond forbidding dating by coworkers and adopt policies that prevent spouses from working together; such policies are usually motivated by morale concerns—to avoid coworkers bringing their domestic disputes into the workplace—and to avoid charges of favoritism. In *Harper v. TWA*, 525 F.2d 409 (8th Cir. 1975), the U.S. Court of Appeals upheld a TWA policy that prohibited spouses from working together in the same department; if coworkers married, the employer required that the spouse with less seniority had 30 days to transfer, take a leave, or be terminated. The court held that the policy was neutral on its face and did not have a discriminatory effect on female employees. (TWA subsequently changed the policy to apply only when one spouse supervised the other.)

One of the more controversial issues in society today is the appropriate degree of protection and tolerance the legal system should provide for homosexual behavior. Federal antidiscrimination laws do not include lesbians or homosexuals as a protected class, although a number of state statutes do [California, Connecticut, Delaware, Hawaii, Iowa, Maryland, Massachusetts, Minnesota, Nevada, New Jersey, New Mexico, New York, Oregon, Rhode Island, Vermont, Wisconsin, Illinois, Colorado, Maine, Washington, and the District of Columbia].

SUMMARY

Some of the most difficult legal issues in employment law today involve job security, drug testing, and other employee privacy concerns. Employers faced with the pressures of global competition and the need to increase efficiency and make their workers more productive are placing increased demands on employees; some employees resent the pressures and requirements of the workplace that intrude into their personal lives. The social changes in the workforce and the rapid increase in technology have created new tensions and pressures. The courts are called upon to attempt to strike some balance; employers who go too far face extensive liability, and employees who oppose such intrusions and pressures too much may lose their jobs. Much of the law in these areas comes through development of older common law principles on a case-by-case basis.

It is crucial that employers and employees understand each other's needs and goals and the principles of law that apply to such situations. The ever-increasing worldwide competition faced by U.S. businesses makes it unlikely that such problems will disappear in the future—if anything, they are likely to intensify. In time, there may be calls for more laws regulating the workplace, although the current antiregulatory mood of the public makes increased government involvement in employment unlikely in the near future. Thus, the courts will need to resolve legal disputes and update common law legal theories as employees bring actions concerning job security, privacy, drug testing, surveillance of workers, and other infringements on their rights both on and off the job. Employment law will necessarily develop to meet the new problems arising from the changing nature of employment in the 21st century.

CHAPTER QUESTIONS

1. John Roe was a San Diego police officer for seven years; he was fired when the San Diego Police Department discovered that he was selling sexually-explicit videos through the adults-only section of eBay. The videos showed Roe masturbating while wearing a generic police uniform; Roe sold the videos under the name "Code3stud." Roe filed suit against the San Diego Police Department, claiming that his off-duty activities were protected by the First Amendment of the U.S. Constitution, and he could not be disciplined for those activities. How should the court rule—for Roe or for the police department? Explain your answer. [*Roe v. City of San Diego*, 543 U.S. 77 (2004)].

2. Kramer worked for Rite-Aid in downtown Baltimore. His supervisor became concerned about "inventory shrinkage" that she suspected was caused by employee theft. The supervisor requested that Kramer take a polygraph test, according to company policy. Kramer refused to take the test, and in response, the supervisor cut back Kramer's work hours and arranged to transfer him to a store 50 miles away. The supervisor hoped that such changes would force Kramer to quit; Kramer did quit two weeks later. Maryland state law prohibits employers from requiring employees to take polygraph tests and forbids discharging employees who refuse to take such tests. Kramer files a wrongful discharge against Rite-Aid and the supervisor. What arguments can Kramer make to challenge Rite-Aid's actions? Under which of the exceptions to the at will rule can he base his suit? What defense can Rite-Aid make to those claims? Who is likely to win the suit? Why? Explain. [*Moniodis v. Cook*, 494 A.2d 212, 64 Md. App. 1 (1985)]

3. Catherine Wagenseller, a nurse at an Arizona hospital, went on an eight-day rafting trip with several coworkers. Prior to the trip she had established a superior work record and had a very good relationship with her supervisor, Ms. Smith. During the trip, she became increasingly uncomfortable with certain activities such as nude bathing and heavy drinking. During the trip, members of the group, including her boss, created and performed a skit to the tune "Moon River," which ended with the group "mooning" the audience. After returning from the trip, the group performed the skit twice back at the hospital. Ms. Wagenseller chose not to participate in any of these activities. Upon her return to work, her relationship with her supervisor deteriorated sharply, and she was eventually fired. Although she was an employee at will, she sued for wrongful discharge. Should any of the exceptions apply? What should the result be? [*Wagenseller v. Scottsdale Memorial Hospital*, 710 P.2d 1025 (Ariz. 1985)]

4. Homer Simpson was employed as an instrument panel monitor at a nuclear power plant operated by Giant Electrical Utility Co. of Springfield, Pennsylvania. Giant required all of its power-plant employees to sign a form consenting to random drug testing as a condition of employment; the form stated that refusal to submit to such tests would result in termination of employment. After 10 months on the job, Mr. Simpson was requested to take a drug test; he refused, claiming he did not use drugs and that there was no reasonable basis to suspect him of drug use. Giant terminated Mr. Simpson, and he filed for unemployment compensation. Giant contested his unemployment compensation claim. What arguments can Mr. Simpson make to support his claim for unemployment compensation? What arguments can Giant make to oppose his claim? What is the likely outcome of the case? Why? Explain. [See *Moore v. Unemployment Compensation Board of Review*, 134 Pa. Cmwlth. 274, 578 A.2d 606 (1990).]

5. Pacific Bell issued its "Management Employment Security Policy" in 1986; the policy stated that Pacific Bell would attempt to protect the jobs of all management personnel who continued to meet performance expectations in the event of business changes or reorganizations. Pacific Bell stated that the policy would be in force as long as there was no change that will materially affect Pacific Bells' achievement of its business plan. In 1992, Pacific Bell

notified its managers that it was forced to discontinue the policy because of changing industry conditions. It replaced the policy with a new, more flexible, layoff policy. Asimus was a manager who was affected by the termination of the Management Employment Security Policy; he filed suit against Pacific Bell for breach of contract and fraud by discontinuing the Management Employment Security Policy. Is Asimus's suit likely to be successful? Explain your answer. [*Asimus v. Pacific Bell*, 23 Cal. 4th 1 (Ca. Sup. Ct. 2000).]

6. Mr. and Mrs. Spears owned a package store in Arkansas that had been burglarized. Suspecting that one of their employees was involved, they installed a recording device on the business telephone extension in their mobile home and secretly listened to and recorded 22 hours of the conversations of the employee over the next two months. Much of the conversation involved "sexually provocative" exchanges between the employee and a married man with whom she was having an affair. Later, Mr. and Mrs. Spears told the employee's husband and the other man's wife about the conversations. The employee sued for damages. What should the result be? [*Deal v. Spears*, 980 F.2d 1153 (8th Cir. 1992)]

7. The U.S. Customs Service is the government agency responsible for processing and inspecting people and goods coming into the country. One important role it has is stopping and seizing illegal drugs. In 1986 the Customs Service announced that drug tests would thereafter be given to all persons seeking employment or promotion to positions that have the following responsibilities: (1) deal with drug enforcement, (2) involve the carrying of firearms, and (3) handle "classified" materials. The employees' union filed suit to block the program, claiming that it violated the Fourth Amendment. What should be the result and why? [*National Treasury Employees Union v. Von Raab*, 489 U.S. 656 (1989)]

8. United Parcel Service, Inc., fired a manager in Mississippi who violated the company's "no dating between managers and subordinates" policy. Mississippi has no law prohibiting employers from terminating employees for actions that are not illegal in that state. The manager sued, claiming that the company's regulation of his off-duty actions invaded his privacy. What should be the result? Why? [*Watkins v. United Parcel Service, Inc.*, 979 F.2d 1535 (5th Cir. 1992)]

9. Cort and Pincus had worked for Bristol Meyers Co. as sales representatives in the Boston area for a number of years; they were at will employees. After a period of reduced sales in the region, the company's sales manager sent the sales representatives a lengthy questionnaire containing questions that could be used for making a psychological evaluation of the sales force. Cort and Pincus objected to a number of the questions on the grounds that they were highly personal, offensive, and were not related to job performance in any way. They either left such questions blank or gave frivolous answers to them. They subsequently received poor job performance reviews and were later terminated. They argued that the poor sales performance was due to Bristol Meyer's difficulties in producing one drug and the loss of a customer bid on another drug. When Bristol Myers refused to reinstate them, they sued for wrongful discharge and invasion

of privacy. Under which of the exceptions to the at will rule should they sue? Explain. What arguments can they use to support their invasion of privacy claim? What arguments can the employer make to defend against its suit? What is the likely outcome of their suit? Why? Explain. [*Cort v. Bristol Meyers Co.*, 431 N.E.2d 908 (Ma. 1982)]

10. Richard Delloma was fired by Consolidation Coal Company when he was accused of sexual harassment; he had been superintendent of a mine and allegedly made sexual advances to female employees and offered to excuse their absences in return for having sex with him. After his termination, he applied for a job with Arch Minerals, another mining firm. The human resource manager of Arch telephoned the president of Consolidation for information about Delloma. In response to the question of why Delloma was fired, the president replied that "there had been some record-keeping irregularities" involving employee attendance. Delloma was not hired by Arch, and filed suit against Consolidation and its president. What claims can Delloma make against the company and its president? Is his suit likely to be successful? Explain your answer. [*Delloma v. Consolidation Coal Co.*, 996 F.2d 168 (7th Cir. 1993)].

PRACTICAL EXERCISE

Steven suspects that the employees at his book store are cheating him on workers compensation. He has had 5 of his 25 employees collect workers compensation in the past year for various injuries they allegedly incurred while working. Some claimed back strains from lifting heavy boxes, one broke an arm after slipping on a wet floor, and one claimed stress-related disability. Steven does not agree with the stress claim and thinks some of the injuries were the result of off-time activities. Rather than work on eliminating workplace hazards, Steven has decided to hire a private detective to monitor secretly his employees on and off the job.

Steven's private eye follows one employee, Elyse, who is currently receiving workers compensation for a back injury, to her fitness club, and shoots videotape of her sitting in the hot tub, talking with friends, doing aerobics, and swimming with her two-year-old child. The detective then follows Elyse to her home, which she shares with another woman and child. He later places a tap on her phone. After monitoring 25 hours of her private conversations, the investigator learns that she is involved in a romantic relationship with the other woman. He also learns that Elyse really did hurt her back lifting a box at work, and her doctor has urged her to swim on a regular basis to build up her back. Elyse also has talked on the phone about smoking marijuana at least once.

You have just been hired as a consultant for Steven's bookshop. He asks you to meet with his private eye and then prepare a memo to him (Steven) regarding: (1) whether he can fire Elyse—or refuse to reinstate her when she "recovers"—due to her apparent lesbian activity, (2) whether he should confront Elyse with the evidence he has about her personal life, (3) whether he can require her to take a lie detector test or a drug test before returning to work. Also include in your memo a discussion of whether Steven has incurred any liability to Elyse due to his actions.

FURTHER INFORMATION

www.aclu.org/
   The American Civil Liberties Union.
www.shrm.org/
   The Society for Human Resource Management.
www.epic.org/
   The Electronic Privacy Information Center.
www.amanet.org/
   The American Management Association.

CHAPTER 21

EQUAL EMPLOYMENT OPPORTUNITY LAW: TITLE VII

After you have read this chapter, you should be able to:

1. Explain the coverage, administration, and enforcement of Title VII of the Civil Rights Act of 1964.

2. Describe the concepts of unintentional and intentional discrimination, disparate treatment and impact, race-norming, and seniority and their applications under Title VII.

3. Discuss the issues raised by the concept of affirmative action.

4. Analyze Title VII's application to sex discrimination issues, including payment concerns, pension benefits, and sexual harassment.

5. Discuss how Title VII applies to discrimination based on religion or national origin.

CHAPTER OUTLINE

I. Title VII of the Civil Rights Act of 1964

II. Title VII and Sex Discrimination

III. Discrimination Based on Religion or National Origin

IV. Remedies Under Title VII

You are an employer whose manufacturing business has expanded in the past few years because you were successful in winning government contracts; but as those contracts expire, your business is shrinking. You may have to lay off some employees—whom you had hired to work on the government contracts; a large percentage of those employees are Latinos and African-Americans. If you use inverse seniority ("last hired, first fired") to lay off the employees, the minority employees will lose their jobs. How do you decide which employees to lay off without getting sued for employment discrimination? After studying this chapter, you should be able to decide how to proceed with the layoffs.

INTRODUCTION

Chapters 21 and 22 discuss the law of employment discrimination, usually known as Equal Employment Opportunity (or EEO) law. This chapter focuses on the primary law addressing employment discrimination: Title VII of the Civil Rights Act of 1964 (referred to simply as Title VII). Chapter 22 will discuss other EEO legislation and related employment issues.

Prior to the passage of the Title VII, no legal prohibition existed against race, sex, or other discrimination by private sector employers. (The Equal Protection and Due Process provisions of the U.S. Constitution dealt with discrimination by public sector employers.) The Civil Rights Movement of the late 1950s and early 1960s was the moving force behind the development of Title VII and the Civil Rights Act. In the summer of 1963, Dr. Martin Luther King Jr. led a massive march on Washington to press for passage of civil rights legislation, and President Kennedy made such legislation a priority. When Lyndon Johnson became President after Kennedy was assassinated, he mobilized all of his legislative and persuasive skills to push the law through Congress, despite stiff opposition from Southern legislators. A member of the House of Representatives from Virginia offered an amendment to the bill, extending the prohibition against the forms of employment discrimination covered in the bill to include sex discrimination, hoping that such a change would scuttle the bill. He was wrong—the Civil Rights Act was passed by Congress and signed into law by President Johnson in 1964. Title VII of the Act, which deals with employment discrimination, took effect July 2, 1965.

Title VII was amended in 1968 to modify the procedures for enforcing the law; the 1972 amendments extended the law to cover public sector employers at the state and local level. The Pregnancy Discrimination Act of 1978 amended Title VII to include pregnancy within the definition of sex discrimination. Also, the Civil Rights Act of 1991 made substantial changes to the law. Specifically, the Act provides for jury trials and extends the types of damages available. The 1991 legislation was passed to overturn several decisions by the Supreme Court that were perceived as making it more difficult for plaintiffs to sue under the Title VII.

TITLE VII OF THE CIVIL RIGHTS ACT OF 1964

Title VII of the Civil Rights Act prohibits employment discrimination based on race, color, religion, sex, and national origin. Any discrimination in the terms or conditions of employment, such as the refusal or failure to hire, the discharge of any individual, or the discrimination against any individual with respect to compensation, privileges, or benefits of employment because of that individual's race, color, religion, sex or national origin, is illegal under Title VII. Title

VII also prohibits retaliation against employees who avail themselves of procedures under the act or who oppose practices illegal under the act.

COVERAGE OF TITLE VII

Title VII applies to employers with at least 15 employees who are engaged in an industry affecting interstate commerce. The Supreme Court decision in *Walters v. Metropolitan Education Enterprises, Inc.* [519 U.S. 202 (1997)] upheld the use of the "payroll method" for determining the number of employees—are there at least 15 employees on the payroll for each working day of 20 or more weeks in the current or preceding calendar year? State and local governments are also covered by Title VII; the federal government and wholly owned federal corporations are covered under separate provisions of Title VII. Coverage was extended in 1995 to include the employees of Congress and such bodies as the Government Printing Office, the General Accounting Office, and the Congressional Budget Office. The 1991 amendments also extend Title VII to cover U.S. employers that employ U.S. citizens abroad; however, if compliance with Title VII would force the employer to violate the law of the country in which the workplace is located, then the employer need not comply.

Title VII also applies to employment agencies and to labor unions that either operate a hiring hall or have at least 15 members. Employment agencies are prohibited from discriminating on any of the prohibited grounds (race, color, religion, sex, or national origin) in announcing openings, interviewing candidates, or in referring applicants to employers. Title VII prohibits labor unions from discriminating in employment opportunities or in the status of members or applicants.

ADMINISTRATION AND ENFORCEMENT OF TITLE VII

The *Equal Employment Opportunity Commission (EEOC)* administers and enforces Title VII. The EEOC investigates and litigates complaints under the Act. The EEOC also has the power to initiate enforcement actions on its own if it finds a "pattern or practice" of discrimination in employment. The EEOC is empowered to issue binding regulations and nonbinding guidelines for interpreting and complying with the legislation. The regulations under Title VII require employers, unions, and employment agencies to post notices summarizing the act's requirements; failure to display the notice is punishable by a fine of not more than $100 per violation. The Act also requires that employers must maintain payroll records and other records relating to applicants and to employee promotion, demotion, transfer, and discharge.

Enforcement Procedures   Section 706(c) of Title VII requires that an individual seeking to file a complaint under the Act must first file with the state or local agency authorized to handle employment discrimination, if one exists. Sixty days after filing with the state or local agency, or upon termination if the state or local agency terminates its proceedings prior to 60 days, the individual may file the complaint with the EEOC. If an individual is required to go to the state or local agency first, the limitations period under Title VII requires that a complaint be filed with the EEOC within 300 days from the alleged act of discrimination. If no state or local agency exists, then the individual must file the complaint with the EEOC within 180 days of the alleged act of discrimination.

When Does a Violation Occur?   The time limit for filing a complaint under Title VII makes it important to determine when the alleged act of discrimination took place. In most situations, it will not be difficult to determine the date of the violation. However, some cases present problems in determining when the alleged violation actually occurred. For example, in *Delaware State College v. Ricks* [449 U.S. 250 (1980)], a professor alleged that he was denied tenure because of his race; after he was informed of the college's decision to deny him tenure, he was given a final, one-year contract. At the expiration of the one-year contract, he was terminated; he then filed a complaint with the EEOC, alleging race discrimination. The Supreme Court held that the time limit for a Title VII violation starts on the date that the individual becomes aware of, or should be aware of, the alleged violation (in Ricks' case, the date he learned that he was denied tenure), and not from the date on which the alleged violation begins to have an adverse effect on the individual (the date Ricks was discharged).

Continuing Violations   Some violations of Title VII may be continuing violations—actions that are ongoing. In *Bazemore v. Friday* [478 U.S. 385 (1986)], the plaintiffs alleged that the employer paid African-American employees less than white employees. The pay policy had originated prior to the date that Title VII applied to the employer, but the Supreme Court held that the violation was a continuing one—a new violation occurred each time the employees received a paycheck based on the racially discriminatory policy. However, the Supreme Court in *Ledbetter v. Goodyear Tire and Rubber Co.* [127 S.Ct.2162 (2007)] held that the time limit to challenge pay discrepancies based on a sexually-discriminatory performance evaluation began when the evaluation is made, not when paychecks reflecting that discriminatory evaluation were received. However, the Ledbetter decision was overruled by federal legislation—Congress passed the Lilly Ledbetter Fair Pay Act of 2009 [P.L. 111-2 (January 29, 2009), now codified as 42 U.S.C. § 2000e-5(e)]. That law amended Title VII of the Civil Rights Act of 1964, the Age Discrimination in Employment Act, the Americans with Disabilities Act, and the Rehabilitation Act to provide that the time limit for filing suit alleging discrimination in pay begins either:

- When the discriminatory pay practice or policy is adopted;
- When the employee becomes subject to the discriminatory pay practice of policy; or
- When the employee is affected by the application of the discriminatory pay practice or policy.

The law also makes it clear that each payment of wages, benefits, or other compensation (that is, each time the employee receives the discriminatory pay) are paid is a separate violation. Employees filing suits for pay discrimination under Title VII can recover back pay for up to two years from the date they filed a complaint with the Equal Employment Opportunity Commission.

Seniority-Related Violations   Section 706(e)(2) of the act states that in cases involving claims that a seniority system was adopted for discriminatory reasons, the date on which the violation occurs will be either the date the seniority system was adopted, the date on which the complainant became subject to the system, or the date on which the complainant is injured by the application of the seniority system.

Hostile Environment Harassment   For claims of hostile environment harassment, the employee must file a complaint with the EEOC within 300 days (if there is an appropriate state or local EEO agency) or 180 days (if there is no state or local agency) of the most recent discrete incident of harassment, according to the Supreme Court decision in *National Railroad Passenger Corp. v. Morgan* [536 U.S. 101 (2002)]. If a complaint is filed within that time period, the defendant may be held liable for all the actions making up the pattern of hostile environment discrimination, even if some occurred beyond the limitations period for filing a claim.

EEOC Procedure for Handling Complaints   The EEOC, as noted previously, may file suit on its own initiative when it finds a pattern or practice of discrimination; however, most EEOC actions are initiated by individual complaints. Upon receipt of a complaint, the EEOC serves a notice upon the respondent (the employer, union, or employment agency alleged to have engaged in illegal employment discrimination); the EEOC staff then conducts an investigation to determine whether there is reasonable cause to believe that the allegations of the complaint are true. If the investigation does not reveal any reasonable cause, the complaint is dismissed. If the investigation indicates that there is reasonable cause, the EEOC attempts to settle the complaint through voluntary negotiation. If, within 30 days, the voluntary procedures are not successful in settling the complaint to the satisfaction of the parties involved, the EEOC may then choose to file suit in federal court.

If the complaint is dismissed by the EEOC, or if it decides not to file suit, the EEOC notifies the complainant that he or she may personally file suit. The complainant must file suit within 90 days of receiving the right-to-sue notice. If the EEOC has neither dismissed the complaint nor filed suit within 180 days of its filing, the complainant may request a right-to-sue letter from the EEOC. The complainant then has 90 days from receipt of that letter to file suit. If the EEOC decides to file suit at a later date, the suits are joined and are tried together by the court. Suits under Title VII may be filed in either federal district court or in the appropriate state court, according to the Supreme Court decision in *Yellow Freight System, Inc. v. Donnelly* [494 U.S. 820 (1990)].

Relationship Between State and Federal Courts   Because the procedures under Title VII require the complainant to file first with a state or local agency, if one exists, it is possible that the complainant's case may proceed to a trial under the relevant state legislation as well as under Title VII. In *Kremer v. Chemical Construction Co.* [456 U.S. 461 (1982)], the Supreme Court held that a decision by a state court dismissing a suit alleging discrimination in employment is binding on the federal courts; in other words, the complainant may not file suit, based on the same facts, under Title VII in federal court. The holding in *Kremer* is limited only to the effect of state court decisions; a negative determination by a state administrative agency does not affect the complainant's right to sue in federal court, according to *University of Tennessee v. Elliot* [478 U.S. 788 (1986)].

Following the *Elliot* rationale, the courts have held that decisions by other administrative agencies do not affect the ability of the complainant to sue under Title VII. For example, National Labor Relations Board decisions on unfair labor practice complaints involving discrimination do not affect the complainant's right to file suit over the same actions under Title VII. However, if the complainant accepted reinstatement with back pay in settlement of the complaint, the courts have held that the employee then waives his or her right to sue for the same facts under Title VII.

Arbitration and EEO Claims   Businesses increasingly are turning to alternative dispute resolution instead of litigation to resolve disputes, and that includes employment disputes. [See the discussion of ADR, and the arbitration of employment disputes, in Chapter 3.] A growing number of employers require employees to agree, as a condition of employment, to arbitrate any dispute growing out of their employment. How does such an agreement to arbitrate affect an employee's right to bring suit under the EEO laws?

Individual agreements to arbitrate. In *Gilmer v. Interstate/Johnson Lane Corp.* [500 U.S. 20 (1991)], the Supreme Court held that an employee who had signed an agreement to arbitrate all disputes arising from his employment was required to arbitrate, rather than litigate, his age discrimination claim. Subsequent cases applied that *Gilmer* decision to claims under Title VII and other EEO legislation. In *Circuit City Stores, Inc. v. Adams* [532 U.S. 105 (2001)], the Court held that an employer may require employees to sign, as a condition of employment, an agreement to arbitrate all disputes growing out of the employment relationship. The arbitration agreement must have been voluntarily agreed to by the employee, *Prudential Insurance Co. v. Lai* [42 F.3d 1299 (9th Cir. 1994)]. As well, an arbitration agreement signed by an individual employee does not prevent the EEOC from bringing suit against an employer to enforce the EEO statutes and the EEOC may also seek remedies for the individual employees who have signed arbitration agreements, according to the Supreme Court decision in *EEOC. v.* Because employers can require that employees agree to arbitrate all employment-related claims, courts asked to enforce agreements to arbitrate will closely scrutinize those arbitration provisions to ensure that they are fair to both parties and are not being used by the employer to deny or restrict the employee's statutory remedies. According to *Brisentine v. Stone & Webster Engineering Corp.* [117 F.3d 519 (11th Cir. 1997)], in order for an arbitration agreement to be enforced, it must meet three requirements: (1) the employee must have individually agreed to the arbitration provision, (2) the arbitration agreement must authorize the arbitrator to resolve the statutory EEO claims, and (3) the agreement must give the employee the right to insist on arbitration if the statutory EEO claim is not resolved to his or her satisfaction in any grievance procedure or dispute resolution process of the employer. As a result, an agreement to arbitrate, knowingly and voluntarily agreed to by an employee, is binding and requires the employee to arbitrate EEO claims instead of taking them to court. The courts will refuse to enforce arbitration agreements that are onesided, deny employees' rights or limit remedies available to them, *Circuit City Stores, Inc. v. Adams* [279 F.3d 889 (9th Cir. 2002), cert. denied, 535 U.S. 1112 (June 3, 2002)]. In *Ingle v. Circuit City Stores* [328 F.3d 1165 (9th Cir. 2003)], the Ninth Circuit struck down Circuit City's form arbitration agreement, calling it "presumptively unconscionable." The agreement contained provisions requiring employees to forego statutory rights and remedies, and granted the employer benefits not afforded to the employee. In *Hooters of America v. Phillips* [173 F.3d 933 (4th Cir. 1999)] the Fourth Circuit Court of Appeals refused to enforce an arbitration agreement imposed on employees by Hooters Restaurants. The agreement gave Hooters control over the choice of arbitrators and allowed the company to change the arbitration rules at any time. The Court refused enforcement of the arbitration agreement, finding it "so onesided as to undermine the neutrality of the proceeding." In *AT&T Mobility LLC v. Concepcion* [—— S.Ct. ——, 2011 WL 1561956 (U.S. April 27, 2011)] the Supreme Court held that the Federal Arbitration Act pre-empted California law holding that arbitration agreements which prohibit class action arbitrations were not enforceable. The Supreme Court's decision means that employees can be required to arbitrate only their single claim if the arbitration agreement so provides.

    Arbitration under Collective Bargaining Agreements. For employees who are in a union and subject to a collective bargaining agreement between the union and their employer, what is the effect of an arbitration clause in the collective agreement on the ability of the individual employee to bring an EEO suit? In *14 Penn Plaza LLC v. Pyett* (129 S.Ct. 2009), the U.S. Supreme Court held that the arbitration clause of a collective agreement between a union and employer required the individual union members covered by the agreement to arbitrate their claims of age discrimination under federal and state laws. The court held that the arbitration provision, which specifically mentioned that discrimination claims under the various federal and state civil rights laws, was a clear and unmistakable waiver of the individual members' right to sue, and required that they submit such claims to arbitration under the collective agreement. However, the court also held that where the union controlled access to arbitration under the agreement, and could prevent the members from arbitrating their discrimination claims, the arbitration provision of the collective agreement would not preclude the individual members from litigating their claims.

DISCRIMINATION UNDER TITLE VII

Discrimination means making a choice—an employer discriminates among the several applicants when choosing which person to hire for the job, and a professor discriminates upon the basis of performance when grading exams. It must be emphasized that not all discrimination is illegal—discriminating in favor of the most qualified applicant is acceptable. Title VII prohibits discrimination in terms or conditions of employment when that discrimination is based on race, color, religion, sex, or national origin.

bona fide occupational qualification [BFOQ]: Requirement, based on business necessity, that only employees of a specific gender, religion, or national origin will be hired.

    In certain limited instances, Title VII does allow an employer to select employees on the basis of sex, religion, or national origin when the employer can establish that such a distinction is a **bona fide occupational qualification (BFOQ)**. In order to establish a BFOQ, the employer must demonstrate that business necessity—the safe and efficient operation of the business—requires that employees be of a particular sex, religion, or national origin. Note that race or color can never serve as the basis of a BFOQ under Title VII. (BFOQs will be discussed more fully later in this chapter.)

Intentional Discrimination—Disparate Treatment. It should be clear that Title VII prohibits intentional discrimination in employment based on race, color, religion, sex, or national origin. An employer that refuses to hire Hispanic Americans, for example, or that will only hire women for certain limited positions, is in violation of Title VII. Such intentional discrimination is known as **disparate treatment**. (The particular individual is subjected to different treatment because of his or her race, color, religion, sex, or national origin.)

> **disparate treatment** Intentional discrimination based on race, color, religion, sex, or national origin.

In the years immediately following the passage of Title VII, some people believed that the legislation was intended only to protect minority employees. The Supreme Court, however, in the case of *McDonald v. Santa Fe Trail Transportation Co.* [427 U.S. 273 (1976)], held that Title VII applied to employees of all races. In this case, an employer that discharged two white employees for stealing, but only suspended an African-American employee involved in the same incident, was held to be in violation of Title VII—the employer had treated the white employees differently because of their race.

Unintentional Discrimination—Disparate Impact Does Title VII, in addition to forbidding intentional discrimination, also prohibit unintentional discrimination in employment based on the prohibited grounds? An employer may specify certain requirements for a job that effectively disqualify otherwise capable prospective employees. However, what if the requirements in effect disqualify a large proportion of minority applicants? The discriminatory effect of apparently neutral job requirements is known as **disparate impact**.

> **disparate impact:** The discriminatory effect of apparently neutral job requirements.

An employer may frequently use a test for screening job applicants. Although Title VII does permit the use of employment testing, Section 703(h) provides that employers may legally give and act upon the results of any professionally developed ability test only when such tests do not discriminate because of race, color, religion, sex, or national origin.

The following case addressed the legality under Title VII of an employer's use of job requirements that have a disparate impact.

GRIGGS V. DUKE POWER COMPANY

401 U.S. 424 (1971)

FACTS

Prior to the passage of the Civil Rights Act of 1964, Duke Power had openly discriminated in hiring on the basis of race. The workforce was organized into five departments: Labor, Coal Handling, Operations, Maintenance, and Laboratory and Test. African-Americans were employed only in the Labor department, which paid less than any of the other departments. In 1955, the company began to require a high school diploma as a requirement for hiring in any department except Labor. When the Civil Rights Act took effect in 1965, the company abandoned its policy of racial discrimination in hiring and job assignment; the company did require a high school diploma, however, in order to transfer from Labor to any other department. At the same time, white employees hired before the institution of the high school diploma requirement continued to perform satisfactorily and to be promoted in the other departments. The company also required new employees, hired after July 2, 1965, to pass two aptitude tests as well as have a high school diploma in order to be assigned to any department other than Labor. The tests were developed to measure general intelligence and mechanical aptitude; neither was directed or intended to measure the ability to learn to perform a particular job or category of jobs. The scores used for passing the two tests were approximately the national median scores achieved on the tests by high school graduates. Griggs (after going through the required procedures with the EEOC) filed suit alleging that Duke Power violated Title VII by using the high school diploma and testing requirements as a condition of employment when neither requirement was significantly related to successful job performance, and both requirements operated to exclude African-Americans at a substantially higher rate than white applicants.

The trial court found that Duke Power had stopped intentionally discriminating against African-Americans when Title VII took effect and that the company's present requirements did not violate Title VII. The Court of Appeals agreed, holding that there was no intentional discrimination. Griggs appealed to the U.S. Supreme Court on the issue of whether the use of job requirements that are not related to job performance but that have a disparate impact on minority applicants violates Title VII.

DECISION

The Supreme Court held that the objective of Title VII was to achieve equality of employment opportunities and to remove barriers that have operated in the past to favor white applicants over minorities. Under Title VII, "practices, procedures and tests neutral on their face, and even neutral in terms of intent, cannot be maintained if they operate to 'freeze' the status quo of prior discriminatory employment practices." Whites faired far better on the company's requirements than did African Americans; such consequences would appear to be directly traceable to race. Title VII prohibits not only overt or intentional discrimination but also practices that are fair in form but discriminatory in operation. "The touchstone is business necessity," stated the Court. "If an employment practice which operates to exclude Negroes cannot be shown to be related to the job performance, the practice is prohibited." Neither the high school diploma requirement nor the testing requirement was shown to bear a demonstrable relationship to

successful performance of the jobs for which they were required. Both requirements were adopted without any meaningful study of their relationship to job performance. "The evidence, however, shows that employees who have not completed high school or taken the tests have continued to perform satisfactorily and make progress in departments for which the high school and test criteria are now used."

The Court held that "good intent or the absence of discriminatory intent does not redeem employment procedures or testing mechanisms that operate as 'built-in headwinds' for minority groups and are unrelated to measuring job capability." Title VII was directed against the consequences of employment practices, not simply the motivation behind the practices; "Congress has placed on the employer the burden of showing that any given requirement must have a manifest relationship to the employment in question . . . . Far from disparaging job qualifications as such, Congress has made such qualifications the controlling factor, so that race, religion, nationality, and sex become irrelevant. What Congress has commanded is that any test used must measure the person for the job and not the person in the abstract." The Supreme Court reversed the Court of Appeals decision.

CASE QUESTIONS

1. What was the effect of the company's high school diploma requirement on African-American employees? What was the effect of the test requirement?
2. When did the employer establish the diploma and testing requirements?
3. Were employees hired prior to the adoption of the requirements less able to perform the job than those hired after the adoption of the requirements? What other evidence indicates that the requirements were not job related?
4. Why does the Court feel that the employer's lack of intent to discriminate is not relevant to whether the requirements violate Title VII?

The job requirements in *Griggs* were both objective criteria—having a high school diploma and attaining a passing score on a particular exam. Can subjective criteria, such as supervisors' post-interview rankings of job applicants, also be challenged under disparate impact analysis? In *Watson v. Fort Worth Bank & Trust* [487 U.S. 977 (1988)], the Supreme Court held that subjective employment selection practices were also subject to disparate impact analysis. In the *Watson* case, the employer promoted employees based on supervisors' recommendations; Watson, an African-American female, was continually passed over for promotions because her white supervisors rated her lower than other employees who were white. The Supreme Court said that disparate impact analysis could be applied to the promotion practices. A second Supreme Court decision, *Wards Cove Packing Co. v. Atonio* [490 U.S. 642 (1989)], held that the plaintiff raising a disparate impact argument must identify a specific employment practice that allegedly caused the disparate impact. Section 703(k), inserted in Title VII by the 1991 amendments, provides that when a plaintiff has demonstrated that an employment practice has a disparate impact, the defendant-employer must then show that the employment practice is job-related.

Showing a Disparate Impact   To argue successfully a claim of disparate impact, a plaintiff must prove that a protected group is adversely affected by an employment practice or requirement. Hence, the plaintiff's prima facie case must necessarily involve evidence of a statistical nature. While the Supreme Court has not identified any specific statistical formulation that is required, the courts have allowed several different means of proof to be used. One method involves a simple comparison between the workforce of the employer in question, and another method is known as the **four-fifths rule**.

The workforce comparison method involves a statistical comparison of the representation of the relevant protected group in the employer's workforce with the protected group's representation in the relevant labor market (the area from which the employer draws most of its employees—it may be local or even national, depending on the job in question). What does this comparison prove? When a marked discrepancy exists between the percentage of the protected group in the workforce and the percentage in the relevant labor market, that discrepancy likely is due to the effect of the challenged employment practice or requirement.

If the job in question requires specific skills and training, the population used for the comparison may be limited to available qualified individuals within the relevant labor market, according to the Supreme Court decision in *Wards Cove*. Defining the relevant labor market, however, is a question of fact in each case, and may be a major issue in contention between the parties to the case, as was evident in the Supreme Court decision in *Hazelwood School District v. U.S.* [433 U.S. 299 (1977)].

Four-Fifths Rule   A second means of showing a disparate impact is the four-fifths rule set out in the *Uniform Guidelines on Employee Selection Procedures*, a set of regulations adopted by the EEOC and other federal agencies. The four-fifths rule compares the selection rates (the rates at which applicants meet the requirements or pass the selection procedure) for the various groups protected under Title VII. The rule states that a disparate impact will be demonstrated

four-fifths rule: A method of showing that an employment practice has a disparate impact.

when the proportion of applicants from the protected group with the lowest selection rate is less than 80 percent of the selection rate of the group with the highest selection rate. Stating the rule in equation form, a disparate impact exists when:

$$\frac{\text{Pass rate of the group with the lowest selection rate}}{\text{Pass rate of the group with the highest selection rate}} < .80$$

For example, suppose a municipal fire department requires that applicants for firefighter positions be at least five feet, six inches tall and weigh at least 130 pounds. Of the applicants for the positions, 5 of the 25 Hispanic-American applicants meet the requirements, while 30 of 40 of the white applicants meet the requirements. The selection rate for Hispanic-American applicants is 20 percent (5/25), or .20; the selection rate for whites is 75 percent (30/40). To determine whether the requirements have a disparate impact on Hispanic-Americans, we need to divide .20 (the selection rate for Hispanic-Americans) by .75 (the selection rate for whites); if the result is less than .80, a disparate impact exists. Here, .20/.75 = .266, and .266 < .80; therefore a disparate impact exists, establishing a prima facie case of employment discrimination.

Section 703(k) of Title VII addresses disparate impact claims; it states that the plaintiff has the burden of proof to show that the challenged employment practice causes an impact on one of the bases prohibited by Title VII. Using the example discussed previously, a Hispanic-American challenging the use of the minimum height and weight requirements by the fire department must show that such requirements disproportionately disqualify Hispanic-Americans. If the plaintiff makes such a showing, the employer must then demonstrate that the employment practice is job-related for the position in question; the fire department must convince the court that only persons who meet the height and weight requirements are capable of performing the job satisfactorily. If the employer is able to show that the challenged employment practice does not have a disparate impact, then there is no need to demonstrate that the practice is required by job-related factors.

Even if the employer is able to show the employment practice is job related, if the plaintiff can then demonstrate that an alternative employment practice—one that does not have a disparate impact but serves the same job-related purpose—is available, and the employer refuses to adopt it, the employer is still in violation of the Act. For example, the fire department may try to justify the height and weight requirements on the basis that they indicate upper body strength needed by firefighters. Although height and weight may be related to a person's strength, the plaintiff may be able to demonstrate that an upper body strength test serves the same purpose and does not have a disparate impact on Hispanic-Americans. If the fire department refuses to adopt the strength test and continues to use the height and weight requirements, it is in violation of Title VII.

Section 703(k) also states that work rules that bar the employment of persons using or possessing illegal drugs are exempted from disparate impact analysis; such rules are a violation of Title VII only if they were adopted or applied with the intention to discriminate on grounds prohibited by Title VII.

The employer may continue to use an employment practice that has been shown to be sufficiently job related or required by business necessity, and the plaintiff has not shown that an alternative practice without a disparate impact is available. Nothing in Title VII prohibits an employer from hiring those people best able to do the job. If an employer is intentionally discriminating in employment, the fact that an employment practice may be job related is not a defense to a claim of disparate treatment discrimination under Title VII. For example, it is no defense for an employer who deliberately refuses to hire qualified female accountants to show that CPA certification is necessary for the job and that female CPAs are less common than male CPAs.

PROVING DISCRIMINATION—BURDENS OF PROOF

When a suit under Title VII has been filed, the question of the burden of proof arises—what must a plaintiff demonstrate to establish a valid claim of discrimination, and what must the defendant show to defeat a claim of discrimination?

The Supreme Court has consistently held, in a number of cases, that the plaintiff always has the burden of persuasion; that is, the plaintiff must persuade the judge (or jury, if it is a jury trial) that there has been employment discrimination in violation of Title VII. In order to do this, the plaintiff must establish a **prima facie case** of discrimination—enough evidence to raise a presumption of discrimination. If the plaintiff fails to establish a prima facie case of discrimination, then the case will be dismissed—the plaintiff will lose the suit. The plaintiff may use factual evidence or statistical evidence to establish the prima facie case. The specific elements of a prima facie case, and the means to establish it, will vary depending on whether the complaint involves disparate treatment or disparate impact.

prima facie case: Establishing facts sufficient to raise a presumption of discrimination.

Defendant's Burden.   After the plaintiff has successfully demonstrated a prima facie case, the defendant must overcome the plaintiff's claims. As the Supreme Court initially noted in *McDonnell Douglas Corp. v. Green* [411 U.S. 792 (1973)] and reemphasized in *Texas Department of Community Affairs v. Burdine* [450 U.S. 248 (1979)], in disparate treatment cases, the defendant is not required to disprove the plaintiff's claims. The defendant is only required to produce some evidence that offers a legitimate, nondiscriminatory reason for its actions, or, in the words of the Court, "to articulate a legitimate justification" for its actions. For example, the employer may demonstrate that the plaintiff was not hired because he or she was not sufficiently qualified for the job in question. In disparate impact cases, as noted previously, once a plaintiff shows that an employment selection practice has a disparate impact, §703(k) requires the employer to prove that the selection practice is job related.

Plaintiff's Burden of Showing Pretext.   When the defendant has offered a legitimate justification for the challenged conduct, the plaintiff must be afforded the opportunity to show that the offered justification is a mere pretext, a false claim used to cover up the real reason for the actions. This can be shown either directly, by persuading the court that a discriminatory reason probably motivated the defendant, or indirectly, by showing that the justification is not worthy of credence. The Supreme Court, in the decision of *St. Mary's Honor Center v. Hicks* [509 U.S. 502 (1993)], held that the plaintiff has the burden of proof to persuade the court that illegal discrimination has occurred even when the plaintiff can show that the reasons offered by the defendant are false. That is, even when the plaintiff demonstrates that the employer's offered reason for the action is a pretext, the plaintiff, in order to prevail, must also convince the court that the employer's decision was based on an illegal ground of discrimination. When the plaintiff has established a prima facie case of discrimination, and in so doing has provided enough evidence for the judge (or jury) to reject the employer's offered justification as false, there was sufficient evidence to support a finding that the employer had intentionally discriminated against the plaintiff, *Reeves v. Sanderson Plumbing Products, Inc.* [530 U.S. 133 (2000)]. [Note that *Reeves* involved the Age Discrimination in Employment Act, but the analysis is applicable to claims under Title VII as well.]

MIXED MOTIVES

The 1991 amendments to Title VII added §703(m) to the act, which states "an unlawful employment practice is established when the complaining party demonstrates that race, color, religion, sex or national origin was a motivating factor for any employment practice, even though other factors also motivated the practice." Thus, an employer violates Title VII when an illegal factor (race, color, religion, sex, or national origin) is considered, even though other factors or reasons may motivate the decision or practice as well. If the employer in such a situation is able to demonstrate that it would have reached the same decision in the absence of the illegal factor, then the employer's liability for remedies for the violation is limited by §706(g)(2)(B), also added in 1991. This section states that the employer is subject to a court order to cease violating Title VII and is liable for the plaintiff's legal fees. However, the employer is not required to pay damages or to reinstate or hire the plaintiff.

THE "BOTTOM LINE" AND DISCRIMINATION

The case of *Connecticut v. Teal* [457 U.S. 440 (1982)] addressed whether promotion of a greater percentage of successful minority applicants than successful white applicants was a sufficient defense to a claim that the test used to qualify for promotion had a disparate impact on African-American applicants. The plaintiffs showed that the test had a disparate impact under the four-fifths rule, and the employer had not validated the test. The Supreme Court held that using the test to determine which applicants were qualified for promotion was in violation of Title VII, despite the fact that a greater percentage of African-Americans than whites who had qualified were promoted. The problem did not concern the actual promotions; rather, the problem concerned the means used to determine who was qualified for promotion—the test really did not measure or select for ability to perform the job in question. Therefore, the actual percentages of the different groups who were promoted (known as the "bottom line") were irrelevant, because potentially qualified African-Americans were screened out by the use of the test. As a result of the *Teal* case, the bottom line is not a viable defense to a claim of discrimination against an individual employee.

RACE-NORMING

race-norming:
The practice of setting different passing scores for different races or other protected groups; race-norming is prohibited by Title VII.

Section 703(l), added to Title VII by the 1991 amendments, prohibits the practice of **race-norming**, which is the use of different cutoff or passing scores for different protected groups under Title VII. The same section also prohibits adjusting the scores or altering the results of employment tests on the basis of race, color, religion, sex, or national origin. Prior to the addition of that section, some employers had adjusted scores for minority applicants, or had used different passing scores for different groups, in an effort to avoid any disparate impact that might result from the use of the employment tests. The prohibition of such practices now means that the employer must ensure that any employment tests used are validated under the Uniform Guidelines on Employee Selection.

SENIORITY AND TITLE VII

Seniority, or the length of service on the job, is frequently used to determine entitlement or eligibility for certain job benefits, promotions, transfers, and even job security itself. Seniority systems usually provide that layoffs will be conducted on the basis of inverse seniority—the last employee hired is the first to be laid off.

Seniority may have a discriminatory effect on employees when an employer has, in the past, discriminated against women or minority workers. If the employer had refused to hire women or minorities in the past but now does hire them, those employees will have less seniority than white male employees. In the event of a layoff, the women and minorities will be the first to lose their jobs, whereas the white males retain their jobs. The layoffs by inverse seniority, therefore, have a disparate impact on women and minorities. Does that mean that the seniority system violates Title VII, as in the *Griggs* case?

Section 703(h) of Title VII contains an exemption for bona fide seniority systems; it states, in part, the following:

> Notwithstanding any other provision of this title, it shall not be an unlawful employment practice for an employer to apply different standards of compensation or different terms, conditions, or privileges of employment pursuant to a bona fide seniority or merit system provided that such differences are not the result of an intention to discriminate because of race, color, religion, sex, or national origin.

In the *International Brotherhood of Teamsters v. United States* [451 U.S. 324 (1977)], the Supreme Court defined a "bona fide seniority system" as being one that was neutral on its face, and applied equally to all employees. If the seniority system was bona fide, then actions pursuant to it are protected under §703(h) even if the seniority system perpetuated the effects of prior discrimination. In considering whether a seniority system is bona fide within the meaning of §703(h), a court should consider the following factors: 1) does the seniority system apply equally to all employees subject to it?; 2) is the seniority system rational and in accord with industry practices?; 3) did the seniority system originate free from an intention to discriminate illegally?; and 4) has the seniority system been negotiated and maintained free from an intention to discriminate illegally?

Subsequent to the *Teamsters* decision, Supreme Court decisions have further interpreted the provisions of §703(h). In *American Tobacco Co. v. Patterson* [456 U.S. 63 (1982)], the Court ruled that §703(h) applies to seniority systems that were adopted after the passage of Title VII as well as those in operation at the time Title VII was adopted. The term "seniority system" in §703(h) should be interpreted broadly, to encompass rules that determine eligibility for various classifications under a seniority system, according to the decision in *California Brewers Association v. Bryant* [444 U.S. 598 (1980)].

As a result of these decisions, together with the *Teamsters* case, a seniority system and its ancillary rules will be bona fide within the meaning of §703(h) if the system is neutral on its face, applies equally to all employees, and is not intentionally used to discriminate. The court will consider whether the system had its origin in discrimination, whether it has been negotiated and maintained free from discriminatory intent, and whether the basis of the seniority system is reasonable in light of industry practice. If a seniority system is bona fide under §703(h), then actions taken pursuant to the seniority system can only be challenged under Title VII if the employer is intentionally discriminating; in other words, disparate impact claims may not be brought against actions based on bona fide seniority systems.

AFFIRMATIVE ACTION AND TITLE VII

As noted previously, Title VII protects all individuals from employment discrimination on the prohibited bases. Affirmative action programs usually involve giving preference in hiring or promotion to qualified female or minority applicants or employees; persons who are not members of the group given preference may be at a disadvantage in hiring or promotion decisions. (Recall that *McDonald v. Santa Fe Trail Transportation Co.* [427 U.S. 273 (1976)] held that all employees, not just minority employees, are protected by Title VII.) Does such preferential treatment, pursuant to an affirmative action program, violate Title VII?

Affirmative action continues to be a controversial issue. California and several other states have ended all state affirmative action programs. A number of court decisions have dealt with the legality of affirmative-action programs. Employers are not required by Title VII to set up affirmative-action programs; the courts have, however, often ordered affirmative action after an employer has been found guilty of violating Title VII. The Supreme Court, in the case of *Local 28, Sheet Metal Workers Int'l. Ass'n. v. EEOC* [478 U.S. 421 (1986)], held that affirmative action may be ordered to remedy "persistent or egregious discrimination" even if the affirmative action has the result of benefiting individuals who were not themselves victims of discrimination. The Supreme Court also held that affirmative action should only be ordered as a last resort and should be tailored "to fit the nature of the violation" the court seeks to correct. More recent Supreme Court decisions on the constitutionality of affirmative action have involved cases not specifically dealing with employment. *Adarand Constructors, Inc. v. Pena* [515 U.S. 200 (1995)], dealt with the legality of a set-aside program that required that at least 10 percent of federally funded public work projects must be done by minority-owned contractors. The Supreme Court held that government-required racial preferences must be justified under the **strict scrutiny test**. That test requires that the government show a compelling government interest or purpose to justify the program, and that the program must be narrowly tailored to accomplish that purpose. According to *Wygant v. Jackson Board of Education* [476 U.S. 267 (1986)] (which was an employment case), an affirmative action program that requires the layoff of non-minority employees while retaining minority employees with less seniority was not "narrowly tailored" within the require-

strict scrutiny test: A judicial test requiring that the government show that its action is required by a compelling government purpose or interest, and is narrowly tailored to achieve that interest or purpose.

ments of the strict scrutiny test. In cases involving affirmative action programs for admissions to the University of Michigan, *Gratz v. Bollinger* [539 U.S. 244 (2003)], and the University of Michigan School of Law, *Grutter v. Bollinger* [539 U.S. 306 (2003)] the Court held that achieving the educational benefits of a diverse student body was a compelling governmental purpose; however, the affirmative program should use race (or gender) as only one of various factors to be considered rather than making it the determinative factor.

Although court-ordered, or remedial, affirmative-action programs are acceptable under Title VII, what about voluntary affirmative-action programs—programs adopted voluntarily by employers who have not violated Title VII? In *United Steelworkers of America v. Weber* [443 U.S. 193 (1979)], the Supreme Court held that voluntary affirmative programs were legal under Title VII if (1) the purposes of the plan are consistent with those of Title VII—if the plan was designed to break down old patterns of job segregation, and (2) the plan does not "unnecessarily trammel the interests" of the persons not subject to the preference under the plan—the nonpreferred group is not severely disadvantaged. For example, in the *Weber* case, the employer and union set up an affirmative action program to train more minority employees for skilled jobs because very few minority employees held skilled positions. A white male was not accepted into the training program, while an African American with less seniority was; the white employee was not permanently barred from the program and was eligible to apply for admission to the program the next year. In other cases, laying off employees because of their race, so that white employees lose their jobs while less senior minority employees retain their jobs, was not acceptable because the burden on the nonpreferred white employees was substantial.

What must an employer seeking to justify an affirmative-action program show to meet the *Weber* criteria? What kind of evidence must an individual seeking to challenge decisions made under an affirmative-action program demonstrate to establish a claim under Title VII? Those issues were addressed by the Supreme Court in *Johnson v. Transportation Agency, Santa Clara County* [480 U.S. 616 (1987)]. The majority in *Johnson* held that an employer may justify a voluntary affirmative-action plan under Title VII by showing that the plan was adopted to remedy the existence of a "manifest imbalance" reflecting the underrepresentation of women or minorities in "traditionally segregated job categories." In determining whether an imbalance exists, the employer should compare the percentage of women or minorities in the employer's workforce with the percentage in the area labor market. Where the jobs require no special expertise, a comparison with the general population is appropriate; but when the jobs require special training or qualifications, the comparison should be to those in the labor force who possess the relevant qualifications. The manifest imbalance need not be such that it would make out a prima facie case that the employer had violated Title VII. The Court also noted in *Johnson* that the person claiming the employer had illegally discriminated has the burden of proving that the voluntary affirmative-action plan is not valid under Title VII.

Several other points regarding affirmative action have been addressed by the Supreme Court and by Congress. In *Local 93, International Ass'n of Firefighters v. Cleveland* [478 U.S. 501 (1986)], the Court held that an employer admitting to discrimination in violation of Title VII may agree to set up an affirmative-action program pursuant to a consent decree.

Also §703(n), added to Title VII by the 1991 amendments, states that affirmative-action programs resulting from judicial decisions or consent decrees may not be challenged later by persons who had notice of such decisions or decrees and had an opportunity to present objections to the plan at the time it was ordered or adopted. The same section also applies to persons whose interests were adequately represented by another person who had previously challenged the decision or decree on the same legal grounds and with a similar factual situation. Section 703(n) does not preclude subsequent challenges to decisions or decrees that were obtained through fraud or collusion, are "transparently invalid," or were entered by a court that lacked proper jurisdiction over the case.

BONA FIDE OCCUPATIONAL QUALIFICATIONS

As mentioned previously, Title VII does allow employers to restrict their hiring for certain positions to members of one sex or of a particular religion or national origin if that trait is a BFOQ for the job. For example, a Baptist church seeking to hire a new pastor would certainly want to restrict the selection to Baptists rather than to Catholics or Buddhists. An employer seeking to justify a BFOQ must show that it is necessary for the safe and efficient operation of the business. The courts have interpreted the business necessity requirement very strictly—customer preference or employer convenience are not sufficient to justify a BFOQ. Section 703(e)(1) defines the BFOQ exception as follows:

> . . . [I]t shall not be an unlawful employment practice for an employer to hire and employ employees, for an employment agency to classify, or refer for employment any individual, for a labor organization to classify its membership or refer for employment any individual . . . on the basis of his religion, sex, or national origin in those certain instances where religion, sex, or national origin in a bona fide occupational qualification reasonably necessary to the normal operation of that particular business or enterprise . . .

The language of §703(e)(1) prohibits using race or color as a BFOQ. What must an employer do to meet the business necessity requirement in order to establish a BFOQ? In *Dothard v. Rawlinson* [433 U.S. 321 (1977)], the Supreme Court upheld Alabama's requirement that guards in maximum security prisons who have direct contact with male prisoners must be male, because the threat of assault on female guards would pose a danger not only to the female guard herself, but also to the basic control and protection of the inmates and other security personnel.

In dealing with claims of BFOQs, the courts have also recognized BFOQs based on sex when community standards of morality or propriety require that employees be of a particular gender, such as only hiring men as fitting room attendants in a men's clothing store or hiring only females as locker room attendants for the women's locker room of an athletic club.

TITLE VII AND SEX DISCRIMINATION

Title VII prohibits any discrimination in terms or conditions of employment because of an employee's sex, unless it is a BFOQ. Title VII prohibits advertising for male or female employees in help-wanted ads (unless the employer demonstrates that it is a BFOQ) and maintaining separate seniority lists for male and female employees. Unions that negotiate separate seniority lists or that discriminate in membership because of sex also violate Title VII. Sex discrimination in employment may take various different forms, as are discussed in the following sections. Title VII does not prohibit discrimination based on sexual orientation or sexual preference, and some courts have held that Title VII does not protect transsexuals or transvestites.

STEREOTYPING

It is illegal sex discrimination for an employer to apply different standards for promoting female employees than for male employees when those standards reflect sex stereotyping. In *Price Waterhouse v. Hopkins* [490 U.S. 228 (1989)], the Supreme Court held that a female employee who was considered "difficult, abrasive, and unfeminine" for behavior that was perceived as acceptable if engaged in by a male was the victim of sex discrimination when she was denied a partnership. The employer held her to a different standard than the employer used for male employees, and consequently was in violation of Title VII. After *Price Waterhouse,* some transsexuals have argued that they were being discriminated against because they did not match the common stereotype of "maleness". The following case deals with this question – does Title VII's prohibition on sex discrimination extend to such "stereotyping" discrimination against transsexuals?

In the Language of the Court

SMITH V. CITY OF SALEM, OHIO

378 F.3d 566 (6th Cir. 2004)

COLE, Circuit Judge.

Plaintiff-Appellant Jimmie L. Smith appeals from a judgment of the United States District Court for the Northern District of Ohio dismissing his claims against his employer, Defendant-Appellant City of Salem, Ohio, and various City officials, and granting judgment on the pleadings to Defendants . . . Smith, who considers himself a transsexual and has been diagnosed with Gender Identity Disorder, alleged that Defendants discriminated against him in his employment on the basis of sex. He asserted claims pursuant to Title VII of the Civil Rights Act of 1964 . . . . The district court dismissed those claims.

I. BACKGROUND

. . . Smith is—and has been, at all times relevant to this action—employed by the city of Salem, Ohio, as a lieutenant in the Salem Fire Department (the "Fire Department"). Prior to the events surrounding this action, Smith worked for the Fire Department for seven years without any negative incidents. Smith—biologically and by birth a male—is a transsexual and has been diagnosed with Gender Identity Disorder ("GID"), which the American Psychiatric Association characterizes as a disjunction between an individual's sexual organs and sexual identity. After being diagnosed with GID, Smith began "expressing a more feminine appearance on a full-time basis"—including at work—in accordance with international medical protocols for treating GID. Soon thereafter, Smith's co-workers began questioning him about his appearance and commenting that his appearance and mannerisms were not "masculine enough." As a result, Smith notified his immediate supervisor, Defendant Thomas Eastek, about his GID diagnosis and treatment. He also informed Eastek of the likelihood that his treatment would eventually include complete physical transformation from male to female. Smith had approached Eastek in order to answer any questions Eastek might have concerning his appearance and manner and so that Eastek could address Smith's co-workers' comments and inquiries. Smith specifically asked Eastek, and Eastek promised, not to divulge the substance of their conversation to any of his superiors, particularly to Defendant Walter Greenamyer, Chief of the Fire Department. In short order, however, Eastek told Greenamyer about Smith's behavior and his GID.

Greenamyer then met with Defendant C. Brooke Zellers, the Law Director for the City of Salem, with the intention of using Smith's trans-sexualism and its manifestations as a basis for terminating his employment. On April 18, 2001, Greenamyer and Zellers arranged a meeting of the City's executive body to discuss Smith and devise a plan for terminating his employment. The executive body included Defendants Larry D. DeJane, Salem's mayor; James A. Armeni, Salem's auditor; and Joseph S. Julian, Salem's service director. Also present was Salem Safety Director Henry L. Willard . . . who was never a named defendant in this action.

Although Ohio [law] . . . sets forth the state procedures pursuant to which Ohio municipal officials may meet to take employment action against a municipal employee – [and] provides that officials "may hold an executive session to consider the appointment, employment, dismissal, discipline, promotion, demotion, or compensation of a public employee only after a majority of a quorum of the public body determines, by a roll call vote, to hold an executive session and only at a regular or special meeting for the sole purpose of [considering such matters]," the City did not abide by these procedures at the April 18, 2001 meeting.

During the meeting, Greenamyer, DeJane, and Zellers agreed to arrange for the Salem Civil Service Commission to require Smith to undergo three separate psychological evaluations with physicians of the City's choosing. They hoped that Smith would either resign or refuse to comply. If he refused to comply,

Defendants reasoned, they could terminate Smith's employment on the ground of insubordination. Willard, who remained silent during the meeting, telephoned Smith afterwards to inform him of the plan, calling Defendants' scheme a "witch hunt."

Two days after the meeting, on April 20, 2001, Smith's counsel telephoned DeJane to advise him of Smith's legal representation and the potential legal ramifications for the City if it followed through on the plan devised by Defendants during the April 18 meeting. On April 22, 2001, Smith received his "right to sue" letter from the U.S. Equal Employment Opportunity Commission ("EEOC"). Four days after that, on April 26, 2001, Greenamyer suspended Smith for one twenty-four hour shift, based on his alleged infraction of a City and/or Fire Department policy.

At a subsequent hearing before the Salem Civil Service Commission (the "Commission") regarding his suspension, Smith contended that the suspension was a result of selective enforcement in retaliation for his having obtained legal representation in response to Defendants' plan to terminate his employment because of his transsexualism and its manifestations. At the hearing, Smith sought to elicit testimony from witnesses regarding the meeting of April 18, 2001, but the City objected and the Commission's chairman, Defendant Harry Dugan, refused to allow any testimony regarding the meeting, despite the fact that Ohio [law] . . . permitted Smith to introduce evidence of disparate treatment and selective enforcement in his hearing before the Commission.

The Commission ultimately upheld Smith's suspension. Smith appealed to the Columbiana County Court of Common Pleas, which reversed the suspension, finding that "[b]ecause the regulation [that Smith was alleged to have violated] was not effective[,] [Smith] could not be charged with violation of it."

Smith then filed suit in the federal district court . . . [alleging] . . . Title VII claims of sex discrimination and retaliation . . . the district court dismissed the federal claims and granted judgment on the pleadings to Defendants . . .

II. ANALYSIS

On appeal, Smith contends that the district court erred in holding that: (1) he failed to state a claim of sex stereotyping; (2) Title VII protection is unavailable to transsexuals; (3) even if he had stated a claim of sex stereotyping, he failed to demonstrate that he suffered an adverse employment action . . .

A. TITLE VII

The parties disagree over two issues pertaining to Smith's Title VII claims: (1) whether Smith properly alleged a claim of sex stereotyping, in violation of the Supreme Court's pronouncements in *Price Waterhouse v. Hopkins,* 490 U.S. 228 (1989); and (2) whether Smith alleged that he suffered an adverse employment action. . . .

We turn now to examining whether Smith properly alleged a claim of sex stereotyping, in violation of the Supreme Court's pronouncements in *Price Waterhouse v. Hopkins,* 490 U.S. 228, 109 S.Ct. 1775, 104 L.Ed.2d 268 (1989), and whether Smith alleged that he suffered an adverse employment action.

1. SEX STEREOTYPING

. . . In his complaint, Smith asserts Title VII claims of retaliation and employment discrimination "because of . . . sex." The district court dismissed Smith's Title VII claims on the ground that he failed to state a claim for sex stereotyping pursuant to *Price Waterhouse v. Hopkins,* 490 U.S. 228 (1989). The district court implied that Smith's claim was disingenuous, stating that he merely "invokes the term-of-art created by *Price Waterhouse,* that is, 'sex-stereotyping,'" as an end run around his "real" claim, which, the district court stated, was "based upon his transsexuality." The district court then held that "Title VII does not prohibit discrimination based on an individual's transsexualism."

Relying on *Price Waterhouse*—which held that Title VII's prohibition of discrimination "because of . . . sex" bars gender discrimination, including discrimination based on sex stereotypes—Smith contends on appeal that he was a victim of discrimination "because of . . . sex" both because of his gender non-conforming conduct and, more generally, because of his identification as a transsexual. We find both bases of discrimination actionable pursuant to Title VII.

We first address whether Smith has stated a claim for relief, pursuant to *Price Waterhouse's* prohibition of sex stereotyping, based on his gender non-conforming behavior and appearance. . . . As Judge Posner has pointed out, the term "gender" is one "borrowed from grammar to designate the sexes as viewed as social rather than biological classes." [Richard A. Posner, Sex and Reason, 24-25 (1992).] The Supreme Court made clear that in the context of Title VII, discrimination because of "sex" includes gender discrimination: "In the context of sex stereotyping, an employer who acts on the basis of a belief that a woman cannot be aggressive, or that she must not be, has acted on the basis of gender." The Court emphasized that "we are beyond the day when an employer could evaluate employees by assuming or insisting that they matched the stereotype associated with their group."

Smith contends that the same theory of sex stereotyping applies here. His complaint sets forth the conduct and mannerisms which, he alleges, did not conform with his employers' and co-workers' sex stereotypes of how a man should look and behave. Smith's complaint states that, after being diagnosed with GID, he began to express a more feminine appearance and manner on a regular basis, including at work. The complaint states that his co-workers began commenting on his appearance and mannerisms as not being masculine enough; and that his supervisors at the Fire Department and other municipal agents knew about this allegedly unmasculine conduct and appearance. The complaint then describes a high-level meeting among Smith's supervisors and other municipal officials regarding his employment. Defendants allegedly schemed to compel Smith's resignation by forcing him to undergo multiple psychological evaluations of his gender non-conforming behavior. The complaint makes clear that these meetings took place soon after Smith assumed a more feminine appearance and manner and after his conversation about this with Eastek. In addition, the complaint alleges that Smith was suspended for twenty-four hours for allegedly violating an unenacted municipal policy, and that the suspension was ordered in retaliation for his pursuing legal remedies after he had been informed about Defendants' plan to intimidate him into resigning. In short, Smith claims that the discrimination he experienced was based on his failure to conform to sex stereotypes by expressing less masculine, and more feminine mannerisms and appearance.

Having alleged that his failure to conform to sex stereotypes concerning how a man should look and behave was the driving force behind Defendants' actions, Smith has sufficiently pleaded claims of sex stereotyping and gender discrimination.

In so holding, we find that the district court erred in relying on a series of pre-*Price Waterhouse* cases from other federal appellate courts holding that transsexuals, as a class, are not entitled to Title VII protection because "Congress had a narrow view of sex in mind" and "never considered nor intended that [Title VII] apply to anything other than the traditional concept of sex." . . . In this earlier jurisprudence, male-to-female transsexuals . . . as biological males whose outward behavior and emotional identity did not conform to socially-prescribed expectations of masculinity—were denied Title VII protection by courts because they were considered victims of "gender" rather than "sex" discrimination.

However, the approach in [those earlier cases]—and by the district court in this case— has been eviscerated by *Price Waterhouse.* By holding that Title VII protected a woman who failed to conform to social expectations concerning how a woman should look and behave, the Supreme Court established that Title VII's reference to "sex" encompasses both the biological differences between men and women, and gender discrimination, that is, discrimination based on a failure to conform to stereotypical gender norms. . . .

After *Price Waterhouse,* an employer who discriminates against women because, for instance, they do not wear dresses or makeup, is engaging in sex discrimination because the

discrimination would not occur but for the victim's sex. It follows that employers who discriminate against men because they *do* wear dresses and makeup, or otherwise act femininely, are also engaging in sex discrimination, because the discrimination would not occur but for the victim's sex. . . .

Yet some courts have held that this latter form of discrimination is of a different and somehow more permissible kind. For instance, the man who acts in ways typically associated with women is not described as engaging in the same activity as a woman who acts in ways typically associated with women, but is instead described as engaging in the different activity of being a transsexual (or in some instances, a homosexual or transvestite). Discrimination against the transsexual is then found not to be discrimination "because of . . . sex," but rather, discrimination against the plaintiff's unprotected status or mode of self-identification. In other words, these courts superimpose classifications such as "transsexual" on a plaintiff, and then legitimize discrimination based on the plaintiff's gender non-conformity by formalizing the non-conformity into an ostensibly unprotected classification.

Such was the case here: despite the fact that Smith alleges that Defendants' discrimination was motivated by his appearance and mannerisms, which Defendants felt were inappropriate for a male, the district court expressly declined to discuss the applicability of *Price Waterhouse.* The district court therefore gave insufficient consideration to Smith's well-pleaded claims concerning his contra-gender behavior, but rather accounted for that behavior only insofar as it confirmed for the court Smith's status as a transsexual, which the district court held precluded Smith from Title VII protection.

Such analyses cannot be reconciled with *Price Waterhouse,* which does not make Title VII protection against sex stereotyping conditional or provide any reason to exclude Title VII coverage for non sex-stereotypical behavior simply because the person is a transsexual. As such, discrimination against a plaintiff who is a transsexual—and therefore fails to act like and/or identify with the gender norms associated with his or her sex—is no different from the discrimination directed against Ann Hopkins in *Price Waterhouse,* who, in sex-stereotypical terms, did not act like a woman. Sex stereotyping based on a person's gender non-conforming behavior is impermissible discrimination, irrespective of the cause of that behavior; a label, such as "transsexual," is not fatal to a sex discrimination claim where the victim has suffered discrimination because of his or her gender non-conformity. Accordingly, we hold that Smith has stated a claim for relief pursuant to Title VII's prohibition of sex discrimination.

Even if Smith had alleged discrimination based only on his self-identification as a transsexual—as opposed to his specific appearance and behavior—this claim too is actionable pursuant to Title VII. By definition, transsexuals are individuals who fail to conform to stereotypes about how those assigned a particular sex at birth should act, dress, and self-identify. *Ergo,* identification as a transsexual is the statement or admission that one wishes to be the opposite sex or does not relate to one's birth sex. Such an admission—for instance the admission by a man that he self-identifies as a woman and/or that he wishes to be a woman—itself violates the prevalent sex stereotype that a man should perceive himself as a man. Discrimination based on transsexualism is rooted in the insistence that sex (organs) and gender (social classification of a person as belonging to one sex or the other) coincide. This is the very essence of sex stereotyping. Accordingly, to the extent that Smith also alleges discrimination based solely on his identification as a transsexual, he has alleged a claim of sex stereotyping pursuant to Title VII. As noted above, Smith's birth sex is male and this is the basis for his protected class status under Title VII even under this formulation of his claim.

Finally, we note that, in its opinion, the district court repeatedly places the term "sex stereotyping" in quotation marks and refers to it as a "term of art" used by Smith to disingenuously plead discrimination because of transsexualism. Similarly, Defendants refer to sex stereotyping as "the *Price Waterhouse* loophole." These characterizations are almost identical to the treatment that Price Waterhouse itself gave sex stereotyping in its briefs to the U.S. Supreme Court. As we do now, the Supreme Court noted the practice with disfavor, stating:

"In the specific context of sex stereotyping, an employer who acts on the basis of a belief that a woman cannot be aggressive, or that she must not be, has acted on the basis of gender. Although the parties do not overtly dispute this last proposition, the placement by Price Waterhouse of "sex stereotyping" in quotation marks throughout its brief seems to us an insinuation either that such stereotyping was not present in this case or that it lacks legal relevance. We reject both possibilities." . . .

2. ADVERSE EMPLOYMENT ACTION

. . . the district court erred in concluding that, because the Court of Common Pleas overturned the suspension, it was not an adverse employment action. There is no legal authority for the proposition that reversal by a *judicial* body—as opposed to the employer—declassifies a suspension as an adverse employment action.

Accordingly, Smith has stated an adverse employment action and, therefore, satisfied all of the elements necessary to allege a *prima facie* case of employment discrimination and retaliation pursuant to Title VII. We therefore reverse the district court's grant of judgment on the pleadings to Defendants with respect to those claims.

. . .

III. CONCLUSION

Because Smith has successfully stated claims for relief pursuant to both Title VII . . . the judgment of the district court is REVERSED and this case is REMANDED to the district court for further proceedings consistent with this opinion.

CASE QUESTIONS

1. Was Smith subjected to sex discrimination or gender discrimination? Is there a difference between sex discrimination and gender discrimination? Explain.
2. How was the decision in the *Price Waterhouse v. Hopkins* case applicable to Smith's case? Did Smith's employer discriminate against him based on stereotypes? Explain.
3. Does Title VII prohibit discrimination against transsexuals? Explain.

"SEX-PLUS" DISCRIMINATION

Employers who refuse to hire women with preschool-aged children but will hire men with preschool-aged children are guilty of sex discrimination in violation of Title VII. This is the result of the Supreme Court decision in *Phillips v. Martin Marietta Corp.* [400 U.S. 542 (1971)]. In that case, female employees were subjected to an additional requirement (no preschool-aged children) because of their sex. An employer who places additional requirements on employees of one sex, and not the other, violates Title VII. Such discrimination is known as "sex-plus" discrimination. It should be noted that the *Phillips* case was decided before the *Price Waterhouse v. Hopkins* case; the "no pre-school aged children" requirement applied only to female employees also reflects a stereotypical assumption that female, rather than male. employees would be responsible for childcare arrangements.

SEX-BASED PAY DIFFERENTIALS

Both Title VII and the Equal Pay Act of 1963 prohibit sex discrimination in pay (paying different wages to men and women performing the same job in the same location). Both laws allow for exceptions when the pay differentials are due to a bona fide seniority system, a merit pay system, a productivity pay system, or a "factor other than sex." Those four defenses are set out in §703(h) of Title VII and in the Equal Pay Act. The Equal Pay Act applies only when the work performed by the male and female employees is *substantially equivalent*, as determined by the required skills, effort, responsibility, and working conditions of the job.

Title VII, rather than the Equal Pay Act, can be used to challenge pay differentials due to intentional sex discrimination *even when the work being performed is not equivalent*, according to the Supreme Court holding in *County of Washington v. Gunther* [452 U.S. 161 (1981)]. In this case, female guards in the Washington County jail guarded female inmates, while the male prisoners were guarded by male guards. The male guards supervised up to 10 times more prisoners than the female guards, who spent much of their time performing clerical duties. Although a job evaluation study rated the female guard positions at 90 percent of the male guard positions, the county paid the female guards only 70 percent of the male guards' pay. The pay differential was allegedly due to intentional sex discrimination on the part of the county. The Supreme Court held that Title VII applied to the situation—it prohibited intentional sex discrimination in pay by the county, even though the jobs involved were not equivalent.

Subsequent to the *Gunther* decision, the U.S. Court of Appeals for the Ninth Circuit held that *Gunther*-type claims are restricted to cases of disparate treatment discrimination; in these cases, plaintiffs need to show that the pay differentials are due to intentional sex discrimination. That court rejected disparate impact claims of sex-based pay discrimination in *Spalding v. University of Washington* [740 F.2d 686 (1984)], in which the plaintiffs alleged that the university's pay policy discriminated against professors in female-dominated fields such as nursing. The court held that statistical evidence alone was not sufficient to establish intentional discrimination as required by *Gunther*.

The Equal Pay Act   The coverage of the Equal Pay Act is greater than that of Title VII; it applies to all employers engaged in interstate commerce and covers all employees of an enterprise engaged in commerce. A plaintiff claiming a violation of the Equal Pay Act must show that an employer paid lower wages to employees of one gender who are performing work substantially equal to the work performed by employees of the opposite gender in the same establishment. Note that the act requires "equal pay for equal work" rather than "equal pay for work of equal value," also known as comparable worth.

The Equal Pay Act is administered by the EEOC, but there is no requirement that plaintiffs suing on their own must first file with the EEOC before filing suit in federal court. If the EEOC files suit, it precludes an individual suit on the same complaint. An individual suit must be filed within two years of the alleged violation; a violation will be held to be continuing for each payday in which unequal pay is received for equal work.

Plaintiffs suing under the Equal Pay Act may recover the unpaid wages due and also may receive an equal amount as liquidated damages; in addition, plaintiffs can recover legal fees and court costs. The trial court has discretion to deny recovery of liquidated damages if it finds that the employer acted in good faith. The back pay awarded to a successful plaintiff can be awarded for the period going back two years prior to the filing of the suit; that period is extended to three years prior to filing the suit if the court finds that the violation was "willful." A violation is willful if the employer was aware of the appreciable possibility that its actions might violate the act. Remedies in suits by the EEOC include injunctions and back pay with interest; the act does not provide for the recovery of liquidated damages in a suit by the government.

COMPARABLE WORTH

Some commentators believe that the decision in *Gunther* was an endorsement of the concept of **comparable worth**, the idea that employees performing work of equal value should receive equal pay. (Note that comparable worth's idea of equal pay for work of equal value differs from the Equal Pay Act requirement of equal pay for equal work.) Comparable worth would require that an employer set pay according to the value of the job to the employer; for example, a school system might be required to pay secretaries and janitors equally if their jobs were evaluated equally under the employer's job evaluation system. The Supreme Court in *Gunther,* however, emphasized that it was not endorsing comparable worth; it was simply prohibiting intentional sex discrimination in pay. The courts have consistently maintained that Title VII does not require comparable worth—where the work at issue is not equivalent, the employer need not pay equally for work of equal value, as long as the pay differentials are not due to intentional sex discrimination. Although federal law does not require comparable worth in pay, a number of states have adopted comparable worth, or pay equity, policies for public sector employees.

comparable worth: The concept that persons performing work of equal value should be paid equally—"equal pay for work of equal value."

SEX-BASED PENSION BENEFITS

Women, on average, live longer than men do; such differences in average life expectancy are used by actuaries in determining premiums and benefit levels for insurance policies and annuities purchased by individuals. Sex-based actuarial tables used to determine premiums and benefits for pensions may require that women pay higher premiums than men of the same age in order to receive the same benefit. When insurance and pension annuities are employment-related benefits, they are subject to Title VII. An employer's use of sex-based actuarial tables in determining pension premiums, requiring women to pay higher monthly premiums for the same pension benefit payments as men, was held by the U.S. Supreme Court in *City of Los Angeles v. Manhart* [435 U.S. 702 (1978)] to be in violation of Title VII's prohibition of sex discrimination. The Court stated that because the actuarial tables used the sex of an employee as a predictor of longevity, the basis for differentiating between employees was sex rather than actual longevity and, therefore, the practice constituted sex discrimination in employment benefits. Any benefits offered to employees by an employer must be free from sex discrimination in order to comply with Title VII.

PREGNANCY DISCRIMINATION

The Pregnancy Discrimination Act of 1978 added §701(k) to Title VII. Section 701(k) states that:

> The terms "because of sex" or "on the basis of sex" include, but are not limited to, because of or on the basis of pregnancy, childbirth, or related medical conditions; and women affected by pregnancy, childbirth, or related medical conditions shall be treated the same for all employment-related purposes, including receipt of benefits under fringe benefit programs, as other persons not so affected but similar in their ability or inability to work. . . .

The amendment requires that pregnant employees be treated the same as other employees suffering non–pregnancy-related temporary disabilities. If an employer's benefit plan covers temporary disabilities, it must also cover pregnancy-related leaves. If the employer's medical plan covers 80 percent of hospital costs for conditions other than pregnancy, then it must provide equal coverage for pregnancy-related conditions as well, according to the Supreme Court decision in *Newport News Shipbuilding and Dry Dock Co. v. E.E.O.C.* [462 U.S. 669 (1983)].

An employer may feel that some jobs may expose women to substances or working conditions that may be hazardous to the developing fetus carried by pregnant employees. The employer may seek to avoid such potential health problems by prohibiting women of childbearing age from working in such jobs. Does such a restriction violate Title VII, or can it be justified as a BFOQ? In *U.A.W. v. Johnson Controls* [499 U.S. 187 (1991)], the Supreme Court held that the employer may restrict pregnant women from particular jobs only when the pregnancy actually interferes with the employee's ability to perform the job. The employer cannot use concerns about the health of future children to justify a BFOQ; the Court noted "an employer must direct its concerns about a woman's ability to perform her job safely and efficiently to those aspects of the woman's job-related activities that fall within the 'essence' of the particular business."

SEXUAL HARASSMENT

Employees on the job may be subjected to unwelcome sexual remarks, advances, or requests for sexual favors by coworkers or supervisors. Such conduct is known as *sexual harassment*. Although Title VII does not specifically mention sexual harassment, the guidelines adopted by the EEOC under Title VII provide that sexual harassment constitutes sex discrimination in violation of Title VII. The guidelines were upheld by the U.S. Supreme Court in *Meritor Savings Bank v. Vinson* [477 U.S. 57 (1986)]. The Court agreed that conditioning job status, such as hiring, promotion, or other benefits, on submission to requests for sexual favors (known as **quid pro quo** sexual harassment) was prohibited by Title VII. The Court also held that harassment that creates a hostile environment that interferes with an employee's job performance constitutes sex discrimination, even though job status may not be linked to the harassment. Such harassment, known as **hostile environment** sexual harassment, also violates Title VII. The key to what constitutes sexual harassment is "unwelcome" comments, taunts, requests for sexual favors, and other conduct of a sexual nature; an isolated comment probably does not amount to harassment, but repeated acts or comments, especially after the target of such conduct has indicated that they are unwelcome, is harassment. (In addition to sexual harassment, Title VII also prohibits harassment based on race, color, religion, or national origin.) Title VII's prohibition of sexual harassment includes "same-sex" sexual harassment—that is, harassment of a sexual nature in which the harasser and the victim are of the same sex ("male on male" or "female on female" harassment), according to *Oncale v. Sundowner Offshore Services, Inc.* [523 U.S. 75 (1998)].

A plaintiff need not establish that the hostile environment sexual harassment caused her or him psychological trauma; the Supreme Court decision in *Harris v. Forklift Systems, Inc.* [510 U.S. 17 (1993)] held that harassment creating an environment that is reasonably perceived, and is perceived, as being hostile or abusive is prohibited by Title VII. Factors to consider when determining whether the harassment creates a hostile environment include the frequency and severity of the harassment, whether it is physically threatening or humiliating, and whether it unreasonably interferes with employees' work performance.

quid pro quo: Sexual harassment where job status or benefits are conditioned on submission to requests for sexual favors.

hostile environment: Sexual harassment that has the effect of creating a hostile or offensive work environment.

Employers' Liability for Sexual Harassment. Employers may be held liable for harassment by supervisors or managerial employees, by coworkers of the victim of the harassment, or even by nonemployees. The employer may be liable for sexual harassment by the victim's coworkers (who are neither managerial nor supervisors) if the employer knew or should have known of such harassment and failed to take effective corrective action. Where the harassment is done by nonemployees (such as clients or visiting salespersons), the employer may be held liable if it had some measure of control or influence over the harasser and if the employer failed to take corrective action when it knew or should have known of the harassment.

The following Supreme Court decision discusses when an employer will be held liable for sexual harassment by supervisors or managerial employees.

FARAGHER V. CITY OF BOCA RATON

524 U.S. 775 (1998)

FACTS

From 1985 to 1990, Beth Ann Faragher worked part-time and summers during college as an ocean lifeguard for the Parks and Recreation Department of the City of Boca Raton, Florida (City). Faragher's immediate supervisors were Bill Terry, David Silverman, and Robert Gordon. In June 1990, Faragher resigned.

The lifeguards and supervisors were stationed at the city beach and had no significant contact with higher city officials. The lifeguards reported to lieutenants and captains, who reported to Terry; Terry was supervised by the Recreation Superintendent, who in turn reported to a Director of Parks and Recreation, answerable to the City Manager.

The City adopted a sexual harassment policy in 1986 and revised it in 1990, but it failed to disseminate its policy among employees of the Marine Safety Section—Terry, Silverman, Gordon, and many lifeguards were unaware of it. Faragher claimed that Terry and Silverman created a sexually hostile atmosphere at the beach by repeatedly subjecting Faragher and other female lifeguards to uninvited and offensive touching, lewd remarks, and by speaking of women in offensive terms. During Faragher's five years as a lifeguard, Silverman and Terry repeatedly touched the bodies of female employees without invitation, and asked female lifeguards to have sex with them. Faragher did not complain to higher management about Terry's or Silverman's conduct. She did speak about it to Gordon, but she regarded these discussions as personal conversations with a colleague rather than formal complaints to a supervisor. Other female lifeguards had similarly informal talks with Gordon, but he did not report these complaints to Terry or to other city officials. Gordon told one lifeguard that "the City just [doesn't] care."

In April 1990, two months before Faragher's resignation, Nancy Ewanchew, a former lifeguard, wrote to the City's Personnel Director, complaining that Terry and Silver-man had harassed her and other female lifeguards. The City then investigated the complaint, reprimanded Terry and Silverman and required them to choose between a suspension without pay or the forfeiture of annual leave. Faragher filed a suit under Title VII against Terry, Silverman, and the City in 1992; she claimed that Terry and Silverman, as supervisors, were acting as agents of the City, and that their conduct amounted to discrimination in the "terms, conditions, and privileges" of her employment.

The trial court held that the conduct of Terry and Silverman was discriminatory harassment sufficiently serious to alter the conditions of Faragher's employment and constitute an abusive working environment, and that the City was liable for the harassment by its supervisory employees. The court noted that the harassment was pervasive enough to support an inference that the City knew or should have known of it, and the City was liable because Terry and Silverman were acting as its agents when they committed the harassing acts. Finally, the court observed that Gordon's inaction, given his knowledge of the harassment, was a further basis for holding the City liable. The trial court awarded Faragher nominal damages under Title VII.

On appeal by the City, the Court of Appeals for the Eleventh Circuit reversed the judgment against the City, holding that Terry and Silverman were not acting within the scope of their employment when they engaged in the harassment, that they were not aided in their actions by the agency relationship, and that the City had no constructive knowledge of the harassment by virtue of its pervasiveness or Gordon's actual knowledge. Faragher appealed to the U.S. Supreme Court.

DECISION

The Supreme Court reversed the Court of Appeals' decision. Justice Souter, writing the majority opinion, stated that hostile environment sexual harassment by supervisors and coworkers is now recognized as a persistent problem in the workplace. The employer is in the best position to prevent such harassment; therefore, it makes sense, given the rationale of Title VII, to hold the employer liable for harassing conduct of a supervisor when such conduct is possible by the abuse of the supervisor's authority. When a supervisor harasses or discriminates in the terms and conditions of subordinates' employment, his or her actions necessarily draw upon the supervisor's position over the people who report to him or her, or those who work under them—an employee generally cannot avoid a supervisor's abusive conduct the same way that he or she might deal with abuse from a coworker. When a coworker harasses, the victim can walk away or tell the offender where to go, but it may be difficult to offer such responses to a supervisor, who controls the victim's working conditions and may have the power to fire, demote, or reduce pay. The victim may well be reluctant to accept the risks of blowing the whistle on a superior. Employers have a greater opportunity to guard against misconduct by supervisors than by common workers; employers have greater opportunity and incentive to screen supervisors, train them, and monitor their performance.

Although there are good reasons for holding the employer liable for harassment by supervisors, employers are not always automatically liable for all harassing conduct by supervisors. An employer is liable to a victimized employee for sexual harassment by a supervisor of an employee when the harassment causes the employee to suffer some tangible negative employment action—demotion,

transfer, pay or benefit reduction, termination, and so on. Where the harassment causes a hostile work environment but the employee does not suffer any negative employment consequences, the employer may raise an affirmative defense by showing that the employer exercised reasonable care to prevent and correct promptly any sexually harassing behavior and that the employee victim unreasonably failed to take advantage of any preventive or corrective opportunities provided by the employer or to avoid harm otherwise. The employer's defense goes both to liability and the amount of damages. Such a defense is not available to the employer when the supervisor's harassment results in some negative employment consequence. In Faragher's case, it is clear that the harassers were her supervisors, the harassment created a hostile work environment, and the City failed to take reasonable steps to prevent sexual harassment. Therefore, the decision of the Court of Appeals was reversed and the trial court's decision was reinstated. [Justices Scalia and Thomas dissented.]

CASE QUESTIONS

1. Why should an employer be held responsible for the actions of a supervisor?
2. Is an employer always liable for a supervisor's sexual harassment? When can an employer establish a defense to being held liable for sexual harassment by a supervisor?
3. Does Faragher's failure to make a formal complaint about the harassing conduct prevent the City from being held liable for that conduct? Explain.

WALL STREET FIRM SETTLE SEX DISCRIMINATION SUIT

Wall Street brokerage firm Morgan Stanley agreed to a $54 million settlement with the EEOC in a suit that had accused the firm of discriminated against women in pay and promotions. The settlement was reached as the suit was about to go to trial in the federal courthouse in Manhattan. The case began with a complaint filed with the EEOC in November, 1998, by Allison Schieffelin, a former Morgan Stanley broker. She claimed that the firm had tolerated and condoned a hostile workplace environment in which male employees made sexist comments and organized outings to topless bars and strip clubs. As an example, Ms. Schieffelin said that she had organized a group dinner with an important client at an exclusive restaurant in New

York, but after the dinner, she was ushered into a cab while the male co-workers and the client went to a strip club. She was fired in 2000 after she complained about being passed over for a promotion; she claimed that the firing was in retaliation for her complaints. Morgan Stanley claimed that she was fired for insubordination because she became hostile and disrespectful toward her female supervisor, who received the promotion Schieffelin had sought.

In addition to Ms. Schieffelin, the EEOC was prepared to call as witnesses more than 20 other female employees with similar complaints. The settlement sets up a $40 million fund to cover claims by female employees of Morgan Stanley's institutional equities division who claim sex discrimination in employment since 1995; the fund will be overseen by a former federal judge, Abner J. Mikva. Morgan Stanley agreed to set aside $2 million to fund diversity training and anti-discrimination programs. The EEOC recommended that Ms. Schieffelin, who earned $1.35 million in 1998, receive $12 million under the settlement.

The Morgan Stanley settlement is just the latest in a series of sex discrimination claims filed against Wall Street firms. Merrill Lynch and Smith Barney have already paid out more than $200 million to female employees of their brokerage operations; and a panel of arbitrators held that Merrill Lynch had engaged in sex discrimination against Hydie Sumner, a former broker and awarded her $2.2 million. In 2003, Deutsche Bank reached a "multi-million dollar" settlement in a case filed by Virginia Gambale, a managing director who alleged that she was twice denied promotions because of her gender.

Wall Street firms are still male-dominated at the top levels; female employees hold most lower-level jobs such as sales assistant. Data compiled by the EEOC indicate that men made up more than two-thirds of the officials and managers in the securities industry in 2002. According to the Securities Industry Association, white males fill almost 80% of executive management positions and more than 70% of investment bankers, traders and brokers.

The sex discrimination complaints in the securities industry are not limited to the U.S. In England, Stephanie Villalba, who had been in charge of the European division of Merrill Lynch's International Private Client Group, filed a claim of sex discrimination, unequal pay and unfair dismissal against her former employer. She claimed that the other Merrill executives heading regional divisions were paid between $725,000 to $1 million, while she was paid $549,997 ($150,000 as base salary and the rest as bonus) in 2002. She alleged that she had earned about $150,000 more than her 2002 pay, in 2001, before she was promoted; employees who she recruited to work for her were paid $600,000 to $800,000. The claim, seeking $13 million, is being heard by a British Employment Tribunal, a three-person panel; the tribunal's decision is legally binding on the parties, but can be appealed to the U.K. courts.

Sources: Sue Calian, "Merrill Sex-Bias Suit Highlights the Issue Of Global Pay Scales," The Wall Street Journal Online, June 16, 2004; "Frustration: Sex Discrimination on Wall Street," *The Economist,* July 17, 2004; Patrick Mcgeehan, "Morgan Stanley Settles Bias Suit with $54 Million," *The New York Times,* July 13, 2004, page A-1; "Morgan Stanley Settles Discrimination Suit for $54 Million," *New York Law Journal,* July 13, 2004; Carrie Mason-Draffen, "Sex Discrimination Settlement," *Newsday,* July 13, 2004, page A-5; Patrick Mcgeehan, "Discrimination on Wall Street? The Numbers Tell the Story," *The New York Times,* July 14, 2004, page C-1.

DISCRIMINATION BASED ON RELIGION OR NATIONAL ORIGIN

RELIGIOUS DISCRIMINATION

What if an employee claims that he or she is unable to work after sundown on Fridays because of religious beliefs, or if an employee insists that religious beliefs require him to wear a turban and a beard: must the employer grant these requests? The Title VII prohibition against employment discrimination based on religion is broad in scope; the EEOC regulations state that "religion" under Title VII includes an individual's personal moral and philosophical beliefs when those beliefs are held with the strength of traditional religious belief. Title VII has also been held to protect atheists from discrimination because of their beliefs.

However, Title VII's prohibition against discrimination in employment based on religion is not absolute. Religion, as with sex or national origin, may be used as a BFOQ when the employer demonstrates that business necessity requires hiring individuals of a particular religion. In addition, §702(a) and §703(e)(2) of Title VII allow religious corporations or educational institutions to give preference to hiring employees who are members of that religion. Section 703(e)(2) allows a Catholic university, such as the University of Notre Dame, to require that the university president be Catholic, or a Hebrew day school to require that its teachers be Jewish. Some religious organizations may carry on activities that are not specifically "religious" in character: Does the §702(a) exemption apply to these activities as well? In *Corporation of Presiding Bishops of the Church of Jesus Christ of Latter-day Saints v. Amos* [483 U.S. 327 (1987)], the Supreme Court held that the §702(a) exemption extends to the not-for-profit activities of religious organizations, not just to the activities that are "religious" in character. The *Amos* case involved a community gymnasium run by the Church of Jesus Christ of Latter-day Saints (known as the Mormons); all employees of the gymnasium were required to be members of that church.

Reasonable Accommodation. Even if the employer is not able to establish religion as BFOQ, and if §702(a) does not apply, the prohibition against religious discrimination in employment is still not absolute. Title VII prohibits an employer from discriminating against an employee because of religious belief, practice, or observance unless the employer demonstrates that it is unable to accommodate such belief, practice, or observance without undue hardship on the conduct of the employer's business. An employer must make a reasonable attempt to accommodate the religious beliefs or practices; but if such attempts at accommodation fail or involve undue hardship, then the employer's obligation ends.

In *Trans World Airlines v. Hardison* [432 U.S. 63 (1977)], an employee transferred to a job that required him to work weekends; his religion prohibited working from sundown Friday to sundown Saturday. The employer insisted that the job was too important to leave vacant, and it was too expensive to pay another employee overtime to work for Hardison. Hardison wanted to arrange a swap of jobs with another employee on Friday evenings, but the collective agreement covering the jobs used employee seniority for bidding on jobs. Hardison had too little seniority to transfer into a job that would not require

de minimis:
Small or minimal,
insignificant.

him to work Friday evenings, and the union would not waive the seniority system to let Hardison swap jobs. The employer fired Hardison when he refused to work Friday evenings. Consequently, he filed suit under Title VII. The Supreme Court held that the employer's actions did not violate Title VII; the duty to make reasonable accommodation did not require the regular payment of overtime wages or bearing more than a **de minimis** cost, nor did it require the employer to override the seniority provisions of a collective agreement.

When there are several ways to accommodate an employee's beliefs, Title VII does not require that the employer offer the accommodation preferred by the employee; according to *Ansonia Board of Education v. Philbrook* [479 U.S. 60 (1986)], the court requires only that the accommodation offered to the employee must be reasonable. In *Philbrook,* the Court upheld the employer's practice of allowing the employee to take unpaid leave for religious holidays rather than using paid sick days.

SOCIAL/ETHICAL ISSUE

You are the Human Resource Associate at a small manufacturing company in Dearborn, Michigan. A number of your employees are Muslims—followers of Islam. A group of the Muslim employees approach you to request permission to conduct religious prayer services in the plant lunch room during their lunch break and coffee breaks. They are good workers and you don't want to do anything that might affect their morale and productivity. But you are also concerned that other employees who are "born-again" Christians, Buddhists and Hindus may also seek to conduct religious or prayer services in the plant. Should you allow the Muslim employees to hold the prayer services? What arguments can you make for allowing the services? What arguments can you make against allowing the services? Would it be possible to allow the Muslims to hold services, but to deny other groups the right to hold religious services? How would you advise the CEO to proceed on the employees' request? Why?

NATIONAL ORIGIN DISCRIMINATION

Title VII protects all individuals, both citizens and noncitizens, from employment discrimination based on national origin. The prohibition against national origin discrimination under Title VII includes discrimination because of a person's ethnic background, membership in groups associated with particular ethnic backgrounds, or a person's accent. Harassment because of a person's national origin is also prohibited. National origin, however, may be used as a BFOQ under §703(e)(1) where required by business necessity.

After the terrorist attacks of September 11, 2001, the EEOC experienced a great increase in complaints of discrimination against persons of Middle Eastern or Arab origin. In one case, the EEOC agreed to a $1.1 million settlement of a complaint by four Pakistani-American employees against Stockton Steel. The employees alleged that they were repeatedly called derogatory names such as "camel jockeys" and "ragheads". The firm also agreed to conduct training to prevent future discrimination and to implement a policy to guarantee employees' right to request accommodations for their religious beliefs.[1]

[1]EEOC Press Release, March 19, 2003.

Other examples of national-origin discrimination include the use of English language tests when English language skill is not a requirement for the work to be performed, and the refusal to recognize degrees from foreign universities. One area of controversy has been the use of "English-only" rules—rules that require all employees to speak only English while on the job. The EEOC regulations state that employees who work in public contact positions (such as sales clerks or receptionists) may be required to speak English on the job; however, a "blanket" English-only rule covering all employees during working hours may violate Title VII. However, in *Garcia v. Spun Steak* [998 F. 2d 1480 (9th Cir. 1993), *cert. denied*, 512 U.S. 1228 (1994)], the U.S. Court of Appeals for the Ninth Circuit held that an employer's English-only rule, based on job safety concerns, did not have an adverse impact on bilingual employees—they may have preferred to speak Spanish but were capable of speaking English and were not adversely affected by the English-only rule.

Title VII does not prohibit discrimination on the basis of citizenship, according to the Supreme Court in *Espinoza v. Farah Mfg. Co.* [414 U.S. 86 (1973)]. This case held that an employer may refuse to hire persons who are not U.S. citizens because the Title VII prohibition against national origin discrimination does not prohibit discrimination based on citizenship. The EEOC regulations under Title VII, however, state that using a citizenship requirement with the intent to discriminate on the basis of national origin violates the act.

RETALIATION UNDER TITLE VII

In addition to prohibiting discrimination, Section 704 (a) of Title VII prohibits retaliation by an employer, union, or employment agency against an employee or applicant because that person has opposed any practice that is prohibited by Title VII (known as the "opposition clause") or because that person has taken part in or assisted any investigation, hearing, or proceeding under Title VII (known as the "participation clause"). To demonstrate a case of retaliation under §704(a), plaintiffs must demonstrate that (1) they were engaged in an activity or activities protected under Title VII; (2) they suffered an adverse employment decision; and (3) there was a causal link between the protected activity and the adverse employment decision. The "protected activity" must be related to either the participation clause or the opposition clause of §704. An employee who voluntarily cooperated with an employer's internal investigation of a sexual harassment complaint was protected under the opposition clause of §704 even though she did not make a complaint to the employer or file a formal charge under Title VII; the Supreme Court held that her subsequent discharge by the employer violated Title VII, according to *Crawford v. Metropolitan Govt. of Nashville & Davidson City* [555 U.S. 271 (2009)]. In *Burlington Northern & Santa Fe Railroad Co. v. White* [548 U.S.53 (2006)], the Supreme Court held that retaliation under Title VII is not limited to ultimate employment decisions such as promotion or termination, but rather includes any action that a reasonable employee would find to be materially adverse—such that it might dissuade a reasonable worker from making or supporting a charge under Title VII. Section 704(a) also protects former employees from retaliation, according to *Robinson v. Shell Oil Company* [519 U.S. 337 (1997)]. In that case an employer who gave a former employee a negative reference because the employee had filed a Title VII charge against the employer; the

Supreme Court ruled that giving the negative reference was retaliation in violation of §704(a). In *Thompson v. North American Stainless Steel, LP* [131 S.Ct. 863 (2011)], the Supreme Court held that an employer who fired the fiancée of an employee who had filed a sex discrimination claim was guilty of retaliation in violation of Title VII.

REMEDIES UNDER TITLE VII

Remedies available under Title VII include the following: court orders requiring hiring or reinstatement of employees; awards of back pay, seniority, and other benefits; injunctions against unlawful employment practices; punitive damages; legal fees; and "such affirmative action as may be appropriate." In cases where reinstatement may not be appropriate, the court may award the plaintiff "front pay" – monetary damages in lieu of hiring or reinstatement. The amount of front pay awarded depends upon factors such as the employability of the plaintiff and the likely duration of the employment. In *Pollard v. E.I. du Pont de Nemours & Co.* [532 U.S. 843 (2001)], the Supreme Court held that **front pay** is separate from any compensatory and punitive damages awarded, and is not subject to the statutory limits on such damages,

> **front pay:** A monetary settlement paid in lieu of reinstatement or hiring.

The 1991 amendments to Title VII added the right to recover compensatory and punitive damages against defendants, apart from government agencies or other public sector employers, that have engaged in an intentional violation of Title VII. Claims for punitive and compensatory damages are brought under 42 U.S.C. §1981A, which allows for damages in addition to any remedies recoverable under §706(g) of Title VII. The punitive damages available under §1981A are limited by the size of the defendant employer, ranging from $50,000 against employers with fewer than 101 employees to $300,000 against employers with more than 500 employees.

In *Kolstad v. American Dental Association* [527 U.S. 526 (1999)], the Supreme Court held that an employer may not be liable for punitive damages because of the conduct of a supervisory or managerial employee if the employer demonstrates that the supervisor or manager acted contrary to the employer's good faith efforts to comply with Title VII. Simply having a policy is not enough. The employer must demonstrate that its policies clearly prohibited the discriminatory conduct, and that it took prompt and effective corrective action when it became aware of the discriminatory conduct, in order to escape liability for punitive damages. As with the *Faragher* defense to sexual harassment claims, the employer must make sure employees are aware of the policy and that the policy is enforced. Individual employees are not personally liable under Title VII; only employers, unions, or employment agencies are subject to liability under Title VII. However, individuals may be held personally liable for damages, including punitive damages, under state EEO and tort laws.

Legal fees are available under §706(k), in the court's discretion, to the prevailing party, other than to the United States or the EEOC. Section 706(k) does not require that legal fees be awarded but leaves such an award to the trial court's discretion. In *Christiansburg Garment Co. v. EEOC* [434 U.S. 412 (1978)], the Supreme Court held that a prevailing plaintiff should "ordinarily recover an attorney's fees unless special circumstances would render such an award unjust," while a prevailing defendant should recover legal fees only when the plaintiff's claims were held to be "frivolous, unreasonable or groundless. . . ." In *New York Gaslight Club v. Carey* [447 U.S. 54 (1980)], the Supreme Court held that a prevailing plaintiff in a suit under Title VII may also recover legal fees for work done at state or local agency proceedings when the complainant is required to file with that agency by §706(c).

SUMMARY

The purpose of EEO legislation is to eliminate discrimination that prevents capable and qualified individuals from being employed or from performing effectively on the job. The scope of the protection of the EEO laws has been expanding, from Title VII's initial prohibition of discrimination because of race, color, sex, religion, and national origin, to age and disability discrimination. Some state legislation protects against discrimination based on marital status and sexual orientation as well. The U.S. workforce is becoming more diverse, and employees are becoming more aware of the EEO legislation and sensitive to real or perceived discrimination than ever before. More employment discrimination litigation, with potentially greater liability for employers, is one result of these trends. Managers of today and tomorrow, therefore, must understand the EEO laws thoroughly and must practice the principles of equal employment in their workplace.

CHAPTER QUESTIONS

1. Dr. Pronting, an Emergency Room Supervisor at Inner City Hospital, was having an affair with Nurse Harper, who worked in the Emergency Room. When the position of Head Nurse in the Emergency Room became vacant, several nurses, including Harper, applied for the position. The other nurses had more Emergency Room experience, more seniority, and were more qualified than Harper, but Pronting promoted Harper because of her relationship with him. Were the other, more qualified nurses victims of sexual harassment? Explain your answer. [*King v. Palmer,* 778 F. 2d 878 (D.C. Cir. 1985)]

2. McGinnis worked as a clerk for the U.S. Postal Service. The Postal Service distributes the draft registration materials for the Selective Service to young men required to register for the draft. McGinnis had a longtime association with the Society of Friends (Quakers), although she was not formally a member of the Society. Because of her personal religious beliefs, McGinnis refused to distribute the draft registration materials while she was working. The Postal Service fired her. Was her refusal to distribute the draft registration materials protected by Title VII? Explain your answer. [*McGinnis v. U.S. Postal Service,* 512 F.Supp. 517(N.D.Cal.1980)]

3. Madeline O'Hara was a professor in the religion and theology department at Aquinas College, a Catholic institution. Half of the 15 members of her department were ordained priests; only one other member of the department was female. O'Hara was denied tenure because of her personal pro-choice views favoring abortion, which were in conflict with the Catholic Church's position strictly opposing all abortions. Was the denial of tenure to O'Hara in violation of Title VII? Explain. [*Maguire v. Marquette University,* 814 F. 2d 1213 (7th Cir. 1987)]

4. Childress was a cook for the Pennsylvania Department of Corrections; she was the only female cook at Walburg Prison. Although she was paid the same wage rate as the male cooks, she earned less money than they did because she was denied the opportunity to work overtime. Childress filed a complaint under the Equal Pay Act. How should the court rule on her case? Explain. Is there a violation of Title VII here? [*True v. N.Y. Dept. of Correctional Services,* 613 F.Supp. 27 (W.D. N.Y. 1984)]

5. Ally McBee applied for a job as a prison guard with the Arkansas State Board of Corrections. The Board of Corrections required that applicants for guard positions be at least 5'2" tall and no taller than 6'10", and weigh no less than 120 lbs. and no more than 300 lbs. McBee was only 5'1" and was therefore rejected. She filed suit under Title VII. On what basis should she make her claim? Is her suit likely to be successful? What must the Board of Corrections show to counter her claim? Explain. [*Dothard v. Rawlinson,* 433 U.S. 321 (1977)]

6. Elana Back, a school psychologist in New York City, was denied tenure because her bosses questioned her ability to "do her job and be a mother at the same time." Her performance reviews were very favorable, but the employer assumed that the demands of motherhood would prevent her from being fully dedicated to her job. Has Back been the victim of sex discrimination prohibited under Title VII? Why or why not? Explain.

7. Nyugen Ang Mai operates a Vietnamese restaurant in downtown Bakersfield. Mai has restricted hiring for the restaurant to his family and relatives; he now employs 17 people at the restaurant. Smith, an African American, applies for a job at the restaurant; there are waiter and kitchen help positions available. Mai refuses to hire Smith; he says that customers expect Vietnamese, or at least Asian, waiters at a Vietnamese restaurant. Mai also explains that his Vietnamese customers, who constitute a significant portion of his business, would be reluctant to be waited on by an African American, because that might bring up memories of the war in Vietnam. Smith files a claim with the EEOC, alleging race discrimination. Has Mai established a BFOQ, or is Smith likely to prevail? Explain.

8. Michelle Swanson worked as a waitress at the Michigan City Holiday Inn. Fred Lubber, the manager at the Holiday Inn restaurant, was a fundamentalist Christian, as were many of the other restaurant employees. Swanson, who was not married, discovered that she was pregnant; she considered having an abortion and discussed the matter with some of the other employees. She was subsequently fired by Lubber, who claimed that the other employees became very upset by her discussion of abortion and the resulting uproar was very disruptive to the restaurant's operations. Swanson filed a claim under Title VII, challenging her discharge. To what kind(s) of discrimination has Swanson been subjected here? How should the court rule on her suit? Explain. [*Turic v. Holland Hospitality Inc.* (85 F.3d 1211 (6th Cir. 1996)].

9. Maurice Reign worked as a waiter at the MGM Grand Hotel. Reign was a homosexual, and was continually singled out for harassing conduct, including repeated physical contact, grabbing and poking him in the anus, by his male supervisors and coworkers. Reign resigned as a result of the repeated conduct; he then filed a suit against the employer, alleging sexual harassment in violation of Title VII. Is his suit likely to be successful? Explain your answer. [*Rene v. MGM Grand Hotel,* 305 F.3d 1061 (9th Cir. 2002)].

10. Helio Inc., is a company that provides charter helicopter services. Helio signed a contract with the Saudi Arabian government to provide helicopter flights to Muslims who make pilgrimages to Mecca. The flights involved traveling over the sacred shrines and sites of Islam, such as the Kaaba. Islamic law, in effect in Saudi Arabia, forbids non-Muslims from entering such holy sites; the penalty for violating this law is death by beheading. For the Saudi Arabian flights, Helio, Inc., decides to hire only pilots who were Muslims or who were willing to convert to the Islamic faith before starting the flights. Kern, a qualified helicopter pilot, applied for a job with Helio but was refused because he was not a Muslim. Kern claimed that Helio discriminated against him because of his religion; Helio claimed that being a Muslim was a BFOQ for the job. Who is likely to prevail if Kern files suit? Explain your answer. [*Kern v. Dynaelectron Corp.,* 577 F. Supp. 1196 (N.D. Tex., 1983)]

PRACTICAL EXERCISE

Don Franks owns a manufacturing company that makes machine parts for automotive equipment. Business had been slow until the company successfully bid on a large contract to produce tank tread sprockets for the U. S. Army. The three-year contract significantly increased Franks' business. To meet the production demands of the contract, Franks expanded his workforce by 30 percent. Most of the new employees Franks hired for the contract were African-Americans and Latinos; prior to the new hiring, the workforce was predominantly made up of white males.

Now that the tank tread contract has expired, Franks' business has slowed down significantly. Unless new orders can be found, he may be forced to lay off a number of production employees. If Franks uses inverse seniority (last hired, first fired) as the basis of the layoff, most of the employees who lose their jobs will be minorities. Franks feels that having a racially balanced workforce may help him to win more government contracts, so he is reluctant to lay off the minority workers. At the same time, Franks is afraid that some of the more senior white workers will file an employment discrimination suit if he lays them off instead of the more junior minority workers.

How should Franks determine which employees should be laid off? You are Franks' Human Resource Director; he asks you to prepare a memo outlining the various choices and their pros and cons. What arguments can you make for retaining the minority employees? What arguments can you make for using inverse seniority for the layoffs? Which option would you recommend? Would your answer change if the employees are unionized, and the collective agreement covering them requires that employment decisions be based on seniority? Weighing the various options and explaining why you recommend a particular choice, answer these queries in a memo.

FURTHER INFORMATION

www.eeoc.gov/
  The Equal Employment Opportunity Commission's Web site.
www.eeac.org/
  The Equal Employment Advisory Council's Web site.
www.shrm.org/
  The Society for Human Resource Management's Web site.
http://hr.monster.com/
  Human resource management and general employment information.

CHAPTER 22

OTHER STATUTORY REGULATION OF EMPLOYMENT

One of the surgical technicians at your hospital is HIV positive but has no real symptoms of AIDS. The supervisor of the operating room wants you to transfer the technician in order to protect patients and other employees. The technician claims that he can take adequate precautions to avoid accidentally infecting a patient or coworker during surgery. As the employer, what steps can you take to protect patients and coworkers? What are the legal rights of the technician? After studying this chapter, you will be able to decide how to proceed legally.

INTRODUCTION

One of the most significant trends in labor and employment law in the past 25 years has been the shift in emphasis from collective bargaining as a means of regulating conditions in the workplace to regulation by means of expanding statutory and common law definitions of individual legal rights. The percentage of U.S. employees represented by labor unions has dropped from about 33 percent to approximately 13 percent over that time. In place of the union representation, the worker is increasingly being protected by new federal and state laws and the development of new legal principles from older laws.

In addition to Title VII of the Civil Rights Act (as examined in Chapter 21), which prohibits discrimination on the basis of race, color, sex, religion, or national origin in any aspect of employment, a number of other important federal and state laws regulate aspects of employment. The Family and Medical Leave Act allows some employees to take time off for the birth or adoption of a child, or to care for a spouse, child, or parent who has a serious medical condition. Two laws enacted right after the Civil War can be used to redress the victims of race discrimination. Federal laws also prohibit discrimination in employment based on factors such as age or disability. Other laws require workplaces to maintain a certain level of safety for their employees and to compensate workers for injuries and illnesses arising out of employment. Federal statutes establish a minimum wage that employers are required to pay employees, and set hours and safety requirements for the employment of children and youth. Another federal law regulates pension plans established by employers and enacts certain duties on those who set up and maintain such retirement programs. Each of these federal and state laws is discussed in the following sections.

PARENTAL AND FAMILY LEAVE: THE FAMILY AND MEDICAL LEAVE ACT

One of the most striking employment trends over the past 40 years is the huge increase in the number of women who are employed outside the home. As we saw in Chapter 21, Title VII of the Civil Rights Act of 1964 prohibits discrimination in employment based on race, color, sex, religion, or national origin. Title VII's prohibitions against sex discrimination include discrimination based on pregnancy, childbirth, or related condition. In its *U. A. W. v. Johnson Controls* [499 U.S. 187 (1991)] decision, the U.S. Supreme Court held that a woman should not be forced to choose between her right to a job and her right to have a family. But what happens after a female employee has a family—and is torn between the demands of her job and the need to care for her newborn child, or a seriously ill child, spouse, or parent?

For many years, the United States was alone in the industrialized world in having no national legislation requiring companies to grant leave to new parents. Most European countries have laws requiring employers to grant paid leave of several months for childbirth. Several bills were introduced into Congress in the 1980s, but, because of the opposition of the Reagan and George H.W. Bush Administrations, were not enacted into law. Finally, Congress passed the *Family and Medical Leave Act* (*FMLA*), and it was signed into law by President Clinton in early 1993.

The FMLA provides that **eligible employees** are entitled to take up to 12 weeks of unpaid leave during any 12-month period *to care for a newborn or newly adopted child or a spouse, parent, or child with a serious health problem or because of the employee's own serious health condition.* Eligible employees are those who have been employed for at least 12 months and have worked at least 1,250 hours during the preceding year. The FMLA applies to employers with 50 or more employees and to public employers regardless of the number of employees. The Supreme Court held that the FMLA provisions apply to state government employers, *Nevada Dept. of Human Resources v. Hibbs* [538 U.S. 721 (2003)]; the Court rejected the argument that sovereign immunity granted to the states by the Eleventh Amendment prevented the application of the FMLA to the states.

eligible employees: Under the FMLA, employees who have been employed for at least 12 months and who worked at least 1,250 hours during the past year.

The FMLA requires the employee to provide 30 days' advance notice of the leave to the employer unless such notice is not "practicable." Employers may require employees to use their paid vacation and personal or sick leave as the first part of their 12-week leave, before beginning the unpaid portion. Employers may also require employees to present certification from a health-care provider in a timely manner when requesting leave under the Act. *Key employees* may be denied leave under the FMLA. Key employees are those employees whom it would be necessary for the employer to replace in order to prevent substantial and serious economic injury to the operation of the business; no more than 10 percent of the employees at a worksite can be designated as key employees, and they must be given written notice of their status as key employees when they request a leave.

The FMLA was amended, effective January 28, 2008, to provide for additional leave for FMLA-eligible employees with a family member serving in the armed forces. The amendments create "Servicemember Family Leave" of up to 26 weeks of unpaid leave over a 12-month period for an employee who is the spouse, son, daughter, parent or next of kin of a member of the armed forces (including the National Guard) who is undergoing medical treatment, recuperation, or therapy or is otherwise on temporary disability for an illness or injury incurred on active duty. The amendments also created an additional leave for FMLA-eligible employees of up to 12 weeks unpaid leave to deal with "any qualifying exigency" arising out of the fact that a son, daughter or parent of the employee is on active duty, or has been notified of an impending call to active duty.

The employer must restore the employee to *the same or an "equivalent" position* upon expiration of the leave. This provision requires equivalent benefits, pay, and other terms and conditions of employment. The employee cannot be stripped of any employment benefits he or she accrued prior to the leave. Health benefits must be continued throughout the leave period, but the employer can recover the premiums paid for employees who fail to return from leave, unless due to a serious health condition.

Although 11 states had laws and many companies already had policies that required that employees' jobs be held for them when a child or an elderly parent needed care, the majority of U.S. companies did not. The FMLA provides that state laws that afford greater rights to employees are not to be superseded by the Act.

The FMLA covers about 5 percent of all employers in the United States, and only about 40 percent of U.S. employees. The FMLA is intended to create greater peace of mind for those employees who need some time off to care for a newborn or adopted child, or an aging parent, or to deal with their own health difficulties. Of course, implementing the law requires dealing with many complex issues, often through litigation.

The following case involves the question of what constitutes a "serious health condition" under the FMLA.

RUSSELL V. NORTH BROWARD HOSPITAL

346 F.3d 1335 (11th Cir. 2003)

FACTS

Margaret Russell worked as a Patient Accounts Adjustment Representative at North Broward Hospital; her duties included computer work, typing, filing, and telephone work. As of mid-January 2000, Russell had been disciplined three times for unscheduled absences; under the hospital's discipline policy, she risked being fired for any more unexcused absences. On May 31, 2000, Russell slipped and fell at work; she was diagnosed with a fractured right elbow and a sprained ankle (which she later learned was actually fractured). She also aggravated an existing wrist condition for which she had been receiving medical treatment before she fell. The treating physician gave Russell a sling for her arm and prescribed Darvocet for her pain. The physician told Russell that she could return to work, but restricted the use of her right arm. Russell then returned to work and finished out her shift. The next day (June 1), she reported to work at 8:00 A.M. but left at 10:00 A.M. to go back to the clinic because she was experiencing severe pain. The examining doctor told her that she needed to consult an orthopaedist about her injuries. Russell, still in pain, called her supervisor, Marsha Miller, to tell her that she would not be returning to work that day. She also asked for the following day off, but Miller refused. Russell was paid for two hours of work and six hours of sick leave that day. On June 2 Russell again reported to work at 8:00 A.M., but soon began to feel ill and started vomiting (because she had taken her pain medication on an empty stomach). Russell informed her supervisor that she could not continue working that day and she went home at 9:05 A.M. Also on June 2, Luane Rutt, the Hospital's workers' compensation agent, authorized Russell to see an orthopaedist

and scheduled her an appointment for Monday, June 5. Over the weekend of June 3 and 4, she was in "excruciating pain." On June 5, Russell went to see an orthopaedist, Dr. Boutin, who certified that she could return to work but indicated that she should have "light duty" because she "cannot use [her] right arm." Dr. Boutin also told Russell to keep taking the Darvocet for her pain, and to return for a follow-up appointment for a week later. After her appointment on June 5, Russell went to work for the remainder of her shift, from about 11:20 A.M. to 4:30 P.M. Because she was having trouble performing her duties, she requested the use of a speakerphone, but the hospital never provided her with one. On June 6 Russell reported to work at 8:00 A.M. but, because she was in pain, she asked Miller if she could leave early. Miller allowed her to do so, and Russell left work at 2:00 P.M. On June 7 Russell was scheduled for another appointment with the clinic, but Rutt called her at home the evening before, and again that morning, and told her not to go to the clinic, but instead to wait for Rutt to schedule an appointment for Russell to see Dr. Boutin that day. Russell did not go in to work, but instead waited at home for Rutt's call. When Rutt finally called back at 2:30 P.M. she told Russell that Dr. Boutin's office would be calling her with an appointment time. Dr. Boutin's office did call and tell Russell she had an appointment for 3:30 that afternoon. Russell said she did not have enough time to get to that appointment and would not be going. She did not go to the appointment or to work, but she did call Miller and explain why she had failed to report to work. The next day, June 8, Russell worked a full day. On June 9 Russell returned to see Dr. Boutin, and one of his assistants placed her arm in a cast. She left the doctor's office at 11:15 A.M.

and went home to get her medicine and change clothes. She fell asleep, did not go to work that day, and did not call to inform Miller that she was going to be out. On Monday, June 12, Miller called Russell into her office shortly after Russell reported to work. Miller told her to go home, that human resources would contact her. The next day, Miller called Russell and asked her to come in for a meeting; at the meeting, Russell was informed that her employment was being terminated because of her excessive absenteeism. Russell then filed suit under the FMLA, claiming that the hospital had retaliated against her for exercising a protected FMLA right. The protected right she claimed was the right to be absent from work during the period between May 31 and June 9, 2000, for a serious health condition. At trial, the district court judge, over Russell's objection, instructed the jury that more than three consecutive calendar days of incapacity are required to constitute a "serious health condition" necessary to qualify for protection under the FMLA. During its deliberations, the trial jury submitted several questions to the judge about the definition of a "serious health condition"; the last question was whether three consecutive partial days of incapacity could constitute a "serious health condition." The district court told the jury that the FMLA required "three consecutive calendar days, 72 hours or more." Shortly thereafter, the jury returned a verdict in favor of the hospital. The district court entered final judgment for the hospital, and Russell filed a motion for judgment as a matter of law or, in the alternative, a new trial. The district court denied that motion. Russell then appealed to the U.S. Court of Appeals for the Eleventh Circuit.

DECISION

Russell argued that the district court should have granted her motion for judgment as a matter of law because no reasonable jury could have found that she did not meet the requirement of incapacity for more than three consecutive calendar days. She argues that she established seven consecutive partial days of incapacity and maintains that partial days of incapacity always, as a matter of law, meet the regulatory definition's requirements.

The FMLA provides that "an eligible employee shall be entitled to a total of 12 workweeks of leave during any 12-month period . . . [b]ecause of a *serious health condition* that makes the employee unable to perform the functions of the position of such employee." 29 U.S.C. §2612(a)(1)(D) (emphasis added). Employees who take leave to which they are entitled under that provision must be reinstated to the position they held before the leave; they cannot be fired for taking the leave. 29 U.S.C. §2614(a). The FMLA defines a "serious health condition" as "an illness, injury, impairment, or physical or mental condition that involves—(A) inpatient care in a hospital, hospice, or residential medical care facility; or (B) continuing treatment by a health care provider." §2611(11). The second part of the definition of "serious health condition," the one involving "continuing treatment by a health care provider" is at issue in this case. The FMLA does not define "continuing treatment by a health care provider," but the U.S. Department of Labor has issued a regulation defining that phrase, in relevant part, as follows:

(2) Continuing Treatment by a health care provider. A serious health condition involving continuing treatment by a health care provider includes any one or more of the following:

(i) *A period of incapacity* (*i.e.,* inability to work, attend school or perform other regular daily activities due to the serious health condition, treatment therefor, or recovery therefrom) of *more than three consecutive calendar days,* and any subsequent treatment or period of incapacity relating to the same condition, that also involves:

(A) Treatment two or more times by a health care provider, by a nurse or physician's assistant under direct supervision of a health care provider, or by a provider of health care services (*e.g.,* physical therapist) under orders of, or on referral by, a health care provider; or

(B) Treatment by a health care provider on at least one occasion which results in a regimen of continuing treatment under the supervision of the health care provider . . . . 29 C.F.R. §825.114(a)(2)(i) (emphasis added).

Russell stated that she was incapacitated from May 31 to June 6, which satisfies the requirement that she be incapacitated for more than three consecutive calendar days. She does not contend, that at any point in time she suffered from an incapacity lasting three consecutive full days or more. Instead, she argues that partial days of incapacity are enough to satisfy the regulation, and it is undisputed that she was incapacitated for parts of more than three consecutive calendar days during the period from May 31 to June 6. Russell has not cited to us any judicial or administrative interpretation of §825.114 supporting the proposition that partial days of incapacity can ever, much less will always, satisfy the regulation's requirement of more than three consecutive days of incapacity.

The plain language of §825.114—"a period of incapacity . . . of more than three consecutive calendar days"—points the way to resolution of this issue. A "period," in the sense relevant here, means "any specified division or portion of time." [Random House Unabridged Dictionary 1440 (2d ed.1993)] The specified portion of time in §825.114 is "more than three consecutive calendar days," and a "calendar day" has a simple and universally understood meaning: "[T]he period from one midnight to the following midnight." A "calendar day" thus refers to a whole day, not to part of a day, and it takes some fraction more than three whole calendar days in a row to constitute the "period of incapacity" required under §825.114.

Interpreting §825.114 as requiring full days of incapacity will ensure that "serious health conditions" are in fact serious, and are ones that result in an extended period of incapacity, as Congress intended. This interpretation of the regulation sets forth an objective rule defining the period of incapacity necessary to invoke the protections of the FMLA. The language of §825.114 indicates the Secretary of Labor has chosen an objective standard of more than three consecutive full days of incapacity to establish a serious health condition. Partial days do not count, except at the beginning or end of the "period of incapacity" in order to make up the "more than" element.

The court of appeals rejected Russell's position that partial days of incapacity satisfy the regulation's requirements, and rejected her argument that the district court erred by instructing the jury that the regulation required "three consecutive calendar days, 72 hours or more." The court affirmed the trial court's judgment in favor of North Broward Hospital.

CASE QUESTIONS

1. What was the medical condition from which Russell suffered? Was it a "serious medical condition" that entitled her to the protection of the FMLA? Explain.
2. Does the FMLA define "serious medical condition"? Where did the court look for a definition of "serious medical condition"?
3. What must an employee demonstrate in order to be entitled to a leave under the FMLA?

The FMLA only protects about 40 percent of the nation's employees—those who work for small businesses (with less than 50 employees) are not covered by the FMLA, although they may be covered by state legislation. But even if employees are protected under the FMLA, they may be reluctant to take leave to which they are legally entitled because their employer may question their commitment to their job. If they are viewed as less dedicated to their job, they may be passed over for promotions or raises, and their progression through the employer's ranks could be slowed—they could be shunted aside to the "mommy track." Note that the FMLA does not require that the leave granted be paid leave – it only requires that the employee be granted up to 12 weeks of unpaid leave. Employers may require that the employees use any vacation of other leave time as part of the family and medical leave. As of July 1, 2004, California now requires that employees covered by the state's disability insurance program are eligible for up to 6 weeks of paid family or medical leave in a twelve month period. The employees can recover up to 55% of their normal pay, subject to a maximum payment of $728 per week.

With both parents or the sole parent working, conflicts between the family and work are bound to occur. Obtaining quality childcare at affordable prices is a real challenge for many working parents. Parents may also be unable to attend conferences with their children's teachers or to be present at other school functions or activities. President Clinton had proposed expanding the FMLA to grant parents time off for such purposes, but opposition in Congress and by employers makes such legislation unlikely. Some employees may already have that right—several states have laws that allow working parents unpaid time off work to attend school functions: California requires employers with 25 or more employees to allow employees unpaid time off, up to 40 hours per year, to participate in school activities; Illinois allows employees up to 8 hours unpaid leave per year to attend school functions; Minnesota allows up to 16 hours unpaid leave in any 12 month period; North Carolina allows up to 4 hours unpaid leave per year; and Nevada simply prohibits employers from discharging employees because of absences to attend school conferences or meetings.

OTHER FEDERAL STATUTES PROHIBITING DISCRIMINATION

Hiring the best possible employees—employees who are able, productive, and honest—is an important matter for any business. Employers may want to hire young, physically fit persons, who are perceived by the employer as being more productive than older applicants. Such policies, however, may raise legal concerns under equal employment laws prohibiting discrimination because of age or against otherwise qualified persons with a disability.

Some laws prohibiting employment discrimination actually predate Title VII. For example, the Civil Rights Acts of 1866 and 1871, passed during the Reconstruction Era after the Civil War, were intended to safeguard the rights of the newly freed slaves. However, they have been interpreted by the courts as applying to employment discrimination as well. The U.S. Constitution may also be used to prohibit employment discrimination by public sector employers. Most equal opportunity employment legislation, though, was passed after Title VII. The Age Discrimination in Employment Act, passed in 1967, prohibits discrimination in terms or conditions of employment based on age against employees over 40 years. The Rehabilitation Act of 1973 and the Americans with Disabilities Act, passed in 1990, both prohibit employment discrimination against otherwise qualified handicapped individuals. Executive Order 11246, promulgated by President Johnson in 1965 and revised under President Nixon in 1969, requires that companies doing business with the federal government must be equal opportunity employers. Lastly, most states have their own equal employment laws, similar to Title VII, that apply to employers operating in those states.

THE CIVIL RIGHTS ACTS OF 1866 AND 1871

Section 1981 of the *Civil Rights Act* of 1866 provides, in part, that "All persons within the jurisdiction of the United States shall have the same right in every State and Territory to make and enforce contracts . . . as is enjoyed by white citizens. . . ." The courts have held that §1981 gives plaintiffs the right to sue for damages for intentional race discrimination in terms or conditions of employment. The Civil Rights Act of 1991 extended the protection of §1981 to the "making, performance, modification, and termination of contracts, and the enjoyment of all benefits, privileges, terms and conditions of the contractual relationship."

The Supreme Court has indicated that "race" will be interpreted broadly. For example, in *Saint Francis College v. Al-Khazraji* [481 U.S. 604 (1987)], the court held that a professor who alleged denial of tenure because he was an Arab could sue under §1981. The Civil Rights Act of 1991 also added §1981A, which gives persons the right to sue for punitive and compensatory damages for intentional violations of Title VII, the Rehabilitation Act, and the Americans with Disabilities Act.

Section 1983 of the Civil Rights Act of 1871 also allows claims for damages against intentional discrimination. Unlike §1981, however, it is not limited to race discrimination. In *Maine v. Thiboutot* [448 U.S. 1(1980)], the Supreme Court held that §1983 encompasses claims based on deprivation of rights granted under the U.S. Constitution and federal statutory law. Consequently, §1983 can be used to challenge intentional discrimination on grounds prohibited by federal law, such as age, sex, religion, national origin, disability, and so forth. The wording of §1983 restricts claims under it to cases in which the alleged discrimination is by someone acting (or claiming to act) under government authority. Thus, courts have interpreted §1983 to mean that it can be used only to challenge discrimination by public sector employers (and private sector employers acting pursuant to state action).

THE AGE DISCRIMINATION IN EMPLOYMENT ACT

The federal *Age Discrimination in Employment Act* (*ADEA*), passed in 1967, prohibits discrimination based on age in any terms or conditions of employment. The Act was intended to protect older workers who were more likely subject to such discrimination; thus, its provisions cover only age discrimination against employees aged 40 years and above. State and local laws may provide greater protection from age discrimination. For example, New York State's Human Rights Law prohibits age discrimination against employees 18 years or older.

The act covers employers engaged in commerce with 20 or more employees, labor unions that either operate a hiring hall or have more than 25 members and represent the employees of an employer covered by the act, and employment agencies. State and local governments are included in the definition of *employers* under the ADEA. However, in *Kimel v. Florida Board of Regents* [528 U.S. 62 (2000)], the U.S. Supreme Court held that state governments are immune from suits under the ADEA by reason of the Eleventh Amendment of the U.S. Constitution.

The ADEA prohibits the refusal or failure to hire, the discharge, or any other discrimination in terms, conditions, or privileges of employment because of an individual's age (40 years and over). The mandatory retirement of employees because of their age is also prohibited, but the act does not affect voluntary retirement by employees. The ADEA also does not prohibit an employer eliminating certain employment benefits for employees under fifty years of age while continuing to provide such benefits for employees over fifty, *General Dynamics Land Systems, Inc. v. Cline* [540 U.S. 581 (2004)].

Exceptions and Defenses Under the ADEA The ADEA does provide for some limited exceptions and recognizes that age may be a bona fide occupational requirement (BFOQ) for certain jobs. Age can be a BFOQ when the employer can demonstrate that it is reasonably necessary to the safe and efficient operation of the employer's business to refuse to hire employees over a certain age. For example, the courts have upheld the requirement that New York State Police troopers must retire at age 55 years because of the strenuous nature of their police work. The ADEA was amended in 1996 to allow state and local governments to pass laws setting retirement ages for police or firefighters, provided that the retirement age is at least 55 years.

The ADEA also states that employees who are in executive or high policy-making positions may be retired at age 65 years if they have been in such a position for at least two years and are entitled to retirement benefits of at least $44,000 per year. This provision was inserted into the ADEA to allow employers to ensure that senior executives do not remain in their jobs indefinitely; by providing for turnover in senior jobs, employers can retain talented junior executives by offering them the prospect of advancement into top jobs.

An employer is also permitted to observe the terms of a bona fide seniority system or employee benefit plan (such as a retirement or pension plan) as long as it is not "a subterfuge to evade the purpose" of the act and does not require the involuntary retirement of any individual. That means that an employer may treat employees differently under a benefit plan, as long as the differential is cost justified. For example, the cost of insurance generally increases with the age of the person to be insured. An employer providing life insurance as a benefit to employees can provide reduced coverage for older employees, as long as that reduced coverage costs the same as the insurance coverage provided for younger employees.

In *Smith v. City of Jackson, Mississipi* [544 U.S. 228 (2005)], the U.S. Supreme Court held that an employee may bring a disparate impact claim of age discrimination under the ADEA; however, the scope of employer liability for disparate impact age discrimination is narrower than disparate impact liability under Title VII. The plaintiff must identify a specific employment practice or action that has a disparate impact on older workers; however, the employer is not liable under the ADEA if the disparate impact is based on a "reasonable factor other than age."

In addition, an employer may differentiate between employees as long as the different treatment is based on a factor other than age. For example, an employer may use a productivity-based pay plan even if older employees produce less and earn less than younger employees. In this case, the pay is based on each employee's productivity, a factor other than age. Also note that in *Hazen Paper Co. v. Biggins* [507 U.S. 604 (1993)], the Supreme Court held that discharging an employee because the person would be entitled to a pension was not the same as discharging him because of age. Although such conduct might violate another law, such as the Employment Retirement Income Security Act, the conduct did not violate the ADEA.

In *Gross v. FBL Financial Services, Inc.* [129 S.Ct. 2343 (2009)], the Supreme Court held that the ADEA does not allow "mixed motive" claims— the plaintiff must demonstrate that age was the determining factor in the employer's action. Plaintiffs must show that, but for their age, the employer would not have taken the allegedly discriminatory action against them.

The ADEA does not prohibit voluntary retirement, and an employer may offer incentives to employees to get them to participate voluntarily in an early retirement program. Employers may also require employees to sign waivers of possible ADEA claims as a condition of receiving such early retirement incentives, but the waivers must comply with the specific requirements set out in the ADEA, according to the Supreme Court decision in *Oubre v. Entergy Operations, Inc.* [522 U.S. 422 (1998)].

ADEA Procedures   The ADEA is enforced and administered by the Equal Employment Opportunity Commission (EEOC), but the act also allows for private suits as well. An individual alleging a violation of the ADEA must file a written complaint with the EEOC and with the state or local EEOC agency if one exists. Unlike under Title VII, the complaint may be filed with the EEOC and state agency simultaneously. The complaint must be filed with the EEOC within 180 days of the alleged violation, if no state or local agency exists, or within 300 days if a state or local agency does exist. After filing with the EEOC and state or local agency, the individual must wait at least 60 days before filing suit in federal court; even though the suit may be filed at least 60 days from filing with the EEOC and state agency, the suit must be filed no later than 90 days from receipt of a right to sue notice from the EEOC. If the EEOC chooses to file suit, the EEOC suit supersedes any ADEA suit filed by the individual or by the state or local agency.

If the individual has agreed to submit any employment disputes to arbitration, she or he can be required to submit an ADEA claim to arbitration rather than sue in court, according to the Supreme Court decision in *Gilmer v. Interstate/Johnson Lane Corp.* [500 U.S. 20 (1991)]. [Recall the discussion of arbitration of EEO claims in Chapter 3, and of Title VII claims in Chapter 21.]

Remedies Under the ADEA   The remedies available under the ADEA are similar to those under the Equal Pay Act. Successful plaintiffs can be granted an injunction and may recover any back wages owed, as well as legal fees and court costs. Double damages in the amount equal to any wages owed may be recovered if the employer acted "willfully" (note the difference from the Equal Pay Act). According to the Supreme Court, an employer acts "willfully" under the ADEA when the employer either knows or shows reckless disregard for the matter of whether its conduct is prohibited by the ADEA [see *Trans World Airlines v. Thurston,* 469 U.S. 111 (1985)]. In suits brought by the EEOC, possible remedies include injunctions and back pay. Liquidated damages, however, are not available in such suits.

THE AMERICANS WITH DISABILITIES ACT AND THE REHABILITATION ACT

Two legislative provisions prohibit discrimination because of disability or handicap against otherwise qualified persons in employment. First, the Americans with Disabilities Act, passed in 1990, is a comprehensive law that protects the rights of disabled persons in employment and public accommodations. Second, the Rehabilitation Act of 1973 applies only to employees of the federal government or activities that receive federal funding.

Title I of the *Americans with Disabilities Act (ADA)* addresses employment; it prohibits discrimination in any aspect of employment against an otherwise qualified individual with a disability because of such disability. The ADA defines **"otherwise qualified individual with a disability"** as "an individual with a disability who, with or without reasonable accommodation, can perform the essential functions of the employment position that such individual holds or desires." An employee who has applied for, or received, disability benefits under

otherwise qualified individual with a disability: Individuals who, despite their disability, or with reasonable accommodation to their disability, are capable of performing the essential functions of a particular job.

Social Security or some other disability benefit program is not automatically disqualified from bringing suit under the ADA, according *to Cleveland v. Policy Management Systems Corp.* [526 U.S. 795 (1999)]. The Supreme Court held that the states were immune from individual suits for damages under the ADA, because of sovereign immunity under the Eleventh Amendment of the U.S. Constitution, *Board of Trustees of the University of Alabama v. Garrett* [531 U.S. 356 (2001)]. However, the public accommodation provisions of the ADA (Title II), requiring that public facilities be accessible to the disabled, do apply to state governments, *Tennessee v. Lane* [541 U.S. 509 (2004)].

The *Rehabilitation Act* imposes on employers or organizations or activities that do business with the federal government or receive federal funding an obligation not to discriminate against "otherwise qualified individuals with a disability." Section 503 requires that firms having contracts or subcontracts with the federal government for more than $10,000 must agree not to discriminate in employment against otherwise qualified handicapped individuals. Section 504, which has much broader application than §503, applies to any program, activity, or organization receiving federal funding. There is no minimum level of funding required under §504—any organization, activity, or program receiving federal funding, no matter how small, is subject to §504. Specifically, this section prohibits the denial to a qualified individual with a disability the chance to participate in a program, activity, or organization or receive the benefits of a program, activity, or organization that receives federal funding. *Consolidated Rail Corp. v. Darrone* [465 U.S. 624 (1984)] held that in particular, §504 may be used to challenge discrimination in employment against an otherwise qualified individual with a disability.

In general, both acts define *disability* with respect to an individual broadly. *Disability* means:

(a) a physical or mental impairment that substantially limits one or more of the major life activities of such individual;

(b) a record of such an impairment; or

(c) being regarded as having such an impairment.

The ADA was amended, effective January 1, 2009 [Pub. L. 110-325, 122 Stat. 3553 (2008)], to indicate that the definition of disability should be interpreted in favor of broad coverage of individuals under the ADA. Specifically, the amendments expanded the definition of "major life activities" to include, but not be limited to: caring for oneself, performing manual tasks, seeing, hearing, eating, sleeping, walking, standing, lifting, bending, speaking, breathing, learning, reading, concentrating, thinking, communicating, and working. The amended ADA also states that "major life activity" also includes the operation of a major bodily function, including but not limited to: functions of the immune system, normal cell growth, digestive, bowel, bladder, neurological, brain, respiratory, circulatory, endocrine, and reproductive functions.

Plaintiffs can show that they are "regarded as having such an impairment" if they show that they have been subjected to discriminatory treatment because of an actual or perceived physical or mental impairment, whether or not the impairment limits or is perceived to limit a major life activity. The 2009 amendments were intended to overrule several earlier Supreme Court decisions limiting the interpretation of the ADA's definition of disability. In *Sutton v. United Air Lines, Inc.* [527 U.S. 471 (1999)], the court held that the existence of corrective, mitigating, or remedial measures that may reduce the effect of the disability must be considered when determining whether an individual has a disability that substantially limits one or more major life activities. In *Toyota Motor Manufacturing, Kentucky, Inc. v. Williams* [534 U.S. 184 (2002)], the court stated that a court should inquire whether the individual is unable to perform the variety of tasks central to most people's daily lives, when assessing the impact of a disability on the major life activities, and should not consider whether the individual is unable to perform the tasks associated with her specific job. The 2009 amendments specifically overruled those two decisions. The ADA now provides that "[a]n impairment that substantially limits one major life activity need not limit other major life activities in order to be considered a disability" and that "[a]n impairment that is episodic or in remission is a disability if it would substantially limit a major life activity when active." The amendments also state that when determining whether an impairment substantially limits a major life activity, the court is not to consider the ameliorative effects of mitigating measures, assistive devices, or aids, other than eyeglasses or contact lenses.

By court interpretation, the definition of disability under both acts also includes contagious diseases such as tuberculosis and AIDS [see *School Board of Nassau County, Florida v. Arline,* 480 U.S. 273 (1987) and *Chalk v. U.S. District Court,* 840 F.2d 701 (9th Cir. 1987)]. Neither act, however, protects individuals whose use of illegal drugs prevents those individuals from performing the duties of their jobs or whose employment would present a direct threat to the property or safety of others. Nothing under either the ADA or the Rehabilitation Act prevents private employers from instituting drug testing programs. The ADA does protect individuals who are former drug users or recovering drug users, individuals enrolled in a supervised rehabilitation program, and individuals who are "erroneously regarded" as using drugs. The act also protects alcoholics who do not use alcohol at work or who are not under the influence of alcohol at the workplace.

Employers are permitted to ask about an individual's ability to perform the functions and requirements of the job in question but are prohibited from asking about the existence, nature, or severity of a disability. Employers also cannot require a preemployment medical examination of applicants, but may require such an exam once a job offer has been extended, provided that the exam is required of all entering employees.

The ADA and the regulations under the Rehabilitation Act impose on employers the duty to make *reasonable accommodation* for qualified individuals with a disability, unless such accommodation would impose undue hardship on the employer. Failure to make reasonable accommodation, or the failure to hire an individual because of the need to make accommodation for that individual, is included in the definition of illegal discrimination prohibited by the ADA. The ADA defines "undue hardship" in a complicated definition that includes a number of factors for consideration, such as the nature and cost of the accommodation needed, the financial resources of the facility involved, the number of persons employed at the facility, the size of the business or the entity involved, and the type of operations of the covered entity. The definition of undue hardship is intended to be flexible and determined on a case-by-case basis.

Employers are not required to create a new position for the disabled applicant, nor are they required to offer the individual the most expensive means of accommodation. Reasonable accommodation includes the minimal realignment or reassignment of job duties or the provision of certain assistance devices. An employer, for example, could reassign certain filing or reception duties from the requirements of a typist job in order to accommodate a person requiring the use of a wheelchair, or telephones could be fitted with amplifiers to accommodate an individual's hearing disability. The regulations state, and the courts have held, that the extent of the accommodation required must be determined on a case-by-case basis; drastic realignments of job requirements or imposition of severe financial costs would be considered unreasonable and would not be required. The fact that a requested accommodation may conflict with the seniority system under a collective agreement generally excuses the employer from making such an accommodation; however, the employee requesting the accommodation may present evidence of special circumstances that would make an exception to the seniority system reasonable, according to *U.S. Airways, Inc. v. Barnett* [535 U.S. 391 (2002)].

Defenses   In addition to the "undue hardship" defense, the ADA lists four other possible defenses for employers:

1. Employers may refuse to hire or accommodate an individual when that person's condition poses a direct threat to the safety or health of others in the workplace, such as a person with a contagious or infectious disease. The Rehabilitation Act also provides that a person with a contagious disease or infection who, because of that condition, presents a direct threat to the health or safety of others or is unable to perform the duties of the job, is excluded from the Act's protection.

2. Employers are permitted to hire, select, or promote individuals based on tests, standards, or criteria that are job related or consistent with business necessity; a disabled individual who was unable to meet such job-related standards need not be hired.

3. Employers in the food service industry may refuse to hire individuals who have infectious or communicable diseases that can be transmitted to others through the handling of food, when the risk of infection cannot be eliminated by reasonable accommodation. The ADA directs the Secretary of Health and Human Services to develop a list of diseases that can be transmitted through food handling; only the diseases on that list may be used as a basis for refusing to hire individuals under this defense.

4. Religious corporations, associations, or societies are permitted to give preference to individuals who are members of that particular religion when hiring for positions involved in carrying on the activities of the religious corporation, association, or society.

Enforcement   The enforcement of the ADA is assigned to the EEOC; the act provides that the procedures and remedies under Title VII of the Civil Rights Act shall be used for the ADA. An individual complaining of a violation of the Act must first file a complaint with the appropriate state or local agency, if one exists.

After 60 days or the termination of proceedings by the state or local agency, the individual can file with the EEOC; the EEOC, then, or the individual if the EEOC declines to do so, may file suit against the employer. Remedies available under the ADA are the same as under Title VII—injunctions, hiring or reinstatement orders, back pay, and legal fees. Punitive damages under 42 U.S.C. §1981A are available for cases of intentional discrimination violating the ADA.

Section 503 of the Rehabilitation Act is enforced by the Office of Federal Contract Compliance Programs (OFCCP) of the Department of Labor. An individual alleging a violation of §503 must take the complaint to the OFCCP, which will pursue administrative remedies against the employer. There is no individual right to sue under §503.

Enforcement of §504 of the Rehabilitation Act is coordinated by the federal Department of Education, but the particular agency or department administering the federal funding is the primary enforcement agency for complaints against the recipient of such funding. An individual alleging a violation must first file a complaint with the agency administering the funding; that agency may use administrative or judicial proceedings to pursue the complaint. If the agency determines that there is a violation, it may suspend, terminate, or refuse to grant federal assistance to a recipient found in violation of §504. If the agency fails to act on the complaint, the individual can file suit to challenge the alleged violation of §504.

EXECUTIVE ORDER 11246

Firms doing business with the federal government are required to agree not to discriminate in employment on the basis of race, color, religion, sex, or national origin by *Executive Order 11246*. Firms doing at least $10,000 worth of business with the federal government must include a nondiscrimination clause in their contract or subcontract. Firms doing more than $50,000 worth of business and having more than 50 employees are required to develop and maintain written affirmative action plans for the utilization of women and minorities in their workforce. The OFCCP in the U.S. Department of Labor enforces the obligations of E.O.11246; individuals alleging a violation of the requirements must file a written complaint with the OFCCP within 180 days of the alleged violation. The OFCCP may refer the complaint to the EEOC for investigation or may initiate its own administrative enforcement proceedings. There is no individual right to sue under E.O.11246. Firms found to be in violation of E.O.11246 may be subject to injunctions to cease the violation and may be required to hire, with back pay and remedial seniority, affected individuals. The firm in violation may also have its government contracts canceled or suspended and may be declared ineligible for future government contracts.

THE U.S. CONSTITUTION AND EMPLOYMENT DISCRIMINATION

Public sector employees are protected by the requirements of the U.S. Constitution. The main provision of the Constitution addressing discrimination is the equal protection clause, found in the 14th Amendment, which has also been applied to federal employees through the Fifth Amendment's due process requirement. The equal protection clause prohibits intentional discrimination that is not justified by a compelling government purpose (see Chapter 4 for a more thorough discussion of constitutional law issues).

In considering claims of discrimination under the Constitution, the Court will first consider the basis of discrimination. Some bases of discrimination, or "classifications" by public sector employers, will be considered "suspect classes"—that is, there is little or no legitimate reason for the government to subject persons to different treatment because they are members of a particular class. The courts have consistently held that race, color, and religion are suspect classes. For example, racial discrimination involves treating persons differently because of their race or color; such conduct can rarely ever by justified. However, some government employers have instituted affirmative action programs to hire female or minority employees to remedy the effects of prior discrimination. [See the discussion of affirmative action by public sector employers in Chapter 21.] The court will require that the government employer show that the conduct is required by some compelling government interest and that no less-discriminatory alternatives exist. For example, in *U.S. v. Paradise* [480 U.S. 149 (1987)], the Supreme Court upheld an affirmative action plan requiring the Alabama State Police to promote to corporal one African-American trooper for every white trooper promoted, until a new promotion policy was instituted. The Court imposed the requirement in order to remedy past "pervasive" discrimination against African-Americans by the State Police. Conversely, in *Wygant v. Jackson Board of Education* [476 U.S. 267 (1986)], the Supreme Court held that an affirmative action provision in a collective agreement, requiring that senior white teachers be laid off rather than junior minority teachers in certain situations, violated the 14th Amendment because there were other alternatives available that would not have such a severe effect on the senior teachers. While reaffirming that the constitutionality of any government affirmative action policy must be subject to the "strict scrutiny" test, the Supreme Court held that a federal set-aside program requiring that a certain percentage of contracts under any federally funded highway construction projects be awarded to minority-owned businesses was unconstitutional in *Adarand Constructors, Inc. v. Pena* [515 U.S. 200 (1995)]. But, in cases involving affirmative action programs for admissions to the University of Michigan, *Gratz v. Bollinger* [123 S.Ct. 2411 (2003)], and the University of Michigan School of Law, *Grutter v. Bollinger* [123 S.Ct. 2325 (2003)] the Court held that achieving the educational benefits of a diverse student body was a compelling governmental purpose to justify the adoption of the affirmative action program; however, the affirmative program should use race (or gender) as only one of various factors to be considered rather than making it the determinative factor.

STATE EQUAL EMPLOYMENT OPPORTUNITY LAWS

Most states, and a number of cities, have their own equal employment opportunity legislation. Many such laws go beyond the protection of Title VII and other federal legislation; they also apply to smaller employers who may not be covered by Title VII. For example, the New York Human Rights Law prohibits discrimination in employment on the basis of race, color, religion, sex, national origin, disability, marital status, age (18 or older), sexual orientation or sexual preference, and criminal record. Connecticut state law prohibits employers that the employee is using drugs. Some states, such as Minnesota, Connecticut, Wisconsin, Massachusetts, Rhode Island, New Jersey, California, Vermont, Nevada, the District of Columbia, Maryland, New York, Illinois, Maine, Washington, Hawaii, Delaware, Iowa, New Mexico, and Oregon prohibit discrimination because of sexual orientation or sexual preference. The specific procedures and requirements of the law vary from state to state; most of the laws involve some sort of administrative procedure by a state enforcement agency before the individual may file suit in the state courts. Recall that Title VII and the ADA require an individual filing a complaint with the EEOC first to have filed with the appropriate state or local agency, if one exists.

LEGAL PROTECTIONS FOR GAYS INCREASING

Although neither Title VII nor other federal EEO legislation prohibits discrimination based on sexual preference or sexual orientation, the legal protections afforded to homosexuals have been increasing. Several states (Vermont, Massachusetts, Connecticut, Rhode Island, New Jersey, Wisconsin, Minnesota, Nevada, California, Hawaii, Maryland, Illinois, Maine, Washington, New York, Delaware, Iowa, New Mexico, and Oregon) and the District of Columbia have laws that prohibit discrimination against gays or lesbians in employment, housing or public accommodations. But the coverage of, and protection granted by, such laws varies, and is subject to judicial interpretation. The New Jersey Supreme Court held that the Boy Scouts are a public accommodation under the New Jersey Law Against Discrimination [NJLAD], which prohibits the Boy Scouts of America from dismissing a gay Assistant Scoutmaster, but the U.S. Supreme Court reversed that decision, *Boy Scouts of America v. Dale* [530 U.S. 640 (2000)]. The Court held that requiring the Boy Scouts to hire a gay scoutmaster would undermine the Boy Scouts' mission of instilling values in young people. The California Supreme Court reached the same conclusion, deciding that the Boy Scouts were not subject to California's Unruh Civil Rights Act, and allowing a Boy Scout council to exclude a gay male from serving as a Scoutmaster, *Curran v. Mount Diablo Council of Boy Scouts of America* [17 Cal. 4th 670, 952 P.2d 218 (1998)].

But even apart from legislation, gays and lesbians have been winning some legal rights through the courts. The Vermont Supreme Court held that the Vermont State Constitution requires the state to give the same benefits and protections to gay or lesbian couples as it provides to heterosexual married couples, *Baker v. State of Vermont,* [170 Vt. 194, 744 A.2d 864 (1999)]. The Vermont Supreme Court stopped short of legally recognizing gay marriages, stating that it was up to the state legislature to decide whether to issue marriage licenses to gay or lesbian couples or to set up a domestic partnership registration system. The state legislature created a civil union registration system in 2000. The Supreme Court of Massachusetts held that denying marriage licenses to same-sex couples lacked a rational basis and violated the state constitution's equal protection requirements, *Goodridge v. Dept. of Public Health* [440 Mass. 309, 798 N.E.2d 941 (2003)]. The same court later held that proposed legislation prohibiting same-sex marriage but allowing civil unions (as in Vermont) was in violation of the state constitution's due process and equal protection requirements. Those Massachusetts decisions ignited a political controversy; George W. Bush called for an amendment to the U.S. Constitution that would prohibit same-sex marriages, but the Senate refused to approve the proposed amendment. Bush and the Republicans sought to use the issue of same-sex marriages as a "wedge" issue against Democrats in the 2004 presidential election; many Democrats and even some conservative Republicans took the position that the decision whether to allow same-sex marriages ought to be left to the states, and a federal constitutional amendment was unnecessary.

At the federal government level, the U.S. military forces have had the "don't ask, don't tell" policy for gays in the military since 1993; the policy represented a political compromise between the Clinton administration and Congress. Under the policy, gays were not automatically disqualified from serving in the military, but those who participate in homosexual practices, or demonstrate a propensity to engage in such practices, are disqualified. The "don't ask, don't tell" policy had consistently been held to be constitutional by the federal courts. The Obama Administration was committed to ending the "don't ask, don't tell" policy, and Congress passed the *Don't Ask, Don't Tell Repeal Act of 2010* in December of 2010. The law creates a process to repeal the policy in December, 2010; it requires the president, the Secretary of Defense, and the chairman of the Joint Chiefs of Staff to certify that the Department of Defense has prepared the necessary regulations to carry out the change in policy, and that the change will not damage the military's ability to recruit or to fight. The "don't ask, don't tell" policy will be repealed sixty days after the required certification is made.

In Canada, a number of provincial courts have held that the Canadian Charter of Rights guarantees the right of same-sex couples to marry. The Ontario Court of Appeal legalized same-sex marriages in the Province of Ontario in 2003; subsequently, courts in Quebec, British Columbia, and the Yukon Territory also upheld the legality of same-sex marriages. In 2005, a federal law allowing same-sex marriage was passed, making same-sex marriage legal in all Canadian provinces and territories.

In Europe, Belgium and the Netherlands allow for same-sex marriages. France, Germany Sweden, Finland, and Denmark provide for a legal registration of civil unions (also known as "registered cohabitation" or "registered partnerships") which grant same-sex couples some, but not all, legal rights of married couples. Spain passed legislation to allow similar civil unions. In July, 2004, a French court ruled that French law does not allow same-sex couples to marry.

Sources: David Gram, "Church Launches Trial Liturgy for Same-sex Unions," *Associated Press State & Local Wire*, June 17, 2004; "The Senate Gets It Right," *The Times Union* (Albany, N.Y.), July 19, 2004, p. A-6; "The Unnecessary Chaos on Gay Marriage," *The Ottawa Citizen*, July 26, 2004, p.A-12; "Lesbian Couple Has Filed for Canada's First Same-sex Divorce," *The Associated Press International News*, July 22, 2004; "Court Voids France's First Gay Marriage," *Agence France Presse–English–International News*, July 27, 2004; "Gay Weddings Are on the Way," *Hull (U.K.) Daily Mail*, June 22, 2004, p.16; "A Look at Gay Marriage in Some Countries," *The Associated Press, International News*, March 4, 2004; Dale Fuchs, "Spain's Left Draws Ire of Church," *The International Herald Tribune*, May 31, 2004, p.3. 1 "Vermont Court Backs Gay-Couple Benefits," *The Washington Post* (December 21, 1999); "For Gays, Tolerance Translates to Rights," *The Washington Post* (November 5, 1999); "Don't Lie: Clinton Admits Don't Ask, Don't Tell Is a Policy Failure," *The Plain Dealer* (Cleveland), December 20, 1999. John Schwartz, "Don't Ask, Don't Tell Remains in Effect Months After Passage of Law to End It," *The New York Times,* Feb. 23, 2011.

OCCUPATIONAL SAFETY AND HEALTH

In the year 2002, approximately 5,524 American workers were killed in job-related accidents; and approximately 4.7 million workers suffered from work-related illnesses or injuries. In addition to the human pain and suffering, these workplace accidents cost the nation an estimated $128 billion in 2002.

Congress enacted the *Occupational Safety and Health Act* in 1970 to attempt to make American workplaces safer. The purpose of the act was to "assure, so far as possible every working man and woman in the nation safe and healthful working conditions and to preserve our human resources." The law established a new agency, the Occupational Safety and Health Administration, within the Department of Labor. Both the law and the agency are known by the acronym "OSHA." As part of a line agency, the OSHA administrator is appointed by the President and carries the actual title of Assistant Secretary of Labor for Occupational Safety and Health. The agency had 2,220 employees in 2004, and an annual budget of $457.5 million. Although OSHA has often been controversial, it is a relatively small federal agency. By comparison, in 2004 the Environmental Protection Agency had more than 18,000 employees and a budget in excess of $7 billion.

The OSHA covers virtually all private employees, perhaps as many as 80 million, in the United States. In addition, many public employees are also covered in some way. Federal employees are not directly covered by OSHA, but the federal agencies employing them are required to give them protection equal to the standards set by OSHA. However, only eight agencies have set up such plans, and most of those are inadequate, according to experts. No fines or penalties can be assessed against federal agencies by OSHA.

Workers in mines, railroads, nuclear facilities, and the maritime industry are not covered by OSHA, but they are protected by other laws. Also, the approximately 7 million local and state employees are exempted from the federal OSHA. Many of these workers are covered by occupational safety laws enacted in their states. Together the federal and state programs are responsible for protecting the health and safety of an estimated 100 million workers at almost 6.5 million workplaces.

HEALTH AND SAFETY STANDARDS

specific standards: Regulations setting particular limits for exposing employees to workplace hazards or toxic substances.

general duty clause: The OSHA provision that requires employers to provide a safe workplace for employees.

The law authorizes OSHA to establish **specific standards** for various industries, and standards applicable to all types of employment. Rules and regulations have been promulgated over the past 24 years addressing noise, dust, air, heat, toxic substances, types of protective equipment, ladders, scaffolds, and many other aspects of the workplace.

The OSHA statute also includes the so-called **general duty clause**, which requires employers "to furnish a workplace free from recognized hazards that have caused or are likely to cause death or serious physical harm to employees." This broad language authorizes OSHA to take action against an employer for failing to correct any "recognized hazard," without the need to cite any specific OSHA regulation if none covers the specific dangerous condition.

The OSHA statute began its existence under considerable public pressure to set immediately health and safety standards. As a result, OSHA adopted hundreds of standards established by private industry groups and trade associations. Many of these regulations were originally intended by their organizations as "consensus" standards, which were benchmarks that businesses were to attempt to reach. When OSHA made them regulations—minimum standards that must be met in order to avoid sanctions—it caused a great deal of anger and resistance in the business community. Today, OSHA develops most standards following recommendations of the National Institute for Occupational Safety and Health (NIOSH), a part of the Department of Health and Human Services. These proposed standards are then subject to comment from representatives of both labor and industry, as well as the general public, before they are legally enacted.

The standards adopted by OSHA are rules limiting or prohibiting the exposure of employees to toxic materials or harmful physical agents. The act states that the standards must ensure, to the extent feasible on the basis of the best available evidence, that no employee will suffer material impairment of health or functional capacity because of exposure to the hazard. The feasibility of a standard must be examined from both a technological perspective and a financial perspective. The Secretary of Labor, acting through OSHA, has to establish that the standard is both technologically and economically feasible; but, according to the Supreme Court decision in *American Textile Manufacturers' Institute v. Donovan* [452 U.S. 490 (1981)], the Secretary does not have to show that the benefits of a standard bear a reasonable relationship to its costs.

Employees under OSHA have the right to a workplace free from recognized hazards and are also protected from any employer discrimination because they have exercised any right granted by the act. Employees are also given the **"right to refuse,"** the right to refuse to work in the face of a dangerous condition; employees can exercise that right only if they have reasonable grounds to conclude that they face a real and immediate danger of death or serious injury.

> **right to refuse:** Right granted to employees by OSHA to refuse to work in a dangerous situation.

ENFORCEMENT

Once a regulation has come into effect, OSHA has the duty and power to inspect all businesses to determine if the standards are being met. Federal OSHA has only about 1,000 inspectors on its staff (called Compliance Officers [COs]) for the whole country. In 2003 these COs performed over 39,000 inspections. The inspections resulted in the issuance of 83,562 violation notices, of which 59,899 were listed as "serious," 2,152 were "repeat," and 406 were "willful" (that is "intentional," the most serious category). Following these inspections, OSHA proposed penalties in excess of $82 million in 2003. Prior to 1991, the maximum fine was $1,000 for a serious violation and $10,000 for a willful violation. As part of the Budget Reconciliation Act of 1990, Congress authorized OSHA to increase the maximum fines for a violation sevenfold.

At the completion of an inspection, the compliance officer and a representative of the employer sit down and discuss any violations noted. Then OSHA mails a notice informing the employer of violations and proposing penalties of a specific amount. Employers can request informal conferences in the next 15 days to discuss the problems, and many cases are settled during this time. If the employer wants to contest the violation, a notice must be filed by the end of the 15-day period. The case will subsequently be heard by an administrative law judge (ALJ). Following the ALJ's decision, an appeal is possible to the three-member Occupational Safety and Health Review Commission, which is independent from OSHA.

In the late 1980s and early 1990s OSHA began to use a new tactic, called the "egregious case" policy, to deal with particularly serious health and safety situations. Instead of counting numerous violations of one standard as one violation, OSHA decided in some cases to count each violation as a separate illegal act. For example, if an inspection showed that 200 employees in one plant were not wearing hard hats as required or that 200 injuries had not been properly recorded on OSHA forms, the inspector might assess penalties based on 200 violations rather than one. National OSHA officials made the decision on whether to use the "egregious" policy in each case based on a number of factors, including the following: the seriousness of the problems, the amount and extent of deaths and injuries, the company's attitude toward the problem, and the company's previous record for workplace safety and OSHA violations. The use of this policy led to imposition of some of the largest penalties in OSHA history.

Over the years businesspersons have told numerous "horror stories" about OSHA inspectors looking for small, technical, "nitpicky" violations to cite—such as the width of toilet seats or the spacing between ladder steps. Particularly in the early days of OSHA, when the first group of inspectors was hired from the maritime industry, there was probably good reason for businesses' complaints. As OSHA has matured, the inspectors appear to have developed more tact and experience and now focus more attention on serious problems. Complaints have decreased somewhat, though there are still unhappy individuals. After all, having a safety inspector arrive unannounced at your facility to thoroughly look for safety violations will never be one of life's great pleasures.

Search Warrant Requirements   The OSHA law specified that the inspections could be done by surprise, without a warrant. Why? The COs may arrive at the inspection site and immediately go through the facility before any hazardous conditions could be altered or cleaned up. However, as we have previously mentioned, the U.S. Supreme Court held in *Marshall v. Barlow's Inc.* that the Fourth Amendment of the Constitution requires OSHA to obtain a search warrant when the owner of the business demands one. Most owners and managers permit an OSHA inspector to enter the premises without a warrant, but some troublesome situations do still arise, as in the following case.

NATIONAL ENGINEERING & CONTRACTING CO. V. OSHA REVIEW COMM.

45 F.3d 476 (D.C. 1995)

FACTS

OSHA chooses to inspect construction sites using a randomly generated list from a computer at the University of Tennessee. The list itself is based on a commercially published list of current construction projects known as the "Dodge Reports." Pursuant to this policy, OSHA chose in April 1992 to inspect a bridge construction site near Cincinnati, on which National Engineering was the general contractor.

Compliance Officer John Collier was assigned to do the inspection. Believing that National had a policy of refusing inspections without a warrant, Collier applied and was granted a warrant by a federal magistrate. In his application, Collier stated that he believed a warrant was necessary because of National's policy. He also attached a copy of OSHA's written policy regarding random inspections of construction sites.

Due to changes in Collier's schedule, CO James Denton actually carried out the inspection a few days later. When he arrived at the site, the National representative refused him entry, then asked him to wait one hour until National's attorneys arrived. After consulting with his supervisor, Denton refused this request, then showed the warrant, and began his inspection. After the inspection, Denton issued several citations for violations of OSHA law and regulations. National contested the violations before an ALJ acting for the Occupational Safety and Health Review Commission. Two of the violations, the first concerning a slight worn place on an electrical extension cord and the other a lack of a ground on a plug on an office fax machine, were held to be "not serious" and no penalty was assessed. The other violation, a line of exposed vertical steel bars (rebar), posed the hazard of impalement to workers who might fall. The ALJ found this violation "serious" and assessed a $400 penalty. National appealed to the District of Columbia Circuit Court of Appeals.

DECISION

National challenged the violations, arguing that the warrant was not sufficient. National claimed that OSHA must include information in its warrant request specifically demonstrating how National was chosen for inspection, and that in the absence of such information, there was a lack of probable cause to support the warrant.

In *Marshall v. Barlow's Inc.* [436 U.S. 307 (1978)], the Supreme Court held that a warrant for an OSHA inspection must be obtained when requested by the business. The Court went on to explain that the showing needed to establish probable cause for a routine regulatory inspection is less than that required for a search warrant in a criminal case. OSHA merely needs to "demonstrate that its inspection program is a neutral one and that, using those criteria, it selected National for inspection."

Since Collier had attested in his request for a warrant that the inspection was to be conducted in accordance with OSHA's written policy (which was attached), the *Barlow's* test was met. National's request for more specific details on the selection process was refused. The court noted one case in which a court required more documentation, but several in which the exact OSHA policy used here was upheld. The court stated that "the absence of an encoded establishment list will only be fatal to a warrant application where the target company can make a factual showing that it was placed on the list for reasons other than the application of specific, neutral criteria." National had not alleged that it was selected on other than neutral criteria, so this test was not met.

Thus the court upheld the citations and the penalty assessed by the ALJ against National Engineering.

CASE QUESTIONS

1. Why do you suppose Congress wrote the law in a way that allowed inspectors to enter businesses without a warrant? Has the law been made ineffective by the cases requiring warrants where the business so demands?

2. What is the standard that OSHA must meet to obtain a warrant? Will OSHA be able to justify every inspection?

3. How might a business show that it was placed on the list for reasons other than the application of specific, neutral criteria?

STATE PROGRAMS

Some 25 states and territories (Puerto Rico, for example) have established their own occupational safety and health programs that operate under approval from OSHA. Two of the states (New York and Connecticut) only cover public sector employees, whereas the others cover both public and private sector employees. In order to "opt out" of the federal OSHA, the state must pass a law and issue regulations to establish standards that are "at least as effective" as federal OSHA and enforce them in an equivalent manner to gain exemption. The federal government monitors these programs and will reimburse the state for up to one-half the costs of the state program. Of course, the state regulations may be more strict than OSHA, but normally the states simply adopt the regulation issued by OSHA. In 2003, state inspectors conducted over 59,000 inspections, and found a total of 144,075 violations. Of the violation notices issued, 59,693 were for serious violations, 2,686 were for repeat violations, and 196 were for willful violations; penalties assessed for the violations were in excess of $71 million.

OCCUPATIONAL SAFETY: A SERIOUS PROBLEM IN CHINA

Occupational safety is a worldwide problem; and is particularly serious in developing countries such as China. The agency responsible for worker safety in China, the State Administration of Work Safety, announced that 426,283 workplace incidents involving injuries occurred during the first half of 2004, and that more than 63,000 persons were killed in occupational accidents. Those figures represented an improvement over the same period in 2003—injuries declined by 12.8%, while occupational deaths declined by 0.2%. The energy sectors, including coal mining and the oil and gas industries, are among the most dangerous, as production is constantly being increased to meet China's rising energy demands while safety standards remain poor. Coal mining caused more than 7,200 deaths in the first 10 months of 2003, according to official statistics; some critics claim that the real figures are even higher, because mine operators refrain from reporting many accidents to avoid fines and shutdowns. A blowout in a gas field near Chongqing in December, 2003, killed 243 people, injured more than 4,000, and resulted in the evacuation of more than 60,000 as toxic fumes were spread over a wide area.

Sources: "Trial Underway over China Gas Blowout that Killed 243," *Agence France Presse–English*, July 14, 2004; "China Says Worker Safety Situation Stable," *United Press International*, July 20, 2004; "Twenty-eight Dead or Missing in China Coal Mine Accidents," *Agence France Presse–English*, July 15, 2004; "12 Killed in Three Mine Accidents on Mainland," *South China Morning Post*, July 16, 2004.

SOCIAL/ETHICAL ISSUES

The Occupational Safety and Health Administration has never been funded at anywhere near the level necessary to inspect more than a fraction of workplaces in the United States. State enforcement varies, but in many cases it is even less vigorous due to low state funding. The chances are very good that a facility that does not engage in construction, meat-packing, logging, mining, or other high-hazard industrial manufacturing will rarely be visited by OSHA and may never be inspected at all.

What is the ethical duty of an employer to provide workers with a safe working environment by improving working conditions (that already meet minimum OSHA legal requirements), at potentially substantial cost, without the likely threat of OSHA penalties?

EMPLOYEE DUTIES AND RIGHTS

The OSHA law, while directing employees to follow all OSHA rules and regulations, contains no penalties for workers; it puts the primary responsibility for meeting the standards (and the penalties) on employers. Why? Apparently employers have the power, without involving the government in enforcement, to discipline workers who refuse to follow job safety rules, just as employers can with respect to any other rule of the workplace.

But what if the employer directs employees to do a job that they have good reason to believe is unsafe and hazardous? The OSHA law itself does not address this problem, but an OSHA regulation does give workers the right to refuse to perform an assignment in very limited situations. The requirements are the following: (1) the employee must reasonably believe that the job poses an imminent risk of death or serious bodily injury and (2) there is not sufficient time to seek redress from the employer or OSHA before the task must be performed. In this limited situation, the worker justifiably can refuse to perform the task. In all other cases, OSHA must be called in to determine whether or not the job is safe.

CRIMINAL PENALTIES

The Occupational Safety and Health Act is primarily enforced by inspections and the issuance of civil monetary penalties. OSHA also provides, in limited situations, the power to refer cases to the Justice Department for the filing of criminal charges. Lying to an OSHA inspector, falsifying records, and the willful (intentional) violation of health and safety regulations that results in the death of a worker are subject to criminal penalties under the act. The administration, however, has only rarely used this power to institute criminal charges, and few people have ever served any jail time for OSHA violations.

Because of the lack of criminal enforcement by federal officials, local prosecutors in cities such as Los Angeles, Chicago, New York, Milwaukee, and Austin, Texas, have filed murder and/or manslaughter charges against companies (and individual managers) when it was apparent that a worker's death was caused by a dangerous condition that the company knew about and could have prevented. The prosecutors were frustrated by the fact that employers were aware that conditions in the workplace put workers at risk of death or serious physical danger but chose to do nothing about it.

Several of these cases resulted in convictions of employers and managers, although some of them were reversed for various technical reasons on appeal. In these cases, the prosecution argued that the defendant, although not specifically intending to kill anyone, acted with total reckless disregard for the consequences of his or her dangerous actions. Therefore, because this conduct resulted in the death of another, she or he can be held criminally responsible for that death. This argument resembles that used to charge with negligent homicide a driver who becomes so drunk that she or he does not know or care what she or he is doing and then causes an accident that kills another motorist. Similarly, a manager who knowingly sends workers into an unshored trench, demands that they use defective machinery, or causes them to breathe cyanide fumes continuously without respirators, may be charged with negligent homicide if a worker dies from those avoidable conditions.

The filing and prosecution of these cases received considerable national publicity. In response, OSHA began to refer more cases of willful violations resulting in death to the U.S. Attorney General for possible prosecution. However, the Justice Department brought only a few of them to court. Federal prosecutors were reluctant to ask for more referrals or spend too much time on these cases because the maximum criminal penalty for conviction on this charge is only six months in jail. By the early 1990's, the number of criminal referrals had dropped again. However, commentators hope that the few criminal cases brought on the federal and state level are enough to awaken managers to their responsibilities regarding worker safety, leading companies to increase their efforts to correct workplace safety problems before accidents occur.

WORKERS' COMPENSATION

Although the purpose of OSHA is to make workplaces safer, the law does not provide aid or compensation to those employees who actually suffer work-related injuries. In the early part of this century, workers who were hurt on the job were forced to sue their employers in a tort action to obtain compensation. The burden of proof was on the employee to show that the employer was negligent in a way that directly caused the injury. Remember from our study of negligence that the plaintiff must prove that the defendant was "at fault" in order to prevail. Thus, in an occupational injury case, the worker would have to demonstrate that the employer's conduct fell below the standard of the mythical "reasonable employer," given the particular factual situation, and that this failure directly caused the worker's injury. This burden proved difficult for employees to meet, especially since the courts recognized several defenses that the employer could raise to avoid liability. For example, if the employee was negligent at all in causing the injury, the *contributory negligence* defense allowed the employer to win. If the accident was caused at least in part by the negligence of another worker, the **fellow-servant rule** barred the worker's claim. If the employee knowingly took on a risky job and was injured, sometimes the doctrine of *assumption of risk* barred recovery. The application of these common law theories resulted in the total denial of damages to many employees who suffered serious injuries at work.

fellow-servant rule: A common law defense of the employer that barred an employee from suing an employer for injuries caused by a fellow employee.

The public demanded a better system, and by the 1930s most states had enacted some form of workers' compensation program. These laws, while differing slightly from state to state, have similar basic features and provide that employees who are injured or become ill in the course of their work will be entitled to compensation. The costs of the system are primarily placed on the employers, who may be able to pass at least a portion of them along to their customers as a cost of production and who have a financial incentive to take actions to decrease workplace injuries (and thus lower their costs). All states now have such laws.

COVERAGE AND BENEFITS

Unlike lawsuits, in which a plaintiff can ask a jury for any amount of damages, including a large sum for "pain and suffering," the maximum compensation that may be awarded injured employees under workers' compensation is set forth in and limited by the governing state law.

Generally, employees who are unable to work due to a covered injury will receive the following:

1. Monetary compensation for their wage loss, usually some percentage of the worker's average wage, for the period of time he or she is disabled from working;

2. All reasonable medical and hospital expenses connected with the injury;

3. A fixed sum for a permanent injury or disability, such as the loss of an arm or an eye;

4. In many states, some type of rehabilitation assistance or compensation to help the worker recover physically and mentally so she or he can get back to work (and thus get off workers' compensation); and

5. A death benefit awarded to the family if the worker is killed.

Most employers purchase insurance to cover the expenses of workers' compensation, although some states may allow them to be "self-insured." In all states, there is some administrative agency that administers the program. This agency receives applications for compensation from workers, determines eligibility, and processes payments to workers. Often the employer will contest the worker's claim, arguing that the worker was not injured "in the course of employment" or that the injury does not really disable the person from working. The administrative agency will assign a referee or administrative law judge (ALJ) to hear evidence and make a decision in contested cases. After the case has been heard and appealed within the administrative system, it can be appealed to the regular court system.

ELIGIBILITY

Note that compensation is due to workers whose injuries *"arise out of"* and occur *"in the course of"* employment. Thus, the system is called "no-fault" because coverage does not depend on whether the injured worker (or coworker) was at fault (that is, negligent). As a result, the common law defenses once available to the employer have been basically eliminated. (Some state programs may vary.)

For example, if an automobile factory worker is injured in the plant when his hand is caught in a machine, the determination is simple: The employee is entitled to compensation. However, many workers, such as salespersons or regional managers of a retail business, travel from place to place in connection with their jobs. If the employee is injured in a car accident, 1,000 miles from her home office while driving to lunch, the determination as to whether the injury is covered by workers' compensation is tougher. More difficult still, suppose the worker breaks a leg while dancing at a sales convention in Las Vegas to which he was sent by his employer?

In general, employees are not covered when going to and from their work, but they are covered during lunch and other normal breaks on the job. Court decisions have developed a broad view toward what is "on the job," including some slightly "off task" activities within workers' compensation coverage if the activities are normal types of things that employees do. Some "goofing around" or "horseplay" while on the job is probably a fact of life in most employment situations. For example, an employee who jumped and broke an arm after another employee put a bug down his shirt, and a worker who fell down while swatting a cockroach in the company shower, were both held to be covered by the state workers' compensation system. However, most state workers' compensation laws take a hard line against drug and alcohol abuse—workers who were under the influence of drugs or alcohol at the time they were injured are generally denied benefits.

On the other hand, when it can be said that the employee has really "abandoned the job," or gone on a "frolic," injuries that occur will not be covered. For example, one employee of a steel factory was seriously injured when he was caught in a conveyer belt while he was attempting to cook a pot pie in one of the factory ovens. This act was so unrelated to his job that he was denied compensation. Another employee was refused compensation when she was injured in an auto accident while visiting her sister who lived 50 miles away from the city the employee had traveled to on a business trip.

In order to resolve difficult cases, the courts often look at the following factors: (1) whether the injury occurred during the time of employment and at the place of employment; (2) whether the employee was reasonably performing her or his duties, or at least doing something "incidental to" her or his employment; and (3) whether the activity was of any benefit to the employer or was an activity knowingly allowed by the employer. Courts weigh all these factors in each case and then decide if the injury is covered by workers' compensation.

EXCLUSIVE REMEDY

When an injury or illness is covered by workers' compensation, the worker may not sue the employer for damages—that is, workers' compensation is the *exclusive* remedy the employee has against the employer. However, the employee may still be able to institute a lawsuit against a third party who caused the injury (e.g., a manufacturer of the machine that caused the injury or the driver of the other automobile that caused the crash). If a recovery is obtained against a third party, generally the law requires the employee to reimburse the state workers' compensation system for the benefits previously paid.

CURRENT ISSUES

In recent years the "exclusive remedy" theory has begun to develop some exceptions as employees attempt to "get around" the general rule and sue their employers in court. Several cases around the country have held that a worker may sue an employer in court if the injury resulted from some "intentional" act by the employer.

Similarly, controversy has arisen in many states concerning the amount of workers' compensation benefits. Generally, the amount of the wage loss benefits the worker receives is quite a bit lower than what the worker would have received in actual wages. Many states put the figure at two-thirds of the worker's average weekly wage, but some use a much lower number. A tort lawsuit, for example, would likely result in much higher rewards, including damages for pain and suffering, attorneys' fees, and sometimes a large award of punitive damages. Unions and worker groups argue that since the employee has lost the right to sue the employer through the adoption of workers' compensation, the benefits should be more realistic.

Business associations, on the other hand, have lobbied their state legislatures for other reforms of the workers' compensation system. They complain that the overly broad and generous interpretations regarding what types of injuries are "work-related" (such as swatting a cockroach in the shower) have greatly increased the employer's costs of doing business. Employers also argue that the system makes it difficult to "cut off" malingerers—those workers who are really able to go back to work but would rather stay on workers' compensation. In addition, since each state program is slightly different, multistate employers must deal with a variety of standards, timelines, benefits, and administrative matters, thus adding significant cost to the employer.

UNEMPLOYMENT COMPENSATION

Another type of compensation program for workers is unemployment insurance. This system, created by the federal Social Security law and administered by the states, provides temporary financial support to certain workers who are "ready, willing, and able" to work but cannot find employment.

Employers pay a tax of at least 3 percent of the payroll to support this system, but the employer's percentage will increase if the "experience rating"— that is, the number of ex-employees who collect—is high. Employers who have one or more employees working a total of 20 weeks a year are subject to the law.

In order to qualify for benefits, the person claiming compensation must have been employed for a certain period of time during the preceding 52 weeks, must have earned a specific average wage, and must not have quit the job "without good reason attributable to the employer" or have been fired for serious misconduct. Employees who were fired for failing or refusing to take a drug test are generally denied unemployment benefits. In each state, the claimant must report to the unemployment office on a regular basis and verify that she or he is seeking work and has not turned down suitable employment. The benefits are fairly modest, and usually last for a maximum of 26 weeks, although in times of high unemployment federal legislation sometimes extends this period.

As with workers' compensation, an administrative agency in each state determines eligibility, hears contested cases, and pays benefits. A claimant for unemployment compensation, however, must be able to work and must actively be seeking work. Special federal programs provide compensation and retraining funds to workers who lose their jobs because of international competition or as a result of the NAFTA free trade agreement; those special programs are generally administered by the state unemployment programs.

THE FAIR LABOR STANDARDS ACT

Until the 1930s the federal government was not significantly involved in regulating labor and employment issues. The first wage and hour and child labor laws enacted by Congress were held unconstitutional by the courts. However, in 1938 the *Fair Labor Standards Act (FLSA)* was enacted and upheld by the Supreme Court. The act established a minimum wage for covered employees, required that those employees be paid extra for overtime work, and set forth protections for younger employees.

BASIC COVERAGE

The FLSA covers all employers if any aspect of their business affects, or is involved in, interstate commerce, which thus includes most employers. Civilian federal employees and state and local government workers are also covered. A few specific industries, such as fishing, agriculture, and some retail establishments, are not covered. "Executive, professional, and managerial" positions (including salespersons) are not covered if they involve "discretion."

Contrary to what many people believe, the FLSA does not contain provisions addressing lunch hours, break times, vacation or holiday periods, sick leave, or fringe benefits. Those matters are left to state regulation or to the employer and employees to work out.

The Fair Labor Standards Act was amended [by adding 29 U.S.C.A. §§ 207(r) (1)–(4)] to require employers to provide unpaid break time for nursing or expressing breast milk by mothers nursing a child up to one year old, and employers must provide a place other than a bathroom that is shielded from view and free from intrusion—subject to an exception for employers with fewer than 50 employees, where the requirement would impose an undue hardship on the employer.

MINIMUM WAGE AND OVERTIME

When Congress enacted the FLSA in 1938, the *minimum wage* was set at 25 cents an hour. In the years since then, the minimum wage has been raised a number of times; most recently, it was raised to $7.25 per hour on July 24, 2009. Because raising the minimum wage requires legislative action by Congress and must be approved by the President, attempts to raise the minimum wage often become involved in partisan political disputes. (For example, in 1999, Congressional Republicans proposed raising the minimum wage but included large tax breaks for employers as well, which were opposed by President Clinton; as a result, the minimum wage remained at $5.15 per hour.) Covered employees must be paid at least minimum wage for the first 40 hours of work per week. For additional hours, employees are to receive *overtime pay* at one and one-half times the regular rate, although there are many technical aspects to this standard. The overtime provisions exempt certain professional employees, managerial employees, and sales people. The George W. Bush Administration enacted sweeping changes intended to simplify the tests for determining which employees fall within those exceptions and are not eligible for overtime. Those proposals, which took effect in August, 2004, were criticized by labor groups as being overly restrictive and likely to eliminate overtime for several million workers.

In general, each week of employment is treated separately. For example, if an employee works 50 hours in one week, he or she must receive 50 percent additional pay per hour for the extra 10 hours. The employer cannot average an employee's 30 hours one week with 50 hours the next week to make two 40-hour weeks. A worker who is paid on a commission or piecework basis must still receive at least the minimum wage for whatever hours worked. Employers whose workers regularly receive tips may credit up to 40 percent against the minimum wage if the employees actually receive that much in tips. Food and lodging provided to employees may also count as partial credit against the minimum wage.

CHILD LABOR PROVISIONS

The FLSA includes provisions designed to prohibit the employment of children in hazardous occupations and to prevent their working excessive amounts of time during their schooling years. The requirements of the law apply to those workers under the age of 18 years only. Some of the provisions are as follows:

1. Persons of 14 and 15 years of age may not work during school hours at all and may only work three hours on a school day and eight hours on a non–school day. These persons may not work more than 18 hours in a school week or 40 hours in a non–school week. They may not start work before 7:00 A.M. or end after 7:00 P.M. (9:00 P.M. in the summer). They may not be employed in hazardous jobs (as defined next).

2. Persons 16 and 17 years of age are not covered by the hour restrictions for younger workers. However, they may not work in "hazardous" occupations, such as mining, logging, roofing, excavation, the operation of certain types of power machines, or those involving radioactive substances.

The law, like most laws, provides for some exceptions. Younger workers employed by their parents, who work as actors, in entertainment, or who deliver newspapers are exempt from the child labor requirements of the FLSA.

The following case, decided by an ALJ in the U.S. Department of Labor, concerns the enforcement of the child labor provision of the FLSA.

MARSHALL V. GENERAL MOTORS CORP.

23 Wage & Hours Cases 1133

FACTS

LaVera Palice Holmes applied to a job with the Frigidaire Division of General Motors Corporation on Feb. 25, 1976. She listed her birth date on the application as March 2, 1957; she listed the same birth date on the medical insurance and benefits forms. The employer relied on her statements as to her age and made no efforts to verify her statements. She was hired and started employment March 1, 1976; her work involved the operation of a punch press. On March 9, 1976, she suffered an injury on the job, which resulted in the amputation of her left arm below the elbow. She was hospitalized and underwent surgery because of the injury. She later made an application for benefits under the GM medical insurance plan; on that application she listed her birth date as March 2, 1958. During her hospitalization, her supervisor at Frigidaire began an effort to determine her true age. They contacted her high school to determine if her educational records showed her date of birth. The school replied that its records indicated her birth date as March 2, 1959. The supervisor then contacted the Health Department for Abbeville County, South Carolina, where she was born, to request a copy of her birth certificate. The certificate listed March 2, 1959 as her date of birth.

Upon learning of the accident that injured Holmes, the U.S. Department of Labor cited Frigidaire for violating the regulations under the FLSA that prohibit the employment of minors in dangerous occupations and assessed a penalty of $1,000 for the violation. (The operation of a punch press was one of the hazardous occupations identified in the regulations.)

DECISION

Frigidaire argued that it should not be held in violation of the child labor regulations, or in the alternative that it should not be subject to any penalty for the violation, because Holmes deliberately falsified her birth date and her age. Frigidaire also claimed that Holmes' appearance and her personal history indicated that she was at least 18 at the time she was hired. The ALJ held that Frigidaire had violated the child labor prohibitions of the FLSA by employing Holmes, a minor under the age of 18, in a dangerous occupation. Such conduct, whether intentional or unintentional, was a violation of the FLSA and the child labor regulations under FLSA. In considering whether to impose a penalty, the ALJ considered the employer's size, its past history of any violations, the seriousness of the violation, whether the act was willful, and whether any injury resulted from the violation. In this case, despite the fact that the violation was not willful, the minor (Holmes) suffered a serious injury that resulted in permanent disability. Although the ALJ did not condone Holmes' actions in falsifying her birth date and age, he upheld the penalty of $1,000 assessed against Frigidaire because the employer failed to take any steps to verify Holmes' age.

CASE QUESTIONS

1. Why should Frigidaire be subject to a penalty under FLSA when it was not aware of the fact that Holmes was a minor?
2. Can you think of any reasons why the FLSA prohibitions of child labor apply to both intentional and unintentional violations?
3. What steps, if any, could Frigidaire have taken to verify Holmes' age?

ENFORCEMENT

The FLSA is administered by the Wage and Hour Division of the Department of Labor, with offices in many cities across the country. The act requires employers to keep records and other documentation regarding their workers, ages, and hours worked and make such data available to inspectors. Civil and criminal fines may be assessed for violations of the FLSA, and surprise inspections do sometimes occur. Individual employees may also file suit on their own to recover back wages, overtime pay, and liquidated damages; they can also recover legal fees. Violations of the child labor laws, whether intentional or not, carry a penalty of $1,000 per violation. Employees who feel they may not have been paid the minimum wage or received the correct amount of overtime pay should contact their local Wage and Hour Division office.

PENSIONS AND RETIREMENT

THE EMPLOYEE RETIREMENT INCOME SECURITY ACT

Many, but certainly not all, employees accrue retirement and pension benefits through their employment. The employer often sets up a private retirement plan, and a certain amount of the employee's pay is withheld (often matched by a contribution from the employer) and sent to the pension administrator to hold and invest. When the worker retires, a sum of money, called a pension, will be paid to him or her on an annual or monthly basis, depending on how much is in his or her account. In a large company, these funds hold millions of dollars. The investment and use of this substantial fund of money is a very important and complex task.

In the past years incidents occurred in which these funds were not maintained carefully—the persons or companies controlling them used large amounts of money for their own purposes or abused them in other ways not in the best interests of the employees. Employees who had worked for a company for years were deprived of the pension benefits that they had earned. In 1974, in response to numerous instances of such pension fund mismanagement and abuse, Congress passed the *Employee Retirement Income Security Act (ERISA)* to protect the retirement pensions of workers. The act does not require that employers provide pensions for employees, but it does impose standards of conduct for persons having authority or control over pension fund assets. Such persons are known as **fiduciaries**; they must exercise their duties under the pension plan solely in the interests of the participants of the plan and their beneficiaries for the exclusive purpose of providing them with benefits. The fiduciaries are prohibited from dealing with the pension plan assets for their own interests and are prohibited from receiving any consideration or benefit personally from persons who do business with the plan. They are also required to disclose relevant financial information to employees and the Department of Labor. The act also specifies certain standards that pension plans must meet in order to entitle the employer to tax deductions for contributions to the pension plans.

> **fiduciaries:** Persons with control of financial assets owned by others; the law imposes a duty on the fiduciary to act in the interest of the asset owners.

The ERISA standards apply to all employee welfare benefit plans, such as those providing medical coverage, disability benefits, death benefits, vacation pay, or unemployment benefits for employees, but the main focus of the act concerns pensions. ERISA sets minimum requirements for **vesting** of persons—that is, how long a pension plan participant must contribute before being entitled to a nonforfeitable right to payments from the plan. The act requires that pension plans meet one of two vesting schedules based on employees' length of service with the employer: (1) Employees must either become entirely vested after completing five years of service or (2) The company must vest gradually beginning after three years of service and becoming fully vested

> **vesting:** Becoming entitled to a nonforfeitable pension upon retirement.

after seven years. ERISA also sets minimum funding standards, requiring employers to set aside a sufficient amount of funds each year to cover the benefit liabilities that have accrued, or accumulated, under the plan during that year.

The act created the Pension Benefit Guarantee Corporation (PBGC) to insure employees against the loss of pension benefits when an employer terminates a **defined-benefit pension plan**—that is, one that ensures participants a specified monthly income upon their retirement. (The other type of pension plan is called a **defined contribution plan**; under such a plan, employees pay a specified amount each month during their employment. Upon retirement, the employees receive the income generated by their contributions. Such plans are not subject to the PBGC insurance provisions because they do not present underfunding problems.) PBGC will pay a monthly benefit to plan participants, up to a maximum monthly amount. It finances this pension insurance program by charging a premium to employers offering defined-benefit pensions. An employer who terminates an insufficiently funded pension plan is liable to the PBGC for 100 percent of the underfunding, subject to a limit of 30 percent of the employer's net worth; this liability is treated as a tax lien against the property of the employer. In one well-publicized example, LTV, a steel company experiencing financial difficulties, terminated an underfunded pension plan. PBGC began to make payments to the affected participants. The steel company subsequently set up a new pension plan for existing employees. The PBGC then ruled that LTV was also liable for all the benefits due to participants under the terminated plan. LTV sued to challenge that ruling. The Supreme Court upheld the PBGC ruling holding LTV liable [*PBGC v. LTV Corp.,* 496 U.S. 633 (1990)].

The reporting and disclosure requirements of ERISA and the duties and obligations of fiduciaries are enforced by the Department of Labor. The Internal Revenue Service enforces the vesting and funding requirements. Individual participants in pension plans may sue to enforce their rights under the act. ERISA also provides for criminal penalties for willful violations of the fiduciary requirements and the reporting and disclosure provisions; persons may be fined up to $5,000 and receive up to one year in jail, and corporations and unions are subject to fines up to $100,000. Suits to enforce ERISA provisions may be brought in federal or state courts, but any state laws that relate to pensions or benefit plans are preempted by §514 of ERISA.

defined-benefit pension plan: Plan paying employees a specified amount each month upon retirement.

defined contribution pension plan: Pension plan in which employees or the employer pay a specified amount into the employee's pension account.

AIRLINE INDUSTRY WOES THREATEN WORKERS' PENSIONS

The end of the stock market boom, increased foreign and low-cost competition, and rising oil prices have all contributed to problems with pension plan contributions. The Pension Benefit Guaranty Corporation [PBGC], the federal agency that insures pension plans, had a deficit of $9.7 billion in 2004. The deficit stems from the PBGC being saddled with the pension liabilities of a number of American companies that filed for bankruptcy under Chapter 11. In recent years, American steel firms such as Bethlehem Steel and Wheeling-Pittsburgh Steel sought the protection of the bankruptcy courts in order to divest themselves of "legacy costs" of retiree pensions in the face of intense foreign competition. More recently, U.S. airlines have sought Chapter 11 protection to weather the difficult business conditions caused by post-9/11 travel woes, competition from low cost carriers, and record-high fuel prices.

United Airlines announced that it would stop contributing to its pension programs as of July, 2004; the troubled firm stated that an interim $ 1 billion funding package provided to it prohibited and pension plan payments before it emerged from bankruptcy protection. United had previously sought, but was denied, federal funding under a program set up after 9/11 to ease the financial burdens of the airline industry. The PBGC claimed that United's actions were illegal. The International Association of Machinists and Aerospace Workers, the union that represents many of United's employees, filed suit to force the company to resume making pension payments; the union claims that United's actions were in breach of a concessions agreement the parties reached in 2003.

The problems at United come despite the passage of legislation designed to ease pension burdens; President George W. Bush signed the Pension Funding Equity Act of 2004, which was designed to lower firms' pension fund contributions by using a lower discount rate, and to allow the steel and airline industries to defer deficit reduction contributions over to their pension plans, for the next two years. The lower discount rate means that required pension contributions would be lowered by $80 billion, and the deferred contributions represented an additional $1.6 billion in relief.

Sources: Ronald J. Ryan, "Funding Law Could Hurt More Than Help,", *Pensions and Investments*, July 26, 2004; "Losing Altitude: Occupational Pensions," *The Economist* (U.S. Edition), July 31, 2004; David Armstrong, "United Faces Pension Lawsuit,' *The San Francisco Chronicle*, July 30, 2004, p. C-1; "New Loans Forbid Pension Payments b United Airlines," *Los Angeles Times*, July 24, 2004, p. C-2; James Bernstein, "Airline Workers' Union Acts," *Newsday*, July 30, 2004, p. A-72; "James F. Peltz, "Retirees' Futures Up in Air," *Los Angeles Times*, July 30, 2004, p. C-1

SUMMARY

Federal and state statutes regulate a myriad of elements of employment in U.S. workplaces. Since the 1960s federal law has prohibited discrimination in all aspects of employment based on race, and recent statutes ban any discrimination based on age or disability. From the moment that an employee begins work, the OSHA controls the standards of safety and health protection that must be provided by the employer, and workers' compensation laws establish the compensation and medical benefits to which workers are entitled if they are injured or become sick due to work-related causes. The federal FLSA regulates the minimum wages that must be paid to most employees and imposes restrictions on the number of hours and conditions under which children and youth may work. Pensions and retirement plans offered by employers are regulated by the federal ERISA.

CHAPTER QUESTIONS

1. El Paso Natural Gas Company required that the company pilots who flew the firm's fleet of private jets, upon reaching age 60, either take a nonflying job, if one was available, or retire. El Paso claimed that it was impractical to monitor the health of pilots after age 60 and based its rule on the Federal Aviation Authority requirement that commercial pilots retire at age 60. Does the El Paso Company's rule violate the ADEA? Is it a BFOQ? Explain. [*EEOC v. El Paso National Gas Co.,* 626 F. Supp. 182 (W.D. Tex. 1985)]

2. Lorraine Gargiul was employed as a kindergarten teacher by the Liverpool, New York, Central School District. In November 1994, she took an extended sick leave because of a back problem. In February 1995, she was contacted by the superintendent of schools, Virgil Tompkins, and told to report to Dr. Paul Wadsworth, the school district physician, for a physical examination. Gargiul informed Tompkins that she would be able to return to work on March 17, 1995, and submitted a certificate from her own physician. She also informed Tompkins that she had always gone to a female physician and that it was against her personal beliefs to be examined by a male physician. She refused to report to Dr. Wadsworth but instead offered to make an appointment with any female physician selected by Tompkins. In response, the Liverpool District School Board adopted a resolution requiring that Gargiul be examined by Dr. Wadsworth to determine whether she was physically able to return to work and suspending her without pay until she was examined by Dr. Wadsworth. The School Board again directed Gargiul to report to Dr. Wadsworth for an examination, and she again refused. The School Board then fired her for insubordination. She filed suit to challenge her firing. On what legal provisions can she base her suit? What legal arguments can she make to challenge the firing? Is she likely to win her suit? Explain your answer. [*Gargiul v. Tompkins,* 704 F. 2d 661 (2d Cir. 1983), vacated and remanded on other grounds, 465 U.S. 1016 (1984)]

3. Carolyn Humphrey was a medical transcriptionist for Memorial Hospital; her performance was consistently rated excellent. She began to have problems getting to work on time because she felt compelled to engage in a series of obsessive rituals such as washing and combing her hair for up to three hours, to dress very slowly and repeatedly check for papers and items she needed for work. She was given a disciplinary warning because of her tardiness, but her obsessive rituals grew worse. She saw a physician, who diagnosed her as having obsessive-compulsive disorder [OCD]. Her physician wrote a letter to her employer, explaining that her OCD directly contributes to her tardiness. Humphrey met with her supervisor and requested that she be able to work from her home, but the supervisor instead suggested that she work under a flexible starting time arrangement. Humphrey agreed to the flexible starting time arrangement, but she continued to miss work. Humphrey again requested that she be able to work from her home, but the supervisor refused to agree, because of Humphrey's disciplinary warnings caused by her tardiness. When Humphrey was absent from work again, she was terminated. She filed suit under the ADA, claiming that the employer had refused to make a reasonable accommodation to her condition. Is

Humphrey's suit likely to be successful? Why? Explain your answer. [*Humphrey v. Memorial Hospitals Association,* 239 F.3d 1128 (9th Cir. 2001)]

4. An employer at a public works facility in Connecticut allowed workers to purchase a ping pong (table tennis) table and put it in the garage where they gathered before starting work. The employer allowed them to play one-half hour before work and after work and during their lunch hour. One of the employees seriously injured his ankle playing ping pong about five minutes before starting the working day. He was unable to work for a while and incurred medical expenses. Was he covered by workers' compensation? [*McNamara v. Town of Hamden,* 176 Conn.547 (1979)]

5. Global Home Products Enterprise manufactured cookies and candy and sold them through local groups, retail stores, and door-to-door salespeople. Charles Thomas was one of the door-to-door salespeople employed by Global in Charlotte, North Carolina. Thomas would hire children between the ages of 14 to 18 to sell Global products. Thomas then picked up the children at their homes, drove them to a neighborhood, and assigned them streets on which to sell cookies and candy. The children turned over all the proceeds from the sales to Thomas and in return, were paid $0.60 per box sold (out of the $3 purchase price). Thomas then drove the children home. On school nights, Thomas frequently kept the children out after 7 P.M., often returning them after 9 P.M. On weekends, the children often did not return to their homes until 11:30 P.M. or 12 midnight. Parents complained the children returned home tired and hungry; one parent filed a complaint with the Department of Labor. Has Thomas violated the child labor provisions of the FLSA? Has Global? Explain. [*Thomas v. Brock,* 615 F. Supp. 553 (W.D.N.C. 1985)]

6. Whirlpool Corp. manufactures household appliances at a plant in Ohio. Overhead conveyers transport various components throughout the plant. A mesh screen some 20 feet above the floor catches objects that fall off the conveyers. Maintenance workers are assigned to retrieve the objects from time to time. In June 1974, one worker fell through the screen and was killed. Certain repairs were then made to the screen, and workers were told to stand on the steel supports and not the screen. About a week later two other employees were told to retrieve objects from the screen and refused to do so, believing that it was still unsafe. They called OSHA, but no CO was available to come immediately. They were then told to punch out without being paid for the rest of their shift and that letters would be placed in their files. OSHA filed suit on their behalf to clear their records. Who should win this suit and why? [*Whirlpool Corp. v. Marshall,* 445 U.S. 1 (1980)]

7. Tom Zenor was employed as a hospital pharmacist by El Paso Healthcare, Inc.; he was also addicted to cocaine. After injecting cocaine one evening, he was unable to report for work the next day. He called his supervisor and told him that he was unable to report for work because he was under the influence of drugs; the supervisor told him to arrange for treatment under the employer's Employee Assistance Program, with Zenor's personal physician. Zenore contacted his doctor and then checked into a detox center for nine days. While at the detox center, he contacted his supervisor and said he would enroll in a rehabilitation program and wanted to keep his job. The supervisor told Zenor that he was entitled to a leave under the FMLA, and Zenor enrolled in a residential rehabilitation program. While Zenor was

in the rehabilitation program, his supervisors decided to fire him; he was told that he could complete the rehabilitation program, but would be fired upon completion of his FMLA leave. Zenor filed suit, alleging that the employer had violated the ADA. Has the employer violated the ADA? Explain you answer. [*Zenor v. El Paso Healthcare System, Ltd.*, 176 F.3d 847 (5th Cir. 1999)].

8. Fe Castro Marchisheck was a single mother, raising her 14 year old son; she was a medical technologist at San Mateo General Hospital. She suspected that her son was involved with a gang, and was abusing drugs and alcohol. She decided to send her son to live with relatives in the Philippine Islands, and asked her supervisor for five weeks leave to travel with her son to the Philippines. Her supervisor refused, because he was unable to cover her shifts. Marchisheck again asked for leave, and was again refused; she presented a letter from her son's therapist to support her request. The employer offered her five weeks of unpaid leave at the end of September, or two weeks with pay in early September. She made travel arrangements for August, and left for the Philippines on August 18th. Her employer informed her that she was terminated for insubordination and being absent without leave; she filed suit under the FMLA. How should the court rule on her suit? Explain your answer. [*Marchisheck v. San Mateo County*, 199 F.3d 1068 (9th Cir. 1999)]

9. Robert E. McCrocklin was employed as an engineering writer by Butler Service Group. He worked in an unventilated room containing numerous partially enclosed cubicles; each cubicle was six feet wide and five feet deep and open at the top. Three of the nine people in the work area where McCrocklin worked were smokers; the smoke they produced entered McCrocklin's cubicle. McCrocklin was not allergic to smoke, but he found it unpleasant and offensive; he objected to the carcinogenic effect of breathing smoke produced by other people in an enclosed room. McCrocklin made complaints about the smoke and ventilation problems in his workspace soon after he was hired. He was promised that conditions would be improved by the installation of an air circulation system, ceiling partitions, and doors on the cubicles. Despite the promises, the situation remained unchanged. McCrocklin tried to use portable fans to avoid the smoke, but it did not alleviate the problem. McCrocklin requested to be able to work at his home, but his request was denied. After four years, McCrocklin quit his job. His application to the California Employment Department (CED) for unemployment compensation was denied because CED held that he had quit his job voluntarily, without good cause. McCrocklin filed suit to challenge the denial of benefits. What arguments can McCrocklin make to support his position that he should receive unemployment benefits? What arguments can the CED make to support its position that McCrocklin quit without good cause? How should the court decide the case? Explain your answer. [*McCrocklin v. Employment Development Dept. (Butler Service Group, Inc.)*, 156 Cal. App. 3d 1067 (Cal Ct. of App., 2nd Dist., 1984)]

10. The State of Wyoming had a series of laws requiring all law enforcement officers to retire at the age of 55 years. The laws apply even to Game Wardens, who enforce the state's hunting and fishing laws and regulations. The state justified the laws on the basis that by nature law enforcement

jobs require possible strenuous physical exertion, and the physical conditioning of individuals starts to decline around age 55. Wyoming also argued that it is too difficult to screen all individuals to determine their level of fitness and conditioning, and therefore, a blanket retirement age is appropriate. Posby was a Game Warden who just reached his 55th birthday. He felt that the retirement law was in violation of the federal ADEA. Can he successfully file and win an ADEA complaint? Explain. [*Kimel v. Florida Board of Regents,* 528 U.S. 62 (2000)]

PRACTICAL EXERCISE

Adam Bradley is a surgical technician—he assists surgeons during operations—at the Harrington Cancer Clinic in Dallas. During an interview with a local paper, Bradley admitted that he is HIV positive—he is infected with the virus that causes AIDS. Upon learning that he is HIV positive, the operating room supervisor asks the clinic's chief administrator to transfer Bradley from the surgical technician position to a clerical position. The supervisor claims that Bradley poses a risk of accidentally infecting a patient during an operation. Although the possibility of such an incident may be slight, the consequences of such an incident would be catastrophic. The supervisor argues that the clinic should not take any chances that such an incident may occur. Bradley claims that the risk of infecting patients is very small and can be prevented by taking reasonable precautions during surgery. You are the executive assistant for the clinic's chief administrator. She has asked you to advise her regarding the decision of whether to transfer Bradley. What factors should be considered in making the decision? What recourse would Bradley have to challenge the transfer? Under what legislation could he bring suit? What would be the legal and ethical consequences of a patient being infected while undergoing surgery? What defenses could the clinic demonstrate? Prepare a memorandum outlining your recommended decision, addressing and discussing all of these questions. See *Bradley v. University of Texas,* 510 U.S. 1119 (1994).

FURTHER INFORMATION

www.9to5.org/
  9 to 5 National Association of Working Women.
www.worknwoman.com/
  Women in the World of Work.
www.eeoc.gov/
  The Equal Employment Opportunity Commission.
www.eeac.org/
  The Equal Employment Advisory Council.
www.osha.gov/
  The Occupational Safety and Health Administration.
www.dol.gov/elaws/flsa.htm
  The U.S. Department of Labor Wage and Hour Division FLSA Advisor.

CHAPTER 23

LABOR–MANAGEMENT LAW AND REGULATION

After you have read this chapter, you should be able to:

1. Chronicle the development of labor relations law.
2. Describe the organization and procedures of the National Labor Relations Board and other provisions of the National Labor Relations Act.
3. List several unfair labor practices set out by the NLRA.
4. Discuss bargaining procedures and the administration and enforcement of collective arguments.
5. Compare labor relations in the public and private sectors.

CHAPTER OUTLINE

I. The Development of Labor Relations Law

II. Coverage of the NLRA

III. Provisions of the NLRA

IV. Unfair Labor Practices

V. Public Sector Employees

This chapter discusses labor management relations—the laws under which employees organize and join unions, and bargain collectively with their employers to determine wages and conditions of their employment. Are university faculty members able to organize in a union and bargain with the university over their working conditions? Are there reasons to treat full-time faculty differently than part-time or adjunct faculty? Should faculty have the right to strike?

Should it matter whether the university is public or private? After reading this chapter, you should be able to answer those questions.

INTRODUCTION

Although the percentage of U.S. employees who are union members has been steadily declining over the past 50 years, the importance of labor relations and employment-related legal issues has been increasing (as noted in Chapter 21). Labor relations law remains a significant aspect of U.S. employment policy—the relevant legislation defines rights and duties for employers, whether their employees are unionized or not, and for employees whether they are or are not members of a union.

Workers join unions in order to have a voice in determining the terms and conditions of their employment. Collective bargaining between a union and employer is the primary means for such involvement. The rights of employees to join or organize unions and to bargain collectively with their employer are guaranteed under the *National Labor Relations Act* (*NLRA*). This chapter focuses on the NLRA, and the rights, duties, and obligations that it creates for both employees and employers.

THE DEVELOPMENT OF LABOR RELATIONS LAW

The rationale behind the at will doctrine (discussed in Chapter 20) is that the employer and employee are free to negotiate for a contract for a specific term if they so desire. However, in reality, most employees have very little bargaining power in relation to the employer. The employer's position in negotiating for a job is generally "take it or leave it." By acting jointly, however, employees can counter the employer's advantage. That is why employees join unions—there is strength in numbers, and their joint action creates bargaining power for the employees.

The first unions were craft guilds—groups of skilled employees who agreed to work under certain terms and conditions and for certain wages. All the members of the guild were bound by its rules and agreed not to work for employers who paid less than the specified wage. Employers were forced to pay the going wage or to face boycotts by the skilled workers.

Employers argued that the guilds' actions were conspiracies to increase wages and to interfere with the freedom of workers to contract with employers. Most courts in the early- to mid-19th century agreed with the employers' position; hence, unions were held to be criminal conspiracies. It was not until the 1842 case of *Commonwealth of Mass. v. Hunt* [45 Mass. (4 Met.) 111], that the Massachusetts Supreme Court held that unions were not per se illegal conspiracies; the court's opinion reflected an awareness of the growing public support of unions.

Although the years following the *Hunt* case were marked by a grudging tolerance on the part of the courts toward unions, employers still had several legal weapons to use against unions: the injunction, yellow dog contracts, and the antitrust laws.

injunctions: Court orders directing persons either to refrain from or perform certain activity.

ex parte: A court proceeding in which only the party asking for the court action is present.

yellow dog contracts: Contracts requiring employees to agree not to join unions.

Injunctions are court orders directing persons either to refrain from certain activity or, occasionally, to perform certain activity. Employers facing strikes or union boycotts would ask courts for injunctions against the union's activity; the courts, moreover, did not require the employer to show that the strike or boycott actually harmed its business. Often the injunctions were issued *ex parte*, that is, with only the employer appearing before the court— the union would not have a chance to present its side to the court. Once an injunction was issued, it would be enforced by officers of the court. Union members who resisted were subject to fines and jail terms for contempt of court. The injunction effectively stopped the strike but failed to address the problem that caused the strike. The injunction prevented the union from taking any action against the employer, and the employer was free to continue the conduct that provoked the union.

Yellow dog contracts were contracts of employment that required the employee to agree not to join a union. Because the contract made the promise not to join a union a condition of employment, the employer could legally fire any worker who joined a union for breach of his or her employment contract. The Supreme Court upheld the legality of yellow dog contracts in *Hitchman Coal Co. v. Mitchell* [245 U.S. 229 (1917)].

The antitrust laws (discussed in Chapter 17) also provided employers with another means to attack unions. In several celebrated cases, the courts held that union boycotts of employers' products were "combinations or conspiracies in restraint of trade" in violation of the Sherman Act. In *Loewe v. Lawlor* [208 U.S. 274 (1908)], the Supreme Court upheld a decision finding individual members of the United Hatters' Union liable for $240,000 in damages for a boycott of the products of D.E. Loewe Co. In response to the *Loewe* case, Congress amended the Clayton Act to provide that " . . . the labor of a human being is not a commodity or article of commerce . . . " and that labor unions and their members shall not be held to be "combinations or conspiracies in restraint of trade." Despite Congress's intention to exempt union activities from the antitrust laws, the Supreme Court held that there was no general grant of immunity for union activities and upheld, in *Duplex Printing Press Co. v. Deering* [254 U.S. 443 (1921)], an injunction against a union for organizing a national boycott of an employer's products.

LABOR LEGISLATION

Not until the Great Depression of the 1930s did Congress legislatively endorse the activities of labor unions. Part of Roosevelt's New Deal included recognition of unions and collective bargaining as a means to improve the economic lot of workers.

The first piece of labor legislation was the *Norris-LaGuardia Act*, passed in 1932. The Norris-LaGuardia Act limited the ability of federal courts to issue injunctions in labor disputes: Injunctions could only be issued after both parties appeared before the court and only if the court was convinced that irreparable harm to property was likely to occur and the police were unwilling or unable to protect the property. The act also made yellow dog contracts unenforceable in any federal court. The Norris-LaGuardia Act had the effect of ensuring that the federal judiciary played a neutral role in any labor dispute. Although the act only applied to federal courts, a number of states passed similar laws (known as "little Norris-LaGuardia acts") applying the same restrictions to their state courts.

The second major piece of labor legislation was the *National Labor Relations Act* [*NLRA*], also known as the Wagner Act, passed in 1935. The Wagner Act establishes a legislative framework for industrial relations; specifically, it provides for legal recognition of unions and imposes on employers a duty to bargain with the unions representing their employees. The most important provision of the act concerns the right of employees to join unions and to engage in collective bargaining and other concerted activity for mutual aid and protection. Employer actions that interfere with or restrain those rights are **unfair labor practices**. (Although the Wagner Act only defined unfair labor practices by employers, later legislation added a list of unfair union labor practices.) The Act created the National Labor Relations Board (NLRB), an administrative agency to enforce and administer the act's provisions.

Under the protection of the Wagner Act, unions flourished; many commentators, however, criticized the act and the NLRB as being too pro-union. Public and Congressional concern over union power led to the passage of the *Labor Management Relations Act*, also known as the *Taft-Hartley Act*, in 1947. Taft-Hartley amended the NLRA by creating a list of union activities that are unfair labor practices and also providing that employees also have the right to refrain from joining unions or engaging in concerted activities. The act outlawed the **closed shop**, a contract provision that requires the employer to hire only union members. Lastly, the act also empowered the President to forestall strikes that threaten the national health or safety.

The third major piece of labor legislation was the *Labor-Management Reporting and Disclosure Act*, or the *Landrum-Griffin Act*, passed in 1959. Landrum-Griffin was passed in response to concerns about union racketeering and abusive practices aimed at union members. The act establishes specific rights for individual union members against the union and prohibits financial abuses, manipulation of union election procedures, and racketeering by union officials.

These laws provide the legislative framework for private sector labor relations in the United States.

> **unfair labor practices:** Actions that violate the rights granted under the labor regulations legislation.

> **closed shop agreements:** Contract provisions requiring the employer to hire only employees who are already union members.

NATIONAL LABOR RELATIONS BOARD

The NLRB is the administrative agency that administers and enforces the provisions of the National Labor Relations Act.[1] The NLRB is really made up of two independent authorities within the same administrative structure: the five-member National Labor Relations Board and the Office of the General Counsel. The General Counsel is the chief administrative officer in charge of the day-to-day operation of the agency and is appointed by the President, subject to confirmation by the Senate. The General Counsel also oversees the prosecutorial efforts of the agency to enforce the provisions of the act. The NLRB has 33 regional offices, headed up by regional directors, who report to the General Counsel.

---

[1] For the purposes of this chapter, we will refer to the legislation resulting from the Wagner Act and the Taft-Hartley Act as the National Labor Relations Act [NLRA]. Scholars and labor lawyers differ in whether the legislation should be referred to as the NLRA or the Labor Management Relations Act, or both.

The five-member National Labor Relations Board is the judicial branch of the agency and acts as a specialized court of appeals. Its members are appointed by the President and must be confirmed by the Senate. They hear appeals from decisions by the agency's administrative law judges (ALJs), who act as the agency's trial judges. The ALJs are independent of both the General Counsel and the Board; they decide unfair labor practice complaints filed under the NLRA. The ALJs' decisions involve both findings of fact and of law together with a recommended remedial order; the decisions are subject to review by the Board, which can affirm, amend, reverse, or vary an ALJs' decision.

Procedures   The NLRB handles two kinds of cases: those involving allegations of unfair labor practices and those involving **representation questions**. The NLRB does not initiate proceedings; rather, it responds to complaints of unfair labor practices and to petitions for elections.

representation questions: Cases dealing with employees seeking to join unions or unions seeking to represent employees.

Unfair Labor Practice Cases.   Unfair labor practice cases are initiated by the filing of a complaint within six months of the alleged violation, with the regional director of an NLRB regional office. The regional director and office staff investigate the complaint and may dismiss it if it lacks merit. If the complaint is valid, the regional office will attempt to settle the dispute; failing that, the regional director will issue a formal complaint. The complaint is served on the alleged violator, and a formal hearing on the complaint is held before an ALJ. After the ALJ issues a decision, either party has 20 days to file exceptions to the decision. If there are no exceptions, the decision becomes final; if there are exceptions, they are reviewed by the Board, which then issues its decision and remedial order.

The Board's orders are subject to judicial review by the federal courts of appeals; any party to the case may seek review, and the Board may seek enforcement of its order before the courts of appeals. The Board may also seek injunctions in federal courts to prohibit conduct violating the NLRA. Upon review, the court examines whether the NLRB was acting within its jurisdiction under the Act and whether the NLRB's decision is supported by substantial evidence on the record as a whole. (See Chapter 5 for a discussion of judicial review.) After the court of appeals issues its decision, any affected party may seek a further appeal by petitioning the U.S. Supreme Court to review the decision. The Supreme Court generally grants review only to cases involving novel issues of law or when the courts of appeals are divided on the issue; hence, only a very small percentage of cases reach this final step.

Representation cases.   Representation cases involve employees choosing whether to be represented by a union as their exclusive bargaining agent. A union or group of employees may petition a regional office of the NLRB to hold an election to determine whether the employees of an employer wish to be represented by a union. The NLRB also considers **decertification petitions** filed by employees who no longer wish to be represented by a union. The petitions must be supported by evidence that at least 30 percent of the employees in the appropriate group support the union (or the decertification effort). The regional office staff investigates the petition to determine if the employer and employees are subject to the NLRA and whether an election can be held—an election cannot be held if a valid election took place within the past 12 months or if a valid collective bargaining agreement covering the employees exists. If

decertification petitions: Petitions by employees seeking to revoke a union's right to represent them.

an election is appropriate, the regional director will hold a hearing to determine the appropriate **bargaining unit**—the particular group of employees seeking union representation, the eligibility of employees to vote in the election, and the administrative details of holding the election (the date for the vote, the location of ballot boxes, and so on).

The employer and the union campaign to influence how the employees should vote during the period prior to the actual election. The purpose of the election is to determine the employees' choice; conduct that coerces, intimidates, or threatens the employees will invalidate the election results. Because the employees are dependent on the employer for their economic livelihood, the NLRB takes the position that they will be susceptible to employer threats, either explicit or implicit, of dire consequences such as firings, plant closing, or relocation if the union wins the election. Unfair labor practices committed by either party during the campaign may also invalidate the election. When such conduct occurs, the other party can file an objection to such conduct with the NLRB. Objections must be filed no later than five days after the election.

The election is by secret ballot, and the employees vote on whether they wish to be represented by a union. There may also be two or more unions seeking representation rights; voters must choose among the unions or choose for no union representation. The choice receiving a majority of votes cast is declared the winner; if no choice receives a majority, then a runoff election is held between the top two choices. After the votes are counted, the results are certified by the regional director. If a union wins, it becomes the exclusive bargaining agent for that group of employees; if employees choose no union representation, the employer is free from another election for at least 12 months.

If either party has filed objections, the regional office's staff will investigate the objections and hold a hearing on them. If the objections are upheld, the election results will be set aside; if the objections are rejected by the regional director, the election results will be certified.

bargaining unit:
The group of employees that is represented by a union—the basic unit of constituency for labor relations.

COVERAGE OF THE NLRA

The NLRA gives the NLRB authority to deal with labor disputes "in or affecting commerce"; the NLRB has adopted jurisdictional guidelines that require a firm or operation to involve commerce (sales or purchases of goods) of at least $50,000 yearly to ensure that a firm has at least a minimal effect on commerce. The Act also excludes certain employers and employees from its coverage. Section 2(2) of the NLRA excludes all public section employers (federal, state, or local) and railroads and airlines (which are both subject to the Railway Labor Act instead). Section 2(3) of the NLRA excludes the following employees: agricultural laborers, persons employed as domestic servants within another person's home, persons employed by their parent or spouse, supervisors (who have the power to hire, fire, direct, or discipline other employees), independent contractors, and persons working for employers covered by the Railway Labor Act. In addition to the statutory exceptions to NLRA coverage, the courts have created other exceptions. The courts have held that parochial schools and employers closely identified with, or operated by, foreign governments are outside the NLRB's jurisdiction, and that persons who are managerial employees—those who formulate or carry out management policies—and confidential employees—those whose jobs give them access to confidential labor relations information of the employer—are excluded from the act's definition of employee. The Supreme Court ruled that full-time faculty at a private university were managerial employees because they exercised control over academic policies, curriculum matters and, hiring, tenure and promotion of faculty, *NLRB v. Yeshiva University* [444 U.S. 672 (1980)].

The Supreme Court, in *NLRB v. Town & Country Electric, Inc.* [516 U.S. 85 (1995)] held that union organizers hired by construction contractors but also being paid by a union to help unionize the contractor's workers are employees under §2(3) and enjoy the protections of the NLRA.

The following case involves the question of whether certain nurses, who direct other nursing personnel as part of their work to care for patients, were supervisors as defined in §2(11) of the NLRA.

NLRB V. HEALTH CARE & RETIREMENT CORPORATION OF AMERICA

511 U.S. 571 (1994)

FACTS

The NLRB held that Health Care & Retirement Corp. (HCRC), which operated the Heartland Nursing Home, committed unfair labor practices in disciplining four staff nurses. The staff nurses, who are the senior ranking employees on duty after 5 P.M. during the week and at all times on weekends, are responsible to ensure adequate staffing, make daily work assignments, monitor and discipline aides (who directly provide patient care) to ensure proper performance, resolve aides' problems and grievances, and evaluate aides' performances. HCRC argued that the four nurses involved in this case were supervisors and were therefore excluded from the protection of the NLRA. The ALJ concluded that the nurses were not supervisors, because their supervisory work did not "equate to responsibly directing the aides in the interest of the employer," noting that "the nurses' focus is on the well-being of the residents rather than of the employer." The NLRB affirmed the ALJ's decision, holding that the nurses' direction of less-skilled employees, in the exercise of the nurses' professional judgment for the treatment of patients, is not authority exercised "in the interest of the employer." The NLRB takes that position because professional employees, especially registered nurses, would otherwise be generally excluded from the right to organize and bargain under the NLRA. The attorneys for HCRC argued that the NLRB position contradicts the plain language of §2(11).

Section 2(11) defines a supervisor as: "[a]ny individual having authority, in the interest of the employer, to hire, transfer, suspend, lay off, recall, promote, discharge, assign, reward, or discipline other employees, or responsibly to direct them, or to adjust their grievances, or effectively to recommend such action, if in connection with the foregoing the exercise of such authority is not of a merely routine or clerical nature, but requires the use of independent judgment."

The attorneys for HCRC sought judicial review of the NLRB's decision, and the U.S. Court of Appeals for the Sixth Circuit reversed, holding that the four licensed practical nurses involved in this case were supervisors. The NLRB then appealed to the U.S. Supreme Court.

DECISION

Because the NLRA does not grant the rights to organize unions and bargain collectively to supervisory employees, the statutory definition of supervisor is essential in determining which employees enjoy those rights.

The Supreme Court stated that deciding whether a worker is a supervisor under §2(11) requires the resolution of three questions, which must each be answered in the affirmative if an employee is to be deemed a supervisor. First, does the employee have authority to engage in one of the 12 listed activities?

Second, does the exercise of that authority require "the use of independent judgment"? Third, does the employee hold and exercise that authority "in the interest of the employer"?

This case concerns only the third question: Do the charge nurses exercise their authority to direct other employees "in the interest of the employer"? The NLRB's position sets up a false split between acts taken in connection with patient care and acts taken in the interest of the employer. That split, or dichotomy, makes no sense. Patient care is the business of a nursing home, and it follows that attending to the needs of the nursing home patients, who are the employer's customers, is in the interest of the employer. There is no basis for the NLRB's blanket assertion that supervisory authority exercised in connection with patient care is somehow not in the interest of the employer. The NLRB's test is inconsistent with the ordinary meaning of the phrase "in the interest of the employer," and would render portions of the statutory definition in §2(11) meaningless. The NLRA is to be enforced according to its own terms, not by creating legal categories inconsistent with its meaning, as the NLRB has done in nurse cases. The Court held that the Court of Appeals was correct in deciding that the NLRB's position was inconsistent with the language of the statute.

Justices Ginsburg, Blackmun, Stevens, and Souter dissented, arguing that the NLRB position was necessary to ensure that professional employees are able to exercise the right to join unions and to bargain collectively under the NLRA.

CASE QUESTIONS

1. What is the test to determine whether an employee is a supervisor under the NLRA?
2. Why does the NLRB take the position that the staff nurses exercise their duties in the interest of the residents' health care rather than in the employer's interest? What is the basis of the NLRB's position? Explain.
3. What is the significance of the determination that the staff nurses are supervisors under the NLRA? What implications does this case have for other professional employees such as doctors and lawyers? Explain.

The Supreme Court again rejected the NLRB's interpretation of §2(11) as it related to health care professionals in *NLRB v. Kentucky River Community Care, Inc.* [532 U.S. 706 (2001)]. The NLRB had taken the position that employees who draw upon their professional expertise or technical training in directing less-skilled employees in their duties were not exercising "independent judgment" in the interests of the employer; the Court held that professionally or technically informed judgment could never the less be independent judgment, making the person giving the direction a supervisor under §2(11).

NLRB FLIP-FLOPS ON POLICY DECISIONS

The NLRB is a political institution; because the president appoints the members of the NLRB, the NLRB decisions reflect the political philosophy of the current administration. That means that the NLRB often reverses its decisions, reflecting the changing political composition of the NLRB. Two recent examples of such policy reversals involve the questions of "Weingarten rights" and whether graduate students are employees under the NLRA.

Weingarten Rights: In *NLRB v. J. Weingarten* [420 U.S. 251 (1975)], the U.S. Supreme Court upheld an NLRB decision that union employees were entitled under §7 of the National Labor Relations Act to have a union representative present during meetings with the employer if those meetings were likely to result in disciplinary action against the employee. Since that decision, the NLRB has struggled with the question of whether non-union employees are also entitled to exercise the "Weingarten rights" by having a representative of their choosing present at meetings with the employer. In the case of *Epilepsy Foundation of Northeast Ohio* [331 NLRB 676 (2000)], enforced by the D.C. Circuit Court of Appeals [268 F.3d 1095 (2001)], the NLRB held that non-union employees were entitled to the exercise of Weingarten rights. The Epilepsy Foundation decision reversed the NLRB's prior position that Weingarten rights were only available to unionized employees, *E.I. DuPont & Co.* [289 NLRB 627 (1988)], which in turn had reversed the prior NLRB precedent of *Materials Research Corp.* [262 NLRB 1010 (1982)] extending such rights to all employees under the NLRA. The *Epilepsy Foundation* decision reflected the attitudes of the "Clinton NLRB". However, the "Bush NLRB" reversed *Epilepsy Foundation* in the IBM Corp. case. The NLRB reversed itself once again, and overruled *Epilepsy Foundation* in its decision in *IBM Corporation* [341 NLRB No. 148 (June 9, 2004)].

In the *IBM Corp.* case, three employees who were to be interviewed by employer officials regarding allegations of harassment had requested to have an attorney or a co-worker present during the interview. The IBM officials denied that request. The IBM workers are not represented by a union. A month after the interviews, the three workers were fired by IBM. The employees then filed a complaint with the NLRB, claiming that IBM had violated §8(a)(1) of the NLRA by denying them their Weingarten rights. The administrative law judge hearing the case applied the *Epilepsy Foundation* decision and held that IBM had committed an unfair labor practice. IBM sought review of that decision with the NLRB; on review, the NLRB overruled *Epilepsy Foundation* by a 3-2 vote. The majority rejected the policy considerations underlying the *Epilepsy Foundation* decision. The majority argued that the Weingarten rights flow from the nature of the role of a union as an exclusive bargaining agent under §9(a) of the NLRA; and the *Epilepsy Foundation* decision inappropriately attempted to transfer that analysis to a non-union setting. They reasoned that employers should be allowed to conduct workplace investigations in a thorough, sensitive and confidential manner, and that can best be accomplished in a non-union setting by permitting employers to investigate employees without a co-worker present.

Graduate Teaching Assistants as Employees: Just as with the issue of Weingarten rights for non-union employees, the NLRB has reversed itself several times on the question of whether graduate teaching assistants at private universities, who work as part of their educational program, can be considered employees within the definition of the NLRA. In *Brown University* [342 N.L.R.B. No. 42 (July 13, 2004)], the "Bush NLRB," again by a 3-2 vote, reversed the "Clinton NLRB" decision in *New York University* [332 N.L.R.B. 1205 (2000)]. The *NYU* decision itself reversed prior NLRB decisions that had consistently held that even though graduate teaching assistants received payment for their teaching duties, they were primarily students, and therefore could not be considered employees within the meaning of the NLRA. The "Clinton NLRB" rejected that position in the *NYU* decision; they reasoned that the NLRA does not exclude students from its coverage, and that the teaching assistants provide services to the university, are under the control of the university, and receive payment from the university for their services. Therefore, the teaching assistants at private sector universities should be considered employees, with the right to unionize under the NLRA.

In *Brown University,* the majority reasoned that the teaching assistants are students rather than employees: their status as teaching assistants is contingent upon their continued enrollment as students, and the pay they receive for their services is essentially financial aid to them as students rather than payment for their work. The teaching assistants at private sector universities therefore are not employees within the meaning of the NLRA, and are not entitled to unionize under the provisions of the act. [Note that the NLRB decisions deal only with private universities–public universities are subject to the relevant state legislation for public sector employers rather than the NLRA.]

In reaching its decision in *NYU,* the "Clinton NLRB" relied upon its prior decision in *Boston Medical Center* [330 N.L.R.B. No. 30 (1999)], which held that medical residents and interns were employees under the NLRA. The *Boston Medical Center* decision reversed the NLRB's prior position in *St. Clare's Hospital* [229 N.L.R.B. 1000 (1977)] and *Cedars-Sinai Medical Center* [223 N.L.R.B. 251 (1976)], which held that interns and medical residents were students and not employees under the NLRA. The Brown University decision involved only teaching assistants, and not residents and interns, so the "Bush NLRB" did not specifically overrule the *Boston Medical Center* decision.

PROVISIONS OF THE NLRA

The basic provision of the NLRA is contained in §7, which states:

> Employees shall have the right to self-organization, to form, join or assist labor organizations, to bargain collectively through representatives of their own choosing, and to engage in other concerted activities for the purpose of collective bargaining or other mutual aid or protection, and shall also have the right to refrain from any and all such activities . . .

SECTION 7 RIGHTS

Section 7 gives rights to all employees under the NLRA; employees need not be members of labor unions in order to enjoy such rights. Section 7 requires that the conduct of employees be "concerted" for the purpose of collective bargaining or other mutual aid or protection, in order to be protected. The effect of §7 protection means that the employees cannot be disciplined or discharged for their conduct. Such protected conduct includes discussing the need for a union or the need to improve working conditions with other employees, and attempts to get fellow employees to join a union. But the protection of §7 extends to other conduct as well—in one case, a group of non-union employees who walked off the job to protest the extremely cold temperatures inside the shop were protected under §7, as was an employee who circulated a petition about the management of the company's credit union.

There are limits to the protection under §7. Employees acting individually, without the support or authorization of fellow employees or for purposes unrelated to collective bargaining, mutual aid, or protection, may not be protected. The following case involves the question of whether an employee, acting alone to exercise a right under the collective agreement, is within the protection of §7.

NLRB V. CITY DISPOSAL SYSTEMS

465 U.S. 822 (1984)

FACTS

James Brown was employed as a truck driver by City Disposal Systems, a trash-hauling and disposal firm. The employees of City Disposal were members of Local 247 of the International Brotherhood of Teamsters Union. The collective agreement covering the employees provided that the employer would not require employees to operate any vehicle or equipment that was not in safe operating condition; employees were given the right to refuse to operate unsafe equipment. When the truck he usually drove needed repairs, Brown was ordered to drive a truck that had had brake problems the previous day. Brown refused to drive that truck, stating that there was something wrong with its brakes; Brown did not specifically refer to the collective agreement for his refusal. His supervisor again directed Brown to drive the truck, and when Brown again refused, he angrily directed Brown to go home. Later that day, Brown was notified that he had been fired; he immediately returned to work to seek reinstatement but was unsuccessful.

Brown filed an unfair labor practice complaint with the NLRB against City Disposal, challenging his discharge. The ALJ hearing the complaint held that the discharge violated Brown's rights under §7 of the NLRB and that Brown's refusal to drive the unsafe truck was concerted action under the language of §7. The NLRB affirmed the ALJ's decision and ordered that Brown be reinstated with back pay. City Disposal sought judicial review of the NLRB decision by the Court of Appeals; the Court of Appeals held that Brown's action was not concerted activity because he acted solely on his own behalf. The NLRB appealed to the U.S. Supreme Court on the issue of whether an individual employee's actions could be "concerted" within the meaning of §7.

DECISION

The Supreme Court referred to the language of §7 of the NLRA, which grants employees the right to " . . . form, join or assist labor organizations, to bargain collectively through representatives of their own choosing, and to engage in other concerted activities for the purpose of collective bargaining or other mutual aid or protection . . . ." The Court then looked to the NLRB ruling in the *Interboro Contractors, Inc.* case, which held that an individual employee's assertion of a right granted under a collective bargaining agreement is recognized as concerted activity and is protected under §7. The board's rationale for the *Interboro* doctrine was that exercising a right granted under a collective agreement is an extension of the concerted process of collective bargaining that produced the agreement and that the exercise of a right under a collective agreement affects the rights of all employees covered by that agreement. The Court agreed that the assertion of a right granted under a collective agreement was "unquestionably an integral part of the process that gave rise to the agreement . . . . Moreover, when an employee invokes a right grounded in the collective bargaining agreement, he does not stand alone. Instead, he brings to bear on his employer the power and resolve of all his fellow employees." The Court held that the NLRB's *Interboro* doctrine preserved the integrity of the entire collective bargaining process, which includes the invoking of rights under the agreement by individual employees. "As long as the employee's actions are based on a reasonable and honest belief that he is being, or has been, asked to perform a task that he is not required to perform under his collective bargaining agreement, and the statement or action is directed toward the enforcement of a collectively bargained right, there is no justification for overturning the Board's judgment that the employee is engaged in concerted activity . . . ." The Court therefore reversed the decision of the Court of Appeals and upheld the NLRB determination that Brown had been engaged in concerted activity protected under §7.

CASE QUESTIONS

1. What right was Brown attempting to exercise? What was the source of that right?
2. How is seeking to enforce a collective agreement perceived to be "an extension of the bargaining process"?
3. Would an individual employee who was not a union member be protected by §7 in acting alone to enforce a right to a safe workplace?

UNFAIR LABOR PRACTICES

The NLRA sets out a list of actions by employers and unions that interfere with employees' rights under the act; these unfair labor practices are prohibited by the act. Section 8(a) lists unfair labor practices by employers, and §8(b) lists unfair labor practices by unions. Section 8(e) also prohibits certain conduct by unions. The following discussion of unfair labor practices focuses on the conduct, whether by union or employer, prohibited by §8.

SECTIONS 8(A)(1) AND 8(B)(1): INTERFERENCE WITH §7 RIGHTS

Sections 8(a)(1) and 8(b)(1) prohibit any conduct that interferes with, coerces, or restrains employees in the exercise of their rights under §7 of the NLRA. The NLRB has held that any conduct that has the natural tendency to restrain or coerce employees in the exercise of the §7 rights is prohibited. Actual coercion or restraint of employees need not be shown for a violation, nor is intention to coerce or restrain employees required. Employer threats to fire employees who join unions, threats to close the plant if the employees vote for a union, employer or union threats of violence, interrogation of employees as to their union sympathies, union attempts to force employees to join, and actual violence directed against employees are all examples of conduct that violate §8(a)(1) or §8(b)(1). Such conduct often occurs during union organizing campaigns. Unreasonable restrictions on employees' organizing activities also violate §8(a)(1) and §8(b)(1). Employers may restrict such efforts by employees to nonworking times (such as lunch break or coffee breaks) and to nonworking areas (e.g., washrooms, locker rooms, cafeteria, parking lots); total prohibitions on employees' organizing activities on the employer's property violate §8(a)(1). Under some circumstances, the employer may also be required to allow union organizers who are not employees onto the property to contact employees. The following Supreme Court decision discusses that requirement.

LECHMERE, INC. V. NLRB

502 U.S. 527 (1992)

FACTS

Lechmere operated a retail store located at a shopping plaza in Newington, Connecticut. Lechmere owns the property on which the store is located, along with the parking lot adjacent to the store. A grassy strip of land separates the parking lot from an adjacent highway; the grassy strip is public property. Lechmere company policy prohibited solicitation or distribution of handbills or leaflets of any kind on its property; the policy was posted in all entrances to the store and was consistently enforced against all groups, including the Girl Scouts and the Salvation Army.

Local 919 of the United Food and Commercial Workers Union sought to unionize the employees of Lechmere. After a full-page newspaper ad by the union drew little response, union organizers entered Lechmere's parking lot and placed handbills on the windshields of the cars parked in the corner of the lot used by employees. Lechmere's manager confronted the organizers, informed them of the company policy, and ordered them to leave; Lechmere employees removed the handbills. The union organizers attempted to distribute handbills several other times but each time were asked by store officials to leave, and the handbills were removed. The union later attempted to distribute handbills from the grassy strip of land and picketed there as well. The union then filed an unfair labor practice complaint with the NLRB, alleging that Lechmere had violated §8(a)(1) by barring the organizers from company property. The ALJ upheld the union complaint; the NLRB affirmed and ordered Lechmere to cease and desist from barring the organizers from the parking lot. The U.S. Court of Appeals for the First Circuit enforced the NLRB decision, and Lechmere appealed to the U.S. Supreme Court.

DECISION

The Court referred to the language of §7 of the NLRA, which, it held, granted rights only to employees, not to unions or to nonemployee union organizers. In some instances, the Court held, an employer may be required to allow the nonemployee organizers onto its property when it is necessary to allow employees to exercise their §7 right to organize or to join unions.

The Court then looked to its decision in *NLRB v. Babcock & Wilcox Co.,* which considered the circumstances in which the employer is required to allow organizers access to its property. *Babcock & Wilcox* held that, as a rule, an employer is not required to allow nonemployee organizers to distribute union literature on its property; however, when "the location of a plant and the living quarters of the employees place the employees beyond the reach of reasonable union efforts to communicate with them," the employer may be required to allow the organizers access to "permit communication of information on the right to organize . . . ."

The court stated that its prior cases determined that the employer was required to allow access to the nonemployee organizers when "unique obstacles" prevented other means of communication with the employees. The NLRB, in deciding in favor of the union against Lechmere, considered the availability of "reasonably effective alternative means of communication with the employees." The Court held that the NLRB had erred by focusing on whether other available means of communication were reasonably *effective*; *Babcock & Wilcox* required focus on whether other means of communication were reasonably *available*—did the "inaccessibility of the employees make ineffective the reasonable attempts by nonemployees to communicate with them through the usual channels?" Where reasonable alternative means of access to the employees exist, the employer is not required to allow nonemployee organizers onto its property. Classic examples of when an employer will be required to allow access to the organizers include, according to the court, cases in which employees work in logging camps, mining camps, or resort hotels, where employees are isolated from the reach of usual means of communication.

Because Lechmere's employees did not reside on company property, the court held that they were not beyond the reach of usual means of communication; the employees were not "inaccessible" in the sense required by *Babcock & Wilcox*. The Court emphasized that *"access to employees, not success in winning them over, is the critical issue"* [emphasis added]; because the union failed to establish that there were unique obstacles frustrating its access to the Lechmere employees, the NLRB erred in finding that Lechmere had committed an unfair labor practice by denying the union organizers access to its property. The Court reversed the Court of Appeals decision and refused enforcement of the NLRB's order.

CASE QUESTIONS

1. Why would the employer want to prohibit all solicitation and distribution of literature by nonemployees?
2. Why would the union want to solicit employees at their workplace? What other means might be available to the union to reach the employees?
3. Under what circumstances must an employer allow nonemployee organizers on the employer's property? Give some examples of such situations.
4. Was Lechmere required to allow the organizers to solicit on its property? Explain.

SECTION 8(A)(2): EMPLOYER DOMINATION OF UNIONS

In order for employees to exercise their right to organize or join a union, the union must be free to represent those employees effectively. For that reason, employer interference, support, domination, or assistance of a labor organization is prohibited. An employer who helps a union to solicit membership or who agrees to recognize a union that does not have the support of a majority of employees also violates §8(a)(2). The union agreeing to such an unlawful recognition violates §8(b)(1). Employers who organize employee work groups may run afoul of §8(a)(2) if the work group discusses wages or working conditions with the employer. Remedies for violations of §8(a)(2) involve directing the employer to cease recognizing or supporting the union and canceling any agreement that may have resulted from it.

Section 8(a)(2) was originally aimed at "company unions"—unions organized and controlled by the employer; such company unions were common in the first years of the NLRA. More recent issues arising under §8(a)(2) have involved employee participation programs and innovative workplace arrangements. In *Electromation, Inc.* [309 N.L.R.B. No. 163, 142 L.R.R.M. 1001 (1992)], affirmed by the U.S. Court of Appeals for the Seventh Circuit [35 F.3d 1148 (7th Cir.1994)], the employer set up a series of action committees, comprised of employees and management representatives, to handle matters such as absenteeism, bonuses, pay progression, and a no-smoking policy. The committee members could propose new policies, but management had final authority to adopt any recommendations. The NLRB held that the committees were labor organizations because they acted in a representative capacity and dealt with the employer regarding terms and conditions of employment. Because the committees were established and controlled by the employer, the employer was held to have violated §8(a)(2).

The NLRB addressed the same issue in *E.I. DuPont de Nemours & Co.* [311 N.L.R.B. No. 88 (1993)]. The company created several union–management safety and fitness committees to discuss matters and submit recommendations to management. The NLRB held that the committees were labor organizations under the NLRA because they dealt with the employer on terms and conditions of employment. DuPont decided which employee volunteers served on the committees, reserved the right to abolish any committee, and in some cases sought to use the committees to avoid dealing with the union on the same issues; DuPont therefore was held to have violated §8(a)(2).

SECTIONS 8(A)(3) AND 8(B)(2)

Section 8(a)(3) prohibits employers from discriminating with regard to any terms or conditions of employment in order to encourage or discourage union membership. Section 8(b)(2) prohibits unions from causing or attempting to cause an employer to discriminate against an employee in violation of §8(a)(3). The purpose of the sections is to ensure that an employee does not suffer economically because of the employee's decision to join, or not to join, a union. If employees are to have the free choice, under §7, to join or refrain from joining a union, then they must be protected from being fired, laid off, or refused a job because of their choice. Violations of §§8(a)(3) or 8(b)(2) have two elements: Discrimination must occur against an employee in terms or conditions of employment, and the discrimination must be for the purpose of encouraging or discouraging union membership. Firing employees who have joined a union is a clear violation of §8(a)(3); moreover, a union that seeks to have an employee fired for joining a rival union violates §8(b)(2). An employer who closes a plant because the workers have voted to be represented by a union violates §8(a)(3), according to the Supreme Court decision in *Textile Workers Union v. Darlington Mfg. Co.* [380 U.S. 263 (1965)].

union security agreements: Contract provisions that require an employee to join, or at least pay dues to, a union.

Union Security Agreements   Several specific issues arising under these sections deserve more detailed discussion. The first issue involves **union security agreements**. Union security agreements are contract provisions between a union and employer that require an employee, in order to remain employed, to either join the union or at least pay union dues. Union security agreements clearly have the effect of encouraging union membership. *Closed shop agreements*, which require the employer to hire only union members— that is, in order to be hired, an employee must already be a member of the union—are illegal. However, **union shop agreements**, which require that the employee join the union after completing a probationary period of at least 30 days, or an **agency shop agreement**, which requires that the employee pay union dues and fees but need not actually join the union, are permissible under the sections. Such agreements are possible because of a specific exception contained in §§8(a)(3) and 8(b)(2).

union shop agreements: Contract provisions that require employees to join a union after completing a probationary period.

agency shop agreements: Contract provisions requiring employees to pay union dues and fees.

Where a union security agreement is in effect, the employer must fire, upon the union's request, an employee who is denied union membership or expelled from the union for failing to pay the required union dues or fees. If an employee is expelled from the union or refused union membership for any reason other than failing to pay required dues or fees, then the employer is not required to fire that employee. This protects employees from union discrimination.

right to work laws: State laws that prohibit union security agreements.

Right to Work Laws   Section 14(b) of the NLRA permits states to pass **right to work laws** that prohibit union security agreements. In states that have such laws, union shop and agency shop agreements are illegal. A number of states, mainly in the South and West, have passed such laws.

The Right to Strike   The second issue that arises under these sections concerns the right to strike. Employees enjoy the right to strike under §7. (A *strike* is the essence of concerted action for purposes of collective bargaining or mutual aid and protection.) Strikes under the NLRA are classified as either economic strikes—strikes arising out of negotiations over wages or conditions of employment—or unfair labor practice strikes—strikes to protest illegal action by the employer. Employers are forbidden to fire employees for going on either unfair labor practice strikes or economic strikes; however, in the event of an economic strike, the employer is free to hire permanent replacements for the workers who went on strike. After the strike is over, the striking workers are not guaranteed to get their jobs back if those jobs have been filled by replacement workers and no other positions are available. As long as the former strikers indicate their intent to return to their jobs, the employer is required to rehire them when positions become available. Recent proposed legislation attempted to outlaw the permanent replacement of workers on economic strikes, but Congress failed to pass it. In an unfair labor practice strike, employers are not permitted to permanently replace strikers—to do so would allow the employer to provoke the workers by illegal action and then capitalize upon that wrongdoing by getting rid of the unionized workers.

In recent years, unionized employees have seemed less willing to go on strike and to risk permanent replacement. The percentage of the workforce that is unionized has been decreasing since the 1950s, and employers are more likely during the strike to hire permanent replacements. For these reasons, unions have been developing alternative tactics to striking; these alternatives include consumer boycotts, publicity campaigns, and shareholder resolutions.

Hiring Halls   In some industries, employers do not maintain a permanent workforce but rather hire employees as needed for a particular project or period. In those situations, the employer may rely on the union to refer prospective employees. Such arrangements are known as **hiring halls**. Sections 8(a)(3) and 8(b)(2) require that hiring halls must not discriminate on the grounds of union membership in referring prospective employees and that employers have the right to refuse any applicant the union refers. It is legal for the union to set specific skill requirements necessary for being referred, such as having completed an apprenticeship program. Hiring halls are common in the construction, shipping, and longshore industries.

hiring halls: Arrangements where a union refers employees to an employer.

SECTIONS 8(D), 8(A)(5), AND 8(B)(3): THE DUTY TO BARGAIN IN GOOD FAITH

When a union has the support of a majority of employees in a bargaining unit, it becomes the exclusive bargaining agent for those employees. (The usual method for demonstrating such majority support is by winning a representation election, but that is not the only way—the NLRA requires that an employer with knowledge of the union's majority support, independent of the union's claim of such support, must recognize and bargain with the union.) Thus, the employer must recognize and bargain, in good faith, with the union with regard to wages, hours, terms, and conditions of employment for those employees. The union is also under a duty to bargain in good faith with the employer. Bargaining in good faith does not require the parties to reach an agreement; rather, they are only required to meet and negotiate.

Bargaining in Good Faith   Section 8(d) defines the duty to bargain in good faith as:

> [T]he performance of the mutual obligation of the employer and the representative of the employees to meet at reasonable times and confer in good faith with respect to wages, hours, and other terms and conditions of employment, or the negotiation of an agreement or any question arising thereunder . . .

Once a union has the support of a majority of employees in a bargaining unit, the employer may no longer negotiate with individual employees (unless the collective agreement so allows); the union is now the exclusive bargaining agent of all the employees in the bargaining unit, and matters relating to the wages, hours, terms, and conditions of employment of those employees must be negotiated with the union. Section 9(a) of the NLRA does allow the employer to address individual grievances of the employees, as long as it is done in a manner consistent with the collective agreement and the union has been given notice of such matters.

Bargaining Procedures   A union or employer seeking to bargain with the other party must give notice to that party at least 60 days prior to the expiration of an existing collective agreement; if no agreement presently exists, then the notice is to be given at least 60 days prior to the date it proposes the agreement to go into effect. Section 8(d) requires that any current agreement must be continued in effect from the date of the notice to bargain, for 60 days or until the agreement expires, whichever comes later. During that 60-day-period, the union is prohibited from going on strike, and the employer is forbidden to lock out the employees. When the employer is a health care institution, the notice period is 90 days, and the ban on strikes or lockouts is extended to 90 days. If a union seeks to strike or picket at a health care institution, it must give the employer at least 10 days notice prior to taking such action to give the institution time to make arrangements to ensure that patient care is not disrupted.

Nature of the Duty   The duty of the parties to bargain in good faith is enforced by §§8(a)(5) and 8(b)(3), which make it an unfair labor practice for an employer or union to refuse to bargain in good faith. Section 8(d) also states that the obligation to bargain "does not compel either party to agree to a proposal or require the making of a concession . . . ." In other words, neither party has an obligation to reach an agreement, only the obligation to bargain in good faith. The NLRB regulates the process of collective bargaining but not the results of the process. Hard bargaining is not illegal; but a position of "take it or leave it," with no willingness to bargain, is bargaining in bad faith.

mandatory bargaining subjects: Matters relating to wages, hours, terms, and conditions of employment of the members of the bargaining unit, and over which the parties are required to bargain by the NLRA.

Bargaining Subjects   Although the NLRB does not regulate the results of collective bargaining, it does exert some control over the subject bargained over. Why? This control helps to prevent the parties from making a charade of the process by holding to arbitrary or frivolous positions. The NLRB distinguishes between mandatory bargaining subjects, permissive subjects, and illegal subjects.

Mandatory bargaining subjects are those that relate to wages, hours, terms, and conditions of employment of the employees in the bargaining unit. In the case of *Allied Chemical & Alkali Workers v. PPG* [404 U.S. 157 (1971)], the Supreme Court held that mandatory subjects are those matters "that vitally affect the terms and conditions of employment" of the bargaining unit. The NLRB and the courts broadly interpret the matters subject to mandatory bargaining. "Wages," for example, have been held to include all forms of employee compensation and fringe benefits, including stock options, employee discounts, pensions, and incentive plans. "Hours and other terms and conditions" of employment have received similar broadening. Why label an item a mandatory bargaining subject? To do so ensures that the parties must negotiate over it when the issue is raised by either party. Remember, however, they still need not reach an agreement. Parties, when the negotiations are deadlocked, may insist on a mandatory subject to the point of impasse; the parties may strike or lock out over mandatory subjects. Either party can only make a unilateral change in a mandatory subject after first bargaining in good faith to an impasse. For example, once an existing collective agreement expires, an employer may not unilaterally make changes in wages until it has negotiated to impasse with the union over this issue. Making a unilateral change in mandatory subjects without bargaining to impasse is a violation of §8(a)(5) or §8(b)(3).

Permissive bargaining subjects are those matters that are neither mandatory subjects nor illegal subjects—they are matters not directly related to wages, hours, terms, and conditions of employment of the bargaining unit. Examples of such matters are union and management participation in social or charitable activities and industry promotion activities. Either party is free to raise such matters at the bargaining table but cannot insist on them to the point of impasse. If the other party refuses to accept the permissive matter proposal, then it must be dropped. Insisting on permissive subjects to the point of impasse or conditioning agreement on mandatory subjects upon agreement to permissive matters violates §8(a)(5) or §8(b)(3).

Illegal bargaining subjects are those proposals that involve matters that would violate the NLRA or other laws. For example, a union attempt to negotiate a closed shop agreement would be an illegal bargaining subject. Other examples include negotiating separate wage scales for men and women or agreeing to exclude minorities from certain jobs. Any attempt to bargain over illegal subjects violates §8(a)(5) or §8(b)(3), and any agreement reached on such matters is null and void. Illegal subjects may not be insisted upon to the point of impasse.

The following case discusses whether an employer must bargain with the union over a decision to close a plant (i.e., is this a mandatory bargaining subject?).

permissive subjects: Those matters that are neither mandatory nor illegal; the parties may, but are not required to, bargain over them.

illegal bargaining subjects: Matters that would violate the NLRA or other laws; any attempt to bargain over such matters is a violation of the duty to bargain in good faith under the NLRA.

FIRST NATIONAL MAINTENANCE CORP. V. NLRB

452 U.S. 666 (1981)

FACTS

First National Maintenance (FNM) performed the maintenance and housekeeping work at Greenpark Care Center, a nursing home in Brooklyn, and employed approximately 35 employees at Greenpark. It became aware that it was losing money at the Greenpark location and informed Greenpark that it wished to increase its weekly fee to $500 per week; FNM then informed Greenpark that it would cease its operations at Greenpark on August 1, 1977, if the increase was not granted. On 25 July 1977,

FNM gave Greenpark final notice of termination of its services.

While FNM was experiencing difficulties with Greenpark, District 1199, National Union of Hospital and Health Care Employees (Dist. 1199), was conducting an organizing campaign among the FNM workers at Greenpark. The FNM employees selected Dist. 1199 as their bargaining agent and representative in a representation election held March 31, 1977. Dist. 1199 gave notice to FNM, but FNM did not respond to, or consult with, the union. On July 28, 1977, FNM notified its employees at Greenpark that they would be discharged on August 1. The company only engaged in perfunctory discussions with the union and shut down its Greenpark operations on July 31; the employees were discharged. District 1199 then filed an unfair labor practice complaint, alleging that FNM had violated §§8(a)(1) and (5) by refusing to bargain over the decision to cease operations at Greenpark. The ALJ held in the union's favor, and the NLRB adopted the ALJ's decision ordering FNM to bargain in good faith with the union. The U.S. Court of Appeals for the Second Circuit enforced the NLRB's order, and FNM appealed to the U.S. Supreme Court.

DECISION

The Court noted that the Courts of Appeals had taken different positions on the duty of an employer to bargain with a union over decisions involving "a major commitment of capital investment" or a "basic operational change" in the scope or direction of the enterprise. Although the parties (employer and union) are free to bargain about any legal subject, the NLRA only mandates bargaining over "wages, hours, and other terms and conditions of employment"; Congress, noted the Court, had no intention that the union representing employees of an enterprise would become an equal partner in the running of that enterprise. Some management decisions, such as advertising and promotion strategy, have only an indirect effect on the employment relationship, whereas other management decisions, such as layoffs and recall and work rules, are clearly an aspect of the employment relationship. The decision to cease operations, noted the Court, involved a third type of management decision—one that had a direct effect on the employment relationship, but one that focused on the profitability of the contract with Greenpark, a concern "wholly apart from the employment relationship." Although the decision to cease operations touched on the continued employment of the employees, a matter of central concern to the union, it involved a change in the scope and direction of the enterprise.

The purpose of labeling a matter as a mandatory bargaining subject is to "promote the fundamental purpose" of the NLRA by bringing labor and management together "within the framework established by Congress as most conducive to industrial peace." The rationale behind mandatory bargaining is that the process will result in decisions that are better for both labor and management. "This will be true, however, only if the subject proposed for discussion is amenable to resolution through the bargaining process. Management must be free from the constraints of the bargaining process to the extent essential for the running of a profitable business." The Court concluded that, "in view of an employer's need for unencumbered decision making, bargaining over management decisions that have a substantial impact on the continued availability of employment should be required only if the benefit, for labor–management relations and for the collective bargaining process, outweighs the burden placed on the conduct of the business." If labor costs are an important factor in a failing operation and the decision to close, management will have an incentive to bargain with the union to seek concessions that may make continuing the business profitable. The Court concluded that "the harm likely to be done to an employer's need to operate freely in deciding whether to shut down part of its business purely for economic reasons outweighs the incremental benefit that might be gained through the union's participation in making the decision." Therefore, the Court held that the decision to cease operations was not a mandatory bargaining subject.

Even if a decision is not a mandatory bargaining subject, it is clear that the employer is required by §8(a)(5) to bargain with the union over the effects of that decision on the employees in the bargaining unit; examples include severance pay, retraining allowances, transfer rights, and preferential hiring at other locations.

CASE QUESTIONS

1. Why was FNM planning to cease operations at the Greenpark Care Center?

2. How could the union have affected FNM's decision to cease operations at Greenpark?

3. What test does the Supreme Court set out for determining when a management decision, such as a plant closing, is a mandatory bargaining subject?

NLRB Actions Raise Political Controversies

Two recent actions by the National Labor Relations Board have ignited political controversies by announcing recent legal actions against Boeing and the States of Arizona and South Dakota.

On April 20, 2011, NLRB Acting General Counsel Lafe Solomon announced that the NLRB had filed an unfair labor practice complaint [19-CA-32431] against the Boeing Company alleging that Boeing violated federal labor law by deciding to transfer some production operations to a non-union facility in South Carolina for discriminatory reasons. The complaint grew out of a charge filed by the International Association of Machinists and Aerospace Workers, District Lodge 751, which represents the Boeing workers at its plants in Washington State. The union claimed that Boeing made the decision to transfer a production line accounting for thirty percent of the production of the 787 Dreamliner airplane to its Charleston, South Carolina facilities in retaliation against the union workers for having engaged in strikes against Boeing in the past, and to "chill" the workers from engaging in future strikes. The union has engaged in four strikes against Boeing's Washington operations since 1989. The legality of the decision to shift the second production line to Charleston from Washington depends upon Boeing's intent—and the NLRB has based its complaint on statements made by Boeing officials that it believes indicate retaliation. One executive told the Seattle Times that the decision to move production to South Carolina "was not the business climate. And it was not the wages we're paying today. It was that we cannot afford to have a work stoppage, you know, every three years." The NLRB investigation found that Boeing officials made multiple statements to employees and the media indicating the unlawful motivation to retaliate for past strikes and chill future strike activity, and that statements were coercive. To remedy the alleged unfair labor practices, the Acting General Counsel is seeking an order that would require Boeing to maintain the second production line in Washington state. The complaint does not seek closure of the South Carolina facility, nor does it prohibit Boeing from assembling planes there.

A worker's right to strike is a fundamental right guaranteed by the National Labor Relations Act," Mr. Solomon said. "We also recognize the rights of employers to make business decisions based on their economic interests, but they must do so within the law. I have worked with the parties to encourage settlement in the hope of avoiding costly litigation, and my door remains open to that possibility."

The NLRB decision to issue the unfair labor practice complaint caused immediate political reactions; business groups in Washington accused the Obama Administration of pushing a "radical, pro-union agenda." South Carolina Governor Nikki Haley has made public statements that unions were not welcome in that state, and South Carolina voters approved an amendment to the state constitution to make it harder for unions to organize.

In a related, second action, the NLRB has filed suit against the States of Arizona and South Dakota, seeking to have constitutional amendments similar to those adopted in South Carolina declared unconstitutional under the federal constitution's Supremacy Clause because they are pre-empted by the federal law. The NLRB indicated that it was suing those two states to establish precedents to invalidate the South Carolina amendment and a similar amendment adopted by Utah.

Sources: Steven Greenhouse, "Labor Board Plans to Sue 2 States Over Union Rules," *The New York Times,* April 26, 2011; "Being and the NLRB: Is a Move to South Carolina a Way to Avoid Unions or Retaliate against Them?," *The New York Times,* April 26, 2011; Steven Pearlstein, *The Washington Post,* April 27, 2011; "NLRB Claim vs. Boeing Could Ground 787 Plans," Metal Bulletin Daily Alerts, April 15, 2011; NLRB News Release, "National Labor Relations Board issues complaint against Boeing Company for unlawfully transferring work to a non-union facility," April 20, 2011 [available at http://www.nlrb.gov/news/national-labor-relations-board-issues-complaint-against-boeing-company-unlawfully-transferring-].

Plant Closing Legislation   The Worker Adjustment and Retraining Act (WARN), passed by Congress in 1988, requires employers with 100 or more employees to give at least 60 days notice prior to any plant closing or "mass layoffs." The employer must give advance written notice to the employees or their representative (union), to the state economic development officials, and to the chief elected local government official. Two exceptions to the notice requirement exist: (1) the "failing firm" exception—when giving the required notice would prevent the firm from obtaining capital or business necessary to maintain the operation of the firm and (2) when the work loss is due to "unforeseen circumstances"—such as when the plant is damaged by fire or disaster. The WARN notice requirements do not include the obligation to bargain over the decision to close; the duty to bargain is governed by the *First National Maintenance* decision.

The Duty to Furnish Information   The duty to bargain in good faith also includes the duty of the employer to furnish information to the union in certain situations. When the employer pleads inability to pay in response to union demands, the employer must provide financial information that supports this claim. The information must be requested by the union, and though it need not be in the form requested by the union, the information must be in a reasonably accessible and usable form. Note that the duty to furnish information is not a "truth in bargaining" requirement; it relates only to claims of financial inability to meet union demands.

The employer also has a continuing obligation to provide the union with information relating to the administration and enforcement of the collective agreement that is necessary for the union to perform its role as exclusive bargaining representative for the bargaining unit. Such information includes wage scales, factors entering into compensation, job classifications, and a list of names and addresses of the employees in the bargaining unit.

Remedies for the Duty to Bargain   When the violation of the duty to bargain involves specific practices, such as the refusal to provide information, the NLRB orders the offending party to comply; when a party has made illegal unilateral changes to mandatory subjects, the NLRB requires that the prior conditions be restored. However, when the violation involves the refusal to recognize or to negotiate seriously with the other party, the NLRB is limited to a **cease and desist order** and a **bargaining order** directing, respectively, the offending party to stop the illegal conduct and to negotiate in good faith. The NLRB cannot require either party to reach an agreement or to offer concessions. Such orders only require the parties to return to the bargaining table and make a serious effort to explore the basis for an agreement.

SECTIONS 8(B)(4) AND 8(E): SECONDARY ACTIVITY

Union picketing directed against parties other than the employer with whom it has a dispute may be an unfair labor practice. When a union directs a strike or picket line against a neutral employer, such conduct is called **secondary picketing**. Because the neutral party is not involved in the labor dispute, it is entitled to be free from economic pressure; a union targeting a neutral employer with a strike or picketing violates §8(b)(4). Picketing at a neutral location that is merely intended to inform consumers of the existence of a labor dispute, however, is not a violation. Union picketing against an employer who is an ally of the employer against whom the union is striking is also not a violation. An ally relationship arises when the other employer is performing the work usually done by the striking employees.

The NLRB is required to seek a court injunction against conduct that violates §8(b)(4) when such a complaint is filed with it; the injunction is to prevent the illegal conduct while the NLRB holds a hearing on the alleged unfair labor practice. If the NLRB determines that the conduct is in violation of the act, it will issue a cease and desist order against it. Unions engaging in illegal secondary activity are also subject to damage suits under §303 of the act—employers injured by such conduct can sue the union for damages and legal fees.

Contract provisions that purport to allow a union to engage in secondary conduct are known as **hot cargo clauses**. Section 8(e) prohibits a union from negotiating or attempting to negotiate such clauses. Any agreement containing a hot cargo clause is null and void. [Note, too, that a union attempting to negotiate a hot cargo clause also violates §8(b)(3).]

Not all union activity directed at neutral, or secondary, employers is illegal. An exception to §8(b)(4), known as the *publicity proviso*, states that the

cease and desist order: An order directing a party to stop the illegal conduct and to refrain from such conduct in the future.

bargaining order: NLRB order directing a party to bargain in good faith.

secondary picketing: Picketing directed against an employer that is not a party to the labor dispute.

hot cargo clauses: Contract provisions that would purport to allow unions to engage in secondary picketing; they are illegal under the NLRA.

union does have the right to engage in "publicity picketing"—picketing done peacefully that is intended to advise the public that the products of the employer against whom the union is striking (the primary employer) are being sold or distributed by the secondary employer. In addition, union conduct that is outside the publicity proviso may also be protected under the First Amendment's guarantee of free speech. In *Edward J. DeBartolo Corp. v. Florida Gulf Coast Building Trades Council* [485 U.S. 568 (1988)], the Supreme Court held that a union's peaceful distribution of handbills calling upon consumers to boycott the stores in a mall, because of a labor dispute with one of the stores, was not picketing; such conduct was therefore not subject to §8(b)(4) and was protected by the First Amendment.

OTHER UNFAIR LABOR PRACTICE PROVISIONS

Reprisals   Section 8(a)(4) prohibits an employer from discharging or otherwise discriminating against an employee who has filed charges or has given testimony in proceedings under the NLRA. This section is intended to protect employees exercising their rights under the act from any employer reprisals for such protected action. Reprisals by a union would violate §8(b)(1).

Excessive Union Dues or Fees   Section 8(b)(5) prohibits a union from requiring excessive dues or membership fees of employees covered by a union security agreement. This section is intended to protect employees from union abuse or exploitation. In deciding whether dues or fees are excessive, the NLRB is directed to consider "the practices and customs of labor organizations in the particular industry, and the wages currently paid to the employees affected."

featherbedding:
The union practice that requires an employer to pay for work that is not actually performed.

Featherbedding   It is an unfair labor practice under §8(b)(6) to cause an employer to pay for services that are not actually performed. The practice of getting paid for services not actually performed is called **featherbedding**. For example, if the local musicians' union requires an employer to pay wages for a minimum of three musicians, even if only two actually perform, that is featherbedding. When the work is actually performed, although not really needed by the employer (e.g., the employer agrees to hire three musicians even though only two were desired), it is not featherbedding. Featherbedding at one time was a common occurrence where unions had great power in an industry; now that unionized firms face stiff economic competition from nonunion firms and because of labor-saving technology, featherbedding complaints are relatively rare today.

REMEDIES FOR UNFAIR LABOR PRACTICES

The NLRB has broad discretion under §10(c) of the NLRA to remedy unfair labor practice violations. The remedies for unfair labor practices usually involve a cease and desist order, directing the wrongdoer to stop the illegal act and to refrain from it in the future. The remedy may also include an order to reinstate or hire of employees illegally fired or applicants illegally refused a job, the payment of compensation for lost wages and benefits, a grant of remedial seniority, and the payment of legal fees. The NLRB also may seek an injunction in federal court to stop the alleged unfair practices pending the NLRB hearing on the complaint. The NLRB does not have the power to award punitive damages—only compensation for actual losses can be awarded. What happens when the victim of an employer's unfair labor practices is an illegal alien—does the NLRB have the power to award the alien back pay or order reinstatement? That is the question addressed in the following case:

In the Language of the Court

HOFFMAN PLASTIC COMPOUNDS, INC V. NLRB

535 U.S. 142 (2002)

Chief Justice REHNQUIST:

. . . Hoffman Plastic Compounds, Inc. (petitioner or Hoffman), custom-formulates chemical compounds for businesses that manufacture pharmaceutical, construction, and household products. In May 1988, petitioner hired Jose Castro to operate various blending machines that "mix and cook" the particular formulas per customer order. Before being hired for this position, Castro presented documents that appeared to verify his authorization to work in the United States. In December 1988, the United Rubber, Cork, Linoleum, and Plastic Workers of America, AFL-CIO, began a union-organizing campaign at petitioner's production plant. Castro and several other employees supported the organizing campaign and distributed authorization cards to co-workers. In January 1989, Hoffman laid off Castro and other employees engaged in these organizing activities.

Three years later, in January 1992, respondent Board found that Hoffman unlawfully selected four employees, including Castro, for layoff "in order to rid itself of known union supporters" in violation of § 8(a)(3) of the National Labor Relations Act (NLRA). To remedy this violation, the Board ordered that Hoffman (1) cease and desist from further violations of the NLRA, (2) post a detailed notice to its employees regarding the remedial order, and (3) offer reinstatement and back pay to the four affected employees. Hoffman entered into a stipulation with the Board's General Counsel and agreed to abide by the Board's order.

In June 1993, the parties proceeded to a compliance hearing before an Administrative Law Judge (ALJ) to determine the amount of back pay owed to each discriminatee. On the final day of the hearing, Castro testified that he was born in Mexico and that he had never been legally admitted to, or authorized to work in, the United States. He admitted gaining employment with Hoffman only after tendering a birth certificate belonging to a friend who was born in Texas. . . . Based on this testimony, the ALJ found the Board precluded from awarding Castro back pay or reinstatement as such relief would be contrary to *Sure-Tan, Inc. v. NLRB,* 467 U.S. 883 (1984), and in conflict with [the Immigration Reform and Control Act] IRCA, which makes it unlawful for employers knowingly to hire undocumented workers or for employees to use fraudulent documents to establish employment eligibility.

In September 1998, four years after the ALJ's decision, and nine years after Castro was fired, the Board reversed [the ALJ's decision] with respect to back pay . . . the Board determined that "the most effective way to accommodate and further the immigration policies embodied in [IRCA] is to provide the protections and remedies of the [NLRA] to undocumented workers in the same manner as to other employees." The Board thus found that Castro was entitled to $66,951 of back pay, plus interest. It calculated this back pay award from the date of Castro's termination to the date Hoffman first learned of Castro's undocumented status, a period of 4 1/2 years. . . .

Hoffman filed a petition for review of the Board's order in the Court of Appeals. A panel of the Court of Appeals denied the petition for review. After rehearing the case en banc, the court again denied the petition for review and enforced the Board's order. We granted certiorari . . .

This case exemplifies the principle that the Board's discretion to select and fashion remedies for violations of the NLRA, though generally broad, is not unlimited . . .

Our decision in *Sure-Tan* . . . set aside an award closely analogous to the award challenged here. There we confronted for the first time a potential conflict between the NLRA and federal immigration policy, as then expressed in the Immigration and Nationality Act (INA). Two companies had unlawfully reported alien-employees to the Immigration and Naturalization Service (INS) in retaliation for union activity. Rather than face INS sanction, the employees voluntarily departed to Mexico. The Board investigated and found the companies acted in violation of §§ 8(a)(1) and (3) of the NLRA. The Board's ensuing order directed the companies to reinstate the affected workers and pay them six months' back pay.

We affirmed the Board's determination that the NLRA applied to undocumented workers, reasoning that the immigration laws "as presently written" expressed only a " 'peripheral concern' " with the employment of illegal aliens. "For whatever reason," Congress had not "made it a separate criminal offense" for employers to hire an illegal alien, or for an illegal alien "to accept employment after entering this country illegally." Therefore, we found "no reason to conclude that application of the NLRA to employment practices affecting such aliens would necessarily conflict with the terms of the INA."

With respect to the Board's selection of remedies, however, we found its authority limited by federal immigration policy . . . .

. . . The parties and the lower courts focus much of their attention on *Sure-Tan,* particularly its express limitation of back pay to aliens "lawfully entitled to be present and employed in the United States. All agree that as a matter of plain language, this limitation forecloses the award of back pay to Castro. Castro was never lawfully entitled to be present or employed in the United States, and thus, under the plain language of *Sure-Tan,* he has no right to claim back pay. The Board takes the view, however, that read in context, this limitation applies only to aliens who left the United States and thus cannot claim back pay without lawful reentry. . . .

. . . In 1986, two years after *Sure-Tan,* Congress enacted IRCA, a comprehensive scheme prohibiting the employment of illegal aliens in the United States. As we have previously noted, IRCA "forcefully" made combating the employment of illegal aliens central to "[t]he policy of immigration law." It did so by establishing an extensive "employment verification system," designed to deny employment to aliens who (a) are not lawfully present in the United States, or (b) are not lawfully authorized to work in the United States. This verification system is critical to the IRCA regime. To enforce it, IRCA mandates that employers verify the identity and eligibility of all new hires by examining specified documents before they begin work. If an alien applicant is unable to present the required documentation, the unauthorized alien cannot be hired. . . .

Similarly, if an employer unknowingly hires an unauthorized alien, or if the alien becomes unauthorized while employed, the employer is compelled to discharge the worker upon discovery of the worker's undocumented status. Employers who violate IRCA are punished by civil fines, and may be subject to criminal prosecution. IRCA also makes it a crime for an unauthorized alien to subvert the employer verification system by tendering fraudulent documents. It thus prohibits aliens from using or attempting to use "any forged, counterfeit, altered, or falsely made document" or "any document lawfully issued to or with respect to a person other than the possessor" for purposes of obtaining employment in the United States. Aliens who use or attempt to use such documents are subject to fines and criminal prosecution. There is no dispute that Castro's use of false documents to obtain employment with Hoffman violated these provisions. . . .

The Board contends that awarding limited back pay to Castro "reasonably accommodates" IRCA, because, in the Board's view, such an award is not "inconsistent" with IRCA. The Board argues that because the back pay period was closed as of the date Hoffman learned of Castro's illegal status, Hoffman could have employed Castro during the back pay period without violating IRCA. The Board further argues that while IRCA criminalized the misuse of documents, "it did not make violators ineligible for back pay awards or other compensation flowing from employment secured by the misuse of such documents." . . . What matters here, and what sinks both of the Board's claims, is that Congress has expressly made it criminally punishable for an alien to obtain employment with false documents. There is no reason to think that Congress nonetheless intended to permit back pay where but for an employer's unfair labor practices, an alien-employee would have remained in the United States illegally, and continued to work illegally, all the while successfully evading apprehension by immigration authorities. Far from "accommodating" IRCA, the Board's position, recognizing employer misconduct but discounting the misconduct of illegal alien employees, subverts it.

Indeed, awarding back pay in a case like this not only trivializes the immigration laws, it also condones and encourages future violations. . . . We therefore conclude that allowing the Board to award back pay to illegal aliens would unduly trench upon explicit statutory prohibitions critical to federal immigration policy, as expressed in IRCA. It would encourage the successful evasion of apprehension by immigration authorities, condone prior violations of the immigration laws, and encourage

future violations. However broad the Board's discretion to fashion remedies when dealing only with the NLRA, it is not so unbounded as to authorize this sort of an award.

Lack of authority to award back pay does not mean that the employer gets off scot-free. The Board here has already imposed other significant sanctions against Hoffman—sanctions Hoffman does not challenge. These include orders that Hoffman cease and desist its violations of the NLRA, and that it conspicuously post a notice to employees setting forth their rights under the NLRA and detailing its prior unfair practices. Hoffman will be subject to contempt proceedings should it fail to comply with these orders. We have deemed such "traditional remedies" sufficient to effectuate national labor policy regardless of whether the "spur and catalyst" of back pay accompanies them. . . . As we concluded in *Sure-Tan,* "in light of the practical workings of the immigration laws," any "perceived deficienc[y] in the NLRA's existing remedial arsenal" must be "addressed by congressional action," not the courts. In light of IRCA, this statement is even truer today.

The judgment of the Court of Appeals is reversed.

CASE QUESTIONS

1. Did Hoffman Plastics commit an unfair labor practice when it laid off Castro for trying to organize a union? What section of the NLRA was allegedly violated by Hoffman's conduct?
2. Could Hoffman Plastics legally hire Castro? Why? Explain. Is Castro entitled to back pay or reinstatement under the NLRA? Why?
3. What is the relevance of the Immigration Reform and Control Act to this case? How does it affect the NLRB's power to award Castro back pay or reinstatement?
4. What penalties can the NLRB impose on Hoffman as sanctions for its unfair labor practices here?

ADMINISTRATION AND ENFORCEMENT OF COLLECTIVE AGREEMENTS

During the term of a collective agreement, disputes over the interpretation or administration of a collective agreement occasionally may arise. The disputes may involve questions of a worker's entitlement to several hours of overtime, the employer's liability for cost of living adjustments, or the employer's right to change job requirements. The parties to the agreement have several options for resolving the dispute. The union may choose to strike, or the employer may choose to lock out the employees to try to force the other party to accept its position. Alternatively, either party may choose to sue in court for breach of contract; §301 of the NLRA allows court suits to enforce agreements between unions and employers. Lastly, the parties may choose to pursue arbitration of their dispute; that is, they submit the dispute to a neutral adjudicator (in effect, a private judge) chosen by the parties. For a number of reasons, arbitration is the usual method chosen. Arbitration of the type discussed here is known as **rights arbitration**, because it deals with the rights of the parties under the collective agreement—the arbitrator interprets and applies the agreement. (You may be familiar with another type of arbitration, in which the arbitrator actually defines the terms of the agreement—usually the wages or salary provisions. That type of arbitration is known as **interest arbitration** and is used to resolve salary disputes of professional baseball players and public sector employees who are forbidden to strike.)

Employees are reluctant to go on strike, and suffer a resulting loss of wages and risk of permanent replacement, over relatively minor matters; employers, likewise, are not usually willing to lock out and lose the profits from production over such disputes. Lawsuits are relatively expensive and may take a long time to resolve; the parties are not likely to sue unless there is an extremely important matter—or a lot of money—at stake. Thus, arbitration is a wise solution. Arbitration is not required by law, but more than 90 percent of all collective agreements contain rights arbitration provisions.

Arbitration is popular because it is created by the parties to the agreement, and they are free to tailor the arbitration process to fit their particular situation or desires. Arbitration provisions are usually included in an agreement as part of a **grievance procedure** (a method for dealing with grievances or complaints that a party has violated the agreement). The first steps of the grievance procedure usually involve conferences between union and management officers. If the parties are unable to negotiate a settlement, either side may submit the grievance to arbitration.

Arbitration provisions in collective agreements also usually contain **no-strike clauses** (in which the parties agree not to strike or lock out over a matter that is subject to arbitration). When an agreement contains an arbitration provision, and either party refuses to submit to arbitration a dispute that is within the scope of that provision, the other party can bring a court action under §301 seeking a court order forcing the reluctant party to arbitrate. Similarly, when a union strikes or an employer locks out over an issue subject to arbitration, the other party can use §301 to seek a court order stopping the strike or lockout. If the strike or lockout does not involve a matter subject to arbitration, the courts will not order an end to it. (The Norris-LaGuardia Act prohibits federal courts from enjoining such labor disputes.)

rights arbitration: Arbitration used to resolve disputes over the rights and duties of the parties to a collective agreement.

interest arbitration: Arbitration used to determine rates of pay and other terms of a collective agreement.

grievance procedure: Process set out in a collective agreement for resolving disputes under the agreement.

no-strike clause: A contract provision by which the parties agree not to engage in a strike or lockout during the term of the collective agreement.

When a party files a breach of contract suit over a matter that is subject to arbitration, the courts will defer to arbitration rather than hear the suit itself. In *United Steelworkers of America v. Warrior & Gulf Navigation Co.* [363 U.S. 574 (1960)], the Supreme Court held that if the parties have agreed to an arbitration clause, they have agreed to let the arbitrator, and not the court, decide the dispute. The court, by ordering arbitration, is simply giving the parties that to which they have already agreed. The court, therefore, is not to rule on the merits of the dispute, but rather simply to determine if the subject of the dispute is within the scope of the arbitration provision; if so, then the dispute must be sent to arbitration. After the arbitrator has decided the dispute, either party may also file an action under §301 to force the other party to abide by that decision. A court being asked to enforce the arbitrator's decision is not to substitute its own judgment for that of the arbitrator; rather, the court is simply to consider whether the arbitrator acted within the scope of authority granted under the collective agreement. If so, then the court is to enforce the decision. The court should refuse to enforce the arbitrator's decision only when the arbitrator has exceeded his or her authority granted under the agreement or when the decision conflicts with a "clearly defined" public policy, that is, a policy defined by "reference to the laws and legal precedents," according to the Supreme Court decision in *United Paperworkers International Union v. Misco, Inc.* [484 U.S. 29 (1987)]. In *Eastern Associated Coal Corp. v. United Mine Workers of America, Dist. 17* [531 U.S. 57 (2000)], the Court enforced an arbitration award that reinstated an employee who had twice failed drug tests; the Court held that the arbitration award did not violate any legislation or regulations, and therefore was not in violation of public policy.

As with the courts, the NLRB also defers its unfair labor practice procedures to arbitration between the parties when the dispute is subject to arbitration and does not involve antiunion motives. Examples include complaints alleging that an employer made a unilateral change to a collective agreement. In these cases, the union could allege that the unilateral change violated §8(a)(5) in addition to seeking arbitration over the alleged breach of the agreement. Some courts of appeals decisions have criticized the NLRB's policy of deferring to arbitration; in *Hammontree v. NLRB* [894 F.2d 438 (D.C.Cir., 1990)], the court held that the deferral policy improperly forces complaining employees to give up rights under the NLRA simply because the employer and union have established contractual procedures for resolving similar disputes.

PUBLIC SECTOR EMPLOYEES

Although there are a few significant differences, labor relations in the public sector—whether federal or state, local or municipal—are similar in many respects to private sector labor relations under the NLRA. The U.S. Constitution and the various state constitutions regulate the relationship of government and its citizens. Actions by government employers may raise constitutional issues because public sector employees are also citizens and retain their rights under the relevant constitutions.

A major difference involves the idea of government sovereignty. The government is under specific legal obligations to provide certain services and perform certain functions, and government officials are authorized by law to take certain actions and to make certain decisions. Collective bargaining involves shared decision making between the employer and the union. For public employers, collective bargaining may involve delegating to the union the authority relating to the employer's statutory obligations, or it may affect the employer's financial condition, requiring tax increases or cutbacks in services provided. Because of these concerns, public sector labor relations statutes may narrowly define the matters that are subject to collective bargaining; some state public sector labor relations statutes do not provide for collective bargaining but rather simply require consultation or "meeting and conferring" on working conditions.

A second major difference between public and private sector labor relations involves the right to strike. The federal courts have held that no constitutional right to strike exists; such a right may be created by statute, as §7 of the NLRA does for private sector employees. But in the public sector, most statutes prohibit strikes by public employees; impasses in negotiations over wages or working conditions are resolved by interest arbitration instead. Federal employees who strike are subject to losing their jobs, and unions calling such strikes are subject to losing their right to represent federal employees. The federal air traffic controllers went on strike in 1981, in violation of the Federal Service Labor–Management Relations Act, and consequently lost their jobs. Moreover, the representative union was decertified. Some state statutes only prohibit strikes by employees directly involved in public safety and health—such as police officers, prison guards, and firefighters—while allowing other public workers, such as teachers, to strike. Workers who cannot legally strike sometimes engage in nonstrike pressure tactics such as "working to rule" (doing only what is specifically required by their contracts and job descriptions), "blue flu" (whole groups of police officers or firefighters calling in sick), or work slowdowns (reducing the amount of work actually performed), in order to force the employer to address their concerns.

Public sector employees are not covered by the federal National Labor Relations Act; labor relations and collective bargaining by state and local employees is subject to the laws of the respective state. With state governments facing huge budget deficits due the recent economic recession, some state governments have sought to curtail the power of public sector unions. Supporters of such restrictions on unions claim that public employees' relatively generous retirement and medical insurance benefits are a major source of financial pressures on governments. As a result, there have been well-publicized efforts to restrict the power of unions by limiting the scope of issues subject to collective bargaining and making it more difficult for unions to organize in states such as Wisconsin, Ohio, Indiana, and Massachusetts. Critics of such legislation argue that the unions are being made scapegoats for the economic problems of their government employers, and point to the willingness of unions to accept reductions in pay and benefits to ease financial pressures on the states. Those critics charge that the additional restrictions on union organizing and bargaining are politically motivated, and seek to reduce the bargaining power and the political influence of the public sector unions.

SUMMARY

The percentage of the U.S. private sector workforce that is unionized is presently around 10 percent; that figure has been declining steadily since the early 1950s. Some commentators attribute this decline to the failure of organized labor to adapt to the changing attitudes of U.S. workers and to the country's change from a manufacturing-based economy to one based on service and information industries. Although the importance and influence of unions have been declining as membership declines, labor law remains an important concern for both employers and employees. Employees will continue to seek a role in determining the conditions of their employment; for many employees, unions will continue to provide that role through collective bargaining. For employees who choose not to join unions, labor law is still essential to protect their rights in the workplace. All employees and employers should have an awareness of the provisions of the NLRA and an understanding of their rights and obligations under it.

CHAPTER QUESTIONS

1. Sandra Connor was a dental hygienist in Dr. Callahan's dental office. At a staff meeting, where Dr. Callahan was discussing work-related problems, Connor and a co-worker interrupted Dr. Callahan to ask questions and make critical comments. After the meeting, Connor was reprimanded by the office manager. Later that week, Connor presented the office manager with a list of grievances that she (Connor) had discussed with her co-workers. The office manager fired Connor. Was the firing of Connor an unfair labor practice? Why? Explain your answer. [*Joseph DeRario, D.M.D., P.A..,* 283 NLRB No. 86 (1987)]

2. AmeriHealth Corp. is a health maintenance organization [HMO] that contracts with doctors to provide medical services to the patients who are enrolled in AmeriHealth's medical insurance plan. The doctors are independent medical practitioners who treat patients in their own offices. AmeriHealth pays the doctors a set fee, depending upon the type of care provided, and the doctors were responsible for covering the various expenses of their medical practices, such as rent, wages and benefits. The doctors are dissatisfied with what they regard as the low fees paid to them by AmeriHealth. They seek to form a union and bargain collectively with AmeriHealth over the fees for patient care. The doctors file a petition for a representation election with the NLRB, seeking certification as a collective bargaining agent. Are the doctors employees of AmeriHealth? Are they able to unionize under the NLRA? Explain. [*AmeriHealth and United Food and Commercial Workers Union, Local 56,* 329 NLRB No. 76 (1999)]

3. The employer had established a recreation fund to provide the employees with recreational opportunities; the employer had administered the fund for the benefit of the employees. The union sought to bargain over the allocation of funds from the recreation fund, but the employer refused; the employer claimed that it had total control over the fund, so there was no obligation to bargain over it. The union filed a §8(a)(5) complaint with the

NLRB. Was the refusal to bargain over the recreation fund a violation of the NLRA? Explain your answer. [*Getty Ref. & Mktg. Co.*, 279 N.L.R.B. No. 126, 122 L.R.R.M. 1150 (1986)]

4. The Teamsters Union, Local 572, went on strike against Silver Linen Supply, an industrial laundry supply company. During the strike, the customers normally supplied by Silver were supplied by Puritan Laundry Service. The union also began to picket at the Puritan plant, attempting to stop the Puritan trucks from making deliveries. After several days of the picketing, Puritan stopped supplying the customers of Silver but did not inform the union that they had stopped supplying the Silver customers. The union continued to picket at Puritan, and Puritan filed a §8(b)(4) complaint with the NLRB. Was the union picketing at Puritan an unfair labor practice, both before and after Puritan stopped supplying the Silver customers? Explain your answers. [*Laundry Workers Int., Local No. 259*, 164 NLRB 426 (1967)]

5. Mahon, an employee of Alpha Beta Corp., was fired for refusing to follow a supervisor's order. Mahon claimed that the order violated the work rules set out in the collective agreement. The union filed a grievance over the discharge, and Mahon also filed a complaint alleging a violation of §§8(a)(1) and (3). During discussions pursuant to the grievance procedure, the union and employer agreed to a settlement reinstating Mahon, subject to a two-week suspension. Mahon asked the NLRB to reinstate him with full back pay; the employer argued that the NLRB should defer to the grievance settlement like it defers to an arbitration award. What arguments should Mahon make to urge the NLRB to decide his complaint? What arguments should the employer make to urge the NLRB to defer to the grievance settlement? Should the NLRB hear the complaint, or should it defer to the settlement? Why? [*Alpha Beta Corp.*, 273 N.L.R.B. No. 194, 118 L.R.R.M. 1202 (1985), *aff'd sub nom Mahon v. NLRB*, 808 F.2d 1342 (9th Cir. 1987)]

6. In a bargaining unit of 100 employees, only 65 voted in a representation election, and the union won the election by a vote of 45 to 20. The employer objected to the results of the election, claiming that the number of voters was not substantial in light of the overall number of employees in the unit. Should the election be set aside because of the relatively low voter turnout? Explain your answer. [*Lemco Construction, Inc.*, 283 N.L.R.B. No. 68, 124 L.R.R.M. 1329 (1987)]

7. Callaghan was employed by Smiths Transportation until he became one of the leaders of an effort to unionize Smiths' employees. On January 15, 1999, when his supervisor discovered Callaghan's involvement, Callaghan was fired. On July 29, 1999, Callaghan filed a complaint with the NLRB, alleging that his discharge violated §§8(a)(1) and 8(a)(3) of the NLRA. How should the NLRB rule on Callaghan's complaint? Explain. [*United States Postal Service*, 271 N.L.R.B. No. 61, 116 LRRM 1417 (1984)]

8. While negotiating with Mercy Hospital for renewing a collective bargaining agreement, the union representing the hospital employees proposed that the hospital open the hospital cafeteria for all employees during the hours of 6 A.M.–8 P.M. and 2 A.M.–4 A.M. There were approximately 175 workers on the overnight shift, and many of them used the cafeteria for their lunch

break. The hospital had operated the cafeteria during those hours for the past 10 years but was now considering closing the cafeteria overnight because it was losing money during the overnight hours. One week after the union made its proposal, the hospital closed the cafeteria overnight and installed some vending machines, a toaster, and a microwave oven for use by the employees. The union filed an unfair labor practice complaint with the NLRB over the hospital's actions. Has the hospital violated the NLRA? Why? Is the decision to close the cafeteria overnight a mandatory bargaining subject under the NLRA? Explain. [*Mercy Hospital of Buffalo*, 311 NLRB 869 (1993)]

9. Potter Manufacturing Co. laid off 15 employees, claiming there was a lack of work due to economic conditions. The union representing the employees at Potter subsequently discovered that the employer laid off the employees it believed were most likely to honor a picket line in the event of a strike. The union filed an unfair labor practice charge with the NLRB. On which sections of the NLRA should the union base its charge? Why? What arguments can Potter make to support the layoffs? How is the NLRB likely to rule on the charge? Explain. [*National Fabricators,* 295 N.L.R.B. No. 126, 131 LRRM 1761 (1989)]

10. James Zentgraf, a truck driver for Way Bakery, was a member of the Truck Drivers Union Local 164. The employer suspended him after he made a racial remark to an African-American coworker. He filed a grievance under the collective agreement, protesting the suspension, but the employer denied the grievance. Way Bakery then fired Zentgraf because his conduct violated the company's equal employment opportunity [EEO] policy. The union then submitted Zentgraf's grievance to arbitration. After a hearing, the arbitrator ordered that Zentgraf be reinstated, subject to a six month suspension, without pay. The arbitrator also placed Zentgraf under probation for five years, during which any repeat of such conduct, any racial harassment or racially abusive conduct would be grounds for immediate discharge. Way Bakery filed suit in federal court to vacate the arbitration award. Should the court enforce, or vacate, the arbitration award? Why? Explain your answer. [*Way Bakery v. Truck Drivers Local No. 164,* 2004 WL 736996 (April 7, 2004)]

PRACTICAL EXERCISE

Adjunct and part-time faculty at the School of Management of Farber University (a private university) are concerned over what they regard as inadequate pay and benefits. They are paid on a per-course basis, and are paid considerably less than full-time faculty who teach a similar course load. The adjuncts and part-time faculty do not receive benefits such as medical insurance, dependent tuition and free parking. Some adjunct and part-time faculty members approached the dean of the Management School with their concerns, but the dean refused to take any action. As a result, the adjunct and part-time faculty have decided to explore the possibility of forming a union in order to force the School of Management to bargain with them over workloads, pay scales and benefits.

The dean of the School of Management argues that the part-time and adjunct faculty are not covered by the NLRA and legally are not able to unionize. The part-time and adjunct faculty insist that they are covered by the NLRA and are free to unionize.

Write position papers that do the following:

1. Argue the case that the adjunct and part-time faculty should be considered employees under the NLRA.
2. What arguments can you make for the dean's position, that the part-time and adjunct faculty are not employees under the NRLA.
3. Discuss what steps the adjunct and part-time faculty need to take to get the NLRB to decide this question.
4. Discuss how the NLRB is likely to rule on this issue.
5. Discuss how your answer to #4 would be different if Farber University were a state school rather than a private one. Explain all your answers.

FURTHER INFORMATION

www.nlrb.gov/
The National Labor Relations Board Web site.
www.aflcio.org/
The American Federation of Labor Web site.
www.shrm.org/
The Society for Human Resource Management Web site.
http://hr.monster.com/
Human Resource Management Information (and job listings).

CASE INDEX